Mary T. W. Bourke
February 1970

EQUITY

Equity

GEORGE W. KEETON

M.A., LL.D. (Cantab.), Hon. LL.D. (Sheffield), F.B.A.

of Gray's Inn, Barrister-at-Law
Professor of English Law, University of Notre Dame
and Director of the Notre Dame Centre in London
Professor Emeritus of the University of London

AND

L. A. SHERIDAN

LL.D. (London), Ph.D. (Belfast), Hon. LL.D. (Singapore)

of Lincoln's Inn, Barrister-at-Law
Professor of Comparative Law, Queen's University
of Belfast

Belfast

NORTHERN IRELAND LEGAL QUARTERLY INC.

London

Sir Isaac Pitman and Sons Ltd.

First published 1969

Published in Ireland by the Northern Ireland Legal Quarterly Inc.

SIR ISAAC PITMAN AND SONS LTD.
Pitman House, Parker Street, Kingsway, London, W.C.2
P.O. Box 6038, Portal Street, Nairobi, Kenya

SIR ISAAC PITMAN (AUST.) PTY. LTD.
Pitman House, Bouverie Street, Carlton, Victoria 3053, Australia

PITMAN PUBLISHING COMPANY S.A. LTD.
P.O. Box 9898, Johannesburg, S. Africa

PITMAN PUBLISHING CORPORATION
6 East 43rd Street, New York, N.Y. 10017, U.S.A.

THE CARSWELL COMPANY LTD., TORONTO

SBN: 273 43935 9

Printed by W. & S. MAGOWAN LTD., Belfast and Newry
F.9—(L.26)

PREFACE

ALTHOUGH this volume is founded upon *An Introduction to Equity*, of which six editions have appeared, it is essentially a new work. The original purpose of *An Introduction to Equity*, as the title implied, was to serve as an introduction to a series of volumes, each dealing with some major branch of equity. Of this series, volumes on Trusts and Wills were published, and several others were projected, but the outbreak of war in 1939 indefinitely postponed the preparation of others. With the abandonment of the original plan in 1945, successive editions of *An Introduction to Equity* included additional topics, but they did not attempt to cover the whole field of equity. The authors therefore decided that the time had arrived for the preparation of a volume which included all the main branches of equitable jurisdiction, except the Law of Trusts and Wills. It was also decided to make a further change. To recent editions of *An Introduction to Equity*, there was added an Irish supplement. The present work incorporates the development of equity in Ireland, and also the effect of the Irish decisions, differences between English and Irish practice being noted.

This volume is a joint work, and although its preparation has necessarily involved each author in writing particular chapters, both share responsibility for its form and content.

G. W. KEETON

L. A. SHERIDAN

CONTENTS

Chapter		Page
	Preface	v
	Table of Statutes	ix
	Table of Cases	xxi
I	The Nature of Equity	1
II	The Development of Equity in the Court of Chancery	44
III	The Judicature Acts	73
IV	Equity in Ireland	128
V	Public and Private Uses and Trusts	143
VI	Mortgages	164
VII	The Administration of the Estates of Deceased Persons	263
VIII	Assignment of Choses in Action	292
IX	Fraud	329
X	Powers of Appointment	357
XI	Conversion and Reconversion	375
XII	Election	395
XIII	Satisfaction and Performance	412
XIV	Marshalling	432
XV	The Married Woman's Separate Estate	440
XVI	Procedure	448
XVII	Injunctions	457
XVIII	Specific Performance	482
XIX	The Appointment of a Receiver	509
XX	Tracing	518
XXI	Other Equitable Remedies	530
	Index	565

TABLE OF STATUTES

ACTS OF THE IMPERIAL PARLIAMENT

		PAGE
52 Hen. III, c. 1	(Statute of Marlborough, 1267)	80, 463
6 Edw. I, c. 8	(Statute of Gloucester, 1278)	463
13 Edw. I, c. 18	(Statute of Westminster II, 1285)	3
17 Edw. II, c.11 (Ruffhead, c. 9)	(Crown prerogative in preservation of lands of idiots)	129
25 Edw. III, st. 5, c. 5	(Executors of executors) (1351)	268
1 Ric. III, c. 1	(Uses and trusts) (1483)	147
3 Hen. VII, c. 1	(Star Chamber) (1487)	46
27 Hen. VIII, c. 10	(Statute of Uses, 1535)	66, 130, 147, 150, 359-60
32 Hen. VIII, c.1	(Statute of Wills, 1540)	130, 148
34 & 35 Hen. VIII, c. 5	(Wills) (1542)	
	s. 14	440
43 Eliz. I, c. 4	(Statute of Charitable Uses, 1601)	154-7
1 Jac. I, c. 15	(Bankrupts) (1603)	294
21 Jac. I, c. 16	(Statute of Limitations, 1623)	104, 170, 196
29 Car. II, c. 3	(Statute of Frauds, 1677)	8, 26-7, 54, 68, 96-7, 186, 482, 495, 502, 520, 538, 539, 540
	s. 1	84
	s. 2	84
	s. 4	54, 182, 493, 496
	s. 7	120
	s. 8	120
	s. 9	120
3 W. & M., c. 14	(Fraudulent devises) (1691)	264
1 Anne, st. I, c. 32	(Purchasers of forfeited estates, Ireland) (1702)	
	ss. 7-9	137
6 Geo. I, c. 5	(Dependency of Ireland on Great Britain) (1719)	136
23 Geo. III, c. 28	(Irish appeals) (1783)	136
26 Geo. III, c. 58	(Returns of charitable donations) (1786)	157
39 & 40 Geo. III, c. 67	(Union with Ireland Act, 1800)	132, 136
41 Geo. III, c. 25	(Master of the Rolls, Ireland) (1801)	73, 133, 134
52 Geo. III, c. 102	(Charitable Donations Registration Act, 1812)	157
53 Geo. III, c. 24	(Administration of justice) (1813)	455
10 Geo. IV, c. 7	(Roman Catholic Relief Act, 1829)	137
11 Geo. IV & 1 Will. IV, c. 46	(Illusory Appointments Act, 1830)	365
1 & 2 Will. IV, c. 56	(Bankruptcy Court) (1831)	73
2 & 3 Will, IV, c. 45	(Representation of the People Act [Reform Act], 1832)	73, 160
3 & 4 Will. IV, c. 94	(Court of Chancery) (1833)	73
3 & 4 Will. IV, c. 104	(Administration of Estates Act, 1833)	266
7 Will. IV & 1 Vict., c. 26	(Wills Act, 1837)	
	s. 9	27, 366
	s. 10	366
1 & 2 Vict., c. 74	(Small Tenements Recovery Act, 1838)	
	s. 1	234
5 Vict., c. 5	(Court of Chancery Act, 1841)	73
5 & 6 Vict., c. 69	(Perpetuation of Testimony Act, 1842)	556
5 & 6 Vict., c. 103	(Court of Chancery Act, 1842)	73
7 & 8 Vict., c. 97	(Charitable Donations and Bequests (Ireland) Act, 1844)	158
8 & 9 Vict., c. 18	(Lands Clauses Consolidation Act, 1845)	380, 381

Statute	Title / section	PAGE
8 & 9 Vict., c. 106	(Real Property Act, 1845)	
	s. 3	84, 89
12 & 13 Vict., c. 26	(Leases Act, 1849)	228
	s. 2	366
	ss. 4-7	366
12 & 13 Vict., c. 106	(Bankrupt Law Consolidation Act, 1849)	
	s. 166	276
13 & 14 Vict., c. 17	(Leases Act, 1850)	228
	s. 2	366
	s. 3	366
13 & 14 Vict., c. 35	(Court of Chancery Act, 1850)	
	s. 1	560
	ss. 13-16	560
13 & 14 Vict., c. 51	(Exchequer equitable jurisdiction, Ireland) (1850)	73
14 & 15 Vict., c. 83	(Court of Chancery Act, 1851)	74,455
15 & 16 Vict., c. 76	(Common Law Procedure Act, 1852)	
	s. 2	450
	s. 3	450
15 & 16 Vict., c. 80	(Court of Chancery Act, 1852)	74
15 & 16 Vict., c. 86	(Court of Chancery procedure) (1852)	75
	s. 48	246
	s. 50	560
16 & 17 Vict., c. 78	(Commissioners for oaths) (1853)	74
16 & 17 Vict., c. 137	(Charitable Trusts Act, 1853)	157-8
17 & 18 Vict., c. 113	(Real Estate Charges Act, 1854)	381
17 & 18 Vict., c. 125	(Common Law Procedure Act, 1854)	75
	s. 50	453, 454
	s. 51	452, 454
	s. 78	454
	s. 79	110-11, 453, 454
	s. 80	110-11
	s. 82	453
	s. 83	454
18 & 19 Vict., c. 124	(Charitable Trusts Amendment Act, 1855)	158
19 & 20 Vict., c. 92	(Chancery Appeal Court (Ireland) Act, 1856)	74, 455
19 & 20 Vict., c. 102	(Common Law Procedure Amendment Act (Ireland), 1856)	75
	s. 81	110
	s. 82	110
19 & 20 Vict., c. 120	(Leases and sales of settled estates) (1856)	380
20 & 21 Vict., c. 60	(Irish Bankrupt and Insolvent Act, 1857)	73
	s. 249	276
	s. 251	117, 278
	s. 260	277, 278
	s. 273	79, 279
	s. 298	79, 279
	s. 313	79, 279
21 & 22 Vict., c. 27	(Chancery Amendment Act, 1858 [Lord Cairns' Act])	75, 463, 466, 508
	s. 2	454
	s. 5	452, 453
22 & 23 Vict., c. 35	(Law of Property Amendment Act, 1859)	
	s. 12	366
23 & 24 Vict., c. 136	(Charitable Trusts Act, 1860)	
	s. 2	158
23 & 24 Vict., c. 145	(Trustees' and mortgagees' powers) (1860)	
	s. 11	239, 249
	ss. 12-15	249
	ss. 17-23	239
23 & 24 Vict., c. 154	(Landlord and Tenant Law Amendment Act, Ireland, 1860)	
	s. 1	90
	s. 3	89, 90
	s. 4	89, 90
	s. 104	89

		PAGE
24 & 25 Vict., c. 114	(Wills Act, 1861)	394
30 & 31 Vict., c. 44	(Chancery (Ireland) Act, 1867)	73, 74
	s. 4	455
	s. 27	131
	s. 155	560
30 & 31 Vict., c. 54	(Charitable Donations and Bequests (Ireland) Act, 1867)	158
30 & 31 Vict., c. 69	(Real Estate Charges Act, 1867)	381
30 & 31 Vict., c. 144	(Policies of Assurance Act, 1867)	326
31 & 32 Vict., c. 4	(Sales of Reversions Act, 1867)	354-6
31 & 32 Vict., c. 40	(Partition Act, 1868)	380
32 & 33 Vict., c. 46	(Administration of Estates Act, 1869)	265, 281
32 & 33 Vict., c. 62	(Debtors Act, 1869)	
	s. 6	561
33 & 34 Vict., c. 93	(Married Women's Property Act, 1870).	140, 444
34 & 35 Vict., c. 22	Lunacy Regulation (Ireland) Act, 1871)	516
	s. 66	380
	s. 67	380
34 & 35 Vict., c. 31	(Trade Union Act, 1871)	
	s. 3	477, 478
	s. 4	478
35 & 36 Vict., c. 57	(Debtors (Ireland) Act, 1872)	
	s. 7	561
35 & 36 Vict., c. 58	(Bankruptcy (Ireland) Amendment Act, 1872)	277
	s. 49	276
	s. 52	279
	s. 53	79, 279
36 & 37 Vict., c. 66	(Supreme Court of Judicature Act, 1873)	1, 8, 9, 15, 35, 36, 37, 72, 75, 141, 317, 324, 325, 332, 442, 448, 461
	s. 16	508
	s. 24	76, 538
	s. 25	78, 104, 142, 315, 509
	s. 25(1)	78-9
	s. 25(2)	80
	s. 25(3)	80-1
	s. 25(4)	81, 193
	s. 25(5)	81, 224
	s. 25(6)	81, 326-8
	s. 25(7)	18, 81-3, 505
	s. 25(8)	83, 111, 240
	s. 25(9)	83
	s. 25(10)	83
	s. 25(11)	77, 78, 83-127
	s. 34	76, 263
37 & 38 Vict., c. 37	(Powers of Appointment Act, 1874)	366
37 & 38 Vict., c. 57	(Real Property Limitation Act, 1874)	
	s. 8	287
37 & 38 Vict., c. 78	(Vendor and Purchaser Act, 1874)	
	s. 7	218
38 & 39 Vict., c. 77	(Supreme Court of Judicature Act, 1875)	75, 448
	s. 10	78, 79, 275, 278
	s. 21	110
38 & 39 Vict., c. 87	(Land Transfer Act, 1875)	
	s. 129	218
40 & 41 Vict., c. 18	(Settled Estates Act, 1877)	380
40 & 41 Vict., c. 34	(Real Estate Charges Act, 1877)	381
40 & 41 Vict., c. 56	(County Officers and Courts (Ireland) Act, 1877)	140
	s. 33	140-1
	s. 34	141
	s. 35	141
	s. 36	141
	s. 37	141
	s. 43	141
	s, 45	141

		PAGE
40 & 41 Vict., c. 57	(Supreme Court of Judicature (Ireland) Act, 1877)	1, 8, 9, 15, 35, 36, 37, 72, 75, 141, 247, 324, 332, 442, 448, 497
	s. 21	76
	s. 27	76, 141, 458, 538
	s. 28	78, 104, 141-2, 325
	s. 28(1)	78, 278
	s. 28(2)	80
	s. 28(3)	80, 464
	s. 28(4)	81, 193
	s. 28(5)	81, 224
	s. 28(6)	81, 326
	s. 28(7)	18, 81, 505
	s. 28(8)	83, 111, 240, 465, 509
	s. 28(9)	83
	s. 28(10)	83
	s. 28(11)	77, 78, 83, 121
	s. 34	76
	s. 36	76,263
	s. 37	76
	s. 67	110
41 & 42 Vict., c.31	(Bills of Sale Act, 1878)	
	s. 6	232-3
44 & 45 Vict., c. 41	(Conveyancing Act, 1881)	
	s. 2	93
	s. 5	253
	s. 6	93
	s. 10	87, 223
	s. 14	88
	s. 15	191, 192
	s. 17	197-9, 201
	s. 18	224, 225
	s. 19	232, 236, 239, 240, 249, 250, 513
	s. 20	250
	s. 21	250, 251, 252, 253, 256
	s. 22	250
	s. 24	240-2, 511, 513
	s. 25	192
	s. 39	447
	s. 42	357
	s. 43	357
	s. 52	363
	s. 61	262
45 & 46 Vict., c. 38	(Settled Land Act, 1882)	357, 512
	s. 22	385, 393
	s. 53	470
45 & 46 Vict., c. 39	(Conveyancing Act, 1882)	
	s. 3	214
	s. 6	363
	s. 12	191, 192
45 & 46 Vict., c. 61	(Bills of Exchange Act, 1882)	
	s. 36	308
45 & 46 Vict., c. 75	(Married Women's Property Act, 1882)	104, 442-3
	s. 1	443
	s. 2	443
	s. 19	445
46 & 47 Vict., c. 49	(Statute Law Revision and Civil Procedure Act, 1883)	508
47 & 48 Vict., c. 18	(Settled Land Act, 1884)	357
50 & 51 Vict., c. 30	(Settled Land Acts (Amendment) Act, 1887)	357
51 & 52 Vict., c. 59	(Trustee Act, 1888)	
	s. 8	80
52 & 53 Vict., c. 36	(Settled Land Act, 1889)	357

		PAGE
52 & 53 Vict., c. 60	(Preferential Payments in Bankruptcy (Ireland) Act, 1889)	276
	s. 4	280
53 & 54 Vict., c. 5	(Lunacy Act, 1890)	
	s. 123	379-80
53 & 54 Vict., c. 39	(Partnership Act, 1890)	5-6
	s. 3	277
	s. 22	377
53 & 54 Vict., c. 64	(Directors' Liability Act, 1890)	329
53 & 54 Vict., c. 69	(Settled Land Act, 1890)	357
54 & 55 Vict., c. 66	(Local Registration of Title (Ireland) Act, 1891)	
	s. 22	384
	s. 84	384
	s. 85	384
55 & 56 Vict., c. 13	(Conveyancing and Law of Property Act, 1892)	
	s. 5	88
56 & 57 Vict., c. 53	(Trustee Act, 1893)	
	s. 1	161
	s. 12	259
	s. 17	106
	s. 24	160
	s. 45	31
56 & 57 Vict., c. 63	(Married Women's Property Act, 1893)	445
	s. 2	447
56 & 57 Vict., c. 71	(Sale of Goods Act, 1893)	
	s. 52	490
59 & 60 Vict., c. 25	(Friendly Societies Act, 1896)	
	s. 35	276
59 & 60 Vict., c. 35	(Judicial Trustees Act, 1896)	
	s. 3	272
59 & 60 Vict., c. 47	(Land Law (Ireland) Act, 1896)	
	s. 32	383
60 & 61 Vict., c. 65	(Land Transfer Act, 1897)	
	s. 1	267
60 & 61 Vict., c. 66	(Supreme Court of Judicature (Ireland) (No. 2) Act, 1897)	142
61 & 62 Vict., c. 22	(Statute Law Revision Act, 1898)	508
63 & 64 Vict., c. 51	(Money-lenders Act, 1900)	32
3 Edw. VII, c. 37	(Irish Land Act, 1903)	
	s. 24	384
6 Edw. VII, c. 41	(Marine Insurance Act, 1906)	
	ss. 17-19	551
	s. 50	326
7 Edw. VII, c. 18	(Married Women's Property Act, 1907)	445
1 & 2 Geo. V, c. 37	(Conveyancing Act, 1911)	
	s. 1	253
	s. 3	224, 227, 242, 513
	s. 4	250
	s. 5	251, 253
	s. 7	447
1 & 2 Geo. V, c. 57	(Maritime Conventions Act, 1911)	
	s. 9	83
4 & 5 Geo. V, c. 59	(Bankruptcy Act, 1914)	79, 280
	s. 30	277
	s. 31	117, 278
	s. 33	275-7, 280
	s. 36	277
	s. 38	79, 279
	s. 42	79, 277, 279
	s. 44	79, 279
	s. 52	447
	s. 63	277
	s. 66	277, 278
13 Geo. V, c. 2	(Irish Free State (Consequential Provisions) Act, 1922)	142

		PAGE
15 & 16 Geo. V, c. 18	(Settled Land Act, 1925)	257, 469, 512
	s. 11	431
	s. 16	470
	s. 75	383
	s. 107	470
15 & 16 Geo. V, c. 19	(Trustee Act, 1925)	5, 42, 159, 160, 326
	s. 1	161
	s. 23	106, 160
	s. 30	160
	s. 31	357
	s. 32	357
	s. 33	367
	s. 40	259
	s. 61	272
	s. 62	31
15 & 16 Geo. V, c. 20	(Law of Property Act, 1925)	12, 42, 166, 180, 184, 187, 317, 360, 394, 507
	s. 1	360
	s. 2	86
	s. 13	217
	s. 23	271
	s. 24	271
	s. 25	18, 271, 385
	s. 26	18, 271
	s. 27	271
	s. 28	271, 392
	s. 29-33	271
	s. 40	26, 182, 493, 502
	s. 41	83, 505
	s. 50	253
	s. 52	84
	s. 53	26, 120, 299
	s. 54	84
	s. 62	93
	s. 84	469
	s. 85	179, 236
	s. 86	179, 180
	s. 87	180
	s. 88	243, 250, 252
	s. 89	243, 250, 252
	s. 90	253
	s. 91	192, 246
	s. 92	250
	s. 93	197-9, 201
	s. 94	218, 221-2
	s. 95	191, 192
	s. 97	211, 212
	s. 98	81, 223-4
	s. 99	224-7, 242, 513
	s. 100	227, 513
	s. 101	232, 236, 239-40, 249-51, 513
	s. 102	250
	s. 103	250-1
	s. 104	251-2
	s. 105	256-7
	s. 106	250, 252, 253
	s. 107	250
	s. 109	240-2, 511, 513
	s. 110	240, 250
	s. 111	262
	s. 115	192, 193, 196
	s. 116	192, 261
	s. 135	80, 464
	s. 136	326
	s. 137	211, 303, 304, 307
	s. 141	223

		PAGE
15 & 16 Geo. V, c. 20	(Law of Property Act, 1925)	
	s. 146	88
	s. 152	228, 366
	s. 155	363
	s. 156	363
	s. 157	373-4
	s. 158	365, 366
	s. 159	366
	s. 169	447
	s. 170	445-6
	s. 174	354
	s. 175	290-1
	s. 185	81, 193
	s. 198	214
	s. 199	214-5
	s. 205	93, 102, 386
	1st sch.	236
15 & 16 Geo. V, c. 21	(Land Registration Act, 1925)	218, 222
	s 29	211
	s. 102	303
15 & 16 Geo. V, c. 22	(Land Charges Act, 1925)	12, 27-8, 108, 180, 211, 214
	s. 10	86, 209-10, 431, 469
	s. 13	86, 210, 212, 431, 469
	s. 14	210
	s. 20	212
	s. 22	211
15 & 16 Geo. V, c. 23	(Administration of Estates Act, 1925)	5, 263, 266-7, 279, 280, 285
	s. 1	267
	s. 4	267
	s. 7	268
	s. 9	267
	s. 12	268
	s. 28	268
	s. 32	268
	s. 33	269-70, 376
	s. 34	78-9, 275, 278, 281, 438
	s. 35	381
	s. 36	286
	s. 38	287
	s. 39	270-1
	s. 40	271
	s. 41	271-2
	s. 42	272
	s. 45	386
	s. 46	270, 376, 431
	s. 55	268, 269, 409
	1st sch.	78, 267, 275, 282, 283, 287, 438
	2nd sch.	277
15 & 16 Geo. V, c. 49	(Supreme Court of Judicature (Consolidation) Act, 1925)	
	s. 4	448
	ss. 36-40	76
	s. 41	76, 458
	ss. 42-3	76
	s. 44	76, 83, 538
	s. 45	111, 240, 464-5, 509
16 & 17 Geo. V, c. 7	(Bankruptcy (Amendment) Act, 1926)	
	s. 2	276
17 & 18 Geo V, c. 21	(Moneylenders Act, 1927)	
	s. 9	277
18 & 19 Geo. V, c. 26	(Administration of Justice Act, 1928)	
	s. 6	76

		PAGE
23 & 24 Geo. V, c. 36	(Administration of Justice (Miscellaneous Provisions) Act, 1933)	
	s. 6	453
24 & 25 Geo. V, c. 41	(Law Reform (Miscellaneous Provisions) Act, 1934)	82-3
	s. 1	277
25 & 26 Geo. V, c. 30	(Law Reform (Married Women and Tortfeasors) Act, 1935)	391, 446, 447
2 & 3 Geo. VI, c. 21	(Limitation Act, 1939)	
	s. 12	196
	s. 16	196
	s. 19	80
	s. 26	28-9, 105
8 & 9 Geo. VI, c. 28	(Law Reform (Contributory Negligence) Act, 1945	83
9 & 10 Geo. VI, c. 49	(Acquisition of Land (Authorisation Procedure) Act, 1946)	29
9 & 10 Geo. VI, c. 62	(National Insurance (Industrial Injuries) Act, 1946)	276
9 & 10 Geo. VI, c. 67	(National Insurance Act, 1946)	276
10 & 11 Geo. VI, c. 14	(Exchange Control Act, 1947)	278
10 & 11 Geo. VI, c. 47	(Companies Act, 1947)	
	s. 91	276
	s. 115	276
10 & 11 Geo. VI, c. 48	(Agriculture Act, 1947)	226
11 & 12 Geo. VI, c. 38	(Companies Act, 1948)	211
	s. 38	551
	s. 333	511
11 & 12 Geo. VI, c. 63	(Agricultural Holdings Act, 1948)	
	s. 23	233
	s. 95	226
	7th sch.	226
12, 13 & 14 Geo. VI, c. 78	(Married Women (Restraint upon Anticipation) Act, 1949)	391, 403, 447
15 & 16 Geo. VI & 1 Eliz. II, c. 64	(Intestates' Estates Act, 1952)	376
2 & 3 Eliz. II, c 34	(Law Reform (Enforcement of Contracts) Act, 1954)	26, 493
2 & 3 Eliz. II, c. 53	(Housing Repairs and Rents Act, 1954)	28-9
2 & 3 Eliz. II, c. 56	(Landlord and Tenant Act, 1954)	91-2
	s. 36	224, 226
4 & 5 Eliz. II, c. 74	(Copyright Act, 1956)	
	s. 17	474
5 & 6 Eliz II, c. 35	(Rent Act, 1957)	
	s. 16	234
6 & 7 Eliz. II, c. 53	(Variation of Trusts Act, 1958)	35, 161-2, 371
7 & 8 Eliz. II, c. 72	(Mental Health Act, 1959)	272
	s. 105	516
	s. 106	516
	s. 107	380
8 & 9 Eliz. II, c. 58	(Charities Act, 1960)	153, 158, 159
9 & 10 Eliz. II, c. 62	(Trustee Investments Act, 1961)	161
10 & 11 Eliz. II, c. 37	(Building Societies Act, 1962)	
	s. 36	254
	s. 37	192
1963, c. 44	(Wills Act 1963)	15, 394
1964, c. 55	(Perpetuities and Accumulations Act 1964)	
	s. 1	364
	s. 3	364
	s. 7	364
	s. 9	382
	s. 10	382
	s. 12	364
1965, c. 66	(Hire-Purchase Act 1965)	
	ss.27-9	20

		PAGE
1965, c. 66	(Hire-Purchase Act 1965)	
	ss. 43-5	20
1967, c. 7	(Misrepresentation Act 1967)	330
	s. 1	545, 546-7
	s. 2	545-6
	s. 3	546
	s. 4	547
1967, c. 75	(Matrimonial Homes Act 1967)	104
	s. 1	38
1967, c. 88	(Leasehold Reform Act 1967)	383

ACTS OF THE PARLIAMENT OF IRELAND

10 Hen. VII, c. 2	(Tenure of offices of chancellor, treasurer and judges) (1495)	132
10 Car. I, sess. 2, c. 1	(Statute of Uses, 1634)	130, 147, 359, 360
10 Car. I, sess. 2, c. 2	(Statute of Wills, 1634)	130, 148
	s. 16	440
10 Car. 1, sess. 2, c. 6	(Limitation Act, 1634)	104
10 Car. I, sess. 3, c. 1	(Statute of Charitable Uses, 1634)	154
7 Will III, c. 6	(Statute of Distributions, 1695)	
	s. 11	268
7 Will. III, c. 12	(Statute of Frauds, 1695)	26-7, 482, 497
	s. 1	84, 89
	s. 2	90, 182, 493
	s. 4	120
	s. 5	120
	s. 6	120, 299
9 Will. III, c. 3	(Marriages between Protestants and Papists) (1697)	137
4 Anne, c. 5	(Relief of creditors) (1705)	264
6 Anne, c. 2	(Registration of Deeds Act, 1707)	12, 28, 108, 218, 222
	s. 3	212
	s. 4	212
	s. 5	212
8 Anne, c. 3	(Growth of Popery) (1709)	
	s. 30	137

ACTS OF THE OIREACHTAS

1933, No. 36	(Moneylenders Act, 1933)	
	s. 16	277
1954, No. 30	(Exchange Control Act, 1954)	278
1957, No. 5	(Married Women's Status Act, 1957)	391, 445, 446, 447
	s. 6	391, 403
	s. 8	38, 486
1957, No. 6	(Statute of Limitations, 1957)	
	s. 34	196
	s. 35	196
	s. 43	80
	s. 44	80
	s. 71	28, 105
1958, No. 8	(Trustee (Authorised Investments) Act, 1958)	161
1959, No. 8	(Administration of Estates Act, 1959)	267
1961, No. 17	(Charities Act, 1961)	153, 158
	s. 49	38
1961, No. 38	(Courts (Establishment and Constitution) Act, 1961)	142
1961, No. 39	(Courts (Supplemental Provisions) Act, 1961)	142
1961, No. 41	(Civil Liability Act, 1961)	
	s. 10	277
1963, No. 10	(Copyright Act, 1963)	
	s. 22	474

		PAGE
1963 No. 33	(Companies Act, 1963)	
	s. 44	551
	s. 298	511
1964, No. 11	(Courts Act, 1964)	142
1965 No. 27	(Succession Act, 1965)	263, 267, 285, 394
	s. 1	267
	s. 10	269
	s. 11	376
	s. 13	367
	s. 16	267
	s. 19	268
	s. 23	268
	s. 45	268
	s. 46	78, 278, 281, 438, 439
	s. 47	277, 381
	s. 50	270
	s. 52	286
	s. 55	271
	s. 56	269
	s. 57	272
	s. 59	287
	s. 60	270
	s. 66	270, 376
	s. 67	431
	s. 78	27, 366
	s. 79	366
	s. 85	27
	ss. 102-8	15
	s. 111	431
	1st sch.	275, 282, 438

ACTS OF THE PARLIAMENT OF NORTHERN IRELAND

20 Geo. V, c. 1	(Bankruptcy Amendment Act, 1929)	
	s. 12	79, 277, 279
	s. 13	79, 279
	s. 18	447
23 & 24 Geo. V, c. 23	(Moneylenders Act, 1933)	
	s. 9	277
1 Edw. VIII & 1 Geo. VI, c. 9	(Law Reform (Miscellaneous Provisions) Act, 1937)	82, 267, 391, 446, 447
	s. 14	277
1946, c. 21	(National Insurance (Industrial Injuries) Act, 1946)	276
1946, c. 23	(National Insurance Act, 1946)	276
1948, c. 23	(Law Reform (Miscellaneous Provisions) Act, 1948)	83
1952, c. 19	(Married Women (Restraint upon Anticipation) Act, 1952)	391, 403, 447
1954, c. 26	(Law Reform (Miscellaneous Provisions) Act, 1954)	
	s. 1	26, 493
	s. 2	493
1955, c 24	(Administration of Estates Act, 1955)	263, 267, 285
	s. 1	267, 376
	s. 2	269
	s. 3	267
	s. 6	270, 376
	s. 7	431
	s. 29	268
	s. 30	78, 278, 281, 438
	s. 31	277, 381
	s. 32	270
	s. 34	286

		PAGE
1954 c. 24	(Administration of Estates Act, 1955)	
	s. 37	271
	s. 38	272
	s. 39	287
	s. 40	270
	s. 45	269
	1st sch.	275, 282, 438
1958, c. 10	(Statute of Limitations, 1958)	
	s. 36	196
	s. 37	196
	s. 44	80
	s. 45	80
	s. 70	28, 105
1958, c. 23	(Trustee Act, 1958)	
	s. 1	161
	s. 24	106, 160
	s. 31	160
	s. 32	357
	s. 33	357
	s. 34	367
	s. 39	259
	s. 57	35, 161
	s. 61	272
	s. 62	31
1960, c. 22	(Companies Act, 1960)	
	s. 38	551
	s. 299	511
1962, c. 10	(Trustee (Amendment) Act, 1962)	161
	s. 5	161
1964, c. 23	(Law Reform (Husband and Wife) Act 1964)	446
	s. 4	38
	s. 5	38, 486
	s. 6	38
1964, c. 32	(Preferential Payments (Bankruptcies and Arrangements) Act 1964)	276, 280
1964, c. 33	(Charities Act 1964)	153, 158
	s. 24	38, 42
1964, c. 36	(Business Tenancies Act 1964)	
	s. 17	224, 226
1966, c. 2	(Perpetuities Act 1966)	
	s. 1	364
	s. 3	364
	s. 7	364
	s. 9	382
	s. 10	382
	s. 13	364
	s. 14	364
1966, c. 42	(Hire Purchase Act 1966)	
	ss. 27-9	20
	ss. 43-5	20
1967, c. 14	(Misrepresentation Act 1967)	330, 545
	s. 1	547
	s. 4	547
1967, c. 30	(Registration of Deeds (Amendment) Act 1967)	
	s. 7	28
1967, c. 31	(Building Societies Act 1967)	
	s. 36	254

TABLE OF CASES

PAGE

Abbey National Building Soc., *Ex parte—see* R. *v.* Briant (Judge Dutton); R. *v.* Willes (Judge).

Abbott *v.* Stratten (1846), 3 Jo. & Lat. 603; *sub. nom.* Abbott *v.* Stratton, 9 Ir. Eq. Rep. 233; 72 R.R. 136 184

Abdeen (Abdul Cader) *v.* Thaheer (Abdul Careem Mohamed), [1958] A.C. 116; [1958] 2 W.L.R. 350; 102 S.J. 159 491

Ackroyd *v.* Smithson (1780), 1 Bro. C.C. 503; 28 E.R. 1262; [1775-1802] All E.R. Rep. 227; *sub nom.* Akeroid *v.* Smithson, Dick. 566; 21 E.R. 390; 3 P. Wms. 22n; 24 E.R. 953 . . . . 65, 386, 387-8

Adam *v.* Newbigging—*see* Newbigging *v.* Adam.

Adams *v.* Andrews (1850), 15 Q.B. 284; 117 E.R. 466; 20 L.J.Q.B. 33; 15 L.T.O.S. 499; *sub nom.* Andrews *v.* Adams, 15 Jur. 149 . . 98

Adams *v.* Angell (1877), 5 Ch.D. 634; 46 L.J.Ch. 54, 352; 36 L.T. 334 . 195

Adams *v.* Weare (1784), 1 Bro. C.C. 567; 28 E.R. 1301 501

Adlard, *Re,* Taylor *v.* Adlard, [1954] Ch. 29; [1953] 3 W.L.R. 914; [1953] 2 All E.R. 1437; 97 S.J. 814 309

Adney *v.* Field (1767), Amb. 654; 27 E.R. 425 366

Agra and Masterman's Bank, *Re, Ex parte* Asiatic Banking Corp. (1867), L.R. 2 Ch. App. 391; 36 L.J.Ch. 222; 16 L.T. 162; 15 W.R. 414 . 308

Agra Bank Ltd. *v.* Barry (1874), L.R. 7 H.L. 135 28

Ahearn *v.* Ahearn (1910), 45 I.L.T.R. 28 334

Ahearne *v.* Hogan (1844), Dru. t. Sug. 310 341

Akeroid *v.* Smithson—*see* Ackroyd *v.* Smithson.

Alcock, *Re,* Prescott *v.* Phipps (1883), 23 Ch.D. 372; 49 L.T. 240 . . 189

Alder *v.* Moore, [1961] 2 Q.B. 57; [1961] 2 W.L.R. 426; [1961] 1 All E.R. 1; 105 S.J. 280; [1960] 2 Lloyd's R. 325 19

Alder *v.* Ward (1843), 5 Ir. Eq. Rep. 367 . . . . . 560, 561

Alderson *v.* White (1858), 2 De G. & J. 97; 44 E.R. 924; 30 L.T.O.S. 297; 4 Jur. N.S. 125; 6 W.R. 242; 119 R.R. 38 179

Aldrich *v.* Cooper (1803), 8 Ves. 382; 32 E.R. 402; [1803-13] All E.R. Rep. 51; 7 R.R. 86 433

Aldridge *v.* Duke (1679), Rep. t. Finch 439; 23 E.R. 239 214

Aldridge *v.* Forbes (1839), 9 L.J. Ch. 37; 4 Jur. 20; 52 R.R. 243 . . 436

Alexander *v.* Crosbie (1835), Ll. & G. t. Sug. 145 530

Alison, *Re,* Johnson *v.* Mounsey (1879), 11 Ch. D. 284; 40 L.T. 234; 27 W.R. 537 179

Allan *v.* Allan (1808), 15 Ves. 130; 33 E.R. 704 556

Allcard *v.* Skinner (1887), 36 Ch.D. 145; 56 L.J.Ch. 1052; 58 L.T. 61; 36 W.R. 251; 3 T.L.R. 751; [1886-90] All E.R. Rep. 90 . 33, 337-8, 342

Allen, *Ex parte, Ex parte* Page, *Re* Middleton (1870), L.R. 11 Eq. 209; 40 L.J. Bcy. 17; 19 W.R. 274 302-3

Allen (Samuel) & Sons Ltd., *Re,* [1907] 1 Ch. 575; 76 L.J.Ch. 362; 96 L.T. 660; 14 Mans. 144; [1904-7] All E.R. Rep. 785 213

Allen's Estate, *Re,* Prescott *v.* Allen & Beaumont, [1945] 2 All E.R. 264; 114 L.J.Ch. 298; 173 L.T. 198; 89 S.J. 316 . . . . 400, 409-10

Alley *v.* Deschamps (1806), 13 Ves. 225; 33 E.R. 278 486

Allhusen *v.* Brooking (1884), 26 Ch.D. 559; 53 L.J Ch. 520; 51 L.T. 57; 32 W.R. 657 87

Alliance Bank Ltd. *v.* Broom (1864), 2 Dr. & Sm. 289; 62 E.R. 631; 5 New R. 69; 34 L.J.Ch. 256; 11 L.T. 332; 10 Jur. N.S. 1121; 13 W.R 127; 143 R.R. 120 185

Alliance Building Soc. *v.* Pinwill, [1958] Ch. 788; [1958] 3 W.L.R. 1; [1958] 2 All E.R. 408; 102 S.J. 455 234

Allison *v.* Clayhills (1907), 97 L.J. 709; [1904-7] All E.R. Rep. 500 . . 339-40

Alston, *Ex parte, Re* Holland (1868), L.R. 4 Ch. App. 168; 19 L.T. 542; 17 W.R. 266 438

Alston, *Re,* Sinclair *v.* Willes, [1917] 2 Ch. 226; 86 L.J.Ch. 564; 117 L.T. 222; 33 T.L.R. 410; 61 S.J. 525 380

PAGE

Amalgamated Soc. of Railway Servants *v.* Osborne, [1910] A.C. 87; 79 L.J.Ch. 87; 101 L.T. 787; 26 T.L.R. 177; 54 S.J. 215; [1908-10] All E.R. Rep. 368 . . . 477
Anderson *v.* Stather (1845), 2 Coll. 209; 63 E.R. 702; 14 L.J.Ch. 377; 5 L.T.O.S. 368; 9 Jur. 806 . . . 245
Anderson-Berry, *Re*, Harris *v.* Griffith, [1928] Ch. 290; 97 L.J.Ch. 111; 138 L.T. 354; [1927] All E.R. Rep. 143 . . . 558
Andrews *v.* Adams—*see* Adams *v.* Andrews.
Andrews *v.* City Permanent Benefit Building Soc. (1881), 44 L.T. 641 . 201
Angel *v.* Jay, [1911] 1 K.B. 666; 80 L.J.K.B. 458; 103 L.T. 809; 55 S.J. 140; [1908-10] All E.R. Rep 470 . . . 546
Angell *v.* Angell (1822), 1 Sim. & St. 83; 57 E.R. 33; 1 L.J.O.S. Ch. 6; 24 R.R. 149 . . . 555-6
Anglo Auto Finance Co. Ltd. *v.* James, [1963] 1 W.L.R. 1042; [1963] 3 All E.R. 566; 107 S.J. 534 . . . 20
Annesley *v.* Annesley (1893), 31 L.R.Ir. 457 . . . 531
Anon. (1313-14), Y.B. 6 & 7 Edw. II, 29 Sel. Soc. 85 . . . 167
Anon. (1679), 2 Ch. Cas. 4; 22 E.R. 819 . . . 65
Anon. (1682), 1 Vern. 45; 23 E.R. 298 . . . 235
Anon. (1687)—*see* Gale *v.* Lindo.
Anon. (1701)—*see* Jory *v.* Cox.
Anon. (1705)—*see* Toller *v.* Carteret.
Anon. (1729), Mos. 248; 25 E.R. 377 . . . 172
Anon. (1741), 2 Atk. 210; 26 E.R. 530 . . . 560
Anon. (1748), 1 Atk. 521; 26 E.R. 329 . . . 561
Anon. (unrep.), cit. (1780), Dougl. 384; 99 E.R. 247 . . . 531
Anon. (1797), 3 Ves. 515; 30 E.R. 1134 . . . 516
Anstis, *Re*, Chetwynd *v.* Morgan (1886), 31 Ch.D. 596; 54 L.T. 742; 34 W.R. 483; 2 T.L.R. 335 . . . 366
Antrim County Land, Building, and Investment Co. Ltd. *v.* Stewart, [1904] 2 I.R. 357; 37 I.L.T.R. 95, 101; 3 N.I.J.R. 137, 236 . 231, 247
Archbold *v.* Lord Howth (1866), 1 I.L.T. 760 . . . 89
Archer *v.* Preston (prior to 1682), 1 Eq. Cas. Abr. 133, pl. 3; 21 E.R. 938; 1 Vern. 77 n.; 23 E.R. 323 . . . 14
Archer's Estate, *Re*, [1914] 1 I.R. 285; 49 I.L.T.R. 82 . . . 437
Ardglasse (Earl of) *v.* Muschamp (1682-4), 1 Vern. 75, 135, 237; 23 E.R. 322, 369, 438; *sub nom.* Ardglas (Earl) *v.* Muschampe, 2 Ch. Rep. 266; 21 E.R. 675 . . . 136
Argyll (Duchess of) *v* Duke of Argyll, [1967] Ch. 302; [1965] 2 W.L.R. 790; [1965] 1 All E.R. 611 . . . 31-2, 461
Armitage *v.* Metcalf (1666), 1 Ch. Cas. 74; 22 E.R. 701 . . . 65
Armstrong *v.* Armstrong (1873), I.R. 8 Eq. 1 . . . 345, 351
Arnold, *Re*, Arnold *v.* Arnold (1880), 14 Ch.D. 270; 42 L.T. 705; 28 W.R. 635 . . . 507
Ascherson *v.* Tredegar Dry Dock and Wharf Co. Ltd., [1909] 2 Ch. 401; 78 L.J.Ch. 697; 101 L.T. 519; 16 Mans. 318; [1908-10] All E.R. Rep. 510 . . . 558
Ash *v.* Abdy (1678), 3 Swanst. 664; 36 E.R. 1014 . . . 54
Ashburner *v.* Macguire (1786), 2 Bro. C.C. 108; 29 E.R. 62 . . . 288
Ashby *v.* Palmer (1816), 1 Mer. 296; 35 E.R. 684; 15 R.R. 116 . . . 393
Ashton, *Re*, Ingram *v.* Papillon, [1897] 2 Ch. 574; 66 L.J.Ch. 731; 77 L.T. 49; 46 W.R. 138; 41 S.J. 677 . . . 419
Ashton *v.* Corrigan (1871), L.R. 13 Eq. 76; 41 L.J.Ch. 96 . . . 185
Ashworth *v.* Munn (1880), 15 Ch.D. 363; 50 L.J.Ch. 107; 43 L.T. 553; 28 W.R. 965 . . . 377
Asiatic Banking Corp., *Ex parte*—*see* Agra and Masterman's Bank, *Re*.
Aslatt *v.* Southampton Corp. (1880), 16 Ch. D. 143; 50 L.J. Ch. 31; 43 L.T. 464; 45 J.P. 111; 29 W.R. 117 . . . 112
Assemblers Ltd., *Application of*—*see* Nolan, *Re*.
Associated Distributors Ltd. *v.* Hall, [1938] 2 K.B. 83; [1938] 1 All E.R. 511; 107 L.J.K.B. 701; 158 L.T. 236; 54 T.L.R. 433; 82 S.J. 136 21-2, 23, 24
Atkins *v.* Hill (1775), 1 Cowp. 284; 98 E.R. 1088 . . . 64
Atkinson *v.* Leonard (1791), 3 Bro. C.C. 218; 29 E.R. 499 . . . 560
Atkinson *v.* Webb (1704), 2 Vern. 478; 23 E.R. 907; Prec. Ch. 236; 24 E.R. 115; 1 Eq. Cas. Abr. 203, pl. 3; 21 E.R. 991 . . . 415

PAGE

Attenborough & Son *v.* Solomon, [1913] A.C. 76 ; 82 L.J. Ch. 178 ; 107 L.T. 833 ; 29 T.L.R. 79 ; 57 S.J. 76 ; [1911-13] All E.R. Rep. 155 . 286
Attorney-General *v.* Ailesbury (Marquis of) (1887), 12 App. Cas. 672 ; 57 L.J.Q.B. 83 ; 58 L.T. 192 ; 36 W.R. 737 ; 3 T.L.R. 830 . 378-9, 391
Attorney-General *v.* Ashborne Recreation Ground Co., [1903] 1 Ch. 101 ; 72 L.J.Ch. 67 ; 87 L.T. 561 ; 67 J.P. 73 ; 51 W.R. 125 ; 19 T.L.R. 39 ; 47 S.J. 50 ; 1 L.G.R. 146 480
Attorney-General *v.* Bastow, [1957] 1 Q.B. 514 ; [1957] 2 W.L.R. 340 ; [1957] 1 All E.R. 497 ; 121 J.P. 171 ; 101 S.J. 192 ; 55 L.G.R. 122 . 480
Attorney-General (at the relation of Tamworth Corp.) *v.* Birmingham, Tame and Rea Drainage Board, [1910] 1 Ch. 48 ; 79 L.J.Ch. 137 ; 101 L.T. 796 ; 74 J.P. 57 ; 26 T.L.R. 93 ; 54 S.J. 198 ; 8 L.G.R. 110 ; [1911-13] All E.R. Rep. 926 480
Attorney-General *v.* Harris, [1960] 1 Q.B. 31 ; [1959] 3 W.L.R. 205 ; [1959] 2 All E.R. 393 ; *on appeal*, [1961] 1 Q.B. 74 ; [1960] 3 W.L.R. 532 ; [1960] 3 All E.R. 207 ; 104 S.J. 704 ; 58 L.G.R. 242 480
Attorney-General *v.* Jackson, [1932] A.C. 365 ; 48 T.L.R. 261 ; 76 S.J. 146 ; [1932] All E.R. Rep. 936 ; *sub nom. Re* Cockell, A.-G. *v* Jackson, 101 L.J.Ch. 186 ; [1931] B. & C.R. 167 ; *sub nom. Re* Cockell, Jackson *v.* A.-G., 146 L.T. 450 ; 16 T.C. 681 . . . . 79, 281
Attorney-General *v.* Morgan (1826), 2 Russ. 306 ; 38 E.R. 351 ; 26 R.R. 81 554
Attorney-General *v.* Newry No. 1 R.D.C., [1933] N.I. 50 . . . 466
Attorney-General *v.* P.Y.A. Quarries Ltd., [1957] 2 Q.B. 169 ; [1957] 2 W.L.R. 770 ; [1957] 1 All E.R. 894 ; 121 J.P. 323 ; 101 S.J. 338 ; 55 L.G.R. 208 465
Attorney-General (Boswell) *v.* Rathmines & Pembroke Joint Hospital Board, [1904] 1 I.R. 161 460
Attorney-General *v.* Sharp, [1931] 1 Ch. 121 ; 99 L.J.Ch. 441 ; 143 L.T. 367 ; 94 J.P. 234 ; 46 T.L.R. 554 ; 74 S.J. 504 ; 28 L.G.R. 513 ; [1930] All E.R. Rep. 741 479
Attorney-General *v.* Smith, [1958] 2 Q.B. 173 ; [1958] 3 W.L.R. 81 ; [1958] 2 All E.R. 557 ; 122 J.P. 367 ; 102 S.J. 490 ; 56 L.G.R. 295 . . 480
Attorney-General *v.* Wimbledon House Estate Co. Ltd., [1904] 2 Ch. 34 ; 73 L.J.Ch. 593 ; 91 L.T. 163 ; 68 J.P. 341 ; 20 T.L.R. 489 ; 2 L.G.R.826 . 480
Attorney-General for Newfoundland *v.* Newfoundland Railway Co.—*see* Newfoundland (Government of) *v.* Newfoundland Railway Co.
Attwood *v.* Lamont, [1920] 3 K.B. 571 ; 90 L.J.K.B. 121 ; 124 L.T. 108 ; 36 T.L.R. 895 ; 65 S.J. 25 ; [1920] All E.R. Rep. 55 471-2
Austerberry *v.* Oldham Corp. (1885), 29 Ch.D. 750 ; 55 L.J.Ch. 633 ; 53 L.T. 543; 49 J.P. 532 ; 33 W.R. 807 ; 1 T.L.R. 473 467
Australian Hardwoods Pty Ltd. *v.* Commissioner for Railways, [1961] 1 W.L.R. 425 ; [1961] 1 All E.R. 737 ; 105 S.J. 176 484
Aylesford (Earl of) *v.* Morris (1873), L.R. 8 Ch. App. 484 ; 42 L.J.Ch. 546 ; 28 L.T. 541 ; 37 J.P. 227 ; 21 W.R. 424 ; [1861-73] All E.R. Rep. 300 60, 354-5
Ayliffe *v.* Murray (1740), 2 Atk. 58 ; 26 E.R. 433 341
Aynsley, *Re*, Kyrle *v.* Turner, [1914] 2 Ch. 422 ; 83 L.J.Ch. 807 ; 111 L.T. 525 ; 30 T.L.R. 664 ; *on appeal*, [1915] 1 Ch. 172 ; 84 L.J.Ch. 211 ; 112 L.T. L.T. 433 ; 31 T.L.R. 101 ; 59 S.J. 128 425

Bache *v.* Proctor (1780), Dougl. 382 ; 99 E.R. 247 533
Bacon *v.* Vesey (1677/8), Nottingham's Chancery Cases, 79 Sel. Soc. 660 (case 838) 176
Baden's Deed Trusts, *Re*, Baden *v.* Smith, [1969] 3 W.L.R. 12 ; [1969] 1 All E.R. 1016 ; 113 S.J. 149 363
Baglioni *v.* Cavalli (1900), 83 L.T. 500 ; 49 W.R. 236 ; 45 S.J. 78 . . 435
Bagnall, *Re*, Scale *v.* Willett, [1949] L.J.R. 1 ; 92 S.J. 485 428
Bagnall *v.* Villar (1879), 12 Ch.D. 812 ; 48 L.J.Ch. 695 ; 28 W.R. 242 . 230
Bagnell *v.* Edwards (1876), I.R. 10 Eq. 215 488
Bailey *v.* Barnes, [1894] 1 Ch. 25 ; 63 L. J. Ch. 73 ; 69 L.T. 542; 42 W.R. 66 ; 38 S.J. 9 ; 7 R. 9 219
Baillie *v.* Butterfield (1787), 1 Cox C.C 392 ; 29 E.R. 1217 427
Bainbridge *v.* Smith (1889), 41 Ch.D. 462 ; 60 L.T. 879 ; 37 W.R. 594 ; 5 T L.R. 375 476
Bains *v.* Tweddle, [1959] Ch. 679 ; [1959] 3 W.L.R. 291 ; [1959] 2 All E.R. 724 ; 103 S.J. 563 543

PAGE

Baker v. Monk (1864), 4 De G. J. & S. 388 ; 46 E.R. 968 ; 10 Jur. N.S. 691 ; 12 W.R. 779 ; 146 R.R. 361 335
Baker v. Paine (1750), 1 Ves. Sen. 456 ; 27 E.R. 1140 530
Baldwin v. Belcher (1842), 3 Dr. & War. 173 ; 61 R.R. 39 ; *sub nom. Re* Cornwall, 2 Con. & L. 131 ; 6 Ir. Eq. Rep. 65 433
Baldwin v. Roche (1842), 5 Ir. Eq. Rep. 110 373
Ballman, *Re—see* Garland, *Ex parte*.
Bamfield v. Vaughan (1675), Nottingham's Chancery Cases, 73 Sel. Soc. 183 (case 270) 168
Bank of Montreal v Stuart, [1911] A.C. 120 ; 80 L.J.P.C. 75 ; 103 L.T. 641 ; 27 T.L.R. 117 . . . . 345, 348
Bank of New South Wales v. O'Connor (1889), 14 App. Cas. 273 ; 58 L.J.P.C. 82 ; 60 L T. 467 ; 38 W.R. 465 ; 5 T.L.R. 342 ; [1886-90] All E.R. Rep. 672 188
Bankrupt (*Ex parte* The Trustee of the Property of the) v. Solomon—*see* Solomon, *Re* ; Trytel, *Re*.
Banks v. Ripley, [1940] Ch. 719 ; [1940] 3 All E.R. 49 ; 109 L.J.Ch. 345 ; 163 L.T. 419 ; 56 T.L.R. 731 ; 84 S.J. 358 532
Bannatyne v. MacIver, [1906] 1 K.B. 103 ; 75 L.J.K B. 120 ; 94 L.T. 150 ; 54 W.R. 293 ; [1904-7] All E.R. Rep. 425 115
Bannister v. Bannister, [1948] 2 All E.R. 133 ; 92 S.J. 377 27
Bannon (No. 2), *Re*, Callanan v. Ryan, [1934] I.R. 701 422
Banque Belge pour l'Etranger v. Hambrouck, [1921] 1 K.B. 321 ; 90 L.J.K.B. 322 ; 37 T.L.R. 76 ; 65 S.J 74 ; 25 Com. Cas. 72 . . 10
Barclays Bank Ltd. v. Bird, [1954] Ch. 274 ; [1954] 2 W.L.R. 319 ; [1954] 1 All E.R. 449 ; 98 S.J. 145 . . . . . . 104, 213, 231
Barclay's Bank Ltd. v. Kiley, [1961] 1 W.L.R. 1050 ; [1961] 2 All E.R. 849 ; 105 S.J. 569 229
Barclay's Bank Ltd. v. Quistclose Investments Ltd., [1968] 3 W.L.R. 1097 ; [1968] 3 All E.R. 651 ; 112 S.J. 903 521
Barclays Bank Ltd. v. Stasek, [1957] Ch. 28 ;]1956] 3 W.L.R. 760 ; [1956] 3 All E.R. 439 ; 100 S.J. 800 229-30
Barker, *Re* (1881), 17 Ch.D. 241 ; 50 L.J.Ch. 334 ; 44 L.T. 33 ; 29 W.R. 873 380
Barker v. Illingworth, [1908] 2 Ch. 20 ; 77 L.J.Ch. 581 ; L.T. 187 . . 250
Barnardo's (Dr.) Homes National Incorporated Assoc. v. Commissioners for Special Purposes of the Income Tax Acts, [1921] 2 A.C. 1 ; 90 L.J.K.B. 545 ; 125 L.T. 250 ; 37 T.L.R. 540 ; 65 S.J. 433 ; *sub nom.* R. v. Income Tax Acts Special Purposes Commissioners, *Ex parte* Barnardo's Homes National Incorporated Assoc., 7 T.C. 646 286
Barnes v. Racster (1842), 1 Y. & C.C.C. 401 ; 62 E.R. 944 ; 11 L.J. Ch. 228 ; 6 Jur. 595 ; 57 R.R. 401 . . . . 435, 436, 437
Barnhart v. Greenshields (1853), 9 Moo. P.C. 18 ; 14 E.R. 204 ; 2 Eq. R. 1217 ; L.T.O.S. 178 ; 105 R.R. 1 179
Barr's Contract, *Re*, Moorwell Buildings Ltd. v. Barr, [1956] Ch. 551 ; [1956] 1 W L.R. 918 ; [1956] 2 All E.R. 853 ; 100 S.J. 550 . . 505
Barratt v. Gough-Thomas, [1951] 2 All E.R. 48 ; [1951] 2 T.L.R. 106 ; [1951] W.N. 309 ; 95 S.J. 381 188
Barrell v. Sabine (1684), 1 Vern. 268 ; 23 E.R. 462 171
Barret v. Beckford (1750), 1 Ves. Sen. 519 ; 27 E.R. 1179 415
Barrow v. Isaacs & Son, [1891] 1 Q.B. 417 ; 60 L.J. Q.B. 179 ; 64 L.T. 686 ; 55 J.P. 517 ; 39 W.R. 338 ; 7 T.L.R. 175 547
Barton v. Bank of New South Wales (1890), 15 App. Cas. 379 . . . 179
Barton Thompson & Co. Ltd. v. Stapling Machines Co., [1966] Ch. 499 ; [1966] 2 W.L.R. 1429 ; [1966] 2 All E.R. 222 25
Bassett v. Nosworthy (1673), Rep. t. Finch 102 ; 23 E.R. 55 . . . 120
Battersby's Estate, *Re* (1887), 19 L.R. Ir. 359 417-18
Baxter v. Conolly (1820), 1 Jac. & W. 576 ; 37 E.R. 487 . . . 492
Baxter v. Manning (1684), 1 Vern. 244 ; 23 E.R. 441 62
Baxter v. West (1858), 28 L.J.Ch. 169 ; 32 L.T. O.S. 155 ; 118 R.R. 811 . 509
Baynham v. Baynham, [1968] 1 W.L.R. 1890 ; [1969] 1 All E.R. 305 ; 112 S.J. 839 104
Beaman v. A.R.T.S. Ltd., [1949] 1 K.B. 550 ; [1949] 1 All E.R. 465 ; 65 T.L.R. 389 ; 93 S.J. 236 28
Beanland v. Bradley (1854), 2 Sm. & G. 339 ; 65 E.R. 427 ; 2 W.R. 602 ; 97 R.R. 228 345

PAGE

Bearcroft *v.* Geery—*see* Geary *v.* Bearcroft.
Beauchamp (Earl) *v.* Winn (1873), L.R. 6 H.L. 223 550
Beauclerk *v.* Duke of St. Albans—*see* St. Albans (Duke of) *v.* Beauclerk.
Beaumont's Trusts, *Re* (1863), 32 Beav. 191 ; 55 E.R. 75 385
Beckett *v.* Cordley (1784), 1 Bro. C.C. 353 ; 28 E.R. 1174 213
Beckford *v.* Kemble (1822), 1 Sim. & St. 7 ; 57 E.R. 3 ; 24 R.R. 143 . 14
Beckley *v.* Newland (1723), 2 P. Wms. 182 ; 24 E.R. 691 . . 356, 487
Beddoes *v.* Shaw, [1937] Ch. 81 ; [1936] 2 All E.R. 1108 ; 106 L.J. Ch. 4 ; 155 L.T. 348 ; 80 S.J. 594 211
Beesty's Will Trusts, *Re*, Farrar *v.* Royal Alfred Merchant Seamen's Soc., [1966] Ch. 223 ; [1964] 3 W.L.R. 689 ; [1964] 3 All E.R. 82 ; 108 S.J. 481 374
Beetham, *Re*—*see* Broderick, *Ex parte.*
Belchier *v.* Renforth (1764), 5 Bro. P.C. 292 ; 2 E.R. 686 173
Bell *v.* Cundall (1750), Amb. 101 ; 27 E.R. 63 530
Bellasis *v.* Uthwatt (1737), 1 Atk. 426 ; 26 E.R. 271 ; West t. Hard. 273 ; 25 E.R. 934 ; *sub. nom.* Billingsley *v.* Eckershall, 2 Eq. Cas. Abr. 570, pl. 2 22 E.R. 481 . . . .; 420
Bellew *v.* Russel (1809), 1 Ba. & B. 96 351-2
Belton *v.* Bass, Ratcliffe and Gretton Ltd., [1922] 2 Ch. 449 ; 91 L.J. Ch. 216 ; 127 L.T. 357 . . . . 253, 257
Bendall *v.* McWhirter, [1952] 2 Q.B. 466 ; [1952] 1 All E.R. 1307 ; [1952] 1 T.L.R. 1332 ; 96 S.J. 344 . . . . 37, 103, 470
Bengough *v.* Walker (1808), 15 Ves. 507 ; 33 E.R. 847 ; 10 R.R. 106 . . 421
Bennet *v* . Davis (1725), 2 P. Wms. 316 ; 24 E.R. 746 . . . 151-2
Bennet *v.* Vade ; Bennet *v.* Wade—*see* Bennet *v.* Wade.
Bennett *v.* Bennett, [1952] 1 K.B. 249 ; [1952] 1 All E.R. 413 ; [1952] 1 T.L.R. 400 490
Bennett *v.* Vade (1742), 9 Mod. 312 ; 88 E.R. 474 ; *sub nom.* Bennett *v.* Vade, 2 Atk. 324 ; 26 E.R. 597 ; *sub nom.* Bennet *v.* Wade, Dick. 84 ; 21 E.R. 200 348
Bentley *v.* Mackay (1862), 4 De G. F. & J. 279 ; 45 E.R. 1191 ; 31 L.J. Ch. 697 ; 7 L.T. 143 ; 8 Jur. N.S. 1001 ; 10 W.R. 873 ; 135 R.R. 145 . . 537
Beresford *v.* A.-G., [1918] P. 33 ; 87 L.J.P. 40 ; 118 L.T. 133 ; 34 T.L.R. 100 ; 62 S.J. 103 556
Bernard's (Lord) Case—*see* Vane *v.* Lord Barnard.
Berrey's Will Trusts, *Re*, Greening *v.* Waters, [1959] 1 W.L.R. 30 ; [1959] 1 All E.R. 15 ; 103 S.J. 34 283
Berry *v.* Berry, [1929] 2 K.B. 316 ; 98 L.J.K.B. 748 ; 141 L.T. 461 ; 45 T.L.R. 524 ; [1929] All E.R. Rep. 281 . . . . . 121-2, 123
Berwick & Co. *v.* Price, [1905] 1 Ch. 632 ; 74 L.J. Ch. 249 ; 92 L.T. 110 213, 215
Berwick upon Tweed Corp. *v.* Oswald (1853), 1 E. & B. 295 ; 118 E.R. 447 ; 22 L.J.Q.B. 129 ; 20 L.T.O.S. 306 ; 17 J.P. 230 ; 17 Jur. 1148 . . 120
Beswick *v.* Beswick, [1966] Ch. 538 ; [1966] 3 W.L.R. 396 ; [1966] 3 All E.R. 1 ; 110 S.J. 507 ; *on appeal*, [1968] A.C. 57 ; [1967] 3 W.L.R. 932 ; [1967] 2 All E.R. 1197 ; 111 S.J. 540 . . . . . .38, 486
Bettesworth *v.* Dean and Chapter of St. Paul's (1728), 1 Bro. P. C. 240 ; 1 E.R. 541 482
Bettyes *v.* Maynard (1883), 49 L.T. 389 ; 31 W.R. 461 . . 253, 257
Bewick, *Re*, Ryle *v.* Ryle, [1911] 1 Ch. 116 ; 80 L.J. Ch. 47 ; 103 L.T. 634 ; 55 S.J. 109 387
Beynon *v.* Cook (1875), L.R. 10 Ch. App. 389 ; 32 L.T. 353 ; 23 W.R. 531 355
Biddulph *v.* Lord Camoys (1855), 20 Beav. 402 ; 52 E.R. 658 . . 556
Biel's Estate, *Re*, Gray *v.* Warner (1873), L.R. 16 Eq. 577 ; 42 L.J. Ch. 556 ; 28 L.T. 835 ; 21 W.R. 808 341
Biggerstaff *v.* Rowatt's Wharf Ltd., [1896] 2 Ch. 93 ; 65 L.J. Ch. 536 ; 74 L.T. 473 ; 44 W.R. 536 308
Biggs *v.* Hoddinott, [1898] 2 Ch. 307 ; 67 L.J. Ch. 540 ; 79 L.T. 201 ; 47 W.R. 84 ; 14 T.L.R. 504 ; [1895-9] All E.R. Rep. 625 208
Billage *v.* Southee (1852), 9 Hare 534 ; 68 E.R. 623 ; 89 R.R. 654 ; *sub nom.* Billing *v.* Southee, 21 L.J. Ch. 472 ; 16 Jur. 188 341
Billingsby *v.* Eckershall—*see* Bellasis *v.* Uthwatt.
Bilston Corp. *v.* Wolverhampton Corp., [1942] Ch. 391 ; [1942] 2 All E.R. 447 ; 111 L.J. Ch. 268 ; 167 L.T. 61 ; 106 J.P. 181 ; 40 L.G.R. 167 . 480-1
Birmingham and District Land Co. *v.* London and North Western Railway Co. (1888), 40 Ch. D. 268 ; 60 L.T. 527 ; [1886-90] All E.R. Rep. 620 . 124

PAGE

Birmingham Citizens Permanent Building Soc. *v.* Caunt, [1962] Ch. 883 ; [1962] 2 W.L.R. 323 ; [1962] 1 All E.R. 163 ; 106 S.J. 96 230

Biss *v.* Hygate, [1918] 2 K.B. 314 ; 87 L.J.K.B. 1101 ; 119 L.T. 284 . . 495

Blackburn Building Soc. *v.* Cunliffe, Brooks & Co. (1882), 22 Ch.D. 61 ; 52 L.J. Ch. 92 ; 48 L.T. 33 ; 31 W.R. 98 115

Blake, *Re*—*see* Steward, *Ex parte.*

Blake *v.* Foster (1813), 2 Ba. & B. 387 169

Blakely *v.* Brady (1839), 2 Dr. & Wal 311 ; 56 R.R. 240 . . . 312

Blakely, *Ex parte*—*see* Threlfall, *Re.*

Blandy *v.* Widmore (1715), 1 P. Wms. 324 ; 24 E.R. 408, 2 Eq. Cas. Abr. 352, pl. 11 ; 22 E.R. 300 ; 2 Vern. 709 ; 23 E.R. 1066 . . . 431

Blest *v.* Brown (1862), 4 De G. F. & J. 367 ; 45 E.R. 1225 ; 6 L.T. 620 ; 8 Jur. N.S. 602 ; 10 W.R. 569 ; 135 R.R. 188 552

Bligh *v.* Martin, [1968] 1 W.L.R. 804 ; [1968] 1 All E.R. 1157 ; 112 S.J. 189 349

Blundell, *Re*, Blundell *v.* Blundell, [1906] 2 Ch. 222 ; 75 L.J. Ch. 561 ; 94 L.T. 818 ; 22 T.L.R. 570 420

Boards, *Re*, Knight *v.* Knight, [1895] 1 Ch. 499 ; 64 L.J. Ch. 305 ; 72 L.T. 220 ; 43 W.R. 472 ; 13 R. 278 ; [1895-9] All E.R. Rep. 994 . . . 287

Boazman *v.* Johnston (1830), 3 Sim. 377 ; 57 E.R. 1039 ; 30 R.R. 172 . 435

Bodenham *v.* Halle (1456), 10 Sel. Soc. (Sel. Cas. in Ch. 1364-1471) 137 (case 141) 168

Bolton Building Soc. *v.* Cobb, [1966] 1 W.L.R. 1 ; [1965] 3 All E.R. 814 ; 109 S.J. 852 228

Bond *v.* Hopkins (1802), 1 Sch. & Lef. 413 68

Bonham *v.* Newcomb—*see* Newcomb *v.* Bonham.

Bonhote *v.* Henderson, [1895] 1 Ch. 742 ; [1895] 2 Ch. 202 ; 72 L.T. 814 ; 43 W.R. 580 531

Bonithon *v.* Hockmore (1685), 1 Vern. 316 ; 23 E.R. 492 ; 1 Eq. Cas. Abr. 7, pl. 1 ; 21 E.R. 833 241

Bonnard *v.* Perryman, [1891] 2 Ch. 269 ; 60 L.J. Ch. 617 ; 65 L.T 506 ; 39 W.R. 435 ; 7 T.L.R. 453 ; [1891-4] All E.R. Rep. 965 . . . 462

Bonsor *v.* Musicians' Union, [1956] A.C. 104 ; [1955] 3 W.L.R. 788 ; [1955] 3 All E.R. 518 ; 99 S.J. 814 478

Borman *v.* Griffith ,[1930] 1 Ch. 493 ; 99 L.J. Ch. 295 ; 142 L.T. 645 . 92-3

Borrowes *v.* Delaney (1889), 24 L.R. Ir. 503 531

Borthwick *v.* Evening Post (1888), 37 Ch.D. 449 ; 57 L.J. Ch. 406 ; 58 L.T. 252 ; 36 W.R. 434 ; 4 T.L.R. 234 474

Bosanquett *v.* Dashwood (1734), Cas t. Talb. 38 ; 25 E.R. 648 . . 113

Bosworthick *v.* Bosworthick, [1927] P. 64 ; 95 L.J.P. 171 ; 136 L.T. 211 ; 42 T.L.R. 719 ; 70 S.J. 857 ; [1926] All E.R. Rep. 198 . . 470

Botibol, *Re*, Botibol *v.* Botibol, [1947] 1 All E.R. 26 515

Boughton *v.* Boughton (1750), 2 Ves. Sen. 12 ; 28 E.R. 8 . . 396, 398

Boughton *v.* Hazlehurst (1678/9), Nottingham's Chancery Cases, 79 Sel. Soc. 754 (case 956) 177

Boulton's Settlement Trust, *Re*, Stewart *v.* Boulton, [1928] Ch. 703 ; 97 L.J. Ch. 243 ; 139 L.T. 288 . . . . 367, 368

Bovey *v.* Skipwith (1671), 1 Ch. Cas. 201 ; 22 E.R. 762 ; 3 Ch. Rep. 67 ; 21 E.R. 731 173

Bovill *v.* Endle, [1896] 1 Ch. 648 ; 65 L.J. Ch. 542 ; 44 W.R. 523 . . 189

Bowden, *Re*, Hulbert *v.* Bowden, [1936] Ch. 71 ; 105 L.J. Ch. 23 ; 154 L.T. 157 ; 79 S.J. 625 ; [1935] All E.R. Rep. 933 309

Bowen *v.* Edwards (1661), 1 Ch. Rep. 221; 21 E.R. 555 . . . 168

Bowersbank *v.* Colasseau (1796), 3 Ves. 164 ; 30 E.R. 949 . . . 517

Bowes, *Re*—*see* Jackson, *Ex parte.*

Bowlby, *Re*, Bowlby *v.* Bowlby, [1904] 2 Ch. 685 ; 73 L.J. Ch. 810 ; 91 L.T. 573 ; 53 W.R. 270 ; 48 S.J. 698 290

Bowles, *Re*—*see* Underwood, *Re.*

Bowman *v.* Taylor (1834), 2 Ad. & El. 278 ; 111 E.R. 108 ; 4 Nev. & M. 264 ; 4 L.J.K.B. 58 ; [1824-34] All E.R. Rep. 485 ; 41 R.R. 437 . . 126

Box *v.* Barrett (1866), L.R. 3 Eq. 244 ; 15 W.R. 217 404

Boyle *v.* Bishop of Peterborough (1791), 1 Ves. Jun. 299 ; 30 E.R. 353 ; 3 Bro. C.C. 243 ; 29 E.R. 514 ; 2 R.R. 108 365

Boynton *v.* Helena Rubinstein Ltd. (1960), 176 Est. Gaz. 443 . . . 466

Brace *v.* Duchess of Marlborough (1728), 2 P. Wms. 491 ; 24 E.R. 829 ; Mos. 50 ; 25 E.R. 264 . . . . 120, 172, 175

PAGE

Bradbury *v.* Enfield Corp., [1967] 1 W.L.R. 1311 ; [1967] 3 All E.R. 434 ; 111 S.J. 701 481
Bradford *v.* Gammon, [1925] Ch. 132 ; 94 L.J. Ch. 193 ; 132 L.T. 342 ; 69 S.J 160 ; [1924] All E.R. Rep. 766 . . . . . . 558, 559
Bradford (Earl of) *v.* Earl of Romney (1862), 30 Beav. 431 ; 54 E.R. 956 ; 31 L.J. Ch. 497 ; 6 L.T. 208 ; 8 Jur. N.S. 403 ; 10 W.R. 414 ; 132 R.R. 342 . 532
Bradford Banking Co. Ltd. *v.* Henry Briggs, Son & Co. Ltd. (1886), 12 App. Cas. 29 ; 56 L.J. Ch. 364 ; 56 L.T. 62 ; 35 W.R. 521 ; 3 T.L.R. 170 . 221
Bradley *v* Carritt, [1903] A.C. 253 ; 72 L.J.K.B. 471 ; 88 L.T. 633 ; 51 W.R. 636 ; 19 T.L.R. 466 ; 47 S.J. 534 ; [1900-3] All E.R. Rep. 633 . . 207-8
Bradshaw, *Re*, Bradshaw *v.* Bradshaw, [1902] 1 Ch. 436 ; 71 L.J. Ch 230 ; 86 L.T. 253 404
Brady, *Re*, Brady *v.* Brady, [1936] I.R. 431 384
Branca *v.* Cobarro, [1947] K.B. 854 ; [1947] 2 All E.R. 101 ; [1948] L.J.R. 43 ; 177 L.T. 332 ; 63 T.L.R. 408 498
Brandlyn *v.* Orr (1738), 1 Atk. 571 ; 26 E.R. 359 555
Brandt's (William) Sons & Co. *v.* Dunlop Rubber Co. Ltd., [1905] A.C. 454 ; 74 L.J.K.B. 898 ; 93 L.T. 495 ; 21 T.L.R. 710 ; 11 Com. Cas. 1 ; [1904-7] All E.R. Rep. 345 . . . . . . 299, 315, 324, 328
Bree *v.* Holbech (1781), 2 Dougl. 654 ; 99 E.R. 415 104
Brenchley *v.* Higgins (1900), 70 L.J. Ch. 788 ; 83 L.T. 751 355-6
Brice *v.* Bannister (1878), 3 Q.B.D. 569 ; 47 L.J.Q.B. 722 ; 38 L.T. 739 ; 26 W.R. 670 328
Bridge *v.* Campbell Discount Co. Ltd., [1962] A.C. 600 ; [1962] 2 W.L.R. 439 ; [1962] 1 All E.R. 385 ; 106 S.J. 94 23-4
Bridgeman *v.* Green (1757), Wilm. 58 ; 97 E.R. 22 349
Brisco *v.* Kenrick (1832), Coop. t. Cott. 371, 372 ; 47 E.R. 901, 902; 1 L.J. Ch. 116 . . . . 245, 246
Bristol (Earl of) *v.* Hungerford (1705), 2 Vern. 524 ; 23 E.R. 938 ; 1 Eq. Cas. Abr. 142, pl. 5 ; 21 E.R. 944 . . . . . . 172, 174, 175
Bristow *v.* Warde (1794), 2 Ves. Jun. 336 ; 30 E.R. 660 ; [1775-1802] All E.R. Rep. 369 . . . . 365, 396, 403
Britain *v.* Rossiter (1879), 11 Q.B.D. 123 ; 48 L.J.Q.B. 362 ; 40 L.T. 240 ; 43 J.P. 482 ; 27 W.R. 482 . . . . 36, 493
Britains Ltd. *v.* M. Morris & Co. (London) Ltd., [1961] R.P.C. 217 . . 470
British Actors Film Co. Ltd. *v.* Glover, [1918] 1 K.B. 299 ; 87 L.J.K.B. 689 ; 118 L.T. 626 ; 34 T.L.R. 162 ; 62 S.J. 192 102
British Nylon Spinners Ltd. *v.* Imperial Chemical Industries Ltd., [1955] Ch. 37 ; [1954] 3 W.L.R. 505 ; [1954] 3 All E.R. 88 ; 98 S.J. 699 ; 71 R.P.C. 327 491
British South Africa Co. *v.* Companhia de Moçambique, [1893] A.C. 602 ; 63 L.J.Q.B. 70 ; 69 L.T. 604 ; 10 T L.R. 7 ; 37 S.J. 756 ; 6 R. 1 ; [1891-4] All E.R. Rep. 640 ; *reversing* Companhia de Moçambique *v.* British South Africa Co., [1892] 2 Q.B. 358 . . . . . . 13, 16
Broad *v.* Selfe (1863), 9 L.T. 43 ; 9 Jur. N.S. 885 ; 11 W.R. 1036 ; 2 New R. 541 ; 132 R.R. 873 205
Broadbent *v.* Barlow (1861), 3 De G. F. & J. 570 ; 45 E R. 999 ; 30 L.J. Ch. 569 ; 4 L.T. 193 ; 7 Jur. N.S. 479 ; 130 R.R. 256 438
Broadwood, *Re*, Lyall *v.* Broadwood, [1911] 1 Ch. 277 ; 80 L.J. Ch. 202 ; 104 L.T. 49 439
Brocker *v.* Hamilton (1751), Dick. 154 ; 21 E.R. 228 560
Broderick, *Ex parte*, *Re* Beetham (1887), 18 Q.B.D. 766 ; 56 L.J.Q.B. 635 ; 35 W.R. 613 ; 3 T.L.R. 489 186
Bromley *v.* Hamond (1679), 2 Ch. Cas. 23 ; 22 E.R. 828 176
Bromley *v.* Holland (1802), 7 Ves. 3 ; 32 E.R. 2 ; G. Coop. 9 ; 35 E.R. 458 ; 6 R.R. 58 554
Brook's Settlement, *Re*, Brook *v.* Brook, [1968] 1 W.L.R. 1661 ; [1968] 3 All E.R. 416 ; 112 S J. 845 371
Brooke *v.* Haymes (1868), L.R. 6 Eq. 25 126
Brookes, *Re*, Brookes *v.* Taylor, [1914] 1 Ch. 558 ; 83 L.J. Ch. 424 ; 110 L.T. 691 ; 58 S.J. 286 272
Brooking *v.* Maudslay, Son, & Field (1888), 38 Ch. D. 636 ; 57 L.J. Ch. 1001 ; 58 L.T. 852 ; 36 W.R. 664 ; 4 T.L.R. 421 ; 6 Asp. M.L.C. 296 . 554-5
Brooksbank, *Re*, Beauclerk *v.* James (1886), 34 Ch.D. 160 ; 56 L.J. Ch. 82 ; 55 L.T. 595 ; 35 W.R. 101 395

PAGE

Broun *v.* Kennedy (1864), 4 De G. J. & S. 217 ; 46 E.R. 901 ; 140 R.R. 47 . 341
Brown *v.* Barkham (1720), 1 P. Wms. 652 ; 24 E.R. 555 . . . 178
Brown *v.* Cole (1845), 14 Sim. 427 ; 60 E.R. 424 ; 14 L.J. Ch. 167 ; 5 L.T.O.S. 2 ; 9 Jur. 290 ; 65 R.R. 618 187
Brown *v.* Dudbridge (1788), 2 Bro. C.C. 31 ; 29 E.R. 176 557
Brown *v.* Higgs (1803), 8 Ves. 561 ; 32 E.R. 473 ; [1803-13] All E.R. Rep. 146 ; *on appeal* (1813), 18 Ves. 192 ; 34 E.R. 290 ; 4 R.R. 323 ; 79 R.R. Preface x 362-3
Brown *v.* Howard (1820), 2 Brod. & Bing. 73 ; 129 E.R. 885 ; 4 Moo. C.P. 508 104
Brown *v.* Howden (1900), 34 I.L.T.R. 159 366
Brown *v.* Peto, [1900] 2 Q.B. 653 ; 69 L.J.Q.B. 869 ; 83 L.T. 303 ; 49 W.R. 324 ; 16 T.L.R. 561 225
Brown *v.* Raphael, [1958] Ch. 636 ; [1958] 2 W.L.R. 647 ; [1958] 2 All E.R. 79 ; 102 S.J. 269 545
Brown's Trust, *Re* (1865), L R. 1 Eq. 74 368
Browne *v.* Duffy (1889), 24 L.R. Ir. 13 458
Browne *v.* Ryan [1901] 2 I.R. 653 ; 35 I.L.T.R. 6 ; 1 N.I.J.R. 25 . . 205
Bruce *v.* Brophy, [1906] 1 I.R. 611 247
Brunker, *Ex parte* (1734), 3 P. Wms. 312 ; 24 E.R. 1079 560
Brymer *v.* Thames Haven Dock and Railway Co. (1848), 2 Ex 549 ; 154 E.R. 609 ; 18 L.J. Ex. 110 ; *on appeal*, *sub nom.* Thames Haven Dock and Railway Co. *v.* Brymer (1850), 5 Ex. 696 ; 155 E.R. 305 ; 19 L.J. Ex. 321 ; 15 L.T. O.S. 366 ; 82 R.R. 839 120
Buckley *v.* Irwin, [1960] N.I. 98 . . . . 335-6, 500
Bugden *v.* Bignold (1843), 2 Y. & C.C.C. 377 ; 63 E.R. 167 ; 60 R.R. 202 . 435
Bulfin *v.* Dunne (1861), 12 Ir. Ch. Rep. 67 ; 6 I.J.N.S. 230 182
Bulli Coal Mining Co. *v.* Osborne, [1899] A.C. 351 ; 68 L.J.P.C. 49 ; 80 L.T. 430 ; 47 W.R. 545 ; 15 T.L.R. 257 ; [1895-9] All E.R. Rep. 506 . . 105
Bullock *v.* Lloyds Bank Ltd., [1955] Ch. 317 ; [1955] 2 W.L.R. 1 ; [1954] 3 All E.R. 726 ; 99 S.J. 28 . . . . 342, 344, 349, 350
Burden *v.* Sinclair (1961), 105 S.J. 586 476
Burge, Woodall & Co., *Re*, *Ex parte* Skyrme, [1912] 1 K.B. 393 ; 81 L.J.K.B. 721 ; 106 L.T. 47 ; 20 Mans. 11 438
Burgess *v.* Booth, [1908] 2 Ch. 648 ; 78 L.J. Ch. 32 ; 99 L.T. 677 . 377, 390
Burgess *v.* Eve (1872), L.R. 13 Eq. 450 ; 41 L.J. Ch. 515 ; 26 L.T. 540 ; 20 W.R. 311 553
Burgess *v.* Wheate (1759), 1 Eden 177 ; 28 E.R. 652 ; 1 Black. W. 123 ; 96 E.R. 67 . . . . 151, 152
Burgh *v.* Francis (1673), Rep. t. Finch 28 ; 23 E.R. 16 ; 3 Swanst. 529n ; 36 E.R. 971 ; 1 Eq. Cas. Abr. 320, pl. 1 ; 21 E.R. 1074 . . 171-2, 260
Burgh *v.* Langton (1724), 5 Bro. P.C. 213 ; 2 E.R. 635 ; 2 Eq. Cas. Abr. 609, pl. 5 ; 22 E.R. 511 248
Burgis *v.* Constantine, [1908] 2 K.B. 484 ; 77 L.J.K.B. 1045 ; 99 L.T. 490 ; 24 T.L.R. 682 ; 11 Asp M.L.C. 130 ; 13 Com. Cas. 299 527
Burke's Estate, *Re* (1881), 9 L.R. Ir. 24 212
Burrough *v.* Cranston (1840), 2 Ir. Eq. Rep. 203 187
Burrowes *v.* Molloy (1845), 2 Jo. & Lat. 521 ; 8 Ir. Eq. Rep. 482 ; 69 R.R. 358 245
Burton, *Re*—*see* Tongue, *Re*.
Burton *v.* Slattery (1725), 5 Bro. P.C. 233 ; 2 E.R. 648 178
Burton's Settlements, *Re*, Scott *v.* National Provincial Bank Ltd., [1955] Ch. 82 ; [1954] 3 W.L.R. 581 ; [1954] 3 All E.R. 193 ; 98 S.J. 734 . 369, 370-1
Bush, *Re*, B. Lipton Ltd *v.* Mackintosh, [1930] 2 Ch. 202 ; 99 L.J. Ch. 503 ; 143 L.T. 700 ; [1929] B. & C.R. 216 ; [1930] All E.R. Rep. 605 . 278, 279
Bushby *v.* Munday (1821), 5 Madd. 297 ; 56 E.R. 908 ; [1814-23] All E.R. Rep. 304 ; 21 R.R. 294 15-16
Butler *v.* Butler (1880), 7 L.R. Ir. 401 368
Butler *v.* Miller (1867), I.R. 1 Eq. 195 ; 15 W.R. 779 ; 1 I.L.T. 794 . . 334
Butler *v.* Mountview Estates Ltd., [1951] 2 K.B. 563 ; [1951] 1 All E.R. 693 ; [1951] 1 T.L.R. 524 531
Butler *v.* Standard Telephones & Cables Ltd., [1940] 1 K.B. 399 ; [1940] 1 All E.R. 121 ; 109 L.J.K.B. 238 ; 163 L.T. 145 ; 56 T.L.R. 273 ; 84 S.J. 189 466
Buttery *v.* Pickard (1946), 174 L.T. 144 ; 62 T.L.R. 241 ; [1946] W.N. 25 ; 90 S.J. 80 123

PAGE

Buxton *v.* Lister (1746), 3 Atk. 383 ; 26 E.R. 1020 . . . . 489, 493
Byde *v.* Byde (1761), 1 Cox. C.C. 44 ; 29 E.R. 1055 ; 2 Eden 19 ; 28 E.R. 802 415
Byrne *v.* Kinematograph Renters Soc. Ltd., [1958] 1 W.L.R. 762 ; [1958] 2 All E.R. 579 ; 102 S.J. 509 477
Byrne *v.* Reid, [1902] 2 Ch. 735 ; 71 L.J. Ch. 830 ; 87 L.T. 507 ; 51 W.R. 52 489

Calow, *Re*, Calow *v.* Calow, [1928] Ch. 710 ; 97 L.J. Ch. 253 ; 139 L.T. 235; 72 S.J. 437 ; [1928] All E.R. Rep. 518 382
Calthorpe *v.* May (1707), 7 Bro. P.C. 413 ; 3 E.R. 269 139
Campbell *v.* Holyland (1877), 7 Ch.D. 166 ; 47 L.J. Ch. 145 ; 38 L.T. 128 ; 26 W.R. 160 . . . . 244, 248
Capital Finance Co. Ltd. *v.* Stokes [1969] 1 Ch. 261 ; [1968] 3 W.L.R. 899 ; [1968] 3 All E.R. 625 ; 19 P. & C. R. 791 184
Carberry *v.* M'Carthy (1881), 7 L.R. Ir. 328 363
Card *v.* Jaffray (1805), 2 Sch. & Lef. 374 184
Carew *v.* Johnston (1805), 2 Sch. & Lef. 280 241
Carl Bros. Ltd. *v.* Webster—*see* Curl Bros. Ltd. *v.* Webster.
Carlis Ware *v.* Radford, [1959] R.P.C. 38 474
Carlton Contractors Ltd. *v.* Bexley Corp. (1962), 60 L.G.R. 331 ; 106 S.J. 391 542
Carmichael *v.* Greenock Harbour Trustees, [1910] A.C. 274 ; 102 L.T. 297 ; 54 S.J. 391 ; 26 T.L.R. 332 515
Carpenters Estates Ltd. *v.* Davies, [1940] Ch. 160 ; [1940] 1 All E.R. 13 ; 109 L.J. Ch. 92 ; 162 L.T. 76 ; 56 T.L.R. 269 ; 83 S.J. 960 . . 491
Carr *v.* Eastabrooke (1797), 3 Ves. 561 ; 30 E.R. 1156 . . . 415, 416
Carr *v.* Ellison (1786), 2 Bro. C.C. 56 ; 29 E.R. 480 ; 2 Dick. 796; 21 E.R. 480 390
Carrington, *Re*, Ralphs *v.* Swithenbank, [1932] 1 Ch. 1 ; 100 L.J. Ch. 299 ; 145 L.T. 284 ; [1931] All E.R. Rep. 658 383
Carshalton Park Estate Ltd., *Re*, Graham *v.* The Co., [1908] 2 Ch. 62 ; 77 L.J. Ch. 550 ; 99 L.T. 12 ; 24 T.L.R. 547 ; 15 Mans. 228 . . . 517
Carson *v.* Sloane (1884), 13 L.R.Ir. 139 . . . . . . 519, 520
Carter, *Ex parte* (1773), Amb. 733 ; 27 E.R. 474 176
Carter *v.* Wake (1877), 4 Ch.D. 605 ; 46 L.J. Ch. 841 244
Cartwright, *Re*, Avis *v.* Newman (1889), 41 Ch.D. 532 ; 58 L.J. Ch. 590 ; 60 L.T. 891 ; 37 W.R. 612 ; 5 T.L.R. 482 80
Cartwright, *Re*, Cartwright *v.* Smith, [1939] Ch. 90 ; [1938] 4 All E.R. 209 ; 108 L.J. Ch. 51 ; 159 L.T. 538 ; 55 T.L.R. 69 ; 82 S.J. 930 . . . 394
Cartwright *v.* Pettus (1675), 2 Ch. 214 ; 22 E.R. 916 ; *sub nom.* Carterett *v.* Pettie, Rep. t. Finch 242 ; 23 E.R. 133 ; *sub nom.* Carteret *v.* Petty, 2 Swanst. 323 n ; 36 E.R. 639 14
Casberd *v.* Ward (1819), 6 Price 411 ; 146 E.R. 850 ; Dan. 238 ; 20 R.R. 671 182
Casborne *v.* Scarfe (1738), 1 Atk. 603 ; 26 E.R. 377 ; *sub nom.* Casburne *v.* Inglis, West t. Hard. 221 ; 25 E.R. 905 ; 2 Jac. & W. 194 ; 37 E.R. 600 ; Lee t. Hard. 399 ; *sub nom.* Cashborn *v.* Inglish, 2 Eq. Cas. Abr. 728, pl. 6 ; 22 E.R. 613 . . . . 62, 169, 257-8
Cason *v.* Round (1703), Prec. Ch. 226 ; 24 E.R. 110 ; 2 Eq. Cas. Abr. 594, pl. 4 ; 22 E.R. 499 172
Caton *v.* Caton (1866), L.R. 1 Ch.App. 137 ; (1867), L.R. 2 H.L. 127 ; 36 L.J. Ch. 886 ; 16 W.R. 1 495
Catt *v.* Tourle (1869), L.R. 4 Ch.App. 654 ; 38 L.J. Ch. 665 ; 21 L.T. 188 ; 33 J.P. 659 ; 17 W.R. 939 472
Caunce *v.* Caunce, [1969] 1 W.L.R. 286 ; [1969] 1 All E.R. 722 ; 113 S.J. 204 . . . . 104, 106, 214
Caunter's Charge, *Re*, Bishop *v.* Southgate Corp., [1960] Ch. 491 ; [1959] 3 W.L.R. 822 ; [1959] 3 All E.R. 669 ; 124 J.P. 37 ; 57 L.G.R. 353 ; 103 S.J. 874 257
Cavan (Lady) *v.* Pulteney (1795), 2 Ves. Jun. 544 ; 30 E.R. 768 ; 3 R.R. 8 398, 400
Cave *v.* Cave (1880), 15 Ch.D. 639; 28 W.R. 798; *sub nom.* Chaplin *v.* Cave, 49 L.J. Ch. 505 ; 42 L.T. 730 ; 214, 527
Cavendish *v.* Strutt (1903), 19 T.L.R. 483 . . . . . . 348, 351
Central London Property Trust Ltd. *v.* High Trees House Ltd., [1947] K.B. 130 ; [1947] L.J.R. 77 ; 175 L.T. 332 ; 62 T.L.R. 557 . . . 40-2, 122-4
Central Railway Co. of Venezuela *v.* Kisch (1867), L.R. 2 H.L. 99 ; 36 L.J. Ch. 849 ; 16 L.T. 500 ; 15 W.R. 821 551

PAGE

Chambers *v.* Goldwin (1804), 9 Ves. 254 ; 32 E.R. 600 ; 1 Smith K.B. 252 ; [1803-13] All E.R. Rep. 255 ; 7 R.R. 181 241
Chancey's Case (1717), 1 P.Wms. 408 ; 24 E.R. 448 ; *sub nom.* Chancy *v.* Wooton (1725), 2 Eq. Cas. Abr. 354, pl. 18 ; 22 E.R. 301 ; *sub nom.* Chancy *v.* Wootton, Sel. Cas. t. King 44 ; 25 E.R. 213 . . 413, 416
Chaplin *v.* Cave—*see* Cave *v.* Cave.
Chaplin & Co. Ltd. *v.* Brammall, [1908] 1 K.B. 233 ; 77 L.J.K.B. 366 ; 97 L.T. 860 . . . . 348, 349
Chapman *v.* Chapman, [1954] A.C. 429 ; [1954] 2 W.L.R. 723 ; [1954] 1 All E.R. 798 ; 98 S.J. 246 ; [1954] T.R. 93 ; 33 A.T.C. 94 ; 47 R. & I.T 310 . . . . 35, 38, 161
Chapman *v.* Smith, [1907] 2 Ch. 97 ; 76 L.J. Ch. 394 ; 96 L.T. 662 ; 51 S.J. 120 232
Chapman *v.* Westerby, [1913] W.N. 277 ; 58 S.J. 151 473
Chapple *v.* Mahon (1870), I.R. 5 Eq. 225 206
Chaproniere *v.* Lambert, [1917] 2 Ch. 356 ; 86 L.J. Ch. 726 ; 117 L.T. 353 ; 33 T.L.R. 485 ; 61 S.J. 592 ; [1916-17] All E.R. Rep. 1089 495
Charles *v.* Jones (1887), 35 Ch.D. 544 ; 56 L.J. Ch. 745 ; 56 L.T. 848 ; 35 W.R. 645 256
Chesham (Lord), *Re*, Cavendish *v.* Dacre (1886), 31 Ch.D. 466 ; 55 L.J. Ch. 401 ; 54 L.T. 154 ; 34 W.R. 321 ; 2 T.L.R. 265 . . . . 400, 403
Cheslyn *v.* Dalby (1836), 2 Y. & C. Ex. 170 ; 160 E.R. 357 ; 47 R.R. 384 . 339
Chess (Oscar) Ltd. *v.* Williams, [1957] 1 W.L.R. 370 ; [1957] 1 All E.R. 325 ; 101 S.J. 186 544
Chesterfield (Earl of) *v.* Janssen (1750), 1 Atk. 301 ; 26 E.R. 191 ; 2 Ves. Sen. 125 ; 23 E.R. 82 . . . . 60, 331-2, 337, 352
Chesters, *Re*, Whittingham *v.* Chesters, [1935] Ch. 77 ; 104 L.J. Ch. 65 ; 152 L.T. 210 ; 78 S.J. 634 ; [1934] All E.R. Rep. 319 193
Chichester *v.* Bickerstaff (1693), 2 Vern. 295 ; 23 E.R. 791 389
Chichester (Lord) *v.* Coventry (1867), L.R. 2 H.L. 71 ; 36 L.J. Ch. 673 ; 17 L.T. 35 ; 15 W.R. 849 . . . . 420, 421
Chichester Diocesan Fund and Board of Finance (Inc.) *v.* Simpson, [1944] A.C. 341 ; [1944] 2 All E.R. 60 ; 113 L.J. Ch. 225 ; 171 L.T. 141 ; 60 T.L. R. 492 ; 88 S.J. 246 7-8
Chilcott *v.* Tucker (1675/6), Nottingham's Chancery Cases, 73 Sel. Soc. 263 (case 387) 168
Chitton *v.* Burt—*see* Clifton *v.* Burt.
Chomley *v.* Countess Dowager of Oxford (1741), 2 Atk. 267 ; 26 E.R. 565 . 243
Cholmondeley (Marquis) *v.* Lord Clinton (1817), 2 Mer. 171 ; 35 E.R. 905 ; 16 R.R. 167 230
Cholmondeley (Marquis) *v.* Lord Clinton (1820), 2 Jac. & W. 1 ; 37 E.R. 527 ; 22 R.R. 84 ; (1821), 4 Bligh 1 ; 4 E.R. 721 ; 22 R.R. 83 . 230, 258-9
Christie *v.* Taunton, Delmard, Lane & Co., [1893] 2 Ch. 175 ; 62 L.J. Ch. 385 ; 68 L.T. 638 ; 41 W.R. 475 ; 37 S.J. 304 ; 3 R. 404 308
Church *v.* Church (1877), 11 I.L.T.R. 163 194
Churcher *v.* Street, [1959] Ch. 251 ; [1959] 2 W.L.R. 66 ; [1959] 1 All E.R. 23 ; 103 S.J. 55 . . . . 103, 470
Churchill, *Re*, Hiscock *v.* Lodder, [1909] 2 Ch. 431 ; 79 L.J. Ch. 10 ; 101 L.T. 380 ; 53 S.J. 697 290
Churston Settled Estates, *Re*, [1954] Ch. 334 ; [1954] 2 W.L.R. 386 ; [1954] 1 All E.R. 725 ; 98 S.J. 178 357
Cityland and Property (Holdings) Ltd. *v.* Dabrah, [1968] Ch. 166 ; [1967] 3 W.L.R. 605 ; [1967] 2 All E.R. 639 ; 111 S.J. 518 . 24, 168, 206-7
Clack *v.* Holland (1854), 19 Beav. 262 ; 52 E.R. 350 ; 24 L.J. Ch. 13 ; 24 L.T O.S. 49 ; 18 Jur. 1007 ; 2 W.R. 402 ; 105 R.R. 134 308
Clark *v.* Malpas (1862), 4 De G.F. & J. 401 ; 45 E.R. 1238 ; 31 L.J. Ch. 696 ; 6 L.T. 596 ; 8 Jur. N.S. 734 ; 10 W.R. 677 ; 135 R.R. 212 . . . 335
Clark *v.* Sewell (1744), 3 Atk. 96 ; 26 E.R. 858 290
Clark *v.* Woor, [1965] 1 W.L.R. 650 ; [1965] 2 All E.R. 353 ; 109 S.J. 251 . 28
Clarke *v.* Abbot (1741), Barn. C. 457 ; 27 E.R. 718 ; 2 Eq. Cas. Abr. 606, pl. 41 ; 22 E.R. 509 172
Clarke *v.* Franklin (1858), 4 K. & J. 257 ; 70 E.R. 107 ; 27 L.J.Ch. 567 ; 31 L.T.O.S. 381 ; 6 W.R. 836 ; 116 R.R. 325 387
Clayton's Case, Devaynes *v.* Noble (1816), 1 Mer. 572 ; 35 E.R. 781 ; [1814-23] All E.R. Rep. 1 ; 15 R.R. 161 . . . . . .521-2, 525, 528

PAGE

Clayton *v.* Blakey (1798), 8 T.R. 3 ; 101 E.R. 1234 84
Clayton *v.* Illingworth (1853), 10 Hare 451 ; 68 E.R. 1003 ; 90 R.R. 431 . 487
Clench *v.* Witherley (1678), Rep. t. Finch 376 ; 23 E.R. 206 168
Clibborn *v.* Horan, [1921] 1 I.R. 93 ; 55 I.L.T.R. 49 363
Clifton *v.* Burt (1720), 1 P.Wms. 678 ; 24 E.R. 566 ; *sub nom.* Chitton *v.* Burt, Prec. Ch. 540 ; 24 E.R. 242 65
Clore *v.* Theatrical Properties Ltd., [1936] 3 All E.R. 483 103
Clough *v.* Ratcliffe (1847), 1 De G. & Sm. 164 ; 63 E.R. 1016 ; 16 L.J. Ch. 476 ; 9 L.T.O.S. 264 ; 11 Jur. 648 559
Clout and Frewer's Contract, *Re*, [1924] 2 Ch. 230 ; 93 L.J. Ch. 624 ; 132 L.T. 483 ; 68 S.J. 738 ; [1924] All E.R. Rep. 798 267
Cloutte *v.* Storey, [1911] 1 Ch. 18 ; 80 L.J. Ch. 193 ; 103 L.T. 617 . 369, 373
Clydebank Engineering and Shipbuilding Co. *v.* Don Jose Ramos Yzquierdo y Castaneda, [1905] A.C. 6 ; 74 L.J.P.C. 1 ; 91 L.T. 666 ; 21 T.L.R. 58 ; [1904-7] All E.R. Rep. 251 . . . . 19, 20
Coates, *Re*, Ramsden *v.* Coates, [1955] Ch. 495 ; [1954] 3 W.L.R. 959 ; [1955] 1 All E.R. 26 ; 98 S.J. 871 362
Coates *v.* Kenna (1872), I.R. 7 Eq. 113 530
Coatsworth *v.* Johnson (1886), 55 L.J.Q.B. 220 ; 54 L.T. 520 ; 2 T.L.R. 351 ; [1886-90] All E.R. Rep. 547 89
Cochrane *v.* Cochrane, [1922] 2 Ch. 230 ; 91 L.J.Ch. 605 ; 127 L.T. 737 ; 38 T.L.R. 607 ; 66 S.J. 522 ; [1922] All E.R. Rep. 614 373
Cock *v.* Ravie (1801), 6 Ves. 283 ; 31 E.R. 1053 561
Cockell, *Re*—*see* Attorney-General *v.* Jackson.
Cogan *v.* Stephens (1835), 1 Beav. 482n. ; 48 E.R. 1027 ; 5 L.J. Ch. 17 ; 42 R.R. 258 388
Cohen, *Re*, National Provincial Bank Ltd. *v.* Katz, [1960] Ch. 179 ; [1959] 3 W.L.R. 916 ; [1959] 3 All E.R. 740 ; 103 S.J. 961 439
Cohen *v.* Rothfield, [1919] 1 K.B. 410 ; 88 L.J.K.B. 468 ; 120 L.T. 434 ; 63 S.J. 192 ; [1918-19] All E.R. Rep. 260 459
Cokayn *v.* Hurst (1458), 10 Sel. Soc. (Sel. Cas. in Ch. 1364-1471) 141 (case 142) 482
Colchester Corp. *v.* Lowten (1813), 1 V. & B. 226 ; 35 E.R. 89 ; [1903-13] All E.R. Rep. 388 ; 12 R.R. 216 554
Coleman *v.* Fry (1873), I.R. 7 C.L. 247 543
Collen Bros. *v.* Dublin C.C., [1908] 1 I.R. 503 540
Collins *v.* Hare (1828), 2 Bligh N.S. 106 ; 4 E.R. 1071 ; 1 Dow. & Cl. 139 ; 6 E.R. 476 338
Collins's Estate, *Re*, Collins *v.* Collins, [1924] 1 I.R. 72 ; 58 I.L.T.R. 41, 84 384
Collinson *v.* Pattrick (1838), 2 Keen 123 ; 48 E.R. 575 ; 7 L.J. Ch. 83 ; 44 R.R. 207 312
Collyer *v.* Isaacs (1881), 19 Ch.D. 342 ; 51 L.J. Ch. 14 ; 45 L.T. 567 ; 30 W.R. 70 ; [1881-5] All E.R. Rep. 828 431
Colson *v.* Williams & Co. (1889), 58 L.J. Ch. 539 ; 61 L.T. 71 ; [1886-90] All E.R. Rep. 1040 253
Colverson *v.* Bloomfield (1885), 29 Ch.D. 341 ; 54 L.J. Ch. 817; 52 L.T. 478 ; 33 W.R. 889 . . . . 561, 562
Colyer *v.* Colyer (1863), 3 De G. J. & S. 676 ; 46 E.R. 799 ; 9 L.T. 214 ; 11 W.R. 1051 ; 142 R.R. 214 191
Colyer *v.* Finch (1856), 5 H.L.C. 905 ; 10 E.R. 1159 ; 26 L.J. Ch. 65 ; 28 L.T.O.S. 27 ; 3 Jur. N.S. 25 ; [1843-60] All E.R. Rep. 1020 ; 101 R.R. 442 217
Colyer *v.* Finch (1856), 5 H.L.C. 905 ; 10 E.R. 1159 ; 26 L.J.Ch. 65 ; 28 L.T. O.S. 27 ; 3 Jur. N.S. 25 ; [1843-60] All E.R. Rep. 1020 ; 101 R.R. 442 . 217
Combe, *Re*, Combe *v.* Combe, [1925] Ch. 210 ; 94 L.J.Ch. 267 ; [1925] All E.R. Rep. 159 ; *sub nom.* *Re* Coombe, 133 L.T. 473 ; 69 S.J. 397 . . 363
Combe *v.* Combe, [1951] 2 K.B. 215 ; [1951] 1 All E.R. 767 ; [1951] 1 T.L.R. 811 ; 95 S.J. 317 . . . . 41, 124, 490
Comfort *v.* Betts, [1891] 1 Q.B. 737 ; 60 L.J.Q.B. 656 ; 64 L.T. 685 ; 55 J.P. 630 ; 39 W.R. 595 ; 7 T.L.R. 475 327
Coming, *Ex parte* (1803), 9 Ves. 115 ; 32 E.R. 545 ; 7 R.R. 149 . . . 183
Commissioner of Public Works *v.* Hills, [1906] A.C. 368 ; 75 L.J.P.C. 69 ; 94 L.T. 833 ; [1904-7] All E.R. Rep. 919 20
Commissioners for Inland Revenue *v.* Earl of Derby, [1914] 3 K.B. 1186 ; 84 L.J.K.B. 248 ; 109 L.T. 827 . . . . 91, 92

PAGE

Commissioners of Church Temporalities of Ireland *v.* Harrington (1883), 11 L.R. Ir. 127 511
Commissioners of Public Works, *Re, Ex parte* Rice (1896), 30 I.L.T.R. 57 . 532
Companhia de Moçambique *v.* British South Africa Co.—*see* British South Africa Co. *v.* Companhia de Moçambique.
Compania Colombiana de Seguros *v.* Pacific Steam Navigation Co., [1965] 1 Q.B. 101 ; [1964] 2 W.L.R. 484 ; [1964] 1 All E.R. 216 ; 108 S.J. 75 ; [1963] 2 Lloyd's R. 479 298
Comyns *v.* Comyns (1871), I.R. 5 Eq. 583 237
Condon, *Re—see* James, *Ex parte.*
Coni *v.* Robertson, [1969] 1 W.L.R. 1007 ; [1969] 2 All E.R. 609 . 450, 453
Conlan *v.* Carlow C.C., [1912] 2 I.R. 535 ; 46 I.L.T.R. 183 . . . 327
Conlon *v.* Murray, [1958] N.I. 17 . . . . . . 485, 500-1
Connolly Bros. Ltd., *Re*, Wood *v.* Connolly Bros. Ltd., [1911] 1 Ch. 731, 80 L.J. Ch. 409 ; *sub nom. Re* Conolly Bros. Ltd., 104 L.T. 693 . . 459
Connor *v.* M'Carthy (1878), 12 I.L.T. 336 33
Connor *v.* Potts, [1897] 1 I.R. 534 507
Conolly Bros., *Re—see* Connolly Bros., *Re.*
Cooden Engineering Co. Ltd. *v.* Stanford, [1953] 1 Q.B. 86 ; [1952] 2 All E.R. 915 ; [1952] 2 T.L.R. 822 ; 96 S.J. 802 22
Cook *v.* Fearn (1878), 48 L.J. Ch. 63 ; 39 L.T. 348 ; 27 W.R. 212 . . 536
Cook *v.* Fountain (1672), 3 Swanst. 585 ; 36 E.R. 984 . . . 53, 54
Cook *v.* Gregson (1856), 3 Drew. 547 ; 61 E.R. 1012 ; 25 L.J. Ch. 706 ; 27 L.T.O.S. 332 ; 2 Jur. N.S. 510 ; 4 W.R. 581 ; 106 R.R. 425 . . 265-6
Cooke, *Re—see* Warner, *Ex parte.*
Cookson *v.* Reay (1842), 5 Beav. 22 ; 49 E.R. 494 ; *on appeal, sub nom.* Cookson *v.* Cookson (1845), 12 Cl. & Fin. 121 ; 8 E.R. 1344 ; 9 Jur. 499 ; 69 R.R. 66 385
Coombe, *Ex parte* (1810), 17 Ves. 369 ; 34 E.R. 142 ; 1 Rose 268 . . 183
Coombe, *Ex parte* (1819), 4 Madd. 249 ; 56 E.R. 698 ; 20 R.R. 294 . . 184
Coombe, *Re—see* Combe, *Re.*
Coomber, *Re*, [1911] 1 Ch. 723 ; 80 L.J. Ch. 399 ; 104 L.T 517 . 338, 350
Cooper *v.* Cooper (1873), L.R. 8 Ch. App. 813 ; 43 L.J. Ch. 158 ; 29 L.T. 321 ; 21 W.R. 921 421
Cooper *v.* Cooper (1874), L.R. 7 H.L. 53 ; 44 L.J. Ch. 6 ; 30 L.T. 409 ; 22 W.R., 713 ; [1874-80] All E.R. Rep. 307 . . . 404, 405, 407
Cooper *v* . Joel (1859), 1 De G. F. & J. 240 ; 45 E.R. 350 ; 1 L.T. 351 ; 125 R.R. 432 552
Cooper *v.* Phibbs (1867), L.R. 2 H.L. 149 ; 16 L.T. 678 ; 15 W.R. 1049 550, 552
Coote *v.* Gordon (1877), I.R. 11 Eq. 279 408
Corbett, *Re*, Corbett *v.* Lord Cobham, [1903] 2 Ch. 326 ; 72 L.J. Ch. 775 ; 88 L.T. 591 ; 52 W.R. 74 425
Corbett *v.* Inland Revenue Commissioners, [1938] 1 K.B. 567 ; [1937] 4 All E.R. 700 ; 107 L.J.K.B. 276 ; 158 L.T. 98 ; 54 T.L.R. 279 ; 82 S.J. 34 ; 21 T.C. 449 286
Corcoran, *The Goods of*, [1934] I.R. 571 33
Cordeaux *v.* Fullerton (1879), 41 L.T. 651 ; 28 W.R. 320 536
Cork & Youghal Railway Co., *Re* (1869), L.R. 4 Ch. App. 748 ; 39 L.J. Ch. 277 ; 21 L.T. 735 ; 18 W.R. 26 115
Cork Corp. *v.* Rooney (1881), 7 L.R. Ir. 191 458
Cork Harbour Docks and Warehouse Co. Ltd.'s Estate, *Re* (1885), 17 L.R. Ir. 515 194
Corley *v.* Lord Stafford (1857), 1 De G. & J. 238 ; 44 E.R. 714 ; 26 L.J. Ch. 865 ; 30 L.T.O.S. 77 ; 33 Jur. N.S. 1225 ; 5 W.R. 646 ; 118 R.R. 104 . 341
Cornish *v.* Brook Green Laundry Ltd., [1959] 1 Q.B. 394 ; [1959] 2 W.L.R. 215 ; [1959] 1 All E.R. 373 ; 103 S.J. 130 91-2
Cornish *v.* Stubbs (1870), L.R. 5 C.P. 334 ; 39 L.J.C.P. 202 ; 22 L.T. 21 ; 18 W.R. 547 ; [1861-73] All E.R. Rep. 218 98
Cornwall, *Re—see* Baldwin *v.* Belcher.
Cory *v.* Eyre (1863), 1 De G. J. & S. 149 ; 46 E.R. 58 ; 137 R.R. 184 . 213
Cotterell *v.* Price, [1960] 1 W.L.R. 1097 ; [1960] 3 All E.R. 315 ; 104 S.J. 763 . . . . 189, 190, 192
Cotterell *v.* Purchase (1734), Cas. t. Talb. 61 ; 25 E.R. 663 168
Coubrough *v.* James Panton & Co. Ltd., [1965] I.R. 272 476
Couch *v.* Stratton (1799), 4 Ves. 391 ; 31 E.R. 199 ; 4 R.R. 230 . . 431

PAGE

Coulson *v.* Allison (1860), 2 De G. F. & J. 521 ; 45 E.R. 723 ; 3 L.T. 763 ; 129 R.R. 176 345
Coulson (William) & Sons *v.* James Coulson & Co. (1887), 3 T.L.R. 846 . 462
Courtier, *Re*, Coles *v.* Courtier (1886), 34 Ch.D. 136 ; 56 L.J. Ch. 350 ; 55 L.T. 574 ; 51 J.P. 117 ; 35 W.R. 85 385
Courtney, *Re*, *Ex parte* Pollard (1840), Mont. & Ch. 239 ; 4 Jur. 1018 ; 4 Deac. 27 ; 1 Mont., D. & De G. 264; [1835-42] All E.R. Rep. 415 . 13-14
Coutts & Co. *v.* Somerville, [1935] Ch. 438 ; 104 L.J. Ch. 243 ; 153 L.T. 216 ; [1935] All E.R. Rep. 478 225
Cowell *v.* Rosehill Racecourse Co. Ltd. (1937), 56 C.L.R. 605 ; 11 A.L.J. 32 ; [1937] A.L.R. 273 102
Cowper *v.* Earl Cowper (1734), 2 P.Wms. 720 ; 24 E.R. 930 ; [1558-1774] All E.R. Rep. 216 485
Craddock Bros. *v.* Hunt, [1923] 2 Ch. 136 ; 92 L.J. Ch. 378 ; 129 L.T. 228 ; 67 S.J. 593 ; [1923] All E.R. Rep. 394 539
Cradock *v.* Scottish Provident Institution (1894), 70 L.T. 718 . . 186
Craig *v.* Elliott (1885), 15 L.R. Ir. 257 89
Cranmer's Case (1701), 2 Salk. 508 ; 91 E.R. 434 415
Crawshay, *Re*, Hore-Ruthven *v.* Public Trustee, [1948] Ch. 123 ; [1948] 1 All E.R. 107 ; [1948] L.J.R. 586 ; 64 T.L.R. 67 ; 92 S.J. 95 . 369-70, 371, 372, 373
Crichton *v.* Crichton, [1896] 1 Ch. 870 ; 65 L.J. Ch. 491 ; 74 L.T. 357 . 415
Crickmore *v.* Freeston (1870), 40 L.J. Ch. 137 201
Cripps *v.* Jee (1793), 4 Bro. C.C. 472 ; 29 E.R. 994 168
Croft *v.* Powel (1738), 3 Comyns 603 ; 92 E.R. 1230 168
Crofton *v.* Ormsby (1806), 2 Sch. & Lef. 583 ; 9 R.R. 107 506
Croker *v.* Croker (1870), 4 I.L.T. 181 342
Crompton *v.* Sale (1729), 2 P.Wms. 553 ; 24 E.R. 858 ; 1 Eq. Cas. Abr. 205, pl. 9 ; 21 E.R. 992 415
Crompton & Co. Ltd., *Re*, Player *v.* Crompton & Co. Ltd., [1914] 1 Ch. 954 ; 83 L.J. Ch. 666 ; 110 L.T. 759 ; 58 S.J. 433 ; 21 Mans. 200 . 513
Cromwell Property Investment Co. Ltd. *v.* Western, [1934] Ch. 322 ; 103 L.J. Ch. 168 ; 150 L.T. 335 ; [1933] All E.R. Rep. 440 188-9
Crone *v.* Hegarty (1879), 3 L.R. Ir. 50 ; 13 I.L.T.R. 84 179
Crosley *v.* Marriot (1783), Dick. 609 ; 21 E.R. 408 560
Crosse *v.* Smith (1806), 7 East 246 ; 103 E.R. 94 ; 3 Smith K.B. 203 . . 105
Crowder *v.* Tinkler (1816), 19 Ves. 617 ; 34 E.R. 645 ; [1814-23] All E.R. Rep. Rep. 549 ; 13 R.R. 267 460
Crowley *v.* O'Sullivan, [1900] 2 I.R. 478 . . . . 489, 493, 496-7
Crump *v.* Temple (1890), 7 T.L.R. 120 87
Cruttwell *v.* Lye (1810), 17 Ves. 335 ; 34 E.R. 129 ; 1 Rose 123 ; [1803-13] All E.R. Rep. 189 ; 11 R.R. 98 . . . . **474**
Cud *v.* Rutter (1719), 1 P. Wms. 570 ; 24 E.R. 521 ; 2 Eq. Cas. Abr. 18, pl. 8 ; 22 E.R. 14 ; *sub nom.* Cuddee *v.* Rutter, 5 Vin. Abr. 538 ; *sub nom.* Scould *v.* Butter, Prec. Ch. 534 ; 24 E.R. 239 487
Cull *v.* Showell (1773), Amb. 727 ; 27 E.R. 470 399
Cullen *v.* Cullen, [1962] I.R. 268 461
Cumberland Court (Brighton) Ltd. *v.* Taylor, [1964] Ch. 29 ; [1963] 3 W.L.R. 313 ; [1963] 2 All E.R. 536 ; 107 S.J. 594 193
Cummins *v.* Fletcher (1880), 14 Ch.D. 699 ; 49 L.J. Ch. 563 ; 42 L.T. 859 ; 28 W.R. 772 ; [1874-80] All E.R. Rep. 1274 202
Cundy *v.* Lindsay (1878), 3 App. Cas. 459 ; 38 L.T. 573 ; 42 J.P. 483 ; 26 W.R. 506 ; 14 Cox C.C. 93 ; [1874-80] All E.R. Rep. 1149 ; *sub nom.* Lindsay & Co. *v.* Cundy, 47 L.J.Q.B. 481 548-9
Curl Bros. Ltd. *v.* Webster, [1904] 1 Ch. 685 ; 73 L.J. Ch. 540 ; 90 L.T. 479 ; *sub nom.* Carl Bros. Ltd. *v.* Webster, 52 W.R. 413 474
Curling *v.* May (1734), cit. 3 Atk. 255 ; 26 E.R. 948 385
Curry *v.* Pile (1787), 2 Bro. C.C. 225 ; 29 E.R. 126 428
Curteis *v.* Wormald (1878), 10 Ch.D. 172 ; 40 L.T. 108 ; 27 W.R. 419 . 388
Curtin *v.* Evans (1872), I.R. 9 Eq. 553 422
Curtis *v.* Chemical Cleaning and Dyeing Co., [1951] 1 K.B. 805 ; [1951] 1 All E.R. 631 ; [1951] 1 T.L.R. 452 ; 95 S.J. 253 547
Curtis *v.* Sheffield (1882), 21 Ch.D. 1 ; 51 L.J. Ch. 535 ; 46 L.T. 177 ; 30 W.R. 581 559
Custance *v.* Cunningham (1851), 13 Beav. 363 ; 51 E.R. 140 347

PAGE

Cutliffe's Will Trusts, *Re*, Brewer *v.* Cutliffe, [1940] Ch. 565 ; [1940] 2 All E.R. 297 ; 109 L.J. Ch. 192 ; 163 L.T. 284 ; 56 T.L.R. 537 ; 84 S.J. 303 394

D. & C. Builders Ltd. *v.* Rees [1966] 2 Q.B. 617 ; [1966] 2 W.L.R. 288 ; [1965] 3 All E.R. 837 ; 109 S.J. 971 . . . . 41-2, 124-5
Dagenham (Thames) Dock Co., *Re*, *Ex parte* Hulse (1873), L.R. 8 Ch. App. 1022 ; 43 L.J.Ch. 261 ; 38 J.P. 180 ; 21 W.R. 898 25
Dale *v.* Hamilton (1846), 5 Hare 369 ; 67 E.R. 955 ; 16 L.J.Ch. 126 ; 11 Jur. 163 ; *on appeal* (1847), 2 Ph. 266 ; 41 E.R. 945 ; 71 R.R. 127 . . 489
Dale *v.* Smithwick (1690), 2 Vern. 151 ; 23 E.R. 704 186
Dallas, *Re*, [1904] 2 Ch. 385 ; 73 L.J. Ch. 365 ; 90 L.T. 177 ; 52 W.R. 567 ; 48 S.J. 260 303
Dalton *v.* Hayter (1844), 7 Beav. 313 ; 49 E.R. 1085 ; 3 L.T O.S. 72 ; 64 R.R. 95 246
Danby *v.* Read (1675), Rep. t. Finch. 226 ; 23 E.R. 124 168
D'Angibau, *Re*, Andrews *v.* Andrews (1879), 15 Ch.D. 228 ; 49 L.J.Ch. 182 ; 41 L.T. 645 ; 28 W.R. 311 ; *affirmed* (1880), 15 Ch.D. 228 ; 49 L.J.Ch. 756 ; 43 L.T. 135 ; 28 W.R. 930 ; [1874-80] All E.R. Rep. 1184 . 360-1
Darkin *v.* Cecil (1679/80), Nottingham's Chancery Cases, 79 Sel. Soc. 804 (case 1005) 168
Darley *v.* Nicholson (1841), 1 Dr. & War. 66 561
Darrel *v.* Whitchcott (1673/4), Nottingham's Chancery Cases, 73 Sel. Soc. 27 (case 58) 57
Dashwood *v.* Blythway (1729), 1 Eq. Cas. Abr. 317, pl. 3 ; 21 E.R. 1072 . 248
Daubeny *v.* Cockburn (1816), 1 Mer. 626 ; 35 E.R. 801 ; [1814-23] All E.R. Rep. 604 ; 15 R.R. 174 369
Daubuz *v.* Lavington (1884), 13 Q.B.D. 347 ; 53 L.J.Q.B. 283 ; 51 L.T. 206; 32 W.R. 772 ; Bitt. Rep. in Ch. 211 234
Daun *v.* City of London Brewery Co. (1869), L.R. 8 Eq. 155 ; 38 L.J.Ch. 454 ; 20 L.T. 601 ; 33 J.P. 547 ; 17 W.R. 663 221
Daveron, *Re*, Bowen *v.* Churchill, [1893] 3 Ch. 421 ; 63 L.J.Ch. 54 ; 69 L.T. 752 ; 42 W.R. 24 ; 9 T.L.R. 570 ; 37 S.J. 631 ; 3 R. 685 . 387, 389, 390
Davey *v.* Durrant (1857), 1 De G. & J. 535 ; 44 E.R. 830 ; 26 L.J.Ch. 830 ; 6 W.R. 405 ; 118 R.R. 213 257
Davidson, *Re*, Martin *v.* Trimmer (1879), 11 Ch.D. 341 ; 40 L.T. 726 . 392
Davies, *Re*, Davies *v.* Mackintosh, [1957] 1 W.L.R. 922 ; [1957] 3 All E.R. 52 ; 101 S.J. 611 427
Davies *v.* Ashford (1845), 15 Sim. 42 ; 60 E.R. 531 ; 14 L.J.Ch. 473 ; 6 L.T.O.S. 30 ; 9 Jur. 612 ; 74 R.R. 11 393
Davies *v.* Davies (1863), 4 Giff. 417 ; 66 E.R. 769 ; 9 L.T. 162 ; 9 Jur. N.S. 1002 ; 11 W.R. 1040 ; 2 New R. 384 ; [1861-73] All E.R. Rep. 937 ; 141 R.R. 260 352
Davies *v.* Fitton (1842), 2 Dr. & War. 225 ; 4 Ir. Eq. Rep. 612 . . 538
Davies *v.* Vaughan (1676), Nottingham's Chancery Cases, 73 Sel. Soc. 391 (case 524) 168
Davis *v.* Dendy (1818), 3 Madd. 170 ; 56 E.R. 473 ; 18 R.R. 209 . . 241
Davis *v.* Marlborough (Duke of) (1819), 2 Swanst. 108 ; 36 E.R. 555 ; 2 Wils. Ch. 130 ; 37 E.R. 258 ; [1814-23] All E.R. Rep. 13 . . . 554
Davis *v.* Symons, [1934] Ch. 442 ; 103 L.J.Ch. 311 ; 151 L.T. 96 ; 78 S.J. 297 ; [1934] All E.R. 136 203
Davis *v.* Thomas (1831), 1 Russ. & M. 506 ; 39 E.R. 195 ; 9 L.J.O.S. Ch. 232 ; 32 R.R. 257 179
Davis & Co., *Re*, *Ex parte* Rawlings (1888), 22 Q.B.D. 193 ; 37 W.R. 203 ; 5 T.L.R. 119 298
Davis's Estate, *Re*, [1912] 1 I.R. 516 532
Dawes, *Re*—*see* Kendall, *Ex parte*.
Dawson, *Re*, Swainson *v.* Dawson, [1919] 1 Ch. 102 ; 88 L.J.Ch. 73 ; 120 L.T. 189 ; 63 S.J. 25 ; [1918-19] All E.R. Rep. 866 419
Dawson *v.* Beeson (1882), 22 Ch.D. 504 ; 52 L.J. Ch. 563 ; 48 L.T. 407 ; 31 W.R. 537 475
Dawson *v.* Dawson (1803), 7 Ves. 173 ; 32 E.R. 71 561
Day *v.* Brownrigg (1878), 10 Ch.D. 294 ; 48 L.J.Ch. 173 ; 39 L.T. 553 ; 27 W.R. 217 . . . . 112, 460, 461
Deacon *v.* Smith (1746), 3 Atk. 323 ; 26 E.R. 988 430

PAGE

Deane, *Re* Bridger *v.* Deane (1889), 42 Ch.D. 9 ; 61 L.T. 492 ; 37 W.R. 786 . 31
Dearle *v.* Hall (1823), 3 Russ. 1 ; (1828), 3 Russ. 48 ; 38 E.R. 475, 492 ; [1824-34] All E.R. Rep. 28 ; 27 R.R. 1 . . . . . 211, 300-6
Debenham *v.* Ox (1749), 1 Ves. Sen. 276 ; 27 E.R. 1029 . . 552
Debtor, *Re*, Trustee *v.* Solomon—*see* Solomon, *Re*, *Ex parte* The Trustee of the Property of the Bankrupt *v.* Solomon.
De Costa *v.* Scandret (1723), 2 P. Wms. 170 ; 24 E.R. 686 . . . 552
Deeks *v.* Strutt (1794), 5 T.R. 690 ; 101 E.R. 384 64
Deering *v.* Earl of Winchelsea—*see* Dering *v.* Earl of Winchelsea.
De Francesco *v.* Barnum (1890), 45 Ch.D. 430 ; 60 L.J.Ch. 63 ; 63 L.T. 438 ; 39 W.R. 5 ; 6 T.L.R. 463 ; [1886-90] All E.R. Rep. 414 . . 492
De Freyne's Estate, *Re* (1871), 5 I.L.T.R. 193 179
De la Rochefoucauld *v.* Boustead—*see* Rochefoucauld *v.* Boustead.
Demerara Bauxite Co. Ltd. *v.* Hubbard, [1923] A.C. 673 ; 92 L.J.P.C. 148 ; 129 L.T. 517 . . . . 350, 351
De Nicols *v.* Curlier, [1900] A.C. 21 ; 69 L.J. Ch. 109 ; 81 L.T. 733 ; 48 W.R. 269 ; 16 T.L.R. 101 410
Denmark Productions Ltd. *v.* Boscobel Productions Ltd., [1969] 1 Q.B. 699 ; [1968] 3 W.L.R. 841 ; [1968] 3 All E.R. 513 563
Dennant *v.* Skinner, [1948] 2 K.B. 164 ; [1948] 2 All E.R. 29 ; [1948] L.J.R. 1576 548
Dent *v.* Bennett (1839), 4 My. & Cr. 269 ; 41 E.R. 105 ; 8 L.J.Ch. 125 ; 3 Jur. 99 ; 48 R.R. 94 341
Denton *v.* Donner (1856), 23 Beav. 285 ; 53 E.R. 112 ; 113 R.R. 143 . 341
Dering *v.* Earl of Winchelsea (1787), 1 Cox C.C. 318 ; 29 E.R. 1184 ; [1775-1802] All E.R. Rep. 140 ; 1 R.R. 41 ; *sub nom.* Deering *v.* Earl of Winchelsea, 2 Bos. & P. 270 ; 126 E.R. 1276 30-1
Derry *v.* Peek (1889), 14 App. Cas. 337 ; 58 L.J.Ch. 864 ; 61 L.T. 265 ; 54 J.P. 148 ; 38 W.R. 33 ; 5 T.L.R. 625 ; 1 Meg. 292 ; [1886-90] All E.R. Rep. 1 . . . . 329, 330, 332
Deschamps *v.* Miller, [1908]1 Ch. 856 ; 77 L.J. Ch. 416 ; 98 L.T. 564 . 13, 16
Desmond, *Re*, Creed *v.* Kearney, [1943] I.R. 534 ; 78 I.L.T.R. 145 . . 384
De Sommery, *Re*, Coelenbier *v.* De Sommery, [1912] 2 Ch. 622 ; 82 L.J.Ch. 17 ; 107 L.T. 253, 823 ; 57 S.J. 78 364
Dicey, *Re*, Julian *v.* Dicey, [1957] Ch. 145 ; [1956] 3 W.L.R. 981 ; [1956] 3 All E.R. 696 ; 100 S.J. 874 407-8
Dick, *Re*, Knight *v.* Dick, [1953] Ch. 343 ; [1953] 2 W.L.R. 477 ; [1953] 1 All E.R. 559 ; 97 S.J. 149 370
Dickinson *v.* Barrow, [1904] 2 Ch. 339 ; 73 L.J.Ch. 701 ; 91 L.T. 161 . 496
Dighton *v.* Withers (1862), 31 Beav. 423 ; 54 R. 1202 ; 135 R.R. 501 . 185
Dillon *v.* Coppin (1839), 4 My & Cr. 647 ; 41 E.R. 249 ; 9 L.J.Ch. 87 ; 4 Jur. 427 313
Dillon *v.* Parker (1818), 1 Swanst. 359 ; 36 E.R. 422 ; 18 R.R. 72 ; *on appeal* (1822), Jac. 505 ; 37 E.R. 941 ; *on further appeal* (1833), 7 Bligh N.S. 325 ; 5 E.R. 796 ; 1 Cl. & Fin. 303 ; 6 E.R. 930 ; 36 R.R. 123 397, 398, 405
Dimsdale *v.* Dimsdale (1856), 3 Drew. 556 ; 61 E.R. 1015 ; 25 L.J.Ch. 806 ; 27 L.T.O.S. 317 ; 106 R.R. 428 344
Dingle *v.* Coppen, [1899] 1 Ch. 726 ; 68 L.J. Ch. 337 ; 79 L.T. 693 ; 47 W.R. 279 188
Diplock, *Re*, Diplock *v.* Wintle, [1947] Ch. 716 ; [1947] 1 All E.R. 522 ; [1947] L.J.R. 1158 ; 177 L.T. 40 ; 91 S.J. 248 ; *on appeal*, [1948] Ch. 465 ; [1948] L.J.R. 1670 ; 92 S.J. 409, 484 ; *sub nom.* *Re* Diplock's Estate, Diplock *v.* Wintle, [1948] 2 All E.R. 318 ; *on appeal sub nom.* Ministry of Health *v.* Simpson, [1951] A.C. 251 ; [1950] 2 All E.R. 1137 ; 66 T.L.R. Pt. 2, 1015 ; *sub. nom.* *Re* Diplock, Minister of Health *v.* Simpson, 94 S.J. 777 . . . . . . 7-8, 9-11, 38, 162-3, 525, 527-9
Dixon *v.* Muckleston (1872), L.R. 8 Ch. App. 155 ; 42 L.J. Ch. 210 ; 27 L.T. 804 ; 21 W.R. 178 . . . . 183, 213
Dobson *v.* Land (1850), 8 Hare 216 ; 68 E.R. 337 ; 19 L.J. Ch. 484 ; 14 Jur. 288 ; 85 R.R. 286 ; *subsequent proceedings* (1851), 4 De G. & Sm. 575 ; 64 E.R. 963 ; 87 R.R. 483 258
Doe d. Rigge *v.* Bell (1793), 5 T.R. 471 ; 101 E.R. 265 ; 2 Sm. L.C. 119 . 84
Doe d. Thomson *v.* Amey (1840), 12 Ad. & El. 476 ; 113 E.R. 892 ; 4 Per. & Dav. 177 85

PAGE

Doherty *v.* Allman (1878), 3 App. Cas. 709 ; 39 L.T. 129 ; 42 J.P. 788 ; 26 W.R. 513 464
Doleman & Sons *v.* Ossett Corp., [1912] 3 K.B 257 ; 81 L.J.K.B. 1092 ; 107 L.T. 581 ; 76 J.P. 457 ; 10 L.G.R. 915 490
Dolphin *v.* Aylward (1870), L.R. 4 H.L. 486 ; 23 L.T. 636 ; 19 W.R. 49 . 436
Dominion Coal Co. Ltd. *v.* Dominion Iron and Steel Co. Ltd., [1909] A.C. 293 ; 78 L.J.P.C. 115 ; 100 L.T. 245 ; 25 T.L.R. 309 . . 492
Donaldson *v.* Donaldson (1854), Kay 711 ; 69 E.R. 303 ; 23 L.J. Ch. 788 ; 23 L.T.O.S. 306 ; 1 Jur. N.S. 10 ; 2 W.R. 691 ; [1843-60] All E.R. Rep. 200 ; 101 R.R. 833 309
Donmar Productions Ltd. *v.* Bart (1964), [1967] 1 W.L.R. 740 ; [1967] 2 All E.R. 338 458
Dorset (Duke of) *v.* Girdler (1720), Prec. Ch. 531 ; 24 E.R. 238 ; 2 Eq. Cas. Abr. 181, pl. 2 ; 22 E.R. 155 555
Douglas *v.* Culverwell (1862), 4 De G. F. & J. 20 ; 45 E.R. 1089 ; 31 L.J.Ch. 543 ; 6 L.T. 272 ; 10 W.R. 327 ; 135 R.R. 11 179
Douglas and Powell's Contract, *Re,* [1902] 2 Ch. 296 ; 71 L.J. Ch. 850 . 391, 393
Douglas-Menzies *v.* Umphelby, [1908] A.C. 224 ; 77 L.J.P.C. 64 ; 98 L.T. 509 ; 24 T.L.R. 344 410-11
Dowle *v.* Saunders (1864), 2 H. & M. 242 ; 71 E.R. 456 ; 4 New R. 478 ; 34 L.J. Ch. 87 ; 10 L.T. 840 ; 10 Jur. N.S. 901 ; 12 W.R. 1074 ; 144 R.R. 140 213
Downs *v.* Collins (1848), 6 Hare 418 ; 67 E.R. 1228 ; 12 L.T.O.S. 102 ; 77 R.R. 171 488
Downshire (Marquis of) *v.* Lady Sandys (1801), 6 Ves. 107 ; 31 E.R. 962 . . . . 80, 464
Dowse *v.* Gorton, [1891] A.C. 190 ; 60 L.J. Ch. 745 ; 64 L.T. 809 ; 40 W.R. 17 ; [1891-4] All E.R. Rep. 1230 274
Doyle's Estate, *Re,* [1907] 1 I.R. 204 ; 41 I.L.T.R. 47 384
Drewe *v.* Corp (1804), 9 Ves. 368 ; 32 E.R. 644 506
Driscoll *v.* Church Commissioners for England, [1957] 1 Q.B. 330 ; [1956] 3 W.L.R. 996 ; [1956] 3 All E.R. 802 ; 100 S.J. 872 469
Drought *v.* Eustace (1828), 1 Mol. 328 334
Drover *v.* Beyer (1879), 13 Ch.D. 242 ; 49 L.J. Ch. 37 ; 41 L.T. 393 ; 28 W.R. 110 560-1
Dudley and District Benefit Building Soc. *v.* Emerson, [1949] Ch. 707 ; [1949] 2 All E.R. 252 ; [1949] L.J.R. 1441 ; 65 T.L.R. 444 ; 93 S.J. 512 . 228
Dudley and District Benefit Building Soc. *v.* Gordon, [1929] 2 K.B. 105 ; 98 L.J.K.B. 486 ; 141 L.T. 583 ; 93 J.P. 186 ; 45 T.L.R. 424 ; 27 L.G.R. 448 ; [1929] All E.R. Rep. 528 234
Duggan *v.* Duggan (1880), 7 L.R. Ir. 152 369
Dunbar-Buller, *Re,* [1923] 2 I.R. 143 357
Duncan *v.* Worrall (1822), 10 Price 31 ; 147 E.R. 232 ; 24 R.R. 695 . 554
Duncan, Fox & Co. *v.* North and South Wales Bank (1880), 6 App. Cas. 1 ; 50 L.J. Ch. 355 ; 43 L.T. 706 ; 29 W.R. 763 437-8
Duncombe, *Ex parte* (1774), Dick. 503 ; 21 E.R. 365 560
Duncuft *v.* Albrecht (1841), 12 Sim. 189 ; 59 E.R. 1104 ; 56 R.R. 46 383, 487
Dunlop Pneumatic Tyre Co. Ltd. *v.* New Garage and Motor Co. Ltd., [1915] A.C. 79 ; 83 L.J.K.B. 1574 ; 111 L.T. 862 ; 30 T.L.R. 625 ; [1914-15] All E.R. Rep. 739 19-20
Durham (Earl of) *v.* Wharton (1836), 10 Bligh N.S. 526 ; 6 E.R. 194 ; 3 Cl. & Fin. 146 ; 6 E.R. 1392 ; 39 R.R. 13 ; *sub nom.* Wharton *v.* Lord Durham, 6 L.J. Ch. 15 423-4
Durham Bros. *v.* Robertson, [1898] 1 Q.B. 765 ; 67 L.J.Q.B. 484 ; 78 L.T. 438 . . . . 298, 326
Durham Fancy Goods Ltd. *v.* Michael Jackson (Fancy Goods) Ltd., [1968] 2 Q.B. 839 ; [1968] 3 W.L.R. 225 ; [1968] 2 All E.R. 987 . . 41, 125
Dursley (Lord) *v.* Fitzhardinge Berkeley (1801), 6 Ves. 251 ; 31 E.R. 1036 ; 5 R.R. 285 555
Du Sautoy *v.* Symes, [1967] Ch. 1146 ; [1967] 2 W.L.R. 342 ; [1967] 1 All E.R. 25 ; 111 S.J. 133 504
Dykes' Estate, *Re* (1869), L.R. 7 Eq. 337 ; 20 L.T. 292 ; 17 W.R. 658 . 366

PAGE

E.P. Finance Co. Ltd. *v.* Dooley, [1963] 1 W.L.R. 1313 ; [1964] 1 All E.R. 527 ; 107 S.J. 982 20
Eales *v.* England (1702), Prec. Ch. 200 ; 24 E.R. 96 ; *on appeal, sub nom.* Eeles *v.* England (1704), 2 Vern. 466 ; 23 E.R. 901 152
Eastwood *v.* Vinke (1731), 2 P. Wms. 613 ; 24 E R. 883 415
Eddis *v.* Chichester Constable, [1969] 1 W.L.R. 385 ; [1969] 1 All E.R. 546 ; *on appeal,* [1969] 3 W.L.R. 48 ; (1969), *The Times* newspaper, 24th April 28
Edge *v.* Worthington (1786), 1 Cox C.C. 211 ; 29 E.R. 1133 ; 1 R.R. 20 . 182
Edgeworth *v.* Johnston (1877), I.R. 11 Eq. 326 422
Edmondson *v.* Copland, [1911] 2 Ch. 301 ; 80 L.J. Ch. 532 ; 105 L.T. 8 ; 27 T.L.R. 446 ; 55 S.J. 520 ; [1911-13] All E.R. Rep. 592 . . 188, 189
Edmunds *v.* Low (1857), 3 K. & J. 318 ; 69 E.R. 1130 ; 26 L.J. Ch. 432 ; 30 L.T.O.S. 31 ; 3 Jur. N.S. 598 ; 5 W.R. 444 ; 112 R.R. 161 . . 416
Edmunds *v.* Povey (1683), 1 Vern. 187 ; 23 E.R. 404 . . . 173
Educational Co. of Ireland Ltd. *v.* Fitzpatrick, [1961] I.R. 323 . . 458
Edwards, *Re*, Macadam *v.* Wright, [1958] Ch. 168 ; [1957] 3 W.L.R. 131 ; [1957] 2 All E.R. 495 ; 101 S.J. 515 . . . . . 400, 407
Edwards *v.* Bingham (1879), 28 W.R. 89 536
Edwards *v.* Martin (1856), 25 L.J. Ch. 284 ; 27 L.T.O.S. 164 ; 4 W.R. 219 ; 105 R.R. 279 ; *subsequent proceedings* (1858), 28 L.J. Ch. 49 . . 245
Edwards *v.* Meyrick (1842), 2 Hare 60 ; 67 E.R. 25 ; 12 L.J. Ch. 49 ; 6 Jur. 924 ; 62 R.R. 23 352
Edwards *v.* West (1878), 7 Ch.D. 858 ; 47 L.J. Ch. 463 ; 38 L.T. 481 ; 26 W.R. 507 382
Edwards's Estate, *Re* (1861), 11 Ir. Ch. Rep. 367 205
Eeles *v.* England—*see* Eales *v.* England.
Ellard *v.* Phelan, [1914] 1 I.R. 76 416
Ellerman Lines Ltd. *v.* Read, [1928] 2 K.B. 144 ; 97 L.J.K.B. 366 ; 138 L.T. 625 ; 44 T.L.R. 285 ; 17 Asp. M.L.C. 421 ; 33 Com. Cas. 219 ; [1928] All E.R. Rep. 415 458
Ellice *v.* Roupell (No. 1) (1863), 32 Beav. 299 ; 55 E.R. 117 ; 2 New R. 3 ; 32 L.J. Ch. 563 ; 9 Jur. N.S. 530 ; 11 W.R. 579 555
Ellice *v.* Roupell (No. 2) (1863), 32 Beav. 308 ; 55 E.R. 121 ; 2 New R. 3 ; 32 L.J. Ch. 624 ; 8 L.T. 191 ; 9 Jur. N.S. 530 ; 11 W.R. 579 . . 555
Ellice *v.* Roupell (No. 3) (1863), 32 Beav. 318 ; 55 E.R. 125 ; 2 New R. 150 ; 32 L.J. Ch. 778 ; 8 L.T. 486 ; 9 Jur. N.S. 533 ; 11 W.R. 679 . . 555
Elliotson *v.* Knowles (1842), 11 L.J. Ch. 399 ; 6 Jur. 549 . . . 559
Elliott (Harold) and H. Elliott (Builders) Ltd. *v.* Pierson, [1948] Ch. 452 ; *sub. nom.* Elliott *v.* Pierson, [1948] 1 All E.R. 939 ; [1948] L.J.R. 1452 ; 92 S.J. 271 . . . . 504, 542
Elliston *v.* Reacher, [1908] 2 Ch. 374 ; *on appeal,* [1908] 2 Ch. 665 ; 78 L.J. Ch. 87 ; 99 L.T. 701 ; [1908-10] All E.R. Rep. 612 33
Elphinstone (Lord) *v.* Monkland Iron and Coal Co. (1886), 11 App. Cas. 332 ; 35 W.R. 17 20
Emanuel College *v.* Evans (1625), 1 Ch. Rep. 18 ; 21 E.R. 494 . . . 169
Emery's Investment Trusts, *Re*, Emery *v.* Emery, [1959] Ch. 410 ; [1959] 2 W.L.R. 461 ; [1959] 1 All E.R. 577 ; 103 S.J. 257 31
Emuss *v.* Smith (1848), 2 De G. & Sm 722 ; 64 E.R. 323 ; 79 R.R. 346 . 382
Endacott, *Re*, Corpe *v.* Endacott, [1960] Ch. 232 ; [1959] 3 W.L.R. 799 ; [1959] 3 All E.R. 562 ; 58 L.G.R. 25 ; 103 S.J. 918 38
England *v.* Codrington (1758), 1 Eden 169 ; 28 E.R. 649 . . . 168
England *v.* Curling (1844), 8 Beav. 129 ; 50 E.R. 51 ; 68 R.R. 39 . 488-9
English Hop Growers Ltd. *v.* Dering, [1928] 2 K.B. 174 ; 97 L.J.K.B. 569 ; 139 L.T. 76 ; 44 T.L.R. 443 ; [1928] All E.R. Rep. 396 20
Ensworth *v.* Griffiths (1706), 5 Bro. P.C. 184 ; 2 E.R. 615 . . 177-8, 260
Epstein *v.* Gluckin (1922), 233 N.Y. 490 ; 135 N.E. 861 503
Erlanger *v.* New Sombrero Phosphate Co. (1878), 3 App. Cas. 1218 ; 39 L.T. 269 ; 27 W.R. 65 ; [1874-80] All E.R. Rep. 271 ; *sub nom.* New Sombrero Phosphate Co. *v.* Erlanger, 48 L.J. Ch. 73 . . 34, 543, 544
Errington *v.* Errington, [1952] 1 K.B. 290 ; [1952] 1 All E.R. 149 ; [1952] 1 T.L.R. 231 ; 96 S.J. 119 . . . . 37, 103, 470
Esso Petroleum Co. Ltd. *v.* Harper's Garage (Stourport) Ltd., [1966] 2 Q.B. 514 ; [1966] 2 W.L.R. 1043 ; [1966] 1 All E.R. 725 ; 110 S.J. 265 ; *on appeal,* [1968] A.C. 269 ; [1967] 2 W.L.R. 871 ; [1967] 1 All E.R. 699 ; 111 S.J. 174 . . . . 1, 208

PAGE

Etches *v.* Lance (1802), 7 Ves. 417 ; 32 E.R. 169 561
Eustace *v.* Keightley (1713) 4 Bro. P.C. 588 ; 2 E.R. 401 . . . 139
Evans *v.* Bicknell (1801), 6 Ves. 174 ; 31 E.R. 998 ; 5 R.R. 245 . 217, 329
Evans *v.* Bremridge (1856), 8 De G. M. & G. 100 ; 44 E.R. 327 ; 25 L.J. Ch. 334 ; 27 L.T.O.S. 8 ; 2 Jur. N.S. 311 ; 4 W.R. 350 ; [1843-60] All E.R. Rep. 170 ; 110 R.R. 156 552
Evans *v.* Cook (1874), 8 I.L.T.R. 118 345
Evans *v.* Llewellin (1787), 1 Cox C.C. 333 ; 29 E.R. 1191 ; *sub nom.* Evans *v.* Llewellyn, 2 Bro. C.C. 150 ; 29 E.R. 86 ; 1 R.R. 49 . . . 334
Ewing *v.* Orr-Ewing (1883), 9 App. Cas. 34 ; 53 L.J. Ch. 435 ; 50 L.T. 401 ; 32 W.R. 573 15
Exall *v.* Partridge (1799), 8 T.R. 308 ; 101 E.R. 1405 ; 3 Esp. 8 ; 170 E.R. 520 ; [1775-1802] All E.R. Rep. 341 115
Exton *v.* Greaves (1682), 1 Vern. 138 ; 23 E.R. 371 ; 1 Eq. Cas. Abr. 317, pl. 1 ; 21 E.R. 1072 169
Eyre, *Re*, Johnson *v.* Williams, [1917] 1 Ch. 351 ; 86 L.J. Ch. 257 ; 116 L.T. 469 ; 61 S.J. 336 290
Eyre *v.* McDowell (1861), 9 H.L.C. 619 ; 11 E.R. 871 ; 1 I.J.N.S. 41 ; 131 R.R. 373 184

Fairclough *v.* Marshall (1878), 4 Ex.D. 37 ; 48 L.J.Q.B. 146 ; 39 L.T. 389 ; 27 W.R. 145 ; [1874-80] All E.R. Rep. 1261 223
Fairclough *v.* Swan Brewery Co. Ltd., [1912] A.C. 565 ; 81 L.J.P.C. 207; 106 L.T. 931 ; 28 T.L.R. 450 ; [1911-13] All E.R. Rep. 397 . . 203-4
Falcke *v.* Gray (1859), 4 Drew. 651 ; 62 E.R. 250 ; 29 L.J. Ch. 28 ; 33 L.T.O.S. 297 ; 5 Jur. N.S. 645 ; 7 W.R. 535 ; 113 R.R. 493 . . 490
Faraday *v.* Tamworth Union (1916), 86 L.J. Ch. 436 ; 81 J.P. 81 ; 15 L.G.R. 258 541
Farebrother *v.* Wodehouse (1856), 23 Beav. 18 ; 53 E.R. 7 ; 26 L.J. Ch. 81 ; 28 L.T.O.S. 94 ; 2 Jur. N.S. 1178 ; 5 W.R. 12 ; 113 R.R. 10 ; *on appeal* (1857), 26 L.J. Ch. 240 202
Farey *v.* Cooper, [1927] 2 K.B. 384 ; 96 L.J.K.B. 1046 ; 137 L.T. 720 ; 43 T.L.R. 803 ; [1927] All E.R. Rep. 311 475
Farmer *v.* Curtis (1829), 2 Sim. 466 ; 57 E.R. 862 ; 29 R.R. 140 . 245
Farmer *v.* Pitt, [1902] 1 Ch. 954 ; 71 L.J. Ch. 500 ; 50 W.R. 453 ; 46 S.J. 379 198
Farrand *v.* Yorkshire Banking Co. (1888), 40 Ch. D. 182 ; 58 L.J. Ch. 238 ; 60 L.T. 669 ; 37 W.R. 318 213
Farrar *v.* Farrars Ltd. (1888), 40 Ch.D. 395 ; 58 L.J. Ch. 185 ; 60 L.T. 121 ; 37 W.R. 196 ; 5 T.L.R. 164 . . . . 253, 255
Fector *v.* Philpott (1823), 12 Price 197 ; 147 E.R. 697 ; 26 R.R. 650. . 184, 260
Fee *v.* Cobine (1847), 11 Ir. Eq. Rep. 406 179
Fell *v.* Brown (1787), 2 Bro. C.C. 276 ; 29 E.R. 151 245
Fells *v.* Read (1796), 3 Ves. 70 ; 30 E.R. 899 ; [1775-1802] All E.R. Rep. 525 ; 3 R.R. 47 . . . . 67, 484
Felton *v.* Callis, [1969] 1 Q.B. 200 ; [1968] 3 W.L.R. 951 ; [1968] 3 All E.R. 673 ; 112 S.J. 672 . . . . 560, 561
Fenner *v.* Blake, [1900] 1 Q.B. 426 ; 69 L.J.Q.B. 257 ; 82 L.T. 149 ; 48 W.R. 392 123
Ferrand *v.* Wilson (1845), 4 Hare 344 ; 67 E.R. 680 ; 15 L.J. Ch. 41 ; 9 Jur. 860 ; 67 R.R. 70 559
Ferris *v.* Weaven, [1952] 2 All E.R. 233 ; [1952] W.N. 318 ; 96 S.J. 414 103, 470
Feversham (Earl of) *v.* Watson (1677), 2 Freem. 35 ; 22 E.R. 1042 ; Rep. t Finch 445 (date given as 1680) ; 23 E.R. 242 ; *on appeal* (1681), 1 Vern 83; 23 E.R. 326 ; *on appeal* (1678), Nottingham's Chancery Cases, 79 Sel. Soc. 637 (case 823) 54, 55
Ffrench's Estate, *Re* (1887), 21 L.R. Ir. 283 213
Field *v.* Boland (1837), 1 Dr. & Wal. 37 ; 56 R.R. 150 552
Field *v.* Sowle (1827), 4 Russ. 112 ; 38 E.R. 747 345
Financings Ltd. *v.* Baldock, [1963] 2 Q.B. 104 ; [1963] 2 W.L.R. 359 ; [1963] 1 All E.R. 443 ; 107 S.J. 15 23
Finegan's Estate, *Re*, Mathews *v.* Donegan, [1925] 1 I.R. 201 . . 431
Fisher *v.* Hughes (1820), Coop. t. Cott. 329 ; 47 E.R. 879 . . . 557
Fisherwick *v.* Lowe (1787), 1 Cox C.C. 411 ; 29 E.R. 1225 . . . 245
Fitch *v.* Dewes, [1921] 2 A.C. 158 ; 90 L.J. Ch. 436 ; 125 L.T. 744 ; 37 T.L.R. 784 ; 65 S.J. 626 ; [1921] All E.R. Rep. 13 471

PAGE

Fitch *v.* Weber (1848), 6 Hare 145 ; 67 E.R. 1117 ; 17 L.J. Ch. 361 ; 11 L.T.O.S. 83 ; 12 Jur. 645 ; 77 R.R. 56 388
Fitzgerald *v.* Fitzgerald, [1902] 1 I.R. 477 ; 36 I.L.T.R. 18 . . 532
Fitzgerald *v.* Jervoise (1820), 5 Madd. 25 ; 56 E.R. 804 ; 21 R.R. 268 . 386
Fitzgerald *v.* National Bank Ltd., [1929] 1 K.B. 394 ; 98 L.J.K.B. 382 ; 140 L.T. 406 ; [1928] All E.R. Rep. 596 . . . . . 415, 416
Fitzgerald's Trustee *v.* Mellersh, [1892] 1 Ch. 385 ; 61 L.J. Ch. 231 ; 66 L.T. 178 ; 40 W.R. 251 ; 8 T.L.R. 237 ; 36 S.J. 216 ; [1891-4] All E.R. Rep. 979 189
Fitzroy *v.* Cave, [1905] 2 K.B. 364 ; 74 L.J.K.B. 829 ; 93 L.T. 499 ; 54 W.R. 17 ; 21 T.L.R. 612 ; [1904-7] All E.R. Rep. 194 . . . 296
Fitzroy *v.* Gwillim (1786), 1 T.R. 153 ; 99 E.R. 1025 ; 1 R.R. 167 . . 113
Fitzsimon, *Ex parte—see* Ulster Land, Building and Investment Co., *Re.*
Flack *v.* Holm (1820), 1 Jac. & W. 405 ; 37 E.R. 430 ; 21 R.R. 202 . . 561
Fletcher, *Re*, Gillings *v.* Fletcher (1888), 38 Ch.D. 373 ; 57 L.J. Ch. 1032 ; 59 L.T. 313 ; 36 W.R. 841 ; 4 T.L.R. 486 414-15
Fletcher, *Re*, Reading *v.* Fletcher, [1917] 1 Ch. 339 ; 86 L.J. Ch. 317 ; 116 L.T. 460 ; 61 S.J. 267 . . . . 81, 194
Fletcher *v.* Ashburner (1779), 1 Bro. C.C. 497 ; 28 E.R. 1259 . 65, 375, 386
Flight *v.* Bolland (1828), 4 Russ. 298 ; 38 E.R. 817 ; [1824-34] All E.R. Rep. 372 ; 28 R.R. 101 503
Flight *v.* Booth (1834), 1 Bing. N.C. 370 ; 131 E.R. 1160 ; 1 Scott 190 ; 4 L.J.C.P. 66 ; [1824-34] All E.R. Rep. 43 507
Flight *v.* Cook (1755), 2 Ves. Sen. 619 ; 28 E.R. 394 557
Flint *v.* Howard, [1893] 2 Ch. 54 ; 62 L.J. Ch. 804 ; 68 L.T. 390 ; 2 R. 386 435
Fluker *v.* Taylor (1855), 3 Drew. 183 ; 61 E.R. 873 563
Foley *v.* Hill (1848), 2 H.L.C. 28; 9 E.R. 27 ; [1843-60] All E.R. Rep. 16 ; 81 R.R. 14 521
Forbes (Lord) *v.* Deniston (1722), 4 Bro. P.C. 189 ; 2 E.R. 129 ; 2 Eq. Cas. Abr. 482, pl. 19 ; 22 E.R. 409 . . . . 28, 212
Forbes *v.* Jackson (1882), 19 Ch.D. 615 ; 51 L.J. Ch. 690 ; 48 L.T. 722 ; 30 W.R. 652 ; [1881-5] All E.R. Rep. 863 193
Forbes *v.* Moffatt (1811), 18 Ves. 384 ; 34 E.R. 362 ; [1803-13] All E.R. Rep. 460 ; 11 R.R. 222 193-4
Ford *v.* Tynte (No. 2) (1864), 2 H. & M. 319 ; 71 E.R. 487 ; 144 R.R. 155 ; *on appeal* (1865), 2 De G. J. & S. 557 ; 46 E.R. 492 ; 6 New R. 51 ; 34 L.J. Ch. 452 ; 12 L.T. 512 ; 11 Jur. N.S. 402 ; 13 W.R. 643 ; 144 R.R. 155 421
Ford *v.* Tynte (No. 3) (1864), 2 H. & M. 324 ; 71 E.R. 489 ; 5 New R. 73 ; 11 L.T. 367 ; 10 Jur. N.S. 1193 ; 144 R.R. 161 421
Ford *v.* Wastell (1847), 2 Ph. 591 ; 41 E.R. 1071 ; *on appeal from* 6 Hare 229 ; 67 E.R. 1151 ; 16 L.J. Ch. 372 ; 9 L.T.O.S. 372 ; 11 Jur. 537 ; 77 R.R. 95 248
Ford Motor Co. Ltd. *v.* Amalgamated Union of Engineering and Foundry Workers, [1969] 1 W.L.R. 339 ; [1969] 2 All E.R. 481 ; 113 S.J. 203 . 479
Forrer *v.* Nash (1865), 35 Beav. 167 ; 55 E.R. 858 ; 6 New R. 361 ; 11 Jur. N.S. 789 ; 14 W.R. 8 ; 147 R.R. 92 504
Forrester *v.* Cotton (1760), 1 Eden 531 ; 28 E.R. 792 ; *sub nom.* Forrester *v.* Cotten, Amb. 388 ; 27 E.R. 259 399
Forster *v.* Baker, [1910] 2 K.B. 636 ; 79 L.J.K.B. 664 ; 102 L.T. 522 ; 26 T.L.R. 421 ;]1908-10] All E.R. Rep. 554 327
Forster *v.* Hale (1798), 3 Ves. 696 ; 30 E.R. 1226 ; *on appeal* (1800), 5 Ves. 308 ; 31 E.R. 603 ; [1775-1802] All E.R. Rep. 49 ; 4 R.R. 128 . 68
Fortescue *v.* Barnett (1834), 3 My. & K. 36 ; 40 E.R. 14 ; 3 L.J. Ch. 106 ; [1824-34] All E.R. Rep. 361 ; 41 R.R. 5; *previous proceedings* (1833), Coop. t. Cott. 367 ; 47 E.R. 899 313
Foster *v.* Cockerell (1835), 3 Cl. & Fin. 456 ; 6 E.R. 1508 ; 9 Bligh N.S. 332 ; 5 E.R. 1315 ; 39 R.R. 24 ; *on appeal from* Foster *v.* Blackstone (1833), 1 My. & K. 297 ; 39 E.R. 694 ; 1 L.J. Ch. 84 303
Foster *v.* Foster (1875), 1 Ch.D. 588 ; 45 L.J. Ch. 301 ; 24 W.R. 185 . 380
Foster *v.* Reeves, [1892] 2 Q.B. 255 ; 61 L.J.Q.B. 763 ; 67 L.T. 537 ; 57 J.P. 23 ; 40 W.R. 695 . . . . 90, 93, 448-9
Four-Maids Ltd. *v.* Dudley Marshall (Properties) Ltd., [1957] Ch. 317 ; [1957] 2 W.L.R. 931 ; [1957] 2 All E.R. 35 ; 101 S.J. 408 230

PAGE

Fowke *v.* Draycott (1885), 29 Ch.D. 996 ; 54 L.J. Ch. 977 ; 52 L.T. 890 ; 33 W.R. 701 442
Fowler *v.* Fowler (1735), 3 P. Wms. 353 ; 24 E.R. 1098 ; [1558-1774] All E.R. Rep. 579 417
Fowler *v.* Fowler (1859), 4 De G. & J. 250 ; 45 E.R. 97 ; 124 R.R. 234 . 537
Fox's Estate, *Re* (1856), 5 Ir. Ch. Rep. 541 433
Frame *v.* Dawson (1807), 14 Ves. 387 ; 33 E.R. 569 ; 9 R.R. 304 . . 495
Francklyn *v.* Fern (1740), Barn. C. 30 ; 27 E.R. 542 168
Franco *v.* Bolton (1797), 3 Ves. 368 ; 30 E.R. 1058 553
Frank *v.* Lady Standish (1772), 15 Ves. 391 n. ; 33 E.R. 803 398
Fraser *v.* Evans, [1969] 1 Q.B. 349 ; [1968] 3 W.L.R. 1172 ; [1969] 1 All E.R. 8 ; 112 S.J. 805 461
Frazer *v.* Jones (1816), 5 Hare 475 ; 67 E.R. 999 ; 71 R.R. 184 ; *on appeal* (1848), 17 L.J. Ch. 353 ; 12 Jur. 443 213
Frearson *v.* Loe (1878), 9 Ch. D. 48 ; 27 W.R. 182 474
Freeman *v.* Cooke (1848), 2 Ex. 654 ; 154 E.R. 652 ; 6 Dow & L. 187 ; 18 L.J. Ex. 114 ; 12 L.T.O.S. 66 ; 12 Jur. 777 ; [1843-60] All E.R. Rep. 185 ; 76 R.R. 711 39
Freeman *v.* Laing, [1899] 2 Ch. 355 ; 68 L.J. Ch. 586 ; 81 L.T. 167 ; 48 W.R. 9 ; 43 S.J. 625 306
Freeman-Thomas Indenture, *Re*, *Re* Ratton Estate, [1957] 1 W.L.R. 560 ; [1957] 1 All E.R. 532 ; 121 J.P. 189 ; 101 S.J. 320 ; 55 L.G.R. 232 . 469
French *v.* Baron (1740), 2 Atk. 120 ; 26 E.R. 475 241
Frere *v.* Moore (1820), 8 Price 475 ; 146 E.R. 1267 ; 22 R.R. 759 . 172
Frith, *Re*, Newton *v.* Rolfe, [1902] 1 Ch. 342 ; 71 L.J. Ch. 199 ; 86 L.T. 212 273
Frith *v.* Cartland (1865), 2 H. & M. 417 ; 71 E.R. 525 ; 34 L.J. Ch. 301 ; 12 L.T. 175 ; 11 Jur. N.S. 238 ; 13 W.R. 493 ; [1861-73] All E.R. Rep. 608; 144 R.R. 206 520
Frogley *v.* Earl of Lovelace (1859), Johns. 333 ; 70 E.R. 450 ; 123 R.R. 147 99, 101
Fry, *Re*, Chase National Executors and Trustees Corp. *v.* Fry, [1946] Ch.312; [1946] 2 All E.R. 106 ; 115 L.J. Ch. 225 ; 175 L.T. 392 ; 62 T.L.R. 414 ; 90 S.J. 346 . . . . 318-21, 322, 323
Fry *v.* Lane (1888), 40 Ch. D. 312 ; 58 L.J.Ch. 113 ; 60 L.T. 12 ; 37 W.R. 135 ; 5 T.L.R. 45 ; *sub nom. Re* Fry, Fry *v.* Lane, [1886-90] All E.R. Rep. 1084 333
Fryer *v.* Bernard (1724), 2 P. Wms. 261 ; 24 E.R. 722 136
Fuller's Contract, *Re*, [1933] Ch. 652 ; 102 L.J. Ch. 255 ; 149 L.T. 237 . 377
Fullerton *v.* Provincial Bank of Ireland, [1903] A.C. 309 ; 72 L.J.P.C. 79 ; 89 L.T. 79 ; 52 W.R. 238 ; [1903] 1 I.R. 483 ; 37 I.L.T.R. 188 ; 3 N.I.J.R. 409 212
Fullwood *v* Fullwood (1878), 9 Ch.D. 176 ; 47 L.J. Ch. 459 ; 26 W.R. 435 ; *sub. nom.* Fulwood *v.* Fulwood, 38 L.T. 380 460
Fulthrope *v.* Foster (1687), 1 Vern. 476 ; 23 E.R. 602 235
Furness, *Re*, Furness *v.* Stalkartt, [1901] 2 Ch. 346 ; 70 L.J. Ch. 580 ; 84 L.T. 680 ; 45 S.J. 557 423
Furness *v.* Bond (1888), 4 T.L.R. 457 87

Gainsford *v.* Dunn (1874), L.R. 17 Eq. 405 ; 43 L.J. Ch. 403 ; 30 L.T. 283 ; 22 W.R. 499 365
Gaisberg *v.* Storr, [1950] 1 K.B. 107 ; [1949] 2 All E.R. 411 ; 65 T.L.R. 485 ; 93 S.J. 600 490
Galbraith *v.* Mitchenall Estates Ltd., [1965] 2 Q.B. 473 ; [1964] 3 W.L.R. 454 ; [1964] 2 2 All E.R. 653 ; 108 S.J. 749 24-5
Gale *v.* Lindo (1687), 1 Vern. 475 ; 23 E.R. 601 ; *sub nom.* Gay *v.* Wendow, 2 Freem. 101 ; 22 E.R. 1084 ; Anon., 2 Eq. Cas. Abr. 478 ; pl. 1 ; 22 E.R. 406 39
Gallagher *v.* Tuohy (1924), 58 I.L.T.R. 134 458
Gallie *v.* Lee, [1969] 2 W.L.R. 901 . . . . . . 119, 549
Garland, *Ex parte* (1804), 10 Ves. 110 ; 32 E.R. 786 ; [1803-13] All E.R. Rep. 750 ; 7 R.R. 352 ; *sub nom. Re* Ballman, 1 Smith K.B. 220 . . 273
Garland *v.* Garland (1793), 2 Ves. Jun. 137 ; 30 E.R. 561 517
Garrahan *v.* Garrahan, [1959] I.R. 168 511
Garrard *v.* Frankel (1862), 30 Beav. 445 ; 54 E.R. 961 ; 31 L.J. Ch. 604; 8 Jur. N.S. 985 ; 26 J.P. 727 ; 132 R.R. 352 533-4

PAGE

Garth *v.* Meyrick (1779), 1 Bro. C.C. 30 ; 28 E.R. 966 428
Garthshore *v.* Chalie (1804), 10 Ves. 1 ; 32 E.R. 743 ; [1803-13] All E.R. Rep. 239 ; 7 R.R. 311 431
Gascoigne *v.* Gascoigne, [1918] 1 K.B. 223 ; 87 L.J.K.B. 333 ; 118 L.T. 347; 34 T.L.R. 168 31
Gay *v.* Wendow—*see* Gale *v.* Lindo.
Geary *v.* Bearcroft (1666), Cart. 57 ; 124 E.R. 822 ; Bridg. O. 484 ; 124 E.R. 702 ; *sub nom.* Geary *v.* Barecroft, 1 Sid. 346 ; 82 E.R. 1148; *sub nom.* Bearcroft *v.* Geery, 2 Keb. 285 ; 84 E.R. 177 152
Gee *v.* Pritchard (1818), 2 Swanst. 402 ; 36 E.R. 670 ; 19 R.R. 87 . . 71-2
George's Will Trusts, *Re* Barclay's Bank Ltd. *v.* George, [1949] Ch. 154 ; [1948] 2 All E.R. 1004; 92 S.J. 689 423
German *v.* Yates (1915), 32 T.L.R. 52 . . . 315-7, 318, 320, 321
Gestetner Settlement, *Re*, Barnett *v.* Blumka, [1953] Ch. 672 ; [1953] 2 W.L.R. 1033 ; [1953] 1 All E.R. 1150 ; 97 S.J. 332 . . 362, 363
Ghana Commercial Bank *v.* Chandiram, [1960] A.C. 732 ; [1960] 3 W.L.R. 328 ; [1960] 2 All E.R. 865 ; 104 S.J. 583 192-3
Ghey and Galton's Application, *Re*, [1957] 2 Q.B. 650 ; [1957] 3 W.L.R. 562 ; [1957] 3 All E.R. 164 ; 101 S.J. 679 469
Gibbard's Will Trusts, *Re*, Public Trustee *v.* Davis, [1967] 1 W.L.R. 42 ; [1966] 1 All E.R. 273 ; 110 S.J. 871 362
Gibbs, *Re*, Midland Bank Executor and Trustee Co. Ltd. *v.* Inland Revenue Commissioners, [1951] Ch. 933 ; [1951] 2 All E.R. 63 ; [1951] T.R. 113 ; 30 A.T.C. 129 286
Gibson *v.* Jeyes (1801), 6 Ves. 266 ; 31 E.R. 1044 ; [1775-1802] All E.R. Rep. 325 ; 5 R.R. 295 340
Gibson *v.* Kinven (1682), 1 Vern. 66 ; 23 E.R. 315 365
Gibson *v.* Russell (1843), 2 Y. & C.C.C. 104 ; 63 E.R. 46 ; 7 Jur. 875 ; 60 R.R. 60 341
Gibson *v.* Seagrim (1855), 20 Beav. 614 ; 52 E.R. 741 ; 24 L.J. Ch. 782 ; 26 L.T.O.S. 65 ; 109 R.R. 556 433
Gilchrist, *Ex parte*, *Re* Armstrong (1886), 17 Q.B.D. 521 ; 55 L.J.Q.B. 578 ; 55 L.T. 538 ; 51 J.P. 292 ; 34 W.R. 709 ; 2 T.L.R. 745 . . . 359
Gilford Motor Co. Ltd. *v.* Horne, [1933] Ch. 935 ; 102 L.J. Ch. 212 ; 149 L.T. 241 ; [1933] All E.R. Rep. 109 471
Gillett's Will Trusts, *Re*, Barclays Bank Ltd. *v.* Gillett, [1950] Ch. 102 ; [1949] 2 All E.R. 893 ; 65 T.L.R. 727 ; 93 S.J. 742 282
Gilligan *v.* National Bank Ltd., [1901] 2 I.R. 513 ; 35 I.L.T.R. 67 ; 1 N.I.J.R. 145 182
Gillins, *Re*, Inglis *v.* Gillins, [1909] 1 Ch. 345 ; 78 L.J. Ch. 244 ; 100 L.T. 226 ; 15 Mans. 74 287-8
Gillman *v.* Gillman (1946), 174 L.T. 272 ; 110 J.P. 177 ; 44 L.G.R. 105 ; 90 S.J. 105 345
Gillott's Settlement, *Re*, Chattock *v.* Reid, [1934] Ch. 97 ; 102 L.J.Ch. 332 ; 149 L.T. 419 ; 77 S.J. 447 ; [1933] All E.R. Rep. 334 297
Gissing *v.* Gissing, [1969] 2 W.L.R. 525 ; [1969] 1 All E.R. 1043 . . 104
Gleeson, *Re*, Smyth *v.* Gleeson, [1911] 1 I.R. 113 . . . . 418, 420
Glegg *v.* Bromley, [1912] 3 K.B. 474 ; 81 L.J.K.B. 1081 ; 106 L.T. 825 ; [1911-13] All E.R. Rep. 1138 . . . . 297, 298, 299
Goddard *v.* Carlisle (1821), 9 Price 169 ; 147 E.R. 57 ; 23 R.R. 654 . . 349
Goddard *v.* Complin (1669), 1 Ch. Cas. 119 ; 22 E.R. 722 175
Godfrey *v.* Watson (1747), 3 Atk. 517 ; 26 E.R. 1098 241
Godley's Estate, *Re*, [1896] 1 I.R. 45 194
Going *v.* Farrell (1814), Beat. 472 . . . . 245, 433
Goldie *v.* Helena Rubinstein Ltd.—*see* Boynton *v.* Helena Runbinstein Ltd.
Goldsmid *v.* Goldsmid (1818), 1 Swanst. 211 ; 36 E.R. 361 ; 1 Wils. Ch. 140 ; 37 E.R. 63 ; 18 R.R. 60 . . . . 429, 431
Goodier *v.* Edmunds (No. 2), [1893] 3 Ch. 455 ; 62 L.J.Ch. 649 ; 37 S.J. 526 387
Goodman *v.* Grierson (1813), 2 Ba. & B. 274 ; 12 R.R. 82 179
Goodman *v.* Whitcomb (1820), 1 J. & W. 589 ; 37 E.R. 492 ; 21 R.R. 244 . 515, 516
Goodwin *v.* Waghorn (1835), 4 L.J. Ch. 172 ; 41 R.R. 208 184
Goold Adams's Estate, *Re*, [1965] I.R. 57 532
Gordon, *Re*, Watts *v.* Rationalist Press Assoc. Ltd., [1940] Ch. 769 ; [1940] 3 All E.R. 205; 109 L.J. Ch. 289 ; 163 L.T. 308 ; 56 T.L.R. 860 ; 84 S.J. 415 284

PAGE

Gorringe *v.* Irwell India Rubber and Gutta Percha Works (1886), 34 Ch.D. 128 ; 56 L.J. Ch. 85 ; 55 L.T. 572 ; 35 W.R. 86 317
Gossip *v.* Wright (1869), 21 L.T. 271 ; 17 W.R. 1137 179
Goswell's Trusts, *Re*, [1915] 2 Ch. 106 ; 84 L.J.Ch. 719 ; 113 L.T. 319 ; 59 S.J. 579 386
Goy & Co. Ltd., *Re*, Farmer *v.* Goy & Co. Ltd., [1900] 2 Ch. 149 ; 69 L.J. Ch. 481 ; 83 L.T. 309 ; 48 W.R. 425 ; 16 T.L.R. 310 ; 8 Mans. 221 . 308
Graham *v.* Seal (1918), 88 L.J. Ch. 31 ; 119 L.T. 526 188
Graigola Methyr Co. Ltd. *v.* Swansea Corp., [1929] A.C. 344 ; 98 L.J. Ch. 233 ; 140 L.T. 505 ; 45 T.L.R. 219 ; 93 J.P. 121 ; 27 L.G.R. 243 ; 73 S.J. 109 462-3
Grangeside Properties Ltd. *v.* Collingwoods Securities Ltd., [1964] 1 W.L.R. 139 ; [1964] 1 All E.R. 143 ; 108 S.J. 14 180
Grant (Gordon) & Co. Ltd. *v.* Boos, [1926] A.C. 781 ; 95 L.J.P.C. 167 ; 135 L.T. 740 ; 42 T.L.R. 694 190
Grave *v.* Earl of Salisbury (1784), 1 Bro C.C. 425 ; 28 E.R. 1218 . . 420
Graves *v.* Budgel (1737), 1 Atk. 444 ; 26 E.R. 283 451-2
Gray, *Re*, Dresser *v.* Gray (1887), 36 Ch.D. 205; 56 L.J. Ch. 975 ; 57 L.T. 132 ; 35 W.R. 795 288
Gray *v.* Mathias (1800), 5 Ves. 286 ; 31 E.R. 591 ; [1775-1802] All E.R. Rep. 534 ; 5 R.R. 48 553
Gray *v.* Spyer, [1922] 2 Ch. 22 ; 91 L.J. Ch. 512 ; 127 L.T. 277 ; 66 S.J. 387 92
Grealish *v.* Murphy, [1946] I.R. 35 ; 80 I.L.T.R. 111 336
Great Northern Railway Co. *v.* Manchester, Sheffield and Lincolnshire Railway Co. (1851), 5 De G. & Sm. 138 ; 64 E.R. 1053 ; 18 L.T.O.S. 344 ; 16 Jur. 146 ; 90 R.R. 39 499
Greaves, *Re*, Public Trustee *v.* Ash, [1954] Ch. 434 ; [1954] 2 W.L.R. 557 ; [1954] 1 All E.R. 771 ; 98 S.J. 214 374
Green *v.* Burns (1879), 6 L.R. Ir. 173 230
Green *v.* Gardner (1675), Rep. t. Finch 225 ; 23 E.R. 123 . . . 214
Green *v.* Green (1816), 19 Ves. 665 ; 34 E.R. 662 ; 2 Mer. 86 ; 35 E.R. 873 ; 13 R.R. 277 . . . . 396, 399
Green *v.* Marsh, [1892] 2 Q.B. 330 ; 61 L.J.Q.B. 442 ; 66 L.T. 480 ; 56 J.P. 839 ; 40 W.R. 449 ; 8 T.L.R. 498 ; 36 S.J. 412 233
Green *v.* Pigot (1781), 1 Bro. C.C. 103 ; 28 E.R. 1013 ; Dick. 585 ; 21 E.R. 398 557
Greenhill *v.* North British & Mercantile Insurance Co., [1893] 3 Ch. 474 ; 62 L.J. Ch. 918 ; 69 L.T. 526 ; 42 W.R. 91 ; 37 S.J. 632 ; 3 R. 674 . . 408
Greenwood *v.* Greenwood (1863), 2 De G. J. & S. 28 ; 46 E.R. 285 ; 139 R.R. 13 551
Greer *v.* Kettle, [1938] A.C. 156 ; [1937] 4 All E.R. 396 ; 107 L.J. Ch. 56 ; 158 L.T. 433 ; 54 T.L.R. 143 ; 82 S.J. 133 125-7
Gregg *v.* Kidd, [1956] I.R. 183 . . . . 347, 350, 351
Gresham Life Assurance Soc. *v.* Crowther, [1915] 1 Ch. 214 ; 84 L.J. Ch. 312 111 L.T. 887 ; 59 S.J. 103 ; [1914-15] All E.R. Rep. 991 . . . 302
Gretton *v.* Haward (1819), 1 Swanst. 409 ; 36 E.R. 443 ; 18 R.R. 95 . . 398
Grey *v.* Inland Revenue Commissioners, [1960] A.C. 1 ; [1959] 3 W.L.R. 759 ; [1959] 3 All E.R. 603 ; 103 S.J. 896 ; [1959] T.R. 311 ; 38 A.T.C. 313 299
Griffin, *Re*, Griffin *v.* Griffin, [1899] 1 Ch. 408 ; 68 L.J. L.J. Ch. 220 ; 79 L.T. 442 ; 15 T.L.R. 78 ; 43 S.J. 96 . . . . . . 313, 317
Griffith *v.* Bourke (1887), 21 L.R. Ir. 92 425
Griffith *v.* Pound (1889), 45 Ch.D. 553 ; 59 L.J. Ch. 522 202
Griffith *v.* Ricketts (1849), 7 Hare 299 ; 68 E.R. 122; 19 L.J. Ch. 399 ; 15 L.T.O.S. 43 ; 14 Jur. 325 ; 82 R.R. 111 387
Griffith *v.* Tower Publishing Co. Ltd., [1897] 1 Ch. 21 ; 66 L.J. Ch. 12 ; 75 L.T. 330 ; 45 W.R. 73 ; 13 T.L.R. 9 ; 41 S.J. 29 ; [1895-9] All E.R. Rep. 323 . 298
Griffiths *v.* Robins (1818), 3 Madd. 191 ; 56 E.R. 480 . . . 347
Grigby *v.* Cox (1750), 1 Ves. Sen. 517 ; 27 E.R. 1178 345
Griggs, *Re*, *Ex parte* London School Board, [1914] 2 Ch. 547 ; 83 L.J. Ch. 835 ; 111 L.T. 931 ; 80 J.P. 35 ; 58 S.J. 796 ; 13 L.G.R. 27 267
Grimthorpe (Lord), *Re*, Beckett *v.* Lord Grimthorpe, [1908] 2 Ch. 675 ; 78 L.J. Ch. 20 ; 99 L.T. 679 ; 25 T.L.R. 15 . . . . . 387, 389
Grist *v.* Bailey, [1967] Ch. 532 ; [1966] 3 W.L.R. 618 ; [1966] 2 All E.R. 875 ; 110 S.J. 791 549

PAGE

Grove *v.* Bastard (1848), 2 Ph. 619 ; 41 E.R. 1082 ; 17 L.J. Ch. 351 ; 12 Jur. 385 ; 78 R.R. 223 559
Grundy *v.* Broadbent, [1918] 1 I.R. 433 324
Guaranty Trust Co. of New York *v.* Hannay & Co., [1915] 2 K.B. 536 ; 84 L.J.K.B. 1465 ; 113 L.T. 98 ; 21 Com. Cas. 67 ; [1914-15] All E.R. Rep. 24 . . . . 559, 560
Grove *v.* Bastard (1848), 2 Ph. 619 ; 41 E.R. 1082 ; 17 L.J. Ch. 351 ; 12 Jur. 385 ; 78 R.R. 223 559
Grundy *v.* Broadbent, [1918] 1 I.R. 433 324
Guaranty Trust Co. of New York *v.* Hannay & Co., [1915] 2 K.B. 536 ; 84 L.J.K.B. 1465 ; 113 L.T. 98 ; 21 Com. Cas. 67 ; [1914-15] All E.R. Rep. 24 . . . . 559, 560
Guest *v.* Homfray (1801), 5 Ves. 818 ; 31 E.R. 875 ; 5 R.R. 176 . . 504
Gulbenkian's Settlement Trusts, *Re* (1958)—*see* Whishaw *v.* Stepehns.
Gulbenkian's Settlement Trusts, *Re*, Hacobian *v.* Maun (1969), *The Times* newspaper, 23rd May 358
Gun *v.* M'Carthy (1884), 13 L.R. Ir. 304 . . . . . 534, 555
Gunter *v.* Halsey (1739), Amb. 586 ; 27 E.R. 381 ; West t. Hard. 681 ; 25 E.R. 1147 495
Gwelo (Matabeleland) Exploration and Development Co. Ltd., *Re* (Williamson's Claim), [1901] 1 I.R. 38 307
Gwynne *v.* Heaton (1778), 1 Bro. C.C. 1 ; 28 E.R. 949 334

Haddington Island Quarry Co. Ltd. *v.* Huson, [1911] A.C. 722 ; 81 L.J.P.C. 94 ; 105 L.T. 467 253
Haedicke and Lipski's Contract, *Re*, [1901] 2 Ch. 666 ; 70 L.J. Ch. 811 ; 85 L.T. 402 ; 50 W.R. 20 ; 17 T.L.R. 772 ; 45 S.J. 738 . . . 504
Haffey *v.* Haffey (1807), 14 Ves. 261 ; 33 E.R. 521 561
Haigh, *Ex parte* (1805), 11 Ves. 403 ; 32 E.R. 1143 ; 8 R.R. 189 . . 182
Hailes and Hutchinson's Contract, *Re*, [1920] 1 Ch. 233 ; 89 L.J. Ch. 130 ; 130 ; 122 L.T. 459 ; 36 T.L.R. 130 ; 64 S.J. 209 504
Hain's Settlement, *Re*, Tooth *v.* Hain, [1961] 1 W.L.R. 440 ; [1961] 1 All E.R. 848 ; 105 S.J. 154 362
Hales *v.* Hales (1636), 1 Ch. Rep. 105 ; 21 E.R. 520 169
Halkett *v.* Earl of Dudley, [1907] 1 Ch. 590 ; 76 L.J.Ch. 330 ; 96 L.T. 539 ; 51 S.J. 290 ; [1904-7] All E.R. Rep. 465 . . . . . 502, 504
Hall, *Ex parte*, *Re* Whitting (1878), 10 Ch.D. 615 ; *sub nom. Re* Whitting, *Ex parte* Rowell, 48 L.J. Bcy. 46 186
Hall, *Re*, Nolan *v.* O'Brien (1880), 7 L.R. Ir. 180 306
Hall *v.* Hall (1850), 3 Mac. & G. 79 ; 42 E.R. 191 ; 20 L.J. Ch. 585 ; 17 L.T.O.S. 11 ; 15 Jur. 363 ; 87 R.R. 15 515
Hall *v.* Heward (1886), 32 Ch.D. 430 ; 55 L.J. Ch. 604 ; 54 L.T. 810 ; 34 W.R. 571 191
Hall *v.* Hill (1841), 1 Dr. & War. 94 ; 4 Ir. Eq. Rep. 27 ; 1 Con. & L. 120 ; 58 R.R. 223 417
Hall's Will Trusts, *Re*, Sheil *v.* Clark, [1899] 1 I.R. 308 363
Hall (William) (Contractors) Ltd., *Re*, [1967] 1 W.L.R. 948 ; [1967] 2 All E.R. E.R. 1150 ; 111 S.J. 472 165
Hallas *v.* Robinson (1885), 15 Q.B.D. 288 ; 54 L.J.Q.B. 364 ; 33 W.R. 426 ; 1 T.L.R. 309 108
Hall-Dare *v.* Hall-Dare (1885), 31 Ch.D. 251 ; 55 L.J. Ch. 154 ; 54 L.T. 120 ; 24 W.R. 82 ; 2 T.L.R. 100 . . . . 540, 541
Hallet & Co., *Re*, *Ex parte* Blane, [1894] 2 Q.B. 237 ; 63 L.J.Q.B. 573 ; 42 W.R. 305 ; 10 T.L.R. 287 ; 9 R. 278 ; 1 Mans. 25 ; *sub nom. Re* Hallett, *Ex parte* Trustee, 70 L.T. 361 524
Hallett's Estate, *Re*, Knatchbull *v.* Hallett, (1880), 13 Ch.D. 696 ; 49 L.J. L.J. Ch. 415 ; 42 L.T. 421 ; 28 W.R. 732 ; [1874-80] All E.R. Rep. 793 . . . . 7, 58-9, 162, 522-3, 525, 528
Hallifax (Marquis of) *v.* Higgins (1690), 2 Vern. 134 ; 23 E.R. 694 ; 1 Eq. Cas. Abr. 28, pl. 4 ; 21 E.R. 849 178
Halsey *v.* Grant (1806), 13 Ves. 73 ; 33 E.R. 222 ; 9 R.R. 143 . . . 486
Hambro's Marriage Settlements, *Re*, Hambro *v.* Hambro, [1949] Ch. 484 ; [1949] L.J.R. 1062 367
Hamerton *v.* Stead (1824), 3 B. & C. 478 ; 107 E.R. 811 ; 5 Dow. & Ry. K.B. 206 ; 27 R.R. 407 ; *sub nom.* Hammerton *v.* Stead, 3 L.J.O.S. K.B. 33 . 84

PAGE

Hampshire *v.* Wickens (1878), 7 Ch.D. 555 ; 47 L.J. Ch. 243 ; 38 L.T. 408 ; 26 W.R. 491 498
Hamzeh Malas & Sons *v.* British Imex Industries Ltd., [1958] 2 Q.B. 127 ; [1958] 2 W.L.R. 100 ; [1958] 1 All E.R. 262 ; 102 S.J. 68 ; [1957] Lloyd's R. 549 461
Hanbury *v.* Hanbury (1788), 2 Bro. C.C. 352 ; 29 E.R. 197 ; (1789), 2 Bro. C.C. 529 ; 29 E.R. 290 420
Hancock, *Re*, Hancock *v.* Pawson, [1905] 1 Ch. 16 ; 74 L.J. Ch. 69 ; 91 L.T. 737 ; 53 W.R. 89 396
Hancock *v.* Smith (1889), 41 Ch.D. 456 ; 58 L.J. Ch. 725 ; 61 L.T. 341 ; 5 T.L.R. 459 ; [1886-90] All E.R. Rep. 306 525
Handcock's Trusts, *Re* (1889), 23 L.R. Ir. 34 404
Hands *v.* Hands (1881), 13 L.T. 750 562
Hankey *v.* Vernon (1788), 2 Cox C.C. 12 ; 30 E.R. 6 182
Hanley *v.* Pearson (1879), 13 Ch.D. 545; 41 L.T. 673 536
Hannay *v.* M'Entire (1805), 11 Ves. 54 ; 32 E.R. 1008 561
Hansard *v.* Hardy (1812), 18 Ves. 455 ; 34 E.R. 389 243
Harding, *Re*, Westminster Bank Ltd. *v.* Laver, [1934] Ch. 271 ; 103 L.J. Ch. 121 ; 150 L.T. 277 ; 77 S.J. 853 380
Harding *v.* Glyn (1739), 1 Atk. 469 ; 26 E.R. 299 362
Harding *v.* Harding (1886), 17 Q.B.D. 442 ; 55 L.J.Q.B. 462 ; 34 W.R. 775 ; 2 T.L.R. 856 309
Harding *v.* Hardrett (1673), Rep. t. Finch 9 ; 23 E.R. 5 170
Harding *v.* Metropolitan Railway Co. (1872), L.R. 7 Ch. App. 154 ; 41 L.J. Ch. 371 ; 26 L.T. 109 ; 36 J.P. 340 ; 20 W.R. 321 381
Hargreave *v.* Everard (1856), 6 Ir. Ch. Rep. 278 345
Hargreaves *v.* Hutchinson (1834), 2 Ad. & El. 12 ; 111 E.R. 5 ; 4 Nev. & M.K.B. 11 ; 4 L.J.K.B. 17 113-14
Hargrove, *Re*, Hargrove *v.* Pain, [1915] 1 Ch. 398 ; 84 L.J. Ch. 484 ; 112 L.T. 1062 ; 59 S.J. 364 402
Hargrove's Trusts, *Re* (1873), I.R. 8 Eq. 256 362
Harman Pictures N.V. *v.* Osborne, [1967] 1 W.L.R. 723 ; [1967] 2 All E.R. 324 ; 111 S.J. 434 458
Hargrove, *Re*, Hargrove *v.* Pain, [1915] 1 Ch. 398 ; 84 L.J. Ch. 484 ; 112 L.T. 1062 ; 59 S.J. 364 402
Hargrove's Trusts, *Re* (1873), I.R. 8 Eq. 256 362
Harman Pictures N.V. *v.* Osborne, [1967] 1 W.L.R. 723 ; [1967] 2 All E.R. 324 ; 111 S.J. 434 458
Harnett *v.* Yielding (1805), 2 Sch. & Lef. 549 ; 9 R.R. 98 485
Harper *v.* Aplin (1886), 54 L.T. 383 223
Harper *v.* Kawse (1678/9), Nottingham's Chancery Cases, 79 Sel. Soc. 718 (case 900) 170-1, 174, 261
Harper *v.* Secretary of State for the Home Department, [1955] Ch. 238 ; [1955] 2 W.L.R. 316 ; [1955] 1 All E.R. 331 ; 119 J.P. 148 ; 99 S.J. 95 ; 53 L.G.R. 244 481
Harpham *v.* Shacklock (1881), 19 Ch.D. 207 ; 45 L.T. 569 ; 30 W.R. 49 . 220
Harris *v.* Beauchamp Bros., [1894] 1 Q.B. 801 ; 63 L.J. Q.B. 480 ; 70 L.T. 636 ; 42 W.R. 451 ; 9 R 653 . . . . 111, 510
Harris *v.* Pepperell (1867), L.R. 5 Eq. 1 ; 17 L.T. 191 ; 32 J.P. 132 ; 16 W.R. 68 533
Harrison *v.* Guest (1860), 8 H.L.C. 481 ; 11 E.R. 517 ; [1843-60] All E.R. Rep. 797 ; 106 R.R. 129 335
Harrison (W.F.) & Co. Ltd. *v.* Burke, [1956] 1 W.L.R. 419 ; [1956] 2 All E.R. 169 ; 100 S.J. 300 328
Harrold *v.* Plenty, [1901] 2 Ch. 314 ; 70 L.J. Ch. 562 ; 85 L.T. 45 ; 49 W.R. 646 ; 17 T.L.R. 545 ; 8 Mans. 304 244
Hart *v.* Herwig (1873), L.R. 8 Ch. App. 860 ; 42 L.J. Ch. 457 ; 29 L.T. 47 ; 21 W.R. 663 ; 2 Asp. M.L.C. 63 487
Hartopp *v.* Hartopp (1856), 21 Beav. 259 ; 52 E.R. 858 ; 25 L.J. Ch. 471; 27 L.T.O.S. 37 ; 2 Jur. N.S. 794 ; 111 R.R. 87 344
Harvey, *Re*, Banister *v.* Thirtle, [1950] 1 All E.R. 491 ; 66 (pt.1) T.L.R. 609 358
Harvey *v.* Mount (1845), 8 Beav. 439 ; 50 E.R. 172 ; 14 L.J. Ch. 233 ; 9 Jur. 741 ; 68 R.R. 146 347-8
Harwood *v.* Tooke (1812), 2 Sim. 192 ; 57 E.R. 761 ; 29 R.R. 81 . . 356

PAGE

Hatch *v.* Hatch (1804), 9 Ves. 292 ; 32 E.R. 615 ; 1 Smith K.B. 226 ; [1803-13] All E.R. Rep. 74 ; 7 R.R. 195 344
Hatton *v.* Hooley—*see* Hooley *v.* Hatton.
Hayes, *Re*, Hayes *v.* Hayes, [1951] 2 All E.R. 928 ; [1951] 2 T.L.R. 982 ; [1951] W.N. 550 ; 95 S.J. 728 417
Hawkes *v.* Saunders (1782), 1 Cowp. 289 ; 98 E.R. 1091 64
Hawkins *v.* Taylor (1687), 2 Vern. 29 ; 23 E.R. 628 175
Hawthorne, *Re*, Graham *v.* Massey (1883), 23 Ch.D. 743 ; 52 L.J. Ch. 750 ; 48 L.T. 701 ; 32 W.R. 147 13
Hayes *v.* Hayes (1674), 1 Ch. Cas. 223 ; 22 E.R. 772 ; Rep. t. Finch 231 ; 23 E.R. 127 ; 1 Eq. Cas. Abr. 78, pl. 4 ; 21 E.R. 892 ; 2 Freem. 138 ; 22 E.R. 1113 557
Haynes *v.* Foster, [1901] 1 Ch. 361 ; 70 L.J. Ch. 302 ; 84 L.T. 139 ; 49 W.R. 327 ; 45 S.J. 257 . . . . 398, 399, 402
Haynes *v.* Haynes (1861), 1 Dr. & Sm. 426 ; 62 E.R. 442 ; 30 L.J. Ch. 578 ; 4 L.T. 199 ; 7 Jur. N.S. 595 ; 9 W.R. 497 ; 127 R.R. 176 381
Haynes *v.* Mico (1781), 1 Bro. C.C. 129 ; 28 E.R. 1031 ; Rom. 41 . . 431
Hayward, *Re*, Kerrod *v.* Hayward, [1957] Ch. 528 ; [1957] 3 W.L.R. 50 ; [1957] 2 All E.R. 474 ; 101 S.J. 502 418
Hayward *v.* Dimsdale (1810), 17 Ves. 111 ; 34 E.R. 43 554
Haywood *v.* Cope (1858), 25 Beav. 140 ; 53 E.R. 589 ; 27 L.J.Ch. 468 ; 31 L.T.O.S. 48 ; 4 Jur. N.S. 227 ; 6 W.R. 304 ; 119 R.R. 360 . 29-30, 485
Heales *v.* M'Murray (1856), 23 Beav. 401 ; 53 E.R. 157 ; 113 R.R. 195 . 231
Heard *v.* Wadham (1801), 1 East 619 ; 102 E.R. 239 120
Hearle *v.* Greenbank (1749), 3 Atk. 695 ; 26 E.R. 1200 ; 1 Ves. Sen. 298 ; 27 E.R. 1043 ; [1558-1774] All E.R. Rep. 190 361
Hearne *v.* Tenant (1807), 13 Ves. 287 ; 33 E.R. 301 486
Heartley *v.* Nicholson (1875), L.R. 19 Eq. 233; 44 L.J. Ch. 277; 31 L.T. 822; 23 W.R. 374 . . . . 311, 313
Heath *v.* Crealock (1874), L.R. 10 Ch. App. 22 ; 44 L.J. Ch. 157 ; 31 L.T. 650 ; 23 W.R. 95 120
Heath *v.* Pugh (1881), 6 Q.B.D. 345 ; 50 L.J.Q.B. 473 ; 44 L.T. 327 ; 29 W.R. 904 244
Heather, *Re*, Pumfrey *v.* Fryer, [1906] 2 Ch. 230 ; 75 L.J. Ch. 568 ; 95 L.T. 352 ; 54 W.R. 625 422
Hedley Byrne & Co. Ltd. *v.* Heller & Partners Ltd., [1964] A.C. 465 ; [1963] 3 W.L.R. 101 ; [1963] 2 All E.R. 575 ; 107 S.J. 454 ; [1963] 1 Lloyd's R. 485 . . . . 307, 330
Hedworth *v.* Primate (1663), Hard. 318 ; 145 E.R. 476 . . . . 62, 173
Heming *v.* Clutterbuck (1827), 1 Bligh N.S. 479 ; 4 E.R. 951 ; 30 R.R. 56 ; *sub nom.* Hemming *v.* Gurrey, 1 Dow & Cl. 35 ; 6 E.R. 438 . . 427
Henderson *v.* Astwood, [1894] A.C. 150 ; 6 R. 450 . . . . 237, 255
Henderson's Conveyance, *Re*, [1940] Ch. 835 ; [1940] 4 All E.R. 1 ; 109 L.J. Ch. 332 ; 56 T.L.R. 952 ; 84 S.J. 477 469
Henkle *v.* Royal Exchange Assurance Co. (1749), 1 Ves. Sen. 317 ; 27 E.R. 1055 ; [1558-1774] All E.R. Rep. 450 530
Hercy *v.* Birch (1804), 9 Ves. 357 ; 32 E.R. 640 488
Hermann *v.* Hodges (1873), L.R. 16 Eq. 18 ; 43 L.J. Ch. 192 ; *sub nom.* Herrmann *v.* Hodges, 21 W.R. 57 185
Herne (Lady) *v.* Herne (1706), 2 Vern. 555; 23 E.R. 959; 1 Eq. Cas. Abr. 203, pl. 2 ; 21 E.R. 991 413
Hewitt *v.* Loosemore (1851), 9 Hare 449 ; 68 E.R. 586 ; 21 L.J. Ch. 69 ; 18 L.T.O.S. 133 ; 15 Jur. 1097 ; 89 R.R. 526 214
Hewlins *v.* Shippam (1826), 5 B. & C. 222 ; 108 E.R. 82 ; 7 Dow. & Ry. K.B. 783 ; 4 L.J.O.S.K.B. 241 ; [1824-34] All E.R. Rep. 276 . . 97
Hewson, *Re*, D'Almaine *v.* Moseley (1854), 23 L.J.Ch. 256 405
Heyman *v.* Dubois (1871), L.R. 13 Eq. 158 ; 41 L.J.Ch. 224 ; 25 L.T. 558 . 437
Hibernian Bank *v.* Yourell (No. 2), [1919] 1 I.R. 310 242
Hibernian Fire and General Insurance Co. Ltd. *v.* Dorgan, [1941] I.R. 514 ; 75 I.L.T.R. 232 558
Hiern *v.* Mill (1806), 13 Ves. 114 ; 33 E.R. 237 ; 9 R.R. 149 182
Higgins *v.* Higgins, [1951] Ir. Jur. Rep. 29 511
Higgins (W.) Ltd. *v.* Northampton Corp., [1927] 1 Ch. 128 ; 96 L.J. Ch. 38 ; 136 L.T. 235 ; 90 J.P. 82 539-41

PAGE

Hill *v.* Gomme (1839), 5 My. & Cr. 250 ; 41 E.R. 366 ; 9 L.J. Ch. 54 ; 4 Jur. 165 ; [1835-42] All E.R. Rep. 118 ; 49 R.R. 438 . . . 121
Hill *v.* O'Hanlon (1840), 2 Ir. Eq. Rep. 463 . . . . . 560, 561
Hill *v.* Peters, [1918] 2 Ch. 273 ; 87 L.J. Ch. 584 ; 119 L.T. 613 ; 62 S.J. 717 302
Hill *v.* Rowlands, [1897] 2 Ch. 361 ; 66 L.J. Ch. 689 ; 77 L.T. 34 ; 46 W.R. 26 ; 41 S.J. 639 189
Hilton *v.* Barrow (1791), 1 Ves. Jun. 284 ; 30 E.R. 345 553
Hinchcliffe *v.* Hinchcliffe (1797), 3 Ves. 516 ; 30 E.R. 1134 ; 4 R.R. 89 . 413, 420
Hinckley and Country Building Soc. *v.* Henny, [1953] 1 W.L.R. 352 ; [1953] 1 All E.R. 515 ; 97 S.J. 114 233
Hindley *v.* Hindley, [1957] 1 W.L.R. 898 ; [1957] 2 All E.R. 653 ; 101 S.J. 593 . . . . 461, 470
Hoare *v.* Bremridge (1872), L.R. 8 Ch. App. 22 ; 42 L.J. Ch. 1 ; 27 L.T. 593 ; 21 W.R. 43 553
Hobart *v.* Abbot (1731), 2 P.Wms. 643 ; 24 E.R. 897 ; 2 Eq. Cas. Abr. 169, pl. 24 ; 22 E.R. 144 245
Hobday *v.* Peters (No. 1) (1860), 28 Beav. 349 ; 54 E.R. 400 ; 29 L.J. Ch. 780 ; 2 L.T. 590 ; 6 Jur. N.S. 794 ; 8 W.R. 512 ; 126 R.R. 162 . . 346-7
Hodson, *Re*, Williams *v.* Knight, [1894] 2 Ch. 421 ; 63 L.J. Ch. 609 ; 71 L.T. 77 ; 42 W.R. 531 ; 10 T.L.R. 471 ; 38 S.J. 457 ; 8 R. 346 . . 408
Hodson *v.* Deans, [1903] 2 Ch. 647 ; 72 L.J. Ch. 751 ; 89 L.T. 92 ; 52 W.R. 122 ; 19 T.L.R. 596 ; 47 S.J. 750 255-6
Hodson and Howes' Contract, *Re* (1887), 35 Ch.D. 668 ; 56 L.J. Ch. 755 ; 56 L.T. 837 ; 35 W.R. 553 252
Hoghton *v.* Hoghton (1852), 15 Beav. 278 ; 51 E.R. 545 ; 21 L.J. Ch. 482 ; 17 Jur. 99 ; 92 R.R. 421 344
Holder *v.* Holder, [1968] Ch. 353 ; [1968] 2 W.L.R. 237 ; [1968] 1 All E.R. 665 ; 112 S.J. 17 33
Holford, *Re*, Holford *v.* Holford, [1894] 3 Ch. 30 ; 63 L.J.Ch. 637 ; 70 L.T. 777 ; 42 W.R. 563 ; 10 T.L.R. 496 ; 38 S.J. 512 ; 7 R. 304 . . 291
Holland, *Re—see* Alston, *Ex parte*.
Holles (Lady) *v.* Wyse (1693), 2 Vern. 289 ; 23 E.R. 787 178
Holloway *v.* Radcliffe (1857), 23 Beav. 163 ; 53 E.R. 64 ; 26 L.J. Ch. 401 ; 28 L.T.O.S. 301 ; 3 Jur. N.S. 198 ; 5 W.R. 271 ; 113 R.R. 76 . . 392
Holmes *v.* Holmes (1783), 1 Bro. C.C. 555 ; 28 E.R. 1295 ; 1 Cox C.C. 39 ; 29 E.R. 1052 423
Holmes *v.* Millage, [1893] 1 Q.B. 551 ; 62 L.J.Q.B. 380 ; 68 L.T. 205 ; 57 J.P. 551 ; 41 W.R. 354 ; 9 T.L.R. 331 ; 37 S.J. 338 ; 4 R. 332 . . 509
Holohan *v.* Friends Provident and Century Life Office, [1966] I.R. 1 . 254
Holroyd *v.* Marshall (1862), 10 H.L.C. 191 ; 11 E.R. 999 ; 33 L.J. Ch. 193 ; 7 L.T. 172 ; 9 Jur. N.S. 213 ; 11 W.R. 171 ; [1861-73] All E.R. Rep. 414 ; 138 R.R. 108 297
Holt *v.* Heatherfield Trust Ltd., [1942] 2 K.B. 1 [1942] 1 All E.R. 404 ; 111 L.J.K.B. 465 ; 166 L.T. 251 ; 58 T.L.R. 274 ; 86 S.J. 174 . 317-18, 319, 320
Holt *v.* Mill (1692), 2 Vern. 279 ; 23 E.R. 781 173
Hood Barrs *v.* Heriot, [1896] A.C. 174 ; 65 L.J.Q.B. 352 ; 74 L.T. 353 ; 60 J.P. 612 ; 44 W.R. 481 . . . . 446, 447
Hooley *v.* Hatton (1773), 1 Bro. C. C. 390 n. ; 28 E.R. 1197 ; 2 Dick. 461 ; 21 E.R. 349 ; *sub nom.* Hatton *v.* Hooley, Lofft 122 ; 98 E.R. 566 . 426, 428
Hooper, *Ex parte* (1815), 19 Ves. 477 ; 34 E.R. 593 ; 1 Mer. 7 ; 34 E.R. 580 ; 2 Rose 328 ; 13 R.R. 244 183
Hopkins *v.* Hemsworth, [1898] 2 Ch. 347 ; 67 L.J. Ch. 526 ; 78 L.T. 832 ; 47 W.R. 26 ; 42 S.J. 611 302
Hopkinson *v.* Richardson, [1913] 1 Ch. 284 ; 82 L.J. Ch. 211 ; 108 L.T. 501 ; 57 S.J. 265 380
Hopkinson *v.* Rolt (1861), 9 H.L.C. 514 ; 11 E.R. 829 ; 34 L.J. Ch. 468 ; 5 L.T. 90 ; 7 Jur. N.S. 1209 ; 9 W.R. 900 ; 131 R.R. 313 . . . 221
Hopton *v.* Dryden (1701), Prec. Ch. 179 ; 24 E.R. 87 ; 2 Eq. Cas. Abr. 450, pl. 2 ; 22 E.R. 384 63
Horlock, *Re*, Calham *v.* Smith, [1895] 1 Ch. 516 ; 64 L.J. Ch. 325; 72 L.T. 223 ; 43 W.R. 410 ; 39 S.J. 284 ; 13 R. 356 415-16
Horlock *v.* Smith (1853), 17 Beav. 572 ; 51 E.R. 1157 ; 23 L.J. Ch. 962 ; 22 L.T.O.S. 232 ; 2 W.R. 117 ; 99 R.R. 294 430
Horlock *v.* Wiggins (1888), 39 Ch.D. 142 ; 58 L.J. Ch. 46; 59 L.T. 710 ; [1886-90] All E.R. Rep. 1125 . . . . 415, 416

PAGE

Horwood *v.* Underhill—*see* Underhill *v.* Horwood.
How *v.* Vigures (1628), 1 Ch. Rep. 32 ; 21 E.R. 499 170
Howard *v.* Harris (1681), 1 Vern. 33 ; 23 E.R. 288 ; (1683), 1 Vern. 190 ; 23 E.R. 406 ; 2 Ch. Cas. 147 ; 22 E.R. 888 ; 1 Eq. Cas. Abr. 312, pl. 11, 12 ; 21 E.R. 1068 ; 2 Freem. 86 ; 22 E.R. 1074 ; [1558-1774] All E.R. Rep. 609 . . . . 61, 177
Howard *v.* Norfolk (Duke of) (1681), 2 Swanst. 454 ; 36 E.R. 690 ; 3 Ch. Cas. 1 ; 22 E.R. 931 ; 2 Freem. 72, 80 ; 22 E.R. 1066, 1070 ; Poll. 223 ; 86 E.R. 568 ; 2 Ch. Rep. 230 ; 21 E.R. 665 . . . . . 53, 56
Howard's Estate, *Re* (1892), 29 L.R.Ir. 266 194
Howe *v.* Hall (1870), I.R 4 Eq. 242 ; 4 I.L.T. 382 495
Howes *v.* Bishop, [1909] 2 K.B. 390 ; 78 L.J.K.B. 796 ; 100 L.T. 826 ; 25 T.L.R. 523 345
Hudson *v.* Temple (1860), 29 Beav. 536 ; 54 E.R. 735 ; 30 L.J. Ch. 251 ; 3 L.T. 495 ; 7 Jur. N.S. 248 ; 9W.R. 243 ; 131 R.R. 699 82
Hudston *v.* Viney, [1921] 1 Ch. 98 ; 90 L.J.Ch. 149 ; 124 L.T. 305 ; 65 S.J. 59 216
Hughes *v.* Britannia Permanent Benefit Building Soc., [1906] 2 Ch. 607 ; 75 L.J. Ch. 739 ; 95 L.T. 327 ; 22 T.L.R. 806 . . . . 198, 199
Hughes *v.* Metropolitan Railway Co. (1877), 2 App. Cas. 439 ; 46 L.J.Q.B. 583 ; 36 L.T. 932 ; 42 J.P. 421 ; 25 W.R. 680 ; [1874-80] All E.R. Rep. 187 . . . . 124, 125
Hughes *v.* Pump House Hotel Co. Ltd., [1902] 2 K.B. 190 ; 71 L.J.K.B. 630 ; 86 L.T. 794 ; 50 W.R. 660 ; 18 T.L.R. 654 ; [1900-3] All E.R. Rep. 480 327
Hughes *v.* Waite, [1957] 1 W.L.R. 713 ; [1957] 1 All E.R. 603 ; 101 S.J. 405 228
Hughes *v.* Williams (1806), 12 Ves. 493 ; 33 E.R. 187 ; 8 R.R. 364 . . 236
Huguenin *v.* Baseley (1806), 13 Ves. 105 ; 33 E.R. 234 512
Huguenin *v.* Baseley (1807), 14 Ves. 273 ; 33 E.R. 526 ; [1803-13] All E.R. Rep. 1 ; 9 R.R. 276 . . . . 337, 347, 351
Hulme *v.* Tenant (1778), 1 Bro. C.C. 16 ; 28 E.R. 958 ; (1779), 2 Dick. 560 ; 21 E.R. 388 443-4
Hulse, *Ex parte*—*see* Dagenham (Thames) Dock Co., *Re.*
Humphreys *v.* Harrison (1820), 1 Jac. & W. 581 ; 37 E.R. 489 ; 21 R.R. 238 223
Hunt *v.* Silk (1804), 5 East 449 ; 102 E.R. 1142 ; 2 Smith K.B. 15 ; [1803-13] All E.R. Rep. 655 ; 7 R.R. 739 543
Hunt's Settled Estates, *Re*, Bulteel *v.* Lawdeshayne, [1905] 2 Ch. 419 ; [1906] 2 Ch. 11 ; 75 L.J. Ch. 496 ; 94 L.T. 747 470
Hunter *v.* Atkins (1834), 3 My. & K. 113 ; 40 E.R. 43 ; Coop. t. Brough. 464 ; 47 E.R. 166 ; 41 R.R. 30 352
Hunter *v.* Gibbons (1856), 1 H. & N. 459 ; 156 E.R. 1281 ; 26 L.J. Ex. 1 ; 28 L.T. O.S. 290 ; 2 Jur. N.S. 1249 ; 5 W.R. 91 ; 108 R.R. 672 . . 104
Hunter *v.* Lord Langford (1828), 2 Mol. 572 185
Hunter's Will Trusts, *Re*, Gilks *v.* Harris, [1963] Ch. 372 ; [1962] 3 W.L.R. 1442 ; [1962] 3 All E.R. 1050 ; 106 S.J. 938 368
Hurst *v.* Beach (1820), 5 Madd. 351 ; 56 E.R. 929 ; [1814-23] All E.R. Rep. 523 ; 21 R.R. 304 . . . . 427, 428
Hurst *v.* Picture Theatres Ltd., [1915] 1 K.B. 1 ; 83 L.J.K.B. 1836 ; 111 L.T. 972 ; 30 T.L.R. 642 ; 58 S.J. 739 ; [1914-15] All E.R. Rep. 836 . 37, 98-102
Hutchins *v.* Hutchins (1876), I.R. 10 Eq. 453 369
Hyde *v.* Whitfield (1815), 19 Ves. 342 ; 34 E.R. 544 ; 13 R.R. 215 . . 561
Hyett *v.* Mekin (1884), 25 Ch.D. 735 ; 53 L.J. Ch. 241 ; 50 L.T. 54 ; 32 W.R. 513 385
Hylton *v.* Hylton (1754), 2 Ves. Sen. 547 ; 28 E.R. 349 344
Hyman *v.* Hyman, [1929] A.C. 601 ; 98 L.J.P. 81 ; 141 L.T. 329 ; 93 J.P. 209 ; 45 T.L.R. 444 ; 27 L.G.R. 379 ; 73 S.J. 317 ; [1929] All E.R. Rep. 245 490

Ibbitson's Exstate, *Re* (1869), L.R. 7 Eq. 226 ; 21 L.T. 163 . . . 385
Imperial Gas Light and Coke Co. *v.* Broadbent (1859), 7 H.L.C. 600 ; 11 E.R. 239 ; 29 L.J. Ch. 377 ; 34 L.T.O.S. 1 ; 23 J.P. 675 ; 5 Jur. N.S. 1319 ; 115 R.R. 295 466
Imperial Gas Light & Coke Co. *v.* London Gas Light Co. (1854), 10 Ex. 39 ; 156 E.R. 346 ; 2 C.L.R. 1230 ; 23 L.J. Ex. 303 ; 18 Jur. 497 ; 2 W.R. 527 104

PAGE

Imperial Tobacco Co. (of Great Britain and Ireland) Ltd. *v.* Parslay, [1936] 2 All E.R. 515 ; 52 T.L.R. 585 ; 80 S.J. 464 19
Inche Noriah *v.* Shaik Allie bin Omar, [1929] A.C. 127 ; 98 L.J.P.C. 1 ; 140 L.T. 121 ; 45 T.L.R. 1 ; [1928] All E.R. Rep. 189 . . 345, 346, 350, 351
" Independent " Newspapers Ltd. *v.* " Irish Press " Ltd., [1932] I.R. 615 ; 66 I.L.T.R. 205 475-6
Ingram *v.* Little, [1961] 1 Q.B. 31 ; [1960] 3 W.L.R. 504 ; [1960] 3 All E.R. 332 ; 104 S.J. 704 548-9
Inland Revenue Commissioners *v.* Broadway Cottages Trust, [1955] Ch. 20 ; [1954] 3 W.L.R. 438 ; [1954] 3 All E.R. 120 ; 98 S.J. 588 ; 35 T.C. 577, 585 362
Inland Revenue Commissioners (*Ex parte*) *v.* Phillips—*see* Pratt, *Re.*
Inman *v.* Wearing (1850), 3 De G. & Sm. 729 ; 64 E.R. 680 ; 84 R.R. 416 . 246
International Life Assurance Soc., *Re* (1876), 2 Ch.D. 476 ; 45 L.J. Ch. 766 ; 34 L.T. 782 ; 24 W.R. 627 433-4
Inwards *v.* Baker, [1965] 2 Q.B. 29 ; [1965] 2 W.L.R. 212 ; [1965] 1 All E.R. 446 ; 109 S.J. 75 . . . . 37, 39-40
Ireson *v.* Denn (1796), 2 Cox C.C. 425 ; 30 E.R. 197 ; 2 R.R. 97 . . 176
Irish Shell and BP Ltd. *v.* Ryan, [1966] I.R. 75 208
Iron Trades Employers' Insurance Assoc. *v.* Union of House and Land Investors Ltd., [1937] Ch. 313 ; [1937] 1 All E.R. 481 ; 106 L.J. Ch. 206 206 ; 156 L.T. 322 ; 53 T.L.R. 341 ; 81 S.J. 159 . . . 228, 229
Isaacs, *Re*, Isaacs *v.* Reginall, [1894] 3 Ch. 506 ; 63 L.J. Ch. 815 ; 71 L.T. 386 ; 42 W.R. 685 ; 38 S.J. 662 ; 8 R. 660 381-2
Isherwood, *Ex parte*, *Re* Knight (1882), 22 Ch.D. 384 ; 52 L.J. Ch. 370 ; 48 L.T. 398 ; 31 W.R. 442 ; [1881-5] All E.R. Rep. 120 . . 233
Ives (E.R.) Investment Ltd. *v.* High, [1967] 2 Q.B. 379 ; [1967] 2 W.L.R. 789 ; [1967] 1 All E.R. 504 ; 110 S.J. 963 . . . . . 27-8, 33

Jackman *v.* Mitchell (1807), 13 Ves. 581 ; 33 E.R. 412 ; 9 R.R. 229 . . 554
Jackson, *Ex parte*, *Re* Bowes (1880), 14 Ch.D. 725 ; 43 L.T. 272 ; 29 W.R. 253 232
Jackson, *Re*, Smith *v.* Sibthorpe (1887), 34 Ch.D. 732 ; 56 L.J. Ch. 593 ; 56 L.T. 562 ; 35 W.R. 646 262
Jackson *v.* Butler (1742), 2 Atk. 306 ; 26 E.R. 587 ; 9 Mod. 297 ; 88 E.R. 464 68
Jackson *v.* Jackson (1853), 1 Sm. & G. 184 ; 65 E.R. 80 ; 22 L.J. Ch. 873 ; 21 L.T.O.S. 98 ; 1 W.R. 264 ; 96 R.R. 369 498
Jackson *v.* Petrie (1804), 10 Ves. 164 ; 32 E.R. 807 561
Jackson *v.* Stopford, [1923] 2 I.R. 1 ; 56 I.L.T.R. 137 533
Jackson *v.* Turnley (1853), 1 Drew. 617 ; 61 E.R. 587 ; 1 Eq. R. 328 ; 22 L.J. Ch. 949 ; 21 L.T.O.S. 216 ; 17 Jur. 643 ; 1 W.R. 461 . . 559, 560
Jackson and Haden's Contract, *Re*, [1906] 1 Ch. 412 ; 75 L.J. Ch. 226 ; 94 L.T. 418 ; 54 W.R. 434 ; 50 S.J. 256 543
Jacobs *v.* Revell, [1900] 2 Ch. 858 ; 69 L.J. Ch. 879 ; 83 L.T. 629 ; 49 W.R. 109 507
James, *Ex parte*, *Re* Condon (1874), L.R. 9 Ch. App. 609 ; 43 L.J. Bcy. 107 ; 30 L.T. 773 ; 22 W.R. 937 ; [1874-80] All E.R. Rep. 388 . . . 279
James, *Re*, Lloyd's Bank Ltd. *v.* Atkins, [1947] Ch. 256 ; [1947] 1 All E.R. 402 ; [1947] L.J.R. 735 ; 176 L.T. 370 ; 63 T.L.R. 246 ; 91 S.J. 236 . 284
James *v.* Biou (1819), 3 Swanst. 234 ; 36 E.R. 844 ; 19 R.R. 200 . . 190
James *v.* James (1873), L.R. 16 Eq. 153 ; 42 L.J. Ch. 386 ; 21 W.R. 522 . 244
James *v.* Kerr (1889), 40 Ch.D. 449 ; 58 L.J. Ch. 355 ; 60 L.T. 212 ; 53 J.P. 628 ; 37 W.R. 279 ; 5 T.L.R. 174 . . . . . 207, 356
Jaques, *Re*, Hodgson *v.* Braisby, [1903] 1 Ch. 267 ; 72 L.J. Ch. 197 ; 88 L.T. 210 ; 51 W.R. 229 ; 47 S.J. 145 . . . . . 420, 423
Jaques *v.* Lloyd D. George & Partners Ltd., [1968] 1 W.L.R. 625 ; [1968] 2 All E.R. 187 ; 112 S.J. 211 547
Jared *v.* Clements, [1903] 1 Ch. 428 ; 72 L.J. Ch. 291 ; 88 L.T. 97 ; 51 W.R. 401 ; 19 T.L.R. 219 ; 47 S.J. 435 214
Jason *v.* Eyres (1681), 2 Freem. 69 ; 22 E.R. 1064 ; 2 Ch. Cas. 33 ; 22 E.R. 833 177
Jeffreys *v.* Jeffreys (1841), Cr. & Ph. 138 ; 41 E.R. 443 ; [1835-42] All E.R. Rep. 81 ; 54 R.R. 249 17
Jenkins *v.* Jones (1860), 2 Giff. 99 ; 66 E.R. 43 ; 29 L.J. Ch. 493 ; 2 L.T. 128 ; 6 Jur. N.S. 391 ; 8 W.R. 270 ; 128 R.R. 41 . . . 254, 256

PAGE

Jenkins *v.* Parkinson (1833), 2 My. & K. 5 ; 39 E.R. 846 560
Jenkins and H. E. Randall & Co.'s Contract, *Re*, [1903] 2 Ch. 362 ; 72 L.J. Ch. 693 ; 88 L.T. 628 390
Jennings *v.* Jordan (1881), 6 App. Cas. 698 ; 51 L.J. Ch. 129 ; 45 L.T. 593 ; 30 W.R. 369 ; [1881-5] All E.R. Rep. 475 200-1
Jennings *v.* Ward (1705), 2 Vern. 520 ; 23 E.R. 935 . . . . 177, 209
Jervis *v.* White (1802), 7 Ves. 413 ; 32 E.R. 167 ; 6 R.R. 26 . . 554
Jesus College *v.* Bloom (1745), 3 Atk. 262 ; 26 E.R. 953 ; Amb. 54 ; 27 E.R. 31 563
Job *v.* Job (1877), 6 Ch. D. 562 ; 26 W.R. 206 105-6
John, *Re*, Jones *v.* John, [1933] Ch. 370 ; 102 L.J. Ch. 72 ; 148 L.T. 450 ; [1932] All E.R. Rep. 556 284-5
John *v.* John, [1898] 2 Ch. 573 ; 67 L.J. Ch. 616 ; 79 L.T. 362 ; 47 W.R. 52 ; 14 T.L.R. 583 ; 42 S.J. 731 . . . . 267, 510
Johnson, *Re*, Cowley *v.* Public Trustee, [1915] 1 Ch. 435 ; 84 L.J. Ch. 393 ; 112 L.T. 935 ; 59 S.J. 333 385
Johnson *v.* Bragge, [1901] 1 Ch. 28 ; 70 L.J. Ch. 41 ; 83 L.T. 621 ; 49 W.R. 198 538-9
Johnson *v.* Evans (1889), 61 L.T. 18 188
Johnson *v.* Mills (1749), 1 Ves. Sen. 282 ; 27 E.R. 1033 557
Johnson (B.) & Co. (Builders) Ltd., *Re*, [1955] Ch. 634 ; [1955] 3 W.L.R. 269 ; [1955] 2 All E.R. 775 ; 99 S.J. 490 511
Joicey, *Re*, Joicey *v.* Elliot, [1915] 2 Ch. 115 ; 84 L.J. Ch. 613 ; 113 L.T. 437 368
Jolland,—*v.* (1802), 8 Ves. 72 ; 32 E.R. 278 516
Jolly *v.* Arbuthnot (1859), 4 De G. & J. 224 ; 45 E.R. 87 ; 28 L.J. Ch. 547 ; 33 L.T.O.S. 263 ; 5 Jur. N.S. 689 ; 23 J.P. 677 ; 7 W.R. 532 ; 124 R.R. 222 233
Jones, *Re*, Christmas *v.* Jones, [1897] 2 Ch. 190 ; 66 L.J. Ch. 439 ; 76 L.T. 454 ; 45 W.R. 598 ; [1895-9] All E.R. Rep. 1084 307
Jones, *Re*, Public Trustee *v.* Jones, [1945] Ch. 105 ; 115 L.J. Ch. 33 ; 173 L.T. 357 ; 61 T.L.R. 120 ; 89 S.J. 22 358
Jones *v.* Alephsin (1810), 16 Ves. 470 ; 33 E.R. 1063 561
Jones *v.* Bennett (1713), 1 Bro. P.C. 528 ; 1 E.R. 735 139
Jones *v.* Frost (1818), 3 Madd. 1 ; 56 E.R. 410 ; *on appeal* (1822), Jac. 466 ; 37 E.R. 926 554
Jones *v.* Humphreys, [1902] 1 K.B. 10 ; 71 L.J.K.B. 23 ; 85 L.T. 488 ; 50 W.R. 191 ; 18 T.L.R. 54 ; 46 S.J. 70 327
Jones *v.* Jones (1838), 8 Sim. 633 ; 59 E.R. 251 ; 7 L.J. Ch. 164 ; 2 Jur. 589 ; 42 R.R. 249 . . . . 213, 303
Jones *v.* Kenrick (1727), 5 Bro. P.C. 244 ; 2 E.R. 655 248
Jones *v.* Lipman, [1962] 1 W.L.R. 832 ; [1962] 1 All E.R. 442 ; 106 S.J. 531 504
Jones *v.* Matthie (1847), 11 Jur. 504 ; *sub nom.* Matthie *v.* Edwards, 16 L.J. Ch. 405 ; 73 R.R. 776 253
Jones *v.* Sampson (1803), 8 Ves. 593 ; 32 E.R. 485 561
Jones (James) & Sons Ltd. *v.* Earl of Tankerville, [1909] 2 Ch. 440 ; 78 L.J. Ch. 674 ; 101 L.T. 202 ; 25 T.L.R. 714 100
Jorden *v.* Money (1854), 5 H.L.C. 185 ; 10 E.R. 868 ; 23 L.J. Ch. 865 ; 24 L.T.O.S. 160 ; [1843-60] All E.R. Rep. 350 ; 101 R.R. 116 . . 38, 39, 40, 41, 123
Jory *v.* Cox (1701), Prec. Ch. 160 ; 24 E.R. 77 ; Anon., 2 Eq. Cas. Abr. 611, pl. 3 ; 22 E.R. 513 178
Joseph *v.* Lyons (1884), 15 Q.B.D. 280 ; 54 L.J.Q.B. 1 ; 51 L.T. 740 ; 33 W.R. 145 ; 1 T.L.R. 16 107-8
Judd *v.* Green (1875), 45 L.J. Ch. 108 ; 33 L.T. 597 355
Jump, *Re*, Galloway *v.* Hope, [1903] 1 Ch. 129 ; 72 L.J. Ch. 16 ; 87 L.T. 502 ; 51 W.R. 266 391
Jupp, *Re*, Harris *v.* Grierson, [1922] 2 Ch. 359 ; 91 L.J. Ch. 572 ; 127 L.T. 360 ; 66 S.J. 539 425

Kasumu *v.* Baba-Egbe, [1956] A.C. 539 ; [1956] 3 W.L.R. 575 ; [1956] 3 All E.R. 266 ; 100 S.J. 600 32
Kaye *v.* Waghorn (1809), 1 Taunt. 428 ; 127 E.R. 900 ; 10 R.R. 558 . 120
Keays *v.* Gilmore (1874), I.R. 8 Eq. 290 429

PAGE

Keech *v.* Sandford (1726), Sel. Cas. t. King 61 ; 25 E.R. 223 ; 2 Eq. Cas. Abr. 741, pl. 7 ; 22 E.R. 629 ; [1558-1774] All E.R. Rep. 230 . . . 57, 260
Keighley Rugby Football Club Ltd. *v.* Cunningham (1960), *The Times* newspaper, 25th May 476
Kekewich *v.* Manning (1851), 1 De G. M. & G. 176 ; 42 E.R. 519 ; 21 L.J. Ch. 577 ; 18 L.T.O.S. 263 ; 16 Jur. 625 ; 91 R.R. 53 . 118-19, 309
Kelland *v.* Fulford (1877), 6 Ch.D. 491 ; 47 L.J. Ch. 94, 25 W.R. 506 . 380
Kelly *v.* Bellew (Lord) (1707), 4 Bro. P.C. 495 ; 2 E.R. 338 . . 139
Kelly *v.* Kelly, [1917] 1 I.R. 51 ; 51 I.L.T.R. 17 555
Kelsen *v.* Imperial Tobacco Co. (of Great Britain and Ireland) Ltd., [1957] 2 Q.B. 334 ; [1957] 2 W.L.R. 1007 ; [1957] 2 All E.R. 343 ; 101 S.J. 446 ; 169 Est. Gaz. 593 465
Kemble *v.* Farren (1829), 6 Bing. 141 ; 130 E.R. 1234 ; 3 Moo. & P. 425 ; 7 L.J.O.S.C.P. 258 ; [1824-34] All E.R. Rep. 641 ; 31 R.R. 366 . . 20
Kemp *v.* Pryor (1802), 7 Ves. 237 ; 32 E.R. 96 554
Kempson *v.* Ashbee (1874), L.R. 10 Ch. App. 15 ; 44 L.J. Ch. 195 ; 31 L.T. 525 ; 39 J.P. 164 ; 23 W.R. 38 349
Kempthorne, *Re*, Charles *v.* Kempthorne, [1930] 1 Ch. 268 ; 99 L.J. Ch. 107, 177 ; 142 L.T. 111 ; 46 T.L.R. 15 ; [1929] All E.R. Rep. 495 . 284, 394
Kendall, *Ex parte* (1811), 17 Ves. 514 ; 34 E.R. 199 ; [1803-13] All E.R. Rep. 295 ; 11 R.R. 122 ; *sub nom. Re* Dawes, *Ex parte* Kendall, 1 Rose 71 434
Kenealy *v.* O'Keeffe (1900), 34 I.L.T.R. 75 511
Kennedy, *Ex parte—see* Willis, *Re.*
Kennedy *v.* De Trafford, [1897] A.C. 180 ; 66 L.J. Ch. 413 ; 76 L.T. 427 ; 45 W.R. 671 ; [1895-9] All E.R. Rep. 408 253-4
Kensington, *Ex parte* (1813), 2 V. & B. 79 ; 35 E.R. 249 ; 2 Rose 138 ; [1803-13] All E.R. Rep. 398 ; 13 R.R. 32 183
Keogh's Estate, *Re* (1889), 23 L.R. Ir. 257 . . . . 414, 415
Keogh's Estate, *Re*, [1895] 1 I.R. 201 221
Ker's Settlement Trusts, *Re*, [1963] Ch. 553 ; [1963] 2 W.L.R. 1210 ; [1963] 1 All E.R. 801 ; 107 S.J. 415 14-15
Kerchiss *v.* Colora Printing Inks Ltd., [1960] R.P.C. 235 . . 472
Kernohan Estates Ltd. *v.* Boyd, [1967] N.I. 27 511
Kerr's Trusts, *Re* (1877), 4 Ch.D. 600 ; 46 L.J. Ch. 287 ; 36 L.T. 356 ; 25 W.R. 390 368
Kerrison v. Smith, [1897] 2 Q.B. 445 ; 66 L.J.Q.B. 762 ; 77 L.T. 344 ; [1895-9] All E.R. Rep. 215 . . . . . . 94, 95, 98
Kettleby *v.* Atwood (1684), 1 Vern. 298 ; 23 E.R. 481 . . 65, 376
Kevans *v.* Joyce, [1896] 1 I.R. 442 ; [1897] 1 I.R. 1 ; 30 I.L.T.R. 46, 73 336, 355
Keys *v.* Williams (1838), 3 Y. & C. Ex. 55 ; 160 E.R. 612 ; 7 L.J. Ex. Eq. 59 ; 2 Jur. 611 ; 51 R.R. 339 182
Kidderminster Mutual Benefit Building Soc. *v.* Haddock, [1936] W.N. 158 ; 80 S.J. 466 245
King, *Ex parte* (1750), 1 Atk. 300 ; 26 E.R. 191 176
King, *Re*, Sewell *v.* King (1879), 14 Ch.D. 179 ; 49 L.J. Ch. 73 ; 28 W.R. 344 312
King *v.* Allen (David) & Sons, Billposting Ltd., [1916] 2 A.C. 54 ; 85 L.J.P.C. 229 ; 114 L.T. 762 ; [1916-17] All E.R. Rep. 268 . . 103
King *v.* Anderson (1874), I.R. 8 Eq. 625 341
King *v.* Bird [1909] 1 K.B. 837 ; 78 L.J.K.B. 499 ; 100 L.T. 478 . 224, 225
King *v.* King (1833), 1 My. & K. 442 ; 39 E.R. 749 ; 36 R.R. 349 . . 553
King *v.* King-Harman (1873), I.R. 7 Eq. 446 532
King *v.* Smith (1843), 2 Hare 239 ; 67 E.R. 99 ; 7 Jur. 694 ; 62 R.R. 93 . 223
King *v.* Victoria Insurance Co. Ltd., [1896] A.C. 250 ; 65 L.J.P.C. 38 ; 74 L.T. 206 ; 44 W.R. 592 ; 12 T.L.R. 285 327
Kingsland (Viscount) *v.* Barnewall (1706), 4 Bro. P.C. 154 ; 2 E.R. 105 138-9, 352
Kingswood Estate Co. Ltd. *v.* Anderson, [1963] 2 Q.B. 169 ; [1962] 3 W.L.R. 1102 ; [1962] 3 All E.R. 593 ; 106 S.J. 651 . . . . 90, 449, 496
Kinnaird *v.* Trollope (1888), 39 Ch.D. 636 ; 57 L.J. Ch. 905 ; 59 L.T. 433 ; 37 W.R. 234 ; 4 T.L.R. 697 . . . . 190, 191
Kirkwood *v.* Thompson (1865), 2 De G. J. & S. 613 ; 46 E.R. 513 ; 6 New R. 367 ; 34 L.J. Ch. 501 ; 12 L.T. 811 ; 13 W.R. 1052 ; [1861-73] All E.R. Rep. 714 ; 144 R.R. 189 . . . . . . 256, 260
Kirwan *v.* Cullen (1854), 4 Ir. Ch. Rep. 322 352

PAGE

Kitchen *v.* Royal Air Force Association, [1958] 1 W.L.R. 563 ; [1958] 2 All E.R. 241 ; 102 S.J. 363 28
Knapman, *Re*, Knapman *v.* Wreford (1881), 18 Ch.D. 300 ; 50 L.J. Ch. 629 ; 45 L.T. 102 ; 30 W.R. 395 307
Knight, *Re* (1810)—*see* Langston, *Ex parte*.
Knight, *Re* (1882)—*see* Isherwood, *Ex parte* ; Voisey, *Ex parte*.
Knight *v.* Marjoribanks (1849), 2 Mac. & G. 10 ; 42 E.R. 4 ; 2 H. & Tw. 308 ; 47 E.R. 1700 ; 83 R.R. 166 260
Knights *v.* Atkyns (1687), 2 Vern. 20 ; 23 E.R. 624 ; 2 Ch. Rep. 400 ; 21 E.R. 699 . . . . 65, 376
Knightsbridge Estates Trust Ltd. *v.* Byrne, 1939] Ch. 441 ; 1938] 4 All E.R. 618 ; 108 L.J. Ch. 105 ; 160 L.T. 68 ; 55 T.L.R. 196 ; 82 S.J. 989 ; *on appeal*, [1940] A.C. 613 ; [1940] 2 All E.R. 401 ; 109 L.J. Ch. 200 ; 162 L.T. 388 ; 56 T.L.R. 652 ; 84 S.J. 488 204
Kores Manufacturing Co. Ltd. *v.* Kolok Manufacturing Co. Ltd., [1959] Ch. 108 ; [1958] 2 W.L.R. 858 ; [1958] 2 All E.R. 65 ; 102 S.J. 362 ; [1958] R.P.C. 200 471
Kreglinger *v* New Patagonia Meat and Cold Storage Co. Ltd., [1914] A.C. 25 ; 83 L.J. Ch. 79 ; 109 L.T. 802 ; 30 T.L.R. 114 ; 58 S.J. 97 ; [1911-13] All E.R. Rep. 970 208-9

Lacon, *Re*, Lacon *v.* Lacon, [1891] 2 Ch. 482 ; 60 L.J. Ch. 403 ; 64 L.T. 429 ; 39 W.R. 514 ; 7 T.L.R. 457 ; [1891-4] All E.R. Rep. 286 . . 418
Lacon *v.* Allen (1856), 3 Drew. 579 ; 61 E.R. 1024 ; 26 L.J. Ch. 18 ; 4 W.R. 693 ; 106 R.R. 443 183
Lacon *v.* Mertins (1743), 3 Atk 1 ; 26 E.R. 803 ; Dick. 664 ; 21 E.R. 430 483
Lacy *v.* Anderson (1581-3), 1 Swanst. 445(A) ; 36 E.R. 458 . . 396
Lahay *v.* Brown (1957), 8 D.L.R. (2d) 728 ; [1957] O.W.N. 210 . . 416
Lainson *v.* Tremere (1834), 1 Ad. & El. 792 ; 110 E.R. 1410 ; 3 Nev. & M. K.B. 603 ; 4 L.J.K.B. 207 ; 40 R.R. 426 125-6
Lake *v.* Simmons, [1927] A.C. 487 ; 96 L.J.K.B. 621 ; 137 L.T 233 ; 43 T.L.R. 417 ; 71 S.J. 369 ; 33 Com. Cas. 16 ; [1927] All E.R. Rep. 49 . 548
Lamb, *Re*, Vipond *v.* Lamb, [1929] 1 Ch. 722 ; 98 L.J. Ch. 305 ; 141 L.T. 60 ; 45 T.L.R. 190 ; 73 S.J. 77 ; [1929] All E.R. Rep. 82 282-3
Lamb *v.* Sambas Rummer & Gutta Percha Co. Ltd., [1908] 1 Ch. 845 ; 77 L.J. Ch. 386 ; 98 L.T. 633 ; 15 Mans. 189 476
Lambert's Estate, *Re* (1884), 13 L.R. Ir. 234 213
Lampet's Case (1613), 10 Co. Rep. 46b ; 77 E.R. 994 293
Lancashire Loans Ltd. *v.* Black, [1934] 1 K.B. 380 ; 103 L.J.K.B. 129 ; 150 L.T. 304 ; [1933] All E.R. Rep. 201 . . . . . 343-4, 349
Lane *v.* Dighton (1762), Amb. 409 ; 27 E.R. 274 520
Lanesborough (Lady) *v.* Ockshott (1719), 1 Bro. P.C. 151 ; 1 E.R. 479 ; *sub nom.* Lady Lanesbury *v.* Ockshoth, 2 Eq. Cas. Abr. 207, pl. 2 ; 22 E.R. 176 121
Langdale (Lady) *v.* Briggs (1856), 8 De G. M. & G. 391 ; 44 E.R. 441 ; 26 L.J. Ch. 27 ; 28 L.T.O.S. 73 ; 2 Jur. N.S. 982 ; 4 W.R. 703 ; 114 R.R. 154 560
Langdale Chemical Manure Co. *v.* Ginty (1907), 41 I.L.T.R. 40 . . 511
Langham *v.* Nenny (1797), 3 Ves. 467 ; 30 E.R. 1109 440
Langstaffe *v.* Fenwick (1805), 10 Ves. 405 ; 32 E.R. 902 ; [1803-13] All E.R. Rep. 534 ; 8 R.R. 8 241
Langston, *Ex parte* (1810), 17 Ves. 227 ; 34 E.R. 88 ; [1803-13] All E.R. Rep. 767 ; 11 R.R. 66 ; *sub nom. Re* Knight, *Ex parte* Langston, 1 Rose 26 182
Lanoy *v.* Duke and Dutchess of Athol (1742), 2 Atk. 444 ; 26 E.R. 668 ; 9 Mod. 398 ; 88 E.R. 532 ; [1448-1774] All E.R. Rep. 279 . . 65, 433
Lant *v.* Crispe (1719), 5 Bro. P.C. 200 ; 2 E.R. 626 ; *sub nom.* Lant *v.* Crisp, 2 Eq. Cas. Abr. 599, pl. 20 ; 22 E.R. 503 248
Larios *v.* Bonany Y Gurety (1873), L.R. 5 P.C. 346 185
Latta's Marriage Settlement Trusts, *Re*, Public Trustee *v.* Latta, [1949] Ch. 490 ; [1949] 1 All E.R. 665 ; [1949] L.J.R. 892 ; 93 S.J. 182 . . 368
Lavery *v.* Pursell (1888), 39 Ch.D. 508 ; 57 L.J. Ch. 570 ; 58 L.T. 846 ; 37 W.R. 163 ; 4 T.L.R. 353 . . . . 487, 496
Law *v.* Chartered Institute of Patent Agents, [1919] 2 Ch. 276 ; 88 L.J. Ch. 319 ; 121 L.T. 50 ; 35 T.L.R. 385 ; 63 S.J. 447 ; 36 R.P.C. 163 . . 477

PAGE

Law *v.* Law (1735), 3 P. Wms. 391 ; 24 E.R. 1114 ; Cas. t. Talb. 140 ; 25 E.R. 705 552
Lawder's Estate, *Re* (1861), 11 Ir. Ch. Rep. 346 436
Lawes, *Re*, Lawes *v.* Lawes (1881), 20 Ch.D. 81 ; 45 L.T. 453 ; 30 W.R. 33 423
Lawes *v.* Bennett (1785), 1 Cox C.C. 167 ; 29 E.R. 111 ; 1 R.R. 10 . . 381-3
Lawless's Will Trusts, *Re*, Miley *v.* Carty, [1927] I.R. 541 . . . 384
Lawrance *v.* Galsworthy (1857), 30 L.T.O.S. 112 ; 3 Jur. N.S. 1049 ; 108 R.R. 953 433
Lawrence *v.* Brasier (1666), 1 Ch. Cas. 72 ; 22 E.R. 701 552-3
Lazarus Estates Ltd. *v.* Beasley, [1956] 1 Q.B. 702 ; [1956] 2 W.L.R. 502 ; [1956] 1 All E.R. 341 ; 100 S.J. 131 28-9
Leaf *v.* International Galleries, [1950] 2 K.B. 86 ; [1950] 1 All E.R. 693 ; 66 (pt. 1) T.L.R. 1031 546
Leahy, *Re*, Leahy *v.* Payne, [1920] 1 I.R. 260 368
Leahy *v.* De Moleyns, [1896] 1 I.R. 206 527
Lechmere *v.* Earl of Carlisle (1733), 3 P. Wms. 211 ; 24 E.R. 1033 ; *sub nom.* Lechmere *v.* Lady Lechmere, 2 Eq. Cas. Abr. 31, pl. 42 ; 22 E.R. 27 ; [1558-1774] All E.R. Rep. 137 ; *on appeal* (1735), 3 P. Wms. 228 ; 24 E.R. 1039 ; Cas. t. Talb. 80 ; 25 E.R. 673 ; 2 Eq. Cas. Abr. 501, pl. 35 ; 22 E.R. 425 ; [1558-1774] All E.R. Rep. 144 375-6
Lechmere *v.* Lady Lechmere (1735), Cas. t. Talb. 80 ; 25 E.R. 673 ; 3 P. Wms. 228 ; 24 E.R. 1039 ; 2 Eq. Cas. Abr. 501, pl. 35 ; 22 E.R. 425 ; [1558-1774] All E.R. Rep. 144 429-30
Lecky *v.* Walter, [1914] 1 I.R. 378 546
Ledingham *v.* Bermejo Estancia Co. Ltd., [1947] 1 All E.R. 749 . . 124
Lee *v.* Magrath (1882), 10 L.R. Ir. 313 309
Lee *v.* Smith (1854), 9 Ex. 662 ; 156 E.R. 284 ; 2 C.L.R. 1079 ; 23 L.J.Ex. 198 ; 23 L.T.O.S. 70 ; 96 R.R. 903 ; *sub nom.* Lees *v.* Smith, 2 W.R. 377 85
Leeds Industrial Co-operative Building Soc. Ltd. *v.* Slack, [1924] A.C. 851 ; 93 L.J. Ch. 436 ; 131 L.T. 710 ; 40 T.L.R. 745 ; 68 S.J. 715 ; [1924] All E.R. Rep. 259 . . . . 463, 508
Leek, *Re*, Darwen *v.* Leek, [1969] 1 Ch. 563 ; [1968] 2 W.L.R. 1385 ; [1968] 1 All E.R. 793 362
Lees *v.* Patterson (1878), 7 Ch.D. 866 ; 47 L.J.Ch. 616 ; 38 L.T. 451 ; 26 W.R. 399 562
Lees *v.* Smith—*see* Lee *v.* Smith.
Legard *v.* Hodges (1792), 1 Ves. Jun. 477 ; 30 E.R. 447 ; 3 Bro. C.C. 531 ; 29 E.R. 684 297
Leicester Permanent Building Soc. *v.* Butt, [1943] Ch. 308 ; [1943] 2 All E.R. 523 ; 112 L.J. Ch. 289 ; 169 L.T. 261 ; 59 T.L.R. 361 ; 87 S.J. 298 242
Leith *v.* Irvine (1833), 1 My. & K. 277 ; 39 E.R. 686 ; 36 R.R. 319 . 241, 259
Lench *v.* Lench (1805), 10 Ves. 511 ; 32 E.R. 943 520
Le Neve *v.* Le Neve (1747), 3 Atk. 646 ; 26 E.R. 1172 ; Amb. 436 ; 27 E.R. 291 ; 1 Ves. Sen. 64 ; 27 E.R. 893 28
Leng, *Re*, Tarn *v.* Emmerson, [1895] 1 Ch. 652 ; 64 L.J. Ch. 468 ; 72 L.T. 407 ; 43 W.R. 406 ; 11 T.L.R. 286 ; 39 S.J. 329 ; 12 R. 202 . . 275
Lenton *v.* Tregoning, [1960] 1 W.L.R. 333 ; [1960] 1 All E.R. 717 ; 104 S.J 287 459
Leslie *v.* Crommelin (1867), I.R. 2 Eq. 134 ; 1 I.L.T. 744 507
Lester *v.* Foxcroft (1700), Coll. 108 ; 1 E.R. 205 68
Letts *v.* Inland Revenue Commissioners, [1957] 1 W.L.R. 201 ; [1956] 3 All E.R. 588 ; 101 S.J. 130 ; [1956] T.R. 337 ; 35 A.T.C. 367 ; 49 R. & I. T. 782 300
Lever *v.* Koffler, [1901] 1 Ch. 543 ; 70 L.J. Ch. 395 ; 84 L.T. 584 ; 49 W.R. 506 ; 45 S.J. 326 487
Lever Finance Ltd. *v.* Needleman's Trustee, [1956] Ch. 375 ; [1956] 3 W.L.R. 72 ; [1956] 2 All E.R. 378 ; 100 S.J. 400 ; 167 Est. Gaz. 449 229, 242
Lewis *v.* Lewis (1876), I.R. 11 Eq. 340 408
Lewis *v.* Lewis (1893), 68 L.T. 198 ; 37 S.J. 268; 3 R. 346 . . . 562
Lewis *v.* Love (Frank) Ltd., [1961] 1 W.L.R. 261 ; [1961] 1 All E.R. 446 ; 105 S.J. 155 205-6
Liggett (B.) (Liverpool) Ltd. *v.* Barclays Bank Ltd., [1928] 1 K.B. 48 ; 97 L.J.K.B. 1 ; 137 L.T. 443 ; 43 T.L.R. 449 ; [1927] All E.R. Rep. 451 114-17
Lighton, *Re* (1851), 4 Ir. Jur. 35 188

PAGE

Lincoln *v.* Wright (1859), 4 De G. & J. 16 ; 45 E.R. 6 ; 28 L.J. Ch. 705 ; 33 L.T.O.S. 35 ; 5 Jur. N.S. 1142 ; 7 W.R. 350 ; 124 R.R. 133 . 27, 179
Lind, *Re*, Industrials Finance Syndicate Ltd. *v.* Lind, [1915] 2 Ch. 345 ; 84 L.J. Ch. 884 ; 113 L.T. 956 ; 59 S.J. 651 ; [1915] H.B.R. 204 ; [1914-15] All E.R. Rep. 527 297
Lindsay *v.* Earl of Wicklow (1873), I.R. 7 Eq. 192 194
Lindsay & Co. *v.* Cunday—*see* Cundy *v.* Lindsay.
Lindsay Petroleum Co. *v.* Hurd (1874), L.R. 5 P.C. 221 ; 22 W.R. 492 . 34
Lingen *v.* Sowray (1711), 1 P. Wms. 172 ; 24 E.R. 343 ; *sub nom.* Linguen *v.* Souray, Prec. Ch. 400 ; 24 E.R. 179 ; *sub nom.* Lingen *v.* Souroy, 10 Mod. 38 ; 88 E.R. 615 ; *sub nom.* Lingen *v.* Souray, Gilb. 91 ; 25 E.R. 63 ; 1 Eq. Cas. Abr. 175, pl. 5 ; 21 E.R. 968 ; *sub nom.* Shorer *v.* Shorer, 2 Eq. Cas Abr. 327, pl. 2 ; 22 E.R. 279 . . . . 65, 376
Liquidation Estates Purchase Co. Ltd. *v.* Willoughby, [1898] A.C. 321 ; 67 L.J. Ch. 251 ; 78 L.T. 329 ; 46 W.R. 589 ; 14 T.L.R. 295 . . 194
Lisle *v.* Liddle (1795), 3 Anst. 649 ; 145 E.R. 995 553-4
Lissenden *v.* C.A.V. Bosch Ltd., [1940] A.C. 412 ; [1940] 1 All E.R. 425 ; 109 L.J.K.B. 350 ; 162 L.T. 195 ; 56 T.L.R. 347 ; 31 B.W.C.C. 401 . 396
Litchfield-Speer *v.* Queen Anne's Gate Syndicate (No. 2) Ltd., [1919] 1 Ch. 407 ; 88 L.J. Ch. 137 ; 120 L.T. 565 ; 35 T.L.R. 253 ; 63 S.J. 390 ; [1918-19] All E.R. Rep. 1075 460
Littlewood, *Re*, Clark *v.* Littlewood, [1931] 1 Ch. 443 ; 100 L.J. Ch. 243 ; 144 L.T. 718 ; 47 T.L.R. 79 ; [1930] All E.R. Rep. 151 284
Liverpool Household Stores Assoc. *v.* Smith (1887), 37 Ch.D. 170 ; 57 L.J.Ch. 85 ; 58 L.T. 204 ; 36 W.R. 485 ; 4 T.L.R. 93 462
Livesey, *Re*, Livesey *v.* Livesey, [1953] 1 W.L.R. 1114 ; [1953] 2 All E.R. 723 ; 97 S.J. 572 418
Lloyd, *Re*, Lloyd *v.* Lloyd, [1903] 1 Ch. 385 ; 72 L.J. Ch. 78 ; 87 L.T. 541 ; 51 W.R. 177 ; 19 T.L.R. 101 ; 47 S.J. 128 188
Lloyd *v.* Attwood (1859), 3 De G. & J. 614 ; 44 E.R 1405 ; 29 L.J. Ch. 97 ; 33 L.T.O.S. 209 ; 5 Jur N.S. 1322 ; 121 R.R. 252 . . 341, 351
Lloyd *v.* Banks (1868), L.R. 3 Ch. App. 488 ; 37 L.J. Ch. 881 ; 16 W.R. 988 304
Lloyd *v.* Cox, Nottingham's Chancery Cases, 79 Sel. Soc. 531 (case 707) . 176
Lloyd *v.* Dimmack (1877), 7 Ch.D. 398 ; 47 L.J. Ch. 398 ; 38 L.T. 173 ; 26 W.R. 458 558
Lloyd *v.* Loaring (1802), 6 Ves. 773 ; 31 E.R. 1302 484
Lloyds Bank Ltd., *Re*, Bomze *v.* Bomze, [1931] 1 Ch. 289 ; 100 L.J. Ch. 45 ; 144 L.T. 276 ; 47 T.L.R. 38 345
Lloyds Bank Ltd. *v.* Oliver's Trustee, [1953] 1 W.L.R. 1460 ; [1953] 2 All E.R. 1443 ; 97 S.J. 832 104
Lloyd's Bank *v.* Pearson, [1901] 1 Ch. 865 ; 70 L.J. Ch. 422 ; 84 L.T. 314 ; 45 S.J. 378 302
Lloyd's Estate, *Re*, Waters *v.* Lloyd, [1911] 1 I.R. 153 ; 45 I.L.T.R. 151 . 247
Lock *v.* Bell, [1931] 1 Ch. 35 ; 100 L.J. Ch. 22 ; 144 L.T. 108 ; [1930] All E.R. Rep. 635 82
Lockhart *v.* Hardy (1846), 9 Beav. 349 ; 50 E.R. 378 ; 15 L.J. Ch. 347 ; 10 Jur. 532 ; 73 R.R. 379 . . . . 238, 249
Locking *v.* Parker (1872), L.R. 8 Ch. App. 30 ; 42 L.J. Ch. 257 ; 27 L.T. 635 ; 21 W.R. 113 179
Lodge *v.* National Union Investment Co. Ltd., [1907] 1 Ch. 300 ; 76 L.J. Ch. 187 ; 96 L.T. 301 ; 23 T.L.R. 187 ; [1904-7] All E.R. Rep. 333 . 32, 114
Lomax *v.* Bird (1683), 1 Vern. 182 ; 23 E.R. 402 190
Lombank Ltd. *v.* Excell, [1964] 1 Q.B 415 ; [1963] 3 W.L.R. 700 ; [1963] 3 All E.R. 486 20
Lombank Ltd. *v.* Kennedy, [1961] N.I. 192 22
London and Blackwall Railway Co. *v.* Cross (1886), 31 Ch.D. 354 ; 55 L.J. Ch. 313 ; 54 L.T. 309 ; 34 W.R. 201 ; 2 T.L.R. 231 . . 112
London and County Banking Co. *v.* Goddard, [1897] 1 Ch. 642 ; 66 L.J. Ch. 261 ; 76 L.T. 277 ; 45 W.R. 310 ; 13 T.L.R. 223 ; 41 S.J. 295 . . 260
London & Midland Bank *v.* Mitchell, [1899] 2 Ch. 161 ; 68 L.J.Ch. 568 ; 81 L.T. 263 ; 47 W.R. 602 ; 15 T.L.R. 420 ; 43 S.J. 586 . . 244
London and Yorkshire Bank (Ltd.) *v.* White (1895), 11 T.L.R. 570 ; 39 S.J. 708 299-300

PAGE

London, Chatham and Dover Railway Co. *v.* South Eastern Railway Co., [1892] 1 Ch. 120 ; 61 L.J. Ch. 294 ; 65 L.T. 722 ; 40 W.R. 194 ; 8 T.L.R. 82 ; 36 S.J. 77 ; *on appeal*, [1893] A.C. 429 ; 63 L.J. Ch. 93 ; 69 L.T. 637 ; 58 J.P. 36 ; 1 R. 275 . . . 562-3
London (City of) *v.* Nash (1747), 1 Ves. Sen. 12 ; 27 E.R. 859 ; 3 Atk. 512 ; 26 E.R. 1095 . . . 501
London Corp. *v.* Riggs (1880), 13 Ch. D 798 ; 49 L.J. Ch. 297 ; 42 L.T. 580 ; 44 J.P. 345 ; 28 W.R. 610 . . . 469
London Permanent Benefit Building Soc. *v.* de Baer, [1969] 1 Ch. 321 ; [1968] 2 W.L.R. 465 ; [1968] 1 All E.R. 372 ; 111 S.J. 946 . . . 230
London School Board, *Ex parte—see* Griggs, *Re*.
Long *v.* Donegan (1873), 21 W.R. 830 ; 7 I.L.T.R. 162 . . . 352
Long *v.* Lloyd, [1958] 1 W.L.R. 753 ; [1958] 2 All E.R. 402 ; 102 S.J 488 . 546
Longmate *v.* Ledger (1860), 2 Giff. 157 ; 66 E.R. 67 ; 2 L.T. 256 ; 6 Jur. N.S. 481 ; 8 W.R. 386 ; 128 R.R. 72 ; *affirmed* (unrep.), cit. 4 De G. F. & J. 402 ; 45 E.R. 1239 ; 128 R.R. 72 . . . 334-5
Lord's Estate, *Re*, Lord *v.* Lord (1867), L.R. 2 Ch. App. 782 ; 36 L.J. Ch. 533 ; 17 L.T. 105 ; 15 W.R. 1118 . . . 290
Loveridge *v.* Cooper (1823), 3 Russ. 30 ; 38 E.R. 486 ; [1824-34] All E.R. Rep. 41 ; 27 R.R. 1 . . . 300, 302
Lovesy *v.* Smith (1880), 15 Ch.D. 655 ; 49 L.J.Ch. 809 ; 43 L.T. 240 ; 28 W.R. 979 . . . 536
Low *v.* Bouverie, [1891] 3 Ch. 82 ; 60 L.J. Ch. 594 ; 65 L.T. 533 ; 40 W.R. 50 ; 7 T.L.R. 582 ; [1891-4] All E.R. Rep. 348 . . . 307
Lowe *v.* Adams, [1901] 2 Ch. 598 ; 70 L.J. Ch. 783 ; 85 L.T. 195 ; 50 W.R. 37 ; 17 T.L.R. 763 . . . 98
Lowe & Sons *v.* Dixon & Sons (1885), 16 Q.B.D. 455 . . . 109
Lowry *v.* Reid, [1927] N.I. 142 . . . 495
Lowther *v.* Heaver (1889), 41 Ch.D. 248 ; 58 L.J. Ch. 482 ; 60 L.T. 310 ; 37 W.R. 465 . . . 87
Lucan (Earl of), *Re*, Hardinge *v.* Cobden (1890), 45 Ch.D. 470 ; 60 L.J. Ch. 40 ; 63 L.T. 538 ; 39 W.R. 90 . . . 309-10
Lucas *v.* Hall, [1899] W.N. 92 . . . 498
Lugunda *v.* Service Hotels Ltd., [1969] 2 W.L.R. 1056 . . . 457
Lumley *v.* Wagner (1852), 1 De G. M. & G. 604 ; 42 E.R. 687 ; 21 L.J. Ch. 898 ; 19 L.T.O.S. 264 ; 16 Jur. 861 ; [1843-60] All E.R. Rep. 368 ; 91 R.R. 193 . . . 472-3
Lydon *v.* Lydon (1874), 8 I.L.T.R. 85 . . . 33
Lyle (B.S.) Ltd. *v.* Rosher, [1959] 1 W.L.R. 8 ; [1958] 3 All E.R. 597 ; 103 S.J. 15 . . . 304-5
Lynch's Estate, *Re* (1867), I.R. 1 Eq. 396 . . . 436
Lyndsay *v.* Lyndsay (1849) 1 Ir. Jur. Rep. 289 . . . 555
Lynn *v.* Bamber, [1930] 2 K.B. 72 ; 99 L.J.K.B. 504 ; 143 L.T. 231 ; 46 T.L.R. 367 ; 74 S.J. 298 . . . 105
Lyon *v.* Home (1868), L.R. 6 Eq. 655 ; 37 L.J. Ch. 674 ; 18 L.T. 451 ; 16 W.R. 824 . . . 348
Lysaght, *Re*, Hill *v.* Royal College of Surgeons, [1966] Ch. 191 ; [1965] 3 W.L.R. 391 ; [1965] 2 All E.R. 888 ; 109 S.J. 577 . . . 362
Lysaght *v.* Lysaght (1851), 4 Ir. Jur. 110 . . . 194
Lysaght's Estate, *Re*, [1903] 1 I.R. 235 . . . 436

M. & S. Drapers *v.* Reynolds, [1957] 1 W.L.R. 9 ; [1956] 3 All E.R. 814 ; 101 S.J. 44 . . . 471
McArdle, *Re*, [1951] Ch. 669 ; [1951] 1 All E.R. 905 ; 95 S.J. 284 . . . 310
Macartney, *Re*, Macfarlane *v.* Macartney, [1918] 1 Ch. 300 ; 87 L.J. Ch. 143 ; 118 L.T. 174 . . . 408-9
M'Carthy *v.* M'Cartie (No. 2), [1904] 1 I.R. 100 ; 38 I.L.T.R. 3 . . . 433
Macarty *v.* Bayly (1707), 7 Bro. P.C. 218 ; 3 E.R. 142 . . . 139
M'Causland *v.* Murphy (1881), 9 L.R. Ir. 9 . . . 89-90
M'Causland *v.* O'Callaghan (1903), 3 N.I.J.R. 144 . . . 511
McCausland *v.* Young, [1948] N.I. 72 ; *on appeal*, [1949] N.I. 49 . . . 33
McCombe *v.* Read, [1955] 2 Q.B. 429 ; [1955] 1 W.L.R. 635 ; [1955] 2 All E.R. 458 ; 99 S.J. 370 . . . 466
M'Cormack *v.* M'Cormack (1877), 1 L.R. Ir. 119 . . . 533

PAGE

Macdonald *v.* Irvine (1878), 8 Ch.D. 101 ; 47 L.J. Ch. 494 ; 38 L.T. 155 ; 26 W.R. 381 288
M'Donnell *v.* Stenson, [1921] 1 I.R. 80 ; 56 I.L.T.R. 61 . . . 384
M'Donough *v.* Shewbridge (1814) 2 Ba. & B. 555 . . . 246, 247
McEneaney *v.* Shevlin, [1912] 1 I.R. 32, 278 ; 46 I.L.T.R. 137 . . 325
McEvoy *v.* Belfast Banking Co. Ltd., [1935] A.C. 24 ; 103 L.J.P.C. 137 ; 151 L.T. 501 ; 40 Com. Cas. 1 ; [1934] All E.R. Rep. 800 . . . 325
M'Fadden *v.* Jenkyns (1842), 1 Ph. 153 ; 41 E.R. 589 ; 12 L.J.Ch. 146 ; 7 Jur. 27 ; [1835-42] All E.R. Rep. 206 ; 65 R.R. 354 312
M'Gauran *v.* Furnell (1837), S. & Sc. 263 561
McGillicuddy of the Reeks (The) *v.* Joy, [1959] I.R. 189 . . . 27
McGregor *v.* McGregor (1888), 21 Q.B.D. 424 ; 57 L.J. Q.B. 591 ; 52 J.P. 772 ; 37 W.R. 45 ; 4 T.L.R. 760 490
McIlraith *v.* Grady, [1968] 1 Q.B. 468 ; [1967] 3 W.L.R. 1331 ; [1967] 3 All E.R. 625 ; 111 S.J. 583 459
M'Intosh *v.* Great Western Railway Co. (1850), 2 Mac. & G. 74 ; 42 E.R. 29; 2 H. & Tw. 250 ; 47 E.R. 1676 ; 19 L.J.Ch. 374 ; 15 L.T.O.S. 321 ; 14 Jur. 819 ; 79 R.R. 359 562
McKee, *Re*, Public Trustee *v.* McKee, [1931] 2 Ch. 145 ; 100 L.J.Ch. 325; 145 L.T. 605 ; 47 T.L.R. 424 ; 75 S.J. 442 269
Mackender *v.* Feldia A.G., [1967] 2 Q.B. 590 ; [1967] 2 W.L.R. 119 ; [1966] 3 All E.R. 847 ; 110 S.J. 811 551
Mackenzie *v.* Coulson (1869), L.R. 8 Eq. 368 . . . 537-8, 539, 541
McKenzie *v.* Hesketh (1877), 7 Ch.D. 675 ; 47 L.J.Ch. 231 ; 38 L.T. 171 ; 26 W.R. 189 507
Mackenzie *v.* Johnston (1819), 4 Madd. 373 ; 56 E.R. 742 . . . 560
McKeown *v.* Boudard-Peveril Gear Co. (1896), 65 L.J. Ch. 735 ; 74 L.T. 712 45 W.R. 152 ; 40 S.J. 565 551
Mackey *v.* Jones (1958), 93 I.L.T.R. 177 495
McLuskey *v.* Cole [1922] 1 Ch. 7 ; 91 L.J. Ch. 242 ; 126 L.T. 269 ; [1921] All E.R. Rep. 315 479
M'Mackin *v.* Hibernian Bank, [1905] 1 I.R. 296 ; 39 I.L.T.R. 133 ; 5 N.I.J.R. 260 . . . . 342, 349
McManus *v.* Cooke (1887), 35 Ch.D. 681 ; 56 L.J.Ch. 662 ; 56 L.T. 900 ; 51 J.P. 708 ; 35 W.R. 754 ; 3 T.L.R. 622 . . . . . 101, 493
M'Mechan *v.* Warburton, [1896] 1 I.R. 435 531
Macnamara's Estate (1884), 13 L.R. Ir. 158 221
Maddison *v.* Alderson (1883), 8 App. Cas. 467 ; 52 L.J.Q.B. 737 ; 49 L.T. 303 ; 47 J.P. 821 ; 31 W.R. 820 ; [1881-5] All E.R. Rep. 742 . . 493-5
Maddison *v.* Chapman (1861), 1 J. & H. 470 ; 70 E.R. 831 ; 128 R.R. 475 . 405
Madell *v.* Thomas & Co., [1891] 1 Q.B. 230 ; 60 L.J.Q.B. 227 ; 64 L.T. 9 ; 39 W.R. 280 ; 7 T.L.R. 170 179
Magee *v.* Pennine Insurance Co. Ltd., [1969] 2 W.L.R. 1278 ; [1969] 2 All E.R. 891. 549
Magneta Time Co. Ltd., *Re*, Molden *v.* The Co. (1915), 84 L.J.Ch. 814 ; 113 L.T. 986 192
Mainland *v.* Upjohn (1889), 41 Ch.D. 126 ; 58 L.J.Ch. 361 ; 60 L.T. 614 ; 37 W.R. 411 207
Maitland *v.* Irving (1846), 15 Sim. 437 ; 60 E.R. 688 ; 16 L.J.Ch. 95 ; 8 L.T.O.S. 312 ; 10 Jur. 1025 ; 74 R.R. 115 349
Malone *v.* Harris (1859), 11 Ir. Ch. Rep. 33 ; Dru. t. Nap. 655 . . . 98
Manchester and Liverpool District Banking Co. Ltd. *v.* Parkinson (1888), 22 Q.B.D. 173 ; 58 L.J.Q.B. 262 ; 37 W.R. 264 ; 5 T.L.R. 135 . . 510
Manchester and Milford Railway, *Re* (1881), 45 L.T. 129 . . . 509
Manchester Brewery Co. *v.* Coombs, [1901] 2 Ch. 608 ; 70 L.J.Ch. 814 ; 82 L.T. 347 ; 16 T.L.R. 299 . . . . . 87-8, 101, 327, 328, 487
Manchester, Sheffield and Lincolnshire Railway Co. *v.* North Central Wagon Co. (1888), 13 App. Cas. 554 ; 58 L.J.Ch. 219 ; 59 L.T. 730 ; 37 W.R. 305 ; 4 T.L.R. 728 179
Mangles *v.* Dixon (1852), 3 H.L.C. 702 ; 10 E.R. 278 ; 19 L.T.O.S. 260 ; [1843-60] All E.R. Rep. 770 ; 88 R.R. 296 . . . . . 307, 308
Manlove *v.* Bale (1688), 2 Vern. 84 ; 23 E.R. 664 171
Mann *v.* Lovejoy (1826), Ry. & M. 355 ; 4 L.J.O.S.K.B. 172 . 84
Manners, *Re*, Public Trustee *v.* Manners, [1949] Ch. 613 ; [1949] 2 All E.R. 201 ; [1949] L.J.R. 1574 416

PAGE

Manning *v.* Turner, [1957] 1 W.L.R. 91 ; [1956] 3 All E.R. 641 ; 101 S.J. 46 504, 542
March *v.* Lee (1670), 1 Ch. Cas. 162 ; 22 E.R. 743 ; 3 Ch. Rep. 62 ; 21 E.R. 729 ; *sub nom.* Marsh *v.* Lee, 2 Vent. 337 ; 86 E.R. 473 . . 62, 173-4
Margrave *v.* Le Hooke (1690), 2 Vern. 207 ; 23 E.R. 734 . . . 176
Marks *v.* Lilley, [1959] 1 W.L.R. 749 ; [1959] 2 All E.R. 647 ; 103 S.J. 658 . 485
Marlay, *Re*, Duke of Rutland *v.* Bury, [1915] 2 Ch. 264 ; 84 L.J.Ch. 706 ; 113 L.T. 433 ; 31 T.L.R. 422 ; 59 S.J. 494 382
Marlborough (Duke of), *Re*, Davis *v.* Whitehead, [1894] 2 Ch. 133 ; 63 L.J.Ch. 471 ; 70 L.T. 314 ; 42 W.R. 456 ; 10 T.L.R. 296 ; 38 S.J. 289 ; 8 R. 242 179
Marsden's Trust, *Re* (1859), 4 Drew. 594 ; 62 E.R. 228 ; 28 L.J.Ch. 906 ; 33 L.T.O.S. 217 ; 5 Jur. N.S. 590 ; 7 W.R. 520 ; [1843-60] All E.R. Rep. 393 ; 113 R.R. 171 . . . 370
Marsh *v.* Lee—*see* March *v.* Lee.
Marshall *v.* Cave (1824), 3 L.J.O.S. Ch. 57 . . . . 236, 237
Marshall *v.* Charteris, [1920] 1 Ch. 520 ; 89 L.J.Ch. 354 ; 123 L.T. 162 . 510
Marshall *v.* Shrewsbury (1875), L.R. 10 Ch.App. 250; 44 L.J.Ch. 302; 32 L.T. 418 ; 23 W.R. 803 . . . . 243, 244, 261
Martin, *Re*, Midland Bank Executor and Trustee Co. Ltd. *v.* Marfleet, [1955] Ch. 698 ; [1955] 2 W.L.R. 1029 ; [1955] 1 All E.R. 865 ; 99 S.J. 318 282
Martin *v.* Bannister (1879), 4 Q.B.D. 491 ; 28 W.R. 143 ; *sub nom.* R. *v.* Harington, 48 L.J.Q.B. 677 ; 43 J.P. 829 459
Martinson *v.* Clowes (1882), 21 Ch.D. 857 ; 51 L.J.Ch. 594 ; 46 L.T. 882 ; 30 W.R. 795 ; *on appeal* (1885), 52 L.T. 706 255
Mary Ann, The (1845), 9 Jur. 94 434
Mason *v.* Armitage (1806), 13 Ves. 25 ; 33 E.R. 204 ; 9 R.R. 131 . . 30, 487
Mason *v.* Gardiner (1793), 4 Bro. C.C. 436 ; 29 E.R. 976 . . . 113
Mason *v.* Provident Clothing and Supply Co. Ltd., [1913] A.C. 724 ; 82 L.J.K.B. 1153 ; 109 L.T. 449 ; 29 T.L.R. 727 ; 57 S.J. 739 ; [1911-13] All E.R. Rep. 400 471
Masters *v.* Masters (1718), 1 P. Wms. 421 ; 24 E.R. 454 ; 2 Eq. Cas. Abr. 352, pl. 12 ; 22 E.R. 300 ; 8 Vin. Abr. 312, pl. 29 ; [1558-1774] All E.R. Rep. 483 427
Mathews *v.* Saurin (1893), 31 L.R. Ir. 181 ; 27 I.L.T.R. 25 . . . 558
Mathieson's Trustee *v.* Burrup, Mathieson & Co., [1927] 1 Ch. 562 ; 96 L.J. Ch. 148; 136 L.T. 796; [1927] B. & C.R. 47; [1927] All E.R. Rep. 172 117
Mathison *v.* Clark—*see* Matthison *v.* Clarke.
Matthews *v.* Cartwright (1742), 2 Atk. 347 ; 26 E.R. 611 . . . 173
Matthews *v.* Goodday (1861), 31 L.J.Ch. 282 ; 5 L.T. 572 ; 8 Jur. N.S. 90 ; 10 W.R. 148 ; 136 R.R. 379 253
Matthews' Will Trusts, *Re*, Bristow *v.* Matthews, [1961] 1 W.L.R. 1415 ; [1961] 3 All E.R. 869 ; 105 S.J. 888 ; [1961] T.R. 345 439
Matthie *v.* Edwards—*see* Jones *v.* Matthie.
Matthison *v.* Clarke (1854), 3 Drew. 3 ; 61 E.R. 801 ; 106 R.R. 270 ; *sub nom.* Mathison *v.* Clark, 24 L.J. Ch. 202 ; 3 Eq. R. 127 ; 24 L.T.O.S. 105 ; 18 Jur. 1020 ; 3 W.R. 2 256
Maughan, *Re*, *Ex parte* Monkhouse (1885), 14 Q.B.D 956 ; 54 L.J.Q.B. 128 ; 33 W.R. 308 ; 2 Morr. 25 87
Maunder *v.* Lloyd (1862), 2 J. & H. 718 ; 70 E.R. 1248 ; 11 W.R. 141 ; 1 New R. 123 ; 134 R.R. 405 14
Maunsell *v.* Maunsell (1877), 1 L.R. Ir. 529 530
Maxwell *v.* Lady Montacute ; Maxwell *v.* Lady Mountacute ; Maxwell's Case—*see* Montacute (Viscountess) *v.* Maxwell.
Maxwell *v.* Tipping, [1903] 1 I.R. 498 205
May *v.* Platt, [1900] 1 Ch. 616 ; 69 L.J.Ch. 357 ; 83 L.T. 123 ; 48 W.R. 617 534, 538, 539
Maynard *v.* Maynard, [1969] 2 W.L.R. 22 ; [1969] 1 All E.R. 1 ; 112 S.J. 690 104
Measures Bros. Ltd. *v.* Measures, [1910] 2 Ch. 248 ; 79 L.J.Ch. 707 ; 102 L.T. 794 ; 26 T.L.R. 488 ; 54 S.J. 521 ; 18 Mans. 40 460
Meechett *v.* Bradshaw (1633), Nels. 22 ; 21 E.R. 779 296
Meek *v.* Devenish (1877), 6 Ch.D. 566 ; 47 L.J.Ch. 57 ; 36 L.T. 911 ; 25 W.R. 688 392
Meek *v.* Kettlewell (1842), 1 Hare 464 ; 66 E.R. 1114 ; 11 L.J.Ch. 293 ; 6 Jur. 550 ; 58 R.R. 137 ; *on appeal* (1843), 1 Ph. 342 ; 41 E.R. 662 ; 13 L.J.Ch. 28 ; 2 L.T.O.S. 205 ; 7 Jur. 1120 ; 58 R.R. 137 309

PAGE

Meeking *v.* Meeking, [1917] 1 Ch. 77 ; 86 L.J.Ch. 97 ; 115 L.T. 623 ; [1916-17] All E.R. Rep. 776 . . . . 540, 541
Melbourne Banking Corp. Ltd. *v.* Brougham (1882), 7 App. Cas. 307 ; 51 L.J.P.C. 65 ; 46 L.T. 603 ; 30 W.R. 925 260
Mellor *v.* Lees (1742), 2 Atk. 494 ; 26 E.R. 698 177
Mengel's Will Trusts, *Re*, Westminster Bank Ltd. *v.* Mengel, [1962] Ch. 791; [1962] 3 W.L.R. 311 ; [1962] 2 All E.R. 490 ; 106 S.J. 510 . . 400-1, 410
Menzies *v.* Lightfoot (1871), L.R. 11 Eq. 459 ; 40 L.J.Ch. 561 ; 24 L.T. 695; 19 W.R. 578 221
Mercantile Bank of London Ltd. *v.* Evans, [1899] 2 Q.B. 613 ; 68 L.J.Q.B. 921 ; 81 L.T. 376 ; 15 T.L.R. 535 327
Mercantile Investment and General Trust Co. *v.* River Plate Trust, Loan, and Agency Co., [1892] 2 Ch. 303 ; 61 L.J.Ch. 473 ; 66 L.T. 711 ; 36 S.J. 427 17
Merton, *Re*, Public Trustee *v.* Wilson, [1953] 1 W.L.R. 1096 ; [1953] 2 All E.R. 707 ; 97 S.J. 572 370
Meux *v.* Bell (1841), 1 Hare 73 ; 66 E.R. 955 ; 11 L.J.Ch. 77 ; 6 Jur. 123 ; 58 R.R. 41 303
Meux *v.* Cobley, [1892] 2 Ch. 253 ; 61 L.J.Ch. 449 ; 66 L.T. 86 ; 8 T.L.R. 173 464
Meux's Brewery Co. *v.* City of London Electric Lighting Co.—*see* Shelfer *v.* City of London Electric Lighting Co.
Mexborough U.D.C. *v.* Harrison, [1964] 1 W.L.R. 733 ; [1964] 2 All E.R. 109 ; 128 J.P. 317 ; 108 S.J. 218 ; 62 L.G.R. 287 . . . . 190, 231
Middleton, *Re*—*see* Allen, *Ex parte*.
Miles *v.* Bull, [1969] 1 Q.B. 258 ; [1968] 3 W.L.R. 1090 ; [1968] 3 All E.R. 632 104
Miller *v.* Cook (1870), L.R. 10 Eq. 641 ; 40 L.J.Ch. 11 ; 22 L.T. 740 ; 35 J.P. 245 ; 18 W.R. 1061 . . . . 354, 355
Millett *v.* Davey (1862), 31 Beav. 470 ; 54 E.R. 1221 ; 32 L.J. Ch. 122 ; 7 L.T. 551 ; 9 Jur. N.S. 92 ; 11 W.R. 176 ; 135 R.R. 516 . . . 236-7
Milltown (Earl of) *v.* Stewart (1837), 3 My. & Cr. 18 ; 40 E.R. 830 . . 552
Milnes *v.* Gery (1807), 14 Ves. 400 ; 33 E.R. 574 ; [1803-13] All E.R. Rep. 369 ; 9 R.R. 307 498
Milroy *v.* Lord (1862), 4 De G. F. & J. 264 ; 45 E.R. 1185 ; 31 L.J.Ch. 789 ; 7 L.T. 178 ; 8 Jur. N.S. 806 ; [1861-73] All E.R. Rep. 783 ; 135 R.R. 135 . . . . 311, 313-4, 319, 322, 323
Milward *v.* Earl Thanet (1801), 5 Ves. 720n. ; 31 E.R. 824 ; 5 R.R. 150n. . 505
Ministry of Health *v.* Simpson, [1951] A.C. 251 ; [1950] 2 All E.R. 1137 ; 66 T.L.R. (Pt. 2) 1015 ; *sub nom. Re* Diplock, Minister of Health *v.* Simpson, 94 S.J. 777 . . . . 64, 162, 163
Mirfield *v.* Morley, Nottingham's Chancery Cases, 79 Sel Soc. 474 (case 627) 172
Moat House Farm, *Re*—*see* Young *v.* Clarey.
Moggridge *v.* Thackwell (1792), 1 Ves. Jun. 464 ; 30 E.R. 440 ; 3 Bro. C.C. 517 ; 29 E.R. 677 ; [1775-1802] All E.R. Rep. 218 ; 2 R.R. 140 . . 427
Mogul Steamship Co. Ltd. *v.* McGregor, Gow & Co., [1892] A.C. 25 ; 61 L.J.Q.B. 295 ; 66 L.T. 1 ; 56 J.P. 101 ; 40 W.R. 337 ; 8 T.L.R. 182 ; 7 Asp. M.L.C. 120 ; [1891-4] All E.R. Rep. 263 7
Molony *v.* Kernan (1842), 2 Dr. & War. 31 ; 59 R.R. 635 349
Molton Finance Ltd., *Re*, [1968] Ch. 325 ; [1967] 3 W.L.R. 1561 ; [1967] 3 All E.R. 843 ; 111 S.J. 791 184
Molyneux *v.* Hawtrey, [1903] 2 K. B. 487 ; 72 L.J.K.B. 873 ; 89 L.T. 350 ; 52 W.R. 23 ; [1900-3] All E.R. Rep. 472 504
Molyneux *v.* Richard, [1906] 1 Ch. 34 ; 75 L.J.Ch. 39 ; 93 L.T. 698 ; 54 W.R. 177 ; 22 T.L.R. 76 491
Monaghan C.C. *v.* Vaughan, [1948] I.R 306 . . . . 534-5, 541
Monck *v.* Lord Monck (1810), 1 Ba. & B. 298 ; 12 R.R. 33 425
Monkhouse, *Ex parte*—*see* Maughan, *Re*.
Monson *v.* Madame Tussaud Ltd., [1894] 1 Q.B. 671 ; 63 L.J.Q.B. 454 ; 70 L.T. 335 ; 58 J.P. 524 ; 10 T.L.R. 227 ; 9 R. 177 ; [1891-4] All E.R. Rep. 1051 462

PAGE

Montacute (Viscountess) *v.* Maxwell (1720), 1 P. Wms. 618 ; 24 E.R. 541 ; *sub nom.* Maxwell *v.* Lady Mountacute, Prec. Ch. 526 ; 24 E.R. 235 ; *sub nom.* Maxwell *v.* Lady Montacute (1719), 1 Eq. Cas. Abr. 19 ; pl. 4 ; 21 E.R. 842 ; *sub nom.* Mountacue (Countess Dowager of) *v.* Maxwell, 1 Str. 236 ; 93 E.R. 494; *sub nom.* Maxwell's Case (1719), 1 Eq. Cas. Abr. 20, pl. 5 ; 21 E.R. 842 26
Montefiori *v.* Montefiori (1762), 1 Wm. Bl. 363 ; 96 E.R. 203 . . 39
Montgomery *v.* Montgomery (1845), 3 Jo. & Lat. 47 ; 72 R.R. 17 . . 66
Moody, *Re*, Woodroffe *v.* Moody, [1895] 1 Ch. 101 ; 64 L.J.Ch. 174 ; 72 L.T. 190 ; 43 W.R. 462 ; 13 R. 13 290
Moore *v.* Butler (1805), 2 Sch. & Lef. 249 399
Moore *v.* Moore (1874), L.R. 18 Eq. 474 ; 43 L.J.Ch. 617 ; 30 L.T. 752 ; 38 J.P. 804 ; 22 W.R. 729 313
Moore *v.* Ulster Banking Co. (1877), I.R. 11 C.L. 512 ; 12 I.L.T.R. 5 . 311
Morgan *v.* Hart, [1914] 2 K.B. 183 ; 83 L.J.K.B. 782 ; 110 L.T. 611 ; 30 T.L.R. 286 509
Morgan *v.* Jeffreys, [1901] 1 Ch. 620 ; 79 L.J.Ch. 360 ; 74 J.P. 154 ; 26 T.L.R. 324 204
Morley, *Re, Ex parte* Morley, Scott *v.* Morley—*see* Scott *v.* Morley.
Morley *v.* Bird (1798), 3 Ves. 628 ; 30 E.R. 1192 ; [1775-1802] All E.R. Rep. 108 ; 4 R.R. 106 262
Morley *v.* Loughnan, [1893] 1 Ch. 736 ; 62 L.J.Ch. 515 ; 68 L.T. 619 ; 9 T.L.R. 214 ; 3 R. 592 348
Morphett *v.* Jones (1818), 1 Swanst. 172 ; 36 E.R. 344 ; 1 Wils. Ch. 100 ; 37 E.R. 45 ; [1814-23] All E.R. Rep. 612 ; 18 R.R. 48 . . . 495
Morrell *v.* Wootten (1852), 16 Beav. 197 ; 51 E.R. 753 ; 96 R.R. 95 . . 299
Morret *v.* Paske (1740), 2 Atk. 52 ; 26 E.R. 429 . . 174, 175
Morris's Settlement Trusts, *Re*, Adams *v.* Napier, [1951] 2 All E.R. 528 ; 95 S.J. 609 368
Morris (Herbert) Ltd. *v* Saxelby, [1916] 1 A.C. 688 ; 85 L.J.Ch. 210 ; 114 L.T. 618 ; 32 T.L.R. 297 ; 60 S.J. 305 ; [1916-17] All E.R. Rep. 305 . 471
Morris Motors Ltd. *v.* Lilley, [1959] 1 W.L.R. 1184; [1959] 3 All E.R. 737 ; 103 S.J. 1003 470
Morris Motors Ltd. *v.* Phelan, [1960] 1 W.L.R. 352 , 566 ; [1960] 2 All E.R. 208 ; 104 S.J. 310 ; [1960] R.P.C. 209 470
Morrison *v.* Arnold (1817), 19 Ves. 670 ; 34 E.R. 664 ; 2 Russ. & M. 145 ; 39 E.R. 349 556
Morrison *v.* Barking Chemicals Co. Ltd., [1919] 2 Ch. 325 ; 88 L.J.Ch. 314 ; 122 L.T. 423 ; 35 T.L.R. 196 ; 63 S.J. 302 558
Morrison, Jones & Taylor Ltd., *Re*, Cookes *v.* Morrison Jones & Taylor Ltd., [1914] 1 Ch. 50 ; 83 L.J.Ch. 129 ; 109 L.T. 722 ; 30 T.L.R. 59 ; 58 S.J. 80 213
Morse *v.* Faulkner (1792), 3 Swanst. 400n.; 36 E.R. 936 ; 1 Anst. 11 ; 145 E.R. 784 ; [1775-1802] All E.R. Rep. 556 487
Mortimer *v.* Beckett, [1920] 1 Ch. 571 ; 89 L.J.Ch. 245 ; 123 L.T. 27 ; 64 S.J. 341 ; [1920] All E.R. Rep. 179 473
Mortimer *v.* Shortall (1842), 2 Dr. & War. 383 ; 1 Con. & L. 417 ; 59 R.R. 730 530
Mortlock *v.* Buller (1804), 10 Ves. 292 ; 32 E.R. 857 ; [1803-13] All E.R. Rep. 22 ; 7 R.R. 417 501
Mosely *v.* Virgin (1796), 3 Ves. 184 ; 30 E.R. 959 491
Moses *v.* Macferlan (1760), 2 Burr. 1005 ; 97 E.R. 676 ; [1558-1774] All E.R. Rep. 581 ; *sub nom.* Moses *v.* Macpherlan, 1 Black. W. 219 ; 96 E.R. 120 114
Mountacue (Countess Dowager of) *v.* Maxwell—*see* Montacute (Viscountess *v.* Maxwell.
Mountford *v.* Scott (1823), Turn. & R. 274 ; 37 E.R. 1105 ; 24 R.R. 55 . 183
Mountfort, *Ex parte* (1808), 14 Ves. 606 ; 33 E.R. 653 ; 9 R.R. 359 . . 182-3
Mower's Trusts, *Re* (1869), L.R. 8 Eq. 110 ; 20 L.T. 838 . . . 436
Moxon *v.* Berkeley Mutual Benefit Building Soc. (1890), 59 L.J.Ch. 524 ; 62 L.T. 250 435
Moxon *v.* Payne (1873), L.R. 8 Ch. App. 881 ; 43 L.J. Ch. 240 . . 347
Mumford *v.* Collier (1890), 25 Q.B.D. 279 ; 59 L.J.Q.B. 552 ; 38 W.R. 716 234
Municipal Permanent Investment Building Soc. *v.* Smith (1888), 22 Q.B.D. 70 ; 58 L.J.Q.B. 61 ; 37 W.R. 42 ; 5 T.L.R. 17 235

PAGE

Murphy *v.* Taylor (1850), 1 Ir. Ch. Rep. 92 ; 3 Ir. Jur. 85 179
Murphy (Thomas) & Co. Ltd. *v.* Marren, [1933] I.R. 393 225
Murray *v.* Lord Elibank (1804), 10 Ves. 84 ; 32 E.R. 775 ; 7 R.R. 346 . 441
Murray, Bull & Co. Ltd. *v.* Murray, [1953] 1 Q.B. 211 ; [1952] 2 All E.R. 1079 ; [1952] 2 T.L.R. 1003 ; 96 S.J. 852 37
Mutlow *v.* Bigg (1875), 1 Ch.D. 385 ; 45 L.J.Ch. 282 ; 34 L.T. 273 ; 24 W.R. 409 . . . . 391, 393

Nash, *Re*, Cook *v.* Frederick, [1910] 1 Ch. 1 ; 79 L.J.Ch. 1 ; 101 L.T. 837 ; 26 T.L.R. 57 ; 54 S.J. 48 404
Nash *v.* Armstrong (1861), 10 C.B.N.S. 259 ; 142 E.R. 451 ; 30 L.J.C.P. 286 ; 7 Jur. N.S. 1060 ; 9 W.R. 782 ; 128 R.R. 702 . . 120, 122
Nash *v.* Eads (1880), 25 S.J. 95 253
National Bank Ltd. *v.* Barry (1965), 100 I.L.T.R. 185 511
National Bank Ltd. *v.* M'Govern, [1931] I.R. 368 182
National Bank of Australasia *v.* United Hand-in-Hand and Band of Hope Co. (1879), 4 App. Cas. 391 ; 48 L.J.P.C. 50 ; 40 L.T. 697 ; 27 W.R. 889 . 236
National Provincial Bank Ltd. *v.* Hastings Car Mart Ltd., [1964] Ch. 9 ; [1963] 2 W.L.R. 1015 ; [1963] 2 All E.R. 204 ; 107 S.J. 295 ; *on appeal*, [1964] Ch. 665 ; [1964] 3 W.L.R. 463 ; [1964] 3 All E.R. 93 ; *on further appeal, sub nom.* National Provincial Bank Ltd. *v.* Ainsworth, [1965] A.C. 1175 ; [1965] 3 W.L.R. 1 ; [1965] 2 All E.R. 472 ; 109 S.J. 415 . 38, 104
National Provincial Bank of England *v.* Jackson (1886), 33 Ch.D. 1 ; 55 L.T. 458 ; 34 W.R. 597 119-20
National Sailors' and Firemen's Union of Great Britain and Ireland *v.* Reed, [1926] Ch. 536 ; 95 L.J.Ch. 192 ; 135 L.T. 103 ; [1926] All E.R. Rep. 381 ; *sub nom.* National Seamen's and Firemen's Union of Great Britain and Ireland *v.* McVey, 42 T.L.R. 513 . . . . . 477, 479
Nedby *v.* Nedby (1852), 5 De. G. & Sm. 377 ; 64 E.R. 1161 ; 21 L.J.Ch. 446 ; 19 L.T.O.S. 294 ; 90 R.R. 105 345
Nesbitt and Potts' Contract, *Re*—*see* Nisbet and Potts' Contract, *Re*.
Neville *v.* Wilkinson (1782), 1 Bro. C.C. 543 ; 28 E.R. 1289 39
Newbiggin-by-the-Sea Gas Co. *v.* Armstrong (1879), 13 Ch.D. 310 ; 49 L.J.Ch. 231 ; 41 L.T. 637 ; 28 W.R. 217 110
Newbigging *v.* Adam (1886), 34 Ch.D. 582 ; 56 L.J.Ch. 275 ; 55 L.T. 794 ; 35 W.R. 597 ; [1886-90] All E.R. Rep. 975 ; *on appeal, sub nom.* Adam *v.* Newbigging (1888), 13 App. Cas. 308 ; 57 L.J.Ch. 1066 ; 59 L.T. 267 ; 37 W.R. 97 546
New Brunswick and Canada Railway and Land Co. *v.* Muggeridge (1860), 1 Dr. & Sm. 363 ; 62 E.R. 418 ; 30 L.J.Ch. 242 ; 3 L.T. 651 ; 7 Jur. N.S. 132 ; 9 W.R. 193 ; 127 R.R. 142 551
Newcomb *v.* Bonham (1681), 2 Ch. Cas. 58 ; 22 E.R. 845 ; 1 Vern. 7 ; (1683) 1 Vern. 214 ; (1684) 1 Vern. 232 ; (1689) 1 Vern. 233n.; 23 E.R. 266 , 422, 435 ; 1 Eq. Cas. Abr. 312, pl. 13 ; 21 E.R. 1068 ; *sub nom.* Bonham *v.* Newcomb, 2 Vent. 364 ; 86 E.R. 488 176-7
Newfoundland (Government of) *v.* Newfoundland Railway Co. (1888), 13 App. Cas. 199 ; 57 L.J.P.C. 35 ; *sub nom.* A.-G. for Newfoundland *v.* Newfoundland Railway Co., 58 L.T. 285 ; 4 T.L.R. 292 309
New Sombrero Phosphate Co. *v.* Erlanger—*see* Erlanger *v.* New Sombrero Phosphate Co.
Newton *v.* Langham (1675-6), 2 Ch. Rep. 108 ; 21 E.R. 630 169
Nicholls *v.* Maynard (1747), 3 Atk. 519 ; 26 E.R. 1100 178
Nicholls *v.* Nicholls (1737), West t. Hard. 192 ; 25 E.R. 890 ; 1 Atk. 409 ; 26 E.R. 259 348
Nichols *v.* Gould (1752), 2 Ves. Sen. 422 ; 28 E.R. 270 356
Nicholson's Settlement, *Re*, Molony *v.* Nicholson, [1939] Ch. 11 ; 107 L.J.Ch. 338 ; 159 L.T. 314 ; 54 T.L.R. 1060 ; 82 S.J. 603 372
Nisbet and Potts' Contract, *Re*, [1906] 1 Ch. 386 ; 75 L.J.Ch. 238 ; 22 T.L.R. 233 ; 50 S.J. 191 ; [1904-7] All E.R. Rep. 865 ; *sub nom. Re* Nesbitt and Potts' Contract, 94 L.T. 297 ; 54 W.R. 286 . . . . 468, 504
Noakes & Co. Ltd. *v.* Rice, [1902] A.C. 24 ; 71 L.J.Ch. 139 ; 86 L.T. 62 ; 66 J.P. 147 ; 50 W.R. 305 ; 18 T.L.R. 196 ; 46 S.J. 136 ; [1900-3] All E.R. Rep. 34 207-9
Nocton *v.* Lord Ashburton, [1914] A.C. 932 ; 83 L.J.Ch. 784 ; 111 L.T. 641 ; 30 T.L.R. 602 ; [1914-15] All E.R. Rep. 45 . 60, 329, 330, 331, 336

PAGE

Nolan, *Re*, *Application of* Assemblers Ltd., [1949] I.R. 197 522
Nolan *v.* Graves, [1946] I.R. 376 ; 81 I.L.T.R. 9 539
Nolan *v.* Nolan (1957), 92 I.L.T.R. 94 535
Nordenfelt *v.* Maxim Nordenfelt Guns and Ammunition Co Ltd., [1894] A.C. A.C. 535 ; 63 L.J. Ch. 908 ; 71 L.T. 489 ; 10 T.L.R. 636 ; 11 R. 1 ; [1891-4] All E.R. Rep. 1 471
Norris *v.* Chambres (1861), 29 Beav. 246 ; 54 E.R. 621 ; 30 L.J.Ch. 285 ; 3 L.T. 720 ; 7 Jur. N.S. 59 ; 9 W.R. 259 ; 131 R.R. 551 ; *on appeal* (1861), 3 De G.F. & J. 583 ; 45 E.R. 1004 ; 4 L.T. 345 ; 7 Jur. N.S. 689 ; 9 W.R. 794 ; 131 R.R. 551 . . . . 13, 17
Norris *v.* Wilkinson (1806), 12 Ves. 192 ; 33 E.R. 73 183
North-Eastern Railway Co. *v.* Martin (1848), 2 Ph. 758 ; 41 E.R. 1136 ; 16 L.T.O.S. 61 ; *sub nom.* South-Eastern Railway Co. *v.* Martin, 1 H. & Tw. 69 ; 47 E.R. 1330 ; 5 Ry. & Can. Cas. 478 ; 18 L.J. Ch. 103 ; 12 L.T.O.S. 345 ; 13 Jur. 1 563
Northern Banking Co. Ltd. *v.* Carpenter, [1931] I.R. 268 182
Northern Counties of England Fire Insurance Co. *v.* Whipp (1884), 26 Ch.D. 482 ; 53 L.J.Ch. 629 ; 51 L.T. 806 ; 32 W.R. 626 ; [1881-5] All E.R. Rep. 941 216-17
North London Railway Co. *v.* Great Northern Railway Co. (1883), 11 Q.B.D. 30 ; 52 L.Q.B. 380 ; 48 L.T. 695 ; 31 W.R. 490 . . . 111-12
Nottidge *v.* Prince (1860), 2 Giff. 246 ; 66 E.R. 103 ; 29 L.J.Ch. 857 ; 2 L.T. 720 ; 24 J.P. 726 ; 6 Jur. N.S. 1066 ; 8 W.R. 742 ; [1843-60] All E.R. Rep. 764 ; 128 R.R. 111 348
Noyes *v.* Mordant—*see* Noys *v.* Mordaunt.
Noyes *v.* Pollock (1886), 32 Ch.D. 53 ; 55 L.J. Ch. 513 ; 54 L.T. 473 ; 34 W.R. 383 231
Noys *v.* Mordaunt (1706), 2 Vern. 581 ; 23 E.R. 978 ; Prec. Ch. 265 ; 24 E.R. 128 ; *sub nom.* Noyes *v.* Mordant, Gilb. Ch. 2 ; 25 E.R. 2 . 396, 397
Nunn's Estate, *Re* (1888), 23 L.R. Ir. 286 194
Nutbrown *v.* Thornton (1804), 10 Ves. 159 ; 32 E.R. 805 487
Nutt *v.* Easton, [1899] 1 Ch. 873 ; 68 L.J.Ch. 367 ; 80 L.T. 353 ; 47 W.R. 430 ; 43 S.J. 333 ; *on appeal*, [1900] 1 Ch. 29 ; 69 L.J.Ch. 46 ; 81 L.T. 530 255
Nwakobi *v.* Nzekwu, [1964] 1 W.L.R. 1019 ; 108 S.J. 518 34

Oatway, *Re*, Hertslet *v.* Oatway, [1903] 2 Ch. 356 ; 71 L.J.Ch. 575 ; 88 L.T. 622 523
O'Byrne's Estate, *Re* (1885), 15 L.R. Ir. 373 222
O'Connor *v.* Foley, [1905] 1 I.R. 1 ; [1906] 1 I.R. 20 344
O'Connor *v.* Spaight (1804), 1 Sch. & Lef. 305 563
Oelkers *v.* Ellis, [1914] 2 K.B. 139 ; 83 L.J.K.B. 658 ; 110 L.T. 332 . . 105
Official Receiver, *Ex parte*—*see* S.P., *Re* ; Watson, *Re*.
Ogdens Ltd. *v.* Weinberg (1906), 95 L.T. 567 ; 22 T.L.R. 729 . . . 298
Ogilvie *v.* Foljambe (1817), 3 Mer. 53 ; 36 E.R. 21 ; [1814-23] All E.R. Rep. 262 ; 17 R.R. 13 497
O'Grady *v.* Wilmot, [1916] 2 A.C. 231; 85 L.J.Ch. 386 ; 32 T.L.R. 456 ; 60 S.J. 456 ; *sub nom. Re* O'Grady, O'Grady *v.* Wilmot, 114 L.T. 1097 265, 285
Oldham *v.* Hand (1751), 2 Ves. Sen. 259 ; 28 E.R. 167 339
Oliver *v.* Brickland (1732), cit. 3 Atk. 422 ; 26 E.R. 1044 431
Oliver *v.* Hinton, [1899] 2 Ch. 264 ; 68 L.J. Ch. 583 ; 81 L.T. 212 ; 48 W.R. 3 ; 15 T.L.R. 450 ; 43 S.J. 622 215-16
Olley *v.* Fisher (1886), 34 Ch.D. 367 ; 56 L.J.Ch. 208 ; 55 L.T. 807 ; 35 W.R. 301 . . . . 538, 539
O'Neill, *Re*, [1967] N.I. 129 231
Onions *v.* Cohen (1865), 2 H. & M. 354 ; 71 E.R. 501 ; 5 New R. 400 ; 34 L.J.Ch. 338 ; 12 L.T. 15 ; 11 Jur. N.S. 198 ; 13 W.R. 426 ; 144 R.R. 175 553
O'Reilly *v.* O'Donoghue (1875), I.R. 10 Eq. 73 179
Orion Property Trust Ltd. *v.* Du Cane Court Ltd. [1962] 1 W.L R. 1085 ; [1962] 3 All E.R. 466 ; 106 S.J. 689 458
Ormsby *v.* Dodwell (1702), 6 Bro. P.C. 41 ; 2 E.R. 919 138
O'Rorke *v.* Bolingbroke (1877), 2 App. Cas. 814 ; 26 W.R. 239 . . . 355
O'Rourke's Estate, *Re* (1889), 23 L.R. Ir. 497 229
Orr-Lewis *v.* Orr-Lewis, [1949] P. 347 ; [1949] 1 All E.R. 504 ; [1949] L.J.R. 682 ; 65 T.L.R. 269 459

PAGE

Osborne *v.* Amalgamated Soc. of Railway Servants, [1911] 1 Ch. 540 ; 80 L.J.Ch. 315 ; 104 L.T. 267 ; 27 T.L.R. 289 ; [1911-13] All E.R. Rep. 102 477
Osmond *v.* Fitzroy (1731), 3 P. Wms. 129 ; 24 E.R. 997 348
Otter *v.* Lord Vaux (1856), 6 De G.M. & G. 638 ; 43 E.R. 1381 ; 26 L.J.Ch. 128 ; 29 L.T.O.S. 59 ; 3 Jur. N.S. 169 ; 5 W.R. 188 ; 106 R.R. 235 195, 196
Ottley's Estate, *Re*, [1910] 1 I.R. 1 540
Oughtred *v.* Inland Revenue Commissioners, [1960] A.C. 206 ; [1959] 3 W.L.R. 898 ; [1959] 3 All E.R. 623 ; 103 S.J. 896 ; [1959] T.R. 319 ; 38 A.T.C. 317 299
Owen, *Re*, [1894] 3 Ch. 220 ; 63 L.J.Ch. 749 ; 71 L.T. 181 ; 43 W.R. 55 ; 38 S.J. 617 ; 8 R. 566 . . . . 186, 244
Owen *v.* Peacock —*see* Peacock's Estate, *Re*.
Owen *v.* Thomas (1834), 3 My. & K. 353 ; 40 E.R. 134 ; 3 L.J.Ch. 205 ; [1824-34] All E.R. Rep. 427 ; 41 R.R. 88 497
Oxford's (Earl of) Case (1615), 1 Ch. Rep. 1 ; 21 E.R. 485, 576 . 51-2, 459
Oxley, *Re*, John Hornby & Sons *v.* Oxley, [1914] 1 Ch. 604 ; 83 L.J.Ch. 442; 110 L.T. 626 ; 30 T.L.R. 327 ; 58 S.J. 319 ; [1914-15] All E.R. Rep. 505 . 274

Padbury *v.* Clark (1850), 2 Mac. & G. 298 ; 42 E.R. 115 ; 2 H. & Tw. 341 ; 47 E.R. 1714 ; 19 L.J. Ch. 533 ; 86 R.R. 116 405
Paddington Corp. *v.* A.-G., [1906] A.C. 1 ; 75 L.J. Ch. 4 ; 93 L.T. 673 ; 70 J.P. 41 ; 54 W.R. 317 ; 22 T.L.R. 55 ; 50 S.J. 41 ; 4 L.G.R. 19 ; [1904-7] All E.R. Rep. 362 480
Padwick *v.* Stanley (1852), 9 Hare 627 ; 68 E.R. 664 ; 22 L.J.Ch. 184 ; 19 L.T.O.S. 293 ; 16 Jur. 586 558
Page, *Ex parte*—*see* Allen, *Ex parte*.
Page *v.* Horne (1848), 11 Beav. 227 ; 50 E.R. 804 ; 17 L.J.Ch. 200 ; 11 L.T.O.S. 121 ; 12 Jur. 340 ; 83 R.R. 146 345
Page *v.* Linwood (1837), 4 Cl. & Fin. 399 ; 7 E.R. 154 246
Page One Records Ltd. *v.* Britton, [1968] 1 W.L.R. 157 ; [1967] 3 All E.R. 822 ; 111 S.J. 944 472
Paget *v.* Ede (1874), L.R. 18 Eq. 118 ; 43 L.J.Ch. 571 ; 30 L.T. 228 ; 22 W.R. 625 ; [1874-80] All E.R. Rep. 902 14
Paget *v.* Marshall (1884), 28 Ch.D. 255 ; 54 L.J. Ch. 575 ; 51 L.T. 351 ; 49 J.P. 85 ; 33 W.R. 608 ; [1881-5] All E.R. Rep. 290 533
Paget's Settlement, *Re*, Baillie *v.* De Brossard, [1965] 1 W.L.R. 1046 ; [1965] 1 All E.R. 58 ; 109 S.J. 577 14
Pain *v.* Smith (1833), 2 My. & K. 417 ; 39 E.R. 1003 253
Palk *v.* Lord Clinton (1805), 12 Ves. 48 ; 33 E.R. 19 ; 8 R.R. 283 . . 245
Palliser *v.* Gurney (1887), 19 Q.B.D. 519 ; 56 L.J.Q.B. 546 ; 51 J.P. 520 ; 35 W.R. 760 ; 3 T.L.R. 778 445
Palmer *v.* Hendrie (1859), 27 Beav. 349 ; 54 E.R. 136 ; 122 R.R. 426 . 238, 249
Palmer *v.* Hendrie (No. 2) (1860), 28 Beav. 341 ; 54 E.R. 397 ; 122 R.R. 426 249
Palmer *v.* Wheeler (1811), 2 Ba. & B. 18 ; 12 R.R. 60 369
Park, *Re*, Public Trustee *v.* Armstrong, [1932] 1 Ch. 580 ; 101 L.J.Ch. 295 ; 147 L.T. 118 ; [1931] All E.R. Rep. 633 358
Parkash *v.* Irani Finance Ltd., [1969] 2 W.L.R. 1134 196
Parker *v.* Appleton (1792), 3 Bro. C.C. 427 ; 29 E.R. 623 561
Parker *v.* Braithwaite, [1952] 2 All E.R. 837 ; [1952] 2 T.L.R. 731 ; [1952] W.N. 504 . . . . 228, 229
Parker *v.* Housefield (1834), 2 My. & K. 419 ; 39 E.R. 1004 ; 4 L.J. Ch. 57 244
Parker *v.* Taswell (1858), 2 De G. & J. 559 ; 44 E.R. 1106 ; 27 L.J.Ch. 812 ; 31 L.T.O.S. 226 ; 22 J.P. 432 ; 4 Jur. N.S. 1006 ; 6 W.R. 608 ; 119 R.R. 230 85
Parker's Will, *Re*, [1966] I.R. 309 362
Parkin, *Re*, Hill *v.* Schwarz, [1892] 3 Ch. 510 ; 62 L.J.Ch. 55 ; 67 L.T. 77 ; 41 W.R. 120 ; 36 S.J. 647 ; 3 R. 9 366
Parkin *v.* Thorold (1852), 16 Beav. 59 ; 51 E.R. 698 ; 22 L.J. Ch. 170 ; 16 Jur. 959 ; 89 R.R. 196 . . . . 17-18, 29, 30
Parkinson *v.* Hanbury (1867), L.R. 2 H.L. 1 ; 36 L.J.Ch. 292 ; 16 L.T. 243 ; 15 W.R. 642 236
Parkinson's Estate, *Re* (1865), 13 L.T. 26 ; 10 I.J.N.S. 82 184
Parnell *v.* Hingston (1856), 2 Sm. & G. 337 ; 65 E.R. 684 ; 28 L.T.O.S. 217 ; 2 Jur. N.S. 854 ; 4 W.R. 794 ; 107 R.R. 107 312
Parnell's Estate (1901), 1 N.I.J.R. 168 . . . . 194, 196

PAGE

Parrington v. Parrington, [1951] 2 All E.R. 916 ; [1951] 2 T.L.R. 918 ; [1951] W.N. 534 470
Pasley v. Freeman (1789), 3 T.R. 51 ; 100 E.R. 450 ; [1775-1802] All E.R. Rep. 31 ; 1 R.R. 634 329
Patch v. Ward (1867), L.R. 3 Ch. App. 203 ; 18 L.T. 134 ; 16 W.R. 441 . 248
Patten, *Re*, Official Receiver v. Patten—*see* S.P., *Re*.
Patteson v. Thompson (1676), Rep. t. Finch 272 ; 23 E.R. 149 . . 172
Paul, *Re*, Public Trustee v. Pearce, [1921] 2 Ch. 1 ; 90 L.J. Ch. 446 ; 125 L.T. 566 364
Pauling's Settlement Trusts, *Re*, Younghusband v. Coutts & Co., [1964] Ch. 303 ; [1963] 3 W.L.R. 742 ; [1963] 3 All E.R. 1 ; 107 S.J. 492 . 33, 350, 352
Pawlet v. Pawlet (1748), 1 Wils. K.B. 224 ; 95 E.R. 586 368
Pawlett v. A.-G. (1668), Hard. 465 ; 145 E.R. 550 . . . 177, 258
Pawson v. Revell, [1958] 2 Q.B. 360 ; [1958] 3 W.L.R. 474 ; [1958] 3 All E.R. 233 ; 102 S.J. 632 228
Payne v. Cardiff R.D.C., [1932] 1 K.B. 241 ; 100 L.J.K.B. 626 ; 145 L.T. 575 ; 95 J.P. 173 ; 47 T.L.R. 532 ; 29 L.G.R. 507 ; [1931] All E.R. Rep. 479 250
Peacock v. Burt (1834), 4 L.J. Ch. 33 ; 41 R.R. 199 220
Peacock's Estate, *Re* (1872), L.R. 14 Eq. 236 ; *sub nom.* Owen v. Peacock, 27 L.T. 472 424
Peacock's Trusts, *Re* (1879), 10 Ch.D. 490 ; 48 L.J.Ch. 265 ; 39 L.T. 661 ; 27 W.R. 500 444
Peake v. Highfield (1826), 1 Russ. 559 ; 38 E.R. 216 554
Pearce v. Morris (1869), L.R. 5 Ch. App. 227 ; 39 L.J.Ch. 342 ; 22 L.T. 190; 18 W.R. 196 191
Pearne v. Lisle (1749), Amb. 75 ; 27 E.R. 47 560
Pearse and Prothero, *Ex parte*, *Re* Price (1820), Buck 525 . . . 183
Pearson v. Amicable Assurance Office (1859), 27 Beav. 229 ; 54 E.R. 89 ; 7 W.R. 629 ; 122 R.R. 386 312
Pearson v. Pearson (1802), 1 Sch. & Lef. 10 ; 9 R.R. 1 290
Pedder's Settlement Trusts, *Re* (1854), 5 De G. M. & G. 890 ; 43 E.R. 1116 ; 24 L.J.Ch. 313 ; 3 Eq. R. 157 ; 3 W.R. 136 ; 104 R.R. 333 . . 393
Pegler v. White (1864), 33 Beav. 403 ; 55 E.R. 423 ; 33 L.J.Ch. 569 ; 10 L.T. 84 ; 10 Jur. N.S. 330 ; 12 W.R. 455 ; 3 New R. 557; 140 R.R. 192 . . 501
Pemberton v. Jackson (1845), 5 L.T.O.S. 17 371-2
Penn v. Lord Baltimore (1750), 1 Ves. Sen. 444 ; 27 E.R. 1132 ; [1558-1774] All E.R. Rep. 99 . . . . 14, 61
Pennefather v. Pennefather (1873), I.R. 7 Eq. 300 366
Perfect v. Lane (1861), 3 De G. F. & J. 369 ; 45 E.R. 921 ; 31 L.J.Ch. 489 ; 6 L.T. 8 ; 8 Jur. N.S. 547 ; 10 W.R. 197 356
Performing Right Soc. Ltd. v. London Theatre of Varieties Ltd., [1924] A.C. 1 ; 93 L.J.K.B. 33 ; 130 L.T. 450 ; 40 T.L.R. 52 ; 68 S.J. 99 . . 324
Perkins v. Ede (1852), 16 Beav. 193 ; 51 E.R. 751 ; 1 W.R. 10 ; 96 R.R. 94 . 507
Perowne, *Re*, Perowne v. Moss, [1951] Ch. 785 ; [1951] 2 All E.R. 201 ; [1951] 1 T.L.R. 1135 363
Perry v. Barker (1803), 8 Ves. 527 ; 32 E.R. 459 ; 9 R.R. 171 ; (1806), 13 Ves. 198 ; 33 E.R. 269 ; 9 R.R. 171 249
Pettitt v. Pettitt, [1969] 2 W.L.R. 966 ; [1969] 2 All E.R. 385 . . . 104
Petty, *Re*, Holliday v. Petty, [1929] 1 Ch. 726 ; 98 L.J.Ch. 207 ; 141 L.T. 31 ; [1929] All E.R. Rep. 493 283
Phelan, *Re*, Duggan v. A.-G., [1946] I.R. 451 383
Philips v. Carew (1709), 1 P. Wms. 117 ; 24 E.R. 318 556
Phillips, *Re*, Lawrence v. Huxtable, [1931] 1 Ch. 347 ; 100 L.J.Ch. 65 ; 144 L.T. 178 ; [1930] All E.R. Rep. 165 285
Phillips v. Brooks Ltd., [1919] 2 K.B. 243 ; 88 L.J.K.B. 953 ; 121 L.T. 249 ; 35 T.L.R. 470 ; 24 Com. Cas. 263 ; [1918-19] All E.R. Rep. 246 . . 548-9
Phillips v. Foxall (1872), L.R. 7 Q.B. 666 ; 41 L.J.Q.B. 293 ; 27 L.T. 231 ; 37 J.P. 37 ; 20 W.R. 900 553
Phillips v. Phillips (1852), 9 Hare 471 ; 68 E.R. 596 ; 22 L.J.Ch. 141 . . 562
Phillips v. Phillips (1862), 4 De G. F. & J. 208 ; 45 E.R 1164 ; 31 L.J.Ch. 321 ; 5 L.T. 655 ; 8 Jur. N.S. 145 ; 10 W.R. 236 ; 135 R.R. 97 . . 120
Phillips' Trusts, *Re*, [1903] 1 Ch. 183 ; 72 L.J.Ch. 94 ; 88 L.T. 9 . . 306

PAGE

Phipps *v.* Lovegrove (1873), L.R. 16 Eq. 80 ; 42 L.J.Ch. 892 ; 28 L.T. 584 ; 21 W.R. 590 307
Phonographic Equipment (1958) Ltd. *v.* Muslu, [1961] 1 W.L.R. 1379 ; [1961] 3 All E.R. 626 ; 105 S.J. 947 20
Pickard *v.* Sears (1837), 6 Ad. & El. 469 ; 112 E.R. 179 ; 2 Nev. & P.K.B. 488 ; Will. Woll. & Dav. 678 ; 45 R.R. 538 39
Pickersgill *v.* Rodger (1876), 5 Ch.D. 163 407
Pike *v.* Hoare (1763), 2 Eden 182 ; 28 E.R. 867 ; Amb. 428 ; 27 E.R. 286 . 15
Pilcher *v.* Rawlins (1872), L.R. 7 Ch. App. 259 ; 41 L.J. Ch. 485 ; 25 L.T. 921 ; 20 W.R 281 . . . . 106-7, 214, 527
Pilkington *v.* Inland Revenue Commissioners, [1964] A.C. 612 ; [1962] 3 W.L.R. 1051 ; [1962] 3 All E.R. 622 ; 106 S.J. 834 ; 40 T.C. 416 ; *sub nom. Re* Pilkington's Will Trusts, [1962] T.R. 265 ; 41 A.T.C. 285 . 365
Pilkington *v.* York (City of)—*see* York Corp. *v.* Pilkington.
Pink, *Re*, Elvin *v.* Nightingale, [1927] 1 Ch. 237 ; 96 L.J. Ch. 202 ; 136 L.T. 399 ; 70 S.J. 1090 275
Pisani *v.* A.-G. for Gibraltar (1874), L.R. 5 P.C. 516 ; 30 L.T. 729 ; 22 W.R. 900 ; [1874-80] All E.R. Rep. 971 352
Pledge *v.* White, [1896] A.C. 187 ; 65 L.J.Ch. 449 ; 74 L.T. 323 ; 44 W.R. 589 ; [1895-9] All E.R. Rep. 615 199-201
Plowman, *Re*, Westminster Bank Ltd. *v.* Plowman, [1943] Ch. 269 ; [1943] 2 All E.R. 532 ; 112 L.J. Ch. 229 ; 169 L.T. 118 ; 59 T.L.R. 335 ; 87 S.J. 248 269
Plowright *v.* Lambert (1885), 52 L T. 646 341
Plumb *v.* Fluitt (1791), 2 Anst. 432 ; 145 E.R. 926 ; 3 R.R. 605 . . . 214
Plummer *v.* Webb —*see* Webb *v.* Paternoster.
Plunkett *v.* Lewis (1844), 3 Hare 316 ; 57 E.R. 403 ; 13 L.J.Ch. 295 ; 2 L.T.O.S. 457 ; 8 Jur. 682 ; 64 R.R. 312 417
Pole *v.* Pole, [1924] 1 Ch. 156 ; 93 L.J.Ch. 145 ; 130 L.T. 333 ; 68 S.J. 184 . 377
Pollard, *Ex parte*—*see* Courtney, *Re.*
Pollock, *Re*, Pollock *v.* Worrall (1885), 28 Ch.D. 552 ; 54 L.J.Ch. 489 ; 52 L.T. 718 . . . . 415, 424-5
Pomfret (Earl of) *v.* Lord Windsor (1752), 2 Ves. Sen. 472 ; 28 E.R. 302 . 172
Pool *v.* Pool (1676/7), Nottingham's Chancery Cases, 79 Sel. Soc. 522 (case 700) 169
Pope, *Re* (1886), 17 Q.B.D. 743 ; 55 L.J.Q.B. 522 ; 55 L.T. 369 ; 34 W.R. 693 ; 2 T.L.R. 826 515
Pope *v.* Onslow (1692), 2 Vern. 286 ; 23 E.R. 784 176
Porter *v.* Emery (1637), 1 Ch. Rep. 97 ; 21 E.R. 518 169
Porter (William) & Co. Ltd., *Re*, [1937] 2 All E.R. 361 123
Portland (Duke of) *v.* Lady Topham (1864), 11 H.L.C. 32 ; 11 E.R. 1242 ; 34 L.J.Ch. 113 ; 10 L.T. 355 ; 10 Jur. N.S. 501 ; 12 W.R. 697 ; [1861-73] All E.R. Rep. 980 ; 145 R.R. 20 369
Port Line Ltd. *v.* Ben Line Steamers Ltd., [1958] 2 Q.B. 146 ; [1958] 2 W.L.R. 551 ; [1958] 1 All E.R. 787 ; 102 S.J. 232 ; [1958] 1 Lloyd's R. 290 469
Portman Building Soc. *v.* Young, [1951] 1 All E.R. 191 ; [1951] 2 T.L.R. 369; [1951] W.N. 10 ; 95 S.J. 61 234
Potter *v.* Edwards (1857), 26 L.J.Ch. 468 ; 5 W.R. 407 ; 112 R.R. 418 . 207
Powell *v.* Brodhurst, [1901] 2 Ch. 160 ; 70 L.J.Ch. 587 ; 84 L.T. 620 ; 49 W.R. 532 ; 17 T.L.R. 501 ; 45 S.J. 502 121
Powell *v.* Powell, [1900] 1 Ch. 243 ; 69 L.J.Ch. 164 ; 82 L.T. 84 ; 44 S.J. 134 . . . . 342, 350, 351
Powell Duffryn Steam Coal Co. *v.* Taff Vale Railway Co. (1874), L.R. 9 Ch. App. 331 ; 43 L.J. Ch. 575 ; 30 L.T. 208 492
Powys *v.* Blagrave (1854), 4 De G. M. & G. 448 ; 43 E.R. 582 ; 24 L.J.Ch. 142 ; 2 Eq. R. 1204 ; 24 L.T.O.S. 17 ; 2 W.R. 700 ; 102 R.R. 203 . . 464
Powys *v.* Mansfield (1837), 3 My. & Cr. 359 ; 40 E.R. 964 ; 7 L.J. Ch. 9 ; 1 Jur. 861 ; 45 R.R. 277 . . . . 419, 425
Pratt, *Re*, *Ex parte* Inland Revenue Commissioners *v.* Phillips, [1951] Ch. 225 ; [1950] 2 All E.R. 994 ; 66 T.L.R. (Pt. 2) 847 ; 94 S.J. 803 . . 276
Previtè, *Re*, Sturges *v.* Previtè, [1931] 1 Ch. 447 ; 100 L.J.Ch. 286 ; 145 L.T. 40 287
Price, *Re* (1820)—*see* Pearse and Prothero, *Ex parte.*
Price, *Re*, Tomlin *v.* Latter, [1900] 1 Ch. 442 ; 69 L.J.Ch. 225 ; 82 L.T. 79 ; 48 W.R. 373 ; 16 T.L.R. 189 ; 40 S.J. 242 410

PAGE

Price *v.* Blakemore (1843), 6 Beav. 507 ; 49 E.R. 922 ; 63 R.R. 163 . . 519
Price *v.* Perrie (1702), 2 Freem. 258 ; 22 E.R. 1195 177
Pride of Derby and Derbyshire Angling Assoc. Ltd. *v.* British Celanese Ltd., [1953] Ch. 149 ; [1953] 2 W.L.R. 58 ; [1953] 1 All E.R. 179 ; 117 J.P. 52 ; 51 L.G.R. 121 ; 97 S.J. 28 465
Priscilla, The (1859), Lush. 1 ; 167 E.R. 1; 1 L.T. 272 ; 5 Jur. N.S. 1421 . 434
Property & Bloodstock Ltd. *v.* Emerton, [1968] Ch. 94 ; [1967] 3 W.L.R. 973 ; [1967] 3 All E.R. 321 ; 111 S.J. 414 . . . . 250, 253
Proud *v.* Buzzard (1678/9), Nottingham's Chancery Cases, 79 Sel. Soc. 721 (case 906) 174, 260
Prout *v.* Cock, [1896] 2 Ch. 808 ; 66 L.J. Ch. 24 ; 75 L.T. 409 ; 45 W.R. 157 190
Provincial Bank of Ireland *v.* McKeever, [1941] I.R. 471 . . 341, 350
Pryor *v.* Pryor (1864), 2 De G. J. & S. 205; 46 E.R. 353 ; 4 New R. 82 ; 33 L.J.Ch. 441 ; 10 L.T. 360 ; 10 Jur. N.S. 603 ; 12 W.R. 781 ; [1861-73] All E.R. Rep. 616 ; 139 R.R. 90 369
Pryse, *The Goods of*, [1904] P. 301 ; 73 L.J.P. 84 ; 90 L.T. 747 ; 48 S.J. 474 267
Prytherch, *Re*, Prytherch *v.* Williams (1889), 42 Ch.D. 590 ; 59 L.J.Ch. 79 ; 61 L.T. 799 ; 38 W.R. 61 . . . . 513, 516
Public Trustee *v.* Lawrence, [1912] 1 Ch. 789 ; 81 L.J. Ch. 436; 106 L.T. 791 ; 56 S.J. 504 ; [1911-13] All E.R. Rep. 670 226
Puddephatt *v.* Leith, [1916] 1 Ch. 200 ; 85 L.J. Ch. 185 ; 114 L.T. 454 ; 32 T.L.R. 228 ; 60 S.J. 210 ; [1914-15] All E.R. Rep. 260 . . . 476
Pulbrook *v.* Richmond Consolidated Mining Co. (1878), 9 Ch.D. 610 ; 48 L.J.Ch. 65 ; 27 W.R. 377 476
Pulteney *v.* Earl of Darlington (1783), 1 Bro. C.C. 223 ; 28 E.R. 1095 ; *on appeal* (1796), 7 Bro. P.C. 530 ; 3 E.R. 344 . . . . 389, 393
Purchase *v.* Lichfield Brewery Co., [1915] 1 K.B. 184 ; 84 L.J.K.B. 742 ; 111 L.T. 1105 92
Purefoy *v.* Purefoy (1681), 1 Vern. 28 ; 23 E.R. 283 175
Pusey *v.* Pusey (1684), 1 Vern. 273 ; 23 E.R. 465 . . . . . 67, 484
Putsman *v.* Taylor, [1927] 1 K.B. 741 ; 96 L.J.K.B. 726 ; 137 L.T. 291; 43 T.L.R. 392 ; [1927] All E.R. Rep. 356 471
Pybus *v.* Smith (1791), 3 Bro. C.C. 340 ; 29 E.R. 570 446
Pye, *Ex parte* (1811), 18 Ves. 140 ; 34 E.R. 271 ; [1803-13] All E.R. Rep. 96 ; 11 R.R. 173 . . . . 419, 422
Pyle, *Re*, Pyle *v.* Pyle, [1895] 1 Ch. 724 ; 64 L.J. Ch. 477 ; 72 L.T. 327 ; 43 W.R. 420 ; 39 S.J. 346 ; 13 R. 396 382
Pym *v.* Blackburn (1796), 3 Ves. 34 ; 30 E.R. 878 68

Quarrell *v.* Beckford (1816), 1 Madd. 269 ; 56 E.R. 100; [1814-23] All E.R. Rep. 618 ; 16 R.R. 214 261
Queen's Benefit Building Soc., *Re*—*see* Threlfall, *Re*.
Quin *v.* Armstrong (1876), I.R. 11 Eq. 161 426
Quistclose Investments Ltd. *v.* Rolls Razor Ltd.—*see* Barclays Bank Ltd. *v.* Quistclose Investments Ltd.

R. *v.* Briant (Judge Dutton), *Ex parte* Abbey National Building Soc., [1957] 2 Q.B. 497 ; [1957] 3 W.L.R. 249 ; [1957] 2 All E.R. 625 ; 101 S.J. 555 . 230
R. *v.* Harington—*see* Martin *v.* Bannister.
R. *v.* Income Tax Acts Special Purposes Commissioners—*see* Barnardo's (Dr.) Homes National Incorporated Assoc. *v.* Commissioners for Special Purposes of the Income Tax Acts.
R. *v.* R. and I., [1961] 1 W.L.R. 1334 ; [1961] 3 All E.R. 461 461
R. *v.* Willes (Judge), *Ex parte* Abbey National Building Soc., [1954] 1 W.L.R. 136 ; 98 S.J. 44 230
Radcliffe *v.* Price (1902), 18 T.L.R. 466 341
Rae *v.* Joyce (1892), 29 L.R. Ir. 500 355
Raggett, *Re*, *Ex parte* Williams (1880), 16 Ch.D. 117 ; 50 L.J.Ch. 187 ; 44 L.T. 4 ; 29 W.R. 314 ; [1874-80] All E.R. Rep. 1015 . . . 198, 201-2
Raine, *Re*, Tyerman *v.* Stansfield, [1929] 1 Ch. 716 ; 98 L.J. Ch. 244 ; 141 L.T. 25 291
Ramm *v.* Cartwright—*see* Rand *v.* Cartwright.
Ramsbottom *v.* Wallis (1835), 5 L.J. Ch. 92 ; 42 R.R. 278 189
Ramsden *v.* Dyson (1866), L.R. 1 H.L. 129 ; 12 Jur. N.S. 506 ; 14 W.R. 926 39

PAGE

Rancliffe (Lord) *v.* Lady Parkyns (1818), 6 Dow 149; 3 E.R. 1428; 19 R.R. 36 . . . 397
Rand *v.* Cartwright (1664), Nels. 101; 21 E.R. 800; 1 Ch. Cas. 59; 22 E.R. 694; *sub nom.* Ramm [Rand] *v.* Cartwright, 2 Freem. 183; 22 E.R. 1148 . . . 169
Ranelaugh (Earl of) *v.* Hayes (1683), 1 Vern. 189; 23 E.R. 405; 2 Ch. Cas. 146; 22 E.R. 888; *sub nom.* Lord Ranelagh *v.* Hayes, 1 Eq. Cas. Abr. 17, pl. 6; 21 E.R. 839 . . . 558
Rattenberry, *Re*, Ray *v.* Grant, [1906] 1 Ch. 667; 75 L.J.Ch. 304; 94 L.T. 475; 54 W.R. 311; 22 T.L.R. 249; 50 S.J. 240 . . . 290, 416
Ratton, *Re—see* Freeman-Thomas Indenture, *Re.*
Rauson *v.* Sacheverel—*see* Rayson *v.* Sacheverel.
Ravald *v.* Russell (1830), You. 9; 159 E.R. 884; 34 R.R. 257 . . . 190
Rawlings, *Ex parte—see* Davis & Co., *Re.*
Rawlins *v.* Powel (1715), 1 P.Wms. 297; 24 E.R. 397 . . . 416
Rawlinson *v.* Ames, [1925] Ch. 96; 94 L.J.Ch. 113; 132 L.T. 370; 69 S.J. 142 . . . 496
Raybould, *Re*, Raybould *v.* Turner, [1900] 1 Ch. 199; 69 L.J.Ch. 249; 82 L.T. 46; 48 W.R. 301 . . . 273
Rayson *v.* Sacheverel (1682), 1 Vern. 41; 23 E.R. 295; *sub nom.* Rauson *v.* Sacheverel, 2 Ch. Cas. 98; 22 E.R. 864 . . . 176
Read *v.* Read (1668), 1 Ch. Cas. 115; 22 E.R. 720 . . . 560
Reading *v.* A.-G. [1951] A.C. 507; [1951] 1 T.L.R. 480; [1951] 1 All E.R. 617; 95 S.J. 155; [1951] W.N. 144 . . . 353
Redgrave *v.* Hurd (1881), 20 Ch.D. 1; 51 L.J.Ch. 113; 45 L.T. 485; 30 W.R. 251; [1881-5] All E.R. Rep. 77 . . . 545
Redington *v.* Redington (1809), 1 Ba. & B. 131; 12 R.R. 5 . . . 194
Redland Bricks Ltd. *v.* Morris, [1969] 2 W.L.R. 1437; [1969] 2 All E.R. 576 . . . 457, 466-7
Reeve *v.* Lisle, [1902] A.C. 461; 71 L.J.Ch. 768; 87 L.T. 308; 51 W.R. 576; 18 T.L.R. 767 . . . 205
Refuge Assurance Co. Ltd. *v.* Pearlberg, [1938] Ch. 687; [1938] 3 All E.R. 231; 107 L.J. Ch. 393; 159 L.T. 453; 54 T.L.R. 950; 82 S.J. 544 232, 239, 513
Regent Oil Co. Ltd. *v.* J. A. Gregory (Hatch End) Ltd., [1966] Ch. 402; [1965] 3 W.L.R. 1206; [1965] 3 All E.R. 673; 109 S.J. 833 . . . 234-5
Reid *v.* Reid (1858), 25 Beav. 469; 53 E.R. 716; 119 R.R. 491 . . . 403
Reliance Permanent Building Soc. *v.* Harwood-Stamper, [1944] Ch. 362; [1944] 2 All E.R. 75; 113 L.J. Ch. 290; 171 L.T. 132; 60 T.L.R. 480; 88 S.J. 273 . . . 254
Rely-A-Bell Burglar and Fire Alarm Co. Ltd. *v.* Eisler, [1926] Ch. 609; 95 L.J. Ch. 345; 135 L.T. 286; 70 S..J. 669 . . . 473
Reuter, Hufeland & Co. *v.* Sala & Co. (1879), 4 C.P.D. 239; 48 L.J.Q.B. 492; 40 L.T. 476; 27 W.R. 631; 4 Asp. M.L.C. 121 . . . 82, 83
Reversion Fund and Insurance Co. Ltd. *v.* Maison Cosway Ltd., [1913] 1 K.B. 364; 82 L.J.K.B. 512; 108 L.T. 87; 57 S.J. 144; 20 Mans. 194 . 115
Reynard *v.* Spence (1841), 4 Beav. 103; 49 E.R. 277; 5 Jur. 478; 55 R.R. 27 407
Reynolds, *Re*, M'Mahon *v.* Fetherstonhaugh, [1895] 1 I.R. 83 . . . 522
Rhodes *v.* Bate (1866), L.R. 1 Ch. App. 252; 35 L.J. Ch. 267; 13 L.T. 778; 12 Jur. N.S. 178; 14 W.R. 292; [1861-73] All E.R. Rep. 805 . 339
Rice, *Ex parte—see* Commissioners of Public Works, *Re.*
Rice *v.* Gordon (1848), 11 Beav. 265; 50 E.R. 818; 83 R.R. 153 . . . 552
Rice *v.* Rice (1854), 2 Drew. 73; 61 E.R. 646; 23 L.J.Ch. 289; 2 Eq. R. 341; 22 L.T.O.S. 298; 2 W.R. 139; 100 R.R. 43 . . . 213
Rich *v.* Cockell (1804), 9 Ves. 369; 32 E.R. 644; 7 R.R. 227 . . . 444
Richards, *Re*, Humber *v.* Richards (1890), 45 Ch.D. 589; 59 L.J. Ch. 728; 63 L.T. 451; 39 W.R. 186 . . . 302
Richards *v.* Cooper (1842), 5 Beav. 304; 49 E.R. 595; 59 R.R. 510 . . 246
Richardson *v.* Gifford (1834), 1 Ad. & El. 52; 110 E.R. 1127; 3 Nev. & M.K.B. 325; 3 L.J.K.B. 122; 40 R.R. 253 . . . 84
Richardson *v.* Smith (1870), L.R. 5 Ch. App. 648; 39 L.J.Ch. 877; 19 W.R. 81 . . . 498
Richerson, *Re*, Scales *v.* Heyhoe [1892] 1 Ch. 379; 61 L.J.Ch. 202; 66 L.T. 174; 40 W.R. 233; 36 S.J. 200 . . . 388
Richmond *v.* North London Railway Co. (1868), L.R. 5 Eq. 352; 37 L.J.Ch. 273; 18 L.T. 8; 16 W.R. 449; *on appeal* (1868), L.R. 3 Ch. App. 679; 37 L.J.Ch. 886; 33 J.P. 86 . . . **381**

PAGE
Rickett v. Green, [1910] 1 K.B. 253 ; 79 L.J K.B. 193 ; 102 L.T. 16 . . 87
Rickman v. Morgan (1779), 1 Bro. C.C. 63 ; 28 E.R. 986 ; (1788), 2 Bro. C.C. 394 ; 29 E.R. 220 421
Rico v. Gaultier (1747), 3 Atk. 501 ; 26 E.R. 1088 561
Ridges v. Morrison (1784), 1 Bro. C.C. 389 ; 28 E.R. 1195 427
Ridley, *Re*, Nicholson v. Nicholson, [1950] Ch. 415 ; [1950] 2 All E.R. 1 ; 66 T.L.R. (Pt. 1) 981 ; 94 S.J. 338 284
Riley v. Hall (1898), 79 L.T. 244 ; 42 S.J. 702 200
Roberts v. Cooper, [1891] 2 Ch. 335 ; 60 L.J. Ch. 377 ; 64 L.T. 584 . 442-3
Roberts v. Croft (1857), 2 De G. & J. 1 ; 44 E.R. 887 ; 27 L.J. Ch. 220 ; 30 L.T.O.S. 111 ; 3 Jur. N.S. 1069 ; 6 W.R. 144 ; 119 R.R. 1 . . 213
Roberts (A.) & Co. Ltd. v. Leicestershire C.C., [1961] Ch. 555 ; [1961] 2 W.L.R. 1000 ; [1961] 2 All E.R. 545 ; 59 L.G.R. 349 ; 105 S.J. 425 . 535-6
Robertson v. Abrahams, [1930] W.N. 79 ; 169 L.T. Jo. 305 ; *sub nom.* Robertson v. Adams, 69 L. Jo. 301 469
Robertson v. Minister of Pensions, [1949] 1 K.B. 227 ; [1948] 2 All E.R. 767 ; [1949] L.J.R. 323 ; 64 T.L.R. 526 ; 92 S.J. 603 124
Robertson v. Morrice (1845), 4 L.T.O.S. 430 ; 9 Jur. 122 ; 72 R.R. 766 . 524
Robertson v. Norris (1857), 1 Giff. 421 ; 65 E.R. 983 ; 30 L.T.O.S. 253 ; 4 Jur. N.S. 155 ; 114 R.R. 486 ; *on appeal* (1858), 4 Jur. N.S. 443 ; 114 R.R. 491 ; *subsequent proceedings* (1859), 1 Giff. 428 ; 65 E.R. 986 ; 1 L.T. 123 ; 5 Jur. N.S. 1238 ; 114 R.R. 495 . . . . 253, 255
Robertson's Will Trusts, *Re*, [1960] 1 W.L.R. 1050 ; [1960] 3 All E.R. 146 ; 104 S.J. 726 371
Robinson v. Davison (1779), 1 Bro. C.C. 63 ; 28 E.R. 986 175
Robinson v. Robinson (1854), 19 Beav. 494 ; 52 E.R. 442 ; 105 E.R. 222 . 390
Robophone Facilities Ltd. v. Blank, [1966] 1 W.L.R. 1428 ; [1966] 3 All E.R. 128 ; 110 S.J. 544 . . . . 20, 24
Roche's Estate, *Re* (1890), 25 L.R. Ir. 58 213
Rochefoucauld v. Boustead, [1897] 1 Ch. 196 ; 66 L.J. Ch. 74 ; *sub nom.* De la Rochefoucauld v. Boustead, 75 L.T. 502 ; 45 W.R. 272 ; 13 T.L.R. 118; 118 ; 41 S.J. 156 . . . . 14, 27
Roddy's Estate, *Re* (1861), 11 Ir. Ch. Rep. 369 433
Roe d. Kaye v. Soley (1771), 2 Black. W. 726 ; 96 E.R. 426 176
Rogers v. Challis (1859), 27 Beav. 175 ; 54 E.R. 68 ; 29 L.J.Ch. 240 ; 6 Jur. N.S. 334 ; 7 W.R. 710 ; 122 R.R. 361 185
Rolfe v. Gregory (1865), 4 De G.J. & S. 576 ; 46 E.R. 1042 ; 34 L.J.Ch. 274 ; 12 L.T. 162 ; 11 Jur. N.S. 98 ; 13 W.R. 355 ; 146 R.R. 463 . . . 105
Rooke's Case (1598), 5 Co. Rep. 99b ; 77 E.R. 209 485
Rooke v. Lord Kensington (1856), 2 K. & J. 753 ; 69 E.R. 986 ; 25 L.J.Ch. 795 ; 28 L.T.O.S. 62 ; 2 Jur. N.S. 755 ; 4 W.R. 829 ; 110 R.R. 456 532-3, 560
Rookes v. Barnard, [1964] A.C. 1129 ; [1964] 2 W.L.R. 269 ; [1964] 1 All E.R. 367 ; 108 S.J. 93 ; [1964] 1 Lloyd's R. 28 479
Roome v. Roome (1744), 3 Atk. 181 ; 26 E.R. 906 425
Rooper v. Harrison (1855), 2 K. & J. 86 ; 69 E.R. 704 ; 110 R.R. 112 . 120
Roscarrick v. Barton (1672), 1 Ch. Cas. 217 ; 22 E.R. 769 170
Roscoe (James) (Bolton) Ltd. v. Winder, [1915] 1 Ch. 62 ; 84 L.J. Ch. 286 ; 112 L.T. 121 ; 1915] H.B.R. 61 523-4
Rose, *Re*, Midland Bank Executor and Trustee Co. Ltd. v. Rose, [1949] Ch. 78 ; [1948] 2 All E.R. 971 ; [1949] L.J.R. 208 ; 92 S.J. 661 . . 321-3
Rose, *Re*, Rose v. Inland Revenue Commissioners, [1952] Ch. 499 ; [1952] 1 All E.R. 1217 ; [1952] 1 T.L.R. 1577 ; [1952] T.R. 175 ; 31 A.T.C. 138 . 323-4
Rose v. Page (1829), 2 Sim. 471 ; 57 E.R. 864 ; 29 R.R. 142 246
Rose (Frederick E.) (London) Ltd. v. William H. Pim Jnr. & Co. Ltd., [1953] 2 Q.B. 450 ; [1953] 3 W.L.R. 497 ; [1953] 2 All E.R. 739 ; 97 S.J. 556 ; 70 R.P.C. 238 537
Rossiter v. Miller (1878), 3 App. Cas. 1124 ; 48 L.J. Ch. 10 ; 39 L.T. 173 ; 42 J.P. 804 ; 26 W.R. 865 ; [1874-80] All E.R. Rep. 465 . . . 497-8
Rourke v. Robinson, [1911] 1 Ch. 480 ; 80 L.J.Ch. 295 ; 103 L.T. 895 188, 191
Rowe, *Re*, Bennets v. Eddy, [1941] Ch. 343 ; [1941] 2 All E.R. 330 ; 110 L.J. Ch. 145 ; 165 L.T. 76 ; 57 T.L.R. 592 ; 85 S.J. 264 287
Rowel v. Walley (1662), 1 Ch. Rep. 218 ; 21 E.R. 555 169
Rowley v. Rowley (1854), Kay 242 ; 69 E.R. 103 ; 23 L.J.Ch. 275 ; 2 Eq. R. 241 ; 23 L.T.O.S. 55 ; 18 Jur. 306 ; 101 R.R. 574 373
Roxburgh v. Fuller (1864), 11 L.T. 587 ; 13 W.R. 39 ; 145 R.R. 732 . . 427

PAGE

Roxburghe *v.* Cox (1881), 17 Ch.D. 520 ; 50 L.J.Ch. 772 ; 45 L.T. 225 ; 30 W.R. 74 307
Royce's Will Trusts, *Re*, Tildesley *v.* Tildesley, [1959] Ch. 626 ; [1959] 3 W.L.R. 254 ; [1959] 3 All E.R. 278 ; 103 S.J. 675 428
Rushbrooke *v.* O'Sullivan, [1908] 1 I.R. 232 491
Russ and Brown's Contract, *Re*, [1934] Ch. 34 ; 103 L.J.Ch. 12 ; 150 L.T. 125 ; 50 T.L.R. 19 ; 77 S.J. 749 ; [1933] All E.R. Rep. 997 . . . 506
Russel *v.* Russel (1783), 1 Bro. C.C. 269 ; 28 E.R. 1121 182-3
Russell *v.* Amalgamated Soc. of Carpenters and Joiners, [1912] A.C. 421 ; 81 L.J.K.B. 619 ; 106 L.T. 433 ; 28 T.L.R. 276 ; 56 S.J. 342 ; [1911-13] All E.R. Rep. 550 478
Russell *v.* Dickson (1853), 4 H.L.C. 293 ; 10 E.R. 475 ; 21 L.T.O.S. 161 ; 17 Jur. 307 ; 94 R.R. 116 427
Russell *v.* Norfolk (Duke of), [1949] 1 All E.R. 109 ; 65 T.L.R. 225 ; 93 S.J. 132 477
Russell *v.* St. Aubyn (1876), 2 Ch.D. 398 ; 46 L.J.Ch. 641 ; 35 L.T. 395 . 420
Russell's Estate, *Re* (1887), 19 L.R.Ir. 418 414
Rust *v.* Goodale, [1957] Ch. 33 ; [1956] 3 W.L.R. 749 ; [1956] 3 All E.R. 373 ; 100 S.J. 786 228
Rutherford *v.* Acton-Adams, [1915] A.C. 866 ; 84 L.J.P.C. 238 ; 113 L.T. 931 507
Ryan *v.* Daniel (1841), 1 Y. & C.C.C. 60 ; 62 E.R. 790 487
Ryan *v.* Mackmath (1789), 3 Bro. C.C. 15 ; 29 E.R. 380 553
Rynd's Estate, *Re*, [1916] 1 I.R. 230 ; 51 I.L.T.R. 15 384

S.P., *Re*, *Ex parte* Official Receiver, [1936] Ch. 735 ; 105 L.J.Ch. 371 ; 156 L.T. 31 ; [1936-37] B. & C.R. 8 ; *sub nom. Re* Patten, Official Receiver *v.* Patten, [1936] 2 All E.R. 1119 ; 80 S.J. 673 79
Sadlier *v.* Butler (1867), I.R. 1 Eq. 415 ; 1 I.L.T. 612 408
Said *v.* Butt, [1920] 3 K.B. 497 ; 90 L.J.K.B. 239 ; 124 L.T. 413 ; 36 T.L.R. 762 ; [1920] All E.R. Rep. 232 102
St. Albans (Duke of) *v.* Beauclerk (1743), 2 Atk. 636 ; 26 E.R. 780 . . 426
St. John (Lord) *v.* Lady St. John (1805), 11 Ves. 526 ; 32 E.R. 1192 . . 554
Salmon, *Re*, *Ex parte* the Trustee, [1903] 1 K.B. 147 ; 72 L.J.K.B. 125 ; 87 L.T. 654 ; 51 W.R. 288 ; 10 Mans. 22 198
Salt *v.* Marquess of Northampton, [1892] A.C. 1 ; 61 L.J.Ch. 49 ; 65 L.T. 765 ; 40 W.R. 529 ; 8 T.L.R. 104 ; 36 S.J. 150 . . . . 179, 205
Salting, *Ex parte*, *Re* Stratton (1883), 25 Ch.D. 148 ; 53 L.J.Ch. 415 ; 49 L.T. 694 ; 32 W.R. 450 438
Samuel *v.* Jarrah Timber and Wood Paving Corp. Ltd., [1904] A.C. 323 ; 73 L.J.Ch. 526 ; 90 L.T. 731 ; 52 W.R. 673 ; 20 T.L.R. 536 ; 11 Mans. 276 205
Sanders *v.* Henden (1676), Nottingham's Chancery Cases, 73 Sel. Soc. 343 (case 482) 193
Sandiford, *Re* (No. 2), Italo-Canadian Corp. Ltd. *v.* Sandiford, [1935] Ch. 681 ; 104 L.J.Ch. 335 ; 154 L.T. 7 ; [1935] All E.R. Rep. 364 . . 279
Sandon *v.* Hooper (1843), 6 Beav. 246 ; 49 E.R. 820 ; 12 L.J.Ch. 309 ; 63 R.R. 72 ; *on appeal* (1844), 14 L.J.Ch. 120 . . . . . . 236, 237
Sands to Thompson (1883), 22 Ch.D. 614 ; 52 L.J.Ch. 406 ; 48 L.T. 210 ; 31 W.R. 397 261
Santley *v.* Wilde, [1899] 2 Ch. 474 ; 68 L.J.Ch. 681 ; 81 L.T. 393 ; 48 W.R. 90 ; 15 T.L.R. 528 207
Sargant *v.* Read (1876), 1 Ch.D. 600 ; 45 L.J. Ch. 206 ; 2 Char. Pr. Cas. 81 516
Saul's Trust, *Re*, Saul *v.* Saul, [1951] Ir. Jur. Rep. 34 408
Saunders *v.* Shafto, [1905] 1 Ch. 126 ; 74 L.J. Ch. 110 ; 91 L.T. 789 ; 53 W.R. 424 ; 49 S.J. 100 373
Saxone Shoe Co. Ltd.'s Trust Deed, *Re*, Abbott *v.* Pearson, [1962] 1 W.L.R. 943 ; [1962] 2 All E.R. 904 ; 106 S.J. 687 362
Say *v.* Barwick (1812), 1 V. & B. 195 ; 35 E.R. 76 335
Sayer, *Re*, MacGregor *v.* Sayer, [1957] Ch. 423 ; [1957] 2 W.L.R. 261 ; [1956] 3 All E.R. 600 ; 101 S.J. 130 362
Sayers *v.* Collyer (1884), 28 Ch.D. 103 ; 54 L.J. Ch. 1 ; 51 L.T. 723 ; 49 J.P. 244 ; 33 W.R. 91 ; 1 T.L.R. 45 ; [1881-5] All E.R. Rep. 385 . . 508
Schoole *v.* Sall (1803), 1 Sch. & Lef. 176 238
Scott, *Re*, Langton *v.* Scott, [1903] 1 Ch. 1 ; 72 L.J. Ch. 20 ; 87 L.T. 574 ; 51 W.R. 182 ; 47 S.J. 70 ; [1900-3] All E.R. Rep. 221 418

PAGE

Scott *v.* Morley (1887), 20 Q.B.D. 120 ; 57 L.J.Q.B. 43 ; 57 L.T. 919 ; 52 J.P. 230 ; 36 W.R. 67 ; 4 T.L.R. 56 ; *sub nom. Re* Morley, *Ex parte* Morley, Scott *v.* Morley, 4 Morr. 286 445
Scott *v.* Rayment (1868), L.R. 7 Eq. 112 ; 38 L.J. Ch. 48 ; 19 L.T. 481 . 489
Scott *v.* Scott, [1924] 1 I.R. 141 ; 58 I.L.T.R. 137 . . 519, 522, 527
Scott's Estate, *Re* (1863), 14 Ir. Ch. Rep. 63 436
Scould *v.* Butter—*see* Cud *v.* Rutter.
Scroggs *v.* Scroggs (1755), Amb. 272, 812 ; 27 E.R. 182, 513 . . 60
Seabrook, *Re*, Gray *v.* Baddeley, [1911] 1 Ch. 151 ; 80 L.J. Ch. 61 ; 103 L.T. 587 285
Seagrave *v.* Eustace (1705), 3 Bro. P. C. 11 ; 1 E.R. 1144 . . . 138
Sealey *v.* Stawell (1875), I.R. 9 Eq. 499 417
Searle *v.* Law (1846), 15 Sim. 95 ; 60 E.R. 553 ; 15 L.J. Ch. 187 ; 7 L.T.O.S. 78 ; 10 Jur. 191 ; 74 R.R. 27 311
Seddon *v.* North Eastern Salt Co. Ltd., [1905] 1 Ch. 326 ; 74 L.J. Ch. 199 ; 91 L.T. 793 ; 53 W.R. 232 ; 21 T.L.R. 118 ; 49 S.J. 119 ; [1904-7] All E.R. Rep. 817 546
Seeley *v.* Jago (1717), 1 P. Wms. 389 ; 24 E.R. 438 . . 390, 391
Sefton (Earl of), *Re*, [1898] 2 Ch. 378 ; 67 L.J. Ch. 518 ; 78 L.T. 765 ; 47 W.R. 49 ; 14 T.L.R. 466 ; 42 S.J. 570 405
Selby *v.* Pomfret (1861), 3 De G. F. & J. 595 ; 45 E.R. 1009 ; 30 L.J. Ch. 770 ; 4 L.T. 314 ; 7 Jur. N.S. 835 ; 9 W.R. 583 ; 128 R.R. 402 . 202
Senanayake *v.* Cheng, [1966] A.C. 63 ; [1965] 3 W.L.R. 715 ; [1965] 3 All E.R. 296 ; 109 S.J. 756 546
Sergie, *Re*, Shribman *v.* Hall, [1954] N.I. 1 . . . . 12, 180
Seton *v.* Slade (1802), 7 Ves. 265 ; 32 E.R. 108 ; [1775-1802] All E.R. Rep. 163 ; 6 R.R. 124 82
Seton *v.* Smith (1840), 11 Sim. 59 ; 59 E.R. 796 405
Sevier *v.* Greenway (1815), 19 Ves. 413 ; 34 E.R. 570 198
Seymour *v.* Tyndall (1676/7), Rep. t. Finch 284 ; 23 E.R. 156 . . 177
Shakel *v.* Duke of Marlborough (1819), 4 Madd. 463 ; 56 E.R. 776 . 240
Shanahans Stamp Auctions Ltd. *v.* Farrelly, [1962] I.R. 386 . 520-1, 525
Sharp *v.* Rickards, [1909] 1 Ch. 109 ; 78 L.J. Ch. 29 ; 99 L.T. 916; [1908-10] All E.R. Rep. 480 198-9
Sharp *v.* St. Sauveur (1871), L.R. 7 Ch. App. 343 ; 41 L.J. Ch. 576 ; 26 L.T. 142 ; 20 W.R. 269 393
Shaw, *Re*—*see* Whitbread, *Ex parte*.
Shaw *v.* Bunny (1865), 2 De G. J. & S. 468 ; 46 E.R. 456 ; 34 L.J. Ch. 257 ; 11 L.T. 645 ; 11 Jur. N.S. 99 ; 13 W.R. 374 ; 139 R.R. 190 . . 256
Shaw *v.* Lawless (1838), 5 Cl. & Fin. 129 ; 7 E.R. 353 ; 1 Dr. & Wal. 512 ; 47 R.R. 41 139
Shaw *v.* Shaw, [1954] 2 Q.B. 429 ; [1954] 3 W.L.R. 265 ; [1954] 2 All E.R. 638 ; 98 S.J. 509 28
Shaw (Tom) & Co. *v.* Moss Empires (Ltd.) (1908), 25 T.L.R. 190 . 298
Shea *v.* Moore, [1894] 1 I.R. 158 186
Sheffield *v.* Earl of Coventry (1833), 2 Russ. & M. 317 ; 39 E.R. 415 . 423
Sheffield Gas Consumers' Co. *v.* Harrison (1853), 17 Beav. 294 ; 51 E.R. 1047 ; 99 R.R. 155 488
Sheffield Nickel and Silver Plating Co. Ltd. *v.* Unwin (1877), 2 Q.B.D. 214 ; 46 L.J.Q.B. 299 ; 36 L.T. 246 ; 25 W.R. 493 543
Shelburne (Countess Dowager of) *v.* Earl of Inchiquin (1784), 1 Bro. C.C. 338 ; 28 E.R. 1166 ; *on appeal, sub nom.* Earl of Inchiquin *v.* Fitzmaurice (1785), 5 Bro. P.C. 166 ; 2 E.R. 603 . . . . . 530, 531
Shelfer *v.* City of London Electric Lighting Co., [1895] 1 Ch. 287 ; 65 L.J. Ch. 216 ; 72 L.T. 34 ; 43 W.R. 238 ; 11 T.L.R. 137 ; 39 S.J. 132 ; 12 R. 112 ; *sub nom.* Meux's Brewery Co. *v.* City of London Electric Lighting Co., [1891-4] All E.R. Rep. 838 . . . . . 463, 466
Shelley's Case (1581), 1 Co. Rep. 88b ; 76 E.R. 199 ; Moore K.B. 136 ; 72 E.R. 490 66
Shepard *v.* Jones (1882), 21 Ch.D. 469 ; 47 L.T. 604 ; 31 W.R. 308 ; [1881-5] All E.R. Rep. 608 237
Shephard, *Re*, Atkins *v.* Shephard (1889), 43 Ch.D. 131 ; 59 L.J. Ch. 83 ; 62 L.T. 337 ; 38 W.R. 133 ; 6 T.L.R. 44 . . . . . 510, 515
Sherlock *v.* Annesley (1709), 2 O'Flanagan's *Lives of the Lord Chancellors of Ireland* 15 129

PAGE

Sherlock's Estate, *Re*, [1899] 2 I.R. 561 384
Sherman, *Re*, Trevenen *v.* Pearce, [1954] Ch. 653 ; [1954] 2 W.L.R. 903 ; [1954] 1 All E.R. 893 ; 98 S.J. 302 383
Sherman *v.* Cox (1672-3), Nels. 71 ; 21 E.R. 792 ; (1674), 3 Ch. Rep. 83 ; 21 E.R. 736 ; *sub nom.* Shermer *v.* Robbins (1679), Rep. t. Finch 406 ; 23 E.R. 221 170
Shields, *Re*, Corbould-Ellis *v.* Dales, [1912] 1 Ch. 591 ; 81 L.J. Ch. 370 ; 106 L.T. 748 423
Shipley U.D.C. *v.* Bradford Corp., [1936] Ch. 375 ; 105 L.J. Ch. 225 ; *on appeal*, 154 L.T. 444 541
Shirley *v.* Earl Ferrers (1730), 3 P. Wms. 77 ; 24 E.R. 976 ; *sub nom.* Shirley *v.* Ferrars, Mos. 389 ; 25 E.R. 456 556
Shoe Machinery Co. Ltd. *v.* Cutlan (1894-5), 12 R.P.C. 342, 357 ; *on appeal*, [1896] 1 Ch. 667 ; 65 L.J. Ch. 314 ; 74 L.T. 166 ; 40 S.J. 336 ; 131 R.P.C. 141 474
Shore *v.* Shore (1960), *The Times* newspaper, 13th October 470
Shorer *v.* Shorer—*see* Lingen *v.* Sowray.
Shuttleworth *v.* Laycock (1694), 1 Vern. 245 ; 23 E.R. 443 . . . 62
Sichel *v.* Mosenthal (1862), 30 Beav. 371 ; 54 E.R. 932 ; 31 L.J. Ch. 386 ; 5 L.T. 784 ; 8 Jur. N.S. 275 ; 10 W.R. 283 ; 132 R.R. 312 . . . 488
Sichel *v.* Raphael (1861), 4 L.T. 114 561
Silsby *v.* Holliman, [1955] Ch. 552 ; [1955] 2 W.L.R. 1090 ; [1955] 2 All E.R. 373 ; 99 S.J. 355 246-7
Silva, *Re*, Silva *v.* Silva, [1929] 2 Ch. 198 ; 98 L.J. Ch. 459 ; 141 L.T. 452 ; [1929] All E.R. Rep. 546 . . . . 379, 380
Sim *v.* H. J. Heinz & Co. Ltd., [1959] 1 W.L.R. 313 ; [1959] 1 All E.R. 547 ; 103 S.J. 238 ; [1959] R.P.C. 80 462
Simpson, *Re*, Chadderton *v.* Simpson, [1952] Ch. 412 ; [1952] 1 All E.R. 963 ; [1952] 1 T.L.R. 868 ; 96 S.J. 262 . . . . . 369, 370
Simpson, *Re*, Coutts & Co. *v.* Church Missionary Soc., [1916] 1 Ch. 502 ; 85 L.J. Ch. 329 ; 114 L.T. 835 410
Simpson *v.* Lord Howden (1837), 3 My. & Cr. 97 ; 40 E.R. 862 ; 1 Ry. & Can. Cas. 326 ; 6 L.J. Ch. 315 ; 1 Jur. 703 ; 45 R.R. 225 . . . 553
Sinclair *v.* Brougham, [1914] A.C. 398 ; 83 L.J. Ch. 465 ; 111 L.T. 1 ; 30 T.L.R. 315 ; 58 S.J. 302 ; [1914-15] All E.R. Rep. 622 . 10, 525-6
Sinclair *v.* Gogarty, [1937] I.R. 377 462
Sinfield *v.* Sweet, [1967] 1 W.L.R. 1489 ; [1967] 3 All E.R. 479 ; 111 S.J. 889 . . . . 238, 258
Skelton *v.* Flanagan (1867), I.R. 1 Eq. 362 ; 1 I.L.T. 533 373
Skyrme, *Ex parte*—*see* Burge, Woodall & Co., *Re.*
Slade *v.* Rigg (1843), 3 Hare 35 ; 67 E.R. 286 ; 64 R.R. 204 . . . 244
Slater, *Re*, Slater *v.* Slater, [1907] 1 Ch. 665 ; 76 L.J. Ch. 472 ; 97 L.T. 74 ; 51 S.J. 426 288
Slater's Trusts, *Re* (1879), 11 Ch.D. 227 ; 48 L.J. Ch. 473 ; 40 L.T. 184 ; 27 W.R. 448 354
Slator *v.* Nolan (1876), I.R. 11 Eq. 367 335
"Slogger" Automatic Feeder Co. Ltd., *Re*, Hoare *v.* Slogger Automatic Feeder Co. Ltd., [1915] 1 Ch. 478 ; 84 L.J. Ch. 587 ; 112 L.T 579 ; 59 S.J. 272 ; [1915] H.B.R. 138 514
Smith (Mary), *Re* (1897), 33 I.L.T.R. 69 384
Smith *v.* Casper (E.A.), Edgar & Co.—*see* Tigurds, The.
Smith *v.* Claxton (1820), 4 Madd. 484 ; 56 E.R. 784 ; 20 R.R. 320 . . 388
Smith *v.* Cooke (1746), 3 Atk. 378 ; 26 E.R. 1018 563
Smith *v.* East Elloe R.D.C., [1956] A.C. 736 ; [1956] 2 W.L.R. 888 ; [1956] 1 All E.R. 855 ; 120 J.P. 263 ; 54 L.G.R. 233 ; 100 S.J. 282 . . 29
Smith *v.* Green (1844), 1 Coll. 555 ; 63 E.R. 541 ; 66 E.R. 180 . . . 189
Smith *v.* Hancock, [1894] 2 Ch. 377 ; 63 L.J. Ch. 477 ; 70 L.T. 578 ; 58 J.P. 638 ; 42 W.R. 465 ; 10 T.L.R. 433 ; 38 S.J. 416 ; 7 R. 200 . . 471
Smith *v.* Harrison (1857), 26 L.J. Ch. 412 ; 29 L.T.O.S. 11 ; 2 Jur. N.S. 287 ; 5 W.R. 408 ; 112 R.R. 412 500
Smith *v.* Harvey (1675), Nottingham's Chancery Cases, 73 Sel. Soc. 227 (case 333) 173
Smith *v.* Iliffe (1875), L.R. 20 Eq. 666 ; 44 L.J. Ch. 755 ; 33 L.T. 200 ; 23 W.R. 851 536-7

PAGE

Smith *v.* Johnston (1863), 4 Giff. 632 ; 66 E.R. 859 ; 33 L.J. Ch. 137 ; 9 L.T. 437 ; 9 Jur N.S. 1223 ; 12 W.R. 122 ; 3 New R. 108 . . 474
Smith *v.* Jones, [1954] 1 W.L.R. 1089; [1954] 2 All E.R. 823; 98 S.J. 540 307, 530
Smith *v.* Lynn, [1951] N.I. 69 ; *sub nom.* Smyth *v.* Lynn, 85 I.L.T.R. 57 . 507-8
Smith *v.* Masterman—*see* Smith *v.* Smith
Smith *v.* Pincombe (1852), 3 Mac. & G. 653 ; 42 E.R. 411 ; 20 L.T.O.S. 10 ; 16 Jur. 205 ; 87 R.R. 239 551
Smith *v.* Smith (1833), 2 Cr. & M. 231; 149 E.R. 745 ; 4 Tyr. 52 ; 39 R.R. 762 ; *sub nom.* Smith *v.* Masterman, 3 L.J. Ex. 42 . . . 306
Smith *v.* Warde (1845), 15 Sim. 56 ; 60 E.R. 537 ; 15 L.J. Ch. 105 ; 6 L.T.O.S. 234 ; 9 Jur. 981 ; 74 R.R. 16 313
Smith *v.* "Zigurds" (Steamship) and her Freight (Owners of the)—*see* Zigurds, The.
Smyth *v.* Lynn—*see* Smith *v.* Lynn.
Smyth *v.* Toms, [1918] 1 I.R. 338 ; 52 I.L.T.R. 145 . . . 437
Snow *v.* Boycott, [1892] 3 Ch. 110 ; 61 L.J. Ch. 591 ; 66 L.T. 762 ; 40 W.R. 603 81
Sobey *v.* Sobey (1873), L.R. 15 Eq. 200 ; 42 L.J. Ch. 271 ; 27 L.T. 808 ; 21 W.R. 309 562
Société Générale de Paris *v.* Walker (1885), 11 App. Cas. 20 ; 55 L.J.Q.B. 169 ; 54 L.T. 389 ; 34 W.R. 662 303
Solle *v.* Butcher, [1950] 1 K.B. 671 ; [1949] 2 All E.R. 1107 ; 66 T.L.R. (Pt. 1), 448 . . . . 534, 546, 549-50
Solomon, *Re*, Ex *parte* The Trustee of the Property of the Bankrupt *v.* Solomon, [1967] Ch. 573 ; [1967] 2 W.L.R. 172 ; 110 S.J. 978 ; *sub nom.* *Re* Debtor, Trustee *v.* Solomon, [1966] 3 All E.R. 255 . . . 38
Somerset (Duke of) *v.* Cookson (1735), 3 P. Wms. 390 ; 24 E.R. 1114 67, 484
Somes, *Re*, Smith *v.* Somes, [1896] 1 Ch. 250 ; 74 L.T. 49 ; 44 W.R. 236 ; 12 T.L.R. 152 ; 40 S.J. 210 ; *sub nom.* *Re* Somes, Somes *v.* Somes, 65 L.J. Ch. 262 374
Sopwith *v.* Maughan (1861), 30 Beav. 235 ; 54 E.R. 879 ; 132 R.R. 251 . 407
South *v.* Bloxam (1865), 2 H. & M. 457 ; 71 E.R. 541 ; 34 L.J. Ch. 369 ; 12 L.T. 204 ; 11 Jur. N.S. 319 ; 5 New R. 506 ; 144 R.R. 230 . . 433
South-Eastern Railway Co. *v.* Martin—*see* North-Eastern Railway Co. *v.* Martin.
Sowden *v.* Sowden (1785), 1 Bro. C.C. 582 ; 28 E.R. 1311 ; 1 Cox C.C. 165 ; 29 E.R. 1111 430
Soya Margareta, The, Cargo lately laden on board the Soya Lovisa (Owners) *v.* Soya Margareta (Owners), [1961] 1 W.L.R. 709 ; [1960] 2 All E.R. 756 ; 105 S.J. 406 ; [1960] 1 Lloyd's R. 675 458
Spence *v.* Healey (1853), 8 Ex. 668 ; 155 E.R. 1520 ; 1 C.L.R. 857 ; 91 R.R. 696 ; *sub nom.* Healey *v.* Spence, 22 L.J. Ex. 249 . . . 120
Spencer (Earl) *v.* Peek (1867), L.R. 3 Eq. 415 ; 15 W.R. 478 . . 555
Speyside Estate and Trust Co. Ltd. *v.* Wraymond Freeman (Blenders) Ltd., [1950] Ch. 96 ; [1949] 2 All E.R. 796 ; 65 T.L.R. 681 ; 93 S.J. 773 . 526
Spiller *v.* Bolton (1947), 149 Est. Gaz. 450 500
Spirett *v.* Willows (1866), L.R. 1 Ch. App. 520 ; 35 L.J. Ch. 755 ; 14 L.T. 720 ; 12 Jur. N.S. 538 ; *subsequent proceedings* (1869), L.R. 4 Ch. App. 407 443
Spread *v.* Morgan (1865), 11 H.L.C. 588 ; 11 E.R. 1461 ; 13 L.T. 164 ; 6 New. R. 269 ; 145 R.R. 315 406
Spurgeon *v.* Collier (1758), 1 Eden 55 ; 28 E.R. 605 . . 168, 177
Spurrier *v.* Hancock (1799), 4 Ves. 667 ; 31 E.R. 344 . . . 504
Spurway *v.* Glynn (1804), 9 Ves. 483 ; 32 E.R. 689 ; 7 R.R. 279 . . 290
Stanfield *v.* Gibbon, [1925] W.N. 11 514
Stanhope *v.* Manners (1763), 2 Eden 197 ; 28 E.R. 873 . . . 178
Stanhope *v.* Verney (Earl) (1761), 2 Eden 81 ; 28 E.R. 826 . . 301
Stanley *v.* English Fibres Industries Ltd. (1889), 68 L.J.Q.B. 839 . . 328
Stapylton *v.* Scott (1807), 13 Ves. 425 ; 33 E.R. 353 ; *subsequent proceedings* (1809), 16 Ves. 272 ; 33 E.R. 988 ; 10 R.R. 179 507
Statutory Trusts Declared by Section 105 of the Law of Property Act, 1925, *Re* The—*see* Young *v*' Clarey.
Steed *v.* Preece (1874), L.R. 18 Eq. 192 ; 43 L.J. Ch. 687 ; 22 W.R. 432 . 377
Steedman *v.* Drinkle, [1916] 1 A.C. 275 ; 85 L.J.P.C. 79 ; 114 L.T. 248 ; 32 T.L.R. 231 ; [1914-15] All E.R. Rep. 298 . . . . . 25, 82

PAGE

Steeds *v.* Steeds (1889), 22 Q.B..D. 537 ; 58 L.J.Q.B. 302 ; 60 L.T. 318 ; 37 W.R. 378 ; [1886-90] All E.R. Rep. 1021 121
Steel Wing Co. Ltd., *Re* ,[1921] 1 Ch. 349 ; 90 L.J. Ch. 116 ; 124 L.T. 664 ; 65 S.J. 240 ; [1920] B. & C.R. 160 ; [1920] All E.R. Rep. 292 . . 327
Stenning, *Re*, Wood *v.* Stenning, [1895] 2 Ch. 433 ; 73 L.T. 207 ; 13 R. 807 525, 528
Sterne *v.* Beck (1863), 1 De G. J. & S. 595 ; 46 E.R. 236 ; 32 L.J. Ch. 682 ; 8 L.T. 588 ; 11 W.R. 791 ; 2 New R. 346 ; 137 R.R. 307 . . 206
Stevens *v.* Theatres Ltd., [1903] 1 Ch. 857 ; 72 L.J. Ch. 764 ; 88 L.T. 458 ; 51 W.R. 585 ; 19 T.L.R. 334 253
Stevenson's Estate, *Re*, [1902] 1 I.R. 23 ; 36 I.L.T.R. 49 ; 2 N.I.J.R. 49 ; *on appeal, sub nom.* Fullerton *v.* Provincial Bank of Ireland . . 212
Steward, *Ex parte*, *Re* Blake (1843), 3 Mont. D. & De. G. 265 ; 7 Jur. 116 . 299
Stewart, *Re*, Stewart *v.* Stewart, [1956] N.I. 82 384
Steyning and Littlehampton Building Soc. *v.* Wilson, [1951] Ch. 1018 ; [1951] 2 All E.R. 452 ; [1951] 2 T.L.R. 424 ; 95 S.J. 514 . . 233
Stibbe, *Re*, Cleverley *v.* Stibbe (1946), 175 L.T. 198 414
Stickney *v.* Keeble, [1915] A.C. 386 ; 84 L.J. Ch. 259 ; 112 L.T. 664 ; [1914-15] All E.R. Rep. 73 . . . . 82, 505
Stillwell, *Re*, Stillwell *v.* Stillwell, [1936] Ch. 637 ; [1936] 1 All E.R. 757 ; 105 L.J. Ch. 217 ; 155 L.T. 17 ; 52 T.L.R. 377 ; 80 S.J. 288 . . 380
Stoakes *v.* Verrier—*see* Stokes *v.* Verrier.
Stockloser *v.* Johnson, [1954] 1 Q.B. 476 ; [1954] 2 W.L.R. 439 ; [1954] 1 All E.R. 630 ; 98 S.J. 178 25
Stockton Iron Furnace Co., *Re* (1879), 10 Ch. D. 335 ; 48 L.J. Ch. 417 ; 40 L.T. 19 ; 27 W.R. 433 . . . . 232, 233
Stoddart *v.* Union Trust Ltd., [1912] 1 K.B. 181 ; 81 L.J.K.B. 140 ; 105 L.T. 806 307
Stoer, *Re* (1884), 9 P.D. 120 ; 51 L.T. 141 ; 32 W.R. 1005 . . 556
Stogdon *v.* Lee, [1891] 1 Q.B. 661 ; 60 L.J.Q.B. 669 ; 64 L.T. 494 ; 55 J.P. 533 ; 39 W.R. 467 445
Stokes *v.* Verrier (1677), 3 Swanst. 634 ; 36 E.R. 1003 ; *sub nom.* Stoakes *v.* Verrier, Rep. t. Finch 292 ; 23 E.R. 160 168
Stratford (J.T.) & Son Ltd. *v.* Lindley, [1965] A.C. 269 ; [1964] 3 W.L.R. 541 ; [1964] 3 All E.R. 102 ; 108 S.J. 636 ; [1964] 2 Lloyd's R. 133 . 479
Strathcona (Lord) Steamship Co. Ltd. *v.* Dominion Coal Co. Ltd., [1926] A.C. 108 ; 95 L.J.P.C. 71 ; 134 L.T. 227 ; 42 T.L.R. 86 ; 16 Asp. M.L.C. 585 ; 31 Com. Cas. 80 468-9
Stratton, *Re*—*see* Salting, *Ex parte*.
Streatfield *v.* Streatfield (1736), Cas. t. Talb. 176 ; 25 E.R. 724 ; 1 Swanst. 433n. ; 36 E.R. 455 ; [1558-1774] All E.R. Rep. 497 . 395, 398, 405
Street *v.* Denham, [1954] 1 W.L.R. 624 ; [1954] 1 All E.R. 532 ; 98 S.J. 253 103
Strode *v.* Blanchard (1676/7), Nottingham's Chancery Cases, 79 Sel. Soc. 496 (case 659) 174
Strode *v.* Parker (1694), 2 Vern. 316 ; 23 E.R. 804 178
Strong *v.* Bird (1874), L.R. 18 Eq. 315 ; 43 L.J. Ch. 814 ; 30 L.T. 745 ; 22 W.R. 788 ; [1874-80] All E.R. Rep. 230 316
Stroud Building Soc. *v.* Delamont, [1960] 1 W.L.R. 431 ; [1960] 1 All E.R. 749 ; 104 S.J. 329 229
Stroughill *v.* Buck (1850), 14 Q.B. 781 ; 117 E.R. 301 ; 19 L.J.Q.B. 209 ; 15 L.T.O.S. 22 ; 14 Jur. 741 ; 80 R.R. 395 126
Sturgis *v.* Champneys (1839), 5 My. & Cr. 97 ; 41 E.R. 308 ; 9 L.J. Ch. 10 ; 3 Jur. 1096 ; 48 R.R. 243 442
Sturt, *Re*, De Bunsen *v.* Hardinge, [1922] 1 Ch. 416 ; 91 L.J. Ch. 289 ; 126 L.T. 460 ; 66 S.J. 236 392
Sudeley (Lord) *v.* A.-G., [1897] A.C. 11 ; 66 L.J.Q.B. 21 ; 75 L.T. 398 ; 61 J.P. 420 ; 45 W.R. 305 ; 13 T.L.R. 38 286
Suffolk (Earl of) *v.* Greenvill (1631), 2 Freem. 146 ; 22 E.R. 1119 ; Nels. 15 ; 21 E.R. 778 ; 3 Ch. Rep. 89 ; 21 E.R. 738 296
Suggitt's Trusts, *Re* (1868), L.R. 3 Ch. App. 215 ; 37 L.J. Ch. 426 ; 16 W.R. 551 443
Suisse *v.* Lord Lowther (1843), 2 Hare 424 ; 67 E.R. 175 ; 7 Jur. 252 ; 62 R.R. 170 ; *on appeal*, 12 L.J. Ch. 315 ; 7 Jur. 407, 808 ; 62 R.R. 179 . 423
Sullivan, *Re*, Sullivan *v.* Sullivan, [1917] 1 I.R. 38 408

PAGE
Super Rax Ltd. *v.* Broadfoot, [1961] R.P.C. 61 474
Sutton *v.* Jones (1809), 15 Ves. 584 ; 33 E.R. 875 516
Swain *v.* Ayres (1888), 21 Q.B.D. 289 ; 57 L.J.Q.B. 428 ; 36 W.R. 798 ; 4 T.L.R. 609 . . . . 88-9, 93
Sweeney *v.* Denis (1883), 17 I.L.T.R. 76 89
Sweetman *v.* Sweetman (1868), I.R. 2 Eq. 141 ; 2 I.L.T. 136 . . 405-6
Swinburne, *Re*, Swinburne *v.* Pitt (1884), 27 Ch.D. 696 ; 54 L.J. Ch. 229; 33 W.R. 394 368
Sykes *v.* Hastings (1805), 11 Ves. 363 ; 32 E.R. 1128 . . . 516-7
Symmes *v.* Symonds (1703), 4 Bro. P.C. 328 ; 2 E.R. 222 . . 172

Taafe *v.* Merrick (1931), 65 I.L.T.R. 36 338
Taddy & Co. *v.* Sterious & Co., [1904] 1 Ch. 354 ; 73 L.J. Ch. 191 ; 89 L.T. 628 ; 52 W.R. 152 ; 20 T.L.R. 102 ; 48 S.J. 117 . . 103, 468
Taff Vale Railway Co. *v.* Nixon (1847), 1 H.L.C. 111 ; 9 E.R. 695 . 563
Tailby *v.* Official Receiver (1888), 13 App. Cas. 523 ; 58 L.J.Q.B. 75 ; 60 L.T. 162 ; 37 W.R. 513 ; 4 T.L.R. 726 ; [1886-90] All E.R. Rep. 486 297, 309
Talbot *v.* Braddill (1683), 1 Vern. 183 ; 23 E.R. 402 ; *sub nom.* Talbot *v.* Braddil (1686), 1 Vern. 394 ; 23 E.R. 539 177
Talbot (Earl) *v.* Hope Scott (1858), 4 K. & J. 96 ; 70 E.R. 40 ; 27 L.J. Ch. 273 ; 31 L.T.O.S. 392 ; 4 Jur. N.S. 1172 ; 6 W.R. 269 . . 510
Talbot *v.* Shrewsbury (Duke of)—*see* Talbott *v.* Duke of Shrewsbury.
Talbot *v.* Talbot, [1968] 1 Q.B. 1 ; [1967] 3 W.L.R. 438 ; [1967] 2 All E.R. 920 ; 111 S.J. 278 498
Talbott *v.* Duke of Shrewsbury (1714), Prec. Ch. 394 ; 24 E.R. 177 ; *sub nom.* Talbot *v.* Duke of Shrewsbury, Gilb Ch. 89 ; 25 E.R. 62 ; 2 Eq. Cas. Abr. 352, pl. 10 ; 22 E.R. 299 . . . . . . 413-14, 415
Tancred *v.* Delagoa Bay and East Africa Railway Co. (1889), 23 Q.B.D. 239 ; 58 L.J.Q.B. 459 ; 61 L.T. 229 ; 38 W.R. 15 ; 5 T.L.R. 587 . . 327
Tanfield *v.* Davenport (1638-9), Tot. 114 ; 21 E.R. 140 . . . 441
Tanistry (the Case of) (1608), Davis 78 ; 80 E.R. 516 134
Tankard, *Re*, Tankard *v.* Midland Bank Executor and Trustee Co. Ltd., [1942] Ch. 69 ; [1941] 3 All E.R. 458 ; 111 L.J. Ch. 70 ; 166 L.T. 65 ; 58 T.L.R. 56 ; 85 S.J. 475 274-5
Taplin *v.* Florence (1851), 10 C.B. 744 ; 138 E.R. 294 ; 20 L.J.C.P. 137 ; 17 L.T.O.S. 63 ; 15 Jur. 402 ; 84 R.R. 773 98
Tarn *v.* Turner (1888), 39 Ch.D. 456 ; 57 L.J. Ch. 1085 ; 59 L.T. 742 ; 37 W.R. 276 ; 4 T.L.R. 735 . . . . 190, 228
Tasker (W.) & Sons Ltd., *Re*, Hoare *v.* W. Tasker & Sons Ltd., [1905] 2 Ch. 587 ; 74 L.J. Ch. 643 ; 93 L.T. 195 ; 54 W.R. 65 ; 21 T.L.R. 736 ; 49 S.J. 700 ; 12 Mans. 302 196
Tate *v.* Crewdson, [1938] Ch. 869 ; [1938] 3 All E.R. 43 ; 107 L.J. Ch. 328 ; 159 L.T. 512 ; 54 T.L.R. 857 ; 82 S.J. 454 . . . 558-9
Tate *v.* Williamson (1866), L.R. 2 Ch. App. 55 ; 15 L.T. 549 ; 15 W.R. 321 351
Taunton *v.* Morris (1879), 11 Ch.D. 779 ; 48 L.J.Ch. 408 ; 41 L.T. 259; 27 W.R. 718 442
Tayler *v.* Waters (1816), 7 Taunt. 374 ; 129 E.R. 150 ; 2 Marsh. 551 . . 96-7
Taylor *v.* A.-G. (1837), 8 Sim. 413 ; 59 E.R. 164 559
Taylor *v.* Ellis, [1960] Ch. 368 ; [1960] 2 W.L.R. 509 ; [1960] 1 All E.R. 549 ; 104 S.J. 249 229
Taylor *v.* Emerson (1834), 4 Dr. & War. 117 ; 6 Ir. Eq. Rep. 224 ; 2 Con. & L. 558 ; 65 R.R. 676 179
Taylor *v.* Johnston (1882), 19 Ch.D. 603 ; 51 L.J.Ch. 798 ; 46 L.T. 219 ; 30 W.R. 508 345
Taylor *v.* London and County Banking Co., [1901] 2 Ch. 231 ; 70 L.J. Ch. 477 ; 84 L.T. 397 ; 49 W.R. 451 ; 17 T.L.R. 413 ; 45 S.J. 394 . 219-20
Taylor *v.* Meads (1865), 4 De G. J. & S. 597 ; 46 E.R. 1050 ; 34 L.J. Ch. 203; 12 L.T. 6 ; 11 Jur. N.S. 166 ; 13 W.R. 394 ; 5 New R. 348 ; 146 R.R. 471 444
Taylor *v.* Obee (1816), 3 Pri. 83 ; 146 E R. 198 ; 17 R.R. 548 . . 347
Taylor *v* Plumer (1815), 3 M. & S. 562 ; 105 E.R. 721 ; 2 Rose 457 ; [1814-23] All E.R. Rep. 167 ; 16 R.R. 361 519-20
Taylor *v.* Portington (1855), 7 De G. M. & G. 328 ; 44 E.R. 128 ; 3 Eq. R 781 ; 1 Jur. N.S. 1057 ; 19 J.P. 627 ; 109 R.R. 147 . . . 499
Taylor *v* Russell, [1892] A.C. 244 ; 61 L.J.Ch. 657 ; 66 L.T. 565 ; 41 W.R. 43 ; 8 T.L.R. 463 ; 36 S.J. 379 . . . . . . 218-19, 258

PAGE

Taylor *v.* Taylor (1853), 10 Hare 475 ; 68 E.R. 1014 ; 90 R.R. 440 . . 379
Taylor *v.* Taylor (1853), 3 De G. M. & G. 190 ; 43 E.R. 76 ; 22 L.J.Ch. 742 ; 1 Eq. R. 239 ; 21 L.T.O.S. 213 ; 17 Jur. 583 ; 1 W.R. 398 ; 98 R.R. 104 . 388
Taylor *v.* Taylor (1875), L.R. 20 Eq. 155 ; 44 L.J.Ch. 718 ; 23 W.R. 719 . 418
Taylor's Estate, *Re*, Taylor *v.* Taylor, [1969] 2 W.L.R. 1371 269
Tebb *v.* Hodge (1869), L.R. 5 C.P. 73 ; 39 L.J.C.P. 56 ; 21 L.T. 499 . 184
Teevan *v.* Smith (1882), 20 Ch.D. 724 ; 51 L.J.Ch. 621 ; 47 L.T. 208 ; 30 W.R. 716 . . . . 192, 261
Terry and White's Contract, *Re* (1886), 32 Ch.D. 14 ; 55 L.J. Ch. 345 ; 54 L.T. 353 ; 34 W.R. 379 ; 2 T.L.R. 327 507
Thames Haven Dock and Railway Co. *v.* Brymer—*see* Brymer *v.* Thames Haven Dock and Railway Co.
Thames Launches Ltd. *v.* Trinity House Corp. (Deptford Strond), [1961] Ch. 197 ; [1961] 2 W.L.R. 16 ; [1961] 1 All E.R. 26 ; 105 S.J. 16 . . 459
Tharpe *v.* Tharpe (1806), 12 Ves. 317 ; 33 E.R. 121 517
Thin *v.* Thin (1650), 1 Ch. Rep. 162 ; 21 E.R. 538 530
Thomas *v.* Sorrell (1674), Vaughan 330 ; 124 E.R. 1098 ; 1 Freem. 85, 137 ; 89 E.R. 63, 100 ; *sub nom.* Thomas *v.* Sorrel, 3 Keb. 264 ; 84 E.R. 712 ; 1 Lev. 217 ; 83 E.R. 376 ; [1558-1774] All E.R. Rep. 107 . . . 93, 94
Thompson, *Re* (1877)—*see* Williams, *Ex parte*.
Thompson, *Re*, Public Trustee *v.* Husband, [1936] Ch. 676 ; [1936] 2 All E.R. 141 ; 105 L.J.Ch. 289 ; 155 L.T. 474 ; 80 S.J. 466 287
Thompson, *Re*, Thompson *v.* Thompson, [1906] 2 Ch. 199 ; 75 L.J. Ch. 599 ; 95 L.T. 97 ; 64 W.R. 613 364
Thompson *v.* Hickman, [1907] 1 Ch. 550 ; 76 L.J.Ch. 254 ; 96 L.T. 454 ; 23 T.L.R. 311 539
Thompson *v.* Park, [1944] K.B. 408 ; [1944] 2 All E.R. 477 ; 113 L.J.K.B. 561 ; 170 L.T. 207 464
Thompson-Schwab *v.* Costaki, [1956] 1 W.L.R. 335 ; [1956] 1 All E.R. 652 ; 100 S.J. 246 ; 167 Est. Gaz. 218 457
Thomson's Mortgage Trusts, *Re*, Thomson *v.* Bruty, [1920] 1 Ch. 508 ; 89 L.J. Ch. 213 ; 123 L.T. 138 ; 64 S.J. 375 ; [1920] All E.R. Rep. 664 . 257
Thorn *v.* Commissioners of H.M. Works and Public Buildings (1863), 32 Beav. 490 ; 55 E.R. 192 ; 138 R.R. 838 490
Thornborough *v.* Baker (1675), 3 Swanst. 628 ; 36 E.R. 1000 ; 2 Eq. Cas. Abr. 428, pl. 2 ; 22 E.R. 364 ; 2 Freem. 143 ; 22 E.R. 1117 ; *sub nom.* Thornbrough *v.* Baker, 1 Ch. Cas. 283 ; 22 E.R. 802 61
Thorne *v.* Cann, [1895] A.C. 11 ; 64 L.J.Ch. 1 ; 71 L.T. 852 ; 11 R. 67 . 194
Thorne *v.* Heard, [1895] A.C. 495 ; 64 L.J.Ch. 652 ; 73 L.T. 291 ; 44 W.R. 155 ; 11 T.L.R. 464 ; 11 R. 254 257
Thornhill *v.* Manning (1851), 1 Sim. N.S. 451 ; 61 E.R. 174 ; 20 L.J.Ch. 604 ; 17 L.T.O.S. 208 ; 89 R.R. 160 248
Thornton *v.* Hawley (1804), 10 Ves. 129 ; 32 E.R. 793 ; 7 R.R. 359 . . 386
Thornton *v.* Knight (1849), 16 Sim. 509 ; 60 E.R. 972 ; 13 Jur. 180 ; 80 R.R. 137 553
Thorpe *v.* Fasey, [1949] Ch. 649 ; [1949] 2 All E.R. 393 ; [1949] L.J.R. 1613 ; 65 T.L.R. 561 ; 93 S.J. 552 543
Threlfall, *Re*, *Ex parte* Queen's Benefit Building Soc. (1880), 16 Ch.D. 274 ; 44 L.T. 74 ; 29 W.R. 128 ; *sub nom. Re* Threlfall, *Ex parte* Blakey, 50 L.J.Ch. 318 232
Thurlow *v.* Mackeson (1868), L.R. 4 Q.B. 97 ; 9 B. & S. 975 ; 38 L.J.Q.B. 57 ; 19 L.T. 448 ; 17 W.R. 280 257
Thursby *v.* Eccles (1900), 70 L.J.Q.B. 91 ; 49 W.R. 281 ; 17 T.L.R. 130 . 495
Thynne (Lady) *v.* Earl of Glengall (1848), 2 H.L.C. 131 ; 9 E.R. 1042 ; 12 Jur. 805 ; 81 R.R. 77 420
Tibbits *v.* Tibbits (1815), 2 Mer. 96n. ; 35 E.R. 877 ; (1816), 19 Ves. 656 ; 34 E.R. 659 ; (1821), Jac. 317 ; 37 E.R. 871 ; 23 R.R. 79 . . 396, 400, 407
Tidd *v.* Lister (1852), 10 Hare 140 ; 68 E.R. 872 ; *on appeal* (1854), 3 De G. M. & G. 857 ; 43 E.R. 336 ; 23 L.J.Ch. 249 ; 23 L.T.O.S. 101 ; 18 Jur 543 ; 2 W.R. 184 ; 98 R.R. 335 442
Tighe *v.* Dolphin, [1906] 1 I.R. 305 436-7
Tillett *v.* Nixon (1883), 25 Ch.D. 238 ; 52 L.J.Ch. 199 ; 49 L.T. 598 ; 32 W.R. 226 ; [1881-5] All E.R. Rep. 427 241
Tilley *v.* Thomas (1867), L.R. 3 Ch. App. 61 ; 17 L.T. 422 ; 32 J.P. 180 ; 16 W.R. 166 82

PAGE

Tilley's Will Trusts, *Re*, Burgin *v.* Croad, [1967] Ch. 1179 ; [1967] 2 W.L.R. 1533 ; [1967] 2 All E.R. 303 ; 111 S.J. 237 523
Tipton Green Colliery Co. *v.* Tipton Moat Colliery Co. (1877), 7 Ch.D. 192 ; 47 L.J.Ch. 152 ; 26 W.R. 348 237
Toller *v.* Carteret (1705), 2 Vern. 494 ; 23 E.R. 916 ; 1 Eq. Cas. Abr. 134, pl. 5 ; 21 E.R. 938 ; Anon., 1 Salk. 404 ; 91 E.R. 351 14
Tollet *v.* Tollet (1728), 2 P. Wms. 489 ; 24 E.R. 828 ; 2 Eq. Cas. Abr. 663, pl. 10 ; 22 E.R. 557 ; *sub nom.* Tollet's Case, Mos. 46 ; 25 E.R. 262 . 366
Tomlin *v.* Luce (1889), 43 Ch.D. 191 ; 59 L.J.Ch. 164 ; 62 L.T. 18 ; 54 J.P. 486 ; 38 W R. 323 ; 6 T.L.R. 103 254
Tomlinson *v.* Harrison (1802), 8 Ves. 32 ; 32 E R. 262 561
Tong, *Re*, Hilton *v.* Bradbury, [1931] 1 Ch. 202 ; 100 L.J.Ch. 132 ; 144 L.T. 260 ; [1930] All E.R. Rep. 262 282
Tongue, *Re*, Burton, *Re*, Higginson *v.* Burton, [1915] 1 Ch. 390 ; 84 L.J. Ch. 378 ; 112 L.T. 685 ; *on appeal,* [1915] 2 Ch. 283 ; 84 L.J.Ch. 933 ; 113 L.T.839 402
Took *v.* — (1784), Dick. 785 ; 21 E.R. 476 ; *sub nom.* Tooke *v.* Hartley (1786), 2 Bro. C.C. 125 ; 29 E.R. 73 249
Torkington *v.* Magee, [1902] 2 K.B. 427 ; 71 L.J.K.B. 712 ; 87 L.T. 304 ; 18 T.L.R. 703 ; [1900-3] All E.R. Rep 991 ; *on appeal,* [1903] 1 K.B. 644 ; 72 L.J.K.B. 336 ; 88 L.T. 443 ; 19 T.L.R. 331 327-8
Torquay Hotel Co. Ltd. *v.* Cousins, [1969] 2 W.L.R. 289 ; [1969] 1 All E.R. 522 ; 6 K.I.R. 15 479
Torrance *v.* Bolton (1872), L.R. 8 Ch. App. 118 ; 42 L.J.Ch. 177 ; 27 L.T. 738 ; 37 J.P. 164 ; 21 W.R. 134 330
Tourville *v.* Naish (1734), 3 P. Wms. 307 ; 24 E.R. 1077 . . . 301
Townley, *Re*, Public Trustee *v.* Allder, [1922] 1 Ch. 154 ; 91 L.J.Ch. 258 ; 126 L.T. 591; 66 S.J. 157 ; [1921] All E.R. Rep. 586 . . . 435
Townley *v.* Bedwell (1808), 14 Ves. 591 ; 33 E.R. 648 ; 9 R.R 352 . . 382
Townley *v.* Sherborne (1634), Bridg. J. 35 ; 123 E.R. 1181 ; *sub nom.* Townley *v.* Chalenor, Cro. Car. 312 ; 79 E.R. 872 ; *sub nom.* Townley *v.* Shurborne, Tot. 88 ; 21 E.R. 132 150
Townshend (Marquis) *v.* Stangroom (1801), 6 Ves. 328 ; 31 E.R. 1076 ; [1775-1802] All E.R. Rep. 145 ; 5 R.R. 312 . . . 530, 531
Townshend (Lord) *v.* Windham (1750), 2 Ves. Sen. 1 ; 28 E.R. 1 ; [1558-1774] All E.R. Rep. 428 285
Trafford *v.* Boehm (1746), 3 Atk. 440 ; 26 E.R. 1054 ; [1558-1774] All E.R. Rep. 470 392
Tredennick *v.* Tredennick, [1900] 1 I.R. 354 368
Trego *v.* Hunt, [1896] A.C. 7 ; 65 L.J.Ch. 1 ; 73 L.T. 514 ; 44 W.R. 225 ; 12 T.L.R. 80 ; [1895-9] All E.R. Rep. 804 474-5
Tregoning *v.* Attenborough (1830), 7 Bing. 97 ; 131 E.R. 37 ; 4 Moo. & P. 722 ; 9 L.J.O S.C.P. 28 ; 33 R.R. 397 114
Triffitt's Settlement, *Re*, Hall *v.* Hyde, [1958] Ch. 852 ; [1958] 2 W.L.R. 927; [1958] 2 All E.R. 299 ; 102 S.J. 382 368
Troughton *v.* Binkes (1801), 6 Ves. 573 ; 31 E.R. 1202 ; 5 R.R. 401 . . 190
Truckell *v.* Stock, [1957] 1 W.L.R. 161 ; [1957] 1 All E.R. 74 ; 101 S.J. 108 . . . . 457, 465
Truman, Hanbury, Buxton & Co. Ltd.'s Application, *Re*, [1956] 1 Q.B. 261 ; [1955] 3 W.L.R. 704 ; [1955] 3 All E.R. 559 ; 99 S.J. 796 . 469
Trytel, *Re*, *Ex parte* Trustee of the Property of the Bankrupt *v.* Performing Right Soc. Ltd., [1952] 2 T.L.R. 32 ; [1952] W.N. 355 . . . 324
Tucker *v.* Bennett (1887), 38 Ch.D. 1 ; 57 L.J.Ch. 507 ; 58 L.T. 650 ; 344, 533
Tuckey *v.* Henderson (1863), 33 Beav. 174 ; 55 E.R. 33 ; 9 Jur. N.S. 1306 ; 11 W.R. 1013 ; 140 R.R. 76 427
Tulk *v.* Moxhay (1848), 2 Ph. 774 ; 41 E.R. 1143 ; 1 H. & Tw. 105 ; 18 L.J.Ch. 83 ; 13 L.T.O.S. 21 ; 13 Jur. 89 ; [1843-60] All E.R. Rep. 9 ; 78 R.R. 289 . . . . 11, 235, 468
Turner, *Re*, Barker *v.* Ivimey, [1897] 1Ch. 536; 66 L.J.Ch. 282; 76 L.T. 116; 45 W.R. 495 ; 13 T.L.R. 249 ; 41 S.J. 313 31
Turner *v.* Collins (1871), L.R. 7 Ch. App. 329 ; 41 L.J. Ch. 558 ; 25 L.T. 779 ; 20 W.R. 305 344
Turner *v.* Green, [1895] 2 Ch. 205 ; 64 L.J.Ch. 539 ; 72 L.T. 763 ; 43 W.R. 537 ; 13 R. 551 ; 39 S.J. 484 30

PAGE

Turner *v.* Richmond (1688), 2 Vern. 81 ; 23 E.R. 663 174
Turner *v.* Walsh, [1909] 2 K.B. 484 ; 78 L.J.K.B. 753 ; 100 L.T. 832 ; 25 T.L.R. 605 ; [1908-10] All E.R. Rep. 822 223
Turton *v.* Benson (1718), 1 P Wms. 496 ; 24 E.R. 488 ; 2 Vern. 764 ; 23 E.R. 1099 ; 1 Eq. Cas. Abr. 45, pl. 5 ; 21 E.R. 862 ; *on appeal* (1719), Prec. Ch. 522 ; 24 E.R. 234 ; 10 Mod. 445 ; 88 E.R. 803 ; 1 Stra. 240 ; 93 E.R. E.R. 498 ; 1 Eq. Cas. Abr. 88, pl. 2 ; 21 E.R. 900 307
Twentieth Century Fox Film Corp. *v.* Gala Film Distributors Ltd., [1957] R.P.C. 105 470
Twining *v.* Morrice (1788), 2 Bro. C.C. 326 ; 29 E.R. 182 ; [1775-1802] All E.R. Rep. 494 501
Twisden *v.* Twisden (1804), 9 Ves. 413 ; 32 E.R. 661 ; 7 R.R. 251 . . 421
Twopeny's Settlement, *Re*, Monro *v.* Twopeny, [1924] 1 Ch. 522 ; 93 L.J.Ch. 323 ; 130 L.T. 816 ; 68 S.J. 402 385
Tyler, *Re*, Graves *v.* King, [1967] 1 W.L.R. 1269 ; *sub nom. Re* Tyler's Fund Trusts, [1967] 3 All E.R. 389 ; 111 S.J. 794 299
Tyler *v.* Goodwin (1888), 23 L.R. Ir. 13 458
Tyler *v.* Lake (1831), 2 Russ. & M. 183 ; 39 E.R. 364 ; 34 R.R. 53 . . 444
Tyler *v.* Yates (1871), L.R. 6 Ch. App. 665 ; 40 L.J.Ch. 768 ; 25 L.T. 284 ; 36 J.P. 180 ; 19 W.R. 909 354
Tyler's Fund Trusts, *Re—see* Tyler, *Re*.
Tyrrel's (Jane) Case (1557), 2 Dyer 155a ; 73 E.R. 336 149

Ulster Land, Building and Investment Co., *Re*, *Ex parte* Fitzsimon (1889), 25 L.R. Ir. 24 523
Underhill *v.* Horwood (1804), 10 Ves. 209 ; 32 E.R. 824 ; [1803-13] All E.R. Rep. 122 ; *sub nom.* Ware *v.* Horwood (1807), 14 Ves. 28 ; 33 E.R. 432 ; *sub nom.* Horwood *v.* Underhill (1808), 10 East 123 ; 103 E.R. 722 ; (1812), 4 Taunt. 346 ; 128 E.R. 364 554
Underwood, *Re*, *Re* Bowles, U. *v.* W. (1903), 51 W.R. 335 ; 47 S.J. 256 . 561
Underwood (A.L.) Ltd. *v.* Bank of Liverpool, [1924] 1 K.B. 775 ; 93 L.J.K.B. 690 ; 131 L.T. 271 ; 40 T.L.R. 302 ; 68 S.J. 716 ; 29 Com. Cas. 182 ; [1924] All E.R. Rep. 230 115-16
Union *v.* M'Dermott (1921), 55 I.L.T.R. 194 89
Union Bank of London *v.* Ingram (1882), 20 Ch.D. 463 ; 51 L.J. Ch. 508 ; 46 L.T. 507 ; 30 W.R. 375 246
United Dominions Trust (Commercial) Ltd. *v.* Ennis, [1968] 1 Q.B. 54 ; [1967] 3 W.L.R. 1 ; [1967] 2 All E.R. 345 ; 111 S.J. 191 . . . . 23, 24
United States of America *v.* Motor Trucks Ltd., [1924] A.C. 196 ; 93 L.J.P.C. 46 ; 130 L.T. 129 ; 39 T.L.R. 723 539
Usborne *v.* Usborne (1740), Dick. 75 ; 21 E.R. 196 223
Uvedale *v.* Halfpenny (1723), 2 P. Wms. 151 ; 24 E.R. 677 532

Van den Bergh's Will Trusts, *Re*, Van den Bergh *v.* Simpson, [1948] 1 All E.R. 935 ; 92 S.J. 324 414
Van der Linde *v.* Van der Linde, [1947] Ch. 306 ; [1947] L.J.R. 592 ; 176 L.T. 297 ; 91 S.J. 131 531
Vanderpant *v.* Mayfair Hotel Co. Ltd., [1930] 1 Ch. 138 ; 99 L.J. Ch. 84 ; 142 L.T. 198 ; 94 J.P. 23 ; 27 L.G.R. 752 ; [1929] All E.R. Rep. 296 . 465
Vandervell *v.* Inland Revenue Commissioners, [1967] 2 A.C. 291 ; [1967] 2 W.L.R. 87 ; [1967] 1 All E.R. 1 ; 110 S.J. 910 ; 45 A.T.C. 394 . . 299
Vandervell Products Ltd. *v.* McCleod, [1957] R.P.C. 185 472
Vanderzee *v.* Aclom (1799), 4 Ves. 771 ; 31 E.R. 399 365
Vane *v.* Lord Barnard (1716), 2 Vern. 738 ; 23 E.R. 1082 ; *sub nom.* Vane *v.* Lord Bernard, 1 Salk. 161 ; 91 E.R. 150 ; 1 Eq. Cas. Abr. 399, pl. 3 ; 21 E.R. 1131 ; *sub nom.* Lord Bernard's Case, Gilb. Ch. 127 ; 25 E.R. 89 ; Prec. Ch. 454 ; 24 E.R. 203 . . . . 67, 80, 464
Van Grutten *v.* Foxwell, [1897] A.C. 658 ; 66 L.J.Q.B. 745 ; 77 L.T. 170 ; 46 W.R. 426 66
Van Lynn Developments Ltd. *v.* Pelias Construction Co. Ltd., [1969] 1 Q.B. 607 ; [1968] 3 W.L.R. 1141 ; [1968] 3 All E.R. 824 ; 112 S.J. 819 . . 326
Vardon's Trusts, *Re* (1885), 31 Ch.D. 275 ; 44 L.J.Ch. 259 ; 53 L.T. 895 ; 34 W.R. 185 ; 2 T.L.R. 204 . . . . 400, 401
Vatcher *v.* Paull, [1915] A.C. 372 ; 84 L.J.P.C. 86 ; 112 L.T. 737 ; [1914-15] All E.R. Rep. 609 369

PAGE

Vaux, *Re*, Nicholson *v.* Vaux, [1939] Ch. 465 ; [1938] 4 All E.R. 297, 703 ; 108 L.J.Ch. 60, 211 ; 160 L.T. 65 , 74 ; 55 T.L.R. 92, 230 ; 82 S.J. 949, 1048 . . . . 419, 423
Venning, *Re* (1947), 63 T.L.R. 394 124
Vernon *v.* Bethell (1762), 2 Eden 110 ; 28 E.R. 838 177
Vickery, *Re*, Vickery *v.* Stephens, [1931] 1 Ch. 572 ; 100 L.J.Ch. 138 ; 144 L.T. 168 ; 47 T.L.R. 242 ; [1931] All E.R. Rep. 562 . . 106, 160
Voisey, *Ex parte*, *Re* Knight (1882), 21 Ch.D. 442 ; 52 L.J.Ch. 121 ; 47 L.T. 362 ; 31 W.R. 19 232

W. *v.* B. (1863), 32 Beav. 574 ; 55 E.R. 226 ; 138 R.R. 874 ; *sub nom.* Willyams *v.* Bullmore, 33 L.J.Ch. 461 ; 9 L.T. 216 ; 9 Jur. N.S. 1115 ; 11 W.R. 506 552
Wake *v.* Wake (1791), 1 Ves. Jun. 335 ; 30 E.R. 372 ; 3 Bro. C.C. 255 ; 29 E.R. 521 407
Wakeham *v.* Mackenzie, [1968] 1 W.L.R. 1175 ; [1968] 2 All E.R. 783 ; 112 S.J. 504 495
Walker, *Ex parte*, *Re* Shrewsbury and Hereford Railway (1853), 1 Drew. 508 ; 61 E.R. 546 ; 94 R.R. 760 ; *sub nom. Re* Walker's Estate, 22 L.J. Ch. 888 ; 1 Eq. R. 247 ; 21 L T.O.S. 148 ; 17 Jur. 706 ; 1 W.R. 378 . . 381
Walker, *Re*, Goodwin *v.* Scott, [1921] 2 Ch. 63 ; 90 L J.Ch. 433 ; 125 L.T. 764 ; 65 S.J. 534 ; [1921] All E.R. Rep. 163 380
Walker *v.* Armstrong (1856), 8 De G.M. & G. 531 ; 44 E.R. 495 ; 25 L.J. Ch. 738 ; 27 L.T.O.S. 329 ; 2 Jur. N.S. 959 ; 4 W.R. 770 ; 114 R.R. 234 . 531
Walker *v.* Denne (1793), 2 Ves. 170 ; 30 E.R. 577 ; [1775-1802] All E.R. Rep. 245 ; 2 R.R. 185 391
Walker *v.* Jones (1866), L.R. 1 P.C. 50 ; 3 Moo. P. C. N. S. 397 ; 16 E.R. 151 ; 35 L.J.P.C. 30 ; 14 L.T. 686 ; 12 Jur. N.S. 381 ; 14 W.R. 484 ; 146 R.R. 114 . . . . 188, 191
Walker *v.* Linom, [1907] 2 Ch. 104 ; 76 L.J.Ch. 1500 ; 97 L.T. 92 ; 51 S.J. 483 215
Walker's Estate, *Re—see* Walker, *Ex parte*.
Wallace's Settlements, *Re*, Fane *v.* Wallace, [1968] 1 W.L.R. 711 ; [1968] 2 All E.R. 209 ; 112 S.J. 381 371
Waller *v.* Fowler (1837), S. & Sc. 274 562
Walpole, *Re*, Public Trustee *v.* Canterbury, [1933] Ch. 431 ; 102 L.J. Ch. 209 ; 148 L.T. 526 ; [1933] All E.R. Rep. 988 388
Walpole (Lord) *v.* Lord Orford (1797), 3 Ves. 402 ; 30 E.R. 1076 ; 4 R.R. 38 493
Walsh *v.* Lonsdale (1882), 21 Ch.D. 9 ; 52 L.J.Ch. 2 ; 46 L.T. 858 ; 31 W.R. 109 . . . . 17, 36, 85-93, 448
Walton *v.* Cook (1888), 40 Ch.D. 325 ; 58 L.J.Ch. 180 ; 60 L.T. 91 ; 37 W.R. 189 554
Ward *v.* Buckingham (Duke of) (1725), 3 Bro. P.C. 581 ; 1 E.R. 1511 . 552
Ward *v.* Duncombe, [1893] A.C. 369 ; 62 L.J.Ch. 881 ; 69 L.T. 121 ; 42 W.R. 59 ; 1 R. 224 . . . . 302, 305, 306
Ward *v.* Kirkland, [1967] Ch. 194 ; [1966] 1 W.L.R. 601 ; [1966] 1 All E.R. 609 ; 110 S.J. 289 40
Ware *v.* Horwood (1807), 14 Ves. 28 ; 33 E.R. 432 554
Waring (Lord) *v.* London and Manchester Assurance Co. Ltd., [1935] Ch. 310 ; 104 L.J. Ch. 201 ; 152 L.T. 390 ; 78 S.J. 860 ; [1934] All E.R. Rep. 642 253
Warner, *Ex parte* (1812), 19 Ves. 202 ; 34 E.R. 493 ; 12 R.R. 169 ; *sub nom. Re* Cooke, *Ex parte* Warner, 1 Rose 286 183
Warner *v.* Jacob (1882), 20 Ch.D. 220 ; 51 L.J. Ch. 642 ; 46 L.T. 656 ; 46 J.P. 436 ; 30 W.R. 731 253
Warner Bros. Pictures Inc. *v.* Nelson, [1937] 1 K.B. 209 ; [1936] 3 All E.R. 160 ; 106 L.J.K.B. 97 ; 155 L.T. 538 ; 53 T.L.R. 14 ; 80 S.J. 855 . . 473
Warren *v.* Warren (1783), 1 Bro. C.C. 305 ; 28 E.R. 1149 ; 1 Cox C.C. 41 ; 29 E.R 1053 419
Wasdale, *Re*, Brittin *v.* Partridge, [1899] 1 Ch. 163 ; 68 L.J Ch. 117 ; 79 L.T. 520 ; 47 W.R. 169 ; 15 T.L.R. 97 ; 43 S.J. 126 306
Waterford (Marquis of) *v.* Knight (1844), 11 Cl. & Fin. 653 ; 8 E.R. 1250 ; 9 Jur. 335 74
Watson, *Re*, *Ex parte* Official Receiver in Bankruptcy (1890), 25 Q.B.D. 27 ; 59 L.J.Q.B. 394 ; 63 L.T. 209 ; 38 W.R. 567 ; 6 T.L.R. 332 ; 7 Morr. 155 179

PAGE

Watson *v.* Burton, [1957] 1 W.L.R. 19 ; [1956] 3 All E.R. 929 . . . 507
Watson *v.* Mid Wales Railway Co. (1867), L.R. 2 C.P. 593 ; 36 L.J.C.P. 285 ; 17 L.T. 94 ; 15 W.R. 1107 309
Watt *v.* Mortlock, [1964] Ch. 84 ; [1963] 2 W.L.R. 626 ; [1963] 1 All E.R. 388 ; 107 S.J. 235 558
Watts *v.* Symes (1851), 1 De G.M. & G. 240 ; 42 E.R. 544 ; 21 L.J.Ch. 713 ; 18 L.T.O.S. 216 ; 16 Jur. 114 ; 91 R.R. 69 202
Weall *v.* Rice (1831), 2 Russ. & M. 251 ; 39 E.R. 390 ; 9 L.J.O.S.Ch. 116 ; 34 R.R. 83 420
Webb *v.* Crosse, [1912] 1 Ch. 323 ; 81 L.J.Ch. 259 ; 105 L.T. 867 ; 56 S.J. 177 . . . . 188, 191
Webb *v.* Hewitt (1857), 3 K. & J. 438 ; 69 E.R. 1181 ; 29 L.T.O.S. 225 ; 112 R.R. 224 121
Webb *v.* Paternoster (1619), Poph. 151 ; 79 E.R. 1250 ; 2 Rolle 143 ; 81 E.R. 713 ; Godb. 282 ; 78 E.R. 165 ; *sub nom.* Webbe *v.* Paternoster, 2 Rolle 152 ; 81 E.R. 719 ; *sub nom.* Web *v.* Pater noster, Palm. 71 ; 81 E.R. 983 ; *sub nom.* Plummer *v.* Webb, Noy 98 ; 74 E.R. 1064 97
Webb *v.* Smith (1885), 30 Ch.D. 192 ; 55 L.J.Ch. 343 ; 53 L.T. 737 ; 1 T.L.R. 225 434
Webster *v.* Bosanquet, [1912] A.C. 394 ; 81 L.J.P.C. 205 ; 106 L.T. 357 ; 28 T.L.R. 271 20
Wedgerfield *v.* De Bernardy (1908), 25 T.L.R. 21 355
Weekes' Settlement, *Re*, [1897] 1 Ch. 289 ; 66 L.J.Ch. 179 ; 76 L.T. 112 ; 45 W.R. 265 ; 41 S.J. 225 363
Weir Hospital, *Re*, [1910] 2 Ch. 124 ; 79 L.J.Ch. 723 ; 102 L.T. 882 ; 26 T.L.R. 519 ; 54 S.J. 600 ; [1908-10] All E.R. Rep. 690 158
Weld *v.* Petre, [1929] 1 Ch. 33 ; 97 L.J.Ch. 399 ; 139 L.T. 596 ; 44 T.L.R. 739 ; 72 S.J. 569 ; *sub nom.* Weld-Blundell *v.* Petre, [1928] All E.R. Rep. 564 196-7
Weld-Blundell *v.* Wolseley, [1903] 2 Ch. 664 ; 73 L.J. Ch. 45 ; 89 L.T. 59 ; 51 W.R. 635 ; 47 S.J. 653 80
Wellesley (Lady) *v.* Earl of Mornington (1855), 2 K. & J. 143 ; 69 E.R. 728 ; 1 Jur. N.S. 1202 ; 110 R.R. 143 371
Wellesley *v.* Lord Mornington (1869), 17 W.R. 355 435
Wells, *Re*, Swinburne-Hanham *v.* Howard, [1933] Ch. 29 ; 101 L.J. Ch. 346 ; 148 L.T. 5 ; 48 T.L.R. 617 ; [1932] All E.R. Rep. 277 . . 187
Welwood *v.* Grady, [1904] 1 I.R. 388 527
Wenham, *Re*, Hunt *v.* Wenham, [1892] 3 Ch. 59 ; 61 L.J.Ch. 565 ; 67 L.T. 648 ; 40 W.R. 636 ; 36 S.J. 540 280
Wenlock (Baroness) *v.* River Dee Co. (1887), 19 Q.B.D. 155 ; 56 L.J.Q.B. 589 57 L.T. 320 ; 35 W.R. 822 ; 3 T.L.R. 603 115
West *v.* Sackville (Lord), [1903] 2 Ch. 378 ; 72 L.J.Ch. 649 ; 88 L.T. 814 ; 51 W.R. 625 ; 19 T.L.R. 541 ; 47 S.J. 581 . . . . . 555, 556
West *v.* Williams, [1899] 1 Ch. 132 ; 68 L.J. Ch. 127 ; 79 L.T. 575 ; 47 W.R. 308 221
West (Richard) and Partners (Inverness) Ltd. *v.* Dick, [1969] 2 W.L.R. 383 ; [1969] 1 All E.R. 289 ; *on appeal*, [1969] 2 W.L.R. 1190 ; [1969] 1 All E.R. 943 ; 113 S.J. 165 14
Westerton, *Re*, Public Trustee *v.* Gray, [1919] 2 Ch. 104 ; 88 L.J. Ch. 392 ; 63 S.J. 410 328
West London Commercial Bank *v.* Reliance Permanent Building Soc. (1885), 29 Ch.D. 954 ; 54 L.J.Ch. 1081 ; 53 L.T. 442 ; 33 W.R. 916 ; 1 T.L.R. 609 257
Westminster Bank Ltd. *v.* Lee, [1956] Ch. 7 ; [1955] 3 W.L.R. 376 ; [1955] 2 All E.R. 883 ; 99 S.J. 562 . . . . 103, 104
West Penwith R.D.C. *v.* Gunnell, [1968] 1 W.L.R. 1153 ; [1968] 2 All E. R. 1005 ; 113 S.J. 442 230
Westropp's Estate, *Re*, *Ex parte* Westropp (1903), 37 I.L.T.R. 183 . . 368
Wetherell, *Ex parte* (1805), 11 Ves. 398 ; 32 E.R. 1141 182
Wharton *v.* Lord Durham—*see* Durham (Earl of) *v.* Wharton.
Wheatley, *Re*, Smith *v.* Spence (1884), 27 Ch.D. 606 ; 54 L.J.Ch. 201 ; 51 L.T. 681 ; 33 W.R. 275 401
Whelan *v.* Palmer (1888), 39 Ch.D. 648 ; 57 L.J.Ch. 784 ; 58 L.T. 937 ; 36 W.R. 587 ; 4 T.L.R. 486 373
Whishall *v.* Short—*see* Wichalse *v.* Short.

PAGE

Whishaw *v.* Stephens, [1968] 3 W.L.R. 1127 ; 112 S.J. 882 ; *sub nom. Re* Gulbenkian's Settlement Trusts, Whishaw *v.* Stephens, [1968] 3 All E.R. 785 362
Whistler *v.* Webster (1794), 2 Ves. Jun. 367 ; 30 E.R. 676 ; 2 R.R. 260 403, 404
Whitaker, *Re*, Whitaker *v.* Palmer, [1901] 1 Ch. 9 ; 70 L.J.Ch. 6 ; 83 L.T. 449 ; 49 W.R. 106 ; 17 T.L.R. 24 ; 45 S.J. 43 . . . 79, 278-9
Whitbread, *Ex parte* (1812), 19 Ves. 209 ; 34 E.R. 496 ; *sub nom. Re* Shaw, *Ex parte* Whitbread, 1 Rose 299 182
White *v.* City of London Brewery Co. (1889), 42 Ch.D. 237 ; 58 L.J. Ch. 855 ; 61 L.T. 741 ; 38 W.R. 82 ; 5 T.L.R. 553 . . . . 236, 261
White *v.* Metcalf, [1903] 2 Ch. 567 ; 72 L.J.Ch. 712 ; 89 L.T. 164 ; 52 W.R. 280 241
White *v.* White (1882), 22 Ch.D. 555 ; 31 W.R. 451 404
White's Settlement, *Re*, Pitman *v.* White, [1930] 1 Ch. 179 ; 99 L.J.Ch. 49 ; 142 L.T. 279 ; 46 T.L.R. 30 385
Whitehouse *v.* Partridge (1818), 3 Swanst. 365 ; 36 E.R. 896 ; 19 R.R. 216 . 562
Whiteley *v.* Delaney, [1914] A.C. 132 ; 83 L.J.Ch. 349 ; 110 L.T. 434 ; 58 S.J. 218 . . . . 194-5, 261
White Rose Cottage, *Re*, [1965] Ch. 940 ; [1965] 2 W.L.R. 337 ; [1965] 1 All E.R. 11 ; 108 S.J. 917 252
Whitting, *Re*, *Ex parte* Rowell—*see* Hall, *Ex parte*.
Whittingham *v.* Thornburgh (1690), 2 Vern. 206 ; 23 E.R. 734 ; *sub nom.* Wittingham *v.* Thornborough, Prec. Ch. 20 ; 24 E.R. 11 ; 2 Eq. Cas. Abr. 635, pl. 1 ; 22 E.R. 533 552
Whitwood Chemical Co. *v.* Hardman, [1891] 2 Ch. 416 ; 60 L.J.Ch. 428 ; 64 L.T. 716 ; 39 W.R. 433 ; 7 T.L.R. 325 473
Wichalse *v.* Short (1713), 3 Bro. P.C. 558 ; 1 E.R. 1497 ; *sub nom.* Whishall *v.* Short, 2 Eq. Cas. Abr. 177, pl. 1 ; 22 E.R. 151 248
Wickham, *Re* (1917), 34 T.L.R. 158 ; [1917] H.B.R. 272 . . . 123
Wigsell *v.* Wigsell (1825), 2 Sim. & St. 364 ; 57 E.R. 385 ; 4 L.J.O.S. Ch. 84 ; 25 R.R. 224 193
Wilks, *Re*, Keefer *v.* Wilks, [1935] Ch. 645 ; 104 L.J.Ch. 297 ; 153 L.T. 255 ; 51 T.L.R. 489 269
Willes *v.* Greenhill (1860), 29 Beav. 376, 387 ; 54 E.R. 673, 677 ; 30 L.J. Ch. 808 ; 9 W.R. 217 ; 131 R.R. 624, 631 ; *on appeal* (1861), 4 De G. F. & J. 147 ; 45 E.R. 1139 ; 31 L.J.Ch. 1 ; 5 L.T. 336 ; 7 Jur. (N.S.) 1134 ; 10 W.R. 33 ; 131 R.R. 636 . . . . 306, 308
Willes *v.* Levett (1847), 1 De G. & Sm. 392 ; 63 E.R. 1119 238
Willett *v.* Winnell (1687), 1 Vern. 488 ; 23 E.R. 611 177
Williams, *Ex parte*, *Re* Thompson (1877), 7 Ch.D. 138 ; 47 L.J. Bcy. 26 ; 37 L.T. 764 ; 26 W.R. 274 232
Williams, *Ex parte* (1880)—*see* Raggett, *Re*.
Williams, *Re*, Richards *v.* Williams, [1930] 2 Ch. 378 ; 99 L.J. Ch. 476 ; 143 L.T. 630 ; [1930] All E.R. Rep. 642 282
Williams *v.* Atlantic Assurance Co. Ltd., [1933] 1 K.B. 81 ; 102 L.J.K.B. 241 ; 148 L.T. 313 ; 37 Com. Cas. 304 ; 18 Asp. M.L.C. 334 ; [1932] All E.R. Rep. 32 327
Williams *v.* Bayley (1866), L.R. 1 H.L. 200 ; 35 L.J. Ch. 717 ; 14 L.T. 802 ; 12 Jur. N.S. 875 ; [1861-73] All E.R. Rep. 227 552
Williams *v.* Greatrex, [1957] 1 W.L.R. 31 ; [1956] 3 All E.R. 705 ; 101 S.J. 43 506
Williams *v.* Kenneally (1912), 46 I.L.T.R. 292 499
Williams *v.* Morgan, [1906] 1 Ch. 804 ; 75 L.J. Ch. 480 ; 94 L.T. 473 ; 50 S.J. 420 244
Williams *v.* Owen (1840), 5 My. & Cr. 303 ; 41 E.R. 386 ; 12 L.J. Ch. 207 ; 5 Jur. 114 ; 48 R.R. 322 179
Willie *v.* Lugg (1761), 2 Eden 78 ; 28 E.R. 825 176
Willis, *Re*, *Ex parte* Kennedy (1888) 21 Q.B.D. 384 ; 57 L.J.Q.B. 634 ; 59 L.T. 749 ; 36 W.R. 793 ; 4 T.L.R. 637 ; [1886-90] All E.R. Rep. 820 ; *sub nom. Re* Willis, *Ex parte* Willoughby de Eresby (Lady), 5 Morr. 189 . 233
Willis *v.* Barron, [1902] A.C. 271 ; 71 L.J. Ch. 609 ; 86 L.T. 805 ; 18 T.L.R. 602 ; [1900-3] All E.R. Rep. 876 341
Willoughby *v.* Willoughby (1756), 1 T.R. 763 ; 99 E.R. 1366 ; 2 Ves. Sen. 684 ; 28 E.R. 437 ; Ves. Sen. Supp. 465 ; 28 E.R. 571 ; Amb. 282 ; 27 E.R. 190 ; [1558-1774] All E.R. Rep. 335 ; 1 R.R. 397 172
Willoughby de Eresby (Lady), *Ex parte*—*see* Willis, *Re*.

PAGE

Wills, *Ex parte* (1790), 1 Ves. Jun. 162 ; 30 E.R. 281 184
Wills' Trust Deeds, *Re*, Wills *v.* Godfrey, [1964] Ch. 219 ; [1963] 2 W.L.R. 1318 ; [1963] 1 All E.R. 390 ; 107 S.J. 475 363
Willyams *v.* Bullmore—*see* W. *v.* B.
Wilmot *v.* Pike (1845), 5 Hare 14 ; 67 E.R. 808 ; 14 L.J. Ch. 469 ; 9 Jur. 839 213
Wilson, *Re*, Wilson *v.* Holloway, [1893] 2 Ch. 340 ; 62 L.J.Ch. 781 ; 68 L.T. 785 ; 41 W.R. 684 ; 37 S.J. 386 ; 3 R. 525 377
Wilson *v.* O'Leary (1871), L.R. 12 Eq. 525 ; 40 L.J. Ch. 709 ; 25 L.T. 327 ; 20 W.R. 28 ; *on appeal* (1872), L.R. 7 Ch. App. 448 ; 41 L.J.Ch. 342 ; 26 L.T. 463 ; 20 W.R. 501 427
Wilson *v.* Wilson (1848), 1 H.L.C. 538 ; 9 E.R. 870 ; 12 Jur. 467 ; 73 R.R. 158 490
Wilson *v.* Wilson (1854), 5 H.L.C. 40 ; 10 E.R. 811 ; 23 L.J.Ch. 697 ; 23 L.T.O.S. 134 ; 101 R.R. 25 531
Winchester (Bishop of) *v.* Beavor (1797), 3 Ves. 314 ; 30 E.R. 1029 . . 245
Winchester (Bishop of) *v.* Fournier (1752), 2 Ves. Sen. 445 ; 28 E.R. 284 . 552
Winchester (Bishop of) *v.* Knight (1717), 1 P. Wms. 406 ; 24 E.R. 447 . 563
Winchester (Bishop of) *v.* Paine (1805), 11 Ves. 194 ; 32 E.R. 1062 ; 8 R.R. 131 245
Winter Garden Theatre (London) Ltd. *v.* Millennium Productions Ltd., [1948] A.C. 173 ; [1947] 2 All E.R. 331 ; [1947] L.J.R. 1422 ; 177 L.T. 349 ; T.L.R. 529 ; 91 S.J. 504 . . . . 37, 94-6, 102
Wintour *v.* Clifton (1856), 8 De G. M. & G. 641 ; 44 E.R. 537 ; 26 L.J. Ch. 218 ; 28 L.T.O.S. 194 ; 3 Jur. N.S. 74 ; 5 W.R. 129 ; 111 R.R. 159 . 405
Wiseman *v.* Roper (1646), 1 Ch. Rep. 158 ; 21 E.R. 537 ; 1 Eq. Cas. Abr. 16, pl. 1 ; 21 E.R. 838 487
With *v.* O'Flanagan, [1936] Ch. 575 ; [1936] 1 All E.R. 727 ; 105 L.J. Ch. 247 ; 154 L.T. 634 ; 80 S.J. 285 545
Withrington *v.* Banks (1725), Sel. Cas. t. King 30 ; 25 E.R. 205 . . 236
Wittingham *v.* Thornborough—*see* Whittingham *v.* Thornborough.
Witty, *Re*, Wright *v.* Robinson, [1913] 2 Ch. 666 ; 83 L.J. Ch. 73 ; 109 L.T. 590 ; 58 S.J. 30 ; [1911-13] All E.R. Rep. 1009 368
Wollaston *v.* King (1869), L.R. 8 Eq. 165 ; 38 L.J.Ch. 61 ; 20 L.T. 1003 ; 17 W.R. 641 396
Wolmershausen *v.* Gullick, [1893] 2 Ch. 514 ; 62 L.J.Ch. 773 ; 68 L.T. 753 ; 9 T.L.R. 437 ; 3 R. 610 ; [1891-4] All E.R. Rep. 740 . . . 558
Wolstan *v.* Aston (1670), Hard. 511 ; 145 E.R. 573 168
Wolverhampton and Walsall Railway Co. *v.* London and North-Western Railway Co. (1873), L.R. 16 Eq. 433 ; 43 L.J. Ch. 131 484
Wolverhampton Corp. *v.* Emmons, [1901] 1 K.B. 515 ; 70 L.J.K.B. 429 ; 84 L.T. 407 ; 49 W.R. 553 ; 17 T.L.R. 234 ; 45 S.J. 256 . . . 491
Wood, *Re*, Tullett *v.* Colville, [1894] 3 Ch. 381 ; 63 L.J. Ch. 790 ; 71 L.T. 413 ; 7 R. 495 387
Wood *v.* Abrey (1818), 3 Madd. 417 ; 56 E.R. 558 ; 18 R.R. 264 . . 334
Wood *v.* Gaynon (1761), Amb. 395 ; 27 E.R. 263 464
Wood *v.* Lake (1751), Say. 3 ; 96 E.R. 783 97
Wood *v.* Leadbitter (1845), 13 M. & W. 838 ; 153 E.R. 351 ; 14 L.J. Ex. 161; 4 L.T.O.S. 433 ; 9 J.P. 312 ; 9 Jur. 187 ; [1843-60] All E.R. Rep. 190 ; 67 R.R. 831 94-102
Woodall *v.* Clifton, [1905] 2 Ch. 257 ; 74 L.J. Ch. 555 ; 93 L.T. 257 ; 54 W.R. 7 ; 21 T.L.R. 581 ; [1904-7] All E.R. Rep. 268 382
Woodcock (Jess B.) & Sons Ltd. *v.* Hobbs, [1955] 1 W.L.R. 152 ; [1955] 1 All E.R. 445 ; 99 S.J. 129 . . . . 103, 470
Woodhouse *v.* Newry Navigation Co., [1898] 1 I.R. 161 457
Woodleys, *Re* (1892), 29 L.R. Ir. 304 408
Woodward *v.* Lord Darcy (1557), 1 Plow. 184 ; 75 E.R. 282 . . . 280
Woldridge *v.* Norris (1868), L.R. 6 Eq. 410 ; 37 L.J.Ch. 640 ; 19 L.T. 144 ; 16 W.R. 965 558
Woollam *v.* Hearn (1802), 7 Ves. 211 ; 32 E.R. 86 ; [1775-1802] All E.R. Rep. 587 ; 6 R.R. 113 538
Woolridge *v.* Woolridge (1859), John. 63 ; 70 E.R. 340 ; 28 L.J. Ch. 689 ; 33 L.T.O.S. 254 ; 5 Jur. N.S. 566 ; 123 R.R. 25 404
Woolwich Equitable Building Soc. *v.* Preston, [1938] Ch. 129 ; 107 L.J.Ch. 63 ; 54 T.L.R. 80 ; 81 S.J. 943 ; *sub nom.* Woolwich Equitable Building Soc. *v.* Oriston, 158 L.T. 216 233

PAGE

Wootton, *Re*, Trotter *v.* Duffin, [1968] 1 W.L.R. 681 ; *sub nom. Re* Wootton's Will Trusts, Trotter *v.* Duffin, [1968] 2 All E.R. 618 ; 112 S.J. 174 . 362
Workingman's Benefit Building Soc. *v.* Dixon, [1908] 1 I.R. 582 . . 220
Workingmen's Benefit Building Soc. *v.* Higgins, [1945] Ir. Jur. Rep. 38 . 212
Worthing Corp. *v.* Heather, [1906] 2 Ch. 532 ; 75 L.J.Ch. 761 ; 95 L.T. 718 ; 22 T.L.R. 750 ; 50 S.J. 668 ; 4 L.G.R. 1179 ; [1904-7] All E.R. Rep. 530 382
Worthington & Co. Ltd. *v.* Abbott, [1910] 1 Ch. 588; 79 L.J.Ch. 252 ; 110 L.T. 895 ; 54 S.J. 83 249
Wortley *v.* Birkhead (1754), 2 Ves. Sen. 571 ; 28 E.R. 364 ; 3 Atk. 809 ; 26 E.R. 1262 . . . . .62, 175
Wright, *Re*, Hegan *v.* Bloor, [1920] 1 Ch. 108 ; 88 L.J.Ch. 542 ; 121 L.T. 549 ; 64 S.J. 21 ; [1918-19] All E.R. Rep. 825 . 373
Wright *v.* Carter, [1903] 1 Ch. 27 ; 72 L.J.Ch. 138 ; 87 L.T. 624 ; 51 W.R. 196 ; 19 T.L.R. 29 ; [1900-3] All E.R. Rep. 706 . . . 338, 351
Wright *v.* Goff (1856), 22 Beav. 207 ; 52 E.R. 1087 ; 25 L.J.Ch. 803 ; 27 L.T.O.S. 179 ; 2 Jur. N.S. 481 ; 4 W.R. 522 ; 111 R.R. 330 . 372, 373
Wright *v.* Macadam, [1949] 2 K.B. 744 ; [1949] 2 All E.R. 565 ; 93 S.J. 646 ; 93
Wright *v.* New Zealand Farmers Co-operative Assoc. of Canterbury Ltd., [1939] A.C. 439 ; [1939] 2 All E.R. 701 ; 108 L.J.P.C. 86 ; 55 T.L.R. 673 ; 83 S.J. 522 253
Wright *v.* Proud (1806), 13 Ves. 136 ; 33 E.R. 246 345
Wright *v.* Wright (1750), 1 Ves. Sen. 409 ; 27 E.R. 1111 ; [1558-1774] All E.R. Rep. 528 487
Wright's Estate, *Re* (1930), 64 I.L.T.R. 195 384
Wyatt *v.* Cook (1868), 16 W.R. 502 ; 18 L.T. 12 . . . 354, 355
Wyles, *Re*, Foster *v.* Wyles, [1938] Ch. 313 ; [1938] 1 All E.R. 347 ; 107 L.J. Ch. 164 ; 54 T.L.R. 336 ; 82 S.J. 95 ; *sub nom. Re* Wyles, Porter *v.* Wyles, 158 L.T. 147 289
Wynne *v.* Callander (1826), 1 Russ. 293 ; 38 E.R. 113 552
Wyse *v.* Russell (1882), 11 L.R. Ir. 173 ; 17 I.L.T.R. 31 498

Yager *v.* Musa, [1961] 2 Q.B. 214 ; [1961] 3 W.L.R. 170 ; [1961] 2 All E.R. 561 ; 105 S.J. 568 459
Yellowly *v.* Gower (1855), 11 Ex. 274 ; 156 E.R. 833 ; 24 L.J.Ex. 289 ; 105 R.R. 522 463
Yerburgh, *Re*, Yerburgh *v.* Yerburgh, [1928] W.N. 208 . . 269, 272
Yockney *v.* Hansard (1844), 3 Hare 620 ; 67 E.R. 527 ; 8 Jur. 822 . . 428
York Corp. *v.* Pilkington (1742), 2 Atk. 302 ; 26 E.R. 584 ; 9 Mod. 273 ; 88 E.R. 447 ; *sub nom.* Pilkington *v.* City of York, Dick. 84 ; 21 E.R. 199 . 459
Yorkshire Miners' Assoc. *v.* Howden, [1905] A.C. 256 . . . 478
York Union Banking Co. *v.* Artley (1879), 11 Ch.D. 205 ; 27 W.R. 704 244, 253
Young *v.* Clarey, *Re* The Statutory Trusts Declared by Section 105 of the Law of Property Act, 1925, Affecting the Proceeds of Moat House Farm, Thurlsby, [1948] Ch. 191 ; [1948] 1 All E.R. 197 ; [1948] L.J.R. 812 ; 64 T.L.R. 93 ; 92 S.J. 96 257
Young *v.* Ladies' Imperial Club Ltd., [1920] 2 K.B. 523 ; 89 L.J.K.B. 563 ; 123 L.T. 191 ; 36 T.L.R. 392 ; 64 S.J. 374 ; [1920] All E.R. Rep. 223 . 476
Young *v.* Raincock (1849), 7 C.B. 310 ; 137 E.R. 124 ; 18 L.J.C.P. 193 ; 13 L.T.O.S. 401 ; 13 Jur. 539 ; 78 R.R. 652 126

Zamet *v.* Hyman, [1961] 1 W.L.R. 1442 ; [1961] 3 All E.R. 933 ; 105 S.J. 911 345-6
Zigurds, The, [1934] A.C. 209 ; 103 L.J.P. 28 ; 150 L.T. 303 ; 39 Com. Cas. 178 ; 18 Asp. M.L.C. 475 ; 50 T.L.R. 162 ; [1933] All E.R. Rep. 717 . 300

CHAPTER I

THE NATURE OF EQUITY

EQUITY is no longer the source of law it was in the early days of the Court of Chancery. Equity as a body of principles and rules lives on. Nearly a century after the unification of judicature,[1] it is still of practical significance (though by no means as important as it once was) whether a rule applied in litigation derives from the common law or is equitable in origin. An example of this practical significance is that an equitable proprietary right is often overreached by sale of the legal title to a bona fide purchaser for value without notice of that equitable right; whereas a common law proprietary right is not generally so overreached. The derivation of a rule is not of practical significance in relation to its capacity for development. Judicial inventiveness is no greater in matters of equity than in matters of common law. Possibly the most striking achievement of case-law in the twentieth century has been the development of the tort of negligence. Some people have even claimed to emend equity with the improving virtues of common law. In *Esso Petroleum Co. Ltd.* v. *Harper's Garage* (*Stourport*) *Ltd.*,[2] Diplock, L.J., said: " I am not persuaded that mortgages of land are condemned today to linger in a jurisprudential cul-de-sac built by the Courts of Chancery before the Judicature Acts from which the robust doctrines of the common law are barred."

PRECEDENT AND THE IDEA OF EQUITY

The process of deciding a dispute between antagonists involves determining who is to win and why. The reason for a decision contains within it the germ of a rule of law, because it will be recorded or remembered and referred to in later disputes resembling the earlier dispute in some particular. When a series of precedents has come into existence, a rule of law is extracted from them by quoting the facts and decisions in abstract form, such as, *a person claiming as beneficiary to enforce an incompletely constituted trust will fail unless he has given consideration.* When the rule has become accepted, it is possible

[1] Judicature Acts, 1873 and 1875 (England); Judicature (Ireland) Act, 1877.
[2] [1966] 2 Q.B. 514, 577-8. See p. 208, *post*.

that a case will arise in which its application, owing to the particular circumstances, will result in injustice. In that case the judge may either exercise an equitable jurisdiction so as not to apply the rule (or so as to apply it in modified form) or stick to the rule in its full rigour.

In the formative period of the common law, every judge of the King's courts was considered to have authority to administer the common law, and also, if he thought fit, to by-pass the common law in the particular case and administer equity. With the emergence of Parliament, and also with the establishment of a monopoly by the common lawyers of appointments to judicial office in the King's courts, during the fourteenth century these discretionary powers of the judges were abandoned. Certainty is a virtue in the law, for people regulate their affairs by what they think the law is. But justice in individual cases is also a virtue in the law and justice may become scarcer if certainty is overdone and turned into cussed rigidity.

When the judges stick to the rules, refusing, come what may, to temper them with equity, dissatisfied citizens may react by seeking alternative adjudicative machinery, by lobbying the sovereign to change the rules or, in extreme cases, by promoting revolution. The second is the typical modus operandi of the twentieth century and accounts for the creation of the Law Commission. The first was the predominant reaction in fourteenth century England when statutory law reform was rare. Gradually a number of courts, and particularly the Court of Chancery, emerged as distinct tribunals in which equity, which was no longer available in common law courts, could be obtained. In this way it came about that equity, well known in many legal systems of the world as the power of the judges to modify their own rules, came to have a special meaning in the English legal system, namely the body of rules applied in courts of equity so as to achieve results different from those which would have ensued in trials of the same cases in a common law court. Equitable rules of this kind developed for dealing with particular topics. Equity never became a set of general principles to provide a basis for legal development to occur whenever the common law was defective or archaic. Moreover, this administration in a distinct court had the consequence that equity was extensively concerned with procedure and remedies. Indeed, these are often what give rules of equity their distinctive character.

Courts of equity started their long careers with much the same conception of equity as that which had prevailed in the common law courts before the age of rigidity set in. Gradually, however, the equity of the Chancery turned into a body of rules, authorised by sets of reported precedents. By the time of the unification of judicature in the 1870s it had become very difficult to advance a proposition in the Court of Chancery without the same apparatus of statutory and judicial authority, without the same disadvantage attaching to novelty, as was the case in the common law courts. Meanwhile, the common law itself had become more flexible. Partly as a result of judicial valour, more particularly as a result of reforming legislation in the nineteenth century, the common law had ceased to be hidebound by the forms of action. The common law and equity faced the threshhold of their matrimonial home on equal terms. Both have developed since the institution of the High Court of Justice, but neither has shown a greater capacity to do so than the other. Equity as a source of law is dead. The creativeness of the judges persists.

From the Chancellor's Foot to Standard-sized Shoes

When the common law became rigidly dominated by a writ system which, after the Statute of Westminster II in 1285, was kept within somewhat narrow bounds, the equity to correct the injustices produced by the common law fell into the hands of the Lord Chancellor. This functionary issued the writs to start common law proceedings and was well aware of the limitations of the system. He was an ecclesiastic, learned in another legal system, canon law, and therefore conversant with notions of natural law or the law of God. He was the legal member of the King's Council, to which those aggrieved by the operation of the common law addressed their petitions. Thus he was an obvious official to take over the equitable jurisdiction lately abandoned by the common law judges.

The early functions of the Lord Chancellor have never been more clearly defined than in the language of a Year Book of Edward IV—

> In the Chancery a man shall not be prejudiced by mispleading or by defects of form, but he shall be judged according to the truth of his case; and we must judge according to conscience and not according to things alleged by the parties. And there are two manners of powers and processes in the Chancery—the Ordinary and the Absolute power. The Ordinary power is the power in which a certain order is observed just as it is observed in positive law; but the law of nature has no certain order, but it acts by any means that the truth may be known, and therefore is its procedure called Absolute.

Maitland[3] draws attention to this characteristic of early equity in his first lecture, where he states: "I do not think that in the fourteenth century the Chancellors considered that they had to administer any body of substantive rules that differed from the ordinary law of the land. They were administering the law but they were administering it in cases which escaped the meshes of the ordinary courts."

So long as equity was administered by the medieval ecclesiastical Chancellors it differed neither from the earlier equity of the common law judges nor from the equity of foreign systems of law. St. Germain, whose two *Dialogues between a Doctor of Divinity and a Student of Common Law* appeared in the earlier half of Henry VIII's reign, regarded equity in his day as founded on reason and conscience—as being, in fact, the means through which the principles of natural and divine law were applied to particular cases, to correct injustices over which the common law abdicated jurisdiction. Selden,[4] in the seventeenth century, put it more rudely, that it was as if equity were measured by the length of the Chancellor's foot.

At the close of the middle ages the Chancellor ceased to be a cleric and by the seventeenth century he was almost invariably a lawyer — frequently a common lawyer. The decline of the scholastic tradition and the secularisation of equity had their effect. Then the spirit of English law began to have a perceptible influence upon the development of equity. Equitable jurisdiction started to be exercised in accordance with settled principles and its boundaries became reasonably clearly defined. Holdsworth pointed out[5] that the formulation of the rules of equity by St. Germain in 1523-1531 facilitated their later development on orthodox English lines, for the later Chancellors were able to turn to his writings for inspiration. Also in the seventeenth century, reports of equity cases began to make their appearance and then, most curious of paradoxes, the doctrine of judicial precedent turned the principles of fair dealing into a settled system as technical as the common law. This process may be regarded as having its culmination in the long tenure of the Woolsack by Lord Eldon during the first quarter of the nineteenth century. In general, the merits of the actual cases were subordinated to the intricacies of doctrine and the

[3] *Equity*, 2nd ed. (rev. Brunyate) (1936), p. 5.

[4] According to the *Table Talk of John Selden* (ed. Pollock) (1927), p. 43, he said: "Equity is a roguish thing, for law we have a measure, know what to trust to. Equity is according to the conscience of him that is Chancellor, and as it is larger or narrower so is equity. It is all one as if they should make the standard for the measure we call a foot to be the Chancellor's foot; what an uncertain measure would this be; one Chancellor has a long foot, another a short foot, a third an indifferent foot; it is the same thing in the Chancellor's conscience."

[5] *A History of English Law*, vol. V (1924), pp. 267-9.

rules of equity assumed the shape of a second body of judge-made law, existing side by side with the common law and complementary to it. The process, though, is as incomplete as it was gradual and at all times the relative emphasis given to precedent and to fairness can be seen to vary (within fairly narrow limits) from one judge to another.

The Subject-matter of Equity

Equity offered relief where the common law shoe pinched, primarily in the sphere of property transactions. Its most valuable creation is the trust, whereby the management of property could be separated from its enjoyment by regarding as owner in equity someone other than the person in whom the legal title was vested. The trust has proved a singularly adaptable institution. Used as a means of evading feudal dues in the fifteenth century, it is widely employed for the avoidance of estate duty in the twentieth. Before statutory intervention the trust made possible the development of joint stock trading enterprises. It allows property to be used for purposes where there is no single owner, for example for the holding of property for charitable purposes or for a club. It allowed medieval friars, vowed to poverty, to be endowed. It allows the twentieth century small investor to plant (through unit trusts) a small but nevertheless sturdy stake in the growth of ordinary share values.

Equity's second most spectacular creation is the mortgage. The idea of transferring land as security for repayment of a loan was known to the common law, but our modern sophisticated structure of rules is principally the product of Chancery protection of the mortgagor against the mortgagee.

Both mortgages and trusts are now largely, though not entirely, governed by statute. Where a statute covers all or much of the field, it is of no practical value to know that the previous law was equitable rather than common law. For this reason it is nowadays a matter of infrequent recollection that partnership, for example, was a product of equity. Moreover, the statutes often draw from both common law and equity and introduce innovations of their own. Much the same comment applies to notice, perpetuities, married women's property, the assignment of debts, the management of the property of persons suffering from mental illness and the administration of estates.

Administration of estates is bound up with the law of trusts; indeed, in many respects the office of personal representative is a variety of trusteeship. Neither the Trustee Act nor the Administration of Estates Act has attempted comprehensiveness in the way the Partnership Act has done. There are a number of specialised equitable doctrines currently in operation which affect the estates of deceased persons, such as the doctrine of conversion which was designed to prevent a certain type of accidental diversion of property from one class of intestate successor to another.

The equitable jurisdiction to protect infants, though not dependent on property disputes, is also in contact at points with the law of trusts. Wardship of court, despite its Dickensian (or Gilbertian) aura, is booming today as the average age of marriage goes down and occasionally takes the form of protecting the infant by sending her to jail.

Most of the rest of equitable activity can be grouped under two heads: (1) relief from fraud and (2) auxiliary remedies. As to the first, most transactions, such as contracts and transfers of property, though voidable at common law for deception, can be rescinded only in equity if improperly obtained in subtler ways such as undue influence or even, in certain cases, as a result of an honest mistake. As to the second, while the common law provided money compensation as the panacea for nearly all legal wrongs, equity concentrated on the development of specific relief. The most useful of the equitable remedies is the injunction—an order not to do, stop doing or undo something that should not be done. Another is the decree of specific performance, to compel the carrying out of a contract.

This is not exhaustive of the subject-matter of equity. It makes no mention of the many detailed doctrines, such as that governing the situation where a contract is varied by an agreement unsupported by consideration. It makes no mention of the evolution of rights from remedies, such as the rights against third parties under a restrictive covenant. It makes no mention of equity's contribution to procedure in litigation, such as allowing a party to give evidence. But it should be apparent that equity jurisdiction is widespread and diverse, even if focused on property. At the same time there are parts of the legal system upon which the finger of equity has been laid with but the lightest of touches. The Court of Chancery scarcely concerned itself with torts, except to grant injunctions when damages were not an adequate remedy. In respect of crimes even an injunction is obtainable only in the rarest circumstances. The validity and terminability of marriages, a major part of modern litigation, have never concerned equity at all.

The Equitable Approach: Natural Justice

It is not possible to regard the difference between equity and the common law as one of legal method, in the broadest sense. For several centuries equity has been built up in precisely the same way as the common law, by the analytical reasoning and analogies which are the distinctive characteristics of the doctrine of judicial precedent, interrupted with increasing frequency in modern times by legislation. It is no longer possible to say that equity differs from common law in that equity is an imperfect realisation of the conception of natural justice. A good deal of the common law is also based on natural justice. (Look in a digest of case law under the heading " Natural Justice " and the cases will be found to be concerned with common law rules of procedure.) Both common law and equity set limits to their application of principles of natural justice, though in recent years these limits have been extended.[6] Even within the acknowledged areas of equity jurisdiction, such as actions for breach of contract, defects in the common law have been left unremedied by equity, sometimes to be dealt with eventually by Parliament. For example, there is no action at common law or in equity for trade competition, even though conducted with the plain result of ruining an opponent,[7] nor for striking down agreements for price maintenance, monopolies or other restrictive practices. Moreover, there are some positive rules of equity which are not based on natural justice. Specific performance will not be granted where the court cannot control the execution of the contract (e.g. a contract for personal services). This is expediency, not natural justice. Indeed, the surprising thing about the remedy of specific performance is not the equitable jurisdiction to grant it but that the court should confine its use within the narrow boundaries which the precedents have established.

Nowadays courts make no claim to remedy in equity all injustices that the common law leaves unredressed. Twenty years ago, in *Re Diplock*,[8] the Court of Appeal said—

> . . . if the claim in equity exists it must be shown to have an ancestry founded in history and in the practice and precedents of the courts administering equity jurisdiction. It is not sufficient that because we may think that the " justice " of the present case requires it, we should invent such a jurisdiction for the first time.

Re Diplock itself was a striking illustration of this approach. In that case, money had been paid by the executors of a will to certain charities which, the House of Lords subsequently held, were not entitled to it

[6] See Newman, " The Hidden Equity " (1967), 19 *Hastings Law Journal*, 147.

[7] *Mogul S.S. Co. Ltd.* v. *McGregor, Gow & Co.*, [1892] A.C. 25.

[8] [1948] Ch. 465, 481-2. Cf. the observations of Jessel, M.R., in *Re Hallett's Estate* (1880), 13 Ch.D. 696, 710, quoted pp. 58-9, *post*.

because the bequest was void. When the next of kin sought to reclaim the money from the charities it was contended on behalf of the plaintiff that, independently of the decided cases, it was in any event inequitable for the charities to retain sums of money to which they had been shown to have no title. On this, the Court of Appeal observed[9]—

> It was said . . . that the formulation of any equitable claim against any of the respondents must at least postulate that the consciences of the respondents must in some degree be affected by their retention of the moneys paid to them which should properly have been paid to the appellants and other next-of-kin of the testator. Mr. Gray sought to defeat these claims, as it were, in limine, by denying altogether the postulate: for, said he, notwithstanding the formal invalidity of the bequest, at least it must be taken that Mr. Caleb Diplock intended the respondents or similar institutions to enjoy the residuary estate in preference to his blood relations and it does not lie, accordingly, in the mouths of the next-of-kin to allege any unconscientiousness on the part of those whose claim is in accordance with the wishes that the testator had expressed, albeit ineffectually. This argument appears to us to be wholly untenable. It is in our opinion impossible to contend that a disposition which according to the general law of the land is held to be entirely invalid can yet confer upon those who, ex hypothesi, have improperly participated under the disposition, some moral or equitable right to retain what they have received against those whom the law declares to be properly entitled.

This conservative attitude towards the possibilities of effectuating the intentions of parties, while not universal among judges, has been fairly typical of equity adjudication during the last century and this one. It is a long way removed from the adventurousness of the seventeenth century as exemplified in the invention of the doctrine of secret trusts by Lord Jeffreys, L.C., so as to uphold a disposition taking effect on death despite the absence of the testamentary formalities required by the Statute of Frauds. This conservative attitude tends to push in the direction of defining equity in the second half of the twentieth century as the application or evolution of doctrines administered in the separate courts of equity prior to the Judicature Acts. That is neither edifying nor useful. Fortunately, it is not the whole story. If it were, the continuance in modern English law of the dualism of common law and equity would be indefensible.

9 [1948] Ch. 476.

The Equitable Approach: Acting In Personam

(1) *General*

It is in the method of operation that one finds the distinction between common law and equity: that equity acts in personam. The caution shown by the framers of the Judicature Acts, in amalgamating the courts but not purporting to abolish all distinctions between the types of law the new single court was to administer, was probably justified and wise. A fusion of the two systems was attempted by Lord Mansfield in the eighteenth century, but the attempt failed, and Lord Mansfield's decisions were overruled, because, according to Holdsworth,[10] they were based on the fallacy of ignoring the characteristic of equity of acting in personam and of underrating the substantive differences produced by procedural differences. The difference between the two systems can be illustrated by comparing the right of a principal to recover property or its proceeds from his agent at common law with the complex remedy of a cestui que trust to follow trust property in equity. The right at common law disappears when the thing can no longer be identified, either through destruction or through conversion into some non-identifiable form. " On the other hand, the basis of the equitable right of a *cestui que trust* to follow trust property, is the right of an equitable owner to assert his equitable ownership over any property, which has come to represent the property of which he once had equitable ownership, but of which he has ceased to have equitable ownership, because it has been wrongfully disposed of by his trustee. In effect, he is allowed to assert his proprietary right, not to the original *res* which has disappeared and cannot be identified, but to a different *res* which represents it."[11] The Court of Appeal, in *Re Diplock*,[12] gave a full explanation of this difference in attitude of equity and the common law—

> The common law approached [these questions] in a strictly materialistic way. It could only appreciate what might almost be called the " physical " identity of one thing with another. It could treat a person's money as identifiable so long as it had not become mixed with other money. It could treat as identifiable with the money other kinds of property acquired by means of it, provided that there was no admixture of other money. It is noticeable that in this latter case the common law did not base itself on any known theory of tracing such as that adopted in equity. It proceeded on the basis that the unauthorized act of purchasing was one capable

[10] " Blackstone's Treatment of Equity " (1929), 43 *Harvard Law Review*, 1, 13-24.

[11] Holdsworth, review of Ashburner's *Principles of Equity*, 2nd ed. (1933), 49 *Law Quarterly Review*, 576, 578.

[12] [1948] Ch. 465, 518-20.

of ratification by the owner of the money. . . . Certain words of Lord Haldane in *Sinclair* v. *Brougham*[13] may appear to suggest a further limitation, i.e. that " money " as we have used that word was not regarded at common law as identifiable once it had been paid into a banking account.[14] We do not, however, think it necessary to discuss this point at length. We agree with the comments of Wynn-Parry J. upon it[15] and those of Atkin L.J. (as he then was) in *Banque Belge pour l'Etranger* v. *Hambrouck*.[16] If it is possible to identify a principal's money with an asset purchased exclusively by means of it we see no reason for drawing a distinction between a chose in action such as a banker's debt to his customer and any other asset. If the principal can ratify the acquisition of the one, we see no reason for supposing that he cannot ratify the acquisition of the other.

We may mention three several matters which we think are helpful in understanding the limitation of the common law doctrine and the reasons why equity was able to take a more liberal view. They are as follows:

(1) The common law did not recognize equitable claims to property, whether money or any other form of property. Sovereigns in A's pocket either belonged in law to A or they belonged in law to B. The idea that they could belong in law to A and that they should nevertheless be treated as belonging to B was entirely foreign to the common law. This is the reason why the common law doctrine finds its typical exemplification in cases of principal and agent. If B, a principal, hands cash to A, his agent, in order that it may be applied in a particular manner, the cash, in the eyes of the common law, remains the property of B. If, therefore, A, instead of applying it in the authorized manner, buries it in a sack in his garden or uses it for an unauthorized purchase, B can, in the former case, recover the cash as being still his own property and, in the latter case, affirm the purchase of something bought with his money by his agent. If, however, the relationship of A and B was not one which left the property in the cash in B but merely constituted a relationship of debtor and creditor between them, there could, of course, have been no remedy at law under this head, since the property in the cash would have passed out of B into A.

(2) The narrowness of the limits within which the common law operated may be linked with the limited nature of the remedies available to it. Specific relief as distinct from damages (the normal

13 [1914] A.C. 398.
14 [1914] A.C. 419.
15 [1947] Ch. 716, 745-6.
16 [1921] 1 K.B. 321, 335.

remedy at common law) was confined to a very limited range of claims as compared with the extensive uses of specific relief developed by equity. In particular the device of a declaration of charge was unknown to the common law and it was the availability of that device which enabled equity to give effect to its wider conception of equitable rights.

(3) It was the materialistic approach of the common law coupled with and encouraged by the limited range of remedies available to it that prevented the common law from identifying money in a mixed fund. Once the money of B became mixed with the money of A its identification in a physical sense became impossible; owing to the fact of mixture there could be no question of ratification of an unautorized act; and the only remedy of B, if any, lay in a claim for damages.

Equity adopted a more metaphysical approach. It found no difficulty in regarding a composite fund as an amalgam consituted by the mixture of two or more funds each of which could be regarded as having, for certain purposes, a continued separate existence. Putting it another way, equity regarded the amalgam as capable in proper circumstances, of being resolved into its component parts.

Adapting, for the sake of contrast, the phraseology which we have used in relation to the common law, it was the metaphysical approach of equity coupled with and encouraged by the far-reaching remedy of a declaration of charge that enabled equity to identify money in a mixed fund. Equity, so to speak, is able to draw up a balance sheet on the right-hand side of which appears the composite fund and on its left-hand side the two or more funds of which it is to be deemed to be made up.

The equitable right may thus have a wider orbit than the legal right, although this is not invariably the case. The differences are due to the evolution of equitable rights as rights in personam and not in rem.[17] As a result of legislation, however, even this distinction between the two sets of rules tends to be diminished or become obscured. In the nineteenth century, for example, courts of equity steadily built up, from *Tulk* v. *Moxhay*[18] onwards, the conception of the restrictive covenant. This doctrine was firmly based on notice. In its developed form the doctrine permitted a vendor of part of his land to restrain, by injunction, breach by a successor in title of the purchaser of a convenant entered into by the purchaser, restricting the use of the land transferred for the benefit of the land retained. But an injunction

17 See, further, Keeton, *Elementary Principles of Jurisprudence*, 2nd ed., pp.142-5.
18 (1848), 2 Ph. 774.

could not be obtained against a successor in title of the purchaser if that successor was a bona fide purchaser of a legal estate for value without notice of the covenant. That is still the position in Ireland, but in England since 1925 the enforceability of a restrictive covenant entered into after 1925 depends, not upon notice but upon registration under the Land Charges Act of that year. If the covenant is registered, it binds everyone; if not, no one. At this point the conception of an equitable right as a right in personam breaks down. Conversely, one occasionally finds legal rights placed on the same footing as equitable rights. In England, the Law of Property Act, 1925, permits successive legal mortgages of land, but all of these except the first, which is protected by custody of the title deeds, are inoperative against a purchaser of a legal estate in the land unless registered under the Land Charges Act, 1925.[19] In Ireland, the system of registration of memorials of deeds and conveyances under the Registration of Deeds Act (Ireland), 1707, goes a long way towards equating legal and equitable mortgages in relation to priorities.

When this equation occurs, and especially when a new legal interest is expressly created by legislation and then placed upon exactly the same footing as many equitable interests, it becomes increasingly difficult to differentiate equity from the common law, either historically or analytically. Nevertheless, there are large fields of equity still dominated by the conception of the equitable right as a right in personam, particularly in relation to trusts, and the entire system of equitable remedies seems to be based upon the theory that equity scrutinises conduct and operates against the person, not against the property. It may be that we are steadily (or probably unsteadily) approaching the day when fusion of common law and equity will be necessary, but until that happens an appreciation of the differing

[19] The 1925 property legislation does not apply in Ireland, where there is no equivalent legislation. So, for example, there is no principle of registration corresponding to that of the Land Charges Act. Nor can there be successive legal mortgages of land, except by demise or sub-demise—a method not used in practice, at any rate for freeholds not held at a rent: see, e.g., *Re Sergie*, [1954] N.I. 1. See also Sheridan, " Some Aspects of Legal Mortgages " (1950), 52 *Journal of the Institute of Bankers in Ireland*, 114; " Notice and Registration " (1950), 9 *Northern Ireland Legal Quarterly*, 33.

A general survey of Irish real property law will be found in *The United Kingdom* (ed. Keeton and Lloyd), ch. 20 (Sheridan), and in the Northern Ireland section of the Preliminary Note to title Real Property, Halsbury's *Statutes of England*, 2nd ed., vol. 20, p. 352. An Irish Supplement (Sheridan) bringing the law up to date to 1956 is available with Challis's *Real Property*, 3rd ed. See also Sheridan, " Irish Private Law and the English Lawyer " (1952), 1 *International and Comparative Law Quarterly*, 196, 206-11.

On Irish equity generally, see Kiely, *Principles of Equity as applied in Ireland;* Lord MacDermott, " Law and Practice in Northern Ireland " (1953), 10 *Northern Ireland Legal Quarterly*, 47, 54-6; 1 *Int. & Comp. L.Q.* 201-6. Short articles on all sorts of legal topics, including aspects of equity, are to be found in the *Irish Law Times and Solicitors' Journal* and in the *Irish Jurist.*

approaches of the two to legal problems is the safest guide to the distinction between them. In fact, as Lord Evershed pointed out,[20] true fusion between law and equity will occur only when there is either " some codification of our laws and equity or some such restatement of the law as will indirectly if not directly cut at the roots of the division of our system between Equity and Common Law."

(2) *Equity Jurisdiction Affecting Matters Abroad*

An abiding practical consequence of equity acting in personam is that courts exercising equitable jurisdiction have always been able to take cognisance of trusts, mortgages and contracts relating to land situated abroad, provided that the defendant or some property of his is within the territory over which the court has jurisdiction. No court in England or Ireland will entertain an action relating to title to foreign land: that is a matter for the court of the country in which the land is situated.[21] This limitation of jurisdiction is an aspect of international comity. In *Norris* v. *Chambres*,[22] where a bill in equity to establish a charge on a mine in Prussia was dismissed on the grounds (*a*) of lack of privity of contract between the plaintiff and the defendant and (*b*) that a competent Prussian court was already dealing with the dispute, Lord Campbell, L.C., said—

> An English Court ought not to pronounce a decree, even *in personam*, which can have no specific operation without the intervention of a foreign Court, and which in the country where the lands to be charged by it lie would probably be treated as *brutum fulmen*.

Equitable jurisdiction being in personam, the court can act if the plaintiff can prove an equitable right against the defendant and the latter either is within the territory or can be served with process abroad. Any equitable decree will be against the defendant personally, not a determination of title to foreign land. In *Ex parte Pollard*,[23] where he held that a deposit of title deeds between parties in England amounted to a mortgage of land situated in Scotland although it was found

[20] " Equity after Fusion: Federal or Confederate " (1948), 1 *Journal of the Society of Public Teachers of Law*, 171, 181. See also Evershed, " Reflections on Fusion of Law and Equity after 75 Years " (1954), 70 *Law Quarterly Review*, 326; Crane, " Equitable Interests in Land: Some Problems of Priority " (1956), 20 *Conveyancer and Property Lawyer*, 444; Delany, " Equity and the Law Reform Committee " (1961), 24 *Modern Law Review*, 116. For further discussion of the nature of equitable interests see Nathan, *Equity through the Cases*, 4th ed. (Marshall), ch. 2.

[21] *Re Hawthorne* (1883), 23 Ch. D. 743; *British South Africa Co.* v. *Companhia de Moçambique*, [1893] A.C. 602; *Deschamps* v. *Miller*, [1908] 1 Ch. 856.

[22] (1861), 3 De G.F. & J. 583, 584-5.

[23] (1840), Mont. & Ch. 239, 250-1.

as a fact that no lien or mortgage on the estate in question had been created according to the law of Scotland, Lord Cottenham, L.C., observed—

> . . . contracts respecting land in countries not within the jurisdiction of these courts . . . can only be enforced by proceedings *in personam*, which courts of equity here are constantly in the habit of doing; not thereby in any respect interfering with the *lex loci rei sitae*. If indeed the law of the country where the land is situate should not permit or not enable the defendant to do what the court might otherwise think it right to decree, it would be useless and unjust to direct him to do the act; but when there is no such impediment the courts of this country, in the exercise of their jurisdiction over contracts made here, or in administering equities between parties residing here, act upon their own rules, and are not influenced by any consideration of what the effect of such contracts might be in the country where the lands are situate, or of the manner in which the courts of such countries might deal with such equities.

In *Penn* v. *Lord Baltimore*[24] Lord Hardwicke, L.C., decreed specific performance of a contract relating to the fixing of the boundaries of land in North America, in *Richard West and Partners (Inverness) Ltd.* v. *Dick*[25] Megarry, J., made a similar order in respect of a contract for the sale of land in Scotland and in *Rochefoucauld* v. *Boustead*[26] the Court of Appeal enforced a trust relating to land in Ceylon. The court has also made orders for the foreclosure or redemption of mortgages of property abroad[27] and decreed the winding-up of a Haitian partnership.[28] In *Cartwright* v. *Pettus*[29] a bill was sustained in the English court for an account of rent and profits (though not for partition) of an estate in Ireland; in *Re Ker's Settlement Trusts*[30] the English court approved a variation of a settlement drawn up in Nor-

24 (1750), 1 Ves. Sen. 444. See also *Archer* v. *Preston* (prior to 1682), 1 Eq. Cas. Abr. 133, pl. 3.

25 [1969] 2 W.L.R. 383, affirmed by the Court of Appeal: [1969] 2 W.L.R. 1190.

26 [1897] 1 Ch. 196.

27 *Toller* v. *Carteret* (1705), 2 Vern. 494 (decree by Wright, L.K., foreclosing a mortgage of Sark); *Paget* v. *Ede* (1874), L.R. 18 Eq. 118 (decree by Bacon, V.-C., foreclosing a mortgage of land in Nevis); *Beckford* v. *Kemble* (1822), 1 Sim. & St. 7 (injunction granted by Leach, V.-C., to restrain foreclosure of a mortgage of land in Jamaica).

28 *Maunder* v. *Lloyd* (1862), 2 J. & H. 718.

29 (1675), 2 Ch. Cas. 214.

30 [1963] Ch. 553. Ungoed-Thomas, J., said (at p. 555): "In the execution of trusts, an English court executes the trusts of a foreign settlement in accordance with the foreign law. Variation, however, does not carry out the trusts of a settlement but varies or alters them in accordance with the powers conferred by English law." See also *Re Paget's Settlement*, [1965] 1 W.L.R. 1046, where Cross, J., approved a variation of trusts of property in the United States of America.

thern Ireland, and of which the proper law may well have been the law of Northern Ireland, though the trust property was, at the time of the variation, in England; and in *Ewing* v. *Orr-Ewing*[31] the House of Lords decided that there was equitable jurisdiction in England to administer assets, real and personal, of a testator who had died domiciled in Scotland, these assets being situated mainly in Scotland. No English court, however, would consider the validity of a will of lands situated abroad. This is illustrated by *Pike* v. *Hoare*,[32] where Lord Northington, L.C., said: " As to inconveniences, if the law is clear, they afford no argument of weight with the judge. The legislature alone can remedy them." The hint was taken in the bicentenary year.[33]

In exercising this equitable jurisdiction to affect things extra-territorial, an English court does not interfere with the decisions of any foreign court, any more than the Court of Chancery before the Judicature Acts interfered with judgments of courts of common law. It acts upon the defendant by punishment for his contempt should he disobey the order of the court and, if the defendant should carry contumaciousness to the extent of obtaining judgment in a foreign court, by protecting the plaintiff in the English suit from the consequences of the foreign judgment. This was pointed out by Leach, V.-C., in *Bushby* v. *Munday*.[34] In that case two actions were brought, one in the Court of Session in Scotland and one in the Court of Chancery in England, both involving the question whether, by the law of England, one Cloves could recover on a bond for £5,000 given by Bushby. Leach, V.-C., decided that the Court of Chancery was the more convenient court for settling the question because of evidentiary considerations and because: " The plaintiff . . . may succeed in his defence in Scotland, and still be exposed to future proceedings upon the bond. But if [he] establish his case here, the bond itself will be delivered up to be cancelled, and he will be absolutely relieved from all future proceedings."[35] He also pointed out that if the Court of Session came to the conclusion that Cloves could recover under English law—

> . . . it would be in vain to urge that this Court ought to be concluded by that judgment. The substantial ends of justice would require that this Court should pursue its own better means of determining

[31] (1883), 9 App. Cas. 34.

[32] (1763), 2 Eden 182, 184.

[33] Wills Act 1963, applying in England and Northern Ireland. In the Republic of Ireland, the Succession Act, 1965, Sects. 102-8, makes similar but not identical provision.

[34] (1821), 5 Madd. 297, 307.

[35] 5 Madd. 308.

> both the law and the fact of the case; and it would necessarily follow that it must bind the interests of the parties by its own conclusions. If the opinion of this Court did not concur with that of the Court of Session, the Defendant Cloves must be restrained by the injunction of this Court from taking the fruit of his judgment there. And if the opinion of this Court did concur with that of the Court of Session, the Defendant would have the fruit of that judgment, not by the proper force of that judgment, but because he was entitled to it by the opinion of this Court.[36]

Accordingly, the Vice-Chancellor granted an injunction to restrain Cloves from prosecuting the suit in Scotland pending the proceedings in England, but he bound Bushby to submit to such steps in Scotland, by judgment or otherwise, as would secure to Cloves the benefit of a lien, which he might by his Scottish action have acquired in respect of land in Scotland, if he should eventually establish in the Court of Chancery his claim arising out of the bond. The same principles apply wherever the foreign court may be—" foreign " here means any territory outside that in which the court exercising equitable jurisdiction is situated. In the words of Leach, V.-C.[37]—

> Over the Court of Session in Scotland this Court has not, nor can pretend to have, any authority whatsoever. . . . and the question in this Court is the same, and must depend upon the same principles as if the foreign Court thus exercising its independent jurisdiction were sitting, not at Edinburgh, but at Paris or Vienna.

From the standpoint of the general principles of the conflict of laws, the extension of equitable jurisdiction to immovables situated outside the territory of the court is sometimes regarded as anomalous, and has from time to time provoked criticism from both judges[38] and academic commentators.[39] The obligations which the court enforces " depend upon the existence between the parties to the suit of some personal obligation arising out of contract or implied contract, fiduciary relationship or fraud, or other conduct which, in the view of a Court of Equity in this country, would be unconscionable, and do not depend for their existence on the law of the locus . . . "[40]

36 5 Madd. 308-9.

37 5 Madd. 306-7.

38 E.g. Lord Esher, M.R., in the Court of Appeal in *Companhia de Moçambique* v. *British South Africa Co.*, [1892] 2 Q.B. 358, 404-5, obiter, in a dissenting judgment upheld in the House of Lords, expressed " the strong objection that the Court is doing indirectly what it dare not do directly."

39 E. G. Corry (1933), 11 *Canadian Bar Review*, 211.

40 See *Deschamps* v. *Miller*, [1908] 1 Ch. 856, 863, *per* Parker, J.

The jurisdiction cannot be exercised if the lex situs prohibits the enforcement of the decree, nor can the jurisdiction be exercised if the court cannot effectively supervise the execution of the decree nor if it would for any other reason be in vain. It depends always upon a personal equity between the parties to the suit, and it cannot be exercised against strangers to the equity unless they have become personally affected by it.[41]

The Equitable Approach: Preference for Substance over Form

(1) *General*

Common law courts were disposed to pay attention to matters of formality, to the wording of what was expressed in a documentary transaction and to what arrangement was arrived at rather than how the negotiations proceeded. In equity, on the other hand, greater attention was devoted to matters of substance, to the intention of the parties and to the methods used in arriving at an arrangement.

The common law attention to form reaches its nadir in the qualities attached to a seal—nowadays usually a cheap adhesive red wafer affixed to a document. For example, while a contract generally requires consideration in order to be valid at common law, a written promise under seal is fully enforceable by an action for damages even if it is gratuitous. The attitude of equity is different: the court will not grant specific performance of a voluntary covenant but will leave the covenantee to his remedy at common law.[42] So, too, is the attitude of equity different in cases where, at law, a seal is required even if there is consideration, for example a conveyance or the grant of an easement. If there is consideration but no seal the transaction will be upheld as the equitable equivalent of what purported to be done at law, even if this means denying the grantor a common law remedy he would have had on the footing of the common law position.[43]

The general principle was expressed in this way by Romilly, M.R., in *Parkin* v. *Thorold*[44]—

> . . . Courts of Equity made a distinction in all cases between that which is matter of substance and that which is matter of form; and

[41] *Norris* v. *Chambres* (1861), 29 Beav. 246; *Mercantile Investment and General Trust Co.* v. *River Plate Trust, Loan, and Agency Co.*, [1892] 2 Ch. 303. See, further, Keeton, "Trusts in the Conflict of Laws" (1951), 4 *Current Legal Problems*, 107.

[42] *Jefferys* v. *Jefferys* (1841), Cr. & Ph. 138.

[43] *Walsh* v. *Lonsdale* (1882), 21 Ch. D. 9, discussed fully pp. 85-93, *post*.

[44] (1852), 16 Beav. 59, 66-7.

> if it find that by insisting on the form, the substance will be defeated, it holds it to be inequitable to allow a person to insist on such form and thereby defeat the substance.

The Master of the Rolls then illustrated this principle by referring to the treatment of stipulations as to time in contracts at common law and in equity, one of the situations in which the common law was concerned with the words of the agreement and equity with the substance. If the parties fixed a time for performance, failure to perform at that time was a breach of contract in the eyes of the common law, but in equity this failure constituted a breach only if the delay in performance really injured the promisee or time was expressly made of the essence of the contract. This disparity has now been resolved by the Judicature Act.[45]

Exactly the same principle formed the basis of equity jurisdiction respecting mortgages of land.[46] In a mortgage of a freehold estate at common law, it was usual to convey the estate to the mortgagee with a provision for redemption by the mortgagor if he repaid the mortgagee in full on a specified date. It appeared that the mortgagee owned the land, subject only to a contractual right in the borrower to get it back and that if payment was not made on the due date the mortgagor had lost his land for ever. In equity, however, not only was the mortgagor allowed to redeem after the contractual date but he was regarded as the substantial owner of the land subject only to its standing as security for the loan. This had many practical consequences, including hostile scrutiny by the court of any advantages conferred on the mortgagee beyond what was necessary for the protection of his security. This position still pertains in Ireland, but in England a mortgagor no longer transfers his title to the mortgagee so he remains the estate owner at law.[47]

(2) *Penalties*

Relief from penalties is another equity jurisdiction illustrating the same principle. It is selected for detailed consideration here as an example of modern controversy as to the nature of equity. Generally a contract does not specify what is to happen on its own breach, in which case any damages awarded for a breach of contract are assessed by the court so as to compensate the injured party for his actual loss. Sometimes the contract states the amount payable on breach, in which

[45] Judicature Act, 1873, Sect. 25 (7); Judicature (Ireland) Act, 1877, Sect. 28 (7). See pp. 81-3, *post*.

[46] See pp. 166-71, 187-8, *post*.

[47] Law of Property Act, 1925, Sects. 85-6.

case, at common law before it was affected by equitable principles, this sum would have been recoverable by the plaintiff. In equity this is not necessarily the case. The question is asked whether the amount stated is the result of a genuine attempt to pre-estimate the damage the breach would cause (in which case that amount is recoverable, even if not an exact estimate) or whether it was made larger than the amount of the probable damage so as to threaten the party into performing (in which case it is a penalty and equity relieves the defendant from having to pay it, leaving the plaintiff to recover the actual loss assessed by the court).

In *Dunlop Pneumatic Tyre Co. Ltd.* v. *New Garage and Motor Co. Ltd.*[48] the House of Lords reviewed the earlier authorities. Retailers agreed to sell motor tyres and tubes at list prices and to pay the manufacturers £5 for every sale at a lower price. This was held to be a stipulation for liquidated damages, and therefore enforceable, and not a penalty because, although the damage on a sale at too low a price might not be the same as on another such sale, the provision in the contract must be taken to refer to a single obligation to maintain prices generally. Lord Dunedin stated[49] the various propositions he thought deducible from the authorities—

1. Though the parties to a contract who use the words " penalty " or " liquidated damages " may prima facie be supposed to mean what they say, yet the expression used is not conclusive.[50] The Court must find out whether the payment stipulated is in truth a penalty or liquidated damages. This doctrine may be said to be found passim in nearly every case.

2. The essence of a penalty is a payment of money stipulated as in terrorem of the offending party; the essence of liquidated damages is a genuine covenanted pre-estimate of damage (*Clydebank Engineering and Shipbuilding Co.* v. *Don Jose Ramos Yzquierdo y Castaneda*).[51]

3. The question whether a sum stipulated is penalty or liquidated damages is a question of construction to be decided upon the terms and inherent circumstances of each particular contract, judged of

[48] [1915] A.C. 79. See also *Imperial Tobacco Co. (of Great Britain and Ireland) Ltd.* v. *Parslay*, [1936] 2 All E.R. 515.
[49] [1915] A.C. 86-8.
[50] See also *Alder* v. *Moore*, [1961] 2 Q.B. 57.
[51] [1905] A.C. 6.

as at the time of the making of the contract, not as at the time of the breach (*Public Works Commissioner* v. *Hills*[52] and *Webster* v. *Bosanquet*).[53]

4. To assist this task of construction various tests have been suggested, which if applicable to the case under consideration may prove helpful, or even conclusive. Such are: (*a*) It will be held to be a penalty if the sum stipulated for is extravagant and unconscionable in amount in comparison with the greatest loss that could conceivably be proved to have followed from the breach. (Illustration given by Lord Halsbury in *Clydebank Case*.)[54] (*b*) It will be held to be a penalty if the breach consists only in not paying a sum of money, and the sum stipulated is a sum greater than the sum which ought to have been paid (*Kemble* v. *Farren*).[55] This though one of the most ancient instances is truly a corollary to the last test. . . . (*c*) There is a presumption (but no more) that it is a penalty when " a single lump sum is made payable by way of compensation, on the occurrence of one or more or all of several events, some of which may occasion serious and others but trifling damage " (Lord Watson in *Lord Elphinstone* v. *Monkland Iron and Coal Co.*).[56] On the other hand: (*d*) It is no obstacle to the sum stipulated being a genuine pre-estimate of damage, that the consequences of the breach are such as to make precise pre-estimation almost an impossibility.[57]

The jurisdiction to relieve from penalties is a very lively one nowadays, frequently in relation to minimum payment provisions in hire-purchase contracts.[58] These provide for amounts to be paid by the hirer to the owner if the arrangement should be terminated before the purchase is completed. Should the arrangement end in breach of

[52] [1906] A.C. 368. The Privy Council in this case held the sum in question to be a penalty because it was not a definite sum but was liable to great fluctuation in amount dependent on events not connected with the fulfilment of the contract.

[53] [1912] A.C. 394, where the Privy Council held the sum payable on breach of contract by selling tea to third parties without consent recoverable as liquidated damages because loss was probable, difficult to pre-estimate and hard to prove when it occurred.

[54] [1905] A.C. 6.

[55] (1829), 6 Bing. 141. Tindal, C.J., held penal a stipulation to pay £1000 on any breach of a contract for performances at Covent Garden, one of the obligations being payment of £3 6*s*. 8*d*. on each night the theatre was open.

[56] (1886), 11 App. Cas. 332, 342. See also *Anglo Auto Finance Co. Ltd.* v. *James*, [1963] 1 W.L.R. 1042; *E. P. Finance Co. Ltd.* v. *Dooley*, [1963] 1 W.L.R. 1313; *Lombank Ltd.* v. *Excell*, [1964] 1 Q.B. 415. Cf. *Phonographic Equipment* (1958) *Ltd.* v. *Muslu*, [1961] 1 W.L.R. 1379; *Robophone Facilities Ltd.* v. *Blank*, [1966] 1 W.L.R. 1428.

[57] See also *English Hop Growers Ltd.* v. *Dering*, [1928] 2 K.B. 174.

[58] Restrictions on such provisions are enacted by the Hire-Purchase Act 1965, Sects. 27-9 and 43-5, and the Hire Purchase Act (Northern Ireland) 1966, Sects. 27-9 and 43-5. There is no such legislation in the Republic of Ireland.

contract by the hirer, no special question arises and the ordinary rules apply to determine whether the stipulation for payment is to be enforced as one for liquidated damages or is to be ignored as a penalty. Sometimes, however, the contract is drafted in such a way as to make out that the defaulting hirer is exercising an option to terminate the contract, rather than committing a breach of it, or so that the stipulation is made to appear as a payment due under the contract for depreciation of the article rather than as compensation by way of damages. These devices have given rise to controversy among judges as to whether the rules governing relief from penalties are applicable.

Against giving relief it can be urged that on principle people ought to be made to carry out what they have promised in a contract. Equity does not set out to reform agreements, to rescue people from improvident bargains or to help out when a risk voluntarily undertaken materialises, unless there is fraud or some other such vitiating element. The court has already gone to lengths some judges find difficult to justify in relieving from penalties in cases of breach of contract and if the jurisdiction were to be extended to cases, not of breach, but of payments due as performance of contracts, there would be no end to courts amending people's bargains if they turned out badly.

On the other side it can be argued that if equity truly looks to the intent and not to the form it will scrutinise the nature of the payment and not the way in which the contract is expressed. It is possible to draft any contract so as to make any conduct of a party an alternative mode of performance instead of a breach and so as to make any payment a sum due under the contract instead of compensation for not fulfilling its terms. This kind of term could be scrutinised without opening up the way to endless revision of contracts by confining the scrutiny to cases where the stipulation is for payment in lieu of some primary mode of performance and by asking the orthodox question whether the stipulation is a genuine pre-estimate of the plaintiff's loss or is meant to be held in terrorem over the defendant to make him perform the primary obligation. The cases demonstrate the tension between the view of equity as a body of rules like the common law and the view of equity as embodying a different kind of method.

In *Associated Distributors Ltd.* v. *Hall*[59] there was a contract for the hire-purchase of a bicycle. The hirer exercised an option to terminate the contract whereupon, according to its terms, he had to make payments to the owner so as to bring up the total money passing under the

59 [1938] 2 K.B. 83.

contract to half the price of the bicycle. The Court of Appeal enforced payment, holding it to be neither a penalty nor liquidated damages because there had been no breach of contract.

Later courts have differed as to the correctness of the principle, but they have tended to relieve the hirer without challenging it directly. This they have sometimes done by finding as a fact a breach of contract rather than the exercise of a option to terminate the hiring. But the first slight relaxation of the principle occurred in *Cooden Engineering Co. Ltd.* v. *Stanford*,[60] where a contract for the hire-purchase of a car was breached by the hirer. The Court of Appeal (Jenkins, L.J., dissenting) held that the sum stipulated for payment on that event, being claimed in respect of a breach of contract, was a penalty, even though the same sum was also expressed to be payable as compensation on other events not constituting breaches of contract, for example for agreed depreciation in the value of the car. A few years later, judges of the Northern Ireland Court of Appeal disagreed about whether a sum payable otherwise than on an actionable breach of contract could be irrecoverable as a penalty in *Lombank Ltd.* v. *Kennedy*,[61] also involving hire-purchase of cars. All the judges agreed with the decision in the *Cooden* case, but the majority (Black and Curran, L.JJ.) followed *Associated Distributors Ltd.* v. *Hall* where the sum was not claimed in respect of an actionable breach. Lord MacDermott, L.C.J., who dissented, said[62]—

> The typical instance may be of such a breach when actionable per se; but, in my view, the nature and purpose of the rule do not necessarily call for more than a breach by way of non-performance by the promisor, be that non-performance actionable in itself or otherwise. The kind of stipulation struck at by the rule is one which seeks to enforce performance by a sanction out of proportion to the loss suffered by the promisee through non-performance. If the contract is so drawn as to make the non-performance not in itself an actionable breach the mischief which the rule seeks to control may not be any less.

Earlier,[63] the learned Lord Chief Justice had commented: " . . . the penalty rule, as a rule of equity, is not to be circumvented by drafting devices . . . "

[60] [1953] 1 Q.B. 86.
[61] [1961] N.I. 192.
[62] [1961] N.I. 207.
[63] [1961] N.I. 206.

When the matter came before the House of Lords in *Bridge* v. *Campbell Discount Co. Ltd.*[64] there was complete disagreement. Under a contract for hire-purchase of a car, the hirer made a down-payment of £105, paid one instalment, wrote to the owner that he could not keep payment up and returned the car. One clause of the agreement allowed the hirer to terminate the hiring by written notice to the owner and another provided that if the agreement was terminated for any reason before the car became the hirer's property the hirer had to pay the owner " by way of agreed compensation for depreciation of the vehicle " an amount to bring the receipts of the owner under the contract up to two-thirds of the purchase price. Lord Simonds held that the hirer, having exercised his option, had committed no breach of contract and that therefore there was no equitable jurisdiction to relieve him from making the stipulated payment. Lords Morton of Henryton, Radcliffe and Devlin held, and Lord Denning was prepared to hold if necessary, that the hirer had not intended to exercise his option but had repudiated the contract and, there being a breach, the stipulation for payment was to be struck down as a penalty.[65] Lord Morton said[66] that in his opinion—

> . . . *Associated Distributors Ltd.* v. *Hall*[67] was rightly decided and, if I had thought that in the present case the appellant exercised his option under . . . the agreement . . . , I should have agreed with the decision of the Court of Appeal in the present case. In that event the present appellant would have been bound to pay the stipulated sum . . . , not by way of penalty or liquidated damages but simply because payment of that sum was one of the terms upon which the option could be exercised.

Lord Radcliffe left open the question of relief under the penalty rule where there was no breach of contract, but said[68]—

> " Unconscionable " must not be taken to be a panacea for adjusting any contract between competent persons when it shows a rough edge to one side or the other, and equity lawyers are, I notice, sometimes both surprised and discomfited by the plenitude of jurisdiction, and the imprecision of rules that are attributed to " equity " by their more enthusiastic colleagues. Since the courts of equity never undertook to serve as a general adjuster of men's bargains, it was inevitable that they should in course of time evolve definite rules

[64] [1962] A.C. 600.
[65] See also *Financings Ltd.* v. *Baldock*, [1963] 2 Q.B. 104; *United Dominions Trust (Commercial) Ltd.* v. *Ennis*, [1968] 1 Q.B. 54.
[66] [1962] A.C. 614-5.
[67] [1938] 2 K.B. 83. See pp. 21-2, *ante*.
[68] [1962] A.C. 626.

as to the circumstances in which, and the conditions under which, relief would be given, and I do not think that it would be at all an easy task, and I am not certain that it would be a desirable achievement to try to reconcile all the rules under some simple general formula.

Lord Devlin[69] thought that if the hirer had exercised his option he would still have been able to get relief because if the provision for payment was not a genuine pre-estimate of loss on breach it could not be a genuine figure for depreciation on termination under a provision of the contract. He agreed with Lord Denning that *Associated Distributors Ltd.* v. *Hall*[70] was wrongly decided. That was the central theme of Lord Denning's speech:[71] even if the hirer had exercised his option he was entitled to relief on the same principle as that by which equity invented a right to redeem a mortgage after the contractual date for redemption had passed and as that by which equity relieved from a simple bond to pay a sum of money on not doing something (which the bondsman had not promised to do). The stipulation was not really for " agreed depreciation " but compensation for loss of instalments. Otherwise it would mean that the respondent had to pay two-thirds of the purchase price of the car for two months' use of it, upon which Lord Denning commented[72]—

> Let no one mistake the injustice of this. It means that equity commits itself to this absurd paradox: it will grant relief to a man who breaks his contract but will penalise the man who keeps it. If this be the state of equity today, then it is in sore need of an overhaul so as to restore its first principles. But I am quite satisfied that such is not the state of equity today.

But post-1962 cases suggest that such might be the state of equity today. In the latest reported English case on the subject Harman, L.J., said:[73] " . . . I do not think you can have a penalty without a breach of contract, for which the penalty may be the result." In *Galbraith* v. *Mitchenall Estates Ltd.*[74] there was a contract for hire (not hire-purchase) of a caravan for five years. The retail price of the caravan was £1,050. The hirer made an initial payment of £550 10*s*. and

69 [1962] A.C. 633-4.
70 [1938] 2 K.B. 83. See pp. 21-2, *ante*.
71 [1962] A.C. 626-31. Lord Denning reiterated this view of *Associated Distributors Ltd.* v. *Hall* in *United Dominions Trust* (*Commercial*) *Ltd.* v. *Ennis*, [1968] 1 Q.B. 54, 64.
72 [1962] A.C. 629.
73 *United Dominions Trust* (*Commercial*) *Ltd.* v. *Ennis*, [1968] 1 Q.B. 54, 67. Cf. *Cityland and Property* (*Holdings*) *Ltd.* v. *Dabrah*, [1968] Ch. 166.
74 [1965] 2 Q.B. 473. See also *Robophone Facilities Ltd.* v. *Blank*, [1966] 1 W.L.R. 1428 (C.A., Lord Denning, M.R., dissenting).

agreed to a monthly rent of £12 10*s*. He lived in the caravan for about four months but paid no rent. The owners repossessed the caravan, then worth about £800, and under the contract of hire they were entitled to retain the initial payment. The hirer sued for his £550 10*s*. back but Sachs, J., held that the penalty rule did not apply to it as it was not a sum payable on breach of contract.

(3) *Forfeiture*

Similar theoretical difficulties about interfering with freedom of contract seem to inhibit courts from granting relief from forfeiture of deposits when sales are not completed. These sums are paid under contracts, not for breach of them. They are similar to the initial payment on the caravan in the *Galbraith* case in that the money has passed to the owner under the contract before a breach occurs and the plaintiff is the payer seeking his money back not the promisee trying to exact payment. In *Stockloser* v. *Johnston*[75] there was provision in a contract for the sale of land that the deposit paid by the purchaser was to be forfeited to the vendor if (as happened) the purchaser did not complete the deal. Denning, L.J., (with whom Somervell, L.J., substantially concurred) would not grant relief because, although he considered the forfeiture penal, it was not inequitable for the vendor to retain the money. For relief, in his opinion, one had to show not only disproportion between the deposit and the vendor's loss but also unconscionableness in the retention, viewing the circumstances at the time of the retention. Romer, L.J., went further and thought relief could not be granted unless the purchaser was ready and willing to perform.

Relief from forfeiture of leases for non-payment of rent or for breach of condition or covenant was worked out in equity but is now principally governed by statute. No legislation governs relief from forfeiture of chattels personal, but it seems from *Barton Thompson & Co. Ltd.* v. *Stapling Machines Co.*[76] that there is an equitable jurisdiction to grant it.

(4) *Other Preferences for Substance over Form*

Another divergence between the common law and equity in this respect is to be found in the equitable preference for substance over wording in construing documents. The absence (or presence) of technical words in a will or contract does not produce the marked effect attributed to their presence or absence in a common law con-

[75] [1954] 1 Q.B. 476. See also *Re Dagenham (Thames) Dock Co.* (1873), L.R. 8 Ch. App. 1022; *Steedman* v. *Drinkle*, [1916] 1 A.C. 275.

[76] [1966] Ch. 499.

veyance. Greater emphasis is given to ascertaining the intention of the testator or promisor by attempting to give words the meanings he intended them to have.[77]

Yet another is in the attention given by courts of equity to the manner in which apparent agreements were arrived at. At common law, if parties appeared to have arrived at a bargain intended to be legally binding the courts took it at its face value and enforced it unless it could be proved to be the result of force or threats or deception. But in the Court of Chancery a contract could be rescinded if the agreement was not freely arrived at by virtue of undue influence, advantage having been taken of gross inequality in the bargaining position of the parties, innocent misrepresentation or mistake. Equity takes an expansive view of fraud.[78] It has even been pushed to the length of approaching statutes differently from the common law approach, evolving an equitable principle that " In cases of fraud, equity should relieve, even against the words of the statute . . ."[79]

(5) *Preventing Use of Statutes as Instruments of Fraud*

The principle is that, where a statute has been enacted with the object of preventing frauds, a person who seeks to take advantage of some provision of the Act so as to further a fraud will not get away with it but will be charged on the equities arising out of his fraud. This principle has been applied to (*a*) statutes requiring a particular type of evidence for proof of a transaction; (*b*) statutes establishing registers of transactions; and (*c*) statutes providing for limitation of actions.

(*a*) *Statutes governing evidence.* The principal Act is the Statute of Frauds, 1677,[80] making certain types of contract, and trusts of land, unenforceable unless evidenced in writing. In equity, despite the absence of written evidence, (i) contracts will be enforced under the doctrine of part performance[81] and (ii) contracts and trusts of land will be enforced where property has been acquired which it would be inequitable for the acquirer to keep. It is so inequitable when the property is vested in a person apparently beneficially, but he knows at the time of the vesting that he is not meant to keep it beneficially.

[77] See Keeton, *The Law of Trusts*, 9th ed., pp. 80-4, and Irish Supplement (Sheridan), pp. 10-11.

[78] See ch. IX.

[79] *Per* Lord Parker, L.C., *Viscountess Montacute* v. *Maxwell* (1720), 1 P. Wms. 618, 620.

[80] In Ireland, the Statute of Frauds, 1695, in part repealed by the Law Reform (Miscellaneous Provisions) Act (Northern Ireland), 1954, Sect. 1. In England, part of the relevant portion of the 1677 Act has been replaced by the Law of Property Act, 1925, Sects. 40 and 53, and part repealed by the Law Reform (Enforcement of Contracts) Act, 1954.

[81] See pp. 493-6, *post*.

In *Lincoln* v. *Wright*[82] there was a conveyance of land which, the plaintiff alleged, was orally agreed to be by way of mortgage; while the defendant claimed the property as beneficial owner. The plaintiff proved the oral agreement, and the Court of Appeal in Chancery held that the defendant's claim to hold as beneficial owner, when he knew that was not the intended arrangement, was fraudulent, and that therefore the Statute of Frauds was no bar to enforcement of the mortgage agreement. The same principle was employed in *Rochefoucauld* v. *Boustead.*[83] There, land was conveyed to the defendant. The plaintiff alleged that the defendant took as trustee for her. The defendant claimed the estates beneficially for himself, but there was adequate parol evidence of the trust. The Court of Appeal held it a fraud on the part of the defendant to claim the land beneficially when he knew of the trust, and that he must duly hold on trust even if there was no writing to satisfy the Statute of Frauds.

Secret trusts also proceed on the same principle. The Wills Act, 1837, Section 9,[84] provides that all dispositions on death must be in a will executed and attested in accordance with certain formalities. Nevertheless, if the testator leaves property to a legatee apparently beneficially and, before he dies, the testator informs the legatee that he really wants the legatee to hold the property on trust for (say) the testator's illegitimate child, the trust is enforced. The legatee is not allowed to keep the property beneficially by setting up the absence of a document of trust executed in accordance with the Wills Act.[85]

(*b*) *Registration statutes.* In *E. R. Ives Investment Ltd.* v. *High,*[86] there was an oral agreement, for consideration, between the owners of two adjoining plots of land that one would have a right of way over the land of the other. There was written evidence of this agreement, but the right was not registered under the Land Charges Act, 1925, as either an estate contract or an equitable easement. The dominant owner having exercised his right for some time, and the servient owner having taken his benefit under the bargain, the servient land was sold to a purchaser subject to the right of way. According to the Land Charges Act, a registrable interest which is unregistered is void as

[82] (1859), 4 De G. & J. 16.

[83] [1897] 1 Ch. 196. See also *Bannister* v. *Bannister*, [1948] 2 All E.R. 133; *The McGillicuddy of the Reeks* v. *Joy*, [1959] I.R. 189.

[84] Replacing the Statute of Frauds. The 1837 Act is in force in Northern Ireland, but in the Republic of Ireland it has been replaced by the Succession Act, 1965, Sects. 78 and 85(1).

[85] See, further, Keeton, *The Law of Trusts*, 9th ed., pp. 66-80, and Irish Supplement (Sheridan), pp. 9-10.

[86] [1967] 2 Q.B. 379. See also Crane, "Estoppel Interests in Land" (1967), 31 *Conveyancer and Property Lawyer*, 332; Poole, "Equities in the Making" (1968), 32 *Conv.*, 96; Jackson, "Equitable Easements" (1969), 33 *Conv.*, 135.

against a purchaser, but the Court of Appeal held the purchaser bound. They put the dominant owner's equitable right of way on the basis of estoppel or acquiescence or the doctrine that the purchaser, having the benefit of the agreement, must shoulder the burden, and regarded none of these kinds of equity as registrable. Nothing was actually said about using statutes as instruments of fraud, but the approach is similar: to apply the statute would be inequitable so an equity outside the statute is enforced.

Problems of a similar kind arose a long time ago under legislation providing for registration of memorials of written dispositions of land and providing for registered dispositions to prevail over unregistered ones even of earlier date. It was settled very early, in *Lord Forbes* v. *Deniston*[87] by the House of Lords, that where the person registering under the Registration of Deeds Act (Ireland), 1707, or his agent had actual notice of a prior deed they would be using the statute as a cloak for fraud were they then to claim priority, and that therefore the unregistered deed prevailed.

(*c*) *Limitation Acts.* The impact of statutes imposing a time limit within which actions had to be brought was diminished by the equitable doctrine of concealed fraud. It was not clear before modern legislation what the limits of the doctrine were, but at least if the cause of action was fraud, or if the existence of any other equitable cause of action was fraudulently concealed, time was held by courts of equity not to run, as the statute would have it, from the accrual of the cause of action, but from its discovery or the date on which due diligence would have led to its discovery. In England, in litigation covered by the Limitation Act, 1939, the position has been clarified by Section 26 of that Act.[88] Other limitation statutes contain no such provision.

In *Lazarus Estates Ltd.* v. *Beasley*[89] a tenant who was served with a notice of increase of rent under the Housing Repairs and Rents Act, 1954, failed to apply to the county court challenging the accompanying declaration as to the value of repairs done by the landlord. Under the Act, twenty-eight days was the period allowed for such an application. Long after this period had expired, when sued for the rent,

[87] (1722), 4 Bro. P.C. 189. See also *Agra Bank Ltd.* v. *Barry* (1874), L.R. 7 H.L. 135 (Ireland); *Le Neve* v. *Le Neve* (1747), 3 Atk. 646 (Middlesex); Registration of Deeds (Amendment) Act (Northern Ireland) 1967, Sect. 7.

[88] See also *Beaman* v. *A.R.T.S. Ltd.*, [1949] 1 K.B. 550; *Shaw* v. *Shaw* [1954] 2 Q.B. 429; *Kitchen* v. *Royal Air Force Association*, [1958] 1 W.L.R. 563; *Clark* v. *Woor*, [1965] 1 W.L.R. 650; *Eddis* v. *Chichester Constable*, [1969] 1 W.L.R. 385, affirmed by the Court of Appeal: (1969), *The Times* newspaper, 24th April. Corresponding legislation is the Statute of Limitations, 1957, Sect. 71 (Republic of Ireland), and the Statute of Limitations (Northern Ireland), 1958, Sect. 70. See also pp. 104-5, *post*.

[89] [1956] 1 Q.B. 702.

the tenant pleaded that the declaration contained a fraudulent misrepresentation. The Court of Appeal (Morris, L.J., dissenting) held that this was a good defence. The majority did not refer to the doctrine of concealed fraud, but the decision seems to be based on such a general equity having survived the Limitation Act, 1939. In *Smith* v. *East Elloe R.D.C.*,[90] on the other hand, a case on the Acquisition of Land (Authorisation Procedure) Act, 1946, which provided for a limit of six weeks on applications to court to challenge compulsory purchase orders, Lord Somervell of Harrow alone among five law lords adopted this approach.[91]

THE EQUITABLE APPROACH: DISCRETIONARY REMEDIES

(1) *General*

" The jurisdiction of equity in the execution of the specific performance of contracts . . . is eminently discretionary . . . "[92] Once a common law right has been proved to have been infringed, the person aggrieved is entitled as a matter of course to his common law remedy. Before an equitable remedy is granted, not only the infringement of a right must be demonstrated, but also that the case is one to which equitable relief is applicable. No relief will be obtained, for example, where an adequate common law remedy is available; nor will equitable relief be given if the conduct of the applicant has been inequitable; and if relief is given, it may be given on terms. This does not mean that equitable remedies are a matter of grace depending upon the favour of the court.[93] The principles have been worked out in considerable detail by the courts. As Romilly, M.R., said in *Haywood* v. *Cope*,[94] where non-disclosure by the lessor of unprofitability, ignorance of mining on the part of the lessee and inadequacy of consideration were all held by him no grounds for refusing the lessor specific performance of a contract for a lease of a coal mine—

> . . . it is most important that the profession, and those who have to advise in reference to this subject, should understand the rule which is adopted in this and the other Courts, which is, that the discretion of the Court must be exercised according to fixed and settled rules; you cannot exercise a discretion by merely considering what, as between the parties, would be fair to be done; what one person may

[90] [1956] A.C. 736.
[91] See, further, Sheridan, *Fraud in Equity*, ch. IX.
[92] *Per* Romilly, M.R., *Parkin* v. *Thorold* (1852), 16 Beav. 59, 67. See also pp. 17-18, *ante*.
[93] See Pomeroy, *Specific Performance*, 3rd ed. (1926), para. 46.
[94] (1858), 25 Beav. 140, 151.

consider fair, another person may consider very unfair; you must have some settled rule and principle upon which to determine how that discretion is to be exercised.

Examples were given by the same learned Master of the Rolls in *Parkin* v. *Thorold*[95]—

> . . . it will not enforce a contract where doing so would be productive of peculiar hardship on one party to it . . . Neither will equity enforce a contract, where, though the Court considers the title good, yet considers it sufficiently doubtful that it might reasonably give rise to litigation hereafter between the purchasers and persons not bound by the decree of the Court in the suit for specific performance.

(2) *Requirement of Clean Hands*

The principle that equitable relief will be refused to a party who has behaved unconscionably was first formulated as a requirement that a man coming into a court of equity must come with clean hands by Eyre, L.C.B., in *Dering* v. *Earl of Winchelsea*,[96] where in fact the equitable relief claimed was granted. In that case, Thomas Dering was appointed collector of customs duties, and was required to furnish three sureties for the due performance of his office. The three sureties were his brother (Sir Edward Dering), the Earl of Winchelsea and Sir John Rous. Thomas Dering defaulted to the extent of £3,883 14*s*. and the Crown obtained judgment against Sir Edward Dering for that sum. Sir Edward then claimed contribution from his co-sureties. This was resisted by the Earl of Winchelsea on two grounds, one of which was that the conduct of Sir Edward Dering had deprived him of that right. On this the Lord Chief Baron commented[97]—

> The misconduct imputed to Sir Edward is, that he encouraged his brother in gaming and other irregularities; that he knew his brother had no fortune of his own, and must necessarily be making use of the public money, and that Sir Edward was privy to his brother's breaking the orders of the Lords of the Treasury, to keep the money in a particular box, and in a particular manner, etc. This may all be true, and such a representation of Sir Edward's conduct certainly places him in a bad point of view; and perhaps it is not a very decorous proceeding in Sir Edward to come into this Court, under these circumstances: he might possibly have involved his brother in some measure, but yet it is not made out to the satisfaction of the

[95] (1852), 16 Beav. 59, 67. Chitty, J., in *Turner* v. *Green*, [1895] 2 Ch. 205, 208, used similar language with regard to non-disclosure. See also the judgment of Lord Erskine, L.C., in *Mason* v. *Armitage* (1806), 13 Ves. 25, 37.

[96] (1787), 1 Cox C.C. 318.

[97] 1 Cox C.C. 319-20.

> Court, that these facts will constitute a defence. It is argued that the author of the loss shall not have the benefit of a contribution; but no cases have been cited to this point, nor any principle which applies to this case. It is not laying down any principle to say that his ill conduct disables him from having any relief in this Court. If this can be founded on any principle, it must be, that a man must come into a Court of Equity with clean hands; but when this is said, it does not mean a general depravity; it must have an immediate and necessary relation to the equity sued for; it must be a depravity in a legal as well as in a moral sense. In a moral sense, the companion, and perhaps the conductor, of Mr. Dering, may be said to be the author of the loss, but to legal purposes, Mr. Dering himself is the author of it; and if the evil example of Sir Edward led him on, this is not what the Court can take cognizance of. Cases indeed might be put in which the proposition would be true. If a contribution were demanded from a ship and cargo for goods thrown overboard to save the ship, if the plaintiff had actually bored a hole in the ship, he would in that case be certainly the author of the loss, and would not be entitled to any contribution. But speaking of the author of the loss is a mere figure of speech as applied to Sir Edward Dering in this case.

There are several illustrations of this principle in the law of trusts. One is that if trustees commit a breach of trust, relying on the advice of one of their number who is a solicitor, the ordinary rule of contribution among trustees is replaced by a right in the others to indemnity from the solicitor-trustee.[98] So long as a trustee is in default to the trust estate, he cannot obtain equitable relief. Nor can a beneficiary who concurs in a breach of trust sue the trustee in respect of it.[99]

The principle requiring clean hands has been invoked to negative a trust in favour of the husband i.e. to stop him rebutting the presumption of advancement) where he had placed property in his wife's name with the object of defrauding creditors[1] and where he had done so in order to evade foreign revenue laws.[2] In *Duchess of Argyll* v. *Duke of Argyll*[3] the doctrine was considered in relation to injunctions. The plaintiff, who had been divorced by the defendant, obtained an injunc-

[98] *Re Turner*, [1897] 1 Ch. 536. See, further, Keeton, *The Law of Trusts*, 9th ed., p. 382.

[99] *Re Deane* (1889), 42 Ch. D. 9. See also the Trustee Act, 1925, Sect. 62; Trustee Act (Northern Ireland), 1958, Sect. 62; Trustee Act, 1893, Sect. 45 (Republic of Ireland); Keeton, *The Law of Trusts*, 9th ed., pp. 406-7.

[1] *Gascoigne* v. *Gascoigne*, [1918] 1 K.B. 223.

[2] *Re Emery's Investment Trusts*, [1959] Ch. 410.

[3] [1967] Ch. 302.

tion to restrain him from publishing articles about their married life. It had been contended that the plaintiff should fail because she had had an immoral attitude towards the marriage while it lasted. Ungoed-Thomas, J., took the view that that undermined confidence for the future but did not betray the confidences of the past. He said[4]—

> A person coming to Equity for relief—and this is equitable relief which the plaintiff seeks—must come with clean hands; but the cleanliness required is to be judged in relation to the relief that is sought.

(3) *He Who Seeks Equity Must Do Equity*

A person applying for an equitable remedy must be prepared, or may be forced, to act in an equitable manner himself. For example, a contract cannot be rescinded for undue influence without making restitution of anything received under it. This principle underlies the development of several important branches of equity. It was the direct origin of the married woman's separate estate in equity and of the wife's equity to a settlement. These branches of equity are obsolete, but the principle is still of great importance. It is the root of the process of marshalling,[5] as well as of the twin principle of consolidation.[6] It is also the basis of the equitable doctrine of set-off; and it underlay the old jurisdiction of the court with respect to moneylending transactions.[7] Again, it is the foundation of the modern doctrine of equitable estoppel.[8]

Analogous to the idea of putting an applicant on terms is that of mutuality: that what is sauce for the goose is sauce for the gander. Normally, specific performance will not be granted of a contract to pay money, as damages constitute an adequate remedy. If, however, the obligation of the creditor is specifically enforceable, so is payment of the debt. A vendor under a specifically enforceable contract for the sale of land can obtain specific performance against the purchaser. Similarly, equity does not allow people to approbate and reprobate. This is at the root of the doctrine of election, and especially of some of the extensions of this doctrine;[9] of the mutual

[4] [1967] Ch. 332.
[5] See ch. XIII, *post*.
[6] See pp. 175-6, 197-202, *post*.
[7] If a debtor sought the recovery of securities, on a transaction which he wished the court to avoid as unconscionable, this relief would be given only on equitable terms, that the debtor repay the loan, usually with five per cent interest. Such terms seem to have been imposed sometimes by common law courts as well. The equitable jurisdiction to impose terms does not seem to have survived the Moneylenders Act, 1900. See *Kasumu* v. *Baba-Egbe*, [1956] A.C. 539, where the Privy Council, in a Nigerian case, declined to follow the decision of Parker, J., in *Lodge* v. *National Union Investment Co. Ltd.*, [1907] 1 Ch. 300.
[8] See pp. 123-5, *post*.
[9] See pp. 408-11, *post*.

enforceability of restrictive covenants among purchasers under a building scheme;[10] and of the new type of non-registrable equity of way discovered in *E. R. Ives Investment Ltd.* v. *High.*[11] In this case, an agreement was made that A might leave the foundations of his block of flats under B's land in return for B getting a right of way over A's land. A having the benefit of this agreement, it was held by the majority of the Court of Appeal (Lord Denning, M.R., and Danckwerts, L.J., Winn, L.J., agreeing with the result for different reasons) that B had an equitable right of way, binding on A's successor in title with notice of it.

(4) *Laches and Acquiescence*

Acquiescence in a breach of equitable duty at or before the time of its commission precludes relief for the person acquiescing.[12] Acquiescence in it after the breach of duty also precludes relief, on a principle akin to estoppel. So does quiescence. Mere lapse of time may provide a statutory bar to suit under legislation governing limitation of actions, in which case the equitable doctrine of laches is not in point, but not all equitable relief is governed by such legislation. In respect of actions for breach of fiduciary duty, such as actions to recover property in the hands of a trustee and actions to set aside transactions for undue influence,[13] there is no statutory period of limitation. Here the doctrine of laches applies. Laches is lapse of time and acquiescence is confirmation of the transaction, but the two cannot always be separated. Slight indications of acquiescence may be strengthened as a defence by lapse of time while the defence of laches based on lapse of a relatively short time may be strengthened by acts of acquiescence. Something of the confusion is shown by the Northern Ireland courts in *McCausland* v. *Young*. Black, J., the trial judge, evidently regarded laches and acquiescence as identical;[14] Andrews, L.C.J., referred to acquiescence as " an element in laches operating by way of estoppel ";[15] Babington, L.J., said[16] that the answer to the plaintiff's claim " must be either that he has by his acts shown a ' fixed deliberate and unbiassed determination ' to abide by [the settlement], or that he has so dealt with the property as to make it impossible for the court to grant him relief."

[10] *Elliston* v. *Reacher*, [1908] 2 Ch. 374, 384, *per* Parker, J., approved by the Court of Appeal: [1908] 2 Ch. 665.

[11] [1967] 2 Q.B. 379.

[12] See p. 28, *ante*.

[13] See *Allcard* v. *Skinner* (1887), 36 Ch. D. 145, p. 342, *post*; *Re Pauling's Settlement Trusts*, [1964] Ch. 303; *Holder* v. *Holder*, [1968] Ch. 353.

[14] [1948] N.I. 72, 100-12. See also *Lydon* v. *Lydon* (1874), 8 I.L.T.R. 85; *Connor* v. *M'Carthy* (1878), 12 I.L.T. 336; *The Goods of Corcoran*, [1934] I.R. 571.

[15] [1949] N.I. 49, 88-9.

[16] [1949] N.I. 106-8.

In *Lindsay Petroleum Co.* v. *Hurd,*[17] where a company seeking (with considerable dispatch) to set aside a purchase of land for fraud was unsuccessfully met by a plea of laches, Sir Barnes Peacock, giving the opinion of the Privy Council, said—

> . . . the doctrine of laches in Courts of Equity is not an arbitrary or a technical doctrine. Where it would be practically unjust to give a remedy, either because the party has, by his conduct, done that which might fairly be regarded as equivalent to a waiver of it, or where by his conduct and neglect he has, though perhaps not waiving that remedy, yet put the other party in a situation in which it would not be reasonable to place him if the remedy were afterwards to be asserted, in either of these cases, lapse of time and delay are most material. But in every case, if an argument against relief, which otherwise would be just, is founded upon mere delay, that delay of course not amounting to a bar by any statute of limitations, the validity of that defence must be tried upon principles substantially equitable. Two circumstances always important in such cases, are, the length of the delay and the nature of the acts done during the interval, which might affect either party and cause a balance of justice or injustice in taking the one course or the other, so far as relates to the remedy.

EQUITY TODAY: JUDICIAL INVENTIVENESS v. DEMOCRATIC LEGISLATURE

Development of the law has always been partly by legislation and partly by the judges laying down new principles for the decision of new cases. At times, both methods have been equally acceptable. At other times, legislation has been viewed as an unwelcome intrusion upon the purity of case law. During the nineteenth and early twentieth centuries, as Parliament gradually became more representative, the view has tended to gain ground that it was for the elected representatives of the people to deal with policy, including policy as to what the law ought to be, and that the judges, unrepresentative experts answerable to no one, were confined to ascertainment of the law and its application to cases in accordance with pre-existing authorities. This division cannot be pressed to a complete dichotomy without absurdity, and it has not been, but it is clear that in the first half of the twentieth century, as compared with the seventeenth century, more judges were willing to say, the law is such and such, and if that is unsatisfactory then it is

[17] (1874), L.R. 5 P.C. 221, 239-40. See also the observations of Lord Blackburn in *Erlanger* v. *New Sombrero Phosphate Co.* (1878), 3 App. Cas. 1218, 1279, and those of Lord Radcliffe, giving the opinion of the Privy Council, in *Nwakobi* v. *Nzekwu,* [1964] 1 W.L.R. 1019, 1024-5.

up to Parliament to do something about it. For its part, Parliament rarely responded swiftly and even more seldom systematically. Law reform by statute is now gathering pace and permanent machinery has been created which could lead to it being done scientifically. But at no time has development of the law by judicial process been entirely abandoned and in the field of equity a number of innovations have been made by the present Master of the Rolls.[18]

Upon occasion, a judicial decision that an equitable jurisdiction does not exist or is restricted has been followed by legislation creating or extending that jurisdiction. This has even happened where the judges have denied themselves a discretion. For example, the restricted view taken by the House of Lords in *Chapman* v. *Chapman*[19] as to the court's power to vary beneficial interests under trusts was followed by the conferment of wide powers of doing so by the Variation of Trusts Act, 1958.[20] This and other Acts indicate that a judicial discretion is acceptable to Parliament. Judicial development of the law may be acceptable too, at least outside the criminal law. The real problem regarding law-making by judges is not their unrepresentative capacity but the need to reconcile the requirements of justice in the particular case with certainty in the legal system in general.

Equity Today: Development of Injunctions

Since the Judicature Acts there has been an important change in the use of injunctions. They are much more often asked for and much more often granted. They are available in respect of a much wider range of torts than before. For example, injunctions in libel cases were virtually unknown before the establishment of the Supreme Court of Judicature whereas now they are commonplace.[21] These orders are also commonly made in labour disputes and have been used for such purposes as helping to break up the general strike of 1926 and securing to members of trade unions compliance with union rules and the rules of natural justice in disciplinary proceedings. In some countries, the injunction figures prominently in statutory systems of industrial arbitration and adjudication. The injunction is also frequently used in public law, particularly for the restraint of ultra vires administration, though when it comes to controlling the errors of administrative tribunals the common law remedy of an order of certiorari has proved more useful, having taken on a new lease of life.

[18] See pp. 38-42, *post*.

[19] [1954] A.C. 429.

[20] Similar legislation is the Trustee Act (Northern Ireland), 1958, Sec. 57. The Republic of Ireland has not followed suit.

[21] For details, see ch. XVI.

Injunctions may be said also to have played a vital role in the evolution of new substantive rights. The development of the law of restrictive covenants between vendor and purchaser is based on the injunction. This development began before the Judicature Acts but has since attained a high degree of sophistication and provided a much used part of our modern mechanism of conveyancing. So, too, is the injunction at the root of the development of the licence to use or occupy land,[22] though in its extended applications to the protection of the deserted wife's occupation of the matrimonial home (when the title was in the husband) a false start was made.

Equity Today: Fusion and Confusion

The fusion of the administration of common law and equity in one superior court has sometimes led to the creation of a new doctrine out of a sort of amalgam of common law rules and rules of equity. At other times, this result has been avoided. For example, the common law rule that contracts of service are enforceable has not been added to the rule that the normal equitable remedy for breach of a positive contractual duty is specific performance so as to produce a new rule that contracts of service can be enforced by specific performance.[23]

An amalgam was made in *Walsh* v. *Lonsdale*.[24] The plaintiff was in possession under a specifically enforceable contract to grant a lease. The landlord distrained for rent that would have been payable in advance under the lease had it been granted in accordance with the contract. This distress would have constituted the tort of trespass because at common law when a person was in possession at a rent without a lease rent was payable in arrear. On the other hand, an injunction to restrain the tort would not be granted because an equitable remedy would not issue to restrain something that could at any time be made lawful by another equitable remedy, namely specific performance of the contract to grant a lease. The doctrine of *Walsh* v. *Lonsdale* appears to be that there could be no common law remedy for the trespass either. Although that was not in issue in the Court of Appeal, Jessel, M.R., used language[25] showing that in his view, since the Judicature Acts, the same person could not be simultaneously a tenant from year to year at law and a tenant for seven years in equity: only the rule of equity now applied.

22 See pp. 102-4, *post*.
23 See *Britain* v. *Rossiter* (1879), 11 Q.B.D. 123, p. 493, *post*.
24 (1882), 21 Ch. D. 9. For a full consideration of this case, see pp. 85-93, *post*.
25 21 Ch. D. 14, quoted pp. 85-6, *post*.

Hurst v. *Picture Theatres Ltd.*[26] carries the same process further: in that case there did not purport to be a contract to make a grant. The contract was sale of a ticket for an unreserved seat in a cinema. At common law, a licence (even for value) to enter premises was revocable unless coupled with an interest in land. At common law, there could have been no grant of an interest, for a right to sit in an unspecified seat cannot be a leasehold estate (for lack of identified land to be demised) nor can it be an easement (for lack of a dominant tenement). Yet the Court of Appeal (Buckley and Kennedy, L.JJ., Phillimore, L.J., dissenting) took the view that specific performance could have been granted (presumably of an obligation to execute some document making the licensee secure at law), that an injunction could have been granted to restrain revocation of the licence pending specific performance (presumably by speedy proceedings before the film had ended) and that the ejected cinemagoer could get damages for assault. The result appears to be to use the Judicature Acts to make a common law remedy available by founding a doctrine that licences for value are irrevocable save in accordance with their own terms.[27]

Equity Today: Capacity for Parthenogenesis

The cases on penalties and minimum payment clauses[28] indicate that there are both possibilities for development of equitable doctrines and possibilities of holding these doctrines to their traditional limits.[29] An equitable doctrine may prove malleable in the hands of Lord Denning but intractable in the hands of Lord Justice Harman.

The twentieth century has witnessed many changes. The licence to occupy land[30] has become an important method of protecting occupiers from ejection, sometimes avoiding for the licensor the shackles of the Rent Acts.[31] The doctrine was extended by an enterprising Court of Appeal to protect deserted wives, living in houses owned by their husbands, from eviction by the husbands or their successors in title (except bona fide purchasers of the legal estate for value without notice of the wife's interest)[32] only for a diffident House

26 [1915] 1 K.B. 1. For a full consideration of this case, see pp. 98-102, *post*.

27 See *Winter Garden Theatre* (*London*) *Ltd.* v. *Millennium Productions Ltd.*, [1948] A.C. 173.

28 See pp. 20-5, *ante*.

29 See Denning, " The Need for a New Equity " (1952), 5 *Current Legal Problems*, 1; Evershed, " Equity Past Childbearing ? " (1953), 1 *Sydney Law Review*, 1 ; Sugerman, " Equity's Capacity for Childbearing " (1953), 1 *Sydney L.R.*, 174; Marshall, " The Reform of Equity " (1967), *Law, Justice and Equity*, 66.

30 See pp. 103-4, *post*.

31 See *Errington* v. *Errington*, [1952] 1 K.B. 290; *Murray, Bull & Co. Ltd.* v. *Murray*, [1953] 1 Q.B. 211; *Inwards* v. *Baker*, [1965] 2 Q.B. 29.

32 *Bendall* v. *McWhirter*, [1952] 2 Q.B. 466.

of Lords to dismantle most of the edifice in the following decade.[33] The right of third parties to enforce contracts for their benefit was given a major boost by the Court of Appeal in *Beswick* v. *Beswick*,[34] but the House of Lords in the same case left those rights suspended in mid-air by affirming the decision on a limited ground. A man sold his business for a price which included a promise by the purchaser to pay, after the vendor's death, an annuity to the vendor's widow. It was ultimately held that the vendor's personal representative (his widow) could get specific performance against the purchaser, but it may well turn out to be the case that the widow, had she not been the personal representative, could not have compelled the personal representative to take action. The remedy of tracing has been extended, especially by *Re Diplock*.[35] Remarkable use has been made of extended ideas of estoppel.[36] These innovations and retreats and doubts have been accompanied by refusals to move, as in the refusal of the House of Lords to allow the courts a flexible jurisdiction to vary trusts,[37] so that legislation had to intervene, and in the failure of the Court of Appeal, so far unremedied by legislation in England,[38] to recognise any mechanism whereby a man may give his property for the attainment of non-charitable purposes.[39]

Lord Denning's work in developing equity is well illustrated by recent cases on, or related to, estoppel. The orthodox doctrine, of long standing, is that—

> . . . if a person makes any false representation to another, and that other acts upon that false representation, the person who has made it shall not afterwards be allowed to set up that what he said was false, and to assert the real truth in place of the falsehood which has so misled the other.[40]

33 *National Provincial Bank Ltd.* v. *Hastings Car Mart Ltd.*, [1965] A.C. 1175. See also *Re Solomon*, [1967] Ch. 573; Matrimonial Homes Act 1967, Sect. 1; p. 104, *post*.

34 [1966] Ch. 538; [1968] A.C. 57 (H.L.). But see the Married Women's Status Act, 1957, Sect. 8 (Republic of Ireland); Law Reform (Husband and Wife) Act (Northern Ireland) 1964, Sects. 4-6.

35 [1948] Ch. 465. See pp. 7-11, *ante*. As to tracing generally, see ch. XX.

36 See pp. 122-5, *post*.

37 *Chapman* v. *Chapman*, [1954] A.C. 429. See p. 35, *ante*.

38 For some relief in Ireland, see the Charities Act (Northern Ireland) 1964, Sect. 24, and the Charities Act, 1961, Sect. 49 (Republic of Ireland).

39 See *Re Endacott*, [1960] Ch. 232; Keeton, *The Law of Trusts*, 9th ed., ch. XI, and Irish Supplement (Sheridan), pp. 17-21; Sheridan, " Power to Appoint for a Non-Charitable Purpose: A Duologue or Endacott's Ghost " (1964), 13 *De Paul Law Review*, 210.

40 *Jorden* v. *Money* (1854), 5 H.L.C. 185, 210, *per* Lord Cranworth, L.C.

Such a person, in fact, will be treated as if the representation were true, and will be compelled to make it good in so far as a court has power to compel him.

This principle of estoppel by representation was recognised by the Court of Chancery as early as the seventeenth century,[41] and has been consistently acted on. In *Jorden* v. *Money*[42] itself, however, the House of Lords refused to extend the doctrine to declarations of intention, as distinct from representations of existing fact. This is not an exclusively equitable doctrine: it also exists at common law, where the treatment of it is similar.[43]

In *Ramsden* v. *Dyson*[44] estoppel by representation was considered in relation to cases in which a person builds on the land of another, the landowner standing by without asserting his rights. In such a case, if the builder thought the land was his own when he began to build, equity will treat the true owner's conduct as estopping him from subsequently asserting his title to the detriment of the builder. If, on the other hand, the builder knew he was building on the land of another, without that other's permission, equity will permit the true owner to assert his title to the land. But if the landowner led the builder to expect to be allowed to stay there will be an equity in the builder. In *Inwards* v. *Baker*[45] a father who owned land invited his son to build a bungalow on it. This was done, partly at the son's expense, and the son lived in the bungalow. When the father died the title to the land passed, under a will made before the land was bought or the bungalow built, to the father's mistress and other children. The Court of Appeal held that the son had a right to remain as against them. Lord Denning, M.R., (with whom Danckwerts and Salmon, L.JJ., agreed) said[46]—

> . . . if the owner of land requests another, or indeed allows another, to expend money on the land under an expectation created or encouraged by the landlord that he will be able to remain there, that raises an equity in the licensee such as to entitle him to stay. He has a licence coupled with an equity. . . . even though there is no

41 *Gale* v. *Lindo* (1687), 1 Vern. 475. And see *Neville* v. *Wilkinson* (1782), 1 Bro. C.C. 543.

42 (1854), 5 H.L.C. 185.

43 *Pickard* v. *Sears* (1837), 6 Ad. & El. 469; *Freeman* v. *Cooke* (1848), 2 Ex. 654. The legal doctrine may have been imported from equity by Lord Mansfield: see Ashburner, *Principles of Equity*, 2nd ed., p. 446; *Montefiori* v. *Montefiori*(1762), 1 Wm. Bl. 363.

44 (1866), L.R. 1 H.L. 129.

45 [1965] 2 Q.B. 29.

46 [1965] 2 Q.B. 36-7.

> binding contract to grant any particular interest to the licensee, nevertheless the court can look at the circumstances and see whether there is an equity arising out of the expenditure of money. All that is necessary is that the licensee should, at the request or with the encouragement of the landlord, have spent the money in the expectation of being allowed to stay there. If so, the court will not allow that expectation to be defeated where it would be inequitable to do so. . . . I think that any purchaser who took with notice would clearly be bound by the equity.

In *Ward* v. *Kirkland*[47] Ungoed-Thomas, J., applied this doctrine to give a permanent equitable right to keep drains in position on a neighbour's land. The neighbour was a limited owner who could not dispose of his land without permission. Of that difficulty, the learned judge said[48]—

> It is the expenditure on the property in inserting drains with the knowledge of the rector on the footing that there is no time limitation to their remaining on the property . . . that gives rise to the equity; and it seems to me that the action of the court fastening as it does on the conscience of the fee simple owner, does not constitute a disposition of the land by the rector without the necessary consents . . . . It is true . . . that such an equity may, in effect, take effect as an interest in property, but that is merely the consequence of the court's action in recognising an equity by reason of its being unconscionable in the circumstances to do otherwise.

The decision of Denning, J., in *Central London Property Trust Ltd.* v. *High Trees House Ltd.*[49] was a bold escape from the limitations imposed by the House of Lords in *Jorden* v. *Money*,[50] by treating the promisor in the later case as legally bound because he intended the promisee to rely on his expression of intention. In that case there was a parol agreement to reduce the rent due under a lease, there being no consideration to support the variation. Although the efficacy of this agreement was not directly in issue, Denning, J., held that it was binding. This was expressly not on the basis of estoppel, but because of the circumstances surrounding the promise.[51] Dealing with earlier limitations on this type of equitable doctrine, the learned judge said[52]—

47 [1967] Ch. 194.
48 [1967] Ch. 241-2.
49 [1947] K.B. 130. See, further, Sheridan, " Equitable Estoppel Today " (1952), 15 *Modern Law Review*, 325. See also pp. 122-5, *post*.
50 (1854), 5 H.L.C. 185.
51 [1947] K.B. 134.
52 [1947] K.B. 134-5.

> The law has not been standing still since *Jorden* v. *Money.* There has been a series of decisions over the last fifty years which, although they are said to be cases of estoppel, are not really such. They are cases in which a promise was made which was intended to create legal relations and which, to the knowledge of the person making the promise, was going to be acted on by the person to whom it was made, and which was in fact so acted on. In such cases, the courts have said that the promise must be honoured. . . . *Jorden* v. *Money* can be distinguished, because there the promisor made it clear that she did not intend to be legally bound, whereas in the cases to which I refer the proper inference was that the promisor did intend to be bound. In each case the court held the promise to be binding on the party making it, even though under the old common law it might be difficult to find any consideration for it. The courts have not gone so far as to give a cause of action in damages for the breach of such a promise, but they have refused to allow the party making it to act inconsistently with it. . . . the time has now come for the validity of such a promise to be recognized. The logical consequencc, no doubt is that a promise to accept a smaller sum in discharge of a larger sum, if acted upon, is binding notwithstanding the absence of consideration: and if the fusion of law and equity leads to this result, so much the better. . . . At this time of day however, when law and equity have been joined together for over seventy years, principles must be reconsidered in the light of their combined effect.

The doctrine of the *High Trees* case provides a defence to an action on the original contract for a defendant relying on a voluntary variation. It does not provide a cause of action for a plaintiff relying on a gratuitous promise[53] (but it is not confined to cases where there is a contract; provided there is a legal relationship which could give rise to liabilities and penalties).[54] Nor does it supply a defence if it would not be inequitable for the plaintiff to succeed. In *D. & C. Builders Ltd.* v. *Rees*[55] the plaintiffs had agreed, when intimidated by threats, to accept

[53] *Combe* v. *Combe*, [1951] 2 K.B. 215. Denning, L.J., with whom Asquith and Birkett, L.JJ., agreed, said (at p. 219): " Much as I am inclined to favour the principle stated in the *High Trees* case, it is important that it should not be stretched too far, lest it should be endangered. That principle does not create new causes of action where none existed before. It only prevents a party from insisting upon his strict legal rights, when it would be unjust to allow him to enforce them, having regard to the dealings which have taken place between the parties."

[54] *Durham Fancy Goods Ltd.* v. *Michael Jackson* (*Fancy Goods*) *Ltd.*,[1968] 2 Q.B. 839, 847, *per* Donaldson, J.

[55] [1966] 2 Q.B. 617.

£300 in settlement of their bill for £482 13*s*. 1*d*. The Court of Appeal held the balance recoverable. Lord Denning, M.R., said[56] that the *High Trees* case—

> . . . caused at the time some eyebrows to be raised in high places. But they have been lowered since. The solution was so obviously just that no one could well gainsay it.
>
> In applying this principle, however, we must note the qualification: The creditor is only barred from his legal rights when it would be *inequitable* for him to insist upon them. Where there has been a *true accord*, under which the creditor voluntarily agrees to accept a lesser sum in satisfaction, and the debtor *acts upon* that accord by paying the lesser sum and the creditor accepts it, then it is inequitable for the creditor afterwards to insist on the balance. But he is not bound unless there has been truly an accord between them.

The *High Trees* doctrine may look like a revival of old ideas of equity as a kind of residuary natural justice to remedy defects in the common law. But new common law principles have been brought forth too. In the end, it is the approach of the individual judge that matters, and new rules will tend to be evolved, when needed, by judges with the enterprise required, from equitable ancestry, common law ancestry or a mixture of the two, as convenient.

Statutory Equity

Statutory intervention in the field of equity has already been mentioned in two of its aspects: the expression or modification in statutory form of what were previously rules of equity, as in parts of the Trustee Act, 1925, and the creation of new discretions in the judges, as in the Charities Act (Northern Ireland) 1964, Section 24. There is a third kind of legislation affecting equity: that which uses the distinction between common law and equity as a basis for a new set of proprietary interests. The scheme of the English 1925 property legislation, for example, relies on this division of English law. The Law of Property Act, 1925, could not have stipulated for only one legal estate in freehold land—the fee simple absolute in possession—without the possibility having been understood of continuing to have interests for life, pur autre vie and in tail as equitable interests. Nor could the 1925 mechanism of the trust for sale and the strict settlement have been made, overreaching the beneficiaries' interests in favour of a purchaser, had it not been for the doctrine that the conscience of a bona fide purchaser for value without notice of them was unaffected by equitable interests.

56 [1966] 2 Q.B. 624-5.

The idea of equity in English law is a gradually but constantly changing one. At present we are in a curious half way stage when the division between common law and equity remains of vast practical importance and when at the same time changes in doctrine are taking place as a result of the breaking down of this division. Fusion of administration is bringing about fusion of ideas and of method; but the process has a long way to go yet before it will be complete.

Chapter II

THE DEVELOPMENT OF EQUITY IN THE COURT OF CHANCERY

In the first chapter of his *Lives of the Chancellors*, Campbell gives a picturesque account of various eminent Saxons who are traditionally supposed to have held the office of Chancellor before the Conquest. Modern research however, has found little to support such legends, although it is established that Edward the Confessor employed a body of royal clerks to conduct his administration, and the chief of them may have held the great seal which the Confessor is known to have employed. Such a person performed many of the functions which in later times came to be associated with the Chancellorship, and one of the last to hold such an office before the Conquest was one Regenbald, or (as Campbell styles him) Reimbaldus, who received grants from William.

In France, the Carolingian Kings had regularly employed a cleric as *Cancellarius*, who was also keeper of the King's seal, and who headed the chancery of clerks who conducted the King's business. In Normandy, the Dukes immediately prior to the Conquest were developing a similar system, although as yet the office of Chancellor had not been created. Chief among the Dukes' chaplains to be employed in the ducal administration was Herfast who, after the Conquest, was the first to whom the title of Chancellor can, with certainty, be attributed in England. Thereafter, appointments to the office were continuous, and the occupants were usually clerics who were either already bishops, or became so shortly afterwards. Herfast was consecrated Bishop of Elmham in 1070, his successor became Bishop of Salisbury in 1078, and the third Chancellor, Maurice, was Bishop of London. Until 1340, almost every Chancellor held high ecclesiastical office, departure from this rule being made only for very exceptional reasons. In 1253, on the eve of his departure to Gascony, Henry III made his Queen, Eleanor, Lady Keeper of the Great Seal, but the experiment proved highly unpopular and Parliament compelled her to surrender the office within the year.

There were strong reasons for this ecclesiastical monopoly of the office. The Chancellor's duties were extremely varied, and Stubbs described him as " the secretary of state for all departments," but first and foremost, he was the head of the secretariat which issued the royal writs. This had been so in the reign of Edward the Confessor, and the number and variety of royal writs increased greatly after the Conquest. He was a leading member of the Council, giving advice on every branch of Government: he assisted in the despatch of judicial business, both in the Exchequer and in the Curia Regis, and even as an itinerant justice. For some time, he was subordinate in power and importance to the Chief Justiciar, but when this office was discontinued in Henry III's reign, he came to exercise, in addition to more specific functions, the authority of a modern Prime Minister who, at the same time, also presided over a separate department, the Chancery, for which a separate set of rolls was instituted as early as 1199. From the middle of Henry III's reign, the Chancery was organised as a distinct department, separated from the royal household, with its chaplains and clerks on the one hand, and from the Exchequer on the other. Naturally, the influence of the Chancellor varied. Some were by temperament administrators, under whom the secretariat functioned smoothly. Others exercised a general influence upon government, and were in the centre of the political activities of the period. Occasionally, in disturbed times, the expedient might be adopted of appointing as Chancellor someone who was not a cleric, but these deviations from the usual pattern were of brief duration, and were not strikingly successful.

This pattern was not peculiarly English. Throughout the middle ages, influential members of the clergy are to be found at the elbow of many of the princes of western Europe, advising, administering, negotiating treaties and taking a leading part in political life. They were selected primarily because of their training, which cultivated a knowledge of civil and canon law, in the terminology of which was expressed much of the diplomatic and political activity of the age. A contributing factor was that the clerk, being celibate, was capable of greater dedication to the King's service than a baron, and was less directly influenced by the desire for aggrandisement of his family. This is not to say that the cleric was never influenced by family considerations. George Neville, Archbishop of York, and Chancellor for a period in the reign of Edward IV, was an important element in the political activities of his brother, Warwick, and other examples could be given—for example, Henry Beaufort, Bishop of Winchester in Henry VI's reign—but being without a family for which provision must be made, the loyalties of the cleric were a degree less likely to be divided, more especially as a successful career in the King's service was likely to be accompanied by ecclesiastical preferment.

It was not until the latter part of the fourteenth century that anything resembling a Court of Chancery, administering equity, emerged. As Baildon has pointed out, petitions to the Chancellor appear at a very early period, but they were not "proceedings." For a petition to amount to a proceeding, Baildon suggests there must be (*a*) a petition addressed to the Chancellor or Keeper by a petitioner or plaintiff, complaining of (*b*) an alleged wrong done by a specified person, and asking (*c*) that the person complained of may be sent for to answer the complaint, and (*d*) finally, that a remedy may be provided.[1] In this sense, although petitions were always to the Chancellor, decrees were for a lengthy period the decrees of the Council, or of the Council and the Chancellor, and possibly even the Justices, sitting jointly. In a statute of 1340, the Chancery is mentioned among the courts of the realm, and in 1349 a royal proclamation in the form of a letter from the King to the Sheriffs of London appears to refer to the Chancellor's separate jurisdiction in matters of grace. Further, several petitions of the Commons refer to the jurisdiction of the Chancellor as something separate from that of the Council,[2] but it was not until the middle of the fifteenth century that the two courts became entirely distinct, and that the Chancellor's equity jurisdiction was firmly established. It is during the reign of Henry VI that we can first clearly perceive the application of equitable principles in cases which come before the Chancellor's court, as it has now become, and Baildon suggests[3] that the well-known statute of 1487,[4] defining the Council's jurisdiction in matters which shortly came to be regarded as Star Chamber matters, was probably passed to make a final distinction between the court of the Chancellor and the Council.

From the beginning, the Court of Chancery exercised jurisdiction in two quite distinct classes of case. The first was that which arose from the limitations of the common law, which resulted from the rigidity of its principles and practice. This was the origin of the Chancellor's equity jurisdiction. The second class of case was that which arose from the situation of the parties in cases that would otherwise have come before the common law courts. Not infrequently these cases involved denials of justice because of the power or influence of the person against whom a remedy was sought. These were frequent during the troubled years of the fifteenth century, when the Chancellor's court was first formally establishing itself, but during the sixteeth century, under the firm government of the Tudors, such

[1] *Select Cases in the Chancery*, p. xii.
[2] *Ibid.*, p. xvii.
[3] *Ibid.*, pp. xx-xxi.
[4] 3 Henry VII, c. 1.

cases ceased to come before the Chancellor. They were, in any event, more suitably dealt with by the Council in the Star Chamber. On the other hand, at the same period, the equitable jurisdiction of the Chancery greatly increased.

It was during the formative period of the Chancery's development, in the first half of the fifteenth century, that the characteristic procedure by bill took shape. After the reign of Henry V, bills were in English. The great writ of subpoena, by which the appearance of the defendant before the court was secured, traditionally owes its invention to John Weltham, Master of the Rolls from 1381 to 1386.[5] It replaced an earlier writ, sometimes known as the *quibusdam certis de causis*, in which the penalty for failure to comply was indefinite. In the writ of *subpoena* a definite pecuniary penalty was included.

The procedure of the Chancery was utterly different from that of the common law courts, where the parties stood on an equal footing, conducting a judicial combat in accordance with strict rules, for rights to which, if they were established, they were thereby entitled. In Chancery, the parties came as petitioner and respondent, claiming the Chancellor's intervention as a matter of grace. The petition was contained in the bill. If this disclosed a prima facie case, the writ of subpoena issued, commanding the respondent to appear and answer. However informal, and even oral, the pleadings may have been initially, by the beginning of the seventeenth century they had assumed a more formal shape, but there was no attempt to establish an issue between the parties—The successive statements, petition, or bill, answer, and reply—each recited the facts.[6] Further, the function of the Court of Chancery differed sharply from that of the common law courts, which contented themselves with the role of umpire in the judicial combat between the parties. Proceedings in the Chancery involved the examination of the respondent upon his conduct in respect of the petition. The Chancery, moreover, had no jury. It was for the court to pronounce its decision upon the whole of the facts and the law, the decree of the court was in personam, enforced, if necessary, by the imprisonment of the defendant until he complied with the court's decree. It was these characteristics derived from the origin of the court as an offshoot of the Council, and giving its procedure a marked resemblance to that of the Court of Star Chamber, which so frequently provoked criticism from common lawyers.

5 There exist, however, slightly earlier instances of its use: Baildon, *op. cit.*, pp. xiv-xv.

6 See p. 451, *post*.

During the period (1364-1471) in which the Chancery cases collected by Baildon were decided, the Chancellor was almost invariably an ecclesiastic, usually a Bishop or an Archbishop, and the long line of ecclesiastical chancellors persisted until the Reformation.[7] The majority of them were statesmen. Some, such as Cardinal Beaufort, Cardinal Morton and Cardinal Wolsey, were the leading statesmen of their age, but all of these, and a number of others, for example, Thomas Chichele, Archbishop of Canterbury and the first of Henry V's Chancellors, were also celebrated for their learning, especially in the canon law. This is not without importance in determining the extent of the influence of civil and canon law upon the development of equitable principles. Although many of the cases included in Baildon's collection would have been proper matters for the Court of Chancery at a later time, there were also others which were not. Little by little, such remedies as specific performance, the taking of accounts and rendering up and cancellation of documents make their appearance, and infants, widows and ignorant and weak persons are regarded as within the special protection of the court, and matters arising out of the administration of the estates of deceased persons frequently arise. In addition, there are many examples of the enforcement of uses and trusts.

Since equity is a gloss upon many different parts of the common law, its activities are difficult to describe in general terms. There is a couplet of doggerel, attributed to Sir Thomas More, although it may be older, which says—

> Three things are to be judged in Court of Conscience,
> Covin, accident, and breach of confidence.

In *Doctor and Student*, the serjeant of the laws of England had explained that a subpoena would lie on the Chancery for:

(1) Discovery of documents;

(2) Perfecting imperfect conveyances where valuable consideration had been given;

(3) Recovery of rents reserved in conveyances of the whole estate of the grantor, where, since the grantor had conveyed his whole estate, and therefore had no reversion, he could not reserve a rent, although he could have created, in the technical common law form, a rentcharge;

(4) Defence against unconscionable claims ("accident" in the couplet);

[7] After the Reformation, there were three more: Stephen Gardiner (1553-1555), Archbishop Heath (1555-1558) and Bishop Williams (Lord Keeper 1621-1625). The reversion to ecclesiastics in Mary's reign is not without significance.

(5) The enforcement of uses.

The couplet did not purport to be, and was not, a comprehensive description of equity's province. It did not include, for example, the range of equitable remedies; nor did it specify the supervisory jurisdiction which the Court of Chancery long exercised over the affairs of infants, lunatics, married women, poor persons and, in a slightly different context, borrowers. The history of the Court of Chancery's intervention between mortgagor and mortgagee can be traced to its care for the weaker party, and its determination to check oppression which followed from his weakness.

Covin, or fraud, was a comprehensive head of equitable jurisdiction.[8] It was the basis of equity's intervention in cases of oppressive bonds, or bargains or transactions entered into through undue influence. The common law courts were slow to admit the plea of fraud in cases of contract, and they were even slower in granting a remedy for fraud as a separate tort. When they did, they defined fraud as a misrepresentation of fact, made with the intent that it should be acted upon, either with knowledge that it was false, or without belief in its truth. Such a conception of fraud left many cases of wrongful conduct resulting in loss to another beyond the reach of redress at common law, and equity progressively intervened. In equity, the essence of fraud was unconscientious conduct, i.e., conduct which failed to reach equitable standard of fair dealing, and resulting in loss to another. The typical illustration of this was the person in a fiduciary position who exercised the influence which that position gave him, to induce the weaker party to undertake some act, or part with some property, to his detriment. This jurisdiction has links with the Chancery's supervisory jurisdiction over classes of weaker persons on the one hand, and with its intervention in cases of breach of confidence on the other. Of course, the great contribution which the Court of Chancery made in the sphere of breach of confidence was in the enforcement of uses and trusts, and in the development of the extensive body of law which arose from it.

" Accident " was a vague term which covered many situations, in their nature unforeseen, and it could, in particular situations, shade off into fraud. The law of mistake, particularly in relation to contracts and conveyances, is included under this head, and it led in turn to the development of the equitable rules governing the rectification of contracts and other instruments, and the rescission of documents of all kinds.

[8] See ch. IX.

As yet it is too early to say that there is a settled body of equitable principles. The Chancellor does what appears to be right and necessary in the individual case, and Selden's aphorism that " equity varies as the length of the Chancellor's foot " would be a not inappropriate description. A variety of expressions is used to describe the relief sought, including " conscience," " law, right, and good conscience," and " reason and good faith." In one highly interesting (undated) case from the fifteenth century, the petitioner concludes—

> And so it is, most reverend Lord that the said suppliant cannot have any remedy in this behalf by the law of Holy Church,[9] nor by the common law of the land: May it please your most gracious Lordship, in honour of God and on account of righteousness, to grant writs to cause the said Walter and Reginald to come before you in the King's Chancery, which is the Court of Conscience, there to answer as reason and conscience demand, otherwise the said suppliant is and will be without remedy, which God forfend.[10]

The Court of Chancery, therefore, is a court of conscience, and it is that because it decides cases in accordance with reason and conscience. A century later, St. Germain, in *Doctor and Student*, said very much the same thing. As Sir Carleton Kemp Allen has shown,[11] the ideas there expounded are derived ultimately from John Gerson; they were extremely influential, and they were based upon the principles animating the canon law, which in turn was founded upon the great body of mediaeval learning in which the law of reason transcended human law, and served as a corrective as well as an ideal. The Chancellors, therefore, in giving redress in cases which lay outside the common law or any other system of law applied in English courts, were seeking to give practical application to the principles of reason, as understood by the Church, and as systematised in the law of nature. As Barbour has pointed out,[12] although the Chancellor did not consciously apply canon law—

> He tended to give effect to principles derived from it. " This indirect reception of canon law is not demonstrated with mathematical precision; it seems to me, however, that the whole line of decision in equity points unequivocably towards the Canon Law."

Directly in accord with this is the forceful remark of Archbishop Morton, L.C., in 1489,[13] that " every law should be in accordance

[9] Because it was not a testamentary matter.
[10] Baildon, case 223.
[11] *Law in the Making*, 7th ed., p. 408.
[12] *Oxford Studies in Social and Legal History*, vol. IV, p. 168.
[13] Hil. 4 Hen. 7, 415, pl. 8 (cited Yale 1 *Nottingham's Chancery Cases*, p. xxxix).

with the law of God, and the law of God is that an executor who fraudulently misapplied the goods and does not make restitution will be damned in Hell, and to remedy this is to accord with conscience as I understand it."

As yet, only the procedure of the Court of Chancery was fixed, and it was the varying interpretations which could be given to the rules of conscience which frequently evoked criticism. Even in 1615, in the *Earl of Oxford's Case*,[14] Lord Ellesmere, L.C., asserted—

> The Cause why there is a Chancery is, for that Men's Actions are so divers and infinite. That it is impossible to make any general Law which may aptly meet with every particular Act, and not fail in some Circumstances. The Office of the Chancellor is to correct Men's Consciences for Frauds, Breach of Trusts, Wrongs and Oppressions, of what Nature soever they be . . .

The Reformation produced a decisive change in the selection of the Chancellors, symbolised by the replacement of Wolsey by Sir Thomas More. From the Reformation to the Restoration the Chancellors and Lord Keepers, with three exceptions, were no longer clerics. They were usually lawyers, although sometimes they could be politicians. Some of them were of lesser stature than their predecessors. Some, such as Ellesmere and Bacon, could be the reverse. It was a transitional period, in which the traditional habits of legal thinking were slowly replacing those of the mediaeval Church, even though scholasticism was still influential in the England of the early seventeenth century. One evidence of this change was the appearance of the first imperfect and scrappy reports of Chancery cases. They were not of great value, more particularly since there was no suggestion of a doctrine of judicial precedent in Equity. On the other hand, there was an uninterrupted habit of seeking the assistance of the common law judges to despatch the constantly increasing business of the court, and in course of time this would have an influence upon both the content and the method of equity.

As the business of the Court of Chancery increased, the overlap between equity and common law also increased, and so did the chances of friction. Complaints of Chancery encroachments are found upon the Parliament Roll in the reign of Edward IV. They were renewed at the time of Wolsey's fall, and they were frequent in the latter part of Elizabeth's reign, and again in the opening years of the reign of James I. Eventually, the conflict between the Common Law Courts and the Court of Chancery came to a head in the *Earl of Oxford's Case*.[15]

[14] 1 Ch. Rep. 1, 6-7.
[15] (1615), 1 Ch. Rep. 1.

Coke, then Chief Justice of the Court of King's Bench, held in several cases that imprisonment for disobedience to Chancery injunctions restraining proceedings at common law, or restraining parties from acting upon a common law judgment, was unlawful. For the Chancery, it was argued that the injunctions in no way affected the common law courts. They were merely directed to the conduct of the parties. The quarrel was referred to Bacon, then Attorney-General, who advised that there was a strong current of authority in favour of the issue of injunctions after judgment. James I, therefore, decided in favour of the Chancery, and this decision in effect established the situation that where the rules of common law and the rules of equity were in conflict, the rules of equity were to prevail. Implicit in this decision was the hypothesis that both jurisdictions would adhere to their traditional limits, and in substance this has occurred.

As a prerogative court, the Chancery was for a time under attack during the Commonwealth, but it escaped the fate of the Court of Star Chamber, and was re-established at the Restoration. The first two Chancellors of Charles II's reign, Clarendon (1660-1667) and Shaftesbury (1672-1673), were politicians, who frequently invoked the assistance of the judges when deciding cases in the Chancery. From 1667 until 1672, the Chancery was presided over by Sir Orlando Bridgeman, as Lord Keeper. He had been Chief Justice of the Court of Common Pleas, and was a learned common lawyer, but by general consent he was a failure as an equity judge. " In his time " says Roger North, " the Court of Chancery run out of order into delays and endless motions in causes, so that it was like a field overgrown with briars."

The picture changed completely with the appointment of Lord Nottingham, first as Lord Keeper in 1673, and from 1675 until 1682 as Lord Chancellor. Heneage Finch, first Earl of Nottingham, the son of another Heneage Finch, at one time Recorder of London, was a member of a family which produced a number of distinguished lawyers. All of them were adherents of the Crown, and since the Lord Chancellor's tenure of office and his earlier services as Law Officer covered the period of acute conflict between Charles II and the Whigs, as well as the Popish Plot trials, his services to Charles, whilst free from fanaticism, were extensive, and have not escaped criticism. They are, however, completely overshadowed by his work in the re-establishment of the Court of Chancery, in the delimitation of its jurisdiction, and the elucidation of the principles upon which modern equity is based. A common lawyer by training, he came to be known as " the Father of Equity," and the title is amply justified by his decisions, the clarity of which is equalled by the acuteness of their reasoning. In addition, as Holdsworth has pointed out, for all his mastery of legal principle, Nottingham never lost sight of the practical consequences which would follow from his decisions. Yale[16] suggests that the supreme example of this is *Howard* v. *Duke of Norfolk*[17], in which the whole of the tangled law relating to perpetuities was examined, and the modern rule was formulated, but it is equally well exemplified by *Cook* v. *Fountain*,[18] in which he defines the scope of trusts which arise by implication of law—

> In the case in question there is no pretence of any proof that there was a trust declared either by word or in writing; so the trust, if there be any, must either be implied by the law, or presumed by the Court. There is one good, general, and infallible rule that goes to both these kinds of trusts; it is such a general rule as never deceives; a general rule to which there is no exception, and that is this; the law never implies, the Court never presumes a trust, but in case of absolute necessity. The reason of this rule is sacred; for if the Chancery do once take liberty to construe a trust by implication of law, or to presume a trust, unnecessarily, a way is opened to the *Lord Chancellor* to construe or presume any man in *England* out of his estate . . .

Lord Nottingham's work in recreating the law of trusts has been discussed elsewhere,[19] but there is scarcely a main branch of equity in which a decision of Lord Nottingham is not the starting-point.[20] Perhaps his most important service of all was to complete the secularisation of equity, and to initiate its development by techniques derived from the common law. In many of his decisions, one can discern a determination to settle a rule, and to embody it in a precedent to which equity lawyers and judges in the future could appeal. The first collections of notes of Chancery cases extending over the period from 1557-1650 had already appeared during the Commonwealth. From Lord Nottingham's time, the equity reports increase in number, and improve in quality, as the citation of earlier decisions gradually becomes the rule. Curiously, it was at first thought that a precedent should mature before it could be regarded as an authority. Nevertheless, in the latter part of the seventeenth century, the court would frequently direct a search for precedents. At this early date, this would often

16 *Nottingham's Chancery Cases* (79 Sel. Soc.), p. 1.
17 (1681), 2 Swanst. 454.
18 (1672), 3 Swanst. 585, 591-2.
19 Keeton, *Law of Trusts*, 9th ed., ch. II.
20 As to his development of the principles governing mortgages, see pp. 170-7, *post*.

involve a search of the records of the court, and particularly of the books of decrees and orders. Lord Nottingham's influence upon the transition from arbitrary discretion based on reason and conscience to reasoned judgments, founded upon earlier precedents, is of paramount importance, and he frequently refers to it in his judgments, more especially in *Earl of Feversham* v. *Watson*[21] and in *Cook* v. *Fountain*.[22] Nevertheless, for Lord Nottingham, as for Coke, sixty years earlier, a precedent was not a binding authority. It was evidence of the course of the court, illustrating the manner in which the principles of law were applied.[23] Precedents, in his view, were good servants, but bad masters, and he did not hesitate, for what seemed to him good reason, to disregard a bad one.

Also of considerable importance for the future of equity was Nottingham's consistent application of the maxim: " Equity follows the law." In the middle ages, equity had frequently followed the canon law. For this, there was now substituted the common law. Where the rule of law was satisfactory, equity would apply it. Where the rule was defective, or operated harshly, equity would evolve another solution.

Very similar is Lord Nottingham's attitude to the Statute of Frauds, 1677, of which he claimed to be the author.[24] Section 4 provided that, to be enforceable, some contracts, including contracts for the sale or other disposition of lands, must be evidenced by some note or memorandum in writing, signed by the party to be charged or his agent. Before the statute was passed, the Court of Chancery had granted specific performance of oral contracts for the sale of interests in land, provided they had been part performed. Lord North, Nottingham's successor, and following him all subsequent judges in equity, regarded this jurisdiction as completely unaffected by the statute, and it is clear that, in doing so, they were following Nottingham's own view of the effect of the statute.

Yale interestingly links the development of equity, as a system of legal rules, in Nottingham's Chancellorship, with the appearanec of various collections of maxims of equity.[25] The first of these, by Richard Francis, appeared in 1728, and passed through several editions. Other collections quickly followed, not all of which were published. They are attempts to organise the various rules of equity into a coherent system, and they may have had some value as media of instruction for

21 (1677), 2 Freem. 35.
22 (1676), 3 Swanst. 585, 600.
23 This was his opinion whilst still a Law Officer. See Yale, *op. cit.*, p. xxix.
24 *Ash* v. *Abdy* (1678), 3 Swanst. 664.
25 *Op. cit.*, vol. I, p. ix.

students. Yale suggests,[26] however, that some of the maxims are to be found in elementary form in some of Lord Nottingham's decisions, and even in those of his immediate predecessors. His general conclusion is that whilst the maxims had a more creative role during the eighteenth century (when they were consciously used as sources of new equitable rules), at any earlier date they were used as justifications, or explanations arrived at of principles not yet clearly formulated. It is possibly relevant to notice that in a debate in the House of Lords on 8th July 1678, in an appeal from a decision of Lord Nottingham in *Earl of Feversham* v. *Watson*,[27] Nottingham's predecessor, Shaftesbury, commented on the speech of the Treasurer, Danby, " that his Lordship had spoke like a great statesman, for statesmen always proceed by maxims, and if he could agree with the maxim which makes equity unbounded here, he would agree with the conclusion." On the whole, therefore, it would seem reasonable to conclude that the maxims emerged not later than Nottingham's Chancellorship.

To attempt to summarise the value and extent of Nottingham's contribution to equity in short compass is an impossible task, but his general attitude has been well stated, by Sir Matthew Hale—

> He did look upon equity as a part of the Common Law, and one of the grounds of it; and therefore, as near as he could, he did always reduce it to certain rules and principles, that men might study it as a science, and not think the administration of it had anything arbitrary in it.

After Nottingham's Chancellorship, no-one could again affirm that equity varied as the length of the Chancellor's foot. Nevertheless, Nottingham regarded it as a flexible system, capable of extension. Unlike the common law, it was not presumed to have existed from time immemorial, and since he regarded precedents as evidence of principles, where they spoke with an uncertain voice, he would mould them into a rule, or if this were impossible, he would disregard them altogether. Again, as Yale pointed out[28] in concluding his survey of Nottingham's tenure of the Chancellorship—

> There seems to be a dilemma in equitable development which flows from what is just as between the parties being not necessarily just if erected into a rule of general application, and this is even more pronounced when, in the reverse case, the general rule is qualified by an equitable gloss. Equity indeed strove to do as complete justice

[26] Vol. I, pp. lxi-lxiii.

[27] Nottingham's Chancery Cases, 79 Sel. Soc. 637 (case 823).

[28] *Op. cit.*, p. cxxii.

as possible by drawing into the suit all parties likely to be affected by the decree, but for the purpose of the general antithesis this is scarcely relevant. Another attempt to avoid injustice is seen in the practice of rehearing cases which was already in Lord Nottingham's time giving indications of the dangers inherent in it. Lord Nottingham was rather liberal in this respect but he probably had his doubts.

Rigidity, delay, over-formalism and the ruinous expense of Chancery suits—all these complaints were to be heard in the future. In substantial measure they were derived from the over-zealous application of common law techniques to equitable principles; but before these charges had substance, equity was to enjoy a golden age, in which it became for a time the chief instrument of law reform.

Between Nottingham's resignation in 1682 and the Revolution in 1688, there were only two heads of the Chancery, each holding office for three years. The first, Francis North, Lord Keeper Guilford, was a common lawyer who enjoyed a considerable reputation for learning and, not unnaturally, his judgments reflect his common law bias. North, as Chief Justice of the Court of Common Pleas, had sat frequently with Nottingham in the Chancery, and he was one of the three common law judges whose views did not prevail with the Chancellor in the *Duke of Norfolk's Case*.[29] When the case was reheard by North as Chancellor, he reversed Nottingham's decree, ignoring its far-reaching significance and affirming that "the rules of law must be observed." Fortunately, an unusually full House of Lords, after a lengthy debate, restored it, and thus ensured the rational development of a rule of the very first importance in our property law.

In the proceedings in the House of Lords, important parts had been played by Nottingham's son, Daniel, who had succeeded to the Earldom on his father's death at the end of 1682, and by Lord Jeffreys, who was appointed Chancellor in succession to North. Jeffreys, like North and Nottingham, was primarily a common lawyer, but he quickly made himself familiar with the rules of equity, and in his Chancery judgments he showed a plain disposition to follow where Nottingham had led. Like Nottingham too, he regarded precedents as evidence of equitable rules, and he frequently directed a search for them. It is worthy of note that, after the Revolution, only exceptionally were his decrees reversed by the House of Lords.

[29] (1681) 2 Swanst. 454.

Although the Revolution of 1688 and the accession of the House of Hanover in 1714 did not directly affect the development of equity by the Court of Chancery, it adversely affected appointments to the office of Chancellor. Immediately after the Revolution, and again in 1710, 1718 and 1725, the Great Seal was put into Commission, happily for only brief periods. Other Chancellors and Lord Keepers were chosen rather for their adherence to the Whigs than for their legal attainments, and on their appointment as Chancellors they added little to equity. A similar criticism can be made of Harcourt (1710-1714), who became Lord Keeper during the Tory reaction towards the end of the war of the Spanish Succession. The fame of Lord Keeper King rests principally upon his decision upon constructive trusts in *Keech* v. *Sandford*,[30] but at least one decision of the House of Lords in the time of Lord Nottingham anticipates it.[31] The outstanding Chancellor of the first three decades of the eighteenth century was Thomas Parker, Lord Macclesfield, who had been appointed Chief Justice of the Court of King's Bench in 1710, and who refused the Great Seal in 1711. When it was again offered to him in 1718, with the Whigs firmly established in office, he accepted and held office until 1725, when he was impeached for selling offices in his gift and for concealing the misconduct of Masters in Chancery. As a Chancery judge, however, he had mastered the decisions of his predecessors, and traced out the lines of future development.[32]

Equity by this date had become a system, the boundaries of which could be defined with reasonable certainty. This was due in large measure to the marked improvement in quality of the equity reports, as well as the number of decisions reported. There were also other indications: the appearance of Richard Francis's *Maxims of Equity* in 1728 has already been mentioned. The appearance in 1737 of *A Treatise of Equity* (the first of any note) by Henry Bellow is of more general importance, for it has a surprisingly modern appearance. Divided into six books, the first deals with the general rules of equity, and their application to agreements and covenants. The second is divided into two parts, the first dealing with private uses and trusts, and with the office of trustee. The second part discusses charitable trusts, and the jurisdiction of equity in respect of the estates of infants and lunatics. Book III is devoted to mortgages and pledges; Book IV to wills, legacies and the rights and duties of executors. Book V is occupied with a discussion of damages and interest, and Book VI

30 (1726) Sel. Cas. t. King 61.

31 *Darrel* v. *Whitchcott* (1673/4), Nottingham's Chancery Cases, 73 Sel. Soc. 27 (case 58).

32 For illustrations, see Holdsworth, *H.E.L.*, vol. VII, pp. 208-210.

comprises three chapters on evidence in equity. Possibly the most important omissions from this work are (1) a systematic discussion of the treatment of fraud in equity, for although this was not embodied in a judgment until Lord Hardwicke's Chancellorship, Lord Nottingham had frequently discussed it; and (2) an exposition of equitable remedies.

Holdsworth points out[33] that Bellow's treatise sums up the development in equity which had taken place between the time of Nottingham's Chancellorship and that of Hardwicke. This was the first period of a continuous development of equitable principles which extended to the third decade of the nineteenth century.

> Because Bellow's *Treatise* comes at the end of the earlier part of this period of rapid development, we can see in his book both the connection between the later fixed principles and rules of equity and the original basis upon which equitable modifications of and additions to the law rested, and the manner in which these principles and rules were developed from isolated modifications of and additions to the law in particular cases on grounds of fairness and justice.

Eighteenth century Chancellors were much concerned with the philosophic principles underlying their jurisdiction, and they paid a good deal of attention to natural rights, natural obligations and natural justice. For example, although the rules relating to the satisfaction of portions by legacies, and of legacies by portions, may seem to work awkwardly today, they were developed in the eighteenth century under the influence of theories of natural rights, and of the duty of a property-owning parent to provide for all the children impartially.

It is of this period of continuous development that Jessel, M.R., was thinking, when he said in *Re Hallett's Estate*[34]—

> . . . the rules of Courts of Equity are not, like the rules of the Common Law, supposed to have been established from time immemorial. It is perfectly well known that they have been established from time to time—altered, improved, and refined from time to time. In many cases we know the names of the Chancellors who invented them. No doubt they were invented for the purpose of securing the better administration of justice, but still they were invented. Take such things as these: the separate use of a married woman, the restraint on alienation, the modern rule against perpetuities, and the rules of equitable waste. We can name the Chancellors who first invented them, and state the date when they were first introduced

[33] *Op. cit.*, p. 222.
[34] (1880), 13 Ch. D. 696, 710.

into Equity jurisprudence; and therefore, in cases of this kind, the older precedents in Equity are of very little value. The doctrines are progressive, refined, and improved; and if we want to know what the rules of Equity are, we must look, of course, rather to the more modern than to the more ancient cases.

Not all innovations were sound. Some, after experiment, were ultimately discarded. Others were developed to a state of almost intolerable complexity, Possibly the outstanding example of the latter is the *rule against perpetuities.* Nevertheless, the Chancery judges, unlike their common law colleagues, readily accepted the fact that they were making new law, although they were careful to explain the grounds on which they did so, and it was for this reason that, during the eighteenth century, equity largely replaced legislation as the instrument of law reform.

The Chancellorship of Philip Yorke, Lord Hardwicke, follows immediately upon the earlier period of development which Bellow expounds, and it extended for nearly twenty years from 1737 to 1756. Hardwicke's influence is written largely upon his age, for he was not only an influential statesman, but a commanding intellect, who maintained close contact with the principal thinkers and writers of his day. On many occasions, he expressed his admiration for the balanced constitution and public institutions of Great Britain, as they existed in the middle of the eighteenth century, but, unlike Eldon, he had a basic liberalism which led him to support numerous reforms and to defend individual liberties. Hardwicke, however, held office in a period when the stability of English institutions, like her national security, was exposed to no serious threat. Eldon's Chancellorship extended over the difficult years of the Napoleonic Wars, in which both were directly threatened.

Holdsworth[35] emphasises that Hardwicke, during his lengthy Chancellorship, settled many of the main principles of equity in their final form, and his influence has been an enduring one in every main branch of equitable jurisdiction. His judgments were usually directed to the elucidation of the principle applicable, he frequently overruled precedents which appeared to conflict with it, and he recognised that the application of principles could produce hardships and anomalies in particular cases, which equity could no longer redress, as it had done at an earlier time, in the particular case. On the other hand, equity must remain flexible. Possibly his most famous judgment is that

[35] *Op. cit.*, p. 257.

which he delivered in *Earl of Chesterfield* v. *Janssen*,[36] in which he surveyed the extent of equitable jurisdiction in relation to the various kinds of fraud. Here, in gathering together and classifying many kinds of conduct in respect of which equity will give redress, he affirms that "this Court has undoubted jurisdiction to relieve against every kind of fraud," and in a well-known letter to Lord Kames,[37] he explains his meaning more fully. He says—

> But as to relief against frauds, no invariable rules can be established. Fraud is infinite, and were a Court of Equity once to lay down rules, how far they would go, and no farther, in extending their relief against it, or to define strictly the species or evidence of it, the jursidiction would be cramped, and perpetually eluded by new schemes, which the fertility of man's invention would contrive.

A hundred and sixty-four years later, Lord Haldane, L.C., paraphrased and amplified these observations in his speech in *Nocton* v. *Lord Ashburton*,[38] and Lord Selborne, L.C., in *Earl of Aylesford* v. *Morris*,[39] explained them as follows—

> Fraud does not here mean deceit or circumvention; it means an unconscientious use of the power arising out of these circumstances and conditions; and when the relative position of the parties is such as *primâ facie* to raise this presumption, the transaction cannot stand unless the person claiming the benefit of it is able to repel the presumption by contrary evidence, proving it to have been in point of fact fair, just, and reasonable.

The emphasis, it will be seen, is upon *unconscientious* conduct, and Hardwicke's judgments frequently affirm the proposition that the Court of Chancery is a court of conscience. For example, in *Scroggs* v. *Scroggs*,[40] he says—

> This Court is a Court of conscience, I shall give my opinion in this case according to my conscience . . .

This, nevertheless, did not imply that the Chancellor's decision was arbitrary. In exercising his discretion, he was limited by the rules of equity. These rules, in his view, were both comprehensive and flexible, since equitable remedies were discretionary and the conduct of the parties was a material factor in deciding whether, and to what extent that discretion should be exercised.

[36] (1750), 1 Atk. 301, 351-3. See pp. 331-2, *post*.
[37] Reproduced by Parkes, *History of the Court of Chancery*, pp. 506-9.
[38] [1914] A.C. 932, 954, quoted p. 331, *post*.
[39] (1873), L.R. 8 Ch. App. 484, 491. See also pp. 354-5, *post*.
[40] (1755), Amb. 812, 814.

Conscience is the thread which links many of Lord Hardwicke's most notable judgments. Thus, in *Penn* v. *Lord Baltimore*,[41] in which he decreed the specific performance of articles in England, defining the boundaries of two provinces in America, he said—

> The conscience of the party was bound by this agreement; and being within the jurisdiction of this court, which acts *in personam*, the court may properly decree it as an agreement . . .

It was the flexibility of equitable principles, and their capacity to give birth to new rules, that made them the apt instrument for law reform in a settled age. Yet it was Hardwicke's great achievement that the tremendous advances which occurred during his Chancellorship were accompanied by logical development from the past and by increased certainty and precision in the application of equitable rules.

Something must now be written of some of the principal developments in equity in the period between the Restoration and the Chancellorship of Lord Eldon. Equity had already intervened between mortgagor and mortgagee, to protect the interest of the former, at the beginning of the seventeenth century.[42] By Lord Nottingham's time, the jursidiction was well established, and in *Howard* v. *Harris*[43] he formulated the principle " once a mortgage always a mortgage," which not only proved the starting point of a continuous development of the rules of equity governing the mortgagor's equity of redemption, but also gave rise to a comprehensive body of doctrine relating to " clogging the equity." It was in Nottingham's time that the equity of redemption gradually changed from a personal right to redeem after the appointed date, derived from " conscience," to an equitable interest in the land itself.[44] It is not yet an equitable estate, but the way to such a view of it was now open, more especially since Lord Nottingham, in *Thornborough* v. *Baker*,[45] also decided that on the death of the mortgagee in fee, the mortgage-debt was payable to the executor, and not to the heir, thereby emphasing that a mortgage is not to be regarded as the grant of an estate, but a conveyance by way of security for money borrowed. From the point of view of the mortgagee the recovery of the money was the object sought.

[41] (1750), 1 Ves. Sen. 444.

[42] There were occasional instances of relief at the end of the sixteenth century: Turner, *The Equity of Redemption*, pp. 26-7. See pp. 167-8, *post*.

[43] (1681), 1 Vern. 33.

[44] Yale, *op. cit.*, vol. II, p. 37.

[45] (1675), 3 Swanst. 628.

There was a good deal of development in the law of mortgages at this period, for in *Hedworth* v. *Primate*[46] and in *March* v. *Lee*[47] the doctrine of tacking had been formulated, and this was followed by the recognition of the doctrine of consolidation in *Shuttleworth* v. *Laycock*[48] by Lord Keeper Guilford. Four days previously Lord Guilford in *Baxter* v. *Manning*[49] had accepted the tacking of further advances.

By the time of Lord Hardwicke, these developments were all firmly established, and on the nature of an equity of redemption, he says in *Casborne* v. *Scarfe*[50]—

> . . . An equity of redemption has always been considered as an estate in the land, for it may be devised, granted, or entailed with remainders, and such entail and remainders may be barred by a fine and recovery, and therefore cannot be considered as a mere right only, but such an estate whereof there may be a seisin . . .

Development had proceeded so far by this time in respect of tacking and consolidation, that his powerful mind was directed towards the conditions under which either could occur; and in *Wortley* v. *Birkhead*,[51] after pointing out that in *March* v. *Lee*[47] Hale had explained that, in cases of tacking, the legal estate was the creditor's *tabula in naufragio*, he continued—

> . . . as courts of equity break in upon the common law, when necessity and conscience require it, still they allow superior force and strength to a legal title to estates; and therefore where there is a legal title and equity on one side, this court never thought fit, that by reason of a prior equity against a man, who had a legal title, that man should be hurt, and this by reason of the force this court necessarily and rightly allows to the common law and to legal titles. But if this had happened in any other country, it could never have made a question; for if the law and equity are administered by the same jurisdiction, the rule, *qui prior est tempore potior est jure*, must hold.

From Lord Nottingham's time to that of Hardwicke, the development of the law of trusts had been very considerable, and each Chancellor and Lord Keeper had added something to it. Hardwicke gave it a very modern appearance, many rules applicable to the powers,

46 (1663), Hard. 318.
47 (1670), 1 Ch. Cas. 162.
48 (1684), 1 Vern. 245.
49 (1684), 1 Vern. 244.
50 (1738), 1 Atk. 603, 605.
51 (1754), 2 Ves. Sen. 571, 574.

rights and liabilities being expressed in a form that has remained up to the present time. The separation of the trustee's estate from his personal estate, and the elaboration of the beneficiary's rights in respect of it, had already taken place.

Possibly the most spectacular and continuous intervention of equity during the entire period was in the body of rules which the Chancellors developed to protect the separate estate of the married woman.[52] In this major development of policy, the Chancellors were incorporating into the law some of the more enlightened views of the eighteenth century upon the relations of the parties to a marriage, which gained added force from the abuses to which the transfer of the property of the married woman to the husband's legal ownership had given rise.

Closely approaching in importance to equity's creation of the married woman's separate estate was its acquisition of jurisdiction in respect of the administration of the estates of deceased persons.[53] The story of this development is long and complicated. From early times, the common law courts, and especially the Court of Common Pleas, had excluded all other courts from all questions relating to the devolution of freehold property on death, and even in the limited cases in which a creditor could recover payment of his debt from the real estate of the deceased debtor, the action in respect of it must be brought in the common law courts. On the other hand, all testamentary matters, and the administration of estates of deceased persons, where the subject matter was personal property, were brought in the Church courts. The procedure of these became feeble, uncertain and dilatory after the Reformation, so that progressively actions by creditors to recover their debts out of the personal estates of the deceased, and administrative actions in which a legatee sought to recover his legacy, were brought in the common law courts. Since an executor could not sue himself at common law, the court allowed him the important right of *retainer*, by virtue of which the executor was allowed to retain a debt due to him from the testator in priority to other creditors of equal degree. This was established by the decision of Wright, L.K., in *Hopton* v. *Dryden*.[54] Equity also developed the second right of *preference*, which allows him to pay one creditor in priority to others of the same degree.

Apart from these matters, jurisdiction in all questions of probate, as well as the general administrative jurisdiction over the personal representative in all successions to personal property on death, remained with the ecclesiastical courts, but if either a creditor or a legatee

[52] See ch. XV.

[53] See ch. VII.

[54] (1701), Prec. Ch. 179.

required any special assistance in securing the payment of his debt or legacy, he was compelled to have recourse to the Court of Chancery. This was particularly the case where the proceedings included the taking of an account of the estate of the deceased.

The decline of the Church courts was accelerated by the Commonwealth, and from 1660 onwards, their loss of jurisdiction over the administration of the estates of deceased persons was continuous, although that in probate matters remained. For a time, there was competition between the common law courts and the Chancery, and in the long run, the superior procedure of the Chancery, which included discovery and the taking of accounts, prevailed, although not until after Lord Mansfield in *Atkins* v. *Hill*[55] and *Hawkes* v. *Saunders*[56] had energetically reasserted the claim of the common law courts. These decisions were overruled by Lord Kenyon, C.J., in *Deeks* v. *Strutt*.[57] He pointed out that when equity permitted an action for a legacy to be brought by a husband in right of his wife, it could secure that provision should be made for the family. Since a common law court could not direct that such provision should be made—

> . . . the whole of this admirable system, which has been founded in a Court of Equity, will fall to the ground, if a Court of Law can enforce the payment of a legacy.

Holdsworth[58] points out that the intervention of the Chancery and its supersession of the common law courts was the product of considerations of justice and equity. The Chancery was able to take a comprehensive view of the estate and the various claimants of it. It could in consequence adjust the relations of heirs, devisees and personal representatives, and between creditors and beneficiaries. It also progressively assimilated the office of personal representative with that of trustee, although even today the two have not been completely merged as both the decision in *Ministry of Health* v. *Simpson*,[59] and the views there expressed on the development of this Chancery jurisdiction, sufficiently show. Both in the House of Lords and in the Court of Appeal, the nature of the redress which the Court of Chancery developed from the time of Lord Nottingham onwards to enable the legatee to recover his legacy is exhaustively discussed.

Closely connected with equity's extension to include the administration of the assets of deceased persons was its development of the doc-

55 (1775), 1 Cowp. 284.
56 (1782), 1 Cowp. 289.
57 (1794), 5 T.R. 690, 692.
58 *H.E.L.*, vol. VI, pp. 6, 54-5.
59 [1951] A.C. 251.

trines of marshalling, conversion, election, satisfaction and performance.[60] There could be marshalling either between creditors or between beneficiaries. The foundations of the doctrine appear in cases decided by Lord Clarendon in 1664,[61] and by Lord Nottingham in 1679.[62] The leading cases were decided in the seventeenth century, *Clifton* v. *Burt*[63] by Lord Macclesfield, and *Lanoy* v. *Duke and Dutchess of Athol*[64] by Lord Hardwicke.

In the leading case of *Fletcher* v. *Ashburner*[65] Sir Thomas Sewell, M.R., defined the equitable doctrine of conversion in terms which have become classical—

> . . . he observed that nothing was better established than this principle, that money directed to be employed in the purchase of land, and land directed to be sold and turned into money, are to be considered as that species of property into which they are directed to be converted; and this in whatever manner the direction is given: whether by will, by way of contract, marriage articles, settlement, or otherwise, and whether the money is actually deposited or only covenanted to be paid, whether the land is actually conveyed or only agreed to be conveyed. The owner of the fund or the contracting parties may make land money, or money land. The cases established this rule universally.

At this date the doctrine was of the very first importance, as the basis upon which the trust for sale, or " trader's settlement," had been built up. In the following year, a most important qualification to it was added by Lord Thurlow, L.C., in response to the persuasive eloquence of John Scott, the future Lord Eldon, in *Ackroyd* v. *Smithson*,[66] viz., that conversion, when directed in a will, is for the purpose of the will only; but the doctrine had been taking shape for a century. Its existence had been recognised both by Lord Guilford[67] and Lord Jeffreys[68] before the Revolution, and by Lords Harcourt and Cowper in 1711.[69]

The three doctrines of satisfaction, performance and election all emerged at the beginning of the eighteenth century, and each of them

[60] See Ch. XI-XIV.
[61] *Armitage* v. *Metcalf* (1666) 1, Ch. Cas. 74.
[62] *Anon.* (1679), 2 Ch. Cas. 4.
[63] (1720), 1 P. Wms. 678.
[64] (1742), 2 Atk. 444.
[65] (1779), 1 Bro. C.C. 497, 499.
[66] (1780), 1 Bro. C.C. 503.
[67] *Kettleby* v. *Atwood* (1684), 1 Vern. 298.
[68] *Knights* v. *Atkyns* (1687), 2 Vern. 20.
[69] *Lingen* v. *Sowray* (1711), 1 P. Wms. 172.

owes its origin to the desire of equity to deal equally with beneficiaries, so long as this is consistent with the testator's presumed intention. They depend upon a succession of decisions during the tenure of office of Lords Cowper, Harcourt, Macclesfield and Talbot.

This limited survey by no means indicates all the advances which were being made in equity during the eighteenth century. Charities, and the law of guardianship of infants and lunatics, all received notable additions, but no survey, however brief, would be satisfactory which did not mention the effect of equitable intervention in the law of settlements. These could arise in various ways; and they could operate either at common law, under the Statute of Uses, or in equity through the intervention of a trust or a will. The consequence was that the law, especially that branch of it which governed future interests, became progressively more complex, and it was here that equity, whilst in general following the law, at the same time attempted to introduce more flexibility than was possible under the old common law rules. Unfortunately, the result was sometimes even greater complexity. Possibly the most famous illustration of this is the treatment of the *Rule in Shelley's Case*[70] by courts of equity. The rule provided that where an ancestor by any gift or conveyance takes an estate of freehold, and in the same gift or conveyance an estate is limited either mediately or immediately to his heirs, either in fee simple or in fee tail, the words of remainder to the " heirs " are words of limitation of the estate of the ancestor. They are not words of purchase, conferring any separate interest on the heir.

In his classic speech in *Van Grutten* v. *Foxwell*[71] Lord Macnaghten points out the uncertain origins of the rule, which had existed since the reign of Edward II, and the differences of opinion upon its mode of operation, held by leading writers. With classic irony, he examines the needless complications which successive decisions, both at common law and in equity had introduced. Even Ireland contributed something to the enveloping obscurity, with the decision of Sir Edward Sugden, L.C., in *Montgomery* v. *Montgomery*.[72] "His observations," says Lord Macnaghten[73]—

> . . . were made " with a view to clear up the doubts on this branch of the law." The result was unfortunate. No difficulties were cleared up—no doubtful points explained

and the darkness was even more impenetrable than before.

[70] (1581), 1 Co. Rep. 88b.
[71] [1897] A.C. 658, 670-671.
[72] (1845), 3 Jo. & Lat. 47.
[73] [1897] A.C. 673.

There were, nevertheless, other spheres in which the reforming activities of the Chancery in the eighteenth century showed to greater advantage. In the law of charities, for example, although the procedure for the enforcement of charitable trusts remained cumbrous and dilatory, a conscientious effort was being made to reflect the prevailing attitude of greater toleration in the decisions upon the nature of a charity, especially where the trust was for the advancement of religion. Before the end of the century, Protestant dissenters, Quakers, Jews and others had profited from this more enlightened attitude. In the sphere of trusts and settlements, the trust for sale had been developed to meet the needs of an extended and wealthier middle class, and something had been done to mitigate the rigidity of the common law in its application to strict settlements. To mention only one illustration, the decision in *Vane* v. *Lord Barnard*[74] had established the equitable principle that a tenant for life who was unimpeachable for waste at common law could nevertheless be restrained by injunction if he sought to make an unconscientious use of his legal rights by committing acts of wanton destruction upon the settled estate.

There had also been notable advances in the availability of equitable remedies. Possibly the most important advance of all in this sphere was the establishment of the principle that, though the award of equitable remedies was discretionary, the exercise of that discretion depended upon settled principles, which could be discovered from earlier chancery decisions. Three decisions, extending over a century, had firmly established the remedy of specific restitution. In *Pusey* v. *Pusey*[75] Lord Keeper Guilford had decreed restitution of the famous Pusey horn, but in doing so, he had intimated that he would only do so in cases of heirlooms or of chattels of particular rarity. Lord Talbot, L.C., in *Duke of Somerset* v. *Cookson*,[76] went a step further. In that case, the object to be restored was an old silver altar-piece. Finally, in *Fells* v. *Read*[77] Lord Loughborough, L.C., ordered restitution in respect of some ornamental boxes, without inquiring into their value, and added—

> In all cases, where the object of the suit is not liable to a compensation by damage, it would be strange, if the law of this country did not afford any remedy. It would be great injustice, if an individual cannot have his property without being liable to the estimate of people, who have not his feelings upon it.

[74] (1716), 2 Vern. 738.
[75] (1684), 1 Vern. 273.
[76] (1735), 3 P. Wms. 390.
[77] (1796), 3 Ves. 70, 71-2.

By an extension of the same principle Lord Hardwicke, in *Jackson* v. *Butler*,[78] ordered the delivery of mortgage deeds to a person who was entitled to principal and interest, but who had pawned them to a person who refused to return them.

It was during the eighteenth century that great extensions in the issue of specific performance were undertaken by the Court of Chancery, one of the earliest and most important of them being in respect of parol agreements for leases which under the Statute of Frauds, 1677, should have been in writing. This extension was based on the fact of part performance by the person seeking the aid of equity. The first case in which this occurred was *Lester* v. *Foxcroft* in 1700,[79] a decision of Wright, L.K., which was affirmed by the House of Lords. In *Bond* v. *Hopkins*,[80] an Irish decision, Lord Redesdale, L.C., emphasised that the basis of this relief was conscience—

> The statute of frauds says, that no action or suit shall be maintained on an agreement relating to lands which is not in writing, signed by the party to be charged with it; and yet the Court is in the daily habit of relieving, where the party seeking relief has been put into a situation which makes it against conscience in the other party to insist on the want of writing so signed, as a bar to his relief . . . . It was against conscience to suffer the party who had entered and expended his money on the faith of a parol agreement to be treated as a trespasser, and the other party to enjoy the advantage of the money he had laid out: . . . it appears . . . that Courts of Equity have decided on equitable grounds, in contradiction to the positive enactment of the statute of frauds, though their proceedings are in words included in it . . .

A perusal of *Vesey's Reports*, and particularly *Forster* v. *Hale*[81] and the notes which follow the decision in *Pym* v. *Blackburn*,[82] will show that, by the end of the century, the courts were anxious to limit the availability of a remedy which, in the opinion of Lord Eldon and some of his contemporaries, had been made rather too freely available.

A substantial part of the eighteenth century advance was the consequence of Lord Hardwicke's breadth of view and judicial audacity. His judgments have a ring of certainty, and he was, as Holdsworth has pointed out, our first great judicial comparative lawyer. The eighteenth century also produced a second in Lord Mansfield, and it is interesting

[78] (1742), 2 Atk. 306.
[79] Coll. 108.
[80] (1802), 1 Sch. & Lef. 413, 433-4.
[81] (1798), 3 Ves. 696.
[82] (1796), 3 Ves. 34.

to speculate how posterity would have assessed their respective contributions, had Lord Mansfield been able to follow Lord Hardwicke's example, and to pass from the Chief Justiceship to the Woolsack. As it is, the reforms which he sought to introduce were largely rejected by his successors, and it is only in our own day that common lawyers have turned, with renewed interest, to his objectives.

William Murray, Earl of Mansfield, was Lord Chief Justice from 1756 until 1788, and during that long term he had influenced almost every branch of the common law. Like Hardwicke, his brilliant mind had been moulded by the study of the Year Books, and the early literature of the common law, but also by the study of equity, of Scottish law, of international law, and by the classical French and Dutch writers upon Roman law, and in his judgments he not infrequently resorted to a comparison of English rules with those of Roman law. The breadth of view which this induced led him into an attempt to infuse equitable doctrines into the substance of the common law, in a sustained attempt to adapt the common law to changing social conditions. This was the motive for much of the development which he initiated in the sphere of mercantile law. But Mansfield aimed also at far reaching changes in the relation of law to equity. Holdsworth points out[83] that in the eighteenth century this question was much discussed, and the correspondence between Lord Kames, a Scottish judge who published a volume on equity in 1760, and Lord Hardwicke, has already been mentioned.[84] Lord Kames not unnaturally considered the Scottish system, under which law and equity were administered in the same tribunal, superior to the English. Hardwicke remained convinced of the merits of the English system. Mansfield, a Scotsman, educated in England, but having enjoyed a wide practice both in Scots law and in the English Court of Chancery, before Hardwicke, whom he greatly admired, in this instance sought to influence English law in the direction of fusion. This, he thought, would not only lighten the burdens of the litigant, who under the existing system was compelled to bring two actions, where one should have sufficed, but would also lead to the future development of English law as a unified and rational system. These views did not prevail, and they were repudiated by his successors, perhaps because their inspiration was so plainly drawn from Scottish law, perhaps because other judges were incapable of rising to Mansfield's intellectual height. Even Blackstone, his pupil and admirer, failed to understand his outlook fully, and, as Holdsworth has shown,[85] this led to him, as a common lawyer, to treat

[83] *H.E.L.*, vol. XII, pp. 583-4.
[84] See p. 60, *ante*.
[85] *Op. cit.*, pp. 591 *et seq.*

equity in an ambiguous and unsatisfactory fashion in his *Commentaries*. Indeed, his general conclusion is that the distinction between law and equity is largely accidental, and is due primarily to the different methods of administering justice in each jurisdiction (i.e., differences in modes of proof, the mode of trial and the mode of relief). Holdsworth has little difficulty in pointing out that both Mansfield and Blackstone ignored the fundamental difference in point of view between the two jurisdictions. " Equity, from the first, had always acted *in personam*. It always took all the circumstances of the case and the conduct of the parties into consideration; and its remedies were, for that reason, always discretionary. The courts of law gave, as they were bound to give, the judgment to which the parties were entitled, taking into consideration only the facts pleaded and proved by the evidence. They could not travel outside the record. In the second place, both Mansfield and Blackstone underrated the effect upon substantive rules of the working, for several centuries, of the differences in the mode of proof, the mode of trial, and the mode of relief. These procedural differences had accentuated the fundamental difference between law and equity. They had given rise to many substantial differences, which tended to grow more fundamental as the variant effects of the two procedures were worked out in detail."

Holdsworth's conclusion was therefore the reassuring one that the bulk of the judges were right when they rejected Mansfield's innovations, and that partnership between the two jurisdictions was preferable to fusion. This, however, tends to prove too much. If partnership was the true solution in the eighteenth century, it is difficult to see why it became the false solution in the nineteenth. Again, it is open to question whether the artificial distinction between legal and equitable rights is a necessary one. Further, it is permissible to doubt the value of classifying specific performance and injunction as equitable remedies. The fact that the award of them depends upon special principles, which are well-settled by judicial decisions, seems to be no more difficult for the common law to assimilate than the conception of quasi-contract—or even of negligence. Finally, it should be mentioned that the trust, the greatest of all equity's creations, has been introduced into a large number of legal systems which have never heard of the distinction between legal and equitable rights and interests. In spite of Holdsworth's defence of those who destroyed Mansfield's work, it is possible to regret that the close association of law and equity was not carried out by the inspiration of philosophic judges of the eighteenth century, with their knowledge of other legal systems, rather than by the technicians who accomplished limited changes in the nineteenth, and who have made necessary a fresh investigation of this question in the twentieth.

The failure of Mansfield's enlightened efforts to fuse law and equity helps to place the Chancellorship of Lord Eldon in perspective. John Scott, Lord Eldon, was Lord Chancellor from 1801 (having been Lord Chief Justice of the Court of Common Pleas for two years) until 1805, and again from 1807 until 1827. His Chancellorship therefore extended over the whole of the Napoleonic Wars, and the years of repressive government which followed it, and even as Attorney-General it had been one of his tasks to draft the repressive measures which Pitt had considered necessary to preserve internal order in the struggle with Revolutionary France. The fear of sudden and far-reaching change which this engendered was carried over into his administration of the Court of Chancery, and into his general outlook upon law and government, so that his name is inseparably linked with opposition to practically every measure of reform, legal and political. In his view, the fabric of society had been too profoundly shaken for the enlightenment of the eighteenth century to be a safe guide, and once the threat of Napoleon had passed, every effort should be made to restore the situation which had existed in 1789. So far as the law was concerned, this involved an abandonment of all attempts to introduce major changes in the relation of law to equity. The provinces of each had been established by judicial precedent, and it was his duty to preserve that relationship. Even the eighteenth century policy of reform by equity should now be abandoned. His attitude is very clearly expressed in a letter which he wrote to Sugden in 1826—

> Great alterations in our system of law, I confess, I do not think are likely to improve our law or our lawyers . . . Indulge the appetite for alteration in the law, which we hear so much of nowadays, and in a reign or two more we shall not have a lawyer—a well-grounded lawyer—left.[86]

That Eldon himself was a *well-grounded lawyer* cannot be questioned. His erudition, both in the common law and in equity, was immense, and it was matched by his industry; but it was not matched by breadth of view. For Eldon, English law was a closed system, which could derive no benefit from external influences, even though, in Scottish appeals to the House of Lords, it was apparent that he had taken great pains to master the principles of Scottish law. In so far as equity was concerned, whilst he did not deny the possibility of development, it must henceforth be along lines traced out by earlier decisions, and one of his best-known opinions was expressed in *Gee* v. *Pritchard*,[87] where he said—

[86] Twiss, *Life of Eldon*, vol. III, p. 438; Holdsworth, *H.E.L.*, vol. XIII, p. 607.
[87] (1818), 2 Swanst. 402, 414.

> The doctrines of this Court ought to be as well settled and made as uniform almost as those of the common law, laying down fixed principles, but taking care that they are to be applied according to the circumstances of each case.

It was consciousness of the fact that he was settling what those principles were which directed his exhaustive examination of the precedents, in an attempt to reconcile precedents and to settle a rule; and this was often the cause of lengthy delay in giving judgment. As he himself said, he had undertaken this labour in the hope of saving the time and purses of litigants and their legal advisers in the future. His contemporaries (including those who were opposed to his conservatism) were at one in paying tribute to his legal abilities, his erudition and his powers of analysis, and above all, his anxiety to do justice in the cases which came before him, and several authors (whose views Holdsworth adopts) have compared his labours in equity with those of Coke at common law. Holdsworth aptly sums up his work[88]—

> Eldon is the third of the three great Chancellors who have created our modern system of equity. Nottingham is its father; Hardwicke settled its leading principles and many of its subordinate rules; Eldon worked out in detail the scope and application of those principles and rules, harmonised conflicting interpretations of them, and thus completed the task of making it almost as systematic as the common law.

Except where legislation has intervened, neither the form nor the content of equity has been fundamentally changed since Eldon's day, and in spite of the Judicature Acts, the rules as he settled them still govern the work of a modern equity judge.[89]

[88] *H.E.L.*, vol. XIII, p. 627.
[89] As to equity since the Judicature Acts, see pp. 18-25, 34-43, *ante*, 78-127, *post.*

CHAPTER III

THE JUDICATURE ACTS

INTRODUCTION

THE end of Eldon's long Chancellorship coincided with the rise of a formidable movement in favour of parliamentary reform, which culminated in the Reform Act of 1832. This in turn released a strong impulse in favour of legal reform. Although, as a result mainly of Eldon's influence, the Chancery Commission of 1826 did not report in favour of far-reaching changes in the Court of Chancery, these could not be long delayed. Its abuses and delays were pilloried by Dickens in the famous suit of *Jarndyce* v. *Jarndyce* in *Bleak House*[1] and the attention of Parliament was repeatedly directed to the unsatisfactory position. As a minor improvement, the office of Vice-Chancellor had been established in 1813 (1867 in Ireland), so that the occupant could assist in clearing off the arrears of business, but this failed to improve the position greatly, since an appeal lay from him to the Chancellor, and accordingly delays continued. From 1830, the tide at last turned. In 1831, bankruptcy jurisdiction was transferred from the Chancery to the Chief Judge in Bankruptcy, although the right of ultimate appeal to the Chancellor was preserved.[2] Two years later, the jurisdiction of the Master of the Rolls was extended, the appointment of the Masters was vested in the Crown, their salaries were fixed, the receipt of fees by them was forbidden, and the six clerks were progressively reduced to two.[3] In 1842, the six clerks were finally abolished, and the new office of Taxing Master was established,[4] while the equity jurisdiction of the Court of Exchequer was transferred to the Chancery, two new Vice-Chancellors being appointed.[5] In 1851, the Court of Appeal in Chancery was created. This included the Lord Chancellor and the two Lords Justices in Chancery, and it was instituted for the purpose of hearing appeals from the decisions of the Master

[1] See Holdsworth, *Dickens as a Legal Historian.*

[2] 1 & 2 Will. IV, c. 56. In 1869 the London Court of Bankruptcy was established, with an appeal to the Lords Justices in Chancery. Ireland: Irish Bankrupt and Insolvent Act, 1857.

[3] 3 & 4 Will. IV, c. 94. Ireland: 41 Geo. III, c. 25; Chancery (Ireland) Act, 1867.

[4] Court of Chancery Act, 1842. Ireland: Chancery (Ireland) Act, 1867.

[5] Court of Chancery Act, 1841. Ireland: 13 & 14 Vict., c.51.

of the Rolls, the Vice-Chancellors, and the Chief Judge in Bankruptcy. From the Court of Appeal in Chancery there might be a further appeal to the House of Lords.[6] A year later, the Masters were abolished, their duties in dealing with business which was not transacted in court being transferred to Chief Clerks, the procedure being modelled upon that of the court, not upon the old procedure before the Masters.[7] Since 1873, the Chief Clerks have been styled Masters, but their duties are of modern creation, and they do not resemble those of the old Masters. In 1853, the Masters Extraordinary were abolished, their duties being henceforth discharged by commissioners to administer oaths.[8]

So, in a little over twenty years, the entire complexion of the Court of Chancery had been changed from a respository of ancient offices, many of them little more than sinecures, with a cumbrous and corrupt administration, to a well-equipped and efficient court. There remained still one further reform to undertake. The reform of the Chancery, coinciding as it did with the reform of the common law courts, emphasised the anomaly of two distinct bodies of law, administered in two separate sets of courts. Frequently, if a litigant wished to secure complete legal protection, it was necessary to institute actions in both courts. Had not the time come to put an end to this unscientific and wasteful system ? As the century progressed, the demands of the reformers grew increasingly insistent.

Although the days of conflict between the Court of Chancery and the common law courts were long past, there were many cases which lay upon the frontier of the two jurisdictions. If an action was brought in one jurisdiction, it might be brought up to the House of Lords, only for the parties to discover that the action should have been brought in the other jurisdiction. In *Marquis of Waterford* v. *Knight*[9] (an Irish case), fourteen years of litigation merely produced this negative result. There was a similar vagueness in respect of the limits of common law and admiralty jurisdiction, so that it was common for simultaneous proceedings to be initiated at common law and in the Court of Admiralty. Nevertheless, the greatest problem, resulting in the infliction of the most serious hardships, was that which arose out of the separate administration of law and equity. Legal writers had consistently commented on it. There are several Royal Commissions, each of which suggested changes intended to lead to the ultimate union of the two jurisdictions, but the first step was to give each system of courts

[6] Court of Chancery Act, 1851. Ireland: Chancery Appeal Court (Ireland) Act, 1856.

[7] Court of Chancery Act, 1852. Ireland: Chancery (Ireland) Act, 1867, Part II.

[8] 16 & 17 Vict., c. 78.

[9] (1844), 11 Cl. & Fin. 653.

some of the powers of the other. By the Common Law Procedure Act, 1854,[10] the common law courts, for the first time, were empowered to compel discovery of documents in all cases in which a court of equity could do so, and they were also given a limited power to grant injunctions, and to allow equitable defences to be pleaded. By the Chancery Amendment Act, 1852, the Court of Chancery was enabled to decide all questions of common law, without, as before, seeking the aid of a common law court, and by the Chancery Amendment Act, 1858, it was also given a limited power to award damages. The Court of Chancery was also empowered for the first time to take evidence orally in open court, and to empanel a jury.

These were important steps towards the amalgamation of the common law and equity jurisdictions, although their effect was less than had been anticipated, especially as the Court of Chancery retained its power to use injunctions to stay proceedings at law. In part, the reluctance to change was attributable to the growing conviction that partial change was merely delaying a more comprehensive scheme for fusion. The question acquired a new urgency with the rise of limited liability companies for directors were regarded as both agents and trustees. As agents, they could be pursued in the common law courts and as trustees, simultaneously in the Court of Chancery. This was one of the more important reasons for the appointment of the Royal Commission on Judicature in 1867. Its two reports presented in the following years were the foundation upon which the Judicature Acts, 1873-5, were constructed.

By the Judicature Act of 1873,[11] the Courts of Chancery, Queen's Bench, Common Pleas, Exchequer, Admiralty, Probate, Divorce, and the London Court of Bankruptcy were amalgamated into the Supreme Court of Judicature, which was divided into two parts, the High Court of Justice, and the Court of Appeal. For the more efficient discharge of business, the High Court of Justice was organised into five divisions, reduced in 1881 to three, by the merging of the Queen's Bench Division, the Common Pleas Division, and the Exchequer Division into the Queen's Bench Division. The other two divisions are the Chancery Division, and the Probate, Divorce and Admiralty Division.[12] Furthermore, the determination of certain classes of case was committed, for convenience, to the Chancery Division. These are—

[10] Ireland: Common Law Procedure Amendment Act (Ireland), 1856.

[11] Ireland: Judicature (Ireland) Act, 1877.

[12] In the Republic of Ireland, there are no longer Divisions of the High Court; appeals go to the Supreme Court. In Northern Ireland there are two: Chancery Division and Queen's Bench Division, appeals going to the Court of Appeal.

(1) All causes and matters which by any Act of Parliament may be assigned to the Court of Chancery.

(2) The administration of the estates of deceased persons.

(3) The dissolution of partnerships or the taking of partnership or other accounts.

(4) The redemption or foreclosure of mortgages.

(5) The raising of portions or other charges on land.

(6) The sale and distribution of the proceeds of property subject to any lien or charge.

(7) The execution of trusts, charitable or private.

(8) The rectification, setting aside or cancellation of deeds or other written instruments.

(9) The specific performance of contracts between vendors and purchasers of real estates, including contracts for leases.

(10) The partition or sale of real estates.

(11) The wardship of infants, and the care of infants' estates.[13]

These are substantially the matters dealt with in the Court of Chancery before 1873, and it might therefore seem that the changes of 1873 were changes in the organisation of the court only. This is not so, and the changes effected by the Judicature Acts are fundamental. All jurisdiction is vested in the High Court of Justice as a whole, and may therefore belong to all Divisions.[14] Furthermore, every judge of every Division must recognise and give effect to all equitable rights, obligations and defences and, subject to the supremacy of equity, to all legal rights and obligations, and must grant all such remedies as the parties may be entitled to in respect of any legal or equitable claim, so that, as far as possible, all matters in controversy between the parties may be completely and finally determined, and all multiplicity of legal proceedings avoided.[15] Thus, every judge of the High Court of Justice now administers both systems concurrently, and the benefits of both systems are available to every litigant in every action wherever tried. Hence, since 1873, there has no longer been any possibility of conflict between the two systems, and therefore the Judicature Act also abolished the common injunction by means of which the Court of

[13] Sect. 34. Ireland: 1877 Act, Sect. 36.

[14] Administration of Justice Act, 1928, Sect. 6. Ireland: 1877 Act, Sects. 21, 34 and 37.

[15] Supreme Court of Judicature (Consolidation) Act, 1925, Sects. 36-44 (re-enacting Sect. 24 of the Judicature Act, 1873). Ireland: 1877 Act, Sect. 27.

Chancery had been in the habit of restraining parties to actions at common law; but now, where a party might previously have relied upon an injunction from the Chancery, he may raise every matter of equity by way of defence to the proceedings, and the court may, if it thinks fit, stay them.

From these provisions it might perhaps be assumed that there has at length been a fusion of law and equity. This, however, is not the case. The two systems still preserve their distinct identities, but there has been a union of formerly distinct administrations. The High Court of Justice now administers both systems. But although there were no serious conflicts between the law and equity after 1615, there certainly was variation in the legal consequences derived from the same set of facts at common law and in equity. These differing interpretations are provided for in Section 25[16] of the Judicature Act, 1873—

> In all matters not hereinbefore particularly mentioned, in which there is any conflict or variance between the rules of equity and the rules of common law, with reference to the same matter, the rules of equity shall prevail.

This was an advance on the settlement of 1615 in that, while the courts of common law and the Court of Chancery were free to go their separate ways, and apply differing rules, so long as they did not come into conflict, after 1873, there is only one High Court, sitting in separate Divisions, and only one rule is applicable to the same matter, though it may be the legal rule or the equitable rule; but if before 1873 the rules of common law and equity conflicted *with reference to the same matter*, then the equitable rule now prevails.

It will be clear that the principal consequences of the Judicature Acts are two—

(1) Although there has been no fusion of the two systems, there has been a fusion of the administration of them.

(2) Where there was direct variance between law and equity before 1873, there is now variance no longer. The two systems have adopted a common rule in that particular, the common rule being the equitable rule. This necessarily implies that in one or two instances a common law rule has been abandoned.

Maitland was of the opinion that, after 1873, the importance of the distinction between law and equity would be greatly reduced, and that the distinction would ultimately disappear. It is true that no practitioner can now learn and practise one system and ignore the other; although

[16] Ireland: Sect. 28 of the Act of 1877.

it may be questioned whether any Chancery practitioner ever understood his subject without first mastering the common law. It is also true that to-day the line between common law and equity tends to become blurred, yet the distinction between common law and equity is not only one of history, but also one of attitude.[17] The equitable conception of property and its protection was fundamentally different from that of the common law; and this distinction has been accepted and employed anew in England[18] in the property legislation of 1925, so that it is not an overstatement to say that equity has acquired a fresh value since 1925. An appreciation of the statutory conception of equitable rights and duties is essential for an understanding of the modern practice of conveyancing, and that statutory conception of equity is a direct derivative of the doctrines evolved in the Court of Chancery, although with important modifications and extensions.

The Effect of the Judicature Acts

General

The Judicature Acts did not in any way alter the nature of legal and equitable rights. They remained distinct conceptions as before 1873. Nevertheless, Section 25[19] endeavoured to remove a number of cases of conflict which had occasioned difficulty before the Acts. The first ten subsections deal with particular types of conflict, while the eleventh contains the general provision already set out.[20]

Subsection (1) incorporates the bankruptcy rules into the administration of the estate of a person who has died insolvent. This subsection was repealed by Section 10 of the Judicature Act, 1875, which has now been replaced by the Administration of Estates Act, 1925, Section 34 and Part I of the First Schedule, which provides that funeral, testamentary and administration expenses have priority, and " subject as aforesaid, the same rules shall prevail and be observed as to the respective rights of secured and unsecured creditors and as to debts and liabilities provable and as to the valuation of annuities and future and contingent liabilities respectively, and as to the priorities of debts and liabilities as may be in force for the time being under the law of bankruptcy with respect to the assets of persons adjudged bankrupt."[21]

[17] Cf. Evershed, " Equity after Fusion: Federal or Confederate " (1948), 1 *Journal of the Society of Public Teachers of Law*, 171.

[18] The 1925 property legislation is inapplicable to Ireland, where there is no equivalent.

[19] Ireland: Judicature (Ireland) Act, 1877, Sect. 28.

[20] See p. 77, *ante*. The subsection is considered in detail pp. 84-127, *post*.

[21] Sect. 28 (1) of the Judicature (Ireland) Act, 1877, has been replaced by the Succession Act, 1965, Sect. 46 (Republic of Ireland), and the Administration of Estates Act (Northern Ireland), 1955, Sect. 30 (1). See Leitch, *Handbook on the Administration of Estates Act* (*Northern Ireland*), 1955.

These provisions represent an attempt to simplify a very confusing branch of Chancery practice, some intricacies of which were discussed by Maitland.[22] In the nineteenth century, the Court of Chancery established a certain order for the payment of the debts of a deceased insolvent by a personal representative, which had to be followed when the estate was administered out of court. Courts of bankruptcy, however, had established a different order of payment of debts for an insolvent who was still alive. In *Re Whitaker*,[23] the Court of Appeal decided that the effect of Section 10 of the Judicature Act, 1875, was that the bankruptcy order was introduced into the administration of an insolvent estate of a deceased, where that administration took place in court. Thus, a confusing distinction had been introduced, and further slight differences were possible, according to whether the insolvent estate of the deceased was administered in Chancery or in bankruptcy.[24]

Section 34 of the Administration of Estates Act, 1925, however, has introduced a common order of payment in the administration of all insolvent estates, where the deceased dies after 1925, whether the estate is administered in or out of court, or in bankruptcy. The section did not quite solve all problems, however. It did not explicitly settle the question whether the executor still possessed rights of retainer and preference, enjoyed under the Chancery rules, nor did it settle what were the rights of the Crown in such an administration. In *Attorney-General* v. *Jackson*[25] the House of Lords held that an executor can still retain or prefer in respect of debts of equal or lower degree, and also that the Crown is a preferred creditor to-day only in respect of such debts as are preferred, either by the Bankruptcy Act, 1914, or by the Administration of Estates Act, 1925.[26] A few bankruptcy rules even to-day have not been introduced into the administration of insolvent estates, e.g. rules which go to swell the assets. Thus, the " reputed ownership " clause[27] does not apply, nor do the rules relating to the avoidance of voluntary settlements,[28] nor those relating to fraudulent preferences.[29]

22 *Equity*, Lecture XVI.

23 [1901] 1 Ch. 9.

24 See the Irish cases noted to Sect. 10 of the Judicature Act, 1875, Halsbury's *Statutes of England*, 2nd ed., vol. 9, p. 705.

25 [1932] A.C. 365. And see *Re S. P.*, [1936] Ch. 735.

26 See, further, pp. 275-6, *post*.

27 Bankruptcy Act, 1914, Sect. 38. Ireland: Irish Bankrupt and Insolvent Act, 1857, Sects. 273, 298 and 313. See also Halsbury's *Statutes of England*, 2nd ed., vol. 2, p. 375, for Irish cases.

28 Bankruptcy Act, 1914, Sect. 42. Ireland: Bankruptcy Amendment Act (Northern Ireland), 1929, Sect. 12; no equivalent legislation in the Republic of Ireland.

29 Bankruptcy Act, 1914, Sect. 44. Ireland: Bankruptcy (Ireland) Amendment Act, 1872, Sect. 53; and Bankruptcy Amendment Act (Northern Ireland), 1929 Sect. 13.

Section 25 (2) of the Judicature Act, 1873,[30] provides that a claim by a cestui que trust against an express trustee cannot be barred by any statute of limitations. This subsection was merely declaratory of the existing equitable rule on this topic, and was greatly modified by Section 8 of the Trustee Act, 1888 (now the Limitation Act, 1939, Section 19).[31]

Section 25 (3)[32] deals with the topic of waste, and enacts that an estate for life without impeachment of waste shall not confer or be deemed to have conferred upon the tenant for life any legal right to commit waste of the description known as equitable waste, unless an intention to confer such right shall expressly appear by the instrument creating such estate. This provision has now been replaced in England by a similar one in Section 135 of the Law of Property Act, 1925. At common law, waste was damage to real property tending to the permanent and lasting loss of the person entitled to the inheritance, and it was divided into voluntary and permissive waste. Voluntary waste involved the commission of some wrongful positive act, e.g. pulling down houses, cutting timber, or opening mines for the extraction and sale of minerals. Permissive waste, on the other hand, involved a wrong of omission, and usually took the form of allowing property to fall to ruin through failure to repair. The Statute of Marlborough, 1267, as explained in later decisions, provided that if the grantor of an estate for life expressly made the tenant unimpeachable for waste, no action lay against him for either type of waste, but if no such permission was given the tenant for life was liable for voluntary, but not for permissive, waste unless the instrument expressly imposed upon the tenant the obligation to keep the property in repair.[33] From this, it might appear that a tenant for life unimpeachable for waste might deal with the property exactly as an absolute owner could do, and so at common law he could. Equity, however, would restrain by injunction a tenant for life from committing acts of wanton destruction, even though he was unimpeachable for waste. In *Vane* v. *Lord Barnard*[34] the tenant for life was restrained from dismantling the principal mansion-house, at the instance of the remainderman; and at other times, the felling of ornamental timber has been similarly prevented.[35] Acts so restrained only in equity acquired the oddly-

[30] Ireland: Sect. 28 (2) of the 1877 Act.

[31] See Keeton, *The Law of Trusts*, 9th ed., pp. 407-15, and Irish Supplement (Sheridan), pp. 48-9; Nathan and Marshall, *A Casebook on Trusts*, 5th ed., pp. 481-8. Ireland: Statute of Limitations, 1957, Sects. 43-4 (Republic of Ireland); Statute of Limitations (Northern Ireland), 1958, Sects. 44-5.

[32] Ireland: Sect. 28 (3) of the 1877 Act.

[33] *Re Cartwright* (1889), 41 Ch.D. 532.

[34] (1716), 2 Vern. 738.

[35] *Marquis of Downshire* v. *Lady Sandys* (1801), 6 Ves. 107; *Weld-Blundell* v. *Wolseley*, [1903] 2 Ch. 664.

inappropriate name of " equitable waste." The subsection expressly recognises the validity of the equitable rule, though it provides for the possibility of a settlor expressly granting the right to commit equitable waste in the settlement.

Section 25 (4)[36] (now replaced by Section 185 of the Law of Property Act, 1925) provided that there shall not be any merger by operation of law only of any estate the beneficial interest in which would not be deemed to be merged or extinguished in equity. Here again there was an important variance between common law and equity, to which the Judicature Act put an end. At common law, wherever two estates were united in the same person, the lesser estate was merged in the greater, irrespective of the intent of the parties concerned, provided that the estates united without any intervening estate, and that the person who held them both held them in the same right. Equity adopted a different attitude, however, for where the question of merger depended upon the operation of equitable principles, equity looked at the intent. Where an intention not to merge was declared, no merger occurred. Even where no intent was declared, equity would infer an intention against merger if it was to the interest of the person in whom the estates were united, or if it was in accordance with his duty that no merger should occur.[37] Since 1875 the equitable rule, depending upon intent, express or presumed, has prevailed. If such an intent can be gathered, there will be no merger; otherwise merger will still occur when the two estates are united in the same person.

Section 25 (5) of the Judicature Act[38] dealt with suits for possession of land by mortgagors. It has now been replaced in England by Section 98 of the Law of Property Act, 1925, which provides that until a mortgagee gives notice of his intention to take possession, the mortgagor may bring an action in his own name for the recovery of possession, or of the rents, or for damages in respect of any trespass or wrong relating to the land.

Section 25 (6)[39] deals with the question of the assignment of choses in action.[40]

Section 25 (7)[41] declares that stipulations in contracts as to time or otherwise, which would not before the passing of the Act have been deemed to be or to have become of the essence of such contracts in a

[36] Ireland: Sect. 28 (4) of the 1877 Act.

[37] *Snow* v. *Boycott*, [1892] 3 Ch. 110; *Re Fletcher*, [1917] 1 Ch. 339.

[38] Ireland: Sect. 28 (5) of the 1877 Act.

[39] Ireland: Sect. 28 (6) of the 1877 Act.

[40] Ch. VIII is devoted to this subject.

[41] Ireland: Sect. 28 (7) of the 1877 Act.

court of equity, shall receive in all courts the same construction as they would have received in equity. If before 1875 the parties to a contract fixed a time for the performance of the obligation, the common law treated this as an essential part of the contract, and if performance did not take place at the time stated, the common law regarded the contract as broken, so that the other party could rescind. At common law, that is, time was always of the essence of the contract.

In equity, a different rule prevailed. Equity distinguished on the one hand those terms which were merely formal, a breach of which would not be permitted to bar rights arising under the contract, and those terms which were of the essence of the contract. Prima facie all stipulations as to time were not of the essence of the contract, although in three cases, special circumstances might make them so. For example, if the contract itself expressly declared that time was of the essence of the contract,[42] or if, though time was not originally of the essence of the contract, one party gave the other notice that it should be so treated, after that other had been guilty of unreasonable delay[43] (the time specified being, in the circumstances, reasonable), or thirdly, where from the nature of the contract, time may be considered to be of the essence of the contract—in these three types of cases, equity would regard time as of the essence of the contract, and withhold its remedies from the party at fault. The third class of cases is one which it is impossible to define in general terms. Illustrations are afforded by contracts for sale of leaseholds,[44] several types of businesses as going concerns,[45] and the sale or lease of a house for immediate occupation.[46] The most important contracts of all, however, within this class, were mercantile contracts, arising out of negotiable instruments.[47]

In adopting this attitude, equity was simply generalising the practice already developed in relation to mortgages,[48] and the practice would appear to be connected with the fact that, whilst at common law, in general, interest was not payable upon an overdue debt, equity in the case of mortgages and also in the case of sales of land permitted the creditor to recover interest on sums due. Since the Law Reform (Miscellaneous Provisions) Act, 1934,[49] the court has now in all cases a discretion to award interest upon the debt or damages recovered,

[42] *Steedman* v. *Drinkle*, [1916] 1 A.C. 275 (P.C., Saskatchewan).

[43] *Stickney* v. *Keeble*, [1915] A.C. 386 (H.L., E.).

[44] *Hudson* v. *Temple* (1860), 29 Beav. 536.

[45] *Lock* v. *Bell* [1931] 1 Ch. 35.

[46] *Tilley* v. *Thomas* (1867), L.R. 3 Ch. App. 61.

[47] *Reuter, Hufeland & Co.* v. *Sala & Co.* (1879), 4 C.P.D. 239 (C.A.).

[48] *Seton* v. *Slade* (1802), 7 Ves. 265. See pp. 168-71, 187-8, *post*.

[49] Ireland: Law Reform (Miscellaneous Provisions) Act (Northern Ireland), 1937; no corresponding legislation in the Republic of Ireland.

except that interest upon interest may not be recovered, while the discretion may not affect the position where interest is payable as of right, nor does it affect the damages recoverable for the dishonour of a bill of exchange.

By Section 25 (7) of the Judicature Act, 1873, re-enacted in England in Section 41 of the Law of Property Act, 1925, the rule of equity has now become the rule of law, but only in respect of those contracts which, before 1873, could come before the Court of Chancery for decision. Thus the rule even to-day does not apply to mercantile contracts, where the general rule is that stipulations to time, except as to time of payment, are of the essence of the contract.[50]

Section 25 (8)[51] provides that a mandamus or an injunction may be granted or a receiver appointed by interlocutory order by any Division of the High Court. This was a necessary consequence of the conferring of legal and equitable jurisdiction on all Divisions of the High Court.[52]

Section 25 (9)[53] provided that "in any cause or proceeding for damages arising out of a collision between two ships, if both ships shall be found to have been in fault, the rules hitherto in force in the Court of Admiralty, so far as they have been at variance with the rules in force in the courts of common law, shall prevail." This section, which has nothing to do with the relations of law and equity, has now been replaced by the Maritime Conventions Act, 1911, Section 9 (3). At common law there could be no division of loss where there was contributory negligence, but the Court of Admiralty applied a different rule of very ancient origin,[54] and this by the Judicature Act prevailed.

Section 25 (10)[55] enacted that the equity rules as to the custody and education of infants should prevail. This subsection and subsection (11) are now replaced in England by Section 44 of the Judicature Act, 1925.

There remains now for consideration subsection (11)[56] (now Section 44 of the Judicature Act, 1925). This provided—

[50] *Reuter, Hufeland & Co.* v. *Sala & Co.* (1879), 4 C.P.D. 239 (C.A.).

[51] Ireland: Sect. 28 (8) of the 1877 Act.

[52] As to the effect of the Judicature Act on the principles relating to the grant of injunctions, see pp. 110-13, *post*.

[53] Ireland: Sect. 28 (9) of the 1877 Act.

[54] See Marsden, *Collisions at Sea*, 10th ed., ch. VI. The maritime rule has now been extended to common law actions by the Law Reform (Contributory Negligence) Act, 1945 (Ireland: Law Reform (Miscellaneous Provisions) Act (Northern Ireland), 1948; no corresponding legislation in the Republic of Ireland). Marsden points out that in the original draft of the Act of 1873, it was provided that the common law rule should prevail but the Admiralty rule was restored during the passage of the bill, at the instance of the Admiralty registrar. (p. 156, n. 27).

[55] Ireland: Sect. 28 (10) of the 1877 Act.

[56] Ireland: Sect. 28 (11) of the 1877 Act.

Generally in all matters not hereinbefore particularly mentioned, in which there is any conflict or variance between the rules of equity and the rules of common law with reference to the same matter, the rules of equity shall prevail.

The subsection does not attempt to enumerate any specific cases of conflict or variance. It merely provides for any which may arise, leaving its precise scope indeterminate. In consequence, differing views of its application have been held, and today in some cases continue to be held. One thing is clear. The subsection effected no radical alteration in the relations of law and equity, and indeed, the effect of the decisions has been, on the whole, to confine its effect within narrow limits, which can best be appreciated by studying the operation of the section upon a number of cases of conflicts or variances which are merely illustrations not intended to serve as an exhaustive enumeration of the cases of conflicts or variances which existed before 1873.

Effect of a Written Lease

The Statute of Frauds, 1677, Section 1,[57] enacted that all leases made by parol and not by writing, " should have the force and effect of leases or estates at will only," an exception being made in Section 2[57] in favour of leases for not more than three years, at a rent of at least two-thirds of the full value (now by the Law of Property Act, 1925, Section 54, in England, at the best rent). The Real Property Act, 1845, Section 3, provided that " a lease required by law to be in writing . . . shall be void at law unless also made by deed."[58]

Thus, with the exception of leases under the Statute of Frauds, 1677, Section 2, all leases had to be made by deed. The Real Property Act, 1845, however, said other leases should be " void at law." The question then arose: Had a written lease, not under seal, any, and if so, what effect? Different answers to this were given at common law and in equity. At common law, it was decided that a tenant who held under a written lease, and who had gone into possession, and had paid rent on a yearly basis, was to be regarded as a tenant from year to year, and furthermore, that he held on such terms in his written lease as were not inconsistent with the common law rules relating to yearly tenancies.[59] If the rent was not paid on a yearly basis, the tenant was a

[57] Ireland: Statute of Frauds, 1695, Sect. 1.

[58] These two statutes have been re-enacted in England in the Law of Property Act, 1925, Sects. 54 (1) and 52 (1) and (2).

[59] *Doe dem. Rigge* v. *Bell* (1793), 5 T.R. 471; *Clayton* v. *Blakey* (1798), 8 T.R. 3; *Hamerton* v. *Stead* (1824), 3 B. & C. 478; *Mann* v. *Lovejoy* (1826), Ry. & M. 355; *Richardson* v. *Gifford* (1834), 1 Ad. & El. 52.

mere tenant at will. Equity interpreted the situation differently. It held that a written lease was in fact an agreement for a lease, enabling either party to call at any time for specific performance, so that a formal lease under seal was executed, upon terms corresponding with those in the written lease.[60]

The effect of the Judicature Act upon this variance was considered in the leading case of *Walsh* v. *Lonsdale*,[61] wherein Lonsdale agreed in writing to grant a seven years' lease of a mill to Walsh, one year's rent always being payable in advance. No lease under seal was executed, and Walsh entered into possession, paying rent quarterly, but not in advance. After eighteen months, Lonsdale demanded a year's rent in advance, and when Walsh refused to pay it, he distrained. Walsh brought an action for illegal distraint, and for specific performance of the lease. He rested his claim for damages for illegal distraint upon the argument that at common law, having been let into possession and having paid rent measurable by reference to a year, he was a tenant from year to year, holding on the terms of a written lease which were not inconsistent with the terms of common law yearly tenancies; but payment of a year's rent in advance was inconsistent with such a tenancy. It would seem that payment of rent in advance is not inconsistent with the terms of a common law yearly tenancy,[62] but in *Walsh* v. *Lonsdale*[61] the rent of the property (a weaving shed) was fixed by reference to the number of looms actually worked during the year, thus making the payment of rent in advance difficult of assessment, and presumably making the term unenforceable at common law (though this is not clear). The landlord argued simply that in equity, the written lease could be turned into a lease by specific performance[63] whereupon the provision for rent in advance would be fully enforceable. Since equity regards as done that which ought to be done, the parties were in the same position as if the formal lease had been executed, and further, since 1873, the equitable rule prevailed over the common law rule. This view of the matter was accepted by the court, and Jessel, M.R., said[64]—

> There are not two estates as there were formerly, one estate at common law by reason of the payment of the rent from year to year, and an estate in equity under the agreement. There is only one Court, and the equity rules prevail in it. The tenant holds under

[60] *Doe dem. Thomson* v. *Amey* (1840), 12 Ad. & El. 476; *Parker* v. *Taswell* (1858), 2 De G. & J. 559.

[61] (1882), 21 Ch.D. 9.

[62] *Lee* v. *Smith* (1854), 9 Ex. 662.

[63] See ch. XVIII.

[64] (1882), 21 Ch.D. 14-15.

> an agreement for a lease. He holds, therefore, under the same terms in equity as if a lease had been granted, it being a case in which both parties admit that relief is capable of being given by specific performance. That being so, he cannot complain of the exercise by the landlord of the same rights as the landlord would have had if a lease had been granted. On the other hand, he is protected in the same way as if a lease had been granted; he cannot be turned out by six months' notice as a tenant from year to year. He has a right to say, "I have a lease in equity, and you can only re-enter if I have committed such a breach of covenant as would if a lease had been granted have entitled you to re-enter according to the terms of a proper proviso for re-entry." That being so, it appears to me that being a lessee in equity he cannot complain of the exercise of the right of distress merely because the actual parchment has not been signed and sealed.

This is the rule in *Walsh* v. *Lonsdale*, and it might seem that the decision, in making an agreement for a lease almost as effective as a duly sealed lease itself, has made the equitable interest existing under the agreement as good as a legal estate. This, however, is not so. Maitland has put the distinction clearly—

> An equitable right is not equivalent to a legal right; between the contracting parties an agreement for a lease may be as good as a lease; just so between the contracting parties an agreement for the sale of land may serve as well as a completed sale and conveyance. But introduce the third party and then you will see the difference. I take a lease; my lessor then sells the land to X; notice or no notice my lease is good against X. I take a mere agreement for a lease, and the person who has agreed to grant the lease then sells and conveys to Y, who has no notice of my merely equitable right. Y is not bound to grant me a lease.[65]

If the lessee has entered into possession, this, before 1926, was constructive notice of the equitable interest to the assignee of the lessor; but in England since 1925, an agreement for a lease is an estate contract under the Law of Property Act, 1925, Section 2 (3) (iv), and as such is registrable as a land charge under the Land Charges Act, 1925, Section 10(1), C(iv), and 13(2). If it is registered, it binds all assignees of the lessor, whether the lessee has gone into possession or not. If it is not registered, it is void against a purchaser of a legal estate for money or money's worth,[66] whether there was notice or not.

[65] *Equity*, 2nd ed., p. 158.
[66] Land Charges Act, 1925, Sect. 13 (2).

The distinction emphasised by Maitland was not always clearly appreciated in the courts, and expressions were sometimes used implying that a lease and an agreement for a lease were equal in value and effect since 1873. Thus, Field, J., observed[67]—

> Since the Judicature Acts there is now no distinction that I can see, between a lease and an agreement for a lease, because equity looks upon that as done which ought to be done.

Actually, the view of the Court of Appeal in *Walsh* v. *Lonsdale*, and of all the judges who expressed themselves in similar terms, was based upon the assumption which was expressed in plain terms in Jessel, M.R.'s judgment in that case, that whereas before the Judicature Act, there were two estates, one at law, and the other in equity, since the Judicature Act, there was only one estate, the equitable estate, and that the written lease was simply an agreement to grant a lease upon the same terms. This, as the later cases were to show, was a fallacy. It applied only where the agreement would be specifically enforced, and if, for any reason, the remedy of specific performance was not available, then the parties would be governed by the common law relating to written agreements. Even in *Walsh* v. *Lonsdale* itself, there were some uncertainties relating to the rent payable which, had they been more fundamental, might have proved fatal to the grant of specific performance, and which would have resulted in the application of the rules of common law to the problem.

Other judges expressed their view that a written lease was, since 1873, as good as a lease, for example, Manisty, J., in *Furness* v. *Bond*,[68] Chitty, J., in *Allhusen* v. *Brooking*[69] and Cotton, L.J., in *Lowther* v. *Heaver*.[70] It may be admitted that for many purposes, the two are unquestionably the same. Thus, in *Crump* v. *Temple*,[71] Charles, J., held that a tenant under an agreement for a lease, of which specific performance will be granted, is subject to the same right of distress as if a lease under a seal had been executed. Still, the two are not identical, and a timely check to the mistaken view was given in Farwell, J.'s judgment in *Manchester Brewery Co.* v. *Coombs*,[72] in the course of which he observed—

[67] *Re Maughan* (1885), 14 Q.B.D. 956, 958.

[68] (1888), 4 T.L.R. 457.

[69] (1884), 26 Ch. D. 559, 565.

[70] (1889), 41 Ch.D. 248, 264 (C.A.).

[71] (1890), 7 T.L.R. 120. Again, in *Rickett* v. *Green*, [1910] 1 K.B. 253, a Divisional Court decided that a specifically enforceable agreement for lease was a "lease" within Sect. 10 of the Conveyancing Act, 1881.

[72] [1901] 2 Ch. 608, 617.

> Although it has been suggested that the decision in *Walsh* v. *Lonsdale*[73] takes away all differences between the legal and equitable estate, it, of course, does nothing of the sort, and the limits of its applicability are really somewhat narrow. It applies only to cases where there is a contract to transfer a legal title, and an act has to be justified or an action maintained by force of the legal title to which such contract relates. It involves two questions: (1) Is there a contract of which specific performance can be obtained? (2) If Yes, will the title acquired by such specific performance justify at law the act complained of, or support at law the action in question? It is to be treated as though before the Judicature Acts there had been, first, a suit in equity for specific performance, and then an action at law between the same parties; and the doctrine is applicable only in those cases where specific performance can be obtained between the same parties in the same court, and at the same time as the subsequent legal question falls to be determined.

The importance of the learned judge's emphasis of the fact that the rule is applicable only to cases where specific performance of the agreement will be granted is well illustrated by *Swain* v. *Ayres*.[74] In that case the parties entered into an agreement for a lease, which equity would not have specifically enforced, since there had been breaches of covenant by the tenant. The landlord claimed forfeiture, to which the tenant replied that he was protected by Section 14 of the Conveyancing Act, 1881, which provides that where the parties hold under " a lease," in which there is a right of re-entry or forfeiture for breach of a covenant or condition, such a right of re-entry or forfeiture shall not be enforceable until a certain notice has been served by the lessor. The Court of Appeal held that an agreement for a lease, of which specific performance will not be granted, is not a lease within the section. This particular point has now apparently been altered, for in Section 5 of the Conveyancing Act of 1892, which extended Section 14 of the Act of 1881, the terms " lease " and " underlease " were made to include for this purpose any agreement for a lease or underlease *where the lessee is entitled to have the lease or underlease granted*, and this has been re-enacted in England in the Law of Property Act, 1925, Section 146 (5) (*a*). But it is arguable that these words mean " where the agreement is specifically enforceable," in which event the decision in *Swain* v. *Ayres*[74] remains good.

[73] (1882), 21 Ch.D. 9.
[74] (1888), 21 Q.B.D. 289.

In the course of his decision in *Swain* v. *Ayres*, Lopes, L.J., said[75]—

> It seems to me that the legal position of the defendant in this case was that he was tenant from year to year on the terms of the agreement for a lease.

From this it follows that where there is an agreement for a lease, of which equity will not give specific performance, the old common law rule applies to it, even after the Judicature Act. Since the Judicature Act, that is, there are not two estates, one in law, and another in equity. There must be either one or the other. It is usually the equitable estate, but there are occasions (and *Swain* v. *Ayres* is one example) where the common law estate still exists.

In Ireland, *Walsh* v. *Lonsdale* does represent the law, though there are statutory differences. Section 3 of the Real Property Act, 1845 has been amended by Section 104 of the Landlord and Tenant Law Amendment Act, Ireland, 1860 (known as Deasy's Act). One effect of Sections 3 and 4 of Deasy's Act is that a lease for more than three years, like a shorter one, may be in writing not under seal. When reading a contract between landlord and tenant, it can be difficult to tell whether it is a lease or an agreement for a lease. Nevertheless, there remains a distinction between the two.[76] In *McCausland* v. *Murphy*[77] an agent, not authorised in writing, agreed on behalf of his principal to grant a lease to start at a future date. By Section 4 of Deasy's Act, an agent can grant a lease only if authorised in writing. It was held that this provision did not require an agent who made such an agreement for a lease to be authorised in writing. Sullivan, M.R., said[78] that—

> The Act of 1860 made a great alteration in the law, and one would expect to find its provisions plain and clear, if the intention was to put an end to the distinction between an actual lease and an agreement. But no such intention was expressed in the Act. The 1st section of the Statute of Frauds is repealed by the schedule, and the

[75] 21 Q.B.D. 296. In *Coatsworth* v. *Johnson* (1886), 55 L.J.Q.B. 220, the plaintiff entered into possession of a farm under a contract for a lease, but did not pay any rent. On account of his failure to perform the terms of the intended lease, the defendant treated him as a tenant at will and ejected him. The plaintiff sued in trespass, but it was found as a fact that the terms of the intended lease had been broken, and therefore the Court of Appeal found for the defendant, on the ground that this was an agreement of which specific performance would not be granted.

[76] See Sheridan, "*Walsh* v. *Lonsdale* in Ireland" (1952), 9 *Northern Ireland Legal Quarterly*, 190.

[77] (1881), 9 L.R. Ir. 9. See also *Archbold* v. *Lord Howth* (1866), 1 I.L.T. 760; *Sweeney* v. *Denis* (1883), 17 I.L.T.R. 76; *Craig* v. *Elliott* (1885), 15 L.R. Ir. 257; *Union* v. *M'Dermott* (1921), 55 I.L.T.R. 194 (C.A., Southern Ireland).

[78] 9 L.R. Ir. 15.

> provisions of the 4th section of the Act of 1860 are substituted for it as to actual leases. But the 2nd section of the Statute of Frauds is not repealed, though by the 1st and 3rd sections of the Act of 1860 the relation of landlord and tenant is founded on the express or implied contract of the parties; and a lease means any instrument in writing containing a contract of tenancy. In this case there was authority to make a preliminary agreement for a future tenancy, and a lease was to be executed.

Thus, while an agreement to grant a lease immediately operates as a lease, an agreement to grant a lease at some future date is a contract to which the doctrine of *Walsh* v. *Lonsdale* would apply. Indeed, it is not possible to make an agreement for a lease just as binding as a lease on the lessor's assigns, there being no provision in Ireland for registration of estate contracts.

Foster v. *Reeves*[79] is another example of differences that may still result from the fact that a lease is not under seal. In that case the defendant entered into an agreement in writing to lease premises of a value exceeding £500. Later, he gave six months' notice and left, and the landlord sued him for rent due after the expiration of the notice, on the grounds that the agreement was as good as an executed lease (which would have given the tenant no such right). The action was tried in the county court, which had no equity jurisdiction in cases where the value of the property involved exceeded £500. The Court of Appeal held that the rule that a person who holds under an agreement for a lease is entitled to be considered as holding under an executed lease on the same terms is applicable only if the court in which the action is brought can give specific performance of the agreement; and the landlord was unable to recover.

Lord Esher, M.R., observed[80]—

> The position of the judge was, therefore, like that in which a common law judge would formerly have been. He could not entertain the equitable doctrine and apply it to the case before him, and treat it as if there had had been a lease granted. Consequently the plaintiff could not recover . . .

This, therefore, constitutes a limitation upon Maitland's proposition that, between the parties, an agreement for a lease is as good as a lease.

79 [1892] 2 Q.B. 255.

80 [1892] 2 Q.B. 258. It would have been otherwise had the equitable doctrine been put forward by way of defence: *Kingswood Estate Co. Ltd.* v. *Anderson*, [1963] 2 Q.B. 169 (C.A.).

Several other cases illustrate further differences between a lease, and an agreement for a lease. In *Commissioners for Inland Revenue* v. *Earl of Derby*,[81] a tenant under a lease under seal wished to surrender it and obtain a new one; and an agreement was made between lessor and lessee that, on the performance of certain conditions by the tenant by a specified date, he should be granted a new one. The required conditions were not performed at the specified time, but the lessee discharged his obligations on 29th April 1911, and thereupon obtained a new lease under seal. The court held that until 29th April, the lessee was not entitled to specific performance, and so was not within the scope of the rule of *Walsh* v. *Lonsdale*.[82] Accordingly, the agreement for the new lease, not being equivalent to a lease, did not operate as a surrender by operation of law of the old lease, and the old lease was not determined by the new one.

Both these two cases required consideration in *Cornish* v. *Brook Green Laundry Ltd*.[83] Originally, the Brook Green Laundry and the predecessor in title of Mrs. Cornish had occupied two adjoining shops, 23A and 23, as tenants of the Westminster Estate. In 1949 the Estate leased both shops to the laundry for seven years, and the laundry sub-let No. 23 to Mrs. Cornish's predecessor for seven years less three days. When the Landlord and Tenant Act, 1954,[84] came into force, both parties held over under the Act, and in January 1957 the Estate offered the laundry a new lease of No. 23 for ten and a half years, provided that certain repairs were carried out. This offer was accepted by the laundry, who then offered Mrs. Cornish (who was in occupation of No. 23) a sublease of No. 23A, which she rejected on the ground that No. 23A was too small. Mrs. Cornish then applied to the county court under the Landlord and Tenant Act for the determination of the terms of a new sublease of No. 23. The laundry, as landlords, opposed this on the ground that (as provided by Section 30 (1) of the Act) they proposed to occupy No. 23 themselves, and had offered suitable alternative accommodation. They contended that they had an equitable tenancy of the premises under the agreement of January 1957, on the principle of *Walsh* v. *Lonsdale*.[85] Later, they argued alternatively that they were tenants under the lease of 1949, as continued by the Act of 1954, and that the repairs which the Estate had required them to execute had been deferred, with the concurrence of the Estate. The county court judge held that the laundry was holding under an equitable

[81] [1914] 3 K.B. 1186.
[82] (1882), 21 Ch.D. 9.
[83] [1959] 1 Q.B. 394.
[84] No equivalent legislation in Ireland.
[85] (1882), 21 Ch.D. 9.

tenancy, in accordance with the principle in *Walsh* v. *Lonsdale*,[86] the equitable tenancy arising from the agreement of January 1957. They therefore could not rely on Section 30 (1) of the Act of 1954. He also held that the alternative accommodation which they offered was insufficient, and he therefore granted to Mrs. Cornish a sublease of No. 23. Both parties appealed and the Court of Appeal held that the laundry's tenancy was a holding over from the lease of 1949, prolonged by the Act of 1954, and not an equitable tenancy arising from the agreement of January 1957, because the lease was subject to a condition precedent, i.e. the execution of repairs, which the landlord had not waived. This is an example of the general principle that he who seeks equity must do equity, and it is in accordance with the decision of Horridge, J., in *Commissioners for Inland Revenue* v. *Earl of Derby*.[87]

In *Purchase* v. *Lichfield Brewery Co.*,[88] a tenant of a house under an agreement for a lease purported to assign the term by deed to assignees who accepted the assignment, but never executed the deed, and never entered into possession. The court held that there was neither privity of estate nor privity of contract between the landlord and the assignees, and the former could therefore not recover rent from the latter.

Horridge, J., observed[89]—

> In my opinion an assignee of a mere agreement for a lease who never took possession and never attorned tenant could not before the Judicature Acts and cannot now in his own right enforce specific performance against the landlord. He could not establish such a direct relation between himself and the landlord as would induce a Court of Equity, regarding that as done which ought to be done, to treat him as a person in whom a lease had been vested.

Further, it would seem that specific performance must be expressly claimed,[90] and in all these cases the availability or the non-availability of specific performance is the decisive factor.[91]

Yet another illustration of the *Walsh* v. *Lonsdale*[86] rule is afforded by *Borman* v. *Griffith*.[92] There, A agreed in writing to demise property to B for seven years from 29th September 1923. The property was not approached by a public road, and no right of way had expressly been

[86] (1882), 21 Ch.D. 9.
[87] [1914] 3 K.B. 1186.
[88] [1915] 1 K.B. 184.
[89] [1915] 1 K.B. 187-8.
[90] *Gray* v. *Spyer*, [1922] 2 Ch. 22 (C.A.).
[91] See ch. XVIII.
[92] [1930] 1 Ch. 493.

reserved to B. There was a drive belonging to A, which B used, claiming a right of way over the drive. Maugham, J., held that a contract for a lease exceeding a term of three years does not come within the meaning of the phrase " assurance of property or of an interest therein " under the Law of Property Act, 1925, Section 205 (1) (ii)[93] so that Section 62[94] of that Act whereby such a conveyance would pass " ways . . . reputed to appertain to the land " would not apply.[95]

From the cases considered above, it will be evident that even since 1873, (1) there are still considerable differences between a lease and an agreement for a lease; and (2) the equitable rule has not entirely superseded the common law rule, which was shown to be surviving in *Foster* v. *Reeves*[96] and again in *Swain* v. *Ayres*.[97]

Licences

The rule in *Walsh* v. *Lonsdale*[98] has unfortunately been associated by references in the decisions with an entirely separate branch of the law, which deals with the position of licences at law and in equity before and after the Judicature Acts. In *Thomas* v. *Sorrell*,[99] Vaughan, C.J., defined a licence as follows—

> A dispensation or licence properly passeth no interest, nor alters or transfers property in any thing, but only makes an action lawful, which without it had been unlawful. As a licence to go beyond the seas, to hunt in a mans park, to come into his house, are only actions, which without licence, had been unlawful.
>
> But a licence to hunt in a mans park, and carry away the deer kill'd to his own use to cut down a tree in a mans ground, and to carry it away the next day after to his own use, are licences as to the acts of hunting and cutting down the tree but as to the carrying away of the deer kill'd, and the tree cut down, they are grants.
>
> So to licence a man to eat my meat, or to fire the wood in my chimney to warm him by, as to the actions of eating, fireing my wood and warming him, they are licences; but it is consequent necessarily to those actions that my property be destroyed in the meat eaten, and in the wood burnt, so as in some cases by consequent and not directly, and as its effect, a dispensation or licence may destroy and alter property.

93 Ireland: Conveyancing Act, 1881, Sect. 2 (v).

94 Ireland: Conveyancing Act, 1881, Sect. 6 (1).

95 For the position in the case of an agreement for a lease not exceeding three years, see *Wright* v. *Macadam*, [1949] 2 K.B. 744 (C.A.).

96 [1892] 2 Q.B. 255 (C.A.).

97 (1888), 21 Q.B.D. 289 (C.A.).

98 (1882), 21 Ch.D. 9.

99 (1674), Vaughan 330, 351.

A licence is not an easement or profit, which is an interest in land. So too in a different way is a lease, which also confers exclusive possession for a limited period of the land demised. Both easement and lease must therefore be excluded in considering licences. Moreover, a licence may be gratuitous, or it may be granted in furtherance of a contract for valuable consideration, e.g. the purchase of a ticket for a race meeting or a cinema. The peculiarity of a mere licence, whether gratuitious or for valuable consideration, at common law, was that it could be revoked at any time, and the licensee had no remedy *in respect of his licence*, even though ejected by the licensor before the end of the specified period. Of course, if valuable consideration was given for the licence, a contract has been broken, and the disturbed licensee will have an action for breach of contract.[1] Finally, as Viscount Simon pointed out in *Winter Garden Theatre* (*London*) *Ltd.* v. *Millennium Productions Ltd.*,[2] since the effect of granting a licence is to prevent the licensee from being regarded as a trespasser, then when the licence is revoked, the licensee must be allowed a reasonable time to withdraw.

On the other hand, Vaughan, C.J., points out that a licence may be coupled with an interest, e.g. the licence to enter may be a necessary incident to the enjoyment or destruction of something situated on the land, which has also been granted to the licensee. In such a case, *provided that the interest has been created in the proper manner prescribed by law for that interest*, the licence which is ancillary to it is irrevocable, even though granted verbally. This important general common law principle is expressed by Alderson, B., in *Wood* v. *Leadbitter*[3] as follows—

> A mere license is revocable: but that which is called a license is often something more than a license; it often comprises or is connected with a grant, and then the party who has given it cannot in general revoke it, so as to defeat his grant, to which it was incident.
>
> It may further be observed, that a license under seal (provided it be a mere license) is as revocable as a license by parol; and, on the other hand, a license by parol, coupled with a grant, is as irrevocable as a license by deed, provided only that the grant is of a nature capable of being made by parol. But where there is a license by parol, coupled with a parol grant, or pretended grant, of something which is incapable of being granted otherwise than by deed, there the license is a mere license; it is not an incident to a valid grant, and it is therefore revocable. Thus, a license by A to hunt in his park,

[1] *Kerrison* v. *Smith*, [1897] 2 Q.B. 445.
[2] [1948] A.C. 173 (H.L., E.).
[3] (1845), 13 M. & W. 838, 844-5.

whether given by deed or by parol, is revocable; it merely renders the act of hunting lawful, which, without the license, would have been unlawful. If a license be, as put by Chief Justice Vaughan, a license not only to hunt, but also to take away the deer when killed to his own use, this is in truth a grant of the deer, with a license annexed to come on the land: and supposing the grant of the deer to be good, then the license would be irrevocable by the party who had given it; he would be estopped from defeating his own grant, or act in the nature of a grant. But suppose the case of a parol license to come on my lands, and there to make a watercourse, to flow on the land of the licensee. In such a case there is no valid grant of the watercourse, and the license remains a mere license, and therefore capable of being revoked. On the other hand, if such a license were granted by deed, then the question would be on the construction of the deed, whether it amounted to a grant of the watercourse; and if it did, then the license would be irrevocable.

In *Wood* v. *Leadbitter*,[4] the plaintiff bought a ticket for admission to the grandstand of a racecourse, which entitled him to remain there and see the races. Before the end of the races, a person acting on behalf of the licensor ordered him to leave, and when he refused, he was ejected. In an action for assault, it was argued on behalf of the licensor that he had a right to revoke the licence at any time, and once the licence had been revoked, the licensee became a trespasser whom the licensor was entitled to eject by the use of reasonable force. The Court of Exchequer upheld this contention and dismissed the action.

In *Winter Garden Theatre* (*London*) *Ltd.* v. *Millennium Productions Ltd.*[5] Viscount Simon suggested that the decision in *Wood* v. *Leadbitter* turned on the old system of pleading. The action was in tort for assault and false imprisonment, and it was not open to the plaintiff to join a cause of action for breach of contract to the action in tort. Collins, J., in *Kerrison* v. *Smith*[6] had already made the same point, and Viscount Simon added[7]—

Wood's position really was that Lord Eglintoun had agreed with him for reward, not to treat him as a trespasser till the races were over, and till he had a reasonable time after that to withdraw, but this was not the issue directly raised by the pleadings. It is enough to say that, at any rate since the fusion of law and equity, no court in

4 (1845), 13 M. & W. 838.
5 [1948] A.C. 173.
6 [1897] 2 Q.B. 445.
7 [1948] A.C. 191.

this country would refuse to a plaintiff in Wood's situation the remedy for which he asked, and the case, in my opinion, should no longer be regarded as an authority.

Lord Porter, however, was unable to accept the view that *Wood* v. *Leadbitter* turned upon the pleadings, and he was of opinion that the underlying assumption was that a licence is prima facie revocable.

The only case prior to *Wood* v. *Leadbitter*[8] which seems in conflict with the principles there expressed is *Tayler* v. *Waters*.[9] This was an action against the doorkeeper of the opera house, for preventing the plaintiff from entering during the performance of an opera. It appeared that Tayler, being lessee of the opera house, by a deed of 24th August 1792, assigned his interest to trustees for creditors and other claimants, and ultimately for himself. After the execution of the deed, Tayler remained in possession and managed the theatre. In March 1799, he granted to Gourgas, by deed, for valuable consideration, six silver tickets, entitling the holders to admission to the theatre. One of the tickets was sold by Gourgas to the plaintiff in July 1799, but no deed of assignment was executed. In 1800, Tayler's trustees took possession of the theatre, but the plaintiff continued to attend, in virtue of his ticket, until 1814, when the defendant Waters, as servant of the trustees, prevented him from entering. The plaintiff thereupon brought an action for obstruction, and Gibbs, C.J., found for the plaintiff, the decision being subsequently upheld by the Court of Common Pleas on the ground that the right under the silver ticket was not an interest in land, but an irrevocable licence to the plaintiff to enjoy certain privileges thereon; and that it was not required by the Statute of Frauds to be in writing, and, consequently, might be granted without a deed.

This common law decision failed to win the approval of the common law courts, and Alderson, B., said of it in *Wood* v. *Leadbitter*[10] that the authorities—

> . . . all state in the most distinct manner that every license is and must be in its nature revocable, so long as it is a mere license. Where, indeed, it is connected with a grant, there it may, by ceasing to be a naked license, become irrevocable; but then it is obvious that the grant must exist independently of the license, unless it be grant capable of being made by parol, or by the instrument giving the license. Now in *Tayler* v. *Waters*[11] there was no grant of any right

[8] (1845), 13 M. & W. 838.
[9] (1816), 7 Taunt. 374.
[10] 13 M. & W. 852-3.
[11] Above.

at all, unless such right was conferred by the license itself. C. J. Gibbs gives no reason for saying that the license was a license irrevocable, and we cannot but think that he would have paused before he sanctioned a doctrine so entirely repugnant to principle and to the earlier authorities, if they had been fully brought before the Court. Again, the Chief Justice is represented as saying that the interest of the plaintiff was not an interest in land within the Statute of Frauds, and that consequently it might be granted without deed. How the circumstance, that the interest was not an interest in land within the Statute of Frauds shewed it to be grantable without deed, we cannot discover. The precise point decided in *Webb* v. *Paternoster*[12] is not adverted to, and it is assumed, without discussion, that the license there must have been a parol license, and a naked license, unconnected with an interest, capable of being created by parol. The action was not, as it may have been in *Wood* v. *Lake*,[13] an action founded on the contract. It was an action on the case for the obstruction, and was founded on the supposition that an actual right to enter and remain in the theatre had vested in the plaintiff, under the license conferred by the silver ticket. With all deference to the high authority from which the judgment in *Tayler* v. *Waters* proceeded, we feel warranted in saying that it is to the last degree unsatisfactory; an observation which we have the less hesitation in making, in consequence of its soundness having obviously been doubted by the Court of King's Bench and Mr. Justice Bayley in the case of *Hewlins* v. *Shippam*.[14]

It is accordingly submitted that in view of the observations of the Court in *Wood* v. *Leadbitter*[15] and in *Hewlins* v. *Shippam*,[14] the decision in *Tayler* v. *Waters* could not be supported. A bare licence was always revocable, whether given by deed or by parol. The revocability of a licence coupled with an interest depended upon the validity of the mode of creation of the interest with which the licence was linked. It remains to consider the position of licences in equity before 1873, and the effect of the Judicature Act, 1873, upon the position at law and in equity. There are two distinct ways in which the attitude of equity to licences has differed from the common law attitude. In the first place, equity will, in appropriate circumstances, grant the more efficacious remedy of the injunction to prevent revocation of the licence by the original licensor. Secondly, even when this subject-matter of a licence has been transferred by the licensor to a third party,

[12] (1619), Poph. 151.
[13] (1751), Say. 3.
[14] (1826), 5 B. & C. 222.
[15] (1845), 13 M. & W. 838.

equity, unlike the common law, will sometimes prevent the third party transferee from disregarding the licence. In other words, equity adopted a different attitude to licences both as between the original licensee and licensor and also as between the licensee and a person claiming through the licensor. Dealing first with the attitude of equity as between the original parties to a licence, this received extended consideration in *Hurst* v. *Picture Theatres Ltd.*[16]

In *Hurst* v. *Picture Theatres Ltd.*[16] the plaintiff purchased a ticket for a seat at a cinema show, and was forcibly turned out of his seat, and expelled from the cinema by the manager, acting under the mistaken belief that the plaintiff had not paid for his seat. Channell, J., was of opinion that *Wood* v. *Leadbitter*[17] was no longer good law, and held that a visitor to a theatre who had paid for his seat had a right to retain it so long as the performance lasted, provided he behaved quietly and complied with the regulations laid down by the management. He left to the jury the question whether the plaintiff had paid for his seat. The jury found that he had, and assessed the damages at £150. The defendants appealed, but the Court of Appeal (Buckley, L.J., and Kennedy, L.J., Phillimore, L.J., dissenting) affirmed the decision of Channell, J. For the defendants it was argued that the purchase of a ticket only conferred on the plaintiff a revocable licence, not a licence coupled with an interest. There might be a contract to allow the plaintiff to see the performance, but a breach of it would only give rise to an action for damages. The licence itself was revocable. It was also pointed out that *Wood* v. *Leadbitter*[17] was followed in *Taplin* v. *Florence*,[18] *Adams* v. *Andrews*,[19] and in *Cornish* v. *Stubbs*[20]; and that in *Kerrison* v. *Smith*[21] the principle of *Wood* v. *Leadbitter*[17] was upheld, but the plaintiff was granted damages for breach of contract. Finally, it was argued that the Judicature Acts had not affected the position, although Cozens-Hardy, J., had said in *Lowe* v. *Adams*[22] that, having regard to *Walsh* v. *Lonsdale*,[23] it was doubtful whether *Wood* v. *Leadbitter*[17] was still good law. Nevertheless, it was argued, specific performance would not be granted of a contract such as the present.[24]

16 [1915] 1 K.B. 1.
17 (1845), 13 M. & W. 838.
18 (1851), 10 C.B. 744.
19 (1850), 15 Q.B. 284.
20 (1870), L.R. 5 C.P. 334.
21 [1897] 2 Q.B. 445.
22 [1901] 2 Ch. 598, 600.
23 (1882), 21 Ch.D. 9.
24 *Malone* v. *Harris* (1859), 11 Ir.Ch.Rep. 33, 39, *per* Brady, L.C.

Buckley, L.J., in the course of his judgment, pointed out that in *Wood* v. *Leadbitter*[25] it was affirmed that a mere licence, whether under seal or not (i.e. a licence not coupled with an interest), is revocable. A licence coupled with an interest, or coupled with a grant, is not generally revocable. The learned Lord Justice then pointed out that *Wood* v. *Leadbitter*[25] rests upon one of two grounds—

(1) That the man who bought his ticket for the race meeting had not obtained any grant of the right to come during the currency of the meeting to see any particular spectacle from its commencement to its termination. If that were the true ground of the decision, the learned Lord Justice comments, it would be erroneous.

(2) That no incorporeal hereditament affecting land can be created or transferred otherwise than by deed.

> What Alderson B. was saying there was: this man has got no deed; he has got nothing under seal; he has therefore not got a grant; he cannot in this Court be heard to say he is a grantee, and because he is not a grantee he is a mere licensee, and being a mere licensee (whether it is under seal or not under seal does not make any difference) the licence is revocable.[26]

Wood v. *Leadbitter*,[25] Buckley, L.J., continued, was a common law case. Before the Judicature Acts, he contended, equity would have applied a different principle, and since 1875, the equitable rule has prevailed. This different principle the learned Lord Justice found illustrated in *Frogley* v. *Earl of Lovelace*.[27] In that case the defendant was lessor to the plaintiff of certain lands for twenty-one years; he had executed a lease to the plaintiff, but previously to the execution of the lease, the following memorandum, not under seal, was signed by the parties—

> It is hereby agreed that [lessee] shall have the exclusive right of sporting over, and killing the game upon, the lands included in the within-written lease, and also upon the lands adjacent thereto belonging to the said earl during the continuance of the said term . . .

During the currency of the lease, the lessor served the lessee with a notice that after the date of the notice he would treat the agreement as revoked. The lessee brought in a court of equity a suit for specific performance for the execution of an instrument under seal in the terms of the memorandum, and meanwhile asked for an injunction to preserve his rights until the deed had been executed. The Vice-Chancellor

25 (1845), 13 M. & W. 838.
26 [1915] 1 K.B.6.
27 (1859), Johns. 333.

granted the injunction after noting that according to the decision in *Wood* v. *Leadbitter* the plaintiff could not have obtained a remedy, since the agreement was not under seal.

> He comes into a Court of Equity, and he obtains relief in equity because he would have no remedy at law, and his remedy is given until he has been clothed with such rights under a proper instrument as that he has a remedy at law, and then he is left to his legal rights.[28]

On this supposition, Buckley, L.J. observed that since the Judicature Acts, a court being bound to apply equitable doctrines, *Wood* v. *Leadbitter* is a decision which cannot now be applied in its entirety in a court which is bound to give effect to equitable considerations.[29] He also cited with approval certain observations of Parker, J., in *James Jones & Sons Ltd.* v. *Earl of Tankerville*[30]—

> An injunction restraining the revocation of the licence, when it is revocable at law, may in a sense be called relief by way of specific performance, but it is not specific performance in the sense of compelling the vendor to do anything. It merely prevents him from breaking his contract, and protects a right in equity which but for the absence of a seal would be a right at law, and since the Judicature Act it may well be doubted whether the absence of a seal in such a case can be relied on in any Court . . .

The learned Lord Justice therefore regarded the authority of *Wood* v. *Leadbitter* as now entirely gone, but Miles has pointed out[31] that the jurisdiction mentioned by Parker, J., is limited to cases where the interest coupled with the licence is not a mere contractual right, but an interest in lands or chattels which would have been valid at law if under seal, but the interest in *Hurst* v. *Picture Theatres Ltd.*[32] was neither of these. No interest in lands was dealt with in the agreement. If any interest in lands had been conferred, it could not have been an easement since, there being no dominant tenement, the easement would have been in gross. Neither could it have been a demise, since the seat was unreserved, and the ticket did not therefore relate to any particular land at all. This is, in fact, the point where the application of the rule in *Walsh* v. *Lonsdale*[33] seems to break down completely. As Miles

[28] [1915] 1 K.B. 8-9.
[29] This was also the view of Kennedy, L.J. ([1915] 1 K.B. 14).
[30] [1909] 2 Ch. 440, 443.
[31] "*Hurst* v. *Picture Theatres, Ltd.*" (1915), 31 *Law Quarterly Review*, 217.
[32] [1915] 1 K.B. 1.
[33] (1882), 21 Ch.D. 9.

stated, even if the contract had been under seal, no more than a mere contractual licence would have been created.[34] In strictness, the doctrine in *Walsh* v. *Lonsdale* extends only to agreements for leases where specific performance of such an agreement would be granted in equity. As Farwell, J., pointed out in *Manchester Brewery Co.* v. *Coombs*,[35] the whole doctrine depends upon the availability of specific performance. There is, however, a doctrine analagous to that of *Walsh* v. *Lonsdale* which applies to the informal creation of easements,[36] and it might be, although it is difficult to find authority to support the proposition, that equity would apply similar principles to the informal creation of other interests. In every such case, however, before equity could apply such principles, the availability of specific performance would be a condition precedent. To complete the argument, it may be added that equity would protect the rights of one party against the other, until the agreement had been specifically performed, as in *Frogley* v. *Earl of Lovelace*.[37] It is, however, a novel proposition that an agreement for an unreserved seat at a cinema is an agreement which is specifically enforceable,[38] and if no specific performance is ultimately contemplated, there can be no question of an injunction. Although that in strictness disposes of the matter, it may be pointed out that it is difficult to see how specific performance could ever be of practical assistance to an injured party, when the time for performance of the contract had passed; in such a case he is left to his remedy of damages for breach of contract; and as Miles has pointed out, for an injunction to be effective in such a case, it would be necessary for a judge to be present in a cinema, so that he could grant it on the spot. Accordingly, *Walsh* v. *Lonsdale* has nothing whatever to do with this class of cases. If the equity apparently invoked in *Hurst* v. *Picture Theatres Ltd.*, had any existence before 1873, it had a different origin; but no such origin was assigned to it. It may also be noticed that the second ground for the decision in *Wood* v. *Leadbitter*,[39] as explained by Buckley, L.J., is one from which Alderson, B., would have recoiled; for that learned judge expressly disclaimed any desire to regard the right of the plaintiff as an incorporeal hereditament in land, and therefore, according to Alderson, B.'s own argument, it could be quite validly created without a deed.[40]

[34] (1915), 31 *Law Quarterly Review*, 217-23.

[35] [1901] 2 Ch. 608.

[36] *McManus* v. *Cooke* (1887), 35 Ch.D. 681.

[37] (1859), Johns. 333.

[38] It has been said that equity will not support specific performance of a lease for less than a year: *Lavery* v. *Pursell* (1888), 39 Ch.D. 508, 519, *per* Chitty, J.

[39] (1845), 13 M. & W. 838.

[40] See the extracts from Alderson, B.'s judgment, pp. 94-5, 96-7, *ante*.

The current of textbook authority has in general been strongly opposed to the decision in *Hurst* v. *Picture Theatres Ltd.*[41] It has been accepted, however, by Lush, J., in *British Actors Film Co. Ltd.* v. *Glover*[42] and by McCardie, J., in *Said* v. *Butt.*[43] The decision may be said to have established the principle that a mere licence, granted for value, is irrevocable, and, accordingly, the authority of *Wood* v. *Leadbitter*[44] is now completely gone, or else is confined within exceedingly narrow limits.[45] Commenting upon *Hurst* v. *Picture Theatres Ltd.*,[41] Cross has suggested that it has made a licence as between the parties to it come to look very like a right over land protected in equity, though unaccompanied by any dominant tenement.[46] This is essentially, however, a new departure; and it may be added that in any case, damages were awarded for the breach of an equitable right, and not in lieu of an injunction, for this was not claimed, being, in the circumstances, obviously useless. Most of the members of the House of Lords in *Winter Garden Theatre* (*London*) *Ltd.* v. *Millennium Productions Ltd.*[47] seem to have accepted the view that *Hurst* v. *Picture Theatres Ltd.*[41] represented the position since the Judicature Acts, although Viscount Simon expressly referred to *Wood* v. *Leadbitter*[44] as no longer entitled to authority. Lords Porter and Uthwatt, however, had doubts, and perhaps the position can best be expressed in the words of Evershed that "... the House of Lords seems to me to have left very much in the air what they thought of the merits of Mr. Hurst as opposed to those of Mr. Wood. Some of their Lordships indicated undoubtedly a favourable appreciation of Mr. Hurst, though I find it a little difficult to discern a clear principle for future application."[48]

41 [1915] 1 K.B. 1. See, e.g., Miles (1915), 31 *Law Quarterly Review*, 217; Cheshire, *Modern Law of Real Property*, 10th ed., pp. 477-9; Salmond, *Law of Torts*, 14th ed., pp. 116-18; Hanbury, *Modern Equity*, 8th ed., pp. 429-434; Holdsworth, *History of English Law*, vol. VII, p. 328; Wade, " What is a Licence ? " (1948), 64 *L.Q.R.*, 57. Pollock (1915), 31 *L.Q.R.*, 9, accepted the decision in *Hurst* v. *Picture Theatres Ltd.* as correct. See also Jackson, " Equitable Easements " (1969), 33 *Conveyancer & Property Lawyer*, 135.

42 [1918] 1 K.B. 299, 307.

43 [1920] 3 K.B. 497, 499.

44 (1845), 13 M. & W. 838.

45 See Salmond, *Law of Torts*, 11th ed., pp. 276-9.

46 " A Note on Equitable Easements," (1935), *The Bell Yard*, 26-27. The High Court of Australia, by a majority, refused to follow *Hurst* v. *Picture Theatres Ltd.* in *Cowell* v. *Rosehill Racecourse Co. Ltd.* (1937), 56 C.L.R. 605. (See note in (1937), 53 *L.Q.R.*, 318.) In that case, the majority of the court held that a person who pays to enter a place of public entertainment acquires a mere licence not coupled with any interest. Such a licence is revocable at will, so as to constitute him a trespasser if he refuses to leave after revocation. No action in tort lies for his removal, and no relief in equity is available against the exercise of lawful rights by the proprietor.

47 [1948] A.C. 173.

48 "Equity after Fusion: Federal or Confederate" (1948), 1 *Journal of the Society of Public Teachers of Law*, 171, 177.

This is not another illustration of a conflict or variance between common law and equity being resolved by the Judicature Acts, but a fresh departure based on twentieth-century decisions only. The variance existed before 1873 only in respect of those licences coupled with interests which were informally created, so that the licence remained revocable. If in equity the informal creation would have been implemented by specific performance and the execution of a formal grant, equity would treat the licence as irrevocable, and until specific performance had been granted, would protect by injunction.

With regard to the position of a licensee as against third parties acquiring the subject-matter of the licence, the position at common law is that a licence is, at most, a contract, and since under the rule of privity the burden of a contract cannot be passed on to a third party,[49] third parties were not bound by a licence. This was held to be the position in the leading cases of *King* v. *David Allen and Sons, Bill-posting, Ltd.*[50] and *Clore* v. *Theatrical Properties Ltd.*[51] In a number of recent cases, however, it has been shown that at least in the case of licences to occupy land, equity is prepared, in appropriate circumstances, to grant an injunction against third parties who seek to disregard the licence. In *Errington* v. *Errington*[52] a contractual licensee in occupation of a house was granted an injunction to prevent the devisee of the licensor from disturbing him. In *Bendall* v. *McWhirter*,[53] a licensee in occupation successfully claimed an injunction against the licensor's trustee in bankruptcy. In *Ferris* v. *Weaven*[54] and *Street* v. *Denham*,[55] an injunction was granted against a collusive purchaser of the property over which the vendor had created an occupational licence. The limits and juridical consequences of this equitable jurisdiction have yet to be fully defined,[56] but these cases illustrate the creative powers of equity since 1875 whilst at the same time introducing a crop of new problems. Most of the decisions protected

49 *Taddy & Co.* v. *Sterious & Co.*, [1904] 1 Ch. 354.
50 [1916] 2 A.C. 54 (H.L., I.).
51 [1936] 3 All E.R. 483 (C.A.).
52 [1952] 1 K.B. 290 (C.A.).
53 [1952] 2 Q.B. 466 (C.A.) .See also Jackson, " Equitable Easements " (1969), 33 *Conveyancer & Property Lawyer*, 135.
54 [1952] 2 All E.R. 233.
55 [1954] 1 W.L.R. 624. See also *Westminster Bank Ltd.* v. *Lee*, [1956] Ch. 7.
56 See *Jess B. Woodcock & Sons Ltd.* v. *Hobbs*, [1955] 1 W.L.R. 152 (C.A.); *Churcher* v. *Street*, [1959] Ch. 251.

the right of a deserted wife to continue to live in the matrimonial home,[57] and as yet, there has been little tendency to extend it to other situations.

Concealed Fraud

Section 25 of the Judicature Act, 1873,[58] does not imply that in every case in respect of which different rules were applied at common law and in equity before 1873, there will be applied after 1873 one rule only, and that one will be the equitable rule. In some cases, which could have arisen only in a common law court before 1873, the common law rule has been retained, even though the equitable rule has been preserved in others. Thus, there are contracts which might have been exclusively within the jurisdiction of a common law court before 1873, or exclusively within a court of equity, or which might have been considered in both courts. The effect of the Judicature Act, 1873, upon each of these three types of case must be considered separately, and the distinction will be clearly appreciated from a consideration of the differing application of the Statute of Limitations in the common law courts and in the Court of Chancery.

The Statute of Limitations, 1623,[59] provided that in respect of many types of action arising in contract and tort, the right to sue should be lost if it was not exercised within a period of six years from the time when the cause of action arose. This rule was applied literally by the common law courts, so that an injured person might lose his right to sue without knowing that he had ever enjoyed it, if the guilty party took steps to conceal his wrongdoing from the other for six years after the cause of action arose.[60] The only mitigation to the rule admitted at common law was that if the concealment of the fraud was itself an actionable wrong, time ran from the discovery of the fraud, but this was in respect of the fraud, although it served to keep open the plain-

[57] Based on the Married Women's Property Act, 1882, and elaborated in *Lloyds Bank Ltd.* v. *Oliver's Trustee*, [1953] 1 W.L.R. 1460, *Barclay's Bank Ltd.* v. *Bird*, [1954] Ch. 274 and *Westminster Bank Ltd.* v. *Lee*, [1956] Ch. 7., this right became largely ineffectual against third parties by virtue of the House of Lords decision in *National Provincial Bank Ltd.* v. *Ainsworth*, [1965] A.C. 1175. In England (no equivalent in Ireland), the Matrimonial Homes Act 1967 attempted a remedy. See also *Miles* v. *Bull*, [1969] 1 Q.B. 258; *Baynham* v. *Baynham*, [1968] 1 W.L.R. 1890 (C.A.); *Maynard* v. *Maynard*, [1969] 2 W.L.R. 22; *Caunce* v. *Caunce*, [1969] 1 W.L.R. 286; *Gissing* v. *Gissing*, [1969] 2 W.L.R. 525 (C.A.); *Pettitt* v. *Pettitt*, [1969] 2 W.L.R. 966 (H.L., E.); Crane, "The Matrimonial Homes Act 1967" (1968), 32 *Conveyancer and Property Lawyer*, 85; Tiley, "The More-than-Handy Husband" (1969), 27 *Cambridge Law Journal*, 81; Palley, "Wives, Creditors and the Matrimonial Home" (1969), 20 *Northern Ireland Legal Quarterly*, 132.

[58] Ireland: Judicature (Ireland) Act, 1877, Sect. 28.

[59] Ireland: Limitation Act (Ireland), 1634.

[60] *Bree* v. *Holbech* (1781), 2 Dougl. 654 (cited in *Brown* v. *Howard* (1820), 2 Brod. & B. 73, 75); *Imperial Gas Light & Coke Co.* v. *London Gas Light Co.* (1854), 10 Ex. 39; *Hunter* v. *Gibbons* (1856), 1 H. & N. 459.

tiff's original cause of action, since the loss thereby sustained was an element in the assessment of the extent of the injury resulting from the fraud.

The attitude of equity was different. The rule was developed that the plea of concealed fraud would be a good reply to the Statute of Limitations, so that time would begin to run from the moment when the plaintiff discovered the fraud. The term "concealed fraud" itself requires explanation. It has been held that it includes not only wrongful acts which the defendant took active steps fraudulently to conceal from the knowledge of the plaintiff, but also any wilful wrongdoing which is unknown to the plaintiff at the time when it is committed.[61]

After the Judicature Act, 1873, there was a good deal of uncertainty reflected in the decisions whether the plea of concealed fraud was applicable in *all* actions, or merely in those actions which before the Judicature Acts could have been brought in a court of equity. It is submitted that the latter was the true view, but the question is to-day of mainly historical interest for now by Section 26 of the Limitation Act, 1939,[62] it is provided that in all cases where a cause of action is founded on fraud committed by the defendant or his agent, or where a cause of action is fraudulently concealed by him or his agent, time shall run against the plaintiff only from the time when he discovered the fraud or could with reasonable diligence have discovered it.[63]

Liability of a Personal Representative for Assets

In one class of cases, the effect of the Judicature Acts has been to cause the complete replacement of a common law rule by a varying equitable rule. Before 1873, an executor or administrator was always liable at common law for the loss of assets which had once come into his hands.[64] In equity, however, an executor or administrator was deemed to be in the position of a gratuitous bailee. He could not be charged with the loss unless he was personally at fault, so that if assets were stolen from him, or from a third person to whom he had delivered them for safe custody, he was not liable. In *Job* v. *Job*[65] the court was called upon to consider the effect of the Judicature Acts

[61] *Rolfe* v. *Gregory* (1865), 4 De G. J. & S. 576, 579, *per* Lord Westbury, L.C.; *Bulli Coal Mining Co.* v. *Osborne*, [1899] A.C. 351 (P.C., New South Wales); *Oelkers* v. *Ellis*, [1914] 2 K.B. 139; *Lynn* v. *Bamber*, [1930] 2 K.B. 72.

[62] Ireland: Statute of Limitations, 1957, Sect. 71 (Republic of Ireland); Statute of Limitations (Northern Ireland), 1958, Sect. 70.

[63] The cases on concealed fraud are discussed fully in the first edition of this book and in Sheridan, *Fraud in Equity*, pp. 159-66. See also pp. 28-9, *ante*.

[64] *Crosse* v. *Smith* (1806), 7 East 246, 258, *per* Lord Ellenborough, C.J.

[65] (1877), 6 Ch.D. 562.

upon these varying rules. On the death of the testator, a watchmaker, his executor delivered part of his stock-in-trade to the value of £160, to his son, James Job, who was also a watchmaker and jeweller, for the purpose of being sold in the ordinary course of trade. James Job became bankrupt, and his trustee in bankruptcy took possession of the estate, including the £160 stock, as being within his possession, order, and disposition. It was held that the executor was not liable to the estate for the default, since it was not wilful, the equitable rule having, since 1873, completely replaced the common law rule.

Now, under Section 23 of the Trustee Act, 1925,[66] trustees and personal representatives are given a wider power of appointing agents, and are not responsible for the acts of such agents if employed in good faith. Now, therefore, if an executor has exercised reasonable care, he is not liable if the testator's goods are stolen from his possession, or from the possession of a third party to whose custody he has properly committed them; nor is he liable for loss arising from accidental fire, even though the property has not been insured. The question to be decided is whether the personal representative has consciously or recklessly failed in his duty.[67] Only in such a case will he now be liable for loss.

Distinction between Legal and Equitable Estates

The two maxims, " Where the equities are equal, the law prevails " and " Where the equities are equal, the first in time prevails," form twin pillars on which rest the equitable rules governing the priority of conflicting interests in property. They were firmly established before 1873, and were not affected by the Judicature Acts. This may be illustrated by a consideration of two cases, one decided shortly before, and the other shortly after, the changes of 1873.

In *Pilcher* v. *Rawlins*,[68] P was the sole surviving trustee of a fund of £8,373, for the benefit of A for life, and after his death, for A's children. He lent the money to R on a legal mortgage of land. As a result of this, P held the legal estate in the land, as trustee for A, and the mortgage deed disclosed the trust. R and P then conspired to defraud B by executing a legal mortgage on the land in favour of B in return for

[66] Ireland: Trustee Act (Northern Ireland), 1958, Sect. 24; in the Republic of Ireland, there are no provisions equivalent to subsects. (1) or (2) of Sect. 23 of the 1925 Act, while the Trustee Act, 1893, Sect. 17, corresponds to subsect. (3).

[67] *Re Vickery*, [1931] 1 Ch. 572. On the scope of Sect. 23 of the Trustee Act, 1925, see, further, Keeton, *The Law of Trusts*, 9th ed., pp. 238-42, and (Sheridan) Irish Supplement, p. 34.

[68] (1872), L.R. 7 Ch. App. 259. See also *Caunce* v. *Caunce*, [1969] 1 W.L.R. 286.

£10,000, and to facilitate this, R (a solicitor) prepared an abstract of title which omitted the mortgage to P, so that the fee simple apparently remained in R. Moreover, P reconveyed the legal estate to R in consideration of a repayment of A's trust moneys (which repayment was never made). R then conveyed the legal estate to B by way of mortgage. When the fraud was discovered, the question in issue was whether A or B had the prior right to the land. The court held that as B had acted honestly and reasonably, and as the effect of the reconveyance by P to R was to vest the legal estate in R, and as the whole of the mortgage transaction had been concealed, there was no reason for B to imagine that the mortgage existed, and he was therefore entitled to priority over A, whose interest was equitable only.

In his judgment, James, L.J., said[69]—

> I propose simply to apply myself to the case of a purchaser for valuable consideration, without notice, obtaining, upon the occasion of his purchase, and by means of his purchase deed, some legal estate, some legal right, some legal advantage; and, according to my view of the established law of this Court, such a purchaser's plea of a purchase for valuable consideration without notice is an absolute, unqualified, unanswerable defence, and an unanswerable plea to the jurisdiction of this Court. Such a purchaser, when he has once put in that plea, may be interrogated and tested to any extent as to the valuable consideration which he has given in order to shew the *bona fides* or *mala fides* of his purchase, and also the presence or absence of notice but when once he has gone through that ordeal, and has satisfied the terms of the plea of purchase for valuable consideration without notice, then, according to my judgment, this Court has no jurisdiction whatever to do anything more than to let him depart in possession of that legal estate, that legal right, that legal advantage which he has obtained, whatever it may be. In such a case a purchaser is entitled to hold that which, without breach of duty, he has had conveyed to him.

This decision should be compared with that in *Joseph* v. *Lyons*,[70] for the later decision, being reached after the Judicature Acts, shows that the position of legal and equitable estates is exactly what it was before 1873.

In *Joseph* v. *Lyons*,[70] a jeweller, by bill of sale, assigned to the plaintiff for valuable consideration his after-acquired stock-in-trade, subject to a proviso for redemption; before the plaintiff took possession of the after-

[69] L.R. 7 Ch. App. 268-9.
[70] (1884), 15 Q.B.D. 280 (C.A.).

acquired stock, the jeweller pledged part of it with the defendant, who had no notice of the bill of sale. The court held that the defendant could keep the stock as against the plaintiff, for the grant of future-acquired chattels gives the grantee only an equitable interest in them, so that if, when they come into possession, but before the grantee takes possession, the owner grants the legal title to another, who takes without notice of the equitable interest, he who has received the legal title ranks first in order of priority.

Cotton, L.J., observed[71]—

It has been argued before us that the difference between legal and equitable interests has been swept away by those statutes.[72] But it was not intended by the legislature, and it has not been said, that legal and equitable rights should be treated as identical, but that the Courts should administer both legal and equitable principles. I think that the clause enacting that the rules of equity shall prevail . . . shews that it was not intended to sweep away altogether the principles of the common law. And it was not intended that a conveyance void at common law should, after the passing of those statutes, become valid as a conveyance at common law. . . . I think that this bill of sale, although it was a deed, gave no legal title. Then reliance was placed upon a contract that the after-acquired property should belong to the plaintiff: it was the rule at common law that the property in future-acquired goods should not pass, except, perhaps, where there was a contract that the property in them should pass: that rule still remains in force; and it follows that the legal title remains as it stood at law; only an interest in equity passed to the plaintiff. Then the defendant had the legal title: he had no notice of the equitable title existing in the plaintiff: at least nothing has been proved shewing that he had notice: here the defendant was a pawnbroker, and he was not bound to search the register of bills of sale: he was not bound to inquire as to goods pledged with him in the course of his business. Of course, if he had been informed of the existence of the bill of sale, he would have been bound to search the register in order to inform himself of its contents; but I think that the doctrine as to constructive notice has gone too far, and I shall not extend it.[73]

[71] L.R. 7 Ch. App. 285-6.

[72] The Judicature Acts.

[73] See also *Hallas* v. *Robinson* (1885), 15 Q.B.D. 288 (C.A.), in which *Joseph* v. *Lyons* was followed. In relation to land, the equitable rules as to priorities have been largely superseded by provisions for registration of title (in England and Ireland), under the Land Charges Act, 1925 (in England), and under the Registration of Deeds Acts (in Ireland). See also pp. 209-12, *post*.

Contribution amongst those embarking on a joint adventure

The case of *Lowe & Sons* v. *Dixon & Sons*[74] illustrates a further consequence of the Judicature Act in respect of differing rules upon the same matter in law and in equity. In that case A (the plaintiff) agreed with X that a cargo of wheat should be shipped for their joint account by X's correspondents, Y, at San Franciso, and consigned to A at Liverpool for sale on special terms, the shippers Y to reimburse themselves for the cost of the cargo by drafts on A at sixty days' sight to the extent of 45s. per quarter, less freight, and for the balance of the invoice amount by separate drafts at sixty days' sight upon A, X, and Y, each for one-third of the excess. The cargo was shipped, and a bill was drawn by Y for £29,353 18s. 1d. on account of the invoice price of the wheat upon A, and was accepted and paid by A. When the wheat arrived it was sold by A at a loss. Later X became insolvent, and compounded with his creditors for 30 per cent. A received his percentage in respect of debts due from X, leaving an unpaid balance of £1,760 10s. 9d. due from X for his share in the loss of the adventure. It was held that the purchase and shipment of the wheat was a joint partnership adventure, wherein each of the three firms was to contribute equally, but since one was insolvent, the remaining two were each liable for one-half of the loss. Before 1873, there had been a difference in the attitude of law and equity to this position. At law, each member of the joint adventure was deemed to undertake responsibility to an extent determined by the total amount of liability divided by the number participating in it, and no more. The result was that if there were four adventurers and one adventurer was insolvent, when the creditor recovered in full from one of the remaining three, that one could only recover one-quarter of the liability from the two who were solvent. Equity took a different view. It said that the liability should be shared equally by the partners who were solvent. As Lopes, J., said[75]

> . . . in equity, those who *can* pay must not only contribute their own shares, but they must also make good the shares of those who are unable to furnish their own contribution. Inasmuch, therefore, as the rules of equity prevail, the defendants must make good each one-half . . .

Maitland commented[76] on the former variance—

> . . . the legal rule had become a *caput mortuum* before the Act. The case of *Lowe* v. *Dixon*[77] merely shows that this *caput mortuum* has disappeared altogether.

[74] (1885), 16 Q.B.D. 455.
[75] 16 Q.B.D. 458.
[76] *Equity*, 2nd ed., p. 156.
[77] (1886), 16 Q.B.D. 455.

Practice

The principle that where there is any conflict or variance between the rules of common law and the rules of equity, the latter are to prevail, does not apply to practice. Here the more convenient rule is followed. This is illustrated by *Newbiggin-by-the-Sea Gas Co.* v. *Armstrong.*[78] In that case a solicitor brought an action without his client's authority. There was an application by the defendants that the action should be dismissed, and that the solicitor should pay the plaintiff's costs. Fry, J., made an order dismissing the action, but no order as to costs. On appeal, Jessel, M.R., said[79]—

> The order follows the old practice of the Court of Chancery in such cases, by which the defendant was not served with notice of the application, but was left to get his costs from the person named as plaintiff, who had afterwards to get those costs over from the solicitor. The result was that the nominal plaintiff, who had never given any authority for the use of his name, had to pay the defendant's costs, and might be unable to recover them by reason of the insolvency of the solicitor. On the other hand, according to the practice of the Common Law Courts, the defendant was served with a notice of the application, and the solicitor had to pay the costs of both the plaintiff and the defendant. That appears to me to be better practice. The question is which practice is now to be followed. Since the passing of the *Judicature Act* that must be left to the Court to determine. By the 21st Section of the *Judicature Act*, 1875,[80] it is enacted that in cases where no new method of procedure is prescribed the old practice is to prevail, but where there is a variance in the practice it does not say which practice. I have no hesitation in saying, as I have already said at the Rolls Court, though not with the same authority with which I now say it, that I think the Common Law practice in this case is founded in natural justice, and ought to be followed for the future.

Injunctions

Until the middle of the nineteenth century, the injunction was the peculiar property of the Court of Chancery. By Sections 79-80 of the Common Law Procedure Act, 1854,[81] the common law courts were given power to grant injunctions in certain cases, but the remedy

[78] (1879), 13 Ch.D. 310 (C.A.).
[79] 13 Ch.D. 311.
[80] Ireland: Judicature (Ireland) Act, 1877, Sect. 67.
[81] Ireland: Common Law Procedure Amendment Act (Ireland), 1856, Sects. 81-2.

was not granted generally. By the Judicature Act, 1873, Section 25 (8)[82] (as re-enacted in England in the Supreme Court of Judicature (Consolidation) Act, 1925, Section 45), it is provided that—

> (1) The High Court may grant a mandamus or an injunction or appoint a receiver by an interlocutory order in all cases in which it appears to the court to be just or convenient so to do.
>
> (2) Any such order may be made either unconditionally or on such terms and conditions as the court thinks just.
>
> (3) If, whether before, or at, or after the hearing of any cause or matter, an application is made for an injunction to prevent any threatened or apprehended waste or trespass, the injunction may be granted, if the court thinks fit, whether the person against whom the injunction is sought is or is not in possession under any claim of title or otherwise, or (if out of possession) does or does not claim a right to do the act sought to be restrained under any colour of title, and whether the estates claimed by both or either of the parties are legal or equitable.

The question whether the Judicature Act had in any way extended the availability of the remedy was raised after 1873. In *Harris* v. *Beauchamp Bros.*,[83] Davey, L.J., said—

> We should be sorry to limit by construction the beneficial jurisdiction of the Court to grant an injunction or make an order for a receiver where it is " just or convenient " to do so; but we conceive those well-known words do not confer an arbitrary or unregulated discretion on the Court, and do not authorize the Court to invent new modes of enforcing judgments in substitution for the ordinary modes.

Again, in *North London Railway Co.* v. *Great Northern Railway Co.*,[84] Cotton, L.J., observed of Section 25—

> . . . it did not intend to give the right to an injunction to parties who before had no legal right whatever, but simply to give to the Court, when dealing with legal rights which were under its jurisdiction independently of this section, power, if it should think it just or convenient, to superadd to what would have been previously the remedy, a remedy by way of injunction, altering therefore not in any way the rights of parties so as to give a right to those who had no legal right before, but enabling the Court to modify the principle on which it had previously proceeded in granting injunctions, so

[82] Ireland: Judicature (Ireland) Act, 1877, Sect. 28 (8).
[83] [1894] 1 Q.B. 801, 809 (C.A.).
[84] (1883), 11 Q.B.D. 30, 39-40 (C.A.).

> that where there is a legal right the Court may, without being hampered by its old rules, grant an injunction where it is just or convenient to do so for the purpose of protecting or asserting the legal rights of the parties. That, in my opinion, is the real meaning of this section. In my opinion, all that was done by this section was to give to the High Court power to give a remedy which formerly would not have been given in that particular case, but still only a remedy in defence of or to enforce rights which according to law were previously existing and capable of being enforced in some or one of the different Divisions which are now united in the High Court. It is very true that the High Court does possess jurisdiction in matters which some of the different Courts before did not possess, but then it is the Court which amalgamates in itself all the jurisdictions which had previously existed, and undoubtedly in that sense a new jurisdiction is given now to the Chancery Division in matters which were dealt with previously only by the Common Law Courts. In my opinion the sole intention of the section is this: that where there is a legal right which was, independently of the Act, capable of being enforced either at law or in equity, then, whatever may have been the previous practice, the High Court may interfere by injunction in protection of that right.

Cotton, L.J.'s observations are well illustrated by the decision of Jessel, M.R., in *Aslatt* v. *Southampton Corp.*[85] In that case the plaintiff sought an injunction to restrain the corporation from declaring his office void. There was a remedy at common law by *quo warranto*, and before 1873 an injunction would not have been granted. The injunction was granted.

The Judicature Acts, therefore, have not changed the principles on which the court acts in granting injunctions. The court will not interfere where no legal or equitable right has been violated, even though inconvenience has been suffered.[86] Nor will an injunction be granted in trivial cases, nor where damages are a full and complete remedy.[87] The effect of the Judicature Acts has been to make injunctions available in every Division of the High Court. They have not extended the availability of the injunction to cases in which it would not have been obtainable before 1873; although, since 1873, the court may now grant an injunction where there is a right that can be asserted either at law or in equity, even though that right might not have been protected by injunction before 1873, provided that the

[85] (1880), 16 Ch.D. 143.

[86] *Day* v. *Brownrigg* (1878), 10 Ch.D. 294 (C.A.).

[87] *Per* Lindley, L.J., in *London and Blackwall Railway Co.* v. *Cross* (1886), 31 Ch. D. 354, 369 (C.A.).

court thinks that it should interfere, and that it may do so in harmony with principles already laid down to govern the availability of the remedy. The result has been that injunctions are now granted more frequently and in a greater variety of cases than before 1873.[88]

Other Forms of Equitable Relief

Before 1873, the common law courts and the Court of Chancery applied different rules where a person mortgaged securities to an unregistered moneylender, and then refused to pay the loan, but claimed the securities back as having been given in respect of an illegal contract. Equity declined to assist borrowers in this position unless they were prepared to reimburse the lender.[89] At common law the position has changed somewhat at different periods. Prior to Lord Mansfield's time, the rule seems to have been that the borrower was entitled to the return of the securities, as of legal right, and the court would do nothing to assist the lender. In *Fitzroy* v. *Gwillim*,[90] however, a pawnor brought an action in trover against a pawnbroker with whom she had pledged goods to secure an advance at an illegal rate of interest. She was non-suited by Lord Mansfield, C.J., on the ground that the parties were *in pari delicto*, and therefore the rule *potior est conditio possidentis* ought to prevail. The case clearly shows the influence of equity upon Lord Mansfield's administration of the common law. He observed[91]—

> This is an equitable action brought by the plaintiff in order to be relieved from an usurious contract. She must come therefore with clean hands, according to the principle laid down in the case of *Bosanquet and Dashwood*,[92] that those who seek equity must do equity. It was then determined that a Court of Equity would afford relief in such cases upon payment of principal and interest. A lender upon an usurious contract is precluded from recovering any thing upon such contract; but if the borrower seek relief, he must first do what is right as between the parties.

In the same case Buller, J., gave a decision[91] in the same sense upon the same grounds. The case of *Fitzroy* v. *Gwillim*,[90] however, was doubted upon several occasions in common law courts, if not entirely overruled. In *Hargreaves* v. *Hutchinson*[93] the court refused to impose

88 See ch. XVII.
89 *Mason* v. *Gardiner* (1793), 4 Bro. C.C. 436.
90 (1786), 1.T.R. 153.
91 1 T.R. 154.
92 (1734), Cas. t. Talb. 38.
93 (1834), 2 Ad. & El. 12.

any terms upon the recovery of the securities by the borrower, and in *Tregoning* v. *Attenborough*[94] (which was a similar action) terms were again refused on the ground that trover was a question of strict legal right.

After 1873, the equitable rule prevailed, and in *Lodge* v. *National Union Investment Co. Ltd.*,[95] the court once more had to consider the position of the parties in transactions of this kind. Two forms of relief were claimed, one legal, and the other equitable, and whilst the court held that it had no discretion to refuse the legal relief, it declined to grant equitable relief, except on terms. Parker, J., after citing with approval the observations of Lord Mansfield in *Moses* v. *Macferlan*[96] upon the action for the recovery of money which is not due, has been paid and ought to be repaid, said[97]—

> I do not think it is either aequum or bonum that the plaintiff, who has had the benefit of the £1,075 and who is relying on the illegality of the contract and the exception enabling him to sue notwithstanding such illegality, should have relief without being put on terms by which both parties may be restored to the positions they occupied before the transaction commenced.

Restoration of the securities was therefore refused until the money was repaid.

A further illustration of the operation of this section of the Judicature Act, 1873, is afforded by *B. Liggett (Liverpool) Ltd.* v. *Barclays Bank Ltd.*[98] The bank, negligently and contrary to instructions, had paid the cheques of the plaintiff company (who were customers of the bank) when they were signed by one director only. The cheques were drawn in favour of trade creditors of the company in exchange for goods supplied to the company. The company brought an action for money had and received, but the bank contended that, since the cheques had been devoted to discharging the debts of the company, and had not increased their liabilities in any way, they were entitled to take advantage of the equitable doctrine under which a person who has in fact paid the debts of another without authority is permitted to take advantage of his payment. At common law, before 1873, the position on such facts was that the bank was in the position of a stranger who without the authority of the company paid off the company's debts, and in such circumstances,

94 (1830), 7 Bing. 97.
95 [1907] 1 Ch. 300.
96 (1760), 2 Burr. 1005, 1012.
97 [1907] 1 Ch. 312.
98 [1928] 1 K.B. 48.

the common law had permitted the company to take the benefit, but absolved it from all responsibility in respect of them.[99] Equity followed a different rule, and frequently relieved an agent who borrowed money without authority and applied it to the payment of his principal's debts. Since 1873 this equitable rule has prevailed and has been consistently applied.

In *Blackburn Building Soc.* v. *Cunliffe, Brooks & Co.*,[1] Lord Selborne, L.C., had stated the rules as follows—

> . . . I think the consistency of the equity allowed in the *Cork and Youghal Railway Company's Case*[2] with the general rule of law that persons who have no borrowing powers cannot, by borrowing, contract debts to the lenders, may be shewn in this way. The test is: has the transaction really added to the liabilities of the company? If the amount of the company's liabilities remains in substance unchanged, but there is, merely for the convenience of payment, a change of the creditor, there is no substantial borrowing in the result, so far as relates to the position of the company. Regarded in that light, it is consistent with the general principle of equity, that those who pay legitimate demands which they are bound in some way or other to meet, and have had the benefit of other people's money advanced to them for that purpose, shall not retain that benefit so as, in substance, to make those other people pay their debts. I take that to be a principle sufficiently sound in equity; and if the result is that by the transaction which assumes the shape of an advance or loan nothing is really added to the liabilities of the company, there has been no real transgression of the principle on which they are prohibited from borrowing.

This principle was followed in *Baroness Wenlock* v. *River Dee Co.*[3] and in *Bannatyne* v. *MacIver*.[4] In the latter case the agent was employed, not by a corporation, but by a private individual, and he was permitted to recover. Again, in *Reversion Fund and Insurance Co. Ltd.* v. *Maison Cosway Ltd.*[5] the plaintiff, who lent, actually knew the quasi-borrowing company had no authority to borrow. In *A. L. Underwood Ltd.* v. *Bank of Liverpool*[6] the plaintiff company claimed against the bank for conversion of cheques. The plaintiff was a one-man company, and the one man, as sole director, endorsed some cheques

99 *Exall* v. *Partridge* (1799), 8 T.R. 308.
1 (1882), 22 Ch.D. 61, 71 (C.A.).
2 (1869), L.R.4 Ch. App. 748.
3 (1887), 19 Q.B.D. 155 (C.A.).
4 [1906] 1 K.B. 103 (C.A.).
5 [1913] 1 K.B. 364 (C.A.).
6 [1924] 1 K.B. 775.

of the company and paid them into his own account with the defendants. The Court of Appeal held that this amounted to a conversion, in that the bank were not entitled to collect the proceeds of the cheques and appropriate the proceeds to the personal account of the sole director. That being so, they were misapplying the plaintiff's property, and were liable. But it appeared that the proceeds or some of them were used to discharge the liabilities of the company, and an inquiry was directed to discover to what extent that was so, from which it would appear that the Court of Appeal regarded it as a case to which the equitable doctrine would apply, for Scrutton, L.J., observed[7]—

> But I am not sure that the learned judge had in his mind the equitable doctrines under which a person who had in fact paid the debts of another without authority was allowed the advantage of his payments . . .

After consideration of these cases, Wright, J., observed in *B. Liggett (Liverpool) Ltd.* v. *Barclays Bank Ltd.*[8]—

> That statement of the equity is, I think, wide enough to cover the question which I have to decide in this case, and although there is a technical difference between a claim in conversion and a claim for money had and received such as I have to deal with in the present action, I do not think that that distinction is of such a nature as to prevent the application in the case before me of the same principles as would apply if the claim had been a claim in conversion. The relationship of a banker and customer is that of debtor and creditor; that is, when the customer's account is in credit, the banker is the debtor of the customer and, therefore, it is only by a figure of speech that the banker misapplies money of his customer which he had in his possession. That statement would be perfectly true if what the banker had in his possession was a bag of coins or a bundle of notes, and if acting upon an authority which was invalid the banker quite honestly although erroneously took a number of coins out of a bag or a number of notes out of a bundle and paid them on the faith of such an authority he would be guilty of conversion and, if I understand the judgment of the Court of Appeal in this case, in that event the banker would be entitled to the benefit of the equity. If that be so, and in principle it seems to me that ought to be so, I cannot see why the same result should not apply in a case like the one before me, where the banker does not handle actual cash or notes, chattels capable of conversion, but by reason of the present system of banking

[7] [1924] 1 K.B. 794.
[8] [1928] 1 K.B. 48, 63-4.

> facilities everything is done by way of credit or debit balances. In such a case there is obviously no conversion, but there is misapplication, under an honest mistake as to the validity of the authority, of the credits which constitute the medium of exchange in place of cash. Under these circumstances I think that the equity I have been referred to ought to be extended even in the case where the cheque which was paid was paid out of the credit balance, and was not paid by way of overdraft, so that the banker will be entitled to the benefit of that payment if he can show that that payment went to discharge a legal liability of the customer. The customer in such a case is really no worse off, because the legal liability which has to be discharged is discharged, though it is discharged under circumstances which at common law would not entitle the bank to debit the customer.

Another illustration of the general availability of equitable defences to legal claims since the Judicature Acts is afforded by *Mathieson's Trustee* v. *Burrup, Mathieson & Co.*,[9] in which a defendant sought to set off under Section 31 of the Bankruptcy Act, 1914[10] an equitable debt due to him from a bankrupt against a legal debt claimed by the trustee in bankruptcy. Both debts existed at the date of the receiving order. Clauson, J., held that the defendant could set off the equitable debt against the legal debt, observing[11]—

> The Bankruptcy Act, as I understand it, is an Act regulating the proceedings of a Court which has always been a Court of equity, proceeding on equitable principles, recognizing equitable debts, subject of course to such infirmities as are sometimes present, but drawing no distinction between equitable and legal rights for purposes of administering the estate of the bankrupt. I think, at this time of day, it would be very unfortunate, if it were held that a Court of Bankruptcy is in any way fettered by any such distinctions, except so far as any Court of equity is fettered by the fact that certain infirmities may in certain circumstances attach to equitable rights as compared with corresponding legal rights.

Deeds

The common law attached peculiar sanctity to deeds, and therefore in every case where the common law required writing for a transaction, this necessarily implied a deed.[12] The reason for this is to be found in the fact that the transaction was authenticated, not by signature,

[9] [1927] 1 Ch. 562.
[10] Ireland: Irish Bankrupt and Insolvent Act, 1857, Sect. 251.
[11] [1927] 1 Ch. 569.
[12] Co. Litt. 9.

since many men were illiterate when the rule was established, but by the seal which, from the earliest days of Mesopotamian civilisation onwards, has been regarded as evidence of a person's assent to a transaction. It followed that the affixation of a seal to a writing upon parchment implied some binding transaction of special importance.

The binding effect of a deed in constraining the parties thereto to the strict performance or observance of the terms expressed therein, notwithstanding that they may have received nothing in return, is due to the importance attached in our early law to writing as a mode of proof of a man's intention or consent to make some assurance of property, or to be bound by some promise. In the Middle Ages, when most men were illiterate, peculiar solemnity attached to a written record of a man's intention to make a gift of land or to pay a sum of money or perform some other act; and it was held that, when a writing of this kind was produced, the person purporting to be bound thereby should be obliged to give effect to his intention as expressed therein, unless he could show that the writing was forged, or that his consent thereto had been extorted by using force, causing fear or practising fraud. In times soon after the Norman Conquest it was considered that a writing should have this effect, even if it were unsealed. But afterwards it was required that the seal of the person bound should be affixed to the writing as a guarantee of its authenticity, or else it should not be admitted in evidence against him.[13]

These characteristics of a deed survived the spread of the art of writing, and unsealed documents never acquired in full the characteristics of deeds. This is evidenced by the fact that a contract not under seal requires consideration, while a contract under seal does not, for a " deed imports consideration." In fact, the covenant by deed antedates the evolution of the doctrine of consideration as the test of the enforceability of simple contracts, and has never been reconciled with it.

Equity, the rules of which were formed at a later period than those of the common law, does not regard deeds with the same veneration as the common law. In *Kekewich* v. *Manning*,[14] Knight Bruce, L.J., observed—

> I have been speaking of transactions without any sealed writing. But though it is true that in cases where such an intention, such a promise, is expressed in a deed, it may bind generally at law as a covenant by reason of the light in which the particular kind of instrument called a deed is regarded at law, yet in equity, where at

13 Halsbury's *Laws of England*, 3rd ed., vol. II, p. 324 n.
14 (1851), 1 De G.M. & G. 176, 188.

least the covenantor is living, or where specific performance of such a covenant is sought, it stands scarcely, or not at all, on a better footing than if it were contained in an instrument unsealed.

The scope of the principle must not be misunderstood, however, for with regard to the transfer of legal estates, equity follows the law with regard to the formalities required, and so where a deed is necessary to make a conveyance valid at law, it must also be shown in equity that a deed has been employed. An example of this is afforded by *National Provincial Bank of England* v. *Jackson.*[15] There A, a solicitor, induced his sisters B and C to sign two deeds whereby, in consideration of the release of a debt of £400 and a payment to them of £300, they conveyed their shares of freehold property to A. The property was mortgaged to K. No money was then due to A from either B or C, and no payment was made by him to either of them. The deeds were not read over or explained to B and C, who signed in reliance upon A's statement that he was going to clear off K's mortgage. A then deposited the deeds with the bank as security for an advance, and then absconded. The bank claimed the property as equitable mortgagees, and B and C resisted the claim, urging that since the conveyances had been obtained by fraud and misrepresentation, they were void. The Court of Appeal held that although B and C did not understand the full purport of the deeds, they knew they were executing something affecting their title to the property, and therefore the deeds were not void but voidable. At the same time A had made certain statements to the bank manager at the time of his deposit of the deeds which ought to have put the bank upon inquiry, and which would have led to the detection of the fraud. The bank, through its want of prudence, was therefore affected with the constructive notice of the fraud, and their claim must therefore be postponed to that of B and C.

Cotton, L.J., observed[16]—

> . . . the rule of law is that if a person who seals and delivers a deed is misled by the misstatements or misrepresentations of the persons procuring the execution of the deeds, so that he does not know what is the instrument to which he puts his hand, the deed is not his deed at all, because he was neither minded nor intended to sign a document of that character or class, as, for instance, a release while intending to execute a lease. Such a deed is void. But I cannot come to that conclusion here. The Defendants trusted *Jackson* both as their brother and solicitor, and cannot be said to have been guilty of negligence in so doing. On the evidence it is

15 (1886), 33 Ch. D. 1.
16 33 Ch. D. 10. See also *Gallie* v. *Lee*, [1969] 2 W.L.R. 901 (C.A.).

clear that nothing was said to mislead them as to the nature of the instrument they were executing. It is doubtful how far they understood the nature of the deeds, but it is in my opinion clear upon the evidence that they knew that the deeds dealt in some way with their houses. This contention therefore fails.

There was a further point. B and C also contended that the estate had been reconveyed to them by instrument executed the day before the bank's charge attached. These instruments, however, were never sealed, and so, not being executed as deeds, were inoperative to pass the legal estates. Thus there was no question of a conflict between equitable and legal interests, but merely between two opposing equitable interests.[17]

From the principles already enunciated, it follows that where any voluntary gift (where no declaration of trust occurs) is incomplete for want of formalities required by law, equity will not assist the volunteer, and therefore, where the gift is of the legal estate of freeholds, or of a legal term of years, and no deed is executed, in the absence of a deed this is void in equity as well as at law.

For the transfer of equitable interests, however, no deed is necessary, in the absence of statutory requirement, nor indeed, even writing; although specific statutes (e.g. the Statute of Frauds, 1677, Section 9,[18] and the Law of Property Act, 1925) have made writing necessary for the transfer of certain equitable interests, e.g. those arising under a trust; but by Section 53 of the Law of Property Act, 1925,[19] replacing Sections 7-8 of the Statute of Frauds, all express trusts of land must be evidenced by writing, and signed by the party who is to declare the trust.

Before the Judicature Acts, there was a variance in the rule of common law and equity with regard to contracts made by deed. At common law, obligations arising out of such contracts could only be discharged, before breach, by a deed. Even an agreement for valuable consideration, though it constituted an enforceable contract, would not operate to discharge such an obligation.[20] In equity, however,

17 See also *Bassett* v. *Nosworthy* (1673), Rep. t. Finch, 102, 103; *Brace* v. *Duchess of Marlborough* (1728), 2 P.Wms. 491, 496; *Willoughby* v. *Willoughby* (1756), 1 T.R. 763, 767, 773; *Rooper* v. *Harrison* (1855), 2 K. & J. 86, 108, 109; *Phillips* v. *Phillips* (1862), 4 De G. F. & J. 208, 215; *Heath* v. *Crealock* (1874), L.R. 10 Ch. App. 22, 29, 30.

18 Ireland: Statute of Frauds (Ireland), 1695, Sect. 6.

19 Ireland: Statute of Frauds (Ireland), 1695, Sects. 4-5.

20 *Heard* v. *Wadham* (1801), 1 East 619; *Kaye* v. *Waghorn* (1809), 1 Taunt. 428; *Brymer* v. *Thames Haven Dock & Railway Co.* (1848), 2 Ex. 549; (1850), 5 Ex. 696; *Berwick Corp.* v. *Oswald* (1853), 1 E. & B. 295; *Spence* v. *Healey* (1853), 8 Ex. 668; *Nash* v. *Armstrong* (1861), 10 C.B.N.S. 259.

such an agreement was a valid discharge, and the parties to it were restrained from enforcing the obligation at law.[21] The effect of Section 25(11) of the Judicature Act, 1873,[22] upon the variance was considered in *Steeds* v. *Steeds*[23] wherein Wills, J., observed—

> It is clear that at law accord and satisfaction of a debt due upon a bond is no bar to the action. This is, however, purely the result of a technicality absolutely devoid of any particle of merits or justice, viz., that a contract under seal cannot be got rid of except by performance or by a contract also under seal; so that supposing it had really been the case that in satisfaction of an overdue bond for £1,000 the person liable had given property worth £2,000, which had been accepted in discharge of the obligation, still at law the obligee of the bond might recover his £1,000 without returning the property.
>
> One would have thought that if the Courts of Equity ever interfered at all to prevent a man from enforcing an unconscientious and dishonest demand to which there was no answer at law, they would perpetually restrain an action brought under the circumstances described. Mr. Wood, however, who is an equity lawyer, contended before us that this was a case in which equity would follow the law, and would refuse to interfere, and he laid great stress upon a case of *Webb* v. *Hewitt*,[24] which he said established that proposition. We are glad to say that we are unable to agree with him, and that we think he has done an injustice to a system of which one recommendation has been supposed to be that it was, sometimes at all events, competent to correct some of the worst and most odious technicalities of the common law. The case cited appears to us to lead to the opposite conclusion to that contended for, and we think it perfectly clear that the ratio decidendi of the learned Vice-Chancellor was, that when the plaintiff had accepted money's worth in place of money in discharge of the bond, the debt in equity was gone and there was an end of it.

Since 1875, the equitable rule has replaced the rule of common law. This point is illustrated in the case of *Berry* v. *Berry*.[25] Mr. and Mrs. Berry entered into a deed of separation in 1920, but in 1928, as Mr. Berry found difficulty in making the payments, the parties executed a written agreement whereby some of the terms of the original agreement were varied. After Mrs. Berry had accepted several payments

21 *Lady Lanesborough* v. *Ockshott* (1719), 1 Bro. P.C. 151 (H.L., E.); *Hill* v. *Gomme* (1839), 5 My. & Cr. 250; *Webb* v. *Hewitt* (1857), 3 K. & J. 438.

22 Ireland: Judicature (Ireland) Act, 1877, Sect. 28 (11).

23 (1889) 22 Q.B.D. 537, 539-40. See also *Powell* v. *Brodhurst*, [1901] 2 Ch. 160.

24 (1857), 3 K. & J. 438.

25 [1929] 2 K.B. 316.

under the new agreement, she claimed that she was still entitled to the payments specified in the deed of 1920. At common law, a deed under seal could only be varied or dispensed with by another instrument under seal, but Swift, J., observed[26]—

> . . . although that was the rule of law, the Courts of Equity have always held themselves at liberty to allow the rescission or variation by a simple contract of a contract under seal by preventing the party who has agreed to rescission or variation suing under the deed. In *Nash* v. *Armstrong*[27] it was held that a parol agreement not to enforce performance of a deed and to substitute other terms for some of its covenants was a good consideration for a promise to perform the substituted contract, even although the deed be not thereby released. In the course of the argument, Willes J. said he would have thought " the agreement a good answer " by way of equitable plea. As my brother Acton has pointed out, Willes J. added:[28] " The payment of the £70 under the agreement would surely be ground for an unconditional perpetual injunction against proceeding upon the deed."

Accordingly, since the Judicature Act, 1873, Section 25 (11), when the question arises whether a deed can be varied by any agreement which is not itself contained in a deed, the rules of equity must be applied in consideration of the matter. Mrs. Berry was therefore held to the terms of the written agreement of 1928.

The equitable principle applied in *Berry* v. *Berry*,[29] however, stopped short of an award of relief where there was no consideration for the variations of the terms of the deed. To have held otherwise, indeed, would have implied that equity no longer recognised the necessity for consideration for a simple contract, which such a variation of the original deed undoubtedly was. In *Central London Property Trust Ltd.* v. *High Trees House Ltd.*,[30] however, Denning, J., approached the problem from a new angle. In that case, the plaintiffs, by deed, had granted a lease of a block of flats to the defendants at a rent of £2,500 a year. This was shortly before the outbreak of the war of 1939-45, and the flats were never fully let. Accordingly, in January 1940, the plaintiffs agreed in writing not under seal that they would reduce the rent to £1,250 a year. This was plainly in consequence of the war, although this was not expressly stated. From 1940 to 1945, therefore,

26 [1929] 2 K.B. 319.
27 (1861), 10 C.B.N.S. 259.
28 10 C.B.N.S. 262.
29 [1929] 2 K.B. 316.
30 [1947] K.B. 130. See also pp. 40-2, *ante*.

the defendants paid a rent of £1,250 a year, but in 1945, the plaintiffs announced that henceforth they would require the full rent of £2,500 a year, and in deciding upon this claim the learned judge considered whether they would have been entitled to the full rent of £2,500 for the war years. The equitable doctrine applied in *Berry* v. *Berry* could not assist the defendants, for the plaintiff's original statement that they would accept half the rent had been gratuitous. Again, the statement of the plaintiffs could not be regarded as an estoppel, because it was decided by the House of Lords in *Jorden* v. *Money*[31] that an estoppel must be a representation of an existing fact. A representation as to the future must be part of a contract or else it has no legal effect. However, Denning, J., was able to escape from the restrictions on the doctrine of estoppel which *Jorden* v. *Money*[31] had imposed by applying the principle upon which *Fenner* v. *Blake*,[32] *Re Wickham*,[33] *Re Porter & Co.*[34] and *Buttery* v. *Pickard*[35] are based. These, said Denning, J.,[36] are not cases of estoppel in the strict sense. They are examples of promises intended to be binding, upon which the parties have acted, and which the courts have not then allowed a party to repudiate. He said[37]—

> The courts have not gone so far as to give a cause of action in damages for breach of such a promise, but they have refused to allow the party making it to act inconsistently with it . . . The logical consequence, no doubt is that a promise to accept a smaller sum in discharge of a larger sum, if acted upon, is binding notwithstanding the absence of consideration: and if the fusion of law and equity leads to this result, so much the better.

Accordingly, Denning, J., gave judgment for the defendants, holding that the parties intended the agreement to have temporary effect, until all the flats were let. However, it must be noticed that the actual claim in the case was only for two quarters' rent at a time when the flats were admittedly fully let, and the abnormal war-time conditions had ceased. Learned writers have therefore pointed out that Denning, J.'s, observations, in so far as they relate to the effect of the agreement of the landlords in 1940 to accept a reduced rent, are obiter only—a circumstance which materially affects the present status of the principle discussed in Denning, J.'s judgment.

31 (1854), 5 H.L.C. 185.
32 [1900] 1 Q.B. 426.
33 (1917), 34 T.L.R. 158.
34 [1937] 2 All E.R. 361.
35 [1946] W.N. 25.
36 [1947] K.B. 134.
37 [1947] K.B. 134-5.

In this interesting case, Denning, J., stated that the equitable principle underlying his decision was a development of the past sixty years, i.e., since the passing of the Judicature Acts. An early illustration of it is *Hughes* v. *Metropolitan Railway Co.*[38] In that case, a landlord gave the tenants notice to repair some houses occupied by them within six months. The defendants offered to surrender their interests in the houses for £3,000. This was refused by the landlord, who nevertheless expressed his willingness to give a lesser sum. To this the tenants made no reply, and later, when the landlord's period of notice had practically expired, they said they would execute the repairs. The landlord replied that they had failed to comply with the notice, and sought to forfeit the leases. The House of Lords held that the earlier negotiation for the purchase of the tenants' interests suspended the notice so long as the negotiations were in progress. This, said Lord Cairns, was in accordance with the equitable principle that enforcement of the original obligations is inequitable, so long as negotiations for their modification are in progress. In *Birmingham and District Land Co.* v. *London and North Western Railway Co.*,[39] Bowen, L.J., defined the principle as follows—

> . . . if persons who have contractual rights against others induce by their conduct those against whom they have such rights to believe that such right will either not be enforced or will be kept in suspense or abeyance for some particular time, those persons will not be allowed by a Court of Equity to enforce the rights until such time has elapsed, without at all events placing the parties in the same position as they were before.

It is as yet too early to say whether this principle, in the amplitude given to it by Denning, J., is firmly established. Atkinson, J., accepted it in *Ledingham* v. *Bermejo Estancia Co. Ltd.*,[40] but Somervell, L.J., doubted it in *Re Venning*.[41] In *D. & C. Builders Ltd.* v. *Rees*[42] Lord Denning, M.R., in the Court of Appeal, after referring with approval to *Central London Property Trust Ltd.* v. *High Trees House Ltd.*,[43] said—

> In applying this principle, however, we must note the qualification: The creditor is only barred from his legal rights when it would be *inequitable* for him to insist upon them. Where there has been a *true*

38 (1877), 2 App. Cas. 439 (H.L., E.).

39 (1888), 40 Ch.D. 268, 286 (C.A.).

40 [1947] 1 All E.R. 749. See also the judgment of Denning, J., in *Robertson* v. *Minister of Pensions*, [1949] 1 K.B. 227, and *Combe* v. *Combe*, [1951] 2 K.B. 215 (Denning, L.J., in the Court of Appeal).

41 (1947), 63 T.L.R. 394 (C.A.).

42 [1966] 2 Q.B. 617, 625.

43 [1947] K.B. 130.

> *accord*, under which the creditor voluntarily agrees to accept a lesser sum in satisfaction, and the debtor *acts upon* that accord by paying the lesser sum and the creditor accepts it, then it is inequitable for the creditor afterwards to insist on the balance. But he is not bound unless there has been truly an accord between them.

Donaldson, J., applied the principle in *Durham Fancy Goods Ltd.* v. *Michael Jackson* (*Fancy Goods*) *Ltd.*[44] He said[45]—

> Lord Cairns L.C. in his enunciation of the principle[46] assumed a pre-existing contractual relationship between the parties, but this does not seem to me to be essential, provided that there is a pre-existing legal relationship which could in certain circumstances give rise to liabilities and penalties.

Evershed observed of the decision that " It would appear to have established a right to the extent, but only to the extent, of a right to a specific remedy, namely the remedy of an injunction to prevent the other party recalling his previous promise."[47] Cheshire and Fifoot, in their full discussion of the case, accepted it as a desirable equitable development.[48] Both Wilson and Hanbury stressed that nothing new was actually laid down in the case, even though Denning, J., embraced the opportunity to suggest that there would have been an estoppel from claiming the full rent for 1941-45, since the landlord, though not technically bound for lack of consideration, had expressed his intention to be bound, and the tenant had acted in reliance upon that expressed intention.[49]

Estoppel by Recital

Before the Judicature Acts, the courts of law and equity differed in their treatment of recitals contained in deeds. As Lord Maugham pointed out in *Greer* v. *Kettle*,[50] for over two hundred years a recital in a deed was not considered to be so direct an affirmation as to amount to an estoppel,[51] and the strict common law governing statements in recitals was not established until 1834, when the cases of *Lainson* v.

44 [1968] 2 Q.B. 839.
45 [1968] 2 Q.B. 847.
46 In *Hughes* v. *Metropolitan Railway Co.* (1877), 2 App. Cas. 439, 448.
47 " Equity after Fusion: Federal or Confederate," (1948), 1 *Journal of the Society of Public Teachers of Law*, 171, 176.
48 " *Central London Property Trust Ltd.* v. *High Trees House Ltd.*" (1947), 63 *Law Quarterly Review*, 283.
49 Wilson, " Recent Developments in Estoppel " (1951), 67 *Law Quarterly Review*, 330; Hanbury, *Modern Equity*, 8th ed., pp. 99-101.
50 [1938] A.C. 156, 168 (H.L., E.).
51 Co. Litt. 352.

Tremere[52] and *Bowman* v. *Taylor*[53] were decided. In its developed form, the rule was expressed by Coltman, J., in *Young* v. *Raincock*[54] as follows—

> . . . where it can be collected from the deed, that the parties to it have agreed upon a certain admitted state of facts as the basis on which they contract, the statement of those facts, though but in the way of recital, shall estop the parties to aver the contrary.

In later cases at common law, it was emphasised that the recital must relate to specific facts, it must be certain, clear and unambiguous, and further, in the words of Patterson, J., in *Stroughill* v. *Buck*[55]—

> When a recital is intended to be a statement which all parties to the deed have mutually agreed to admit as true, it is an estoppel upon all. But, when it is intended to be the statement of one party only, the estoppel is confined to that party, and the intention is to be gathered from construing the instrument.

As Lord Maugham said in *Greer* v. *Kettle*[56]—

> The position in equity is and was always different in this respect, that where there are proper grounds for rectifying a deed, e.g., because it is based upon a common mistake of fact, then to the extent of the rectification there can plainly be no estoppel based on the original form of the instrument. It is at least equally clear that in equity a party to a deed could not set up an estoppel in reliance on a deed in relation to which there is an equitable right to rescission or in reliance on an untrue statement or an untrue recital induced by his own representation, whether innocent or otherwise, to the other party. Authority is scarcely needed for so clear a consequence of a rectification order or an admitted or proved right to such an order. The well known rule of the Chancery Court in regard to a receipt clause in a deed not effecting an estoppel if the money has not in fact been paid is a good illustration of the equity view. . . . The decision of Lord Romilly in *Brooke* v. *Haymes*,[57] is even more closely in point, and it may be added that the statement of the law in that case appears never to have been doubted. The headnote begins as follows: " A party to a deed is not estopped in equity from averring

52 1 Ad. & El. 792.
53 2 Ad. & El. 278.
54 (1849), 7 C.B. 310, 338.
55 (1850), 14 Q.B. 781, 787.
56 [1938] A.C. 156, 171-2.
57 (1868), L.R. 6 Eq. 25.

against or offering evidence to contravert a recital therein contrary to the fact, which has been introduced into the deed by mistake of fact, and not through fraud or deception on his part." In a simple case of this kind it would be unnecessary, as that case shows, to counterclaim for rectification, though in a case of any complexity it would certainly be desirable to do so.

Since the Judicature Act, 1873, the rule in equity must prevail.

CHAPTER IV

EQUITY IN IRELAND

THE topic of equity in the Irish courts has suffered from very general neglect from English writers—as has, indeed, Irish legal history generally. Holdsworth, for example, ignores it altogether. Even Pollock and Maitland[1] content themselves with remarking that " a smaller England has been created across the Channel." The fact that the English Judicature Acts were followed a year or two later by a similar transformation in Ireland has passed almost completely unremembered. One reason for this is that Irish law reports before the nineteenth century are fragmentary, and, since 1800, they have formed little more than an appendix to the English reports, especially in equity. Another is that the difficulties of reconstructing Irish legal history were very greatly increased by the loss of the judicial records in the destruction of the Four Courts during the political upheavals which followed the war of 1914-1918. Nevertheless, in spite of close similarities with English law, from which it is derived, Irish law contains distinctive features.

The connection between Irish legal history and that of England begins with Henry II's expedition to Ireland, which was followed by the introduction of Anglo-Norman law and the establishment of legal institutions similar to those which had been created in England in the previous century. For some centuries the common law was applicable only to those Englishmen who had settled in Ireland, and over whom effective and continuous control from Dublin could be exercised. It was not until the end of the sixteenth century that it was progressively extended to all the inhabitants of Ireland, whatever their origin. Because of the circumstances of the English occupation, and the establishment of government through a Viceroy, who was always dependent upon the English government, without whose frequent intervention that viceregal government would have been ineffective, there was no fusion of English and Irish law. Indeed, for some centuries, after the reign of Henry II, the native Irish were habitually described as " enemies," although, from time to time, particular clans were included within the orbit of the common law. It would appear that King John had

[1] *H.E.L.* (2nd ed.), p. 221.

intended that the common law should be extended to the whole of the population of Ireland, but this was frustrated by the Viceroy and the English settlers.[2]

Although the numbers of the population to which English law was applied remained small, until the whole of Ireland was brought within the common law, there were established in Dublin courts which very closely resembled those at Westminster. There were the three common law courts, the Exchequer, the King's Bench and the Common Pleas and, at a later stage, there was the Court of Chancery. As in England, the Exchequer even exercised a limited equity jurisdiction. For example, the great case of *Sherlock* v. *Annesley*, which raised important constitutional questions, was first decided on 24th February 1709 in the Irish Court of Exchequer by a decree in equity.[3] In the late eighteenth century, the Exchequer in Ireland was more resorted to in equity matters than its English counterpart. Although a number of officials, including a Chief Justiciary, or Viceroy, were introduced during the reign of Henry II, there is no mention of a Chancellor, until John de Worchley was appointed to that office in 1219, the third year of Henry III's reign. As with the other great officers of state, the Chancellors were English by birth and training. They were most frequently Prelates. Several Archbishops of Dublin appear in the role of mediaeval Irish Chancellors, but there are also Bishops, an occasional Archdeacon, and Priors. As in England, the Chancellor had custody of the Great Seal, and presided in the House of Peers. As in England, also, there might from time to time be a Lord Keeper, instead of a Lord Chancellor, or even Lord Commissioners for the execution of the office.

The development of the Irish Chancery as a court administering equity closely followed that of the Chancery in England and, during the Middle Ages, the ecclesiastical Chancellors on both sides of the Irish Channel shared a common outlook upon the nature of equity. As early as the reign of Edward II, an English statute[4] provided that the rents and profits of idiots and lunatics should be vested in the Crown and, as a consequence of this, the Chancellor was given jurisdiction in all lunacy matters.

[2] O'Flanagan, *Lives of the Lord Chancellors of Ireland*, vol. I, p. 9.

[3] O'Flanagan, *op cit.*, vol. II, p. 15. O'Flanagan's work (published in 1870) was avowedly modelled on Lord Campbell's *Lives of the Chancellors* and, like that work, contains numerous inaccuracies, but it is the only continuous account of the Irish Chancellors.

[4] 17 Edw. II, c. 9.

Throughout the mediaeval period, however, the equity business of the Chancery remained small, and successive Chancellors were more frequently concerned with political affairs, and even military expeditions, than with the development of equity. There is evidence, nevertheless, that the subpoena was introduced into Irish Chancery procedure at approximately the same time that it makes its appearance in England,[5] and in addition, it is plain that uses and trusts were recognised in Ireland, exactly as they were in England, before the close of the fifteenth century.[6]

> It was not, however, until the reign of Henry VIII that the equitable jurisdiction of this Court [of Chancery] made its greatest stride. Then it became settled law, that there being a feoffment to uses, the person beneficially entitled could not, on violation of the trust, maintain an action at common law. Thereupon the Chancellors determined they would compel the faithless trustee to perform the duty binding upon his conscience, and, in process of time, the remedy was extended against his heir and assignee, with notice of the trust. But it was not considered equitable to extend this remedy against a purchaser of the legal estate for valuable consideration without such notice.[7]

During the reign of Henry VIII, there was a considerable extension of English law to persons of Irish descent, so that the jurisdiction of all the courts was extended. Gradually, the common law replaced the ancient laws of Ireland, the process of assimilation being virtually complete by the reign of James I. Even so, during the reign of Edward VI, only fifty-two decrees were enrolled in the Chancery. The suits were mainly for obtaining quiet possession of land, for an account or for the perpetuation of testimony. In the reign of Mary I, the number had risen to about a hundred, once again mainly in respect of suits for injunctions, for the perpetuation of testimony and for breaches of trust. Perpetuation of testimony was frequently needed where legitimacy was disputed in matters of succession. Both the Statute of Uses, 1535, and the Statute of Wills, 1540, had their counterparts in Irish legislation in 1634.

O'Flanagan, [8] who examined the Calendars of Proceedings in Chancery for the reign of Henry VIII and Elizabeth I, gave the following illustrations of proceedings in the sixteenth century:

5 O'Flanagan, *op. cit.*, vol. I, p. 71.
6 O'Flanagan, *op. cit.* vol. I, p. 146.
7 *Ibid.*, pp. 149-150.
8 *Op. cit.*, vol. I, p. 13.

" For an injunction to stay proceedings at law."

" To compel the defendant as feoffee in trust to make an estate to the plaintiff and his heirs in certain lands and tenements."

" To be relieved from an unjust demand made by the defendant, who is the keeper of a tavern which the plaintiff had visited; and praying a write of *certiorari.*"

" For discovery of deeds alleged to be in the defendant's possession."

" To set aside a deed obtained by fraud, and to obtain an injunction to stay proceedings."

Once again, the parallelism with the work of the English Court of Chancery at this period is very close.

At the accession of Elizabeth I, Hugh Curwen, Archbishop of Dublin, was re-appointed Lord Chancellor, having been appointed in 1554. He was a person of unusual ability, who introduced important changes into the Chancery, whereby its jurisdiction was extended. Sequestration and commissions of rebellion enforced obedience to the procedure, and Curwen followed the English practice by directing issues of fact to be tried before common law judges. The Chancery was now a busy court and, during Elizabeth I's reign, no less than seven hundred and eighty decrees were enrolled.[9] During James I's reign, the number was three hundred and twenty,[10] and during that of his son, the number rose to seven hundred and twenty-six.[11]

The office of Master in Chancery dates from 1532, in which year Cormac Rothe, Archdeacon of Armagh, was appointed. At first the principal function of the Masters was to examine the records and writs which emanated from the Chancery, and to authenticate any writs before they were issued. Occasionally they were appointed to hear causes, and from the reign of Elizabeth I onwards, they gradually became judicial officers, whose duties were to enquire and report upon all cases referred to them by the Chancellor, to audit the accounts of guardians, receivers and committees of idiots and lunatics, to tax costs, to execute conveyances under orders of the courts, approve purchases of stock for trust estates, to undertake the guardianship of minors and lunatics and, finally, to hear causes with one of the judges, when directed by the Chancellor. The office was abolished by the Chancery (Ireland) Act, 1867, Section 27.

[9] O'Flanagan, *op. cit.*, vol. I, p. 294.
[10] *Ibid.*, p. 315.
[11] *Ibid.*, p. 344.

The office of Master of the Rolls was mediaeval in origin, but in the reign of Elizabeth I, the functions attached to it were similar to those of his English counterpart. Thus, on the appointment of Edward Fitz-Symon, in 1578, the Queen gave " full power and authority to our well-beloved Edward Fitz-Symon Esq., our Serjeant-at-Law, not only to sit in our High Court of Chancery, and there hear, decide, decree, and determine such cause and causes as depend in the said Court, or hereafter shall be brought in suit in the said Court, and to do, execute, proceed and set forth, all and every other thing and things in the Court in as large and ample a manner as the said Nicholas White, Master of the Rolls, or any other before him in this office, might and ought to have done in the said Court of Chancery, which pertaineth to the keeping of the Master of the Rolls' office; to have, hold, use, occupy and exercise, the said office of getting, hearing, ordering, decreeing, and determining causes, as aforesaid, and keeping of the rolls, documents, records, files, books, writings, and other premises unto the said Edward."

During the nineteenth century there was a prolonged dispute concerning the status of the Master of the Rolls, and his power to appoint a secretary. Whatever may have been included in the terms of Edward Fitz-Symon's appointment, the office of Master of the Rolls had long ceased to have any judicial functions, and indeed, during the eighteenth century, it became no more than a sinecure. Immediately after the passing of the Act of Union, the Lord Chancellor, John Fitzgibbon, Earl of Clare, proposed to the Chief Secretary for Ireland that there should be a drastic change, which was to coincide with the appointment of Sir Michael Smith, a Baron of the Exchequer in Ireland. Lord Clare wrote—

> By an Act passed in Ireland in the reign of Henry VII[12] the tenure of the office of Master of the Rolls can be during the King's pleasure only, and from every inquiry which I have been enabled to make, the profits of it do not exceed, on the average, eighteen hundred pounds yearly. There has, however, been a shabby perquisite of the office, arising from an open sale of the situations of six clerks and examiners of the Court of Chancery, which certainly ought to be abolished. Under these circumstances, I feel that if the office of Master of the Rolls is to be placed upon a respectable foundation in this country, it ought to be assimilated, as nearly as may be, to that of the Master of the Rolls in England, and if the tenure in that Country is permanent, it ought to be made permanent here; so the profits of the office here ought to be made up to the possessor of it (fees included) three thousand pounds annually, and if the tenure

[12] 10 Hen. VII, c. 2.

is not to be permanent, the King should be empowered to make a concurrent grant to the Master of the Rolls of an annuity equal to that provided by the Act of the late Session for him in case of removal.

Lord Clare also emphasises that if the Lord Chancellor of Ireland is to be able to attend the House of Lords in England, it is essential that there should be an efficient Master of the Rolls, to carry on the work of the Chancery. The result of this was the passing of the Act for the better regulation of the Office of Master of the Rolls in Ireland, 1801,[13] giving the occupant security of tenure, and a salary of £3,500 a year, and making it clear that the office was a judicial one, and " assistant to the Lord High Chancellor of Ireland."

Unfortunately the new arrangement providing for Masters of the Rolls, with legal attainments of higher calibre, did not always work smoothly. On the resignation of Lord Manners (a cadet of the Rutland family) from the Chancellorship in 1827, Sir Antony Hart, the Vice-Chancellor of the English Court of Chancery, was appointed to succeed him over the head of Lord Plunkett, the outstanding Irish equity lawyer of the day. Hart's unfamiliarity with Irish procedure unfortunately led him to comit a serious blunder immediately after taking office. By an order of 7th November 1827, he directed that the Registers of the court should not receive or file any petition, unless it were signed by the Lord Chancellor's secretary. This order covered, and was intended to cover, petitions to be heard in the Rolls Court. On the following day, Sir William McMahon, the Master of the Rolls, replied with an order, directing that, in proceedings before the Master of the Rolls, orders and petitions should be directed to the Master of the Rolls, instead of the Lord Chancellor. He also appointed Mr. Frederick Shaw (later Recorder of Dublin) to be his secretary—an action which was also contested by the Lord Chancellor, and which followed the precedent set by Sir Michael Smith in 1802, when he appointed a secretary to receive petitions of suitors and to take down the orders thereon at the times of the year when the courts were not sitting, and consequently, when the Registers were not in attendance. Immediately on this appointment, the Lord Chancellor's secretary had claimed and received compensation for loss of fees, to the extent of £500 a year for the rest of his life.

Behind this squabble lay the assertion of the Master of the Rolls of a status similar to that of the Master of the Rolls in England, whose secretary was a recognised officer of the Rolls Court. This was com-

[13] 41 Geo. III, c. 25.

pletely rejected by the Lord Chancellor, who referred to the long disuse of the judicial functions of the Master of the Rolls, and their re-establishment by the Statute of 1801. Accordingly, he denied the right of the Master of the Rolls to appoint a secretary, with power to receive petitions.

There the matter remained until the appointment of Lord Plunkett as Lord Chancellor, in December 1830, when the Master of the Rolls renewed his claim. Lord Plunkett, instead of following Hart's order, suggested the matter should be made the subject of an appeal to the House of Lords. Lord Plunkett was in a little difficulty, as he had just appointed his nephew as his own secretary, in addition to the existing occupant of the office, and he added that nothing which the House of Lords might decide should adversely effect the rights of the two secretaries. To this condition, the Master of the Rolls (still Sir William McMahon) demurred. The upshot was the introduction in the House of Commons of the Master of the Rolls (Ireland) Bill in February 1832, to give the Master of the Rolls the desired power. It failed, however, to win the approval of Parliament.

Although there are no regular reports of decisions in the Irish Chancery until the beginning of the nineteenth century, mention should be made of a compilation, printed in 1615, and prepared by Sir John Davies, who served for a time both as Solicitor-General, and then as Attorney-General for Ireland. Davies had a considerable knowledge of the ancient Irish laws, and in his collection of decisions there are a number of decisions which deal with Irish customs and history. Outstanding amongst them is the *Case of Tanistry*.[14] These cases were, however, decided in the Irish Court of King's Bench.

As in England, the Irish Chancery survived the Commonwealth, although the office of Chancellor was vested in three Commissioners, the First Commissioner being Richard Pepys, father of the diarist, and ancester of a Victorian Lord Chancellor of England, Lord Cottenham. The volume of work in the Chancery, at this time, showed little change, three hundred and ninety-four decrees being pronounced during the Commonwealth.[15]

During most of the reign of Charles II, the Irish Woolsack was occupied by Michael Boyle, Archbishop of Dublin and, later, Archbishop of Armagh. Boyle is remarkable in several ways. He was the last of Ireland's ecclesiastical Chancellors and, accordingly, he had no

14 (1608), Davies 78.
15 O'Flanagan, *op. cit.*, vol. I, p. 357.

legal training. He therefore stands in sharp contrast with his English contemporary, Lord Nottingham. Appointed in 1663, he held office until February 1686, when James II replaced him with Sir Charles Porter. Although already an old man, he survived until 1702, having then reached the great age of ninety-two. Although very little is known of his administration of equity, there was published in Dublin in 1673, " A collection of such Orders heretofore used in Chancery, with such alterations and additions thereunto as Michael, Lord Archbishop of Dublin, Lord Chancellor of Ireland hath thought fit at present to ordain and publish for reforming of severe abuses in the said courts, preventing multiplicity of suits, motions and unnecessary charges to the suitors, and for their more expeditious and certain relief."

How far the Archbishop had modified the pre-existing practice is not clear. In any case, although one would have expected the Chancery to be active after the Restoration, only two hundred and fifteen decrees are enrolled from the quarter of a century of the reign. During the short reign of James II nearly a hundred decrees were made, which was almost the exact number for the reign of William III. There was, however, good reason for this small number. John Methuen, a diplomat with no legal training (but the negotiator of the Methuen treaty with Portugal signed in 1701), was selected to act as Lord Chancellor by Lord Summers at the beginning of 1697. The appointment was a thoroughly bad one, and Methuen unsuccessfully sought to conceal his ignorance of equity by delays and periodic absences in England. These visits were successful, for in 1701 he was able to exchange the Great Seal of Ireland for the Ambassadorship to the Portugese Court. He was followed by Sir Richard Cox, an Irish Protestant of English descent, who was called to the bar by Gray's Inn in 1673. His decisions in the Chancery were highly regarded, and were almost invariably affirmed by the Irish House of Lords on appeal.

On 24th February 1709, the Irish Court of Exchequer made a decree in equity in favour of Maurice and John Annesley, and against the complainant, Hester Sherlock. The complainant appealed, and the Irish House of Lords varied the Exchequer decree in a number of important particulars, in June 1716. Maurice Annesley thereupon appealed from the Irish House of Lords to the English House of Lords, who upheld the appeal, and restored the decree of the Irish Court of Exchequer. The next step in what was to become a major constitutional battle was a petition from Mrs. Sherlock in 1717 to the Irish House of Lords, praying them to make an order in her favour. The House, after deliberating the question, ordered the High Sheriff of Kildare to execute the previous decision of the House in Mrs. Sherlock's appeal. The sheriff complied, and put Mrs. Sherlock into possession of the disputed property, whereupon the Irish Exchequer issued an injunction against him, ordering him to dispossess Mrs. Sherlock, and restore Annesley to possession. When the sheriff refused, he was fined by the Exchequer, and was compelled to abscond to avoid arrest. In June 1719, he petitioned the Irish House of Lords, and his petition was referred to the Lords' Committee for the Courts of Justice. The report of this committee supported the sheriff, and censured the Barons of the Exchequer, and the House of Lords adopted it by a majority of thirty-four, Lord Chancellor Midleton dissenting. In consequence of this resolution, the Barons of the Exchequer were taken into custody, and the Irish House of Lords made energetic representations to George I that the right to decide Irish appeals rested with the Irish Parliament. They pointed out that in the reign of Henry III the practice grew of asking the King to advise on the common law, and this was given on the advice of the judges of the King's Bench in England. From this arose the custom of removing causes by writs of error from the King's Bench in Ireland to the King's Bench in England; but they in no way implied that there could be appeals from the Irish to the English House of Lords. So far as the Chancery was concerned, there were only two precedents for appeals to the English House of Lords before the Revolution, one in 1670 and the other in 1679, both when no Irish Parliament was sitting. There were also two after that date. The Lords' representations further pointed out that there existed no machinery for the enforcement of decrees of any English court in Ireland. Whilst this is true, it should be noticed that in *Earl of Ardglasse* v. *Muschamp*[16] Lord Keeper North granted a sequestration in respect of land in Ireland, and this precedent was followed by Lord Macclesfield in *Fryer* v. *Bernard*,[17] although the learned editor of the reports asks to whom the sequestration should be directed, as the defendant had property only in Ireland.

In England, as might have been expected, the House of Lords upheld the proceedings of the Irish Exchequer, and the Parliament of Great Britain passed a statute[18] providing for the subordination of the Irish Parliament to that at Westminster, and removing the appellate jurisdiction of the Irish House of Lords. The effect of this statute remained until, in 1783, a statute of George III[19] restored Irish appeals to the Irish House of Lords. By the Act of Union the appellate jurisdiction returned to the House of Lords at Westminster once more.[20]

16 (1682-4), 1 Vern. 75, 135, 237.
17 (1724), 2 P. Wms. 261.
18 6 Geo. I, c. 5.
19 23 Geo. III, c. 28.
20 39 & 40 Geo. III, c. 67, Art. 8.

One remarkable branch of Irish equity jurisdiction in the early eighteenth century arose out of the penal laws against Roman Catholics. By the principal statute, 9 William III, c.3, of the Irish Parliament, any Protestant woman owning property, whether *real* or *personal*, to the value of £500 or more, who married without a certificate declaring that her husband was a Protestant, was declared along with her husband to be incapable of owning the property, which devolved upon the next Protestant kin of the wife. The statute was put into operation by bills of discovery. By a statute of 1701 of the English Parliament, Papists who failed to take certain oaths were incapable of inheriting or purchasing real property,[21] and another two sections of this statute prohibited Papists from purchasing leaseholds, whether directly or by way of trust.[22] By 8 Anne, c.3, Section 30 (Irish Parliament), any Protestant might prefer a bill of discovery in the Chancery against any person concerned in the sales or incumbrances of any trust property, held in trust for Papists, in order to discover any such trusts. All issues arising on the statute were to be tried by Protestants.

It fell to Lord Chancellor West to construe this savage code. He held (1) that there must be a conviction for Papistry before a forfeiture was incurred; and (2) a Protestant who married a Papist was not only incapable of being a discoverer, but was a constructive Papist. On the other hand, a Protestant trustee for a Papist beneficiary was held to be capable of securing a bill of discovery.[23] All this repressive legislation, and the Chancery practice which arose from it, was abolished by the Roman Catholic Relief Act, 1829.

Early in the second half of the eighteenth century, there were frequent complaints of the length and the expense of Chancery proceedings in Ireland which greatly exceeded anything known at that time in England. One of many reasons for this was the enormous length of pleadings, another was the number of counsel retained by parties to a suit.[24] Howard, whose preface to his *Practice of Chancery* discusses these evils at length, recounts[25] the following—

> A gentleman of eminence at the Bar, had three briefs tied together (one in effect) for a motion in a cause in this Court, which seeming a burden to him led me and some others to enquire about it. They contained one hundred and eighty sheets of quarto paper, so widely

[21] 1 Anne, stat. I, c. 32, Sect. 7.
[22] 1 Anne, stat. I, c.32, Sects. 8 and 9.
[23] O'Flanagan, *op. cit.*, vol. II, pp. 43-44.
[24] Howard, *Practice of the Chancery*, preface, p. xvi.
[25] *Ibid.*, p. xx.

> written that two might well be included in one, and the gentleman who held it said six, or eight at most, might have contained the matter of the whole, and on this motion (I think he said) five Counsel were employed, so that at three shillings and four pence a sheet briefing, and two shillings the copy, the agent's fees for those five briefs came to no less a sum than one hundred and twenty pounds, thirteen shillings and four pence; then what must the five Counsel have had with their briefs ! What fortune could stand it ? If the Masters in taxing costs would excuse the briefs and also the copies thereof, and of pleadings and other proceedings, it might prevent in a great measure these most horrid impositions.

Yet another grievance was the great expense of appeals to the English House of Lords, which only the wealthiest could afford to prosecute. This cause of hardship, it has been mentioned, ceased in 1783.

Before the Chancellorship of Lord Liffard (1767-1789), Irish law reporting was for practical purposes non-existent. A collection of Lord Liffard's judgments, however, was published in 1839, reported by Mr. Wallis, of the Irish bar, and edited by James Line. The sources of our knowledge of the work of earlier Chancellors are fragmentary and scattered, but something can be gleaned from Brown's *Parliamentary Cases*, for the period prior to 1782, when Irish appeals came to Westminster. *Ormsby* v. *Dodwell*[26] was one of the appeals mentioned by the House of Lords, in its controversy with its English counterpart. It arose out of a settlement of 1686 made by the appellant's father of lands in Limerick; and charges for portions in 1689 by two deeds, in favour of his daughters and his two younger sons. Dodwell was the husband of a daughter, Catherine, and with his wife he filed a bill in the Irish Chancery for payment of the portion. On 3rd December 1701, Methuen, L.C., decreed that the defendant should pay the one hundred and fifty pounds with interest from the time of filing the bill, and his decree was affirmed by the House of Lords.

The second appeal in this period was *Seagrave* v. *Eustace*,[27] an appeal from a decision of Sir Richard Cox, L.C., given on 2nd November 1704. Once again the decree was affirmed, on a question relating to succession to personal estate. There were, however, more than two appeals from the Irish Chancery between the Revolution and the controversy which arose in 1709. *Viscount Kingsland* v. *Barnewall*[28] was decided

[26] (1702), 6 Bro. P.C. 41.
[27] (1705), 3 Bro. P.C. 11.
[28] (1706), 4 Bro. P.C. 154.

on 11th December 1705 by Sir Richard Cox, assisted by Doyne, L.C.J., Donnellan, L.C.B., and Dolben and Coote, JJ. Once again their decree, dismissing the plaintiff's claim, was affirmed.

Two others, both decisions of Sir Richard Cox, are *Macarty* v. *Bayly*[29] and *Calthorpe* v. *May*,[30] on both of which the Chancellor's decree was reversed. In *Kelly* v. *Lord Bellew*,[31] Sir Richard Cox's decree was varied, and in *Eustace* v. *Keightley*[32] the decree of Sir Constantine Phipps, L.C., was reversed. In another appeal, *Jones* v. *Bennett*,[33] Phipps, L.C.'s decree in favour of the defendant was affirmed.

It is in fact, from these appeals in Brown's Parliamentary Cases that we can obtain our best impressions of the working of the Irish courts in the eighteenth century, and from them we can draw the conclusion that the work of the Irish Chancery did not differ in nature from the work of the Chancery in England. What is of interest, in view of the complaints of the expense of appeals which appear in many writers, is the number of appeals which are reported from this period, and the parties were by no means always wealthy.

With the continuous appearance of reports of Irish equity cases from Lord Liffard's Chancellorship onwards, citation of them in English courts became frequent, and the two streams of equity completely fused. Further, during the nineteenth century, Irish legal writers made frequent and valuable contributions to the literature of equity through the medium of legal periodicals, and particularly the *Irish Law Times.* Some Irish decisions in the nineteenth century have been landmarks in the history of equity—for example, *Shaw* v. *Lawless*,[34] where the House of Lords affirmed the decree of Lord Plunkett, L.C., and reversed that of his successor, Sir Edward Sugden, and held that precatory words, expressing desire, did not create a binding trust.

It is therefore unnecessary to trace the development of equity in Ireland in the nineteenth century in detail, but one or two general observations may be made. In the first place, the office of Chancellor remained something of a bone of contention between the two countries. There were one or two Irish Chancellors of great ability, e.g., Lord Plunkett. There were one or two other Chancellors who could be similarly described, e.g. Sir Edward Sugden, later Lord St. Leonards, and Lord Redesdale, but these were often destined for office in England,

[29] (1707), 7 Bro. P.C. 218.
[30] (1707), 7 Bro. P.C. 413.
[31] (1707), 4 Bro. P.C. 495.
[32] (1713), 4 Bro. P.C. 588.
[33] (1713), 1 Bro. P.C. 528.
[34] (1838), 5 Cl. & Fin. 129.

and their stay in Ireland was therefore brief. There were other Chancellors—for example Lord Manners, who held office from 1807 until 1827—whose attainments were low and whose appointment was due exclusively to political and family influence. Indeed, the office of Chancellor in Ireland always remained more deeply involved in politics than in England.

A second point of general importance is that, following the Act of Union, the reform of the Irish Chancery kept closely in step with reform in the Court of Chancery in England. There were Irish Common Law Procedure Acts and Chancery Amendment Acts, which corresponded with those which preceded the Judicature Acts in England.[35] Irish County Courts were established shortly after their establishment in England, and they too were given a limited equity jurisdiction. Finally, the English Judicature Acts were followed, in 1877, by two important statutes relating to Ireland. The first, the County Officers and Courts (Ireland) Act, consolidated and modified the organisation and jurisdiction of the Irish Civil Bill Courts, including their equitable jurisdiction. By Section 33, this is defined as extending to:

(*a*) Suits by creditors, legatees, devisees, heirs at law or next of kin, when the value of the estate does not exceed five hundred pounds, if it is personalty, or the annual value of thirty pounds, if it is land.

(*b*) Suits for the execution of trusts where the trust estate does not exceed five hundred pounds, if it is personalty, or the annual value of thirty pounds if it is land.

(*c*) Suits for the foreclosure, sale or redemption of a mortgage or any charge upon land where the charge does not exceed five hundred pounds, and the annual value of the land does not exceed thirty pounds.

(*d*) Suits for specific performance of a contract for the sale or lease of property or for reforming or cancelling such agreement, where the purchase money does not exceed five hundred pounds, or the annual value of the property to be let does not exceed thirty pounds.

(*e*) Proceedings under the Married Woman's Property Act, 1870, where the property does not exceed five hundred pounds in value.

(*f*) Suits for taking a partnership account, again up to a limit of five hundred pounds.

(*g*) Partition actions, up to a five hundred pound limit.

[35] See Keeton, *An Introduction to Equity*, 5th ed., Irish Supplement (Sheridan), p. 3.

(*h*) Proceedings by a landlord against a tenant in respect of waste, where the annual value of the holding does not exceed thirty pounds.

(*i*) Proceedings under the Trustees' Relief Act or other Trustee Acts, again with a limit of five hundred pounds, or if land, thirty pounds annual value.

(*j*) Proceedings relating to the maintenance or advancement or for the protection of an infant, with similar limits.

(*k*) Finally, in proceedings for injunctions, where these are requisite for granting relief in any matter in which jurisdiction is given to the Civil Bill Courts, or for staying proceedings at law to recover any debt proveable under a decree for the administration of an estate made by the court to which the application for the order to stay proceedings is made.

By Section 34, the chairman of the court was given, for the purposes of the Act, all the powers of a judge of the High Court of Chancery, but the Lord Chancellor was given power, if he thought fit, to remove any suit from the Civil Bill Court to the Court of Chancery,[36] and if a suit had been commenced in the Chancery, which might have been commenced in the Civil Bill Court, any party might apply to the judge of the Court of Chancery, for its transfer to the Civil Bill Court.[37] There was also provision for the transfer to the Court of Chancery of suits exceeding the jurisdiction of the Civil Bill Court, which had been commenced in that court.[38] Sections 43 and 45 provided for appeals from decisions in equity of the Civil Bill Courts to the Lord Chancellor or other judge of the Court of Chancery. In the intervals between the sittings of the Civil Bill Courts, the Lord Chancellor was empowered to issue injunctions in respect of proceedings in equity which could properly be brought in them, but the grant of an injunction did not operate to remove the suit from the Civil Bill Court, unless the Lord Chancellor so directed.

The Irish Judicature Act (which is the next Act in the Statute book) follows closely the model of the English Judicature Act of 1873. It unites the existing High Courts into a Supreme Court of Judicature, divided into a High Court (of original jurisdiction) and a Court of Appeal. Section 27 provides that in any cause or matter, law and equity shall be concurrently administered, and Section 28, after dealing with a number of specific matters, such as the administration of assets of insolvent estates, and the assignment of debts and choses in action,

36 Sect. 35.
37 Sect. 36.
38 Sect. 37.

in terms identical with those of the Judicature Act, 1873, Section 25, concludes with a provision that in any conflict or variance between the rules of equity and the rules of common law, the rules of equity are to prevail.

After 1877, the functions of the Court of Chancery in relation to civil bill appeals were assigned to the Chancery Division; and by the Judicature (Ireland) (No. 2) Act, 1897, the number of divisions of the High Court was reduced to two: The Queen's Bench and the Chancery Divisions. This is still the position in Northern Ireland.

In the Irish Free State (now the Republic of Ireland), the system of judicature was changed in 1924. There is now a District Court, a Circuit Court and a High Court (undivided), each with original civil (including equitable) and criminal jurisdiction; and finally, a Supreme Court, whose jurisdiction is, in general, appellate only.[39]

The office of Lord Chancellor of Ireland ceased to exist upon the establishment of the Irish Free State and the creation of Northern Ireland, in 1922,[40] but in both Northern and Southern Ireland the continuity in the development and application of equity has remained unbroken. The functions of the Lord Chancellor of Ireland are now vested in the two Chief Justices.

39 See, now, the Courts (Establishment and Constitution) Act, 1961; Courts (Supplemental Provisions) Act, 1961; Courts Act, 1964.

40 Irish Free State (Consequential Provisions) Act, 1922.

CHAPTER V

PUBLIC AND PRIVATE USES AND TRUSTS

SINCE the law of trusts is the subject of a separate volume, no attempt will be made here to examine it in detail. It will be sufficient to indicate, in general terms, the part which the law of trusts has played in the development of modern equity.

The trust, it has been mentioned, developed out of mediaeval feoffment to uses. The older writers all regarded this as an institution derived from the *fideicommissum* of Roman law, but this theory has long since been abandoned. In the law of Ceylon, both institutions exist side by side, and their differences are sharply contrasted.

Old Germanic law was familiar with the conception of a holding of property on behalf of another. This arose when the Salnan received property for purposes which were to be carried out in the lifetime or, more frequently, on the death of the donor. Many writers, including Mr. Justice Holmes, have seen in the Salnan the prototype of the executor, but he could also have been the forerunner of the feoffee to uses. This institution was well known to Salian Franks and other Teutonic peoples. Apart from this development, however, Pollock and Maitland have shown[1] that, from the time of the Norman Conquest, the idea of a permanent or semi-permanent use is gradually gaining ground. Land might be held in use when the owner was going on a Crusade, the beneficiaries being the crusader's wife and children, or again, land might be given to a religious house and devoted to a particular (charitable) object. Finally, with the advent of the Franciscan friars in the thirteenth century, vowed to poverty, it became common for a benefactor to convey a house or a borough " to the use of " or for the habitation of the Franciscans. These, in the opinion of Pollock and Maitland, were the first persons who employed the use on a large scale. In such transactions, it was intended that the feoffee should be the owner bearing the burden of ownership, but that he should allow the benefits to be enjoyed by another. At first, this was conceived as a religious rather than as a legal obligation, although it may be that land given for the use of the Franciscans might have enjoyed the protection of ecclesiastical courts.

[1] *H.E.L.*, vol. II, p. 231.

Other feoffments might be regarded as gifts upon a condition. In any case, as the use existed outside the purview of the common law, no writ was available to a beneficiary whose feoffee failed to observe the terms of his feoffment, and it was not until the Chancellor recognised and enforced the use that it enjoyed legal protection. There were several reasons for this. One was that the common law was reluctant to admit that anyone who was not seised to an estate of freehold in the land could have an enforceable interest in it, since this would have encouraged the evasion of feudal obligations upon which mediaeval feudal society was based. And there was the difficulty of establishing, by means of a jury, whether a use had been created or not. Nevertheless, in the reigns of Henry II, Richard I, John and Henry III, such questions did come from time to time before common law courts.[2] It was only in the reign of Edward I that considerations of public policy finally included the reform of the common law courts. In 1379, a century later, the judges, upon being asked by Parliament whether a request made by Edward III to the feoffees of his will to perform certain obligations could be recognised by the common law, replied that the common law could not take notice of any limitation upon the estate of feoffees of land, unless it complied with the technical rules relating to common law conditions.

This rigidity of the common law emphasised the need for the Chancellor's intervention, for uses were exceedingly common. The position of the Franciscans has already been noticed; in countries in which the civil law governed the situation, the usufruct or uses of the Franciscans created no theoretical difficulties and, since a Papal Bull of 1279 permitted the Franciscans to hold property on such terms, it can readily be understood that this must have influenced the development of the use in England.

There were, however, numerous other reasons for the protection of the use. Foremost among them was the desire to find a method of making a will of freeholds. On the death of the freeholder, his estate or inheritance passed as an undivided whole to his heir. If, however, in his lifetime he enfeoffed another to the use of himself for the remainder of his life, and afterwards to the uses of his will, a restriction which was felt to be increasingly burdensome was avoided. There were other reasons which were the subject of frequent complaints in Parliament, and which ultimately provoked restrictive legislation. Among them were the evasion of feudal incidents, such as wardship and marriage, the commission of frauds upon creditors and the evasion of the Statutes of Mortmain. So long as the interest of the beneficiary

[2] Holdsworth, *H.E.L.*, vol. IV, pp. 414-5.

was, from the legal point of view, indefinite, it was difficult to prevent abuses, which might also include the repudiation of his obligations by the feoffee. When, at the beginning of the fifteenth century, the Chancellor intervened to recognise and enforce uses, the interest of the beneficiary obtained such recognition and protection in equity and, since his interest now enjoyed legal recognition, it became possible to control and regulate it by legislation. Two points should be noticed, however. The mediaeval use, unlike the modern trust, was almost invariably passive; that is to say, the feoffee was little more than a repository of legal title. The beneficiary entered into possession of the property subject to the use, and dealt with it as if it were his own. The second point is that the doctrines which the Court of Chancery steadily developed in respect of the use were evolved in respect of uses of land. Although there could be uses of chattels, they were of lesser importance, and they had little influence upon the development of the equitable rules applicable to uses. One of the reasons why they occurred more rarely was that there could then be a will of chattels, to be administered by an executor, whose office was recognised and regulated in the ecclesiastical courts in much the same way as the office of feoffee to uses came to be developed in the Court of Chancery.

Uses were not only created by the declarations of the feoffor: they could arise by operation of law or they could be implied from the acts of the parties. If a person gratuitously conveyed land to another, the Court of Chancery held that, unless a use had been expressly declared, there was a resulting use to the feoffor, who could alienate it either by conveyance or by will, as he chose.

A use in favour of a purchaser might be implied from a bargain and sale of land. This was important, for in such cases, the purchaser had no remedy at common law for lack of a deed. In recognising and enforcing this use implied by law, equity was following the analogy of a bargain and sale of goods, which passed the property in the goods. A bargain and sale of land could not pass the title to land, but where the vendor had received the purchase money, he henceforth held to the use of the purchaser, it being unconscientious for a vendor who has obtained the purchase money to hold to his own use.

Between the equitable rule that a feoffment without consideration raised a resulting use to the feoffor, and the rule that in a bargain and sale of land there was implied a use for the purchaser, there lay the problem of consideration sufficient to raise a use. Equity would not enforce a gratuitous agreement under seal to create a use, for " Equity looks at intent and not the form," and therefore did not give special force to deeds, leaving the party who sought to enforce a gratuitous covenant to his remedy at common law. However, during the sixteenth century it was established that a covenant made in consideration of marriage would raise a use, and (later) a covenant made in consideration of natural love and affection of a man for his family. In this respect, equity differed from the common law with its application to contracts, but equity was concerned to a much greater degree with the enforcement of family settlements.

Neither the King nor a corporation could be seised to a use, although both could be beneficiaries. By the sixteenth century, however, a corporation would need a licence in mortmain before it held land as a cestui que use. A use could arise only where the feoffee held an estate in fee simple, because of the technical rules of the feudal land law. Whenever a life estate or a fee tail was created, there was tenure between feoffor and feoffee, and this relationship prevented any presumption that the estate could be held for any other use than the fulfilment of the obligation of tenure.

So long as the use subsisted, the feoffee was compelled in equity to permit the cestui que use to take the profits of the land. He was also compelled to create estates in the land at the latter's direction. Further, the feoffee was obliged to take all proceedings necessary to protect the enjoyment by the cestui que use of his interest and, in return, the feoffee was entitled to be indemnified against all expenses incurred in respect of the use. If the cestui que use died without heirs, the overlord had no claim to his interest and, in this case, the feoffee took the land beneficially. There was not, as with the trust at a later date, a resulting trust for the grantor.

During the fifteenth century, the Chancery very rapidly developed the interest of the cestui que use, from a personal obligation, enforceable against the feoffee, to an interest enforceable against all who claimed through the feoffee, other than a bona fide purchaser for value without notice of the use. Where, however, a person acquired the land not through the feoffee (e.g. a disseisor or the lord who took the estate by escheat), he took free from the use.

Once the wide extent of the interest of the cestui que use had been established, it became possible to create a variety of estates and interests in the use. Here, while in general the Chancellor followed the common law rules, he nevertheless refused to adopt the technicalities which prevailed in the common law. For example, the only future estate known to the common law was the remainder, and many technical rules governed its creation. For example, there could never be a gap in the seisin. If a future interest was to take effect, it must do so on the determination of a prior freehold estate. If a remainder failed, then all estates dependent upon it also failed. Moreover, once a remainder had been created, it must proceed to its natural termination. Equity ignored these technicalities, and at an early date it recognised springing uses (i.e. uses which arose in the future, on the happening of a condition) and shifting uses (i.e. uses which passed from one beneficiary to another on the happening of a specified event). Once these possibilities were realised, landowners could employ the use to achieve a wide variety of purposes, incidental to the creation of a family settlement, free from the restrictions of the common law of the land.

There were other purposes which could be achieved through the intervention of a use which were less meritorious, for example, a feoffment to uses could have the effect of defrauding creditors and there was legislation against such fraudulent feoffments from 1377 onwards. Similarly, successive statutes imposed restrictions upon feoffments to the use of religious foundations and bodies, whether corporate or unincorporate. A problem of steadily increasing importance was that which resulted from the exercise of powers of alienation by a cestui que use, accentuated as it was by the fact that many feoffments to uses were secret. A person might purchase from another, whom he assumed to be the legal owner when in fact he was a cestui que use, and in consequence he was liable to be ejected by the feoffee to uses. It was to protect the interests of such persons that a statute of 1483[3] provided that dispositions by a cestui que use should prevail against the cestui que use himself, his heirs and all persons who had held to the beneficiary's sole use at the time when the disposition occurred. Since this statute did not restrict the powers of alienation of the feoffee to uses, uncertainties were increased by the very fact that the power of alienation of the cestui que use had been extended.

It was, however, the evasion of incidents of tenure, valuable principally to the Crown, which was primarily responsible for the passing of the Statute of Uses in 1535,[4] thereby bringing to an end the first phase in the development of this institution. After an attempt in 1529 to reform the land law, which failed to win the support of the House of Commons, since the proposed changes would have abridged the powers of landowners to make wills and family settlements, Henry VIII was able to induce Parliament to pass the Statute of Uses. Its main provision was that whenever any person or persons were seised in fee simple to the use of another person or persons, or body politic,[5] the beneficiary should henceforth, by the operation of the statute, enjoy a

[3] 1 Ric. III, c. 1.
[4] Ireland: Statute of Uses, 1634.
[5] I.e., a corporation.

legal estate, corresponding to the equitable estate which he would have enjoyed before the passing of the statute. Accordingly if, after the statute, X and Y were seised in fee simple to the use of A for life, then to the use of B in fee tail, and afterwards to the use of C in fee simple, whilst before the statute A, B and C would all have enjoyed equitable estates in the use, after 1535 their estates would be converted into legal estates.

The statute did not abolish all uses, nor was it intended so to do. It did not apply where a person held personal property (including leases, which were technically chattels real) to the use of another. Again it applied only where the feoffor's function was merely that of a repository of title. When active duties were imposed on the feoffee, the statute did not apply.

Even with these limitations, the effect of the statute was extremely far-reaching. So far as passive uses of land were concerned, the estates created, being now legal estates, came within the purview of the common law courts, which were now called upon to consider, alongside their own technical scheme of future interests, the newer and more flexible scheme created by the Chancellors. The result, so far as the land law was concerned, was still greater complexity, for the common law courts elaborated rules governing the question when one set of rules was applicable, and when another. One other major consequence was that the passing of the statute put an end to the practice of making wills to uses. This was very widely resented, and indeed, it was one of the grievances which induced country landowners to give support to Robert, as he and others rebelled in the troubled years which followed the passing of the statute, in which the monasteries were suppressed and the English Church separated from Rome. This grievance was largely removed by the Statute of Wills in 1540,[6] which permitted a landowner to devise by will all his lands held in socage, and two-thirds of the lands which he held in knight service.

To sum up upon the changes in conveyancing which the statute made necessary: (1) the old will to uses was replaced by an instrument which enjoyed full recognition in the common law courts;[7] (2) while feoffments to uses now had the effect of vesting in the beneficiaries legal estates corresponding to the equitable estates they would have enjoyed before 1535, such estates were now recognised and enforced by the common law courts; (3) settlements of freehold estates inter vivos

[6] Ireland: Statute of Wills, 1634.

[7] There was never any suggestion that wills of lands should be within the jurisdiction of the ecclesiastical courts—at which the Reformation had struck such a blow.

could now be of two distinct types: (*a*) settlements made in conformity with the old common law rules, and (*b*) settlements made in a form which took advantage of the provisions of the Statute of Uses and in which therefore the settlor enjoyed greater freedom to fashion the successive interests which he created: for example, springing and shifting uses, previously equitable only, now by virtue of the statutes enjoyed the protection of the common law courts.

For some time after the passing of the Statute of Uses, uses in the old equitable sense could still exist in respect of chattels, and in respect of leases of land (where the lessor was seized of an estate of freehold), and finally, there could be uses in trusts of freehold land, where the feoffor had active duties to perform. One question which was resolved by the decision in *Jane Tyrrel's Case*[8] in 1557, was the effect of limiting a use upon a use—for example, a feoffment to X and Y to the use of A to the use of B. It was plain that the statute operated to pass the legal estate from X and Y to A, but in *Tyrrel's Case* the Court of Wards decided that the second use to B was void, being repugnant to the first use in favour of A. Apart from this technical reason, for a century after the passing of the statute common law judges and Chancellors were at one in believing that if the second use was permitted to take effect in equity again, all the evils which were mentioned in the preamble to the Statute of Uses would arise once more. Even trusts of long terms were disliked because by means of them land could be settled in such a way as to diminish the King's rights in respect of the land held in knight service. Ocassionally, the Chancellor and the common law judges indicated that there might be occasions where the second use might be enforced, e.g. to prevent a fraud, or where the second use was in favour of a charity, but it was not until the military tenures were abolished at the Restoration that the King's rights in respect of land held in knight service disappeared and, with them, the objection to the enforcement of the second use in equity. The modern trust is therefore largely the product of Lord Nottingham's Chancellorship, although there were indications of such a development at an earlier period. Thus, in the edition of Shepherd's *Touchstone*, which appeared in 1651, it is stated that in all cases of uses not affected by the Statute of Uses—

> the law is now as it was before the same statute was made, and all these matters are determinable in Chancery, for as the question of uses and trusts that are within the statute are to be decided and ruled by the judges of the Common Law, so are all other questions of uses and trusts, that are out of the statute to be ruled and decided by the judges of the Chancery.

[8] 2 Dyer 155a.

This being the case, it is not surprising that some of the distinctive features of the later law of trusts have already appeared before 1660. Some distinctions between private and charitable trusts had been recognised, and the courts had consistently declared that they favoured charities. There was some recognition of the distinction between express trusts on the one hand, and implied and constructive trusts on the other. There was some development of the law relating to the duties and liabilities of trustees, as the perusal of Tothill's and Cary's Reports will illustrate. It is, for example, from this period that we have the rule, established in *Townley* v. *Sherborne*,[9] that a trustee is not liable simply for signing for conformity.

As Holdsworth has pointed out,[10] the influence of the trust has been more far-reaching than that of uses executed by the statute. The latter affected only the law of land. The trust has been an important factor in the law of real and personal property, in family law and in parts of public or semi-public law:

(1) The growth of commerce made personal property of many kinds of steadily increasing importance, and the new mercantile classes sought to deal with such property, especially stocks and shares, as landowners dealt with their land. The trust was a flexible instrument whereby this could be done. Even landowners came increasingly to favour the trust as a method of land-holding for the family having a number of advantages over the strict settlement which was created by virtue of the Statute of Uses.

(2) When the Court of Chancery took over from the ecclesiastical courts the administration of the estates of deceased persons, it progressively assimilated the office of personal representative to that of trustee, so giving rise to the modern law governing the administration of estates.

(3) The development of the married woman's separate estate in equity, which has already been mentioned, was made possible through the medium of the trust.

(4) Much of the law relating to the guardianship of infants was developed by the same means.

(5) Finally, the trust was made applicable to property-holding on behalf of many groups of persons, charitable and non-charitable. As Holdsworth points out,[11] the Inns of Court were themselves outstanding examples of unincorporated groups owning substantial property.

9 (1634), Tot. 88.
10 *H.E.L.*, vol. IV, pp. 476-80.
11 *H.E.L.*, vol. IV, p. 478.

There were also unincorporated bodies which participated in local government and, at a later date, trading companies before the use of the modern limited liability company, and finally, trade unions.

All this lay in the future, and it is doubtful whether Lord Nottingham himself was conscious of the almost unlimited possibilities of the institution which he refashioned out of the mediaeval trust of land. It was fully recognised by his successors, however. In *Burgess* v. *Wheate*,[12] Lord Mansfield said—

> In my opinion, trusts were not on a true foundation till Lord *Nottingham* held the great seal. By steadily pursuing, from plain principles, trusts in all their consequences, and by some assistance from the legislature, a noble, rational, and uniform system of law has been since raised. Trusts are made to answer the exigencies of families, and all purposes, without producing one inconvenience, fraud, or private mischief, which the statute of *H.* 8 meant to avoid.

Much of Lord Nottingham's work in the sphere of trusts was devoted to defining the respective interests, rights and duties of trustees and beneficiaries, and in differentiating the trust from the use. One of the restrictive doctrines applicable to uses was that of privity between the feoffee and beneficiary. Thus, if A enfeoffed B to the uses of A's will, and B enfeoffed C without disclosing the use, neither A nor those claiming through him could enforce the use against C, for lack of privity. So far as the legal estate of the feoffee was concerned, privity prevented a use from being enforced against a tenant by the curtesy, a tenant in dower, a tenant by elegit, a disseissor, an abator, a lord taking by escheat, a person taking by title paramount, and finally, a purchaser without notice. On the side of the cestui que use, the heir or an assignee of the beneficiary's interest could enforce the use, but almost no-one else.[13]

Lord Nottingham's immediate predecessors had been inclined to carry over these limitations into the emergent law of trusts, but Lord Nottingham regarded the law relating to uses merely as a starting point, not as a body of rules restricting development. For example, a corporation could not have been enfeoffed to a use, but Lord Nottingham had no difficulty in deciding that they were capable of acting as trustees. He also progressively protected the beneficiary's interest against claims made against the trustee in his personal capacity, and his work in this field reached its logical conclusion in 1725, when in *Bennet* v. *Davis*[14] Jekyll, M.R., decided that the interest of the bene-

[12] (1759), 1 Eden. 177, 223.
[13] Yale, Nottingham's Chancery Cases, 79 Sel. Soc. pp. 88-9.
[14] 2 P.Wms. 316.

ficiary was not adversely affected by the trustee's bankruptcy, so long as the trust property remained. On the other hand, Lord Nottingham devised procedures whereby the creditors of a cestui que use could enforce their claims against his beneficial interest.

One problem upon which the law of trusts was long uncertain was that of the effect of the escheat of the trust estate on the death of the trustee. Shortly after the Restoration, it had been held that the trusts prevailed against the Lord taking by escheat for felony of the trustee, tenant,[15] and in 1702, Trevor, M.R., decided in *Eales* v. *England*[16] that the trust was also enforceable against a lord taking by escheat *propter defectum sangyuini.* In *Burgess* v. *Wheate*,[17] Henley, L.K., and Clarke, M.R., decided against the dissent of Lord Mansfield that the beneficiary's equitable fee simple did not escheat to the lord for want of heirs.

Something must now be said of the place of charities and of charitable gifts and trusts in the work of the Court of Chancery. The law of charities has always been considered to be a distinct branch of equity, containing doctrines not found elsewhere, and in so far as charitable trusts are concerned, they have been classed as public trusts. A public trust is one which exists for the furtherance of some public object and, accordingly, it is apparent that there may be many public trusts which are not charitable, e.g. a trust for the furtherance of the aims of a political party or group. Accordingly, it becomes necessary to explain how a charitable trust differs on the one hand from a private trust, and on the other from a public non-charitable trust.

One of the abiding difficulties of this branch of equity has been the continuing inability of courts and writers to produce a satisfactory definition of a charitable purpose. Historically, the idea of a charitable purpose is a development of the conception of pious uses. The Church encouraged gifts, either inter vivos or by will, for pious uses from the time of Justinian, and when the laws of succession in Western Europe took shape, most of them (including the law of succession applied in the church courts in England) contained provision that on death, a portion of every man's estate (usually one third) should be applied for pious or charitable purposes, and the Ordinary was bound so to apply it. If the deceased, in his will, had expressed the desire to benefit certain specific pious or charitable purposes, the Ordinary would give effect to such desires, so far as was possible, but, if they could not be achieved, the over-riding intention to benefit charity generally must

15 *Geary* v. *Bearcroft* (1666), Carter 57, 67.
16 Prec. Ch. 200.
17 (1759), 1 Eden 177.

still be carried out. In this, there can be detected the beginnings of the doctrine of *cy-près*, a doctrine which is applicable only to charities and which, since the Reformation, has forgotten its ecclesiastical origin, so that the extent of its application has become obscure.

In the period between the Norman Conquest and the creation of the Court of Chancery, gifts for pious and charitable purposes were within the jurisdiction of the ecclesiastical courts and, during this period, they acquired three distinct characteristics which they still retain. These are:

(1) The privilege of indefinite existence, which is sometimes mistakenly described as exemption from the rule against perpetuities.

(2) The privilege of taking effect as a charitable gift, even if it is in general terms only, so long as the gift is devoted solely to charitable purposes. Thus, a gift " for charity," or " for the advancement of education," is good, even though no mode of carrying it into effect is indicated. In such cases, the court will approve a scheme of administration prepared by the trustees.

(3) The privilege of obtaining fresh objects, where the original objects indicated by the donor are either initially incapable of execution, provided that the donor has shown a general intention to benefit charity only, or become so subsequently. This is the *cy-près* doctrine mentioned above.

In contrast to the favour shown to charitable gifts by the eccleciastical courts, the legislature discouraged gifts of land to charitable corporations, because the overlord lost valuable feudal rights, such as wardship, marriage and primer seisin by such a transfer. Beginning with Magna Carta, a succession of statutes prohibited alienations in mortmain without a licence from the Crown. In one form or another, restrictions on alienation in mortmain remained a characteristic of the law of charities until they were finally abolished by the Charities Act, 1960.[18]

Gifts for charitable purposes were at this period frequently made to religious foundations (who themselves were regarded as charitable corporations) or guilds, and the gifts might be made without qualification, or with an express purpose, e.g. for the relief of poverty in the parish or town. Where such purposes were expressed, the ecclesiastical courts sought to ensure that they were carried out. On the other hand, other gifts for charitable purposes made inter vivos were to

[18] Ireland: Charities Act, 1961 (Republic of Ireland); Charities Act (Northern Ireland) 1964.

trustees. A number of such gifts antedate the Reformation. This is not surprising, for the habit of giving to charity for the good of one's soul was strongly entrenched, and in *The Vision of Piers Plowman*, rich merchants are counselled by Truth to obtain remission of sins and a happy death by devoting a substantial part of their fortunes for charitable purposes.

> And therewith repair hospitals,
> help sick people,
> mend bad roads,
> build up bridges that had been broken down,
> help maidens to marry or to make them nuns,
> find food for prisoners and poor people,
> put scholars to school or to some other craft,
> help religious orders, and ameliorate rents or taxes.

The formulation of these charitable objects seemingly anticipates the language of the preamble to the Statute of Charitable Uses in 1601,[19] and the resemblance is too close to be accidental. It shows how little the conception of charity had changed, or had been affected by the religious upheavals of the sixteenth century.

Already before the accession of the Tudors, the Court of Chancery had assumed jurisdiction in respect of charitable trusts and, from this time onwards, the contact of the ecclesiastical courts with charities was only occasional. The machinery of the Chancery was far superior for the purpose of control and, in addition, it was accepted doctrine that the Crown had a special interest in the execution of charitable trusts, which would be manifested by the intervention of the Attorney-General to secure the proper application of the funds. From the Tudor period onwards, it is possible to detect a progressive shift in emphasis from the pious objects of charitable gifts, expressed in *Piers Plowman*, e.g. the achievement of salvation, to the concept of public benefit, which has become the *tabula in naufragio* of the modern law of charities. Nevertheless, until the close of the seventeenth century, where charitable gifts were made by will the conventional expressions of pious objectives were still frequent.

It is an error, demonstrated by Professor Jordan[20] and others, to suppose that the Reformation in any way checked the flow of charitable giving; but there were serious problems of administration. Since the monasteries had been suppressed, and the guilds were in decay, charitable

[19] Ireland: Statute of Charitable Uses, 1634.
[20] *Philanthropy in England* 1480-1660.

trusts became much more common and the problem of their effective supervision has proved extremely difficult to solve, more especially as, until the Brougham Commission reported in the nineteenth century, many charitable trusts were either unknown to the community at large or else were known only to a very small group of persons. The real problem, which has always eluded solution, has been to devise some quick and inexpensive administrative machinery to which the ordinary citizen can appeal, if he feels that a charitable trust is not being properly carried out. What has become clear in the past four centuries is that the procedure of the Court of Chancery is ill-adapted for this purpose.

These considerations will assist in explaining the purpose of the Statute of Charitable Uses, 1601. The object of the statute being to provide an effective method of enforcement, the first point was to define what charities were within its scope. Some charities were excluded: for example, those for the advancement of religion, and the Oxford and Cambridge Colleges, and the great public schools for which the procedure would plainly be inappropriate. The object is exactly explained in the preamble, which provides—

> Whereas lands, tenements, rents, annuities, profits, heriditaments, goods, chattels, money and stocks of money have been given, limited, appointed and assigned as well by the Queen's most excellent majesty, and her most noble progenitors, as by sundry other well-disposed persons. Some for relief of aged, impotent and poor people, some for maintenance of sick and maimed soldiers and mariners, schools of learning, free schools, and scholars in universities. Some for repair of bridges, ports, havens, causeways, churches, sea banks and highways, some for education and preferment of orphans, some for or towards relief, stock or maintenance for houses of correction, some for marriages of poor maids, some for supportation, aid and help of young tradesmen, handicraft men and persons decayed and others for the relief or redemption of prisoners or captives, and for aid in ease of any poor inhabitants concerning payment of fifteens, setting out of soldiers and other taxes, which lands, tenements, rents, annuities, profits, hereditaments, goods, chattels, money and stocks of money, nevertheless have not been employed according to the charitable intent of the givers and founders thereof, by reason of frauds, breaches of trust and negligence in those that should pay, deliver and employ the same: for redress and remedy whereof, be it enacted by authority of this present Parliament,
>
> That it shall and may be lawful to and for the Lord Chancellor or Keeper of the Great Seal of England for the time being, and for the Chancellor of the Duchy of Lancaster for the time being for lands

within the county of Palatine of Lancaster from time to time to award commissions under the Great Seal of England, or the see of the county Palatine, as the case shall require, into all or any part or parts of this realm respectively, according to their several jurisdictions as aforesaid, to the Bishop of every general diocese and his Chancellor, (in case there shall be any Bishop of that diocese, at the time of awarding of the same commissions) and to other persons of good and sound behaviour, authorising them thereby, or any four or more of them to enquire, as well by the oaths of twelve lawful men or more of the county, as by all other good and lawful ways and means, of all and singular such gifts, limitations, assignments and appointments aforesaid, and of the abuses, breaches of trusts, negligences, misemployment, not employing, concealing, defrauding, misconverting or misgovernment of any lands, tenements, rents, annuities, profits, hereditaments, goods, chattels, money or stocks of money, heretofore given, limited, appointed or assigned, or which hereafter shall be given, limited, appointed or assigned, to or for any of the charities and goodly uses before rehearsed;

And after the said Commissioners or any four or more of them (upon calling the parties interested in any such lands, tenements, rents, annuities, profits, hereditaments, goods, chattels, money and stocks of money) shall make enquiry by the oaths of twelve men or more of the said county whereunto the said parties interested shall and may have and take their lawful orders and challenges. And upon such enquiry, hearing and examining thereof, set down such orders, judgments and decrees as the said lands, tenements, rents, annuities, profits, goods, chattels, money and stocks of money may be duly faithfully employed, to and for such of the charitable uses and interests before rehearsed respectively, for which they were given limited, assigned or appointed by the donors and founders thereof; which orders, judgments and decrees not being contrary or repugnant to the orders, statutes or decrees of the donors or founders, shall by the authority of this present Parliament stand firm and good, according to the tenor and purport thereof, and shall be executed accordingly, until the same shall be undone or altered by the Lord Chancellor of England, or Lord Keeper of the Great Seal of England, or the Chancellor of the county Palatine of Lancaster respectively, within their several jurisdictions, upon complaint by any party grieved to be made to them.

Besides the Oxford and Cambridge Colleges, the statute exempts from the jurisdiction of the commissioners the colleges of Westminster, Eton and Winchester, all cathedrals and collegiate churches, every city, town, and all colleges, hospitals and free schools with special visitors, governors or overseers. In such cases, it was assumed that supervision and enquiry were already provided for. The orders of the commissioners were certified to the Court of Chancery, which then executed them. A person aggrieved by a decree of the commissioners should then complain in the Chancery, and the Chancery, after hearing the complaint, could " annul, diminish, alter or enlarge the said orders, judgments and decrees of the said commissioners, or any four of them, as to either of them in their said several jurisdictions shall be thought to stand with equity and good conscience, according to the true intent and meaning of the donors and founders thereof."

It will be noticed that the statute did not, and did not purport to, define what a charity was. It simply enumerated a number of charitable activities to which the procedure by commission was to apply, at the same time excluding a number of others for which a supervisory procedure already existed. Accordingly, though the purposes mentioned were useful guides, they could never be regarded, and they have not been regarded, as defining what a charity is. The test of a charitable purpose is not whether it is within the list set out in the statute, but whether it fulfils a public purpose within the spirit and intendment of the statute of 1601.

Commissioners under the statute were appointed regularly until the outbreak of the Civil War. After the Restoration they functioned only intermittently, and they were virtually obsolete in the eighteenth century.

The failure to make such commissioners a permanent means of enforcing charitable trusts meant that persons aggrieved must apply to the Court of Chancery for redress. This had the consequence that abuses in the administration of charities multiplied even though attempts were ocasionally made by legislation to improve the position. Thus, the Returns of Charitable Donations Act, 1786, and the Charitable Donations Registration Act, 1812, both attempted to provide for the registration of charitable trusts, although without success.

In 1818 Parliament set up the Brougham Commission to investigate and record all charitable trusts in England and Wales. The task proved much bigger and more difficult than the reformers had thought, and the material collected was vast. By 1835, the work of the commission had been completed only in twenty-eight counties, and it was necessary for Parliament to establish a Select Committee to report on the work of the commission and to put forward proposals for the reform of the law. Even then improvement was difficult, mainly because of the stubborn resistance of some of the most powerful organisations to any form of control. Ultimately, the Charitable Trusts Act, 1853, and the Charitable Trusts Amendment Act, 1855, embodied the principal proposals of the Select Committee. They established the Charity Commissioners, in whom powers of supervision were vested, and also the Official Trustee of Charity lands and the Official Trustee of Charitable Funds, in whom charity property could be vested. However, it was not until 1860 that the Commissioners were given jurisdiction, by Section 2 of the Charitable Trusts Act, 1860, to establish or frame schemes for the employment of charitable funds.[21] Thereafter, it was identical with, and additional to the jurisdiction of the Court of Chancery, and the Commissioners, equally with the court, were bound by the rigidity of the law in applying the *cy-près* doctrine,[22] and there could be an appeal from the Commissioners to the Court.

The Commissioners were not responsible to any government department, and although their number usually included a Member of Parliament, he was powerless to secure the passage of legislation to amend the law of charities. Further, because of shortage of staff, the Commissioners were unable to make their supervisory functions in respect of charities sufficiently comprehensive. They could give valuable advice to trustees, when it was sought, but they could only investigate the condition of a charity after a complaint had been made, which meant, in virtually every case, after the damage had been done.

Although criticisms of the law of charities were incessant, it was not until the Charitable Trusts Acts, 1853 and 1855, had been in operation for practically a century, that the Nathan Committee[23] was established to advise what changes in the law and administration of charities might be necessary in the changed social conditions of the second half of the twentieth century. Its principal recommendations are embodied in the Charities Act, 1960,[24] which introduced many important changes. Although the Charity Commissioners have not been absorbed into any government department, they report annually to the Home Secretary, who lays their report before Parliament, and responsibility for the reform of the law of charities will henceforth belong to the Home Secretary. At long last, an effective scheme for the registration of charities has been devised, and charities must send copies of their accounts to the Commissioners. The *cy-près* doctrine has been modified, so that funds of trusts which fulfil no useful purpose may be transferred to other purposes. All trustees have wider powers of

[21] Ireland: the main nineteenth century legislation was the Charitable Donations and Bequests (Ireland) Acts, 1844 and 1867.

[22] *Re Weir Hospital*, [1910] 2 Ch. 124 (C.A.).

[23] Northern Ireland: Newark Committee (the report, 1959, is Cmd. 396).

[24] Ireland: the Acts of 1961 and 1964 referred to p. 153, *ante*, n. 18.

investment since 1961, although if they wish, charity trustees may take advantage of common investment funds established by the Charity Commissioners themselves. Where the Commissioners have reason to think that a charity is not functioning properly they may now institute enquiries and call for documents and, if necessary, they may remove trustees and appoint others. At long last also, the Act of 1960 finally abolished the legislation relating to mortmain; on the other hand, it made no attempt to define what a charitable purpose is.

During the past century there have been far-reaching changes in the law of trusts generally, in response to changing social conditions. Some of the most important of them will be considered under the following heads:—

1. The appointment of agents.
2. The measure of the trustee's responsibility.
3. Tracing.
4. Trustee investments.
5. Trusts and taxation.
6. The variation of trusts.

The Appointment of Agents and the Measure of the Trustee's Responsibility

Although the doctrine of equity was always that a trustee discharged his duties in person, it was also always accepted that a trustee could appoint and pay agents where there was a legal or practical necessity to do so. For example, if the trust was involved in litigation, the trustee could appoint and pay a solicitor, who in turn might employ counsel. The sale or purchase of a house would involve employing a surveyor. Where the trust property included real property which was let, the administration of the trust might involve the appointment of an agent to collect rents or to negotiate new tenancies. In each case, however, the trustee might be called upon to justify his employment of the agent.

In the second half of the nineteenth century, statutes conferred on the trustees powers to appoint agents, and now their power is governed by the Trustee Act, 1925. In considering this power, it should be remembered that the number of professionally qualified agents has increased very greatly during the present century. Architects, surveyors, estate agents, accountants, bankers and brokers, as well as lawyers, may all be called upon at various times by trustees, and the professional competence of each of them will, in general terms, be guaranteed by the agent's possession of the usual professional qualification. On the other hand, the trustee today may not be the man of affairs that his predecessor in the nineteenth or the eighteenth century was assumed to be. He will, therefore, be very much in the hands of his professional advisers, the number of whom has tended to increase. Recognition of these changes underlies the provisions of the Trustee Act, 1925, and particularly of Section 23,[25] which confers a power to appoint agents in wider terms than any previous Act. Today, there is a power to appoint agents (whether professionally qualified or not) to perform any trust *work*, but the trustee himself must still exercise his discretions personally. For example, the trustee himself must appoint a surveyor or valuer and, in so doing, he must assure himself that the agent is professionally qualified, but, once appointed, the agent exercises his professional competence, and the trustee is not expected to supervise his activities. Provided that he has taken care in the original appointment, he is thereafter liable only on the footing of wilful default.[26] Such a reduction in liability is only reasonable, when the number of possible agents and the nature of their professional qualifications are considered.

Trustee Investments

There have also been very considerable alterations in the law relating to trustee investments during the past century. At the beginning of the nineteenth century, virtually the only fields of trustee investment were mortgages of freehold property, with an adequate margin, and certain classes of government stock. With the reform of municipal corporations which followed the Reform Act, 1832, and the development of local government which occurred during the nineteenth century, local government stocks were admitted, subject to conditions which were not onerous, to the trustee list. Later in the century, the development of self-government in the colonies, and later the emergence of Dominions and, in the second half of the present century, of Commonwealth nations, demonstrated the need, again subject to conditions relating to security, for making colonial and Dominion government stocks and also the stocks of colonial and Dominion provinces, towns and cities available to trustees. This was made possible by Colonial Stock Acts. At a somewhat earlier date the stocks of various public utilities, principally of the Metropolitan Water Board and of railways incorporated under special Acts, became trustee investments, although in the case of railways the door was only opened in respect of debenture

[25] No equivalent in the Republic of Ireland. Northern Ireland: Trustee Act, 1958, Sect. 24.

[26] Trustee Act, 1925, Sect. 30; Trustee Act, 1893, Sect. 24 (Republic of Ireland); Trustee Act (Northern Ireland), 1958, Sect. 31. See *Re Vickery*, [1931] 1 Ch. 572.

and preferred stocks and, even then, only so long as a dividend had been paid upon the ordinary stock for a continuous period immediately prior to the investment. All these developments were ultimately collected together in Section 1[27] of the Trustee Act, 1925, but, in spite of public discussion, the door was still firmly closed upon participation by trustees in commercial and industrial enterprises other than public utilities, unless the trust instrument expressly authorised it. Since 1914, however, the experience of trustees in investing in government fixed interest stocks has not always been a happy one. Continuing inflation since 1945 and a steady increase in interest rates has often led to a depreciation of the capital value of trust funds. Accordingly, the demand for a general power to invest in " equities " steadily became more insistent, and in 1961 the Trustee Investments Act[28] was passed, unfortunately too late to save numerous funds, which possessed no special power of investment, from heavy losses. Under the Act of 1961, the trustees may now, after taking expert advice, divide the fund into two equal parts, one part of which must still be invested in the traditional type of fixed interest stock (mainly government) and the other half of which may be invested in the " equities " of commercial and industrial enterprises and in unit trusts, again subject to certain conditions. Here again, the movement towards giving the trustee greater freedom in the administration of the fund is plainly discernible.

Trusts and Taxation and Variation of Trusts

Yet another feature of the modern law of trusts has been its adaptation to the eccentricities of modern taxation. With the present penal incidence of income tax, surtax, capital gains tax and death duties, this has now become a problem of major importance in the settlement of large funds for family and allied purposes. Too quick a succession, for example, could relieve a large trust fund of three-quarters of its capital and, since it is impossible to know in advance how the limitations of a settlement will take effect, efforts were consistently made to secure the maximum flexibility. Not all these efforts were successful, and they were very seriously circumscribed by the decision of the House of Lords in *Chapman* v. *Chapman*.[29] Once again, legislation remedied this unsatisfactory situation and, under the Variation of Trusts Act, 1958,[30] parties to a settlement may now seek the approval

27 Ireland: Trustee Act, 1893, Sect. 1, now as substituted by the Trustee (Authorised Investments) Act, 1958 (Republic of Ireland); Trustee Act (Northern Ireland), 1958, Sect. 1.

28 Adapted to Northern Ireland by the Trustee (Amendment) Act, 1962.

29 [1954] A.C. 429.

30 Northern Ireland: Trustee Act, 1958, Sect. 57, as amended by the Trustee (Amendment) Act, 1962, Sect. 5. No equivalent in the Republic of Ireland.

of the court for variations in the provisions of a settlement. Whilst many of the applications have sought approval for the variation of beneficial interests, mainly with the object of minimising the incidence of taxation, others have asked for other kinds of modification, and in particular, for investment clauses giving powers more extensive than those conferred by legislation.

Tracing

These developments have been the result of statutory intervention, but others have been achieved through judicial decision. One of the most important of these has been the development of tracing in equity. A whole series of decisions, beginning with *Re Hallett's Estate*[31] and culminating in the decision of the House of Lords in *Ministry of Health* v. *Simpson*,[32] have shown this remedy to be capable of application to a variety of situations. Since the equitable principle of tracing is the subject of Chapter XX, it is sufficient at this point to cite two observations from the judgment of the Court of Appeal in the latter case.[33]

> . . . the doctrine of *Hallett's* case [31] . . . now must be regarded not, so to speak, as a genus but as a species in a genus where equity works on the same basic principles but selects what on the particular case is the equitable method of applying them in practice.

Upon the nature of tracing in modern law, the Court of Appeal said—

> The equitable form of relief whether it takes the form of an order to restore an unmixed sum of money (or property acquired by means of such a sum) or a declaration of charge upon a mixed fund (or upon property acquired by means of such a fund) is, of course, personal in the sense that its efficacy is founded upon the jurisdiction of equity to enforce its rules by acting upon the individual. But it is not personal in the sense that the person against whom an order of this nature is sought can be made personally liable to repay the amount claimed to have belonged to the claimant. The equitable remedies pre-suppose the continued existence of the money either as a separate fund or as part of a mixed fund or as latent in property acquired by means of such a fund. If, on the facts of any individual case, such continued existence is not established, equity is as helpless as the common law itself. If the fund, mixed or unmixed, is spent upon a dinner, equity, which dealt only in specific relief and not in damages, could do nothing. If the case was one which at common

31 (1880), 13 Ch.D. 696.
32 [1951] A.C. 251.
33 *Re Diplock*, [1948] Ch. 465, 518, 521.

> law involved breach of contract, the common law could, of course, award damages but specific relief would be out of the question. It is, therefore, a necessary matter for consideration in each case where it is sought to trace money in equity, whether it has such a continued existence, actual or notional, as will enable equity to grant specific relief.

It will be noticed how strongly traditional equitable concepts are emphasized in this formulation. It must be possible to grant specific relief, and further, the concept of equity still acting in personam underlies the development of the modern remedy of tracing, whether as a powerful remedy of a beneficiary against a trustee, or in the wider variety of situations to which the remedy of tracing is now applicable—for example, as in *Ministry of Health* v. *Simpson*,[34] to a legatee against a person to whom the legacy had been wrongly distributed.

[34] [1951] A.C. 251.

Chapter VI

MORTGAGES

Introduction

Nowadays the commonest use of the mortgage is as a device for the hire-purchase of houses to live in. The purchaser pays a deposit to the vendor, the balance of the price is paid to the vendor by a financier by way of loan to the purchaser, the purchaser gets the use of the house and, in England, a legal estate in it (in which respect the transaction differs from hire-purchase of chattels, where the legal ownership is with the finance company or vendor until the final payment is made), and the financier's loan is secured on the property. In house-purchase transactions the loan of the money is most frequently made by a building society, but may be by anybody. Both banks and big employers engage in such lending to their customers and employees respectively. Trustees also lend money on mortgage, this being a trustee investment authorised, subject to safeguards as to amount and so on, by statute.[1]

Other types of premises are also acquired by this process, such as land upon which to conduct a business. Where there is a system of tying retail outlets to producers, importers or distributors, the small retailer often finances the purchase of his business premises by borrowing from the concern to which he is tied. For example, most garages are tied to oil companies (i.e. they are under contract to supply only one company's petrol and lubricating oil) and most public houses are tied to brewers, and the establishment of such garages and public houses is often financed by borrowing on mortgage from the oil company or brewery company concerned.

It is not only upon the acquisition of property that a mortgage is entered into. This device is also used as a means of raising cash without parting with an asset altogether. For example, a person owning in fee simple land worth £10,000, and wishing to raise £3,000 in cash, may find it more convenient to borrow £3,000 from his bank, securing the overdraft on his land, than to sell the land. Nor is it only

1 See Keeton, *The Law of Trusts*, 9th ed., pp. 253-6, and Irish Supplement (Sheridan), pp. 35-7.

land that can be used as security. Chattels personal, unless very valuable like ships, are not normally mortgaged because of the relative formality of the bill of sale, while it is easy to raise money on them by going to a pawnbroker and easy to acquire them on the never-never by hire-purchase. But incorporeal property, such as legal choses in action, equitable interests under trusts and shares in companies are often offered as mortgage security. Indeed, the process of " gearing " by which investment trusts increase their income without sacrificing capital growth in times of cheap money, is that of mortgaging their shareholdings at a lower rate of interest than the yield on their shares and using the money borrowed for the purpose of buying fixed interest securities, such as government stocks or preference shares, which carry a higher rate of interest than the yield on the shares. A trading company may raise new working capital by borrowing on the security of its premises, equipment, goodwill and stock-in-trade (though, so as to allow stock to be dealt with, the latter will normally be used to secure a floating charge, not a mortgage). House purchase is sometimes funded by borrowing on the security of a life insurance policy. Nevertheless, since equity has been more concerned with the mortgage in relation to land than in connection with other types of property, mortgages of land form the principal subject-matter of this chapter.[2]

The meaning of " security " is that (floating charges apart) some specific asset of the debtor is appropriated to repayment of the creditor. If the debtor does not produce cash when he should, then, in addition to suing the debtor for damages for breach of contract, the creditor may proceed to pay himself out of the property on which his debt is secured by one or more of several processes, depending on the nature of the mortgage and of the property, such as selling it, letting it and taking the rent or entering into possession of it and working it at a profit. This is particularly valuable when the debtor is insolvent. In bankruptcy, an unsecured creditor will get only a dividend proportionate to what he is owed, paid out of the proceeds of sale of property not given by the debtor as security. The secured creditor, on the other hand, may satisfy himself in full or as far as possible by realising his security; if he is only partially repaid by this process he may then prove as an unsecured creditor for the balance, on which he will get a dividend.[3] The appropriation of property as security for a debt is carried out by giving some right in it to the creditor so as to make it impossible or improper or difficult for the debtor to deal with it otherwise than subject to the interest of the creditor. The most obvious

[2] As to dealings with choses in action by way of security, see ch. VIII.
[3] See *Re William Hall (Contractors) Ltd.*, [1967] 1 W.L.R. 948.

ways of doing this are to transfer ownership to the creditor (subject to a right to get it back on paying him off), to give the creditor a lesser estate (e.g. a fee simple owner giving his creditor a term of years), to give physical possession to the creditor (the pledge of chattels), to give the creditor documents whose production is essential for transfers (e.g. title deeds to unregistered land) and to give a charge whose efficacy against third parties will depend upon notice or registration. The history of the modern mortgage of freehold land in English law is one of progress from transfer of title to the mortgagee upon condition, the mortgagor having a contractual right to redeem, through transfer of title to the mortgagee at law with the mortgagor regarded as owner in substance, finally to the mortgagor retaining title at law and giving the mortgagee a derivative estate or charge. The second stage was achieved by equity evolving an estate which came to be called the equity of redemption, coupled with an equitable right to redeem after the contractual date for redemption had passed. This is the stage at which Irish law has stopped in relation to unregistered land. In England, the Law of Property Act, 1925, has brought about the third stage: the equity of redemption is rendered obsolete where the whole legal title remains with the mortgagor (though it continues to exist in respect of mortgages by demise).

Although mortgages are normally made to secure repayment of money lent, this is not necessarily the case; a mortgage may be made to secure the payment of any sum due to the mortgagee, however it becomes due, and probably, too, to secure the performance of obligations other than the payment of money.

THE COMMON LAW MORTGAGE AND EQUITABLE INTERVENTION

Origin of the Equity of Redemption

Between the Norman conquest and the time of Littleton a number of forms of mortgage of freehold land were used. The earliest is probably the transfer of the fee to the mortgagee subject to a condition precedent —that the mortgagor should not have paid him off by a specified date. Later, the feoffment came to be made subject to a condition subsequent, i.e., the mortgagee was seised immediately but the mortgagor would have a right of entry (resuming his freehold and determining the estate of the mortgagee) if he repaid on the due date but losing his land for ever if he did not pay on time. At one stage, freeholders commonly mortgaged by granting the mortgagee a term of years, but this fell into comparative disuse until revived in England by the Law of Property Act, 1925. Later still than the invention of the demise, a more popular version was a transfer of the fee to the mortgagee with a covenant by him to reconvey to the mortgagor if the latter repaid him at the stipulated time. This form may have developed under the influence of the growing jurisdiction of the Court of Chancery to order specific performance.[4] According to Turner[5]—

> It appears that the Court of Chancery first took cognizance of mortgages in the reigns of Henry VI and Edward IV. Where property was delivered or conveyed as a security, and the debt was duly paid at the day, or if no day was fixed, when it had been satisfied out of the rents and profits, the Chancellor compelled a redelivery or reconveyance of the property in accordance with the proviso for reconveyance, express or implied, a more potent remedy than that of the ancient common law with its action for damages.[6]

There is no reason to believe that common lawyers were under any delusions about the nature of mortgages. In 1313 or 1314, in the Eyre of Kent, Spigurnel J. said[7]—

> When a man pledges tenements his intention is not to grant an estate of inheritance, but to give security for the repayment of the money he has borrowed and to redeem the tenements; and in such case, if he repay the money, he can enter.

The reason for the common law regarding the land as the mortgagee's if the mortgagor did not repay on the stipulated date was that that was the contract between the parties. The Court of Chancery did not take a different view of the nature of the transaction: it simply used its superior equipment of remedies the better to effectuate treatment of the mortgage as security. Prior to the reign of Elizabeth I, equitable intervention was by way of a decree for reconveyance by the mortgagee to the mortgagor when the latter repaid on the due date (while at com-

4 See Hazeltine, General Preface to Turner, *The Equity of Redemption.* See also Chaplin, " The Story of Mortgage Law " (1890), 4 *Harvard Law Review*, 1 ; Hazeltine, " The Gage of Land in Medieval England " (1904), 17 *H.L.R.* 549 and 18 *H.L.R.* 26; Barton, " The Common Law Mortgage " (1967), 83 *Law Quarterly Review*, 229. " Gage " is provision of property as security. The derivation of "mortgage" is not agreed. According to *Glanvill*, x, 6, the gage is called dead when the rents and profits of the thing gaged do not count towards repayment of the loan. Littleton said: " And it seemeth that the cause why it is called mortgage is, for that it is doubtful whether the feoffor will pay at the day limited such sum or not: and if he doth not pay, then the land which is put in pledge upon condition for the payment of the money, is taken from him for ever, and so dead to him upon condition, etc. And if he doth pay the money, then the pledge is dead as to the tenant, etc." Coke accepts both Glanvill's and Littleton's explanations. (Co. Litt., 18th ed., vol. 2, p. 205a.)

5 *The Equity of Redemption*, p. 21.

6 See also Baildon, *Select Cases in the Court of Chancery* 1364-1471.

7 Y.B. 6 & 7 Edw. II (29 Sel. Soc. 85). See also Hazeltine, " The Early History of English Equity " (1913), *Essays in Legal History* (ed. Vinogradoff), pp. 265-7, as to rudimentary common law equity of redemption and foreclosure.

mon law the mortgagor might have had to be content with damages for breach of covenant) and by way of a similar decree where the repayment was late due to special circumstances, such as fraud by the mortgagee. Under Elizabeth I there appear the first signs of the Court of Chancery allowing redemption on late repayment even without special circumstances—a variety of relief from forfeiture[8]—but this is not the settled practice of the court until the following century.

When the modern mortgage was fashioned by the building of an equitable superstructure on to the common law hull, the Court of Chancery did not distinguish between one legal mechanism and another. The form of the transaction where the mortgagor was the fee simple owner might be a conveyance in fee with a covenant for reconveyance, a lease, a lease coupled with a provision for the fee to pass on non-payment, a conveyance to uses, a trust, or any variant of these. If the proprietary interest transferred was meant by way of security, there was a mortgage. In allowing or not allowing redemption the intent was regarded, not the form.[9]

Paucity of reports makes it impossible to say with precision exactly when the equitable right to redeem, after the legal date for redemption had passed, became a matter of course. The earliest known case appearing to show this as the position was decided in 1625, but either Lord Ellesmere or Lord Chancellor Bacon might have been responsible for earlier such decisions. It is beyond dispute that by the middle of the seventeenth century the equity of redemption as we now know it had acquired a settled status. The equity of redemption may be described as an equitable estate, equivalent in quantity to the legal estate transferred to the mortgagee, regarded as arising in the mortgagor when the mortgage is made and enduring and carrying with it a right to redeem after the stipulated date for redemption, at least for a time.

8 The cases are mentioned by Turner, *The Equity of Redemption*, p. 26. There are some early cases in which the report makes no mention of special circumstances, though these may have been present. See the decision of Bourchier, L.C., in *Bodenham* v. *Halle* (1456), 10 Sel. Soc. 137, where the facts and decision were similar to those in *Cityland and Property* (*Holdings*) *Ltd.* v. *Dabrah*, [1968] Ch. 166, pp. 206-7 *post*.

9 See, e.g. *Bowen* v. *Edwards* (1661/2), 1 Ch. Rep. 221; *Wolstan* v. *Aston* (1670), Hardres 511; *Bamfield* v. *Vaughan* (1675), 73 Sel. Soc. 183; *Danby* v. *Read* (1675), Rep. temp. Finch 226; *Chilcott* v. *Tucker* (1675/6), 73 Sel. Soc. 263; *Davies* v. *Vaughan* (1676), 73 Sel. Soc. 391; *Stokes* v. *Verrier* (1677), 3 Swanst. 634; *Clench* v. *Witherley* (1678), Rep. temp. Finch 376; *Darkin* v. *Cecil* (1679/80), 79 Sel. Soc. 804; *Cotterell* v. *Purchase* (1734), Cas. temp. Talb. 61; *Croft* v. *Powel* (1738), 2 Comyns 603; *Francklyn* v. *Fern* (1740), Barn. C. 30; *Spurgeon* v. *Collier* (1758), 1 Eden 55; *England* v. *Codrington* (1758), 1 Eden 169; *Cripps* v. *Jee* (1793) 4 Bro. C.C. 472; *Sevier* v. *Greenway* (1815), 19 Ves. 413.

In *Emanuel College* v. *Evans*[10] the fee simple owner of land, in 1582 or 1583, mortgaged it by demising it for 500 years. Later the mortgagor created a trust of his interest in the land for Emmanuel College. Later still, he paid the mortgagee off, after the legal date for redemption. Upon this it was said[11]—

> . . . this Court conceived the said Lease being but a Security, and that Money paid, the said Lease had been void, as well against the said College, as against any other; and though the Money not paid at the Day, but afterwards, the said Lease ought to be void in Equity, as well as on a legal Payment, it had been void in Law against them.

Doubt has been expressed, since the report was published sixty years later, as to whether the reporter interpolated later ideas. There seems, however, to be nothing surprising about such an attitude in 1625 and all the reports in volume 1 of *Chancery Reports* seem to have been taken from the Registers' Book. Other cases not much later follow along the same track. In *Porter* v. *Emery*[12] Coventry, L.K., held that the legatee of the estate from the mortgagor could redeem after the contractual date for redemption had passed. The position reached by then was succintly stated by Lord Hardwicke, L.C., a century later, in *Casborne* v. *Scarfe*,[13] where a husband was held entitled to curtesy out of his wife's equity of redemption—

> . . . An equity of redemption has always been considered as an estate in the land, for it may be devised, granted, or entailed with remainders, and such entail and remainders may be barred by a fine and recovery, and therefore cannot be considered as a mere right only, but such an estate whereof there may be a seisin; the person therefore intitled to the equity of redemption is considered as the owner of the land, and a mortgage in fee is considered as personal assets.

Once a mortgagor is allowed to redeem after the contractual date for redemption has passed, he may be allowed to redeem indefinitely or some other time limit has to be devised. During the seventeenth century and later, the Court of Chancery frequently refused redemption to a mortgagor who had let the repayment date pass thirty years or

[10] (1625), 1 Ch. Rep. 18. See also *Hales* v. *Hales* (1636), 1 Ch. Rep. 105; *Rowel* v. *Walley* (1662), 1 Ch. Rep. 218; *Newton* v. *Langham* (1675/6), 2 Ch. Rep. 108; *Pool* v. *Pool* (1676/7), 79 Sel. Soc. 522, 524; *Exton* v. *Greaves* (1682), 1 Vern. 138.

[11] 1 Ch. Rep. 20.

[12] (1637), 1 Ch. Rep. 97. See also *Rand* v. *Cartwright* (1664), Nels. 101, where Lord Clarendon, L.C., held a voluntary conveyance fraudulent as against a subsequent mortgagee, yet valid so as to pass the equity of redemption.

[13] (1738) 1 Atk. 603, 605. Ireland: *Blake* v. *Foster* (1813), 2 Ba. & B. 387, 402, *per* Lord Manners, L.C.

more, by analogy with the Statute of Limitations. Alternatively the mortgagee could go over to the attack by what are now known as foreclosure proceedings. The earliest reported case of this kind is *How* v. *Vigures*,[14] where a mortgage for £340 was made in 1620 and the date stipulated for redemption had passed. The successor in title of the mortgagee got a decree against the successor in title of the mortgagor to pay the plaintiff " £340 with Damages, or in Default, the Premisses mortgaged are decreed to the Plaintiff, to be sold for Satisfaction of his Debt . . ."[15] In *Roscarrick* v. *Barton*,[16] where the owner of an equity of redemption in fee simple settled it on himself for life, with remainder to his wife for life, remainder to his sons successively in tail, remainder to the plaintiff in tail, there was a foreclosure order against the mortgagor. Bridgman, L.K., Wyndham, J., and Hale, C.J., held (Wyld, J., dissenting) that the plaintiff, a volunteer, could not redeem after the mortgagor's death. Had the plaintiff given value for his remainder in tail, the foreclosure proceedings would not have precluded him from redeeming unless he had been a party to them. In *Sherman* v. *Cox*,[17] a similar case, Finch, L.K., showed that the Chancery, while concerned to protect hard-pressed mortgagors against usurious mortgagees, was also concerned that the lengthening of the power of redemption should not lead to an increase of bad debts. He said[18]—

> He would consider of a Way to make Men take Care to redeem Mortgages, either by making it a Rule, 1. That Interest upon Interest should be allowed, etc., Or, 2. By taking away the Rule, that Mortgagees should answer for what they should or might receive without their wilful Default . . .

While the equity of redemption, and hence the equitable right to redeem late, persisted against the mortgagee, and generally against his successors in title, until barred by lapse of time or foreclosure, it was generally lost as against a bona fide purchaser of a legal estate in the land without notice of its existence. This was decided by Finch, L.K., in *Harding* v. *Hardrett*.[19] It would be difficult, though, to take the legal estate without notice that there was an equity of redemption; persons who claimed to do so were not always believed; and the court was anxious to avoid mortgagees paying themselves by being astute to find a bona fide purchaser to sell to. In *Harper* v. *Kawse*[20] the pur-

14 (1628), 1 Ch. Rep. 32.
15 1 Ch. Rep. 33.
16 (1672), 1 Ch. Cas. 217.
17 (1674), 3 Ch. Rep. 83.
18 3 Ch. Rep. 85.
19 (1673) Rep. temp. Finch 9.
20 (1678/9), 79 Sel. Soc. 718. Cf. the rule as to tacking, p. 174, *post*.

chaser bought the legal estate from a mortgagee who had been paid off. It was held by Lord Nottingham, L.C., that the purchaser acquired no right and that the mortgagor was entitled to a reconveyance. The mortgagee was a constructive trustee for the mortgagor and as the trust arose by operation of law ignorance of it was no excuse. Moreover, the purchaser should have made inquiries and would then have found out the state of the accounts between the mortgagor and the mortgagee. Nowadays, a purchaser for value would not be bound by a constructive trust of which he had no notice, but he would be regarded as having notice of anything he would have discovered in the course of inquiries he should have made.

In general, the right of redemption was held to exist only where there was a mortgage, i.e. a transaction which, whatever its form, was intended as provision of security for a debt. In line with this principle is the decision of Lord Guilford, L.K., in *Barrell* v. *Sabine*,[21] that in the case of an absolute sale, with an option reserved to the vendor to re-purchase, the time limit for the exercise of the option must be strictly observed. Four years later, however, in *Manlove* v. *Bale*,[22] Trevor, M.R., came to the contrary conclusion.

Successive Mortgages and Priorities

At common law, a mortgagor could not make a second mortgage during the subsistence of the first unless he had granted the mortgagee a less estate than his own. One of the effects of the invention of the equity of redemption, with all the attributes in equity of an estate equivalent to that of the legal estate granted to the mortgagee, was that even a mortgagor who had conveyed his whole legal estate to the mortgagee could create further mortgages. He could mortgage the equity of redemption. Such further mortgages, being incumbrances on an equitable estate, must be equitable mortgages. Their existence gave rise to problems of priorities when the security was inadequate to pay all lenders in full and the mortgagor was insolvent.

The general principle of the prevalence of the legal estate would give the legal mortgagee priority not only over subsequent equitable mortgagees but even over equitable incumbrancers of whom he had no notice. *Burgh* v. *Francis*[23] shows that even the protection of the legal estate was regarded as having limits. After an equitable mortgage, unsecured loans were made to the mortgagor by persons other than the mortgagee. Then the mortgagor confessed judgments on the land to the unsecured creditors. Holding that the equitable mortgagee had priority

[21] (1684), 1 Vern. 268.
[22] (1688), 2 Vern. 84.
[23] (1673), Rep. temp. Finch 28.

over them, Finch, L.K., said[24] that the equitable mortgage had been meant to be a legal mortgage. It was defective at law, but equity regarded it as effective.[25] Also, there was a covenant for further assurance. So the heir of the mortgagor " is in the Nature of a Trustee for the Mortgagee till the Money is paid, and cannot incumber it and tho' the Creditors had not any Notice of this Mortgage, yet they shall be bound in this Case, because they are not put in a worse Condition than they ought to be, *viz.* to be postponed to the Mortgage . . ." In other words, they had already lent their money without security and at the time of the loan they were a lower order of creditor than the equitable mortgagee.

Equitable incumbrancers among themselves, unless the equities are unequal by virtue of some conduct such as fraud or negligence on the part of one of them, generally take priority in the order of the dates of creation of their incumbrances. This was laid down by Lord Nottingham by analogy (as he generally proceeded) to the attitude at law to successive legal incumbrances. In *Mirfield* v. *Morley*[26] the Lord Chancellor said that had the second assignee obtained a legal title without notice of the first assignment, " this Court would therefore have let him enjoy it and not take the benefit of law from him, but where the question is only between two purchasers of equity, there 'tis all one as between two purchasers of law. Ignorance mends no man's title, but *qui prior est tempore potior est jure.*"

Tacking

One way in which an equitable mortgagee could obtain priority over an earlier equitable mortgage was by getting in the legal estate, provided he had no notice of the prior equitable mortgage when taking his own.[27] He could then hold the legal estate until he was paid anything due on it, and anything due on his equitable security, before the prior equitable mortgagee was payable at all. This plank in the shipwreck, which came to be known as the doctrine of tacking, antedates Lord Nottingham, who in fact found it slightly distasteful. The earliest reported

[24] Rep. temp. Finch 29.

[25] See also *Patteson* v. *Thompson* (1676), Rep. temp. Finch 272; *Anon.* (1729), Mos. 248.

[26] 79 Sel. Soc. 474, 475. See also *Symmes* v. *Symonds* (1703), 4 Bro. P.C. 328; *Earl of Bristol* v. *Hungerford* (1705), 2 Vern. 524; *Brace* v. *Duchess of Marlborough* (1728), 2 P. Wms. 491; *Clarke* v. *Abbot* (1741), Barn. C. 457; *Earl of Pomfret* v. *Lord Windsor* (1752), 2 Ves. Sen. 472; *Willoughby* v. *Willoughby* (1756), 1 T.R. 763; *Frere* v. *Moore* (1820), 8 Price 475.

[27] See *Cason* v. *Round* (1703), Prec. Ch. 226; *Willoughby* v. *Willoughby* (1756), 1 T.R. 763.

case in the Court of Chancery[28] is *March* v. *Lee.*[29] So far as they related to the Wigsel estate (not the only property in issue), the circumstances of this case were that E, the fee simple owner, granted it to D on 4th March 1664 to secure £3,000 borrowed and repayable on 5th June the same year. E covenanted that the Wigsel estate was free from incumbrances. Later, E entered into a recognisance in Chancery with D in respect of a further £2,000. D died on 7th December 1665, having appointed the plaintiffs, EM, C and HM, his executors. Both the mortgage and the recognisance were then unredeemed and overdue. The plaintiffs sued E at common law for ejectment and in Chancery for foreclosure and obtained their judgment at common law. E then got an order of the Court of Chancery staying execution of the common law judgment pending the Chancery hearing. This hearing ended in a decree against E for repayment of £8,530 within a year, failing which he was to be foreclosed. The defendants then appeared for the first time, claiming to hold a mortgage of the Wigsel estate in fee simple, made on 21st June 1665 and repayable on 27th June 1666, and brought proceedings against E and the plaintiffs. The latter then unsuccessfully moved for the removal of the stay of the ejectment, alleging that B had incumbrances prior to them (there being therefore a breach of E's covenant). The defendants thereupon bought out B, getting from him mortgages for £1000 made by E in 1649 and 1656 and a statute[30] made by E in 1656 for £800, and claimed to be paid everything owed to them by E in priority to the plaintiffs. The plaintiffs thought that the defendants should either pay them and take over their security, or accept from them what was due to B, and let them (the plaintiffs) proceed before being paid on the mortgage of 1665, but the defendants refused. When the case came into court, the defendants argued that they took the mortgage of 1665 from E believing him to be beneficially entitled in fee simple and without notice of the plaintiffs' interests. They later heard of the plaintiffs and of B and bought out B on counsel's advice. The plaintiffs objected on the grounds that the defendants were seeking to protect a mortgage, not an absolute estate, and that they had bought from B after the plaintiffs had obtained their judgment for ejectment. It was, however, unanimously decided by Bridgman, L.K., Hale, C.B., and Rainsford, J., that the defendants could tack. That is

28 In *Hedworth* v. *Primate* (1663), Hard. 318, Hale C.B. and the other Barons of the Court of Exchequer had allowed a mortgagee to tack so as to postpone an entail for value of the equity of redemption.

29 (1670), 1 Ch. Cas. 162. See also *Bovey* v. *Skipwith* (1671), 1 Ch. Cas. 201; *Smith* v. *Harvey* (1675), 73 Sel. Soc. 227; *Edmunds* v. *Povey* (1683), 1 Vern. 187, where Somers, L.K., regarded this kind of tacking as the settled course of Chancery; *Holt* v. *Mill* (1692), 2 Vern. 279; *Matthews* v. *Cartwright* (1742), 2 Atk. 347; *Belchier* v. *Renforth* (1764), 5 Bro. P.C. 292, where it was approved by the House of Lords.

30 A money obligation entered into under a statutory procedure.

to say, the defendants, having taken their equitable security in 1665 without notice of the plaintiffs' equitable security of 1664 and having bought B's legal estate, were entitled to be paid all due on the securities they took over from B and all due on the loan of 1665 before anything was paid to the plaintiffs. As it is sometimes put, the intervening incumbrancer was squeezed out.

Another intricate case, not much later, was *Proud* v. *Buzzard*.[31] AC in 1669 granted a lease for 21 years to B, who, in the same year, sublet to F for 19 years. F assigned the underlease to P as security for a mortgage in 1673. Later the same year, F fraudulently got back the underlease from P and purported to assign it to Lee (to whom he handed it over) and to C and M (using forgeries of the underlease). In 1675 the head lease was surrendered by B to AC and AC granted a new lease. B assigned this new lease to Lockwood (C's administrator), who had paid off Lee. The only legal mortgagee of the underlease while the old lease was on foot was, of course, P. Lockwood, however, now had the legal estate in the new lease. Lord Nottingham held that when B got the new lease in 1675 he held it on trust for F for the unexpired portion of the term of 19 years. However, Lockwood took free from all equitable incumbrances as he had the legal estate and C, in 1673, had no notice of prior incumbrances. P's remedy was to sue B for breach of trust.

It was held by Jeffreys, L.C., that an equitable mortgagee could tack even if he acquired the legal estate from a mortgagee who had been fully repaid.[32] This seems difficult to justify, even in 1688, as the legal mortgagee when paid off holds the legal estate on trust for the person redeeming.[33] On the other hand, Lord Nottingham, L.C., held that there could be no tacking where the legal mortgagee acquired a subsequent equitable incumbrance, nor where the equitable incumbrancer who subsequently bought in the legal estate had acquired his equitable incumbrance improperly.[34] He recorded: "I said the case gave the Court a fair opportunity to set some bounds and distinctions to that rule of buying in precedent incumbrances, which was now grown a common practice and very mischievous." In the following century it was determined by Lord Hardwicke, L.C., that a person who acquired his equitable mortgage as trustee could not tack if he later got in the legal estate,[35] and by Wright, L.K., that he could not tack if he acquired

[31] (1678/9), 79 Sel. Soc. 721.

[32] *Turner* v. *Richmond* (1688), 2 Vern. 81.

[33] See *Harper* v. *Kawse* (1678/9), 79 Sel. Soc. 718, pp. 170-1, *ante*. See also *Earl of Bristol* v. *Hungerford*, p. 175, n. 36, *post*.

[34] *Strode* v. *Blanchard* (1676/7), 79 Sel. Soc. 496.

[35] *Morret* v. *Paske* (1740), 2 Atk. 52.

the legal estate after a decree for redemption had been made in respect of it.[36] An equitable mortgagee who got the legal estate from a legal mortgagee against whom proceedings for redemption were pending was held able to tack,[37] but not one who took his equitable mortgage pendente lite, for he then took with notice.[38]

Another variety of tacking is that relating to further advances unsecured by a fresh mortgage. The first (legal) mortgagee lends more money against his original mortgage and claims priority, for the whole amount owed to him, over an equitable mortgagee whose security was created between the granting of the legal mortgage and the making of the additional loan by the first mortgagee. Bridgman, L.K., decided[39] that the further advances could be tacked where they were made without notice of the intervening incumbrance, to which Lord Nottingham, L.C., added [40] that this was so only if the deed of first mortgage provided for the securing of further advances.

Consolidation

Even as between mortgagor and mortgagee, protection was not, in the early days of the modern mortgage, all for the mortgagor. As was shown by Lord Nottingham's concern for making mortgagors pay despite an indefinite right to redeem, the position of the mortgagee was of concern to Chancellors. One positive doctrine to ensure that the mortgagee received equitable treatment came to be known as the doctrine of consolidation (in early cases it was referred to as a variety of tacking). The situation this doctrine was designed to cater for was one in which a mortgagor gave two securities for two debts to the same mortgagee, one of the properties subsequently increasing and the other decreasing in value, and the mortgagor eventually seeking to redeem the more valuable property by paying off one debt, leaving the other debt outstanding against inadequate security. In its developed form, the rule of consolidation is that if the mortgagor seeks to redeem one property the mortgagee can insist on his redeeming both or neither.

36 *Earl of Bristol* v. *Hungerford* (1705), 2 Vern. 524.

37 Jeffreys, L.C., in *Hawkins* v. *Taylor* (1687), 2 Vern. 29; Varny, M.R., in *Brace* v. *Duchess of Marlborough* (1728), 2 P. Wms. 491, the Master of the Rolls saying: "... and this the Lord Chief Justice *Hale* called a *plank* gained by the third mortgagee, or *tabula in naufragio* . . .", and regarding it (pp. 492-3) as harsh on the second mortgagee and not to be extended; Lord Hardwicke, L.C., in *Wortley* v. *Birkhead* (1754), 2 Ves. Sen. 571; *Robinson* v. *Davison* (1779), 1 Bro. C.C. 63.

38 *Per* Lord Hardwicke, L.C., *Morret* v. *Paske* (1740), 2 Atk. 52.

39 *Goddard* v. *Complin* (1669), 1 Ch. Cas. 119.

40 *Purefoy* v. *Purefoy* (1681), 1 Vern. 28.

The germ of this rule is to be seen in Lord Nottingham's decision in *Lloyd* v. *Cox*,[41] but this is not a satisfactory authority because in that case there was alleged to be an agreement by the mortgagor to redeem both or neither. In the late seventeenth and early eighteenth centuries it was common to regard Powle, M.R.'s decision in *Pope* v. *Onslow*[42] as the foundation of the rule, and as late as 1750 Lord Hardwicke, L.C., doubted that case and "was not satisfied that this was the established rule of the court . . ."[43] The doubt was not justified, as there were quite a few cases dealing with the doctrine, including some applying the rule before *Pope* v. *Onslow*.[44] Indeed, the doctrine must have been settled before the first reported cases applying it, for there are earlier reported cases designating its limits. In *Bacon* v. *Vesey*[45] Lord Nottingham, L.C., decided that there was no right to consolidate if the mortgages were originally to two different mortgagees and in *Bromley* v. *Hamond*[46] he decided that there was also no such right if the mortgages were made by different mortgagors. No one seems to have raised doubts as to the very existence of the doctrine after the time of Lord Hardwicke, and Lord Northington, L.C., extended the doctrine to cases where one mortgage had been assigned, before redemption was sought, by the original mortgagee of both.[47]

Clogs on the Equity of Redemption

Early in the development by the Court of Chancery of the equity of redemption the judges had to deal with attempts to limit the right to redeem, to impose penalties or to secure collateral advantages. One such device, quickly struck down, was a provision in the mortgage deed that the right of redemption should be limited to the mortgagor personally. In *Newcomb* v. *Bonham*,[48] Lord Nottingham, L.C., allowed redemption after the death of the mortgagor despite an agreement that no right to redeem should pass to the heir. The Lord Chancellor remarked,[49] '. . . . once a mortgage, and always a mortgage . . ." The case was later reheard by North, L.K.,[50] who refused redemption on the ground that the transaction was not a mortgage, and this decision

41 79 Sel. Soc. 531.

42 (1692), 2 Vern. 286.

43 *Ex parte King* (1750), 1 Atk. 300.

44 *Rayson* v. *Sacheverel* (1682), 1 Vern. 41; *Margrave* v. *Le Hooke* (1690), 2 Vern. 207. See also *Ex parte Carter* (1773), Amb. 733.

45 (1677/8), 79 Sel. Soc. 660.

46 (1679), 2 Ch. Cas. 23.

47 *Willie* v. *Lugg* (1761), 2 Eden. 78. See also *Roe* v. *Soley* (1771), 2 Black. W. 726; *Ireson* v. *Denn* (1796), 2 Cox C.C. 425.

48 (1681), 1 Vern. 7.

49 1 Vern. 8.

50 (1683), 1 Vern. 214; (1684), 1 Vern, 232.

was affirmed by the House of Lords.[51] The principle, however, is not in doubt, having been applied by Lord Nottingham in another case, *Jason* v. *Eyres*,[52] decided in the same year as *Newcomb* v. *Bonham*. There he said:[53] "... if it be once a security, no words in the same conveyance for excluding the redemption, in case of failure to do it by the time thereby limited, can bar a redemption ..."

The converse device is by a contract that the right of redemption shall not arise until some remote time in the future. In general, the equitable right to redeem does not arise until the legal date for redemption has passed. The mortgage in *Talbot* v. *Braddill*[54] was made in 1657 and expressed to be redeemable in 1688. When the mortgagor sought to redeem in 1682, North, L.K., held that he could, the bargain to the contrary being unreasonable, and this decision was affirmed by Jeffreys, L.C.[55]

Options given to a mortgagee to purchase the equity of redemption from the mortgagor were also frowned on. Any such option contained in a mortgage deed was held void from an early date.[56] In *Jennings* v. *Ward*[57] Powle, M.R., explained why they were regarded as unconscionable: "A man shall not have interest for his money, and a collateral advantage besides for the loan of it, or clog the redemption with any by-agreement." Over half a century later, the position was summarised by Lord Northington, L.C., in *Vernon* v. *Bethell*[58]—

> ... I take it to be an established rule, that a mortgagee can never provide at the time of making the loan for any event or condition on which the equity of redemption shall be discharged, and the conveyance absolute. And there is great reason and justice in this rule, for necessitous men are not, truly speaking, free men, but, to answer a present exigency, will submit to any terms that the crafty may impose upon them.

However, the House of Lords held, in *Ensworth* v. *Griffiths*,[59] that after the mortgage the mortgagee could buy the equity of redemption for a

[51] 2 Vent. 364.

[52] (1681), 2 Freem. 69. See also *Pawlett* v. *A.-G.* (1668), Hardres 465; *Howard* v. *Harris* (1681), 1 Vern. 33 (Lord Nottingham, L.C.), (1683), 1 Vern. 191 (North, L.K.); *Price* v. *Perrie* (1702), 2 Freem. 258; *Mellor* v. *Lees* (1742), 2 Atk. 494; *Spurgeon* v. *Collier* (1758), 1 Eden 55.

[53] 2 Freem. 70.

[54] (1683), 1 Vern. 183.

[55] (1686), 1 Vern. 394.

[56] *Seymour* v. *Tyndall* (1676/7), Rep. temp. Finch 284; *Boughton* v. *Hazelhurst* (1678/9), 79 Sel. Soc. 754; *Willett* v. *Winnell* (1687), 1 Vern. 488.

[57] (1705), 2 Vern. 520, 521.

[58] (1762), 2 Eden 110, 113.

[59] (1706), 5 Bro. P.C. 184.

fresh consideration. In that case, the mortgage was made in 1680, for redemption in 1686. The debt not having been repaid, the mortgagor released the equity of redemption to the mortgagee in 1687 for full value.

Some confused thinking led to a strange distinction in relation to penal interest for late payment.[60] In *Holles* v. *Wyse*[61] the mortgage deed provided for interest of 5%, but rising to 6% if payments got into arrears. It was held that the higher rate was void as " nomine poenae " to oblige punctual payment. But in *Jory* v. *Cox*[62] the stipulation was for 6% interest, the mortgagee agreeing to accept 5% if punctually paid. Wright, L.K., held that this was not an " unreasonable penalty " and that the mortgagor, being unpunctual, must pay 6%.

The Modern Mortgage: Equitable Elaboration and Statutory Reform

Legal Mortgages

Despite the development of the equity of redemption by the Court of Chancery in the seventeenth and eighteenth centuries, the common law forms of mortgage remained unchanged. Prior to statutory reform, the mortgage deed of a fee simple owner continued to suggest that if the debt were not repaid on the date mentioned in it, the land became the absolute property of the mortgagee. In equity, it was very difficult for the mortgagee to achieve this position, even if he foreclosed when the debt was substantially overdue. This led Maitland to remark[64]—

> That is the worst of our mortgage deed—owing to the action of equity, it is one long *suppressio veri* and *suggestio falsi.* It does not in the least explain the rights of the parties; it suggests that they are other than really they are.

In determining whether a transaction is a mortgage or not—often turning on the question of whether a person who has parted with an interest in property can redeem it—equity has continued to look to the

[60] See Meredith, " A Nicety in the Law of Mortgage " (1916), 32 *Law Quarterly Review*, 420.

[61] (1693), 2 Vern. 289. Somers, L.K., came to the same conclusion in *Strode* v. *Parker* (1694), 2 Vern. 316. The Lords Commissioners had arrived at the opposite decision in *Marquis of Hallifax* v. *Higgins* (1690), 2 Vern. 134. In *Burton* v. *Slattery* (1725), 5 Bro. P.C. 233, the House of Lords, in an appeal from Ireland, upheld as liquidated damages a provision that if interest of 5% were overdue three months the rate should rise to 8% *from then.*

[62] (1701), Prec. Ch. 160. Despite incomprehension of the distinction, this view was followed by Lord Hardwicke, L.C., in *Nicholls* v. *Maynard* (1747), 3 Atk. 519, and by Lord Northington, L.C., in *Stanhope* v. *Manners* (1763), 2 Eden 197. Cf. *Brown* v. *Barkham* (1720), 1 P. Wms. 652 (Lord Parker, L.C.).

[64] *Equity* (rev. Brunyate), p. 182.

intent and not to the form of the transfer. If the proprietary interest transferred is meant as security, it can be redeemed on fulfilling the obligation secured.[65] What appears to be a conditional sale, or even an absolute transfer, may be shown, as a matter of construction of the document or by evidence from outside the document, to be a mortgage; and vice versa. In *Williams* v. *Owen*,[66] Lord Cottenham, L.C., said—

> That this Court will treat a transaction as a mortgage, although it was made so as to bear the appearance of an absolute sale, if it appear that the parties intended it to be a mortgage, is, no doubt, true; but it is equally clear that, if the parties intended an absolute sale, a contemporaneous agreement for a repurchase not acted upon, will not of itself entitle the vendor to redeem.

This principle has not been affected in England by the introduction, by the Law of Property Act, 1925, of obligatory forms for legal mortgages of land. By Section 85 of that Act, the only permissible legal mortgages of fee simple estates are by demise for a term of years absolute and a charge by deed expressed to be by way of legal mortgage. The section goes on to provide that a purported mortgage by conveyance of the fee simple operates to give the mortgagee a term (of 3000 years, if a first mortgage). Corresponding provisions for mortgages of terms of years absolute are contained in Section 86. The mortgage of a term must be by subdemise or by charge by deed expressed to be by way of legal mortgage, and a purported mortgage by assignment of the term makes the mortgagee a sublessee (for ten days less than the mortgagor's term, if a first mortgage). The equitable principle as to identifying a mortgage would apply in this way: if a deed purported to convey the grantor's fee simple, but on close construction, or as a result of extraneous evidence, it could be seen to be intended merely as security, the grantee would get a term of years. The Court of Appeal have determined that that is so, in relation to an assignment of a term

65 See p. 168, *ante*.

66 (1840), 5 My. & Cr. 303, 306. See also *Davis* v. *Thomas* (1831), 1 Russ. & M. 506; *Barnhart* v. *Greenshields* (1853), 9 Moo. P.C. 18; *Alderson* v. *White* (1858), 2 De G. & J. 97; *Lincoln* v. *Wright* (1859), 4 De. G. & J. 16: see p. 27, *ante*; *Douglas* v. *Culverwell* (1862), 4 De G.F. & J. 20; *Gossip* v. *Wright* (1869), 17 W.R. 1137; *Locking* v. *Parker* (1872), L.R. 8 Ch. App. 30; *Re Alison* (1879), 11 Ch. D. 284; *Manchester, Sheffield, and Lincolnshire Railway Co.* v. *North Central Wagon Co.* (1888), 13 App. Cas. 554; *Re Watson* (1890), 25 Q.B.D. 27; *Barton* v. *Bank of New South Wales* (1890), 15 App. Cas. 379; *Madell* v. *Thomas & Co.*, [1891] 1 Q.B. 230; *Salt* v. *Marquess of Northampton*, [1892] A.C. 1; *Re Duke of Marlborough*, [1894] 2 Ch. 133. The principle is the same in Ireland: *Goodman* v. *Grierson* (1813), 2 Ba. & B. 274; *Taylor* v. *Emerson* (1843), 4 Dr. & War. 117; *Fee* v. *Cobine* (1847), 11 Ir. Eq. Rep. 406; *Murphy* v. *Taylor* (1850), 1 Ir. Ch. Rep. 92; *Re De Freyne's Estate* (1871), 5 I.L.T.R. 193; *O'Reilly* v. *O'Donoghue* (1875), I.R. 10 Eq. 73; *Crone* v. *Hegarty* (1879), 3 L.R. Ir. 50.

of years, in *Grangeside Properties Ltd.* v. *Collingwoods Securities Ltd.*,[67] where Harman, L.J., with whom Donovan and Russell, L.JJ., agreed, said—

> Section 86 (2) cannot have intended to alter the ancient law, which had always been, that Chancery would treat as a mortgage that which was intended to be a conveyance by way of security between A and B. Once a mortgage, always a mortgage and nothing but a mortgage, has been a principle for centuries. " By way of mortgage " must mean that which is in fact intended as a mortgage and it was that which the complainant in Chancery swore in his bill when he asked for an injunction to restrain the landlord from treating the proviso for redemption as exhausted at the end of the six months for which it was usually expressed to exist. It could not be that section 86 (2) is intended to sweep away the view of the law which had always been that if you proved the thing was a mortgage, equity would allow you to have your equity of redemption to redeem on payment of the mortgage money, interest and costs. In my view this document did operate, although expressed as an absolute assignment, by way of sub-demise.

The restrictions in the Law of Property Act, 1925, on the mechanism of legal mortgages in England are important from the point of view of conveyancing but have little impact on the substance of the relations between mortgagor and mortgagee. One noticeable change is that, as the mortgagor retains the legal estate, there can be successive legal mortgages whereas the pre-1926 mortgagor who conveyed his estate to the mortgagee could grant only equitable mortgages (i.e. mortgages of the equity of redemption) thereafter. However, the effect this might have had on priorities is minimised by the system of registration under the Land Charges Act, 1925. Another change is that in a mortgage in the form of a charge the mortgagee gets no estate in the land at all. Section 87 of the Law of Property Act, 1925, puts him in the same position as if he had. On the face of it, though, the mortgagor, having parted with no part of his legal estate, has no equity of redemption. This also makes no practical difference, as he still has the equitable right to redeem after the contractual date for redemption has passed, and it is still customary to refer to restraints on this right as clogs on the equity of redemption.

In Ireland, it is still usual to mortgage land by conveying the mortgagor's title to the mortgagee, though a fee simple held subject to a fee farm rent is sometimes mortgaged by demise,[68] and terms of years are

[67] [1964] 1 W.L.R. 139, 142-3.
[68] See *Re Sergie*, [1954] N.I. 1.

sometimes mortgaged by subdemise. The only use of the charge by way of legal mortgage is in respect of registered land.[69]

Equitable Mortgages

The mortgagor (in England before 1926, in Ireland at any time) who parted with his entire legal estate to the mortgagee could thereafter raise further money on the same land during the currency of the legal mortage only by offering the equity of redemption as security. A mortgage of an equity of redemption, as of any equitable interest, must be equitable. Thus (except in the rare cases where a mortgage was by grant of a legal estate less than that of the mortgagor) any mortgage after a legal mortgage had to be equitable. The fee simple owner who conveyed it to a mortgagee had an equity of redemption: an equitable fee simple. He could mortgage it by conveying it to a second mortgagee, which would leave the mortgagor with an equity of redemption entitling him to redeem his equity of redemption (i.e. the mortgagor still had an equitable fee simple but at one further remove from the legal estate). This process could go on ad infinitum. This is still the position in Ireland. In England, since 1925, an unlimited number of legal mortgages in succession can be granted of the same land, so that mortgaging the equity of redemption is unlikely to occur. But there seems no theoretical objection to it. Suppose a mortgagor who owns the fee simple to grant a mortgagee a term of 3000 years to secure the debt. In raising a further loan, it seems, the mortgagor could either make the second mortgagee a legal mortgage (by legal charge or reversionary term of years) or assign (or subdemise) his equity of redemption (an equitable term of 3000 years), this giving the second mortgagee an equitable mortgage.

It can thus be seen that an equitable mortgage may be given not only by the owner of an equitable interest but also by a person in a position to grant a legal estate. Apart from assignment of the equity of redemption, a number of methods of creating security effective only in equity have been devised.

(i) *Deposit of title deeds.* The equitable mortgage by deposit of title deeds is a startling creation of late eighteenth century equity. It is one of the few ideas in mortgage law that cannot be traced back to the time of Lord Nottingham or earlier. It was invented quite suddenly in 1783 by the Lords Commissioners, and Lord Thurlow is

69 See the Local Registration of Title (Ireland) Act, 1891, Sects. 40, 50 and 51; Sheridan, " Some Aspects of Legal Mortgages " (1949), 52 *Journal of the Institute of Bankers in Ireland*, 114; Sheridan, " Registration and the Priority of Securities " (1950), 53 *J.I.B.I.* 259; Greene, " Law relating to Leaseholds as Security for Bank Adavnces " (1963), 65 *J.I.B.I.* 123.

generally regarded as responsible. What they decided, in *Russel* v. *Russel*,[70] was that a deposit of title deeds with a creditor, unaccompanied by any memorandum, if intended as security for the debt, gives the creditor a security enforceable in equity.

There is a theoretical difficulty in this doctrine: that of reconciling it with the requirement of written evidence before agreements to create interests in land can be enforceable.[71] The deposit of the deeds may be accompanied by a memorandum, which is prudent from the point of view of evidence and necessary if there are to be any special terms of the agreement, though a mortgagee may prefer to have no document so as to escape the need to register to preserve his priority. If there is written evidence, the theoretical difficulty disappears; but the Lords Commissioners said the mortgage was enforceable without it. Their statement that the contract was executed, not executory, and needed explanation, suggests the doctrine of part performance. But neither receipt by the mortgagee of the deeds (for that is not to his detriment) nor the loan to the mortgagor (for payment of money is not necessarily referable to a contract) is part performance in the usual sense of that expression. The enforceability of the mortgage by deposit of title deeds may be anomalous, but it is useful. The arrangement is secure and informal, and therefore popular, and is now well established.

Lord Eldon, who was bothered by the anomaly but unimpressed by the utility of the transaction, lost few opportunities for attacking *Russel* v. *Russel*; though, as it was a precedent, he respected the case and followed it. He regarded *Russel* v. *Russel* as " a decision much to be lamented . . . "[72] and said that he " must always protest, that the doctrine now prevailing ought never to have been established."[73] In 1808, in *Ex parte Mountfort*,[74] he said: " I recollect the first determination, establishing a mortgage by deposit of deeds; which surprised

70 (1783), 1 Bro. C.C. 269. See also *Edge* v. *Worthington* (1786), 1 Cox C.C. 211; *Hankey* v. *Vernon* (1788), 2 Cox C.C. 12, 14, where Kenyon, M.R., said: " . . . it certainly has always been held in this Court that the deposit of title deeds as a security is an equitable mortgage . . . "; *Ex parte Wetherell* (1805), 11 Ves. 398; *Hiern* v. *Mill* (1806), 13 Ves. 114; *Ex parte Langston* (1810), 17 Ves. 227; *Casberd* v. *Ward* (1819), 6 Price 411; *Keys* v. *Williams* (1838), 3 Y. & C. Ex. 55. Ireland: *Bulfin* v. *Dunne* (1861) 12 Ir. Ch. Rep. 67; *Gilligan* v. *National Bank Ltd.*, [1901] 2 I.R. 513; *Northern Banking Co. Ltd.* v. *Carpenter* [1931] I.R. 268; *National Bank Ltd.* v. *M'Govern* [1931] I.R. 368. Corscadden, " Deposit of Title Deeds " (1953), 55 *Journal of the Institute of Bankers in Ireland*, 253.

71 England: Statute of Frauds, Sect. 4, replaced by the Law of Property Act, 1925, Sect. 40; Ireland: Statute of Frauds (Ireland), 1695, Sect. 2.

72 *Ex parte Haigh* (1805), 11 Ves. 403.

73 *Ex parte Whitbread* (1812), 19 Ves. 209, 210.

74 14 Ves. 606, 606-7.

the Bar considerably; and that feeling has been justified by every subsequent case upon the point." The views of Lord Eldon were well epitomised by his dictum in *Ex parte Hooper*[75]—

> With great deference to Lord *Thurlow*, who first held, that the deposit of a deed necessarily implied an agreement for a mortgage, I repeat, that this decision has produced considerable mischief; and that the case of *Russell* v. *Russell* ought not to have been decided, as it was. The vice of that decision is, that it supposes, that the deposit can refer to nothing but an intention to subject the estate. To that I do not agree. A deposit of title-deeds may be of considerable use without any such object. The right to hold them, and so to work out payment, is of great value; and there are many cases, in which that right may be maintained against all the owners of the estate. That decision, however, has been repeatedly followed; and must not be now disturbed.

It was not disturbed. Indeed, Lord Eldon himself extended the scope of this type of mortgage, for example by holding that a deposit of deeds with a memorandum expressing the mortgage to cover further advances was effective to subject the land as security for the additional sums lent later.[76] Kindersley, V.-.C., later introduced more potential mischief by holding[77] that it was not necessary to deposit all the deeds: there was a mortgage if enough were deposited to constitute material evidence of title. Awkward problems of priorities could arise if the landowner deposited some deeds with one mortgagee and others with another. An example offered itself a few years later.[78] A landowner deposited an old deed (without which title to his land was complete) with his aunt, together with a memorandum stating that the deposit was by way of security. The depositee, who was no lawyer, had no reason to believe that the deed was not the story of the title. Later, the landowner deposited all the other title deeds with a bank to secure his overdraft. The bank investigated the title without getting notice of the earlier incumbrance. Lord Selborne, L.C., held that there were two equitable mortgages, that the equities were equal because the aunt had not been negligent and that therefore they had priority in order of the dates of their creation.

[75] (1815), 19 Ves. 477, 478-9. See also *Ex parte Coming* (1803), 9 Ves. 115, 117; *Ex parte Coombe* (1810), 17 Ves. 369, 370-1; *Ex parte Warner* (1812), 19 Ves. 202, 203; *Ex parte Kensington* (1813), 2 V. & B. 79, 83; *Ex parte Pearce* (1820), Buck 525; Grant, M.R., joined in in *Norris* v. *Wilkinson* (1806), 12 Ves. 192, 196-8.

[76] *Ex parte Kensington* (1813), 2 V. & B. 79. Cf. *Ex parte Hooper* (1815), 19 Ves. 477; *Mountford* v. *Scott* (1823), Turn. & R. 274.

[77] *Lacon* v. *Allen* (1856), 3 Drew. 579. But giving the title-deeds to a lender to prepare a mortgage is not itself a mortgage, nor is a deposit of one deed with a promise to deliver the rest: *Ex parte Pearse* (1820), Buck 525.

[78] *Dixon* v. *Muckleston* (1872), L.R. 8 Ch. App. 155.

Despite judicial and other misgivings, this form of mortgage has remained popular. It has been extended to registered land, in respect of which deposit of the certificate of title has a similar effect. It has also been held to have been created by a purchaser depositing with the lender the vendor's receipt for the purchase money, the receipt describing the property and having a plan of it attached.[79] The deposit of deeds may be a first or subsequent mortgage, though it is likely to be a first one because a first legal mortgage is normally protected by handing the title deeds to the mortgagee (who is, incidentally, put in a position to submortgage by deposit if he so wishes). In Ireland, the legal mortgagee is entitled to the deeds at common law if the mortgagor transfers his estate to him, and in England the legal mortgagee is so entitled, under the Law of Property Act, 1925, despite not being a transferee of the mortgagor's estate.

Where there has been a deposit of title deeds intended to be by way of security, the Court of Appeal have decided, in *Re Molton Finance Ltd.*,[80] that the depositee has no common law lien over the deeds separate from the equitable mortgage.

(ii) *Equitable mortgage by agreement for a legal mortgage.* An agreement to grant a legal mortgage itself constitutes an equitable mortgage if there is a debt. This is essentially a nineteenth century doctrine. In *Fector* v. *Philpott*,[81] in the Court of Exchequer, Richards, L.C.B., held that an agreement to mortgage, subject to a prior mortgage, was an equitable mortgage. The House of Lords, in an Irish appeal, *Eyre* v. *McDowell*,[82] regarded a covenant to convey land as security as being an equitable mortgage. In *Tebb* v. *Hodge*,[83] where there was an agreement to grant a lease and for it to be mortgaged to the lessor, the Court of Exchequer Chamber held that there was an equitable mortgage. On the other hand, a parol agreement to deposit a lease when granted was held by Leach, V.-C., to give no title.[84]

To treat the transaction as an equitable mortgage, as opposed to a purely contractual right to have a legal mortgage, is often of practical significance in bankruptcy cases. Damages for breach of contract will rank with other unsecured debts while the equitable mortgagee

79 *Goodwin* v. *Waghorn* (1835) 4 L.J. Ch. 172.

80 [1968] Ch. 325.

81 (1823), 12 Price 197.

82 (1861), 9 H.L.C. 619. See also *Ex parte Wills* (1790), 1 Ves. Jun. 162; *Capital Finance Co. Ltd.* v. *Stokes* [1969] 1 Ch. 261 (C.A.). Ireland: *Card* v. *Jaffray* (1805), 2 Sch. & Lef. 374; *Abbott* v. *Stratten* (1846), 3 Jo. & Lat. 603; *Re Parkinson's Estate* (1865), 13 L.T. 26.

83 (1869), L.R. 5 C.P. 73.

84 *Ex parte Coombe* (1819), 4 Madd. 249.

can look for payment by realising the security. This would not be so important if specific performance could be given of the contract to make a legal mortgage, but this is impossible if the mortgagor has not got the legal estate.

In order to have force as an equitable mortgage the agreement for a legal mortgage must be a legally binding contract (though not necessarily susceptible of specific performance). If the indebtedness precedes the agreement to give security it is not obvious where the consideration for the debtor's promise can be found. In *Dighton* v. *Withers*[85] Romilly, M.R., without referring to this problem, held that a debtor's memorandum, promising to give his creditors a legal mortgage, was an equitable mortgage. Two years later, Kindersley, V.-C., in *Alliance Bank Ltd.* v. *Broom*,[86] while acknowledging that the plaintiff creditors could sue for the debt at any time after the giving of security as well as before, said—

> . . . although there was no promise on the part of the Plaintiffs to abstain for any certain time from suing for the debt, the effect was, that the Plaintiffs did in effect give, and the Defendant received, the benefit of some degree of forbearance; not, indeed, for any definite time, but, at all events, some extent of forbearance.

Where there is a contract to advance money on mortgage, and no advance has been made or security given—in other words the contract is wholly executory—there will be no order for specific performance on either side, as damages are an adequate remedy,[87] and until there is a debt there can be no equitable security for its repayment. But once the loan has been made under such a contract, the lender can have specific performance (if the borrower is in a position to perform),[88] and as soon as the money is advanced there is an equitable mortgage. Once the loan is made, damages are no longer an adequate remedy for the creditor, as such damages rank as an unsecured debt. In order for a contract to make a mortgage of land to be enforceable at all there must be a memorandum in writing or (if purely equitable remedies are sought) some act of part performance or fraud to take the case out

[85] (1862), 31 Beav. 423.

[86] (1864), 2 Dr. & Sm. 289, 292.

[87] *Rogers* v. *Challis* (1859), 27 Beav. 175 (Romilly, M.R.); *Larios* v. *Bonany Y Gurety* (1873), L.R. 5 P.C. 346 (on appeal from Gibraltar).

[88] So held by Wickens, V.-C., with doubts, in *Ashton* v. *Corrigan* (1871), L.R. 13 Eq. 76, and by Lord Selborne, L.C., with no doubts, in *Hermann* v. *Hodges* (1873), L.R. 16 Eq. 18. Ireland: *Hunter* v. *Lord Langford* (1828), 2 Mol. 572 (Hart, L.C.).

of the statute.[89]

(iii) *Security by way of equitable charge.* There may be an express agreement, by which a borrower charges his property in equity with repayment of a loan; and such an equitable charge may be created by will. A defective attempt to grant legal security may also be upheld as an equitable charge.[90] In the case of land, an equitable charge must be evidenced in writing[91] unless there is an equity to take the case outside the statute.

Usage of the terms " mortgage " and " charge " is not uniform and sometimes a charge for repayment of money lent is regarded as a type of mortgage. Sometimes they are distinguished, as, for example, by Walker, C., in the Irish Court of Appeal,[92] saying: " . . . every charge is not an equitable mortgage though every equitable mortgage is a charge." The substantial points are as follows. A legal mortgagee and an equitable mortgagee (by deposit of title deeds or by agreement for a legal mortgage) have available to them, among other remedies, an order for foreclosure.[93] The remedy of an equitable chargee, whether the charge is to secure money lent or not, is " . . . to have the sums mentioned realized by sale or mortgage of the property charged, and not by way of foreclosure . . . "[94] Another term used is " lien." The position of an equitable lienee is the same as that of an equitable chargee. The term " lien " is commonly reserved to designate a charge arising by operation of law, such as a vendor's lien, over property he has transferred, for unpaid purchase money, while " charge " is used for a charge created by agreement. " Pledge " is quite a different type of transaction for, though the ultimate remedies of a pledgee are similar to those of a chargee, no proprietary interest passes under a pledge. There is a bailment of a chattel as security for a debt, the pledgee having merely possession. This is a common law variety of security, most frequently used when borrowing from a pawnbroker. Incidentally, at common law, deposit of title deeds as security for a loan would be a pledge, but this has ceased to be of practical importance since equity started treating it as a mortgage.

89 In *Ex parte Broderick* (1887), 18 Q.B.D. 766, the Court of Appeal held that there was no contract, merely an unaccepted offer to give security to a bank. But they said that, had there been a contract, it would not have been part performed, so as to take it out of the Statute of Frauds, by a conversation between the debtor and the person who held deeds of title of the debtor's property whereby that person agreed to hold the deeds for the bank.

90 *Dale* v. *Smithwick* (1690), 2 Vern. 151 (Lords Commissioners).

91 *Ex parte Hall* (1878), 10 Ch. D. 615 (C.A.).

92 *Shea* v. *Moore*, [1894] 1 I.R. 158, 168. No particular words are necessary; an intention to give security is all that is required: *Cradock* v. *Scottish Provident Institution* (1894), 70 L.T. 718 (C.A.).

93 See pp. 242-9, *post*.

94 *Per* Stirling, J., *Re Owen*, [1894] 3 Ch. 220, 227, a case of a charge by will of a contingent reversionary interest in land. See also Rowley, " Conveyancing and Equitable Charges " (1962), 26 *Conveyancer and Property Lawyer* (*N.S.*), 445.

The Equity of Redemption and the Equitable Right to Redeem

In Ireland, where mortgages are still normally made by transfer of the property to the mortgagee, the equity of redemption is the mortgagor's equitable estate in the land, equivalent in duration to the legal estate granted to the mortgagee.[95] In England, after 1925, the mortgagor still has an equity of redemption where the mortgage is by demise or subdemise, but though this is still regarded as a proprietary interest,[96] it is of less significance in view of the fact that the modern English mortgagor by these methods has a legal estate. The present Irish mortgagor and the pre-1926 English mortgagor who transferred the legal estate could deal with the land by making further mortgages or otherwise creating interests in it by will or inter vivos only by virtue of the equity of redemption coming into existence simultaneously with the making of the mortgage. The modern English mortgagor can deal with his legal estate. Moreover, the mortgage by charge under the Law of Property Act, 1925, in England, or by charge of registered land in England or Ireland, does not give the mortgagee any legal estate and hence the mortgagor does not, strictly speaking, have any equity of redemption.

Probably the most valuable right associated with the equity of redemption is the equitable right to redeem.[97] This does not arise simultaneously with the equity of redemption, but only after the legal date for redemption has passed[98] or, if the legal date for redemption is put unconscionably far in the future, after a reasonable time. This right has been unaffected by changes in forms of legal mortgage. If the mortgagee does not take a legal estate, the equitable right to redeem is still associated with the mortgagor's interest in the mortgaged property. Equally unaffected by such changes are principles invalidating clogs on the equity of redemption, which might with more accuracy but less tradition be styled clogs on the right to redeem.

The Equitable Right to Redeem

A person absolutely entitled to the equity of redemption—the mortgagor or his successor in title—may redeem after the contractual date for redemption has passed,[99] on payment of the principal debt, arrears of

[95] See p. 168, *ante*.
[96] *Re Wells*, [1933] Ch. 29 (C.A.).
[97] See pp. 168-71, *ante*.
[98] *Brown* v. *Cole* (1845), 14 Sim. 427. Ireland: *Burrough* v. *Cranston* (1840), 2 Ir. Eq. Rep. 203.
[99] See pp. 166, 168-71, *ante*.

interest and any legitimate costs of the mortgagee.[1] The payment of interest must include arrears which the mortgagee could not recover in an action on the contract, by reason of lapse of time, on the principle of doing equity when seeking it.[2]

Tender of the correct amount will not put an end to the mortgage, even if the tender is improperly rejected. In *Bank of New South Wales* v. *O'Connor*,[3] where the mortgage was by deposit of title deeds, the Privy Council held that improper rejection by the mortgagee of the correct amount tendered by the mortgagor did not allow the latter to get his deeds back by an action in detinue: he must bring a redemption action. On the other hand, the Privy Council thought that the rejection of the tender would stop interest running and might affect the liability for costs. In *Graham* v. *Seal*[4] the mortgagor offered the right money on condition of the mortgagee there and then executing a reconveyance (previously seen and approved by the mortgagee); on this offer being rejected, the Court of Appeal held that no further interest was payable. But this is only on the basis that the money is not producing income because the mortgagor, in order to tender it, has it in cash or in some other idle form like a current account at a bank. In *Edmondson* v. *Copland*[5] Joyce, J., thought that the mortgagor would be liable to account to the mortgagee for further income (after the rejection of the tender) on the mortgage principal money if he made any; while in *Barratt* v. *Gough-Thomas*[6] Danckwerts, J., allowed interest to continue where the sum tendered was not shown to have been set aside for payment on demand.

The person seeking to redeem must generally give six months notice to the mortgagee or pay six months interest in lieu of notice.[7] The idea behind this is that the mortgagee must be given a fair opportunity to find an alternative investment for his money without an intervening loss of income. The requirement was reviewed by Maugham, J., in *Cromwell Property Investment Co. Ltd.* v. *Western*.[8] He said there was a settled rule of practice that, after default had been made in payment of the principal and interest in accordance with the proviso for re-

[1] *Walker* v. *Jones* (1866), L.R. 1 P.C. 50 (on appeal from New South Wales); *Bank of New South Wales* v. *O'Connor* (1889), 14 App. Cas. 273 (on appeal from Victoria); *Rourke* v. *Robinson*, [1911] 1 Ch. 480; *Webb* v. *Crosse*, [1912] 1 Ch. 323; *Graham* v. *Seal* (1918), 88 L.J.Ch. 31.

[2] *Dingle* v. *Coppen*, [1899] 1 Ch. 726; *Re Lloyd*, [1903] 1 Ch. 385.

[3] (1889), 14 App. Cas. 273.

[4] (1918), 88 L.J. Ch. 31.

[5] [1911] 2 Ch. 301.

[6] [1951] 2 All E.R. 48.

[7] *Johnson* v. *Evans* (1889), 61 L.T. 18 (C.A.).

[8] [1934] Ch. 322. Ireland: *Re Lighton* (1851), 4 Ir. Jur. 35.

demption, the mortgagor must in general give to the mortgagee six calendar months notice of redemption. The learned judge regarded this as harsh, because it takes far less than six months to get a suitable alternative investment, but he did not interfere with the practice. He held, however, that where a proper notice had been given, and payment was not made on the date named, and the mortgagors explained the delay to the mortgagees, only reasonable—here three months—fresh notice had to be given because the mortgagees had agreed in the first place to accept reasonable notice, which they regarded as three months, which was what was given. He refused their claim for a new notice of six months.

Here one sees equity in its rigid aspect, substituting technicality for substance. A rule requiring reasonable notice would be more equitable than a rule requiring six months notice. Judges have kept to the six months rule in general but, like Maugham, J., have given practical expression to their dislike of it by creation of exceptions. The rule has been held to apply only to long term mortgages, not to temporary mortgages, as in the usual case of deposit of title deeds, where reasonable notice (less than six months) was held sufficient.[9] It has been held inapplicable when the mortgagee has demanded repayment, and the mortgagor can then redeem without notice,[10] even if the mortgagor had given and the mortgagee accepted six months notice;[11] and also inapplicable if the mortgagee has entered into possession of the mortgaged premises.[12] But in *Hill* v. *Rowlands*[13] the Court of Appeal held that, even if a mortgagor could redeem without notice when foreclosure proceedings were commenced, once a foreclosure order had been made, with a specified date for the mortgagor to redeem or be foreclosed, the rights of the parties were crystallised by the order of the court and the mortgagor must pay interest up to the specified date.

Limited owner of the equity of redemption. A mortgage can be redeemed by a person with a limited, but present, interest in the equity of redemption. The typical exercise of this power is redemption of the first mortgage by the second mortgagee.[14] Another example is

9 *Per* Chitty, J., *Fitzgerald's Trustee* v. *Mellersh*, [1892] 1 Ch. 385.

10 *Emondson* v. *Copland*, [1911] 2 Ch. 301.

11 *Re Alcock* (1883), 23 Ch.D. 372 (C.A.).

12 *Per* Kekewich, J., *Bovill* v. *Endle*, [1896] 1 Ch. 648.

13 [1897] 2 Ch. 361.

14 *Smith* v. *Green* (1844), 1 Coll. 555. Cf. *Ramsbottom* v. *Wallis* (1835), 5 L.J.Ch. 92, where Lord Langdale, M.R., held that apart from redeeming a second mortgagee had no right to buy out the first mortgagor, and hence a second mortgagee could not proceed where he had contracted with the mortgagor not to enforce his mortgage for a ten-year period which had not yet elapsed; *Cotterell* v. *Price*, p. 190, *post*.

the right, upheld up the Court of Appeal in *Tarn* v. *Turner*,[15] of a lessee of the equity of redemption whose lease is not binding on the mortgagor to redeem.[16] A person interested in the equity of redemption in remainder cannot redeem during the currency of the prior estate;[17] and on this same basis a third mortgagee cannot redeem the first mortgage without also redeeming the second.

Stranger to the equity of redemption. With a single exception, no one without a present interest in the equity of redemption can redeem. He may buy the mortgagee's interest by agreement, but he cannot redeem, i.e. discharge the mortagee whether he likes it or not.[18] In *Cotterell* v. *Price*[19] Buckley, J., held that a second mortgagee whose rights against the mortgagor were statute barred, having no longer any estate or interest in the land or in the equity of redemption, could not redeem the first mortgage.

The one exceptional case is that of the original mortgagor who has assigned his equity of redemption and is subsequently proceeded against to pay off the mortgage under his liability on the covenant to repay the amount lent. Stirling, J., decided this in *Kinnaird* v. *Trollope*.[20] In that case, after the mortgagor assigned his equity of redemption, the assignee received further advances and later become insolvent. The mortgagee sued the mortgagor on the covenant for the sum originally secured. The learned judge held that the mortgagor thereupon got a new right to redeem and, on exercising it, became entitled to a reconveyance subject to an equity of redemption in anyone else.

If the mortgagor is sued on the personal covenant after foreclosure,[21] or after sale in a foreclosure action if the purchaser is the mortgagee,[22] he has a renewed right to redeem.

Duty of mortgagee on redemption. Prior to statutory intervention, if the mortgagor redeemed, the duty of the mortgagee was to reconvey all his interest in the land to the mortgagor or (if the mortgagee had notice) to whomever the mortgagor had assigned the immediate interest

[15] (1888), 39 Ch.D. 456.

[16] As to mortgagors' leases binding on mortgagees, see pp. 224-30, *post*.

[17] *Ravald* v. *Russell* (1830), You. 9; *Prout* v. *Cock*, [1896] 2 Ch. 808.

[18] *Lomax* v. *Bird* (1683), 1 Vern. 182; *Troughton* v. *Binkes* (1801), 6 Ves. 573; *James* v. *Biou* (1819), 3 Swanst. 234.

[19] [1960] 1 W.L.R. 1097.

[20] (1888), 39 Ch.D. 636.

[21] *Mexborough U.D.C.* v. *Harrison*, [1964] 1 W.L.R. 733.

[22] *Gordon Grant & Co. Ltd.* v. *Boos*, [1926] A.C. 781 (Privy Council, on appeal from the West Indian Court of Appeal).

in the equity of redemption (e.g. a second mortgagee).[23] In the case of redemption by a person with a limited interest in the equity of redemption, the reconveyance to him should reserve the equities of others.[24] Apparently the mortgagee could not be required to transfer to anyone not entitled to a reconveyance. In *Colyer* v. *Colyer*,[25] in the Court of Appeal in Chancery, Turner, L.J., said: .". . I am at a loss to see upon what ground the mortgagor can compel the mortgagee to transfer. The contract is, to reconvey to the mortgagor or his assigns; and this is all that the mortgagee is compellable to do."

One might be forgiven for wondering what it could matter to the mortgagee whether he reconveyed or transferred. The arbitrary power of the mortgagee to object to transfer was eliminated by the Conveyancing Act, 1881, Section 15—

> 15.—(1) Where a mortgagor is entitled to redeem, he shall, by virtue of this Act, have power to require the mortgagee, instead of reconveying, and on the terms on which he would be bound to reconvey, to assign the mortgage debt and convey the mortgaged property to any third person, as the mortgagor directs; and the mortgagee shall, by virtue of this Act, be bound to assign and convey accordingly.
>
> (2) This section does not apply in the case of a mortgagee being or having been in possession.
>
> (3) This section applies to mortgages made either before or after the commencement of this Act, and shall have effect notwithstanding any stipulation to the contrary.

This provision was extended by the Conveyancing Act, 1882, Section 12, which provided that the right under Section 15 of the 1881 Act was to belong to and be capable of being enforced by each incumbrancer, or by the mortgagor, notwithstanding any intermediate incumbrance. It also laid down that a requisition of an incumbrancer was to prevail over a requisition of the mortgagor and that, as between incumbrancers, a requisition of a prior incumbrancer was to prevail over a requisition of a subsequent incumbrancer. The Conveyancing Acts are still in force in Ireland, but the same effect is now produced in England by the Law of Property Act, 1925, Section 95.

23 *Walker* v. *Jones* (1866), L.R. 1 P.C. 50; *Rourke* v. *Robinson*, [1911] 1 Ch. 480; *Webb* v. *Crosse*, [1912] 1 Ch. 323.

24 *Pearce* v. *Morris* (1869), L.R. 5 Ch.App. 227 (Lord Hatherley, L.C.); *Hall* v. *Heward* (1886), 32 Ch.D. 430 (C.A.); *Kinnaird* v. *Trollope* (1888), 39 Ch.D. 636, p. 190, *ante*.

25 (1863), 3 De G.J. & S. 676, 693.

These sections have been judicially considered. In *Teevan* v. *Smith*[26] the Court of Appeal pointed out that Section 15 of the 1881 Act only allowed the mortgagor to " require " a transfer " instead of re-conveying." They held that if the mortgagor redeemed the first mortgage, and there was a second mortgage, it was the second mortgagee who was entitled to a reconveyance and so the mortgagor could not make a requisition without the second mortgagee's consent. Jessel, M.R., said:[27] " Where there are first and second mortgagees and the first mortgagee has notice of the second, when he is paid off he becomes a trustee of the legal estate for him." Similarly, on Section 12 of the 1882 Act, Neville, J., thought, but did not decide, that " . . . a mortgagee will not be safe in transferring to the mortgagor, or to a nominee of the mortgagor, without the consent of the puisne incumbrancers, of which he has notice."[28] In *Cotterell* v. *Price*[29] Buckley, J., held that a second mortgagee whose rights against the mortgagor were statute barred could not give directions to the first mortgagee under Section 95 of the Law of Property Act, 1925, as he was no longer an incumbrancer as defined by Section 205 (1) (vii) of the Act.

In England, if the parties so agree, it is no longer necessary to have a reconveyance or transfer on redemption, as an appropriately worded receipt has the same effect.[30]

By the Conveyancing Act, 1881, Section 25,[31] and the Law of Property Act, 1925, Section 91, a person entitled to redeem mortgaged property may have a judgment or order for sale instead of for redemption in an action brought by him either for redemption alone, or for sale alone, or for sale or redemption in the alternative. Furthermore, in a redemption action (as in any other action respecting a mortgage), the court has a discretion to order a sale on the request of the mortgagee, or of any person interested either in the mortgage money or in the right of redemption.

Payment of mortgage debt by person not entitled to redeem. If the mortgagee agrees to accept payment from someone not entitled to redeem, the payer may intend to extinguish the security or to buy it. Unless the contrary appears, it is presumed that the payer intends to keep the mortgage alive for his own benefit. In *Ghana Commercial*

26 (1882), 20 Ch.D. 724.

27 20 Ch.D. 729-30.

28 *Re Magneta Time Co. Ltd.* (1915), 84 L.J.Ch. 814, 816.

29 [1960] 1 W.L.R. 1097. See p. 190, *ante*.

30 Law of Property Act, 1925, Sect. 115. See also the Building Societies Act, 1962, Sect. 37. As to cesser of satisfied terms, see Sect. 116 of the 1925 Act. In Ireland, there is no general equivalent of either Sect. 115 or Sect. 116.

31 Not applying to Ireland, where there is no equivalent legislation.

Bank v. *Chandiram*[32] the third party bank paying off the mortgagee was the mortgagor's creditor but had no security for the debt. The bank had the title deeds to the mortgaged property but held them for the mortgagee, whose mortgage was by deposit of the deeds. After paying the mortgagee, the bank kept the deeds, but there was no express agreement relating to them. The Privy Council held that the bank had become an assignee of the equitable mortgage. The same principle applies (*a*) where the person paying the mortgage debt has an interest in the equity of redemption, but as it is in remainder there is no question of merger,[33] and (*b*) where the payment is not by agreement but by a surety who has been made to pay.[34]

In England, unless there is express provision to the contrary or the payment is from a special trust fund, a receipt by the mortgagee showing the mortgage to have been paid off by a person who is not entitled to the immediate equity of redemption operates to transfer the mortgage to the payer.[35]

Merger. Some intricate problems can arise when, by redemption or otherwise, an interest in an equity of redemption and an interest in a security come into the same hands and it is disputed whether they merge or both remain alive. At common law, whenever two estates in the same land were united in the ownership of the same person, the lesser estate was merged in the greater, irrespective of the intent of the parties concerned, provided that the estates united without any intervening estate, and that the person who held them both held them in the same right. In equity, it was a matter of intention. If merger was intended, it occurred; if continued separate existence was intended, no merger resulted. In the absence of any expressed intention, equity imputed the result most advantageous to the owner of the two interests. These principles were applied to all questions of merger in equity, not just merger of mortgages or charges with equities of redemption. They have now been extended to apply to common law estates as well by the Judicature Act, 1873, Section 25 (4),[36] and the Judicature (Ireland) Act, 1877, Sect. 28 (4).

In *Forbes* v. *Moffatt*[37] Grant, M.R., said—

32 [1960] A.C. 732.

33 *Wigsell* v. *Wigsell* (1825), 2 Sim. & St. 364; *Re Chesters*, [1935] Ch. 77.

34 *Forbes* v. *Jackson* (1882), 19 Ch.D. 615. See also *Sanders* v. *Henden* (1676), 73 Sel. Soc. 343.

35 Law of Property Act, 1925, Sect. 115 (2). See also *Cumberland Court (Brighton) Ltd.* v. *Taylor*, [1964] Ch. 29.

36 Replaced by the Law of Property Act, 1925, Sect. 185.

37 (1811), 18 Ves. 384, 390.

> . . . a person, becoming entitled to an estate, subject to a charge for his own benefit, may, if he chooses, at once take the estate, and keep up the charge. . . . The question is upon the intention, actual or presumed, of the person, in whom the interests are united. In most instances it is, with reference to the party himself, of no sort of use to have a charge on his own estate; and, where that is the case, it will be held to sink, unless something shall have been done to keep it on foot.

In that case the contest was between the party's real representatives—entitled, as the law then stood, to the estate—and his personal representatives—entitled to the charge if still on foot. He had done nothing to show an intention in favour of merger or against it. The matter therefore depended on presumed intention, as to which the Master of the Rolls, holding the charge still subsisting, said[38]—

> With regard to presumptive intention, it was evidently most advantageous to *John Moffatt*, that this mortgage should be kept on foot; for otherwise he would have given priority to the other mortgage and all the debts of his brother. The reasonable presumption therefore is, that he would choose to keep the mortgage on foot. Where no intention is expressed, or the party is incapable of expressing any, I apprehend the Court considers what is most advantageous to him.[39]

An example of an express intention being effectuated is *Thorne* v. *Cann*.[40] The assignee of an equity of redemption paid off a mortgage with a view to assigning it, with its priority, to a new lender. The House of Lords held that there was a transfer, not a reconveyance. If a first mortgage is redeemed after a second mortgage has been made, a subsequent lender will rank after the second mortgagee if he takes a new mortgage, but before him if he is a transferee of the first mortgage. This was illustrated by yet another House of Lords decision, *Whiteley* v. *Delaney*.[41] In that case Lord Haldane, L.C., said[42]—

[38] 18 Ves. 392.

[39] The House of Lords took the same view in *Liquidation Estates Purchase Co. Ltd.* v. *Willoughby*, [1898] A.C. 321.

[40] [1895] A.C. 11.

[41] [1914] A.C. 132. See also *Re Fletcher*, [1917] 1 Ch. 339 (C.A.); Randall, "Merger of Charges" (1912), 28 *Law Quarterly Review*, 348. Ireland: *Redington* v. *Redington* (1809), 1 Ba. & B. 131; *Lysaght* v. *Lysaght* (1851), 4 Ir. Jur. 110; *Lindsay* v. *Earl of Wicklow* (1873), I.R. 7 Eq. 192; *Church* v. *Church* (1877), I.L.T.R. 163; *Re Cork Harbour Docks and Warehouse Co. Ltd.'s Estate* (1885), 17 L.R. Ir. 515; *Re Nunn's Estate* (1888), 23 L.R.Ir. 286; *Re Howard's Estate* (1892), 29 L.R.Ir. 266; *Re Godley's Estate*, [1896] 1 I.R.45; *Parnell's Estate* (1901), 1 N.I.J.R. 168.

[42] [1914] A.C. 145.

> . . . it is now quite plain that a purchaser from a mortgagor and the first mortgagee can always, if he chooses, keep the first mortgage alive, and so protect himself against subsequent incumbrancers, whether he had notice of them or not.

And Lord Dunedin[43]—

> Where by appropriate conveyancing the charge could be preserved (this excludes all cases of which *Otter* v. *Lord Vaux*[44] is a type), then it will be for the party alleging the charge to be dead to shew an intention to that effect. What have been called the presumptions arising from the continued existence of the charge being to the benefit of the person who has paid it off, as, e.g., in the case of payment by a limited owner, are just, I think, other ways of expressing the same rule.

The mortgagor in that case made a first legal mortgage to A, followed by a second equitable mortgage to M. The mortgagor, being pressed by A for repayment, then entered into an arrangement to sell the property, free from incumbrances, to W, who would finance the transaction by borrowing from F to pay off A. F paid off A, A reconveyed to the mortgagor, the mortgagor conveyed " an unencumbered fee simple " to W, and W mortgaged it in favour of F. Then W and F discovered the existence of M, previously concealed by the fraud of the mortgagor. If F had a new mortgage from W, it was subsequent to M's security, but if F was a transferee of A's mortgage he was in front of M. The House of Lords held that F had priority to M either because there was no merger in equity of the mortgagor's and A's interests or because when F paid A, A became trustee for F pro tanto, the mortgagor took from A with knowledge of that trust and so subject to it, W took from the mortgagor in like fashion, and M was a volunteer so far as this transaction was concerned.

It also works the other way round, the mortgagee acquiring the equity of redemption. In *Adams* v. *Angell*[45] the first mortgagee bought the equity of redemption by paying £20 and releasing the debt of £1380 due on that mortgage. There was a second mortgage, but the property was not worth more than £1380. If the first mortgage had ceased to exist, the second mortgage was the first charge on the property. The Court of Appeal held that there was no merger as the intention had been to keep the first mortgage alive so as to retain priority over the second.

[43] [1914] A.C. 151-2.
[44] (1856), 6 De G.M. & G. 638. See p. 196, *post*.
[45] (1877), 5 Ch.D. 634.

The rule as to intention in matters of merger does not allow the mortgagor to play dirty tricks on subsequent mortgagees. In *Otter* v. *Lord Vaux*[46] the mortgagor bought when the first mortgagee sold under his express power of realising his security by selling free from the equity of redemption. The proceeds of sale were insufficient to pay off the first mortgage, but there was a second mortgagee, whose security had evaporated if the equity of redemption was destroyed by the sale, and the mortgagor was sitting pretty with an unencumbered estate. Lord Cranworth, L.C., did not let him get away with it, saying[47]—

> The general principle, that a mortgagor cannot set up against his own incumbrancer any other incumbrance created by himself, is a proposition that I think has never been controverted.

Loss of power of redemption. The equitable right to redeem disappears when the equity of redemption is destroyed by foreclosure by the mortgagee,[48] when the mortgagee exercises an express or statutory power to sell the property free from the equity of redemption,[49] and by long lapse of time after the mortgagee has gone into possession of the mortgaged property.

In the early days of the equity of redemption of land, the Court of Chancery refused redemption after a lapse of thirty years, and by the nineteenth century of twenty years, by analogy with the Statute of Limitations applying to common law actions for recovery of possession of land. This was first put on a statutory footing in 1833 and is now governed in England by the Limitation Act, 1939, Section 12[50]—

> When a mortgagee of land has been in possession of any of the mortgaged land for a period of twelve years, no action to redeem the land of which the mortgagee has been so in possession shall thereafter be brought by the mortgagor or any person claiming through him.

By section 16, when this twelve year period has elapsed, the mortgagor's title is extinguished.[51]

There is no such provision for mortgages of pure personalty. In *Weld-Blundell* v. *Petre*[52] there was a mortgage of shares in 1900. The interest was never paid after 1908 (the mortgagor died in 1901). The

46 (1856), 6 De G.M. & G. 638. See also *Re W. Tasker & Sons Ltd.*, [1905] 2 Ch. 587 (C.A.); *Parkash* v. *Irani Finance Ltd.*, [1969] 2 W.L.R. 1134. Cf. *Parnell's Estate* (1901), 1 N.I.J.R. 168.

47 6 De G.M. & G. 642-3. See also the Law of Property Act, 1925, Sect. 115 (3).

48 See pp. 242-9, *post*.

49 See pp. 249-57, *post*.

50 Corresponding legislation is the Statute of Limitations, 1957, Sect. 34(1)(*a*) (Republic of Ireland); Statute of Limitations (Northern Ireland), 1958, Sect. 36.

51 Similarly under the Statute of Limitations, 1957, Sect. 35 (Republic of Ireland), and the Statute of Limitations (Northern Ireland), 1958, Sect. 37.

52 [1929] 1 Ch. 33.

mortgagee was receiving the income on the shares, which was negligible until things perked up during the First World War. By the time the mortgagee died in 1923 he had received enough in dividends to pay all the interest due and the principal debt. In 1926 the mortgagor's executors suddenly came to life and tried to redeem from the mortgagee's executors. In the absence of a statutory period of limitation, the defendants pleaded laches. This the Court of Appeal thought the applicable doctrine, for they saw no reason to go by analogy to the twelve year period for land. However, the dormancy of the plaintiffs from 1908 until 1926 had not caused the mortgagee to alter his position, so there was no element of acquiescence or estoppel,[53] and the court considered the mere delay not long enough to amount to laches.

Consolidation. The doctrine that a mortgagee of two properties for two debts from the same mortgagor could consolidate them (i.e. insist on the redemption of both or neither)[54] packed the nineteenth century Chancery reports with technicalities, nice distinctions and injustice. Cases conflicted, judges felt themselves bound to support or even extend the doctrine (so as to preserve certainty in conveyancing) while expressing regret at its very existence, and, amid a flurry of House of Lords decisions, a half-hearted abolition took place in 1881. The Conveyancing Act, 1881, Section 17, still operative in Ireland, was replaced in England by the Law of Property Act, 1925, Section 93, which provides—

> (1) A mortgagor seeking to redeem any one mortgage is entitled to do so without paying any money due under any separate mortgage made by him, or by any person through whom he claims, solely on property other than that comprised in the mortgage which he seeks to redeem.
>
> This subsection applies only if and as far as a contrary intention is not expressed in the mortgage deeds or one of them.
>
> (2) This section does not apply where all the mortgages were made before the first day of January, eighteen hundred and eighty-two.
>
> (3) Save as aforesaid, nothing in this Act, in reference to mortgages, affects any right of consolidation or renders inoperative a stipulation in relation to any mortgage made before or after the commencement of this Act reserving a right to consolidate.

[53] See pp. 33-4, *ante*.
[54] See pp. 175-6, *ante*.

As this section allows the parties to a mortgage to stipulate for the doctrine of consolidation to operate, and this is done in practice, the rules worked out by the courts before legislation certainly apply to a person seeking to redeem a post-1881 mortgage, if he is the mortgagor or took his interest in the equity of redemption after the creation of all the mortgages to be consolidated, and in either case one of these mortgages is by a deed expressing " a contrary intention " within the meaning of Section 93 (1).[55] Moreover, the reference to " property other than that comprised in the mortgage which he seeks to redeem " probably means that the section does not apply to successive mortgages of the same property so that these can be consolidated (if at all) without an express reservation of the power. That was the opinion of Wright, J., in *Re Salmon*,[56] on Section 17 of the 1881 Act. It was not necessary for him to decide because the first mortgage in that case excluded the section. There were three mortgages to different people, but the second mortgagee had transfers from the other two. The learned judge held that the mortgagor's trustee in bankruptcy could not redeem the third mortgage without redeeming the other two. This must not be taken as indicating a judicial attitude favouring consolidation in general, for this is not the case. In *Farmer* v. *Pitt*[57] Byrne, J., held that a contract to grant a legal mortgage did not contain an implied term that the mortgage deed would exclude Section 17.

In its early applications, consolidation was permitted only by a common mortgagee against a common mortgagor. Virtually nothing is left of this limitation, except that there can be consolidation only of mortgages originally made by the same mortgagor. In *Re Raggett*[58] James, L.J. (Cotton and Lush, L.JJ., expressing no opinion on this point), held that there could be no consolidation where the first mortgage was made by two people, and the equity of redemption was held on trust for themselves and another, and the second mortgage was made by all three of them. This was the basis of the decision of Neville, J., in *Sharp* v. *Rickards*[59] that mortgages made by different mortgagors could not be consolidated merely because the equities of redemption had come into the same hands by assignment. He held that if a mortgage were carried out by S, the owner of the equity of redemption in property A, conveying property B to C on trust to mortgage it (and C doing so), for consolidation purposes the mort-

[55] *Hughes* v. *Britannia Permanent Benefit Building Society*, [1906] 2 Ch. 607, *per* Kekewich, J.
[56] [1903] 1 K.B. 147.
[57] [1902] 1 Ch. 954.
[58] (1880), 16 Ch.D. 117 (C.A.).
[59] [1909] 1 Ch. 109.

gagor of property B is C, not S. But the doctrine was extended so as to apply in favour of common owners of securities, even if they were originally created in favour of different mortgagees, and so as to apply against owners of equities of redemption, even if they were not the original mortgagors.

Consolidation against assignees of the equity of redemption has been based on the notion that the assignees can be in no better position than the assignor, but has given rise to a number of problems. The result of the authorities seems to be as follows.

(1) A holder of two or more mortgages originally made by the same mortgagor can consolidate as against the holder of an equity of redemption by assignment, even if the assignee holds the equity of redemption in only one of the mortgages to be consolidated. In *Hughes* v. *Britannia Permanent Benefit Building Society*,[60] first, the mortgagor gave a mortgage of property A to X by deed excluding Section 17. Secondly, he gave a mortgage of property B to X. Thirdly, he gave a mortgage of property B to Y (who thus became the owner of the equity of redemption on X's mortgage of that property). Later, the mortgagor granted mortgages of properties C and D to X. Kekewich, J., held that X could consolidate his mortgages of properties A and B so as to compel Y to redeem both or neither, because the equity to consolidate existed against the mortgagor before Y derived his equity from him. On the other hand, he held that X could not also make Y redeem properties C and D because the equity to consolidate these against the mortgagor arose after the assignment of the equity of redemption in property B to Y and after X had notice of Y's equity. (It may be the rule that mortgages made after the assignment of the equity of redemption cannot be consolidated against the assignee even if made to a mortgagee not having notice of the assignment. There is no clear authority on this.)

(2) A holder of two or more mortgages originally made by the same mortgagor to different mortgagees can consolidate as against the assignee of the equities of redemption of both or all of them, even if the union of the mortgages in the hands of a single holder occurred after the assignment of the equities of redemption. In *Pledge* v. *White*,[61] first, the mortgagor mortgaged properties A and B to V. Secondly, he mortgaged property C to W. Thirdly, he mortgaged properties D, E, F and G to other mortgagees. Fourthly, he mortgaged these last four properties to X (who thus acquired the equities of

[60] [1906] 2 Ch. 607.
[61] [1896] A.C. 187.

redemption). Fifthly, he mortgaged all seven to X and another person (who thus now owned all the equities of redemption between them). X and his co-owner later transferrred all seven equities of redemption to Y (the appellant, Pledge). Y was now the owner of third mortgages on properties D, E, F and G, and of second mortgages on A, B and C. X was the second mortgagee of D, E, F and G but had no interest in A, B or C. X later acquired the first mortgages on A, B, D and E. After his death, X's executors had the first mortgage on C transferred to them so that they held mortgages of all seven properties. Y wanted to redeem only the mortgage on B. It was admitted in court that X's executors could consolidate A with B, because these were in the hands of a common mortgagee before Y acquired the equities of redemption. The House of Lords held that X's executors could consolidate all the mortgages because the assignee of the equity of redemption was in the same position as the mortgagor. The result was arrived at without enthusiasm by three law lords, of whom only one went into the case in a speech.[62] Lord Davey, who was the one, summarised the doctrine of consolidation as being applicable[63]—

> . . . where at the date when redemption is sought all the mortgages are united in one hand and redeemable by the same person, or where after that state of things has once existed the equities of redemption have become separated. If the purchaser of two or more equities of redemption desires to prevent consolidation, he has it in his power to redeem any one mortgage before consolidation takes place; but if for his own convenience he delays doing so, he runs the same risk as his assignor ran of the mortgages becoming united by transfer in one hand.

(3) A holder of two mortgages originally made to different mortgagees cannot consolidate them against the assignee of the first equity of redemption alone, if the assignment occurred before the second mortgage was made. In *Jennings* v. *Jordan*,[64] first the mortgagor mortgaged property A to X. Secondly, he assigned the equity of

[62] Lord Halsbury, L.C., who did not go into the matter himself, said ([1896] A.C. 190): " . . . I have had an opportunity of considering the judgment prepared by my noble and learned friend (Lord Davey) and I am not prepared to dissent from it. I use that form of expression because I confess I lament the conclusion to which it has been found necessary to come . . . " The whole of Lord Watson's speech was ([1896] A.C. 191): " My Lords, I also have had an opportunity of carefully considering the judgment about to be delivered by my noble and learned friend opposite. For my own part, I should have desired if possible to decide otherwise; but I am compelled to say that I concur with the reasoning and the conclusion of my noble and learned friend."

[63] [1896] A.C. 198-9. See also *Riley* v. *Hall* (1898), 79 L.T. 244, as to the mortgages being united in one hand.

[64] (1881), 6 App. Cas. 698.

redemption of property A to Y. Thirdly, he mortgaged property B to Z. When the mortgages of X and Z later came into the same hands, the House of Lords held Y could redeem A without redeeming B.

There is no clear authority on the following situation: (*a*) mortgage by A of Blackacre to X; (*b*) assignment of the equity of redemption in Blackacre to Y; (*c*) mortgage by A of Whiteacre to X without notice of the assignment to Y. *Jennings* v. *Jordan*[65] does not preclude X from consolidating against Y because in that case the second mortgage was not to the same person as the first. It suggests no consolidation because the equity of Y to redeem Blackacre alone is prior to any equity claimed by X in respect of redemption of Whiteacre. But that is not conclusive because of *Pledge* v. *White*.[66] There the equity to consolidate was held to prevail over a prior equity to redeem a single mortgage. But *Pledge* v. *White* does not guarantee X consolidation because in that case the person seeking to redeem held all the equities of redemption of all the mortgages consolidated whereas Y holds only that in Blackacre. Moreover, this hypothetical situation does not meet the conditions laid down for consolidation by Lord Davey in that case.[67] Of course, the question can arise in respect of mortgages made after 1881 only if the deed mortgaging Blackacre to X excluded Section 17 or Section 93, as the case may be, and in that event might be governed by the interpretation of the clause creating the right to consolidate.[68]

Only mortgages can be consolidated. In *Crickmore* v. *Freeston*[69] there was a first mortgage, in respect of which there were sureties for the debt. Then the mortgagor made a mortgage of another estate to the same mortgagee. The title deeds of a third estate were deposited with the mortgagee as collateral security for part of the debt due on the second mortgage. After that, the first mortgage was paid off, partly by the sureties (who thereupon acquired a transfer right, pro tanto, in the first mortgage). Finally, the second mortgage was paid off. It was held by the Court of Appeal in Chancery that the mortgagee must redeliver the title deeds of the third estate to their owner. The sureties had no interest in them. They could not consolidate their interest in the first mortgage with the deposit of the deeds because that had been merely a bailment for a purpose that had ended, not an equitable mortgage. In *Re Raggett*[70] the Court of Appeal held that two mortgage

[65] See above.
[66] See pp. 199-200, *ante*.
[67] See p. 200, *ante*.
[68] Cf. *Andrews* v. *City Permanent Benefit Building Society* (1881), 44 L.T. 641.
[69] (1870, 40 L.J.Ch. 137.
[70] (1880), 16 Ch.D. 117.

debts could not be consolidated if one of the properties mortgaged had ceased to exist—in this case a lease forfeited by the landlord. In the same year, in *Cummins* v. *Fletcher*[71] the Court of Appeal also held that there could be no consolidation by way of insisting on the redemption of a mortgage on which there had been no default and the debt was not due.

The doctrine applies to all types of mortgage, legal and equitable, of realty and personalty.[72] It applies, too, whatever the occasion for redemption, whether the owner of the equity of redemption is seeking of his own initiative to redeem one mortgage, or is seeking to redeem in a foreclosure action[73] or is seeking to redeem (and has tendered the money due) after the mortgagee has given notice to pay off the one mortgage so as to make his power of sale exercisable.[74] Consolidation is permitted even if the mortgagee acquired his security in one of the properties after the bankruptcy of the mortgagor.[75] The mortgagee's right of consolidation also overrides the paying surety's right to a transfer of a mortgagee. In *Farebrother* v. *Wodehouse*,[76] first, A mortgaged Blackacre to B for £2000, with C as surety. Secondly, A mortgaged Whiteacre to B for £3000 with no surety. B sued C for £2000, which he paid. Romilly, M.R., held that B could insist on C paying the £3000 as well, as a condition of a transfer of the mortgage on Blackacre. (Of course, if C. paid the £3000 he could have a transfer of the mortgage on Whiteacre too.)

Clogs on the Equity of Redemption

Attempts to fetter the equitable right to redeem were quickly stamped upon.[77] In the seventeenth century, when the equity of redemption was being fashioned, the mortgage was looked upon as a kind of nominate contract, many of whose terms were not variable by the agreement of the parties. Thereafter, while the general English law of contract developed, subject to slender requirements of public policy, as a body of principles for the enforcement of bargains, the Court of Chancery continued to insist that terms in mortgage contracts conform to a basic pattern. This was due in part to the fact that the typical seventeenth and eighteenth century mortgagor was conceived to be a landowner in straitened circumstances and the mortgagee a man of affairs ready

71 (1880), 14 Ch.D. 699.
72 *Watts* v. *Symes* (1851), 1 De G.M. & G. 240 (C.A. in Ch.).
73 *Watts* v. *Symes* (1851), 1 De G.M. & G. 240. See p. 243, *post*.
74 *Griffith* v. *Pound* (1889), 45 Ch.D. 553.
75 *Selby* v. *Pomfret* (1861) 7 Jur. N.S. 835 (C.A. in Ch.).
76 (1856), 23 Beav. 18.
77 See pp. 176-8, *ante*.

to take advantage of the mortgagor's feeble bargaining position. It was also due in part to the spirit of the usury laws, which made the Court of Chancery reluctant to allow a lender any advantage out of his security over and above the return of his capital together with a reasonable payment by the borrower for its use.

Mortgagees sought three main types of additional gain: to become owners of the mortgaged property, to get back more than they advanced, and to secure trade advantages when the mortgaged property consisted of premises used for the manufacture or supply of goods. It was settled very early[78] that the equitable right to redeem could not be made of limited duration and this has never been disputed in modern times. The attitude of the courts to other benefits secured to the mortgagee has fluctuated. In the nineteenth and twentieth centuries (and even, to a less extent, in the eighteenth), there have been judges who regretted the stringent limitations on terms in mortgage contracts and who sought to restrict or overrule the earlier decisions. This is a reflection of the growing equality of mortgagor and mortgagee, especially exemplified in the steadily increasing number of borrowings for commercial purposes between businessmen and companies well equipped to take care of themselves. It is a reflection, too, of the growing dependence of a developing economy on credit finance, the repeal of the usury laws in 1854 being but one of the ways in which the legal system reacted. At the same time, there have continued to be occasional oppressive mortgagees. For this reason and because of a subservience to precedent there have been judges who favoured maintenance of the ancient fetters on freedom of contract in mortgage transactions. The cases on the various types of " clog on the equity of redemption " illustrate the divergences of opinion, sometimes producing a change, sometimes a compromise, and sometimes not being readily susceptible of reconciliation with each other. Today we are probably moving towards a greater degree of freedom of choice of terms in mortgage contracts than has yet been attained.

Postponing the redemption date. It is not permissible to contract for a redemption date so far in the future as to make the security practically irredeemable. In *Fairclough* v. *Swan Brewery Co. Ltd.*[79] a lease having about seventeen and a half years to run was mortgaged. Repayment was to be by instalments lasting until six weeks before the expiry of the term, and therefore no legal right to redeem would arise

[78] See pp. 176-7, *ante*.

[79] [1912] A.C. 565, on appeal from Western Australia. See also *Davis* v. *Symons*, [1934] Ch. 442.

under the contract till then. The Privy Council held that the mortgagor could nevertheless redeem two years after making the mortgage.

Different considerations apply where the equity of redemption is not a wasting asset. In *Morgan* v. *Jeffreys*[80] the mortgagor mortgaged a long lease of a hotel to a brewer. The contract provided that only the mortgagee's beer was to be sold for twenty-eight years in the mortgaged premises and that the security was to be irredeemable for the same period. Presumably the point of the postponement was fear that the restrictive trade agreement would be invalid in respect of any period after redemption. Joyce, J., held this postponement void on the grounds that it was too long and that it was one-sided: there was no obligation on the mortgagee to refrain from calling in the loan for twenty-eight years.

It is impossible to say when a long delay of the right of redemption is too long by reference only to the length of the period. A curtailment, for mortgages, of the general duty of parties entering into contracts to perform what they have promised makes sense only in relation to the special circumstances of mortgages and to the extent that these require special protection for mortgagors. If these special circumstances exist at all nowadays, they would seem to consist of a mortgagor, finding himself in an emergency, being taken advantage of by the lender driving a hard bargain which is oppressive by virtue of depriving the mortgagor of a much greater interest in his property than is necessary for the full protection of the mortgagee's money. If this is to be the criterion, each mortgage transaction must be looked at to see whether the postponement of redemption is oppressive on the facts of that case. The decision of the Court of Appeal in *Knightsbridge Estates Trust Ltd.* v. *Byrne*[81] suggests that this is the modern law. Here, a large freehold estate was mortgaged for £310,000, repayable by instalments over forty years. When the mortgagors claimed to redeem just over five years later, it was held that they could not: the postponement for forty years was valid. It was a commercial arrangement between businessmen, not an oppressive bargain where the borrower was at the mercy of an unscrupulous lender, nor was there anything unreasonable in the mere length of the period. Anyway, the Court of Appeal would not relieve even if it was unreasonable unless it was oppressive or unconscionable.

80 [1910] 1 Ch. 620.

81 [1939] Ch. 441, affirmed by the House of Lords on different grounds, [1940] A.C. 613. See also Bodkin, " Postponement of the Right to Redeem " (1941), 5 *Conveyancer and Real Property Lawyer* (*New Series*), 178.

Making the mortgagor part with his title. In *Browne* v. *Ryan*[82] the defendant mortgaged land to the plaintiff and also agreed to sell the land within a year either through the plaintiff (an auctioneer) or, if not through him still paying the plaintiff 5% commission on the sale. The defendant redeemed and then sold the land through someone other than the plaintiff, who sued for £62 10*s*. (5%) commission and failed. The Irish Court of Appeal held that although the suit was not for redemption or foreclosure, the contract was still void as fettering the equity of redemption because redemption was (if the contract was valid) accompanied by an obligation to get rid of the land.

Similar treatment has been meted out to an option given to the mortgagee to buy the equity of redemption.[83] In *Samuel* v. *Jarrah Timber and Wood Paving Corp. Ltd.*[84] the House of Lords held void such an option contained in the mortgage deed. (Actually it was a case of debenture stock mortgaged by the company but this was considered to make the case no different from that of a mortgage of land.) With regret, their lordships stated that the invalidity of such an option was an absolute rule, regardless of the bargain being a fair one between businessmen. One may be forgiven for wondering at such a rule being approved by the highest court in 1904; nevertheless the rule remains unaltered today. But once a mortgage has been made, there is no objection to a wholly separate subsequent transaction whereby the mortgagee gets the equity of redemption or an option to purchase it.[85] However, the grant of an option is not a transaction separate from the mortgage merely because it is done by a document separate from the mortgage deed. It is in substance a question of whether there is a separate consideration. In *Lewis* v. *Frank Love Ltd.*[86] the option given to the mortgagee to purchase part of the mortgaged property was created at the same time as the mortgage was made but by a separate written contract. The mortgagee would make the loan only if he got the option and the mortgagor would give the option only if he got the loan. Plowman, J., held the option void as a clog on the equity of redemption, regarding the granting of the option and the mortgaging of the property as being in substance all one transaction. He said[87]—

> . . . .the doctrine of clog on the equity is a technical doctrine which is not affected by the question whether in fact there has been oppres-

82 [1901] 2 I.R. 653. See also *Re Edwards's Estate* (1861), 11 Ir. Ch. Rep. 367; *Broad* v. *Selfe* (1863), 11 W.R. 1036; Wyman, " The Clog on the Equity of Redemption " (1908), 21 *Harvard Law Review*, 459.

83 See p. 177, *ante*.

84 [1904] A.C. 323. See also *Salt* v. *Marquess of Northampton*, [1892] A.C. 1.

85 *Reeve* v. *Lisle*, [1902] A.C. 461. See also *Maxwell* v. *Tipping*, [1903] 1 I.R. 498.

86 [1961] 1 W.L.R. 261.

87 [1961] 1 W.L.R. 270.

sion, and which applies just as much where parties are represented, as they were here, by solicitors.

Penalties. Modern law has retained the distinction between valid reduction of interest for punctual payment and void increase for late payment.[88] The courts have also frowned upon provisions to the effect that interest overdue be added to the capital sum so as to carry interest upon interest.

The rise of instalment mortgages, under which the borrower makes a series of periodic payments of which each is compounded partly of interest and partly of a capital repayment, has given rise to a number of legal problems, One early determination of the Court of Appeal in Chancery[89] was that a term of such a mortgage making the whole debt payable on default of payment of one instalment was valid.

Mortgage to secure more than the amount advanced. A mortgage may be made to secure a loan or to secure the payment of any other sum of money however due. But if there is a loan and the mortgage is to secure payment of a greater sum to the mortgagee the court will scrutinise the fairness of the bargain.[90] In *Cityland and Property (Holdings) Ltd.* v. *Dabrah*[91] £2,900 was borrowed, the lender being given a charge on registered land to secure £4,553, no interest being provided for. Payment was to be by instalments spread over a period of six years. The mortgagor having fallen into arrears after a year, the mortgagees claimed the whole sum due and interest of 5%. The defendant mortgagor claimed that he should be made to pay only the sum advanced (£2,900) and 5% interest. Goff, J., held that the plaintiffs could have £2,900 and interest at 7%. The £1,653 was a collateral advantage, void because it was " unfair and unconscionable " or " unreasonable." The learned judge said[92]—

> . . . this was not an unsecured loan: a security was being offered with a reasonable margin, not, it is true, a one-third/two-thirds margin as one usually expects in trustee investments, but still the defendant provided £600 and there was that margin in the property to secure the plaintiffs. I think they would have been entitled to charge a higher rate of interest than the normal market rate, or a reasonable premium comparable therewith, but nothing like the extent of 19 per cent. looked at as an interest rate, or 57 per cent.

[88] See p. 178, *ante*.
[89] *Sterne* v. *Beck* (1863), 32 L.J. Ch. 682.
[90] See p. 168, n. 8, *ante*.
[91] [1968] Ch. 166. See also *Chapple* v. *Mahon* (1870), I.R. 5 Eq. 225.
[92] [1968] Ch. 181.

looked at as a capital sum; and it must be borne in mind that this premium was so large that it forthwith destroyed the whole equity and made it a completely deficient security. If default were made, and all that had been secured was the principal and interest, it was likely that on any exercise of the plaintiffs' powers as mortgagees, there would be a surplus for the mortgagor, but this premium destroyed any possibility of that, and it also made the security which was offered deficient.

The invalidity lies not in the very taking of the premium but in its unconscionableness or unreasonableness. A premium may be valid, if not too great, if taken in lieu of interest or in conjunction with a low rate of interest or, possibly, where the security is hazardous. In *Potter* v. *Edwards*[93] the amount borrowed was £700 and the mortgage was expressed to secure £1000. Kindersley, V.-C., held that the mortgagor must pay £1000 to redeem, but it is not clear why. That was referred to as the agreed sum, as if the matter was thus concluded, and there was a passing reference to the security being hazardous.

A very controversial case is *Santley* v. *Wilde*.[94] It was criticised (not for the propositions of law stated by the judges, but for their application to the facts), by Lords Macnaghten and Davey in *Noakes & Co. Ltd.* v. *Rice*[95] and again by the same two law lords in *Bradley* v. *Carritt*.[96] However, it has never been overruled and Lord Lindley (who presided in the Court of Appeal) several times looked back on it with approval from later cases in the House of Lords. In *Santley* v. *Wilde*, the mortgagor had a lease, of which ten years were unexpired, and borrowed £2000 to carry on a theatre. The lease was mortgaged to secure the £2000, repayable by instalments for five years, and to secure payment to the mortgagee of one-third of the net profit rents to be derived from any underleases. The Court of Appeal held that this additional obligation was not a clog on the equity of redemption and that the mortgage could not be redeemed until all the sums expressed to be secured by it had been paid. There was a reasonable bargain, with no fraud, undue influence, overreaching or hard bargaining.

Covenants in restraint of trade. One of the commonest varieties of collateral arrangement in connection with mortgages is a trade facility in cases where the mortgage is of business premises or a business asset and the mortgagee is engaged in the same trade. Although the existence of the usury laws was one of the factors influencing the early

93 (1857), 26 L.J. Ch. 468. See also *Mainland* v. *Upjohn* (1889), 41 Ch. D. 126.
94 [1899] 2 Ch. 474. Cf. *James* v. *Kerr* (1889), 40 Ch.D. 449.
95 [1902] A.C. 24.
96 [1903] A.C. 253.

attitude of equity judges to collateral advantages and clogs on the equity of redemption, the repeal of these laws in 1854 seems to have had very little effect on these equitable rules.[97] The common law has principles under which contracts in restraint of trade may be void for unreasonableness, inter partes or in the public interest, and these apply to restraints in mortgages as much as to those in a vendor and purchaser or a master and servant contract.[98] Subject to that, the validity of the restraint depends on its not being unconscionable.

In *Biggs* v. *Hoddinott*,[99] approved by the House of Lords in *Noakes & Co. Ltd.* v. *Rice*,[1] a hotelier mortgaged his premises to a brewer and covenanted to sell only the mortgagee's beer during the continuance of the security. The Court of Appeal held that this was a collateral stipulation because there was no clog on the equity of redemption (i.e., the restrictive covenant was expressed to last only until redemption), but nothing seems to depend on this, except perhaps that it tended to show reasonableness. The court held it valid on the ground that it was not unconscionable or oppressive but a reasonable bargain between businessmen.

Noakes & Co. Ltd. v. *Rice*[2] is more difficult to place in the context of the precedents. A publican mortgaged his public house, held on a twenty-six year lease, to a brewery company. The mortgage deed contained a covenant by the mortgagor to sell only the mortgagees' beer during the rest of the mortgaged term (i.e., for twenty-six years, even if redemption took place earlier). Six months later the mortgagor gave notice to redeem, free from the covenant. This was refused by the mortgagees, but the House of Lords granted the mortgagor a declaration that he could so redeem. They said that the mortgagee's advantage was not collateral because it was to continue after redemption, and was therefore a clog on the mortgagor's equity. The borrower mortgaged a free house and so was entitled to redeem a free house. This case cannot have decided that the restraint was invalid merely because it was to continue after redemption, for that is inconsistent with the later House of Lords decision in *Kreglinger* v. *New Patagonia*

97 See Firth, "Freedom of Contract in Mortgages" (1895), 11 *Law Quarterly Review*, 144.

98 *Esso Petroleum Co. Ltd.* v. *Harper's Garage (Stourport) Ltd.*, [1968] A.C. 269 (House of Lords). See also *Irish Shell and BP Ltd.* v. *Ryan* [1966] I.R. 75; Whiteman, "Exclusive Distributorship Agreements in the Petrol Industry" (1966), 29 *Modern Law Review*, 507.

99 [1898] 2 Ch. 307.

1 [1902] A.C. 24.

2 [1902] A.C. 24. See also *Bradley* v. *Carritt*, [1903] A.C. 253.

Meat and Cold Storage Co. Ltd.,[3] where *Noakes* v. *Rice* was not dissented from—where, indeed, it was binding according to the doctrine of precedent as operated in those days. It may be explained on the basis that expression of the restraint to continue after redemption is capable of amounting to oppression (or unfairness or unconscionableness or unreasonableness) and that it was an oppressive restraint in this case because it was expressed to endure for the full term of the mortgagor's interest in the land.

Kreglinger v. *New Patagonia Meat and Cold Storage Co. Ltd.*[3] is the present terminus of the law on this subject. The case involved a floating charge redeemable on one month's notice, but the House of Lords treated the principles of the law of mortgages as applicable. The chargor promised to sell certain goods for five years only to the chargees so long as the latter were willing to buy at the best price offered by anyone. After three years the loan was repaid, but the House held that the chargor was still bound to sell the goods to the chargees until the five years had expired. This obligation was a collateral advantage not clogging the equity of redemption and not unfair or oppressive. Their lordships said that *Jennings* v. *Ward*[4] was no longer correct unless the bargain was unconscionable, and that the change was the result of the repeal of the usury laws and the growth of modern varieties of commercial bargaining. Lord Parker of Waddington said[5]—

> . . . I invite your Lordships to hold, that there is now no rule in equity which precludes a mortgagee, whether the mortgage be made upon the occasion of a loan or otherwise, from stipulating for any collateral advantage, provided such collateral advantage is not either (1.) unfair and unconscionable, or (2.) in the nature of a penalty clogging the equity of redemption, or (3.) inconsistent with or repugnant to the contractual and equitable right to redeem.

Priorities of Successive Mortgages

The Land Charges Act, 1925 (*England*)

By Section 10 of this Act—

> (1) The following classes of charges on, or obligations affecting, land may be registered as land charges in the register of land charges, namely:— . . .

[3] [1914] A.C. 25. See also Glanville Williams, "The Doctrine of Repugnancy III: 'Clogging the Equity' and Miscellaneous Applications" (1944), 60 *Law Quarterly Review*, 190-3.

[4] (1705), 2 Vern. 520. See p. 177, *ante*.

[5] [1914] A.C. 60-1.

Class C :—A mortgage charge or obligation affecting land of any of the following kinds, created either before or after the commencement of this Act, but if created before such commencement only if acquired under a conveyance made after such commencement, namely:—

(i) Any legal mortgage not being a mortgage protected by a deposit of documents relating to the legal estate affected, and (where the whole of the land affected is within the jurisdiction of a local deeds registry) not being registered in the local deeds register (in this Act called a " puisne mortgage "); and . . .

(iii) Any other equitable charge, which is not secured by a deposit of documents relating to the legal estate affected and does not arise or affect an interest arising under a trust for sale or a settlement and is not included in any other class of land charge (in this Act called " a general equitable charge "); and

(iv) Any contract by an estate owner or by a person entitled at the date of the contract to have a legal estate conveyed to him to convey or create a legal estate, including a contract conferring either expressly or by statutory implication a valid option of purchase, a right of pre-emption or any other like right (in this Act referred to as " an estate contract "). . . .

(7) A puisne mortgage created before the commencement of this Act may be registered as a land charge before any transfer of the mortgage is made.

Section 13 (2) provides—

A land charge of . . . Class C . . ., created or arising after the commencement of this Act, shall (except as hereinafter provided) be void as against a purchaser of the land charged therewith, or of any interest in such land, unless the land charge is registered in the appropriate register before the completion of the purchase:

Provided that, as respects . . . an estate contract . . . entered into after the commencement of this Act, this subsection only applies in favour of a purchaser of a legal estate for money or money's worth.

Finally, by Section 14 (2)—

After the expiration of one year from the first conveyance, occurring after the commencment of this Act, of a land charge of . . . Class C created before such commencement, the person entitled thereto shall not be able to enforce or recover the land charge or any part thereof as against a purchaser of the land charged therewith, or of any interest in the land, unless the land charge is registered in the appropriate register before the completion of the purchase.

Registration of a puisne mortgage or charge does not interfere with overreaching by a prior mortgagee selling or foreclosing.[6] The system does, however, largely replace the old equitable structure of priorities of claims against the security based on favouring the best equity, determining the relative quality of equities by reference to notice, giving favoured treatment to the owner of a legal estate as against the owner of an equitable interest, and paying equal equities in the order of their creation. The mdern legislative picture is completed by Section 97 of the Law of Property Act, 1925—

> Every mortgage affecting a legal estate in land made after the commencement of this Act, whether legal or equitable (not being a mortgage protected by the deposit of documents relating to the legal estate affected) shall rank according to its date of registration as a land charge pursuant to the Land Charges Act, 1925.
>
> This section does not apply to mortgages or charges of registered land or of land within the jurisdiction of a local deeds registry.

The following dealings are not governed by the Land Charges Act.

(*a*) Mortgages, legal or equitable, of a legal estate, protected or secured by handing the title deeds of the legal estate to the mortgagee. Normally only one such mortgage can be created in respect of any given land and it is normally the first or only mortgage. Should questions of priority involve such a mortgage, they are determined in accordance with equitable principles.

(*b*) Mortgages of equitable interests. Successive mortgages of this type rank in the order in which the incumbrancers gave notice to the trustee or other person under an obligation to pay.[7]

(*c*) Equitable assignments of legal mortgages. The priority of successive equitable assignments of a legal mortgage is determined in accordance with general equitable principles.[8]

(*d*) Puisne mortgages, registered in the local deeds register, of land in Yorkshire.

(*e*) Land charges registered in another charges register, either that under the Companies Act[9] or that under the Land Registration Act, 1925.[10]

The priority inter se of puisne mortgages and general equitable charges is determined in general by the dates of registration (Law of

[6] Sect. 22 (2).

[7] *Dearle* v. *Hall* (1823), 3 Russ. 1 ; Law of Property Act, 1925, Sect. 137. See pp. 300-6, *post*.

[8] *Beddoes* v. *Shaw*, [1937] Ch. 81.

[9] At present, the Companies Act, 1948, Part III.

[10] See Sect. 29.

Property Act, 1925, Section 97). Nothing depends on their legal or equitable nature. It would seem, however, that if (for example) a puisne mortgage is made of Blackacre, followed by a general equitable charge, followed by registration of the puisne mortgage and finally the general equitable charge is registered, the equitable mortgage may have priority over the legal mortgage despite the order of registration because an unregistered puisne mortgage is void as against a subsequent purchaser (Land Charges Act, 1925, Section 13 (2)) and " purchaser " means any person (including a mortgagee or lessee) who, for valuable consideration, takes any interest in land or in a charge on land " (Land Charges Act, 1925, Section 20 (8)). In this example, one could get the same result with a general equitable charge followed by a puisne mortgage or with two puisne mortgages or two general equitable charges. However, an equitable mortgage consisting of an express contract to make a legal mortgage by demise or by subdemise is an estate contract and, if not registered, is void as against a subsequent legal mortgagee but not as against a subsequent equitable mortgagee (Land Charges Act, 1925, Section 13 (2)). If, therefore, such an estate contract, unregistered, were followed by a general equitable charge, the priorities would depend on the dates of registration or, if neither was ever registered, on general equitable principles.[11]

The Registration of Deeds Act (*Ireland*), 1707

Under Section 3 of this Act, a memorial of any written legal or equitable mortgage of a legal estate in land may be registered. The only type of unregistrable mortgage of a legal estate is therefore the equitable mortgage by deposit of title deeds, unaccompanied by any memorandum. As between two registered mortgages, the priority is in order of registration (Section 4). As between a registered mortgage and an unregistered but registrable one, the registered one prevails (Section 5) unless it was taken fraudulently, i.e. with intent to prevail over an earlier unregistered mortgage known to the subsequent mortgagee.[12] As between a registrable mortgage (whether registered or not) and an unregistrable one, general equitable principles apply.[13] So do they to successive mortgages of an equitable interest.

[11] See, further, Megarry and Wade, *The Law of Real Property*, 3rd ed. (1966), pp. 961-71; Megarry, " Priority after 1925 of Mortgages of a Legal Estate in Land " (1941), 7 *Cambridge Law Journal*, 243; Crane, " Equitable Interests in Land: Some Problems of Priority " (1956), 20 *Conveyancer and Property Lawyer*, 444; Lee, " An Insoluble Problem of Mortgagees' Priorities " (1968), 32 Conv. 325.

[12] *Lord Forbes* v. *Deniston* (1722), 4 Bro. P.C. 189; *Workingmen's Benefit Building Soc.* v. *Higgins*, [1945] Ir. Jur. Rep. 38.

[13] *Re Burke's Estate* (1881). 9 L.R.Ir. 24. See also *Re Stevenson's Estate*, [1902] 1 I.R. 23, *sub nom. Fullerton* v. *Provincial Bank of Ireland*, [1903] A.C. 309.

As in England, there are separate statutory provisions for registration of charges created by companies and for charges over registered land.

The General Principles of Equity

In cases to which registry provisions do not apply, the first principle of equity is that mortgages rank in order of their creation.[14] This principle applies to all mortgages of realty in Ireland, as it did in England prior to 1926. In the case of mortgages of equitable interests under trusts of personalty and, in England after 1925, of realty, the order is that of giving notice to the trustees.[15] For example, if there are two successive deposits of title deeds, each mortgagee getting some of the deeds, the first equitable mortgagee will have priority.[16]

Secondly, if two mortgages are both equitable, but the equities are not equal, the better equity prevails even if created later than the other. In *Rice* v. *Rice*[17] there was a conveyance and, although the purchase-money was unpaid, the deeds were handed to the purchaser, a receipt for the purchase-money being endorsed on the conveyance. The purchaser deposited the deeds with a mortgagee as security for a loan. It was held that the mortgagee had a better equity than the vendor's lien. Kindersley, V.C., said[18]—

> In examining into the relative merits (or equities) of two parties having adverse equitable interests, the points to which the Court must direct its attention are obviously these: the nature and condition of their respective equitable interests, the circumstances and manner of their acquisition, and the whole conduct of each party with respect thereto. And in examining into these points it must apply the test, not of any technical rule or any rule of partial application, but the same broad principles of right and justice which a Court of Equity applies universally in deciding upon contested rights.

14 *Beckett* v. *Cordley* (1784), 1 Bro. C.C. 353; *Jones* v. *Jones* (1838), 8 Sim. 633; *Wilmot* v. *Pike* (1845), 5 Hare 14; *Frazer* v. *Jones* (1846), 5 Hare 475; *Cory* v. *Eyre* (1863), 1 De G.J. & S. 149; *Berwick & Co.* v. *Price*, [1905] 1 Ch. 632; *Barclay's Bank Ltd.* v. *Bird*, [1954] Ch. 274. See also *Re Samuel Allen & Sons Ltd.*, [1907] 1 Ch. 575; *Re Morrison, Jones & Taylor Ltd.*, [1910] 1 Ch. 50; Hollond, "Equitable Liens under Hire-Purchase Agreements" (1928), 3 *Cambridge Law Journal*, 173; Guest and Lever, "Hire-Purchase, Equipment Leases and Fixtures" (1963), 27 *Conveyancer and Property Lawyer* (*N.S.*), 30, 37-41; p. 172, *ante*.

15 See pp. 211, *ante*, 300-6, *post*.

16 *Roberts* v. *Croft* (1857), 2 De G. & J. 1; *Dixon* v. *Muckleston* (1872), L.R. 8 Ch. App. 155.

17 (1854), 2 Drew. 73. See also *Dowle* v. *Saunders* (1864), 2 H. & M. 242; *Re Lambert's Estate* (1884), 13 L.R.Ir. 234; *Re Ffrench's Estate* (1887), 21 L.R.Ir. 283; *Re Roche's Estate* (1890), 25 L.R.Ir. 58.

18 2 Drew. 78-9. See also *Farrand* v. *Yorkshire Banking Co.* (1888), 40 Ch. D. 182.

Thirdly, as between a legal mortgage and a prior equitable mortgage, the legal mortgagee is subject to prior equitable mortgages of which (at the time of the legal mortgage) he has notice,[19] but takes free of those of which (at that time) he is without notice.[20] This doctrine, which had an extended application in tacking,[21] requires some elucidation of the nature of notice. In England, the law is in part altered by Sections 198 and 199 of the Law of Property Act, 1925, which provide—

> 198.—(1) The registration of any instrument or matter under the provisions of the Land Charges Act, 1925, or any enactment which it replaces, in any register kept at the land registry or elsewhere, shall be deemed to constitute actual notice of such instrument or matter, and of the fact of such registration, to all persons and for all purposes connected with the land affected, as from the date of registration or other prescribed date and so long as the registration continues in force.
>
> (2) This section operates without prejudice to the provisions of this Act respecting the making of further advances by a mortgagee,[22] and applies only to instruments and matters required or authorised to be registered under the Land Charges Act, 1925.
>
> 199.—(1) A purchaser shall not be prejudicially affected by notice of—
>
> (i) any instrument or matter capable of registration under the provisions of the Land Charges Act, 1925, or any enactment which it replaces, which is void or not enforceable as against him under that Act or enactment, by reason of the non-registration thereof;
>
> (ii)[23] any other instrument or matter or any fact or thing unless—
>
> (*a*) it is within his own knowledge, or would have come to his knowledge if such inquiries and inspections had been made as ought reasonably to have been made by him; or
>
> (*b*) in the same transaction with respect to which a question of notice to the purchaser arises, it has come to the knowledge of his counsel, as such, or of his solicitor or other

19 *Green* v. *Gardner* (1675), Rep. temp. Finch 225; *Aldridge* v. *Duke* (1679), Rep. temp. Finch 439; *Hewitt* v. *Loosemore* (1851), 9 Hare 449; *Jared* v. *Clements*, [1903] 1 Ch. 428.

20 *Plumb* v. *Fluitt* (1791), 2 Anst. 432; *Pilcher* v. *Rawlins* (1872) L.R. 7 Ch. App. 259; *Cave* v. *Cave* (1880), 15 Ch. D. 639; *Caunce* v. *Caunce*, [1969] 1 W.L.R. 286. See also Albery, "Foul Deeds" (1944), 8 *Conveyancer and Property Lawyer (N.S.)*, 145.

21 See pp. 172-5, *ante*, 218-22, *post*.

22 See pp. 220-2, *post*.

23 Sect. 199 (1) (ii) is to the same effect as the Conveyancing Act, 1882, Sect. 3 (1), which is still in force in Ireland.

agent as such, or would have come to the knowledge of his solicitor or other agent, as such, if such inquiries and inspections had been made as ought reasonably to have been made by the solicitor or other agent.

(2) Paragraph (ii) of the last subsection shall not exempt a purchaser from any liability under, or any obligation to perform or observe, any covenant, condition, provision, or restriction contained in any instrument under which his title is derived, mediately or immediately; and such liability or obligation may be enforced in the same manner and to the same extent as if that paragraph had not been enacted.

(3) A purchaser shall not by reason of anything in this section be affected by notice in any case where he would not have been so affected if this section had not been enacted.

(4) This section applies to purchases made either before or after the commencement of this Act.

Section 199 (1) (ii) refers, though not by name, to what before and after the Act have come to be known as actual, constructive and imputed notice, the first two being covered by paragraph (*a*) and the last by paragraph (*b*). Few problems occur in relation to actual or imputed notice,[24] but awkward questions can arise in relation to constructive notice.If a purchaser has actual notice of a fact, instrument or thing, he may be put on inquiry by that actual notice; if he then fails to inquire, he is deemed to have notice of what he would have found had he sought.[25] If, on the other hand, facts of the class which put a person on inquiry are in existence, but the purchaser does not get to know or get actual notice of them, whether he is affected by anything of which he is ignorant depends on his state of mind or standard of conduct. If he deliberately abstains from inquiry to avoid notice he is fraudulent and affected by constructive notice of what due diligence would have discovered. If he is duly diligent he is unaffected by what he does not know. In between these two extremes, the older cases[26] used to equate the effect of mere negligence to that of diligence and the effect of " gross " or " wilful " negligence to that of fraud. The more recent cases on gross negligence have got away from the notion of fraud and from that of constructive notice. In *Oliver* v. *Hinton*[27] Lindley, M.R., said—

[24] See, however, Sheridan, " Notice and Registration " (1950), 9 *Northern Ireland Legal Quarterly*, 33, 34-6, 39-41.

[25] See Sheridan, *Fraud in Equity* (1957), pp. 52-3.

[26] Discussed in Sheridan, *Fraud in Equity*, pp. 53-5.

[27] [1899] 2 Ch. 264, 273. See also *Walker* v. *Linom*, [1907] 2 Ch. 104; *Berwick & Co.* v. *Price*, [1905] 1 Ch. 632, 640.

> The only person who can [override a prior equitable chargee] is a bona fide purchaser for value without notice of her charge. But this does not include a purchaser for value who is so grossly negligent as to take none of the ordinary precautions which ought to be taken in such a matter. . . . He may be a bonâ fide purchaser for value without notice of a prior charge, but he is not entitled to the protection of the Court. I do not base my judgment upon constructive notice of the plaintiff's charge, nor do I mean to suggest that there was any fraud or any complicity in fraud on the part of either the defendant or her agent . . .

Eve, J., in *Hudston* v. *Viney*,[28] said that this language—

> . . . undoubtedly qualifies what had been said in the earlier cases, but it still leaves open in each case the question whether the degree of negligence has been such as to destroy the protection of the legal estate, for I apprehend that by the words " gross negligence " something more is meant than mere carelessness; it must be at least be carelessness of so aggravated a nature as to amount to the neglect of precautions which the ordinarily reasonable man would have observed and to indicate an attitude of mental indifference to obvious risks. If there are no circumstances suggestive of risk I doubt whether the neglect to make inquiries by which the existence of such risk might have been disclosed would as a general rule amount to " gross negligence".

Finally, where there is a legal mortgage followed by an equitable mortgage, in certain circumstances the equitable mortgage will have priority. After some uncertainty the rules of equity became settled during the nineteenth century to the effect described by Fry, L.J., giving the judgment of the Court of Appeal in *Northern Counties of England Fire Insurance C:o.* v. *Whipp*.[29] In that case, A was the manager of the B. Co., and he mortgaged land to the company, giving them the deeds, which were put in a safe to which A had a key. A later extracted the deeds from the safe, and purported to give a first legal mortgage to C. The contest was between the B Co. and C for priority. Fry, L.J., said[30]—

[28] [1921] 1 Ch. 98, 104.

[29] (1884), 26 Ch.D. 482. The earlier cases are discussed in Sheridan, *Fraud in Equity*, pp. 56-60. See also Ewart, " Priorities in Relation to Estoppel " (1897), 13 *Law Quarterly Review*, 46 and 144.

[30] 26 Ch.D. 489-90.

> The expression[31] " gross negligence that amounts to evidence of a fraudulent intention " is certainly embarrassing, for negligence is the not doing of something from carelessness or want of thought or attention; whereas a fraudulent intention is a design to commit some fraud, and leads men to do or omit doing a thing not carelessly but for a purpose. But Lord Eldon seems to have meant by his words to describe the not doing of something, so ordinarily done by honest men under the circumstances, as to be really attributable not to negligence or carelessness, but to fraudulent intention. In short, it appears to us that in the mouth of Lord Eldon the word " negligence " was used simply to express non-feasance.

The Court of Appeal proceeded[32] to indicate two classes of case where the legal mortgagee would lose his priority to a subsequent equitable incumbrancer. The first is where there is assistance or connivance at fraud, i.e., where the legal mortgagee fraudulently misrepresents that he has not that legal interest, or authorises someone else to do so, or stands by while someone else does so, or supplies someone else with the means of doing so. The second occurs where a mortgagee permits the mortgagor to have the deeds in order to borrow again, in which case the mortgagee must bear the loss if the mortgagor suppresses the existence of the first mortgage. The court made no distinction between not getting the deeds at all and parting with them. They also said that while, in the first class of case, fraud was required before the legal mortgagee would be postponed to a later incumbrancer, the omission to use ordinary care, if not otherwise explained, might be sufficient evidence of assistance or connivance at fraud. The Court of Appeal came to the conclusion that the B Co. were very careless but there was no evidence of fraud and the loss must fall on C.

The Law of Property Act, 1925, Section 13, provides—

> This Act shall not prejudicially affect the right or interest of any person arising out of or consequent on the possession by him of any documents relating to a legal estate in land, nor affect any question arising out of or consequent upon any omission to obtain or any other absence of possession by any person of any documents relating to a legal estate in land.

31 Used by Lord Eldon, in *Evans* v. *Bicknell* (1801), 6 Ves. 174, 190-1, where he said: " The doctrine at last is, that the mere circumstance of parting with the title-deeds, unless there is fraud, concealment, or some such purpose, or that gross negligence, that amounts to evidence of a fraudulent intention, is not of itself a sufficient ground to postpone the first mortgagee. . . . Where there has been mere negligence, though it may have very mischievous consequences, the Court has not charged the party, unless it has been so gross as to amount to evidence of fraud." So also *Colyer* v. *Finch* (1856), 5 H.L.C. 905.

32 26 Ch.D. 494.

Tacking

The tabula in naufragio,[33] whereby an equitable mortgagee who took his security without notice of a prior equitable incumbrance subsequently acquired priority over that incumbrance by getting in the legal estate, was abolished by the Law of Property Act, 1925, Section 94, of which subsections (3) and (4) provide—

(3) Save in regard to the making of further advances as aforesaid, the right to tack is hereby abolished:

Provided that nothing in this Act shall affect any priority acquired before the commencement of this Act by tacking, or in respect of further advances made without notice of a subsequent incumbrance or by arrangement with the subsequent incumbrancer.

(4) This section applies to mortgages of land made before or after the commencement of this Act, but not to charges registered under the Land Registration Act, 1925, or any enactment replaced by that Act.

In Ireland, the possibilities of this type of tacking, though not eliminated, are reduced by the Registration of Deeds Act, 1707, as a result of which an equitable incumbrancer can tack only if his equitable mortgage is unregistrable (by deposit of title deeds) or the prior equitable mortgage over which he seeks to gain priority is unregistered.

The turn of the century saw much elaboration of tacking. Four cases will serve as examples. They go some way towards showing why tacking has been abolished in England, for it is impossible to see the equity in altering the priorities of equal equities by a scramble to buy the legal estate.

In *Taylor* v. *Russell*,[34] M, the fee simple owner, gave a legal mortgage to Legard of many properties, including Blackacre, but Legard did not get the title deeds to Blackacre. Then M sold Blackacre to Toward (who could, of course, get only the equity of redemption). Toward, using forged title deeds, mortgaged Blackacre to Taylor (necessarily an equitable mortgage). Later, using the genuine title deeds, Toward mortgaged Blackacre to Russell (another equitable mortgage), Russell having no notice of Taylor's incumbrance. Finally, Russell bought the legal estate in Blackacre from Legard's personal representatives. The House of Lords held that Russell had thus acquired for his

[33] See pp. 172-5, *ante*. It was abolished by the Vendor and Purchaser Act, 1874, Sect. 7, but this section was repealed, as from the date of its coming into force, by the Land Transfer Act, 1875, Sect. 129 (England), and the Conveyancing Act, 1881, Sect. 73 (Ireland).

[34] [1892] A.C. 244.

equitable mortgage priority over that of Taylor. It did not matter whether Russell had notice of Taylor when he bought from Legard's representatives so long as he was without notice when he took his equitable mortgage.

In *Bailey* v. *Barnes*[35] J, the fee simple owner, gave a legal mortgage of Blackacre to A and then an equitable mortgage of the same premises to Bailey. A transferred his mortgage to Barnes, who improperly exercised his power of sale in favour of M, i.e., purported to convey to M the fee simple free from J's equity of redemption. M then gave a legal mortgage to C, after which he sold the equity of redemption to L. At this stage, the sale by Barnes to M was set aside by the court, which meant that C still had the legal estate, but subject to the original equity of redemption created by J's mortgage to A, which further meant that Bailey's equitable mortgage was restored and was prior in time to L's equitable interest in the property. L, who had no notice of Bailey's equitable incumbrance when he acquired his own, now bought the legal estate from C and was held by the Court of Appeal thus to have postponed Bailey to his (L's) combined equitable and legal interests.

In *Taylor* v. *London and County Banking Co.*[36] the facts were as follows. First, T lent his own money on the security of leaseholds mortgaged to him by subdemise. Secondly, having received money belonging to the B settlement and misappropriated it, he purported to assign the mortgage in satisfaction, but did not pass the legal estate. The cestui que trust of the B settlement found out about the misappropriation and purported reparation, but did nothing. Next, T, sole trustee of the T settlement, appointed N co-trustee and conveyed the mortgage to himself and N but retained possession of the sublease. After that T deposited the sublease with the bank as security for a loan and gave them a power of attorney to deal with the legal estate. T then disappeared. Notice was thereupon given to the bank of the T settlement's interest in the mortgage, after which the bank purported to exercise the power of attorney to acquire the legal estate. The Court of Appeal held that N, as trustee of the T settlement, had priority over both the bank and the B settlement. Stirling, L.J., said[37]—

> An equitable mortgagee, who has made an advance without notice of a prior equitable title, may gain priority by getting in the legal estate, unless there are circumstances which make it inequitable for him to do so. One case which falls within this exception is

[35] [1894] 1 Ch. 25.
[36] [1901] 2 Ch. 231.
[37] [1901] 2 Ch. 256.

where the mortgagee has notice that the legal title, at the time when it is so got in, is held on an express trust in favour of persons who assert a claim to the property.

This rule that an equitable mortgagee cannot tack after notice of a prior incumbrance by getting in the legal estate from a bare trustee for the prior incumbrancer had been approved by the Court of Appeal earlier, in *Harpham* v. *Shacklock*,[38] and was the basis of the later decision of the Irish Court of Appeal in *Workingman's Benefit Building Soc.* v. *Dixon*.[39] In the latter case, X, the fee simple owner of land, agreed orally to grant a lease of it to D. D then executed a mortgage of his interest to the W society, who registered it. This was an equitable mortgage for D's interest, an agreement for a lease, was itself equitable. X then executed the lease in favour of D. At a later date, the W society asked X for the lease but got no reply. The next thing that happened was that D deposited the lease with the Ulster Bank by way of mortgage. The W society discovered this and gave notice of their mortgage to the bank, who then got a legal mortgage from D. It was held that the W society had priority over the Ulster Bank because the bank, when taking the legal estate, had express notice that D was trustee of the lease for the society.

Peacock v. *Burt*,[40] which has been frowned upon but never overruled, represents the opposite extreme. The second mortgagee gave notice of his interest to the first mortgagee. Then the third mortgagee, who had no notice of the second mortgage, came on the scene by paying off the first mortgagee, advancing more money to the mortgagor, and taking as security a transfer of the legal estate from the first mortgagee. Pepys, M.R., held that the third mortgagee came before the second as to the total advanced by him, not just as to the amount paid to the first mortgagee. While this appears to be a fraud upon the second mortgagee by the first, there is no fraud by the third mortgagee. The latter did not have notice of any trust for the second mortgagee: indeed, there was no trust, in all probability, to have notice of.

Apart from the tabula in naufragio, whereby the owner of a sinking equitable incumbrance uses the legal estate as the plank, the Court of Chancery developed the doctrine of tacking further advances.[41] Where a mortgage was expressed to secure not only the amount lent at the time of the mortgage but also further sums that might be lent in the future by the mortgagee to the mortgagor, and the mortgagor gave

[38] (1881), 19 Ch.D. 207.
[39] [1908] 1 I.R. 582.
[40] (1834), 4 L.J. Ch. 33.
[41] See p. 175, *ante*.

someone else a second mortgage before borrowing more money from the first mortgagee, a question of priorities arose. The rule came to be settled that the further advances by the first mortgagee could in general be regarded as repayable as part of the obligation secured by his first incumbrance, i.e., before anything was due on the second mortgage. If, however, the first mortgagee received notice of the existence of the second mortgage, the second mortgagee took priority over any advances made by the first mortgagee after that notice.[42] The Court of Appeal decided in *West* v. *Williams*[43] that after notice of an intervening incumbrance the first mortgagee could not tack further advances to his original security so as to gain priority for them over the intervening incumbrancer even if the first mortgagee was obliged by the terms of his mortgage to make such advances, but they thought that on receiving notice of the later incumbrance the first mortgagee was released from that obligation.

In England, the Law of Property Act, 1925, Section 94,[44] provides—

(1) After the commencement of this Act, a prior mortgagee shall have a right to make further advances to rank in priority to subsequent mortgages (whether legal or equitable)—

(*a*) if an arrangement has been made to that effect with the subsequent mortgagees; or

(*b*) if he had no notice of such subsequent mortgages at the time when the further advance was made by him; or

(*c*) whether or not he had such notice as aforesaid, where the mortgage imposes an obligation on him to make such further advances.

This subsection applies whether or not the prior mortgage was made expressly for securing further advances.

(2) In relation to the making of further advances after the commencement of this Act a mortgagee shall not be deemed to have notice of a mortgage merely by reason that it was registered as a

42 *Hopkinson* v. *Rolt* (1861), 9 H.L.C. 514, Lord Cranworth dissenting, where Lord Campbell, L.C. (pp. 534-5) and Lord Chelmsford (p. 553) stressed that the rule of no priority for advances after notice was based on the fact that if the first mortgagee did not like being postponed he need not make any further advance. See also *Daun* v. *City of London Brewery Co.* (1869), L.R. 8 Eq. 155; *Menzies* v. *Lightfoot* (1871), L.R. 11 Eq. 459; *Bradford Banking Co. Ltd.* v. *Henry Briggs, Son & Co. Ltd.* (1886), 12 App. Cas. 29, applying the same rule to shares. Ireland: *Macnamara's Estate* (1884), 13 L.R. Ir. 158 ; *Re Keogh's Estate*, [1895] 1 I.R. 201.

43 [1899] 1 Ch. 132.

44 And see Rowley, " Tacking Further Advances " (1958), 22 *Conveyancer and Property Lawyer* (*N.S.*), 44.

land charge or in a local deeds registry, if it was not so registered at the date of the original advance or when the last search (if any) by or on behalf of the mortgagee was made, whichever last happened.

This subsection only applies where the prior mortgage was made expressly for securing a current account or other further advances . . .

(4) This section applies to mortgages of land made before or after the commencement of this Act, but not to charges registered under the Land Registration Act, 1925, or any enactment replaced by that Act.

In Ireland there has been no statutory change of this kind, and the rules of equity are in full force with regard to unregistered land. Tacking of further advances is unaffected by the Registration of Deeds Act (Ireland), 1707. The further advance by the first mortgagee is not a disposition of land and so is not registrable. Registration of the intervening incumbrance is not notice of it to the first mortgagee. On these grounds the Irish Court of Appeal held, in *Re O'Byrne's Estate*,[45] that a further advance could be added to the amount secured by the first mortgage so as to squeeze out a registered intervening incumbrance of which the first mortgagee had no notice when making his further advance.

Relation of the Parties to the Property

Mortgagor in Possession

Mortgagees have a right to possession of the mortgaged premises as against their mortgagors. Nevertheless, it is and for a few centuries has been usual for the mortgagor to remain in possession until steps have to be taken by the mortgagee to realise the security or to get arrears of interest paid off. The mortgagee does not lightly enter the mortgaged premises because by doing so he saddles himself with an apparatus of duties and responsibilities.[46] If the mortgage is a legal mortgage and the mortgagor is occupying the premises, in the absence of an express agreement between the parties it is not easy to ascribe the mortgagor's possession to any broader category of possessory capacities. In particular, the mortgagor does not seem to be a tenant at will (though he is in at the pleasure of the mortgagee, not adversely to him) or tenant at sufferance of the mortgagee. Nothing seems to be gained by attempting to describe his position in any other way than as mortgagor in possession.[47]

[45] (1885), 15 L.R. Ir. 373.
[46] See pp. 235-7, *post*.
[47] See, further, Turner, *The Equity of Redemption*, pp. 88-110.

So long as he is left in possession by the mortgagee, the mortgagor has got to manage the property, which he can do in his own interests provided he does not prejudice those of the mortgagee. For example, the mortgagor can cut timber if the land is adequate security without it,[48] but the mortgagee will get an injunction to restrain him if the security is scanty.[49] In *Fairclough* v. *Marshall*[50] the Court of Appeal decided that, the mortgaged property being let, a mortgagor in possession (by receiving the rents and profits) could enforce a restrictive covenant against the lessee. Cotton, L.J., said[51]—

> The exact relation of mortgagor and mortgagee, when the mortgagee is not in possession, is not very clearly defined. But it is sufficient to say that if the mortgagee does not assert his right to possession, and the mortgagor is left to manage the property, he has a right to insist, without reference to the mortgagee, on the observance of any obligations, the non-observance of which would injuriously affect the premises.

The power of the mortgagor to take action is strengthened by statute. Section 141 (1) of the Law of Property Act, 1925, which refers to rent, covenants and provisions in leases binding on the lessee, provides—

> Any such rent, covenant or provision shall be capable of being recovered, received, enforced, and taken advantage of, by the person from time to time entitled, subject to the term, to the income of the whole or any part, as the case may require, of the land leased.

In *Turner* v. *Walsh*[52] the Court of Appeal held that the Conveyancing Act, 1881, Section 10 (which Section 141 of the 1925 Act replaces),[53] enabled a mortgagor in possession to sue his lessee for damages for breach of a covenant to repair. By Section 98 of the 1925 Act—

> (1) A mortgagor for the time being entitled to the possession or receipt of the rents and profits of any land, as to which the mortgagee has not given notice of his intention to take possession or to enter into the receipt of the rents and profits thereof, may sue for such possession, or for the recovery of such rents or profits, or to prevent or recover damages in respect of any trespass or other wrong relative

[48] *King* v. *Smith* (1843), 2 Hare 239.

[49] *Usborne* v. *Usborne* (1740), Dick. 75; *Humphreys* v. *Harrison* (1820), 1 Jac. & W. 581; *Harper* v. *Aplin* (1886), 54 L.T. 383.

[50] (1878), 4 Ex. D. 37.

[51] 4 Ex. D. 48-9.

[52] [1909] 2 K.B. 484.

[53] Sect. 10 of the 1881 Act is still the operative provision in Ireland.

thereto, in his own name only, unless the cause of action arises upon a lease or other contract made by him jointly with any other person.

(2) This section does not prejudice the power of a mortgagor independently of this section to take proceedings in his own name only, either in right of any legal estate vested in him or otherwise.

(3) This section applies whether the mortgage was made before or after the commencement of this Act.

This section replaces the Judicature Act, 1873, Section 25 (5).[54]

Commercially the most important power of a mortgagor, apart from selling or remortgaging, is that of letting the premises. Before 1881, a mortgagor could grant leases of the equity of redemption, but, in the absence of agreement by the mortgagee, no such lease would bind him, i.e., no such lease would impede the mortgagee's right to take physical possession nor would it survive foreclosure. Statutory powers of leasing were introduced by the Conveyancing Acts, 1881, Section 18, and 1911, Section 3, which are still in force in Ireland. In England, they have been replaced by the Law of Property Act, 1925, Section 99, which provides as follows—

99.[55]—(1) A mortgagor of land while in possession shall, as against every incumbrancer, have power to make from time to time any such lease of the mortgaged land,[56] or any part thereof, as is by this section authorised.

(2) A mortgagee of land while in possession[57] shall, as against all prior incumbrancers, if any, and as against the mortgagor, have power to make from time to time any such lease as aforesaid.

(3) The leases which this section authorises[58] are—

[54] The provision in force in Ireland is the Judicature (Ireland) Act, 1877, Sect. 28 (5).

[55] With minor differences and one significant difference (see p. 225, n. 61, *post*), Sect. 18 of the 1881 Act corresponds to Sect. 99 (1)-(17) of the 1925 Act and Sect. 3 (10), (11), of the 1911 Act to Sect. 99 (18), (19), of the 1925 Act.

[56] A single lease of the mortgaged land together with other land at a single rent is not binding on the mortgagee: *King* v. *Bird*, [1909] 1 K.B. 837.

[57] As to the position of the mortgagee in possession generally, see pp. 230-8, *post*.

[58] See also the Landlord and Tenant Act, 1954, Sect. 36 (4), and the Business Tenancies Act (Northern Ireland) 1964, Sect. 17(4), (5), p. 226, n. 65, *post*.

(i) agricultural or occupation[59] leases for any term[60] not exceeding twenty-one years, or, in the case of a mortgage made after the commencement of this Act, fifty years;[61] and

(ii) building leases for any term not exceeding ninety-nine years, or, in the case of a mortgage made after the commencement of this Act, nine hundred and ninety-nine years.[61]

(4) Every person making a lease under this section may execute and do all assurances and things necessary or proper in that behalf.

(5) Every such lease shall be made to take effect in possession not later than twelve months after its date.

(6) Every such lease shall reserve the best rent that can reasonably be obtained, regard being had to the circumstances of the case, but without any fine being taken.[62]

(7) Every such lease shall contain a covenant by the lessee for payment of the rent, and a condition of re-entry[63] on the rent not being paid within a time therein specified not exceeding thirty days.

(8) A counterpart of every such lease shall be executed by the lessee and delivered to the lessor, of which execution and delivery the execution of the lease by the lessor shall, in favour of the lessee and all persons deriving title under him, be sufficient evidence.

(9) Every such building lease shall be made in consideration of the lessee, or some person by whose direction the lease is granted, having erected, or agreeing to erect within not more than five years from the date of the lease, buildings, new or additional, or having improved or repaired buildings, or agreeing to improve or repair buildings within that time, or having executed, or agreeing to execute within that time, on the land leased, an improvement for or in connexion with building purposes.

(10) In any such building lease a peppercorn rent, or a nominal or other rent less than the rent ultimately payable, may be made payable for the first five years, or any less part of the term.

(11) In case of a lease by the mortgagor, he shall, within one month after making the lease, deliver to the mortgagee, or, where there are

59 See *Brown* v. *Peto*, [1900] 2 Q.B. 653 (C.A.).

60 See *King* v. *Bird* [1909] 1 K.B. 837.

61 The periods are still (i) 21 years and (ii) 99 years in Ireland under the Conveyancing Act, 1881, Sect. 18 (3).

62 See *Coutts & Co.* v. *Somerville*, [1935] Ch. 438.

63 See *Thomas Murphy & Co. Ltd.* v. *Marren*, [1933] I.R. 393.

more than one, to the mortgagee first in priority, a counterpart of the lease duly executed by the lessee, but the lessee shall not be concerned to see that this provision is complied with.[64]

(12) A contract to make or accept a lease under this section may be enforced by or against every person on whom the lease if granted would be binding.

(13) This section applies only if and as far as a contrary intention is not expressed by the mortgagor and mortgagee in the mortgage deed, or otherwise in writing, and has effect subject to the terms of the mortgage deed or of any such writing and to the provisions therein contained.[65]

(14) The mortgagor and mortgagee may, by agreement in writing, whether or not contained in the mortgage deed, reserve to or confer on the mortgagor or the mortgagee, or both, any further or other powers of leasing or having reference to leasing; and any further or other powers so reserved or conferred shall be exercisable, as far as may be, as if they were conferred by this Act, and with all the like incidents, effects, and consequences:

Provided that the powers so reserved or conferred shall not prejudicially affect the rights of any mortgagee interested under any other mortgage subsisting at the date of the agreement, unless that mortgagee joins in or adopts the agreement.

(15) Nothing in this Act shall be construed to enable a mortgagor or mortgagee to make a lease for any longer term or on any other conditions than such as could have been granted or imposed by the mortgagor, with the concurrence of all the incumbrancers, if this Act and the enactments replaced by this section had not been passed:

Provided that, in the case of a mortgage of leasehold land, a lease granted under this section shall reserve a reversion of not less than one day.

(16) Subject as aforesaid, this section applies to any mortgage made after the thirty-first day of December, eighteen hundred and eighty-one, but the provisions thereof, or any of them, may, by

64 See *Public Trustee* v. *Lawrence*, [1912] 1 Ch. 789.

65 By the Landlord and Tenant Act, 1954, Sect. 36 (4): " A lease executed or agreement made under this section, in a case where the interest of the lessor is subject to a mortgage, shall be deemed to be one authorised by section ninety-nine of the Law of Property Act, 1925 . . ., and subsection (13) of that section . . . shall not have effect in relation to such a lease or agreement." The Business Tenancies Act (Northern Ireland) 1964, Sect. 17 (4), (5), is to the like effect. There is no such legislation in the Republic of Ireland.

By the Agricultural Holdings Act, 1948, Sect. 95 and 7th sch., para. 2, the Law of Property Act, 1925, Sect. 99 (13), does not apply to a mortgage made after 1st March 1948 of agricultural land within the meaning of the Agriculture Act, 1947. There is no such legislation in Ireland.

agreement in writing made after that date between mortgagor and mortgagee, be applied to a mortgage made before that date, so nevertheless that any such agreement shall not prejudicially affect any right or interest of any mortgagee not joining in or adopting the agreement.

(17) The provisions of this section referring to a lease shall be construed to extend and apply, as far as circumstances admit, to any letting, and to an agreement, whether in writing or not, for leasing or letting.

(18) For the purposes of this section " mortgagor " does not include an incumbrancer deriving title under the original mortgagor.

(19) The powers of leasing conferred by this section shall, after a receiver of the income of the mortgaged property or any part thereof has been appointed by a mortgagee under his statutory power, and so long as the receiver acts, be exercisable by such mortgagee instead of by the mortgagor, as respects any land affected by the receivership, in like manner as if such mortgagee were in possession of the land, and the mortgagee may, by writing, delegate any of such powers to the receiver.

By section 100,[66] a mortgagor in possession and a mortgagee in possession have power to accept a surrender of a lease of the mortgaged land, for the purpose only of granting a lease authorised by Section 99 or by agreement between the parties.

If a mortgagor grants a lease in conformity with the statutory power or in conformity with a power created by agreement with the mortgagee (including a power granted by the mortgage instrument), the tenant is secure against the mortgagee. On the other hand, a lease which is not authorised in one of these ways will not generally interfere with the mortgagee's power to enter the premises and take possession or to foreclose or sell so as to destroy the lessee's interest in the land. A mortgagor's lease may be unauthorised because the mortgagor is not in possession or because the lease does not comply with the statutory requirements or because the statutory powers have been excluded or restricted by agreement between the mortgagor and mortgagee and the lease is outside the restricted power (if any) left with the mortgagor. It is not usual for mortgage deeds to exclude the mortgagor's power of leasing entirely, but it is usual to provide that the power is not to be exercised without the consent of the mortgagee.

[66] Replacing the Conveyancing Act, 1911, Sect. 3 (1)-(7), still in force in Ireland.

Sometimes an unauthorised lease may be saved by Section 152 of the Law of Property Act, 1925,[67] subsection (1) of which provides that, if exercise of a power of leasing was intended, the lease was made in good faith, and the lessee has entered, the invalid lease is to "take effect in equity as a contract for the grant, at the request of the lessee, of a valid lease under the power, of like effect as the invalid lease, subject to such variations as may be necessary in order to comply with the terms of the power . . ." Failing that, the position of the lessee under an unauthorised lease is that he has a lease only of the equity of redemption and his only protection against the mortgagee is to redeem.[68]

In *Rust* v. *Goodale*[69] there was a mortgage (necessarily equitable) of an agreement for a lease, followed by a second mortgage of it. Both mortgages excluded the statutory powers of leasing but, undeterred by this, the mortgagor sublet. After that, the head lease was granted to the mortgagor in accordance with the agreement he had mortgaged. The first mortgagee contracted to sell the mortgaged premises to the second mortgagee subject to the underlease (but with no warranty as to its validity or otherwise). The first mortgagee then got a legal charge from the mortgagor (thus enabling the contract for sale to be performed) and conveyed the premises to the purchaser, but there was no mention of the underlease in the conveyance. On the purchaser suing the subtenant for possession, Harman, J., held: (a) the mortgagee's right to object to the mortgagor's unauthorised tenant was not lost by sale or foreclosure; (b) that right passed to the purchaser without express assignment; (c) an unauthorised lease by a mortgagor was good by estoppel against the mortgagor but was void as between lessee and mortgagee;[70] (d) the defendant subtenant did not get a legal estate before the plaintiff purchaser got one because an unauthorised lease did not create a legal estate at all.[71]

The mortgagee may expressly adopt an unauthorised lease and so part with his right to challenge it. Alternatively, the mortgagee may so conduct himself as to be estopped from denying that the mortgagor's

67 Replacing the Leases Acts, 1849 and 1850, still in force in Ireland. For an example, see *Pawson* v. *Revell*, [1958] 2 Q.B. 360 (C.A.).

68 See *Tarn* v. *Turner* (1888), 39 Ch.D. 456, p. 190, *ante*.

69 [1957] Ch. 33, commented on by Crane, "Equitable Interests in Land: Some Problems of Priority" (1956), 20 *Conveyancer and Property Lawyer*, 444.

70 See also *Iron Trades Employers' Insurance Assoc.* v. *Union of House and Land Investors Ltd.* [1937] Ch. 313; *Parker* v. *Braithwaite*, [1952] 2 All E.R. 837; *Hughes* v. *Waite*, [1957] 1 W.L.R. 713; *Bolton Building Soc.* v. *Cobb*, [1966] 1 W.L.R. 1.

71 See also *Dudley and District Benefit Building Soc.* v. *Emerson*, [1949] Ch. 707 (C.A.); *Bolton Building Soc.* v. *Cobb*, [1966] 1 W.L.R. 1.

unauthorised lessee has a valid tenancy of the premises,[72] but merely refraining for some time from evicting the lessee is not such conduct.[73] If the mortgagee does some confirmatory act, such as receiving rent from the lessee, this merely estops him from denying the tenancy, not necessarily from denying that the tenancy is of the precise kind purported to be created by the unauthorised lease. Unless the mortgagee does acts making it inequitable to challenge the lease, his bare recognition of the tenancy will make the lessee a tenant from year to year, week to week, etc., as appropriate, as against him.

The commonest case in which a mortgagor's lease is alleged to be void as against the mortgagee is one in which the mortgagor is said to have granted the lease without the mortgagee's consent in contravention of a term in the mortgage deed. Should there be a dispute as to whether the mortgagee did consent, the onus of proving consent rests upon the lessee.[74] The absence of consent does not make the lease a breach of covenant by the mortgagor, but merely stops the lease, in normal cases, binding the mortgagee.[75] The mortgage deed (or other agreement between mortgagor and mortgagee) could not restrict the mortgagor's power to let the equity of redemption: any such attempted restriction would be void as a clog on the equity.[76]

Absence of the mortgagee's consent where the mortgage deed requires it does not always even prevent the lease binding the mortgagee. In *Lever Finance Ltd.* v. *Needleman's Trustee* [77] a peculiarly drafted clause led to the mortgagee being estopped. The mortgage contained express provision against leasing by the mortagor without the mortgagee's consent, but provided that it was not necessary to express the consent in the lease and that the lessee was not to be concerned to see that consent had been given. The mortgagor having granted a lease without the mortgagee's consent, the mortgagee was held to be estopped from denying its validity against him. Another unusual case, in which the persons in possession turned out to be validly holding against the mortgagor under one tenancy and against the mortgagee under

[72] *Parker* v. *Braithwaite*, [1952] 2 All E.R. 837; *Taylor* v. *Ellis*, [1960] Ch. 368; *Stroud Building Soc.* v. *Delamont*, [1960] 1 W.L.R. 431. Ireland: *Re O'Rourke's Estate* (1889), 23 L.R. Ir. 497.

[73] *Parker* v. *Braithwaite*, [1952] 2 All E.R. 837; *Taylor* v. *Ellis*, [1960] Ch. 368; *Barclay's Bank Ltd.* v. *Kiley*, [1961] 1 W.L.R. 1050. Ireland: *Re O'Rourke's Estate* (1889), 23 L.R. Ir. 497.

[74] *Taylor* v. *Ellis*, [1960] Ch. 368.

[75] *Iron Trades Employers' Insurance Assoc.* v. *Union of House and Land Investors Ltd.*, [1937] Ch. 313.

[76] See pp. 202-9, *ante*

[77] [1956] Ch. 375.

another, is *Barclays Bank Ltd.* v. *Stasek*.[78] The premises were let before the mortgage, which excluded the mortgagor's power of leasing without the mortgagee's consent. After the mortgage, the mortgagor made a new letting to the same tenants without the mortgagee's consent. Since the new letting superseded the old without the old running out, as against the mortgagor the old tenancy had been surrendered by operation of law. As against the mortgagee, however, the new tenancy was void, and Danckwerts, J., held that therefore there was no surrender of the old tenancy as against the mortgagee.

Mortgagee in Possession

The right to possession. As against the mortgagor, though not always as against another incumbrancer, a mortgagee has a right to go into possession of the mortgaged premises. A chargee who cannot bring foreclosure proceedings has no such right. A mortgagee does not usually take possession unless he wishes to grant a lease or sell with vacant possession, but that is his own choice. In *Four-Maids Ltd.* v. *Dudley Marshall (Properties) Ltd.* [79] Harman, J., said—

> The mortgagee may go into possession before the ink is dry on the mortgage unless there is something in the contract, express or by implication, whereby he has contracted himself out of that right. He has the right because he has a legal term of years in the property or its statutory equivalent.[80] If there is an attornment clause,[81] he must give notice. If there is a provision that, so long as certain payments are made, he will not go into possession, then he has contracted himself out of his rights. Apart from that, possession is a matter of course.

The court has no discretion to keep a legal mortgagee out, but in the action for possession may allow the mortgagor a short adjournment in which to redeem if there is a reasonable prospect of his paying the debt.[82]

78 [1957] Ch. 28, commented on by Megarry (1957), 73 *Law Quarterly Review*, 14. See also Prichard, " Tenancy by Estoppel " (1964), 80 *L.Q.R.*, 370.

79 [1957] Ch. 317, 320. See also *Marquis Cholmondeley* v. *Lord Clinton* (1817), 2 Mer. 171, 359, *per* Grant, M.R.; *Marquis Cholmondeley* v. *Lord Clinton* (1820), 2 Jac. & W. 1, 183, *per* Plumer, M.R.; *Bagnall* v. *Villar* (1879), 12 Ch. D. 812; *R.* v. *Judge Willes*, [1954] 1 W.L.R. 136; *R.* v. *Judge Dutton Briant*, [1957] 2 Q.B. 497, approved by the Court of Appeal in *West Penwith R.D.C.* v. *Gunnell*, [1968] 1 W.L.R. 1153; *Birmingham Citizens Permanent Building Soc.* v. *Caunt*, [1962] Ch. 883; Rudden, "Mortgagee's Right to Possession" (1961), 25 *Conveyancer and Property Lawyer* (*N.S.*), 278. Ireland: *Green* v. *Burns* (1879), 6 L.R. Ir. 173.

80 In Ireland, he may have a freehold estate: see p. 180, *ante*. As to the equitable mortgagee's right to possession, see p. 231, *post*.

81 See pp. 232-5, *post*.

82 *Birmingham Citizens Permanent Building Soc.* v. *Caunt*, [1962] Ch. 883. See also *London Permanent Benefit Building Soc.* v. *de Baer*, [1969] 1 Ch. 321; Megarry (1957), 73 *Law Quarterly Review*, 300.

In *Re O'Neill*,[83] a Northern Ireland case, the mortgagee had obtained a court order for sale of the land, but the bankrupt mortgagor would not leave. The mortgagee successfully sought, from the Queen's Bench Division, possession so as to sell the property vacant. Lowry, J., said[84]—

> . . . the Supreme Court has an inherent jurisdiction to make an order putting a legal or equitable mortgagee into possession and . . . such an order may be made not only in the Chancery Division, but also by a judge exercising bankruptcy jurisdiction in the Queen's Bench Division.

Normally, though, such proceedings are brought in the Chancery Division, to which mortgage business is assigned by statute.

The only difference between a legal mortgagee and an equitable mortgagee, when seeking possession against the mortgagor, appears to be that equitable remedies are discretionary. The legal mortgagee goes in by virtue of his legal estate, or its statutory equivalent, the right to possession being an attribute of his title. The equitable mortgagee goes in by asserting an equitable right to enforce his security by overriding the mortgagor's possession (which is an attribute of his legal title if he has retained it). The court will normally put the equitable mortgagee, in, if he so desires, but will presumably not do so if that would be inequitable (for example if the mortgagee lacks clean hands).[85]

A mortgagee commonly goes into possession by taking over occupation of the premises from the mortgagor, either by agreement or as a result of legal proceedings. But if the mortgagor's lessee is in occupation, the mortgagee may go into possession by requiring the rent to be paid to him, though he does not do so merely by arranging to receive the rent (or that amount) from the mortgagor.[86] The mortgagor also goes into possession if he grants an occupation lease and receives the rent,[87] but on the facts a lease by a mortgagee when the mortgagor is in possession may be, not an occupation lease ousting the mortgagor, but merely a demise of the mortgagee's estate, in which

[83] [1967] N.I. 129.

[84] [1967] N.I. 135.

[85] See *Barclays Bank Ltd.* v. *Bird*, [1954] Ch. 274; Willoughby, "The Rights of Second Mortgagees Regarding Possession" (1908), 24 *Law Quarterly Review*, 297; Wade, "An Equitable Mortgagee's Right to Possession" (1955), 71 *L.Q.R.*, 204. Ireland: *Antrim County Land, Building, and Investment Co. Ltd.* v. *Stewart*, [1904] 2 I.R. 357 (C.A.).

[86] See *Noyes* v. *Pollock* (1886), 32 Ch. D. 53 (C.A.).

[87] *Mexborough U.D.C.* v. *Harrison*, [1964] 1 W.L.R. 733. See also *Heales* v. *M'Murray* (1856), 23 Beav. 401.

case it will cease on redemption.[88] Since the grant of an occupation lease by the mortgagee and his receipt of the rent amount to him taking possession, it may be that the mortgagee is in possession from the outset if, in the mortgage deed, the mortgagor attorns tenant to the mortgagee at a substantial rent.[89]

A mortgagee in possession may go out of possession. One way of doing this, if he is receiving income from the property, is to exercise his power under Section 101(1)(iii) of the Law of Property Act, 1925, to appoint a receiver.[90]

The attornment clause. It has been common (though by no means invariable) for a long time for the mortgage deed, in the case of a legal mortgage, to contain a clause providing that the mortgagor thereby attorned tenant to the mortgagee at a rent. The details of the clause would vary according to the object with which it was inserted, and its usefulness has varied from time to time with changes in the law and procedure.[91] There are various purposes for which one might wish to create the relationship of landlord and tenant between mortgagee and mortgagor. The attornment clause creates this relationship for all purposes consistent with the nature of the mortgage transaction.

One of the early purposes of using the attornment clause was to bring the mortgagor's chattels into the security. By making the mortgagor the tenant of the mortgagee at a substantial rent (often equal to or in lieu of interest on the loan), the mortgagee got the right of a landlord to distrain for arrears of rent by way of securing his income.[92] This is no longer possible by an attornment clause without registering the mortgage as a bill of sale. The Bills of Sale Act, 1878, Section 6, makes a mortgage containing such a clause a bill of sale, with the consequence that the only way a mortgagor can become the tenant of the mortgagee without there being a bill of sale is, under the proviso to that section, by the mortgagee going into possession after the mortgage

[88] See *Chapman* v. *Smith*, [1907] 2 Ch. 97.

[89] This was suggested by James , L.J., in the Court of Appeal in *Re Stockton Iron Furnace Co.* (1879), 10 Ch. D. 335, 356. As to attornment clauses, see below.

[90] *Refuge Assurance Co. Ltd.* v. *Pearlberg*, [1938] Ch. 687 (C.A.). As to the appointment of receivers, see pp. 239-42, *post*. In Ireland the power to appoint a receiver is given by the Conveyancing Act, 1881, Sect. 19.

[91] See Gray, " The Attornment Clause " (1948), 13 *Conveyancer and Property Lawyer (N.S.)*, 31; Megarry (1958), 74 *Law Quarterly Review*, 348.

[92] *Re Stockton Iron Furnace Co.* (1879), 10 Ch. D. 335 (C.A.); *Re Threlfall* (1880), 16 Ch. D. 274 (C.A.); *Ex parte Voisey* (1882), 21 Ch. D. 442 (C.A.). Cf. *Ex parte Williams* (1877), 7 Ch. D. 138 (C.A.); *Ex parte Jackson* (1880), 14 Ch. D. 725 (C.A.).

and granting the mortgagor a lease at a fair and reasonable rent.[93] This being the case, unless it is desired to register it as a bill of sale there is now no point in a mortgage deed containing an attornment clause reserving the mortgagee a substantial rent.[94] Most modern attornment clauses reserved a peppercorn or sixpence a year, if demanded.

It is conceivable that an attornment clause would be put in to protect the mortgagor by specifying the length of notice to be given him to determine his tenancy. An example sometimes to be found is provision that the mortgagor's tenancy can be determined by the mortgagee on seven days notice at any time after his power of sale has become exercisable. This will bind the mortgagee, restricting his right to take possession accordingly.[95] If the only object of the exercise is to give the mortgagor security of tenure an attornment clause is unnecessary because the mortgagee can restrict his right to take possession by contract without becoming the mortgagor's landlord. On the other hand, the attornment clause is not dangerous to the mortgagee, for it creates the landlord and tenant relation only so far as consistent with the mortgagee's rights as such.[96] In the absence of express contract, the mortgagor is not protected by statutory extension of tenants' rights against landlords. *Steyning and Littlehampton Building Soc.* v. *Wilson*[97] was a case where the mortgagor of agricultural land attorned tenant to the mortgagee at a yearly rent of sixpence, if demanded, the tenancy to be terminable by the mortgagee giving three days notice. Danckwerts, J., held that the mortgagor was not protected from eviction as a tenant under the Agricultural Holdings Act, 1948, Section 23(1). The learned judge remarked:[98] " This is a case, which again illustrates the undesirability of retaining in mortgages an attornment clause, which is entirely obsolete and at the present time performs no useful purpose." With respect, the judge's decision removes the particular illustration of undesirability and the attornment clause, though often included unthinkingly, is not completely

93 *Re Willis* (1888), 21 Q.B.D. 384 (C.A.). See also *Green* v. *Marsh*, [1892] 2 Q.B. 330 (C.A.); *Woolwich Equitable Building Soc.* v. *Preston*, [1938] Ch. 129, 131, *per* Clauson, J.; *Hinckley and Country Building Soc.* v. *Henry*, [1953] 1 W.L.R. 352, 354, *per* Upjohn, J.

94 It might even inconvenience the mortgagee by making him accountable as being in possession: *Re Stockton Iron Furnace Co.* (1879), 10 Ch. D. 335, 356, *per* James, L.J.

95 *Hinckley and Country Building Soc.* v. *Henry*, [1953] 1 W.L.R. 352. See also *Jolly* v. *Arbuthnot* (1859), 4 De G. & J. 224, 236, *per* Lord Chelmsford, L.C.

96 See *Ex parte Isherwood* (1882), 22 Ch. D. 384 (C.A.).

97 [1951] Ch. 1018. See also Baker (1965), 81 *Law Quarterly Review*, 341; (1966), 82 *L.Q.R.*, 21.

98 [1951] Ch. 1020.

useless. In *Portman Building Soc.* v. *Young*[99] the attornment clause provided for the tenancy, at £9 16*s*. a month, to be terminable by the mortgagee at any time without notice. The Court of Appeal held there was no tenancy within the Rent Acts because (i) it was not the sort of landlord and tenant relation envisaged by the Act and (ii) the Rent Acts dealt separately with mortgages and if a mortgagor could not bring himself within the protection of those provisions he could not get himself blown into the landlord and tenant provisions by a side wind. On the first point Evershed, M.R., with whom Lord Radcliffe and Singleton, L.J., agreed, said[1]—

> . . . the whole idea and scheme of the [Rent] Acts, so far as they relate to protected dwellings and the right of the person in occupation to continue in occupation, is to deal with premises of which the person in possession is, in a true and sensible meaning of the word, a tenant of them from someone else who is in ordinary language the landlord and their owner. . . . In the present case the true position is that the person in occupation is the owner and the person seeking possession is a chargee wishing to realise his charge.

In *Alliance Building Soc.* v. *Pinwill*[2] the attornment clause provided for seven days notice by the mortgagee to determine the tenancy. Vaisey, J., held the mortgagor entitled to only seven days notice, not the four weeks notice allowed to a tenant by the Rent Act, 1957, Section 16.

Procedural advantages in ejecting a tenant as compared with ejecting a mortgagor were a reason for the attornment clause too. A mortgagee who was his mortgagor's landlord could always, under the Rules of the Supreme Court, specially indorse his writ and proceed to summary judgment.[3] This was so even if the attornment clause was void for non-registration as a bill of sale, as that affected its validity only with regard to chattels and not as to the realty.[4] But for thirty years now, since changes in the Rules of the Supreme Court, this procedure has been available to mortgagees as such without a landlord and tenant relationship. The only remaining procedural advantage of the attornment clause is that it enables the mortgagee to evict the mortgagor under the Small Tenements Recovery Act, 1838, Section 1.[5]

Interest in the attornment clause has been revived by the Court of Appeal decision in *Regent Oil Co. Ltd.* v. *J. A. Gregory* (*Hatch End*)

[99] [1951] 1 All E.R. 191.
[1] [1951] 1 All E.R. 194.
[2] [1958] Ch. 788.
[3] *Daubuz* v. *Lavington* (1884), 13 Q.B.D. 347.
[4] *Mumford* v. *Collier* (1890), 25 Q.B.D. 279.
[5] *Dudley and District Benefit Building Soc.* v. *Gordon*, [1929] 2 K.B. 105.

Ltd.[6] A lease was mortgaged by legal charge, the mortgagor attorning tenant to the chargee at a yearly rent of a peppercorn (if demanded), with a proviso for the chargee to re-enter on seven days notice after the power of sale had become exercisable. The mortgagor also covenanted to buy petrol and oil only from the chargee. Later, the mortgagor assigned the lease to the defendants, who asserted that the restrictive trading covenant was not binding on them. It was held that the attornment clause created the relationship of landlord and tenant—the mortgagor becoming the mortgagee's tenant for the duration of the security, but subject to the proviso for notice—and that the restrictive covenant was one enforceable by a landlord against the assignee of his tenant. Very often, such restrictive covenants may be enforceable against assignees of the equity of redemption under the rule in *Tulk* v. *Moxhay*,[7] as was the case here, even without a landlord and tenant relationship, but the burden of covenants does run with a lease in some circumstances not covered by the rule in *Tulk* v. *Moxhay.*

Power to grant leases. The power of the mortgagee in possession to grant leases of the mortgaged premises is similar to that of the mortgagor in possession.[8] If a mortgagee goes into possession after a lease has been granted by the mortgagor in possession, the mortgagee than takes over the position of landlord and can enforce covenants in the lease against the tenant.[9]

Accountability and allowances. A mortgagee in possession must account for what he receives out of the property, and for no more unless he has been guilty of wilful default.[10] In *Fulthrope* v. *Foster,*[11] where the mortgagee was in possession, the loan was only £90 but the annual profits from the land amounted to £13. Trevor, M.R., held that the mortgagee must account: the profits were too high in relation to the capital sum secured to be in lieu of interest. To say that the mortgagee must account is to mean that, subject to deductions for his allowable expenditure on managing the property, the mortgagee must apply the income from the land to paying himself what is due on the mortgage and, if there is any surplus after that, hand it over to the mortgagor.

6 [1966] Ch. 402.
7 (1848), 2 Ph. 774.
8 See pp. 224-7, *ante*.
9 *Municipal Permanent Investment Building Soc.* v. *Smith* (1888), 22 Q.B.D. 70 (C.A.).
10 *Anon.* (1682), 1 Vern. 45.
11 (1687), 1 Vern. 476.

The mortgagee is accountable not only for actual receipts but for what, but for his wilful default, he might have received.[12] As Lord Erskine, L.C., said in *Hughes* v. *Williams*[13]—

> . . . a mortgagee, taking possession, is to take the fair rents and profits; and is not bound to engage in adventures and speculations for the benefit of the mortgagor; but is liable only for wilful default . . .

If the mortgagee goes into possession of a mortgaged dwelling-house and, instead of letting it, lives in it himself or leaves it unoccupied, he will be accountable for an occupation rent, though he was not so charged in *Marshall* v. *Cave*,[14] where the house was in such ruinous condition that no rent could have been got for it. Nor is the mortgagee accountable for trade profits made out of dealing with a person to whom he lets the mortgaged premises. In *White* v. *City of London Brewery Co.*[15] the mortgagees in possession were brewers and the mortgaged premises were a public house. They let it, the lessee contracting to buy only the mortgagees' beer. The Court of Appeal held the mortgagees not liable to account for the profits on the beer sold to the tenant (though they would have to account for the rent that would have been got by letting the public house as a free house if higher than the rent they actually received).

In *Withrington* v. *Banks*[16] mortgagees in possession cut down and sold timber. Price, B., decreed that an account be taken, the money to be applied (i) to the payment of interest and (ii) to repayment of the loan, and granted an injunction to restrain further cutting. He said[17]—

> Mortgagee in fee, at law, may commit waste, but never in equity; unless it appears the security is defective . . .[18]

In *Sandon* v. *Hooper*[19] Lord Langdale, M.R., held the mortgagor entitled to an account of any loss occasioned by pulling down two of the cottages on the premises. In *Millett* v. *Davey*[20] the mortgagee in

[12] See, e.g., *National Bank of Australasia* v. *United Hand-in-Hand and Band of Hope Co.* (1879), 4 App. Cas. 391, 408-9 (Privy Council, Victoria). Cf. *Parkinson* v. *Hanbury* (1867), L.R. 2 H.L. 1.

[13] (1806), 12 Ves. 493, 495-6.

[14] (1824), 3 L.J.O.S.Ch. 57.

[15] (1889), 42 Ch. D. 237.

[16] (1725), Sel. Cas. t. King 30.

[17] Sel. Cas. t. King 31.

[18] See also the Law of Property Act, 1925, Sect. 85(2), Sch. 1, pt. VII, paras. 1 and 2, and Sect. 101(1)(iv), (3)-(5), to which, in Ireland, the Conveyancing Act, 1881, Sect. 19, corresponds.

[19] (1843), 6 Beav. 246, affirmed on appeal by Lord Lyndhurst, L.C.: (1844), 14 L.J.Ch. 120.

[20] (1862), 31 Beav. 470.

possession granted mining leases. The security being insufficient, Romilly, M.R., charged him only with the net profits. The learned Master of the Rolls said[21]—

> . . . where the security is insufficient, . . . a mortgagee is entitled to make the most of the property for the purpose of realizing what is due to him. He may cut timber, he may open a mine, and this court will not, by injunction, interfere to prevent his doing so, providing he is not committing wanton destruction . . . if he incurs a great loss in working the mine, he cannot charge a penny of that loss against the mortgagor, and if he obtains a great profit, the whole of that profit must go in discharge of his mortgage debt.

As to improvement expenses allowable to the mortgagee out of the income he collects from the land, the principles were reviewed by Lord Langdale, M.R., in *Sandon* v. *Hooper*[22]—

> Such repairs as are necessary for the support of the property he will be allowed for. He will not only be allowed for repairs, but he will be also allowed for doing that which is essential for the protection of the title of the mortgagor. Further, if he has got the consent of the mortgagor, or has given him notice, in which he acquiesces, then he may be allowed for sums of money which are laid out in increasing the value of the property; but he has no right to lay out money in what he calls increasing the value of the property, which may be done in such a way as to make it utterly impossible for the mortgagor, with his means ever to redeem; this is what has been termed, improving a mortgagor out of his estate—an expression which has been used both in this argument, and on former occasions. The mortgagee has not a right to make it more expensive for the mortgagor to redeem than may be required for the purpose of keeping the property in a proper state of repair, and for protecting the title to the property.

In *Marshall* v. *Cave*[23] Leach, V.-C., held a mortgagee not entitled to the cost of replacing old buildings.

Nor is the mortgagee entitled to remuneration for his work when in possession of the property. In *Comyns* v. *Comyns*[24] Sullivan, M.R., held void a stipulation in a mortgage deed that the mortgagee was to have £100 a year for his trouble in managing the lands. There are

[21] 31 Beav. 476.

[22] (1843), 6 Beav. 246, 248. See also *Tipton Green Colliery Co.* v. *Tipton Moat Colliery Co.*. (1877), 7 Ch. D. 192 (Jessel, M.R.); *Shepard* v. *Jones* (1882), 21 Ch. D. 469 (C.A.); *Henderson* v. *Astwood*, [1894] A.C. 150 (Privy Council, Jamaica).

[23] (1824), 3 L.J.O.S.Ch. 57.

[24] (1871), I.R. 5 Eq. 583.

many cases,[25] too, in which the mortgagee has not been allowed payment as if he were a receiver. He may appoint a receiver or go into possession, but he cannot go into possession and claim to be treated as a receiver.

Remedies of the Mortgagee to Enforce his Security

A mortgage usually supports a promise to pay or repay a sum of money to the mortgagee. When this is the case, if the payment is not made when it should be, in addition to realising his security the promisee may sue for the amount in an action for breach of contract.[26] But the remedy in contract, though separate from the remedies in respect of the security, is not wholly independent of them. For example, a mortgagor who pays in full when sued is entitled to have his property freed from the incumbrance because there is no obligation left to secure. In *Palmer* v. *Hendrie*[27] Romilly, M.R., held that a mortgagee who had parted with the estate, and who therefore could not restore it to the mortgagor on redemption, could not sue on the covenant. He said[28]—

> A mortgagee may pursue all his remedies at once; he may bring actions of covenant and ejectment, and at the same time proceed to foreclose the mortgage. If he forecloses it, and afterwards sues on the covenant, he thereby opens the foreclosure; but if he sues on the covenant, and does not get fully paid, he may still go on and foreclose the mortgage. But after he has once been paid in full, under the covenant, he cannot touch the estate, and is precluded from all proceedings afterwards.
>
> . . . the mortgagees must perform their reciprocal obligations:—they are bound, on payment, to restore the property to the mortgagor, and if it appear, from the state of the transaction, that, by the act of the mortgagee, unauthorized by the mortgagor, it has become impossible to restore the estate on payment of all that is due, I am of opinion that this Court will interefere and prevent the mortgagee suing the mortgagor at law.

In *Willes* v. *Levett*,[29] on the other hand, where a mortgagee, in exercise of his power of sale, had contracted to sell part of the mortgaged pro-

[25] See p. 241, n. 48, *post*.

[26] If expenditure by the mortgagee is properly incurred so that it can be added to the amount due on the security, that does not mean it can also be sued for on the covenant in the absence of an express promise by the mortgagor to pay it: *Sinfield* v. *Sweet*, [1967] 1 W.L.R. 1489.

[27] (1859), 27 Beav. 349. See also p. 249, *post*.

[28] 27 Beav. 351. See also *Lockhart* v. *Hardy* (1846), 9 Beav. 349, 354-5, *per* Lord Langdale, M.R. Ireland: *Schoole* v. *Sall* (1803), 1 Sch. & L. 176.

[29] (1847), 1 De. G. & Sm. 392.

perty for more than the total amount due on the mortgage, Knight Bruce, V.-C., would not restrain the mortgagee from suing the mortgagor on the covenant: the contract for sale (the validity of which was being impeached in an action by the mortgagor to have it set aside) might not be performed.

If interest or instalments of repayment should get into arrears, the mortgagee may get his hands directly upon the income of the mortgaged property by going into possession[30] or by appointing a receiver.[31] To secure repayment of a capital sum the mortgagee may either foreclose the mortgage[32] or sell the property free from the equity of redemption.[33]

Appointment of a Receiver

Power to appoint. In England, the Law of Property Act, 1925, Section 101 (1), provides—

> A mortgagee, where the mortgage is by deed, shall, by virtue of this Act, have the following powers, to the like extent as if they had been in terms conferred by the mortgage deed (namely): . . .
>
> (iii) A power, when the mortgage money has become due,[34] to appoint a receiver of the income of the mortgaged property, or any part thereof; or, if the mortgaged property consists of an interest in income, or of a rentcharge or an annual or other periodical sum, a receiver of that property or any part thereof . . .

This replaces a similar power given by the Conveyancing Act, 1881, Section 19 (1) (iii), which is still in force in Ireland, and which in turn replaced a more restricted power conferred by an Act of 1860.[35] The other relevant provisions of Section 101 of the 1925 Act are as follows—

> (3)[36] The provisions of this Act relating to the foregoing powers, comprised either in this section, or in any other section regulating the exercise of those powers, may be varied or extended by the mortgage deed, and, as so varied or extended, shall, as far as may be, operate in the like manner and with all the like incidents, effects and consequences, as if such variations or extensions were contained in this Act.

[30] See pp. 230-8, *ante*.

[31] See below.

[32] See pp. 242-9, *post*.

[33] See pp. 249-57, *post*.

[34] A receiver may be appointed under this section by a mortgagee in possession (which will result in his going out of possession): *Refuge Assurance Co. Ltd.* v. *Pearlberg*, [1938] Ch. 687 (C.A.).

[35] 23 & 24 Vict., c. 145, Sects. 11, 17-23.

[36] Ireland: Conveyancing Act, 1881, Sect. 19(2).

(4)[37] This section applies only if and as far as a contrary intention is not expressed in the mortgage deed, and has effect subject to the terms of the mortgage deed and to the provisions therein contained.

(5)[38] Save as otherwise provided, this section applies where the mortgage deed is executed after the thirty-first day of December, eighteen hundred and eighty-one.

Exercise of the statutory power to appoint a receiver is governed by the Law of Property Act, 1925, Section 110,[39] which relates to the bankruptcy of the mortgagor, and Section 109 (1), (4), (5)[40]—

(1) A mortgagee entitled to appoint a receiver under the power in that behalf conferred by this Act shall not appoint a receiver until he has become entitled to exercise the power of sale conferred by this Act,[41] but may then, by writing under his hand, appoint such person as he thinks fit to be receiver.

(4) A person paying money to the receiver shall not be concerned to inquire whether any case has happened to authorise the receiver to act.

(5) The receiver may be removed, and a new receiver may be appointed, from time to time by the mortgagee by writing under his hand.

Where the mortgage is not by deed, or was made before 1882, the mortgagee will be able to appoint a receiver only under an express power in the mortgage agreement (or under the 1860 Act if applicable). Before 1882 it was usual to include such an express power in terms similar to those of the modern statutory power.

The court also has power to appoint a receiver on the application of a mortgagee.[42] Before the Judicature Acts, the Court of Chancery would appoint a receiver on the application of an equitable mortgagee,[43] but would not help a legal mortgagee who, in the absence of an express power (or power under the 1860 Act) to appoint a receiver, was left to his right to take possession of the mortgaged property. To-day, any mortgagee may get a receiver appointed by the court even if he has power to appoint one himself, but if he goes to court unnecessarily he

[37] Ireland: Conveyancing Act, 1881, Sect. 19(3).

[38] Ireland: Conveyancing Act, 1881, Sect. 19(4).

[39] There is no equivalent legislation in Ireland.

[40] Ireland: Conveyancing Act, 1881, Sect. 24(1), (4), (5).

[41] See pp. 250-1, *post*.

[42] England: Supreme Court of Judicature (Consolidation) Act, 1925, Sect. 45(1), (2), replacing the Judicature Act, 1873, Sect. 25(8). Ireland: Judicature (Ireland) Act, 1877, Sect. 28(8).

[43] For an example, see *Shakel* v. *Duke of Marlborough* (1819), 4 Madd. 463.

may have to pay the costs. Making such an appointment in *Tillett* v. *Nixon*,[44] Pearson, J., came to the conclusion that when an action for foreclosure was pending, and the parties were at arm's length, it was preferable that the appointment should be made by the court.

Functions and position of receiver. The main purpose of appointing a receiver is to intercept the income produced by the mortgaged property, before it reaches the mortgagor, so that it can be used to pay interest on the loan if the mortgagor is not paying up. To this end, a receiver appointed under the statute is given power[45] to get in the income and to give receipts and he may also be delegated additional powers by the mortgagee. He is also placed under a duty,[46] if so directed in writing by the mortgagee, to insure the mortgaged property.

The receiver may be remunerated, by commission on the money he receives.[47] If, however, a mortgagee goes into possession and personally manages the property, he cannot charge the mortgagor for doing the work a receiver might have been appointed to do, even if such a charge is expressly authorised by the mortgage deed.[48]

What such a receiver must do with the money he collects is governed by the Law of Property Act, 1925, Section 109 (8)[49]—

> Subject to the provisions of this Act as to the application of insurance money, the receiver shall apply all money received by him as follows, namely:
>
> (i) In discharge of all rents, taxes, rates, and outgoings whatever affecting the mortgaged property; and
>
> (ii) In keeping down all annual sums or other payments, and the interest on all principal sums, having priority to the mortgage in right whereof he is receiver; and
>
> (iii) In payment of his commission, and of the premiums on fire, life, or other insurances, if any, properly payable under the mortgage deed or under this Act, and the cost of executing necessary or proper repairs directed in writing by the mortgagee;[50] and

[44] (1883), 25 Ch. D. 238.

[45] Law of Property Act, 1925, Sect. 109(3); Conveyancing Act, 1881, Sect. 24(3).

[46] Sect. 109(7) of the 1925 Act; Sect. 24(7) of the 1881 Act.

[47] Sect. 109(6) of the 1925 Act; Sect. 24(6) of the 1881 Act.

[48] *Bonithon* v. *Hockmore* (1685), 1 Vern. 316; *French* v. *Baron* (1740), 2 Atk. 120; *Godfrey* v. *Watson* (1747), 3 Atk. 517, 518; *Chambers* v. *Goldwin* (1804), 9 Ves. 254, 271-2; *Langstaffe* v. *Fenwick* (1805), 10 Ves. 405; *Davis* v. *Dendy* (1818), 3 Madd. 170, 172; *Leith* v. *Irvine* (1833), 1 My. & K. 277. Ireland: *Carew* v. *Johnston* (1805), 2 Sch. & Lef. 280, 301.

[49] In Ireland, the Conveyancing Act, 1881, Sect. 24(8), is to the like effect except that there is no equivalent of para. (v).

[50] See *White* v. *Metcalf*, [1903] 2 Ch. 567, decided on Sect. 24(8)(iii) of the 1881 Act.

(iv) In payment of the interest accruing due[51] in respect of any principal money due under the mortgage;[52] and

(v) In or towards discharge of the principal money if so directed in writing by the mortgagee;

and shall pay the residue, if any, of the money received by him to the person who, but for the possession of the receiver, would have been entitled to receive the income of which he is appointed receiver, or who is otherwise entitled to the mortgaged property.

The old express power to appoint a receiver used to specify that, when appointed, he became the agent of the mortgagor. This provision also appears in the statutory provisions.[53] This makes it quite clear that a mortgagee appointing a receiver is not thereby going into possession of the mortgaged premises. It also probably means, though there is no direct authority on the point, that receipt of rent by a receiver would not estop the mortgagee from challenging an unauthorised tenancy granted by the mortgagor. That was the opinion of Harman, J., in *Lever Finance Ltd.* v. *Needleman's Trustee.*[54] In that case, a mortgagee, having no power (statutory or otherwise) to do so, because he was not at the material time the registered owner in respect of a charge on registered land, purported to appoint a receiver. The learned judge held that the so-called receiver was the mortgagee's agent and that receipt of rent by the receiver constituted recognition by the mortgagee of the tenancy in respect of which it was paid.

Foreclosure

Nature of foreclosure. As developed in England prior to 1926, foreclosure was a judicial proceeding which ended (if the mortgagee was successful) in an order destroying the equity of redemption and leaving the mortgagee beneficial owner of the full estate or interest.[55] To begin with the most straightforward case of a mortgagor who had conveyed the fee simple to the mortgagee, the foreclosure made the mortgagee the beneficial owner in fee simple discharged from any estate

[51] "Due" under Sect. 24(8)(iv) of the 1881 Act means legally enforceable, so a receiver must not pay the mortgagee statute-barred interest: *Hibernian Bank* v. *Yourell* (*No.* 2), [1919] 1 I.R. 310.

[52] In respect of paras. (iv) and (v) the mortgagee is entitled to an account from the receiver: *Leicester Permanent Building Soc.* v. *Butt*, [1943] Ch. 308.

[53] Law of Property Act, 1925, Sect. 109(2): "A receiver appointed under the powers conferred by this Act, or any enactment replaced by this Act, shall be deemed to be the agent of the mortgagor; and the mortgagor shall be solely responsible for the receiver's acts or defaults unless the mortgage deed otherwise provides." Sect. 24(2) of the Conveyancing Act, 1881, is similar. See also Sect. 99(19) of the 1925 Act (Sect. 3(11) of the 1911 Act), p. 227, *ante*.

[54] [1956] Ch. 375.

[55] See p. 170, *ante*.

or interest of the mortgagor. The proceedings might be begun by the mortgagee claiming foreclosure or the mortgagor claiming redemption —in either action the mortgagor would have a chance to redeem and, if he did not do so, would be foreclosed. In either case a date would be set, six months ahead, on which the mortgagor could redeem. If the mortgagor did not redeem on the date, in a mortgagee's action, the court would then make a foreclosure order absolute; if it were a mortgagor's redemption action, the suit would be dismissed. Dismissal of a redemption suit, except when dismissal is for want of prosecution, normally has the same effect as an order of foreclosure absolute.[56] The one exception is the case of an equitable mortgage by deposit of title deeds. In *Marshall* v. *Shrewsbury*[57] James, L.J., with whom Mellish, L.J., agreed, said—

> With regard to an equitable mortgage, I have never met with a bill by an equitable mortgagor for redemption, though such a bill might probably be filed. But how could the dismissal of such a bill operate as a decree for foreclosure? The only thing foreclosed would be the right to redeem certain pieces of parchment. If may be that the Plaintiff would be barred from bringing another bill to redeem those pieces of parchment, but that is all. When an equitable mortgagee files a bill to enforce his security, he does not get a simple decree for foreclosure, but he gets further substantial relief. He is entitled to have a declaration that his deposit operated as a mortgage, and that in default of payment of what may be found due, the mortgagor is a trustee of the legal estate for him; and then the decree goes on to order the mortgagor to convey the estate to him. . . . There is no authority for saying that a mere dismissal is an equivalent to such a comprehensive decree.

In England after 1925 there is no mortgaging of legal estates in land by transfer of the mortgagor's estate to the mortgagee. Nevertheless, a foreclosure order is made to operate so as to transfer beneficially to the mortgagee the legal estate of the mortgagor.[58] In Ireland there has been no such change, but in any case in that country successful foreclosure proceedings end in an order for sale.[59]

Foreclosure, though still sought in appropriate circumstances, has become steadily less popular in England as sale free from the equity of redemption has become easier. Most modern mortgagees have an

[56] *Cholmley* v. *Countess Dowager of Oxford* (1741), 2 Atk. 267; *Hansard* v. *Hardy* (1812), 18 Ves. 455, 460, *per* Grant, M.R.

[57] (1875), L.R. 10 Ch. App. 250, 254 (C.A. in Ch.).

[58] Law of Property Act, 1925, Sects. 88(2), (4)-(6), 89(2), (4)-(6).

[59] See p. 247, *post*.

express or statutory power of selling the mortgagor's interest,[60] whereas foreclosure always means litigation.[61] Moreover, it is inconclusive litigation. If the mortgagee makes out a case in the first place, he gets an order nisi and has to wait six months to see if the mortgagor redeems. During this waiting period the court is inclined to generosity towards mortgagors' applications to extend it. If the mortgagee eventually gets his order absolute, the foreclosure may still be re-opened,[62] i.e., the mortgagor given a renewed opportunity to redeem.

Who may foreclose. Originally, foreclosure was the remedy of a legal mortgagee. It was conceived as a process by which the owner of the estate at law (the mortgagee) destroyed an incumbrance (the equity of redemption). Later, however, after debate and hesitation, it became established that an equitable mortgagee of a legal estate could foreclose. This involved an order under which the legal estate had to be transferred to him.[63] Authority now establishes that every mortgagee, legal or equitable, has the same right of foreclosure. Foreclosure orders have been granted to an equitable mortgagee of land by deposit of title deeds,[64] to an equitable mortgagee of shares by deposit of the share certificate,[65] and to a mortgagee of a reversionary interest in stock.[66] But only a mortgagee can foreclose, that is, only a person whose security consists of the mortgagor's interest in the property or the right to call for it. A pledgee of chattels, having no title, cannot foreclose,[67] nor can a person entitled to a charge created by will.[68]

When a mortgagee may foreclose. There can be no foreclosure if the mortgagor is not in default of any payment due under the mortgage contract.[69] As soon as the legal date for redemption has passed without the mortgagor redeeming, the capital is overdue and the mortgagee can start foreclosure proceedings. Thereafter the right to foreclose remains, even if the right to sue the mortgagor for the debt becomes statute-barred,[70] so long as the mortgagee's interest in the property

60 See pp. 249-57, *post*.

61 For general discussions of the nature of foreclosure, see *Heath* v. *Pugh* (1881), 6 Q.B.D. 345, 359-61, *per* Lord Selborne, L.C. (C.A.), and *Campbell* v. *Holyland* (1877), 7 Ch.D. 166, 171-2, *per* Jessel, M.R.

62 See pp. 248-9, *post*.

63 See the description by James, L.J., in *Marshall* v. *Shrewsbury* (1875), L.R. 10 Ch. App. 250, 254, p. 243, *ante*.

64 *Parker* v. *Housefield* (1834), 2 My. & K. 419; *James* v. *James* (1873), L.R. 16 Eq. 153; *York Union Banking Co.* v. *Artley* (1879), 11 Ch.D. 205.

65 *Harrold* v. *Plenty*, [1901] 2 Ch. 314.

66 *Slade* v. *Rigg* (1843), 3 Hare 35.

67 *Carter* v. *Wake* (1877), 4 Ch.D. 605.

68 *Re Owen*, [1894] 3 Ch. 220.

69 *Williams* v. *Morgan*, [1906] 1 Ch. 804.

70 *London & Midland Bank* v. *Mitchell*, [1899] 2 Ch. 161.

is not itself destroyed either by redemption or the running of the limitation period. Further, a mortgagee may foreclose even if capital repayment is not due, if there has been some other default. In *Edwards* v. *Martin*[71] Kindersley, V.-C., held a mortgagee able to foreclose after interest had become in arrear, though the principal was not due, and even though the mortgagee had entered the mortgaged premises and sold part of them for more than enough to pay off the arrears. In *Kidderminster Mutual Benefit Building Soc.* v. *Haddock*[72] Clauson, J., held, in respect of an instalment mortgage, that the mortgagee could foreclose as soon as an instalment was in arrear although that default was not expressed by the contract to make the balance immediately payable. On the other hand, Sugden, L.C., in *Burrowes* v. *Molloy*,[73] decided that if a mortgagee has covenanted not to call in the principal debt until a specified date, he cannot foreclose before then even if interest is in arrear.

Parties to foreclosure. Primarily the proceedings must be against the mortgagor or his successor in title as owner of the equity of redemption.[74] The mortgagee may find the equity of redemption on his mortgage split among several owners, such as subsequent mortgagees. He must join them all as parties unless they are so numerous as to render that impracticable or, possibly, the mortgagor has deliberately multiplied them so as to embarrass the mortgagee.[75] In *Bishop of Winchester* v. *Paine*[76] Grant, M.R., held that persons who took equitable mortgages after a mortgagee had started foreclosure proceedings need not be made parties as they would be bound by the decree anyway. The persons who must be joined are therefore all persons acquiring an interest in the equity of redemption, of the mortgage being foreclosed, before proceedings are started. In *Anderson* v. *Stather*[77] Knight Bruce, V.-C., held that the mortgagee must join as parties the grandchildren of the mortgagor, who were entitled to portions under a settlement of the equity of redemption made by the mortgagor on his daughter's marriage, and who were resident in the United States of America. When a sub-mortgagee[78] forecloses the head mortgagor he must join the sub-mortgagor (head mortgagee).[79]

71 (1856), 25 L.J.Ch. 284.
72 [1936] W.N. 158.
73 (1845), 2 Jo. & Lat. 521.
74 *Fell* v. *Brown* (1787), 2 Bro. C.C. 276; *Farmer* v. *Curtis* (1829), 2 Sim. 466.
75 *Brisco* v. *Kenrick* (1832), 1 Coop. t. Cott. 371, 372. See also *Bishop of Winchester* v. *Beavor* (1797), 3 Ves. 314. Cf. *Fishwick* v. *Lowe* (1787), 1 Cox 411.
76 (1805), 11 Ves. 194. Ireland: *Going* v. *Farrell* (1814), Beat. 472 (Lord Manners, L.C.).
77 (1845), 2 Coll. 209. See also *Palk* v. *Lord Clinton* (1805), 12 Ves. 48.
78 A sub-mortgage is a mortgage made by a mortgagee. He secures a loan made to him by granting the lender an interest in the property he (as mortgagee) holds as security for the loan he has made.
79 *Hobart* v. *Abbot* (1731), 2 P. Wms. 643.

A mortgagee cannot foreclose a prior mortgagee and so need not join him as a party. For example, if there are three mortgages, and the second mortgagee wishes to foreclose, he may proceed against the mortgagor and the third mortgagee (the two persons interested in the equity of redemption on the second mortgage) without joining the first mortgagee as a party.[80] If he proceeds in this way to a foreclosure order absolute, the second mortgagee will end up by owning an unincumbered equity of redemption on the first mortgage. But the second mortgagee may wish to acquire an unincumbered legal estate. Although he cannot foreclose the first mortgage, he is a partial owner of the equity of redemption on it and so can redeem it. Should he fail to redeem by agreement he may, in his foreclosure proceedings, join the first mortgagee as a party, but the only relief he can claim against that party is redemption.[81]

Sale in lieu of foreclosure. In England by the Chancery Amendment Act, 1852, Section 48, in a foreclosure action the court was empowered to order a sale on the request of any party. Today, this power is contained in the Law of Property Act, 1925, Section 91 (2), (4)-(6).

Generally a mortgagee would not ask for sale in a foreclosure action because he could either sell under a statutory or express power or apply to the court to order a sale. A mortgagor, too, will not commonly apply, for if the value of his interest in the property is greater than the amount of the debt he will prefer to redeem and should be able to raise the necessary money, if he needs to, by further charging the property. A subsequent mortgagee is the most likely person to seek a sale in a foreclosure action.[82]

An example of an unsuccessful request by a mortgagor's successors in title for sale in a foreclosure action is provided by *Silsby* v. *Holliman.*[83] A mortgagor in possession, having made an unauthorised lease, gave the tenant notice to quit, after which the tenant remained in occupation as a statutory tenant under the Rent Acts. After the death of the mortgagor, payment of the debt was required by the mortgagees, and the statutory tenant redeemed (thus becoming the mortgagee). The tenant-mortgagee continued to tender rent to the mortgagor's personal representatives, who rejected it. He then

80 *Rose* v. *Page* (1829), 2 Sim. 471; *Brisco* v. *Kenrick* (1832), 1 Coop. t. Cott. 371; *Richards* v. *Cooper* (1842), 5 Beav. 304.

81 *Dalton* v. *Hayter* (1844), 7 Beav. 313; *Inman* v. *Wearing* (1850), 3 De G. & Sm. 729. Ireland: *M'Donough* v. *Shewbridge* (1814), 2 Ba. & B. 555, 561-2, *per* M'Mahon, M.R.

82 See, e.g., *Union Bank of London* v. *Ingram* (1882), 20 Ch. D. 463 (C.A.).

83 [1955] Ch. 552. See also, as to a mortgagee in possession as tenant, *Page* v. *Linwood* (1837), 4 Cl. & Fin. 399 (House of Lords, England).

brought a foreclosure action, in which the personal representatives asked for a sale with vacant possession, saying that the plaintiff was in possession as mortgagee. (The property would be more valuable with vacant possession than subject to a statutory tenancy.) Upjohn, J., held that the plaintiff, though now the mortgagee, could, if he wished, still stay in possession as statutory tenant rather than as mortgagee, and granted him a foreclosure order.

In Ireland there are no statutory provisions for sale in foreclosure actions because a course of judicial practice has existed, since before law reporting began, of always ordering a sale in such proceedings and never a foreclosure.[84] In *Antrim County Land, Building and Investment Co. Ltd.* v. *Stewart*,[85] in the Court of Appeal, Fitzgibbon, L.J., said—

> Under the old law [i.e., before the Judicature Act], the test of a right of a mortgagee, whether puisne or not, to obtain possession of the land, was whether he had the right to foreclose. In Ireland, foreclosure fell into disuse, because there was here a special procedure for realizing mortgages by Court Receivers, and by sales in the Landed Estates Court; but puisne mortgagees had the same right of foreclosure as in England.

One must, presumably, accept that a foreclosure order could be granted in Ireland, though it is doubtful whether cases are to be found in which this has been done. Fitzgibbon, L.J., was not alone in thinking it possible. In *Bruce* v. *Brophy*[86] the Court of Appeal took the view that it had been the settled practice for centuries to decree a sale, not a foreclosure, but Walker, C., said[87]—

> I do not say that, under special circumstances, and where a special case is made for foreclosure, the Court has not power to grant a decree for foreclosure, and not a sale. No such case has been made here . . .

Reopening foreclosure after order absolute. When the order of foreclosure is made absolute, the mortgagor (and other defendants, if any) has let six months go by without redeeming. Nevertheless, even after foreclosure absolute the mortgagor's right of redemption continues, at lease for a short time. This protraction of the agony

[84] For an early reported statement as to the practice, see *M'Donough* v. *Shewbridge* (1814), 2 Ba. & B. 555, 563, *per* M'Mahon, M.R.

[85] [1904] 2 I.R. 357, 369. See also *Waters* v. *Lloyd*, [1911] 1 I.R. 153, 161-3, *per* Holmes, L.J.

[86] [1906] 1 I.R. 611.

[87] [1906] 1 I.R. 616.

was considered by Jessel, M.R., in *Campbell* v. *Holyland*,[88] where he said—

> An order for foreclosure, according to the practice of the old Court of Chancery, was never really absolute, nor can it be so now. In cases of great hardship a mortgagor might have obtained further time for payment, and the suit was allowed to go on after decree. The decree, though final in terms, was not final in fact, and the suit could not be considered as terminated.

The learned Master of the Rolls said[89] that it was not possible to lay down rules as to when there could be redemption after foreclosure absolute, but the mortgagor must come within a reasonable time, having regard to the nature of the property and to the circumstances in which he failed to redeem in due time. Other relevant circumstances were the value of the property in relation to the amount of the debt and any special value of the property to the parties. He went on to say[90] that if the mortgagee has sold the property after foreclosure absolute, whether the mortgagor can reopen the foreclosure as against the purchaser depends on how long after the decree he bought and the state of his knowledge as to the relative amounts of the value of the property and the mortgage debt. In this case, the foreclosure was re-opened. The mortgagor had not redeemed in the foreclosure proceedings because he thought he had bought the mortgage from the mortgagee. It turned out that someone else, who purchased from the mortgagee after foreclosure nisi but before the order was made absolute, had a better title, and the mortgagor then made his redemption application promptly.

A foreclosure absolute may also be reopened by the mortgagee suing on the contract to pay.[91]

Suing on the covenant after foreclosure absolute. A mortgagee who has foreclosed may come to the conclusion that the value of the property he has acquired by these proceedings is less than the amount of the debt secured by the mortgage. He may then seek to recover the balance by suing the mortgagor on the promise to pay. There is no doubt that, if he still holds the title to the property, the mortgagee can do this, but doing so reopens the foreclosure and the mortgagor

88 (1877), 7 Ch.D. 166, 169. See also *Wichalse* v. *Short* (1713), 3 Bro. P.C. 558 (House of Lords, England); *Lant* v. *Crispe* (1719), 5 Bro. P.C. 200 (H.L., E.); *Burgh* v. *Langton* (1724), 5 Bro. P.C. 213 (H.L., E.); *Jones* v. *Kenrick* (1727), 5 Bro. P.C. 244 (H.L., E.); *Ford* v. *Wastell* (1847), 2 Ph. 591; *Thornhill* v. *Manning* (1851), 1 Sim. (N.S.) 451. Cf. *Patch* v. *Ward* (1867), L.R. 3 Ch. App. 203 (C.A. in Ch.).

89 7 Ch.D. 172-3.

90 7 Ch.D. 173-4.

91 See below.

has a new right to redeem.[92] A mortgagee who has been foreclosed by a prior mortgagee may also seek to sue the mortgagor for payment. In *Worthington & Co. Ltd.* v. *Abbott*[93] Eve, J., held that a puisne mortgagee could do this, though he had been foreclosed by a consent order, not insisting on time to redeem the prior incumbrance. Where the suit is by an incumbrancer other than the one who foreclosed the foreclosure is not reopened.

If the mortgagee has foreclosed and sold the property for less than the amount due on the mortgage, and wishes to get the balance from the mortgagor, a number of possibilities exist. It could be the rule that he can sue and the foreclosure is not reopened, because the sale has established the value of the property and it is not therefore inequitable to make the mortgagor pay without giving him a chance to redeem. It was the opinion of Lord Thurlow, L.C.,[94] that this was the law, but later cases take a different view. The rule could have developed that the mortgagee could sue, but that this reopened the foreclosure so that if the mortgagor redeemed the plaintiff must either get the property back for reconveyance to the defendant or pay damages for breach of his obligation to reconvey on redemption. What was actually determined during the nineteenth century was that if the mortgagee had sold after foreclosure he could not sue the mortgagor on the covenant.[95] This contrasts with the right of a mortgagor to take the initiative to reopen a foreclosure even after sale by the mortgagee.[96]

An analogous case of loss of the right to sue by parting with the property is *Palmer* v. *Hendrie* (No. 2),[97] where Romilly, M.R., said—

> If a man mortgages property and afterwards sells the equity of redemption to a third person, who then sells the property with the concurrence of the mortgagee, such mortgagee cannot, if he has allowed the purchaser of the equity of redemption to receive the purchase-money, sue the original mortgagor for the amount of the money which he has thus allowed to be paid to the purchaser of the equity of redemption. That is one of the first principles of equity.

Sale

By the Law of Property Act, 1925, Section 101 (1) (i)[98]—

92 *Dashwood* v. *Blythway* (1729), 1 Eq. Cas. Abr. 317, pl. 3.

93 [1910] 1 Ch. 588.

94 *Took* v. — (1784), Dick. 785. Indeed, Lord Thurlow thought a mortgagee who had foreclosed could not sue on the covenant until he had sold the property.

95 *Lockhart* v. *Hardy* (1846), 9 Beav. 349. See also *Perry* v. *Barker* (1803), 8 Ves. 527 (Lord Eldon, L.C.), (1806), 13 Ves. 198 (Lord Erskine, L.C.).

96 See p. 248, *ante*.

97 (1860), 28 Beav. 341, 343. See also *Palmer* v. *Hendrie* (1859), 27 Beav. 349.

98 Previously the Conveyancing Act, 1881, Sect. 19(1)(i), still in force in Ireland. The earliest statutory power of sale was conferred on mortgagees by 23 & 24 Vict., c. 145, Sects. 11-15.

A mortgagee, where the mortgage is made by deed, shall by virtue of this Act, have the following powers, to the like extent as if they had been in terms conferred by the mortgage deed, but not further (namely):

(i) A power, when the mortgage money has become due,[99] to sell, or to concur with any other person in selling, the mortgaged property, or any part thereof, either subject to prior charges or not, and either together or in lots, by public auction or by private contract, subject to such conditions respecting title, or evidence of title, or other matter, as the mortgagee thinks fit,[1] with power to vary any contract for sale, and to buy in at an auction, or to rescind any contract for sale, and to re-sell, without being answerable for any loss occasioned thereby . . .[2]

Subsections (3) and (4)[3] provide that the power of sale may be varied or extended by the mortgage deed and that the whole section applies only if the mortgage deed expresses no contrary intention.

By Section 103 of the 1925 Act[4]—

A mortgagee shall not exercise the power of sale conferred by this Act unless and until—

(i) Notice requiring payment of the mortgage money has been served on the mortgagor or one of two or more mortgagors, and default has been made in payment of the mortgage money, or in part thereof, for three months after such service;[5] or

(ii) Some interest under the mortgage is in arrear and unpaid for two months after becoming due; or

[99] Where the mortgagor has to pay by instalments, the mortgagee can sell on default in paying one instalment even if the whole sum does not thus become due: *Payne* v. *Cardiff R.D.C.*, [1932] 1 K.B. 241 (Div. Ct.).

[1] See *Property & Bloodstock Ltd.* v. *Emerton* [1968] Ch. 94 (C.A.).

[2] See also Sects. 88-89, 101(6), making it clear that sale by the mortgagee carries the mortgagor's estate; Sect. 101(2), authorising the imposition of covenants and conditions and authorising separate dealings with the surface and mines or minerals (Ireland: Conveyancing Act, 1911, Sect. 4); Sect. 92, giving the court power to authorise the surface and mines or minerals to be dealt with separately; Sect. 102, as to mortgages of undivided shares in land; Sect. 106(4), which entitles the selling mortgagee to get the title deeds (Ireland: Conveyancing Act, 1881, Sect. 21(7)); Sect. 107(1), providing that a mortgagee's receipt is a sufficient discharge for the purchase-money (Ireland: Conveyancing Act, 1881, Sect. 22(1)), and Sect. 110, as to the effect on the power to sell of the bankruptcy of the mortgagor.

[3] See pp. 239-40, *ante*. Ireland: Conveyancing Act, 1881, Sect. 19(2), (3).

[4] Ireland: Conveyancing Act, 1881, Sect. 20.

[5] See *Barker* v. *Illingworth*, [1908] 2 Ch. 20, a case on Sect. 20 of the 1881 Act.

(iii) There has been a breach of some provision contained in the mortgage deed or in this Act, or in an enactment replaced by this Act, and on the part of the mortgagor, or of some person concurring in making the mortgage, to be observed or performed other than and besides a covenant for payment of the mortgage money or interest thereon.

This distinction between the power to sell *coming into existence* as soon as the legal date for redemption has passed (Section 101 (1) (i)) and the power *not being exercisable* until certain additional conditions are satisfied (Section 103) is a distinction between the effectiveness of a sale and its propriety. If a mortgagee purports to sell before the power arises the sale is a nullity as against the mortgagor. If he sells after the power has become exercisable, the sale is perfect. If he sells after the power has arisen but before it becomes exercisable the sale is effective to carry the estate to the purchaser, free from the equity of redemption, but if the mortgagor has suffered loss by virtue of the sale he can recover damages from the mortgagee. This is made clear by Section 104[6] (especially subsection (2)), which provides—

(1) A mortgagee exercising the power of sale conferred by this Act shall have power, by deed, to convey the property sold, for such estate and interest therein as he is by this Act authorised to sell or convey or may be the subject of the mortgage, freed from all estates, interests, and rights to which the mortgage has priority, but subject to all estates, interests, and rights which have priority to the mortgage.

(2) Where a conveyance is made in exercise of the power of sale conferred by this Act, or any enactment replaced by this Act, the title of the purchaser shall not be impeachable on the ground—

(*a*) that no case had arisen to authorise the sale; or

(*b*) that due notice was not given; or

(*c*) where the mortgage is made after the commencement of this Act, that leave of the court, when so required, was not obtained; or

(*d*) whether the mortgage was made before or after such commencement, that the power was otherwise improperly or irregularly exercised;

and a purchaser is not, either before or on conveyance, concerned to see or inquire whether a case has arisen to authorise the sale, or due notice has been given, or the power is otherwise properly and regular-

6 Ireland: Conveyancing Acts, 1881, Sect. 21(1), (2), and 1911, Sect. 5(1).

ly exercised; but any person damnified by an unauthorised, or improper, or irregular exercise of the power shall have his remedy in damages against the person exercising the power.

(3) A conveyance on sale by a mortgagee, made after the commencement of this Act, shall be deemed to have been made in exercise of the power of sale conferred by this Act unless a contrary intention appears.[7]

By Section 106 (1)[8]—

The power of sale conferred by this Act may be exercised by any person for the time being entitled to receive and give a discharge for the mortgage money.

The statutory power of sale is given to a mortgagee where the mortgage is made by deed, not drawing any distinction between legal and equitable mortgages, but if the mortgage is an equitable one by deed it is not made clear anywhere in the Act that sale by the mortgagee can transfer the mortgagor's legal estate (if he has one). In England, if the equitable mortgage is secured by a legal term of years absolute or by a charge by way of legal mortgage, the equitable mortgagee can sell the mortgagor's legal estate by virtue of Sections 88 (1) and 89 (1) of the Law of Property Act, 1925. If not, it is at least doubtful whether he can do this under the statutory power. The question is what is meant by " such estate and interest therein as . . . may be the subject of the mortgage " in Section 104 (1). This was taken (in respect of similar words in the Conveyancing Act, 1881, Section 21 (1)) by the Court of Appeal, in *Re Hodson and Howes' Contract*,[9] to refer to the estate or interest given to the mortgagee, and it was held that a charge in equity by deed by way of mortgage gave the mortgagee no statutory power to sell the mortgagor's fee. On this view, all sale by such a mortgagee does is to pass to the purchaser whatever interest in the land the mortgagee had, but free from the equity of redemption.[10] On the 1925 Act, the Court of Appeal expressed a different point of view in *Re White Rose Cottage*,[11] but held that an equitable mortgagee selling under a power of attorney in the mortgage deed was not exercising the statutory power of sale but was in effect the mortgagor selling with the consent of the mortgagee and so sold subject to incumbrances subsequent to that of the mortgagee selling.

[7] In Ireland there is no legislation equivalent to Subsect. 2(*c*) nor to Subsect. (3).
[8] Ireland: Conveyancing Act, 1881, Sect. 21(4).
[9] (1887), 35 Ch.D. 668.
[10] In Ireland and pre-1926 England, a mortgagee by demise or subdemise could pass only a term of years or sub-term under the statutory power of sale.
[11] [1965] Ch. 940.

Where the mortgagee has no statutory power of sale (either because the mortgage is not by deed or because the deed excludes it), the court may order a sale. Application for such an order is the equitable mortgagee's normal procedure for realising his security.[12] Conversely, a mortgagee with no statutory power of sale may have an express one, and a mortgagee who has got a statutory power may be given a more extensive power by the mortgage deed.

The statutory power of sale does not affect the right of foreclosure,[13] but an order of foreclosure nisi does render the power of sale temporarily not exercisable without the leave of the court.[14] If the mortgagee enteres into a contract to sell under the statutory power, the mortgagor cannot redeem so long as the contract is in existence.[15]

The mortgagee's duty of care. By the Law of Property Act, 1925, Section 106 (3)[16]—

> The mortgagee shall not be answerable for any involuntary loss happening in or about the exercise or execution of the power of sale conferred by this Act, or of any trust connected therewith, or, where the mortgage is executed after the thirty-first day of December, nineteen hundred and eleven, of any power or provision contained in the mortgage deed.

In general, the mortgagee cannot be attacked in respect of his motives for selling or of the timing of the sale. If he has obtained a fair price, the sale is not wrongful merely because a higher one could have been got. According to the House of Lords,[17] the mortgagee, not being a

12 See *Pain* v. *Smith* (1833), 2 My. & K. 417; *Matthews* v. *Goodday* (1861), 31 L.J. Ch. 282; *York Union Banking Co.* v. *Artley* (1879), 11 Ch. D. 205.
See also the Law of Property Act, 1925, Sect. 90, giving supplementary powers to the court; and Sect. 50, giving the court powers in respect of the discharge of incumbrances (Ireland: Conveyancing Acts, 1881, Sect. 5, and 1911, Sect. 1).
As to orders for sale in foreclosure proceedings, see pp. 246-7, *ante*.

13 Law of Property Act, 1925, Sect. 106(2). Ireland: Conveyancing Act, 1881, Sect. 21(5).

14 *Stevens* v. *Theatres Ltd.*, [1903] 1 Ch. 857.

15 *Waring (Lord)* v. *London and Manchester Assurance Co. Ltd.*, [1935] Ch. 310; *Property & Bloodstock Ltd.* v. *Emerton*, [1968] Ch. 94 (C.A.).

16 Ireland: Conveyancing Acts, 1881, Sect. 21(6), and 1911, Sect. 5(2).

17 *Kennedy* v. *De Trafford*, [1897] A.C. 180. See also *Jones* v. *Matthie* (1847), 11 Jur. 504; *Robertson* v. *Norris* (1857), 1 Giff. 421; affirmed (1858), 4 Jur. N.S. 443; *Nash* v. *Eads* (1880), 25 S.J. 95 (C.A.); *Warner* v. *Jacob* (1882), 20 Ch.D. 220; *Bettyes* v. *Maynard* (1883), 31 W.R. 461 (C.A.); *Farrar* v. *Farrars Ltd.* (1888), 40 Ch.D. 395, 410-1, *per* Lindley, L.J., giving judgment of the Court of Appeal; *Colson* v. *Williams & Co.* (1889), 58 L.J.Ch. 539; *Haddington Island Quarry Co. Ltd.* v. *Huson*, [1911] A.C. 722 (Privy Council, British Columbia); *Belton* v. *Bass, Ratcliffe and Gretton Ltd.*, [1922] 2 Ch. 449; *Waring (Lord)* v. *London and Manchester Assurance Co. Ltd.*, [1935] Ch. 310; *Wright* v. *New Zealand Farmers Co-operative Assoc. of Canterbury Ltd.*, [1939] A.C. 439 (Privy Council).

trustee of his power of sale, is under a duty only to exercise it in good faith, taking reasonable precautions to safeguard the interests of the owners (including subsequent incumbrancers) of the equity of redemption.

Examples of liability, at least where there has been a genuine sale to a stranger, are few. In *Jenkins* v. *Jones*[18] Stuart, V.-C., set aside a sale made after tender of the debt by the mortgagor, the purchaser knowing of the circumstances. In *Tomlin* v. *Luce*[19] the Court of Appeal held first mortgagees liable to the second mortgagees for the loss occasioned by a mistake in the description of the property made by the auctioneer selling it for the first mortgagees. In *Holohan* v. *Friends Provident and Century Life Office*[20] the whole principle was fully considered by the Supreme Court of the Republic of Ireland. In that case the mortgagees proposed to sell under an express power to do so. They entered into a contract to sell the premises as an investment, subject to existing tenancies, and refused to consider the alternative of selling with vacant possession so as to get a higher price. The mortgagor was granted an injunction. Ó Dálaigh, C.J. (with whom Lavery and Walsh, JJ., agreed), said[21] that the test was what a reasonable man would do in the mortgagee's position. Good faith was not enough: there was no reason to doubt the good faith of the reasonable man. The reasonable man would bear in mind the interests of the mortgagor and of subsequent incumbrancers and would try to get the best price. This decision does not seem to go any further than *Kennedy* v. *De Trafford*[22] in imposing duties on the mortgagee, for the defendants' pig-headed refusal to consider a sensible suggestion in the *Holohan* case was conduct falling below what the House of Lords considered acceptable.

In England, the Building Societies Act, 1962, Section 36, imposes on building societies selling as mortgagees the duty " to take reasonable care to ensure that the price at which the estate is sold is the best price which can reasonably be obtained . . . "[23]

The purpose of the mortgagee's power of sale is to enable him to realise his security, not to enable him to lay his hands on the property (which he can do only by the judicial process of foreclosure in England, and in Ireland not at all) nor to enable him to do his friends a favour. A mortgagee may not sell to a nominee with a view to getting the pro-

18 (1860), 2 Giff. 99.
19 (1889) ,43 Ch.D. 191.
20 [1966] I.R. 1.
21 [1966] I.R. 21.
22 [1897] A.C. 180. See p. 253, *ante*, footnote 17.
23 See *Reliance Permanent Building Soc.* v. *Harwood-Stamper*, [1944] Ch. 362. Northern Ireland: Building Societies Act (Northern Ireland) 1967, Sect. 36.

perty himself. In *Robertson* v. *Norris*[24] Stuart, V.-.C., allowed the mortgagor to redeem fifteen years after the mortgagee had sold to his (the mortgagee's) brother, the mortgagee remaining in occupation. A mortgagee will not be allowed to sell to his agent, such as his solicitor, employed in the transaction. However, not all connection is fatal. In *Farrar* v. *Farrars Ltd.*[25] three mortgagees, including F, sold the property to a company promoted by F for the purpose of the purchase. F was solicitor to the mortgagees and to the purchasing company, and a substantial shareholder in the company. The Court of Appeal held that (i) the sale was not to F, in form or substance; (ii) F had a conflict of interest and duty; (iii) the company had notice of this conflict ; (iv) therefore the company was under the burden of upholding the sale ; and (v) the company had discharged this onus: the sale was upheld because reasonable trouble had been taken to get the best price. In *Nutt* v. *Easton*[26] the personal representative of the mortgagee of a reversionary interest sold it to a solicitor for more than its actuarial value. The purchaser was not acting as the vendor's solicitor at the time. Cozens-Hardy, J., held the sale valid on the ground that the vendor was not a trustee and there was no bad faith (and anyway there was laches).

Servants of mortgagee organisations are not allowed to purchase from their employers. In *Martinson* v. *Clowes*,[27] at a sale by auction by a building society, the property was bought by the society's secretary. Despite the absence of proof of undervalue, North, J., set this sale aside, saying[28]—

> It is quite clear that a mortgagee exercising his power of sale cannot purchase the property on his own account, and I think it clear that the solicitor or agent of such mortgagee acting for him in the matter of the sale cannot do so either.

The vendor-mortgagees in *Hodson* v. *Deans*[29] were a friendly society. At the auction, the property was bought at a slight undervalue by a member of the society's management committee. Joyce, J., said that a

24 (1857), 1 Giff. 421. This decision was affirmed by Lord Cranworth, L.C., on appeal: (1858), 4 Jur. N.S. 443. (In *Giffard's Reports* the date of Stuart, V.-C.'s decision is given as 11th November 1858, but it must have been 11th November 1857, as stated in 4 Jur. N.S. 155, published on 6th March 1858, and repeated in the report, 5 Jur. N.S. 1238, 1239, of subsequent proceedings before Stuart, V.-C.). See also *Henderson* v. *Astwood*, [1894] A.C. 150 (Privy Council, Jamaica).

25 (1888), 40 Ch.D. 395.

26 [1899] 1 Ch. 873.

27 (1882), 21 Ch.D. 857, affirmed (1885), 52 L.T. 706 (C.A.).

28 21 Ch.D. 860.

29 [1903] 2 Ch. 647.

mortgagee was not a trustee, but the solicitor or agent managing the sale could not sell to himself: this was not fair and bona fide, so the sale was set aside. On the same principle, an agent may be denied his commission. In *Matthison* v. *Clarke*[30] the mortgagee employed for the sale the firm of auctioneers of which he was a member. Kindersley, V.-C., held that the firm were not entitled to commission. He said that, because the mortgagee is a trustee of surplus purchase-moneys after paying himself off, he places himself in a fiduciary capacity by exercising the power of sale.

A second mortgagee may purchase when the first mortgagee exercises his power of sale,[31] even if the second mortgage is in the form of a trust for sale.[32]

The proceeds of sale. By the Law of Property Act, 1925, Section 105[33]—

> The money which is received by the mortgagee, arising from the sale, after discharge of prior incumbrances to which the sale is not made subject, if any, or after payment into court under this Act of a sum to meet any prior incumbrance, shall be held by him in trust to be applied by him, first, in payment of all costs, charges, and expenses properly incurred by him as incident to the sale or any attempted sale, or otherwise ; and secondly, in discharge of the mortgage money, interest, and costs, and other money, if any, due under the mortgage; and the residue of the money so received shall be paid to the person entitled to the mortgaged property, or authorised to give receipts for the proceeds of the sale thereof.

The curious closing words of this section, despite the fact that the purchaser seems to be the person entitled to the mortgaged property, seem to be designed to reproduce the doctrine of equity that the selling mortgagee is trustee of the residue for the person entitled, immediately before the sale, to the equity of redemption. This money must be handed over, or interest will be payable.[34] The person entitled immediately to the equity of redemption will be the next incumbrancer, if any, after the vendor, or, if there are no later incumbrancers, the mortgagor or his assignee.

30 (1854), 3 Drew. 3.
31 *Shaw* v. *Bunny* (1865), 2 De G.J. & S. 468 (C.A.Ch.).
32 *Kirkwood* v. *Thompson* (1865), 2 De G.J. & S. 613 (C.A.Ch.).
33 Ireland: Conveyancing Act, 1881, Sect. 21(3).
34 *Charles* v. *Jones* (1887), 35 Ch.D. 544. See also *Matthison* v. *Clarke* (1854), 3 Drew. 3, *per* Kindersley, V.-C.; *Jenkins* v. *Jones* (1860), 2 Giff. 99, 108, *per* Stuart, V.-C.

In *Re Thomson's Mortgage Trusts*[35] Eve, J., decided that a first mortgagee, as trustee of the surplus for the second mortgagee, must hand it over to him. It was not permissible to satisfy only the part of the amount owing on the second mortgage that was not statute-barred and then hold the balance for the third mortgagee. But in *Young* v. *Clarey*,[36] where the mortgagor and the puisne mortgagees were all statute-barred when the first mortgagee (in possession) exercised his statutory power of sale under the 1925 Act, Harman, J., held that the first mortgagee could keep all the proceeds of sale because he was the only person entitled to the mortgaged property within the meaning of Section 105.

The Court of Appeal, in *West London Commercial Bank* v. *Reliance Permanent Building Soc.*,[37] held the first mortgagee liable to a subsequent mortgagee, for not handing him the surplus after the first mortgage had been satisfied, where the sale was by the mortgagor with the concurrence of the first mortgagee, the latter having notice of the subsequent incumbrance.

When he sells, the mortgagee may agree to leave all or part of the purchase-money outstanding, secured by a mortgage, on the property sold, by the purchaser to the vendor; but he will have to account to the owners of the equity of redemption in cash just as much as if he had received it.[38]

The Mortgagee as a Trustee

Analogies are dear to the hearts of developers of the law by judicial process. Chancery practitioners and judges seeking to enhance their fees by enhancing the jurisdiction of their court were no exception. One way of developing the mortgage jurisdiction was to draw an analogy with trusts. Lord Hardwicke, L.C., did this in *Casburne* v. *Scarfe*[39]—

> It is true that a mortgagee is not barely a trustee; but . . . he is in fact a trustee. He is owner of the charge or incumbrance upon the mortgaged premises, and is entitled, in his own right, to hold the same as a pledge for his debt; but as to the inheritance descendible,

[35] [1920] 1 Ch. 508. See also *Thorne* v. *Heard*, [1895] A.C. 495 (House of Lords, England); *Re Caunter's Charge*, [1960] Ch. 491.

[36] [1948] Ch. 191.

[37] (1885), 29 Ch.D. 954.

[38] *Davey* v. *Durrant* (1857), 1 De G. & J. 535 (C.A. Ch.); *Thurlow* v. *Mackeson* (1868), L.R. 4 Q.B. 97; *Bettyes* v. *Maynard* (1883), 31 W.R. 461 (C.A.); *Belton* v. *Bass, Ratcliffe and Gretton Ltd.*, [1922] 2 Ch. 449.

[39] (1738), 2 Jac. & W. 194, 196.

> the real estate in the land, he is a trustee for the mortgagor till the equity of redemption is foreclosed, either by decree or by such a length of time as courts of equity allow to bar a redemption.

This is a sample: Lord Hardwicke was not alone. Restrictively viewed, it does no harm. It is just a complicated way of saying that the mortgagor in fee has an equity of redemption in fee, an equitable estate in the land. But taking quotations out of context is one of the peccadilloes of barristers with scanty authority for their arguments; with the result that the helpful analogy of one judgment becomes the dreadful master of another. So it is that other judges have had explicitly to deny that a mortgagee is a trustee.

There is no chronological sequence about this. Denials and assertions are contemporaneous. As early as 1668, in the Court of Exchequer in *Pawlett* v. *A.-G.*,[40] Hale, C.B., said—

> There is a diversity betwixt a trust and a power of redemption; for a trust is created by the contract of the party, and he may direct it as he pleaseth . . . But a power of redemption is an equitable right inherent in the land, and binds all persons in the post, or otherwise. Because it is an ancient right, which the party is entitled to in equity. . . . And it is of such consideration in the eye of the law, that the law takes notice of it, and makes it assignable and devisable.

Some of this is a bit obscure,[41] but the general drift is plain enough. Tougher language fell from the lips of Lord Herschell in the House of Lords two centuries later[42]—

> . . . it is quite a different proposition and one which I think is wholly untenable to assert that a mortgagee is trustee for the mortgagor.

In the abstract like that, or as a generalisation, it is untenable. As a generalisation, a mortgage is a mortgage and the relations between mortgagee and mortgagor are those of mortgagee and mortgagor. In the long course of *Marquis Cholmondeley* v. *Lord Clinton*[43] Plumer, M.R., put several of his fingers on the point—

> Lord *Mansfield*, adverting to the comparisons made in respect to mortgages, has, I think, said there is nothing so unlike as a simile, and nothing more apt to mislead. A mortgagor has had ascribed to him a variety of different characters, in which there existed some

[40] Hardres 465, 469.

[41] For another convoluted denial that a mortgagee is a trustee (or much of one), see *Dobson* v. *Land* (1850), 8 Hare 216, 220, *per* Wigram, V.-C.

[42] *Taylor* v. *Russell*, [1892] A.C. 244, 255. See also *Sinfield* v. *Sweet*, [1967] 1 W.L.R. 1489, 1496, *per* Pennycuick, J.

[43] (1820), 2 Jac. & W. 1, 182-3.

> points of resemblance, when it was not very material to ascertain what his powers or interests were, or to settle with any great precision in what respect the resemblance did, and in what it did not exist. But it would be productive of much error, if it were to be concluded that the resemblance was complete, in every point, to any one of the ascribed characters. . . . The truth is, it is a relation perfectly anomalous and *sui generis*. The names of mortgagor and mortgagee most properly characterise the relation; they are . . . characters well known, and their rights, powers, and interests as well settled, as any in the law. It is only in a secondary point of view, and under certain circumstances, and for a particular purpose, that the character of trustee constructively belongs to a mortgagee. No trust is expressed in the contract; it is only raised by implication in subordination to the main purpose of it, and after that is fully satisfied; its primary character is not fiduciary.

This is not quite true, but it is on the right lines. The analogy-knockers, though, can invent their own counter-analogies, and quite a vivid (and nearly accurate, so far as it goes) four stages of man-the-mortgagee were put forward by Plumer, M.R.,[44] and Lord Brougham, L.C.:[45] (i) before the date for redemption, he is tenant in mortgage; (ii) after default, he is a creditor with a lien; (iii) after taking possession, he is quasi-owner; (iv) after payment off, he is a mere trustee.

He is a mortgagee throughout. Sometimes he is other characters. He is landlord under an attornment clause. He may be an express trustee if that is what the mortgage says. He may, if the mortgage is equitable, be a beneficiary of a trust of the legal estate vested in the mortgagor. He may be a trustee for the mortgagor (after payment or after sale) or for a subsequent incumbrancer or for a co-mortgagee. He may owe a fiduciary duty without being a trustee (as in exercising the power of sale). It is not a mere question of words: it does matter. For example, if a mortgagee is a trustee of the legal estate for the mortgagor, he may be able to assign it by appointing new trustees by deed (which operates, under the Trustee Act, 1925, Section 40,[46] to vest the trust property in them).

The Mortgagee May Buy from the Mortgagor

Once the mortgage has been made, the mortgagee may buy the equity of redemption from the mortgagor for a fresh consideration.[47] A

[44] *Marquis Cholmondeley* v. *Lord Clinton* (1820), 2 Jac. & W. 1, 183-6.

[45] *Leith* v. *Irvine* (1833), 1 My. & K. 277, 287-8.

[46] The same is true under the Trustee Act (Northern Ireland), 1958, Sect. 39, but in the Republic of Ireland the position under the Trustee Act, 1893, Sect. 12, is different.

[47] See pp. 176-8, 202-9, *ante*, as to agreements contained in the mortgage deed restricting the mortgagor's ownership of the equity of redemption.

trustee may buy a beneficiary's interest, but there is a presumption of undue influence in such a transaction. There is no presumption when a mortgagee buys the equity of redemption: the relationship between the parties is regarded as that of an ordinary vendor and purchaser.[48] That is true also when the mortgagee buys from a prior mortgagee, and even if the purchasing mortgagee holds a mortgage in the form of a trust for sale.[49]

Doctrine of Graft

This is the Irish name for what is called in England the rule in *Keech* v. *Sandford*,[50] that any accretion to trust property, even if on the face of it meant for the trustee beneficially, is held on the same trusts as the original trust property. In *Fector* v. *Philpott*[51] Richards, L.C.B., held that depositees of a lease by way of mortgage were bound to seek renewal (on the expiry of the lease) on behalf of the mortgagor, " . . . for, taking it as a deposit of deeds, they make themselves trustees of [the mortgagor], subject to their own debt, which was secured on the property."

If there is indeed a trusteeship in this respect, it cuts both ways. The mortgagor may be subject to the doctrine of graft. Indeed, this doctrine was applied to mortgages in this way long before *Keech* v. *Sandford* was decided in 1726. If a lessee mortgages a lease by depositing it, and then surrenders to the landlord and gets a new lease of the same premises, he will be a trustee of the new lease for the mortgagee of the old one.[52]

The Mortgagor as Trustee for an Equitable Mortgagee

When the owner of a legal estate in land makes an equitable mortgage he sometimes declares himself trustee of the legal estate for the mortgagee.[53] Even without an express declaration, there may be such a trust. For example, if the mortgage purports to be a legal mortgage, but lacks some element so that it operates only in equity, at least if it contains a covenant for further assurance the mortgagor's position in relation to the legal estate " is in the Nature of a Trustee for the Mortgagee till the Money is paid . . . "[54]

48 *Ensworth* v. *Griffiths* (1706), 5 Bro. P.C. 184 (House of Lords, England); *Knight* v. *Marjoribanks* (1849), 2 Mac. & G. 10 (Lord Cottenham, L.C.); *Melbourne Banking Corp. Ltd.* v. *Brougham* (1882), 7 App.Cas.307 (Privy Council, Victoria).

49 *Kirkwood* v. *Thompson* (1865), 2 De G.J. & S. 613 (C.A.Ch.).

50 (1726), Sel. Cas. temp. King 61. See Keeton, *The Law of Trusts*, 9th ed., pp. 207-11, and Irish Supplement (Sheridan), p. 30.

51 (1823) 12 Price 197, 208-9.

52 Cf. *Proud* v. *Buzzard* (1678/9), 79 Sel.Soc. 721 (Lord Nottingham, L.C.). The facts are given on p. 174, *ante*.

53 For an example, see *London and County Banking Co.* v. *Goddard*, [1897] 1 Ch. 642.

54 *Burgh* v. *Francis* (1673), Rep. temp. Finch 28, 29. See pp. 171-2, *ante*.

It is often said that a mortgage by deposit of title deeds makes the mortgagor a trustee of the legal estate for the mortgagee. This is not true (in the absence of an express declaration of trust) except in the sense that in foreclosure proceedings the mortgagee is entitled to a declaration that, in default of payment of what may be found due, the mortgagor is a trustee of the legal estate for him.[55]

Accountability of a Mortgagee in Possession

A mortgagee in possession has to account to the mortgagor not only for all his receipts but also for what he would have received had he not been guilty of wilful default (if he has).[56] This is not on the footing of a trust, however, and has never been so put. In fact, the decision in *White* v. *City of London Brewery Co.*[57] that the mortgagees did not have to account for the profit they made on the sale of beer to the tenant, when they had entered the mortgaged premises and let them as a tied house, was expressly related by Cotton, L.J.,[58] to the mortgagees not being trustees.

In any case, as so often, the duties are mutual. The mortgagor in possession owes a duty to the mortgagee not to deal with the premises in any way that will damage their adequacy as security.[59]

The Satisfied Mortgagee as Trustee

Plumer, V.-C., said, in *Quarrell* v. *Beckford*[60]—

> All the cases treat the mortgagee, as soon as he is paid, as becoming a mere naked trustee, holding the legal estate for the benefit of the *cestui que trust*, the mortgagor.

Bleak as this may seem, it is true, except that the cestui que trust is not always the mortgagor: it is the person with the first claim on the equity of redemption, who may be the mortgagor, his successor in title, or the next incumbrancer after the mortgagee paid off.[61]

Mortgagee's Duty on Sale

When a mortgagee exercises his power of sale so as to override the equity of redemption he owes a duty of care, to act in good faith, to get

55 See *Marshall* v. *Shrewsbury* (1875), L.R. 10 Ch.App. 250, 254, p. 243, *ante*.
56 See pp. 235-8, *ante*.
57 (1889), 42 Ch.D. 237. See p. 236, *ante*.
58 42 Ch.D. 245-6.
59 See p. 223, *ante*.
60 (1816), 1 Madd. 269, 278.
61 See, further, *Harper* v. *Kawse* (1678/9), 79 Sel. Soc. 718, pp. 170-1, *ante; Teevan* v. *Smith* (1882), 20 Ch.D. 724, 729-30, *per* Jessel, M.R., p. 192, *ante*; *Whiteley* v. *Delaney*, [1914] A.C. 132, pp. 194-5, *ante*. Cf. *Sands to Thompson* (1883), 22 Ch.D. 614. See also the Law of Property Act, 1925, Sect. 116.

a reasonable price in the interests of the mortgagor and subsequent incumbrancers. But he is not a trustee of the power.[62] He may not sell to himself or his nominee or agent employed in the sale,[63] and this shows a fiduciary position but not a trust.

After sale, if there is a residue of money after paying himself off, the mortgagee is a trustee of this residue for the person with the highest priority of interest in the equity of redemption.[64] Since 1881,[65] when a mortgagee has sold and discharged prior incumbrances to which the sale was not made subject, the mortgagee is made a statutory trustee of the rest of the money on trust to pay for the sale, and secondly on trust to pay himself what is due to him in respect of the mortgage.

Joint Mortgages

When money is jointly advanced on mortgage, the mortgagees are tenants in common in equity. If they are joint tenants at law they hold on trust for themselves as tenants in common.[66]

Conclusion

Mortgages should be confused with trusts with caution and in moderation. It should be done only when it is useful and only by persons who know what they are doing. Mortgagors and mortgagees are neither always trustees nor never trustees.

62 See pp. 253-4, *ante*.

63 See pp. 254-6, *ante*.

64 See pp. 256-7, *ante*.

65 Conveyancing Act, 1881, Sect. 21(3); Law of Property Act, 1925, Sect. 105. See p. 256, *ante*.

66 See *Morley* v. *Bird* (1798), 3 Ves. 628; *Re Jackson* (1887), 34 Ch.D. 732; Conveyancing Act, 1881, Sect. 61; Law of Property Act, 1925, Sect. 111.

CHAPTER VII

THE ADMINISTRATION OF THE ESTATES OF DECEASED PERSONS

WHEN a person dies, the collection and distribution of his estate is undertaken by his personal representatives. If he leaves a will, and has appointed persons termed " executors " to administer it, and they accept, the administration is undertaken by them. If he has left no will, then he dies intestate, and the court will appoint administrators, who will administer the estate in accordance with the provisions of the Administration of Estates Act, 1925,[1] and the general law relating to intestacy. When the deceased has left a will, and has appointed no executors, or where there are no executors able or willing to act, then administrators " cum testamento annexo " will be appointed to carry out the provisions of the will. In all administrations of the estates of deceased persons, there are three stages:

(1) the estate of the deceased must be collected;
(2) the debts must be paid;
(3) the balance remaining after payment of debts must be distributed to those who are entitled to it, either under the will or by virtue of the law of succession.

Although the law relating to the administration of assets was completely changed by the Administration of Estates Act, 1925,[1] some important doctrines antedating the Judicature Acts survived, and a brief sketch of the earlier and much more complicated law upon this topic will aid in the elucidation of the modern law.

Section 34 of the Judicature Act, 1873[2] made the administration of the estates of deceased persons one of the matters assigned to the Chancery Division, and in so doing it confirmed the equity jurisdiction upon this topic, which had previously been exercised by the Court of Chancery. Although this was often described as part of the exclusive jurisdiction of the Court of Chancery, there were, nevertheless, occasions when those who were interested in the administration of an estate might wish to have recourse to the common law courts; and there were

[1] Ireland: Succession Act, 1965 (Republic of Ireland); Administration of Estates Act (Northern Ireland), 1955. As to the latter Act generally, see Leitch's *Handbook* on it, which examines the Irish cases thoroughly.

[2] Ireland: Judicature (Ireland) Act, 1877, Sect. 36.

also occasions when they were compelled to do so. Something has already been said of the jurisdiction of the ecclesiastical courts in respect of the distribution of the personal estate of a deceased, and it was here, for some centuries, that the legatee enforced his right to receive a legacy from the executor, whose office was the creation of the ecclesiastical courts. These courts, however, had nothing to do with succession to real property, which passed directly to the heir or devisee, and accordingly it could not be made liable for the deceased's debts unless such debts were secured by a charge upon the realty or unless the deceased, in his will, devised and bequeathed all his property to trustees (who were frequently the executors) on trust to pay his creditors out of it. In such a case, the creditor would seek the assistance of the Court of Chancery to enforce the trust, and so to secure payment of his debts. It was in cases such as these that the Court of Chancery, in the early seventeenth century, first came to acquire jurisdiction in such matters.

In such cases the common law courts could not assist the creditor but, at substantially the same period, the common law courts gave a creditor an action to sue the personal representative directly, and he would then be compelled to satisfy the creditor out of the assets of the deceased which had come into his hands. Further, the common law courts would allow a creditor to sue the heir for the recovery of his debt in some circumstances; and although the common law courts did not give the legatee an action to recover a general legacy, or a share of the residue, it would nevertheless entertain an action for a specific legacy or for a legacy charged on land. In some cases, too, statutes aided a creditor. For example by 3 W. & M., c. 14,[3] a creditor was enabled to sue at law the devisee of his debtor.

Ultimately, however, the general jurisdiction in the administration of estates was acquired by the Court of Chancery, primarily because of the superior remedies which it offered. For example, its machinery in the taking of accounts, developed in respect of trusts, was extended to the administration of estates. Further, the Chancery could call upon all the creditors to prove their debts, and then, by injunction, it could prohibit them from enforcing them elsewhere, i.e. at common law. Again, at the instance of a personal representative, a creditor or a legatee, it could decree that the administration of the estate should be undertaken by the court itself and, when it did so, it administered the estate in conformity with the existing common law rules, to which were added the rules which the Court of Chancery itself progressively evolved.

[3] Ireland: 4 Anne, c. 5 (Ir.).

Thus there arose the important distinction between administration out of court (i.e. by personal representatives) and administration by the court. Where the administration was out of court, the common law order of priority for the payment of debts, as modified from time to time by statute, was strictly applicable. The personal representative was bound to adhere to this order, and if he paid them in another order, he was answerable to a creditor thereby prejudiced for the loss. Within each class of debts, the representative could pay as he pleased (with exceptions marked below). This was due to the common law right of the personal representative to prefer one or more creditors of equal degree at the expense of the others, and, as a corollary, and also since he would not sue himself, he had a right of retainer in respect of any debt within the class, for himself. The order of ranking, which is now merely of historical interest, was as follows:—

1. Debts to the Crown by record or specialty.
2. Debts to which a priority was given by particular statutes.
3. Debts due upon judgments obtained in courts of record. (These were to be paid, as between themselves, rateably.)
4. Recognizances.
5. Debts due upon judgments obtained against the personal representative. These ranked for payment in the order of date.
6. Debts due upon specialty or simple contract (originally specialty debts had ranked before simple contract debts, but the distinction was abolished in 1869).[4]
7. Debts upon voluntary convenants and bonds.

(At law, these ranked with other specialty debts, but in equity they were postponed to all obligations for valuable consideration.)

These rules were followed in equity as fully as at common law, but where the administration was in the Court of Chancery, the court from time to time had property to distribute to which these common law rules could never apply—for example, where property was devised on trust to pay debts. In such cases, a court of equity developed its own rules, and showed greater flexibility in ordering payment of debts. It could, and did, ignore the legal order; it could order a rateable payment, and in consequence could prevent the operation of retainer and preference.

This greater flexibility only operated in respect of such property which, in consequence, was termed *equitable assets*. These were described by Kindersley, V.-C., in *Cook* v. *Gregson*[5] as follows—

The general proposition is clear enough that, when assets may be

[4] Administration of Estates Act, 1869.
[5] (1856), 3 Drew. 547, 549-50. See also *O'Grady* v. *Wilmot*, [1916] 2 A.C. 231.

made available in a Court of law, they are legal assets; and when they can only be made available through a Court of Equity, they are equitable assets. This position does not, however, refer to the question whether the assets can be recovered by the executor in a Court of law or in a Court of Equity. The distinction refers to the remedies of the creditor, and not to the nature of the property. The question is not whether the testator's interest was legal or equitable, but whether a creditor of the testator, seeking to get paid out of such assets, can obtain payment thereout from a Court of law, or can only obtain it through a Court of Equity. This, I apprehend, is the true distinction. If a creditor brings an action at law against the executor, and the executor pleads *plene administravit*,[6] the truth of the plea must be tried by ascertaining what assets the executor has received, and whatever assets the Court of law, in trying that question, would charge the executor with must be regarded as legal assets; all others would be equitable assets.

Supposing, however, that distinction to be well founded, there still remains the question, what property come to the hands of the executor would a Court of law consider properly to be taken into account as assets, in trying the truth of the plea of *plene administravit*? I think the general principle is, that a Court of law would treat as assets every item of property come to the hands of the executor which he has recovered, or had a right to recover, merely *virtute officii*, *i.e.*, which he would have had a right to recover if the testator had merely appointed him executor without saying anything about his property or the application thereof. That, I think, is the test which, upon principle, a Court of law would apply.

Historically, the oldest and most important kind of equitable assets was real property the deceased either devised for the payment of his debts, or charged with the payment of them. Equity accepted slight evidence as sufficient to establish such a charge since, before 1833[7] real property was not assets for the payment of simple contract debts. Since 1925 however, the distinction between legal and equitable assets has ceased to be of importance.

In addition to the distinction between the administration of estates by an executor out of court and administration by the court, already mentioned, there were also certain special bankruptcy rules, which might be applicable when the estate was found to be insolvent. Happily, it is not now necessary to consider these rules, since the Administration

6 The defence, to a creditor's claim, that administration is complete and there are no assets left.

7 3 & 4 Will. IV, c. 104.

of Estates Act, 1925,[8] established a uniform set of rules relating to priorities and other matters, however the administration is carried out, and the first Schedule to the Act specifies the rules applicable when the estate is insolvent.

On the death of a person, all his property, including all real estate to which the deceased was entitled for an interest not ceasing on his death, devolves upon his personal representative.[9] This provision reproduces Section 1 of the Land Transfer Act, 1897,[10] but under that Act, it was held that until a legal personal representative was appointed, the real estate still vested in the heir-at-law.[11] Section 9 of the Administration of Estates Act, 1925,[12] now provides, however, that when a person dies intestate, his real and personal estate vest until administration is granted, in the Probate Judge. As soon as administration is granted, the administrator's title relates back to the time of the death.[13] The executor's interest vests in him from death, his title being derived from the will.

Although there are certain acts which can be performed by an executor before probate, the executor first steps in to take out probate of the will, and Section 4 provides that the court has power to summon a person named as executor either to prove the will, or renounce probate.[14] Renunciation must be in respect of the whole office of the executor and, thereafter, his title ceases completely. It need not be made under seal, and in some cases, it may be inferred from conduct. In *Re Clout and Frewer's Contract*[15] a person named as executor did not prove the will, and never acted, dying twenty-nine years after the testator. He had also failed to claim a legacy given to him in his capacity of executor. This was held to amount to disclaimer by conduct.

The executor of a sole or last surviving executor of a testator is also the executor of the testator, and so long as the chain of representation

8 Ireland: Succession Act, 1965 (Republic of Ireland); Administration of Estates Act (Northern Ireland), 1955.

9 Administration of Estates Act, 1925, Sect. 1; Administration of Estates Act (Northern Ireland), 1955, Sect. 1; Succession Act, 1965, Sect. 10 (Republic of Ireland).

10 Ireland: Administration of Estates Act, 1959 (Republic of Ireland); Law Reform (Miscellaneous Provisions) Act (Northern Ireland), 1937.

11 *John* v. *John*, [1898] 2 Ch. 573 (C.A.); *Re Griggs*, [1914] 2 Ch. 547 (C.A.).

12 Ireland: 1965 Act, Sect. 13 (Republic of Ireland) (President of the High Court) 1955 Act, Sect. 3 (Northern Ireland).

13 *In the Goods of Pryse*, [1904] P. 301.

14 Ireland: 1965 Act, Sect. 16 (Republic of Ireland); no Northern Ireland equivalent.

15 [1924] 2 Ch. 230.

is unbroken, the last executor is the executor of every preceding testator. The chain of representation is broken by

(a) an intestacy; or
(b) the failure of the testator to appoint an executor; or
(c) the failure to obtain probate.[16]

Probate or administration may not be granted to more than four persons, and administration must, if there is a minority or a life interest, be granted to not less than two persons or a trust corporation.[17]

Moreover, any person who takes possession of, or intermeddles with, the estate of the deceased, without authority, is treated as an " executor de son tort " so far as liability for death duties is concerned.[18] More generally, Section 28 provides that any person who, either for defrauding creditors or without " full valuable consideration " obtains or holds any real or personal estate of the deceased or who releases any debt or liability due to the estate should be charged as an executor of his own wrong to the extent of the property coming into his hands, after deducting any debt due from the deceased to him, and any payment which such a person might properly have made, had he been a personal representative.[19]

What are Assets for the Payment of Debts

Section 32[20] states that the real and personal estate, whether legal or equitable, of a deceased person, to the extent of his beneficial interest therein, and the real and personal estate of which the deceased in pursuance of any general power (including the statutory power to dispose of entailed interests) disposes by his will, are assets for the payment of his debts and liabilities, and any disposition by will inconsistent with this section is void as against creditors. Such property passes to the personal representative subject to the rights which may be enjoyed by an incumbrancer in respect of it.

If any person to whom such a beneficial interest devolves disposes of it in good faith before an action is brought against him, he is personally liable for the value of the interest of which he has disposed, but the interest itself is not liable to be taken in execution in the action brought against him.

[16] Sect. 7. Ireland: 1965 Act, Sect. 19 (Republic of Ireland), abolishing the chain of representation; 25 Edw. III, st. 5, c. 5 (Northern Ireland).
[17] Sect. 12 (1). No equivalent legislation in Ireland. But see S. R. & O. (N.I.) 1956, No. 29, reg. 16 (administrators).
[18] Sect. 55(i)(xi). Ireland: no equivalent legislation.
[19] Ireland: 1965 Act, Sect. 23 (Republic of Ireland); 7 Will. III, c. 6 (Ir.), Sect. 11 (Northern Ireland).
[20] Ireland: 1965 Act, Sect. 45 (Republic of Ireland); 1955 Act, Sect. 29 (Northern Ireland).

The Trust for Sale on Intestacy

Section 33[21] introduces an important change in the law of intestate succession. It provides that when a person dies intestate, then his property, whether real or personal, is held on trust for sale, with power to pospone such sale and conversion for such period as the personal representatives, without being liable to account, may think proper, but:

(1) a reversionary interest should not be sold until it falls into possession, unless the personal representative sees some special reasons for the sale, and
(2) personal chattels should not be sold except for special reason, unless the sale is required for purposes of administration.

By this section, personal representatives are also made trustees. The two offices, though similar, are not identical, and questions may arise concerning the capacity in which they have acted. In *Re Yerburgh*,[22] it was pointed out that they do not become trustees immediately on appointment. The trust arises only when the administration is complete. So long as there are duties of administration to perform, they retain their powers as administrators.[23]

" Personal chattels," by Section 55 (1) (x),[24] means carriages, horses, stable furniture and effects (not used for business purposes), motor cars and accessories (not used for business purposes), garden effects, domestic animals, plate, plated articles, linen, china, glass, books, pictures, prints, furniture, jewellery, articles of household or personal use or ornaments, musical and scientific instruments and apparatus, wines, liquors, and consumable stores, but the term does not include any chattels used at the death of the intestate for business purposes nor money, nor securities for money.

Section 33 applies also to partial intestacies, but it applies only to cases of intestacy affecting the whole interest in the estate or some part thereof, and not to an intestacy as to a partial interest in the residuary estate, e.g. a life interest or a reversionary interest.[25]

From the proceeds of the sale and conversion of the real and personal estate, and out of the ready money of the deceased, the

[21] Ireland: no equivalent legislation. Cf. 1965 Act, Sect. 10(3) (Republic of Ireland); 1955 Act, Sect. 2(3) (Northern Ireland).

[22] [1928] W.N. 208.

[23] *Re Wilks*, [1935] Ch. 645. See also Keeton, *The Law of Trusts*, 9th ed., pp. 13-14, and Irish Supplement (Sheridan), pp. 1-3.

[24] Ireland: 1965 Act, Sect. 56 (Republic of Ireland) (household chattels); 1955 Act, Sect. 45(1) (Northern Ireland).

[25] *Re McKee*, [1931] 2 Ch. 145 (C.A.); *Re Plowman*, [1943] Ch. 269; *Re Taylor's Estate*, [1969] 2 W.L.R. 1371.

administrators must first pay all funeral, testamentary and administrative expenses, debts and other liabilities, having regard to the rules of administration contained in the Act, and out of the residue, they must then set aside a sum sufficient to pay any pecuniary legacies bequeathed by the will, if any (i.e. on a partial intestacy). During the minority of any beneficiary, or the subsistence of any life interest, and pending the distribution of the whole or any part of the deceased's estate, the personal representatives may invest the residue, or so much as may not have been distributed, in authorised investments, with power to change them, at their discretion, for other authorised investments.

The residue of such money, and any investments representing it, including any unsold part of the estate not required for administration purposes, is distributed in accordance with the provisions of Section 46.[26] By Section 33 (5)[27]—

> The income (including net rents and profits of real estate and chattels real after payment of rates, taxes, rent, costs of insurance, repairs and other outgoings properly attributable to income) of so much of the real and personal estate of the deceased as may not be disposed of by his will, if any, or may not be required for administration purposes aforesaid, may, however such estate is invested, as from the death of the deceased, be treated and applied as income, and for that purpose any necessary apportionment may be made between tenant for life and remainderman.

Administrative Powers of Personal Representatives

Equity has always conceded to personal representatives wide powers of management and disposition over the property of the deceased, for the purposes of administration. These are now defined in the Administration of Estates Act, 1925[28]—

1. Section 39 provides that for purposes of administration, or during the minority of any beneficiary, or whilst there is no life interest, or until the period of distribution arrives, personal representatives possess:

   (i) the same powers and discretions, including the power to raise money by mortgage or charge, as a personal representative had before the Act, so far as personal estate is concerned, and the power of raising money by way of legal mortgages in the case of land;

[26] Ireland: 1965 Act, Sect. 66 (Republic of Ireland); 1955 Act, Sect. 6 (Northern Ireland).
[27] Ireland: No equivalent legislation.
[28] Ireland: 1965 Act, Sects. 50 and 60 (Republic of Ireland); 1955 Act, Sects. 32 and 40 (Northern Ireland).

(ii) all the powers, discretions and duties of trustees for sale holding land upon an effective trust for sale (including the power to overreach equitable interests and powers as if the same affected the proceeds of sale); and

(iii) all the powers conferred by statute on trustees for sale.

This section therefore gives to personal representatives the very wide powers possessed by trustees for sale, which are conferred by the Law of Property Act, 1925, Sections 23-33.[29]

2. *Power to Raise Money by Leasing*

Section 40 provides that for the purpose of giving effect to beneficial interests, the personal representative may grant leases, with or without impeachment for waste, to trustees for raising any principal sums, in respect of which the trust is liable, and may grant a rentcharge for giving effect to any annual or periodical sum for which the land or the income thereof, is liable.

3. *The Power of Appropriation*

Section 41 confers upon the personal representative a wide power of appropriation, whether or not the deceased died intestate.[30] It may be exercised without prejudice to any other power of appropriation conferred by law or by will, and it takes effect with any extended powers conferred by will.[31]

The section provides that the personal representative may appropriate any part of the real or personal estate, including choses in action, in the actual condition of investment at the time of the appropriation, towards the satisfaction of any legacy, or any other interest or share in the property of the deceased, as the personal representatives consider just and reasonable, having referred to the interests of the various persons with interests in the property of the deceased.

The appropriation may only be made under the following conditions:

(i) it may not prejudicially affect any specific devise or bequest;

(ii) it may only be made with the following consents:—

(a) when made for the benefit of a person absolutely and beneficially entitled in possession, with the consent of that person;

(b) when made in respect of a settled legacy, with the consent of the trustee of the legacy, or of the person entitled to the income. Where the person is an infant or a person of

[29] No equivalent legislation in Ireland.

[30] Sect. 41 (9). Ireland: 1965 Act, Sect. 55 (Republic of Ireland); 1955 Act, Sect. 37 (Northern Ireland).

[31] Sect. 41 (6).

unsound mind, the consent of the parent or guardian or committee or receiver or, failing such a person, the consent of the court, is needed;

(iii) no consent (other than that of the trustee) is needed on behalf of an unborn beneficiary;

(iv) if no receiver for a person suffering from mental disorder has been appointed, then no consent is required in respect of such a person;[32]

(v) if, independently of the personal representatives, there is no trustee of a settled legacy, nor is there any person of full age and capacity entitled to the income, no further consent to the appropriation is needed, provided that the appropriation is of an authorised investment.

Once an appropriation has been made, the property is treated as an authorised investment and, accordingly, it may be retained.[33] Before the appropriation is made, the personal representatives may employ a duly qualified valuer to value the property, in any case where it may be necessary. When the property is likely to fluctuate in value, valuation is most desirable for the protection of the personal representatives. For example, in *Re Brookes* [34] a personal representative, with an estate in possession divisible between two beneficiaries, gave one portion, which was valuable, to one beneficiary, and retained the other to satisfy the other share. The retained portion eventually proved to be valueless, and Astbury, J., held that he ought to have ascertained the value of the respective parts of the property at the time when he distributed one part. Since he had not done so, he was liable for breach of trust, and could not claim the protection of the Judicial Trustees Act, 1896, Section 3 (now replaced by Section 61 of the Trustee Act, 1925),[35] as having acted "honestly and reasonably."

4. *Powers to Appoint Trustees for the Property of an Infant*

When an infant is absolutely entitled, either to a legacy under a will or to a share on intestacy, and there are no trustees of the legacy or share, the personal representative may appoint trustees, in whom they may vest the infant's legacy or share, and when he has done so, he is discharged from any further liability in respect of it.[36]

[32] The wording of Sect. 41 (1) (ii) and (iv) has been amended by the Mental Health Act, 1959, Seventh Sched.

[33] Sect. 41 (2).

[34] [1914] 1 Ch. 558.

[35] Ireland: Trustee Act (Northern Ireland), 1958, Sect. 61; no equivalent legislation in the Republic of Ireland.

[36] Sect. 42 The section does not apply where there is a life interest enjoyed by the widow of the deceased, or where the infant is only contingently entitled: *Re Yerburgh*, [1928] W.N. 208. Ireland: 1965 Act, Sect. 57 (Republic of Ireland); 1955 Act, Sect. 38 (Northern Ireland).

5. *Carrying on the Deceased's Business*

Where part of the assets of the deceased was a business, the personal representative has by law a power to carry it on merely for the purpose of sale or winding up. The deceased by his will may, however, give the personal representative power to carry on the business either indefinitely or for a period, e.g. until the personal representative may sell it profitably. Where the personal representative does so for any length of time, some questions arise:

(a) *What part of the deceased's property may be employed in the business?* It would appear that only that part of the property which is employed in the business at his death is available, in the absence of any directions by the testator. The business is regarded as an entity, comprising its assets, and subject to its liabilities.

(b) *The Position of the Personal Representative.* Whenever the personal representatives carry on the business of the deceased, they are personally liable for the debts and liabilities incurred in its conduct. If there is no authorisation in the will to carry on the business, the creditors have a right only against the personal representatives; but if they have been authorised by the will to carry it on, the personal representatives, as such, have a right to recoup themselves out of the assets of the business, and the creditors, in turn, are subrogated to them, to the extent that such assets are properly employed in the conduct of the business. In *Ex parte Garland*[37] the executor who was directed to carry on the deceased's business became bankrupt, so that it became necessary to determine the extent of the rights of the business creditors against the estate. Lord Eldon, L.C., held that they were entitled to recover only from those assets which were declared to be embarked in trade. Moreover, since the creditor's right of subrogation is equitable, he can only exercise it if the personal representative is not himself in default to the assets. If, however, there are several executors, and only one is in default, the trade creditors may proceed in respect of the right of indemnity of those executors who are not in default.[38]

The creditor's right to subrogation extends not only to debts, but also to damages for torts committed by the executor in carrying on the business. In *Re Raybould*[39] a trustee and executor had commenced working a colliery belonging to the trust for its benefit. In so doing he let down the surface of an adjoining owner's land. The adjoining

[37] (1804), 10 Ves. 110.
[38] *Re Frith*, [1902] 1 Ch. 342.
[39] [1900] 1 Ch. 199.

owner sued and recovered £1,092, which Byrne, J., held could be paid directly out of the trust estate, from which the trustee was entitled to an indemnity.

When the executor carries on the business of the deceased in accordance with the directions of the will, and with the assent of the creditors existing at his death, he is entitled to be indemnified out of the estate against liabilities properly incurred in the conducting of the business, in priority to the claims of the testator's creditors. The result is, by the application of the doctrine of subrogation, that the claims of business creditors, whose claims arose subsequent to the testator's death, should be paid in priority to the claims of the other creditors.[40] Such priorities only exist if the testator's creditors have actually assented to the carrying on of the business. If they have not, they are entitled to be paid first out of the assets existing at the time of the testator's death, even though the deceased directed that the business was to be carried on by the executors.[41]

The Payment of the Debts of the Deceased

Once the personal representative has got in the estate, it is his duty to pay the debts of the deceased. In *Re Tankard*[42] Uthwatt, J., defined that duty as follows—

> Apart from any provisions contained in the will of a testator which expressly or impliedly deal with the payment of the debts, it is the duty of the executors, as a matter of the due administration of the estate, to pay the debts of their testator with due diligence having regard to the assets in their hands which are properly applicable for that purpose, and in determining whether due diligence has been shown regard must be had to all the circumstances of the case. It was contended by the defendants that this was not a duty which was owed to the beneficiaries. In my opinion this contention is not correct. The duty is owed not only to the creditors, but also to beneficiaries, for the ultimate object of the administration of an estate is to place the beneficiaries in possession of their interest and that object cannot be fully achieved unless all debts are satisfied.

After pointing out that the duty extended both to debts which bore interest, and to those which did not, the learned judge continued[43]—

> With respect to the period within which debts should be paid, there is, in my opinion, no rule of law that it is the duty of executors to pay such debts within a year from the testator's death. The duty is

40 *Dowse* v. *Gorton*, [1891] A.C. 190.
41 *Re Oxley*, [1914] 1 Ch. 604 (C.A.).
42 [1942] Ch. 69, 72.
43 [1942] Ch. 73.

to pay with due diligence. Due diligence may, indeed, require that payment should be made before the expiration of the year, but the circumstances affecting the estate and the assets comprised in it may justify non-payment within the year, but, if debts are not paid within the year, the onus is thrown on the executors to justify the delay.

The Order of Payment

Reference to those chapters of Maitland's *Equity* which discuss the administration of assets shows how complicated the problems relating to the order of payment formerly were. There were differences as between administration in court and administration out of court, and between the rules administered in the Chancery Division and in bankruptcy. All these differences were abolished in England in 1925, and now, when the estate of a deceased person is insolvent, his real and personal estate is administered in accordance with the rules set out in Part I of the First Schedule of the Administration of Estates Act, 1925,[44] whether the administration is in court or out of court.

Whether an estate is insolvent is a question of fact, determined by the Master after a consideration of its liabilities, which may, for example, include the capitalised value of an annuity payable out of it.[45] Even if the estate is insolvent a landlord may distrain in respect of rent falling due before the making of the order for administration.

Insolvent Estates

If the estate is insolvent, then:—

1. The funeral, testamentary and administration expenses have priority. Testamentary expenses include estate and other duties payable in respect of the estate at death.

2. Subject to the above expenses, then " the same rules shall prevail and be observed as to the respective rights of secured and unsecured creditors and as to debts and liabilities provable and as to the valuation of annuities and future and contingent liabilities respectively, and as to priorities of debts and liabilities as may be in force for the time being under the laws of bankruptcy with respect to the assets of persons adjudged bankrupt."

The Bankruptcy Rules

The order of priority of debts in the administration of an insolvent estate, as in bankruptcy, is set out in Section 33 of the Bankruptcy Act,

[44] Sect. 34 (1). Ireland: 1965 Act, 1st Sched., Part I (Republic of Ireland); 1955 Act, 1st Sched., Part I (Northern Ireland).

[45] *Re Pink*, [1927] 1 Ch. 237. See also *Re Leng*, [1895] 1 Ch. 652 (C.A.), decided on the Judicature Act, 1875, Sect. 10.

1914,[46] as amended. In general, all debts must be paid pari passu (unless they are supported by security), but Section 33 makes a few preferred debts, and there are also one or two preferred debts under special statutes.[47] Preferred debts under Section 33 are:—

(a) All rates and taxes due at the date of the death, and payable within twelve months next before that time, assessed on him up to 5th April next before his death, and not exceeding one year's assessment. If more than one year's taxes are due, the Crown may select for preferential payment the "last year," which is not necessarily the concluding year. As Lord Evershed, M.R., pointed out in *Re Pratt*,[48] until this limited priority was introduced in Section 166 of the Bankruptcy Act, 1849, the Crown had a prerogative right to priority in respect of all assessed taxes, which the words of the section have abridged. It extends, however, to all assessed taxes, including profit tax, purchase tax, selective employment tax and others.

(b) The wages or salary of a clerk or servant for services during the four months preceding the death, to a maximum of £200.[49] There was for some time a doubt whether money paid by way of commission, e.g. to a commercial traveller, was within this subsection. Section 2 of the Bankruptcy (Amendment) Act, 1926,[50] now provides that such payments are entitled to preference.

(c) All wages of any labourer or workman, not exceeding £200, in respect of services rendered during the four months preceding the death, to a maximum of £200.

(d) All amounts due, in respect of contributions payable during the twelve months before the bankruptcy, by the deceased as employed under the National Insurance (Industrial Injuries) Act, 1946,[51] or either as the employer of any person or as a self-employed or non-employed person, under the National Insurance Act, 1946.[52]

These debts rank equally between themselves.[53] When they have been paid, the remainder of the debts, subject to a few exceptions, are

[46] Ireland: Irish Bankrupt and Insolvent Act, 1857, Sect. 249, Bankruptcy (Ireland) Amendment Act, 1872, Sect. 49, Preferential Payments in Bankruptcy (Ireland) Act, 1889 (Republic of Ireland); Preferential Payments (Bankruptcies and Arrangements) Act (Northern Ireland), 1964.

[47] E.g. money owed by the Officer of a Friendly Society to the Society. Friendly Societies Act, 1896, Sect. 35.

[48] [1951] Ch. 225, 228 (C.A.).

[49] Sect. 33 as amended by the Companies Act, 1947, Sects. 91, 115.

[50] Ireland: Preferential Payments (Bankruptcies and Arrangements) Act (Northern Ireland), 1964, Sect. 1 (1) (*b*); no equivalent legislation in the Republic of Ireland.

[51] Ireland: no equivalent legislation in the Republic of Ireland; National Insurance (Industrial Injuries) Act (Northern Ireland), 1946.

[52] Ireland: no equivalent legislation in the Republic of Ireland; National Insurance Act (Northern Ireland), 1946.

[53] Bankruptcy Act, 1914, Sect. 33 (2).

paid pari passu.[54] The exception, making the debts contained in them deferred debts, payable only after all other debts for valuable consideration have been discharged, are contained in the Bankruptcy Act, 1914, Sections 36, 42, 63 and 66;[55] in the Partnership Act, 1890, Section 3; and in the Moneylenders Act, 1927, Section 9.[56]

In the administration of insolvent estates, the bankruptcy rules relating to secured creditors are also applicable.[57] The secured creditor may choose between the following courses of action:—

1. he may rely on his security, and not prove for the debt;
2. he may realise the security and, if there is a deficiency, he may prove for the balance;
3. he may surrender his security, and prove for the whole debt;
4. he may give particulars of his security, and value it, and then prove for the balance, if the security is insufficient.

Debts Provable

In the administration of an insolvent estate, the bankruptcy rules relating to debts provable are also applicable. These are contained in England in Section 30 of the Bankruptcy Act, 1914, which first provides that demands in the nature of unliquidated damages arising otherwise than by contract, promise or breach of trust shall not be provable. To this an important exception was introduced by Section 1 (6) of the Law Reform (Miscellaneous Provisions) Act, 1934[58] which states—

> In the event of the insolvency of an estate against which proceedings are maintainable by virtue of this section, any liability in respect of the cause of action in respect of which the proceedings are maintainable shall be deemed to be a debt provable in the administration of the estate, notwithstanding that it is a demand in the nature of unliquidated damages arising otherwise than by a contract, promise or breach of trust.

With this qualification, all debts and liabilities, present or future, certain or contingent, to which the deceased is subject, or would be

54 1914 Act, Sect. 33 (7).
55 Ireland: The Bankruptcy Amendment Act (Northern Ireland), 1929, Sect. 12, corresponds to Sect. 42 of the Bankruptcy Act, 1914. In the Republic of Ireland, the Bankruptcy (Ireland) Amendment Act, 1872, corresponds, except that there is no equivalent of Sect. 42(3) of the 1914 Act. There is no Irish equivalent of Sect. 63. Throughout Ireland, the Irish Bankrupt and Insolvent Act, 1857, Sect. 260, corresponds to Sect. 66.
56 Ireland: Moneylenders Act (Northern Ireland), 1933, Sect. 9; Moneylenders Act, 1933, Sect. 16 (Republic of Ireland).
57 2nd Schedule, rr. 10-18. Ireland: 1965 Act, Sect. 47 (Republic of Ireland); 1955 Act, Sect. 31 (Northern Ireland).
58 Ireland: Civil Liability Act, 1961, Sect. 10 (Republic of Ireland); Law Reform (Miscellaneous Provisions) Act (Northern Ireland), 1937, Sect. 14.

subject, are provable, and an estimate may be made of the debt or liability, where, because of its nature, its value is not certain. If, in the opinion of the court, the value is incapable of being fairly estimated, it may make an order to that effect, whereupon the debt will be considered to be a debt not provable.

Under the Exchange Control Act, 1947,[57] in the administration of the estate of a deceased person, a claim not payable without the permission of the Treasury, is nevertheless admitted to proof, even though Treasury permission has not been given, or it has been revoked; but the personal representative may not make a payment until such permission has been obtained.

Where the personal representative is administering an estate which is insolvent, the bankruptcy rules in respect of interest on provable debts apply. Accordingly, if the debt carries interest, interest at the rate of 5 per cent per annum is allowed. If the debt carried a higher rate, the excess will be payable only after all the debts proved have been paid in full.[58] So far as insolvent estates are concerned, it had been held in *Re Whitaker*[59] that this rule had been introduced by Section 10 of the Judicature Act, 1875,[60] and in *Re Bush*[61] Luxmoore, J., held that Section 66 of the Bankruptcy Act, 1914[62] had been incorporated into the administration of insolvent estates by virtue of Section 34 of the Administration of Estates Act, 1925.[63]

By virtue of the same section, the bankruptcy rules relating to set-off, contained in Section 31 of the Bankruptcy Act, 1914,[64] are applicable in the administration of an insolvent estate.

One other point which was regarded as settled by all three members of the Court of Appeal in *Re Whitaker*[59] was that Section 10 of the Judicature Act, 1875,[60] had introduced a change from the old Chancery practice in respect of debts provable. Before that Act, it was a well established rule of Chancery practice that, in the administration by the court of an insolvent estate, creditors for valuable consideration took precedence over those whose debts were not founded upon valuable consideration. The bankruptcy rule made no distinction between the two sorts of debt, and the Court of Appeal in that case decided that

57 Sched. IV, para. 5. Republic of Ireland: Exchange Control Act, 1954.
58 Bankruptcy Act, 1914, Sect. 66 (1). Ireland: no equivalent legislation.
59 [1901] 1 Ch. 9.
60 Ireland: Judicature (Ireland) Act, 1877, Sect. 28 (1).
61 [1930] 2 Ch. 202.
62 Ireland: Irish Bankrupt and Insolvent Act, 1857, Sect. 260.
63 Ireland: 1965 Act, Sect. 46 (Republic of Ireland); 1955 Act, Sect. 30 (Northern Ireland).
64 Ireland: Irish Bankrupt and Insolvent Act, 1857, Sect. 251.

this rule was now applicable in the administration of an insolvent estate. In *Re Bush*,[65] Luxmoore, J., points out that the position following the passing of the Administration of Estates Act, 1925, remained the same.

Bankruptcy Rules not Applicable in the Administration of an Insolvent Estate.

1. *Swelling the Assets*

It was well settled, even before the decision of the Court of Appeal in *Re Whitaker*,[66] that the bankruptcy rules relating to the enlargement of the assets of a bankrupt had no application in the administration of an insolvent estate, and here again, there has been no change by rules of the Administration of Estates Act, 1925. The most important of the rules relates to reputed ownership,[67] voluntary settlements by the bankrupt[68] and fraudulent preferences.[69] The personal representatives therefore administer the property which belonged to the deceased at the time of his death.

2. *Unenforceable Claims*

In *Re Sandiford* (No. 2)[70] a barrister sought to prove in the administration of the estate of an insolvent solicitor for fees which the clients had paid to the solicitor on his false representation that he had paid them to counsel, and which he improperly retained. Clauson, J., held that there was no right to prove. No action lies for the recovery of counsel's fees and, although in *Ex parte James*,[71] the Court of Appeal in Chancery held that where a trustee in bankruptcy had received certain moneys which, in the view of the court, it would not be honest of him to retain, he ought to refund them, even though their return could not be legally enforced, nevertheless, an executor is not an officer of the court, and accordingly there was no obligation upon him to pay over counsel's fees, and the court would not order him to do so.

Similarly, where an oral contract was unenforceable for lack of written evidence, where this was required by law, the personal representative could not pay it.

65 [1930] 2 Ch. 9. 202.
66 [1901] 1 Ch. 9.
67 Bankruptcy Act, 1914, Sect. 38. Ireland: Irish Bankrupt and Insolvent Act, 1857, Sects. 273, 298 and 313.
68 1914 Act, Sect. 42. Ireland: Bankruptcy (Ireland) Amendment Act, 1872, Sect. 52 (Republic of Ireland); Bankruptcy Amendment Act (Northern Ireland), 1929, Sect. 12.
69 1914 Act, Sect. 44. Ireland: Bankruptcy (Ireland) Amendment Act, 1872, Sect. 53 (all Ireland); Bankruptcy Amendment Act (Northern Ireland), 1929, Sect. 13.
70 [1935] Ch. 681.
71 (1874), L.R. 9 Ch. App. 609.

Statute Barred Debts

The position of statute-barred debts is different from that of unenforceable claims. Here, provided the claim was originally enforceable, and the remedy merely (not the claim itself) is barred by lapse of time, the personal representative may pay, unless a legatee or some other person interested in the estate objects, or unless an order or judgment for administration has been made.[72]

Distraint by a Landlord

There is nothing in the Bankruptcy Act, 1914, or in the Administration of Estates Act, 1925, to prevent a landlord from distraining in respect of rent falling due after the making of an order for administration. In bankruptcy, the landlord may keep only six months' rent for the period immediately before the bankruptcy, and this rule will apply where the estate is being administered in bankruptcy, but in other cases he may retain six years' back rent. This right is, however, qualified by Section 33 (4) of the Bankruptcy Act, 1914[73]—

> In the event of a landlord or other persons distraining or having distrained on any goods or effects of a bankrupt within three months next before the date of the receiving order[74] the debts to which priority is given by this section shall be a first charge on the goods or effects so distrained on, or the proceeds of sale thereof:
>
> Provided that in respect of any money paid under such charge the landlord or other person shall have the same rights of priority as the person to whom such payment is made.

The effect of the proviso is not clear, but it presumably means that the landlord becomes a preferential creditor, postponed to those who have been paid from the proceeds of the distraint.[75]

Retainer and Preference

An executor has two rights, which are of importance in the administration of an insolvent estate, which have no place in bankruptcy. These rights are the rights of *Retainer* and *Preference*, already well established in the reign of Elizabeth I.[76]

(a) *Retainer.* By virtue of this right, the personal representative may pay a debt due to himself in priority to any debt of an equal degree

[72] *Re Wenham*, [1892] 3 Ch. 59.
[73] Ireland: Preferential Payments in Bankruptcy (Ireland) Act, 1889, Sect. 4 (4) (Republic of Ireland); Preferential Payments (Bankruptcies and Arrangements) Act (Northern Ireland), 1964, Sect. 1 (7), (8).
[74] In the case of the deceased being insolvent, this means the date of death.
[75] Williams, *Bankruptcy*, 18th ed., p. 233.
[76] *Woodward* v. *Lord Darcy* (1557), 1 Plow, 184.

of priority to his own. It may now be exercised in respect of all the assets of the deceased, whether legal or equitable,[77] whereas, before 1926, it could be exercised only in respect of legal assets. It may be exercised only in respect of debts owed to the personal representative in his own right, whether solely or jointly with another person, but it does not extend to debts which have never been legally enforceable (e.g. because of absence of writing, where this is required by law), but it can be exercised in respect of a statute-barred debt.

The right may only be exercised in respect of debts of equal priority to that of the personal representative. For example, he may not retain a simple contract debt as against the Crown's preferential claim for one year's taxes.[78] In the words of Lord Tomlin in *A.-G.* v. *Jackson*,[79] by virtue of modern legislation, and especially by the Administration of Estate Act, 1925—

> The right to retain or prefer has not been altered, but the degrees in which debts are ranged have been changed, and it is in the field as so changed that the rights in question must to-day operate.
>
> The result is that all debts fall within one or other of two degrees. There are no other degrees where the Act of 1925 applies. If, therefore, a legal personal representative is a creditor for a debt in the higher of the two degrees he can retain against all creditors of whichever degree they may be. If, however, his debt falls within the lower degree he can retain against all creditors of such degree, but against none in the higher degree.

The rights of retainer and preference are enjoyed not only by executors, but also by administrators, unless there is included in the bond an understanding not to retain or prefer. Such an undertaking normally appears when a creditor takes out letters of administration.

(b) *Preference.* This right, it has been mentioned, is now, by Section 34 (2) of the Administration of Estates Act, 1925,[80] exerciseable against all the assets of the deceased. It enables the personal representative to prefer a particular creditor to the same extent as he could retain, i.e. against a creditor of equal, but not superior, priority. From this point of view, there is no distinction between a specialty and a simple contract debtor, since the Administration of Estates Act, 1869 (Hinde Palmer's Act), placed the two upon an equal footing so far as payment was concerned.

77 Administration of Estates Act, 1925, Sect. 34(2). Ireland: 1965 Act, Sect. 46(2) (Republic of Ireland); 1955 Act, Sect. 30 (2) (Northern Ireland).

78 *A.-G.* v. *Jackson*, [1932] A.C. 365 (H.L., E.).

79 [1932] A.C. 385.

80 Ireland: 1965 Act, Sect. 46(2) (Republic of Ireland); 1955 Act, Sect. 30(2) (Northern Ireland).

The right to prefer may be exercised, not only by payment of the debt, but by creating a legal charge, or by equitable assignment of the future proceeds of the sale of assets of the deceased.[81]

Unlike the right of retainer, the right to prefer ends whenever the court makes an order for administration, or when a receiver is appointed.

The Application of Assets where the Estate is Solvent

Even where the assets are more than sufficient to pay the debts of the deceased, problems arise relating to the order in which the property of the deceased shall be made available for payment, where the deceased has left a will. Part II of the First Schedule in the Administration of Estates Act, 1925,[82] introduces a new order of availability for the payment of debts and legacies which is, nevertheless, subject to two overriding considerations.

(a) The will of the deceased may vary the order. Thus, in *Re Martin*,[83] the testator failed to dispose of his real estate by will, but provided that the executors should sell and convert his personal estate, and pay thereupon his debts, funeral and testamentary expenses. Danckwerts, J., held that this varied the statutory order in Part II of the First Schedule, and made the personal estate the primary fund to meet his debts and expenses. A directive to vary will not, however, be inferred.

(b) The order contained in Part II does not affect the liability of lands to answer death duty imposed thereon in exoneration of other assets.

Subject to these two limitations, the order of application of assets is now:[84]

1. Property of the deceased, undisposed of by will, subject to the retention thereout of a fund sufficient to meet any pecuniary legacies. In *Re Martin*,[83] had not the testator varied the statutory order, his undisposed of realty would have been the primary fund.

Property undisposed of by will for this purpose includes a lapsed share of residue,[85] as well as undisposed of income,[86] unless there was a contrary intention to the will. Thus, in *Re Lamb*,[87] the testator

81 *Re Williams*, [1930] 2 Ch. 378.
82 Ireland: 1965 Act, 1st Sched., Part II (Republic of Ireland); 1955 Act, 1st Sched., Part II (Northern Ireland).
83 [1955] Ch. 698.
84 See Woodman, "Payment of Debts and Legacies: Proposals for Reform" (1968), 6 *University of Queensland Law Journal*, 84.
85 *Re Gillett's Will Trusts*, [1950] Ch. 102.
86 *Re Tong*, [1931] 1 Ch. 202 (C.A.).
87 *Re Lamb*, [1929] 1 Ch. 722.

directed that, after his debts, funeral and testamentary expenses had been paid his property should be equally divided between his brother, a cousin and his two nephews. The brother predeceased the testator, and his share lapsed, thus becoming the primary fund for the payment of debts and legacies. On the other hand, in *Re Petty*,[88] the testator, after making certain bequests, bequeathed all his real and personal estate to his executors and trustees on trust to sell and convert, and out of the money procured by the sale, to pay his funeral and testamentary expenses and debts, and then to hold the residue in trust for certain persons, one of whom predeceased him, so that the share lapsed. Astbury, J., held[89] that the disposition varied the statutory order—

> . . . [the testator] created a mixed fund for the payment of funeral and testamentary expenses, debts and legacies, and there was no undisposed of moiety of the balance of residue until those expenses and debts were ascertained and paid. In those circumstances the estate must be administered according to the testator's directions, and the expenses and debts are not thrown primarily on the lapsed moiety.

This and subsequent decisions have established the position that, whilst a mere direction to pay debts (as in *Re Lamb*) is insufficient to displace the statutory order, a direction which only establishes the property to be distributed after the payment of debts is in fact a manifestation of a contrary intention, so that if a share of the residue so ascertained lapses, it cannot be regarded as the primary fund. In *Re Berrey's Will Trusts*,[90] one of the more recent applications of this rule, the testator made her own will on a printed form which contained the usual directions, including one that all her debts and funeral expenses should be paid as soon as conveniently possible after her decease. She then gave two legacies of £500 each, and added: " After all my debts, and funeral, and expenses are paid I give and bequeath all the residue of my estate in equal shares " to four named persons, one of whom predeceased her, so that this share lapsed. Danckwerts, J., held that the use of the words " After all my debts, and funeral, and expenses are paid " showed an intention to vary the order of application of assets in Part II of the First Schedule, and, since the testator had referred to " debts," " funeral " and " expenses " separately, all these were to be paid out of the residuary estate before there was any division into shares. Since one of these had lapsed, there was an intestacy in respect of it.

88 [1929] 1 Ch. 726.
89 [1929] 1 Ch. 730.
90 [1959] 1 W.L.R. 30.

2. A residuary gift. This means any property of the deceased not specifically devised or bequeathed, but included in a residuary gift by the testator. If, however, debts are expressly charged upon a specific bequest, they are payable from such a bequest.[91]

In *Re Ridley*[92] the testatrix devised " free of all death duties all my real estate " to a person, and then gave the residue of her property by a separate clause. Harman, J., held that the devise of the realty was a general devise, but it did not form part of the residue.

3. Property specifically appropriated (either by a specific or by a general description) for the payment of debts. It could obviously be suggested that such a specific appropriation of property might in itself be regarded as a variation of the statutory order, making it the primary fund, but the Court of Appeal in *Re Kempthorne*[93] rejected this suggestion. There must be, as Roxburgh, J., pointed out in *Re James*,[94] some reasonably clear indication of an intention to vary. This is clearly shown by a clear intention to exonerate some other fund, for example, the residuary estate, as was the intention in *Re James*.[94] It is otherwise where there is no residuary gift to be exonerated. In such a case, where the fund is appropriated for the payment of debts and expenses, the statutory order will apply.[95]

4. Property charged with, or devised or bequeathed subject to a charge for, the payment of debts. Very much the same considerations apply to property so disposed of as apply to property appropriated under the third head. Something more than a mere direction to pay debts is needed—there must be a charge upon specific property.

5. The fund, if any, retained to meet pecuniary legacies, The establishment of such a fund is one of the first acts of the executors on undertaking administration.

6. Property specifically devised or bequeathed, rateably according to value. " Value " in this context means value to the testator. In *Re John*[96] the testator devised a property subject to a mortgage, and he also devised other real property burdened with the payment of certain specified legacies. The personal estate of the testator was insufficient to pay pecuniary legacies and debts, and it therefore became necessary to value the two gifts of real property. Farwell, J., held that the value of the mortgaged property was the value of the equity of redemption

[91] *Re Littlewood*, [1931] 1 Ch. 443.
[92] [1950] Ch. 415.
[93] [1930] 1 Ch. 268.
[94] [1947] Ch. 256.
[95] *Re Gordon*, [1940] Ch. 769.
[96] [1933] Ch. 370.

(i.e. the value of the property less the mortgage), but that in valuing the real property subject to the payment of the legacies, there should be no deduction from the property of the amount of the legacies.

7. Property appointed by will under a general power, including the statutory power to dispose of entailed interests. These properties are taken rateably, according to value.

If the donee of a general power to appoint a fund by will gives pecuniary legacies and appoints executors, and his estate is insufficient for the payment of debts and legacies, he is deemed to have exercised his power of appointment to the extent necessary for the payment, not only of the legacies, but also of the debts.[97] The gift of the legacies is regarded as to some extent an exercise of the power, and it is also regarded as an exercise of the power necessary to enable that payment to be carried into effect, i.e. by paying the debts first.

The schedule, it will be observed, only includes general powers of appointment exerciseable by will. However, if there is a general power, exerciseable by deed, but taking effect only on the death of the appointor, Lord Hardwicke held in *Lord Townshend* v. *Windham*[98] that if the power were exercised voluntarily in favour of a third person, it was to be considered as part of his assets, and the sum appointed could therefore be recalled for the benefit of the deceased's creditors. Such assets are equitable assets only and, accordingly, if there is anything over after the payment of creditors, the balance remains with the appointors. This decision was approved by the House of Lords in *O'Grady* v. *Wilmot*.[99]

The Distribution of the Assets

Once the debts and other liabilities of the deceased have been discharged, the personal representative's duty is to distribute the assets as provided in the will, or, on intestacy, in accordance with the provisions of the Administration of Estates Act, 1925.[1] It has already been pointed out that a beneficiary cannot proceed to enforce his rights until the expiration of the "executor's year," although the personal representative may distribute sooner, if it is convenient, and he so chooses. Until the property remaining after payment of liabilities has been ascertained, the beneficiary has no right to any actual assets,

97 *Re Seabrook*, [1911] 1 Ch. 151.

98 (1750), 2 Ves. Sen. 1.

99 [1916] 2 A.C. 231. See also *Re Phillips*, [1931] 1 Ch. 347.

1 Ireland: Succession Act, 1965 (Republic of Ireland); Administration of Estates Act (Northern Ireland), 1955.

but merely a right to have the estate administered. In *Re Gibbs*[2] Danckwerts, J., said—

> The argument against the claim of the Inland Revenue was that there cannot be said to be any right or claim to the residuary estate or to the enjoyment of it until the residuary estate is ascertained by process of administration. Until that occurs all that the persons interested in the residuary estate have, according to law, is a right to have the estate of the testator, or it may be in the case of intestacy the estate of the intestate, duly administered. Therefore, when finally the residuary estate is ascertained, and still more when the executors assent to the trusts of the residuary estate and, therefore, put off the character of executors and assume that of trustees, with the consequences which ensue, as, for instance, in *Attenborough* v. *Solomon*,[3] there is a change in the rights, title and position of the persons beneficially interested in the residuary estate. That has been laid down by the House of Lords and other courts in a series of cases, notably *Sudeley* v. *Attorney-General*,[4] *Barnardo's Homes* v. *Special Income Tax Commissioners*,[5] and *Corbett* v. *Inland Revenue Commissioners*,[6] from which it appears that until the residuary estate has been ascertained by administration the beneficiaries entitled under the trusts of the will cannot claim that they have any right to any particular assets forming part of the testator's estate, or that the income which the executors may acquire in respect of the residuary estate is in any way the income of the beneficiaries, at any rate for the purposes of income tax.

Assents

The actual transfer of the property from the personal representative to the beneficiary is accomplished by means of an assent. In the case of personal property passing by delivery, the assent can be oral, or it may simply consist of handing over the property. Before 1926 an oral assent was sufficient for land also, but now Section 36 (4)[7] requires assents of legal estates to be in writing, signed by the personal representative. Any person in whose favour an assent of a legal estate is made may require that notice of this assent be endorsed on the probate or letters of administration. An assent in respect of a legal estate operates in favour of a purchaser, unless notice of a previous

[2] [1951] Ch. 933, 938.
[3] [1913] A.C. 76 (H.L., E.).
[4] [1897] A.C. 11 (H.L., E.).
[5] [1921] A.C. 1 (H.L., E.).
[6] [1938] 1 K.B. 567 (C.A.).
[7] Ireland: 1965 Act, Sect. 52(5) (Republic of Ireland); 1955 Act, Sect. 34(4) (Northern Ireland).

assent affecting that legal estate has been placed on the probate or letters of administration, as sufficient evidence that the person in whose favour the assent has been made is the person entitled to have the legal estate conveyed therein.

An assent by a personal representative to a person other than a purchaser does not prejudice the rights of any person to follow the property to which the assent relates, or any property representing it, into the hands of the person in whom it is vested by the assent, provided that such a person is not a purchaser.[8]

Legacies

A number of points relating to the payment of legacies need brief mention.

(1) It was well settled before 1926 that where a testator bequeathed legacies, and then bequeathed the residue of his real and personal estate, the legacies were charged upon the real estate or its proceeds, but they were payable primarily out of the personalty, unless the testator directed that they were to be paid out of the mixed fund, in which case they were paid rateably out of the realty and the personalty.[9] This rule still operates, and it is unaffected by the provisions of Part II of the First Schedule of the Administration of Estates Act, 1925.[10]

(2) *Types of Legacies.* By general modern usage, " legacy " denotes a gift of personal property only, " devise " being the customary word for a gift of real property; but originally, as in *Termes de la Ley*, " legacy " included both types of property; and sometimes in the context of a particular will,[11] or in some statutes,[12] it may be so construed.

A *general* legacy is a gift of property in such a manner that it can be satisfied by any property of the type described, e.g. a horse, a picture or £100 stock. In *Re Gillins*[13] the testator made a number of bequests of a specified number of shares in the Commercial Union Assurance Company. Warrington, J., said[14]—

> . . . Are these legacies of shares specific or general legacies? As to that I think there can be do doubt. A gift of so much stock, a gift of so many bonds, a gift of so many shares, have in several cases

8 1925 Act, Sect. 38(1). Ireland: 1965 Act, Sect. 59(1) (Republic of Ireland); 1955 Act, Sect. 39 (Northern Ireland).
9 *Re Boards*, [1895] 1 Ch. 499.
10 *Re Thompson*, [1936] Ch. 676; *Re Rowe*, [1941] Ch. 343.
11 *Re Previtè*, [1931] 1 Ch. 447.
12 E.g. Real Property Limitation Act, 1874, Sect. 8.
13 [1909] 1 Ch. 345.
14 [1909] 1 Ch. 348.

been held to be general legacies and not specific. As to stock, that is well-known. So many bonds is the case of *Macdonald* v. *Irvine*,[15] so many shares is the case of *In re Gray*.[16] The legacies, therefore, are not specific legacies, but general, and if the testator had not been possessed of any shares in the Commercial Union Assurance Company there would, I think, be no doubt that it would have been the duty of the executors to buy so many shares as they found them at date of the testator's death, there being shares which could be bought satisfying the words of the testator's will.

If, however, at the date of the will, the company has ceased to exist, then the gift becomes impossible to carry out.[16]

A *specific* legacy is a gift of a particular thing, so that no other thing of that class will satisfy it. Thus, a legacy of " all my shares in the X Company " is specific. Specific legacies, unlike other kinds of legacy, are subject to ademption; that is to say, if the thing named has ceased to exist, or has been changed into something else,[17] or if it is no longer in the testator's possession at the time of the testator's death, then the legatee gets neither the legacy nor anything in place of it. This is particularly the case where the testator bequeaths a debt due to him, and it is subsequently extinguished by the act or concurrence of the testator.

A *demonstrative* legacy is one in which a sum of money, or other property, is directed to be paid out of a larger fund. It is, as Lord Thurlow, L. C., pointed out in *Ashburner* v. *Macguire*,[18] " in its nature a general legacy, but where a particular fund is pointed out to satisfy it. . ." A demonstrative legacy, like a general legacy, is not subject to ademption.

A *pecuniary* legacy is a gift either of a sum of money or of property (e.g. Consols) expressed in terms of a sum of money. Obviously, many pecuniary legacies are general, but they may again be either specific or demonstrative.

If the testator's estate is insufficient for the payment of debts and expenses and also to pay all legacies, then it will be necessary to consider in what order they abate. The residuary gift is the first to abate. Thereafter, the executors will resort to the fund for the general legacies, and only after that has been exhausted will the demonstrative and specific legacies abate.

[15] (1878), 8 Ch. D. 101 (C.A.).
[16] (1887), 36 Ch. D. 205.
[17] *Re Slater*, [1907] 1 Ch. 665 (C.A.).
[18] (1786), 2 Bro. C.C. 108, 109.

So far as the *payment* of legacies is concerned, the specific and demonstrative legacies are paid first, then the general legacies, and finally, the residuary legatee. It may be, however, that the testator has indicated some special priority, and if he has, this will modify the general rule. In such a case, the legacies with the special priority will be paid in full first and, if the estate is insufficient to pay all, the others will abate, but if there has been delay beyond the executor's year, those entitled to priority will not be entitled to interest also at the expense of the other legacies,[19] and there is no residue from which interest can be paid.

Interest on Legacies

As a general rule, interest at the rate of 4 per cent per annum is payable on pecuniary legacies from the date at which they are payable. This is the time mentioned in the will or, if no time is mentioned, then at the end of the executor's year. In *Re Wyles*[20] Farwell, J., explained the rule as follows—

> It is a well established rule that if a pecuniary legacy is for any cause not paid over to the legatee at the end of one year from the testator's death, the legatee is entitled to interest on his legacy from that date up to the date of payment. The reason for that rule is obvious. Where the estate is sufficient to pay the whole of the legacies in full, and there is a residue, it is unjust that the residuary legatees who are entitled to nothing until all the legacies have been paid, should benefit by the delay in paying them which they would do if the interest which the money has been earning in the meantime was paid to them, and therefore the legatees are entitled to interest on their legacies. But it is quite a mistake, in my judgment, to say that the interest payable to a legatee is in any sense a legacy given by the testator. It is a sum given in the course of administration to the legatee because justice requires that owing to the failure to pay his legacy in due time he should be put in the position in which he would have been had it been so paid; but it is not a bounty of the testator in the sense that a gift to the legatee of the amount of the legacy duty payable on the legacy is an additional legacy given by the testator.

Some exceptions to this general rule may be briefly mentioned:

1. It has already been mentioned that the testator may himself indicate some specific event from which payment of interest is to begin.

[19] *Re Wyles*, [1938] Ch. 313.

[20] [1938] Ch. 313, 315-16.

In *Lord* v. *Lord*[21] the testatrix bequeathed property which was the subject of pending litigation to J. Lord upon trust, directing him to pay certain legacies " so soon as proceedings in law and equity shall be terminated, and the same shall come into his possession . . ." The Court of Appeal in Chancery held that the trust to pay the legacies did not arise, and hence, the legacies did not carry interest, until the litigation ended.

2. Where the legacy is given in satisfaction of a debt, then interest is payable from the death of the testator.[22] From this, it follows, as Lord Hardwicke pointed out in *Clark* v. *Sewell*,[22] that if the testator directs payment to be made at a date some time after his death there is no case for satisfaction.

3. When a legacy is charged on land only, and no time is fixed for payment, then payment of interest begins at the date of the testator's death.[23]

4. Where a legacy, whether vested or contingent, is given to an infant child of the testator or testatrix, or to an infant to whom the testator is *in loco parentis*, and no other provision is made in the will for the infant's maintenance, then it is presumed that the testator, being responsible for the infant's maintenance,[24] intended the interest on the legacy to be made available from the date of the testator's death.[25]

5. Where, independently of any relationship, the testator has shown an intention that the legatee shall be maintained, then interest is payable from the testator's death.[26]

Contingent Legacies

Before 1926, the general rule (subject to what has been stated above with regard to legacies to the testator's infant child) was that contingent specific or general legacies did not confer any right to interest until the contingency occurred. Now, by Section 175 of the Law of Property Act, 1925,[27] a contingent or future specific devise or bequest of property, real or personal, a contingent residuary devise of freehold land and a specific or residuary devise of freehold land, to trustees on trust for

[21] (1867), L.R. 2 Ch. App. 782.
[22] *Clark* v. *Sewell* (1744), 3 Atk. 96; *Re Rattenberry*, [1906] 1 Ch. 667.
[23] *Spurway* v. *Glynn* (1804), 9 Ves. 483; Ireland: *Pearson* v. *Pearson* (1802), 1 Sch. & Lef. 10.
[24] *Re Eyre*, [1917] 1 Ch. 351.
[25] *Re Moody*, [1895] 1 Ch. 101; *Re Bowlby*, [1904] 2 Ch. 685 (C.A.).
[26] *Re Churchill*, [1909] 2 Ch. 431.
[27] No equivalent legislation in Ireland.

persons whose interests are contingent or executory, carries the intermediate income of that property from the date of the testator's death, unless he otherwise disposes of that income.

Accordingly, only a contingent pecuniary legatee is now deprived of interest until the contingency occurs,[28] since the Court of Appeal decided in *Re Holford*[29] that a contingent bequest of residuary personalty carries the intermediate income.

[28] *Re Raine*, [1929] 1 Ch. 716.
[29] [1894] 3 Ch. 30.

CHAPTER VIII

ASSIGNMENT OF CHOSES IN ACTION

MEANING OF TERMS

PROPERTY was classified by common lawyers as realty or personalty. This classification was important for a variety of legal purposes, such as succession, in respect of which these two classes of property have now been largely assimilated. It remains important with regard to the methods of transfer. Personal property comprises money, chattels personal (*choses in possession*), leasehold estates in land (*chattels real*) and incorporeal property. Pure personalty of an incorporeal nature could not generally be assigned at common law, and in that sense was not property, but it is valuable and has long been assignable one way or another. In its most extensive sense, the term *chose in action*[1] is used in contradistinction to the term *chose in possession*, which denotes tangible things—things capable of being stolen according to the common law, of which possession and, if intended, ownership will pass by physical delivery, and which may be seized and sold by the sheriff in execution of a judgment in a personal action. A chose in action has no existence in the sphere of material things and it therefore cannot be physically possessed or enjoyed. Choses in action are recoverable only by action; having no physical existence, they cannot be taken in execution by the sheriff.

The typical illustration is a debt, but (in the extensive sense) choses in action comprise a wide residuary class of valuable rights, to which additions are constantly being made. Patents, copyrights and trade marks are now valuable rights of property, created or redefined as to their extent by modern statutes, and they are all choses in action. Goodwill, though not so completely protected as the foregoing, is also a chose in action. The tendency of this class of property is to increase in importance and extent. As an illustration, professional opinion in the United States has been considering for some time whether scientific truths and discoveries (as distinct from new *inventions* in which such truths and discoveries may be applied) may be the subject of individual ownership. If proposals to this end were embodied in legislation, a new chose in action would have been created.

1 On choses in action and their assignment generally, see Marshall, *The Assignment of Choses in Action*.

Chose in action is not a precise expression of agreed meaning. In a narrower sense, the category of chose in action comprises only rights to receive sums of money.[2] Examples are debts, sums payable under contracts and dividends due on stocks and shares. In this sense a share in a limited liability company, for example, though incorporeal, is not a chose in action: it carries rights in the management of the company but not necessarily a right to receive money from the company. So also are copyrights[3] not mere choses in action in this sense, for they include rights of exploitation and licensing of reproduction, and infringement can be prevented by injunction. Similar remarks apply to patents, trade marks and goodwill. Moreover, not every right to recover a sum of money has come to be assignable at all. For example, a bare cause of action in tort or for damages for breach of contract or for adultery is personal to the claimant, and restrictive usage would confine the term *chose in action* to rights to money which, though unassignable in general at common law, became assignable in equity.

Whether taken in a wider or a narrower sense, a chose in action may be either a *legal chose* (i.e. one giving rise to a common law action for its enforcement or recovery), such as an obligation to repay borrowed money, or an *equitable chose* or *chose in equity* (i.e. one giving rise to an equitable remedy for its enforcement or recovery), such as a life interest under a trust of personalty.

Assignment and the Common Law

At common law, the general rule was that no debt or other chose in action could be assigned, unless the debtor assented to the assignment. The reason given by Coke for this rule was that assignments would be ". . . the occasion of multiplying of contentions and suits, of great oppression of the people, . . . and the subversion of the due and equal execution of justice."[4] It is difficult to resist the conclusion that this view is based upon some confusion between a chose in action and a bare right to litigate, e.g. in respect of a tort. Such a right has never been assignable, and is not even today, in either law or equity; nor is a right arising under an agreement for personal service.

Even at common law, however, there were exceptions to this rule against assignment. First, the King could both grant and receive choses in action by way of assignment. Secondly, the rise of capitalism

[2] See, further, Elphinstone, " What is a Chose in Action ?" (1893), 9 *Law Quarterly Review*, 311; Sweet, " Choses in Action " (1894), 10 *L.Q.R.*, 303.

[3] See Brodhurst, " Is Copyright a Chose in Action ?" (1895), 11 *Law Quarterly Review*, 64; Williams, " Property, Things in Action and Copyright " (1895), 11 *L.Q.R.*, 223; Sweet, " Choses in Action " (1895), 11 *L.Q.R.*, 238.

[4] *Lampet's Case* (1613), 10 Co. Rep. 46b, 48a.

and trading in the sixteenth century gave rise to English banking, accompanied by mercantile customs as to the transfer of rights to be paid money. When the rules of the law merchant were incorporated into the common law, there was introduced the rule that mercantile choses in action (e.g. bills of exchange, such as cheques) were not only assignable, but *negotiable.* While an assignee normally takes subject to any flaws in the assignor's title, a holder in due course and for value of a negotiable instrument has a good title even if the person from whom he received it had not.[5] Negotiable instruments are transferable by endorsement, or sometimes by delivery. Thirdly, assignments of one or two choses in action were possible under special statutes.[6]

The rule preventing the assignment of choses in action at common law seems, in fact, to have been based upon the early view of contract that it was a personal obligation existing between the two parties, and therefore not enforceable by persons other than the original contracting parties.[7] Accordingly, if it was desired at common law to shift the obligation from the original contracting party, then except in the cases mentioned in the preceding paragraph, a *novation* was necessary. For example, if A was owed £50 by B, and A wished to transfer the benefit of that obligation to C, then A, B and C had to agree together that the old obligation between A and B should be extinguished, and a new one between B and C substituted for it. This was a cumbrous proceeding, and, therefore, it would appear that to avoid the difficulty at common law in some cases a form of contract was evolved, under which the party bound expressly agreed at the time of the original obligation to perform it in favour of the person named in the contract or of any person to whom he might assign his claim. It was in accordance with this principle that it became possible for the common law to admit the rule of mercantile law governing the negotiability of bills of exchange, for an acceptor of a bill of exchange is deemed to undertake on acceptance to pay the sum, when due, to any bona fide holder who presents it for payment.[8] An alternative method of assignment at common law seems to have been by letter of attorney, authorising the recipient to sue in the name of the person entitled. Such a mode of assignment was distinctly popular until the practice was for a time interrupted, from the fifteenth to the seventeenth centuries, being

5 A bill of exchange is negotiable only if that is consistent with the bill. A cheque crossed " not negotiable " is not negotiable, but can be assigned.

6 E.g. of the debts of a bankrupt under 1 Jac. I, c. 15.

7 Spence, *Equitable Jurisdiction of the Court of Chancery*, vol. II, p. 850; Winfield, "Assignment of Choses in Action in relation to Maintenance and Champerty " (1919), 35 *Law Quarterly Review*, 143.

8 Williams, *Personal Property*, 18th ed., pp. 33-4.

regarded by the courts as bad, as constituting the offence of maintenance. Coke's observation was made while such an attitude on the part of the common law judges existed.[9]

In the course of his interesting researches into the history of the assignment of choses in action, Bailey pointed out[10] that the history of assignment was greatly influenced in its beginnings by the fact that, until their expulsion from England at the end of the thirteenth century, the Jews were the principal sources of loans of money, and they seem to have recognised that assignments of the debts, which were due from Christians, were possible, since Christians were forbidden to lend money at interest; such assignments were at first always to Jews, and the assignments were apparently registered. No questions relating to assignments came before the ordinary courts at this period, however, since the Jews resorted to their own court, the Beth Din, and no royal licence seems to have been required. When a Jewish creditor died, his rights in the debts passed to the Crown, but since the Crown itself was fettered by the prohibition of lending money at interest, it was customary to regrant the debts to a relative of the deceased, after levying a fine. In the thirteenth century, the Jewish Exchequer had been organised as a special branch of the Great Exchequer, and assignment of the benefit of a debt could occur only by novation before chirographers, who retained a record of the transaction. In the second half of the thirteenth century, Christians are found taking assignments of debts from Jews, but only with royal licence. In such a case the Jewish assignor retained nominal title, but he was compelled to agree that he would enforce payment only at the order of the Christian assignee, and on his behalf. Such assignments were not novations, since the consent of the debtor was not required. Already, however, a movement restricting assignments of debts was setting in, and in 1269, it was enacted that all debts could be assigned only with royal licence. Thus, for the first time, an assignment between Jew and Jew required a royal licence. About the same time, the Christian assignee secured additional protection, through his power to serve on the chirographers a notice prohibiting all dealings with the debt by the Jewish assignor,

9 On the early history of assignments of choses in action, see Ames, " Disseisin of Chattels " (1909), *Select Essays in Anglo-American Legal History*, vol. III, p. 580, and (1890), 3 *Harvard Law Review*, 337. See also Kenneson, " Purchase for Value without Notice " (1914), 23 *Yale Law Journal*, 193.

10 "Assignments of Debts in England from the Twelfth to the Twentieth Century " (1931), 47 *Law Quarterly Review*, 516; (1932), 48 *L.Q.R.*, 248 and 547. See also Cook, " The Alienability of Choses in Action " (1916), 29 *Harvard Law Review*, 816; Williston, " Is the Right of an Assignee of a Chose in Action Legal or Equitable ?" (1916), 30 *H.L.R.*, 97; Cook, " The Alienability of Choses in Action: A Reply to Professor Williston " (1917), 30 *H.L.R.*, 449; Williston " The Word ' Equitable ' and its Application to the Assignment of Choses in Action " (1918), 31 *H.L.R.*, 822; Holdsworth, " The History of the Treatment of *Choses* in Action by the Common Law " (1920), 33 *H.L.R.*, 997.

after the assignment. In these assignments between Jewish assignor and Christian assignee, all the material elements of the later equitable assignments can be detected.

Meanwhile, it would seem that the King during the middle ages frequently assigned debts due to the Exchequer in satisfaction of his own debts. In such a case, the assignee sued in the name of the King (with the attendant privileges) but could not reassign the debt unless he was expressly empowered to do so. Following the expulsion of the Jews, assignments between private persons lapsed at common law, becoming entangled with doctrines of maintenance and champerty. Bailey also pointed out[11] that another reason for the dislike of assignment at common law was fear of the debtors' prison. A debtor commonly reposed some confidence in his creditor, that he would normally refrain from proceeding to extremities, and this may account for the common law view of the debt as a personal relation. This " personal " view of the transaction dies hard.[12] Notwithstanding this view, however, it would seem that once the taint of maintenance had gone, from the end of the seventeenth century, the common law courts would enforce assignments of debts *between assignor and assignee*, if made by deed.[13] This provoked some confusion of thought in the Court of Chancery[14] in the nineteenth century, for equity accepted the deed if the assignment was voluntary, and would otherwise have failed. Even at common law, before the end of the eighteenth century, " it was decided that, if a debtor paid his creditor knowing that the latter had assigned the debt, the assignee could sue him even at law by using the creditor's name "—apparently on the ground of fraud.[15]

EQUITABLE ASSIGNMENTS

What may be Assigned

Equity has allowed, at least since the first half of the seventeenth century,[16] the assignment of legal choses in action, of equitable choses in action and of possibilities.

[11] (1932), 48 *Law Quarterly Review*, 550.

[12] See, e.g., *Fitzroy* v. *Cave*, [1905] 2 K.B. 364, 372, *per* Cozens-Hardy, L.J.

[13] Bailey (1932), 48 *Law Quarterly Review*, 574.

[14] See pp. 310–14, *post*.

[15] Bailey (1932), 48 *Law Quarterly Review*, 575.

[16] See *Earl of Suffolk* v. *Greenvill* (1631), 2 Freem. 146 (assignment of legal chose held invalid for lack of consideration); *Meechett* v. *Bradshaw* (1633), Nels. 22 (assignment by deed of legal chose held valid). See also, generally, Tudsbery, *The Nature, Requisites and Operation of Equitable Assignments*.

Possibilities. A possibility differs from a chose in action in that it is not enforceable by action at all. It is a mere expectation that some beneficial interest will be received by the assignor in the future, e.g. under the will of a person still living, the interest therefore being liable to destruction by revocation of the will or the operation of the doctrine of lapse.

An assignment of such future property is possible in the sense that a contract is created immediately under which there is to be automatic transfer of the property when it does come into existence. Specific performance can then be obtained: at that point an interest in the property passes.[17] But an interest of a kind passes immediately. In *Re Lind*[18] a man made two mortgages of his share of his mother's estate on her intestacy (the mother being still alive). The mortgagor went bankrupt, but neither mortgagee proved for his debt. After the mortgagor's discharge, he made a further assignment of his expectancy, and later his mother died intestate. The Court of Appeal held that, as the assignment of an expectancy passed the expected property automatically to the assignee as soon as that property vested in the assignor, such an assignment was not a mere contract pending the property falling in, and therefore the two mortgagees' interests, being treated as mortgages and not contracts, survived the bankruptcy and prevailed over the post-bankruptcy assignment.

The basis of the equitable principle is to be found in the following observations of Lord Macnaghten in *Tailby* v. *Official Receiver*,[19] where an assignment for value of future book debts was held valid—

> Long before *Holroyd* v. *Marshall*[20] was determined it was well settled that an assignment of future property for value operates in equity by way of agreement, binding the conscience of the assignor, and so binding the property from the moment when the contract becomes capable of being performed, on the principle that equity considers as done that which ought to be done, and in accordance with the maxim which Lord Thurlow said he took to be universal, " that whenever persons agree concerning any particular subject, that, in a Court of Equity, as against the party himself, and any claiming under him, voluntarily or with notice, raises a trust:" *Legard* v. *Hodges*.[21]

The analogy of a trust is rather forcibly recalled when the procedure offered by equity to the assignee for the enforcement of his chose in

17 *Glegg* v. *Bromley*, [1912] 3 K.B. 474, 490, *per* Parker, J.
18 [1915] 2 Ch. 345. See also *Re Gillott's Settlement*, [1934] Ch. 97.
19 (1888), 13 App. Cas. 523, 546.
20 (1862), 10 H.L.C. 191.
21 (1792), 1 Ves. Jun. 477.

action is considered. If the assignment were of an equitable chose in action, the assignee was allowed to sue in his own name, since equity recognised the transaction, although the assignor was joined as a party in order to allow him to dispute the assignment if he wished. If, however, the assignment was of a legal chose in action, equity compelled the assignor to lend his name to the action, on receiving an indemnity for costs from the assignee.[22] The function of the assignor in such an action very closely resembled that of the trustee, and everything recovered would be impressed with a trust for the assignee in the hands of the assignor.

Personal contracts. Contracts of personal service are not assignable, nor are personal licences.[23] One cannot assign any contractual right if the substance of that right would be changed by the change of identity of the parties. In *Griffith* v. *Tower Publishing Co. Ltd.*[24] Stirling, J., held that a contract between author and publisher was not assignable by the publisher. Rights to sums of money payable by way of salary for personal services are assignable.[25]

Rights to litigate. A bare right to sue for damages for a civil wrong is not assignable. In *Glegg* v. *Bromley*[26] Parker, J., said—

> Equity on the ground of public policy did not give validity to the assignment of what is in the cases referred to as a bare right of action, and this was so whether the bare right were legal or equitable. . . . The question was whether the subject-matter of the assignment was, in the view of the Court, property with an incidental remedy for its recovery, or was a bare right to bring an action either at law or in equity.

The distinction is between bare rights of action, the assignment of which is stigmatised as maintenance, and rights of action in which the assignee has some substantial interest outside the suits themselves. An example of the latter category is *Ogdens Ltd.* v. *Weinberg*,[27] where the House of Lords held that a right to sue for damages for breach of contract had been successfully assigned. In *Compania Colombiana de Seguros* v. *Pacific Steam Navigation Co.*[28] Roskill, J., held that cargo owners who had been compensated by their insurance company for damage to the cargo could assign to the insurance company their right of action against the tortfeasor who damaged the cargo.

[22] *Per* Chitty, L. J., *Durham Bros.* v. *Robertson*, [1898] 1 Q.B. 765, 769-70.
[23] *Re Davis & Co.* (1888), 22 Q.B.D. 193 (C.A.).
[24] [1897] 1 Ch. 21.
[25] *Shaw & Co.* v. *Moss Empires* (*Ltd.*) (1908), 25 T.L.R. 190.
[26] [1912] 3 K.B. 474, 489-90.
[27] (1906), 95 L.T. 567.
[28] [1965] 1 Q.B. 101. See also Williams, " Is a Right of Action in Tort a Chose in Action ?" (1894), 10 *Law Quarterly Review*, 143.

As distinct from assignment of a bare right to litigate, assignment of the fruits of litigation is valid. In *Glegg* v. *Bromley*[29] the Court of Appeal held valid, as assignment of a possibility, a transfer for value of damages to be recovered in a future slander action.

Formalities and Evidence

No special form is required for an equitable assignment. An oral agreement is valid except when writing is required under some special statute.[30] In *William Brandt's Sons & Co.* v. *Dunlop Rubber Co. Ltd.*[31] Lord Macnaghten said—

> But, says the Lord Chief Justice, " the document does not, on the face of it, purport to be an assignment nor use the language of an assignment." An equitable assignment does not always take that form. It may be addressed to the debtor. It may be couched in the language of command. It may be a courteous request. It may assume the form of mere permission. The language is immaterial if the meaning is plain. All that is necessary is that the debtor should be given to understand that the debt has been made over by the creditor to some third person. If the debtor ignores such a notice, he does so at his peril. If the assignment be for valuable consideration and communicated to the third person, it cannot be revoked by the creditor or safely disregarded by the debtor.

The House of Lords held there had been an assignment where merchants had agreed with their bankers that purchasers of goods from the merchants should pay the purchase price to the bank, and the bank had notified the purchasers to that effect.

A mere mandate from a principal to his agent, not communicated to any third person, does not give the third person any right in the subject-matter of the mandate, and is revoked by any subsequent disposition of property inconsistent with it. In *Morrell* v. *Wootten*[32] P ordered his bankers to pay a sum of money to the plaintiff. Later, before the plaintiff learned of the order and before the bank had paid the plaintiff, P went bankrupt. Romilly, M. R., held that the plaintiff could not insist that the bankers pay him, as there had been no assignment in equity. On the other hand, in *London and Yorkshire Bank (Ltd.)* v. *White*[33] F, on 6th or 7th December 1893, agreed with his

29 [1912] 3 K.B. 474.
30 For example, the Law of Property Act, 1925, Sect. 53, and the Statute of Frauds (Ireland), 1695, Sect. 6, require equitable interests under trusts to be assigned in writing. See *Grey* v. *Inland Revenue Commissioners*, [1960] A.C. 1; *Oughtred* v. *I.R.C.*, [1960] A.C. 206; *Vandervell* v. *I.R.C.*, [1967] 2 A.C. 291; *Re Tyler*, [1967] 1 W.L.R. 1269.
31 [1905] A.C. 454, 462.
32 (1852), 16 Beav. 197.
33 (1895), 11 T.L.R. 570. See also *Ex parte Steward* (1843), 3 Mont. D. & De G. 265; generally, Tudsbery, *The Nature, Requisites and Operation of Equitable Assignments.*

bank manager to assign as security for his overdraft books he had deposited for sale with G. On 9th December, F notified G that he had assigned his interest in the goods to the bank, and requested G to pay the proceeds of sale to the bank. It was held that the conversation of 6th or 7th December constituted a good equitable assignment, of which effective notice was given to G on 9th December.

In *The Zigurds*[34] A & Co., who were acting as ship's agents for that vessel at West Hartlepool, were asked to pay certain sums of money in respect of expenses that the ship had incurred there. Before A & Co. consented to do this, they obtained from the master of the ship, and with the consent of the managing owner of the ship, the following document: " Dear Sirs, Please pay the freight for my vessel the *Zigurds* and all demurrage which may be payable under the charter to my agents . . ." It was admitted that this was a valid equitable assignment, and it was held that title was completed by the following letter from A & Co. to C & Co., the persons liable to pay the freight which the *Zigurds* had earned: " Dear Sirs,—*S.S. Zigurds*—We beg to give you notice that we hold Captain's authority to collect the freight per this steamer's cargo, against which we have made payments. Yours faithfully," A & Co.

In each of the last two cases, the assignee gave notice of the assignment to the debtor. While the assignment is in equity complete from the standpoint of the assignor and assignee without such notice, it does not bind the debtor until he has notice of the agreement, so that if he pays the assignor before he obtains notice, he obtains a good discharge. Accordingly, the assignee should give notice of the assignment to the debtor at the earliest possible moment. He should also do so for another reason. The assignor may again assign the chose in action, and if he does, the rule in *Dearle* v. *Hall*[35] applies.

Priorities of Successive Assignments: the Rule in Dearle v. Hall

The priority of successive assignees in equity of a chose in action depends upon what is generally known as the rule in *Dearle* v. *Hall.*[35] There are indications that the rule may be somewhat older than that, while the rule itself depends for its exposition almost as much upon the decision in *Loveridge* v. *Cooper*[36] as upon the decision in *Dearle* v. *Hall.*

[34] [1934] A.C. 209. For an example of an equitable assignment of the rights of a partner, see *Letts* v. *Inland Revenue Commissioners*, [1957] 1 W.L.R. 201.

[35] (1823), 3 Russ. 1. See Firth, " The Rule in *Dearle* v. *Hall* " (1895), 11 *Law Quarterly Review*, 337.

[36] (1823), 3 Russ. 30.

The rule may be stated as follows: where there are successive assignments in equity of a chose in action, the priority of assignees is determined prima facie by the order in which the assignees gave notice of the assignment to the debtor, and not by the order in which the assignments were made.

In *Dearle* v. *Hall*[37] Plumer, M. R., quoted a passage in Powell's *Law of Mortgages*, in which the learned author observed—

> On the mortgage of a chose in action, it should never be omitted to give notice of the transfer to the trustee; for upon the authority of the cases quoted in the text, *Tourville* v. *Nash*[38] and *Stanhope* v. *Verney*,[39] it has been thought (and indeed, as it should seem, with a great degree of reason), that, if a mortgagee of equitable right neglect to give notice of his incumbrance to the trustee, and such equitable right be afterwards assigned to a second mortgagee, who takes the precaution of giving the trustee proper notice, the first mortgagee will be postponed.

This would seem to make the possible origin of the rule a good deal older than has been generally supposed, although it may be stated with some confidence from the reasoning in *Dearle* v. *Hall* itself, that originally the postponement of a prior assignee would occur only where the failure to give notice earlier was due to the negligence of the prior assignee. In some of the later cases this basis of the rule has been overlooked.

In *Dearle* v. *Hall*, Peter Brown left his property on trust for sale to pay thereout the interest on one moiety to his son Zachariah Brown. The latter then mortgaged his interest, first to Dearle in 1808, then to Sherring in 1809, and then sold it to Hall in 1812. Hall took with no notice of the earlier assignments, and gave notice of the transaction to the trustees of the fund. Several months later, the trustees for the first time received notice of the two earlier assignments. Dearle and Sherring claimed that they were entitled to priority over Hall, but Sir Thomas Plumer, M.R., decided in Hall's favour, observing[40]—

> Where a contract, respecting property in the hands of other persons, who have a legal right to the possession, is made behind the back of those in whom the legal interest is thus vested, it is necessary, if the security is intended to attach on the thing itself, to lay hold of that thing in the manner in which its nature permits it to be laid hold of—that is, by giving notice of the contract to those in whom the legal interest is. By such notice, the legal owners are converted into trustees for the new purchaser, and are charged with responsibility towards him . . .

[37] 3 Russ. 29-30.
[38] *Tourville* v. *Naish* (1734), 3 P. Wms. 307.
[39] *Stanhope* v. *Earl Verney* (1761), 2 Eden 81.
[40] 3 Russ. 12-13.

Continuing, he observed[41] that if there were neglect, resulting in failure to give notice, the cestui que trust would be enabled to commit a fraud, and to obtain thereby " a false and delusive credit," and in the absence of notice, the trustees would be justified in representing the fund as the absolute property of the vendor. Accordingly, if an assignee fails to give notice, he must be held liable, in some degree, for the results of that negligence. In this particular case, Dearle's negligence had extended over three years. As far as the argument that giving notice to the trustees was no part of the equitable assignment was concerned, this was true, if the purchaser intended to rely on his personal remedy against the vendor; but if he wished the right to attach to the subject-matter of the contract, notice was necessary, since without it the purchaser had not done everything towards obtaining the highest degree of possession of which the subject-matter admitted. It was necessary to do all that is equivalent to obtaining possession by placing every person who had an equitable or legal interest in the matter under an obligation to treat it as the assignee's property.[42] This view was upheld by Lord Lyndhurst, L.C., on appeal,[43] and so also was a similar decision in *Loveridge* v. *Cooper*,[44] on appeal in that case.

In origin, the rule is based on the negligence of the prior assignee in failing to give notice. Later decisions tended to obscure this, concentrating simply on the dates when notice was actually given as the key moment, and in *Hill* v. *Peters*[45] Eve, J., indorsing the view of Lord Macnaghten in *Ward* v. *Duncombe*,[46] regarded it as undesirable to extend the doctrine to cases not already covered by it.

Before 1926, the rule applied only to choses in action, including equitable interests in pure personalty, and that is still the position in Ireland. In *Ward* v. *Duncombe*[47] the House of Lords ruled that this included the proceeds of sale of land held on trust for sale, and in *Lloyd's Bank* v. *Pearson*[48] Cozens-Hardy, J., held that the rule also applied to interests in settled realty which reached the beneficiary in the form of personalty. The rule did not formerly extend to equitable interests in realty or to leaseholds not settled by way of trust for sale,[49] nor does it now so extend in Ireland; while in *Ex parte Allen*[50] Bacon,

41 3 Russ. 13-14.
42 3 Russ. 22.
43 (1827), 3 Russ. 48.
44 (1823), 3 Russ. 30.
45 [1918] 2 Ch. 273, 279.
46 [1893] A.C. 369, 394.
47 [1893] A.C. 369. See also *Gresham Life Assurance Soc.* v. *Crowther*, [1915] 1 Ch. 214 (C.A.).
48 [1901] 1 Ch. 865.
49 *Re Richards* (1890), 45 Ch. D. 589; *Hopkins* v. *Hemsworth*, [1898] 2 Ch. 347.
50 (1870), L.R. 11 Eq. 209.

C. J., held that the rule did not extend to bills of sale, and in *Société Générale de Paris* v. *Walker*[51] the House of Lords declined to apply it to assignments of shares in a company.

A new departure was made in England by Section 137 of the Law of Property Act, 1925, Subsection (1) of which provides—

> The law applicable to dealings with equitable things in action which regulates the priority of competing interests therein, shall, as respects dealings with equitable interests in land, capital money, and securities representing capital money effected after the commencement of this Act, apply to and regulate the priority of competing interests therein.
>
> This subsection applies whether or not the money or securities are in Court.

By Subsection (10) it is provided that the section applies only where a trust has been created, while " dealing " includes a disposition by operation of law, e.g. the vesting of a bankrupt's property in the trustee in bankruptcy. As far as equitable interests in registered land are concerned, Section 102(2) of the Land Registration Act, 1925, provides—

> Priorities as regards dealings effected after the commencement of this Act between assignees and incumbrancers of life interests, remainders, reversions and executory interests shall be regulated by the order of the priority cautions or inhibitions lodged (in a specially prescribed form) against the proprietor of the registered estate affected . . .[52]

The foundation of the rule in *Dearle* v. *Hall* is to be discovered in the negligence to be attributed to the assignee who fails to give notice—an omission which means that the first incumbrancer " has not acquired that which, in equity, is equivalent to possession at law . . ."[53] Accordingly it would appear that the rule was at first the consequence of a scrutiny of the conduct of the competing assignees. In *Foster* v. *Cockerell*,[54] however, the House of Lords decided that the rule was independent of the conduct of the assignees; it depended simply upon the date of giving notice, and this has been the accepted view of equity since then. A good illustration of the consequences of applying the rule in this fashion is afforded by *Re Dallas*.[55] In 1897, D charged his

51 (1885), 11 App. Cas. 20.
52 On the effect of these statutory provisions, see Gower, " The Present Position of the Rule in *Dearle* v. *Hall* " (1935), 20 *Conveyancer and Property Lawyer* (*O.S.*), 137 and 153.
53 *Per* Wigram, V.-C., in *Meux* v. *Bell* (1841), 1 Hare 73, 85. See also the observations of Shadwell, V.-C., in *Jones* v. *Jones* (1838), 8 Sim. 633, 643.
54 (1835), 3 Cl. & Fin. 456.
55 [1904] 2 Ch. 385.

expectant interest in a legacy under the will of his father (then living), in favour of S. A year later, he charged it in favour of B. The father died in 1902, and D was the sole executor. In 1903, D renounced probate, and his sister took out letters of administration. B immediately gave her notice of the charge, and a week later S, who then learned of the position for the first time, also gave notice. The Court of Appeal held that although the delay of S in giving notice was not in any way due to his negligence, he must be postponed to B.

The notice need not be formal, and it is sufficient if it reaches the trustee or debtor from any reliable source. In *Lloyd* v. *Banks*[56] the trustee learned of an assignment from reading a newspaper, and it was held that this was sufficient, Lord Cairns, L.C., observing[57]—

> If it can be shewn that in any way the trustee has got knowledge of that kind—knowledge which would operate upon the mind of any rational man, or man of business, and make him act with reference to the knowledge he has so acquired—then I think the end is attained, and that there has been fixed upon the conscience of the trustee, and through that upon the trust fund, a security against its being parted with in any way that would be inconsistent with the encumbrance which has been created.

These rules as to the effectiveness of informal notice still have full vigour in Ireland, but in England they apply only (a) to equitable assignments of legal choses in action, and (b) in the case of assignments of interests under trusts, as between the trustees and a single assignee of the interest so as to oblige the trustees to pay the assignee. Where a question of priority between two or more assignees of an interest under a trust arises, and falls to be determined according to the order of giving notice to the trustees, the matter is now governed in England by the Law of Property Act, 1925, Section 137(3)—

> A notice, otherwise than in writing, given to, or received by, a trustee after the commencement of this Act as respects any dealing with an equitable interest in real or personal property, shall not affect the priority of competing claims of purchasers in that equitable interest.

In order that the rule in *Dearle* v. *Hall* may operate, there must be assignments of interests in the fund. If the person who is alleged to be assignor has no interest, no question of competing priorities arises, and *Dearle* v. *Hall* has no application. This proved fatal to the apparent incumbrancer in *Lyle Ltd.* v. *Rosher*.[58] Under a settlement, Willis and his father had a joint power of appointment over certain funds. When

56 (1868), L.R. 3 Ch. App. 488.
57 L.R. 3 Ch. App. 491.
58 [1959] 1 W.L.R. 8. See also Elphinstone, "The Mischief of Secret Trusts" (1961), 77 *Law Quarterly Review*, 69.

Willis became a member of Lloyd's, funds were deposited with Lloyd's, and these were obtained from the settlement by three deeds, one of which was the execution of the joint power of appointment by Willis and his father, and the other two, between Willis and Lloyd's, transferring the fund to Lloyd's on trust to pay the income to Willis, or as he should direct, and providing that the fund might be used to pay claims, on policies underwritten by Willis, if they should arise. In 1953 Willis purported to charge the funds deposited in favour of Lyle Ltd., who were informed by Lloyd's, on inquiry, that they had no notice of any prior charge. Lyles thereupon gave Lloyd's written notice of their charge. In 1954, Willis was adjudicated bankrupt, and Lyles claimed that their charge took priority over any interest in the fund of the trustees of the settlement. The House of Lords held that the power of appointment was exercised only to the extent necessary to comply with the conditions governing Willis's admission to Lloyd's. Accordingly, no equitable interest in the funds was ever conferred on Willis, so that he never had any interest capable of being assigned. The rule in *Dearle* v. *Hall* therefore never had any application to the transaction with Lyles. The majority view is indicated by the following passage from the speech of Lord Kilmuir, L.C.[59]—

> We were pressed with the argument that, in the classic *Dearle* v. *Hall* case, the assignor has no beneficial interest at the time he makes the second assignment and is, indeed, constructive trustee for the first assignee. I do not think that the rule would be restricted beyond its intendment or present effect if it were held to apply only where, at the time of the assignment, the assignor had a beneficial interest *or* had no beneficial interest only because he had voluntarily divested himself of it. . . . In view of Lord Macnaghten's words in *Ward* v. *Duncombe*[60] I am certainly not disposed to extend the doctrine. It was presented to us as a check—of necessity arbitrary—on the inevitable possible injustices of equitable assignments; all that one can do with an arbitrary rule is to endeavour to clarify its limits.

Lord Reid was unable to accept the significance of the distinction between an " assignor " who had never had an interest and one who had parted with the whole of it.[61] He preferred Lloyd's to Lyles on the ground that the former were cestuis que trust, not assignees, and that the rule in *Dearle* v. *Hall* did not apply to defeat a cestui que trust (who is not required to give notice of the trust in his favour to the person who holds the fund). With respect to their lordships, both grounds are unconvincing and have not clarified an arbitrary rule but added an arbitrary exception to it.

59 [1959] 1 W.L.R. 14, Lords Morton of Henryton and Cohen agreeing.
60 [1893] A.C. 369, 384 *et seq.*
61 [1959] 1 W.L.R. 19-20. Lord Keith of Avonholm agreed with Lord Reid.

Some difficulty has arisen out of cases in which the assignee has given notice only to one of several trustees. It has been laid down in general terms that notice to one trustee is sufficient.[62] In *Ward* v. *Duncombe*[63] a wife executed a marriage settlement, whereby her interest in a fund of personalty was settled. The marriage settlement was known to S, one of the trustees of the fund, but not to E, the other trustee. Later, the wife wished to mortgage her share without disclosing the settlement. The prospective mortgagees asked S and E whether prior incumbrances existed. S replied evasively, and E stated that he knew of none. The mortgagees therefore made the advance, and gave formal notice of it to S and E. Later, S died, and was replaced in the trust by X. The House of Lords held that the trustees of the marriage settlement were entitled to priority over the mortgagees. In *Re Phillips' Trusts*,[64] however, Kekewich, J., held that where only one of three trustees had notice of an assignment, and died without informing either of the others of the assignment, and then a second assignment was made to an assignee who gave notice, the second assignee was entitled to priority. In reaching this decision, Kekewich, J., adopted a dictum of Byrne, J., in *Freeman* v. *Laing*,[65] and he failed to find a satisfactory answer to the difficulty that in such a case, the prior assignee is displaced, not by his fault, but by an accident. In Ireland the rule of equity had earlier been settled in the same sense by Chatterton, V.-C., in *Re Hall.*[66] The principle seems to be that notice to one of several trustees who keeps the information to himself perishes with him. If that is right, the following sequence makes the rule in *Dearle* v. *Hall* unworkable: (1) assignment by B to X of B's interest under a trust of which T_1 and T_2 are the trustees; (2) notice by X to T_1; (3) assignment by B to Y of the same interest, Y having inquired of T_2 and been told there were no prior incumbrances; (4) notice by Y to T_2; (5) death of T_1 without having told T_2 of X's interest; (6) appointment of T_3 as trustee in place of T_1; (7) assignment by B to Z of the same interest; (8) notice by Z to T_2 and T_3. X has priority over Y, Y over Z, and Z over X.

If notice is given to all the trustees priority is retained, even though all the trustees die, and new ones are appointed, who are unaware of it.[67]

[62] *Smith* v. *Smith* (1833), 2 Cr. & M. 231; *Willes* v. *Greenhill* (1861), 4 De G. F. & J. 147.

[63] [1893] A.C. 369.

[64] [1903] 1 Ch. 183.

[65] [1899] 2 Ch. 355, 358.

[66] (1880), 7 L. R. Ir. 180.

[67] *Re Wasdale*, [1899] 1 Ch. 163.

The position of a trustee who replies evasively, or fails to answer, when he is asked by an intending assignee whether there are prior assignments, was discussed by the Court of Appeal in *Low* v. *Bouverie*,[68] and it was then decided that the trustee was under no duty to answer such questions and, in the absence of fraud, the trustee was held to be under no liability to an intending assignee who subsequently discovered that there were prior charges of which he was not informed. In England, Section 137(8) of the Law of Property Act, 1925, provides that " any person interested in the equitable interest may require production of the notice " served on trustees of dealings with a beneficial interest. Whether an intending assignee can be regarded as a " person interested in the equitable interest " has not yet been decided. In England or Ireland, in view of the decision of the House of Lords in *Hedley Byrne & Co. Ltd.* v. *Heller & Partners Ltd.*,[69] a trustee who negligently gave false information to a prospective purchaser of an equitable interest would probably be liable in tort to the purchaser for any consequential loss.

Assignments are Subject to All Equities

Equitable assignments have always been subject to all equities,[70] i.e. all defences which could be raised in respect of the chose against the assignor can be raised also against the assignee, provided that the matters on which they are based occurred before the assignment.[71] For example, if the assignor gives the assignee a bond which is satisfied, or which is void at law, the assignee obtains thereby no right against the debtor.[72] Again, if the debtor can plead against the assignor fraud, misrepresentation, mistake, or some other ground for setting aside the obligation, the same defences are available against the assignee.[73] The debtor also has the same rights of set-off against the assignee as he had against the assignor.[74]

This rule goes so far as to provide that where a trustee is also a beneficiary under the trust, and he assigns his beneficial interest, having previously committed a breach of trust, whereby a debt becomes due to the estate, the assignee cannot claim the trust fund until he has

68 [1891] 3 Ch. 82.

69 [1964] A.C. 465.

70 So also are statutory assignments. See p. 326, *post*. See also *Re Gwelo (Matabeleland) Exploration and Development Co. Ltd.*, [1901] 1 I.R. 38.

71 *Phipps* v. *Lovegrove* (1873), L.R. 16 Eq. 80; *Roxburghe* v. *Cox* (1881), 17 Ch. D. 520. (C.A.).

72 *Turton* v. *Benson* (1718), 1 P. Wms. 496.

73 *Mangles* v. *Dixon* (1852), 3 H.L.C. 702; *Stoddart* v. *Union Trust Ltd.*, [1912] 1 K.B. 181 (C.A.); Lumley, "Assignment of Debts " (1912), 28 *Law Quarterly Review*, 184. Cf. *Smith* v. *Jones*, [1954] 1 W.L.R. 1089.

74 *Re Knapman* (1881), 18 Ch. D. 300 (C.A.); *Re Jones*, [1897] 2 Ch. 190.

repaired the breach of trust by paying the debt due.[75] Similarly, if a beneficiary under a trust has instigated a breach of trust, and then assigns his beneficial interest, the assignee must make good the breach of trust.[76]

However, a debtor may expressly agree that he will not avail himself against an assignee of rights he possesses against the creditor,[77] and even if he does not expressly so agree, the debtor may by his conduct waive his rights against the assignee, or even lose them by neglecting to inform the assignee of some defect to which he was privy.[78]

It is sometimes said that there are exceptions to the rule that assignments are subject to all equities. One example of this, it is suggested, occurs in respect of negotiable instruments, where a holder in due course for value takes a good title, notwithstanding the fact that the transferor's title was defective. This is an illustration of the negotiability which the law merchant has attached to certain classes of commercial paper. Even here, however, an overdue bill or promissory note loses its negotiability and the transferee takes it subject to all defects in the hands of the transferor.[79]

A second exception to the rule that the assignee takes subject to all equities arises in connection with set-off.[80] An assignee takes subject to any right of set-off arising before notice of the assignment is received by the debtor.[81] In *Christie* v. *Taunton, Delmard, Lane & Co.*,[82] however, A held both partly-paid shares and a debenture of the X Co. He assigned his debenture for value to B, who gave notice to the X Co. The company was wound up shortly afterwards, and it was held that in the winding-up, there could be no set-off of the amount of any call on the shares made after the X Co. had received notice of the assignment of the amount of the debenture, since that would prejudice B. In this case, the claim arose out of a contract which was independent of that which created the debenture which was assigned. If, however, the set-off had arisen directly out of the same transaction as the chose assigned, the debtor could have pleaded the set-off against the assignee, even if the right did not accrue to him until after notice of the assignment. This is illustrated by the decision of the Privy Council in

75 *Clack* v. *Holland* (1854), 19 Beav. 262.
76 *Willes* v. *Greenhill* (1860), 29 Beav. 376.
77 *Per* Stirling, J., *Re Goy & Co. Ltd.*, [1900] 2 Ch. 149, 154.
78 *Mangles* v. *Dixon* (1852), 3 H.L.C. 702; *Re Agra and Masterman's Bank* (1867), L.R. 2 Ch. App. 391 (C.A.Ch.).
79 Bills of Exchange Act, 1882, Sect. 36(2).
80 See Snell's *Principles of Equity*, 26th ed., p. 90; Marshall, *The Assignment of Choses in Action*, pp. 182-90.
81 *Biggerstaff* v. *Rowatt's Wharf Ltd.*, [1896] 2 Ch. 93 (C.A.); *Re Goy & Co. Ltd.*, [1900] 2 Ch. 149.
82 [1893] 2 Ch. 175.

Government of Newfoundland v. *Newfoundland Railway Co.*,[83] where Lord Hobhouse, giving the advice of the Board, accepted the reasoning of Bovill, C. J., in *Watson* v. *Mid Wales Railway Co.*[84] Lord Hobhouse said[85]—

> The two claims under consideration have their origin in the same portion of the same contract, where the obligations which gave rise to them are intertwined in the closest manner. The claim of the Government does not arise from any fresh transaction freely entered into by it after notice of assignment by the company.

Consideration

Possibilities. Agreements to assign future property require consideration to support them, otherwise they will no more be enforced in equity than they would be at law. This was stated by the House of Lords in *Tailby* v. *Official Receiver.*[86] In *Lee* v. *Magrath*[87] the holder of a non-negotiable promissory note payable at a future date attempted to transfer it to a volunteer. The " transfer " was ineffectual to pass the legal title. It was held also ineffectual to pass the equitable interest, as there is no equity to perfect an imperfect gift. In *Re Bowden*[88] Bennett, J., held a voluntary assignment of an expectancy to trustees, reinforced by a power of attorney to receive anything due under the will, to be good. Here the trustee had secured the fund and the court refused to help the settlor get it back.

Choses in equity. An assignment of an equitable chose in action places the assignee in exactly the position of the assignor; the gift is perfect and therefore no consideration is required. In *Kekewich* v. *Manning*[89] the assignment was of residuary personalty, the assignment taking the form of a settlement in favour of a volunteer. The Court of Appeal in Chancery held this to be a complete alienation.

On the other hand, a mere agreement to make a future assignment of an equitable chose is operative, if at all, as a contract, and must therefore be for consideration or under seal. A voluntary dealing with such a chose, not purporting to be an assignment, is inoperative to pass a proprietary interest. In *Re Earl of Lucan*[90] X was entitled to a

83 (1888), 13 App. Cas. 199.
84 (1867), L.R. 2 C.P. 593, 598.
85 13 App. Cas. 212.
86 (1888), 13 App. Cas. 523. See the quotation, p. 297, *ante*, from the speech of Lord Macnaghten.
87 (1882), 10 L.R.Ir. 313.
88 [1936] Ch. 71. See also *Re Adlard*, [1954] Ch. 29.
89 (1851), 1 De G. M. & G. 176. See also *Meek* v. *Kettlewell* (1842), 1 Hare 464; *Donaldson* v. *Donaldson* (1854), Kay 711; *Harding* v. *Harding* (1886), 17 Q.B.D. 442.
90 (1890), 45 Ch. D. 470.

reversionary interest in certain stock which he voluntarily charged by deed with an annuity in favour of Y. Chitty, J., held that the effect of the deed was not to transfer the fund, but to create a charge on it, and accordingly the assignment was incomplete. In consequence, Y had no priority over the creditors of X. In *Re McArdle*[91] the residuary estate of a testator was held upon trust for the testator's widow for life and subject thereto upon trust for his five children in equal shares. One of the children, Monty, lived with his wife, Marjorie, in a bungalow forming part of the residuary estate and in 1943-4 Marjorie, at her own expense, executed certain alterations and repairs on the bungalow at a cost of £488. In 1945, the five children signed a document in the following terms: " To Mrs. Marjorie McArdle, Gravel Hill, Wimborne. In consideration of your carrying out certain alterations and improvements to the property . . . at present occupied by you, we the beneficiaries under the Will of William Edward McArdle hereby agree that the Executors . . . shall repay to you from the said estate when so distributed the sum of £488 in settlement of the amount spent on such improvements." The Court of Appeal held that the consideration for the agreement was past and was, therefore, no consideration and held further that it could not be construed as an equitable assignment of a proportionate part of the residuary estate since it was neither intended as such, nor, even if it had been so intended, was it complete and perfect. On the other hand, both Evershed, M. R., and Jenkins, L. J., were prepared to accept the proposition that an equitable assignment of an equitable chose in action which is complete and perfect may be a valid and binding assignment notwithstanding that it is made voluntarily and is in the nature of a mere gift.

Legal choses in action. The question of when consideration is necessary for the validity of an equitable assignment of a legal chose in action was very confused before the Judicature Act, which made such choses assignable at law. Since the Act, answers to this question have become somewhat different.[92]

Consideration for equitable assignments of legal choses in action before the Judicature Act. There seems to have been general agreement about some principles, and a maxim of uncertain content that " equity will not assist a volunteer." The first principle is this: where a trust is completely constituted (or " executed " or " perfect ") then, subject to a few specialised exceptions, a beneficiary who is a volunteer can enforce the trust; on the other hand, where the trust is incompletely constituted (or " in fieri " or " executory " or " imperfect "), a volunteer cannot

91 [1951] Ch. 669. See also Megarry (1951), 67 *Law Quarterly Review*, 295.
92 See Sheridan, " Informal Gifts of Choses in Action " (1955), 33 *Canadian Bar Review*, 284.

enforce it. This rule is not confined to trusts of choses in action: it applies to all property.[93] Similarly well settled is the rule that " there in no equity to perfect an imperfect gift ": an imperfect gift will not be enforced at the instance of a volunteer, but one which is perfect will.[94]

The question of when equity would enforce a voluntary assignment of a chose in action thus becomes: When was a gift or trust perfect ? Marshall, in his book on *Assignment of Choses in Action*, lists six tests of perfection.[95] One of these tests is whether the legal estate has passed. Where that test is applied, the rule that equity will uphold a perfect gift becomes a rule that equity will not impose a resulting trust upon the donee of such a gift. All gifts of choses in action, upon that view, must have been gifts of legal titles, and any disposition leaving the legal title in the assignor could be enforced against him only by someone giving consideration. There could be no equitable voluntary assignment of a chose whose legal title was unassignable, a category which included most choses, But, as Marshall pointed out,[96] "... the test requiring the legal title to be in the trustees is only applied where it is possible so to vest the legal title and even then not in an absolute form." One can thus postulate as the first rule of voluntary assignments before the Judicature Act that, in the case of a chose in action whose legal title was transferable, the assignor was bound only if he transferred the legal title.[97]

If there could be a perfect gift of a chose whose legal title was not assignable, there must have been some other test of perfection. As to this, as Marshall pointed out,[98] there were conflicting opinions. One thing owners of choses in action used to do was to execute a deed purporting to assign the chose, and giving the assignee a power of attorney to sue to recover the money.[99]

Gifts of such choses were held to be perfect in some cases. It was sometimes said that for a perfect gift all that was necessary was that the assignor do all he could towards transferring the legal title. Yet

93 See Anson, "Assignment of Choses in Action" (1901), 17 *Law Quarterly Review*, 90, 94; Bailey, "Assignments of Debts in England from the Twelfth to the Twentieth Century" (1932), 48 *L.Q.R.*, 547, 564.

94 See Jenks, " Consideration and the Assignment of Choses in Action " (1900), 16 *Law Quarterly Review*, 241, 248; Bailey, *op.cit.*, 48 *L.Q.R.*, 564.

95 Pp. 125-7.

96 P. 137.

97 *Searle* v. *Law* (1846), 15 Sim. 95; *Milroy* v. *Lord* (1862), 4 De G. F. & J. 264; *Heartley* v. *Nicholson* (1875), L.R. 19 Eq. 233. Ireland: *Moore* v. *Ulster Banking Co.* (1877), I.R. 11 C.L. 512.

98 Pp. 125-7.

99 See Ames, " Disseisin of Chattels " (1909), *Select Essays in Anglo-American Legal History*, vol. III, p. 580. Cf. Cook, "Alienability of Choses in Action " (1916), 29 *Harvard Law Review*, 816. See also Costigan, " Gifts *Inter Vivos* of *Choses* in Action " (1911), 27 *Law Quarterly Review*, 326, 329.

if the legal title could not be transferred, then he could not do anything towards transferring it. What seems to have been meant is that he should have made such efforts towards (an abortive) transfer as to make it plain to everyone that he meant to transfer the chose. Clearly, he made a good shot at this if he gave a power of attorney (which would enable the assignee to sue the debtor) and executed a deed of transfer (which would at least give the assignee contractual rights against the assignor at common law). A typical example is the following dealing with a life assurance policy on the life of George Townsend. On September 15th 1828, George Townsend executed a voluntary settlement of the policy of assurance and thereby, in consideration of the natural love and affection which he had and bore unto his father and mother and brother and sisters, he assigned the policy of assurance and all benefit and advantage thereof respectively, and all sums and sum of money to be received in respect of the shares in which he had become a member of the society, or otherwise in respect of the policy, to two trustees, upon certain trusts for his father, mother, brother and sisters. The deed contained the usual irrevocable power of attorney from Mr. Townsend to the two trustees. And Mr. Townsend thereby covenanted with the trustees to pay " the annual premium of £97 10s. as and when the same should become due and payable, and do all other acts and things necessary to keep the policy of assurance on foot." And also that he and his heirs, etcetera, at all times thereafter, would " make, do and execute, or cause and procure to be made, done and executed, all and every such further and other acts, deeds, things and assurances, for establishing, corroborating and confirming these presents, and every clause, matter and thing therein contained," and for better enabling the trustees " to perform and execute all the trusts hereby in them reposed," as by the trustees " or any person or persons interested in the permises " should be required. This was held by Romilly, M. R., to be a valid voluntary equitable assignment in *Pearson* v. *Amicable Assurance Office*.[1]

This led Spence[2] to summarise the position as at 1849 in these words—

> As regards choses in action, this much perhaps may be stated to be clear, that if a person, with a view to confer the beneficial interest in a chose in action, in which he has the legal interest, on another, makes an assignment in writing, particularly if by deed, and delivers the assignment and the security to the donee or to a trustee for him, showing an intention to put both the one and the other and con-

1 (1859), 27 Beav. 229. See also *Collinson* v. *Pattrick* (1838), 2 Keen 123; *M'Fadden* v. *Jenkyns* (1842), 1 Ph. 153; *Parnell* v. *Hingston* (1856), 3 Sm. & Giff. 337; *Re King* (1879), 14 Ch. D. 179. Ireland: *Blakely* v. *Brady* (1839), 2 Dr. & Wal. 311.

2 *Equitable Jurisdiction of the Court of Chancery*, vol. 2, p. 907.

sequently the debt out of his control, and also gives notice to the debtor, so as to make the debtor a *quasi* trustee for the donee, then the transaction is complete and binding, and the donor becomes a trustee of the legal interest, which must of course remain in him, for the donee; a clear and explicit verbal declaration, accompanied by the delivery of the securities and notice would, it is presumed, be equivalent to an assignment in writing: but in cases not embracing all these ingredients the authorities are not uniform, and particularly there is, as above mentioned, authority [*Fortescue* v. *Barnett*[3]] for saying that such a transaction may be complete, if by deed, although no notice should have been given to the debtor or person from whom the money is to be recovered.

And Marshall,[4] looking back from 1950, said that the answer seemed to be that, in order to make a perfect gift of a chose whose legal title was not transferable—

> . . . the assignor must have done everything possible to perfect the assignment, as for example, by executing a deed of assignment, or giving the assignee an irrevocable power of attorney, or covenanting to perfect the assignment, so that a Court of Equity would not have to act against the assignor in favour of the volunteer.

This sketch of the position before the Judicature Act is completed by reference to one further rule: that an imperfect voluntary assignment by way of gift or on trust would not be construed as a declaration by the assignor that he himself held as trustee. Courts did sometimes construe abortive transactions in that way, but it was settled by *Milroy* v. *Lord*[5] that this was wrong. In that case, Turner, L. J. said[6]—

> I take the law of this Court to be well settled, that, in order to render a voluntary settlement valid and effectual, the settler must have done everything which, according to the nature of the property comprised in the settlement, was necessary to be done to transfer the property and render the settlement binding upon him. He may of course do this by actually transferring the property to the persons for whom he intends to provide, and the provision will then be effectual, and it will be equally effectual if he transfers the property to a trustee for the purposes of the settlement, or declares that he himself holds it in trust for those purposes . . . . The cases I think

3 (1834), 3 My. & K. 36.
4 *Assignment of Choses in Action*, p. 132.
5 (1862), 4 De G. F. & J. 264 (C.A. Ch.).
6 4 De G. F. & J. 274. See also *Dillon* v. *Coppin* (1839), 4 My. & Cr. 647; *Smith* v. *Warde* (1845), 15 Sim. 56; *Moore* v. *Moore* (1874), L.R. 18 Eq. 474; *Heartley* v. *Nicholson* (1875), L.R. 19 Eq. 233; *Re Griffin*, [1899] 1 Ch. 408; Megarry, "Consideration and Equitable Assignments of Legal Choses in Action" (1943), 59 *Law Quarterly Review*, 58, 60-1.

go further to this extent, that if the settlement is intended to be effectuated by one of the modes to which I have referred, the Court will not give effect to it by applying another of those modes.

The position before the Judicature Act was confused. The main currents of authority, however, seem to give ground for believing in the correctness of the following three principles: (1) where the legal title to the chose was transferable, an assignor was bound in respect of a voluntary assignment only if he transferred the legal title (to the donee or to a trustee for him); (2) where the legal title was not transferable, as in most cases, the assignor was bound in favour of a volunteer if he did everything that he could do to put the chose under the control of the donee or a trustee for him (such as assigning by deed, giving a power of attorney to sue, covenanting for further assurance, handing over evidentiary documents, transferring securities for the chose, or telling the debtor to hold for the donee), or, if not everything, nearly everything; (3) an imperfect trust or gift would not be construed as a declaration of trust.

Consideration for equitable assignments of legal choses in action after the Judicature Act. All legal choses are transferable at law. If the assignor observes the statutory procedure,[7] the assignee gets the legal title and the assignor disappears into thin air. You can give your chose away under the statute, but what of the informal gift ? At least four views could be taken of the impact of the act.

First, applying the old rule that if the legal title was transferable a gift was perfect only on transfer of that legal title, there could never be a voluntary informal assignment.

Secondly, deducing from *Milroy* v. *Lord*[8] that a gift was perfect whenever the assignor had done all that was necessary towards a transfer, and which could be done only by the assignor, the new rule might be that a voluntary equitable assignment bound the assignor whenever the assignee could by his own act acquire the legal title.

Thirdly, it might be argued that the Judicature Act marked such a rift in the law relating to choses in action that an entirely new body of rules relating to informal voluntary transfers would have to be worked out.

Finally, it might be that the old pre-Judicature Act rules continued unaffected by the act directly, but went on developing and altering with time and circumstances, as they would have done had there been no Judicature Act.

[7] See pp. 326-8, *post.*
[8] (1862), 4 De G. F. & J. 264.

All these views have found favour with different people. At the outset, however, it may be said that the basic rule would probably continue to be that a gift (to a donee immediately or on trust) will be recognised as valid by equity unless it is imperfect. The question would then be: What gifts of choses in action are to be regarded as perfect ?[9]

In *German* v. *Yates*[10] Mrs. *G* lent *S.Y.* £100 and took from her an I.O.U. acknowledging receipt. Later, Mrs. *G*, *S.Y.* and *M.Y.* met and agreed that *S.Y.* should pay *M.Y.* instead of paying Mrs. *G.* Thereupon Mrs. *G.* tore up the I.O.U. and *S.Y.* wrote out a new one to *M.Y.* Subsequently Mrs. *G.* died, and *G* became her administrator. In this action, *G* claimed £100 from *S.Y.*, and *M.Y.* was a co-defendant. The case was decided by Lush, J., who gave judgment for the defendants.

The report of the judgment contains the following passage[11]—

> [Counsel] had contended that since the Judicature Act the creditor could make a good legal assignment under the Act, and that if he purported to make an equitable assignment without consideration he was trying to do what could be quite well done in another way and the transaction failed. But he [Mr. Justice Lush] could not accept that view. *Brandts* v. *Dunlop* showed that the Act had not destroyed equitable assignments or impaired their efficiency in any way, and they still existed alongside of the new kind of assignment under section 25. Nor could he accept the view that the assignment here was invalid because it was incomplete; it was perfectly good and complete.
>
> There remained the question whether the assignment was invalid for want of consideration .... It might be that if a creditor ordered his debtor to pay the money to some other person he might revoke the order if it was given without consideration; but if the creditor died without revoking it his executor could not ignore the transaction. He held, therefore, that the plaintiff's action failed.
>
> There was a further answer to it, that in the fact the transfer here was made for good consideration.

9 See Jenks, " Consideration and the Assignment of Choses in Action " (1900), 16 *Law Quarterly Review*, 241; Anson, "Assignment of Choses in Action " (1901), 17 *L.Q.R.*, 90; Costigan, " Gifts *Inter Vivos* of *Choses* in Action " (1911), 27 *L.Q.R.*, 326; Megarry, " Consideration and Equitable Assignments of Legal Choses in Action " (1943), 59 *L.Q.R.*, 58; Hollond, " Further Thoughts on Equitable Assignments of Legal Choses in Action " (1943), 59 *L.Q.R.*, 129; Sheridan, " Informal Gifts of Choses in Action " (1955), 33 *Canadian Bar Review*, 284; Hall, " Gift of Part of a Debt " (1959), *Cambridge Law Journal*, 99; Cullity and Ford, " Gifts of Future Income from Choses in Action " (1966), 30 *Conveyancer and Property Lawyer* (*N.S.*), 286.

10 (1915), 32 T.L.R. 52.

11 32 T.L.R. 53.

Leaving aside the second ground of the decision, the salient features are that (a) there was no consideration; (b) the statutory formalities were not complied with in that there was no written instrument of transfer; and (c) the assignee succeeded against the assignor's personal representative. However, it is far from clear what proposition of law the case can be regarded as authority for. At one stage Lush, J., referred to the assignment as " perfectly good and complete." By this he evidently did not mean that it was binding on the assignor, for in the next couple of sentences he suggested that the assignor might have revoked it. He was therefore not holding that the assignment was immediately a perfect gift. Presumably, then, he meant that the transaction was an intended and purported immediate gift. The position as Lush, J., evidently saw it was that while Mrs. *G* was alive *S.Y.* could please herself whether to pay Mrs *G* or *M.Y.* If *S.Y.* paid Mrs. *G*, there was a discharge, for Mrs. *G* had the legal title, and Mrs. *G* could keep the money as against *M.Y.*, who was a volunteer under an imperfect gift. That would have been an exercise of the power of revocation. If *S.Y.* paid *M.Y.*, there was a discharge, for *S.Y.* would then have carried out Mrs. *G*'s instructions. Whether *M.Y.* could keep the £100 is in doubt. It could be said (a) that the payment perfected the gift, as *M.Y.* now had the legal title to the subject matter of the chose, or (b) that, as *M.Y.* never had a beneficial interest in the debt, so she would not acquire a beneficial interest in the money when paid, but held on a resulting trust for Mrs. *G*. It would appear that Lush, J., would have opted for choice (a), for he seemed to think that the gift of the chose would have been valid until revoked, and one would imagine that revocation would have to take place before the chose was reduced into possession. Then, further, Lush, J., took the view that any power of revocation was personal to the assignor. Thus, when Mrs. *G* died (without having revoked), the legal title to the debt vested in *G* and an indefeasible equitable interest in *M.Y.*

The judgment therefore appears to be concerned, not with the question of when a gift is perfect, but with the attributes of an imperfect gift. It appears to proceed on the basis that an imperfect gift becomes perfect on the death of the donor (without having revoked) or, possibly, on the donee obtaining payment. If that is right, an imperfect gift is effective against a legatee or next of kin; or, rather, a gift is never imperfect as against anyone but the donor. But if that is right, a lot of other decisions are wrong, and such rules as the rule in *Strong* v. *Bird*[12] are superfluous. Incidentally, though it does not affect the analysis, Lush, J.'s, two grounds of decision put the legal title in

12 (1874), L.R. 18 Eq. 315.

different people. So far as the transaction was held effectual without consideration, *G* had the legal title and *M.Y.* the equitable. So far as consideration was held to exist, the transaction was a novation: that is, Mrs. *G* released her debt in consideration of *S.Y.*'s promise to pay *M.Y.*, who thus became the legal owner of a new debt.

In *Holt* v. *Heatherfield Trust Ltd.*,[13] the material facts for present purposes were these: *P* got judgment against *C*. Then *P* assigned the judgment debt to Holt, the assignment complying with all the statutory formalities except that notice of the assignment was not given to *C*. There was no consideration for the assignment.[14] Atkinson, J., held that there had been a valid equitable assignment.

The following passages from the judgment indicate the reasoning.

> Absence of notice does not affect the efficacy of the transaction as between the assignor and assignee. Unless notice be given the assignment is an equitable assignment, but it is an assignment which requires nothing more from the assignor to become a legal assignment. The assignee may himself give notice at any time before action brought, and further than that, even before notice, he may sue in his own name provided that he makes the assignor a party to the action, as plaintiff if he consents, and as defendant if he does not consent.[15]
>
> Therefore, it seems beyond argument that the absence of notice does not affect the efficacy of the transaction as between assignor and assignee. The Supreme Court of Judicature Act, 1873, relieved the assignee from the necessity of applying to equity for help, and therefore, valuable consideration is no longer necessary. Neither the Act of 1873 nor the Act of 1925 says a word about consideration. It is not suggested that valuable consideration is necessary if there is an absolute assignment and notice is given, but it is contended that, although valuable consideration may be unnecessary if notice be given, it is necessary to give validity to the transaction if notice be not given or until notice be given. If A. holds by way of gift an absolute assignment of an existing debt of which notice has not yet been given, it is said to be unenforceable and invalid. Yet, once A. gives notice, the invalidity is destroyed and the invalid becomes valid. It would, indeed, be strange if mere notice of an invalidity

13 [1942] 2 K.B. 1. For general comment, see Megarry, " Consideration and Equitable Assignments of Choses in Action " (1943), 59 *Law Quarterly Review*, 58. See also *Gorringe* v. *Irwell India Rubber and Gutta Percha Works* (1886), 34 Ch. D. 128; *Re Griffin*, [1899] 1 Ch. 408.

14 Hollond, " Further Thoughts on Equitable Assignments of Legal Choses in Action " (1943), 59 *Law Quarterly Review*, 129, argued that there was consideration. He was supported by Megarry (1943), 59 *L.Q.R.*, 208.

15 [1942] 2 K.B. 4.

> could destroy that invalidity, and, so far from being invalid, the assignment entitles the assignee to sue for the debt assigned even before notice is given so long as he joins the assignor on one side or another.[16]

The assignor had done everything necessary towards a transfer of the legal title so far as those things could be done only by him. The gift was perfect because the assignor had put the chose out of his control: he could not stop the assignee giving the debtor notice and so acquiring the legal title.

Atkinson, J., however, was not driven inevitably to his conclusion. He could have held that the assignor could withdraw his gift at any time before notice was given to the debtor. Moreover, some of his reasoning is unconvincing. His reference to the strangeness of notice of the invalidity operating to destroy the invalidity and make the invalid become valid is a play on words. There are lots of ways in which this sort of thing can happen. Signature can often " make the invalid valid." (There is nothing odd in a completed process being effective when to stop part way through would be null.) And Atkinson, J., himself recognised that notice of the legally invalid destroyed the invalidity and gave it legal operation. The intention of the parties, though, being that the gift should operate immediately, and the assignor having done all he alone could do towards passing the legal title, it was correctly held a perfect gift. The alternative would be to encourage a race between the grasping assignee to give notice and the dithering assignor to retract his gift. The results of that could only be arbitrary.

Viewed narrowly, *Holt* v. *Heatherfield Trust Ltd.* decided that a voluntary assignment complying with the statutory formalities, except for notice to the debtor, operates as an equitable assignment. More widely, the case might be regarded as authority for the view that wherever an assignor has done all that only he can do towards transferring the legal title in the chose to the assignee there is a perfect gift. Thus, although in both this case and *German* v. *Yates* the voluntary equitable assignment of a legal chose was held valid, there is a difference, or possible difference, in that on no view of *Holt* v. *Heatherfield Trust Ltd.* did the assignor ever have a power of revocation.

In *Re Fry*,[17] the relevant facts were as follows: *A.F.*, who lived in the United States of America, owned shares in *L. B. Ltd.*, an English company. The share certificates were deposited with the Putney (London) branch of Barclay's Bank. Late in 1940, *A.F.* executed transfers in proper form of the shares (a) in favour of his son *S.F.*,

[16] [1942] 2 K.B. 5.
[17] [1946] Ch. 312.

and (b) in favour of a private company, *C.I.T.* Then *A.F.* sent transfer (a) to the manager of the bank, and transfer (b) to the *C.I.T. Co.'s* accountants. In each case the transfer was a gift. Later, the two transfers, executed by the transferees, were sent together with the share certificates to *L.B. Ltd.* for registration. Under the Defence (Finance) Regulations, 1939, then in force, registration was prohibited without Treasury consent. To obtain this consent various forms and declarations had to be signed both by the transferor and by the transferees, and, in addition, a questionnaire was submitted to the transferor which he had to answer personally. Although the various forms, declarations and other documents were in the end completed, the transferor died (in October 1941) before the requisite consent of the Treasury to either of the transfers had been obtained. Romer, J., held that the shares belonged to *A.F.*'s residuary estate.

The learned judge said[18] that the case was " one where a person, having formed the intention to make a gift, dies before that intention has been fully and completely implemented. The law generally applicable to such a position was stated by Turner, L.J. in *Milroy* v. *Lord* . . . ." He pointed out that *S.F.* and the *C.I.T. Co.* had not acquired legal titles because of the absence of registration. " Had they, however, arrived at the position which entitled them, as against [*L.B. Ltd.*], to be put on the register of members ? Had everything been done which was necessary to put the transferees into the position of the transferor ?" No, because Treasury consent had not been obtained. Therefore the transferees had neither legal title nor a right to it.[19]

Romer, J., went on[20]—

> As no question of trust arises, I must next consider whether there had been a complete gift of an equitable interest in the shares . . . . It was said that the testator executed documents which were appropriate to the subject matter of the gifts, namely, share transfers; that these documents, being under seal, were irrevocable; that he did everything he could, and that was necessary for him to do, to divest himself of his legal and equitable interest in the shares in favour of the transferees; and that even if he failed to succeed in his purpose so far as the legal title was concerned, he must be regarded as having passed to them his equitable interest in the shares.

He then referred to *Holt* v. *Heatherfield Trust Ltd.* as establishing that notice to the debtor was not necessary for a perfect gift, and continued[21]—

18 [1946] Ch. 315.
19 [1946] Ch. 316.
20 [1946] Ch. 316-7.
21 [1946] Ch. 317.

So, here, it is contended, the absence of registration of the share transfers does not affect the efficacy of the transaction as between assignor and assignee, and the transactions must be treated as complete assignments of the testator's equitable interest in the shares.

To this contention Romer, J., found two answers. First[22]—

> Now I should have thought it was difficult to say that the testator had done everything that was required to be done by him at the time of his death, for it was necessary for him to obtain permission from the Treasury for the assignment and he had not obtained it. Moreover, the Treasury might in any case have required further information of the kind referred to in the questionnaire which was submitted to him, or answers supplemental to those which he had given in reply to it; and, if so approached, he might have refused to concern himself with the matter further, in which case I do not know how anyone could have compelled him to do so.

The second answer was that the Defence (Finance) Regulations, 1939, prohibited even an equitable interest from vesting in the transferees.[23]

These two answers were given separately. The second has nothing to do with equity, but is the government's intervention by legislation to keep a check on cases where the assignment of choses in action might affect the interests of others than the parties to the assignment. The first answer, on the other hand, purports to hold good even if all that the regulations prohibited was the passing of the legal title (by registration) without Treasury consent, that is, even if they could be interpreted as not prohibiting equitable assignments.

Re Fry differs from the earlier cases in that the co-operation of someone other than the parties to the assignment was required. Neither *German* v. *Yates* (which was not cited) nor *Holt* v. *Heatherfield Trust Ltd.* (which was distinguished) could supply much guidance. However, *Re Fry* does follow in the line of those two earlier cases in rejecting the pre-Judicature Act rule on choses whose legal title was transferable. And it also accords with *Holt's* case in asking as the test of perfection of the gift the question: Has the assignor done everything that was required to be done by him ? But this test was devised for cases where certain parts of an assignment could be undertaken only by the assignor, and all the other parts either by the assignee alone or equally well by assignor or assignee. *Re Fry* was a case where at least one part—giving Treasury consent—could be carried out neither by assignor nor by assignee. So, in order to apply the test, Romer, J., had to deal with a

22 [1946] Ch. 317-8.
23 [1946] Ch. 318.

stage called obtaining Treasury consent, as though that were something to be done by the assignor. This obscured the reality that what was required was Treasury consent, which is something done by the Treasury.

Looking at it Romer, J.'s, way, it is then said that the assignment was not a perfect gift because the assignor had neither obtained Treasury consent nor done everything within his potential to do so, because the Treasury might have asked for further information. But suppose this had happened, and the assignor had given all the information at his disposal, and Treasury consent had been withheld. The assignor would then have done everything he could towards completing the assignee's title. If it is then said that there was still no perfect gift because the duty of the assignor was to obtain Treasury consent, then one is going back to a rule that was rejected as too harsh before the Judicature Act, namely, that an assignor must do everything necessary to transfer the legal title even when that is impossible.

The substance of the problem, though, was this: the consent of the Treasury to a legal transfer was required. Could there be a perfect gift when that consent was not given ? In other words, is the test of perfection to be whether the assignor had done everything that could be done only by him (in which case the gift would be perfect without the Treasury consent, for the objection that the assignor might have refused to give further information would only arise if the Treasury asked for it), or is it to be whether everything remaining to be done to pass the legal title could be done by the assignee (in which case there would be no perfection without Treasury consent) ? The answer must depend on what is regarded as the object of the rule against imperfect gifts.

The actual decision of Romer, J., that the gift was imperfect may have been influenced by the public policy avoidance of the gift even if perfect. Moreover, he did not seem to share the view of Lush, J., in *German* v. *Yates* that an imperfect gift became perfect if the assignor died without revoking, at least where the imperfection rested in failure to secure a third person's consent.

In *Re Rose* (1949)[24] *T*, by will made in 1943, left 5,000 preference shares in *H.G.S. Ltd.* to *H*, " if such preference shares have not been transferred to him previously to my death." In 1944, *T* executed a voluntary transfer of 5,000 preference shares in *H.G.S. Ltd.* to *H* and delivered the certificates to him. The directors of the company, in the exercise of their powers, refused at first to register the transfer.

[24] [1949] Ch. 78.

T died in January 1946. The directors registered *H* in March 1946. *T*'s executors took out a summons to determine inter alia whether the gift to *H* took effect under the will. Jenkins, J., held that there had been a gift inter vivos.

The learned judge said[25]—

> I was referred to the well known case of *Milroy* v. *Lord*, and also to the recent case of *In re Fry*. Those cases, as I understand them, turn on the fact that the deceased donor had not done all in his power, according to the nature of the property given, to vest the legal interest in the property in the donee. In such circumstances it is, of course, well settled that there is no equity to complete the imperfect gift. If any act remained to be done by the donor to complete the gift at the date of the donor's death the Court will not compel his personal representatives to do that act and the gift remains incomplete and fails.

Referring to *Re Fry*, Jenkins, J., went on[25]—

> Something had to be done by the donor's executors if the gift was to be completed, and that was the execution of further transfers which were not open to the objection of the absence of Treasury consent. In this case, as I understand it, [*T*] had done everything in his power to divest himself of the shares in question to [*H*]. He had executed a transfer. It is not suggested that the transfer was not in accordance with the company's regulations. He handed that transfer together with the certificates to [*H*]. There was nothing else [*T*] could do. It is true that [*H*'s] legal title would not be perfect until the directors passed the transfer for registration, but that was not an act the testator had to do, it was an act which depended on the discretion of the directors. Therefore it seems to me that the present case is not in pari materia with the two cases to which I have referred.

With respect, the gift in *Re Fry* was not imperfect because the executors had to complete it by executing further transfers. The issue was whether the executors should make confirmatory transfers, and that depended on whether the gift was perfect. The gift was held imperfect because Treasury consent had not been obtained. The giving of consent was within the discretion of the Treasury and, so far as the question of perfection was concerned, affected only the location of the legal title. Similarly, in *Re Rose* (1949) the legal title could not pass without registration, which was within the discretion of the

[25] [1949] Ch. 89.

directors. Yet the gift was held perfect without registration. There appear to be only two distinctions of fact between the cases. First, the consenting body in one was the Treasury and in the other a company. It is not apparent why this should be material. Secondly, in *Re Fry* the assignor had a part to play in seeking Treasury consent, while in *Re Rose* (1949) the assignee could apply for registration off his own bat. Yet the assignor had taken the appropriate steps in *Re Fry* towards persuading the Treasury. It was said he might be asked further questions. In *Re Rose* (1949) the directors might have reacted to *H*'s application for registration by sending *T* a questionnaire. What has happened is that Romer, J., and Jenkins, J., have taken up different standpoints on the necessity for a third person's consent. Romer, J., applied implicitly in *Re Fry* as the test of perfection: Can the assignee complete his own title ? This means that where a third person's co-operation is outstanding the gift is imperfect. Jenkins, J., in *Re Rose* (1949) applied as the test: Has anything further to be done by the assignor ? This means that the mere fact that a third person's consent is required does not render a gift imperfect if (a) the consent can be applied for by the assignee (as in *Re Rose*, 1949), or (b) the consent can be and has been applied for by the assignor (as in *Re Fry*).

Re Rose (1952)[26] concerned the following facts: *E.H.R.*, on March 30th 1943, executed a voluntary transfer under seal, in the form required by the company's articles, of 10,000 shares in the *L.E. Co.* to his wife *R.M.R.* By another such document of the same date he made a voluntary transfer of another 10,000 shares in that company to *R.M.R.* and *E.T.X.* on trust for *R.M.R.* and the son of *R.M.R.* and *E.H.R.* The transfers and the settlement were executed by all parties between March 30th and April 5th 1943, and thereafter *E.T.X.*, who was secretary of the *L.E. Co.*, held all the certificates for registration purposes. The directors of the *L.E. Co.* had a discretion whether to register or not. The transfers were stamped on April 12th 1943, and registered by the *L.E. Co.* on June 30th 1943. *E.H.R.* died on February 16th 1947. The question when the gifts were complete was important for death duty purposes. The Court of Appeal held the transfers complete on March 30th 1943.

The decision of Evershed, M.R., and Jenkins and Morris, L.JJ., was unanimous. The Master of the Rolls said the transactions were intended to operate as immediate transfers. He adopted[27] the view of Jenkins, J., in the earlier *Re Rose* (1949) on the effect of *Milroy* v. *Lord* and *Re Fry*. Then Evershed, M.R., held[28] that as *E.H.R.* did all

[26] [1952] Ch. 499.
[27] [1952] Ch. 508-12.
[28] [1952] Ch. 512-3.

he could towards transferring the legal title there was a perfect gift and *E.H.R.* was trustee of the shares pending registration. (Furthermore, there was consideration.)[29] *Re Rose* (1952) thus bestows the approval of the Court of Appeal upon the *Re Rose* of 1949.

In the light of the cases, the following propositions seem supportable:

(1) Where the assignor has done everything necessary and which can be done only by him towards transferring the legal title, the transfer is perfect. If the legal title is still in the assignor because some act yet remains to be done by the assignee or by someone else, nevertheless the transferee, though a volunteer, is entitled in equity to the chose in action. So long as the assignor retains the legal title he holds it on trust for the assignee.

(2) If there is still something to be done towards vesting the legal title in the assignee, and the co-operation of the assignor is required to complete the vesting, then the gift is imperfect and only if he has given consideration can the assignee enforce the assignor's co-operation.

Equitable Assignments After the Judicature Act

A problem which remained unsettled for some years after the Judicature Act, 1873, was the effect of the statute[30] upon equitable assignments. This point was only finally settled in *William Brandt's Sons & Co.* v. *Dunlop Rubber Co. Ltd.*,[31] in which case Lord Macnaghten said—

> The statute does not forbid or destroy equitable assignments or impair their efficacy in the slightest degree. Where the rules of equity and the rules of the common law conflict, the rules of equity are to prevail. Before the statute there was a conflict as regards assignments of debts and other choses in action. At law it was considered necessary that the debtor should enter into some engagement with the assignee. That was never the rule in equity. . . . In certain cases the Judicature Act places the assignee in a better position than he was before.[32]

Accordingly, an assignment which fails to operate as a statutory assignment by reason of some want of form may nevertheless take effect as an equitable assignment to the same extent that it would have been effective in equity prior to 1876.[33]

[29] [1952] Ch. 513. The transferees had executed the transfers and, the shares being in an unlimited company, had thus undertaken obligations.

[30] See p. 326, *post*.

[31] [1905] A.C. 454, 461. Ireland: *Grundy* v. *Broadbent*, [1918] 1 I.R. 433, to the same effect with regard to the Judicature (Ireland) Act, 1877.

[32] See also *Performing Right Soc. Ltd.* v. *London Theatre of Varieties Ltd.*, [1924] A.C. 1.

[33] Cf. *Re Trytel*, [1952] W. N. 355. As to the requirement of consideration in post-1875 equitable assignments, see pp. 314-24, *ante*.

In Ireland, Section 28 of the Judicature Act, 1877, which has otherwise achieved the same results as the 1873 Act in England,[34] has not affected the assignment of deposit receipts.[35] In *McEneaney* v. *Shevlin*[36] S, the owner of a deposit receipt for £900, surrendered it to the bank, and directed a new deposit receipt to be made out in the names of himself and his two nephews (who gave no consideration for the transaction), with the intention that the interest in the property should pass on his death to the nephews. The Court of Appeal held that there had been an effectual transfer of the beneficial interest, and that at the death of S it passed to the two nephews. No reasons are given in the report for their decision, beyond allusion to the judgment in the court below. There,[37] Ross, J., stated the principles relating to the assignment of deposit receipts—

> If the owner directs a new deposit receipt to be taken out in the names of other persons, there is a resulting trust in favour of the owner, and the other persons are merely trustees for him. The *onus* is upon the other persons to show that the beneficial interest also was intended to pass to them. If, however, the owner stands *in loco parentis* to these other persons, the *onus* is the other way, and an advancement is presumed. It is, however, open to the persons in respect of whom the owner does not occupy the relationship indicated by the phrase *in loco parentis* to prove by contemporaneous declarations, or by other evidence, that the beneficial interest was intended to pass. All that is required is the surrender of the deposit receipt and the reception by the owner of the new deposit receipt in the names of the other parties, or in the names of the owner and the other parties. No further writing is necessary.

Since no legal title passes to " the other persons," the principles seem to be in conflict with, or a departure from, the general principle that a voluntary imperfect gift will not be upheld in equity.

[34] See p. 326, *post*.

[35] See Keeton, *The Law of Trusts*, 9th ed., Irish Supplement (Sheridan), pp. 11-13; n. 37, below.

[36] [1912] 1 I.R. 278.

[37] [1912] 1 I.R. 32, 36. Cf. *McEvoy* v. *Belfast Banking Co. Ltd.*, [1935] A.C. 24. The cases on this subject are discussed in: Montrose, " Deposit Receipts and the Doctrine of Consideration " (1935), 39 *Journal of the Institute of Bankers in Ireland*, 232; Corscadden, " Joint Deposit Receipts " (1937), 1 *Northern Ireland Legal Quarterly*, 123 and 174; Sheridan, " Reflections on Irish Deposit Receipts " (1951), 9 *N.I.L.Q.*, 101; Montrose, " Joint Deposit Receipts—A Reconsideration " (1951), 9 *N.I.L.Q.*, 148; Sheridan, " Irish Private Law and the English Lawyer " (1952), 1 *International and Comparative Law Quarterly*, 196, 201-2; Lyons, " The Law relating to Deposit Receipts " (1956), 58 *J.I.B.I.*, 183 and 258; Delany, " Joint Deposit Accounts: Some Misconceptions " (1957), 23 *Irish Jurist*, 31.

Statutory Assignments

When choses in action were either created or regulated by nineteenth century statutes, the same statute usually included provisions governing assignment. For example, before 1867, life assurance policies could not be assigned at law, but by the Policies of Assurance Act, 1867, the assignee of such a policy was enabled to sue in his own name for the recovery of the money, provided that written notice had been given to the company, and priorities of assignees were governed by the date at which notice was given. There are similar provisions in the Marine Insurance Act, 1906.[38]

Section 25(6) of the Judicature Act, 1873, contained the following comprehensive provision, now re-enacted in Section 136(1) of the Law of Property Act, 1925[39]—

> Any absolute assignment by writing under the hand of the assignor (not purporting to be by way of charge only)[40] of any debt or other legal thing in action, of which express notice in writing[41] has been given to the debtor, trustee or other person from whom the assignor would have been entitled to claim such debt or thing in action, is effectual in law (subject to equities having priority over the right of the assignee) to pass and transfer from the date of such notice—
>
> (*a*) the legal right to such debt or thing in action;
> (*b*) all legal and other remedies for the same; and
> (*c*) the power to give a good discharge for the same without the concurrence of the assignor;
>
> Provided that, if the debtor, trustee or other person liable in respect of such debt or thing in action has notice—
> (*a*) that the assignment is disputed by the assignor or any person claiming under him; or
> (*b*) of any other opposing or conflicting claims to such debt or thing in action;
> he may, if he thinks fit, either call upon the persons making claim thereto to interplead concerning the same, or pay the debt or other thing in action into court under the provisions of the Trustee Act, 1925.

This legislation established a new form of assignment under which the legal title passes. A purported assignment failing to comply with

[38] Sect. 50.
[39] The corresponding provision in Ireland is Sect. 28(6) of the Judicature (Ireland) Act, 1877.
[40] See *Durham Bros.* v. *Robertson*, [1898] 1 Q.B. 765 (C.A.).
[41] As to the nature of the notice, see *Van Lynn Developments Ltd.* v. *Pelias Construction Co. Ltd.*, [1969] 1 Q.B. 607. (C.A.).

all the statutory requirements will pass an equitable interest in the chose if the requirements of equitable assignments are complied with; otherwise, it will be a nullity.

The requirement in the statute that the assignment be absolute, and not by way of charge only, means that the assignor must have parted with his entire interest in the property. If he has done this, the assignment is absolute, even if the transfer is by way of mortgage, i.e. subject to a right of redemption,[42] or subject to an implied right to a reassignment,[43] or to a trustee on trust to hold the proceeds of the chose for the assignor himself.[44] If the assignment is conditional only, or purports to give merely a charge, or is indefinite in extent, this is not an absolute assignment within the section.[45] Assignment of part of a debt, existing or future, is not an absolute assignment within the section: to be absolute, the assignment must extend to the whole fund.[46]

The phrase " other legal thing in action " has provided some speculation concerning its scope, and there is some authority for stating that the term includes both assignable choses in action and choses in equity, but not rights, such as a bare right of action, which before the Judicature Act were not assignable at all. In *King* v. *Victoria Insurance Co. Ltd.*[47] the Privy Council considered the following definition of the phrase which had been accepted in the lower court (the Supreme Court of Queensland): " . . . all rights the assignment of which a Court of Law or Equity would before the Act have considered lawful . . . "[48] Their lordships did not express any dissent from the definition, but preferred " to avoid discussing a question not free from difficulty . . ."[49] A few years later, in *Manchester Brewery Co.* v. *Coombs*,[50] Farwell, J., accepted the definition, and held that the phrase was comprehensive enough to include a restrictive covenant in the lease of a hotel that all beer should be purchased from the lessor. The following year, in *Torkington* v. *Magee*,[51] Lord Alverstone, C.J., and Darling and Channell, JJ., decided that the benefit of a contract for the sale of a

42 *Tancred* v. *Delagoa Bay and East Africa Railway Co.* (1889), 23 Q.B.D. 239.
43 *Hughes* v. *Pump House Hotel Co. Ltd.*, [1902] 2 K.B. 190 (C.A.).
44 *Comfort* v. *Betts*, [1891] 1 Q.B. 737 (C.A.).
45 *Mercantile Bank of London Ltd.* v. *Evans*, [1899] 2 Q.B. 613 (C.A.); *Jones* v. *Humphreys*, [1902] 1 K.B. 10.
46 *Forster* v. *Baker*, [1910] 2 K.B. 636 (Bray, J., the decision being affirmed by the Court of Appeal on a different ground); *Re Steel Wing Co. Ltd.*, [1921] 1 Ch. 349; *Williams* v. *Atlantic Assurance Co. Ltd.*, [1933] 1 K.B. 81 (Greer and Slesser, L.JJ., in the Court of Appeal, Scrutton, L.J., expressing no opinion on this point). Ireland: *Conlan* v. *Carlow C. C.*, [1912] 2 I.R. 535. See also Hall, " Gift of Part of a Debt " (1959), *Cambridge Law Journal*, 99.
47 [1896] A.C. 250.
48 [1896] A.C. 254.
49 [1896] A.C. 256.
50 [1901] 2 Ch. 608.
51 [1902] 2 K.B. 427.

reversionary interest could be the subject of a statutory assignment. These cases have sometimes been taken to support the view that the words " other legal thing in action " must be interpreted to mean " any chose in action or chose in equity," though they were in fact concerned with choses carrying a right of action at law, and in none of them did any judge expressly mention the possibility that assignment of a chose in equity might be within the statute. It is submitted, moreover, that such an interpretation goes beyond the words of the section. Even if it had been held that the assignments in *Manchester Brewery Co.* v. *Coombs*[52] and in *Torkington* v. *Magee*[53] were not covered by Section 25(6) of the Judicature Act, 1873, there is no reason why they should not have been valid equitable assignments under which the assignee would be fully protected. As was pointed out in *William Brandt's Sons & Co.* v. *Dunlop Rubber Co. Ltd.*,[54] the purpose of the Judicature Act, 1873, was not to destroy equitable assignments, but rather to provide a statutory method of assignment in addition. This was perhaps not clearly appreciated when *Manchester Brewery Co.* v. *Coombs* and *Torkington* v. *Magee* were before the courts, and this may explain why commentators thought they had discovered a determination of the judges to bring within the statute cases which, on one interpretation, may be outside its ambit; although the use of the term " trustee " hints that equitable choses in action may have been within the contemplation of the draftsman.

The assignment must be in writing, under the hand of the assignor: it need not be by deed, and it is clear that consideration is not required.[55] Further, express notice in writing must be given to the debtor, though the section does not specify who must give it, or the time when it is to be given. On the other hand, it has been decided that if the date of the assignment is wrongly stated in the notice, the notice is invalid.[56] If notice is not given, the assignment is still effectual as between assignor and assignee, but as an equitable assignment only, and the assignor must be joined in the action. Moreover, the rights of the assignee may be defeated by a subsequent statutory assignment. If notice is given, the assignee is subject only to those equities which have arisen before notice of assignment.[57] Finally, if the assignee fails to give notice, he will be postponed to a later assignee who gives notice without at the time of the assignment having notice of the earlier assignment.

[52] [1901] 2 Ch. 608.
[53] [1902] 2 K.B. 427.
[54] [1905] A.C. 454.
[55] *Re Westerton*, [1919] 2 Ch. 104.
[56] *Stanley* v. *English Fibres Industries Ltd.* (1889), 68 L.J.Q.B. 839; *W. F. Harrison*
in action, see pp. 209–22, 300–7, *ante*.
[57] *Brice* v. *Bannister* (1878), 3 Q.B.D. 569 (C.A.), a case of an equitable assignment.

CHAPTER IX

FRAUD

THE relation between the treatment of fraud at common law and its treatment in equity[1] sometimes gives rise to difficulty and has not always been clearly understood. It was traced with great learning by Lord Haldane, L.C., in *Nocton* v. *Lord Ashburton*.[2] In the course of his speech in that case, he pointed out that in cases of actual fraud courts of equity and courts of common law exercised concurrent jurisdiction from the earliest times. In some ways, the Court of Chancery was always the more suitable forum, even in cases where concurrent jurisdiction existed. For one thing, it showed greater freedom in admitting the testimony of the parties. Moreover, its remedies were more elastic. The common law courts gave damages only, but the Court of Chancery, operating in personam, though it could not award damages, could order the defendant to make restitution, e.g. by an account of profits. It was only by stages that the common law courts evolved the action for deceit, and it was not until the decision of the Court of King's Bench, in *Pasley* v. *Freeman*[3] in 1789, that this action was finally established, independently of a special duty arising out of a contract, implied contract or agency. The conception of actual fraud still remained fluid in important particulars, until the decision of the House of Lords in *Derry* v. *Peek*,[4] a decision which, as Lord Haldane noticed, took no account of the treatment of fraud in equity, and which insofar as directors were concerned, produced so many difficulties that it necessitated the passing of the Directors' Liability Act, 1890. In *Derry* v. *Peek*[4] the House of Lords defined deceit, or fraud at common law, as a misrepresentation of fact, made either knowingly, without belief in its truth, or recklessly, not caring whether it was true or false. Although carelessness, or absence of reasonable ground for believing the statement to be true, might be evidence of fraud, the inference could be displaced by showing that it was made with an honest belief in its truth, no matter how naive. Thus, until the legislature intervened in 1890, many directors went

1 See Sheridan, *Fraud in Equity*.

2 [1914] A.C. 932, 946-57.

3 3 T.R. 51. For Lord Eldon's adverse criticism, see *Evans* v. *Bicknell* (1801), 6 Ves. 174, 182-7.

4 (1889), 14 App. Cas. 337.

free. Until the decision of the House of Lords in *Hedley Byrne & Co. Ltd.* v. *Heller & Partners Ltd.*,[5] there was no common law liability for negligent misrepresentation.

To have a fraudulent misrepresentation at common law, there must be a *misrepresentation of fact.* Misstatement of opinion, or of law, is not a ground for liability, and this view of the common law is due to the necessity of placing a clear issue of fact before a jury. Everyone is supposed to know the law; therefore a misstatement of law (in theory, at any rate) cannot deceive; whilst a misstatement of opinion is too intangible a matter for a jury to pronounce upon. Equity, however, looked at the matter differently, and in addition to its concurrent jurisdiction in respect of " actual " (i.e. common law) fraud, developed an exclusive jurisdiction in respect of many other types of fraud, which escaped the meshes of the common law. " In Chancery the term ' fraud ' thus came to be used to describe what fell short of deceit, but imported breach of a duty to which equity had attached its sanction."[6]

Equity, that is to say, was looking, not so much to specific statements or representations of fact, but to *conduct* and the Court of Chancery was particularly fitted to undertake inquiries of this kind, since there was no jury, and ample opportunity to call upon the parties to account for their conduct. Thus " fraud " came to include a wide range of transactions " in which the Court is of opinion that it is unconscientious for a person to avail himself of the legal advantage which he has obtained. Indeed the books are full of cases in which the Court has dealt with contracts of that kind—contracts obtained by persons from others over whom they have dominion, contracts obtained by persons in a fiduciary position, contracts for the sale of shares obtained by directors through misrepresentation contained in the prospectus, in respect of which it was never necessary to allege or prove that the directors were wilfully guilty of moral fraud in what they had done."[7]

This last point, if remembered in *Derry* v. *Peek*, might have turned the decision the other way, notwithstanding the tenderness of the House of Lords at that date towards errant company directors.

[5] [1964] A.C. 465. See also the Misrepresentation Act 1967; Misrepresentation Act (Northern Ireland) 1967; Murdoch, " Some Observations on the Misrepresentation Act 1967 " (1967), 31 *Conveyancer and Property Lawyer* (*N.S.*), 234; Fairest, " Misrepresentation and the Act of 1967 " (1967), *Cambridge Law Journal*, 239.

[6] *Per* Lord Haldane, L.C., *Nocton* v. *Lord Ashburton*, [1914] A.C. 932, 953.

[7] *Per* James, L. J., *Torrance* v. *Bolton* (1872), L.R. 8 Ch. App. 118, 124-5.

Fraud, in the sense in which it was used in equity in its exclusive jurisdiction, was not capable of precise definition. Two centuries ago, Lord Hardwicke said[8] that fraud was infinite.

Over a century and a half later, another Lord Chancellor, Lord Haldane, emphatically reaffirmed this refusal of equity to define fraud, adding—[9]

> . . . when fraud is referred to in the wider sense in which the books are full of the expression, used in Chancery in describing cases which were within its exclusive jurisdiction, it is a mistake to suppose that an actual intention to cheat must always be proved. A man may misconceive the extent of the obligation which a Court of Equity imposes on him. His fault is that he has violated, however innocently because of his ignorance, an obligation which he must be taken by the Court to have known, and his conduct has in that sense always been called fraudulent, even in such a case as a technical fraud on a power. It was thus that the expression " constructive fraud " came into existence. The trustee who purchases the trust estate, the solicitor who makes a bargain with his client that cannot stand, have all for several centuries run the risk of the word fraudulent being applied to them. What it really means in this connection is, not moral fraud in the ordinary sense, but breach of the sort of obligation which is enforced by a Court that from the beginning regarded itself as a Court of conscience.

In spite of the comprehensiveness of the term, equity's exclusive jurisdiction in respect of fraud is capable of being classified under distinct heads. Indeed, Lord Hardwicke's analysis of it in *Earl of Chesterfield* v. *Janssen*[10] has influenced all subsequent development. In his judgment in that case, Lord Hardwicke says—

> This court has an undoubted jurisdiction to relieve against every species of fraud. 1. Then fraud, which is *dolus malus*, may be actual, arising from facts and circumstances of imposition; which is the plainest case. 2. It may be apparent from the intrinsic nature and subject of the bargain itself; such as no man in his senses and not under delusion would make on the one hand, and as no honest and fair man would accept on the other; which are unequitable and unconscientious bargains . . . A 3*d* kind of fraud is, which may be presumed from the circumstances and condition of the parties contracting: and this goes farther than the rule of law; which is,

[8] In a letter to Lord Kames, reproduced by Parkes, *History of the Court of Chancery*, pp. 506-9. See p. 60, *ante*, for an extract from the letter.

[9] *Nocton* v. *Lord Ashburton*, [1914] A.C. 932, 954.

[10] (1750), 2 Ves. Sen. 125, 155-7.

that it must be proved, not presumed; but it is wisely established in this court to prevent taking surreptitious advantage of the weakness or necessity of another: which knowingly to do is equally against the conscience as to take advantage of his ignorance . . . A 4*th* kind of fraud may be collected or inferred in the consideration of this court from the nature and circumstances of the transaction, as being an imposition and deceit on the other persons not parties to the fraudulent agreement . . . The last head of fraud, on which there has been relief, is that, which infects catching bargains with heirs, reversioners, or expectants, in the life of the father, etc. . . .

Of fraudulent misrepresentation, as defined in *Derry* v. *Peek*,[11] nothing more need be said, for although equity has concurrent jurisdiction, and can give different forms of relief, the development of this tort has been essentially a common law matter. However, since the Judicature Act, 1873, and the Judicature (Ireland) Act, 1877, every division of the High Court has been able to give all legal and equitable remedies appropriate to the case, so that to-day the court can (and does) award both damages and an account of profits, where these remedies are appropriate.

Other varieties of actual fraud consist of property frauds affecting priorities and fraud in legal proceedings. As to priorities, a person may (a) be affected with constructive notice of a prior interest, so as to take subject to it, when he deliberately refrains from investigating the title so as to avoid getting actual notice of it; or (b) lose the priority of his interest as against a subsequent incumbrancer, for example the case of a legal mortgagee of shares in a company who allows the mortgagor to have the share certificate with a view to deceiving someone else into lending money on the security of what appears to be a first legal mortgage of the shares.[12] As to fraud in legal proceedings, this usually consists of collusion so as to mislead the court and can give rise to an action, by a person prejudiced by it, to have the judgment set aside.[13]

Apart from cases of " actual fraud," Lord Hardwicke stated that the common law exercised a limited jurisdiction over his second category. However, the normal practice has been to bring suits in respect of these matters in equity. The third, fourth and fifth classes

[11] (1889), 14 App. Cas. 337.

[12] As to priorities of successive mortgages and of successive assignments of choses in action, see pp. 209-22, 300-7., *ante*.

[13] See Sheridan, *Fraud in Equity*, ch. III; " Fraud and Surprise in Legal Proceedings " (1955), 18 *Modern Law Review*, 441; Gordon, " Fraud or New Evidence as Grounds for Actions to Set Aside Judgments " (1961), 77 *Law Quarterly Review*, 358 and 533.

of fraud were described by Lord Hardwicke as being within equity's exclusive jurisdiction. The following types of fraud in equity are discussed in this chapter—

1. Inequitable and unconscientious bargains, made with weak and ignorant persons.

2. Abuse of a fiduciary relationship, including undue influence.

3. Frauds upon third parties.

4. " Catching bargains " with heirs, reversioners and expectants.

There are other contexts in which the word " fraud " has been used by courts of equity. One of these, often in the form of the maxim " Equity will not allow a statute to be used as an instrument of fraud," represents a special approach by the Court of Chancery to the application of Acts of Parliament passed to check frauds.[14] Another is the equitable doctrine of fraud on a power. A power of appointment carries with it no fiduciary duty; nevertheless an exercise of the power, with an ulterior objective, other than one for which the power was created, is voidable as fraudulent.[15]

Inequitable and Unconscientious Bargains

The relief given by equity under this head is frequently connected with the relief given under the head of " catching bargains," for it may well be that an heir or expectant is both poor (in the sense that he is badly in need of money) and ignorant, possibly on account of youth. Nevertheless, there need not necessarily be a " catching bargain " with an heir or expectant for relief to be given, for, as Kay, J., said, in *Fry* v. *Lane*[16]—

> The result of the decisions is that where a purchase is made from a poor and ignorant man at a considerable undervalue, the vendor having no independent advice, a Court of Equity will set aside the transaction.
>
> This will be done even in the case of property in possession, and *à fortiori* if the interest be reversionary.
>
> The circumstances of poverty and ignorance of the vendor, and absence of independent advice, throw upon the purchaser, when the transaction is impeached, the onus of proving, in Lord *Selborne's* words, that the purchase was " fair, just, and reasonable."

[14] See pp. 26-9, *ante*.
[15] See pp. 368-74, *post*.
[16] (1888), 40 Ch.D. 312, 322.

By itself, mere under-value, or over-value, is not a ground for setting aside a sale, for equity has never assumed the right to make bargains. Nevertheless, the under-value or over-value may be so gross as to be evidence of fraud. Lord Thurlow, L.C., in *Gwynne* v. *Heaton*,[17] said—

> To set aside a conveyance, there must be an inequality *so strong, gross, and manifest*, that it must be *impossible to state it* to a man of common sense, *without producing an exclamation at the inequality of it*.

But the inequality is only evidence of the fraud, not proof of it. As Hart, L.C., said in the Irish case of *Drought* v. *Eustace*[18]—

> . . . inadequacy of price is not of itself sufficient, but the Court has got at it by indirect means:—it has been astute, as it is said to infer fraud from inadequacy, so as to raise it indirectly into a ground for relief.

In a later Irish case, *Butler* v. *Miller*,[19] Walsh, M. R., took the view that there was a strong presumption against a sale of property for less than half its value. Furthermore, where there is a purchase from a poor and ignorant person at a considerable undervalue, it is no objection to setting aside the transaction that the vendor was of mature age.[20] As people become more literate and less necessitous the number of cases of this kind diminishes; but they have not disappeared yet. The rule of equity remains that inequality of bargain is some evidence of fraud to be weighed along with the other evidence. Other factors that commonly go to support a case of fraud are mental feebleness, drunkenness, illness, old age, youth, illiteracy, ignorance, poverty and urgent need of money.

In *Evans* v. *Llewellin*[21] an owner of property was induced to sell it at a gross undervalue, and the sale was set aside. The vendor, who did not consult anyone, was poor and ignorant of his rights. The purchaser was affluent and aware of the position. In *Wood* v. *Abrey*[22] a sale for £400 of property worth £1,600 was set aside. The vendors were of a low station in life (one was a common porter and the other a sergeant in the army), ignorant of the value of the property, and in urgent need of money. The only professional person employed in the sale was the purchaser's solicitor. In *Longmate* v. *Ledger*[23] a sale

[17] (1778), 1 Bro. C.C. 1, 9.
[18] (1828), 1 Mol. 328, 335.
[19] (1867) I.R. 1 Eq. 195, 211-2.
[20] *Ahearn* v. *Ahearn* (1910), 45 I.L.T.R. 28.
[21] (1787), 1 Cox C.C. 333.
[22] (1818), 3 Madd. 417.
[23] (1860), 2 Giff. 157.

at a considerable under-value, with one solicitor acting for both parties, by an old, weak and eccentric man, was set aside. In *Clark* v. *Malpas*[24] a poor, illiterate and ill man, not having independent advice, sold his only property at an under-value. The sale was set aside. In *Baker* v. *Monk*[25] cottages were sold, without independent advice, by a poor, elderly and ignorant spinster, to a prosperous tradesman, ex-mayor of the town, in return for a small weekly payment and the right of residence in one of the cottages. This being found a sale at an under-value, it was set aside. *Baker* v. *Monk* was followed and applied in the Irish case of *Slator* v. *Nolan*,[26] where a reckless, improvident and destitute man was taken advantage of by his brother-in-law, who was a man of the world, well versed in business, and induced to part with property for a grossly inadequate consideration; the transaction was set aside.

On the other hand, in *Harrison* v. *Guest*,[27] the offer which led to the impeached sale of land came from the vendor, and the conveyance was allowed to stand. The vendor was old and ignorant, and of a humble station in life; he had no independent advice; the sale was at an under-value; and the purchaser was of a higher station than the vendor. But the under-value was slight, and the vendor's faculties were in no way impaired by his age.

A very astute intoxicator was deprived of the spoils of his activities in *Say* v. *Barwick*.[28] An infant owned land, and the person who led him astray was out to become tenant. The latter managed to get the infant drunk daily during the period immediately preceding the attainment of his majority, ending up with a thorough carousal on the last night of infancy. Early the next morning, his majority a couple of hours old, the landowner was woken up with a hangover, and he signed a lease to the defendant at a little over half an economic rent for the premises, which lease had been the subject of discussion between them for some time. It was set aside.

In *Buckley* v. *Irwin*[29] the transaction was the sale by the defendant of his farm to the plaintiff at a substantial under-value. The defendant was not of unsound mind, but a person who would require protection and guidance in carrying out business affairs, even of a comparatively simple nature. The plaintiff, and his friend who participated in the negotiations, were two sharp-eyed and experienced dealers who had the defendant sized up as one who could be imposed on. They called

24 (1862), 4 De G.F. & J. 401.
25 (1864), 4 De G.J. & S. 388.
26 (1876), I.R. 11 Eq. 367.
27 (1860), 8 H.L.C. 481.
28 (1812), 1 V. & B. 195.
29 [1960] N.I. 98.

on him out of the blue and in half an hour had bought the farm, though the defendant had never previously considered selling it. In addition to refusing the plaintiff specific performance (which may be done on grounds of unfairness not amounting to fraud),[30] McVeigh, J., said[31]—

> . . . I consider that this is a contract which ought not to be allowed to stand. Rescission has not been claimed in the pleadings, but I do not consider that a court of equity should allow damages for breach of contract in a case in which it is of opinion that the contract is vitiated in the way I have described. For this reason I refuse damages.

The question of unconscionableness must be decided by looking at all the circumstances of the particular case.[32] Where circumstances of inequality are present, and the bargain is not fair, just and reasonable, and the weaker party has not had independent competent advice, the transaction will be set aside for fraud. To uphold it on the ground that the other party had advice, the party benefiting must show that this advice was competent and independent in substance as well as in form. For example, in *Grealish* v. *Murphy*,[33] an improvident settlement by a mental defective was set aside, although he was separately advised by an independent solicitor, as his solicitor did not know all the material facts, did not give him a complete explanation of the nature and effect of the settlement, and was unaware of the full extent of his mental deficiency. The plaintiff in *Kevans* v. *Joyce*[34] had declined to have an independent solicitor, and had signed a statement to that effect, but the transaction was nevertheless set aside.

THE ABUSE OF A FIDUCIARY RELATIONSHIP

Such an abuse is not necessarily fraud, but the following breaches of fiduciary duty are generally so regarded:[35] purchase by a trustee of the trust property from himself (and certain similar dealings); purchase by an agent of property he is employed to sell or sale by an agent to his principal when the agent is employed to buy from a third party; making a secret profit out of a fiduciary position; negligence on the part of a fiduciary agent employed to exercise expert skill;[36] and undue influence.

30 See pp. 499-501, *post*.
31 [1960] N.I. 105.
32 See Sheridan, *Fraud in Equity*, ch. IV and VII.
33 [1946] I.R. 35.
34 [1896] 1 I.R. 442.
35 See Keeton, *The Law of Trusts*, 9th ed., pp. 206-11, 307-18, and Irish Supplement (Sheridan), pp. 29-30, 42-3; Sheridan, *Fraud in Equity*, pp. 107-16.
36 *Nocton* v. *Lord Ashburton*, [1914] A.C. 932.

Undue Influence

The doctrine of undue influence, closely associated as it is with the equitable conception of fiduciary relationship, has been of the very greatest importance in the development of equitable conceptions of fraud. Although the doctrine was recognised as a head of fraud in Lord Hardwicke's great judgment in *Earl of Chesterfield* v. *Janssen*,[37] recognition of its extent only came with Lord Eldon's judgment in *Huguenin* v. *Baseley*,[38] and full development of it only occurred in the nineteenth century. In formulating it, it would seem that the Court of Chancery was influenced by Pothier's great treatise, *Traité des donations entre vifs*, which discusses at length the invalidity of gifts on the ground of the relationship of the parties. Pothier argued that not only gifts to *administrateurs* of the property of another were forbidden, but also physicians, surgeons, confessors, and all who exerted influence, could not receive gifts from those subject to that influence, except under stringent conditions. At this period, the Court of Chancery was also struggling with the problem of the undue influence exercised by husbands upon wives to compel them to surrender their property. It therefore lent a ready ear to suggestions that a general principle should be formulated.

Undue influence, however, is not easy to define. It must be distinguished from duress, i.e. the exercise or threat of physical force. It is obviously something more than mere advice, although advice, strongly pressed and often repeated, may be construed as undue influence if the relationship of the parties warrants it. Much turns upon this last point, for every case of undue influence is founded upon the assumption that one party is in a stronger position, or has greater intellectual power or knowledge of affairs than the other and that that other, in consequence, places reliance upon the guidance of the stronger party. Kekewich, J., in his judgment in *Allcard* v. *Skinner*[39] went to the root of the matter. He said—

> The law allows absolute freedom of disposition, and only insists that when challenged, under such circumstances as exist here, the disposition shall be proved to have been absolutely free. What is required by law for the fulfilment of this condition? The law does not exclude influence. Nay, it recognises influence as natural and right. Few, if any, men are gifted with characters enabling them to act, or even think, with complete independence of others, which could not largely exist without destroying the foundations of society. But the law requires that influence, however natural and however

[37] (1750), 2 Ves. Sen. 125.
[38] (1807), 14 Ves. 273.
[39] (1887), 36 Ch. D. 145, 157-8 (affirmed by the Court of Appeal).

> right, shall not be unduly exercised—that is, shall be exercised only in due proportion to the surrounding circumstances and the strength of the person submitting to it. The more powerful influence or the weaker patient alike evokes a stronger application of the safeguard . . .

Undue influence, therefore, is the unconscientious use of power or authority, by one person over another, in such a way that the stronger party acquires a benefit, either for himself or for some person or object indicated by him. Where it exists, the transaction cannot stand. Equity will set it aside on the application of the weaker party.

There are some relationships which are presumed to be relationships of confidence, and these are termed fiduciary relationships, while in other relationships confidence may be proved to have been reposed. Whenever confidence is presumed or proved to exist, there is a presumption that a transaction between the parties, as to the subject-matter of the confidence, has been entered into as a result of the exercise of undue influence: it is up to the party claiming to uphold the deal to show its righteousness.

Fiduciary relationships.[40] These may arise out of a commercial or proprietary relation to another or out of personal or domestic considerations. A may rely on B because of B's expertness, or acumen, or power, or because of A's youth, or illness, or love for B, or for other reasons. But not every fiduciary relation gives rise to a presumption of undue influence.[41] It depends on whether there is dominance. A servant, though owing his employer fiduciary duties, is not presumed to exercise undue influence over him.[42] An agent is sometimes so presumed and sometimes not, according to the nature of the agency.

The fiduciary relationships commonly held to give rise to the presumption are: solicitor and client; trustee and beneficiary; doctor and patient; spiritual adviser and layman; and certain domestic relationships, such as parent and child.

Solicitor and client. Gifts by client to solicitor are viewed with suspicion by the court, but there is no absolute rule against them.[43]

[40] See, generally, Arenson, *Doctrine of Undue Influence in Anglo-American Law;* Vinter, *A Treatise on the History and Law of Fiduciary Relationship and Resulting Trusts;* Scott, " Constructive Trusts " (1955), 71 *Law Quarterly Review*, 39; Sealy, " Fiduciary Relationships " (1962), *Cambridge Law Journal*, 69; Winder, " Undue Influence and Coercion " (1939), 3 *Modern Law Review*, 97; " Undue Influence in English and Scots Law " (1940), 56 *L.Q.R.*, 97; " Undue Influence and Fiduciary Relationship " (1940), 4 *Conveyancer and Property Lawyer (N.S.)*, 274.

[41] See *Re Coomber*, [1911] 1 Ch. 723 (C.A.).

[42] See *Collins* v. *Hare* (1828), 2 Bligh N.S. 106 (H.L., I.).

[43] *Wright* v. *Carter*, [1903] 1 Ch. 27 (C.A.). Ireland: *Taafe* v. *Merrick* (1931), 65 I.L.T.R. 36.

So long as there is the relation of solicitor and client between the parties, however tenuous, and however sporadic its operation, there is a presumption against such a gift. The actual quality of the relation will affect the ease with which the presumption can be rebutted.

The presumption against dealings for value is more restricted. It does not apply where the solicitor buys property from, or makes some other bargain with his client, in respect of which no confidence is reposed and in respect of which the solicitor has no special knowledge. In *Cheslyn* v. *Dalby*[44] it was held that there was no objection to a solicitor taking from his client security for a debt actually due—in this case, professional fees.

A solicitor is not subject to the presumption of undue influence only in respect of dealings affecting matters he is specifically employed by his client to look after. Parker, J., summarised the position as follows, in *Allison* v. *Clayhills*[45]—

> It appears to me to be quite clear that a solicitor is not wholly incapacitated from purchasing or taking a lease from his client, but, where the relationship of solicitor and client exists, the onus of upholding the vitality of such a transaction will rest upon the solicitor. It is, I think, equally clear that, although the relationship of solicitor and client in its strict sense has been discontinued, the same principle applies as long as the confidence naturally arising from such a relationship is proved or may be presumed to continue.[46] There are cases in which it is laid down that this principle only applies when the solicitor is the solicitor of his client in the particular transaction the validity of which is in dispute; but, in my opinion, that only means that when the relationship is of such a nature that it does not impose on the solicitor any duty towards his client in the particular transaction, then the principle has no application. It does not mean, in my opinion, that the principle has no application in any case in which the solicitor is not in the particular transaction actually retained by or actually acting for his client under such circumstances that if he neglected his professional duty he would be liable to an action at law for negligence. Of course, if he be so retained and is so acting, there can be no question that the principle does apply, but, even if he be no longer so retained or acting, his duties in the contemplation of a court of equity may still be such as to throw

[44] (1836), 2 Y. & C. Ex. 170.

[45] (1907), 97 L.T. 709, 711-12.

[46] The same principle applies when any relationship giving rise to the presumption ceases: see *Rhodes* v. *Bate* (1866), L.R. 1 Ch. App. 252. Once the influence can be shown to have ended, a solicitor may deal with impunity with his ex-client; see *Oldham* v. *Hand* (1751), 2 Ves. Sen. 259. (This footnote is not a quotation from the judgment.)

upon him the onus of upholding the validity of a purchase or a lease from his client. In considering whether this onus lies upon him, the test appears to me to be the proper answer to the question whether in the particular transaction, he owes his client any duty in the contemplation of a court of equity. If he owes his client any duty in the particular transaction, the equal footing on which the parties to any bargain should stand is impaired or destroyed, and the solicitor is, I think, solicitor *in hac re* within the meaning of the decisions although not retained to act as solicitor in the transaction or, indeed, in any pending transaction at all. Thus, if a solicitor is actually engaged to conduct or is conducting for his client an action, say, for slander, and, while that action is pending, meets his client in the hunting field and bargains and buys from him a horse, each party relying upon his own knowledge of horseflesh, that transaction will stand on the same footing as a transaction between strangers, because the matter is entirely outside any confidential relationship between the parties, and the solicitor owes his client no duty whatever in the particular matter. On the other hand, if a solicitor has once been employed, say, to manage his client's real estates, then, although the employment may have entirely ceased, yet there may still be a duty on the solicitor's part towards his client—for example, that of possibly advising or possibly communicating information which he has obtained while acting as solicitor—and the existence of such duty may bring the ordinary rule into operation and make the solicitor solicitor *in hac re* if he subsequently purchased the real estates from his client, although as a matter of fact the relationship of solicitor and client in the strict sense had ceased to exist altogether.

Lord Eldon laid down the general principle in *Gibson* v. *Jeyes*[47] that if the solicitor has obtained an advantage which, with due diligence he would have prevented, had he been acting for his client in relation to a third party, he may not retain it. In that case, the transaction under review was the sale of an annuity by the solicitor to the client, and Lord Eldon observed,[48] in respect of the solicitor's action—

Therefore I say, he might contract: but then he should have said, if he was to deal with her [the client] for this, she must get another attorney to advise her as to the value: or, if she would not, then out of that state of circumstances this clear duty results from the rule of this Court, and throws upon him the whole *onus* of the case; that, if he will mix with the character of attorney that of vendor, he shall, if the propriety of the contract comes in question, manifest,

[47] (1801), 6 Ves. 266.

[48] 6 Ves. 278.

that he has given her all that reasonable advice against himself, that he would have given her against a third person. It is asked, where is that rule to be found. I answer, in that great rule of the Court, that he, who bargains in matter of advantage with a person placing confidence in him is bound to shew, that a reasonable use has been made of that confidence; a rule applying to trustees, attornies, or any one else.

It appears from *Corley* v. *Lord Stafford*[49] that a presumption similar to that arising out of the relationship of solicitor and client emerges from the relationship of a barrister to a person for whom he prepares a settlement. In this case, however, the barrister was also the fiancé of the woman who consulted him. In *Broun* v. *Kennedy*[50] it was held that there was undue influence between barrister and litigant, but it is not made clear in the report whether the relation was presumed to be one of confidence: in that case there was overwhelming evidence of actual confidence.

Trustee and beneficiary. This relationship gives rise to the presumption of undue influence,[51] and the trustee's influence, like that of other people, is presumed to continue after he has vacated that office.[52] A similar burden is cast upon the agent of a trustee who deals with the beneficiary,[53] and on an executor dealing with a legatee.[54]

Doctor and patient. This is another such relationship.[55] In *Ahearne* v. *Hogan*[56] a humble, poor man assigned life assurance policies to his doctor at an undervalue. The assignments were set aside (1) because there was actual fraud; and (2) on account of the relationship between the parties, it being confidential. Sugden, L.C., said[57] that there was no general rule against physicians contracting with patients. An eminent physician with a large practice might properly buy a house from a patient. " In such a case the contract proceeds openly and fairly, and the relation of physician and patient has, in reality, no bearing upon it. But that is not the case here, for the relation was continued down to the time of the contract, and the contract, in point of fact, arose out of it." A similar dictum issued from Lord Cottenham, with regard to a surgeon, in *Dent* v. *Bennett*.[58]

49 (1857), 1 De G. & J. 238.
50 (1864), 4 De G.J. & S. 217.
51 *Ayliffe* v. *Murray* (1740), 2 Atk. 58; *Denton* v. *Donner* (1856), 23 Beav. 285; *Lloyd* v. *Attwood* (1859), 3 De G. & J. 614 (C.A. Ch.); *Plowright* v. *Lambert* (1885), 52 L.T. 646; *Willis* v. *Barron*, [1902] A.C. 271 (trustee-solicitor).
52 *Provincial Bank of Ireland* v. *McKeever*, [1941] I.R. 471.
53 *King* v. *Anderson* (1874), I.R. 8 Eq. 625 (C.A. Ch.).
54 *Re Biel's Estate* (1873), L.R. 16 Eq. 577.
55 *Gibson* v. *Russell* (1843), 2 Y. & C.C.C. 104; *Billage* v. *Southee* (1852), 9 Hare 534; *Radcliffe* v. *Price* (1902), 18 T.L.R. 466.
56 (1844), Dru. t. Sug. 310.
57 Dru. t. Sug. 322.
58 (1839), 4 My. & Cr. 269.

Spiritual adviser and layman. In *Allcard* v. *Skinner*[59] the relationship of the mother superior of a convent to an ordinary member of the sisterhood was held to give rise to the presumption. This case is also the classic illustration of laches as a defence to an action to set aside a gift for undue influence. In 1868 Miss Allcard, a lady of twenty-seven years of age, entered a sisterhood, and under the influence of Miss Skinner, the mother superior, she transferred all her property to the sisterhood. These transactions were completed in 1874. In 1879, Miss Allcard left the sisterhood, and in 1885, she sought to set aside the transfers of property. The Court of Appeal found undue influence to have existed, in virtue of the relationship between Miss Allcard and Miss Skinner, but they held that it was too late for Miss Allcard to set aside the transfers of property. For six years, she had delayed to seek the restoration of her property, and independently of any Statute of Limitations, this was a good defence in equity against the claim. It was not only that there was delay (laches). During that period of delay, the plaintiff had acquiesced in the situation created by her transfers of property. That acquiescence, naturally, was only of significance in equity after the undue influence had ceased, and when the plaintiff was, in the words of Bowen, L.J.,[60] "surrounded by persons perfectly competent to give her proper advice." During this time, it was sufficient to bar her rights if she was aware that she had rights, or might have them, to recall the property, but nevertheless decided not to enforce them. What constitutes acquiescence depends upon the facts of each case.[61]

Parent and child, and guardian and ward. In the relationship of parent and child, the undue influence arises out of the presumed inexperience of the child. The presumption will persist so long as the child is an infant, and for an indeterminate time thereafter, so long as the influence can be regarded as remaining. In the words of Farwell, J., in *Powell* v. *Powell*[62]—

> A man of mature age and experience can make a gift to his father or mother because he stands free of all overriding influence except as may spring from what I may call filial piety; but a young person (male or female) just of age requires the intervention of an independent mind and will, acting on his or her behalf and interest solely, in order to put him or her on an equality with the maturer donor who is capable of taking care of himself.

59 (1887), 36 Ch. D. 145.

60 36 Ch. D. 192.

61 *Bullock* v. *Lloyds Bank Ltd.*, [1955] Ch. 317.

62 [1900] 1 Ch. 243, 246. Ireland: *Croker* v. *Croker* (1870), 4 I.L.T. 181; *M'Mackin* v. *Hibernian Bank*, [1905] 1 I.R. 296.

How long the influence can be regarded as continuing depends upon the circumstances of each case. Where a son or a daughter of weak will continued to live at home, it might last for some considerable time after majority was reached. Even marriage might not necessarily end it, if the husband or wife of the child lived under the roof of the child's parents. In *Lancashire Loans Ltd.* v. *Black*[63] a daughter had inherited considerable property under her grandmother's will. She lived with her mother until she married, at the age of eighteen, when she went to live with her husband. Two years later she separated from her husband, and returned to her mother's house. At the mother's request, she then mortgaged her reversionary interests under her grandmother's will to a moneylender, by way of security for further loans by the moneylender to the mother. Later the daughter sought to set aside these transactions on the ground of the mother's undue influence. In considering whether undue influence on the part of the mother existed at this time, Lawrence, L.J., said[64]—

> The fact that a daughter has married and gone to live with her husband is no doubt a circumstance of great importance in determining whether or not the dominion of a mother over her daughter has completely terminated, but it is not conclusive. The relationship between a mother and her daughter is undoubtedly one of the greatest intimacy and confidence, and it is impossible to lay down any general rule for measuring the amount or duration of the dominion which a mother may have acquired over her daughter. I can readily imagine cases in which a husband might truthfully assert that the parental dominion of his mother-in-law over his wife had continued for a considerable time and to a considerable extent after the marriage, and, for aught I know to the contrary, it may be that in the present case the continuance and excercise of that parental dominion was a contributory force to the estrangement between the daughter and her husband. Be that as it may, however, I am of opinion that the true answer to the respondent's contention is that it is a question of fact depending on the particular circumstances of each case whether or not the parental dominion has completely ceased to exist, and that there is no hard and fast rule that in every case where a daughter has married and left the home of her parents the parental dominion must necessarily be taken to have completely ended.
>
> [Counsel for the respondents] stressed the fact that no case is to be found in the reports where in such circumstances a daughter has

[63] [1934] 1 K.B. 380 (C.A.).

[64] [1934] 1 K.B. 410-11.

> been held to be under the dominion of her mother. The absence of any such reported case, however, does not, in my opinion, prevent the Court, if the circumstances warrant it, from coming to the conclusion that a mother's dominion had not completely ceased although the daughter had married and left her home.

The guarantee was held voidable on the ground that, either marriage was not sufficient to " emancipate " the daughter and so put an end to the presumption arising out of the parent-child relationship, or undue influence was proved to have been re-established on her return from the frying-pan to the fire.

The presumption of undue influence which arises between parent and child is not confined to cases in which the influence is exerted to secure a benefit to the parent. Thus, in *Bullock* v. *Lloyds Bank Ltd.*[65] a settlement was set aside which had been made by a young woman, who had then only recently attained her majority, acting on the advice of her father, even though the father was not a beneficiary under the settlement.

The one transaction involving parent and child which is not presumed to be the result of the undue influence of the parent is a family arrangement,[66] i.e. an agreement entered into for the purpose of securing the peace or honour of a family, or for preventing litigation, or for preserving property in the family.[67] Examples are a compromise of claims in connection with a disputed succession, and a resettlement of land. There is also no presumption of undue influence when a father advises his daughter as to the terms of her marriage settlement.[68] But special duties of disclosure exist in making a family arrangement. Besides, undue influence may be proved as a fact.

The rules governing undue influence as between parent and child apply in similar fashion as between guardian and ward[69] and stepfather and stepchild.[70]

Other family relationships. Where there is no special likelihood of dominance or reliance in it, a relationship does not give rise to a

65 [1955] Ch. 317.

66 See, e.g., *Hoghton* v. *Hoghton* (1852), 15 Beav. 278; *Hartopp* v. *Hartopp* (1856), 21 Beav. 259; *Turner* v. *Collins* (1871), L.R. 7 Ch. App. 329; Benas, " Family Arrangements " (1943), 8 *Conveyancer and Property Lawyer* (*N.S.*), 68.

67 *Dimsdale* v. *Dimsdale* (1856), 3 Drew, 556, 569, *per* Kindersley, V.-C.

68 *Tucker* v. *Bennett* (1887), 38 Ch. D. 1 (C.A.).

69 *Hylton* v. *Hylton* (1754), 2 Ves. Sen. 547; *Hatch* v. *Hatch* (1804), 9 Ves. 292. Ireland: *O'Connor* v. *Foley*, [1905] 1 I.R. 1.

70 *Kempson* v. *Ashbee* (1874), L.R. 10 Ch. App. 15.

presumption of undue influence. There has been held to be no presumption between brother and brother,[71] brother-in-law and sister-in-law,[72] grandson and grandfather,[73] or son-in-law and father-in-law.[73] In *Inche Noriah* v. *Shaik Allie bin Omar*,[74] her nephew by marriage lived next to the appellant, who was an aged widow of failing mental powers, and he acquired control of all her affairs. She relied on his judgment, and on his looking after her. When she purported to give him all her property, the disposition was set aside, the Judicial Committee stating that the relationship between the parties gave rise to a presumption of undue influence. Presumably what was meant was not that the presumption arose out of the parties' connection by marriage, but that, a relation of confidence having been proved to exist, a presumption arose that such an improvident gift was made as a result of the exercise of undue influence. In order to raise a presumption of undue influence against anyone, it is irrelevant to show relationship by blood or marriage, and what must be proved is parenthood or guardianship, or that the person impeached is in loco parentis. A person is not a guardian merely because an infant resides with him.[75]

Besides guardians of infants, there may be persons similarly placed in relation to adults. It was held in *Wright* v. *Proud*[76] that there was a presumption of undue influence between the keeper of a lunatic asylum and an inmate.

It has been decided many times that a man is not presumed to have exercised undue influence over his wife.[77] No doubt such influence in individual cases is easy enough to prove, but few would contend that inequality between spouses is so common as to justify a presumption. Probably the same is true as between a man and a woman with whom he is cohabiting without being married to her.[78] With regard to engaged couples, a line of cases beginning with *Page* v. *Horne*[79] in 1848 seemed to have established that the man was presumed to exercise undue influence over the woman. However, in *Zamet* v. *Hyman*[80] the Court of Appeal took a different view. In that case, where a widow aged 71, about to marry a widower of 79, agreed to give up for £600

[71] *Armstrong* v. *Armstrong* (1873), I.R. 8 Eq. 1 (C.A. Ch.).
[72] *Evans* v. *Cook* (1874), 8 I.L.T.R. 118.
[73] *Beanland* v. *Bradley* (1854), 2 Sm. & G. 339.
[74] [1929] A.C. 127 (P.C., Straits Settlements).
[75] *Taylor* v. *Johnston* (1882), 19 Ch. D. 603.
[76] (1806), 13 Ves. 136.
[77] *Grigby* v. *Cox* (1750), 1 Ves. Sen. 517; *Field* v. *Sowle* (1827), 4 Russ. 112; *Nedby* v. *Nedby* (1852), 5 De G. & Sm. 377; *Howes* v. *Bishop*, [1909] 2 K.B. 390; *Bank of Montreal* v. *Stuart*, [1911] A.C. 120 (P.C., Canada); *Re Lloyds Bank Ltd.*, [1931] 1 Ch. 289; *Gillman* v. *Gillman* (1946), 174 L.T. 272.
[78] Compare the Irish case of *Hargreave* v. *Everard* (1856), 6 Ir. Ch. Rep. 278, with the English case of *Coulson* v. *Allison* (1860), 2 De G. F. & J. 521.
[79] 11 Beav. 227.
[80] [1961] 1 W.L.R. 1442.

all her rights in her future husband's estate (which turned out to be worth about £10,000), undue influence was held to exist and the contract was set aside. Donovan, L.J., thought there was never a presumption of undue influence between fiancé and fiancée. Lord Evershed, M.R., with whom Danckwerts, L.J., agreed, said[81] of the older cases—

> . . . taking, I hope, a sensible view of the position of women in modern society, I cannot be persuaded that this court ought now to say that these principles, illustrated in the cases I have mentioned, have ceased altogether to be part of our law. I say only that in modern conditions, at any rate, one should not necessarily assume the existence of such influence in every case. I would put it somewhat thus: that in any transaction of the kind of a deed or arrangement or settlement (and I make that qualification bearing in mind what [counsel for the appellants] put to us of the case of a young man who may be persuaded to give an extravagant engagement ring to his fiancée) made between an engaged couple which upon its face appears much more favourable to one party than the other, then in the circumstances of the case the court may find a fiduciary relationship of the nature I have mentioned so as to cast an onus on the party benefited of proving that the transaction was completed by the other party only after full, free and informed thought about it.

Confidence proved as a fact. Where a disposition of property is made by A to B, and the relation between the parties is not such as to give rise to a presumption that A has reposed confidence in B, who has abused it, A may still prove that a relationship of confidence existed, which can be proved to have been abused, or which it seems from *Inche Noriah* v. *Shaik bin Omar*,[82] will be presumed to have been abused if the disposition is of property which is the subject-matter of the confidence. If the relationship of donor and donee is not one giving rise to a presumption of undue influence, the burden of upsetting the transaction rests upon the party complaining of it. No rules can be laid down as to how undue influence may be proved to have resulted from a relationship.

In some of the cases, there has been an advantage taken by an expert of his special knowledge. In *Hobday* v. *Peters* (*No.* 1),[83] the defendant was the plaintiff's solicitor's clerk, who was asked by his employer to do the plaintiff's legal work gratuitously. The defendant became intimate with the plaintiff, doing a lot of work for her, and acquired a great knowledge of her rights and property. It was held that his was a position of confidence, and that benefits which he had derived from

81 [1961] 1 W.L.R. 1446.
82 [1929] A.C. 127.
83 (1860), 28 Beav. 349.

the position must be held on trust for the plaintiff. In *Taylor* v. *Obee*,[84] a sale of land at an undervalue was set aside, having been made by a widow to a builder who had been on terms of intimacy with her late husband, and who was an expert and knew the value of the property, and whom she trusted,

Similar are cases where one person, for example as friend or as business associate, comes to be relied on by another as the manager of his affairs. In *Moxon* v. *Payne*,[85] a clerk in a business deliberately set out to bring himself into the favour of the owner. He succeeded in getting appointed manager, and later partner. Eventually, the original owner came to place entire confidence in the quondam clerk, especially as this man contrived to show a greater profit than was in fact made. A transaction between these partners was set aside for undue influence. In *Huguenin* v. *Baseley*,[86] the defendant ingratiated himself with a newly bereaved widow. She came, to his knowledge, to repose confidence in him, and she delegated to him the management of her affairs. It was held that he would not be allowed to keep a benefit derived from subordinating her interests to his own. Reliance of this kind comes to be placed, as well as on the manager of a person's affairs, upon those with whom a person resides. In *Custance* v. *Cunningham*,[87] an old woman was induced to make a gift to the man in whose house she lived. It was a gift of stock, said by the recipient to have been made subject to his paying the dividends to the donor for life, but there was no evidence, written or oral, apart from his, as to the terms of the gift. The court set it aside. In *Griffiths* v. *Robins*,[88] a woman aged 84, and nearly blind, was entirely dependent on the kindness and assistance of her niece and the niece's husband. A gift by her to this couple was set aside for undue influence. In *Gregg* v. *Kidd*[89] a settlement by deed in favour of the settlor's nephew was set aside. The settlor was ill and old and helpless, and was living with the nephew and the nephew's mother, who looked after him. It was held that this was a relationship in which influence had been acquired and that the donee had not discharged the burden on him of proving that it had not been abused.

Sometimes one person comes, by one means or another, to acquire complete dominance over a weaker human being. In *Harvey* v. *Mount*[90] two sisters, both owning property, lived together. The elder

[84] (1816), 3 Pri. 83.
[85] (1873), L.R. 8 Ch. App. 881.
[86] (1807), 14 Ves. 273.
[87] (1851), 13 Beav. 363.
[88] (1818), 3 Madd. 191.
[89] [1956] I.R. 183.
[90] (1845), 8 Beav. 439.

was more intelligent, managed the property for both, and generally attained mastery of the household, being described by witnesses as like a mother to the younger. The younger sister made a settlement for the benefit of her elder sister on the occasion of the elder's marriage; this was set aside for undue influence. In *Morley* v. *Loughnan*[91] a man who was weak in body and mind, depressed, and apprehensive of lunacy, paralysis, and various other ailments, went to live with the defendant, who arranged all his affairs—business, domestic, and religious—and kept him in a state of seclusion. This man gave a vast fortune to the defendant, who kept no record of their financial transactions, and indeed made great efforts to hush them up. It was held that undue influence was proved as a fact (there was also a dictum that the relationship gave rise to a presumption of undue influence). In *Lyon* v. *Home*[92] the plaintiff, a widow, consulted the defendant spiritualist medium, who purported to tell her late husband's wishes. These included the adoption of the defendant by the plaintiff, and the settlement on him of a large fortune. All this was done by the plaintiff in the belief that her husband so desired. It was held that the settlement must be set aside.

Again, the control which one obtains over another may be lawfully and expressly granted. In *Osmond* v. *Fitzroy*[93] an infant, who was entrusted to the care of a servant, to guard him from being imposed upon, was induced by the servant to execute a bond: this was set aside. In *Nicholls* v. *Nicholls*[94] a conveyance was set aside, having been made under some pressure by a person properly arrested for debt, the conveyance not having been projected before the arrest.

There are some cases where undue influence has been proved as a fact to have been exercised by husband over wife. In *Chaplin & Co. Ltd.* v. *Brammall*,[95] a wife was pressed by her husband to sign a guarantee which he made no effort to explain to her, and which she did not understand. In *Bank of Montreal* v. *Stuart*[96] a wife, who was a confirmed invalid, divested herself of all her property over a period of several years when she was living with her husband. She did this in order to relieve her husband's financial distress, and acted, as it was found, in passive obedience to his instructions.

Where there is a relationship between parties which gives rise to a presumption of undue influence, but that presumption has ceased, it

91 [1893] 1 Ch. 736. See also *Bennett* v. *Vade* (1742), 9 Mod. 312; *Cavendish* v. *Strutt* (1903), 19 T.L.R. 483.
92 (1868), L.R. 6 Eq. 655. See also *Nottidge* v. *Prince* (1860), 2 Giff. 246.
93 (1731), 3 P. Wms. 129.
94 (1737), West t. Hard. 192.
95 [1908] 1 K.B. 233 (C.A.).
96 [1911] A.C. 120.

may be shown as a fact that the undue influence has revived or continued. This was one of the alternative bases of the decision in *Lancashire Loans Ltd.* v. *Black*.[97]

Third parties. Whether undue influence is presumed or proved, the transaction will be set aside, not only as against a donee who exercised the undue influence, but also as against third parties.[98] Wilmot, L.C.J., said in *Bridgeman* v. *Green*[99]—

> There is no pretence that Green's brother, or his wife, was party to any imposition, or had any due or undue influence over the plaintiff; but does it follow from thence, that they must keep the money ? No: whoever receives it, must take it tainted and infected with the undue influence and imposition of the person procuring the gift; his partitioning and cantoning it out amongst his relations and friends, will not purify the gift, and protect it against the equity of the person imposed upon. Let the hand receiving it be ever so chaste, yet if it comes through a corrupt polluted channel, the obligation of restitution will follow it . . .

Wills. Undue influence is also a doctrine applied, under the probate jurisdiction, to the execution of wills. Here, however, undue influence is not presumed in a fiduciary relation. It must always be established as a fact.

Upholding the transaction. Apart from loss of the equity to rescind, by laches or acquiescence, or by the property coming into the hands of a bona fide purchaser for value without notice of it, the person seeking to uphold a transaction impugned for undue influence may do so by showing: (1) that the person alleged to have been influenced had independent competent advice; or (2) that, in the case of a voluntary disposition, the person alleged to have been influenced had a freely formed intention of making a gift; or (3) that, in the case of a transaction for consideration, the bargain was fair.

There are cases in which it has been held or said that proof of independent competent advice was the only way to rebut a presumption or inference of undue influence. This is a question which was extensively discussed in the nineteenth century, and as Scrutton, L.J., pointed out in *Lancashire Loans Ltd.* v. *Black*,[1] the equity judges tended to

97 [1934] 1 K.B. 380. See pp. 343-4, *ante*.
98 *Goddard* v. *Carlisle* (1821), 9 Pri. 169; *Maitland* v. *Irving* (1846), 15 Sim. 437; *Kempson* v. *Ashbee* (1874), L.R. 10 Ch. App. 15; *Chaplin & Co. Ltd.* v. *Brammall*, [1908] 1 K.B. 233 (C.A.); *Lancashire Loans Ltd.* v. *Black* [1934] 1 K.B. 380 (C.A.); *Bullock* v. *Lloyds Bank Ltd.*, [1955] Ch. 317. Ireland: *Molony* v. *Kernan* (1842), 2 Dr. & War. 31; *M'Mackin* v. *Hibernian Bank*, [1905] 1 I.R. 296.
99 (1757), Wilm 58, 64-5.
1 [1934] 1 K.B. 380, 404.

take the view that independent advice was essential, and the common law judges (when they came to deal with these cases) thought that independent advice was important, but not essential. The equity view was well expressed by Farwell, J., in *Powell* v. *Powell*,[2] whilst the common law view was equally clearly reflected in the observations of the Privy Council in *Inche Noriah* v. *Shaik Allie bin Omar*.[3] Even to-day, therefore, this question cannot be said to be finally settled. The better opinion seems to be that the person supporting the transaction must show that it did not result from undue influence, and that he may do this by any evidence available to him.[4]

Independent competent advice. If the person complaining of a transaction on the score of undue influence can be shown to have had independent competent advice on the transaction, it will stand.[5] The purpose of the advice is to ensure that that person knows and understands what he is doing, and so long as this is seen to, there is no need for advice to be given to him as to whether or not to enter into the transaction at all.[6] Moreover, it is the giving of the advice which rebuts the presumption of undue influence, and there is no need to show that that advice was acted on, provided it was " given with a knowledge of all relevant circumstances and [it] must be such as a competent and honest adviser would give if acting solely in the interests of the donor."[7] The one exception to this principle is the case of undue influence on young persons (e.g. exercised by a parent on his child when just of age), where the presumption cannot be rebutted by proving independent competent advice unless it was actually acted on.[8] In *Bullock* v. *Lloyds Bank Ltd.*,[9] where a person just of age, at the instance of her father executed a rather unusual settlement, Vaisey, J., said—

> Such a settlement as this is can, in my judgment, only be justified after prolonged consideration, being made, as it was, by a young girl only just of age, and can only stand if executed under the advice of a competent adviser capable of surveying the whole field with an absolutely independent outlook, and who explains to the intending settlor, first, that she could do exactly as she pleased, and, secondly, that the scheme put before her was not one to be accepted or rejected

[2] [1900] 1 Ch. 243, 245-6.
[3] [1929] A.C. 127, 133-6. Ireland: *Provincial Bank of Ireland* v. *McKeever*, [1941] I.R. 471, 485-6, *per* Black, J.
[4] See *Re Pauling's Settlement Trusts*, [1964] Ch. 303, 336, *per* Willmer, L.J., giving the judgment of the Court of Appeal.
[5] *Demerara Bauxite Co. Ltd.* v. *Hubbard*, [1923] A.C. 673 (P.C., British Guiana).
[6] *Re Coomber*, [1911] 1 Ch. 723 (C.A.).
[7] *Per* Lord Hailsham, *Inche Noriah* v. *Shaik Allie bin Omar*, [1929] A.C. 127, 135-6. Ireland: *Gregg* v. *Kidd*, [1956] I.R. 183.
[8] *Powell* v. *Powell*, [1900] 1 Ch. 243.
[9] [1955] Ch. 317, 326.

out of hand but to be discussed, point by point, with a full understanding of the various alternative possibilities.

It is uncertain whether what is required is advice or an adviser. It was left open in Ireland in *Armstrong* v. *Armstrong*[10] whether, where there was an apparently independent competent adviser, the court could scrutinise the actual advice given.

The competence required of the adviser has two aspects. First, he must be a qualified person in respect of the subject-matter of the advice: generally, that means a solicitor. In *Demerara Bauxite Co. Ltd.* v. *Hubbard*[11] it was held that advice given by an executor, not having special knowledge, to his co-executor, would not do. Secondly, the qualified person must have before him the material relating to the subject-matter in hand upon which to found an adequate opinion.[12] Therefore the person seeking to uphold the transaction must show not only independent qualified advice, but also either that he (the upholder) disclosed all material facts known to him or that these facts were known to all parties anyway.[13]

Independence is required of the adviser—independence of the person alleged to have exercised undue influence. Advice from a solicitor acting for both parties will not get rid of undue influence,[14] nor will advice from a solicitor acting only for the party complaining, if he has been in some respects the confidential adviser of the alleged influencer,[15] or if he was himself under that influence, or took his instructions from the influencer.[16]

Freely formed intention of giving. Lord Hailsham, in *Inche Noriah* v. *Shaik Allie bin Omar*,[17] said that all that was necessary was for the donee, by some means, " to prove that the gift was the result of the free exercise of independent will." Probably Lord Eldon put the duty too high in *Huguenin* v. *Baseley*,[18] where he held that it was not enough for the grantee to show that the grantor made the disposition voluntarily: he must show that the grantor had such knowledge of its effect, nature, and consequences, as a solicitor would be bound to supply in advising his client. Two years later, in *Bellew* v. *Russel*,[19] it was held in Ireland that all the circumstances might show that, although the donee-donor relation was one giving rise to a presumption

10 (1873), I.R. 8 Eq. 1 (C.A. Ch.).
11 [1923] A.C. 673.
12 *Wright* v. *Carter*, [1903] 1 Ch. 27. Ireland: *Gregg* v. *Kidd*, [1956] I.R. 183.
13 *Tate* v. *Williamson* (1866), L.R. 2 Ch. App. 55.
14 *Powell* v. *Powell*, [1900] 1 Ch. 243.
15 *Lloyd* v. *Attwood* (1859), 3 De G. & J. 614 (C.A. Ch.).
16 *Cavendish* v. *Strutt* (1903), 19 T.L.R. 483.
17 [1929] A.C. 127, 135.
18 (1807), 14 Ves. 273.
19 (1809), 1 Ba. & B. 96.

of undue influence (solicitor and client in this case), there was an uninfluenced intention to make a gift. In this case, the solicitor, a relative, had treated his client very kindly; the client was at loggerheads with his other relatives; and had, by his post-gift conduct, indicated approval of his gift. It was held that, in these circumstances, the solicitor could keep what he had been given. The position was well summed up by Stuart, V.-C., in *Davies* v. *Davies*[20]—

> Freedom from the pressure of influence may be shewn in many ways: it may be shewn that, from a laudable motive, there has been a long-continued intention often expressed to make a gift; or that the donor, perfectly understanding the nature of the transaction, had resolved, perhaps by the advice of unbiassed friends, to make the gift. In all cases where gifts have been supported it has been shewn that nothing equivocal remained in reference to the existence of the influence.

Fair bargain. Where a transaction for consideration is impeached on the ground of undue influence, it may be upheld as a fair bargain: it cannot be supported as partly a bargain and partly a gift. Lord Brougham, in *Hunter* v. *Atkins*,[21] said a bargain could be supported by showing it to be voluntary and fair, and with full warning and perfect knowledge. Transactions have been upheld as being for " full value,"[22] where, on a sale of land, the purchase-money was " nearly equal " to the value of the land;[23] and where it was shown that a greater price could not have been obtained elsewhere.[24] In this last case, which was of a purchase by a solicitor from his client, it was suggested that a solicitor, in such circumstances, should insist, as a matter of prudence, on independent competent advice for his client.

FRAUDS UPON THE PUBLIC OR UPON THIRD PARTIES

In *Earl of Chesterfield* v. *Janssen*[25] illustrations were given of fraudulent conduct affecting persons other than those who were parties to it. Of these, the principal are marriage brokage contracts, a secret agreement to return to a parent or guardian part of a portion agreed to be paid to the trustees of a marriage settlement, private agreements between a debtor who compounds with his creditors and one creditor who is to obtain a special benefit, and finally, premiums given for

[20] (1863), 4 Giff. 417, 420. See also *Re Pauling's Settlement Trusts*, [1964] Ch. 303. Ireland: *Kirwan* v. *Cullen* (1854), 4 Ir. Ch. Rep. 322; *Long* v. *Donegan* (1873), 21 W.R. 830 (C.A. Ch.).

[21] (1834), 3 My. & K. 113, 136.

[22] *Edwards* v. *Meyrick* (1842), 2 Hare 60.

[23] *Viscount Kingsland* v. *Barnewall* (1706), 4 Bro. P.C. 154 (H.L., I.).

[24] *Pisani* v. *A.-G. for Gibraltar* (1874), L.R. 5 P.C. 516.

[25] (1750), 2 Ves. Sen. 125.

preferring a person to a public office. For the most part, this class of cases reflects abuses of eighteenth century society, now of little importance, and when these abuses do occur nowadays the contracts, settlements or other arrangements concerned are held void at common law as being contrary to public policy. Even when the question is not one of validity but of accounting for ill-gotten gains, the tendency of the courts is to ignore the possibility of appeal to Lord Hardwicke's fourth head of fraud, but to achieve, by different processes of reasoning, the same result as would be brought about by such an appeal.[26]

Catching Bargains with Heirs, Reversioners and Expectants

Earl of Chesterfield v. *Janssen*[27] itself was a case of a post obit bond given by an expectant heir. The terms were, in the opinion of the majority of the judges, unconscionable, but the bond was unanimously upheld on account of the subsequent affirmation by the obligor. Equity has always scrutinised bargains with poor and ignorant persons with particular care. Bargains with heirs, reversioners, and expectants are really a particular class of such bargains, although they have been treated separately. Lord Hardwicke himself, in his great judgment, agreed that it is often difficult to separate these bargains from ordinary cases of bargains with poor or ignorant persons. However, in the eighteenth and early nineteenth centuries, such bargains had an especial importance, though relief from them goes back much further, having originated in the Court of Star Chamber. Moreover, although a tenant in tail or reversioner had a definite marketable interest in respect of which he might hope to raise a loan on reasonable terms, the interest of an expectant was much more fragile. He merely hoped to succeed or to receive a legacy, if he survived his kinsman, and was therefore usually able to secure a loan on his expectancy only on exorbitant terms. Accordingly, equity intervened repeatedly in such transactions, whether the subject-matter was a future interest of the ordinary kind, or whether it was merely an expectancy, presuming fraud where the terms were harsh. As *Earl of Chesterfield* v. *Janssen* shows, the relief was not confined to dealings with the reversion or expectancy, but extended to all catching bargains with a reversioner or expectant.[28]

Dealings with Reversions and Expectancies

In the Court of Chancery there were three fairly well defined periods during which different attitudes were taken.[29] First, prior to the mid-nineteenth century, such dealings were set aside if advantage had

[26] See, e.g., *Reading* v. *A.-G.*, [1951] A.C. 507.
[27] (1750), 2 Ves. Sen. 125.
[28] See Sheridan, *Fraud in Equity*, pp. 141-4.
[29] See Sheridan, *Fraud in Equity*, pp. 132-8.

been taken of weakness or distress to drive an unconscionable bargain, or where the purchase price was so grossly inadequate as to " shock the conscience " or as to show that there must have been financial distress to accept such terms. Secondly, there is the short period, of which the 1860's are the main decade, when sales of reversions and expectancies were set aside for any under-value, however slight. Romilly, M.R., was largely responsible for this development. Thirdly, there is the period from the passing of the Sales of Reversions Act, 1867, to the present day.

The 1867 Act is still in force in Ireland, but in England it has been replaced by the Law of Property Act, 1925, Section 174—

(1) No acquisition made in good faith, without fraud or unfair dealing, of any reversionary interest in real or personal property, for money or money's worth, shall be liable to be opened or set aside merely on the ground of under value.

In this subsection " reversionary interest " includes an expectancy or possibility.

(2) This section does not affect the jurisdiction of the court to set aside or modify unconscionable bargains.

This legislation has been construed restrictively. In *Miller* v. *Cook*[30] the plaintiff, a young man in financial difficulties, borrowed money at exorbitant interest and charged his reversionary interest with repayment. He was advised by a solicitor, who, however, was not accurately informed as to the transaction. Stuart, V.-C., held that the circumstances of the case were unaffected by the Act of 1867, and that the security must be set aside except as to what was actually advanced with interest at 5 per cent.

The first case in which the Act was thoroughly considered was *Earl of Aylesford* v. *Morris*,[31] where a young man who had just attained his majority, and who was entitled to estates worth £20,000 a year in tail on the death of his father, borrowed money on bills at over 60 per cent interest. He had no advice, except from those with whom he was dealing. The bills were set aside as being fraudulent, notwithstanding (1) that the offer came from the plaintiff borrower; (2) that several other moneylenders had turned the offer down before the defendant took it up; (3) that the plaintiff's remainder was vested; and (4) that the dealing was not with the expectancy. This last circumstance,

30 (1870), L.R. 10 Eq. 641. See also *Wyatt* v. *Cook* (1868), 16 W.R. 502; *Re Slater's Trusts* (1879), 11 Ch. D. 227.

31 (1873), L.R. 8 Ch. App. 484. See also *Tyler* v. *Yates* (1871), L.R. 6 Ch. App. 665.

however, would clearly take the case out of the Act, and make obiter what was said[32] on that subject: the usury laws—

> proved to be an inconvenient fetter upon the liberty of commercial transactions; and the arbitrary rule of equity as to sales of reversions was an impediment to fair and reasonable, as well as to unconscionable, bargains. Both have been abolished by the Legislature; but the abolition of the usury laws still leaves the nature of the bargain capable of being a note of fraud in the estimation of this Court; and the Act as to sales of reversions (31 Vict. c. 4) is carefully limited to purchases " made *bonâ fide* and without fraud or unfair dealing," and leaves under-value still a material element in cases in which it is not the sole equitable ground for relief. These changes of the law have in no degree whatever altered the *onus probandi* in those cases, which, according to the language of Lord *Hardwicke*, raise " from the circumstances or conditions of the parties contracting—weakness on one side, usury on the other, or extortion, or advantage taken of that weakness "—a presumption of fraud. Fraud does not here mean deceit or circumvention; it means an unconscientious use of the power arising out of these circumstances and conditions; and when the relative position of the parties is such as *primâ facie* to raise this presumption, the transaction cannot stand unless the person claiming the benefit of it is able to repel the presumption by contrary evidence, proving it to have been in point of fact fair, just, and reasonable.

Lord Selborne's explanation has been accepted in the later cases. *Beynon* v. *Cook*[33] concerned a man aged 26, entitled to have £600 paid to him on a bond when his father died, who mortgaged that expectancy at an undervalue and at exorbitant interest when in financial distress. The same view was taken as in *Wyatt* v. *Cook*[34] and *Miller* v. *Cook*[35]. Jessel, M.R., whose decision was summarily affirmed, said that the doctrine was that one dealing with a reversioner must not take advantage of his position with a view to repayment out of the estate. In *O'Rorke* v. *Bolingbroke*[36] the House of Lords approved *Earl of Aylesford* v. *Morris*[37] and suggested also (Lord Hatherley dissenting) that undervalue was not of great importance since the statute. This statement as to undervalue was obiter, and, in *Brenchley* v. *Higgins*,[38]

32 *Per* Lord Selborne, L.R. 8 Ch. App. 490-1.
33 (1875), L.R. 10 Ch. App. 389.
34 (1868), 16 W.R. 502. See p. 354, *ante*.
35 (1870), L.R. 10 Eq. 641. See p. 354, *ante*.
36 (1877), 2 App. Cas. 814, on appeal from Ireland. See also *Rae* v. *Joyce* (1892), 29 L.R.Ir. 500 (C.A.); *Kevans* v. *Joyce*, [1896] 1 I.R. 442 (C.A.).
37 (1873), L.R. 8 Ch. App. 484.
38 (1900), 83 L.T. 751, 752. See also *Judd* v. *Green* (1875), 33 L.T. 597. Cf. *Wedgerfield* v. *De Bernardy* (1908), 25 T.L.R. 21 (C.A.).

there was an obiter dictum by Rigby, L.J., to the effect that undervalue may be enough to show unfair dealing within the meaning of the Act. In this case, a reversion under a trust was sold by a man aged 30 who was not well versed in business. The purchaser dictated a letter for the vendor to send the trustees, asking for information about the property, but giving a false reason for wanting to know, i.e. not saying he was thinking of selling his interest. The sale was set aside by the Court of Appeal.

Under the Act, therefore, it seems that the position is as in the first period. The purchaser must show that he did not take advantage of the weakness of the position of the vendor of a reversion. If he cannot show that there is no substantial undervalue, he will probably fail to uphold the sale; but he need not explain every difference between the price and the market value. He may show that he took no advantage by the fact that he bought at an auction, or (probably) by the approval of a person in loco parentis to the vendor. Proof of other independent competent advice has not been held to have any value, but probably has the same standing as in connection with dealings of the kind discussed earlier in this chapter[39] under the description of " inequitable and unconscientious bargains."

In *James* v. *Kerr*[40] a young man was defendant in an action in which he claimed to be co-heir of a deceased person. He was in a position of poverty and necessity which put him at the mercy of persons from whom he borrowed money on the security of his interest in the deceased's estate, he covenanting to pay back much more than he borrowed. This security was modified, Kay J., expressing the relief to be by way of analogy to the principle relating to expectant heirs.

Bargains will not be set aside merely because they turn out badly. In *Beckley* v. *Newland*[41] specific performance was granted by Lord Macclesfield, where no advantage was taken by one party of the other, of an agreement by two people that they would divide equally whatever was left to them by a third, although, in the event, it was highly advantageous to one, highly detrimental to the other. In *Nichols* v. *Gould*[42] Lord Hardwicke held that a sale of an expectancy whose value depended on a contingency (such as the longevity or fertility of owners of prior estates) would not be set aside merely because, as it turned out, the expectancy vested in possession very speedily.

39 See pp. 333-6, *ante*.

40 (1889), 40 Ch. D. 449.

41 (1723), 2 P. Wms. 182. See also *Harwood* v. *Tooke* (1812), 2 Sim. 192.

42 (1752), 2 Ves. Sen. 422. See also *Perfect* v. *Lane* (1861), 3 De G.F. & J. 369 (C.A. Ch.).

CHAPTER X

POWERS OF APPOINTMENT

HISTORY AND NATURE

THE history of the law relating to powers, and more especially powers of appointment, is a tangled story, in which the common law, equity, and statute have at various times participated, and which, at various times, has been influenced by rules of law relating to the conceptions of property and trusts.[1] In the widest sense of the term, a power is an authority conferred upon a person to determine, by the exercise of his own will, the legal relations of himself or others. Powers may be either public, i.e. conferred by the state upon an agent acting on its behalf, or they may be private, in which case they are conferred by one person on another. Statutes expressly confer numerous powers on many public officials. As far as private persons are concerned, the general law (either statute or case law) confers many powers upon a person occupying a certain office. For example, in England a trustee has powers of maintenance and advancement in respect of beneficiaries conferred upon him by the Trustee Act, 1925.[2] An executor has a power of appropriation, and a mortgagee, if the mortgage is by deed, has a power of sale in respect of the mortgaged property. Under the Settled Land Act, 1925,[3] the tenant for life is invested with a number of powers which exceed in extent those which the common law conferred on limited owners of real property.

A power of appointment is a power given to a person to dispose of property in which he may have no interest.[4] Such a power is termed *general* when the donee of it may make any appointment, including one to himself;[5] and *special* when the donee may appoint the property

1 It is discussed in Holdsworth, *History of English Law*, vol. VII, pp. 149-53. See also Crane, " The Law and Literature of Powers of Appointment, 1916-1966 " (1967), *Law, Justice and Equity*, 76.

2 Sects. 31-32. Northern Ireland: Trustee Act (Northern Ireland), 1958, Sects. 32-33. Republic of Ireland: Conveyancing Act, 1881, Sects. 42-43 (maintenance only, not advancement).

3 Ireland: Settled Land Acts, 1882-90.

4 No formal words are necessary for the creation of a power of appointment. As to construction of documents where it is not clear whether a power of appointment is intended or not, see Keeton, *The Law of Trusts*, 9th ed., pp. 14-16.

5 See *Re Churston Settled Estates*, [1954] Ch. 334; Crane, " Consent Powers and Joint Powers " (1954), 18 *Conveyancer and Property Lawyer* (*N.S.*), 565; Campbell, " The Enigma of General Powers of Appointment " (1956), 7 *Res Judicatae*, 244. Ireland: *Re Dunbar-Buller*, [1923] 2 I.R. 143 (C.A., N.I.).

only to one person or to one or more persons on a list or belonging to a class designated by the donor of the power.[6] This distinction is important for a number of reasons: for example, the rule against perpetuities applies to general powers of appointment in a different way from its application to special powers, and the doctrine of fraud on a power applies only to special powers.

In addition to general and special powers of appointment there are also what have come to be known as *hybrid* powers. These are powers whose objects are stated very extensively but not so as to include the donee.[7] In *Re Park*[8] a woman was given power to appoint property to any person except herself. Holding this valid, Clauson, J., said[9]—

> . . . the division of valid legal powers into general and particular is not exhaustive . . . there is a third class of powers where the donee can appoint to any one with certain exceptions . . .

In *Re Jones*[10] Vaisey, J., upheld a power to appoint to any person or persons living at the death of the donee of the power, saying[11]—

> I construe the words as equivalent to a subtraction from the generality of objects (i.) of all corporate bodies, charities and the like, and (ii.) of all individuals not actually in existence at the moment of the death of the appointor. Accordingly, although it is neither a general power nor a special power, . . . I am bound to hold that it is, nevertheless, a power permissible to be created . . .

The donee being unable to appoint in any manner he chooses, the power is not general and is, presumably, governed by the rules relating to special powers. But in *Re Harvey*[12] Vaisey, J., held that if the exception, mentioned by the donor of the power, from the generality of objects did not and could not exist, or ceased to exist without possibility of replacement, the power became general. The power in that case was given to a woman to appoint to any person not being her husband. She made an appointment by will and died a spinster. The learned judge held that the exercise could be treated as having been of a general power.

[6] In *Re Gulbenkian's Settlement Trusts* (1969), *The Times* newspaper, 23rd May, Plowman, J., decided that an object of the power could, by agreement for valuable consideration, exclude himself from this list or class.

[7] See Fleming, " Hybrid Powers " (1948), 13 *Conveyancer and Property Lawyer* (*N.S.*), 20; Hughes, " The Classification of Powers of Appointment " (1962), 26 *Conv.* & *P.L.* (*N.S.*), 25.

[8] [1932] 1 Ch. 580.

[9] [1932] 1 Ch. 584.

[10] [1945] Ch. 105.

[11] [1945] Ch. 107.

[12] [1950] 1 All E.R. 491.

Powers of appointment, especially general powers, have something of the appearance of property. Nevertheless, the distinction between power and property is fundamental to the law. In the words of Fry, L.J., in *Ex parte Gilchrist*,[13] where the Court of Appeal held that a bankrupt could not be compelled to exercise a general power of appointment in favour of the trustee in bankruptcy—

> A " power " is an individual personal capacity of the donee of the power to do something. That it may result in property becoming vested in him is immaterial; the general nature of the power does not make it property. The power of a person to appoint an estate to himself is, in my judgment, no more his " property " than the power to write a book or to sing a song. The exercise of any one of these three powers may result in property, but in no sense which the law recognises are they " property." In one sense no doubt they may be called the " property " of the person in whom they are vested, because every special capacity of a person may be said to be his property; but they are not " property " within the meaning of that word as used in law. Not only in law but in equity the distinction between " power " and " property " is perfectly familiar . . .

Whilst the common law was familiar with the general conception of powers, and also of powers as incidents of property rights (e.g. powers of disposition), it knew nothing of powers of appointment. A feoffment once made transferred the interest of the grantor, and could not be recalled subsequently by any new disposition. It is true that a condition could be annexed to a feoffment, determining the estate on the happening of a future event, but if that occurred, only the grantor and his heirs could enter, and on re-entry, all estates passing under the feoffment were destroyed.

It was to surmount these limitations that equity intervened, taking advantage of the flexibility of the rules governing uses. Under these rules, a settlor could either reserve to himself or bestow upon others, power to revoke any of the uses which he declared, and to create new uses. When this occurred, the feoffees to uses were compelled to hold the legal estate for the beneficiaries under the newly-declared uses. Coke[14] declared that the insertion of such powers had become very common at the time of the passing of the Statute of Uses, 1535.[15] The effect of that statute was to convert interests, which had formerly been created in equity behind the use by the exercise of powers of appointment, into legal estates. Thus, the common law courts for the

13 (1886), 17 Q.B.D. 521, 531.
14 Co. Litt., 237a.
15 Ireland: Statute of Uses, 1634.

first time had cognisance of powers of appointment, which they classed differently from the limited range of powers, which were little more than mandates, known to the common law before the Statute of Uses; and from an early date after the statute the common law courts began to ascribe to powers of appointment some of the characteristics of proprietary interests.[16]

However, exactly as in equity after the lapse of a century, trusts were created again to replace the uses which had been executed by virtue of the Statute of Uses, so there arose again in equity a new class of equitable powers, operating behind a trust, and giving rise to equitable estates. Moreover, in addition to the common law rules governing powers of appointment operating to create legal estates by virtue of the Statute of Uses, equity gradually developed a number of supplementary rules, governing the exercise of legal powers also.

Further far-reaching changes were brought about in England by the Law of Property Act, 1925, which repealed the Statute of Uses.[17] Sect. 1(7) of that Act provides that every power of appointment in respect of land or any interest therein operates only in equity. Thus, the old dualism between legal and equitable powers of appointment is now at an end.

By long tradition, powers are divisible into those which are:

1. *Simply Collateral.* This is a power given to a person who has no interest in the property over which the power is given.

2. *In Gross.* This is a power given to a person who has an interest in the property over which the power exists, but such an interest as cannot be affected by the exercise of the power, e.g. a power of appointment given to a tenant for life, to take effect after his death.

3. *Appendant or Appurtenant.* This is a power exercisable by a person who has an interest in the property, which interest is capable of being affected (i.e. diminished or disposed of to some extent) by the exercise of the power.[18]

Both the first two classes of powers were sometimes described as powers collateral. The distinction between these powers and powers which were not collateral was important, because powers which were not collateral were regarded as having proprietary characteristics. Some of the differences between these three classes of powers emerge very clearly in *Re D'Angibau.*[19] A female infant had been given a

[16] Holdsworth, *History of English Law*, vol. VII, p. 159.

[17] The Statute of Uses (Ireland), 1634, is still in force.

[18] *Per* Jessel, M.R., in *Re D'Angibau* (1879), 15 Ch. D. 228, 232-3 (affirmed by the Court of Appeal (1880)).

[19] (1880), 15 Ch. D. 228 (C.A.).

power of appointment by deed or will over a fund of personalty. No dispute arose as to the type of power which she possessed, it being agreed that it was in gross. The question in issue was whether an infant could effectively exercise such a power by deed, at any rate in respect of personalty. Where the power was simply collateral, it was settled law that the infant could exercise it, and at first instance, Jessel, M.R., held that where a manifest intention that the infant should exercise it was shown in the settlement, the infant could also exercise a power in gross. This decision was upheld by the Court of Appeal (James and Brett, L.JJ., Cotton, L.J., dissenting), and Brett, L.J., in his judgment, stressed that such a power, equally with a power simply collateral, is to be regarded as " a pure mandate," and he continued[20]—

> Inasmuch as the power is given by a person who had full authority to give that power, who delegated that which he could have most effectively done himself if he had chosen, it seems to me that to say that that power is to be suspended till the infant comes to full age, is, to say the least of it, a most artificial doctrine.

He added that he would have taken the same view of such a power in respect of real property, had it not been for the decision in *Hearle* v. *Greenbank*[21]. As Holdsworth commented, " . . . in the case of powers given to infants over realty, the proprietary aspect of these powers has prevailed, and in the case of powers over personalty their mandatory aspect."[22]

Powers of appointment may also be classified as *bare* powers and *fiduciary* powers, i.e., powers in respect of whose exercise the donee has a complete discretion and powers in respect of whose exercise the donee owes a duty to consider the interests of all potential appointees. Fiduciary powers will often be found as part of a trust mechanism, but the mere fact that the donee is a trustee of the property is not conclusive that it is a fiduciary power. This distinction is not the same as that between *bare powers* and *powers in the nature of a trust*. This is a distinction between powers under which the objects take an interest only when an appointment is made to them and those over property which, in default of appointment, the objects are to share equally. Powers in the nature of a trust[23] may be, but are not necessarily, fiduciary.

In relation to the possibility of invalidity for uncertainty, the rules of equity make a distinction between powers in the nature of a trust on

[20] 15 Ch.D. 243-4.
[21] (1749), 3 Atk. 695.
[22] *History of English Law*, vol. VII, p. 182.
[23] See pp. 362-3, *post*.

the one hand and bare powers, whether fiduciary or not, on the other hand. The former class of power will fail for uncertainty unless all possible objects are ascertainable throughout the duration of the power,[24] while the latter class is valid, notwithstanding that the donee cannot be sure of knowing at any given time who all the objects are, on account of the size of the class, its fluctuating nature or the imprecision of the description;[25] though an appointment under such a power will be invalid if made to a person of whom it cannot be said with certainty that he is an object, and the power itself will be void for uncertainty if the description of the class is so vague that no workable criterion of membership has been provided.

Powers in the Nature of Trusts

The existence of this class of powers in the nature of trusts was first explicitly recognised in the leading case of *Harding* v. *Glyn*.[26] Where such a power existed, and the donee failed to execute it, the court would act on his behalf, and in so doing, would distribute the fund equally between the objects of the appointment. Lord Eldon stated the principle upon which this development is founded in *Brown* v. *Higgs*,[27] as follows—

> . . . there are not only a mere trust and a mere power, but there is also known to this Court a power, which the party, to whom it is given, is intrusted and required to execute; and with regard to that species of power the Court consider it as partaking so much of the nature and qualities of a trust, that if the person, who has that duty imposed upon him, does not discharge it, the Court will, to a certain extent, discharge the duty in his room and place . . . . if the power is a power which it is the duty of the party to execute, made his duty by the requisition of the Will, put upon him as such by the testator, who has given him an interest extensive enough to enable him to

[24] *Inland Revenue Commissioners* v. *Broadway Cottages Trust*, [1955] Ch. 20 (C.A.); *Re Sayer*, [1957] Ch. 423; *Re Hain's Settlement*, [1961] 1 W.L.R. 440 (C.A.); *Re Saxone Shoe Co. Ltd.'s Trust Deed*, [1962] 1 W.L.R. 943; *Re Leek*, [1968] 2 W.L.R. 1385 (C.A.).

[25] *Whishaw* v. *Stephens*, [1968] 3 W.L.R. 1127 (" any person or persons in whose house or apartments or in whose company or under whose care or control or by or with whom the said Nubar Sarkis Gulbenkian may from time to time be employed or residing ") (H.L., E.). See also *Re Gestetner Settlement*, [1953] Ch. 672 (large fluctuating class); *Re Coates*, [1955] Ch. 495 (" any friend "); *Re Sayer*, [1957] Ch. 423 (large fluctuating class, including imprecise expressions —" other infant dependents " and " other dependent relatives "); *Re Lysaght*, [1966] Ch. 191 (" not of the Jewish or Roman Catholic faith "); *Re Gibbard's Will Trusts*, [1967] 1 W.L.R. 42 (" any of my old friends "); *Re Wootton*, [1968] 1 W.L.R. 681 (". . . such other organisation or body not being registered as a charity but in the opinion of my trustees as having charitable objects . . ."). Ireland: *Re Parker's Will*, [1966] I.R. 309 (" my necessitous nieces and nephews . . . and . . . their children ").

[26] (1739), 1 Atk. 469. Ireland: *Re Hargrove's Trusts* (1873), I.R. 8 Eq. 256.

[27] (1803), 8 Ves. 561, 570-1, 574.

discharge it, he is a trustee for the exercise of the power, and not as having a discretion, whether he will exercise it, or not; and the Court adopts the principle as to trusts; and will not permit his negligence, accident, or other circumstances, to disappoint the interests of those, for whose benefit he is called upon to execute it.

A power can be in the nature of a trust only when it is a special power. It is so when the intention of the donor is to benefit the class in any event, appointment or no appointment. This cannot be the case if there is express alternative provision in default of appointment. On the other hand, the absence of such provision, though indicative, is not conclusive that there is a power in the nature of a trust. The contrary proposition was rejected in *Re Weekes' Settlement*,[28] *Re Combe*,[29] and *Re Perowne*.[30]

The Law of Property Act, 1925, Sections 155 and 156[31] allow the donee of a power of appointment to release or contract not to exercise or disclaim the power. This certainly does not apply to a power in the nature of a trust,[32] and probably does not apply to a fiduciary power.[33]

Some Equitable Doctrines Applicable to Powers of Appointment

The Rule Against Perpetuities

As evolved by the courts, this rule governed the vesting of future equitable interests and future legal interests under the Statute of Uses and, in England, but not in Ireland, future common law interests such as contingent remainders. It was concerned with possibilities, not actual events, and was to the effect that a future interest was void ab initio if there was some possibility that the interest in question might not vest within the perpetuity period counted from the date of coming into operation of the instrument creating the interest. This period was

28 [1897] 1 Ch. 289, 292, *per* Romer, J.

29 [1925] Ch. 210, 216, *per* Tomlin, J.

30 [1951] Ch. 785, 789–91, *per* Harman, J. See also *Re Baden's Deed Trusts*, [1969] 1 All E.R. 1016 (C.A.). Ireland: *Carberry* v. *M'Carthy* (1881), 7 L.R. Ir. 328; *Re Hall's Will Trusts*, [1899] 1 I.R. 308; *Clibborn* v. *Horan*, [1921] 1 I.R. 93. See also Gray, " Powers in Trust and Gifts Implied in Default of Appointment " (1911), 25 *Harvard Law Review*, 1; Rood, " The Disposition to be Made of Property the Subject of a Power if the Power is Not Exercised " (1917), 15 *Michigan Law Review*, 386; Marshall, " Trusts and Powers " (1957), 33 *Canadian Bar Review*, 1060; Unwin, " Power or Trust Power " (1962), 26 *Conveyancer and Property Lawyer* (*N.S.*), 92.

31 Replacing the Conveyancing Acts, 1881, Sect. 52(1), and 1882, Sect. 6(1), still in force in Ireland.

32 *Re Wills' Trust Deeds*, [1964] Ch. 219. See also Hawkins, " The Release of Powers " (1968), 84 *Law Quarterly Review*, 64.

33 *Re Gestetner Settlement*, [1953] Ch. 672, 687, *per* Harman, J.

a life or lives in being at that date plus twenty-one years from the dropping of that life or the last of them, counting persons en ventre leures mères as in being.

This is still the position in the Republic of Ireland. However, in England, by the Perpetuities and Accumulations Act 1964, Section 12, and in Northern Ireland, by the Perpetuities Act 1966, Sections 13-14, the rule against perpetuities applies to legal future interests. Considerable changes have been made in the application of the rule in these two jurisdictions. The chief are the introduction of what is known as the " wait-and-see " doctrine,[34] i.e. an interest is not void ab initio under the rule but fails for perpetuity if it does not in fact vest during the period; and secondly, allowing the grantor of the interest to specify a term of years not exceeding eighty instead of the life or lives in being and twenty-one years.[35] The statutory changes affect only instruments coming into operation after the Act.

It was not until the eighteenth century that it was recognised that the perpetuity rule applied to powers of appointment; and when this application was made, a distinction was drawn between general powers which, since they gave a general power of disposition, did not restrict alienability, and special powers, which impose a restriction upon alienability from the time when the power is conferred, since an appointment can only be made to a limited class. A general power fails for perpetuity only if it does not become exercisable within the perpetuity period,[36] while a special power, even if exercisable within the period, becomes void at the end of the period.[37]

When considering the validity, in relation to the rule against perpetuities, of appointments, in the case of the exercise of a general power the period runs from the date of the appointment, while in the case of a special power[38] it runs from the date of the creation of the power,[39] but, in jurisdictions without the wait-and-see doctrine, the facts as they exist at the date of the appointment are taken into consideration.[40]

34 England: Perpetuities and Accumulations Act 1964, Sect. 3; Northern Ireland: Perpetuities Act 1966, Sect. 3.

35 1964 Act, Sect. 1; 1966 Act, Sect. 1.

36 1964 Act, Sect. 3(2); 1966 Act, Sect. 3(2). Republic of Ireland: a general power is void ab initio if it might not become exercisable within the period.

37 1964 Act, Sect. 3(3); 1966 Act, Sect. 3(3). Republic of Ireland: a special power is void ab initio if it might remain exercisable after the end of the period. See *Re De Sommery*, [1912] 2 Ch. 622.

38 1964 Act, Sect. 7; 1966 Act, Sect. 7.

39 *Re Thompson*, [1906] 2 Ch. 199; *Re Paul*, [1921] 2 Ch. 1.

40 See, further, Morris and Leach, *The Rule Against Perpetuities*, 2nd ed., ch. 5, and Supplement (1964).

The rule against perpetuities applies to the statutory power of advancement in England and Northern Ireland as it applies to special powers of appointment.[41]

The Doctrine of Illusory Appointments

The doctrine of illusory appointments had its origin in the anxiety of the Court of Chancery to control donees of powers of appointment, to ensure that as far as possible they carried out the donor's intention. Once again, the anxiety of equity to import doctrines from the law of trusts into the law of powers of appointment is evident. This control was founded upon the distinction between exclusive and non-exclusive powers. An exclusive power was one by whose terms one or more of the objects might receive nothing at all. If a power was non-exclusive, then all the objects must receive something. In such a case, if the donee of the power gave merely a token sum to one or more objects, this was regarded by equity as an illusory appointment, which the Court of Chancery would set aside. In *Gibson* v. *Kinven*[42] Lord Nottingham, L.C., set aside an appointment by a wife, in which only five shillings had been given to one object of the appointment, and the court then divided the fund equally among the objects of the power. This was the starting-point of a good deal of litigation upon what was, and what was not, an illusory appointment. It was a question which was constantly before the courts in the time of Lords Thurlow and Loughborough, who inclined to the view that an apparently illusory share could be accounted for by the circumstances of the appointment.[43] In *Vanderzee* v. *Aclom*[44] Arden, M.R., set out the difficulties which attended the application of this doctrine.

Since the equitable doctrine was so difficult to apply, it was abolished in 1830.[45] However, the statute did not abolish the distinction between exclusive and non-exclusive powers. " The consequence of this remarkable alteration of the law has been this, that where the power is non-exclusive, if the appointor forgets to appoint a shilling, or even a farthing, to every object of the power, the appointment is bad, because some one is left out."[46] As Jessel, M.R., pointed out, " the reasonable mode of altering the law would have been to make every power of appointment exclusive, unless the author of the settlement had pointed

41 *Pilkington* v. *Inland Revenue Commissioners*, [1964] A.C. 612 (H.L., E.).

42 (1682), 1 Vern. 66.

43 *Boyle* v. *Bishop of Peterborough* (1791), 1 Ves. Jun. 299, 310; *Bristow* v. *Warde* (1794), 2 Ves. Jun. 336, 349.

44 (1799), 4 Ves. 771, 784-5. See also Howe, " Exclusive and Nonexclusive Powers and the Illusory Appointment " (1944), 42 *Michigan Law Review*, 649.

45 Illusory Appointments Act, 1830, still in force in Ireland but replaced in England by the Law of Property Act, 1925, Sect. 158.

46 *Per* Jessel, M.R., *Gainsford* v. *Dunn* (1874), L.R. 17 Eq. 405, 407.

out the minimum share which every object was to get." This step was taken in 1874, and full freedom of appointment (unless expressly excluded) was restored to donees of powers of appointment.[47]

Relief Against Defective Execution

The rule of law with regard to the formalities of execution was that whatever formalities were prescribed must be strictly observed. This rule applied to the exercise of many powers in addition to powers of appointment. This strict rule led to the failure of many exercises of powers. In certain cases, statutory relief is now given,[48] but in other cases, the legal rule is still applicable. However, equity has given a limited relief in certain cases. Apart from powers in the nature of trusts, a court of equity will not exercise a power which the donee has failed to exercise, but it will aid a defective execution, on the ground of want of form, provided that the defect is *formal* and not material. Even so, it will intervene only in favour of certain classes of persons—creditors of the donee, charities, purchasers for value from the donee (including mortgagees and lessees), and the donee's wife and legitimate children.[49] Equity will not intervene in favour of a husband, an illegitimate child, remoter relations, or a volunteer.[50] Nor can the court aid a defective execution of a power if the result would be to perpetrate a fraud on the power.[51]

The relief is available only where the defect is formal, and not substantial. For example, if the power requires certain consents as a condition of its exercise, then relief will not be given if the consents have not been obtained. In *Tollet* v. *Tollet*[52] the court relieved when a husband had exercised a power in favour of his wife by will, instead of exercising it by deed. On the other hand, if the power is to be exercised by will, and it is exercised by irrevocable deed, equity will not relieve, because the effect of such a deed is to remove from the donee a discretion as to its exercise which the settlor intended the donee to retain during his lifetime.[53]

47 Powers of Appointment Act, 1874, still in force in Ireland, but replaced in England by the Law of Property Act, 1925, Sect. 158.

48 E.g. Law of Property Act, 1925, Sects. 152, 159; Wills Act, 1837, Sects. 9-10. Ireland: the Leases Act, 1849, Sects. 2 and 4-7, and the Leases Act, 1850, Sects. 2 and 3, correspond to the 1925 Act, Sect. 152; the Law of Property Amendment Act, 1859, Sect. 12, corresponds to Sect. 159 of the 1925 Act. The 1837 Act is in force in Northern Ireland, but Sects. 9-10 of it are replaced in the Republic of Ireland by the Succession Act, 1965, Sects. 78-79.

49 *Tollet* v. *Tollet* (1728), 2 P. Wms. 489; *Re Dykes' Estate* (1869), L.R. 7 Eq. 337. Ireland: *Pennefather* v. *Pennefather* (1873), I.R. 7 Eq. 300 (C.A. Ch.).

50 See *Re Anstis* (1886), 31 Ch.D. 596 (C.A.).

51 *Brown* v. *Howden* (1900), 34 I.L.T.R. 159. As to fraud on a power, see pp. 368-74, *post*.

52 (1728), 2 P. Wms. 489.

53 *Adney* v. *Field* (1767), Amb. 654; *Re Parkin*, [1892] 3 Ch. 510.

In *Re Hambro's Marriage Settlements*,[54] funds were settled, by two marriage settlements, upon trust for the issue of the marriage as the husband and wife should by deed jointly appoint, with or without power of revocation and new appointment. In default of appointment, the fund was to be held on trust for the children of the marriage. There were two sons and two daughters, and by deed of appointment of 11th February 1936, the husband and wife exercised the joint power, appointing the fund to the four children of the marriage, and reserving power to revoke or vary the appointment, such a power to be exercised " by deed during the joint lives or by the survivor " during his or her life. The wife died in 1942 without having joined in exercising the power of revocation, and the husband, by his will dated 14th September 1943, purported to exercise the power of appointment conferred by the settlement, in favour of the two sons. The trustees of the settlement then raised the question whether the appointment in the husband's will operated as a revocation of the previous appointment by deed, and as a variation of the appointment made in the deed. The Court of Appeal held that the settlements and appointments must be read together. So considered, the limitation of the power of revocation in the appointment to a power to revoke by deed was of the essence of the power, and therefore the power of revocation could not be exercised by will. The question of the materiality of the forms to be observed must be decided in reference to the facts of each case.

Excessive Execution

If a donee of a power when making an appointment exceeds the limits of the power conferred upon him, the execution of the power is said to be excessive. An excessive execution may occur in several ways. For example, the donee may appoint to persons who are not within the class specified by the donor. Secondly, the donee may give to one or more persons larger interests than the power permits. Finally, he may appoint, and in doing so, he may impose conditions which are not within the terms of his power.

An appointment to a non-object may be express or by reference. In *Re Boulton's Settlement Trust*[55] an appointment to an object of the power on protective trusts was held void because non-objects might benefit by virtue of the Trustee Act, 1925, Section 33.[56]

In any case, an appointment to a non-object is void. If a severable appointment is made to objects and non-objects, the appointment is

[54] [1949] Ch. 484
[55] [1928] Ch. 703.
[56] Northern Ireland: Trustee Act, 1958, Sect. 34. There is no such provision in the Republic of Ireland.

valid as to the objects and void as to the rest. This is so whether the objects and others are mixed up together,[57] as where an appointor appoints half the fund to an object and half to a non-object, or whether the gifts are substitutionary,[58] as where an appointor appoints to an object until bankruptcy, with remainder to a non-object. If, on the other hand, it is impossible to separate the good from the bad, the whole appointment fails.[59]

In general, if an appointor appoints to an object of the power, but attempts to attach an unauthorised condition to the gift, the appointee will take free from the condition.[60] But such a condition may be valid if it operates in favour of another object of the power.[61]

Apart from the possibility of non-objects benefiting, another successful objection to the validity of the appointment in *Re Boulton's Settlement Trust*[62] was that an appointment on protective trusts would involve the trustees in exercising a discretion as to payments to the object of the power should his life interest determine. The donee of a power of appointment is invested with a personal discretion and may not, by his exercise of the power or otherwise, delegate that discretion,[63] unless the terms of the power expressly or impliedly authorise him to do so.[64]

Fraud on a Power

At the same period when the Court of Chancery was developing the doctrine of illusory appointments, it was also developing the doctrine of fraud upon a power. By this doctrine, equity invalidated appointments which were made with an intention not in accordance with the purpose of the donor. This is an attempt by the appointor to secure the effect of an excessive execution without actually making one.

Bargain. Whatever the nature of the power, except where the appointor is entitled in default of appointment, an exercise is fraudulent if in furtherance of a bargain between the appointor and the appointee

57 *Re Kerr's Trusts* (1877), 4 Ch.D. 600; *Re Swinburne* (1884), 27 Ch.D. 696.

58 *Re Boulton's Settlement Trust*, [1928] Ch. 703; *Re Latta's Marriage Settlement Trusts*, [1949] Ch. 490.

59 *Re Brown's Trust* (1865), L.R. 1 Eq. 74.

60 *Pawlet* v. *Pawlet* (1748), 1 Wils. K.B. 224. Ireland: *Butler* v. *Butler* (1880), 7 L.R. Ir. 401.

61 *Re Witty*, [1913] 2 Ch. 666 (C.A.). Ireland: *Re Leahy*, [1920] 1 I.R. 260.

62 [1928] Ch. 703.

63 *Re Joicey*, [1915] 2 Ch. 115 (C.A.); *Re Boulton's Settlement Trust*, [1928] 1 Ch. 703; *Re Morris's Settlement Trusts*, [1951] 2 All E.R. 528 (C.A.); *Re Hunter's Will Trusts*, [1963] Ch. 372. Ireland: *Tredennick* v. *Tredennick*, [1900] 1 I.R. 354; *Re Westropp's Estate* (1903), 37 I.L.T.R. 183. See also Martin, "Observations on Powers of Appointment" (1917), 33 *Law Quarterly Review*, 256.

64 *Re Triffitt's Settlement*, [1958] Ch. 852.

to benefit out of the appointed property some person not an object of the power, and not entitled in default of appointment, whether that person is the appointor or someone else.[65]

Intention without bargain. If the appointor's dominant intention in exercising the power was to benefit a non-object out of the property appointed, the position of the parties depends on the type of power involved.

First, the power may be " for an appointor to select and define the beneficial interests inter se of the several members of a class of beneficiaries or their issue in a fund which (subject to the exercise of the power of appointment) is to pass in defined proportions to some or all of the members of the class."[66] In *Re Crawshay*[67] certain propositions were put forward by the Court of Appeal as to frauds on this type of power—

> . . . (1.) One case of a fraud on a power is where the donee of a special power of appointment makes an appointment intended to benefit some person not an object of the power. (2.) To establish a fraud on a power it is not necessary to prove a bargain between the donee of the power and the appointee.[68] (3.) What the court looks to is the intention or purpose of the appointor in making the appointment.[69] (4.) It is not necessary that (*a*) the appointee should be a party to or know of the corrupt intention or purpose or (*b*) that the purpose should in fact take effect. (5.) The relevant date as at which the intention of the appointor has to be ascertained is the date of the exercise of the power. (6.) Evidence is admissible as to the state of mind of the appointor, including statements by the appointor which go to show his or her state of mind at the material date. Such statements may be material though they are not contemporaneous with the date of exercise of the power.

Re Crawshay[70] was concerned with an intention on the part of the appointor that the appointee should benefit a non-object out of the appointed property. In that case the exercise of the power was held

[65] *Daubeny* v. *Cockburn* (1816), 1 Mer. 626; *Duke of Portland* v. *Lady Topham* (1864), 11 H.L.C. 32; *Pryor* v. *Pryor* (1864), 2 De G. J. & S. 205 (C.A. Ch.); *Cloutte* v. *Storey*, [1911] 1 Ch. 18 (C.A.). Ireland: *Palmer* v. *Wheeler* (1811), 2 Ba. & B. 18; *Duggan* v. *Duggan* (1880), 7 L.R. Ir. 152 (C.A.).

[66] *Per* Cohen, L.J., giving the judgment of the Court of Appeal in *Re Crawshay*, [1948] Ch. 123, 134.

[67] [1948] Ch. 123, 134-5.

[68] See also *Vatcher* v. *Paull*, [1915] A.C. 372 (P.C., Jersey); *Re Simpson*, [1952] Ch. 412. Cf. *Re Burton's Settlements*, [1955] Ch. 82.

[69] See also *Re Simpson*, [1952] Ch. 412; *Re Burton's Settlements*, [1955] Ch. 82. Ireland: *Palmer* v. *Wheeler* (1811), 2 Ba. & B. 18; *Hutchins* v. *Hutchins* (1876), I.R. 10 Eq. 453.

[70] [1948] Ch. 123.

fraudulent because the appointor intended that the appointee should become subject to strong moral pressure to benefit a non-object. In *Re Dick*[71] the Court of Appeal held that in order for the exercise of a power of appointment to be fraudulent it was not necessary that there be a likelihood of such strong moral suasion as the appointee would be unable to resist.[72] The appointor's intention was the dominant factor, though a mere confident hope would be inadequate. Evershed, M.R., said—[73]

> I should not wish to be thought to lay down that whenever there is any intention, however secreted in the bosom of the appointor, to benefit some non-object in some measure, that therefore the exercise of the power is bad. After all, although the phrase " fraud on the power " does not carry the sense of deceit which the word " fraud " bears in other contexts, it indicates the doing of something which is not right, using those words in their broad sense—at least, a deliberate defeating of what the donor of the power authorized and intended.

Later the Master of the Rolls said[73] that if " the proper inference from all the facts is that what the appointor has deliberately set out to achieve, by means of the appointment he has made, is the benefiting of some non-object, then, as it seems to me, the appointment " is a fraud on the power.

In *Re Burton's Settlements*[74] Upjohn, J., said—

> In my judgment, " the purpose and intention " of the appointor is to be ascertained as a matter of substance and not solely by analysing the effect of the appointment, though, of course, that is important.

The testator in this case had a power of appointment in favour of his children. He made appointments in favour of his daughters, and also gave them some of his own property. The gift of his own property was conditional on the recipient settling her share of the appointed property on herself and her children (the latter not being objects of the power). There was held to be no fraud on the power (there was no excessive execution because the unauthorised condition was not annexed to the appointments). Upjohn, J., said[75]—

> . . . the mere fact that the appointor purports to attach conditions intended to compel the appointees to settle the fund or make certain payments is not, in my judgment, by itself sufficient to constitute a fraud on the power.

71 [1953] Ch. 343. See also *Re Marsden's Trust* (1859), 4 Drew. 594. Cf. *Re Merton*, [1953] 1 W.L.R. 1096.
72 I.e. *Re Crawshay* illustrated, but did not provide an exhaustive formulation of, what constituted frauds on powers.
73 [1953] Ch. 360.
74 [1955] Ch. 82, 100. Cf. *Re Simpson*, [1952] Ch. 412.
75 [1955] Ch. 101.

Here there was evidence that the appointments were intended to benefit the objects. There was no contrary evidence and accordingly the appointments were valid.

Stamp, J., reviewed the recent cases in the light of the older authorities in *Re Brook's Settlement.*[76] A tenant for life, in that case, had power to appoint the remainder among his children. An application was made to the court under the Variation of Trusts Act, 1958,[77] with a view to converting the tenant for life's protected life interest into an absolute one and giving the remainder equally to his only two issue, his son Richard and his infant daughter Ann. A few days before the hearing, the donee of the power exercised it in favour of Richard and Ann. The learned judge held the appointment fraudulent because[78]—

> . . . first, the known effect of the appointment was to produce, by defeating the interests of future children, a state of affairs under which the court might be expected to approve a decision more favourable to the tenant for life than would have been the case if the division had had to be shown to be for the benefit of the after-born children: and secondly, because of the fact that the tenant for life here was anxious to obtain all he could on the division.

There is another class of case: where the appointor intends a non-object to benefit by operation of law. These cases have concerned appointors exercising a power with the intention of succeeding to the appointed property on the appointee's intestacy. In *Lady Wellesley* v. *Earl of Mornington*[79] the appointment was by a father to his ill and lunatic son, knowing the son was likely to die soon—he obliged within the year—so that the property appointed would go to the appointor. The appointment was held a fraud on the power. The intention of the appointor, as in the *Re Crawshay*[80] type of case, is predominantly what the court must look to. If the appointor puts himself in the position of being likely to succeed to the property, but his thoughts when appointing were only of the welfare of the objects of the power, the appointment cannot be impeached. In *Pemberton* v. *Jackson*[81] an appointor having power to appoint among his children and grandchildren, and having only one child aged four days, appointed the property to all his children equally. It was shown that he had no intention to benefit himself. The appointment was held valid

76 [1968] 1 W.L.R. 1661. Cf. *Re Robertson's Will Trusts*, [1960] 1 W.L.R. 1050; *Re Wallace's Settlements*, [1968] 1 W.L.R. 711. See also Cretney (1969), 32 *Modern Law Review*, 317.

77 See Keeton, *The Law of Trusts*, 9th ed., pp. 356-66.

78 [1968] 1 W.L.R. 1669.

79 (1855), 2 K. & J. 143.

80 [1948] Ch. 123. See pp. 369-70, *ante*.

81 (1845), 5 L.T.O.S. 17.

notwithstanding the contingency that the appointor might succeed to the property appointed.

Re Crawshay[82] dealt with a limited type of power which consists of that of varying the shares of members of a class who are to take anyway. If the power is to determine not only the shares of members but also whether any member of the class is to take anything at all, different considerations arise. If the appointor is himself entitled in default of appointment, besides the fact that *Re Crawshay*[82] does not apply, an execution of the power will be valid even if in furtherance of a bargain that the appointee will benefit a third party, a non-object, out of the property.[83] But there is no decision as to a power given to A to appoint to one or more of a class containing B, C, and D, with a gift over to E in default of appointment. Presumably an appointment under a bargain to benefit A or F would be bad as a fraud on E; but it is far from clear that an appointment to D with the intention (without a bargain) that A or F should benefit would be objectionable. *Re Nicholson's Settlement*[84] suggests that it would be valid. That case, however, is usually cited as authority for a different type of power: that to appoint to one person only. According to *Re Nicholson's Settlement*,[84] where there is a power to appoint to one person only, the *Re Crawshay*[82] rules do not apply, and there must be a bargain, not a mere intention, to benefit a non-object. The power in question was given to a spinster to appoint a fund to any husband she might marry, with the property going in default of appointment to some third persons. This is not a power to appoint to one person only, for two reasons. First, there is a power of selection. A power given to a married woman to appoint to her present husband is a power to appoint to one person only, but a power given to a woman to appoint to any husband she might marry enables her to choose the object from a large class or group, i.e. all men able and willing to marry her. She is in a particularly advantageous position to do this if she is a spinster, and the appointor in *Re Nicholson's Settlement*[84] chose her husband on the sole criterion that he was likely, without a bargain, to carry out her intention to benefit non-objects out of the property she appointed. Secondly, the appointor may leave behind her a trail of husbands, each an appointee to some extent. Re *Nicholson's Settlement*[84] ought to have been regarded as a case, not of a power to appoint to one person only, but of a power given to A to appoint to one or more of a class (provided she married each appointee) with a gift over in default of appointment to other people (not A and not within the class).

82 [1948] Ch. 123. See pp. 369-70, *ante*.
83 *Wright* v. *Goff* (1856), 22 Beav. 207.
84 [1939] Ch. 11.

Benefit to appointor not out of property appointed. Where the power is of the *Re Crawshay*[85] type, an appointment in pursuance of a bargain to secure a benefit to the appointor otherwise than out of the appointed property (e.g. out of some other property, or some non-proprietary benefit such as speedy divorce)[86] is fraudulent. It makes no difference whether the bribe is given by the appointee, or by someone else with or without the knowledge of the appointee.[87]

If, on the other hand, the power is of some other type, the position is not clear. It has been decided[88] that, in the case of a power to jointure,[89] an exercise is fraudulent only if in execution of a bargain giving the chargor a benefit out of the jointure property, and that therefore a charge would not be void merely because the man makes his wife pay for it, even if the price is the full value or more. This may be because of the origin of jointuring as a transaction for consideration; there is no authority as to whether the same rule applies to powers of appointment. In the light of *Wright* v. *Goff*,[90] it probably does.

Acquiescence. When all the objects of a power concur in or confirm the transaction, there being no imposition or undue influence, they cannot complain that the transaction is a fraud on the power.[91]

Effect of fraudulent appointment. Where the power is to pass a legal title, a fraudulent exercise is voidable. A bona fide purchaser for value from the appointee without notice of the fraud will then get a good title. Where the power is to pass an equitable interest, a fraudulent appointment is void.[92] If, however, the appointment is severable into an honest and a fraudulent exercise, the honest part of the appointment may be effective.[93]

The Law of Property Act, 1925, Section 157,[94] deals with the position of persons acquiring interests from donees under powers of appointment. The first two subsections provide—

> (1) An instrument purporting to exercise a power of appointment over property, which, in default of and subject to any appointment, is held in trust for a class or number of persons of whom the appointee

[85] [1948] Ch. 123. See pp. 369-70, *ante*.
[86] *Cochrane* v. *Cochrane*, [1922] 2 Ch. 230.
[87] *Rowley* v. *Rowley* (1854), Kay 242; *Re Wright*, [1920] 1 Ch. 108; *Cochrane* v. *Cochrane*, [1922] 2 Ch. 230.
[88] *Saunders* v. *Shafto*, [1905] 1 Ch. 126. Ireland: *Baldwin* v. *Roche* (1842), 5 Ir. Eq. Rep. 110.
[89] Generally this is a power given to trustees to charge settled property with an annuity in favour of the widow of the tenant for life.
[90] (1856), 22 Beav. 207.
[91] *Skelton* v. *Flanagan* (1867), I.R. 1 Eq. 362, 369, *per* Walsh, M.R.
[92] *Cloutte* v. *Storey*, [1911] 1 Ch. 18.
[93] *Whelan* v. *Palmer* (1888), 39 Ch.D. 648.
[94] There is no equivalent legislation in Ireland.

is one, shall not (save as hereinafter provided) be void on the ground of fraud on the power as against a purchaser in good faith:

Provided that, if the interest appointed exceeds, in amount or value, the interest in such property to which immediately before the execution of the instrument the appointee was presumptively entitled under the trust in default of appointment, having regard to any advances made in his favour and to any hotchpot provision, the protection afforded by this section to a purchaser shall not extend to such excess.

(2) In this section " a purchaser in good faith " means a person dealing with an appointee of the age of not less than twenty-five years for valuable consideration in money or money's worth, and without notice of the fraud, or of any circumstances from which, if reasonable inquiries had been made, the fraud might have been discovered.

Release of power. There is no doctrine of fraud on a release of a power.[95]

Revocation of appointment. In general, there is no doctrine of fraud on a revocation of an appointment.[96] It was suggested in *Re Greaves*[97] that a revocation might be avoided if done only to clear the way for a fraudulent reappointment. However, in such a case the revocation (since it enures to the benefit of the person entitled in default of appointment) ought to be valid and only the reappointment impeachable.

If a power of appointment is exercisable only by deed, an appointment is irrevocable unless the instrument exercising the power reserves a right of revocation. If, on the other hand, the power can be and is informally exercised, the appointment can be changed in a similar manner without any reservation, in the first exercise, of a power of change or revocation.[98]

95 *Re Somes*, [1896] 1 Ch. 250.
96 *Re Greaves*, [1954] Ch. 434 (C.A.)
97 [1954] Ch. 434, 450.
98 *Re Beesty's Will Trusts*, [1966] Ch. 223.

CHAPTER XI

CONVERSION AND RECONVERSION

MEANING OF THE DOCTRINE OF CONVERSION

THE equitable doctrine of conversion was formulated by Sir Thomas Sewell, M.R., in the leading case of *Fletcher* v. *Ashburner*,[1] where he said that—

> . . . nothing was better established than this principle, that money directed to be employed in the purchase of land, and land directed to be sold and turned into money, are to be considered as that species of property into which they are directed to be converted; and this in whatever manner the direction is given: whether by will, by way of contract, marriage articles, settlement, or otherwise, and whether the money is actually deposited or only covenanted to be paid, whether the land is actually conveyed or only agreed to be conveyed. The owner of the fund or the contracting parties may make land money or money land. The cases established this rule universally.

The basis of this doctrine is explained in *Lechmere* v. *Earl of Carlisle*,[2] where money was agreed to be laid out in the purchase of land. The covenantor having died before the purchase was made, it was decided that the money passed to the heir, and that it made no difference whether the money to be laid out in the purchase was in the hands of trustees or in the hands of the covenantor. In both cases, the effect of the agreement was to turn money into land and Sir Joseph Jeykll, M.R., added[3]—

> The forbearance of the trustees in not doing what it was their office to have done, shall in no sort prejudice the *cestuy que trusts*, since at that rate it would be in the power of trustees, either by doing, or delaying to do, their duty, to affect the right of other persons; which can never be maintained. Wherefore the rule in all such cases is, that what ought to have been done, shall be taken as done; and a rule so powerful it is, as to alter the very nature of things;

[1] (1779), 1 Bro. C.C. 497, 499.
[2] (1733), 3 P. Wms. 211.
[3] 3 P. Wms. 215.

> to make money land, and on the contrary, to turn land into money; thus money articled to be laid out in land, shall be taken as land, and descend to the heir; and on the other hand, land agreed to be sold, shall be considered as personal estate.

The concluding observations advert to the practical consequence of the rule until 1926. Inasmuch as, on intestacy before 1926, real property devolved in one way, and personalty in another, it was important to discover, by reference to the doctrine of conversion, what property could properly be regarded as realty, and what personalty, before the interests of the heir and of the next-of-kin could be accurately ascertained. By Sections 45-6 of the Administration of Estates Act, 1925,[4] however, descent of realty to the heir was abolished, and a new form of succession, common to both real and personal property, was introduced.[5] Furthermore, by Section 33 of that Act,[6] on intestacy the personal representatives hold on trust for sale, so that the persons entitled under the Act to the property of the intestate will primarily always be entitled to it as personalty. These provisions have robbed the doctrine of its importance in relation to intestacies, but it is still applicable where the testator appoints both a residuary legatee and a residuary devisee; whilst the doctrine has undergone a new, and somewhat unexpected development as a result of a succession of decisions since 1925, which are explained in a later section.

It was, however, the unfairness of allowing trustees prejudicially to affect the interests of beneficiaries by postponing sales or purchases of land which led to the establishment of the doctrine at the beginning of the eighteenth century. Something of its implications may be recognised in *Kettleby* v. *Atwood*[7] and in *Knights* v. *Atkyns*,[8] during the Chancellorships of Lord Guilford and Lord Jeffreys, but it first received formal recognition in *Lingen* v. *Sowray*,[9] where Lord Cowper put it on the ground stated by Sir Joseph Jekyll, M.R., in *Lechmere* v. *Earl of Carlisle*.[10]

THE OCCASIONS WHEN CONVERSION OPERATES

Conversion, either of land into personalty, or of personalty into land, may arise in any of the following cases—

4 Ireland: Succession Act, 1965, Sects. 11, 66 (Republic of Ireland); Administration of Estates Act (Northern Ireland), 1955, Sects. 1, 6.
5 The detailed provisions have been amended by the Intestates' Estates Act, 1952.
6 No equivalent legislation in Ireland.
7 (1684), 1 Vern. 298.
8 (1687), 2 Vern. 20.
9 (1711), 1 P. Wms. 172.
10 (1733), 3 P. Wms. 211.

Partnership Land

Section 22 of the Partnership Act, 1890 (re-enacting an old equitable rule), provides—

> Where land or any heritable interest therein has become partnership property, it shall, unless the contrary intention appears,[11] be treated as between the partners (including the representatives of a deceased partner), and also as between the heirs of a deceased partner and his executors or administrators, as personal or moveable and not real or heritable estate.

The reason for this provision is to be found in the fact that on the dissolution of the partnership, the land will have to be sold, and the proceeds apportioned amongst the partners. Since 1926 partnership land is always held on trust for sale in England.[12]

In *Re Fuller's Contract*,[12] Luxmoore, J., held that where, since 1926, partners hold land as joint tenants as part of the partnership property, such land is held by the partners on a statutory trust for sale for the benefit of themselves as tenants in common, notwithstanding the observations of James, L.J., in *Ashworth* v. *Munn*[13] that the beneficial interests of partners is " not as tenants in common or as joint tenants . . ." It has been suggested that the effect of this decision has been to create some inconvenience, inasmuch as it establishes in respect of partnership property an express trust of land, carrying with it all the implications of duties and liabilities imposed on an express trustee. One of these is obviously the duty of appointing a new trustee before the land is sold.[14]

Order of the Court

Where a court properly directs the sale of realty, there is conversion from the date of the order, and all the consequences of conversion follow, so that any person interested must take the property in the converted form, unless the person entitled has some equity entitling him to direct that property should be reconverted into its original form.[15] It may be, however, that where a sale is directed by a court having competent jurisdiction, the order directs that the property sold, or the money invested shall not be regarded as converted, and if

11 On this, see *Re Wilson*, [1893] 2 Ch. 340.

12 *Re Fuller's Contract*, [1933] Ch. 652. Ireland: there are no statutory trusts for sale, and *Re Fuller's Contract* does not represent the law.

13 (1880), 15 Ch.D. 363, 369 (C.A.).

14 See further Potter, (1934), 50 *Law Quarterly Review*, 19.

15 *Steed* v. *Preece* (1874), L.R. 18 Eq. 192; *Burgess* v. *Booth*, [1908] 2 Ch. 648 (C.A.); *Pole* v. *Pole*, [1924] 1 Ch. 156 (C.A.).

this is the case, then there is no conversion. Thus, in *A.-G.* v. *Marquis of Ailesbury*,[16] money of a lunatic was invested, by order of the Lords Justices having jurisdiction in lunacy, in purchases of land, which under their lordships' direction, were conveyed to trustees upon trust for the lunatic, his executors, administrators and assigns, with a declaration that the lands so conveyed (and all others to be purchased in lieu of them under any exercise of certain powers of sale and reinvestment, which were contained in the deed) should " to all intents and purposes, be considered as part of the personal estate of the lunatic." After the death of the lunatic, who never recovered, the Crown claimed probate duty upon his interest under this trust, as part of his personal estate and effects at the time of his death which, by virtue of the probate of his will (made before the lunacy) became vested in his executors. A Divisional Court of the Queen's Bench Division held the Crown entitled to the duty so claimed; but that judgment was reversed by the Court of Appeal. The House of Lords held, reversing the decision of the Court of Appeal, that the value of the lands was part of the personal estate of the lunatic at his death, and liable to probate duty. In the course of his judgment, Lord Selborne said[17]—

> It is to be observed that in this case the lunatic, to whom the money laid out in these purchases belonged, never himself did, or assented to, any act by which it was or could be converted into realty; he was incapable of doing any such act, or of giving any such consent. And although I do not think it is open to dispute that the Lords Justices, in the due course of the administration of his estate in lunacy, might have done any act which they judged to be for his benefit, it is to me clear that, in this case, they did not judge it necessary, or for his benefit, to do any act which would have the effect of converting his personal right to the money thus invested into a real right to land with the incidents belonging to realty; but that, on the contrary, they intended to prevent the investment which they authorized from having any such consequence, and introduced both into their own order, and into the conveyance which followed thereon, declarations which they considered proper and sufficient to effectuate that intention.
>
> Under these circumstances, I think the present case undistinguishable in principle from those in which trustees without authority, or the guardians of an infant or committees of a lunatic without the sanction of any Court, have invested personalty belonging to the

[16] (1887), 12 App. Cas. 672.
[17] 12 App. Cas. 680-1.

trust, or to the infant, or the lunatic, in the purchase of lands of inheritance, nothing being afterwards done to supply the original want of authority.

The principle last mentioned by Lord Selborne is that where an unauthorised sale is effected by a trustee, guardian of an infant or committee of a lunatic, the property retains its original character. In *Taylor* v. *Taylor*,[18] a testator, who was a shopkeeper, made a will bequeathing his leasehold house and shop and the stock-in-trade to his wife, and disposed otherwise of his residuary estate. The testator then became insane, and no commission of lunacy was taken out, but the wife, not being competent to carry on his business, joined with the persons named as executors and with the residuary legatees in an agreement for the sale of the leasehold premises and stock-in-trade, for a sum to be paid in instalments. After the agreement had been made, and possession had been given to the purchaser, the testator died. The court, in an administration suit, approved of the agreement as beneficial to the estate, and directed it to be carried out. Page Wood, V.-C., held, however, that, notwithstanding the agreement for sale and the transfer of the possession of the property specifically bequeathed, none of the persons having any lawful authority to effect such a sale, both the leasehold estate and the stock-in-trade must be regarded as unconverted at the death of the testator, and they accordingly passed to the specific devisee thereof.

In *Re Silva*[19] real property was purchased by an order of the court out of funds belonging to a person of unsound mind not so found. The real property was intended as a residence for the person of unsound mind, and the order did not contain any direction whether the property was to be regarded as realty or personalty. Later, the house was sold, and the court directed that the proceeds of sale should retain the character of realty, and should pass to the heir at law (since the person of unsound mind had not recovered his sanity since 1926, and had died intestate). Thus, the court directed with respect to the second sale, that the character of the property established by the order for the purchase of the house should be retained.

In general, therefore, the court itself will not alter the condition in which a lunatic's property is, so as adversely to affect the rights of other persons in it, although the court will take as its first principle the promotion of the interests of the lunatic. Further, the Lunacy Act, 1890,

18 (1853), 10 Hare 475.
19 [1929] 2 Ch. 198.

Section 123,[20] provided that the lunatic, his heirs, executors, administrators, next of kin, devisees, legatees, and assigns, should have the same interest in any moneys arising from any sale, mortgage, or other disposition under the powers of that Act as they would have had in the property if no such disposition had been made, and the surplus moneys were to be of the same nature as the property disposed of.[21] The principle of this section, therefore, was directly applied in *Re Silva*[22] to the lunatic's house, in so far as the second sale was concerned, thus preventing conversion from realty to personalty, but it did not apply to the purchase of the house, since that was intended for the lunatic's occupation, and the court, in making the order, omitted the well-known form of declaration which could have directed that the house was still to be regarded as personal property. These rights of persons interested have been preserved in Section 107 of the Mental Health Act, 1959,[23] when the owner is suffering from mental disorder.

The doctrine of conversion applies to sales under an order of the court only in so far as no equity for reconversion exists. Where, before 1926, there was a sale of real property of an infant or lunatic under the Partition Act, 1868, this Act incorporated some of the provisions of the Leases and Sales of Settled Estates Act, 1856 (replaced by the Settled Estates Act, 1877), wherein provision was made for the reinvestment of the proceeds of sale in the purchase of land. In such a case, there was no conversion, and the real property descended to the heir-at-law of the infant or lunatic.[24] Again, where freehold land of an infant is taken compulsorily under the Lands Clauses Consolidation Act, 1845, and the purchase-money is paid into court, the purchase-money is again regarded as real estate, and would before 1926 have descended to the infant's heir-at-law on his death intestate.[25]

Binding Contract for the Sale or Purchase of Land

Where there is a binding contract for the sale or purchase of land, of which specific performance will be ordered, there is conversion from the date of the contract, so that from the standpoint of the purchaser, the property is regarded as realty.[26] On the death of the purchaser, the

[20] Ireland: Lunacy Regulation (Ireland) Act, 1871, Sect. 67.

[21] On this section, see *Re Alston*, [1917] 2 Ch. 226; *Re Walker*, [1921] 2 Ch. 63; *Re Harding*, [1934] Ch. 271; *Re Stillwell*, [1936] Ch. 637.

[22] [1929] 2 Ch. 198.

[23] Ireland: Lunacy Regulation (Ireland) Act, 1871, Sects. 66, 67.

[24] *Foster* v. *Foster* (1875), 1 Ch. D. 588; *Re Barker* (1881), 17 Ch. D. 241 (C.A.); *Hopkinson* v. *Richardson*, [1913] 1 Ch. 284.

[25] *Kelland* v. *Fulford* (1877), 6 Ch. D. 491.

[26] For a discussion of the relationship between vendor and purchaser whilst the contract is executory, see Keeton, *The Law of Trusts*, 9th ed., pp. 195-203.

person who takes the real property will, generally speaking, also be under an obligation to pay the purchase-money, in accordance with Section 35 of the Administration of Estates Act, 1925,[27] replacing the Real Estate Charges Acts, 1854, 1867, and 1877.

In this class of case, conversion depends upon the fact that the contract is one of which specific performance will be ordered, and therefore a mere notice to treat by a railway company, acting under the Lands Clauses Consolidation Act, 1845, to an owner of land, does not give rise to conversion,[28] nor does it where the contract fixes the price, but omits to specify the amount of land to be taken.[29] On the other hand, if the notice to treat is followed by the fixing of the price, either by private agreement, arbitration, valuation by surveyors, or the verdict of a jury, then if the amount of the land to be taken is settled, specific performance would be awarded, and there will accordingly be conversion.[30]

The principle that conversion follows the conclusion of a binding contract for the sale of land has been extended to cover options for the purchase of land. In the leading case of *Lawes* v. *Bennett*,[31] Witterwronge in 1758 leased a farm to Douglas for seven years, and at the same time agreed that if Douglas should give notice in writing before 29th September 1765 of his intention to purchase the freehold for £3000, Witterwronge would sell to him at that figure. The lessor died in 1763, having devised all his realty to Bennett, and all his personalty to Bennett and Mary Lawes equally. Douglas had assigned the lease and the option to Waller in 1762, and on 2nd February 1765, Waller exercised his option, and the land was conveyed to him. Mary Lawes now claimed from Bennett half the purchase price, claiming that at the time of Witterwronge's death it must be considered as personalty, since the exercise of the option related back to the date of the original agreement, from which date, therefore, conversion would operate. This contention was upheld by Kenyon, M.R.

It is now settled that this principle applies even where the option is not exercisable until after the testator's death. In *Re Isaacs*,[32] there was a lease by Isaacs, with an option to purchase within six months of

[27] Ireland: Succession Act, 1965, Sect. 47 (Republic of Ireland); Administration of Estates Act (Northern Ireland), 1955, Sect. 31.

[28] *Haynes* v. *Haynes* (1861), 1 Dr. & Sm. 426; *Richmond* v. *North London Railway Co.* (1868), L.R. 5 Eq. 352.

[29] *Ex parte Walker* (1853), 1 Drew. 508.

[30] *Haynes* v. *Haynes* (1861), 1 Dr. & Sm. 426; *Harding* v. *Metropolitan Railway Co.*, (1872), L.R. 7 Ch. App. 154.

[31] (1785), 1 Cox C.C. 167. See Marshall, "Anachronisms in Equity" (1950), 3 *Current Legal Problems*, 30, at pp. 35-9.

[32] [1894] 3 Ch. 506.

the lessor's death. Isaacs died intestate, the lessee exercised his option, and Chitty, J., held that the purchase-moneys passed to the next-of-kin, and not to the heir-at-law. In all these cases, however, until the option is exercised, any rents and profits of the land pass to the heir or devisee.[33]

In *Re Isaacs*, the lessor died intestate. If, however, the lessor makes a will *after* he has given the option, or if a previous will is confirmed by codicil after the option was given, it may be that the court will infer an intention that the specific devisee should receive the purchase-money when the option is exercised.[34] That is to say, in such a case, there is no conversion until the option is in fact exercised. In *Re Pyle*,[35] the testator made his will in 1886, giving Blackacre by a specific devise to X. By a codicil of June 1895, he confirmed his will; and *on the same day*, he gave an option on Blackacre to Y, who also took a lease of that property. Y exercised the option after the testator's death, but Stirling, J., held that the facts constituted sufficient indication that the principle of *Lawes* v. *Bennett*[36] should not be applicable.

It will be evident, therefore, that the courts have accepted comparatively slight evidence as an indication that the principle of *Lawes* v. *Bennett*[36] should be excluded, and it has been observed in several judgments that the principle will not be extended. In *Woodall* v. *Clifton*[37] the Court of Appeal held that the perpetuity rule applied to options to purchase, though it does not to options to renew a lease. A more direct limitation, however, was imposed by Fry, J., in *Edwards* v. *West*,[38] where the lessor covenanted to insure, and the lessee had an option to purchase. No agreement was concluded in respect of the insurance moneys. When the property was burnt down, the lessee exercised his option and then claimed from the lessor the insurance money, on the ground that the option, when exercised, related back to the original agreement, from which date conversion operated, and the lessee was therefore entitled to the insurance money. Fry, J., however, declined to extend the doctrine so as to imply that conversion existed from the date of the agreement as between vendor and purchaser.

33 *Townley* v. *Bedwell* (1808), 14 Ves. 591; *Re Marlay*, [1915] 2 Ch. 264 (C.A.).

34 *Re Calow*, [1928] Ch. 710; *Emuss* v. *Smith* (1848), 2 De G. & Sm. 722.

35 [1895] 1 Ch. 724.

36 (1785), 1 Cox C.C. 167.

37 [1905] 2 Ch. 257. See also *Worthing Corporation* v. *Heather*, [1906] 2 Ch. 532; Perpetuities and Accumulations Act 1964, Sects. 9 and 10. Ireland: Perpetuities Act (Northern Ireland) 1966, Sects. 9 and 10; no Republic of Ireland equivalent.

38 (1878), 7 Ch. D. 858.

Notwithstanding this general disinclination to extend the doctrine of conversion in relation to options, the Court of Appeal in *Re Carrington*[39] gave a somewhat novel interpretation to the principle. In 1911, a testator specifically bequeathed 420 preference shares in a company to A. Later, he gave an option over those shares, along with a number of others to X, the option to be exercised within one month of the testator's death. When the option was exercised, it was contended that there was conversion from the date when the option was given, so that at the death of the testator, the shares would be deemed to be money and, accordingly, the shares, as a specific bequest, should be regarded as having been adeemed. The Court of Appeal, purporting to apply the principle in *Lawes* v. *Bennett*, accepted this argument. It is submitted, however, that the principle in *Lawes* v. *Bennett* ought to have no application to such a case, (1) because that principle was elaborated to deal with options on leases, and the principle should not now be extended; and (2) because the doctrine of conversion was a doctrine elaborated by equity to govern the devolution of realty and personalty on a person's death. It was not intended to govern, nor had it hitherto governed, the devolution of different classes of personalty on the death of a person. Moreover, the whole basis of the rule in *Lawes* v. *Bennett* is that the contract which exists after the option has been exercised is specifically enforceable. None of the learned judges of the Court of Appeal discussed the question whether the contract in *Re Carrington* was specifically enforceable,[40] although normally contracts for the sale of shares are.

In *Re Sherman*,[41] however, Harman, J., refused to extend the doctrine of conversion to a case where a testator devised an equitable interest in land which had been obtained in breach of trust and which, after the testator's death, had to be given up in return for a payment of £400. It was held that the devisee was entitled to the £400 and not the residuary legatee.

A number of cases arose in Ireland under the Land Purchase Acts, where the death of the vendor or purchaser took place before completion. There are four classes of relevant circumstances.

(1) *Conversion of tenant's chattel real into realty.* By the Land Law (Ireland) Act, 1896, Section 32 (4), the existence of a binding agreement by a tenant for a term of years to buy the freehold under the Acts did not operate to convert the tenant's interest into realty.[42]

[39] [1932] 1 Ch. 1.
[40] See *Duncuft* v. *Albrecht* (1841), 12 Sim. 189.
[41] [1954] Ch. 653.
[42] *Re Phelan*, [1946] I.R. 451. As to similar problems which might arise under English provisions for leasehold enfranchisement, see Tiley, " Conversion and the Leasehold Reform Act 1967 " (1969), 33 *Conveyancer and Property Lawyer*, 43 and 141.

(2) *Conversion of tenant's realty into personalty.* By the Local Registration of Title (Ireland) Act, 1891, Section 22 (1), the title to land dealt with under the Land Purchase Acts must be registered. By Sections 84 and 85, registered land devolved on intestacy as personalty.[43] In *Re Collins' Estate*[44] a tenant of an estate pur autre vie agreed to purchase his holding under the Land Purchase Acts, but died before the land had been vested or registered, though the advance of the purchase-money had previously been sanctioned. The Court of Appeal of the Irish Free State held that, the tenant having died intestate, the land, though freehold, devolved as personalty. In *Re Mary Smith*,[45] on the other hand, the Court of Appeal had held that the fee simple devolved as realty where the purchaser died before registration, since the vesting order was made before the 1891 Act came into operation, and this was followed in the Irish Free State in *Re Brady*[46] and in Northern Ireland in *Re Stewart*.[47] In *Re Desmond*,[48] an Irish Free State case, Overend, J., thought there was a conflict between *Re Mary Smith* and *Re Collins's Estate* and held that the former was to be followed even where the purchase was made after registration became compulsory.

(3) *Conversion of landlord's realty into personalty.* The existence of a binding agreement by a landlord to sell his freehold under the Acts operated to convert his interest in the land into personalty.[49]

(4) *Conversion of real claims against landlord's interest into personal claims.* Where, on the sale of an estate under the Acts, the land was vested in the tenant purchaser, the purchase-money was paid into the bank and an order was made attaching claims thereto under Section 24 (1) of the Irish Land Act, 1903, the claim in respect of a fee simple head rent previously payable out of the lands was thereupon converted into a personal claim.[50]

Under a Trust for Sale or Purchase

The doctrine of conversion is of cardinal importance in relation to trusts for sale and purchase. In such a case, there is conversion from the moment when the instrument comes into force, so that in a

[43] Today, all disposable property devolves in the same way on intestacy: see p. 376, *ante*.

[44] [1924] 1 I.R. 72. See also *M'Donnell* v. *Stenson*, [1921] 1 I.R. 80 (C.A.).

[45] (1897), 33 I.L.T.R. 69.

[46] [1936] I.R. 431.

[47] [1956] N.I. 82.

[48] [1943] I.R. 534.

[49] *Re Doyle's Estate*, [1907] 1 I.R. 204. See also *Re Sherlock's Estate*, [1899] 2 I.R. 561 (C.A.); *Re Lawless's Will Trusts*, [1927] I.R. 541; *Re Wright's Estate* (1930), 64 I.L.T.R. 195.

[50] *Re Rynd's Estate*, [1916] 1 I.R. 230.

trust for sale, the land is deemed to be personalty even though still unsold. The trust for sale must be imperative, however; though the trustees may be given expressly a power to postpone. It must be more than a mere power of sale, which does not effect a conversion;[51] but if there is a power of sale which is held to be in the nature of a trust, then there is conversion from the date when the instrument comes into force.[52] If the settlor gives the trustees a discretion to invest money in the purchase of land or of good securities, the money is not converted until land is actually bought with it.[53] It may be, nevertheless, that although such an option is apparently given to the trustees, the limitations, being such as are apt primarily for real property, indicate that the settlor's true intention was that the money should be invested in the purchase of land. In such a case there is conversion from the date of the instrument, and this is so even though land is not ultimately purchased.[54]

Difficulties arose in construing dispositions coming into force before 1926, if the settlor or testator gave property to the trustees with a direction either to retain or sell.[55] If the instrument showed that it was intended that the land was to remain land, then conversion was excluded and the land was dealt with as settled land. If an intention was shown that the land was to be sold, then the instrument was held to have created a trust for sale, with conversion from the date when such instrument came into force. Now, in England, Section 25 (4) of the Law of Property Act, 1925,[56] states that in dispositions or settlements coming into operation after 1925, a direction to retain or sell shall be construed as a trust to sell the land with power to postpone the sale, with the consequence that there is conversion from the time when the trust for sale becomes operative.

Difficulties sometimes arise where a trust for sale or purchase is only to be exercised at the request or with the consent of some person, frequently the tenant for life. Questions of this kind are regarded by the court as questions of construction. If the provision is inserted with the object primarily of ensuring that a sale does occur, there is conversion from the date of the instrument; if on the other hand, the direction was inserted with the object of giving to the person indicated a

51 *Re Beaumont's Trusts* (1863), 32 Beav. 191; *Hyett* v. *Mekin* (1884), 25 Ch. D., 735; *Re Ibbitson's Estate* (1869), L.R. 7 Eq. 226.

52 *Re Courtier* (1886), 34 Ch. D. 136 (C.A.).

53 *Curling* v. *May* (1734), cit. 3 Atk. 255; *Re Twopeny's Settlement*, [1924] 1 Ch. 522 (C.A.).

54 *Cookson* v. *Reay* (1842), 5 Beav. 22.

55 See *Re Johnson*, [1915] 1 Ch. 435; *Re White's Settlement*, [1930] 1 Ch. 179.

56 Ireland: see the Settled Land Act, 1882, Sect. 22 (5).

discretion whether there should be a sale or not, there is no conversion until actual sale; and if there is a sale by the trustees without the necessary consent, the proceeds will nevertheless be still regarded as land.[57]

Sometimes also the instrument directs that a trust for sale shall not arise until the death of a person, frequently the wife or husband of the testator. Here there will be no conversion until the event contemplated has happened.[58]

The trust for sale is now one of the two great conveyancing devices (the other being the strict settlement) whereby property is settled in trust for a number of persons with limited interests, and the scope of both institutions in England was very greatly extended by the property legislation of 1925. Lightwood[59] has shown that, in its modern form, the trust for sale was the consequence of the far-reaching decisions in *Fletcher* v. *Ashburner*[60] and *Ackroyd* v. *Smithson*[61] which were decided in successive years. Trusts for sale in wills, however, were already common by the middle of the seventeenth century, and there are instances of their insertion into wills so early as the fifteenth century. The trust for sale by deed is, on the other hand, a modern device. It is a nineteenth century invention, representing, no doubt, the desire of the wealthy middle-class industrialist to provide for all his children in roughly similar terms, as distinct from the strict settlement, the primary aim of which was the preservation of the family estate as an undivided whole. When, in the middle of the nineteenth century, trusts for sale came into general use, many settlors, especially by will, wished to insert an ordinary life tenancy in land so long as the first life interest (e.g. of a widow or child) existed. However, conveyancers in general preferred the practice of establishing an immediate trust for sale, with a power to postpone until someone, usually the tenant for life, consents. In both cases, the Law of Property Act, 1925,[62] provides that the trust for sale is still to be regarded as " immediate."

The Effect of Failure of the Objects of Conversion

If the objects for which a conversion has been directed *completely* fail, then, the purpose no longer existing, equity has always held that conversion does not operate. This rule applies whether the conversion

[57] *Thornton* v. *Hawley* (1804), 10 Ves. 129; *Re Goswell's Trusts*, [1915] 2 Ch. 106. As to a trust for sale of land, however, see Sect. 205 (1) (xxix) of the Law of Property Act, 1925. Ireland: there is no such statutory definition.

[58] *Fitzgerald* v. *Jervoise* (1820), 5 Madd. 25.

[59] " Trusts for Sale " (1922), 3 *Cambridge Law Journal*, 39.

[60] (1779), 1 Bro. C.C. 497.

[61] (1780), 1 Bro. C.C. 503.

[62] Sect. 205 (1) (xxix). Ireland: no equivalent legislation.

is directed by deed or will. There is, however, this important distinction between deeds and wills, which was pointed out in *Re Lord Grimthorpe*.[63] In the case of a will, the moment to determine whether the purposes have failed is the testator's death; in the case of a deed, it is the date of the execution of the deed.

Where a trust for sale is directed to be exercised outside the perpetuity period, the trust will fail, and there will be no conversion. If, however, the beneficiaries who were the objects of the trust can be ascertained within the perpetuity period, they will still be entitled to their interests, but they will take the property in the unconverted form. If, however, the class cannot be ascertained within the perpetuity period, their interests will fail, and the property will revert back in its unconverted form to the donor, if the gift is by deed, and if by will, to his residuary legatee or devisee.[64]

Where there is only a partial failure of the objects of conversion, a distinction has been drawn between cases in which conversion has been directed by deed, and cases in which conversion has been directed by will.

Conversion Directed by Deed

Where conversion is directed by deed, and there is a partial failure of the objects of conversion, then whether the conversion is of land into money, or of money into land, the property reverts to the settlor *in its converted form*. For example, if there is a trust for sale arising by deed, with a direction to divide the proceeds for certain objects, some of which have failed before the deed comes into operation, there is a resulting trust for the settlor, who receives back the property in the form of money.[65]

Conversion Directed by Will

Where a trust for sale of real property arises by will, and there is a partial failure of the objects of conversion, the land reverts to the settlor *as realty*, so that it will pass to the testator's residuary devisee or, under the old law, to the heir-at-law. This rule was established in the leading case of *Ackroyd* v. *Smithson*,[66] largely as a result of the persuasive eloquence of Mr. Scott, afterwards Lord Eldon. The substance of his argument was that conversion was directed for the purposes of the will

[63] [1908] 2 Ch. 675 (C.A.).

[64] *Re Daveron*, [1893] 3 Ch. 421; *Goodier* v. *Edmunds*, [1893] 3 Ch. 455; *Re Wood*, [1894] 3 Ch. 381 (C.A.); *Re Bewick*, [1911] 1 Ch. 116.

[65] *Clarke* v. *Franklin* (1858), 4 K. & J. 257; *Griffith* v. *Ricketts* (1849), 7 Hare 299.

[66] (1780), 1 Bro. C.C. 503.

only, and that when those purposes partially failed, conversion also failed to that extent, so that the heir-at-law could take the lapsed share of the realty. This contention was accepted by Lord Chancellor Thurlow.[67]

The rule applies even though the testator states that the real property should be treated for all purposes as personalty.[68]

It has also been decided, however, that where the heir or residuary devisee, in such a case, dies before receiving the lapsed share, this will result to him in the form of personalty so that it will pass under his will to his residuary *legatee* or, before 1926, to the heir-at-law's next of-kin.[69]

Again, where, in a will, a sale of realty is directed for a particular purpose, such as the payment of debts, and there is a surplus, the surplus will be regarded as realty and will devolve accordingly.[70]

Exactly the same rules apply in the converse case. Where in a will it is directed that personalty shall be employed for the purchase of land, and there is a partial failure of the objects of conversion, the rule is that a lapsed share will pass to the residuary legatee, and not to the residuary devisee. This was admitted by Mr. Scott in *Ackroyd* v. *Smithson*, and it was expressly so decided in *Cogan* v. *Stephens*.[71] If, however, the residuary legatee died, before the property had been transferred, it would devolve under his will as realty, whether in fact land had been bought or not.[72]

Reconversion

Reconversion must be distinguished from total or partial failure of the objects of conversion. Under the latter doctrine, the assumption is that the purposes for which conversion was originally directed having failed, there never was any conversion at all. On the other hand, reconversion is an imaginary further step by which an earlier conversion which has in theory taken effect, is reversed, so that, in the view of equity, the property reverts to its original state. Such a reconversion usually occurs at the instance of some person who is competent to call for the transfer of the property in one form or other.

67 The substance of Scott's interesting argument is set out in White and Tudor's *Leading Cases in Equity*, 9th ed., vol. I, pp. 329-32. The rule is excellently explained by Sir John Leach, M.R., in *Smith* v. *Claxton* (1820), 4 Madd. 484, 492-3.

68 *Taylor* v. *Taylor* (1853), 3 De G. M. & G. 190; *Fitch* v. *Weber* (1848), 6 Hare 145.

69 *Re Richerson*, [1892] 1 Ch. 379; *Re Walpole*, [1933] 1 Ch. 431.

70 *Re Richerson*, [1892] 1 Ch. 379.

71 (1835), 1 Beav. 482 n.

72 *Curteis* v. *Wormald* (1878), 10 Ch. D. 172 (C.A.); *Re Richerson* [1892] 1 Ch. 379.

In *Re Lord Grimthorpe*[73] by a marriage settlement of 1845, Lord Grimthorpe conveyed real property to trustees, upon trust to secure certain annual payments to his parents during their lives; and on the death of the survivor of his parents, to the use of Lord Grimthorpe for life; and after his death, to his trustees upon trust that the trustees should sell the property, and invest the proceeds, and to pay Lady Grimthorpe, if then alive, £250 a year, and if she should be dead, then as to £10,000, to hold in trust for such persons as Lord Grimthorpe should appoint; and subject to that, to the children of Lord and Lady Grimthorpe; and finally in default of children, for Lord Grimthorpe absolutely. The survivor of Lord Grimthorpe's parents died in 1874, and in 1901 Lord Grimthorpe executed a will, devising his freehold estates to his successor in the peerage. Lady Grimthorpe died a few months after he had made the will, and Lord Grimthorpe died in 1905, without issue, and without having exercised his power of appointment as to the £10,000. Eve, J., regarded the deed of 1845 as creating an immediate trust for sale, with power to postpone, so that the realty was converted into personalty from the date of the deed. He also held that the property had been reconverted by Lord Grimthorpe's will and, when this took effect, he was then in a position to elect, as his parents and Lady Grimthorpe were dead, and there were no children of the marriage. Accordingly, Lord Grimthorpe's successor in the peerage took the property settled in the deed of 1845 as realty. The Court of Appeal, however, were inclined to regard the case as one in which the objects of conversion had failed.

Reconversion may occur without any direct intervention on the part of such a person at all. This happens where the property is said to be " at home," that is to say is already in the hands of some person who is absolutely entitled. In such a case, the person to whom the property is to be transferred has both the legal interest in it, and also the absolute beneficial interest to have the property in its changed form. Here, equity will not stultify itself, and direct that the property shall be converted. The property is reconverted into the form in which it comes into the owner's hands. He has the absolute right to dispose of it as he pleases, and whatever happens to the property subsequently is not a consequence, direct or indirect, of the original command to convert, but of his own inherent powers as legal and beneficial owner to deal with that property as he pleases.[74]

Reconversion of the property may, however, also occur where the beneficial interest in the property becomes vested in some person who

[73] [1908] 2 Ch. 675.

[74] *Chichester* v. *Bickerstaff* (1693), 2 Vern. 295; *Pulteney* v. *Earl of Darlington* (1783), 1 Bro. C.C. 223; *Re Daveron*, [1893] 3 Ch. 421.

is entitled in possession to the whole of the interest, and is subject to no disability. Such a person may elect to take the property in its unconverted form, since, if the court enforced a conversion, the beneficiary himself might immediately annul its effect by repurchasing or reselling, and " Equity, like nature, does nothing in vain." If the person so entitled does not exercise his right to elect, the conversion stands, although comparatively slight evidence of intention to elect is accepted as sufficient.[75]

In *Re Daveron*,[76] Chitty, J., said—

> It is plain that the trust to sell and pay the proceeds to "A" (a named person) confers an equity on " A " and gives him the whole beneficial title which the testator is entitled to in fee simple. In equity " A " is the beneficial owner, and " A " can come to the trustees and say, " I desire you not to sell, but to convey the estate to me." About that there is no question. It is equally plain that if there is a direction to sell and to pay the proceeds in shares to A, B, and C, then A, B, and C are regarded, in equity, also as the owners of the estate. They can, by the doctrine of election, prevent any sale taking place, and, if they all express their intention, the trustees could lawfully convey the estate to them in the shares in which they are entitled to the purchase money. The difference between the cases I have put of the proceeds going to one person or the proceeds going to several, consists in this: that where there are several they must all concur to stop the sale.

It is essential that the person claiming to elect should have full capacity and, in this connection, the position of one or two special classes of persons requires special notice.

Infant

An infant cannot elect as an ordinary rule.[77] But if it is essential that election should take place before he attains his majority, the court will either elect for him, or sanction his election, the benefit of the infant being the primary consideration of the court.[78] The court will not, however, go any further than a bare election. For example, it will not sanction an alteration in the *size* of an infant's beneficial interest even though such an alteration would be for the infant's benefit.

[75] *Re Jenkins and H. E. Randall & Co.'s Contract*, [1903] 2 Ch. 362.
[76] [1893] 3 Ch. 421, 424.
[77] *Seeley* v. *Jago* (1717), 1 P. Wms. 389; *Carr* v. *Ellison* (1786), 2 Bro. C.C. 56.
[78] *Robinson* v. *Robinson* (1854), 19 Beav. 494; *Burgess* v. *Booth*, [1908] 2 Ch. 648 (C.A.).

Mental Patient

A mental patient may not elect,[79] and here again, the court will avoid electing if it can do so without detriment to his interest.[80] If it is essential to elect, however, the Court of Protection (a branch of the Chancery Division of the High Court)[81] may elect on behalf of the mental patient, having regard here also to the benefit of the mental patient.[82]

Married Woman

A married woman can elect in exactly the same way as a man, in consequence of successive Married Women's Property Acts, of the Law Reform (Married Women and Tortfeasors) Act, 1935, and of the Married Women (Restraint upon Anticipation) Act, 1949.[83]

Chargee

Where a person is entitled to the property subject to a charge, he may elect, provided that the person entitled to the charge assents to, or acquiesces in, the election.[84]

Owner of an Undivided Share

A person entitled to an undivided share can obviously elect with the consent of the other persons who are also entitled to undivided shares, being also of full capacity, since together they are entitled to the entirety of the beneficial interest. Difficulties may arise, however, where one person entitled to an undivided share wishes to convert and the other does not. Here a common-sense rule has been evolved. If money is to be laid out in the purchase of land, then one of the beneficiaries may elect to reconvert into money, even though the other does not, for the residue of the money to be invested may still be invested in the purchase of land without detriment to either beneficiary.[85] Where, however, land is to be converted into money, all those entitled must

[79] *Re Jump*, [1903] 1 Ch. 129.

[80] *Re Douglas and Powell's Contract*, [1902] 2 Ch. 296.

[81] The High Court in the Republic of Ireland and the Chancery Division in Northern Ireland.

[82] *A.-G.* v. *Marquis of Ailesbury* (1887), 12 App. 672 (H. L., E.).

[83] Ireland: the Married Women's Property Acts are still in force in Northern Ireland, but have been replaced in the Republic of Ireland by the Married Women's Status Act, 1957. Legislation equivalent to the English Acts of 1935 and 1949 is to be found in the Law Reform (Miscellaneous Provisions Act (Northern Ireland), 1937, and the Married Women (Restraint upon Anticipation) Act (Northern Ireland), 1952. The law of the Republic of Ireland was brought into line by the Married Women's Status Act, 1957, Sect. 6.

[84] *Mutlow* v. *Bigg* (1875), 1 Ch.D. 385 (C.A.).

[85] *Seeley* v. *Jago* (1717), 1 P. Wms. 389; *Walker* v. *Denne* (1793), 2 Ves. 170.

elect to reconvert, or alternatively conversion proceeds, since otherwise those who dissented would be compelled to sell undivided shares, which the ordinary purchaser will be reluctant to take.[86] This was the rule developed by equity before 1926, but wherever money is directed to be laid out in the purchase of land for the benefit of persons in undivided shares, a statutory trust for sale is now interposed in England, so that the beneficiaries will now always take their interests as personalty. Moreover, under Section 28 (3) of the Law of Property Act, 1925,[87] the statutory trustees for sale may, if the persons beneficially entitled are of full age and absolutely entitled, with the consent of any persons of full age (not being annuitants) who may be interested in possession in the net rents and profits until sale, partition any unsold land and provide by way of mortgage or otherwise for the payment of any equality money, and give effect, by way of conveyance in severalty to such partition. If one of the persons entitled to an undivided share is a mental patient, the consent of his committee or receiver protects the trustees; and if any share is affected by an incumbrance, the trustees for sale may either give effect to it or provide for its discharge by means of the property allotted in respect of that share.

Remainderman

A remainderman is unable to elect so as to cause his choice to operate adversely to the wishes of prior owners, but the weight of authority seems to be in favour of the view that he may elect to this extent, that when his interest, being absolute, vests in possession, that election is then operative.[88] Where, however, the remainderman's interest is contingent, it is essential that the contingency should happen during the remainderman's lifetime, if he is to be competent to elect. If the interest is still contingent at his death, an election by the remainderman's will is inoperative.[89]

Tenant in Tail

A tentant in tail, not in possession, may elect, and the election will bind his own issue. If, however, there are remainders over, it is necessary for the tenant in tail to secure the consent of the remainderman, whose rights can only be barred by a disentailing assurance.[90]

86 *Holloway* v. *Radcliffe* (1857), 23 Beav. 163; *Re Davidson* (1879), 11 Ch. D. 341 (C.A.).
87 There are no statutory trusts for sale in Ireland.
88 *Meek* v. *Devenish* (1877), 6 Ch. D. 566.
89 *Re Sturt*, [1922] 1 Ch. 416.
90 See *Trafford* v. *Boehm* (1746), 3 Atk. 440.

General

Election may be made by a proper person either by express declarations or by acts from which intention will be presumed, provided that in both cases the intent is unequivocally shown. If this is in fact shown, slight declarations or acts will suffice.[91] In *Sharp* v. *St. Sauveur*,[92] a person entitled to elect, in respect of land converted into money, devised it as his " landed property," and this was held to be a sufficient expression of election. Again, mere keeping of land for some time has been held sufficient, where the person absolutely entitled was competent to elect,[93] although not where he or, if there were several, one of them was subject to a disability[94] and obviously this presumption is considerably strengthened where the person competent to elect obtains custody of the title-deeds from the trustees for sale.[95] Where money is to be laid out in the purchase of land, mere receipt of *income*, even for a considerable time, is not sufficient evidence of election.[96]

Conversion under the Settled Land Act, 1925

The notion of conversion has received an important statutory application in England in the Settled Land Act, 1925. Section 75 (5) of that Act provides—

> (5) Capital money arising under this Act while remaining uninvested or unapplied, and securities on which an investment of any such capital money is made shall for all purposes of disposition, transmission and devolution be treated as land, and shall be held for and go to the same persons successively, in the same manner and for and on the same estates, interests, and trusts, as the land wherefrom the money arises would, if not disposed of, have been held and have gone under the settlement.[97]

Subsection (6) states that the income of the securities shall be paid or applied as the income of the land, if unsold, would have been paid or applied. It would seem that immediately on the sale of the settled land, the purchase-money is, *for the purposes of disposition, transmission and devolution*, converted into land.

91 *Pulteney* v. *Earl of Darlington* (1783), 1 Bro. C.C. 223, 237, *per* Lord Thurlow, L.C.
92 (1871), L.R.7 Ch. App. 343.
93 *Ashby* v. *Palmer* (1816), 1 Mer. 296; *Mutlow* v. *Bigg* (1875), 1 Ch. D. 385 (C.A.).
94 *Re Douglas and Powell's Contract*, [1902] 2 Ch. 296.
95 *Davies* v. *Ashford* (1845), 15 Sim. 42.
96 *Re Pedder's Settlement Trusts* (1854), 5 De. G. M. & G. 890 (C.A. Ch.).
97 Ireland: Settled Land Act, 1882, Sect. 22 (5).

These two subsections have no application to the proceeds of sale under a trust for sale, which remain converted into personalty from the moment when the trust becomes operative.[98]

In *Re Cartwright*[99] the Court of Appeal held that certain securities representing the proceeds of sale of land held under a strict settlement must be treated as land, and so were incapable of being disposed of by a will made under the Wills Act, 1861,[1] by a British subject residing in France, and in the French form.

CONVERSION UNDER THE STATUTORY TRUSTS

The establishment of certain statutory trusts by virtue of the provisions of the Law of Property Act, 1925,[2] has given rise to some troublesome problems, raising also the question of the application of the doctrine of ademption.

[98] *Re Kempthorne*, [1930] 1 Ch. 268.
[99] [1939] Ch. 90, followed in *Re Cutcliffe's Will Trusts*, [1940] Ch. 565.
[1] Replaced and extended, in England and Northern Ireland, by the Wills Act 1963. Republic of Ireland: Succession Act, 1965, Part VIII.
[2] No equivalent legislation in Ireland.

CHAPTER XII

ELECTION

NATURE OF THE DOCTRINE

IN the last chapter some mention was made of election by a person absolutely entitled to property which has been subjected to a notional conversion in equity. That type of election should be distinguished from the equitable principle of election which is discussed in the present chapter, and which applies where a person is given property by the donor under a deed or will, and, by the same instrument, some of the recipient's property is also given to a third party. Where these dispositions exist, the original donee must either give up his own property to the third party as directed, or alternatively, out of the fund he receives from the donor, he must compensate the third party for the property that party has failed to receive. Two cases must, however, be distinguished.

(1) X gives, by deed or will, £10,000 to A, on condition that A gives Blackacre to B. Here X has made it clear that A only receives £10,000 if A gives up Blackacre to B. If A does not, then A gets nothing at all from X.

(2) X gives, by deed or will, £10,000 to A, and in the same instrument he gives Blackacre, belonging to A, to B. This is a valid case for election if A accepts the £10,000. A can either keep Blackacre, giving its value out of the £10,000 to B (this is known as taking *against* the instrument), or he can give Blackacre to B, and receive the whole of the £10,000 (this is known as taking *under* the instrument). It is sometimes suggested that the doctrine of election depends upon the implied intention of the donor. Lord Talbot, L.C., put it in *Streatfield* v. *Streatfield*[1]—

> . . . when a man takes upon him to devise what he had no power over, upon a supposition that his will will be acquiesced under, this Court compels the devisee, if he will take advantage of the will, to take intirely, but not partially under it . . . there being a tacit condition annexed to all devises of this nature, that the devisee do not disturb the disposition which the devisor hath made.

[1] (1736), Cas. t. Talb. 176, 182-3. See also *Re Brooksbank* (1886), 34 Ch.D. 160.

Where the donee elects to take against the instrument, he is under an obligation to compensate the third party out of the fund he has received to the extent of the value of the donee's property which the third party has not received. This was plainly put by Lord Loughborough, L.C., in the leading case of *Bristow* v. *Warde*[2]—

> The doctrine of election . . . never can be applied, but where, if an election is made contrary to the will, the interest, that would pass by the will, can be laid hold of, to compensate for what is taken away; therefore in all cases there must be some free disposable property given to the person, which can be made a compensation for what the testator takes away.

This is now the accepted doctrine of equity, although the matter remained somewhat uncertain during Lord Eldon's tenure of the Chancellorship, and it will be seen from his decisions in *Tibbits* v. *Tibbits*[3] and *Green* v. *Green*[4] that he was inclined to draw a distinction between election upon a will and election upon a deed, applying the principle of compensation to the former, and the principle of forfeiture to the latter. Whatever may be said logically for this distinction, it has long been abandoned.

In determining the amount of compensation payable, the value of the properties is ascertained at the date of the testator's death, and not at the time when the election is made.[5] For a case of election to arise, there must be a claim under the will, or other document, and a claim outside the will and adverse to it. Election does not apply as between two clauses in the same will.[6]

Historical Foundations of the Doctrine

The doctrine of election has several times been stated, on the authority of Lord Hardwicke,[7] to have been first formulated in *Noys* v. *Mordaunt*.[8] This may be incorrect. Both Spence[9] and Swanston refer to a case decided in the reign of Elizabeth, in which a widow unsuccessfully sued for her dower, when an annuity had been given to her

[2] (1794), 2 Ves. Jun. 336, 350.

[3] (1816), 19 Ves. 656.

[4] (1816), 19 Ves. 665.

[5] *Re Hancock*, [1905] 1 Ch. 16.

[6] *Wollaston* v. *King* (1869), L.R. 8 Eq. 165, 174, *per* James, V.-C. See also the observations of Viscount Maugham in *Lissenden* v. *C. A. V. Bosch Ltd.*, [1940] A.C. 412, 417-19 (H.L., E.).

[7] *Boughton* v. *Boughton* (1750), 2 Ves. Sen. 12, 14-15.

[8] (1706), 2 Vern. 581.

[9] *Equitable Jurisdiction*, vol. I, p. 413 n. (*b*). See also *Lacy* v. *Anderson* (1581-3), 1 Swanst. 445 (A).

in lieu of it. This, however, seems to be primarily a case of satisfaction. On the other hand, Lord Eldon, L.C., in *Lord Rancliffe* v. *Lady Parkyns*,[10] after stating that *Noys* v. *Mordaunt* is generally regarded as the starting-point of the modern doctrine of election, adds his opinion that it was not the first case on the topic, but unfortunately cites no authority.

A good deal of the early history of the doctrine can be gleaned from Spence,[11] and from Swanston's learned notes to *Dillon* v. *Parker*.[12] Both authors take the view that the doctrine is ultimately derived from Roman law, in which the following rules existed.

(1) A testator could bequeath property to A, knowing that it did not belong to himself but to B. In such a case, A could recover from the heir either the property itself or, if B was unwilling to part with it, its value.[13]

(2) Further, by express direction (originally in a *fideicommissum*, but later by *legatum ab aliquo*), a testator could impose the obligation of providing the bequest or its value on any person deriving a benefit under a will.[14] (Here, however, the closest analogy seems to be, not to the doctrine of election, but to the institution of a trust.)

(3) Generally, however, if a bequest was made in the erroneous belief that the property belonged to the testator, the bequest was void, unless the legatee stood in a certain degree of relationship to the testator, or unless the property already belonged to the heir.[15]

There are unquestionably analogies between the rules of Roman law and those of equity in respect of election, but they must not be pressed too far. Possibly the medieval ecclesiastical Chancellors applied rules more closely approximating to those of Roman law, but by the eighteenth century, when the doctrine appears in the Chancery reports in its modern form, it has already acquired distinctive characteristics. For example, the Roman law rules applied only to wills, but when the doctrine of election makes its appearance in the equity reports covering the first half of the eighteenth century, it is already applied both to deeds and wills.

10 (1818), 6 Dow 149, 179 (H.L., E.).

11 *Op. cit.*, vol. II, p. 585.

12 (1818), 1 Swanst. 359.

13 *Institutes*, II, xx, 4; II, xxiv, 1; *Digest*, XXX, 39, vii; XXX, 104, ii; XXX, 71, iii; XXXII, 30, vi.

14 *Digest*, XXXII, 1, vi; XXXII, 14, ii; *Code* VI, 37, x; VI, 42, ix.

15 *Institutes*, II, 20, iv; *Digest*, XXXI, 67, viii; *Code*, VI, 37, x; *Code* VI, 42, xxv.

Although some cases declare the basis of the doctrine to be the presumed intent of the donor, it is clear that such a basis, if pushed to its logical conclusion, can result in difficulties, and the early decisions ascribe several other possible[16] bases to the doctrine. For example, the doctrine was said to rest upon a tacit condition,[17] or upon a constructive condition.[18] Again it is said to rest simply upon equity—a view which is reflected in the following observations, embodied in Plumer, M.R.'s interesting judgment in *Gretton* v. *Haward*[19]—

> . . . the language of the great judges by whom it has been discussed, proceeds to the extent of ascribing to the Court an equity to lay hold on the estate thus taken from the devisee by the principle of election, and dispose of it in favour of those whom he has disappointed; not merely taking it from one, but, such is the uniform doctrine, bestowing it on the other. A doctrine not confined to instances in which the heir is put to election, and which may be said to bring him within the operation of the general principle, but prevailing as an universal rule of equity, by which the Court interferes to supply the defect arising from the circumstances of a double devise, and the election of the party to renounce the estate effectually devised; and instead of permitting that estate to fall into the channel of descent, or to devolve in any other way, lays hold of it, to use the expression of the authorities, for the purpose of making satisfaction to the disappointed devisee; a very singular office; for in ordinary cases, where a legatee or devisee is disappointed, the Court cannot give relief; but here it interposes to assist the party whose claim is frustrated by election. Such is the language of Lord Chief Justice *de Grey*, cited with approbation by Lord *Loughborough:* " the equity of this Court is to sequester the devised estate *quousque* till satisfaction is made to the disappointed devisee."[20]

This view was approved by Hargrave,[21] but Swanston, in his note to *Dillon* v. *Parker*,[22] points out that Lord Chief Justice de Grey is not really intending to emphasise any distinction between an equity and an implied condition, but between an express condition and an equity arising from an implied condition. Notwithstanding this weighty view to the contrary, it is submitted that such a distinction exists. An

16 Cf. the judgment of Kekewich, J., in *Haynes* v. *Foster*, [1901] 1 Ch. 361.

17 *Streatfield* v. *Streatfield* (1736), Cas. t. Talb. 176, 183; *Frank* v. *Lady Standish* (1772), 15 Ves. 391 n.

18 *Boughton* v. *Boughton* (1750), 2 Ves. Sen. 12, 14.

19 (1819), 1 Swanst. 409, 423.

20 *Lady Cavan* v. *Pulteney* (1795), 2 Ves. Jun. 544, 560.

21 *Jurid. Arg.*, vol. II, pp. 302-3.

22 (1818), 1 Swanst. 359.

equity raised by the court can be confined within what limits the court chooses and, in fact, the courts have set arbitrary boundaries to the doctrine. On the other hand, the theory of presumed intent raises certain logical consequences which it is hard to evade. For example, if the donor knows the true facts when he makes his two gifts, it seems plain enough there is a case for election, but if presumed intent is the guiding principle, what should be the attitude of the court where the donor gives property which he thinks is his own, but which in fact belongs to someone else ? Lord Northington, L.K., thought that for a case of election to arise, it was essential that the donor should know that the property of which he purported to dispose should not be his own,[23] but Lord Eldon rejected this distinction, which is a logical deduction from the doctrine of presumed intent,[24] and held that the doctrine applied whether the donor knew the true facts or not, and this view has been generally accepted since Lord Eldon's time. Sugden, indeed, attempts to defend Lord Eldon's conclusion on the ground of the danger of speculating upon what the testator would have done had he known of the fact,[25] but it is submitted that in cases of election this is exactly what the court purports to do. In fact, the theory that knowledge of the true facts by the donor is essential died hard,[26] and Kekewich, J., in *Haynes* v. *Foster*[27] revived it in a slightly different setting, to decide whether a married woman donee who was given property with a restraint on anticipation, but had become a widow when the instrument came into operation, must elect or not. Once again, however, the strictly logical view was ultimately rejected.[28]

Another logical difficulty resulting from the adoption of the theory of presumed intent affects the consequences of election. It has already been shown that if A gives property to B, upon an expressed condition that B gives Blackacre to C, then B gets nothing unless he in fact transfers Blackacre to C. Why should cases of presumed intent or implied condition be any different? Nevertheless, it is quite clearly established by the modern cases that the principle of election is compensation and not forfeiture. Once again this difficulty is reflected in the eighteenth-century cases, and was by no means finally settled by Lord Eldon. Where the early equity judges regarded the effect of a refusal of the first donee to comply with the donor's intent as being forfeiture of the inter-

23 *Forrester* v. *Cotton* (1760), 1 Eden 531, 535. See also *Cull* v. *Showell* 1773), Amb. 727, 728, *per* Lord Apsley, L.C.

24 *Green* v. *Green* (1816), 19 Ves. 665.

25 *Powers*, 7th ed., vol. II, pp. 147-8.

26 See e.g. *Moore* v. *Butler* (1805), 2 Sch. & Lef. 249, 267, *per* Lord Redesdale, L.C.

27 [1901] 1 Ch. 361.

28 See p. 402, *post*.

est he would have received, they gave the property so lost by the first donee to the second donee, but where this exceeded the amount of the original gift, obviously he was getting more than the donor intended. To take a simple example: If A gives property of £150 value to B, and gives B's property of £100 value to C, if the principle applied is forfeiture, then B will lose the £150, which will be given to C—a curious result. On the face of it, therefore, it is not difficult to see why the principle of compensation ultimately prevailed, although there may be logical difficulties attending its application. Even when Spence published his researches in 1849, the issue was still in doubt, and he sets out at some length the authorities supporting the conflicting views. Even Sugden thought the true principle was forfeiture.[29] However, the doctrine of equity in this instance has returned to the view enunciated by Lord Chief Justice de Grey and cited with approval by Lord Loughborough in *Lady Cavan* v. *Pulteney*[30]—

> . . . the Chief Justice distinguishes the equity of this Court from an express condition; "which," he says, "must be performed as framed; and "if it is not, that will induce a forfeiture; but the equity of this Court is" (as he very well expresses it), "to sequester the devised interest *quousque*, till satisfaction is made to the disappointed devisee."

Lord Eldon's view, as expressed in *Tibbits* v. *Tibbits*,[31] was that the principle upon which the older cases had been decided was compensation, but that the opinions of later judges had shaken it. He himself thought that the principle of compensation should be confined to wills. In the second half of the nineteenth century, however, the courts tacitly ignored this latter qualification.[32]

Today, both the doctrines of presumed intent and implied condition can be regarded as finally discarded, and Buckley, J., has well expressed the modern view in the following terms[33]—

> The doctrine of election does not depend upon the intention of the testator (see *In re Edwards, decd.*[34]) and, indeed, the case in which the testator frames his will with the conscious intention of bringing the doctrine into play must be very rare. In the great majority of cases to which the doctrine is applicable it applies because the testator

[29] *Powers*, 7th ed., vol. II, pp. 144-5.

[30] (1795), 2 Ves. Jun. 544, 560.

[31] (1821), Jac. 317.

[32] *Re Vardon's Trusts* (1885), 31 Ch.D. 275 (C.A.); *Re Lord Chesham* (1886), 31 Ch.D. 466; *Re Allen's Estate*, [1945] 2 All E.R. 264.

[33] *Re Mengel's Will Trusts*, [1962] Ch. 791, 796-7.

[34] [1958] Ch. 168 (C.A.).

has made a mistake. His intention is not in doubt, but he has mistakenly assumed an ability to do something which, in fact, he cannot do of his own volition. The doctrine has been said to relate to the material validity of the relevant will (see Williams on Executors and Administrators, 14th ed., p. 854). For myself I should prefer to say that it is a doctrine by which equity fastens on the conscience of the person who is put to his election and refuses to allow him to take the benefit of a disposition contained in the will, the validity of which is not in question, except upon certain conditions.

SCOPE OF THE MODERN DOCTRINE

The availability of the fund received from the donor for purposes of compensation used to cause some difficulty when the recipient was a married woman restrained from anticipation. In *Re Wheatley*,[35] A gave Blackacre, belonging to X, a married woman, to B, and he also gave £10,000 to trustees on trust to pay the income to X, with a restraint upon anticipation. The question was whether X was compelled to elect, or whether she might keep both Blackacre and the income from the £10,000. Chitty, J., held that the problem must be looked at on the assumption that the woman was going to take against the instrument. If she did, she clearly could not use the capital of the fund for purposes of compensation, since this would defeat the testator's intention, as expressed in the imposition of the restraint. Here, therefore, the implied intention of the testator, that there should be election, must give way to the expressed intention, contained in the imposition of the restraint, that no fund should be available for compensation. Accordingly, X could keep both Blackacre and the fund.

There was a certain amount of doubt about this, until the Court of Appeal, in *Re Vardon's Trusts*[36] held that Chitty, J.'s view was right. However, a further question arising out of the problem of election in respect of restraints upon anticipation still remained to be settled. The problem may be put in this way: Suppose a testator leaves legacies to his daughters, A and B, with a restraint on anticipation, and then, by the same will gives property belonging to A and B to X. Suppose also that both daughters are married at the time when the will is made, and that at the time of the testator's death, A is still married, but B is a widow. Clearly, A will be free from the necessity of election and can can keep both the legacy and her own property. But will B, now a widow, be required to elect? The answer will probably be, no, if the doctrine of presumed intent governs election, for the presumed intent

35 (1884), 27 Ch.D. 606.
36 (1885), 31 Ch.D. 275.

is that of the testator, and the operative time is when he made his will, not when it took effect. But the answer will be, yes, if election depends upon implied condition, for at the time of election, B is free to elect. This is the problem that Kekewich, J., thought he was deciding in *Haynes* v. *Foster*,[37] in favour of the theory of presumed intent.

In *Haynes* v. *Foster*,[37] a testator with land in Turkey devised it on trust for sale, the proceeds to be added to his residuary estate. This estate was to be given to his son, A, and his daughters, B and C, with a restraint upon anticipation. As far as the land in Turkey was concerned, such a disposition was invalid, for the proceeds of sale must be divided, one-half to go to the son, A, and one-quarter each to the daughters, B and C. Accordingly, the daughters would normally have to elect whether they will take against the will (under which they receive more than they would by the operation of Turkish law) or not for, by the will, the testator has given some of the son's property to each of the daughters. Both daughters were married when the will was made, but whereas B was still a wife when the testator died, C was a widow, so that the restraint was then inoperative. B was clearly under no obligation to elect, and the main question to be decided was therefore whether C was under such an obligation. Kekewich, J., held that election depended upon implied intention, and that the testator had shown such an intention when he made his will, by subjecting C's share to a restraint upon anticipation. Accordingly, C, too, was excused from the necessity of electing.

The case bristles with difficulties. Even overlooking the main question, that the case really turned upon the operation of Turkish law, and not upon the application of the doctrine of election, we are still left, *not* with a situation in which the testator gives his own property to A, and in the same instrument, gives A's property to B, but with one in which, in the same instrument, he gives his own property to A, B, and C in a manner not effective by the *lex situs*. The problem, therefore, is of the effect upon the dispositions in the will of another transaction altogether—viz. the operation of Turkish law upon the succession to the testator's property.

However, in *Re Tongue*,[38] Warrington, J., and in *Re Hargrove*,[39] Astbury, J., held that where a woman restrained from anticipation is a spinster or a widow when the instrument under which she has to elect comes into force, she must elect, since the property she receives can be then applied for purposes of compensation.

[37] [1901] 1 Ch. 361.
[38] [1915] 1 Ch. 390.
[39] [1915] 1 Ch. 398.

Since the Married Women (Restraint upon Anticipation) Act, 1949,[40] the particular form which the problem took in these cases will not arise in the future but the cases are still of value as having settled an important point of principle.

The question whether the property which the donor gives to the person otherwise under an obligation to elect is available for compensation may also arise in other situations. In *Re Lord Chesham*,[41] a father by his will gave chattels (which were settled by previous instruments, in strict settlement, to be enjoyed with the mansion house, and of which his eldest son was tenant for life), to trustees for his two younger sons. He also gave his residuary estate to his eldest son, but Chitty, J., held that the eldest son could take the residuary estate free from the necessity of compensating his brothers for the chattels they did not receive, for the eldest brother had only a life interest in the chattels, and had no power to transfer ownership of them to the trustees at all.

If the donee receives a protected life interest, and then the donor gives the donee's property to a third party in the same instrument, the donee will be able to keep both, since the protected life interest is not available for compensation.

It is also clear that where the donor gives A's property to B, but omits to give any of his own property to A, there is again no case for election. Such cases are not always clearly recognisable at first sight. In *Bristow* v. *Warde*,[42] a father had a special power of appointment in favour of his children. He appointed part to his children, and part to strangers. Lord Loughborough, L.C., held that the children might keep the property which the father had validly appointed to them, and further that they could also claim, as on default of appointment, that property which the father had improperly appointed to strangers; for no part of the father's property had been given to the children by the will. If, however, in similar circumstances, the father had given his own property to the children, a valid case for election would have arisen.[43]

There is, however, no case for election where a person, to whom a power of appointment has been given, validly appoints an object of the power, and then adds some condition (not warranted by the terms of the instrument creating the power) whereby the appointee must hold the property, or part of it, for other persons who are not objects of the power. Such a condition is void, and it is none the less void because

40 Ireland: Married Women's Status Act, 1957, Sect. 6 (Republic of Ireland); Married Women (Restraint upon Anticipation) Act (Northern Ireland), 1952.

41 (1886), 31 Ch.D. 466.

42 (1794), 2 Ves. Jun. 336.

43 *Whistler* v. *Webster* (1794), 2 Ves. Jun. 367; *Reid* v. *Reid* (1858), 25 Beav. 469.

the appointee would also be entitled in default of election or appointment and also receives other property under the will.[44] However, in *White* v. *White*,[45] a testator was given power under a settlement to appoint settled lands to children of his first marriage only. He appointed to a son of his first marriage, describing the property as his own, but with a charge in favour of his other children, including the children of his second marriage. He also gave other property of his own to the same son, with similar charges in favour of his other children " so as to equalise the shares of all his children in all his property." Fry, J., held that there was enough to indicate that the son should be put to his election.

There cannot be an election where the exercise of a power of appointment has violated the rule against perpetuities. Where the appointor appoints to a person outside the perpetuity period, and then gives property of his own to the persons entitled in default of appointment, the appointment is regarded as a nullity, and the persons entitled in default of appointment will be able to claim not only the benefits given them by the will but also the property which was subject to the power of appointment.[46]

For a case of election to arise, it is essential that the person giving his property to A, and A's property to B, should intend to dispose of both properties, and apparently it does not matter whether the donor actually had the doctrine of election in mind or not,[47] nor whether he knew that one property was not his own, nor whether he mistakenly supposed it to be his.[48] There must, however, be a clear intention to dispose of that which is not the property of the donor, and if that intention is not shown, there is no case for election. In *Box* v. *Barrett*,[49] X was entitled to a life interest under a settlement, and subject to that, his four daughters, A, B, C, and D were entitled. By his will, X stated that since A and B were entitled under the settlement, he was not giving them so much property as he otherwise would have done. He then gave much larger benefits to C and D. Lord Romilly, M.R., held that C and D could keep both the benefits under the settlement and the larger benefits under the will.

Where the donor gives property which belongs, not only to the recipient of his own property, but to the donor himself also, difficulties some-

44 *Woolridge* v. *Woolridge* (1859), John. 63.

45 (1882), 22 Ch. D. 555.

46 *Re Nash*, [1910] 1 Ch. 1 (C.A.), overruling *Re Bradshaw*, [1902] 1 Ch. 436. Ireland: *Re Handcock's Trusts* (1889), 23 L.R. Ir. 34 (C.A.).

47 *Per* Lord Cairns, L.C., in *Cooper* v. *Cooper* (1874), L.R. 7. H.L. 53, 67.

48 *Whistler* v. *Webster* (1794), 2 Ves. Jun. 367.

49 (1866), L.R. 3 Eq. 244.

times arise in considering whether there is a case for election or not, and the rule which has been adopted is that, wherever possible, the donor must be deemed to have given only that which was his own.[50] If the donor, however, uses words which relate unambiguously to the whole of the property, then if the owner of the other part of the property has also received by the same instrument other property, a case for election has arisen.[51]

Where an infant is called upon to elect, the election will, if possible, be deferred until he comes of age. In *Streatfield* v. *Streatfield*,[52] the infant was given six months after he came of age in which to elect. In other cases, an inquiry into what is most beneficial for the infant will be directed, and the court may, if necessary, elect for him.[53] The committee of a lunatic so found was held able to elect on his behalf, under the direction of the court,[54] although the court could direct that the election be postponed, so that the lunatic's personal representatives may elect after his death.[55]

When the person entitled dies before electing, the person on whom the property devolves must then elect, and if it devolves on several persons, then each has a right of election.[56]

Where a person is called upon to elect, he is entitled to know the relative values of the properties affected, so that if a person elects under the mistaken view that it will not be binding on him, he is entitled to have it set aside, and to make a fresh election after the true values of the properties have been assessed.[57] In *Sweetman* v. *Sweetman*,[58] in Ireland, Chatterton, V.-C., considered the circumstances in which a valid election could take place—

> The requisities for holding a party bound by an election as concluded are, I think, these:—first, he must have a knowledge of his rights, that is to say, he must know that the property, which the testator attempted to give to another person, was not the testator's property, and that it would, upon the testator's decease, become, independently of the testator's will, the property of the party called upon to elect.

[50] *Maddison* v. *Chapman* (1861), 1 J. & H. 470; *Wintour* v. *Clifton* (1856), 8 De G. M. & G. 641.

[51] *Padbury* v. *Clark* (1850), 2 Mac. & G. 298; *Wintour* v. *Clifton, supra.*

[52] (1736), Cas. t. Talb. 176.

[53] *Seton* v. *Smith* (1840), 11 Sim. 59.

[54] *Re Earl of Sefton*, [1898] 2 Ch. 378 (C.A.).

[55] *Re Hewson* (1854), 23 L.J. Ch. 256 (C.A. Ch.).

[56] *Cooper* v. *Cooper* (1874), L.R. 7 H.L. 53.

[57] *Dillon* v. *Parker* (1818), 1 Swanst. 359, 381, *per* Plumer, M.R.

[58] (1868), I.R. 2 Eq. 141, 152-3.

It must be known by him, as a matter of fact, that the testator had not the power to give the property which he purported to devise, and that it belongs, not by the will, but by an earlier title, to the person who is called upon to elect. Next, he must know the relative values of the properties between which he is called upon to elect; and further, he must know, as a matter of fact, and not as a presumption of law, that the rule of equity exists, that he cannot, under such circumstances, take both estates, but must make an election between the two. And, further, the Court must be satisfied that he made a deliberate choice with the intention of making it. That is perfectly ascertained law; and I need not go beyond the case of *Spread* v. *Morgan*[59] for authority, as every one of these propositions was there laid down by the House of Lords.

But when I say that these propositions must be established to the satisfaction of the Court, I do not mean to say that there must be in every case actual, direct evidence of the existence of them. From a long course of dealing, from a series of acts, the Court is at liberty, as an inference of fact, to conclude that the party called upon to elect knew his rights, knew the value of both estates, and knew the rule of equity, that he was bound to elect, and had, with that full knowledge, made his choice, with the intention of making it, and of electing between the two estates. To justify the Court, however, in arriving at that conclusion, there must be a series of acts or dealings, consistent only with the knowledge which I have already mentioned, and with the deliberate intention to elect; or, at least, a series of acts or dealings that preponderates so strongly in the mind of the Court, that no person could come reasonably to any other conclusion; and the *onus* of proof must rest always upon the party who alleges that the knowledge existed, and that the deliberate choice was made.

If, however, a time is set for election, and the person entitled does not elect within that time, he is deemed to have elected against the instrument.

Election may, of course, be by an unequivocal act, following a proper inquiry, but it is clear that it may be accomplished by something less than this, provided that the party is aware of his rights. No strict rule can be laid down as to what amounts to a sufficient act indicating election, for it clearly depends upon the circumstances of each case, and the nature of the property. Mere lapse of time, resulting in the person entitled to elect remaining in the possession of that property of his own which is given in the instrument to someone else is usually not

59 (1865), 11 H.L.C. 588 (from Ireland).

sufficient evidence of an intention to take against the instrument, where no time for election is specified, so that three and five years' enjoyment have been held insufficient.[60] On the other hand, enjoyment of the property for a considerable period may be sufficient to incline the court to the view that the time for election has passed.[61] It does not necessarily follow, because the person who was called upon to elect has not done so during his lifetime, that the right to elect has gone, for the person receiving the properties affected will in turn be entitled to elect,[62] and if they have passed into different hands, then it is presumed that election is *against* the instrument, so that the property given under the original instrument will pass subject to the liability to compensate.[63] For example, suppose A by will gives £5000 of his own to B, and B's picture to C. Suppose that B fails to elect, and by his will gives the £5000 received from A to X, and the picture to Y, but of the £5000 which X receives, X will have to pay C the value of the picture, whilst Y will receive the picture without any liability to pay anything to X.

Two modern cases excellently illustrate the operation of the doctrine of election. In *Re Edwards*,[64] Mrs. Edwards, by her will, dated 8th February 1952, directed that No. 78 Albion Road, Hounslow, together with the remainder of her real and personal property, should be divided among seven named beneficiaries, including her sister Elsie Mary Wright. In May 1952, the testatrix and Elsie Wright orally agreed that in consideration of Elsie Wright coming to reside with the testatrix and performing certain household duties, the testatrix would devise No. 78 Albion Road to her. On 1st June 1952, Elsie Wright came to live with the testatrix, who died on 30th July 1952. Following an order of Danckwerts, J., No. 78 Albion Road was conveyed to Elsie Wright and the executor of Mrs. Edwards' will then raised the question whether Elsie Wright was bound to elect between the one-seventh share of the house and the residue of the estate, bequeathed by the will, and the house, or whether she could take both. The Court of Appeal held that Elsie Wright could take both. The gift of the house to Elsie Wright in the testatrix's lifetime adeemed the specific devise of it in the will. There was therefore no case for election.

In *Re Dicey*[65] a testatrix devised to her grandson, James Julian, by a will made in 1950, " my two freehold houses in Beresford Road." She

[60] *Wake* v. *Wake* (1791), 1 Ves. Jun. 335; *Reynard* v. *Spence* (1841), 4 Beav. 103. In *Sopwith* v. *Maughan* (1861), 30 Beav. 235, sixteen years was held to be not too long.

[61] *Tibbits* v. *Tibbits* (1816), 19 Ves. 656.

[62] *Cooper* v. *Cooper* (1874), L.R. 7 H.L. 53.

[63] See *Pickersgill* v. *Rodger* (1876), 5 Ch.D. 163.

[64] [1958] Ch. 168.

[65] [1957] Ch. 145.

then gave another freehold house in Beresford Road, and the residue of her estate, to her son, Charles Dicey. In fact, the testatrix had no disposable interest in the two houses in Beresford Road, which she occupied under a deed of family arrangement, by which, on her death in 1954, Charles Dicey became entitled to a half share of the beneficial interest in the two houses, the other share being divided equally between James Julian and his brother, Charles Julian.

James Julian claimed that Charles Dicey must elect in terms of the will, in which case he would surrender to him Charles' interest in the houses, or else he must compensate James Julian to the extent of the value of Charles' interest in the two houses, which Charles failed to surrender. To this Charles Dicey replied that he was unable to give effect to the devise, since a quarter share belonged to Charles Julian. The Court of Appeal held that there was a case for election and, if Charles Dicey elected to take under the will, his obligation was to make the disposition of his interest effective in so far as he was able to do so.[66]

It was pointed out at the beginning of this chapter that, in strictness, the doctrine of election applies only where A gives his own property to X, and some of X's property to Y. The principle has, in several cases, been extended beyond its original limits, however, and some illustrations will show the manner in which these extensions have occurred.

(1) Suppose X, a person subject to a disability, in pursuance of an ante-nuptial agreement makes a settlement on the occasion of his or her marriage, in favour of the other party to the marriage and the children thereof. Suppose also the other party does the same, conferring benefits on X. The person subject to the disability cannot avoid his or her settlement and at the same time claim benefits under the settlement, provided by the other party. X cannot " blow hot and cold," or approbate and reprobate. He or she must accept either the settlement as a whole, or renounce all benefits under it.[67] Such cases usually arose in respect of settlements made by married women during coverture, when coverture was a disability, and thus could not arise to-day.

(2) In *Re Macartney*,[68] the testator bequeathed £3000 stock to his daughter, Maggie Macartney. He also gave his shares in the X com-

[66] For Irish illustrations, see *Sadlier* v. *Butler* (1867), I.R. 1 Eq. 415; *Lewis* v. *Lewis* (1876), I.R. 11 Eq. 340 (C.A. Ch.); *Coote* v. *Gordon* (1877), I.R. 11 Eq. 279 (C.A. Ch.); *Re Woodleys* (1892), 29 L.R. Ir. 304 (C.A.); *Re Sullivan*, [1917] 1 I.R. 38 (C.A.); *Re Saul's Trust*, [1951] Ir. Jur. Rep. 34.

[67] *Greenhill* v. *North British and Mercantile Insurance Co.*, [1893] 3 Ch. 474; *Re Hodson*, [1894] 2 Ch. 421.

[68] [1918] 1 Ch. 300.

pany to his seven children, including Maggie. The testator owned 95 per cent of the shares of the X company, and the X company held 90 per cent of the shares of the Y company. In fact, the testator held the £3000 stock simply as trustee for the Y company, and as a result, the shares of the Y company were of increased value. Accordingly the shares of the X company were also of greater value and, as these were bequeathed to the seven children, Neville, J., held that the seven children, including Maggie herself, must make compensation to Maggie for the £3000 stock which she had not received. One difficulty in this case is in identifying the £3000 stock with the shares of the seven children, the existence of the two companies being apparently ignored for this purpose, and the £3000 being treated as belonging to the seven children. Another difficulty is that, even ignoring these circumstances, Macartney would appear to have disposed of the same asset twice, in separate clauses of his will. The title of Maggie to the stock, and the title of all the children to the testator's property, both arose under the will; but for a case of election to arise, the property in respect of which compensation must be given, if the person called upon to elect retains it, must be enjoyed by a title arising outside the will.

(3) In *Re Allen's Estate*,[69] a testator, domiciled in South Africa, made a will appointing an English solicitor to be one of his trustees, and disposing of " all my personal chattels as defined by the Administration of Estates Act, 1925, s. 55 " to his wife. He also gave " the residue of his property " on trust for sale and to hold the proceeds for his wife for life, with remainder over. Most of the property comprised in the testator's estate was in England. On these facts, Cohen, J., held that the ordinary rule that the will was to be construed according to the law of the domicile did not apply. The will was to be construed according to English law, as the testator had given clear indication of his intention that English law should govern the construction. However, the testator's widow being domiciled in South Africia, under South African substantive law she was entitled under the doctrine of community of property to one-half of the proceeds of the estate. The question therefore arose whether she was entitled to one-half of the estate under South African law, together with the additional benefit under the will, or whether she was put to her election. Cohen, J., held that the widow was put to her election, as the testator in disposing of the residue, meant the whole of the residue (including the widow's interest in it) and not merely his one-half interest in it. Cohen, J., held that the widow was bound to elect between her rights under South African law relating to community of property and the benefits which

[69] [1945] 2 All E.R. 264.

she received under the will. This case has been strongly criticised by Morris,[70] on the ground that the doctrine of election is not a rule of construction, but a doctrine which affects the essential validity of the will, so that South African law should have applied. This was the view taken in *De Nicols* v. *Curlier*[71] (not cited in *Re Allen's Estate*), where the applicability of the doctrine of community of goods in French law was under consideration. It was also strongly criticised by Buckley, J., in *Re Mengel's Will Trusts*[72] where the learned judge pointed out that election does not depend upon the testator's intent, and therefore has nothing to do with the construction of the testator's will. He also pointed out that the cases of *Re Price*[73] and *Re Simpson*,[74] to which Cohen, J., referred, were not cases upon the doctrine of election, but they decided questions relating to the exercise of powers of appointment. *Re Allen's Estate* was, however, distinguishable, as in that case, the testator died domiciled in South Africa, whilst in *Re Mengel's Will Trusts*,[72] the testator died domiciled in England. In *Re Mengel's Will Trusts*[72] the testator was a Danish subject, who married a British subject in 1909. In 1921, he became a naturalised British subject, and at his death in 1960 he was domiciled in England. By his will, made in 1958, he bequeathed all his personal effects absolutely and the residue for life to his widow. Since community of goods existed under Danish law in consequence of the marriage in 1909, the question to be decided was whether the widow was bound to elect between the benefits which she received under the will, and the benefits to which she was entitled under the Danish law of community of goods. Buckley, J., held that the testator must have purported to dispose of the whole of the personal effects which would have belonged to him if such property had not been governed by the Danish law of community of property; and therefore, in respect of this property, the doctrine of election applied; but the clause in the will governing the residue must be construed in its literal sense, and therefore, it was not applicable to anything beyond the testator's own property. Accordingly the doctrine of election did not arise in respect of the property, and the testator was only disposing of what was in fact his own.

(4) In *Douglas-Menzies* v. *Umphelby*[75] a testator made two wills, disposing of properties in two different countries. The Privy Council held that they formed one testamentary disposition, and consequently,

[70] (1945), 10 *Conveyancer and Property Lawyer*, 102; Dicey, *Conflict of Laws*, 8th ed., pp. 610-11.
[71] [1900] A.C. 21 (H.L., E.).
[72] [1962] Ch. 791.
[73] [1900] 1 Ch. 442.
[74] [1916] 1 Ch. 502.
[75] [1908] A.C. 224 (P.C., New South Wales).

where a beneficiary elected against one will she could claim under the other only on terms that her interest under the second will should be used to compensate those disappointed by her election under the first. The two wills were therefore read as one for the purpose of election.

CHAPTER XIII

SATISFACTION AND PERFORMANCE

INTRODUCTION

THE essence of the equitable doctrine of satisfaction is that, A being under an obligation to give something to or to provide for B, A gives B *something else*, and the gift is thereupon presumed to be made with the intention of satisfying that prior obligation. This doctrine is obviously based upon the general equitable maxim that " Equity imputes an intention to fulfil an obligation."

(1) The principle of satisfaction has several applications. In the first place A may owe B £50. This debt is not paid by A in his lifetime, and by A's will, it is discovered that A has bequeathed a legacy to B. Is this legacy to be presumed to be given in satisfaction of the debt which A owes B, or can B claim both the debt and the legacy? The answer to this question involved a consideration of the principles governing the *satisfaction of debts by legacies.*

(2) Secondly, a parent may undertake to give one of his children a portion, or to make some other definite provision for him. In fact the father never does so, but on his death, it is found that the father's will includes a gift of a large legacy to that child. Is the obligation to provide a portion satisfied by the provision of a legacy ?

(3) The converse case to the preceding one arises where a father makes a will, and gives a legacy to a child, and then in his lifetime either gives or covenants to give that child a portion. The question for determination here is whether the child can claim both the legacy and the portion, or whether the legacy has been either wholly or partially satisfied by the portion. This doctrine is also frequently referred to as the *ademption of legacies by portions.*

(4) A fourth case, which is frequently grouped with the preceding three, but really rests upon slightly different principles, may for convenience also be considered here, so long as the differences in principle are appreciated. This is what is sometimes known as the doctrine of satisfaction of legacies by legacies—in reality, an illustration of the rules followed by courts of equity in construing wills.

Finally, there is another equitable doctrine very similar to that of satisfaction, and which in the early cases is often referred to as satisfaction, but which is distinct. This is the doctrine of performance. In cases of performance, a person has undertaken a binding obligation to do something—usually to transfer property. Later, he does some act which might be construed as fulfilment of that obligation, and the court must decide whether in fact it amounts to such a fulfilment. The differences between performance and satisfaction are considered more fully later in this chapter, but for the present it is sufficient to point out that in the first three cases of satisfaction (the fourth not being in strictness satisfaction at all) the court has to determine whether something not identical with that which is intended to be done can be regarded as substantially fulfilling an obligation; whilst in performance the court must decide whether substantially the actual thing to be done has in fact been done.

The doctrine of satisfaction seems to have been first elaborated at the beginning of the eighteenth century in the case of *Lady Herne* v. *Herne*.[1] In that case, a husband covenanted by marriage articles that his wife should have, at his death, in addition to her third, a legacy of £800 and certain chattels. It was also agreed that this should not exclude her from benefiting by any other gifts which the husband might confer on her " by will or writing." The husband bequeathed his wife a legacy of £1000 and Lord Cowper held that this must be taken in satisfaction of the legacy of £800, conferred by the marriage articles. The rule was immediately afterwards extended to the satisfaction of debts by legacies in *Talbott* v. *Duke of Shrewsbury*[2] and in *Chancey's Case*,[3] and by the middle of the century it was firmly established, notwithstanding some doubts regarding its value expressed by some equity judges. Indeed, in *Hinchcliffe* v. *Hinchcliffe*[4] Arden, M.R., pointed out that Lord Thurlow was of opinion that the rules of satisfaction relating to portions and legacies had been pressed too far, and on the satisfaction of debts by legacies, the learned Master of the Rolls said that " any little circumstances are laid hold by the Court " to take a case out of the rule.

Satisfaction of Debts by Legacies

The general principle in cases in which a debtor has left his creditor a legacy was agreed by Sir John Trevor, M.R., in *Talbott* v. *Duke of Shrewsbury*[5] to be—

1 (1706), 2 Vern. 555.
2 (1714), Prec. Ch. 394.
3 (1717), 1 P. Wms. 408.
4 (1797), 3 Ves. 516, 527, 529.
5 Prec. Ch. 394-5.

> . . . that if one, being indebted to another in a sum of money, does by his will give him as great, or greater sum of money than the debt amounts to, without taking any notice at all of the debt, that this shall nevertheless be in satisfaction of the debt, so as that he shall not have both the debt and legacy . . .

Thus, the rule is subject at the outset to two limitations: (*a*) the legacy must be equal to or exceed the debt; and (*b*) the testator must not, by his will, show an intention that the creditor should have both the debt and the legacy. All these doctrines considered in this chapter rest upon presumed intention, and therefore if the donor states what he really intends with regard to the two gifts, without ambiguity, no question of the application of any of them can arise.

An illustration of an intention rebutting the presumption of satisfaction is afforded by *Re Stibbe*.[6] By a settlement made in 1939, X (in fulfilment of a covenant made in 1922 on the occasion of his divorce) charged an annuity of £300 on certain property in favour of his first wife. The annuity was payable quarterly. By his will, made in August 1942, X bequeathed an annuity of £400 upon trust for his first wife. By a codicil, he directed his trustees to pay his first wife, as soon as possible after his death, the sum of £150 on account of her annuity of £400. On X's death, the question arose whether the annuity of £400 in the will satisfied the annuity of £300 created by the settlement of 1939. Romer, J., held that it did not. There were three indications in the will that no satisfaction was intended:

1. The settled annuity was payable quarterly, and the first instalment of the annuity by will was payable one year after the testator's death.

2. The settled annuity was secured, whilst the legacy by will was unsecured.

3. The direction in the will to pay debts showed that the annuity in the will was only to be paid after the debts, including the settled annuity, were paid.

Once the presumption has been established, however, its logical consequences are admitted. In *Re Fletcher*,[7] a husband owed his wife £625. He then made a will bequeathing her £625, and later paid the debt. The court held that she was not entitled to the legacy, as it was

[6] (1946), 175 L.T. 198. See also *Re Van den Bergh's Will Trusts*, [1948] 1 All E.R. 935. Ireland: *Re Keogh's Estate* (1889), 23 L.R. Ir. 257. See also *Re Russell's Estate* (1887), 19 L.R.Ir. 418.

[7] (1888), 38 Ch.D. 373.

given simply in satisfaction of an obligation which had been discharged. The identity of the amount made it clear that the legacy was given for a specific purpose.[8]

Although the rule is based upon the theory of presumed intention, it is clear that a strict application of it would in many cases defeat the testator's real intention; and therefore, courts of equity in the eighteenth and nineteenth centuries limited its operation by many exceptions.

(1) If the debt exceeds the legacy in amount, it is held that there is no intention to satisfy, not even part of the debt, and therefore the creditor will be able to claim both debt and legacy.[9] In 1929, however, Talbot, J., held that a debt of £100, carrying 5 per cent interest, which interest was in arrear at the testator's death, was satisfied by a legacy of £100.[10]

(2) The presumption will not operate where the will precedes the debt, or even where the will is made at the same time as the debt was contracted. In both cases it is assumed that the testator would not have intended to fulfil an obligation which did not then exist.[11]

(3) There is no presumption where the gift by will and the debt are different in nature, so that a gift of land by will will not be a satisfaction of a debt of a sum of money,[12] and a legacy of a specific chattel will not satisfy a debt, unless the testator intends this, and the creditor accepts it;[13] nor will a legacy satisfy a negotiable instrument (which may have been transferred to a third party).[14]

(4) It is essential for the presumption to operate that the legacy must be as immediately beneficial as payment of the debt would be. If the legacy is contingent or uncertain in amount (as in a gift of the residue, or a share of it), the creditor can claim both.[15] In *Re Horlock*,[16] the entire principle was in danger of abolition through the invocation of this rule, for Stirling, J., held in that case that since a payment of a legacy cannot in general be enforced by the legatee until

8 Cf. *Re Pollock* (1885), 28 Ch.D. 552 (C.A.), pp. 424-5, *post*.

9 *Atkinson* v. *Webb* (1704), 2 Vern. 478.

10 *Fitzgerald* v. *National Bank Ltd*., [1929] 1 K.B. 394. Presumably the interest was recoverable separately, but the report does not say so.

11 *Cranmer's Case* (1701), 2 Salk. 508; *Horlock* v. *Wiggins* (1888), 39 Ch. D. 142 (C.A.); *Crichton* v. *Crichton*, [1896] 1 Ch. 870 (C.A.).

12 *Eastwood* v. *Vinke* (1731), 2 P. Wms. 613. Ireland: *Re Keogh's Estate* (1889), 23 L.R. Ir. 257.

13 *Byde* v. *Byde* (1761), 1 Cox C.C. 44, 49.

14 *Carr* v. *Eastabrooke* (1797), 3 Ves. 561.

15 *Crompton* v. *Sale* (1729), 2 P. Wms. 553; *Barret* v. *Beckford*, (1750), 1 Ves. Sen. 519. See also *Talbott* v. *Duke of Shrewsbury* (1714), Prec. Ch. 394.

16 [1895] 1 Ch. 516.

the expiration of the executor's year, whilst the debt is immediately recoverable, a legacy could not usually be as beneficial as the debt, and on this ground he held that there was no satisfaction of a debt expressed to be payable within three months of the testator's death. In *Re Rattenberry*,[17] however, Swinfen Eady, J., held that since the legacy carried interest from the date of death, it was as beneficial as the debt, and therefore the presumption would apply, if there were no other circumstances impairing equality of the obligations; and this seems now to be regarded as the better view.[18]

(5) It may sometimes occur that the debt itself is uncertain in amount, and the legacy certain, as where the debt is due on current account, and here there will be no satisfaction,[19] although the mere fact that the debt is liable to decrease through recall of sums from time to time by the creditor is not sufficient to rebut the presumption.[20] Moreover, the person to whom the debt is payable may be uncertain, as where it is due on a negotiable instrument, and here again there will be no satisfaction.[21] An unsatisfactory Irish case is *Ellard* v. *Phelan*,[22] where legacies to servants were held to satisfy amounts due to them in respect of wages although, presumably, the debts were of a kind that fluctuated in amount.

(6) The whole doctrine of satisfaction of debts by legacies, it may be repeated, is based upon the presumed intention of the testator, and therefore it is always open to him to exclude its operation by declaring that both the debt and the legacy shall be payable. In *Chancey's Case*,[23] advantage was taken of this principle to exclude the presumption of satisfaction in those cases where the testator expressly directed that his *debts and legacies* should be payable, and this rule has been followed in many later cases. For some time, however, the same rule did not apply where the testator simply directed his executors to pay his debts,[24] but in *Horlock* v. *Wiggins*[25] the Court of Appeal decided that such a direction was sufficient to exclude satisfaction, and this view seems to have met with general approval. On the other hand, it is

[17] [1906] 1 Ch. 667.
[18] See *Fitzgerald* v. *National Bank Ltd.*, [1929] 1 K.B. 394, p. 415, *ante*.
[19] *Rawlins* v. *Powel* (1715), 1 P. Wms. 297.
[20] *Edmunds* v. *Low* (1857), 3 K. & J. 318.
[21] *Carr* v. *Eastabrooke* (1797), 3 Ves. 561.
[22] [1914] 1 I.R. 76.
[23] (1717), 1 P. Wms. 408.
[24] E.g. *Edmunds* v. *Low* (1857), 3 K. & J. 318.
[25] (1888), 39 Ch.D. 142. See also *Re Manners*, [1949] Ch. 613 (C.A.); *Lahay* v. *Brown* (1957), 8 D.L.R. (2d) 728 (Ontario C.A.).

doubtful whether the presumption will ever be rebutted in the absence of a direction of some sort to pay debts. No such direction was given in *Re Haves*,[26] and the presumption of satisfaction applied.

The presumption being one of law, rules of construction would normally admit extrinsic evidence of intention to rebut it, although, of course, no extrinsic evidence is admissible to contradict an intention appearing on the face of the will. Whilst in *Plunkett* v. *Lewis*[27] extrinsic evidence was admitted to rebut the presumption, the high authority of Lord Talbot and Sir Edward Sugden would seem to be opposed to it.[28]

Satisfaction of Portion-debts by Legacies

This branch of the doctrine of satisfaction has a more restricted operation than the one just considered, for it applies only between a father, or some other person in loco parentis, and those in favour of whom parental obligations exist. Here the general principle is that, wherever a father or person standing in loco parentis to another has undertaken to give a portion, either on marriage or upon some other occasion, and then (not having carried out his promise) gives a legacy to the child in whose favour the obligation was made, there is a presumption that the legacy was given in satisfaction of the obligation to give a portion. This rule is based not only on the general maxim that " Equity imputes an intent to fulfil an obligation," but also upon the further equitable principle that " Equity leans against double portions," a strong presumption which will explain some of the differences in application between this rule and the preceding one. This leaning of the court seems to have had its origin in the favour shown to the heir in equity, as well as at law.[29] In the Irish case of *Re Battersby's Estate*,[30] Monroe, J., said—

> The question whether a portion given by a settlement is satisfied by a legacy in a subsequent will is entirely one of intention to be gathered in the absence of other evidence, from the terms of the two instruments, subject to this consideration, that the presumption of law is against double portions. If the provision made by the latter instrument is equal to or greater than that made by the earlier one,[31]

[26] [1951] 2 T.L.R. 892.

[27] (1844), 3 Hare 316.

[28] *Fowler* v. *Fowler* (1735), 3 P. Wms. 353; *Hall* v. *Hill* (1841), 1 Dr. & War. 94.

[29] Spence, *Equitable Jurisdiction*, vol. II, p. 427.

[30] (1887), 19 L.R.Ir. 359, 363-4. See also *Sealey* v. *Stawell* (1875), I.R. 9 Eq. 499.

[31] There will be satisfaction *pro tanto* by a legacy of a less sum than the portion: see p. 419, *post*.

and the limitations are substantially the same, double portions will not be allowed; the parties entitled will be put to their election. If the limitations are widely different, the presumption is that the provisions were to be cumulative.[32]

The term " portion " is one which has been very often considered by courts of equity, although an exhaustive definition presents difficulties. It may be regarded as a substantial provision for a child, with the object of establishing that child in life, as distinct from a casual payment.[33]

In *Re Lacon*,[34] Bowen, L.J., said—

. . .in order to establish a case for the application of this rule as to double portions, there must be two matters, I think, made out, and it will be seen upon reflection that there are two presumptions really which are to be considered, and not one. In the first place, both of the suggested gifts or donations must be gifts in the nature of a portion. The first presumption here comes under discussion: it is said that, whatever gifts are made by the father, which it may be supposed will have to be distributed among the children, or which are given by the father to one child with a view to establishing him in life, are presumed to be portions within the meaning of the rule. We have, therefore, to ask ourselves, in the first place, were these two shares which were received during the lifetime of the father received under such circumstances as to justify their being treated and considered as a portion? But, supposing both gifts are gifts in the nature of portions, then comes a further question, for the solution of which a further presumption is invoked. That question is, whether it was intended that the former gift or portion should take the place of an advancement of the gift which is given by the will, and there the second presumption which is invoked has to be dealt with—a presumption to the effect that the former gift, the gift *inter vivos*, was intended as an advancement *pro tanto* of the gift under the bequest—a presumption, it is said, which ought to be made in favour of equality amongst children, it being the view of the law that equality is what the father, in dealing with his children, would, in most cases, presumably intend.

32 See *Re Gleeson*, [1911] 1 I.R. 113; p. 420, *post*.

33 *Taylor* v. *Taylor* (1875), L.R. 20 Eq. 155; *Re Lacon*, [1891] 2 Ch. 482 (C.A.); *Re Scott*, [1903] 1 Ch. 1 (C.A.); *Re Livesey*, [1953] 1 W.L.R. 1114; *Re Hayward*, [1957] Ch. 528 (C.A.).

34 [1891] 2 Ch. 482, 497-8 (C.A.).

Bowen, L.J., is here dealing with the situation which arises where a will is made by a father, and the testator subsequently makes a gift to that child in his lifetime; but the same processes of reasoning are applicable to both types of case.

In *Re Vaux*,[35] Green, M.R., said—

> The rule against double portions rests upon two hypotheses: first of all, that under the will the testator has provided a portion and, secondly, that by the gift inter vivos which is said to operate in ademption of that portion either wholly or pro tanto, he has again conferred a portion. . . . When the word " portion " is used in reference to the gift inter vivos, it has a qualitative significance, in this sense, that it is not every gift inter vivos that will cause the rule to come into operation. If a testator gives to a child as pure bounty and by way merely of a present a sum of money, that will not have the character to cause the rule to come into operation. Similarly . . . [the testator] . . . may wish to free him from some embarrassment, or something of that kind. In cases of that sort upon the facts a gift may not be a portion at all, in which case, of course, the rule does not apply.

Where both father and mother are living, and the mother agrees to make a gift to the child, this will not prima facie be regarded as a portion, since the obligation to provide is one imposed primarily upon the father. It is, however, open to the person alleging it to prove affirmatively that the mother was in loco parentis.[36] By this phrase, it is meant that a person not the father has undertaken to provide for the child. Such an undertaking to provide may exist where the father is alive, and the child lives with him.[37]

If the father, or person standing in loco parentis, gives a legacy equal to or greater than the intended portion, there is a presumption that the portion is entirely satisfied. If the legacy is less than the portion, there is a presumption of satisfaction pro tanto.[38] If, however, the gift by will is to a stranger, and the donor (not being in loco parentis) has in his lifetime agreed to give or settle property on the legatee, there is not, in any circumstances, satisfaction, at any rate under this head, so that the stranger may claim both. A grandchild or an illegitimate child is a stranger, unless the donor has put himself in loco parentis.[39]

[35] [1939] Ch. 465, 481-2 (C.A.).
[36] *Re Ashton*, [1897] 2 Ch. 574.
[37] *Powys* v. *Mansfield* (1837), 3 My. & Cr. 359.
[38] *Warren* v. *Warren* (1783), 1 Bro. C.C. 305.
[39] *Re Dawson*, [1919] 1 Ch. 102; *Ex parte Pye* (1811), 18 Ves. 140.

In most cases today this will be determined by establishing whether the person making the provision has legally adopted the person to whom the portion is given.

The doctrine will not apply where the father actually gives property by way of portion to a child, and then makes a will giving that child a legacy, for here the logical conclusion to draw from the facts is that the father intended the child to take both. However, the position is different where the father makes the will first giving the child a legacy, then gives the child a portion.[40]

Slight differences in the nature of the two gifts will not be sufficient to rebut the presumption, although substantial differences will. The presumption against double portions will not prevail where the testamentary portion and the subsequent advancement are not ejusdem generis.[41] Such differences, however, will necessarily relate to the nature of the property or to the mode of user or payment, and not to the amount, which affects only the question whether the portion has been wholly or partially satisfied. In *Lord Chichester* v. *Coventry*,[42] Lord Romilly pointed out that if a father covenanted to settle £10,000 on his daughter for her life, remainder to the children of the marriage, this would be satisfied, as far as the daughter was concerned, by a legacy of £10,000, although this would not affect the interests of the children of the marriage. If the settlement in the father's lifetime gives the son an absolute life interest, and the will gives him a protected life interest, the presumption will arise,[43] and there are many other decisions which illustrate that none but substantial variations between the will and settlement on the child will be allowed to rebut the presumption,[44] as, for example, the fact that the settlement provides for a well-secured gift, while the legacy is hazardous and likely to fluctuate.[45] If the portion is vested and the legacy contingent, the presumption will not arise.[46] Where the portion is of land, and the legacy of money, or vice versa, there is no presumption, this being regarded as sufficiently negatived by the difference in the nature of property.[47] However,

40 See the next section of this chapter.

41 *Re Jaques*, [1903] 1 Ch. 267 (C.A.).

42 (1867) L.R. 2 H.L. 71, 90. See also *Re Blundell*, [1906] 2 Ch. 222.

43 *Russell* v. *St. Aubyn* (1876), 2 Ch.D. 398.

44 *Hinchcliffe* v. *Hinchcliffe* (1797), 3 Ves. 516; *Lady Thynne* v. *Earl of Glengall* (1848), 2 H.L.C. 131; *Weall* v. *Rice* (1831), 2 Russ. & M. 251.

45 *Re Gleeson*, [1911] 1 I.R. 113. Another example, now obsolete, was the settlement providing for a daughter to enjoy property absolutely, while the will gave it to her with a restraint upon anticipation. See *Weall* v. *Rice* (1831), 2 Russ. & M. 251.

46 *Hanbury* v. *Hanbury* (1788), 2 Bro. C.C. 352; (1789), 2 Bro. C.C. 529.

47 *Bellasis* v. *Uthwatt* (1737), 1 Atk. 426; *Grave* v. *Earl of Salisbury* (1784), 1 Bro. C.C. 425.

one form of personalty may be satisfaction for another. In *Bengough* v. *Walker*[48] a share in a powder works, to be made up in value to £10,000 charged with an annuity for life to another person, was held to be satisfaction of a portion of £2000.

Sometimes a settlement states that a gift by a father to his child in his lifetime shall be considered a satisfaction of an obligation to give a portion. If this is so, there is no satisfaction if he leaves the child a legacy,[49] or if the child becomes entitled to a share of the father's estate on intestacy,[50] although the presumption will arise if the father's undertaking is to give a portion during his lifetime, or at the time of his death.[51]

As this presumption is also one of law, and rebuttable, evidence of a different intention on the part of the testator, derived from contemporary declarations, is admissible to negative it.[52] In such circumstances, further evidence may then be brought to restore the presumption. In *Lord Chichester* v. *Coventry*,[53] it was pointed out by Lord Cranworth that if the will is made first, giving the legacy, and then the obligation to give a portion arises, the presumption is that the testator intends the portion to be in lieu of what he has given by will. If, however, the donor enters into an undertaking to give, and then makes a will, he is in effect saying: "I give this in lieu of what I am already bound to give, if those to whom I am so bound will accept it." The second assumption may be rebutted by much less evidence than the first.

Where a parent makes a provision by way of advancement for a child, and *then* makes a will giving that child a legacy, so that a presumption of satisfaction arises, the child may choose whether he will insist upon his rights under the obligation arising in the testator's lifetime or accept what is given in the will in satisfaction, or in part satisfaction, of his rights under the settlement, to that extent renouncing them. Thus, he is called upon to elect. If the father agrees to give him £15,000 by way of advancement, and he receives £20,000 by legacy, he may insist on the advancement, and receive only £5000 under the will, or he may accept the legacy, and renounce his rights under the settlement altogether.[54] Such an election can only affect

48 (1808), 15 Ves. 507.
49 *Cooper* v. *Cooper* (1873), L.R. 8 Ch. App. 813.
50 *Twisden* v. *Twisden* (1804), 9 Ves. 413.
51 *Rickman* v. *Morgan* (1779), 1 Bro. C.C. 63; (1788), 2 Bro. C.C. 394.
52 *Ford* v. *Tynte* (1864), 2 H. & M. 319, 324.
53 (1867), L.R. 2 H.L. 71, 87.
54 *Lord Chichester* v. *Coventry* (1867), L.R. 2 H.L. 71, 87.

the rights of the person electing, and not those of others, e.g. the children of the elector, and no case for election arises where the will comes first, for the subsequent advancement is regarded as a revocation of the will to that extent.

Satisfaction (or Ademption) of Legacies by Portions

This is the complementary rule to the one just considered, and operates within substantially similar limits. The principle was stated by Lord Eldon in *Ex parte Pye*[55] as follows—

> . . . where a father gives a legacy to a child, the legacy coming from a father to his child, must be understood as a portion, though it it not so described in the Will; and afterwards advancing a portion for that child, though there may be slight circumstances of difference between that advance and the portion, and a difference in amount, yet the father will be intended to have the same purpose in each instance; and the advance is therefore, an ademption of the legacy; but a stranger, giving a legacy, is understood as giving a bounty, not as paying a debt: he must therefore be proved to mean it as a portion, or provision, either upon the face of the Will, or, if it may be, and it seems that it may, by evidence, applying directly to the gift, proposed by that Will . . .

The rule, like the preceding one, relates only to gifts by a father or person in loco parentis to the child in respect of whom the obligation is deemed to exist. If a father in a will gives legacies of £10,000 each to his son X, and his nephew Y, to each of whom he subsequently gives in his lifetime £15,000, then, on the testator's death, X's legacy will be regarded as having been adeemed, but Y will be able to claim the whole of his—a result which can hardly be regarded as ideal. It has been decided, however, that a stranger cannot profit by the ademption of a child's legacy by a portion. Thus, if a testator divides his residuary estate between his two children, A and B, and a stranger, and then gives portions to a child, A, and to the stranger, A's third share of the residue will be wholly or party adeemed, but the stranger will receive simply his third share. The portion given to A will be added to the remaining two-thirds of residue and divided equally between the children.[56]

[55] (1811), 18 Ves. 140, 153-4. Ireland: see the statement of the principle by Sullivan, M.R., in *Curtin* v. *Evans* (1872), I.R. 9 Eq. 553, 557-8; *Edgeworth* v. *Johnston* (1877), I.R. 11 Eq. 326. Cf. *Re Bannon* (No. 2), [1934] I.R. 701 (Sup. Ct.).

[56] *Re Heather*, [1906] 2 Ch. 230.

There will be no ademption of a legacy by a subsequent portion, however, if it appears from all the circumstances that the testator intended the child to take both[57] and parol evidence is admissible to rebut or confirm the fact that the testator has a different intention, i.e. that he intended both gifts.[58]

Under this doctrine, a legacy can be adeemed entirely by a portion or advance of equal or greater amount, and is adeemed pro tanto by an advance of lesser amount. However, it is clear that the gift made in the lifetime of the father must be substantial, and must be made with the object of setting up the child in life. Small sums will not be added for the purpose of creating an advancement.[59]

In *Re George's Will Trusts*,[60] the testator, a farmer, had two sons, one of whom assisted him in working two farms. He left his residuary estate to his two sons, but after making his will, he gave to the son who assisted him the live and dead stock on the farm, a valuation being made, following which he let both farms to the same son at a fair rent. Jenkins, J., held this gift to be a portion, which must be set off against the gift in the will.

As in the case of the satisfaction of portions by legacies, the presumption of ademption of legacies by portions is not affected by slight differences in the nature of the gift, e.g. slight differences in the limitations attaching to the two gifts.[61] Where, however, the legacy was of money and the gift was of stock-in-trade, it was held that the presumption did not arise,[62] although it would appear that where the legacy is of money, and the advance is of other personalty, assessed in money, the presumption operates.[63]

The presumption depends upon the presumed intention of the parties, and accordingly, if the donor indicates that the presumption is to be excluded, then the presumption will not be applicable. In *Earl of Durham* v. *Wharton*,[64] W.L. by a will made in 1772 charged a legacy of £5,000 in favour of his niece S.M.A.L. on his freehold lands, which he then devised to his brother J.L. W.L. died in 1774 and J.L. succeeded him. The latter, by a will of 1788, gave his daughter S.M.A.L. £10,000, half to be paid to S.M.A.L. within three years of his death,

57 *Re Vaux*, [1939] Ch. 465 (C.A.).

58 *Re Shields*, [1912] 1 Ch. 591.

59 *Suisse* v. *Lord Lowther* (1843), 2 Hare 424.

60 [1949] Ch. 154.

61 *Sheffield* v. *Earl of Coventry* (1833), 2 Russ. & M. 317; *Re Furness*, [1901] 2 Ch. 346.

62 *Holmes* v. *Holmes* (1783), 1 Bro. C.C. 555.

63 *Re Lawes* (1881), 20 Ch. D. 81 (C.A.); *Re Jaques*, [1903] 1 Ch. 267 (C.A.).

64 (1836), 10 Bligh N.S. 526 (H.L., E.).

the other half within six years. The will provided that interest of 4 per cent should be paid to S.M.A.L. during her life, but the principal should be paid to such of her children as she should appoint. This legacy was stated to be additional to the legacy of £5,000 given to S.M.A.L. in W.L.'s will. On the marriage of S.M.A.L. about 1790, J.L. agreed to give the husband £15,000 as S.M.A.L.'s marriage portion, and this sum was stated to be in full satisfaction of all sums to which S.M.A.L. should be entitled under the will of her uncle W.L. The sum was paid in full in 1793 to trustees of S.M.A.L.'s marriage settlement. J.L. died in 1794, and later S.M.A.L. and her husband sued the Earl of Durham, who had become tenant in tail of the lands settled by the will of J.L. (which had been charged with the payment of the legacy of £10,000 in favour of S.M.A.L.), for the payment of this legacy of £10,000. The Vice-Chancellor decreed that the legacy would be paid, because the portion, unlike the legacy, was to be settled; and the Lord Chancellor upheld the decree. It was, however, reversed by the House of Lords, which held that the legacy had been adeemed and satisfied by the provision of a portion of £15,000 on S.M.A.L.'s marriage. In this case, the marriage portion had been given expressly in satisfaction of the legacy in W.L.'s will, by J.L. who was then bound to pay it.

The presumption does not arise at all where the father pays a sum of money to the child before the will is made, for at the date of the gift there was obviously nothing to adeem,[65] and the child will receive the subsequent legacy in full.

The doctrine under consideration generally operates only where the person making the two types of gift is a father or person in loco parentis. If, however, a stranger gives a legacy to X, and it is expressed to be for a particular purpose, and he then gives a similar sum in his lifetime, the gift being expressed to be for the same purpose, this is regarded as an ademption of the legacy. In *Re Pollock*,[66] Lord Selbourne, L.C., said—

> To constitute a particular purpose within the meaning of that doctrine it is not, in my opinion, necessary that some special use or application of the money, by or on behalf of the legatee (*e.g.* for binding him an apprentice, purchasing for him a house, advancing him upon marriage, or the like), should be in the testator's view. It is not less a purpose, as distinguished from a mere motive of spontaneous bounty, if the bequest is expressed to be made in fulfilment of some moral obligation recognised by the testator, and

[65] *Re Peacock's Estate* (1872), L.R. 14 Eq. 236.
[66] (1885), 28 Ch. D. 552, 556 (C.A.).

originating in a definite external cause, though not of a kind which (unless expressed) the law would have recognised, or would have presumed to exist.

Gifts to charities are within the rule,[67] even if the gift inter vivos is to a person other than the legatee. A legacy to the parish priest of Kilcolman for the erection of a new chapel in Claremorris, Co. Galway, was held to be adeemed by a gift inter vivos by the testator to the Roman Catholic Archbishop of Tuam for the same purpose.[68] However, the presumption will be rebutted by material differences in the nature of the two gifts. In *Re Aynsley*,[69] a testator by his will made in 1904 bequeathed £500 to his trustees to invest in land in the parish of Madley to be used as glebe for the vicarage, declaring that the gift was in pursuance of his wife's wish. In 1905 the testator purchased land in the parish of Madley, and conveyed it to the Diocesan Finance Association upon trust for the endowment of the incumbent of Madley. By a codicil of 1911 the testator bequeathed certain further legacies, and in other respects confirmed his will. Joyce, J., held that the conveyance of 1905 was not an ademption of the legacy in the will, on the ground that the codicil made after the gift of the land showed the testator intended a further gift for the living. The decision is open to criticism for, in other cases, the rule has been applied that a codicil, unless in express terms to that effect, could not set up a legacy which had been adeemed.[70] The Court of Appeal affirmed the decision on different grounds.

In cases of ademption of legacies by portions, there is no question of election by the recipient of the property for the subsequent gift of a portion is regarded as a substitution for the original legacy, which the testator may modify at his pleasure.

SATISFACTION OF LEGACIES BY LEGACIES

This is not strictly a case of satisfaction at all, for it would appear that the object of the court, in determining whether two legacies are cumulative or substantial, is to determine the testator's intention by

67 *Re Corbett*, [1903] 2 Ch. 326; *Re Jupp*, [1922] 2 Ch. 359.

68 *Griffith* v. *Bourke* (1887), 21 L.R. Ir. 92. See also *Monck* v. *Lord Monck* (1810), 1 Ba. & B. 298.

69 [1914] 2 Ch. 422; [1915] 1 Ch. 172.

70 E.g. *Roome* v. *Roome* (1744), 3 Atk. 181, 183; *Powys* v. *Mansfield* (1837), 3 My. & Cr. 359.

ordinary rules governing the construction of wills, which, on this topic, appear to be derived from the rules of Roman law. In the leading case of *Hooley* v. *Hatton*,[71] Aston, J., said—

There are four cases of double legacies:

First, where the same specific thing is given twice.—*Cujacius* takes a distinction between the same *res* and the same quantity. In the first case, it can take place but once, *at eadem quantitas saepius praestari potest.*[72] Secondly, where the like quantity is given twice.—Lord *Hardwicke* (in *Beauclerk* v. the Duke of *St. Alban's*)[73] alluding to the particular circumstances of the case, laid down one only should be taken unless an intention appeared to the contrary.—but nothing can be collected from hence, as the title of the Digest must be attended to,[74] which expressly says *animo adimendi.*—where £100 and £100 legatee intitled to both. The doctrine from repetition of two equal sums, in one will, being bad, and, in a will and codicil, being good, attributing the former to forgetfulness, is strange.—the case of the *Slaves*[75] . . . [is] upon entirely different principles. It would be strange to suppose Lord *Hardwicke* applied this as a general rule, which would be inconsistent with his recognizing (as he did expressly) the authority of Swinburne, 526, 530—but said that the case before him was different, from the internal evidence.

In regard to the cases in the *Roman* law—first, where equal sums are given in two distinct writings, both shall pass by the *Roman* law,[76] and the decisions of this Court are agreeable thereto . . .

3dly, As to a less sum in the latter deed, as £100 by will, and £50 by the codicil, the legatee shall take both . . .

4thly, As to a larger sum after a less, *Ricard*[77] says,—where they are in the same instrument, the two sums are not blended, but the legatee has two legacies; and the heir must shew that the one was meant to be blended with the other, the presumption being in favour of what is written . . .

[71] (1773), 1 Bro. C.C. 389 *n*. There are some exceedingly interesting observations on the growth of this rule in the Court of Chancery in this case. Ireland: see *Quin* v. *Armstrong* (1876), I.R. 11 Eq. 161.

[72] *Digest*, XXII, 3, xii.

[73] (1743), 2 Atk. 636.

[74] *Digest*, XXXIV, 4, ix.

[75] *Digest*, XXXIV, 1, xviii.

[76] *Digest*, XXII, 3, xii.

[77] *Traité des Donations*, vol. I, p. 451.

The law seems to be, and the authorities only go to prove the legacy not to be double where it is given for the same cause in the same act, and *totidem verbis*, or only with small difference; but where in different writings, there is a bequest of equal, greater, or less sums, it is an augmentation . . .

The following examples will illustrate the rules which the courts have laid down.

Legacies in Different Instruments

(1) If legacies of quantity are given to the same person by different testamentary instruments, the presumption is that both are to belong to the legatee, whether the sums are the same or one is larger than the other.[78] This, however, is simply a presumption, and will yield to evidence of a contrary intention. Such a contrary intention will be regarded as being shown where the same amount is given in both cases for exactly the same reason, If no motive is expressed, or different motives for the two gifts, or a motive for one and no motive for the other, the presumption that the legatee is to take both exists, even though the amounts are identical.[79] Similarly, the presumption will arise when, though the motive for the gift is the same in each case, the legacies are of different amounts.

(2) If the two legacies are of different things (e.g. a pecuniary legacy and a share of residue) or are to be paid at different times, the presumption is that they are cumulative.[80]

(3) Where a codicil gives a second legacy of similar amount, and the codicil makes it apparent that the testator is simply revising and explaining his will, this will be evidence that the legacies are to be regarded as substitutional,[81] and the same rule applies where the second instrument repeats the gift in the first instrument in identical terms, especially if other legacies are also repeated in identical terms, thus raising the inference that the codicil is intended to operate in substitution for part of the original will.[82]

Will and codicil are different instruments, if admitted to probate as will and codicil, even if written on the same paper;[83] but where two or more instruments are admitted to probate as one instrument, they are so considered for all purposes.[84]

[78] *Wilson* v. *O'Leary* (1871), L.R. 12 Eq. 525; *Russell* v. *Dickson* (1853), 4 H.L.C. 293 (H.L., I.).; *Re Davies*, [1957] 1 W.L.R. 922.

[79] *Hurst* v. *Beach* (1820), 5 Madd. 351, 358; *Ridges* v. *Morrison* (1784), 1 Bro. C.C. 389.

[80] *Masters* v. *Masters* (1718), 1 P. Wms. 421.

[81] *Moggridge* v. *Thackwell* (1792), 1 Ves. Jun. 464.

[82] *Roxburgh* v. *Fuller* (1864), 13 W.R. 39; *Tuckey* v. *Henderson* (1863), 33 Beav. 174.

[83] *Baillie* v. *Butterfield* (1787), 1 Cox C.C. 392.

[84] *Heming* v. *Clutterbuck* (1827), 1 Bligh N.S. 479 (H.L., E.).

In *Re Bagnall*[85] the testatrix made two wills, one in 1936 and the other in 1943. In the first will, she gave certain legacies, and then disposed of the residue. In the second will (which was incomplete, and which was not a codicil, and did not expressly revoke the first will) the testatrix again provided legacies of similar amounts to those in the first will, for the same beneficiaries. Probate was granted of both wills, and the court held that the second will, as far as it went, was intended to replace the first will, so that any legacies given in the first will, and repeated in the second, were substitutional only in the second will. The court also held that the second will was not entirely intended to supersede the first. Accordingly, the first will effectively disposed of the residue, and also one legacy appearing in the first will and neither repeated nor revoked in the second. Harman, J., in deciding this case, emphasised the point that, in deciding whether gifts in two testamentary documents are cumulative or substitutional, the two wills must be construed as a whole, and the court must decide in each case as a matter of construction what the testator meant, not weighing probabilities too nicely if the effect of this would be to upset the rule.

Legacies in the same Instrument

(1) If legacies of the same amount (or of amounts showing trifling variations) are given in the same instrument to the same person, the presumption is that they are substitutional.[86]

(2) Legacies of different amounts, given to the same person in the same instrument, are presumed to be cumulative,[87] unless it appears from the context that the testator is merely repeating himself.[88]

Extrinsic Evidence

(1) Where a presumption exists that the second legacy, in a *different* instrument, is substitutional, extrinsic evidence is admissible to support the language of the instrument, and thereby to prove that the testator intended the legatee to take both.[89]

(2) If, however, the presumption is that the legacies are cumulative, extrinsic evidence to rebut this is inadmissible, the rule being regarded as one of construction.[89]

Both rules operate in favour of the legatee.

85 [1949] L.J.R. 1.

86 *Hooley* v. *Hatton* (1773), 1 Bro. C.C. 389 *n.*; *Garth* v. *Meyrick* (1779), 1 Bro. C.C. 30.

87 *Curry* v. *Pile* (1787), 2 Bro. C.C. 225; *Re Royce's Will Trusts*, [1959] Ch. 626 (C.A.).

88 *Yockney* v. *Hansard* (1844), 3 Hare 620.

89 *Hurst* v. *Beach* (1820), 5 Madd. 351.

Performance

The basis of the equitable doctrine of performance is the same as the basis of the doctrine of satisfaction, i.e. the maxim " Equity imputes an intent to fulfil an obligation." The difference, is, however, that in satisfaction something other than the act contemplated is given and accepted in discharge of the obligation; while in performance what is done is regarded as a step towards the fulfilment of the obligation itself.[90] In the leading case of *Lechmere* v. *Lady Lechmere*,[91] Lord Lechmere covenanted by marriage articles to lay out £30,000 within a year of his marriage, in the purchase of freehold lands, in fee simple in possession, in the south part of Great Britain, with the consent of the trustees. When purchased, the lands were to be settled upon Lord Lechmere for life, and after his death, to pay a jointure to his wife, remainder to the first and other sons of the marriage in tail, remainder to trustees for 500 years to raise portions for daughters, remainder to Lord Lechmere, his heirs and assigns for ever. The term was to be void if there were no daughters, and until the £30,000 was laid out in land, interest was to be paid at the rate of 5 per cent per annum to the persons entitled to the rents and profits of the land when purchased. Lord Lechmere was seised in fee simple of certain lands at the time of his marriage, and also after the marriage he bought some estates for lives, and also certain reversionary interests in land. He also purchased after the marriage, but not within the year, and without the consent of the trustees, several estates in fee simple in possession, which were not settled in accordance with the covenant. Lord Lechmere died, intestate, leaving considerable real property to devolve upon the heir-at-law. The widow took out administration, and in an action by the heir-at-law to have the covenant carried into execution, it was held—

(1) that the effect of the covenant was that the sum to be laid out in the purchase of land must be regarded as land, and would thus devolve upon the heir;

(2) that purchases of land made *before* the covenant could not be regarded as being made in performance of the subsequent covenant;

(3) that estates for lives, and reversionary estates in fee simple, purchased after the marriage, could also not be regarded as being bought in performance of the covenant, since they did not conform with the description of the lands to be bought appearing in the covenant, viz. estates in fee simple in possession; and

[90] This asserted distinction rests upon the judgment of Plumer, M.R., in *Goldsmid* v. *Goldsmid* (1818), 1 Swanst. 211, 218.

[91] (1735) Cas. t. Talb. 80. Ireland: see *Keays* v. *Gilmore* (1874), I.R. 8 Eq. 290.

(4) that purchases of fee simple estates in possession after the marriage of less value than those described in the covenant could be regarded as being made in part-performance of the covenant, even though the lands were not purchased within the year, or with the consent of the trustees. As Lord Talbot, L.C., observed[92]—

> The Lord Lechmere was bound to lay out the money with the liking of the trustees, but there was no obligation to lay it out all at once, nor was it hardly possible to meet with such a purchase as would exactly tally with it. Parts of the land purchased are in fee simple in possession, in the south part of Great Britain, and near to the family estate. But it is said they are not bought with the liking of the trustees. The intention of naming trustees was to prevent unreasonable purchases, and the want of this circumstance, if the purchases are agreeable in other respects, is no reason to hinder why they should not be bought in performance of the articles.

The dispute was between the two representatives, the one of his real estate (the heir), and the other of his personal estate (the widow). The freehold lands purchased in fee simple in possession after marriage naturally passed to the heir, and the case decided that these must go in part performance of the covenant. Thus it followed that the residue only of the £30,000 had to be made good out of the personal estate.

The position would have been exactly the same if the covenant had directed that the covenantor should pay the money to trustees, so that they might invest it in the purchase of land.[93] It is essential, however, that land of the estate contemplated should be bought, even though of less value than that prescribed in the covenant; so that if a covenantor to purchase lands lays out money in building on land already within the settlement, this will not be regarded as performance.[94]

Performance, like satisfaction, rests on the presumption of the covenantor's intention, and therefore, if lands are bought capable of satisfying the covenant, and the covenantor later sells or mortgages them, this will be evidence that he did not intend to fulfill the covenant by that transaction. In consequence, the position of the purchaser or mortgagee is not adversely affected by the existence of the covenant simply as a result of the operation of the presumption.[95] Accordingly, the covenant creates no lien on lands to be bought subsequently, unless it relates to specific property (or to specific property already held by the

[92] White and Tudor, *Leading Cases in Equity*, 9th ed., vol. 2, p. 355.
[93] *Sowden* v. *Sowden* (1785), 1 Bro. C.C. 582.
[94] *Horlock* v. *Smith* (1853), 17 Beav. 572.
[95] *Deacon* v. *Smith* (1746), 3 Atk. 323.

covenantor), in which case the covenant will be specifically enforceable.[96] By Section 11 of the Settled Land Act, 1925, and Sections 10 and 13 of the Land Charges Act, 1925, a covenant to settle land already belonging to the purchaser made after 1925 must be registered as a land charge, to bind a purchaser.[97]

A further illustration of performance is afforded by a covenant by a person to leave, or that his executors shall pay, a sum of money or personal property to another on the death of the promisor. If, on the death of the promisor, the promisee receives on his intestacy an equal or greater amount, that sum is regarded as being given in performance of the covenant. If it is less than the promised amount, it is regarded as given in partial performance of the covenant.[98] However, the fact that the covenant prescribes that the sum shall be paid within three months of the covenantor's death, and payment of the sum on intestacy cannot be enforced within the "executor's year," is not regarded as evidencing a contrary intention.[99]

This rule, curiously, has not been applied to covenants followed by legacies, on the ground that the intention of the testator is to augment the provision under the covenant and not to perform it;[1] a process of reasoning which seems somewhat illogical. If, however, the gift is by a will which becomes inoperative, so that the recipient takes a share on intestacy, this is regarded as performance.[2]

Secondly, the rule does not apply where the covenantor undertakes to pay the sum in his lifetime, for obviously a gift on death is not within its terms. In such a case, the covenantee could claim under the covenant, and also on intestacy.[3]

Lastly, if the covenant is to pay an annuity, or the interest on a sum of money for life, this was not before 1926 performed in England by a gift on intestacy,[4] although it has been suggested that if the covenantee was a widow, the life interest given her under Section 46 of the Administration of Estates Act, 1925,[5] could now be regarded as performance.[6]

96 *Collyer* v. *Isaacs* (1881), 19 Ch. D. 342 (C.A.).

97 Ireland: no equivalent legislation.

98 *Blandy* v. *Widmore* (1715), 1 P. Wms. 324. Ireland: *Re Finegan's Estate* [1925] 1 I.R. 201.

99 *Garthshore* v. *Chalie* (1804), 10 Ves. 1.

1 *Haynes* v. *Mico* (1781), 1 Bro. C.C. 129.

2 *Goldsmid* v. *Goldsmid* (1818), 1 Swanst. 211.

3 *Oliver* v. *Brickland* (1732), cit. 3 Atk. 422.

4 *Couch* v. *Stratton* (1799), 4 Ves. 391.

5 Ireland: Succession Act, 1965, Sects. 67 and 111 (Republic of Ireland); Administration of Estates Act (Northern Ireland), 1955, Sect. 7.

6 White and Tudor, *Leading Cases in Equity*, 9th ed., vol. 2, p. 366.

CHAPTER XIV

MARSHALLING

ONE of the doctrines of equity designed to relieve against accidents, marshalling is a process by which a person's interest in property is adjusted so as not to be adversely affected by the irrelevant acts of another person interested in the same property. It operates in circumstances in which two persons, A and B, are interested in the same property and A, whose interest has priority to that of B, could equally well deal with his interest in either of two ways, one of which would prejudice B and the other not. Where the doctrine of marshalling applies, B is regarded as having an equity entitling him either to have A act so as not to prejudice him or, if A has prejudiced him, to have the proprietary interests adjusted so as to remove that prejudice. There are two main areas in which the doctrine can operate: (*a*) as between two secured creditors of the same debtor, and (*b*) as between beneficiaries under a will.

MARSHALLING AS BETWEEN CREDITORS

Mortgages

The commonest application of marshalling is as between successive mortgagees. Suppose the fee simple owner of two properties, Blackacre and Whiteacre, to mortgage them both to A to secure £6000, after which he grants a second mortgage of Blackacre alone to B to secure £2000. Suppose, further, that a sale of Blackacre would produce £6000 and a sale of Whiteacre £3000. On the face of it, A may pay himself in full by realising Blackacre and releasing Whiteacre from his security, or by realising both estates and accounting for the surplus of £3000 on Blackacre. If A takes the former course, B's mortgage disappears, but if he takes the latter, A must pay B off out of the £3000 surplus. If the mortgagor is insolvent, the way in which A acts is most material to B, for the former course reduces him on the face of it to the status of an unsecured creditor, while the latter results in B being paid in full before any payment to unsecured creditors. Since neither the mortgagor nor the unsecured creditors are any worse off if B is protected (since A could, if he wished, act so as to preserve B's security), the equitable doctrine protects B.

Marshalling is much older than the middle of the eighteenth century, as appears from the terms in which Lord Hardwicke, L.C., stated it in the earliest clear report[1]—

> Is it not then the constant equity of this court that if a creditor has two funds, he shall take his satisfaction out of that fund upon which another creditor has no lien.
>
> Suppose a person, who has two real estates, mortgages both to one person, and afterwards only one estate to a second mortgagee, who had no notice of the first; the court, in order to relieve the second mortgagee, have directed the first to take his satisfaction out of that estate only which is not in mortgage to the second mortgagee, if that is sufficient to satisfy the first mortgagee, even though the estates descended to two different persons.

Ever since Lord Eldon, L.C.'s statement of the principle in *Aldrich* v. *Cooper*,[2] it has been clear that the doctrine applies even in favour of a second incumbrancer who did have notice of the first.

Marshalling does not interfere with the security of the first mortgagee. Should he pay himself in full out of the property on which the second mortgagee is secured, he is not liable to the second mortgagee, but the latter's position is adjusted by treating him as if he were secured on the other property.[3]

The same principles apply in cases where the second creditor is not a mortgagee, but has some other proprietary interest, even if he is a volunteer. For example, if the fee simple owner of Blackacre and Whiteacre mortgages both to secure a single debt, and then executes a voluntary settlement of Blackacre, the beneficiaries of the settlement have an equity to marshal by throwing the mortgagee primarily on to Whiteacre.

But there is no equity to marshal in favour of a person who has no proprietary interest in one of the properties even if he is compelled to restrict himself to that one property in seeking payment. In *Re International Life Assurance Soc.*[4] the Society's members' liability was unlimited except as to policyholders: in other words, policyholders could look for payment only to the proceeds of calls on members up

1 *Lanoy* v. *Duke of Athol* (1742), 2 Atk. 444, 446.

2 (1803), 8 Ves. 382. See also *Gibson* v. *Seagrim* (1855), 20 Beav. 614. Ireland: *Going* v. *Farrell* (1814), Beat. 472; *Baldwin* v. *Belcher* (1842), 3 Dr. & War. 173; *Re Fox's Estate* (1856), 5 Ir. Ch. Rep. 541 (Privy Council); *Re Roddy's Estate* (1861), 11 Ir. Ch. Rep. 369.

3 *Lawrance* v. *Galsworthy* (1857), 3 Jur. N.S. 1049; *South* v. *Bloxam* (1865), 2 H. & M. 457. Ireland: *M'Carthy* v. *M'Cartie* (No. 2), [1904] 1 I.R. 100 (C.A.).

4 (1876), 2 Ch.D. 476.

to a stipulated amount. The Society mortgaged to a bank the proceeds of future calls on members, the mortgage being to secure repayment of a loan for purposes of the Society's business. On the winding-up of the Society, the Court of Appeal held that policyholders had no right to marshal so as to throw the mortgagee on the unlimited assets. Policyholders were limited to payment out of proceeds of calls but had no proprietary interest in them.

Nor may the second creditor marshal if the first has a proprietary interest in only one of the two funds. In *Webb* v. *Smith*[5] auctioneers held two funds for a client for whom they had sold two properties. They had a lien over fund A for their charges, but had no such lien over fund B: the most they could claim in respect of fund B was a set-off for their charges if sued for the fund by the client. The client charged fund A in favour of the plaintiff, after which the auctioneers paid themselves out of fund A and handed over fund B to their client. The Court of Appeal held that the plaintiff could not marshal. The auctioneers were entitled to use their lien: they could not be obliged to reduce their right to that of an unsecured set-off.

There can also be no marshalling if the first creditor is not equally secured on the two properties. If A is mortgagee of Whiteacre only to the extent that Blackacre is inadequate security for his debt, B as subsequent mortgagee of Blackacre has to put up with A going against that property so far as necessary to pay A's debt.[6] Creditors of different debtors cannot marshal either. In *Ex parte Kendall*[7] there were creditors of five persons and there were other creditors of only four of the five. The four went bankrupt. Lord Eldon, L.C., held that the creditors of the four could not invoke marshalling so as to compel the creditors of the five to proceed first against the (solvent) estate of the deceased fifth debtor. The Lord Chancellor said[8]—

> The equity is clear upon the authorities, that, if two funds of the debtor are liable to one creditor, and only one fund to another, the former shall be thrown upon that fund, to which the other cannot resort; in order that he may avail himself of his only security: where that can be done without injustice to the debtor or the creditor: but that principle has never been pressed to the effect of injustice to the common debtor: much less have persons, who are not common creditors of the same debtor, a right to compel the creditors of both funds to resort to the one: in order to leave a large dividend for those, who can claim only against the other.

5 (1885), 30 Ch.D. 192.
6 See *The Priscilla* (1859), Lush 1. Cf. *The Mary Ann* (1845), 9 Jur. 94.
7 (1811), 17 Ves. 514.
8 17 Ves. 527.

The picture will be changed by the entry of a third mortgagee. If, after the mortgages of Blackacre and Whiteacre to A and of Blackacre to B, the mortgagor mortgages Whiteacre to C, marshalling in favour of B will prejudice C, another secured creditor. It is sometimes said that there is no marshalling in these circumstances; but it is more accurate to say that there is, though with different objectives and adjustments from those in cases of only two secured creditors. The leading authority is *Barnes* v. *Racster*,[9] where, however, the mortgage of the two properties did not come before the mortgage of one of them. Racster mortgaged land known as Foxhall to Barnes. Then he mortgaged Foxhall to H, who had notice of Barnes. Next, Racster mortgaged both Foxhall and another property, known as No. 32, to Barnes (who had notice of H) to secure all sums owed to Barnes on both properties. Finally, Racster mortgaged Foxhall and No. 32 to W, who had notice of all that had gone before. H claimed to throw Barnes entirely on to No. 32 so as to preserve Foxhall for himself. This, however, would prejudice W (who could, perhaps, with equal justice or injustice claim to throw Barnes primarily on to Foxhall). Knight Bruce, V.-C., held that H and W stood on an equal footing. H had no equity to throw Barnes off Foxhall (H's security) so as to leave less of it for W. Barnes must be paid rateably from Foxhall and No. 32.

This insistence that the mortgagee of both properties be paid out of both proportionately to their respective values is not a denial of marshalling to the second mortgagee but an according of it to both the subsequent mortgagees equally. Complete refusal to marshal would leave the first mortgagee's acts of his choice with their prejudicial effect (if any) on subsequent mortgagees unabated. The apportionment rule is well settled. In *Flint* v. *Howard*,[10] where the Court of Appeal so decided, Kay, L.J., said—

> The right of a subsequent mortgagee of one of the estates to marshall—that is, to throw the prior charge on both estates upon that which is not mortgaged to him—is an equity which is not enforced against third parties, that is, against anyone except the mortgagor and his legal representatives claiming as volunteers under him. It is not enforced against a mortgagee or purchaser of the other estate. If both estates are subject to separate second mortgage the Court apportions the first mortgage between them.

9 (1842), 1 Y. & C.C.C. 401, followed in *Bugden* v. *Bignold* (1843), 2 Y. & C.C.C. 377, and *Wellesley* v. *Mornington* (1869), 17 W.R. 355. See also *Boazman* v. *Johnston* (1830), 3 Sim. 377; *Moxon* v. *Berkeley Mutual Benefit Building Soc.* (1890), 59 L.J. Ch. 524; *Re Townley*, [1922] 1 Ch. 154.

10 [1893] 2 Ch. 54, 73. See also *Baglioni* v. *Cavalli* (1900), 83 L.T. 500.

The House of Lords decided, in an Irish case,[11] that there could be no marshalling so as to prejudice a third party even if the third party were a volunteer.

If, however, the third party is not prejudiced, the second has an equity to marshal. This will be so if the third party takes expressly subject to and after payment of the first two.[12] In *Aldridge* v. *Forbes*[13] the owner mortgaged the G and M estates to A; then he charged the G estate in favour of volunteers; next, he mortgaged both estates, subject to the charge on the G estate, to B; finally, A assigned his first mortgages of G and M to B. Lord Cottenham, L.C., held that the chargees could marshal so as to throw the first mortgage as far as possible on the M estate. This might be regarded as overruled by *Barnes* v. *Racster*,[14] but was explained by Ross, J., as being consistent with that case in the Irish decision of *Re Lysaght's Estate*[15]—

> The reason for this decision appears very plainly stated in 4 Jur., p. 20; it was expressly agreed that the last mortgage should not affect or prejudice the rights of those claiming under the voluntary settlement.

Irish courts seem to have had some difficulty in reconciling themselves to *Barnes* v. *Racster*.[14] Even when the Court of Appeal in Chancery expressed themselves to accept it, in *Re Lawder's Estate*,[16] they distinguished it from the case before them. Later,[17] they seem to have regarded the principle as inapplicable to judgment mortgages. In *Tighe* v. *Dolphin*[18] the owner of two estates subject to a mortgage settled one of them on his daughter's marriage. There was no covenant against incumbrances in the settlement, but a verbal representation was made previously to the execution of it by the settlor to the intended husband, that the estate was free from incumbrances, and it was conveyed without reference to incumbrances. The other estate passed under the settlor's will to his widow, who conveyed it to a purchaser for value, with notice of the settlement but not of the verbal representation. Porter, M.R., held that the purchased estate was bound to indemnify the settled estate against the mortgage debt, and that *Barnes* v. *Racster*[14]

[11] *Dolphin* v. *Aylward* (1870), L.R. 4 H.L. 486.

[12] *Re Mower's Trusts* (1869), L.R. 8 Eq. 110.

[13] (1839), 9 L.J. Ch. 37.

[14] (1842), 1 Y. & C.C.C. 401. See p. 435, *ante*.

[15] [1903] 1 I.R. 235, 244.

[16] (1861), 11 Ir. Ch. Rep. 346.

[17] *Re Scott's Estate* (1863), 14 Ir. Ch. Rep. 63. See also *Re Lynch's Estate* (1867), I.R. 1 Eq. 396.

[18] [1906] 1 I.R. 305.

was confined to cases of successive mortgages. If this decision is difficult to accept, *Re Archer's Estate*[20] is even more so. A was entitled to a first charge on two funds, X and Y. B was entitled to a second charge on fund Y only. A subsequently took a further charge on both funds; and after that C acquired a charge on fund X only. Each chargee had notice of all prior charges. If A's first charge were paid rateably out of both funds, the residue of fund Y would be insufficient to pay B's second charge in full. Wylie, J., held that B was entitled to marshal A's first charge, and to have so much of it paid out of fund X as would leave sufficient of fund Y to pay his own second charge in full, notwithstanding the fact that C's charge would thus be prejudiced. *Barnes* v. *Racster*[19] could be distinguished. In this case, B's existing right to marshal could not be altered by the creation of C's charge. In *Smyth* v. *Toms*,[21] on similar facts, Ross, J., disagreed with Wylie, J., and came to the opposite conclusion. This seems in accordance with principle. There is nothing stranger in modifying B's right to marshal, by the subsequent charge to C, than in modifying A's freedom of action by the subsequent charge to B.

Suretyship

A surety may marshal both against the principal debtor and against all persons claiming through him. In *Heyman* v. *Dubois*[22] a person took out a policy on his life from an insurance company, and mortgaged it to the company for £1000. He then took out a second life insurance policy with the same company, and mortgaged it to them for £500. Later, he took out a third policy with the same company, and mortgaged it, with a second mortgage of the first policy, to secure £1,500, there being a surety for this transaction. The insured mortgagor then became bankrupt, and the surety was compelled to pay the company £975. The third policy was forfeited for non-payment of the premium. The insured bankrupt mortgagor died, so that money became payable under the life policies not forfeited. Bacon, V.-C., held the surety entitled to have the securities marshalled against the deceased's trustee in bankruptcy, so that he could claim to be reimbursed out of the policy moneys the sum which he had been compelled to pay to the company.

In *Duncan, Fox & Co.* v. *North and South Wales Bank*[23] the House of Lords applied the equitable principles as between surety and acceptor

19 (1842), 1 Y. & C.C.C. 401. See p. 435, *ante*.
20 [1914] 1 I.R. 285.
21 [1918] 1 I.R. 338.
22 (1871), L.R. 13 Eq. 158.
23 (1880), 6 App. Cas. 1.

of a bill of exchange, so as to entitle the indorser (who was liable on the bill as surety) to the benefit of securities for payment of the bill deposited with the holder by the acceptor.

Principal and Agent

If an agent pledges the goods of his principal, and also goods of his own, to secure a debt due from himself (the agent), the principal may compel the creditors to have recourse in the first place to the agent's own goods.[24]

Marshalling as Between Beneficiaries

Before twentieth century legislation, marshalling used to play a very important part in the administration of assets of deceased persons, where there were specialty creditors and simple contract creditors, and where the assets comprised realty and personalty. Now, since specialty and simple contract creditors are on the same footing, and since realty and personalty are equally available for both types of creditor,[25] marshalling has lost much of its importance in connection with debts (other than mortgage debts) of deceased persons. The principle, however, still has some application between beneficiaries.[26]

The order in which assets are to be applied for the payment of the debts of a solvent estate has been set out in the statute,[27] though it is subject to variation by the testator. If a creditor, or the personal representative in paying a creditor, has recourse to assets out of the order laid down by the statute or by the testator, the interests of the beneficiaries appear to have been affected. For example, if a block of shares bequeathed to someone is sold in order to pay debts out of the proceeds while a fund of property specifically bequeathed for the payment of debts is left untouched (whereas that fund should be used before the shares), unless an adjustment is made the residuary legatee is enriched at the expense of the specific legatee. The principle of marshalling is that a beneficiary whose property has been taken prematurely may have recourse against any property that should have been

24 See *Broadbent* v. *Barlow* (1861), 3 De G.F. & J. 570; *Ex parte Alston* (1868), L.R. 4 Ch. App. 168; *Ex parte Salting* (1883), 25 Ch.D. 148 (C.A.); *Re Burge, Woodall & Co.*, [1912] 1 K.B. 393.

25 Administration of Estates Act, 1925, Sect. 34 (3) and 1st Sch., Pt. II; Administration of Estates Act (Northern Ireland), 1955, Sect. 30 (3) and 1st Sch., Pt. II; Succession Act, 1965, Sect. 46 (3) and 1st Sch., Pt. II (Republic of Ireland).

26 For detailed consideration of marshalling in the administration of estates, see Jarman on *Wills*, 8th ed., vol. 3, pp. 1956-60; Theobald on *Wills*, 12th ed., pp. 716-20; White and Tudor, *Leading Cases in Equity*, 9th ed., vol. 1, pp. 42-59: Williams on *Executors and Administrators*, 13th ed., vol. 2, pp. 989-93.

27 Administration of Estates Act, 1925, Sect. 34 (3) and 1st Sch., Pt. II; Administration of Estates Act (Northern Ireland), 1955, Sect. 30 (3) and 1st Sch., Pt. II; Succession Act, 1965, Sect. 46(3) and 1st Sch., Pt. II (Republic of Ireland). See pp. 282-5, *ante*.

taken before his. If any other beneficiary is disturbed by this marshalling operation, he in turn may have recourse against other property higher up the list.

In the Republic of Ireland these principles have been given a statutory basis. The Succession Act, 1965, Section 46, after specifying in Subsection (3) the statutory order of liability of assets for debts, goes on—

> (4) Nothing in subsection (3) affects the rights of any creditor of the deceased or the legal right of a spouse.
>
> (5) Where a creditor, a person entitled to a legal right or a personal representative applies an asset out of the order mentioned in Part II of the First Schedule, the persons entitled under the will or on intestacy shall have the right to have the assets marshalled so that a beneficiary whose estate or interest has been applied out of its order shall stand in the place of that creditor or person *pro tanto* as against any property that, in the said order, is liable before his own estate or interest.

In England and Northern Ireland, the doctrine still depends on case law. A recent example of its application is *Re Matthews' Will Trusts*.[28] There, Pennycuick, J., ordered marshalling so as to compensate a specific devisee out of residue where sums for which residue was primarily liable had been paid out of the proceeds of sale of the devised property. The learned judge said[29]—

> In the course of his argument, Mr. Abbery treated the right of the legatee in such circumstances as being based on subrogation. I feel great doubt as to whether this is the correct view: see *In re Broadwood*.[30] For the present purpose, I am content to treat the right of the legatee as being simply an equitable right to compensation.

Analogous to the right to marshal is the right to contribution. Should there be, for example, six houses equally liable for the testator's debts, each specifically devised to one of six people, and the proceeds of four are sufficient to clear the debts, the six devisees will share equally in the two remaining houses.[31]

[28] [1961] 1 W.L.R. 1415.
[29] [1961] 1 W.L.R. 1419.
[30] [1911] 1 Ch. 277.
[31] *Re Cohen*, [1960] Ch. 179.

CHAPTER XV

THE MARRIED WOMAN'S SEPARATE ESTATE

ALTHOUGH practically no relics of the former subordinate status of the married woman now remain, it can be asserted that every step in her progressive emancipation was pioneered by equity, and accordingly, a brief survey of the nature and extent of equitable intervention will serve as a classic illustration of the response of the Court of Chancery to changing social conditions.

At common law, the husband was entitled to receive the rents of his wife's real estates during their joint lives, and on the birth of issue capable of inheriting, then if the wife was seised of estates of inheritance, the husband became entitled to them for life, as " tenant " by the curtesy. The husband was also, by marrying, entitled to all the wife's chattels personal in possession, and to her choses in action, provided he reduced them into possession. He also had full power to alienate the wife's chattels real, and to retain the proceeds for himself. If, however, the husband died before the wife, without having reduced the choses in action into possession, or without having disposed of the chattels real, they survived to the wife.[1]

From the day of her marriage, the wife ceased to have an independent power to contract. Any contracts which she purported to make were binding on the husband, only if she was contracting on his behalf. On the other hand, the husband was liable for the wife's ante-nuptial debts, whether or not he received property through her on marriage. He was also liable for her torts, whether committed before or during the marriage. The wife had no power to make a will without her husband's consent, and even with that, it extended only to personalty, for a statute of 1542[2] disabled her from making a will of land in any circumstances.

Until the second half of the nineteenth century, the progressive improvement of the status of the married woman was achieved exclusively by equity, in the Court of Chancery, so that gradually a very considerable body of law was built up. This the court did under two principal heads:

1 *Langham* v. *Nenny* (1797), 3 Ves. 467. See also Holdsworth, *H.E.L.*, vol. III, pp. 520-533.

2 34 & 35 Hen. VIII, c. 5, Sect. 14. Ireland: 10 Car. I, sess. 2, c. 2 (Ir.), Sect. 16.

(1) the wife's equity to a settlement; and
(2) the evolution of the concept of the wife's " separate use," and of the power to enter into binding agreements in respect of it.

Both these concepts had appeared in equity before the Civil War. In particular, the Court of Chancery was prepared to uphold conveyances of property to trustees for the benefit of the woman during marriage, so as to give the wife the sole benefit of it, provided they were fair and reasonable—for example, in cases where the parties were separated, or where the husband was a wastrel. Since her capacity to hold such property by equitable title was thus admitted, so also was her power to dispose of it, even to the husband, or by will, whilst in at least one case[3] the Court of Chancery had already issued an injunction to stay proceedings by a husband in the Ecclesiastical Court for a portion due to his wife until he had made adequate provision for her by jointure.[4]

By the second half of the seventeenth century, these principles were firmly established, and property was regularly settled to the wife's separate use. As yet, such a settlement required the husband's approval, for which consideration would normally be required. If, however, a husband had recourse to the Chancery for the purpose of securing his wife's portion, equity, applying the principle that " He who seeks equity must do equity," would compel him to make some provision for her.[5]

The Wife's Equity to a Settlement

By the beginning of the eighteenth century, as the cases cited in *Cases in Chancery* show,[6] it was settled practice in the Court of Chancery that, if the husband found it necessary to apply to that court for aid to secure possession of the wife's property (e.g. where trustees declined to pay it over to him), the court would compel him to make a settlement in his wife's favour. From the time of Lord Eldon's decision in *Murray* v. *Lord Elibank*,[7] however, the wife was permitted actively to asert her equity as a plaintiff in a suit or, if there were already a suit, by petition in it, at any time before the husband had reduced his wife's equitable property into possession. The wife's equity was regarded not as an obligation upon the property itself, but upon the husband's right to receive it.

3 *Tanfield* v. *Davenport* (1638-9), Tot. 114.
4 Holdsworth, *H.E.L.*, vol. V, pp. 310-315.
5 Holdsworth, *H.E.L.*, vol. VI, pp. 644-5.
6 2nd ed. (1759), pp. 146-7.
7 (1804), 10 Ves. 84.

Since the cases in which the husband would need the assistance of the Court of Chancery to obtain his wife's property were cases in which the property was equitable, it followed that the wife's equity to a settlement usually existed only where the property was equitable, but in *Fowke* v. *Draycott*,[8] North, J., pointed out that since the Judicature Act, 1873,[9] by virtue of which all Divisions of the High Court must take notice of all equities, the court would give effect to the wife's equity whether the subject matter of the action were legal or equitable. Even before 1873, however, there were cases in which the property was legal, but was nevertheless subject to a suit in equity, and to this property the wife's equity was also applicable.[10]

The wife's equity extended to all property other than that limited to her separate use, whether vested in interest in her before or after marriage, and it was applicable as much against a life interest as against an absolute interest. In *Taunton* v. *Morris*,[11] the wife's right was successfully asserted against the husband's assignee in bankruptcy who, the Court of Appeal held, was in the same position as the husband himself. Such an assignee is a general assignee, but in *Tidd* v. *Lister*[12] a married woman, whose husband did not maintain her, was unsuccessful in her claim to a settlement for maintenance out of the income of property to which she was entitled for life in equity, as against a *particular* assignee.

Where the wife was entitled to an absolute interest in property, and she asserted her equity, the court included children in the settlement, and the provision could be extended to her children by a former marriage. The children, in such a case, had no independent rights, and so, if the wife died before asserting her right, the children had no right to a settlement.

Whenever the wife asserted her equity to a settlement, she must herself have acted equitably. This was of particular importance in considering the claim in respect of an assignee of the husband. As Bowen, L.J., pointed out in *Roberts* v. *Cooper*,[13] in discussing the wife's equity as against the husband's assignee for value, there are two questions which must be kept distinct:

(1) What is the wife's position as regards her husband? And

(2) What is her position as regards the assignee?

[8] (1885), 29 Ch. D. 996.

[9] Ireland: Judicature (Ireland) Act, 1877.

[10] *Sturgis* v. *Champneys* (1839), 5 My. & Cr. 97.

[11] (1879), 11 Ch. D. 779.

[12] (1852), 10 Hare 140.

[13] [1891] 2 Ch. 335, 345 (C.A.).

In either case, the court must consider whether there has been any conduct of the wife which would make it unconscionable for her to retain the fund. In that case, the actions of husband and wife were held to have been unconscientious as against the assignees, who had assented to a settlement of one half of the wife's interest, and the Court of Appeal therefore held that she was not entitled to any further provision.

The usual practice was to settle one half of the property which the husband received juri mariti upon the wife and children, leaving the remaining half with the husband,[14] but in particular cases, the court would exercise its discretion, and vary the proportion, where there were special reasons. The court, as Lord Cairns, L.J., pointed out in *Re Suggitt's Trusts*,[15] would only order that the whole of the fund should be settled where there were special circumstances, e.g. adultery or cruelty on the part of the husband, the husband's insolvency or, possibly, the smallness of the property under consideration.

The wife's equity to a settlement was barred where the husband made an adequate settlement upon her, but not if the settlement was of small value. The settlement, if of a personal fund, usually provided that the wife should have the income for life, subject to a restraint on anticipation, and thereafter it should be held in trust for her children, whether by the existing husband or by any future husband. If there were no children, and the husband survived the wife, then he was entitled to the whole of the property.

The Separate Property of a Married Woman

From the Restoration onwards, it was settled equitable practice that property held by trustees for the separate use of the married woman could be dealt with by her, independently of her husband. In *Hulme* v. *Tenant*,[16] Lord Thurlow, L.C., said:

> . . . in respect to a feme covert, determined cases seem to go thus far, that the general engagement of the wife shall operate upon her personal property, shall apply to the rents and profits of her real estate, and that her trustees shall be obliged to apply personal estate, and rents and profits when they arise, to the satisfaction of such general engagement; but this Court has not used any direct process against the separate estate of the wife, and the manner of coming at the separate property of the wife has been by decree to bind the

14 *Spirett* v. *Willows* (1866), L.R. 1 Ch. App. 520; (1869), L.R. 4 Ch. App. 407.
15 (1868), L.R. 3 Ch. App. 215, 217-18.
16 (1778), 1 Bro. C.C. 16, 20-1.

> trustees, as to personal estate in their hands or rents and profits, according to the exigency of justice, or of the engagement of the wife to be carried into execution. . . . I believe there is no instance of a personal decree against a feme covert, for payment of any sum whatever.—Though her separate personal property is liable, yet the decree is to fetch forth her separate estate, and make it liable to her engagement.

These last observations emphasize the most characteristic feature of equity's development of the separate estate of the married woman. Her liability was proprietory, and not personal.

By the eighteenth century, it was established that if property were given to a married woman for her separate use, but with no appointment of trustees, then the Court of Chancery regarded the husband as a trustee for his wife.[17]

Equity did not require any particular form of words to be used for the creation of a married woman's separate estate in equity,[18] and accordingly any words which made plain the intention that the wife should enjoy the property separate from her husband were accepted. Usually the gift for the wife was of a life interest only, but if a fee simple or other heritable property was given to her separate use, then it became her property absolutely, and she could dispose of it by deed or will.[19] In a number of cases, a separate estate for a married woman was held to have been created by implication. For example, in *Re Peacock's Trusts*,[20] the East India Company had granted a pension to the widow of one of its servants " to provide a comfortable maintenance," and with a direction that it should not be disposed of or incumbered directly or indirectly. When the widow remarried, Malins, V.C., held that the pension was held to the wife's separate use.

From the middle of the nineteenth century, a succession of statutes progressively created the separate estate of the married woman *at law*. The first Act of importance was the Married Women's Property Act, 1870, which made the earnings of any married woman acquired after the passing of the Act, in any employment, occupation or trade in which she was engaged, and also anything acquired by her in consequence of her literary, artistic or specific skill, and all investment of such earnings, a separate property. This cautious beginning was superseded by the very wide terms of the Married Women's Property

[17] *Rich* v. *Cockell* (1804), 9 Ves. 369.

[18] *Tyler* v. *Lake* (1831), 2 Russ. & M. 183.

[19] *Taylor* v. *Meads* (1865), 4 De G.J. & S. 597.

[20] (1879), 10 Ch. D. 490.

Act, 1882. Section 1 (1) provided that a married woman should be capable of acquiring and disposing (whether by will or inter vivos) of any real or personal property, as her separate property, without the intervention of any trustee. By Section 1 (2) she was made liable to the extent of her separate property, whether in contract or in tort, as if she were a feme sole, and her husband need not be made a party to the proceedings, " and any damages or costs recovered against her in any such action or proceeding shall be payable out of her separate property, and not otherwise." Section 1 (5) made a married woman carrying on a trade separately from her husband subject to the bankruptcy laws, as if she were a feme sole. Section 2 provided: " Every woman who marries after the commencement of this Act shall be entitled to have and to hold as her separate property and to dispose of in manner aforesaid all real and personal property which shall belong to her at the time of marriage, and shall be acquired by or devolve upon her after marriage " including any savings she may gain.

Although the terms of this Act were wide, it did not make clear the extent of the liability which attached to the wife's separate property. In *Scott* v. *Morley*[21] the Court of Appeal decided that under the Act of 1882, as previously in equity, her contractual and tortious liabilities could only be enforced against her separate estate, and not against the married woman personally, but in *Palliser* v. *Gurney*[22] a Divisional Court held that the liability only attached when the wife had separate estate at the time when she incurred liability. This limitation was removed by the Married Women's Property Act, 1893.[23] Nevertheless, at the end of the nineteenth century, a number of characteristics derived from the common law still survived. A husband was still liable for his wife's ante-nuptial contracts and torts to the extent of property acquired through her, and the husband also remained liable for the torts of his wife committed during marriage. Moreover, although the Act of 1882 had given the married woman wide powers of holding and disposing of real estate, the concurrence of the husband was still necessary for dispositions of it.

This was remedied by the Married Women's Property Act, 1907, and accordingly Section 170 (1), (2), of the Law of Property Act, 1925,[24] provides—

21 (1887), 20 Q.B. D.120.

22 (1887), 19 Q.B. D.519. See also *Stogdon* v. *Lee*, [1891] 1 Q.B. 661 (C.A.).

23 The Married Women's Property Acts have been replaced in the Republic of Ireland by the Married Women's Status Act, 1957.

24 The 1907 Act is still in force in Northern Ireland.

(1) A married woman is able to acquire as well from her husband as from any other person, and hold, any interest in property real or personal either solely or jointly with any other person (whether or not including her husband) as a trustee or personal representative, in like manner as if she were a feme sole; and no interest in such property shall vest or be deemed to have vested in the husband by reason only of the acquisition by his wife.

(2) A married woman is able, without her husband, to dispose of, or to join in disposing of, any interest in real or personal property held by her solely or jointly with any other person (whether or not including her husband) as trustee or personal representative, in like manner as if she were a feme sole.

Finally, the Law Reform (Married Women and Tortfeasors) Act, 1935,[25] made a married woman capable of acquiring and disposing of property, of suing and being sued in respect of any tort, contract, debt or obligation, and of being made bankrupt, exactly as if she were a feme sole, thus substituting for the proprietory liability which had existed for so long, a personal liability. At the same time the Act abolished the husband's liability for his wife's torts and for her ante-nuptial contracts, debts and obligations. By this Act, therefore, the married woman at long last acquired full status *at law*.

The Restraint on Anticipation

Conferring wide powers of disposition upon a married woman in respect of her separate estate might not be to her ultimate advantage. Inexperience may cause her to dissipate her property or cajolery by her husband might induce her to surrender either the whole or a substantial part of it to him. It was to protect her from such consequences that the restraint on anticipation was devised at the end of the eighteenth century. The need for such a clause had been felt for some time, as Lord Macnaghten showed in *Hood Barrs* v. *Heriot*,[26] but early attempts to limit the married woman's powers of alienation had failed. In *Pybus* v. *Smith*[27] Lord Thurlow, L.C., was unable to give redress to a married woman who had made away with all her property in less than three months, so that the object of settling property to her separate estate was defeated.

25 Ireland: Married Women's Status Act, 1957 (Republic of Ireland); Law Reform (Miscellaneous Provisions) Act (Northern Ireland), 1937; Law Reform (Husband and Wife) Act (Northern Ireland), 1964.

26 [1896] A.C. 174, 182 (H.L., E.).

27 (1791), 3 Bro. C.C. 340.

" . . . these decisions " (said Lord Herschell in *Hood Barrs* v. *Heriot*)[28] " suggested to Lord Thurlow, in a case where he was trustee, the introduction of a clause in restraint of anticipation." Until the Married Women's Property Acts, the restraint operated only against the married woman's property in equity, but following those Acts,[29] it could attach also to her statutory property. It was operative only during coverture, so that if a testator imposed a restraint upon the property of his daughter in his will, the restraint did not arise until the daughter married. It ceased if the woman became a widow, although it would revive on a subsequent marriage, unless the testator expressly restricted it to the first marriage.

No special form of words was necessary to create a restraint on anticipation, so long as the intention that the married woman should not alienate capital or anticipate future income was shown.

Nevertheless, in several statutes, the court was given power to lift the restraint on anticipation, so as to make the property alienable to the extent desired by the court,[30] and Section 169 of the Law of Property Act, 1925,[31] gave the court a general discretion to lift the restraint whenever it appeared to the court to be to the woman's benefit to do so. Ten years later, the Law Reform (Married Women and Tortfeasors) Act, 1935, abolished restraints on anticipation in instruments coming into force after 1st January 1936, with the qualification that the will of any testator who died after December 1945 should be deemed to have been executed after 1st January 1936. This gave testators ten years during which existing wills could be altered—possibly by the substitution of a particular trust for a restraint on anticipation. Finally, by the Married Women (Restraint upon Anticipation) Act, 1949, all existing restraints were brought to an end, and their future creation was prohibited.[32]

28 [1896] A.C. 174, 178.

29 E.g. Married Women's Property Act, 1882, Sect. 19; Conveyancing Act, 1911, Sect. 7; Law of Property Act, 1925, Sect. 169.

30 Conveyancing Act, 1881, Sect. 39; Married Women's Property Act, 1893, Sect. 2; Bankruptcy Act, 1914, Sect. 52, to which there was no corresponding provision in the Republic of Ireland, but to which the Bankruptcy Amendment Act (Northern Ireland), 1929, Sect. 18, corresponded.

31 Ireland: corresponding legislation was contained in the Conveyancing Act, 1911, Sect. 7.

32 Ireland: Married Women's Status Act, 1957 (Republic of Ireland); Law Reform (Miscellaneous Provisions) Act (Northern Ireland), 1937 (following the 1935 Act); Married Women (Restraint upon Anticipation) Act (Northern Ireland), 1952 (following the 1949 Act).

Chapter XVI

PROCEDURE

In the unitary High Court of England, set up in the first place by the Judicature Acts of 1873 and 1875,[1] procedure does not vary much according to whether points of common law or points of equity are in issue. In the Republic of Ireland and many other common law countries, the High Court is not even divided into Divisions. In England and Northern Ireland, the bulk of procedural steps are common to the Chancery Division and the Queen's Bench Division. The purpose of this chapter is not to describe practice and procedure in general,[2] but to mention the special features of equity proceedings and to outline the contribution to adjective law of the Court of Chancery.

Where the High Court is divided into Divisions, each judge has the full jurisdiction of the whole court[3] and all cases are tried as a unit. Hence it is possible, for example, for a judge of the Queen's Bench Division to hear an application for an interlocutory injunction (an equitable remedy) in an action to recover possession of land (a common law action in tort); or for a judge of the Chancery Division in an action for specific performance of a contract to determine a counterclaim for damages for breach. Business is assigned to the Divisions according to the nature of the case, not the points to be raised by the parties in the course of it.

In the county courts,[4] too, cases are dealt with on that basis. However, the equity jurisdiction of county courts is more limited than their common law jurisdiction, so that cases may have to be classified to determine the competence of the judge. In *Foster* v. *Reeves*,[5] a county court claim for recovery of rent had to be dealt with according to the common law, i.e. the plaintiff was not allowed to pray in aid the doctrine of *Walsh* v. *Lonsdale*,[6] because the value of the land was above

1 Ireland: Supreme Court of Judicature (Ireland) Act, 1877.

2 For a detailed account, see Daniell, *The Practice of the Chancery Division of the High Court of Justice* (7th ed., 1901, of Daniell's *Chancery Practice*).

3 England: Supreme Court of Judicature (Consolidation) Act, 1925, Sect. 4 (4).

4 Circuit courts in the Republic of Ireland.

5 [1892] 2 Q.B. 255 (C.A.). See p. 90, *ante*.

6 (1882), 21 Ch. D. 9 (C.A.). See pp. 85-93, *ante*.

that limiting the equity jurisdiction of the court. On the other hand, even if the value of the land puts it outside the limits for a claim in equity, the defendant may avail himself of an equitable defence to the plaintiff's common law claim.[7]

In many respects, procedure in the Court of Chancery followed common law ideas of procedure.[8] That was a natural consequence of the staffing, regularly from the early seventeenth century, of the Chancery bench by common lawyers. It was augmented by the Chancery practice, engaged in until the nineteenth century but commoner down to Lord Nottingham's tenure of the Woolsack, of calling in judges or serjeants when important questions of law or fact arose, and by that of sending cases for the opinion of common law judges.[9] On the other hand, some parts of Chancery procedure differed radically from that of the common law courts. Some of these differences have found a lasting place in the modern unified system, while others led to the dead end of dilatoriness that made being in chancery a metaphor for a state of inactivity. For the most part, the special features of Chancery procedure resulted from its position as a court of conscience, seeking to do complete justice between the parties (whereas the common law courts dealt only with specific issues submitted to them), and from its position as a court interfering with but not overriding the common law rights of the parties, acting mainly in personam.

Once the Court of Chancery became secularised, the organisation of the legal profession for cases before it came to be similar to that of practitioners before the common law courts. Barristers (members of a largely separate Chancery bar) undertook advocacy before the court, and they were briefed by solicitors, whose functions corresponded to those of attorneys in respect of common law work.[10] By a process beginning before the fusion of the courts and ending after it, the bar became unified and nowadays, although specialisation in fact occurs in England,[11] all barristers have a right of audience in every court. The same happened with the other branch of the profession, attorneys, proctors and solicitors becoming merged under the last name.

[7] *Kingswood Estate Co. Ltd.* v. *Anderson* [1963] 2 Q.B. 169 (C.A.). See p. 90, *ante*.

[8] As to the development of Chancery procedure from its early informality to its nineteenth century decay and reform, see Holdsworth, *H.E.L.*, vol. 9, pp. 335-411, 433-440; Spence, *Equitable Jurisdiction of the Court of Chancery* (1846), vol. 1, pp. 367-406.

[9] See Spence, *op. cit.*, pp. 383-4.

[10] As to the Sixty Clerks, who duplicated some of the work of solicitors, see Holdsworth, *H.E.L.*, vol. 9, pp. 369-70; Keeton, *An Introduction to Equity*, 5th ed., pp. 27-9, and Irish Supplement (Sheridan), p. 3.

[11] But scarcely at all in either part of Ireland.

The fashion in which proceedings were commenced was one of the striking differences between equity and common law cases. Before the statutory reforms of the nineteenth century,[12] the common law plaintiff had to fit himself into the system of forms of action, and selection of the correct writ was one of the technical prerequisites for success in the suit. In the Court of Chancery, there was generally uniform procedure for all types of cause,[13] and a generally uniform document, called a bill, for the institution of the action. In principle, that is a just system because of its flexibility. Unfortunately, the desire of the Court of Chancery to do complete justice by going into every aspect of the case led to a large and changing number of parties in some types of litigation, such as a suit for the administration of a testator's estate, which, coupled with the development of various types of supplementary bill for various procedural steps, commonly led to there being a multiplicity of bills in a single action.[14] For this reason, among others, the bill in Chancery did not survive the Judicature Acts, but the idea of a single method of instituting proceedings prevailed and spread to all the courts. Now, apart from motions (e.g. for prerogative writs and orders) and petitions under particular statutes (e.g. governing matrimonial causes), all actions are started by either writ of summons or originating summons. The difference between these two is that the writ is available for all types of action[15] while the summons may be used where the sole or principal question at issue is likely to be one of construction of legislation or a document or some other question of law or where there is unlikely to be a substantial dispute of fact. The originating summons is met much more commonly in the Chancery Division than elsewhere in the High Court, but all methods of commencing actions are available for all Divisions. In general,[15] choice of a writ when a summons would be more appropriate, or vice versa, will lead to no more serious setback than a slight increase in the costs.[16]

Pleadings in the Court of Chancery were also different from those at common law. In part, that was due to the different objects: that of common law pleadings being to define the issue to be adjudicated upon and that of equity pleadings being to get before the court all the relevant facts about the relations between the parties. It was also due

12 Common Law Procedure Act, 1852, Sects. 2 and 3.

13 See Holdsworth, *H.E.L.*, vol. 9, pp. 343-4.

14 See Holdsworth, *H.E.L.*, vol. 9, pp. 344-8. See also pp. 358-60 as to motions for all sorts of purposes.

15 But under R.S.C. 1965, O. 5, r. 2, certain types of action must be commenced by writ.

16 As to differences in respect of discovery of documents, see *Coni* v. *Robertson*, [1969] 2 All E.R. 609, p. 455, n. 25, *post*.

in part to the different modes of taking evidence.[17] The bill in equity was the first stage in the pleadings in a suit before the Court of Chancery. It stated the plaintiff's case, was answered by the defendant, was supplemented (or repeated in different words) in answer to the defence, and so on. These papers became voluminous and time-consuming.

> A bill in a Chancery suit was a marvellous document, which stated the plaintiff's case at full length and three times over. There was first the part in which the story was circumstantially set forth. Then came the part which " charged " its truth against the defendant—or, in other words, which set it forth all over again in an aggrieved tone. Lastly came the interrogating part, which converted the original allegations into a chain of subtly framed inquiries addressed to the defendant, minutely dovetailed and circuitously arranged so as to surround a slippery conscience and to stop up every earth. No layman, however intelligent, could compose the ' answer ' without professional aid. It was inevitably so elaborate and so long, that the responsibility for the accuracy of the story shifted, during its telling, from the conscience of the defendant to that of his solicitor and counsel, and truth found no difficulty in disappearing during the operation.[18]

Pleadings in both the Queen's Bench Division and the Chancery Division now follow a common form of statement of claim, defence and reply (possibly followed by further steps), but the substance of a Chancery pleading, in many cases, bears little resemblance to that of a Queen's Bench pleading because the Chancery Division is frequently concerned with construction, administration and continuing supervision (e.g. of a trust) while the Queen's Bench Division is generally faced with adjudicating on a single incident (such as a factory accident).

The most extraordinary feature of proceedings in the Court of Chancery was the embargo on one of the obvious ways of getting evidence, namely the oral examination of witnesses. This could be done, exceptionally, to clear up doubts on the paper evidence or to prove an exhibit. But—

> There never was a case, where witnesses have been allowed to be examined at large at the hearing; and though it might be desirable

[17] See below.

[18] Lord Bowen, " Progress in the Administration of Justice during the Victorian Period " (1907), *Select Essays in Anglo-American Legal History*, vol. 1, pp. 524-5.

> to allow this, yet the fixed and settled proceedings cannot be broke through for it.[19]

Witnesses were in fact examined by a commission which travelled to each witness's district, administered to him a set of prefabricated interrogatories and took down his answers in their (the commission's) own words. No party was present (except at his own examination) nor was he represented by counsel or a solcitor. The end product was a report to the court, published and sent to the parties. A disputed question of fact might then be settled by sending an issue to be tried by a court of law (i.e. by jury), or a new commission might be sent to administer a new set of interrogatories, at new expense, but when the Court of Chancery finally came to the hearing the only evidence would be on paper. Holdsworth wrote[20]—

> . . . a more futile method of getting at the facts of a case, than the system in use in the court of Chancery from the seventeenth century onwards, never existed in any mature legal system . . . it was carried out under such technical forms, and in such a manner, as to be productive of the most unconvincing testimony at the greatest possible expense.

Since the nineteenth century reforms,[21] oral evidence has been available in Chancery suits. Today, written evidence, in the form of affidavits, while available in all courts, predominates in the Chancery Division, but deponents may be called and cross-examined on their affidavits and there is no legal restriction on types of evidence. The absence of juries from the Chancery Division accounts for the lack of addiction to oral testimony. With the jury now seldom used in civil cases in the Queen's Bench Division, it may be wondered why greater use of affidavits is not made there.

Interrogatories, though put to a different purpose, have survived. Indeed, together with discovery of documents, they may be regarded as a major Chancery contribution towards efficiency in preparing for a trial. In all Divisions of the High Court, a party may apply for an order giving him leave to administer interrogatories, relating to any matter in question between him and the other party, and requiring the other party to answer on affidavit.[22] These answers are now used in preparing for trial, or as part of the evidence at the trial, but not as a substitute for other kinds of evidence. Discovery of documents is the

[19] *Per* Lord Hardwicke, L.C., *Graves* v. *Budgel* (1737), 1 Atk. 444, 445.

[20] *H.E.L.*, vol. 9, pp. 353-8. See also Bowen, *op. cit.*, pp. 525-531.

[21] Chancery Amendment Act, 1858, Sect. 5.

[22] See R.S.C. 1965, O. 26. The Common Law Procedure Act, 1854, Sect. 51, allowed for interrogatories in the common law courts.

process of one party informing the other party what documents relevant to the case the former has, and producing those the latter wants to inspect. That was normal procedure in the Court of Chancery, but was not available to parties in common law courts, before the nineteenth century reforms,[23] except by bringing a bill in Chancery to have discovery ordered. Such (general) discovery is generally compulsory nowadays, in all Divisions of the High Court, and without any order of the court.[24] An order will be made if necessary;[25] and must be applied for if one party wants to compel the other party to make an affidavit stating whether he has some specified document which did not appear on the latter's general list.[26] Apart from the passing of information by discovery and answers to interrogatories, an important Chancery contribution to interlocutory proceedings is the injunction,[27] issued on motion (even ex parte, before issue of a writ, in urgent cases) to preserve the status quo pending trial.[28] This type of order has been available in all courts (later, all Divisions) since the nineteenth century reforms.[29]

Procedure at trial in the Court of Chancery differed from procedure in common law cases in the following major respects.

(1) The way evidence was given.[30]

(2) The absence of a jury. Juries are not available in the Chancery Division. In England (but not Ireland), since the second world war, they are rare in civil cases generally, but are still allowable by the court.[31] For a while after the Judicature Acts, issues were sent by the Chancery Division for trial by jury at assizes; but in modern times, in the rare cases where a jury is ordered in the Chancery Division, the whole suit is transferred to the Queen's Bench Division for trial.

(3) The practices of sending an issue of fact to be tried by jury at Nisi Prius and of sending a point of law for the opinion of the common law judges. These practices disappeared under the nineteenth century reforms. Today cases are tried as a whole. In the Chancery Division all issues of fact are determined by the judge.[32] So are issues of com-

23 Common Law Procedure Act, 1854, Sect. 50.

24 R.S.C. 1965, O. 24, rr. 1, 2, 5, 6 and 9 to 11.

25 R.S.C. 1965, O. 24, rr. 3 and 8. Discovery is not automatic in actions begun by originating summons, but it " will be ordered unless there is some good reason why it should not be ordered " (*per* Cross, J., *Coni* v. *Robertson*, [1969] 2 All E.R. 609, 615).

26 R.S.C. 1965, O. 24, rr. 7 and 8.

27 See pp. 459-60, *post*.

28 See, now, R.S.C. 1965, O. 29, r. 1.

29 Common Law Procedure Act, 1854, Sects. 79 and 82.

30 See pp. 451-2, *ante*.

31 See the Administration of Justice (Miscellaneous Provisions) Act, 1933, Sect. 6; R.S.C. 1965, O. 33, r. 5.

32 Since the Chancery Amendment Act, 1858, Sect. 5.

mon law,[33] just as the judge in the Queen's Bench Division determines issues of equity raised before him.[34] Allied to these practices was the point of substance, that a plaintiff would lose in the Court of Chancery if he had, in the opinion of the judge, an adequate remedy at common law.[35] Since the nineteenth century reforms, all courts (later all Divisions) have given both common law and equitable remedies, or either, as appropriate to the case.[36]

(4) The use by the Court of Chancery of motions for all sorts of purposes[37] and of copious references to masters.[38] Modern motions in the High Court bear no relation to the old Chancery motions. In so far as they occur otherwise than to institute proceedings or to initiate consequential steps or appeals after judgment, they are generally brief applications (e.g. for an adjournment) speedily dealt with. Modern masters in the High Court are also quite different in function from their predecessors in the Court of Chancery. They have most of the powers of a judge in chambers,[39] and, in certain cases, assess damages after judgment.[40] Much more work, and more detailed work is done in chambers in the Chancery Division than in the Queen's Bench Division, including orders and the taking of accounts in the administration of trusts and estates. Appeal lies from the master to the judge, but in the Chancery Division there is also a practice, commonly resorted to, of asking the master to adjourn the matter to a judge instead of deciding it himself.

(5) The system of rehearings. This has gone, though a judge may always amend his decision until it is formally recorded. In the Court of Chancery, before the Judicature Acts, enrolment of a decree ended the proceedings in the court of first instance. Enrolment was up to the parties; until it was done, there could be no appeal, but there could be rehearings.[41] There are many instances in the reports of cases re-

[33] Since the Judicature Acts.

[34] Courts of common law never wholly ignored points of equity. The Court of Common Pleas particularly inclined to give effect to equitable defences. This tendency was augmented by statutes (e.g. on relief from penalties) from the late seventeenth century onwards. It was given general impetus by the Common Law Procedure Act, 1854, Sect. 83. The process was not completed until the Judicature Acts.

[35] See pp. 459-60, 486, *post*.

[36] Common Law Procedure Act, 1854, Sects. 50, 51, 78 and 79; Chancery Amendment Act, 1858, Sect. 2.

[37] See Holdsworth, *H.E.L.*, vol. 9, pp. 358-60.

[38] *Op. cit.*, pp. 360-5.

[39] R.S.C. 1965, O. 32, rr. 11 and 14. See the *Annual Practice*, 1967, vol. 1, pp. 433, 442, as to matters dealt with by masters.

[40] R.S.C. 1965, O. 37, r. 1.

[41] As to excessive speed in enrolment, see Sheridan, "Fraud and Surprise in Legal Proceedings" (1955), 18 *Modern Law Review*, 441, 443.

heard, sometime by the successor of the Lord Chancellor who made the first decree, and decisions were sometimes changed many years after first being made.

After a final decision of a judge of any court, there has always been some method in English law of having some sort of review. In respect of the common law courts, review was by the Court of King's Bench (by writs of certiorari and mandamus, limited to procedural or jurisdictional irregularities and errors on the record), and by that court and the Court of Exchequer Chamber (by writ of error, in theory a new action, limited to error of law appearing on the face of the record). There was no appeal from a common law court in respect of the findings of fact or in respect of matters of law not on the record. The Court of Chancery invented the appeal by way of rehearing (i.e. a complete re-examination of the merits, but not a re-taking of the evidence of witnesses). It was, however, an imperfect system for several reasons.[42] First, if the case were heard at first instance by the Lord Chancellor, the only appeal was to the House of Lords (after appeals to that House from the Chancery became established in the 1640s),[43] and the same Lord Chancellor might be the only legally trained member of the House present at the hearing of the appeal. Secondly, if the hearing at first instance were by the Master of the Rolls (or, from the early nineteenth century, a Vice-Chancellor),[44] the appeal to the Lord Chancellor might be to a less learned equity lawyer than the trial judge. The prospects varied arbitrarily. One litigant might be heard by the Master of the Rolls, appeal to the Lord Chancellor and appeal again to the House of Lords with a membership not including judges who had heard him before. Another might be heard by the Lord Chancellor, move for a rehearing before the same judge, then appeal to the House of Lords only to find himself being judged a third time by the same man. The appeal by rehearing has now spread to all civil appeals to the Court of Appeal from all courts, but, since the establishment in the mid-nineteenth century of a regular Court of Appeal in Chancery,[45] it has been the settled course of practice that a judge does not sit on an appeal from one of his own decisions.

Enforcement procedures in the Court of Chancery were directly related to the notion of acting in personam. That meant that the main way of enforcing obedience was by imprisonment until the contumaceous person became co-operative. The same applied to

[42] See Holdsworth, *H.E.L.*, vol. 9, pp. 368-9.

[43] See Spence, *Equitable Jurisdiction of the Court of Chancery* (1846), vol. 1, pp. 395-6.

[44] 53 Geo. 3, c. 24. Ireland: Chancery (Ireland) Act, 1867, Sect. 4.

[45] Court of Chancery Act, 1851. Ireland: Chancery Appeal Court (Ireland Act, 1856.

getting a defendant before the court.[46] Down to the end of the reign of Charles I, decrees were enforced in England by committal to the Fleet prison.[47] However, the fact that a person of determination could, by elusiveness or by accepting imprisonment for life, deprive the plaintiff of the fruits of his judgment, had early to be taken into account. From the time of Elizabeth I, if the defaulting party were not apprehended, could not be found or escaped, sequestration was possible.[47] Sequestration was the taking of possession, by court order, of the defendant's property until he carried out what the Chancery wished him to do. In the case of a decree for land, if the defendant disobeyed, the Court of Chancery could grant an injunction ordering him to deliver up possession. If that injunction, too, was disobeyed, the court could order that the plaintiff be put in possession with the help of the Justices of the Peace and the Sheriff.[48] Times have changed, but not out of all recognition. People are still sent to prison for contempt of court as the primary method of sanctioning obedience to orders of an equitable nature, such as injunctions.[49] However, there are many statutory supplements to sequestration.[50] The High Court, in equity cases, may give effect to its orders by additional orders, of which the most important are: (*a*) the use of the processes previously confined to the common law courts, e.g. writ of fiere facias to satisfy a money judgment; (*b*) orders for sale (e.g. to assist an equitable mortgagee to realise his security); (*c*) vesting orders (e.g. to vest leasehold property in new trustees where the landlord will not consent to the assignment); and (*d*) orders that another person do something in the defendant's stead (e.g. execute a conveyance by way of carrying out a decree of specific performance of a contract for the sale of land).

It will be seen that the Court of Chancery was quite inventive in matters of practice and procedure, but also succeeded in getting itself ensnared in a web of delay and expense. The nineteenth century reforms, the Common Law Procedure Acts and Chancery Amendment Acts, culminating in the Judicature Acts, abolished the abuses and absurdities of both common law and equity proceedings, adopted for all the beneficial institutions of each, and ended up with a single court in which variations from Division to Division correspond to the variations in the type of case tried.

[46] See Holdsworth, *H.E.L.*, vol. 9, pp. 348-53.

[47] See Spence, *Equitable Jurisdiction of the Court of Chancery*, vol. 1, p. 391. As to equitable execution by the imposition of a charging order, see R.S.C. 1965, O. 50, as amended by R.S.C. (Amendment No. 2) 1967; as to equitable execution by the appointment of a receiver, see pp. 510-11, *post*.

[48] *Op. cit.*, p. 392.

[49] See R.S.C. 1965, O. 45, r. 5, and O. 52, r. 4.

[50] See R.S.C. 1965, O. 45, rr. 1, 3-5 and 13. As to sequestration, see O. 46, r. 5.

CHAPTER XVII

INJUNCTIONS

The Various Kinds of Injunction

The remedy of specific performance is one which equity developed exclusively in the field of contract. The remedy of injunction, on the other hand, is one which has been of first-class importance in many fields of private law—in the law of real and personal property, in all branches of the law of torts and also in the fields of industrial law, company law and trusts. Accordingly, a complete account of the use of injunctions would involve an analysis of many of these divisions of law, and this would plainly be beyond the scope of this volume. In the present chapter, therefore, no more will be attempted than a statement of the general equitable principles governing the award of injunctions, together with illustrations of its use drawn from the various divisions of the law.

An injunction is an order of the court restraining the commission or the continuance of some wrongful act, or the continuance of some omission. If the injunction forbids the commission or continuance of an act, e.g. of a trespass on the land of another, it is said to be *prohibitory*; if it directs that a positive act should be done to repair some ommission, it is said to be *mandatory*. Such injunctions are naturally only granted sparingly, but in a suitable case, the court will not hesitate to issue an injunction in mandatory form, even if it directs that buildings shall be pulled down.[1]

Another division of injunctions is into those which are perpetual and those which are interlocutory only. A perpetual injunction is only granted after a judicial decision, when the plaintiff has established the existence of his right in law, and the fact that the defendant has infringed it or is about to do so. An interlocutory injunction, on the other hand, is one which follows as quickly as possible upon the issue of the writ, directing that the acts complained of should cease whilst the issue between the parties is determined.[2] Such an order, naturally,

[1] *Truckell* v. *Stock*, [1957] 1 W.L.R. 161 (C.A.). The principles governing the grant of mandatory injunctions in such cases were discussed by the House of Lords in *Redland Bricks Ltd.* v. *Morris*, [1969] 2 W.L.R. 1437. See also *Lugunda* v. *Service Hotels Ltd.*, [1969] 2 W.L.R. 1056 (C.A.). Ireland: see *Woodhouse* v. *Newry Navigation Co.*, [1898] 1 I.R. 161 (C.A.).

[2] For examples, see *Thompson-Schwab* v. *Costaki*, [1956] 1 W.L.R. 335 (C.A.); *Lugunda* v. *Service Hotels Ltd.*, [1969] 2 W.L.R. 1056.

may involve the defendant in considerable financial loss, and it is therefore granted only after the plaintiff has given an undertaking to indemnify the defendant, if the plaintiff should fail to establish his case.

An interlocutory injunction to maintain the status quo may be granted by a court of first instance, pending an appeal to a higher court.[3]

In such an application, the applicant must establish a probability or a strong prima facie case that he is entitled to the right of whose violation he complains. Subject to this, the main consideration is then the maintenance of the status quo pending the trial.

> It is well established that in deciding whether the matter shall be maintained in statu quo regard must be had to the balance of convenience and to the extent to which any damage to the plaintiffs can be cured by payment of damages rather than by the granting of an injunction. Of course the burden of proof lies on the applicant throughout.[4]

In a proper case, an interlocutory injunction will be granted ex parte; that is to say, before the defendant has had the opportunity to appear to oppose it. This is a measure of extreme urgency (granted, e.g., where an alleged libel is published in a daily newspaper or where continuance of waste would cause great damage to property),[5] and if it is intended that it should endure for any length of time, it is customary for the court to limit its duration until a day on which the matter may be heard on motion.

One type of injunction was abolished by the Judicature Act—the *common injunction* whereby the Court of Chancery restrained persons from enforcing their rights at law in violation of equitable principles. The necessity for such an injunction vanished when the Judicature Act gave all civil courts power to award all legal and equitable remedies.[6] The High Court still has power to restrain by injunction the resort by parties to inferior courts or foreign courts, however,[7] but will

[3] *Orion Property Trust Ltd.* v. *Du Cane Court Ltd.*, [1962] 1 W.L.R. 1085.

[4] *Per* Ungoed-Thomas, J., *Donmar Productions Ltd.* v. *Bart*, [1967] 1 W.L.R. 740, 742. See also the observations of Goff, J., in *Harman Pictures N.V.* v. *Osborne*, [1967] 1 W.L.R. 723. Ireland: *Cork Corp.* v. *Rooney* (1881), 7 L.R.Ir. 191; *Tyler* v. *Goodwin* (1888), 23 L.R.Ir. 13; *Gallagher* v. *Tuohy* (1924), 58 I.L.T.R. 134; *Educational Co. of Ireland Ltd.* v. *Fitzpatrick*, [1961] I.R. 323 (Sup. Ct.).

[5] *Browne* v. *Duffy* (1889), 24 L.R. Ir. 13.

[6] See now, Judicature Act, 1925, Sect. 41. Ireland: Judicature (Ireland) Act, 1877, Sect. 27 (5).

[7] *Ellerman Lines Ltd.* v. *Read*, [1928] 2 K.B. 144 (C.A.); *The Soya Margareta*, [1961] 1 W.L.R. 709.

impose an injunction on a party taking legal proceedings abroad only with great caution.[8] The High Court will grant an injunction against the prosecution of criminal proceedings which raise the same question which is the subject of High Court proceedings.[9]

The breach of an injunction constitutes a contempt of court, for which committal is the appropriate punishment. Committal may be for a specified term, and where there are successive breaches, the terms should become increasingly long.[10]

In matters within its jurisdiction, a county court may grant an injunction,[11] but, if the defendant ignores the injunction, he may be committed for contempt only if the committal order set out specifically " the particular matter of contempt " constituting the breach for which he is to be committed.[12]

Development of the Remedy

The injunction had a forerunner in the common law courts in the writ of prohibition, a writ which could be issued not only to restrain an inferior court from a course of conduct, but also to restrain an individual. However, the Chancery developed the injunction, and made it available in a wide variety of cases, at an early date: there are frequent instances of its use in the fourteenth century. In the following century, the Chancery had established its power to restrain persons from enforcing common law rights in violation of equitable principles by the common injunction. From the beginning, the common law courts resisted this exercise of equitable jurisdiction, and the conflict came to a head in the reign of James I in the *Earl of Oxford's Case.*[13]

The ruling of James I upon the ensuing quarrel between Coke and Ellesmere settled the practice until the Judicature Acts.

The Scope of Injunctions

Since the injunction is the creation of courts of equity, its award had depended upon the application of a number of equitable principles. In the first place, an injunction will not be granted when damages are

8 *Cohen* v. *Rothfield*, [1919] 1 K.B. 410 (C.A.); *Orr-Lewis* v. *Orr-Lewis*, [1949] P. 347.

9 *York Corp.* v. *Pilkington* (1742), 2 Atk. 302; *Re Connolly Bros. Ltd.*, [1911] 1 Ch. 731 (C.A.); *Thames Launches Ltd.* v. *Trinity House Corp.* (*Deptford Strond*), [1961] Ch. 197.

10 *Yager* v. *Musa*, [1961] 2 Q.B. 214 (C.A.). See also *Lenton* v. *Tregoning*, [1960] 1 W.L.R. 333 (C.A.).

11 *Martin* v. *Bannister* (1879), 4 Q.B. D. 491 (C.A.).

12 *McIlraith* v. *Grady*, [1968] 1 Q.B. 468 (C.A.).

13 (1615), 1 Ch. Rep. 1, pp. 51-2, *ante*. On the use of injunctions in the sixteenth century see Holdsworth, *H.E.L.*, vol. V, pp. 323-5.

an adequate remedy; for example when the wrong has been committed, and there is no threat of a repetition. Secondly, the plaintiff must show that some legal or equitable right has been infringed or is threatened.[14] Where injury has not yet occurred, but is feared or threatened, the plaintiff may bring what is known as a quia timet action. A striking example of such a threat is afforded by *Crowder* v. *Tinkler*,[15] when the defendants were restrained from erecting a dangerous powder mill. In the words of P. O. Lawrence, J., in *Litchfield - Speer* v. *Queen Anne's Gate Syndicate* (*No.* 2) *Ltd.*[16]—

> In all cases of apprehended nuisance the authorities show that if the plaintiff proves that he will certainly sustain substantial damage by what the defendant is about to do the Court will restrain the defendant from doing the act and will not wait until the plaintiff has sustained the damage.

In accordance with the principle that the plaintiff who seeks equity must come with clean hands, he must show that he has acted in accordance with equitable principles. For example, a plaintiff who is himself in default upon a contract can never enforce any of its terms by injunction.[17] Again, a plaintiff who has been guilty of laches or acquiescence will be unable to obtain an injunction. Lapse of time is an important element in considering whether there has been acquiescence, although mere delay in the enforcement of a legal right is no bar to the grant of an injunction.[18]

Ordinarily the grant of an injunction, like the grant of any other equitable remedy, is discretionary, but the discretion of the court is one which is exercised in accordance with settled principles, established by judicial precedent. There are, nevertheless, circumstances in which an injunction will not be issued; for example, where the injury complained of has been ended before trial, or where it is impossible to restore the status quo. Thus, where timber has already been cut down, it would be idle to seek an injunction to restrain the felling of it and, in such a case, all that can be done is to leave the plaintiff to his remedy for damages.

It has already been pointed out that the Judicature Act gave the court power to award an injunction wherever it was "just or convenient" to do so, and that this has been interpreted as giving the courts

[14] *Day* v. *Brownrigg* (1878), 10 Ch. D. 294 (C.A.).

[15] (1816), 19 Ves. 617.

[16] [1919] 1 Ch. 407, 412. Ireland: *A.-G.* (*Boswell*) v. *Rathmines & Pembroke Joint Hospital Board*, [1904] 1 I.R. 161 (C.A.).

[17] *Measures Bros. Ltd.* v. *Measures*, [1910] 2 Ch. 248 (C.A.).

[18] *Fullwood* v. *Fullwood* (1878), 9 Ch. D. 176.

jurisdiction to award an injunction wherever the violation of a legal or equitable right has occurred or is threatened.[19] The Act did not, however, confer on the court power to create new heads of actionable wrong. Thus, in *Day* v. *Brownrigg*[20] the court refused to award an injunction against a person who had given his house the same name as the house next door. The effect of the Judicature Act, 1873, was not, said the Court of Appeal, to give the court the legislative power to create new wrongs, which could be restrained by injunction.

A case which comes near the border-line, however, is *R.* v. *R. and I.*[21] Two parties to a marriage had been divorced, the husband having been awarded the custody of the child. Subsequently, after the wife had withdrawn an application for access to the child, she wrote to the child, explaining her reasons, in terms likely seriously to affect him. She sent the letter to the child's headmaster, who retained it in his possession, and the husband was granted an injunction, forbidding the wife from communicating the letter to the child. The foundation for this exercise of jurisdiction was that the matter arose out of problems of custody of, and access to, a child over whom the court had jurisdiction.

Nevertheless, a survey of the decisions at once reveals the fact that there has been an important change in the use of injunctions since 1873. Because all divisions of the High Court now have power to award all legal and equitable remedies, injunctions are asked for oftener than before the Judicature Act, and they are oftener granted. Further, they are granted in respect of a wider variety of torts. Maitland suggested that the only torts in respect of which an injunction could not be obtained were assault and battery, malicious prosecution and false imprisonment. There has been an important change in respect to actions for libel. Before the Judicature Acts, this tort was outside the orbit of the remedy of injunction. The reason was sometimes said to be because libel was a crime; and at other times, it was said to be because libel was essentially a matter for a jury. To-day, however, injunctions for libel are frequently granted, and even an interlocutory injunction will issue where, as in the case of a libel alleged to be published in a daily news-

19 *Ante*. In *Hindley* v. *Hindley*, [1957] 1 W.L.R. 898 the court refused an injunction to a husband who had instituted divorce proceedings to restrain his wife from disposing of property which he had given her. In *Duchess of Argyll* v. *Duke of Argyll*, [1967] Ch. 302, an injunction was granted to restrain a former husband from disclosing marital confidences. In *Frazer* v. *Evans*, [1969] 1 Q.B. 349 (C.A.) an injunction to restrain breach of confidence was refused on the ground that the duty of confidence was not owed to the plaintiff. In *Hamzeh Malas & Sons* v. *British Imex Industries Ltd.*, [1958] 2 Q.B. 127 (C.A.) the court refused to grant an injunction to stop payment under a commercial letter of credit until the rights of the parties to the sale of goods to which the letters of credit related could be ascertained. Ireland: in *Cullen* v. *Cullen*, [1962] I.R. 268 an injunction was refused in respect of a family squabble.

20 (1878), 10 Ch. D.294.

21 [1961] 1 W.L.R. 1334.

paper, the harm threatened could not be adequately redressed by an action some months after publication. This power to award an interim injunction where libel is alleged is only exercised with caution, however. In *William Coulson & Sons* v. *James Coulson & Co.*,[22] Lord Esher, M.R., said that—

> . . . it could not be denied that the Court had jurisdiction to grant an interim injunction before the trial. It was, however, a most delicate jurisdiction to exercise, because, though Fox's Act only applied to indictments and informations for libel, the practice under that Act had been followed in civil actions for libel that the question of libel or no libel was for the jury. It was for the jury and not for the Court to construe the document, and to say whether it was a libel or not. To justify the Court in granting an interim injunction it must come to a decision upon the question of libel or no libel, before the jury decided whether it was a libel or not. Therefore the jurisdiction was of a delicate nature. It ought only to be exercised in the clearest cases, where any jury would say that the matter complained of was libellous, and where if the jury did not so find the Court would set aside the verdict as unreasonable. The Court must also be satisfied that in all probability the alleged libel was untrue, and if written on a privileged occasion that there was malice on the part of the defendant. It followed from those three rules that the Court could only on the rarest occasions exercise their jurisdiction.

These observations have frequently been referred to and acted upon in later cases.[23]

Two further points should be noticed in connection with the extension of the use of injunctions to nearly the entire field of the law of torts. The common law courts could award only damages, and even then, only for damage which had already been suffered. Equity, however, could grant an injunction, not only in respect of damage already sustained, but also for that which was apprehended. An action in respect of threatened injury is termed a *quia timet* action, and it was already in use before the Judicature Acts. An injunction will not be readily granted where injury has not yet been suffered, but is simply apprehended, however. In *Graigola Merthyr Co. Ltd.* v. *Swansea Corp.*,[24] Lord Buckmaster said: " . . . a mere vague appre-

[22] (1887), 3 T.L.R. 846.

[23] E.g. *Liverpool Household Stores Assoc.* v. *Smith* (1887), 37 Ch.D. 170 (C.A.); *Bonnard* v. *Perryman*, [1891] 2 Ch. 269 (C.A.); *Monson* v. *Madame Tussaud Ltd.*, [1894] 1 Q.B. 671 (C.A.). See also *Sim* v. *H. J. Heinz & Co. Ltd.* [1959] 1 W.L.R. 313. Ireland: *Sinclair* v. *Gogarty*, [1937] I.R. 377 (Sup. Ct.).

[24] [1929] A.C. 344, 353.

hension is not sufficient to support an action for a quia timet injunction. There must be an immediate threat to do something . . ." Secondly, under the Chancery Amendment Act, 1858, the court has power to grant damages in lieu of an injunction, and this jurisdiction has survived the Judicature Acts. This, too, is a power which is very rarely exercised, for the court will not allow a wealthy defendant to buy the right to continue a wrong.[25] It is now settled, however, that the court has power under this Act to award damages in lieu of an injunction where the injury is threatened but has not yet been committed (i.e. in lieu of a quia timet injunction).[26]

The Use of Injunctions to Protect Property Rights

The use of the injunction to restrain the infringement of rights in respect of real property is written large in our legal history, and it has played a prominent part in the development of our land law. Some of the main applications of the injunction in this field will be mentioned below.

(*a*) *Waste.* Where land was held, either under a term of years or by a limited owner under a settlement, wide classes of acts which damaged the reversioner's interests were restrained as *waste.* Even in early times, a distinction was drawn between *voluntary waste*, e.g. pulling down buildings, or damaging them, cutting timber, opening pits or mines or changing the course of husbandry, and *permissive waste*, which simply consisted in allowing land to go out of cultivation or in omitting to repair buildings on it. The legislature attempted to grapple with this problem in the reign of Edward I. The Statutes of Marlborough (1267) and Gloucester (1278) made a tenant for a fixed term of years or for life liable for voluntary waste at common law, in the absence of express agreement. The position with regard to permissive waste was less certain. In *Yellowly* v. *Gower*,[27] the court held a tenant for a fixed term of years liable at common law for permissive waste, although the correctness of this decision has been doubted.

However, a lease or a settlement might make a tenant " unimpeachable for waste;" and if this occurred, the reversioner had no remedy at law if the tenant injured the inheritance.

Equity extended the protection granted to the person entitled to the inheritance. Where voluntary waste at common law was committed, and the tenant was impeachable for waste, the Court of Chancery

25 *Per* Lindley, L.J., *Shelfer* v. *City of London Electric Lighting Co.*, [1895] 1 Ch. 287, 315-316 (C.A.).
26 *Leeds Industrial Co-operative Soc. Ltd.* v. *Slack*, [1924] A.C. 851 (H.L., E.).
27 (1855), 11 Ex. 274.

would grant an injunction; but it always declined to extend the use of injunctions to cases of permissive waste.[28] In the leading case of *Doherty* v. *Allman*,[29] however, the House of Lords, on appeal from Ireland, decided that equity would no longer grant an injunction to restrain " meliorating waste," i.e. acts which (like changing the course of husbandry or pulling down ruinous buildings to replace them with dwelling houses) might come technically within the term " waste " at common law, nevertheless improved, rather than damaged, the inheritance.

Moreover, even where a tenant was unimpeachable for waste, so that the common law was powerless to interfere, equity would prevent wanton acts of destruction, such as the dismantling of the mansion-house[30] or the felling of purely ornamental timber.[31] The determination of what is purely ornamental timber is not an easy question to decide, especially as tastes may differ upon whether some trees can be regarded as ornamental at all, and in *Marquis of Downshire* v. *Lady Sandys*,[32] Lord Eldon said—

> The principle, upon which the Court has gone, seems to be, that, if the testator or the author of the interest by deed had gratified his own taste by planting for ornament, though he had adopted the species the most disgusting to the tenant for life, and the most agreeable to the tenant in tail, and upon the competition between those parties the Court should see, that the tenant for life was right, and the other wrong, in point of taste, yet the taste of the testator, like his will, binds them; and it is not competent to them to substitute another species of ornament for that, which the testator designed.

By the Law of Property Act, 1925, Section 135,[33] it is now provided that a tenant for life may not commit that species of waste known as equitable waste unless the intention to confer such a right on him appears in the instrument conferring the interest on him.

(*b*) *Trespass.* An injunction was available in a court of equity to reinforce a claim for damages at common law in respect of a trespass.[34] Not only the tenant for life can claim, but also the reversioner if the trespass threatens the reversion. Now, the Judicature Act, 1925,

[28] *Wood* v. *Gaynon* (1761), Amb. 395; *Powys* v. *Blagrave* (1854), 4 De G. M. & G. 448.
[29] (1878), 3 App. Cas. 709. See also *Meux* v. *Cobley*, [1892] 2 Ch. 253.
[30] *Vane* v. *Lord Barnard* (1716), 2 Vern. 738.
[31] *Marquis of Downshire* v. *Lady Sandys* (1801), 6 Ves. 107.
[32] 6 Ves. 110.
[33] Ireland: Judicature (Ireland) Act, 1877, Sect. 28 (3).
[34] See *Thompson* v. *Park*, [1944] K.B. 408 (C.A.).

Section 45 (3),[35] provides that an injunction may be granted to prevent any threatened or apprehended waste or trespass, whether the person against whom the injunction is sought is or is not in possession under any claim of title or otherwise, or (if out of possession) does or does not claim a right to do the act sought to be restrained under any colour of title; and whether the estates claimed by both or either of the parties are legal or equitable.[36] The installation of a sign which projects into the air space above the property of another is a trespass, and the court will grant a mandatory injunction.[37]

(*c*) *Nuisance.* The Court of Chancery exercised a wide jurisdiction to restrain the commission of a nuisance. Even a public nuisance (e.g. obstruction of the highway) can be restrained at the suit of a person who has suffered damage thereby, but " the private individual who seeks to restrain the obstruction of a public highway must, in order to maintain his suit, prove that he has sustained particular damage other than and beyond the general inconvenience and injury suffered by the public; and moreover he must prove that the particular damage which he has sustained is direct and substantial."[38]

The line between public and private nuisance is sometimes a fine one, and the Court of Appeal has expressed the view that any nuisance which materially affects the comfort and convenience of life of a class of the Queen's subjects is a public nuisance. The question whether the local community in a neighbourhood comprises sufficient persons to constitute a class of the public, so that the nuisance is a public one, is a question of fact in every case.[39]

If a public authority so exercises any of its functions as to cause a private nuisance to any person, the authority is liable, and may be restrained by injunction, unless it can rely upon the words of some statute as a defence.[40]

In so far as private nuisances are concerned, an injunction will only be granted if the injury cannot be adequately compensated by damages, or if, from its continuance and mischievous character, it is a constantly recurring grievance; for example, the continuing nuisance

[35] Ireland: Judicature (Ireland) Act, 1877, Sect. 28 (8).

[36] *Truckell* v. *Stock*, [1957] 1 W.L.R. 161 (C.A.).

[37] *Kelsen* v. *Imperial Tobacco Co.* (*of Great Britain and Ireland*) *Ltd.*, [1957] 2 Q.B. 334.

[38] *Per* Luxmoore, J., in *Vanderpant* v. *Mayfair Hotel Co. Ltd.*, [1930] 1 Ch. 138, 153.

[39] *A.-G.* v. *P.Y.A. Quarries Ltd.*, [1957] 2 Q.B. 169.

[40] *Pride of Derby and Derbyshire Angling Assoc. Ltd.* v. *British Celanese Ltd.*, [1953] 1 Ch. 149 (C.A.).

to property caused by encroachment by the roots of trees growing on the land of another person,[41] or by the noise of large scale building operations.[42] In *Imperial Gas Light and Coke Co.* v. *Broadbent*[43] Lord Kingsdown said—

> The rule I take to be clearly this: if a Plaintiff applies for an injunction to restrain a violation of a common law right, if either the existence of the right or the fact of its violation be disputed, he must establish that right at law; but when he has established his right at law, I apprehend that unless there be something special in the case, he is entitled as of course to an injunction to prevent the recurrence of that violation.

Three points may be made by way of commentary upon these observations—

1. The fact that the grant of an injunction would interfere with, or even bring about, the suspension of a public service is not "something special in the case," so as to cause an injunction to be refused.[44]

2. The award of an injunction depends on general equitable principles and, accordingly, an injunction will be refused where there has been laches and acquiescence.[45]

3. As far as a grant of damages in lieu of an injunction under Lord Cairns' Act is concerned, this Act did not alter the principles governing the award of injunctions, but if the injury to the plaintiff's legal right is small, and is one which is capable of being estimated in money, and is one which can be adequately compensated by a small money payment, and the case is one in which it would be oppressive to the defendant to grant an injunction, damages in lieu of injunction may be awarded under that Act.[46]

If these conditions are not all satisfied, then an injunction—even a mandatory injunction—will be granted. In *Redland Bricks Ltd.* v. *Morris*[47] the plaintiffs, market gardeners, owned and cultivated eight acres of land adjoining land from which the defendants excavated earth and clay, in consequence of which a large pit, which was filled with

[41] *Butler* v. *Standard Telephones and Cables Ltd.*, [1940] 1 K.B. 399; *McCombe* v. *Read*, [1955] 2 Q.B. 429.

[42] *Boynton* v. *Helena Rubinstein Ltd.* (1960), 176 Est. Gaz. 443, 445.

[43] (1859), 7 H.L. C. 600, 612.

[44] *Imperial Gas Light and Coke Co.* v. *Broadbent* (1859), 7 H.L. C. 600, 612.

[45] *A.-G.* v. *Newry No.* 1 *R.D.C.*, [1933] N.I. 50.

[46] *Per* A. L. Smith, L.J., *Shelfer* v. *Cty of London Electric Lighting Co.*, [1895] 1 Ch. 287, 322-3 (C.A.).

[47] [1969] 2 W.L.R. 1437.

water, formed on the plaintiffs' land, which also began to slip. The plaintiffs claimed damages and an injunction in the county court, and the judge awarded £325 damages, and injunctions:

(1) restraining the defendants from further excavations, thus interfering with the support of the plaintiffs' land, and

(2) directing them to take all necessary steps to restore support to the plaintiffs' land.

The Court of Appeal affirmed this decision, notwithstanding the fact that cost of restoring support would substantially exceed the value of the plaintiffs' land, but the House of Lords reversed it because the defendants had only behaved wrongly, not unreasonably, and because the injunction granted had not indicated what work had to be done.

(*d*) *The Enforcement of Restrictive Covenants.* The enforcement of restrictive covenants in equity has been made possible solely by the use of the injunction; and the development of these equitable interests in land was probably the most important contribution made by equity to English law during the nineteenth century, for it filled a notable gap left by the common law. At common law, although the *benefit* of a covenant, whether negative or positive, made with a covenantee with an interest in the land subject to the covenant, might pass to the successor in title of the original covenantor, provided the covenantor had an estate in the land, and the covenant touched and concerned the land, nevertheless the *burden* of the covenant did not run with the land at law. This was finally settled by the decision of the Court of Appeal in *Austerberry* v. *Oldham Corp.* in 1885.[48] Equity, however, permitted the enforcement of covenants which were negative in nature against the successors in title of the original person bound, subject to the following conditions.

1. The covenant must be imposed between vendor and purchaser of a fee simple.

2. The covenant must be negative in substance, i.e. it must be a covenant to refrain from doing something.

3. The covenant must touch and concern the land.

4. The person entitled to the benefit of the covenant must retain land, for the benefit of which the covenant exists, and he must show that the benefit of the covenant has passed to him.

Provided these conditions are fulfilled, then the successors in title of the person entitled to the benefit of the covenant may enforce it, just as much as the original convenantee himself.

48 29 Ch.D. 750.

The first clear case of the application of this great equitable principle is *Tulk* v. *Moxhay*.[49] In that case, the plaintiff, being in 1808 the owner of a piece of land forming the garden of Leicester Square, and being also the owner of several adjoining houses, sold the land, but took a restrictive covenant that he would put a railing round it, and keep it as an open space. The land was subsequently sold several times, until it came into Moxhay's hands, with notice of the covenant. Moxhay then made preparations to build on the land, whereupon the plaintiff sought an injunction. This was granted, with remarkably little discussion of the general principle underlying the case. The gist of the judgment of Lord Cottenham, L.C., is contained in the following observations (taken from 18 L.J. Ch. 87)—

> Without adverting to any question about a covenant running with land or not, I consider this piece of land is purchased subject to an equity created by a party competent to create it: and the present defendant took it with distinct knowledge of such equity existing; and such equity ought to be enforced against him as it would be against the party who originally took the land from Mr. Tulk.

Later judges, extracting a general principle from the decision, regarded it as a logical deduction from the doctrine of notice, but later still, it was settled that the true view is that the restrictive covenant creates an equitable interest enforceable under the usual conditions applicable to equitable interests. This is strikingly illustrated by the decision in *Re Nisbet and Potts' Contract*,[50] in which case the restrictive covenant was enforced against a person who had acquired title to the land by adverse possession. All three members of the Court of Appeal in that case were of opinion that such covenants were in the nature of negative easements in equity, which bound all persons except those who could show they were free of them.

This equitable doctrine does not apply to chattels,[51] but in *Lord Strathcona Steamship Co. Ltd.* v. *Dominion Coal Co. Ltd.*,[52] the Judicial Committee of the Privy Council granted an injunction to restrain a purchaser of a ship from using it in a way inconsistent with the terms of a charterparty of which he had notice. The Privy Council obviously regarded this as a logical extension of the principle underlying the enforcement of restrictive covenants affecting land. The decision

49 (1848), 2 Ph. 774.
50 [1906] 1 Ch. 386.
51 *Taddy & Co.* v. *Sterious & Co.*, [1904] 1 Ch. 354.
52 [1926] A.C. 108 (Nova Scotia).

provoked very considerable criticism, however, and in *Port Line Ltd.* v. *Ben Line Steamers Ltd.*,[53] Diplock, J., came to the conclusion that the Privy Council were wrong.

The property legislation of 1925 introduced important changes in England in respect of restrictive covenants. All covenants between vendor and purchaser, made after 1925, must now be registered. If not registered, they are void even against a purchaser of a legal estate for money or money's worth who had notice of them.[54] Moreover, the Law of Property Act, 1925, has provided machinery whereby restrictive covenants which have ceased to be applicable may be extinguished.[55] Such cases are referred to the Lands Tribunal, but the courts have emphasised that the provisions of the Law of Property Act, 1925, are not to be construed too broadly. " If a case is to be made out under this section, there must be some proper evidence that the restriction is no longer necessary for any reasonable purpose of the person who is enjoying the benefit of it, or that by reason of a change in the character of the property or the neighbourhood, the restriction is one which is no longer to be enforceable or has become of no value."[56]

(*e*) *The enforcement of Easements.* Little needs to be said upon the use of the injunction to restrain the infringement of easements. Very often such an infringement amounts to a nuisance, and can be restrained as such, e.g. an interference with a right of light, or with an easement of support. Even where it does not amount to this, however, an injunction will be granted.[57] Moreover, an owner of land subject to an easement may be entitled to an injunction in respect of excessive user by the person entitled to the easement. In *London Corp.* v. *Riggs*[58] the defendant was restrained from using an implied way of necessity for purposes other than the agricultural purposes which were the sole method of user at the time of the implied grant.

(*f*) *The Restraint of a Tenant for Life or the Trustees of a Settlement.* By virtue of the Settled Land Act, 1925, the tenant for life of settled land occupies a fiduciary position in respect of those entitled to interests

53 [1958] 2 Q.B. 146.

54 Land Charges Act, 1925, Sects. 10 (1) and 13 (2). Ireland: no equivalent legislation.

55 Law of Property Act, 1925, Sect. 84. See also *Re Freeman-Thomas Indenture* [1957] 1 W.L.R. 560. Ireland: no equivalent legislation.

56 *Per* Farwell, J., *Re Henderson's Conveyance*, [1940] Ch. 835, 846. See also *Re Truman, Hanbury, Buxton & Co. Ltd's Application*, [1956] 1 Q.B. 261 (C.A.); *Driscoll* v. *Church Commissioners for England*, [1957] 1 Q.B. 330 (C.A.); *Re Ghey and Galton's Application*, [1957] 2 Q.B. 650 (C.A.).

57 *Robertson* v. *Abrahams*, [1930] W.N. 79.

58 (1880), 13 Ch.D. 798.

in the land in succession to his.[59] Both he and the trustees of land held on trust for sale, as well as trustees of other kinds of property, will be restrained from acting inconsistently with the trust at the suit either of other trustees or of beneficiaries under the settlement.[60]

An injunction will be granted at the suit of a party to a marriage, who is petitioning for divorce, to restrain the other party from disposing of funds arising from an ante-nuptial settlement, where the effect of it would be to stultify the jurisdiction of the Divorce Court in respect of the settlement;[61] and it will also be granted against a husband, against whom a decree has been pronounced on the ground of cruelty, from disposing of his assets, so long as costs and maintenance are unpaid.[62] An injunction will also be issued where a husband commits a breach of an undertaking not to molest his wife.

(*g*) *Licences.* In recent years equity has granted injunctions at the instance of a licensee in occupation of land against certain classes of successors in title of the licensor. An injunction has been granted against a devisee,[63] a trustee in bankruptcy[64] and a collusive purchaser.[65] It therefore seems that the courts have recognised a new equity[66] in the licensee.

(*h*) *Passing-Off.* In *Morris Motors Ltd.* v. *Lilley*,[67] and again in *Morris Motors Ltd.* v. *Phelan*[68] firms were restrained from offering for sale, as new, motor-cars of the plaintiffs which in fact were not new. A more common type of " passing-off " occurs where a firm simulates the appearance or title of goods of another firm, so that a purchaser or customer is likely to be deceived,[69] and applications for injunctions are numerous.

[59] Settled Land Act, 1925, Sects. 107 and 16. Ireland: the Settled Land Act, 1882, Sect. 53, corresponds to Sect. 107 of the 1925 Act; no legislation corresponding to Sect. 16.

[60] See *Re Hunt's Settled Estates*, [1905] 2 Ch. 419; [1906] 2 Ch. 11 (C.A.).

[61] *Bosworthick* v. *Bosworthick*, [1927] P. 64 (C.A.); *Parrington* v. *Parrington* [1951] 2 All E.R. 916; *Hindley* v. *Hindley*, [1957] 1 W.L.R. 898.

[62] *Shore* v. *Shore* (1960), *The Times* newspaper, 13th October.

[63] *Errington* v. *Errington*, [1953] 1 K.B. 290 (C.A.).

[64] *Bendall* v. *McWhirter*, [1952] 2 Q.B. 466 (C.A.).

[65] *Ferris* v. *Weaven*, [1952] 2 All E.R. 233.

[66] *Jess B. Woodcock & Sons Ltd.* v. *Hobbs*, [1955] 1 W.L.R. 152 (C.A.); *Churcher* v. *Street*, [1959] Ch. 251. See pp. 103-4, *ante*.

[67] [1959] 1 W.L.R. 1184.

[68] [1960] 1 W.L.R. 352 and 566.

[69] E.g. *Twentieth Century Fox Film Corp.* v. *Gala Film Distributors Ltd.*, [1957] R.P.C. 105; *Britains Ltd.* v. *M. Morris & Co. (London) Ltd.*, [1961] R.P.C. 217.

The Use of Injunctions in Contract

Exactly as the equitable remedy of specific performance was evolved to enforce the positive stipulations in certain classes of contracts, so the remedy of injunction has been available to restrain breaches of negative stipulations, and the injunctions, if granted, will prevail, not only against the defendant but against any company, or even person, such as a wife, who is sued by the defendant as a mere cloak for his activities.[70]

Because of the nature of the remedy, however, it has been possible to make the remedy of injunction available in a wider range of contracts than the remedy of specific performance. One wide class of agreements in the enforcement of which the injunction plays an important part is those in which the question of " restraint of trade " arises. These are either contracts for the sale of a business or between employer and employee. Whether, in either of these classes of case, the restraint is too wide is a question of public policy, the answer to which depends upon the circumstances of each case.[71] The old common law rule had been that restraints must be limited as to time, space, or both, whilst equity had held that the reasonableness of the restraint depended upon the facts of each case. In *Nordenfelt* v. *Maxim Nordenfelt*,[72] the House of Lords accepted the equitable view, and granted an injunction in respect of a covenant imposing a world-wide restraint. This was a case of vendor and purchaser of a business. There is, however, an important difference between such cases, and those in which restraints are imposed in contracts of employment. This was defined by Younger, L.J., in *Attwood* v. *Lamont*,[73] in the following terms—

> . . . when a purchaser takes over the goodwill of a business, if he is to have all its advantages it must in his hands be immune from its former owner exercising his special knowledge and skill to its detriment, and without a covenant on the part of the vendor against competition a purchaser cannot get what he is contracting to buy, nor can the vendor give what he is intending to sell. But, on the other hand, as is pointed out by Lord Parker in *Morris* v. *Saxelby*,[74]

[70] *Smith* v. *Hancock*, [1894] 2 Ch. 377 (C.A.); *Gilford Motor Co. Ltd.* v. *Horne*, [1933] Ch. 935 (C.A.).

[71] On which, see *Nordenfelt* v. *Maxim Nordenfelt Guns and Ammunition Co. Ltd.*, [1894] A.C. 535 (H.L., E.); *Mason* v. *Provident Clothing and Supply Co.*, [1913] A.C. 724 (H.L., E.); *Herbert Morris Ltd.* v. *Saxelby*, [1916] 1 A.C. 688 (H.L., E.); *Attwood* v. *Lamont*, [1920] 3 K.B. 571 (C.A.); *Fitch* v. *Dewes*, [1921] 2 A.C. 158 (H.L., E.); *Putsman* v. *Taylor*, [1927] 1 K.B. 741 (C.A.); *M. & S. Drapers* v. *Reynolds*, [1957] 1 W.L.R. 9 (C.A.); *Kores Manufacturing Co. Ltd.* v. *Kolok Manufacturing Co. Ltd.*, [1959] Ch. 108 (C.A.); Hedges, *Restraint of Trade*.

[72] [1894] A.C. 724.

[73] [1920] 3 K.B. 571, 590.

[74] [1916] 1 A.C. 688, 709.

> the case is very different when the employer takes such a covenant from his employee. The employer's goodwill is always necessarily subject to the competition of all persons, including the employee, who choose to engage in a similar trade. . . . Accordingly covenants against competition by a former servant are as such not upheld; and the permissible extent of any covenant imposed upon a servant must be tested in every case with reference to the character of the work done for the employer by the servant while in his service and by the consideration whether in that view the covenant taken from him goes further than is reasonably necessary for the protection of the proprietary rights of the covenantee.

A useful illustration of these observations is afforded by the decision of the Court of Appeal (upholding a decision of Gorman, J.) in *Vandervell Products Ltd.* v. *McCleod.*[75] McCleod had been employed by the appellants to do work involving secret processes, and he covenanted not to enter the employment of any competitor of the appellants for two years after the termination of his employment with them. This was held to be unenforceable, being too wide, not only in point of space, but because it would prevent McCleod from entering the employment of any person or company who should, at a future date, when his employment by the appellants ended, then be in competition with the appellants.

The use of the injunction sometimes goes further than in these cases of agreements in restraint of trade. It may have the effect almost of indirect specific performance. Here, however, a distinction must be drawn between contracts of personal service and other contracts. Where the contract is *not* for personal service, equity will enforce it by injunction, if negative in substance, even though it is positive in form. It will, in fact, read the necessary logical negative into the contract. Thus, in *Catt* v. *Tourle*,[76] a publican agreed to take all his beer from a specified brewer. The court granted an injunction to prevent the publican from buying beer from anyone else, reading into the contract the negative stipulation, by way of corollary, that the publican would not buy his beer from anyone else.

In *Lumley* v. *Wagner*,[77] an allied problem arose in respect of the contract of personal service. Miss Wagner agreed to sing at the plaintiff's opera house, and during the existence of the contract, she agreed not to sing anywhere else. When Miss Wagner, after a quarrel,

[75] [1957] R.P.C. 185. Cf. *Kerchiss* v. *Colora Printing Inks Ltd.*, [1960] R.P.C. 235.

[76] (1869), L.R. 4 Ch. App. 654.

[77] (1852), 1 De G.M. & G. 604. See also *Page One Records Ltd.* v. *Britton*, [1968] 1 W.L.R. 157.

announced her intention of singing elsewhere, although specific performance of the positive stipulations could not be obtained, the court granted an injunction preventing her from singing anywhere else. This important use of the injunction in personal service contracts is, however, subject to two important limitations—

1. The court will not read negative terms into a purely positive contract. For example, if an employee agrees to give the whole of his time to his employer during his employment, the court will not read into that an undertaking not to serve anyone else for the duration of the contract.[78]

2. The court will not grant an injunction where the effect of granting it will be that the employee must fulfil his contract or starve. This point is of great importance so far as the form of the negative stipulation is concerned. Thus in *Chapman* v. *Westerby*,[79] there was a contract of employment of a skipper of a trawler, and the negative stipulation provided that the skipper " shall not give his time or personal attention to any other business or occupation." An injunction was refused, for, as Warrington, J., said:[80] " To so enforce it would involve this, that so far as earning his living was concerned the defendant would have to be absolutely idle for the term of ten years or continue this contract of personal service; in other words, it would for all practical purposes be granting specific performance of a contract of service, a thing which the Court would never do." In *Rely-A-Bell Burglar and Fire Alarm Co. Ltd.* v. *Eisler*,[81] Russell, J., applied the same principle to a negative covenant in similar terms. On the other hand, in *Warner Bros. Pictures Inc.* v. *Nelson*,[82] an injunction was granted in respect of the negative stipulation in the contract of a film actress, but only to restrain the film actress from participating in stage or film plays, although the negative covenant had prohibited the actress from these and also "*any other occupation*." It remains to be seen whether the courts will follow the lead given in this later case, in granting an injunction in terms narrower than those of the negative clause, or will prefer the more literal approach of earlier judges to the negative clause.

The Protection of Industrial Property

Historically, the Court of Chancery has played a great part in the development of the conception of property in copyrights, patents and trade marks, as a glance through the pages of the reports of cases in

78 *Whitwood Chemical Co.* v. *Hardman*, [1891] 2 Ch. 416 (C.A.); *Mortimer* v. *Beckett*, [1920] 1 Ch. 571.

79 [1913] W.N. 277.

80 [1913] W.N. 278.

81 [1926] Ch. 609.

82 [1937] 1 K.B. 209.

Chancery during the nineteenth century will show. It was at this period that the main principles underlying the modern statute law upon these rights were elaborated. The usual remedy for an infringement is an injunction and an account of profits.[83] In so far as copyrights are concerned, the court may grant an injunction without proof of actual damage, if it is probable that there will be damage, and that the defendant will continue to infringe.[84] In respect of patents, two kinds of action for an injunction may be brought by the patentee. One is based on actual infringement, and here, either damages or an account, together with an injunction against future infringements, may be claimed. In the other type of action, the claim of the patentee is that the defendant intends or threatens to infringe, and an injunction is sought to restrain the threatened breach.[85]

One type of industrial property, however, has not yet attracted the attention of the legislature. This is goodwill. In *Trego* v. *Hunt*[86] Lord Macnaghten said—

> What " goodwill " means must depend on the character and nature of the business to which it is attached. Generally speaking, it means much more than what Lord Eldon took it to mean in the particular case actually before him in *Cruttwell* v. *Lye*,[87] where he says: " the goodwill which has been the subject of the sale is nothing more than the probability that the old customers will resort to the old place." Often it happens that the goodwill is the very sap and life of the business, without which the business would yield little or no fruit. It is the whole advantage, whatever it may be, of the reputation and connection of the firm, which may have been built up by years of honest work or gained by lavish expenditure of money.

The question to be settled in *Trego* v. *Hunt* was this: Is a person, who has sold the goodwill of his business independently of any covenant, at liberty to set up a rival business and to solicit the old customers of the business? To this the House of Lords replied, Yes, to the first question, but No, to the second, although if the old customers came to him of their own accord, he may deal with them. All the members of the

[83] E.g. *Carlis Ware* v. *Radford*, [1959] R.P.C. 38; *Super Rax Ltd.* v. *Broadfoot*, [1961] R.P.C. 61. See also the Copyright Act, 1956, Sect. 17 (1). Republic of Ireland: Copyright Act, 1963, Sect. 22.

[84] *Smith* v. *Johnson* (1863), 4 Giff. 632; *Borthwick* v. *Evening Post* (1888), 37 Ch. D. 449 (C.A.).

[85] *Frearson* v. *Loe* (1878), 9 Ch. D. 48, 65; *Shoe Machinery Co. Ltd.* v. *Cutlan* (1895) 12 R.P.C. 342, 357.

[86] [1896] A.C. 7, 23-4 (H.L., E.). See also *Curl Bros. Ltd.* v. *Webster*, [1904] 1 Ch. 685.

[87] (1810), 17 Ves. 335, 346.

House of Lords in *Trego* v. *Hunt* regretted that protection of the purchaser of a business, in the absence of a covenant, was so limited, and Lord Macnaghten said[88]—

> . . . authorities, which it is now too late to question, undoubtedly shew that a man who has sold the goodwill of his business may do much to regain his former position, and yet keep on the windy side of the law. The common law has always been jealous of any interference with trade. It was a lighter matter to interfere with freedom of contract and avoid covenants under seal. Courts of Equity could not of course enforce even in a modified form and within reasonable limits an agreement express or implied which the law would have held void on the ground of public policy; nor could they treat the mere non-observance of such an agreement as fraudulent or inequitable. And so it has resulted that a person who sells the goodwill of his business is under no obligation to retire from the field. Trade he undoubtedly may, and in the very same line of business. If he has not bound himself by special stipulation, and if there is no evidence of the understanding of the parties beyond that which is to be found in all cases, he is free to carry on business wherever he chooses. But, then, how far may he go ? He may do everything that a stranger to the business, in ordinary course, would be in a position to do. He may set up where he will. He may push his wares as much as he pleases. He may thus interfere with the custom of his neighbour as a stranger and an outsider might do; but he must not, I think, avail himself of his special knowledge of the old customers to regain, without consideration, that which he has parted with for value. He must not make his approaches from the vantage ground of his former position, moving under cover of a connection which is no longer his. He may not sell the custom and steal away the customers in that fashion.

Even this last restriction, however, extends only to free sales of a business, for in *Dawson* v. *Beeson*[89] a partner who had been expelled from the partnership was allowed to solicit the old customers; and so was a trader who had assigned his business, with the goodwill, to a trustee for his creditors in *Farey* v. *Cooper*.[90]

In Ireland, in "*Independent*" *Newspapers Ltd.* v. "*Irish Press*" *Ltd.*,[91] an injunction was sought to restrain the use by the defendants of a proprietary name which had been bought by the plaintiffs, but never

88 [1896] A.C. 24-5.
89 (1882), 22 Ch.D. 504 (C.A.).
90 [1927] 2 K.B. 384 (C.A.).
91 [1932] I.R. 615.

used by them. It was held that an injunction could be granted, but the court refused to issue a quia timet injunction on the ground that the plaintiffs had not discharged the burden of showing a strong probability of damage.[92]

The Use of the Injunction in the Law of Associations

Deviations from the rules governing the transaction of business by associations, whether corporate or unincorporate, can in many cases be restrained by injunction. Some of the more important associations will be briefly considered below—

(*a*) *Companies.* A director may, by injunction, restrain his fellow directors from excluding him from office.[93] A mandatory injunction may issue to enforce an agreement to vote at a meeting,[94] or to enforce the calling of a meeting.[95] An injunction may also issue for the mala fide exercise by the directors of the power to make calls on shares,[96] and an injunction may also be granted against directors who wrongly seek to forfeit shares.[96] Indeed, the injunction is freely available to those who wish to enforce their rights under the Companies Acts.

(*b*) *Clubs and Unincorporated Associations.* Where clubs and societies are concerned, equity draws a distinction between those which are proprietary (i.e. in which the property is owned by someone other than the members) and those which are non-proprietary (i.e. in which the property is vested in the members of the club themselves). In the first type of club, since the member has no right of property in the club, equity will not interfere if he has been irregularly expelled, and will leave him to his remedy in damages at common law; but in the second case, equity may grant an injunction unless the rules have been strictly complied with, and the forms of natural justice have been adhered to. This means that the members will have an opportunity of being heard,[97] but it does not imply that the association, or its committee, must conduct itself like a court of law. Where the claim is for an injunction for failure to apply the principles of natural justice, there must

[92] As to quia timet injunctions, see pp. 460, 462, *ante*.

[93] *Pulbrook* v. *Richmond Consolidated Mining Co.* (1878), 9 Ch. D. 610. See also *Bainbridge* v. *Smith* (1889), 41 Ch. D. 462 (C.A.); *Burden* v. *Sinclair* (1961), 105 S.J. 586 (C.A.). Ireland: *Coubrough* v. *James Panton & Co. Ltd.*, [1965] I.R. 272.

[94] *Puddephatt* v. *Leith*, [1916] 1 Ch. 200.

[95] Palmer, *Company Law*, 21st ed., ch. 47.

[96] *Lamb* v. *Sambas Rubber and Gutta Percha Co. Ltd.*, [1908] 1 Ch. 845.

[97] *Young* v. *Ladies' Imperial Club Ltd.*, [1920] 2 K.B. 523 (C.A.); *Keighley Rugby Football Club Ltd.* v. *Cunningham* (1960), *The Times* newspaper, 25th May (where Danckwerts, J., declared invalid the suspension of a player without a hearing).

be a contractual basis.[98] Again, in the second type of club, a member may restrain by injunction the use of the property of the club or society, in a way not warranted by the terms of association.

The same principles govern the use of injunctions in respect of professional and trade associations, and friendly societies. A few examples may serve to illustrate these principles:

(i) In *Amalgamated Soc. of Railway Servants* v. *Osborne*,[99] Osborne obtained an injunction to prevent the use of the funds of the union for unlawful purposes. However, his victory was shortlived, for he was expelled from his union, and this time the court refused an injunction against the expulsion.[100]

(ii) In *National Sailors' and Firemen's Union of Great Britain and Ireland* v. *Reed*,[1] members of the trade union obtained an injunction to restrain Reed, the secretary of the Tower Hill branch, and other officials from calling on members to leave their employment without the authority of the executive council of the union. The grant of this injunction by Astbury, J., was one of the main causes leading to the collapse of the general strike of 1926.

(iii) In *Law* v. *Chartered Institute of Patent Agents*,[2] the Institute expelled a member on the ground of misconduct. At a previous inquiry into the same charge before a committee appointed by the Board of Trade, the defendants had put themselves into the position of accusers. Eve, J., therefore held that by acting as accusers before the committee of the Board of Trade, the Institute had acted so as to create in the mind of a reasonable man the suspicion of bias. Accordingly, an injunction was granted to restrain the expulsion.

(*c*) *Trade Unions*. The use of the injunction to regulate the affairs of one most important class of voluntary associations—trade unions—needs particular attention, more especially as it is affected by legislation. Section 3 of the Trade Union Act, 1871 (which affirmed the lawfulness of trade unions) made enforceable at law " any agreement or trust " for the purposes of a trade union. In the general terms in which it was expressed the clause would not only have made enforceable the rules of the union itself, its contracts with its agents and its dispositions of its property, but also any contracts whereby workmen bound themselves not to work, and accordingly, the court might have

[98] *Russell* v. *Duke of Norfolk*, [1949] 1 All E.R. 109 (C.A.); *Byrne* v. *Kinematograph Renters Soc. Ltd.*, [1958] 1 W.L.R. 762.

[99] [1910] A.C. 87 (H.L., E.).

[100] *Osborne* v. *A.S.R.S.*, [1911] 1 Ch. 540 (C.A.).

[1] [1926] Ch. 536.

[2] [1919] 2 Ch. 276.

been called upon by injunction to enforce a strike upon which the union had agreed.[3] This was desired neither by the state nor by the unions themselves, and accordingly, the general effect of Section 3 is limited by Section 4, which provides—

> Nothing in this Act shall enable any court to entertain any legal proceeding instituted with the object of directly enforcing or recovering damages for the breach of any of the following agreements, namely,
>
> 1. Any agreement between members of a trade union as such, concerning the conditions on which any members for the time being of such trade union shall or shall not sell their goods, transact business, employ, or be employed:
>
> 2. Any agreement for the payment by any person of any subscription or penalty to a trade union:
>
> 3. Any agreement for the application of the funds of a trade union,—
>
> (a.) To provide benefits to members; or
>
> (b.) To furnish contributions to any employer or workman not a member of such trade union, in consideration of such employer or workman acting in conformity with the rules or resolutions of such trade union; or
>
> (c.) To discharge any fine imposed upon any person by sentence of a court of justice; or,
>
> 4. Any agreement made between one trade union and another; or,
>
> 5. Any bond to secure the performance of any of the above-mentioned agreements.

There has been a good deal of litigation, and a variety of views has been expressed, upon the extent of the withdrawal of these agreements from the control of the courts under Section 4.[4] It has now been established that, in an important number of cases, the grant of an injunction does not amount to a direct enforcement of the agreement. Accordingly, an injunction will be granted to restrain the misapplication of the funds of a trade union;[5] or to restrain the wrongful expulsion of a member;[6] or to restrain the adoption or enforcement of ultra vires

[3] *Per* Lord Robson, *Russell* v. *Amalgamated Soc. of Carpenters and Joiners*, [1912] A.C. 421, 441 (H.L., E.). See also Citrine, *Trade Union Law*, 2nd ed., p. 91.

[4] Citrine, *op cit.*, pp. 91 *et seq.*

[5] *Yorkshire Miners' Assoc.* v. *Howden*, [1905] A.C. 256 (H.L., E.).

[6] *Bonsor* v. *Musicians' Union*, [1956] A.C. 104 (H.L., E.).

amendments to rules; or to restrain action upon an *ultra vires* resolution. Where, however, the grant would amount substantially to the direct enforcement of an agreement, it will be refused.[7] In *Ford Motor Co. Ltd.* v. *Amalgamated Union of Engineering and Foundry Workers*,[8] after full argument on an application for an interlocutory injunction, Lane, J., held that a collective agreement was not enforceable because the parties had not intended it to be legally binding. The learned judge thought the agreement could have been made to have contractual force but that, having regard to the climate of opinion as to labour relations and having regard to the expressions used by the parties, it had not been intended to have that force in this case.

The Tort of Intimidation

In *Rookes* v. *Barnard*,[9] the House of Lords held that the tort of intimidation was committed when persons in the employment of a firm, being members of a trade union, threatened to withdraw their services in breach of contract, unless the plaintiff (who had ceased to be a member of the union) was dismissed. In this case the plaintiff asked for, and obtained, damages only, but in *J. T. Stratford & Son Ltd.* v. *Lindley*,[10] a case which again raised the question of intimidation arising out of threats by trade union officials to induce a breach of contract by members of their union, the company asked for an injunction, which Marshall, J., granted, the Court of Appeal discharged, and the House of Lords restored.

The Use of the Injunction in Public Law

Not only has the injunction been used very widely over the field of private law. It has also been applied to the field of public law. Some trade union decisions, indeed, are within this field, more especially that given in *National Sailors' and Firemen's Union of Great Britain and Ireland* v. *Reed*[11] in 1926. There have been other applications in the field of public law, however. Thus, in *A.-G.* v. *Sharp*,[12] the Court of Appeal held that it had power to grant an injunction to restrain the breach of a statute, although the statute itself imposed a penalty for breach of it. Lord Hanworth, M.R., in that case cited with approval a passage from Halsbury's *Laws of England*[13] in the following broad terms—

[7] *McLuskey* v. *Cole* [1922] 1 Ch. 7 (C.A.).
[8] [1969] 1 W.L.R. 339.
[9] [1964] A.C. 1129.
[10] [1965] A.C. 269. See also *Torquay Hotel Co. Ltd.* v. *Cousins*, [1969] 2 W.L.R. 289 (C.A.).
[11] [1926] Ch. 536.
[12] [1931] 1 Ch. 121.
[13] 1st ed., vol. 27, p. 191. Cf. 3rd ed., vol. 36, p. 447.

In addition to the common law remedy of indictment, and any specific remedies provided by the statute in question, the Attorney-General may at any time apply to the High Court to exercise its equitable jurisdiction of granting an injunction against the breach of a statutory duty or the infringement or threatened infringement of a public right, and an individual who, save as one of the public, has sustained no special damage can only do so in the Attorney-General's name.

For example, in *A.-G.* v. *Ashborne Recreation Ground Co.*[14] Buckley, J., held that the court could enforce by-laws by an injunction in an action brought by the Attorney-General at the relation of the local authority.

These two decisions, and others of a similar type,[15] open up an interesting vista of the enforcement of public interests by the Attorney General, even where certain acts against the public interest are made crimes by statute. In such actions, the Attorney-General himself exercises his discretion, and he will require to be satisfied that the provisions of the statute or by-law have been broken. Even so, it does not follow that the court will then grant an injunction as a matter of course. The court must also satisfy itself that there has been injury to the public. Even if the injury is small, provided it is real, an injunction may be granted; but if the public has suffered no injury, an injunction will be refused.[16] In *Paddington Corp.* v. *A.-G.*[17] it was pointed out that an individual might sue, apart from the Attorney-General, where (i) the interference with a public right also involves the interference with a private right of the individual or (ii) where the individual has suffered special damage as a result of the interference with the public right.[18]

This, however, is by no means the full extent of possible developments in this field. In *Bilston Corp.* v. *Wolverhampton Corp.*[19] Simonds, J., refused an injunction, at the suit of one local government authority against another, which had agreed not to oppose a private Act of Parliament, and the learned judge observed with respect to the constitutional principle involved—

14 [1903] 1 Ch. 101.

15 E.g. *A.-G.* v. *Wimbledon House Estate Co. Ltd.*, [1904] 2 Ch. 34; *A.-G.* v. *Bastow*, [1957] 1 Q.B. 514; *A.-G.* v. *Smith*, [1958] 2 Q.B. 173.

16 *A.-G.* v. *Birmingham, Tame and Rea Drainage Board*, [1910] 1 Ch. 48, 61 (C.A.); *A.-G.* v. *Bastow*, [1957] 1 Q.B. 514, 520; *A.-G.* v. *Harris*, [1960] 1 Q.B. 31; reversed, [1961] 1 Q.B. 74 (C.A.).

17 [1906] A.C. 1 (H.L., E.).

18 This question is interestingly discussed at length in Hanbury, *Modern Equity*, 8th ed., p. 595.

19 [1942] Ch. 391, 392-3.

> The court clearly has power to enforce a contractual obligation entered into by a person or a corporation that he or it will not apply to Parliament or will not oppose an application to Parliament by another person. That jurisdiction was asserted over and over again by Lord Chancellors in the middle of the last century, but it is significant that the assertion was always accompanied by the statement that it was difficult to conceive a case in which such a jurisdiction should be exercised . . .

The learned judge then pointed out that in determining a dispute between two local authorities concerning the grant of statutory powers to them or one of them, Parliament will have to consider questions of policy in the broadest sense and it would therefore be improper for a court to intervene to prevent those matters being placed before Parliament. He added that there was no difference in this connection between a case where the contractual obligation was not to apply to Parliament, and one where the obligation was not to oppose the application of another party.[20]

Finally, in *Bradbury* v. *Enfield Corp.*[21] the Court of Appeal granted an injunction against a local education authority which failed to carry out its statutory duty to " maintain " a school, which it sought to merge into a comprehensive school, and Lord Denning, M.R., sharply observed that a local authority, as well as the Department of Education, were subject to the rule of law like everyone else, and could be compelled by the courts to observe it.

[20] See on this case, Holdsworth (1943), 59 *Law Quarterly Review*, 2; Sawer (1944), 60 *Law Quarterly Review*, 83; Pollak (1944), 60 *Law Quarterly Review*, 226. For an interesting attempt to restrain the Home Secretary by injunction from presenting a draft Order to the Queen in Council see *Harper* v. *Secretary of State for the Home Department*, [1955] Ch. 238 (C.A.).

[21] [1967] 1 W.L.R. 1311.

CHAPTER XVIII

SPECIFIC PERFORMANCE

INTRODUCTION

AN ORDER of specific performance is an order that the contracting party against whom it is made carry out his obligations under the contract. Specific performance is the great equitable remedy, fashioned by the Court of Chancery, as an alternative remedy for certain classes of contract to the award of damages at common law. Holdsworth pointed out that in the fifteenth century, the Court of Chancery sometimes decreed specific performance of contracts for the sale of chattels, or of a contract to build;[1] but the origin of the modern equitable jurisdiction in respect of specific performance is to be found in the decisions of the following century, for at that period the earlier theories of equity in respect of contracts, based on *laesio fidei* and derived from canon law, had been abandoned in face of the progressive extensions of assumpsit by the common law courts. The Court of Chancery progressively adopted the view that it was necessary to resort to the Court of Chancery only when damages were an inadequate remedy, and when, therefore, some form of specific relief was required.[2] For a time, during the latter part of the seventeenth century, there was a tendency for the Court of Chancery to adopt the restrictive rule that specific performance of executory contracts would only be granted when the plaintiff had recovered damages at law.[3] In 1728, however, the House of Lords in *Bettesworth* v. *Dean and Chapter of St. Paul's*[4] finally rejected this view, thus leaving the way open for the development of the equitable doctrine of part performance for some contracts in respect of which the Statute of Frauds, 1677,[5] required a note or memorandum in writing. This doctrine was at that time regarded as less of an evasion of the terms of the Statute of Frauds than it now appears, inasmuch as the statute itself was intended as a check upon frauds, and the insistence of the Court of Chancery on making the

1 *History of English Law*, vol. I, p. 457, vol. II, pp. 276-7, 290. See also *Cokayn* v. *Hurst* (1458), Sel. Cas. Ch., 10 Sel. Soc. no. 142 (specific performance granted, of marriage articles, so as to order the settlement of land).
2 *History of English Law*, vol. V, pp. 322-3.
3 *History of English Law*, vol. VI, p. 658.
4 1 Bro. P.C. 240.
5 Ireland: Statute of Frauds, 1695.

award of specific performance discretionary, and in so doing, ensuring that the plaintiff had himself satisfied equitable standards of fair dealing, appeared to be in general conformity with the policy of the statute. In the time of Lord Hardwicke, equity's jurisdiction to decree specific performance began to assume a more modern appearance. The remedy remained discretionary, but the discretion was exercised in accordance with principles. By this time, too, the doctrine of part performance was well established. The act relied upon as being part performance must be such an act " as appears to the court would not have been done, unless on account of the agreement . . ."[6] Nevertheless in the same case, Lord Hardwicke also said: " Paying of money has been always held in this court as a part-performance "—a view which was decisively rejected in the nineteenth century decisions. Moreover, Lord Hardwicke followed an earlier practice in awarding damages in some cases where specific performance had been refused. Here again, later equity judges refused to follow him.[7]

In essence, the remedy of specific performance enforces the execution of a contract according to its terms, and it may therefore be contrasted with the remedy of damages, which is compensation for non-execution. In specific performance, execution of the contract is enforced by the power of the court to treat disobedience of its decree as contempt, for which the offender may be imprisoned until he is prepared to comply with the decree. Actually, as Fry[8] points out, it is not strictly accurate to say that the court enforces execution of the contract according to its terms, for the court will not usually intervene until default upon the contract has occurred, so that enforcement by the court is later than the time stipulated in the contract.

At common law, a contract could not be specifically enforced, the appropriate remedy being damages. There were, however, cases where a common law court would give a remedy with somewhat similar effects. (1) Where a public duty arose from a private contract, the prerogative writ of mandamus was available for the enforcement of the public duty. (2) If there were a contract for the delivery of a

[6] *Lacon* v. *Mertins* (1743), 3 Atk. 1, 4.

[7] For examples of the valuable work done on the early history of specific performance, see Ames, " Specific Performance of Contracts " (1889), 1 *Green Bag*, 26; Barbour, " The History of Contract in Early English Equity " (1914), 4 *Oxford Studies in Social and Legal History*, esp. pp. 120-3; Fry, " Specific Performance and Laesio Fidei " (1889), 5 *Law Quarterly Review*, 235; Hazeltine, " The Early History of English Equity " (1913), *Essays in Legal History* (ed. Vinogradoff), 261, esp. pp. 269-70; Hazeltine, " Early History of Specific Performance of Contract in English Law " (1909), *Festgabe für Kohler*, 67; Holdsworth, *History of English Law*, vol. XII, pp. 276-7, 290; Holmes, " Early English Equity " (1908), 2 *Select Essays in Anglo-American Legal History*, 705, esp. pp. 716-21.

[8] Specific Performance, 6th ed., p. 3.

chattel on the payment of a sum of money then if the sum were paid, and the chattel were not delivered, the person entitled to delivery could sue at common law for the detention of the chattel. Here the basis of the action was that the contract had been executed by the payment of the price, so that the chattel was being wrongfully withheld from the new owner. (3) Where the owner covenanted to convey lands to a purchaser, then originally at common law, this could be enforced by a writ of covenant. This took the form of a command to the sheriff that the vendor should fulfil his covenant to the purchaser, and the sheriff placed the purchaser in possession by means of a praecipe quod reddat. All these common law procedures, however, were entirely distinct from the machinery of specific performance evolved by the Court of Chancery, the origin of which is the canon law administered by the ecclesiastical courts, particularly that branch of jurisdiction which dealt with breaches of faith, especially in respect of obligations reinforced by an oath. The remedy was secularised in the sixteenth century. The decisive step was taken in respect of contracts for the conveyance of land, and it was because in these cases the common law remedy of damages was recognised to be inadequate, that the resistance of the common law courts ebbed away.

Specific performance is a remedy which is applicable only to executory contracts. Where a contract is executed, (i.e. nothing more remains to be done to place the parties in their final positions) specific relief may be obtained, but it is not specific performance.[9] Frequently, it is either an injunction or damages against the party who is acting in a way inconsistent with the position established by the executed contract.

Specific performance differs from equitable relief by way of specific restitution of a chattel, which exists independently of contract. In the leading case of *Pusey* v. *Pusey*[10] specific restitution of the famous Pusey horn was decreed to the Pusey heir, since the horn had a special value to the heir which could not be assessed in terms of money. The same remedy has been decreed for an ancient altarpiece with a Greek inscription,[11] for a unique tobacco-box,[12] and for masonic regalia.[13]

Specific performance, being an equitable remedy, shares with other remedies the quality of being discretionary, in contrast with common law remedies which are available as a matter of right. This does not mean, and has not for centuries meant, that a court of equity is free to

9 *Wolverhampton and Walsall Railway Co.* v. *London and North-Western Railway Co.* (1873), L.R. 16 Eq. 433. Cf. *Australian Hardwoods Pty. Ltd.* v. *Commissioner for Railways*, [1961] 1 W.L.R. 425, 433-4 (P.C.).
10 (1684), 1 Vern. 273.
11 *Duke of Somerset* v. *Cookson* (1735), 3 P. Wms. 390.
12 *Fells* v. *Read* (1796), 3 Ves. 70.
13 *Lloyd* v. *Loaring* (1802), 6 Ves. 773.

grant or refuse the remedy arbitrarily. The discretion of the court is exercised in accordance with well-settled principles. Sir Joseph Jekyll said in *Cowper* v. *Earl Cowper*[14]—

> . . . though proceedings in equity are said to be *secundum discretionem boni viri*, yet when it is asked, *vir bonus est quis*? the answer is, *qui consulta patrum, qui leges juraque servat*. And as it is said in *Rook's* case, 5 Rep. 99b, that discretion is a science, not to act arbitrarily according to men's wills and private affections, so the discretion which is exercised here, is to be governed by the rules of law and equity, which are not to oppose, but each, in its turn, to be subservient to the other; this discretion, in some cases, follows the law implicitly, in others, assists it, and advances the remedy; in others again, it relieves against the abuse or allays the rigour of it; but in no case does it contradict or over-turn the grounds or principles thereof, as has been sometimes ignorantly imputed to this Court. That is a discretionary power, which neither this nor any other Court, not even the highest, acting in a judicial capacity, is by the constitution intrusted with.

It has been said that in suits for specific performance, the cause of action is not a breach of the contract, which alone will give rise to an action at law for damages, but it is the duty considered in equity to be incumbent on the defendant of actually doing what he promised to perform. A breach of contract by one party is not necessarily (though it usually is) a condition precedent to a grant of specific performance in favour of the other party.[15] When a vendor refused to complete by the specified date in a contract for the sale of a house and it was clear that there was no defence to a suit for specific performance, although time was not of the essence of the contract, Vaisey, J., held that the purchaser was entitled to an order for costs after taking out a writ, although the vendor was then ready to complete .[16]

Contracts of which Specific Performance can be Granted

General Principles

Fry[17] stated several preliminary propositions:

1. The orbit of the equitable remedy of specific performance in respect of a contract is not identical with the orbit of the common law remedy for damages. A contract could sometimes be specifically

[14] (1734), 2 P. Wms. 720, 753-4. See also *Haywood* v. *Cope* (1858), 25 Beav. 140, 151; pp. 29–30, *ante*. Ireland: *Conlon* v. *Murray*, [1958] N.I. 17.
[15] Williams, *The Contract of Sale of Land*, p. 132.
[16] *Marks* v. *Lilley*, [1959] 1 W.L.R. 749.
[17] *Specific Performance*, 6th ed., pp. 21-42. Ireland: see the discussion of the principles by Lord Redesdale, C., *Harnett* v. *Yielding* (1805), 2 Sch. & Lef. 549, 553-4.

enforced in equity even though strict fulfilment of every term was impossible at common law, or even where a contract was not enforceable at all at common law. An example of the latter would be a contract to assign a chose in action before the Judicature Act. An example of the former would be a contract with a stipulation as to time, which could no longer be fulfilled, but which was not regarded by equity as affecting the substance of the contract.[18]

2. Equity will intervene where there is no adequate remedy at common law, but not where the remedy is adequate. This proposition arises from the fact that the general remedy for loss at common law is money damages. Where this is adequate, equity will not interfere, but where damages will not fully compensate for the injury, specific performance will be granted. In *Beswick* v. *Beswick*[19] the plaintiff was the widow and executrix of a coal merchant who had sold his business to the defendant, his nephew, for a price consisting of an annuity of £6 10s. a week for the vendor for life, and after his death, an annuity for his widow for life of £5 a week. When the vendor died, the defendant paid only one weekly instalment of £5 to the plaintiff and then stopped. The House of Lords held that the plaintiff (as administratrix) could have an order for specific performance, notwithstanding that damages might have been nominal; or even if they would have been substantial, for damages would not have been an adequate remedy on account of instalments having to be sued for as they fell into arrear.[20]

Contracts for the Sale of Land

The main illustration of a contract in respect of which damages is not adequate compensation is one for the sale of an interest in land. From an early date, equity took the view that since the amount of land available was limited, and since estates of equal value might differ very considerably in their worth to a purchaser, contracts for the sale of such interests were especially suitable for the remedy of specific performance.[21] Whether specific performance of a contract to grant a

[18] See the explanation by Lord Erskine, L.C., *Hearne* v. *Tenant* (1807), 13 Ves. 287, 289. See also *Halsey* v. *Grant* (1806), 13 Ves. 73; *Alley* v. *Deschamps* (1806), 13 Ves. 225.

[19] [1968] A.C. 57. In Ireland, the widow would have been able to get a legal or equitable remedy even if she had not been the personal representative: Law Reform (Husband and Wife) Act (Northern Ireland) 1964, Sect. 5; Married Women's Status Act, 1957, Sect. 8 (Republic of Ireland).

[20] For a discussion of the question whether damages are an inadequate remedy, for this purpose, because the defendant is insolvent and so cannot pay them, see Horack, " Insolvency and Specific Performance " (1918), 31 *Harvard Law Review*, 702.

[21] See Clark, " Some Problems in Specific Performance " (1917), 31 *Harvard Law Review*, 271; " Specific Performance in Connection with Receivership " (1919), 33 *H.L.R.*, 64; Keener, " The Burden of Loss as an Incident of the Right to the Specific Performance of a Contract " (1901), 1 *Columbia Law Review*, 1.

tenancy from year to year can be obtained has been questioned, but it would seem that the better view is that specific performance would be granted.[22]

Specific performance can be granted of a contract relating to land abroad, provided the defendant is within the jurisdiction.[23]

Contracts for the Sale of Stocks and Shares and Expectancies

The rule that specific performance will not be granted in respect of government stock has been firmly established since the decision of Lord Parker, L.C., in *Cud* v. *Rutter*,[24] a case in which specific performance was refused in respect of South Sea stock. Shares, however, are treated differently, since their number is limited, and other similar shares may not be available in the open market. It now seems to be settled practice that specific performance will be granted in respect of shares.[25] The effect of the decree is that the vendor will be compelled to complete by execution and registration of a proper transfer. Again, equity will specifically enforce a contract for the sale of an expectancy,[26] although it was not enforceable at all at common law. Such contracts are scrutinised carefully in order to ensure that no undue advantage is taken of the heir's inexperience or impecuniousness,[27] for if that were the true position, specific performance would be refused, and the transaction itself would be set aside.

Partnership Agreements

In general a court of equity will not grant specific performance of a contract to enter into and to carry on a partnership. There are, however, exceptions to this rule. A partner can never obtain specific performance where the proposed partnership was to be at will, or for a term which could be ended at any time by notice, for " Equity, like nature, does nothing in vain," and the defaulting partner could defeat

22 See *Lever* v. *Koffler*, [1901] 1 Ch. 543; *Manchester Brewery Co.* v. *Coombs*, [1901] 2 Ch. 608, 616. Cf. *Clayton* v. *Illingworth* (1853), 10 Hare 451; *Lavery* v. *Pursell* (1888), 39 Ch.D. 508, 519.

23 See p. 14, *ante*. See also *Hart* v. *Herwig* (1873), L.R. 8 Ch. App. 860, where there was held to be jurisdiction to order specific performance of a German contract to sell a German ship to an Englishman, although the defendant vendor was not in England. However, the ship was in Sunderland and the master, being the vendor's agent in the sale, was held to have been properly served with the bill and notice of motion (for an interlocutory injunction).

24 (1719), 1 P. Wms. 570. See also *Nutbrown* v. *Thornton* (1804), 10 Ves. 159, 161, *per* Lord Eldon, L.C.; *Mason* v. *Armitage* (1806), 13 Ves. 25, 37, *per* Lord Erskine, L.C.

25 *Duncuft* v. *Albrecht* (1841), 12 Sim. 189. See also Fry, *Specific Performance*, 6th ed., part V, ch. 1, pp. 678-93.

26 *Wiseman* v. *Roper* (1646), 1 Ch. Rep. 158; *Beckley* v. *Newland* (1723), 2 P. Wms. 182; *Wright* v. *Wright* (1750), 1 Ves. Sen. 409.

27 *Morse* v. *Faulkner* (1792), 3 Swanst. 400n.; *Ryan* v. *Daniel* (1841), 1 Y. & C. C. C. 60. See pp. 353-6, *ante*.

the order of the court by giving immediate notice of dissolution. Lord Eldon observed in *Hercy* v. *Birch*:[28] "... no one ever heard of this Court executing an agreement for a partnership, when the parties might dissolve it immediately afterwards."

There can be no order for specific performance of partnership articles if details of the proposed arrangement are lacking. This is illustrated by *Downs* v. *Collins*.[29] A and B agreed to enter into a partnership as brewers, each undertaking on behalf of himself, his executors and administrators, to continue as partners for twenty-one years. One partner died, and his executors called for immediate dissolution of the partnership, and distribution of the partnership property, whilst the surviving partner brought an action for specific performance against the executors. Wigram, V.-C., held that specific performance could not be enforced against them because the amount of the capital, the manner of providing it and the mode of carrying on the business were not specified in the contract. In *Sichel* v. *Mosenthal*[30] Romilly, M.R., refused specific performance in respect of an agreement to enter into a partnership on a future day, or in default to lend the other party £10,000 for two years. The agreement was too vague; moreover, the demand was a money claim, in respect of which damages would be an adequate remedy. In *Bagnell* v. *Edwards*,[31] Chatterton, V.-C., in the Irish Court of Chancery, declined to order specific performance of a partnership agreement where the sole relief sought was the payment of a sum of money. The plaintiff was left to his remedy for damages at law, which was perfectly adequate.

In respect of a partnership agreement, where it is specified in the memorandum that articles shall be drawn up, Lord Hardwicke observed obiter[32]—

> I should be of opinion, upon a bill brought by the other in this court, for a specific performance, that notwithstanding it is in relation to a chattel interest, yet a specific performance ought to be decreed.

In *England* v. *Curling*,[33] A, B and C agreed to become partners as ship agents for seven, ten or fourteen years, and they initialled the agreement to that effect. A deed was drawn up to give effect to the agreement, but it differed somewhat from the agreement, and was

28 (1804), 9 Ves. 357, 360. See also *Sheffield Gas Consumers' Co.* v. *Harrison* (1853), 17 Beav. 294.
29 (1848), 6 Hare 418.
30 (1862), 30 Beav. 371.
31 (1876), I.R. 10 Eq. 215.
32 *Buxton* v. *Lister* (1746), 3 Atk. 383, 385.
33 (1844), 8 Beav. 129. Ireland: *Crowley* v. *O'Sullivan*, [1900] 2 I.R. 478 (D.C.).

never executed. After carrying on business for eleven years, the partners began to disagree, and C gave notice to dissolve the partnership in three months. He then retired and entered into partnership with other persons, at the old address, in the name of the old firm. Lord Langdale, M.R., held the other partners entitled to a decree of specific performance of the agreement by the execution of the deed, and to an injunction in respect of the activities of the new partnership.

This decision has been discussed and followed in several later cases, and in *Scott* v. *Rayment*,[34] Giffard, V.C., referring to this and another case, said—

> In both those cases there had been part performance, and I do not at all hesitate to say, that in both it was essential to the ends of justice that the *status* of the parties should be ascertained, determined, and fixed; and especially in *England* v. *Curling* is that manifest, when one finds that there was a direction to ascertain, in substance, what the agreement between the parties was.

In *Scott* v. *Rayment*, as there was no part performance, and damages were an adequate remedy, specific performance was refused.

A somewhat different point arose in *Byrne* v. *Reid*.[35] There the articles of partnership permitted a partner to nominate any other person as a partner. He did so, but the other partners declined to give effect to it by allotting the nominee a share in the profits in respect of the capital which the new partner agreed to bring in. The Court of Appeal held that he was entitled to an injunction against the other partners in respect of their attempted exclusion of him, and also to other specific relief appropriate to partnership (but not specific performance).

The last class of cases where specific performance of partnership agreements will be awarded is where persons have agreed to share the profits of a joint enterprise, and when this has terminated, some of the partners have attempted to deprive another partner of his share. An example of this is afforded by *Dale* v. *Hamilton*.[36] In these cases what is really wanted is an account of the profits, and the plaintiff asks for specific performance, so that the profits may be distributed in accordance with the terms of the original agreement.

Separation Deeds

Another type of contract in respect of which a court of equity will grant a decree of specific performance is a separation deed. Prior to

34 (1868), L.R. 7 Eq. 112, 115.
35 [1902] 2 Ch. 735.
36 (1846), 5 Hare 369; *on appeal* (1847), 2 Ph. 266.

the decision of the House of Lords in *Wilson* v. *Wilson*,[37] the status of separation deeds in general was uncertain, but it was settled by that case that an agreement which regulates the rights of parties to a marriage whose separation has occurred or is immediate, pending and inevitable, is not only not contrary to public policy, but will also be specifically enforced in equity. An agreement between husband and wife, whilst they are still living together, to live apart in the future is still invalid as contrary to public policy. However, where litigation on matrimonial affairs has already arisen between them, or serious differences between them exist, a binding contract regulating their rights and duties on separation can be made.[38] But an undertaking to forego any rights which a party may have in matrimonial litigation is sometimes void on the ground of public policy and so is not consideration.[39]

Arbitrators' Awards

A court of equity has also, in a number of cases, decreed specific performance of an award made by an arbitrator. Such a decree will not be made where the award is simply to pay a sum of money. The award must direct an act such as the conveyance of an estate, the assignment of securities, or some similar transaction.[40]

Contracts for the Transfer of Chattels and relating to Patents

In general, a court of equity will not grant a decree of specific performance for the transfer of a chattel, partly because of the difficulty of securing the transfer, or even the continued existence of the chattel, and partly because, for many chattels, damages is a sufficient remedy. Where, however, the chattel is unique, or has a special value to the claimant, then it would seem that specific performance will be granted on substantially the same principles as a decree for specific restitution of a chattel will be granted.[41]

Apart from this equity jurisdiction, Section 52 of the Sale of Goods Act, 1893, provides that where there is a contract to deliver specific or ascertained goods, the court may, if it thinks fit, direct that the contract shall be performed specifically, either unconditionally, or upon such

37 (1848), 1 H.L. C. 538.

38 *McGregor* v. *McGregor* (1888), 21 Q.B.D. 424 (C.A.).

39 See *Hyman* v. *Hyman*, [1929] A.C. 601 (H.L., E.); *Gaisberg* v. *Storr*, [1950] 1 K.B. 107 (C.A.); *Combe* v. *Combe*, [1951] 2 K.B. 215 (C.A.); *Bennett* v. *Bennett*, [1952] 1 K.B. 249 (C.A.).

40 See the observations of Fletcher Moulton, L.J., in *Doleman & Sons* v. *Ossett Corp.*, [1912] 3 K.B. 257, 267-70, as to the refusal of courts of equity to grant specific performance of a contract to go to arbitration.

41 *Falcke* v. *Gray* (1859), 4 Drew. 651; *Thorn* v. *Commissioners of Works* (1863), 32 Beav. 490. See also Treitel, " Specific Performance in the Sale of Goods " (1966), *Journal of Business Law*, 211.

terms as seem just to the court. The courts have taken a cautious view of their powers under this section. Nevertheless, in *British Nylon Spinners Ltd.* v. *Imperial Chemical Industries Ltd.*[42] specific performance was decreed by Danckwerts, J., of a contract relating to patent rights between an English and an American firm.

Building Contracts

It used to be thought that the court would not grant specific performance of building contracts on the ground of difficulty in supervision, but Lord Loughborough, L.C., in *Mosely* v. *Virgin*,[43] expressed a different view, provided the work was defined with sufficient clearness. To-day, the position is that the court will grant specific performance if, in addition to clear definition of the work to be done, the plaintiff has an interest in its execution which cannot be adequately compensated by damages, and if, in addition, the defendant has obtained possession of the land on which the work is to be done.[44]

Restricted Nature of the Remedy

The courts have developed specific performance within comparatively narrow limits. Some other systems admit a remedy closely resembling specific performance in respect of most classes of contract. For example the law of Ceylon, which is founded on Roman-Dutch law, grants to every party who is ready to carry out the contract, a legal right to demand performance by the other, which the court has a discretionary right to refuse in certain cases; and the parties themselves may substitute the alternative remedy of damages.[45]

The limitation on the jurisdiction which flows from the inability of the court to supervise the execution of the contract is often more apparent than real, for the extent of equitable procedure applicable against a party who does not comply with a decree, culminating in his committal for contempt, would render failure to comply with the decree a perilous course. It would seem, therefore, that one must look further for the reasons for the caution of the English courts of equity. One explanation may perhaps be found in the hypothesis that one basic assumption upon which the English law of contracts rests is that the vast majority of contracts will be fulfilled according to their terms.[46] The law is therefore only providing remedies in the exceptional case,

42 [1955] Ch. 37.

43 (1796), 3 Ves. 184.

44 *Wolverhampton Corp.* v. *Emmons*, [1901] 1 K.B. 515 (C.A.); *Molyneux* v. *Richard*, [1906] 1 Ch. 34; *Carpenters Estates Ltd.* v. *Davies*, [1940] Ch. 160. Ireland: *Rushbrooke* v. *O'Sullivan*, [1908] 1 I.R. 232.

45 *Abdeen* v. *Thaheer*, [1958] A.C. 116 (P.C.).

46 See Gebhardt, " Pacta sunt servanda " (1947), 10 *Modern Law Review*, 159.

and in the exceptional case damages will usually be the most convenient and satisfactory remedy. An alternative explanation may also be found in the respect for individual freedom which has been such a striking feature of the development of English law. Even to the extent of declining to generalise remedies which compel the performance of the actual obligations assumed, the courts of equity have normally restricted the remedy of specific performance to those contracts which involved the transfer of property, and have refused to extend it to contracts, such as contracts of service, which would have involved the application of measures of constraint, limiting personal freedom, for extended periods (e.g. a contract of apprenticeship as in *De Francesco* v. *Barnum*).[47] Moreover, the court will not enforce a contract where it is incapable of supervising performance, e.g. a contract involving the performance of continuous acts,[48] or a contract for the sale of goodwill which is unconnected with business premises.[49] The difficulty of supervising them is one of the grounds upon which contracts of personal service cannot be specifically enforced. Again, specific performance will not be decreed where it can be immediately frustrated, for example, an agreement which one of the parties can terminate at once by giving notice.

The general rule that equity will not assist a volunteer debars a person who claims under a voluntary contract from seeking specific performance, even if the obligation has been assumed in a document under seal.

Defences to an Action of Specific Performance

Fry, in his treatise on *Specific Performance*, enumerated no less than twenty-five distinct defences to an action for specific performance of the contract. Some of these, however, such as want of capacity, absence of a binding agreement, mistake and illegality, are equally defences to an action for damages at common law. Moreover, the cases show that a number of the defences tend to shade off into one another, and that many of them are direct applications of the principle that equity, in exercising its discretionary jurisdiction, will insist that the parties conform to equitable standards of worthy conduct, so that want of fairness, or the fact that the decree, if granted, will operate

[47] (1890), 45 Ch.D. 430.

[48] *Powell Duffryn Steam Coal Co.* v. *Taff Vale Railway Co.* (1874), L.R. 9 Ch. App. 331 (injunction refused in these circumstances); *Dominion Coal Co. Ltd.* v. *Dominion Iron and Steel Co. Ltd.*, [1909] A.C. 293 (P.C., Nova Scotia).

[49] *Baxter* v. *Conolly* (1820), 1 Jac. & W. 576.

harshly and oppressively, are grounds for resisting an action for specific performance. In *Buxton* v. *Lister*[50] Lord Hardwicke said—

> Nothing is more established in this court, than that every agreement of this kind ought to be certain, fair, and just in all its parts.
>
> If any of those ingredients are wanting in the case, this court will not decree a specific performance.

Absence of Writing and Part Performance

The Statute of Frauds, 1677, Section 4,[51] required certain types of contract to be evidenced in writing; that is to say, the contracts were unenforceable in the absence of a sufficient memorandum of their terms. The most important class of such contracts, from the point of view of the doctrine of part performance, consisted of contracts for the sale of an interest in land, and in England and Northern Ireland the statutory requirement of written evidence has now been repealed as to all other types of contract except contracts of guarantee.[52]

In the common law courts, neither party could enforce a contract covered by the statute unless the memorandum existed. If, however, a suit were brought in equity for specific performance of a contract for the sale of an interest in land,[53] the contract would be enforced, notwithstanding the absence of a sufficient memorandum, if the plaintiff had part performed his contract.[54] The basis of this intervention was described by Lord Selborne, L.C., in *Maddison* v. *Alderson*[55]—

> That equity has been stated by high authority to rest upon the principle of fraud: " Courts of Equity will not permit the statute to be made an instrument of fraud." By this it cannot be meant that equity will relieve against a public statute of general policy in cases admitted to fall within it; and I agree with an observation made by Lord Justice Cotton, in *Britain* v. *Rossiter*,[56] that this summary way

50 (1746), 3 Atk. 383, 386. So also Lord Loughborough in *Lord Walpole* v. *Lord Orford* (1797), 3 Ves. 402, 420.

51 Now re-enacted in England as to interests in land by the Law of Property Act, 1925, Sect. 40. Ireland: Statute of Frauds, 1695, Sect. 2.

52 Law Reform (Enforcement of Contracts) Act, 1954; Law Reform (Miscellaneous Provisions) Act (Northern Ireland), 1954, Sects. 1 and 2. There is no corresponding legislation in the Republic of Ireland.

53 In *McManus* v. *Cooke* (1887), 35 Ch.D. 681, 697, Kay, J., said that the doctrine applied to a parol agreement for an easement, though no interest in land was intended to be acquired. He thought it applicable to all contracts of which specific performance could be granted. Ireland: the same view was taken by a Divisional Court in *Crowley* v. *O'Sullivan*, [1900] 2 I.R. 478.

54 The validity of the doctrine is expressly recognised in the Law of Property Act, 1925, Sect. 40, which states that it " does not affect the law relating to part performance . . ."

55 (1883), 8 App. Cas. 467, 474-6 (H.L., E.). See, further, Sheridan, *Fraud in Equity*, pp. 151-156.

56 (1879), 11 Q.B.D. 123, 130.

of stating the principle (however true it may be when properly understood) is not an adequate explanation, either of the precise grounds, or of the established limits, of the equitable doctrine of part performance . . . . In a suit founded on such part performance, the defendant is really " charged " upon the equities resulting from the acts done in execution of the contract, and not (within the meaning of the statute) upon the contract itself. If such equities were excluded, injustice of a kind which the statute cannot be thought to have had in contemplation would follow. Let the case be supposed of a parol contract to sell land, completely performed on both sides, as to everything except conveyance; the whole purchase-money paid; the purchaser put into possession; expenditure by him (say in costly buildings) upon the property; leases granted by him to tenants. The contract is not a nullity; there is nothing in the statute to estop any Court which may have to exercise jurisdiction in the matter from inquiring into and taking notice of the truth of the facts. All the acts done must be referred to the actual contract, which is the measure and test of their legal and equitable character and consequences. If, therefore, in such a case a conveyance were refused, and an action of ejectment brought by the vendor or his heir against the purchaser, nothing could be done towards ascertaining and adjusting the equitable rights and liabilities of the parties, without taking the contract into account. The matter has advanced beyond the stage of contract; and the equities which arise out of the stage which it has reached cannot be administered unless the contract is regarded. The choice is between undoing what has been done (which is not always possible, or, if possible, just) and completing what has been left undone. The line may not always be capable of being so clearly drawn as in the case which I have supposed; but it is not arbitrary or unreasonable to hold that when the statute says that no action is to be brought to charge any person upon a contract concerning land, it has in view the simple case in which he is charged upon the contract only, and not that in which there are equities resulting from res gestae subsequent to and arising out of the contract. So long as the connection of those res gestae with the alleged contract does not depend upon mere parol testimony, but is reasonably to be inferred from the res gestae themselves, justice seems to require some such limitation of the scope of the statute, which might otherwise interpose an obstacle even to the rectification of material errors, however clearly proved, in an executed conveyance, founded upon an unsigned agreement.

The act of part-performance must be done by the plaintiff. It is insufficient if it is done by the defendant, since the basis of intervention is that the party suing has prejudiced his position by his conduct, and has thereby acquired an equity to be protected against the destruction of the agreement in virtue of which he acted.[57] To have part performed, the plaintiff must have done such acts as unequivocally denote the existence of a contract between the parties. That is to say, the acts would not have been done if the plaintiff had not possessed excellent reason to suppose that a contract existed between himself and the defendant.[58] In *Maddison* v. *Alderson*[59] an intestate had induced a woman to serve him as housekeeper for years without wages by promising orally to give her a life estate in land by his will. He tried to do so by a will which was invalid because not properly attested. The House of Lords held that there was no act of part performance unequivocally referable to a contract, so that any contract there might have been was not taken out of the Statute of Frauds. A case which makes an instructive comparison is *Lowry* v. *Reid*,[60] where a mother contracted orally to make a will leaving to her son William her two farms in Drumhirk in consideration of William conveying his farm in Ballykeigle to his brother Andrew. The Court of Appeal of Northern Ireland held that the conveyance by William was a sufficient act of part performance to render the mother's undertaking specifically enforceable. Andrews, L.J., said[61] that *Maddison* v. *Alderson* did not decide anything different from the principle of the older cases, viz. " that the act must be of such a nature that if stated, it would of itself infer the existence of some agreement; and then parol evidence is admitted; to shew, what the agreement is."

In *Maddison* v. *Alderson*[62] Lord Selborne pointed out—

> . . . the payment of money is an equivocal act, not (in itself) until the connection is established by parol testimony, indicative of a contract concerning land.

So also, the payment of rent in advance by the tenant under an oral agreement for a lease, unaccompanied by entry into possession, is not enough.[63] Where, however, a prospective tenant under an

[57] *Caton* v. *Caton* (1866), L.R. 1 Ch. App. 137; *Biss* v. *Hygate*, [1918] 2 K.B. 314 (D.C.), would not seem to affect this point.

[58] *Gunter* v. *Halsey* (1739), Amb. 586, *per* Lord Hardwicke, L.C., *Morphett* v. *Jones* (1818), 1 Swanst. 172, 181, *per* Plumer, M.R.

[59] (1883), 8 App. Cas. 467. Cf. *Wakeham* v. *Mackenzie*, [1968] 1 W.L.R. 1175. See also Pettit, " The Statute of Frauds Again " (1968), 32 *Conveyancer and Property Lawyer*, 384.

[60] [1927] N.I. 142. See also *Wakeham* v. *Mackenzie*, [1968] 1 W.L.R. 1175.

[61] [1927] N.I. 158, citing Grant, M.R., in *Frame* v. *Dawson* (1807), 14 Ves. 387-8. There must be clear evidence of a concluded agreement: *Howe* v. *Hall* (1870), I.R. 4 Eq. 242; *Mackey* v. *Jones* (1958), 93 I.L.T.R. 177.

[62] (1883), 8 App. Cas. 467, 479.

[63] *Thursby* v. *Eccles* (1900), 70 L.J.Q.B. 91; *Chaproniere* v. *Lambert*, [1917] 2 Ch. 356 (C.A.).

oral agreement for a lease supervised certain alterations which the landlord undertook at her request, and made suggestions concerning the manner in which the work was to be done (which were accepted), it was held that the landlord had done sufficient acts of part-performance, giving him a right to specific performance when the tenant subsequently attempted to repudiate the agreement.[64] In *Kingswood Estate Co. Ltd.* v. *Anderson*[65] an elderly widow, statutory tenant of a house, agreed to vacate it under an oral agreement by which the landlords undertook to allow her to live for the rest of her life in a flat belonging to them, paying thirty-five shillings a week rent. She moved into the flat and paid the rent, but after a while the landlords tried to eject her. The Court of Appeal held that the widow had done such an act of part performance as to make the agreement specifically enforceable, and this was a good defence to the landlords' claim for possession.

The doctrine of part performance can only be invoked in respect of a contract of which specific performance can be granted. It can be used in order to obtain damages in lieu of specific performance, but not, on the English view, to obtain common law damages for breach of contract,[66] the Judicature Acts having made no difference in this respect. In *Britain* v. *Rossiter*[67] there was a contract for personal service for more than a year, which at that time was covered by the Statute of Frauds, 1677, Section 4. There was no writing, but the plaintiff claimed to have part performed the contract. The Court of Appeal held that the plaintiff could not recover, as the doctrine of part performance was inapplicable, the contract not being one of which specific performance could be ordered. Thesiger, L.J., said[68]—

> I confess that on principle I do not see why a similar doctrine should not be applied to the case of a contract of service, and as the doctrine of Equity is based upon the theory that the Court will not allow a fraud on the part of one party to a contract on the faith of which the other party has altered his position, I do not see why a similar doctrine should not comprehend a contract of service.

But the learned Lord Justice, when he came to regard it as a matter not of principle but of authority, accepted that the doctrine was confined to contracts relating to land.

In Ireland, *Britain* v. *Rossiter* is not doubted, but it seems from the decision of the Divisional Court in *Crowley* v. *O'Sullivan*[69] that part

64 *Rawlinson* v. *Ames*, [1925] Ch. 96. See also *Dickinson* v. *Barrow*, [1904] 2 Ch. 339.
65 [1963] 2 Q.B. 169.
66 See *Lavery* v. *Pursell* (1889), 39 Ch.D. 508, 518, *per* Chitty, J.
67 (1879), 11 Q.B.D. 123.
68 11 Q.B.D. 131.
69 [1900] 2 I.R. 478.

performance will take a contract out of the Statute of Frauds so as to enable common law damages for breach to be given, if it is a contract of which specific performance could be granted (in this case a partnership agreement). Palles, C.B., with whom Andrews and Johnson, JJ., concurred, said[70] that the reply to the defence of the Statute of Frauds in a jury action for damages was—

> . . . that this is a case in which, before the Judicature Act, specific performance of the agreement would have been decreed by a Court of Equity, that therefore part performance may take the case out of the statute, and that that part performance can be relied upon whether the relief which a Court of Equity would have thought proper to have given before the Judicature Act or this Court may now think proper to give, is specific performance or damages.

Incompleteness

A contract is incomplete if it does not include all the essential terms of the bargain. It must specify the subject-matter of the contract with sufficient precision to distinguish it from other things. It must also sufficiently identify the parties to the contract. Where the contract is a sale or lease, the price must be fixed. Finally, if either party relies on any special terms, these must have been in the minds of the parties at the time when the bargain was concluded. All these points, however, must be considered in relation to the maxim *id certum est quod certum reddi potest*, so that if the agreement contains machinery whereby any of these elements of the contract can be discovered with certainty, that element can be regarded as being present in the contract.

For example, in one case, the subject-matter was regarded as sufficiently identified by the phrase " Mr. Ogilvie's house,"[71] and in another by reference to the fact that its title deeds were in the custody of a named person.[72] In both these cases, parol evidence was admitted to free the phrases used from possible ambiguity. Similarly, the parties to the contract must be identified with sufficient particularity, or alternatively the contract must provide means of identifying them. Lord Cairns, L.C., said in *Rossiter* v. *Miller*,[73] where a description of vendors as " the proprietors " was held good enough—

> . . . your Lordships have frequently seen conditions of sale not merely by auction but by private contract, in which it is stated that the sale is made, sometimes by the owners, and sometimes by the

70 [1900] 2 I.R. 485-6.
71 *Ogilvie* v. *Foljambe* (1817), 3 Mer. 53.
72 *Owen* v. *Thomas* (1834), 3 My & K. 353.
73 (1878), 3 App. Cas. 1124, 1140 (H.L., E.).

mortgagees, and a form of contract is annexed in which an agent signs for the vendors, and no other specification upon the vendor's part is inserted, and I never heard up to this time that a contract under those circumstances was invalid.

Where a contract provides a method for ascertaining the price payable, this establishes the price with sufficient certainty. This will normally take the form of allowing a third party to fix the price. If, however, the contract provides that the price shall be fixed by one valuer from each side, and they cannot agree, the contract fails for uncertainty, for the court will not fix the price.[74] This type of case must be distinguished from those in which the parties agree to sell at a fair price. Here, if they fail to agree on the meaning of " a fair price," the court itself will take the necessary steps to determine what a fair price is. This distinction was drawn by Grant, M.R., in *Milnes* v. *Gery*,[75] and it has been applied in a number of later cases.[76]

Sometimes in a lease of real property the lease is said to be with " the usual covenants." These being capable of exact ascertainment, this mode of description is no bar to a grant of specific performance.[77]

A contract is incomplete if, being for a lease, the length of the term is not stated,[78] or some other necessary provision is omitted; nor is it complete if some essential part has been left for future settlement. In such a case, the contract remains incomplete until the parties have decided on it. Closely allied with this point is the rule that where the parties to an agreement for the sale of real property settle the terms " subject to contract," there is no binding contract until the formal contract has been concluded. On the other hand, in *Branca* v. *Cobarro*,[79] there was an agreement in writing for the sale of the lease and goodwill of a mushroom farm. The agreement described itself as " a provisional agreement until a fully legalized agreement, drawn up by a solicitor " was signed. The Court of Appeal held the document to be binding, on the ground that a " provisional " agreement, expressed to be " until " something happened, was intended to be acted on, whilst an agreement " subject to contract " was not.

74 *Milnes* v. *Gery* (1807), 14 Ves. 400.

75 (1807), 14 Ves. 400, 407.

76 *Jackson* v. *Jackson* (1853), 1 Sm. & G. 184; *Richardson* v. *Smith* (1870), L.R. 5 Ch. App. 648; *Talbot* v. *Talbot*, [1968] 1 Q.B. 1 (C.A.).

77 See *Hampshire* v. *Wickens* (1878), 7 Ch.D. 555; *Lucas* v. *Hall*, [1899] W.N. 92.

78 Ireland: in *Wyse* v. *Russell* (1882), 11 L.R. Ir. 173, Flanagan, J., refused specific performance of an agreement for a lease which did not specify when the lease was to commence.

79 [1947] K.B. 854.

Uncertainty

If the contract contains an element of vagueness or uncertainty in regard to an essential term, it will not be enforced. Such a type of uncertainty cannot be described with precision in the abstract. Furthermore, in any contract, an apparently vague term may be cured by applying the test of reasonableness. In *Great Northern Railway Co.* v. *Manchester, Sheffield and Lincolnshire Railway Co.*[80] one railway contracted with another that it should have the right of running passenger and goods trains over the railway of the other. It was objected that this agreement was too vague to be enforced, since it was not stated how many trains could be run over the tracks of the other company; but the court rejected this contention, holding that reasonable user was implied in the contract, and granting an injunction to restrain a breach. Specific performance was not directly in issue. On the other hand, in *Taylor* v. *Portington*[81] the Court of Appeal in Chancery refused specific performance of a contract for a lease of a house, where one party had made an offer for the lease at a rent, if the house were put into thorough repair, and had gone on to state that he would require the drawing-rooms to be handsomely decorated according to the present style, with some further requirements as to painting. These requirements were held to be too uncertain to permit specific performance.

An Irish illustration is provided by *Williams* v. *Kenneally*.[82] In that case, which was an action for specific performance of a parol agreement for a five-year lease of a fishery, the evidence of the plaintiff as to the terms and date of the alleged agreement was indefinite and uncertain, while the evidence of the defendant was that no final agreement for a lease had ever been arrived at, and that the plaintiff had taken the fishery for one season only. Barton, J., was of the opinion that some binding agreement had been entered into between the parties, but refused to decree specific performance.

Want of Fairness

As a ground for refusing specific performance and leaving the plaintiff to his common law remedy of damages, this defence must be distinguished from fraud, which is a ground for rescinding a contract altogether. Unfairness falls short of fraud, and it may arise, either out of the terms of the contract itself, or out of some extrinsic circumstances. For unfairness to be a ground for resisting specific performance, it

[80] (1851), 5 De G. & Sm. 138.
[81] (1855), 7 De G. M. & G. 328.
[82] (1912), 46 I.L.T.R. 292.

must exist at the time when the contract was entered into. It is not sufficient to show that circumstances arising later have made performance of the contract inequitable or specially difficult. An illustration of this defence is afforded by *Smith* v. *Harrison*.[83] The defendant, in administering the affairs of Francis Norton, and his son, F. J. Norton, both of whom were insolvent, put up for auction, " the chattel interest (if any) " of Francis Norton in the lease of premises at No. 1, York Street, St. James's. The sale was held, and the sum of £151 was obtained, but it appeared that Francis Norton in fact had no interest in the lease. There was no fraudulent intention on the part of the defendant, but Page Wood, V.-C., held that the sale must be set aside. In *Spiller* v. *Bolton*[84] Roxburgh, J., refused specific performance and rescinded a contract for the sale of land, sold (by auction) for building purposes, on the ground that the auctioneer failed to make clear (what was known to him), that the land was in an area provisionally zoned for amenity, and if these proposals were confirmed, building within the area would be prohibited.

Want of fairness may also arise from the unequal situation of the parties, e.g. one of them may be poor or inexperienced. If advantage is taken of this inequality in such circumstances as to amount to fraud,[85] the contract will be rescinded; but in cases not sufficiently unfair to be regarded as cases for rescission the unfairness may be enough to cause a refusal of specific performance. In *Conlon* v. *Murray*,[86] in the Northern Ireland Court of Appeal, Black, L.J. (with whom Lord MacDermott, L.C.J., and Sheil, J., concurred), after pointing out that the court's discretion in awarding or refusing specific performance was to be exercised in accordance with principles, said—

> And it is well established that there is a class of cases in which a contract may be such and entered into in such conditions that the court will not order it to be rescinded but, at the same time, looking to the substantial justice of the case, will not order it to be specifically performed. It follows naturally, as observed in Kerr on Fraud and Mistake, 7th ed. (1952) p. 568 that when the aid of a court is sought by way of specific performance of a contract the principles of ethics have a more extensive sway than when a contract is sought to be rescinded.

Specific performance was refused to a purchaser of a house from an old woman, sick and about to go into hospital and with nowhere to

[83] (1857), 26 L.J. Ch. 412.
[84] (1947), 149 Est. Gaz. 450.
[85] See pp. 333-6, *ante*.
[86] [1958] N.I. 17, 25. See also *Buckley* v. *Irwin*, [1960] N.I. 98.

go if she came out (having sold her house), and not independently advised, where the contract had been concluded hastily. This sort of decision shades off into those classified as "hardship."[87] Indeed, Black, L.J., said[88]—

> It was argued on behalf of the plaintiff that cases in which equity refuses the remedy of specific performance fall within one or other of certain defined categories. I cannot accept this view. Certainly equity acts on certain broad and ascertained principles but it has always refused to be forced into rigid categories.[89]

Specific performance will not be decreed where to do so would involve a breach of trust, or a breach of an existing contractual obligation.[90]

Hardship

If special hardship would accompany the execution of the contract, even though this is not due to the act of the other party, then specific performance may be refused. In *Pegler* v. *White*[91] specific performance of a contract to purchase a lease was refused, when litigation was pending to establish to whom the rent was payable. The effect of granting it would have been to thrust a law-suit immediately upon the purchaser. The hardship must probably exist at the date of the contract. It will probably not be a defence if it arises subsequently to the conclusion of the contract.[92]

Inadequacy of consideration, sometimes regarded as a separate defence, is a form of hardship or unfairness. Of itself, it affords no ground for relief, unless the discrepancy between the price paid and the market value is so great as to give rise to an inference, or at least suspicion, of fraud.[93]

Want of Mutuality

Mutuality means that the contract is enforceable by either party indifferently. If one of the parties, because of the personal incapacity

87 See below.
88 [1958] N.I. 26.
89 He quoted with approval the passage to that effect in Story's *Equity Jurisprudence*, 10th ed., vol. 1, p. 739.
90 See *Twining* v. *Morrice* (1788), 2 Bro. C.C. 326 (where the seller's agent bade for the plaintiff); *Mortlock* v. *Buller* (1804), 10 Ves. 292 (breach of trust and inadequacy of consideration).
91 (1864), 33 Beav. 403.
92 In *City of London* v. *Nash* (1747), 1 Ves. Sen. 12, the hardship did arise subsequently, and relief was given by Lord Hardwicke, L.C., but Lord Thurlow, L.C., took a different view in *Adams* v. *Weare* (1784), 1 Bro. C.C. 567.
93 See pp. 333-6, *ante*.

of the other or the nature of the contract, or for some other reason, cannot enforce it, then that party is, in general, immune from the liability to have it enforced against him in equity.

This is the traditional doctrine, as formulated by Fry, and following him, other distinguished writers on the law of contract. It is still accepted apparently by Cheshire and Fifoot.[94] Even as formulated in this way, however, a number of exceptions have always been recognised, and these have been gathered together by Saunders[95] within the single general principle " that the defence of ' want of mutuality ' will not avail to prevent the Court from exercising its beneficial jurisdiction where the contract can be properly enforced without any possible injustice to the defendant, provided a corresponding equitable remedy becomes available against the plaintiff on or before his institution of the action." This asserted general principle, it must be conceded, is at once vague and sufficiently comprehensive to sweep away large parts of the defence of want of mutuality altogether.

Fry, in his treatise on specific performance,[96] gave a number of illustrations of apparent exceptions to the applicability of the defence, of which the following are the chief—

1. Where the contract gives one party a right not enjoyed by the other, e.g. a right on the part of the lessee to obtain a renewal of his lease. Such cases have been regarded as conditional contracts. In reality, said Fry, such rights are simply examples of unilateral rights deliberately conferred by the parties, and no question of mutuality arises. They are therefore fully enforceable.

2. Where a purchaser contracts for the purchase of property from a person with no title, or with a title other than that contracted for, the contract is not mutual.[97] Fry added that if the purchaser investigates title on the footing of this defect or concurs in proceedings for remedying the defect, he may not afterwards set up the want of mutuality.[98] Actually, it is difficult to see in these cases any genuine questions of want of mutuality at all, and they are best considered as examples of a separate defence.

3. Where a contract is required to be evidenced by writing under the Statute of Frauds or the Law of Property Act, 1925, Section 40, a party who has not signed the memorandum may enforce it against a

[94] *Law of Contracts*, 6th ed., p. 533. See also *Anson on Contract*, 22nd ed. (Guest), p. 515; Treitel, *Law of Contract*, pp. 628-9; and the excellent discussion by Hanbury, *Modern Equity*, 8th ed., pp. 547-50.
[95] Reviewing the fourth edition of Fry (1903), 19 *Law Quarterly Review* 340, 341.
[96] 6th ed., pp. 223-8.
[97] See p. 504, post.
[98] See *Halkett* v. *Earl of Dudley*, [1907] 1 Ch. 590.

party who has. Leach, M.R., said[99] that by instituting proceedings, the plaintiff has waived the original want of mutuality and has thus rendered the remedy mutual.

Perhaps the only clear case of want of mutuality is that of an infant. Although he could sue on the contract in many cases at common law, he could not compel specific performance, since the court would never award specific performance against him.[1]

Among English writers, Ashburner[2] expressed himself doubtful of the existence of any general defence of want of mutuality. It has also been subjected to vigorous criticism in the United States. Ames[3] destroyed the alleged historical foundation of the rule, and added that, if pushed to its logical conclusion, the rule would produce absurd results. He restated[4] what was left of it after deducting the numerous exceptions: " Equity will not compel specific performance by a defendant if, after performance, the common law remedy of damages would be his sole security for the performance of the plaintiff's side of the contract." Although even to-day it is difficult to discern a decisive change of attitude in the English decisions towards this question, the influence of the work of Ames and others has been considerable. In America, however, as Judge Cardozo has interestingly described in his *Growth of the Law*,[5] the labours of the legal writers eventually brought about a reconsideration of the question, and a restatement of the modern doctrine by the Court of Appeals of New York in *Epstein* v. *Gluckin.*[6] Eventually the view of Ames was in substance adopted by the *Restatement of the Law of Contracts* in the following terms[7]—

> The fact that the remedy of specific performance is not available to one party is not a sufficient reason for refusing it to the other party.

In the United States, therefore, for practical purposes the rule has gone. In England, it survives to an indeterminate degree, and so many exceptions have been engrafted on it, that it is doubtful whether it serves any useful purpose.

99 *Flight* v. *Bolland* (1828), 4 Russ. 298, 301.
1 *Ibid.*
2 *Principles of Equity*, 2nd ed., pp. 404-5.
3 " Mutuality in Specific Performance " (1903), 3 *Columbia Law Review*, 1. See also Clark, " Some Problems in Specific Performance " (1917), 31 *Harvard Law Review*, 271-5.
4 3 *C.L.R.*, 2-3.
5 P. 42 (*Selected Writings of Benjamin Nathan Cardozo*, ed. Hall, 1947, p. 203).
6 (1922), 135 N.E. 861. The judgment of the court was given by Cardozo, J. See, especially, p. 862, where he substantially adopts views expressed by Durfee, " Mutuality in Specific Performance " (1922), 20 *Michigan Law Review*, 289. For the New York position after *Epstein* v. *Gluckin*, see Cook, " The Present Status of the ' Lack of Mutuality ' Rule " (1927), 36 *Yale Law Journal*, 897.
7 S. 372.

Want of Title

A vendor cannot succeed in an action for specific performance if he fails to show a clear title. This is a logical consequence of a system of private conveyancing, and it ties in with the principle that the court will not force upon a purchaser a title which involves immediate litigation.[8] Moreover, if an investigation reveals restrictive covenants which were not implied or expressed in the contract, the court may give relief to the purchaser, and it adopts the same attitude where there are unusual or onerous covenants in a lease.[9]

A question which has frequently arisen for consideration is the extent to which the court will assist a vendor who, though possessing a defective title, or even no title at all, nevertheless is in a position, or can be in a position, to give a title in accordance with the contract at the date fixed for completion. Here the position is that specific performance will be decreed if the defect has been removed before the purchaser has finally repudiated the contract.[10] In *Harold Elliott and H. Elliott* (*Builders*) *Ltd.* v. *Pierson*,[11] the first plaintiff sold to the defendant a roadhouse, which in fact was owned by the second defendant which was a limited company in which the first plaintiff held all the shares but one. In addition, the company had leased the property to the first plaintiff for forty years. The defendant resisted specific performance on the ground (inter alia) of want of title on the part of the first plaintiff, but Harman, J., held that the defence failed, as the first plaintiff was in a position, whenever it was necessary to do so, by exercising his powers as sole director, or by winding up the company, to ensure that the company should comply with his undertaking to sell.

The Plaintiff's Laches

Specific performance being an equitable remedy, it is subject to the limitation that it is available only to those whose conduct has attained the standards required by equity. Accordingly, if the plaintiff has neglected to pursue his remedy, his claim may fail on the ground of his laches.[12] In Vesey's Reports there appears the following interesting explanatory note[13] upon this bar to the exercise of the discretion—

8 See p. 501, *ante*.

9 See *Re Nisbet and Potts' Contract*, [1906] 1 Ch. 386 (C.A.); *Re Haedicke and Lipski's Contract*, [1901] 2 Ch. 666; *Molyneux* v. *Hawtrey*, [1903] 2 K.B. 487 (C.A.). These were all cases of rescission, not refusal of specific performance.

10 *Forrer* v. *Nash* (1865), 35 Beav. 167; *Halkett* v. *Earl of Dudley*, [1907] 1 Ch. 590; *Re Hailes and Hutchinson's Contract*, [1920] 1 Ch. 233.

11 [1948] Ch. 452. See also *Manning* v. *Turner*, [1957] 1 W.L.R. 91; *Jones* v. *Lipman*, [1962] 1 W.L.R. 832.

12 *Spurrier* v. *Hancock* (1799), 4 Ves. 667; *Guest* v. *Homfray* (1801), 5 Ves. 818. Cf. *Du Sautoy* v. *Symes*, [1967] Ch. 1146.

13 5 Ves. 720 n.

In *Milward* v. *Earl Thanet*, at the Rolls, *March* the 24th, 1801, the bill for specific performance was dismissed. The parties differed as to the construction of the agreement; and the bill was delayed for seven years. Lord *Alvanley*, then *Master of the Rolls*, observed, that Lord *Kenyon* was the first, who set himself against the idea, that had prevailed, that, when an agreement was entered into, either party might come at any time: but that it is now perfectly known, that a party cannot call upon a Court of Equity for a specific performance, unless he has shewn himself ready, desirous, prompt, and eager.

In all these cases, the assumption is that initially equity has not regarded time as of the essence of the contract. This was the general rule in equity before the Judicature Acts, and now, by virtue of the Law of Property Act, 1925, Section 41,[14] this rule is applicable at law. In some cases time may be regarded as being of the essence of the contract, and if this is the case, failure to fulfil the specified conditions will be as fatal in equity as it is at law. These cases may be classified as follows—

(i) Where the contract itself makes time to be of the essence of the contract.

(ii) Where, although the contract did not originally so stipulate, one of the parties, after delay by the other, gives reasonable notice that, from that point he will regard time as of the essence of the contract.[15]

(iii) In certain contracts, e.g. mercantile contracts, or a sale of a house required for immediate occupation, time may be regarded as of the essence of the contract.

In *Stickney* v. *Keeble*,[16] Lord Parker of Waddington, after pointing out that at law, time had always been regarded as of the essence of the contract, continued—

> In such cases, however, equity having a concurrent jurisdiction did not look upon the stipulation as to time in precisely the same light. Where it could do so without injustice to the contracting parties it decreed specific performance notwithstanding failure to observe the time fixed by the contract for completion, and as an incident of specific performance relieved the party in default by restraining proceedings at law based on such failure.

14 Replacing the Judicature Act, 1873, Sect. 25(7). Ireland: Judicature (Ireland) Act, 1877, Sect. 28(7), which is still in force.

15 *Stickney* v. *Keeble*, [1915] A.C. 386 (H.L., E.); *Re Barr's Contract*, [1956] Ch. 551.

16 [1915] A.C. 386, 415-6.

This is really all that is meant by and involved in the maxim that in equity the time fixed for completion is not of the essence of the contract, but this maxim never had any application to cases in which the stipulation as to time could not be disregarded without injustice to the parties, when, for example, the parties, for reasons best known to themselves, had stipulated that the time fixed should be essential, or where there was something in the nature of the property or the surrounding circumstances which would render it inequitable to treat it as a non-essential term of the contract.

In *Williams* v. *Greatrex*[17] there had been a delay of ten years, but the purchaser had paid a deposit, had entered into possession, and had performed acts of ownership. The plea of laches was therefore rejected, and specific performance was granted.

Misdescription

This is a frequent source of difficulty, especially since the remedy of specific performance is most frequently applicable to contracts for the transfer of interests in land. Equity has distinguished between misdescription which is substantial and misdescription which is slight. Where misdescription is substantial, specific performance will not be awarded, and the prospective purchaser will be entitled to rescission of the contract. Where, on the other hand, misdescription is slight, specific performance will be decreed, sometimes with an abatement of the purchase price. Where there has been a substantial misdescription, the party entitled to rescission may choose to go on, but at the same time he may ask for, and get, an abatement of the purchase money by way of compensation. Contracts for the sale of interests in land may be open (that is to say, made without reference to any express conditions) or they may be subject to conditions of sale. Such conditions of sale may either take some standardised form, such as The Law Society's General Conditions of Sale, or the conditions may be special. One special condition which is often met with relates to the length of title to be shown by the vendor.

Misdescription will be regarded as substantial if the interest in the property is different from what it is alleged to be, e.g. where the property is described as freehold, when it is leasehold (even though the lease is for 4,000 years),[18] or where the property is described as leasehold, and it is held on an underlease.[19] Where an investigation of title shows that the vendor has no title to a part (even a small part) of the land

17 [1957] 1 W.L.R. 31. Ireland: *Crofton* v. *Ormsby* (1806), 2 Sch. & Lef. 583, 603-4, *per* Lord Redesdale, L.C.
18 *Drewe* v. *Corp* (1804), 9 Ves. 368.
19 *Re Russ and Brown's Contract*, [1934] Ch. 34 (C.A.).

sold, specific performance will be refused.[20] Other such cases include the non-disclosure of onerous covenants[21] and misstatement of the area of the land.[22] The general principle is that unless the purchaser will get the actual thing contracted for, he will not be compelled to take what the vendor offers; and where the misdescription is substantial, the vendor will not obtain specific performance and the purchaser may rescind, even where the contract provides that errors shall not avoid the sale, but shall be a matter for compensation.[23]

On the other hand, the purchaser may elect to go on with the contract, and ask for an abatement of the purchase price, where the misdescription is substantial, whether the misdescription relates to the extent of the property, or to the nature of the vendor's interest in it, or to the incumbrances on it. If, however, the contract expressly states that no compensation shall be paid, then the purchaser must either resist specific performance and claim rescission, or proceed with the contract without compensation.[24] A condition in these terms now appears in the statutory conditions, drawn up under the Law of Property Act, 1925, applicable to all open contracts by correspondence.[25]

Where the misdescription is slight, the underlying assumption in respect of claims for specific performance is that the purchaser is going to get substantially what he contracted for, e.g. where there is a contract for the sale of a large estate, which is a few acres smaller than the description of it. Here compensation by way of abatement of purchase price will be awarded, unless the possibility has been excluded by a condition in the contract.[26]

Misdescription does not always lead to relief even by way of compensation, and no compensation can be granted where the misdescription is not part of the contract. In *Smith* v. *Lynn*[27] a house riddled with woodworm was described as being " in excellent structural and decorative repair, and ready for immediate owner occupation."

20 *Stapylton* v. *Scott* (1807), 13 Ves. 425; *Perkins* v. *Ede* (1852), 16 Beav. 193.

21 *Flight* v. *Booth* (1834), 1 Bing. N.C. 370.

22 *Re Arnold* (1880), 14 Ch.D. 270; *Jacobs* v. *Revell*, [1900] 2 Ch. 858; *Watson* v. *Burton*, [1957] 1 W.L.R. 19.

23 *Re Arnold* (1880), 14 Ch.D. 270 (C.A.); *Jacobs* v. *Revell*, [1900] 2 Ch. 858; *Watson* v. *Burton*, [1957] 1 W.L.R. 19. See also *Flight* v. *Booth* (1834), 1 Bing. N.C. 370, 376-7, *per* Tindal, C.J.

24 *Re Terry and White's Contract* (1886), 32 Ch.D. 14 (C.A.).

25 There is no equivalent in Ireland to these statutory conditions.

26 See, e.g., *McKenzie* v. *Hesketh* (1877), 7 Ch.D. 675; *Rutherford* v. *Acton-Adams*, [1915] A.C. 866 (P.C., New Zealand). Ireland: *Leslie* v. *Crommelin* (1867), I.R. 2 Eq. 134; *Connor* v. *Potts*, [1897] 1 I.R. 534.

27 [1951] N.I. 69. See also *Rutherford* v. *Acton-Adams*, [1915] A.C. 866; Delany, " Misrepresentation as a Defence to Actions for Specific Performance " (1951), 17 *Irish Jurist*, 51.

Curran, J., in the Northern Ireland Chancery Division, granted specific performance because each party had had equal opportunities of inspecting the house and forming his own opinion and neither had discovered the woodworm.

DAMAGES IN LIEU OF SPECIFIC PERFORMANCE

In Lord Hardwicke's day the Court of Chancery occasionally awarded damages in lieu of specific performance. The practice was discontinued, however, and it was not until the Chancery Amendment Act, 1858, that the Court of Chancery recovered that power. Although that Act has now been repealed in England,[28] the power to award damages in lieu of specific performance has not been affected.[29]

[28] It is still in force in Ireland.

[29] *Sayers* v. *Collyer* (1884), 28 Ch.D. 103 (C.A.); *Leeds Industrial Co-operative Building Soc. Ltd.* v. *Slack*, [1924] A.C. 851 (H.L., E.). These were both cases of damages in lieu of an injunction. The repeal was by the Statute Law Revision and Civil Procedure Act, 1883, which preserved the jurisdiction. See also the Judicature Act, 1873, Sect. 16; Statute Law Revision Act, 1898.

CHAPTER XIX

THE APPOINTMENT OF A RECEIVER

THE jurisdiction of the Court of Chancery to appoint a receiver has a long history, and is an important illustration of the manner in which equity evolved new remedies to supplement the inadequacy of the common law courts. A receiver is an officer of the court who is appointed to preserve property and, where necessary, to collect income for the benefit of those entitled to it. For the achievement of this purpose, he will receive the rent or other income arising from the property, and he will pay the necessary outgoings. A receiver, however, is not a manager of a business, and accordingly, the effect of appointing a receiver to a going concern is that it stops forthwith, its assets are realised, its debts paid, and the surplus distributed to those entitled to it. Therefore, where immediate realisation is not desired, the court will appoint a manager, who has power to continue the business in accordance with the general practice in that trade.[1]

The appointment of a receiver is just as much governed by equitable principles as the grant of any other equitable remedy, and accordingly the conduct of the applicant must have been free from fault.[2]

By virtue of Section 25 of the Judicature Act, 1873 (now Section 45 of the Judicature Act, 1925)[3] any Division of the High Court may now appoint a receiver by interlocutory order in all cases in which it shall appear to the court just and convenient to do so; and the order may be made unconditionally or upon such terms and conditions as the court shall think fit. Whilst the Act has widened the availability of the remedy, and has removed various inconvenient limitations on its use, it is nevertheless the case that the principles governing its exercise are those which were evolved by equity before the Judicature Acts.[4] The position, in fact, is very similar to that which exists in respect of the grant of an injunction. Thus, in *Morgan* v. *Hart*[5] the Court of Appeal refused to appoint a receiver by way of equitable execution, over property the title to which was legal, simply because it was a more convenient mode of payment, as no receiver would have been appointed before 1873.

1 *Re Manchester and Milford Railway* (1881), 45 L.T. 129.
2 *Baxter* v. *West* (1858), 28 L.J. Ch. 169.
3 Ireland: Judicature (Ireland) Act, 1877, Sect. 28 (8).
4 *Holmes* v. *Millage*, [1893] 1 Q.B. 551 (C.A.).
5 [1914] 2 K.B. 183.

The original purpose of appointing a receiver was to preserve property which was the subject of litigation, until that litigation was completed, and the title to it determined. However, prior to the Judicature Act, the court was reluctant to appoint a receiver of land in interlocutory proceedings in an ejectment action. The old equitable practice was discussed by Page Wood, V.-C., in *Earl Talbot* v. *Hope Scott*,[6] where he said—

> . . . it is too clear for any contention in the present day that this Court will not interfere at the instance of a person alleging a merely legal title in himself against other persons in possession of the estates, to grant a receiver and put them out of possession.

In that case, the estates were annexed by private Act to the Earldom of Shrewsbury, to which the plaintiff had a claim pending before the Committee of Privileges of the House of Lords. The defendants were the trustees in possession of parts of the estates for the purposes of the private Act. A receiver was therefore refused.

The effect of the Judicature Act upon this equitable practice was considered by Lindley, M.R., in *John* v. *John*,[7] and it would seem that the court will now take into consideration how long the defendant has been in possession, and the nature of his title, together with any other material circumstances, and in particular the risk to which the tenants of the land may be exposed.

There is also a second, and distinct, use of a receiver. This is by way of equitable execution, where adequate relief is not available at common law. Certain property of a judgment debtor cannot be seized by the sheriff under a writ of fieri facias, to be sold in satisfaction of the debt. A fund in court, an equity of redemption, a beneficiary's interest in a trust fund, a legacy payable in the future, and a share in the proceeds of sale of land not yet sold, are all beyond the reach of the sheriff. It was therefore the practice of the Court of Chancery to permit an equitable substitute for execution at common law in respect of such property. It would direct the appointment of a receiver of rents and profits. Since the Judicature Act, any Division of the High Court can now grant this substitute for execution, but only in accordance with principles settled in equity before. This was not at first fully appreciated, and there was some indication of a belief that equitable execution would be granted irrespective of whether any impediment to legal execution existed. This belief was strongly negatived by all three members of the Court of Appeal in *Re Shephard*.[8]

[6] (1858), 4 K. & J. 96, 111-12.

[7] [1898] 2 Ch. 573, 578 (C.A.). See also *Marshall* v. *Charteris*, [1920] 1 Ch. 520.

[8] (1889), 43 Ch. D. 131. See also *Manchester and Liverpool District Banking Co. Ltd.* v. *Parkinson* (1888), 22 Q.B.D. 173 (C.A.); *Harris* v. *Beauchamp Bros.*, [1894] 1 Q.B. 801 (C.A.).

The question whether a difficulty exists in securing the legal remedy is a question of fact, however, and if the court is satisfied that the judgment debtor intends and is able to make away with property liable to execution at law, in order to defeat his creditors, a receiver may be appointed.

A receiver may be appointed in one of two ways:

1. *Out of Court*—for example, by a mortgagee or by debenture holders, where the trust deed provides for such an appointment. In these cases, the receiver is the agent of the person appointing him, and he therefore incurs no personal liability for acts done within the scope of his authority. If, in the exercise of powers under a debenture, a debenture holder appoints a receiver, the receiver does not become an officer of the company under Section 333(1) of the Companies Act, 1948,[9] nor is he a manager of the company. He is the manager of the company's property only on behalf of the debenture holders.[10] There are also statutory powers of appointing a receiver out of court.[11]

2. *By the Court*—Such a receiver is not an agent for any of the parties. He is an officer of the court, and any interference with him in the performance of his duties may be punished as a contempt, and restrained by injunction.

A receiver appointed by the court is entitled to a proper remuneration which is normally fixed at 5 per cent of the income received. A receiver appointed by debenture holders receives the remuneration provided for in the trust deed. So far as a receiver for a mortgagee is concerned, Section 109 of the Law of Property Act, 1925,[12] provides for the appointment, powers, remuneration and duties of the receiver. In particular, it entitles him to retain out of money received by him a commission not exceeding five per cent of the gross amount of all money received, or where no rate is specified in his appointment, five per cent of the gross amount, or any rate as the court thinks proper to be allowed.

In Ireland, the appointment of receivers is in general governed by the same rules as in England.[13] The Republic of Ireland, however, seems to have a special rule that a public service pension, not alienable by act of the pensioner, can be taken in equitable execution.[14]

9 Ireland: Companies Act (Northern Ireland), 1960, Sect. 299; Companies Act, 1963, Sect. 298 (Republic of Ireland).

10 *Re B. Johnson & Co. (Builders) Ltd.*, [1955] Ch. 634 (C.A.); *Kernohan Estates Ltd.* v. *Boyd*, [1967] N.I. 27.

11 See p. 513, *post*.

12 Ireland: Conveyancing Act, 1881, Sect. 24.

13 See, e.g., *Commissioners of Church Temporalities of Ireland* v. *Harrington* (1883), 11 L.R. Ir. 127; *Kenealy* v. *O'Keeffe* (1900), 34 I.L.T.R. 75 (D.C.); *M'Causland* v. *O'Callaghan* (1903), 3 N.I.J.R. 144 (C.A.); *Langdale Chemical Manure Co.* v. *Ginty* (1907), 41 I.L.T.R. 40 (D.C.); *National Bank Ltd.* v. *Barry* (1965), 100 I.L.T.R. 185 (Sup. Ct.).

14 *Higgins* v. *Higgins*, [1951] Ir. Jur. Rep. 29; *Garrahan* v. *Garrahan*, [1959] I.R. 168.

When a Receiver is Appointed

The use of a receiver to preserve property is very wide, and no exhaustive enumeration of the occasions for appointment can be attempted. Some of the most important occasions may be briefly mentioned, however.

In Executorships and Trusteeships

Wherever an executor or trustee commits such breaches of duty that the trust property is wasted or endangered, the court will appoint a receiver. For example, if a trustee improperly invests in non-trustee securities, or if, being a sole trustee, he becomes bankrupt, a receiver may be appointed, as an alternative to the removal of the trustee. The mere poverty of the trustee or executor is not a sufficient reason for appointing a receiver, but if it is allied to bad character, improvidence or drunkenness, a case for appointment will arise.

Under the Settled Land Act, 1925, the legal estate is now vested in the tenant for life, on trust to give effect to the beneficial interests under the settlement.[15] A receiver will therefore be appointed (as under the old law) in respect of the tenant for life's interest where he fails to discharge his duties as trustee.

The principles applicable to executors and trustees are also applicable to administrators and to all persons who take under implied trusts, and to those who have acquired property in respect of which a constructive trust exists.[16]

Between Vendor and Purchaser

In a suitable case between vendor and purchaser, a receiver might be appointed on the application of either party. Where a sale has been concluded in such circumstances that a strong suspicion of fraud on the part of the purchaser arises, a receiver might be appointed on the application of the vendor or those claiming through him. Conversely if, after the purchase money had been paid, the vendor refused to execute a conveyance and remained in possession, a receiver might be appointed at the suit of the purchaser.

Between Mortgagor and Mortgagee

Before the Judicature Acts, an equitable mortgagee whose security had become enforceable had a right to apply for the appointment of a receiver, as a step towards the realisation of the security, and this

15 In Ireland, under the Settled Land Acts, 1882-90, this is not so.
16 *Huguenin* v. *Baseley* (1806), 13 Ves. 105.

would be granted, unless there was a prior legal mortgagee in possession, as an equitable mortgagee had no right to enter into possession.[17] On the other hand, a receiver would normally be refused, when asked for by a legal mortgagee, since he could always take possession by virtue of his legal title. However, under the Law of Property Act, 1925, Section 101 (1) (iii),[18] wherever a mortgage, whether legal or equitable, is made by deed, the mortgagee enjoys the right to appoint a receiver, at any time after he has become entitled to exercise his power of sale. The receiver is deemed to be the agent of the mortgagor.[19] The great value of appointing a receiver in respect of mortgaged property is that it confers on the mortgagee virtually all the benefits of taking possession, without its disadvantages. The power of appointing a receiver under the Law of Property Act, 1925, belongs to the mortgagee and is regulated by the statute.[20] It extends as of right to both legal and equitable mortgages, and it may be exercised by a mortgagee who has taken possession,[21] but independently of this statutory power, the court, in the exercise of its equitable jurisdiction, still retains the right to appoint a receiver in a proper case between mortgagor and mortgagee. Since the Judicature Act, a receiver will be appointed by the court at the instance of a legal mortgagee, but the court will consider whether the circumstances are appropriate to the appointment. A mortgagee is not debarred from asking for a receiver even if he has entered into possession, although the court will not be disposed to grant his request, and so enable him to go out of possession, without the consent of those who are entitled to the equity of redemption. This point is well illustrated by *Re Prytherch*.[22] Certain property was mortgaged, and Mr Charles Bishop was appointed receiver. Later, he ceased to enjoy that character, and being himself a legal mortgagee, he forthwith entered in possession of the mortgaged property, and he continued in possession for eleven years. At the expiration of this time, he asked for a receiver to be appointed, so that he could go out of possession. North, J., after alluding to the changed practice since the Judicature Acts, took the view that Mr. Bishop was not free to relinquish possession whenever he chose, and was not disposed to accept the contention that it was "just or convenient" to appoint a receiver because the mortgagee had tired of being in possession. He would have been inclined to have refused the application, but it was eventually agreed that Bishop should be appointed receiver without salary and without security.

17 *Re Crompton & Co. Ltd.*, [1914] 1 Ch. 954. See also pp.239-42, *ante*.
18 Ireland: Conveyancing Act, 1881, Sect. 19 (1).
19 See the Law of Property Act, 1925, Sects. 99(19), 100(13), 101(1) (iii) and 109. Ireland: Conveyancing Act, 1911, Sect. 3(1), (11); Conveyancing Act, 1881, Sects. 19(1) and 24.
20 Sect. 109. Ireland: 1881 Act, Sect. 24.
21 *Refuge Assurance Co. Ltd.* v. *Pearlberg*, [1938] Ch. 687 (C.A.).
22 (1889), 42 Ch.D. 590.

Since, as we have seen, a receiver has no power to carry on a business, if the property in respect of which he had been appointed includes a business which is to be continued, a manager must also be appointed.

Between Debenture Holders and Company

Mortgagees or debenture holders of companies incorporated under the Companies Acts may apply to the court for the appointment of a receiver; and it would seem that in cases of mismanagement by the directors, the shareholders can also ask for the appointment of a receiver.[23] The practice with regard to appointment follows closely the practice governing the appointment of a receiver in respect of a mortgage of real property. The debenture holders may obtain the appointment of a receiver—

1. Where either principal or interest is in arrear, or when any other event has happened by which the security has become enforceable.

2. Where the security has crystallised into a specific charge in consequence of a winding-up order or resolution.

3. Where the security is in jeopardy, and particularly where creditors are pressing.[24]

Independently of the court's jurisdiction, the debenture holders themselves may have a power to appoint a receiver under a power conferred by the debentures. If the debenture holders exercise their power, this does not debar the court from making an appointment. In *Re* " *Slogger* " *Automatic Feeder Co. Ltd.*,[25] certain debentures issued by the company contained a condition that at any time after the principal sum borrowed had become due, any debenture holder, with the consent in writing of the holders of a majority in value of the debentures, might appoint a receiver and manager of the company's business. Two hundred debentures were issued, of which X (a bank) held 60, C held 55, L held 65, and T held 20. L had deposited 64 of his debentures with X as security for a loan. C, after obtaining the consent in writing of L and T, but without communicating with X, appointed a receiver and a manager. In a debenture holder's action, Neville, J., held that as X were registered holders of 60 debentures, and were the equitable mortgagees of 64 more, the receiver and manager had not been properly appointed, as X's consent had not been obtained. Accordingly a receiver and manager should be appointed by the court.

23 *Stanfield* v. *Gibbon*, [1925] W.N. 11.

24 Kerr *on Receivers*, 13th ed., pp. 56-9.

25 [1915] 1 Ch. 478.

Where a company or public utility is incorporated under a special Act of Parliament, with borrowing powers, a mortgagee or debenture holder may come to the court and ask for a receiver to be appointed.[26]

Between Debtor and Creditor

In *Re Shephard*[27] it was pointed out that a creditor has a general right to apply to the court for the appointment of a receiver, where he can show some equity upon which the jurisdiction is founded. For example, where there is a danger that assets of a deceased person may be wasted pending the appointment of a personal representative, a creditor may ask for a receiver to be appointed.[28] Again, where a creditor has a right to be paid out of a particular fund, the creditor may secure the appointment of a receiver to prevent the fund from being wasted.

Judgment creditors are in a special position, from the standpoint of equitable relief. Before the Judicature Act, it was necessary for them to show that they had exhausted the possibilities of legal execution, and further, that the debtor possessed an interest which could not be reached by common law process. Since the Act, it is no longer necessary to satisfy the first condition, but the second condition still holds good.[29]

In Partnership Cases

Where a partnership has been dissolved, but the realisation of the assets is being delayed by one of the former partners, a receiver may be appointed at the instance of another former member of the partnership who is being prejudiced. Exceptionally, the court might appoint a receiver where the partnership is still in existence, but the question whether a proper case for appointment has arisen is one of great difficulty, and the court will do the best it can in the matter, in the interests of the partners, without following any settled rule. In fact, it would seem that the court will only appoint a receiver where it is reasonably clear that a dissolution of the partnership will be ordered at the trial.[30] Where this does not appear to be the probable result of the trial, a receiver will be refused, but the court may by injunction restrain the partner from committing acts prejudicial to the partnership.[31]

Even where a dissolution of partnership is claimed, a receiver will only be appointed where a partner has done something inconsistent with his duty as a partner, so that mutual confidence between the

26 See *Carmichael* v. *Greenock Harbour Trustees*, [1910] A.C. 274 (H.L., S.).
27 (1889), 43 Ch.D. 131 (C.A.).
28 On the position of such a receiver, see *Re Botibol*, [1947] 1 All E.R. 26.
29 *Re Pope* (1886), 17 Q.B.D. 743 (C.A.).
30 *Goodman* v. *Whitcomb* (1820), 1 J. & W. 589.
31 See *Hall* v. *Hall* (1850), 3 Mac. & G. 79.

partners has been destroyed, and the affairs of the partnership have been prejudiced. This means more than that partners have disagreed, or that one of them has ceased to be active. On the other hand, if one partner entirely excludes another from the management of the affairs of the partnership, a receiver will be appointed.[32]

In Cases of Mental Infirmity

In cases of mental infirmity, the court has jurisdiction to appoint a receiver of the infirm person's property, even though no action is pending. To-day, however, receivers are appointed under the Mental Health Act, 1959.[33] Such persons have wide powers of administration of the patient's or infirm person's property.

Who may be Appointed Receiver

It is beyond the scope of a general treatise on equity to discuss in detail the effect of appointing a receiver, and the extent of his powers, duties, and liabilities. Something may be said, however, concerning the practice of a court of equity in respect of the persons who may act as receivers. The general rule is that a person who is disinterested in the subject-matter of the appointment should be appointed. This rule, however, may be varied if it can be shown that the appointment will be of benefit in respect of the property. Thus, a partner has frequently been appointed, in an action for the dissolution of the partnership,[34] though he will usually be required to give security. Even a party to the action may be appointed, often without salary.[35] On the other hand, the court will avoid, if possible, appointing a trustee as receiver to a trust estate.[36] In *Sykes* v. *Hastings*,[37] Lord Eldon laid down the principle governing the position of a trustee as follows—

> I do not say, there is any general rule, that will not bend to circumstances; but the general principle is, that the person, who accepts the office of trustee, engages to do the whole duty of receiver without emolument. That is useful; as the Court, appointing a receiver, looks to the trustee to examine with an adverse eye, to see, that the receiver does his duty. The consequence is, the case of appointing a trustee to be receiver is extremely rare; and only, where he will act without emolument. There is no instance of such an appointment with emolument; unless no one else can be procured,

32 See *Goodman* v. *Whitcomb* (1820), 1 J. & W. 589.
32 See *Goodman* v. *Whitcomb, supra*.
33 Sects. 105-6. Ireland: Lunacy Regulation (Ireland) Act, 1871.
34 *Sargant* v. *Read* (1876), 1 Ch.D. 600.
35 E.g. *Re Prytherch* (1889), 42 Ch.D. 590.
36 *Anon* (1797), 3 Ves. 515; —— v. *Jolland* (1802), 8 Ves 72; *Sykes* v. *Hastings* (1805), 11 Ves. 363; *Sutton* v. *Jones* (1809), 15 Ves. 584.
37 (1805), 11 Ves. 363, 364.

who will act with the same benefit to the estate; where there is a necessity; from the circumstance, that by any one else the estate will not be so well managed. The principle of the Court is, that the trustee shall not be the receiver; if any other can be procured.

The principle governing trustees applies to other persons in a fiduciary position, e.g. the solicitor to a party to the action, since in the conduct of it, it will be his duty to check the receiver's accounts.[38] A company may not be a receiver of a company, nor may a director of the company in respect of which the receiver is desired.[39] The overriding consideration is always the suitability and, in general, the absence of bias of the person selected, although where a party to the action is, for convenience, appointed, this rule is departed from.

It was the settled practice of the old Court of Chancery, when the appointment of receivers was made by the Masters in Chancery, never to entertain any objection to the report of the Master which was not founded on principle. As Arden, M.R., pointed out in *Bowersbank* v. *Colasseau*,[40] if any other practice were adopted, " The reasons for the Master's judgment are so nice, that the consequence would be, every appointment would be brought before the Court." Accordingly special reasons and a strong case were required.[41]

The same principle now governs the practice of the Court of Appeal with regard to the appointment of a receiver by a judge.

[38] *Garland* v. *Garland* (1793), 2 Ves. 137.
[39] See *Re Carshalton Park Estate Ltd.*, [1908] 2 Ch. 62.
[40] (1796), 3 Ves. 164, 165.
[41] See *Tharpe* v. *Tharpe* (1806), 12 Ves. 317.

CHAPTER XX

TRACING

INTRODUCTION

WHEN a person goes bankrupt, or an insolvent company goes into liquidation, creditors are rarely paid in full. A person trying to recover something from the wreckage will seek, if possible, to do better than receive a proportion in the general distribution among the creditors, by establishing a claim superior to that of a mere debt. One variety of superior claimant is a secured creditor, such as a mortgagee,[1] who can show that he has a proprietary interest, by way of security, in some specific asset of the insolvent. Another such claim is that by a person who can show that some item of property, apparently belonging to the debtor, really belongs to the claimant. If the owner of a horse stables it with a riding school, he can take it back on the bankruptcy of the owner of the riding school (unless the doctrine of reputed ownership applies) and the bankrupt's creditors have no claim that that horse should swell the assets available for paying them, i.e. no claim that the horse's owner should rank with them.

The equitable doctrine of tracing is an extended application of the notion that what appears to be the insolvent's property does not in reality belong to him, i.e. the notion that someone who appears to be merely a creditor has a claim in respect of specific property. It is given legal effect either by treating some asset as the property of the claimant or by treating the claimant as a creditor secured on that property. It is used to cope with cases of misappropriation. For example, if the riding school owner in the hypothetical case above had, before his bankruptcy, exchanged the horse for a motor car the erstwhile horse-owner, if unable to get his horse back, could trace his property into the car and either (a) take it or (b) have a charge on it for the value of the horse, this charge being realised by sale. Whichever course he chose, if the car was worth less than the horse he could claim as an ordinary creditor for the balance.

The equitable process of tracing is available to anyone who was beneficially entitled to the original property which has been misappro-

[1] See pp. 164-262, *ante*.

priated and transformed. It makes no difference whether the claimant was the legal owner or the owner of an equitable interest. He may be a legal owner who has been a victim of the tort of conversion, as in the case of the horse swopped for a car. He may be a legal owner who has given an agent a power to dispose of the legal title, and who is the victim of misappropriation by the agent of the proceeds. He may be a beneficiary under a trust seeking to trace property misappropriated in breach of trust. These are only examples, not an exhaustive list; but the claimant must, except in one case, claim as beneficial owner. The one exception is that a trustee can trace trust property, on behalf of the beneficiaries, in the hands of someone who should not have it.[2]

The process of tracing in equity can continue through any number of transformations, so long as the thing now claimed can be identified as representing the original property; through mixture or confusion with property of someone other than the claimant, so long as the thing now claimed can be identified as partly representing the original property of the claimant; and through any number of people's hands, so long as so identifiable, except as against a bona fide purchaser of a proprietary interest without notice of the claimant's equity.[3]

Tracing is not an exclusively equitable process, but it is more extensively available in equity than at common law. Its origins both at common law and in equity are respectably ancient, but the present refinements are modern. For a full understanding it is no longer necessary to look further back than the nineteenth century cases.

Tracing Property in a Changed Form in the Hands of the Wrongdoer

Simple Change of Form

Taylor v. *Plumer*[4] shows how the process operates in an uncomplicated case. The defendant (later Master of the Rolls) had got his broker to sell stock, intending to buy land with the proceeds. As the money was not needed immediately to pay for the land, he instructed the broker to buy Exchequer bills with it. The broker, who had paid the money into a bank, drew it out in £1,000 Bank of England notes. The broker then used some of these identical notes to buy himself American shares, stock and bullion and tried to get away to America. There was a dramatic chase by the defendant's attorney and a police officer, who

[2] *Price* v. *Blakemore* (1843), 6 Beav. 507. Ireland: *Carson* v. *Sloane* (1884), 13 L.R.Ir. 139.

[3] Ireland: *Scott* v. *Scott*, [1924] 1 I.R. 141.

[4] (1815), 3 M. & S. 562.

caught the broker at Falmouth where he was waiting for a boat bound for Lisbon to sail. The broker handed the property he was making off with over to the defendant. On the broker's bankruptcy, it was held that the defendant could keep the shares, stock and bullion as against the assignee in bankruptcy. Lord Ellenborough, C.J., said[5]—

> It makes no difference in reason or law into what other form, different from the original, the change may have been made, . . . for the product of or substitute for the original thing still follows the nature of the thing itself, as long as it can be ascertained to be such, and the right only ceases when the means of ascertainment fail . . .[6]

In *Taylor* v. *Plumer* the assignee in bankruptcy failed to get the property back, but the process works in a positive way too. If the property has come into the hands of the wrongdoer's trustee in bankruptcy, the beneficial owner of the original property with which it is identified can claim it.[7] Even if the wrongdoer has bought land with the proceeds of sale of the original property, tracing can proceed in the absence of a memorandum in writing, for a constructive trust, based on fraud, is not within the Statute of Frauds.[8]

A recent example of the application of the doctrine in Ireland is *Shanahans Stamp Auctions Ltd.* v. *Farrelly*,[9] where Budd, J., in an elaborate judgment, reviewed the authorities. A company had advertised a scheme whereby people would subscribe money with which stamps would be bought abroad and brought to the Republic of Ireland. Subscribers would be grouped into syndicates, stamps would be allocated to each syndicate, and after a stated period the stamps would be sold by auction, the proceeds (after the company had received its auctioneer's commission) being divided among the members of the syndicate in proportion to their subscriptions. A profit was assumed, but the company purported to guarantee the return of the capital invested in any event. When the company went into liquidation there was a huge deficit on the subscribers' account and there were ordinary creditors. There were some stamps which had been allocated to syndicates and there were also unallocated stamps and unsyndicated subscribers. On a claim to trace the stamps, Budd, J., held that the money given to buy stamps was held by the company on trust. There

5 3 M. & S. 575.
6 The rest of this sentence is wrong, and is omitted for that reason.
7 *Frith* v. *Cartland* (1865), 2 H. & M. 417, where the wrongdoer, as in *Taylor* v. *Plumer*, acquired the property on the eve of bankruptcy for the purpose of absconding with it.
8 *Lane* v. *Dighton* (1762), Amb. 409. See also *Lench* v. *Lench* (1805), 10 Ves. 511, 517, *per* Grant, M.R. Ireland: *Carson* v. *Sloane* (1884), 13 L.R.Ir. 139.
9 [1962] I.R. 386.

was no trust of the stamps in specie because that was neither intended nor practicable, but they were held on trust for sale. That is to say, the syndicated investors were entitled pro rata to the proceeds of the allocated stamps and the unsyndicated investors to those of the unallocated stamps, in priority to any claim by ordinary creditors.

Mixture of Funds

The commonest case of confusion of two persons' property is that where the property is money or is converted into money and paid into a bank account. Suppose the wrongdoer to have paid in some of his own money and proceeds of sale of misappropriated property. The person who owned the misappropriated property would want to trace it into the bank account, not just rank as ordinary creditor of a bankrupt wrongdoer.

The claim is not against the bank which, unless it has notice of a trust[10] or has made some special arrangement, does not stand in a fiduciary relation to its customer or to persons wronged by its customer.[11] The claim is against the wrongdoer, to take or be secured by charge on one of his assets, namely the debt owed to him by his bank, in priority to unsecured creditors. Therefore, in the normal course of such events, the claimant is not concerned with the relations between the wrongdoer and his bank. However, these can sometimes be relevant, and it is convenient to mention *Clayton's Case*[12] before the later authorities.

When a debtor owes several debts to one creditor and pays less than the total due, the question of appropriating the payment to one or other of the debts is one to be settled by agreement between debtor and creditor. What Grant, M.R., decided in *Clayton's Case*[13] was that, in the absence of agreement, when a bank made a payment to its customer, that was to be debited against the earliest subsisting payment in, because that is how banks work their accounts. " First in, first out " is, in effect, what the Master of the Rolls said. Clayton was a customer of a banking partnership run by Devaynes and four others. At Devaynes's death Clayton's account was in credit to the tune of £1,713. After that, Clayton drew out more than £1,713 (so creating an overdraft) and later paid in sums totalling even more. The surviving partners then became insolvent and Clayton tried to recover from Devaynes's estate. Grant, M.R., held that the sums paid out to Clayton

10 See *Barclays Bank Ltd.* v. *Quistclose Investments Ltd.*, [1968] 3 W.L.R. 1097(H.L.).
11 *Foley* v. *Hill* (1848), 2 H.L.C. 28 (H.L.,E.).
12 (1816), 1 Mer. 572. See also McConville, " Tracing and the Rule in *Clayton's Case* " (1963), 79 *Law Quarterly Review*, 388.
13 (1816), 1 Mer. 572.

after Devaynes's death must be appropriated to the £1,713 then due, and therefore Devaynes's estate was free from liability, while the sums which Clayton subsequently paid in constituted a new debt, for which the surviving partners alone were liable.

The wrongdoer cannot take advantage of this rule of " first in, first out " against the person he has wronged; nor can his ordinary creditors. Take the case of a solicitor who misappropriates a client's funds by paying them into his private bank account. At that moment the client can trace, and is entitled to a charge on the whole debt due from the bank so far as necessary to satisfy the amount due from the solicitor to the client. If the solicitor pays in more money of his own, and later draws out money and spends it, there is no question of applying the rule of " first in, first out " so as to say that the client's money has been spent and the solicitor's own money remains, for the charge remains on the whole debt. This was settled in *Re Hallett's Estate*,[14] where Jessel, M.R., in the Court of Appeal, said[15]—

> The modern doctrine of Equity as regards property disposed of by persons in a fiduciary position is a very clear and well-established doctrine. You can, if the sale was rightful, take the proceeds of sale, if you can identify them. If the sale was wrongful, you can still take the proceeds of the sale, in a sense adopting the sale for the purpose of taking the proceeds, if you can identify them. There is no distinction, therefore, between a rightful and a wrongful disposition of the property, so far as regards the right of the beneficial owner to follow the proceeds. But it very often happens that you cannot identify the proceeds. The proceeds may have been invested together with money belonging to the person in a fiduciary position, in a purchase. He may have bought land with it, for instance, or he may have bought chattels with it. Now, what is the position of the beneficial owner as regards such purchases ? I will, first of all, take his position when the purchase is clearly made with what I will call, for shortness, the trust money, although it is not confined, as I will shew presently, to

14 (1880), 13 Ch.D. 696. Ireland: *Re Reynolds*, [1895] 1 I.R. 83; *Re Nolan*, [1949] I.R. 197. Cf. *Scott* v. *Scott*, [1924] 1 I.R. 141.
See also Williston, " The Right to Follow Trust Property when Confused with Other Property " (1888), 2 *Harvard Law Review*, 28; Brodhurst, " Following Property in the Hands of an Agent " (1898), 14 *Law Quarterly Review*, 272; Ames, " Following Misappropriated Property into its Product " (1906), 19 *H.L.R.*, 511; Scott, " The Right to Follow Money Wrongfully Mingled with Other Money " (1913), 27 *H.L.R.*, 125; Taft, "A Defense of a Limited Use of the Swollen Assets Theory where Money has Wrongfully been Mingled with Other Money " (1939), 39 *Columbia Law Review*, 172; Maudsley, " Restitution in England " (1966), 19 *Vanderbilt Law Review*, 1123, esp. pp. 1136-41; Waters, " The English Constructive Trust: A Look Into the Future " (1966), 19 *Vand. L.R.*, 1215, esp. pp. 1229-50.

15 13 Ch.D. 708-9.

express trusts. In that case, according to the now well-established doctrine of Equity, the beneficial owner has a right to elect either to take the property purchased, or to hold it as a security for the amount of the purchase money laid out in the purchase; or, as we generally express it, he is entitled at his election either to take the property, or to have a charge on the property for the amount of the trust money. But in the second case, where a trustee has mixed the money with his own, there is this distinction, that the *cestui que trust*, or beneficial owner, can no longer elect to take the property, because it is no longer bought with the trust-money simply and purely, but with a mixed fund. He is, however, still entitled to a charge on the property purchased, for the amount of the trust-money laid out in the purchase; and that charge is quite independent of the fact of the amount laid out by the trustee. The moment you get a substantial portion of it furnished by the trustee, using the word " trustee " in the sense I have mentioned, as including all persons in a fiduciary relation, the right to the charge follows. That is the modern doctrine of Equity.

The dependence of tracing on being able to identify the available property as representing in part the misappropriated property can be demonstrated by two variations. The first is illustrated by *Re Oatway*,[16] where a trustee paid trust money into his personal account, and then drew out money and invested it in his own name. After this drawing, there was still more in the account than the amount of the trust money paid in. He subsequently spent the balance without having any property to show for it. The charge on the account was now useless because the credit balance had gone. On the other hand the investment made with the sum first drawn out was there and it was held by Joyce, J., that it could be traced as representing the trust money. The reason is that, when the trust money was paid into the bank, the beneficiary of the trust had a charge on the whole fund. When he bought the investment, the trustee did so with money subject to that charge. Therefore the charge attached to the investment.

The second variation is illustrated by *James Roscoe* (*Bolton*) *Ltd.* v. *Winder*.[17] The defendant agreed to collect debts owed to the plaintiff company and pay them over to the company. He collected the debts (£623-8s.-5d.) and paid £455-18s.-11d. of this into his private bank account (what happened to the rest is not known). He drew out money and spent it until the credit balance of his account was only £25-18s.

16 [1903] 2 Ch. 356. See also *Re Tilley's Will Trusts*, [1967] Ch. 1179.

17 [1915] 1 Ch. 62. Ireland: *Re Ulster Land, Building and Investment Co.* (1889), 25 L.R.Ir. 24.

Later he paid in more of his own money and died with a balance of £358-5s.-5d. Sargant, J., held that Winder was a trustee of the £455-18s.-11d. for the company, but that the Company's charge on the account was only to the extent of £25-18s. This was the only trust money identifiable. The money paid in after the account had sunk to this level was identifiable as not being trust money. The learned judge said[18]—

> . . . it is impossible to attribute to [Winder] that by the mere payment into the account of further moneys, which to a large extent he subsequently used for purposes of his own, he intended to clothe those moneys with a trust in favour of the plaintiffs.

In other words, he had not declared himself express trustee of the later credits. It would certainly have been different if he had. In *Robertson* v. *Morrice*[19] a trustee who held stock in trust, and also similar stock of his own, confused them. He sold parts of the mixed-up stock from time to time so that shortly before his death the amount left was less than what he should have been holding on trust. On his deathbed, he got his clerk to buy more of this stock in order to replace what he had misappropriated from the trust. Lord Langdale, M.R., held that all the stock was held on trust: the balance of the original mixed holding because of the charge that attached on the mixing, and the newly acquired holding because of the declaration that it was to replace the trust property.

Another case of impossibility of identification occurs where there are mere bookkeeping entries and no funds actually change hands. In this way, what a bank does may affect claims on its customers. In *Re Hallett & Co.*,[20] trustees asked their bankers to collect money from a company in which the trustees held debentures. The bankers knew of the trust. The bankers also had to pay larger sums to the same company, these sums being due from other customers of the bank, so they struck a balance, sent a cheque to the company, and credited the trustees' account with £1,600 (the sum due on the debentures). The bankers having gone bankrupt, the Court of Appeal held there was no identifiable trust property as nothing had been paid to their bankers by the trustees nor had anything been paid to the trustees by the bank.

It seems that where a wrongdoer adds to his own bank account money misappropriated from two other people, and then makes drawings so that there is not enough left in the account to satisfy both

[18] [1915] 1 Ch. 69.

[19] (1845), 4 L.T.O.S. 430.

[20] [1894] 2 Q.B. 237.

chargees, the rule in *Clayton's Case*[21] may apply as between these two chargees so as to throw the loss primarily on the one whose property was misappropriated first. There is no imposing authority for this, and it may be doubted as being inequitable as compared with a distribution pari passu, which has the support, in other circumstances, of the House of Lords in *Sinclair* v. *Brougham*[22] and of Budd, J., in the Irish case of *Shanahans Stamp Auctions Ltd.* v. *Farrelly*.[23] However, it has been said[24] that the rule of " first in, first out " applies as between beneficiaries under two separate trusts and as between two or more beneficiaries of the same trust. In *Re Stenning*[25] a solicitor paid clients' money into his personal bank account. This money included £448-18s.-6d. due to Mrs. Sydney Smith. There was always more in the account than that, but there was often less than the total of clients' money paid in. North, J., held, first, that in fact there was not a trust of the money but a loan at interest by agreement; but, secondly, that if the £448-18s.-6d. was trust money, *Clayton's Case*[26] applied as between Mrs. Smith and the other clients whose money had been paid into the account.

The principles were reviewed by the House of Lords in *Sinclair* v. *Brougham*.[27] A building society had been conducting a banking business, which was ultra vires. When it was being wound up, the society had a miscellaneous mass of assets. The question before the House was as to the relative claims of the shareholders in the society and the depositors of money on the ultra vires side of its business. The assets exceeded the amounts contributed by the shareholders. Viscount Haldane, L.C., with whom Lord Atkinson concurred, thought that the two classes of claimant should share pari passu. The claim of the depositors was based on tracing, since the deposits (being ultra vires) did not pass the equitable title to the money. That is to say, no relationship of debtor and creditor was established between the bank and its customers because the banking business was ultra vires. But the depositors could not claim a charge for the whole amount of the deposits, in priority to payment of anything to the shareholders, because the society had not been guilty of a breach of fiduciary duty to the depositors: there was no fiduciary duty, and the society had

21 (1816), 1 Mer. 572. See pp. 521-2, *ante*.
22 [1914] A.C. 398. See below.
23 [1962] I.R. 386. See pp. 520-1, *ante*.
24 See *Re Hallett's Estate* (1880), 13 Ch.D. 696 (C.A.); *Hancock* v. *Smith* (1889), 41 Ch.D. 456 (C.A.). See also *Re Diplock*, [1948] Ch. 465, 553-4, pp. 527-9, *post*.
25 [1895] 2 Ch. 433. Ireland: see *Shanahans Stamp Auctions Ltd.* v. *Farrelly*, [1962] I.R. 386.
26 (1816), 1 Mer. 572. See pp. 521-2, *ante*.
27 [1914] A.C. 398. See also Lord Wright, " *Sinclair* v. *Brougham* " (1938), 6 *Cambridge Law Journal*, 305; Holdsworth, " Unjustifiable Enrichment " (1939), 55 *Law Quarterly Review*, 37; Stoljar, " Re-examining Sinclair *v.* Brougham " (1959), 22 *Modern Law Review*, 21.

applied the money in accordance with the (albeit ultra vires) agreement with the depositors. Lord Dunedin arrived at the same result, but emphasised the element of liability on the part of someone (the shareholders) who would be unjustly enriched in the absence of tracing, rather than the right of the person (the depositors) to trace to support a proprietary right. Lord Parker of Waddington, although arriving at the same result, thought that the society did owe a fiduciary duty to the depositors—that there was a trust because the legal title to the money passed but not the equitable title. The equal rating of the shareholders and the depositors was on the footing that the society had not breached its fiduciary duty. Lords Parker and Sumner agreed that, since the banking business was ultra vires, the officers of the society must have been carrying on the business on their own account (though liable to account to the society for profits). The funds of the depositors and society being mixed, the depositors and shareholders were equal claimants against any legal title that might be in the officers.

A fiduciary relationship between the wrongdoer and the claimant is not an essential prerequisite of tracing. It is essential, however, in cases where the property is, or becomes at some stage, money (or a chose in action). If an express or constructive trust of the money cannot be established, i.e. if no equitable proprietary interest can be set up by the claimant, the whole title to the money passes (unless there is a bailment of specific coins). Then the claimant either has no claim at all (for example, where the transaction is ultra vires) or becomes an ordinary creditor.

If a fiduciary relationship is established, tracing does not depend on abuse of it but upon the identifiability of the misappropriated property as constituting part of the mixed fund. Breach of fiduciary duty by the misappropriator will give the claimant first claim on the mixed fund in the fiduciary's hands. Absence of breach will give him a claim to the fund pari passu with other innocent claimants. Two or more victims of breach of fiduciary duty should also rank pari passu, but the authorities show that the rule of " first in, first out " may apply between them when the claim is to trace into a bank account.[28]

Tracing Property in the Hands of a Third Party

If the third party acquires the legal title to the property, for value and bona fide, without notice of the claim to trace, the process of tracing is no longer available. The person whose property has been

[28] As to the practical difficulties of tracing converted property, and the possibility, in exceptional circumstances, of an order for discovery before delivery of the statement of claim, see *Speyside Estate and Trust Co. Ltd.* v. *Wraymond Freeman (Blenders) Ltd.*, [1950] Ch. 96.

misappropriated is reduced, at worst, to being remediless, and at best, to the status of an ordinary creditor of the wrongdoer.[29] In *Scott* v. *Scott*,[30] in Ireland, it was held that the same applied where the bona fide purchaser acquired only an equitable interest in the property without notice of the claim. This was on the ground that the claim to trace was a mere equity. It is submitted, however, that the claim to trace is an equitable interest in property, being equitable ownership, or an equitable charge, under an express or constructive trust,[31] and therefore ranks in priority to any equitable interest created later.

While a volunteer taking a legal title is liable to the claim of the equitable owner to trace, complications may exist as to the extent of the claimant's charge if the volunteer is no party to any breach of fiduciary duty, is without notice of the claim of the equitable owner, and has mixed the latter's property with his own. The position of the innocent volunteer in these circumstances was exhaustively considered by the Court of Appeal in *Re Diplock*.[32]

In that case, a testator had left his residuary estate to " such charitable institutions or other charitable or benevolent object or objects in England " as the executors should select. The House of Lords decided that the words included non-charitable as well as charitable objects, and the gift therefore failed for uncertainty. Before the decision of the House of Lords was given the executors had distributed most of the residuary estate to a number of charities. The next-of-kin claimed the property from the executors, and after these claims had been compromised with the approval of the court, the next-of-kin sought to recover the balance of the residue from the charities who had wrongly received it. The charities had treated the sums received from the Diplock estate in different ways. In the majority of cases, they had been paid into the general account of the charities. Some of these were in credit, others were overdrawn (either secured or unsecured). In a few cases, payment was made into a special account. In one or two cases, it was earmarked for a particular purpose. The next of kin

29 *Pilcher* v. *Rawlins* (1872), L.R. 7 Ch.App. 259. For detailed consideration of these circumstances, see Keeton, *The Law of Trusts*, 9th ed., pp. 394-400.

30 [1924] 1 I.R. 141.

31 See *Cave* v. *Cave* (1880), 15 Ch.D. 639; *Burgis* v. *Constantine*, [1908] 2 K.B. 484 (C.A.).

32 [1948] 1 Ch. 465; [1951] A.C. 251 (H.L.), *sub nom. Ministry of Health* v. *Simpson*. Ireland: *Leahy* v. *De Moleyns*, [1896] 1 I.R. 206 (C.A.). Cf. *Welwood* v. *Grady*, [1904] 1 I.R. 388.
See also Denning, " The Recovery of Money " (1949), 65 *Law Quarterly Review*, 37; Higgins, " Re Diplock—A Reappraisal " (1964), 6 *University of Western Australia Annual Law Review*, 428; Palmer, " Restitution of Distributions by a Fiduciary to which the Recipient was not Entitled " (1968), 19 *Hastings Law Journal*, 993.

prosecuted two types of claim: (1) in rem, by way of tracing the fund, by virtue of the principal underlying *Re Hallett's Estate*.[33] The Court of Appeal held that the remedy of tracing, or the remedy in rem, as it was termed in that case, was available to recover property wrongfully (even if innocently) transferred by trustee to volunteers, whether or not the volunteer himself has changed the form of the property, or has mixed it with property of his own. Amongst such volunteers are overpaid beneficiaries, or (as in the *Diplock* case) persons or institutions who have received the property upon the erroneous assumption that they are beneficiaries under trusts, and legatees under wills. Where the volunteer retains the property in an unmixed form, it is still impressed by a trust, and it must be restored when the beneficiary claims it. If the volunteer has mixed the property of the trust with his own, the beneficiary has a charge upon the mixed fund for the value of the trust property. The principle applicable to such cases differs from that applicable to trustees, against whom a beneficiary traces, because the volunteer, so long as he has taken innocently, may also set up a claim in respect of his own property and where he does, he and the beneficiary will share the proceeds pari passu. The second type of claim was: (2) in personam, against the charities.[34]

Dealing with the consequences of an innocent volunteer paying the claimant's funds into an active bank account, Lord Greene, M.R., giving the judgment of the Court of Appeal in *Re Diplock* said[35]—

> It might be suggested that the corollary of treating two claimants on a mixed fund as interested rateably should be that withdrawals out of the fund ought to be attributed rateably to the interests of both claimants. But in the case of an active banking account this would lead to the greatest difficulty and complication in practice and might in many cases raise questions incapable of solution. What then is to be done ? In our opinion, the same rule as that applied in *Clayton's* case[36] should be applied. This is really a rule of convenience based upon so-called presumed intention. It has been applied in the case of two beneficiaries whose trust money has been paid into a mixed banking account from which drawings were subsequently made, and, so far as we know, its application has not been adversely criticized (see per Fry J. in *Hallett's* case[37] and per North J. in *In re Stenning*.[38]) In such a case both claimants are innocent, neither is in a fiduciary

33 (1880), 13 Ch.D. 696. See pp. 522-3, *ante*.
34 See Keeton, *The Law of Trusts*, 9th ed., pp. 401-3.
35 [1948] Ch. 553-4.
36 (1816), 1 Mer. 572.
37 (1880), 13 Ch.D. 696.
38 [1895] 2 Ch. 433.

> relation to the other, and if the mixed fund had not been drawn upon they would be entitled to rateable charges upon it. Exactly the same occurs where the claimants are not two beneficiaries but one beneficiary and one volunteer, and we think, accordingly, that the same principle should be adopted.

The court, however, saw no reason for extending the rule of " first in, first out " beyond the case of a banking account.

Chapter XXI

OTHER EQUITABLE REMEDIES

Rectification of Instruments for Mistake

General

The court possesses a power to rectify documents (i.e. to order a change in their wording) to coincide with what was agreed between the parties. It does not modify agreements: the court merely reforms the written expression of them to conform with the intent of the makers. This jurisdiction was originally exercised mainly in respect of marriage settlements which did not correspond with marriage articles, an early reported example being *Thin* v. *Thin*.[1] It has been extended to leases and other conveyances, and even to voluntary deeds. By the time of Lord Hardwicke, the jurisdiction rested on well-settled principles.[2] These principles were discussed in *Maunsell* v. *Maunsell*,[3] where three classes of case were enunciated by Sullivan, M.R.: (1) where settlements are sought to be reformed on the ground of mutual mistake; (2) where a party acting in the transaction and claiming a benefit under it occupied a confidential relationship to the settlor and, having undertaken to have a proper settlement drawn, had an improper one drawn in his favour; and (3) where the grantor under a voluntary deed did not know the precise effect of the deed, and the precise limitations were not authorised by him.

Usually, the instrument of which rectification is asked is bilateral, executed for value. It seems not to have been doubted, since the

1 (1650, 1 Ch. Rep. 162.

2 *Henkle* v. *Royal Exchange Assurance Co.* (1749), 1 Ves. Sen. 317 (rectification of insurance policy so as to cover loss already incurred: refused because of lack of evidence that that was what the parties intended); *Baker* v. *Paine* (1750), 1 Ves. Sen. 456 (contract for sale of goods rectified to conform with minutes made by the parties at the time of agreeing); *Bell* v. *Cundall* (1750), Amb. 101 (no rectification of names in a recovery, "especially after such a length of time . . . and the defendant was a purchaser for a valuable consideration without notice"—p. 102). As to when there is notice of an equity to rectify, see *Smith* v. *Jones*, [1954] 1 W.L.R. 1089. Ireland: in *Coates* v. *Kenna* (1872), I.R. 7 Eq. 113 (C.A.Ch.), rectification was refused as against a bona fide purchaser for value without notice. See also *Alexander* v. *Crosbie* (1835), Ll. & G. t. Sug. 145; *Mortimer* v. *Shortall* (1842), 2 Dr. & War. 363.

Cf. the jurisdiction to admit parol evidence to resolve latent ambiguities in a document: *Countess of Shelburne* v. *Earl of Inchiquin* (1784), 1 Bro. C.C. 338, 341, *per* Lord Thurlow; *Marquis Townshend* v. *Stangroom* (1801), 6 Ves. 328, 332-4, *per* Lord Eldon. See p. 531, *post*.

3 (1877), 1 L.R. Ir. 529, 539-40.

decision of the Court of Appeal in Chancery in *Walker* v. *Armstrong*,[4] that a voluntary covenant will be rectified (though the jurisdiction is approached with caution), if it would otherwise fail to carry out the proved intention of the donor.[5] The court will so rectify at the instance of the donor or in favour of one volunteer against another, but not for a volunteer as against the donor.[6]

Where rectification of a bilateral instrument is granted, the parties have reached an agreement, but the document which they have executed does not express that agreement properly. In cases where the error is apparent on the face of the document, the court will read the document in the sense in which the parties clearly intended it to be read.[7] This is construction rather than rectification, and was apparently the course of action at common law too.[8] In *Annesley* v. *Annesley*,[9] a wife brought an action against her husband for payment of an annuity created by a settlement of which he was trustee. It plainly appeared on the face of the settlement that the annuity was intended to be payable during the joint lives of the husband and wife, and to be secured by an immediate term, but that, by mistake, it was secured by a term not to arise until after the husband's death. The pleadings neither stated the mistake nor claimed rectification. Chatterton, V.-C., held that the court could declare the annuity well charged on the lands without rectifying the settlement. This type of case was treated by Danckwerts, J., in *Butler* v. *Mountview Estates Ltd.*,[10] as being an example of the equitable remedy of rectification.

Rectification can be granted notwithstanding the fact that the agreement affects rights other than those of the parties. Indeed, that will

4 (1856), 8 De G. M. & G. 531. See also the observations of Kekewich, J., *Bonhote* v. *Henderson*, [1895] 1 Ch. 742, 748-9 (C.A., [1895] 2 Ch. 202), and of Evershed, J., *Van der Linde* v. *Van der Linde*, [1947] Ch. 306, 311-2.

5 It so failed in *Walker* v. *Armstrong* in circumstances described by Knight Bruce, L.J. (8 De G. M. & G. 538) as follows: " This litigation owes its origin to the manner in which a series of professional gentlemen in the north of England permitted themselves to transact, or in more accurate phrase to entangle and perplex, some legal business intrusted to their case. These licensed pilots undertook to steer a post-captain through certain not very narrow straits of the law, and with abundance of sea room ran him aground on every shoal they could make. First in 1824, then in 1825, and again some years afterwards, was the gallant officer encumbered with help of a description for which he could perhaps supply a better term than I can."

6 In *M'Mechan* v. *Warburton*, [1896] 1 I.R. 435, a voluntary deed was rectified after the death of the donor and the principles were discussed by Chatterton, V.-C., pp. 439-40.

7 See *Countess of Shelburne* v. *Earl of Inchiquin* (1784), 1 Bro. C.C. 338; *Marquis Townshend* v. *Stangroom* (1801), 6 Ves. 328.

8 See the remarks of Lord St. Leonards, *Wilson* v. *Wilson* (1854), 5 H.L.C. 40, 66-7, referring to an anonymous case cited by Buller, J., *Bache* v. *Proctor* (1780), Dougl. 382, 384.

9 (1893), 31 L.R.Ir. 457. See also *Borrowes* v. *Delaney* (1889), 24 L.R.Ir. 503 (Div. Ct., Ex. Div.).

10 [1951] 2 K.B. 563, 571.

generally be the case with marriage settlements. One of the commonest early uses of rectification was for a marriage settlement showing a discrepancy from the marriage articles. Such settlements will not be rectified, however, even where the discrepancy exists, unless the settlement was expressly made in pursuance of the articles, or is shown by external evidence to have been intended to be made in pursuance of them. In *King* v. *King-Harman*,[11] Sullivan, M.R., rectified a marriage settlement to correspond with the marriage articles, despite the fact that there was no direct evidence to connect the settlement with the prior agreement, there being positive evidence that no other agreement had been made between the parties.

The normal case of rectification is one in which the departure of the document from the agreement between the parties is established by written or oral evidence of what in fact they agreed. In exceptional cases, sufficient evidence of the true intention of the parties may be obtained simply by perusal of the document of which rectification is sought. In *Banks* v. *Ripley*,[12] a marriage settlement provided, but without words of limitation, for interests in freehold land to vest in the children of the marriage. There was a gift over in the event of no child taking a vested interest in the land. The only child of the marriage would have had a life interest in the absence of words of limitation, but Morton, J., having no evidence apart from the document itself, rectified the settlement so as to give her the fee simple. An intention to give it to her was found largely in the terms of the gift over, which was not on her death but on her failing to take any interest in the property.

The Kind of Mistake Required

The whole basis of the equitable jurisdiction to rectify bilateral instruments is that there was a true agreement, but the document does not properly represent it. The usual case for rectification is that where the mistake was common to both parties. Sometimes, judges state the existence of a common mistake as a prerequisite to rectification. In *Rooke* v. *Lord Kensington*,[13] Page Wood, V.-C., said—

> . . . in order to enable this Court to rectify a settlement, it must be proved that it contains something which has been inserted by mistake, contrary to the intention of all the parties. Where a party

[11] (1873), I.R. 7 Eq. 446.

[12] [1940] Ch. 719. See also *Uvedale* v. *Halfpenny* (1723), 2 P. Wms. 151. Ireland: *Ex parte Rice* (1896), 30 I.L.T.R. 57; *Fitzgerald* v. *Fitzgerald*, [1902] 1 I.R. 477 (C.A.); *Re Davis's Estate*, [1912] 1 I.R. 516. Cf. *Re Goold Adams's Estate*, [1965] I.R. 57.

[13] (1856), 2 K. & J. 753, 764. See also *Earl of Bradford* v. *Earl of Romney* (1862), 30 Beav. 431, 438, *per* Romilly, M.R.

has obtained an interest under a deed, especially and above all other considerations, if such party has entered into an irrecoverable condition, such as marriage, upon the faith of that deed, it is not enough to say that the other party who entered into the contract did not intend to part with what the deed purports to convey; but it must be made out that there was a mistake common to all the parties before he can be liberated from his part of the contract. The other parties have a right to say, we understood the contract to be exactly as it appears by the deed, and we have acted upon the faith of it; and if you come to set it aside it can only be done by shewing that we were parties to the mistake, and are now improperly insisting on having the benefit of it.

It is not enough for a party to show that the agreement turned out differently from what he anticipated.[14] According to Bigelow,[15] the cases show that if the parties select one type of transaction (e.g. a letter of attorney, which is revoked by the principal's death), rather than another (e.g. a mortgage, which is not revoked by the death of the mortgagor), to carry out a purpose which could be effectuated in either way, and one party suffers because of the choice made, the court will not rectify so as to turn the dealing into the other type of transaction. Moreover, in rectifying a settlement or agreement, the court is guided by the intention of the parties at the time when it was executed, and not previously expressed intentions, since the parties might have changed their minds before the settlement or agreement was actually executed.[16] However, the court will rectify on parol evidence alone, even after a long time, if a common mistake can be duly proved.[17]

Page Wood, V.-C., in saying[18] that there must be a mistake common to all the parties, went too far. It is correct that such a common mistake is a ground for rectification; it is also correct that there is no ground for rectification if only one party was mistaken as to the terms of the document while the other (being unaware of the mistake) thought it correctly represented the terms of the agreement between them. Between these two extremes come a variety of intermediate cases. One type is exemplified by *Garrard* v. *Frankel*,[19] where a lease, by the

14 *Tucker* v. *Bennett* (1887), 38 Ch.D. 1 (C.A.). Ireland: *Jackson* v. *Stopford*, [1923] 2 I.R. 1 (High Court of Appeal).

15 " Mistake of Law Again " (1886), 2 *Law Quarterly Review*, 78. See also his main article, " Mistake of Law as a Ground of Equitable Relief " (1885), 1 *L.Q.R.*, 298.

16 *Tucker* v. *Bennett* (1887), 38 Ch.D. 1.

17 Ireland: see the remarks of Ball, C., *M'Cormack* v. *M'Cormack* (1877), 1 L.R.Ir. 119, 124.

18 *Rooke* v. *Lord Kensington* (1856), 2 K. & J. 753: see p. 532, *ante*.

19 (1862), 30 Beav. 445. See also *Harris* v. *Pepperell* (1867), L.R. 5 Eq. 1; *Paget* v. *Marshall* (1884), 28 Ch.D. 255.

mistake of the lessor, was granted at a rent of £130 a year, whereas the original agreement was for £230 a year. The case was decided on the footing that the lessee perceived the error in the lease and determined to take advantage of it. Romilly, M.R., said[20] that the mistake—

> was certainly not a mistake committed by [the lessee], and thereupon it is argued that there must be an end of the case, for that, to enable this Court to interfere to rectify a mistake, the mistake must be mutual. But though, as a general rule, this is correct, it does not apply to every case. The Court will, I apprehend, interfere in cases of mistake, where one party to the transaction, being at the time cognizant of the fact of the error, seeks to take advantage of it.

Having come to the belief[21] that the lessee would equally have executed the lease had it stated the rent as £230, the Master of the Rolls said: " . . . but I do not think that I am entitled to found any decree on such a belief." On the other hand, he was quite clear that he could not compel the lessor to be bound by the terms of the lease as it stood, or permit the lessee to derive any advantage from the mistake, and that, in that respect, the lessor was entitled to relief. His way out of the dilemma was to give the lessee the option of rejecting the lease (subject to payment of rent at £230 a year for her period of occupation) or retaining it at £230.[22]

It may be correct to view this type of case as rescission, upon terms, for misrepresentation,[23] rather than as rectification. That was the attitude of Flanagan, J., in *Gun* v. *M'Carthy*,[24] where, in the circumstances, he ordered rescission without the option of retaining the lease in a reformed condition. A similar view was taken by Farwell, J., in *May* v. *Platt*,[25] where, there being no fraud, the learned judge offered neither rectification nor rescission. On the other hand, in *Monaghan C.C.* v. *Vaughan*,[26] Dixon, J., granted rectification without the option of rescission (which would, in any case, have come to the same thing). In that case, there had been an agreement that the defendant would pay the plaintiffs £1,200 for the right to clear one of their sites (the profit coming from sale of material so cleared). The subsequent written contract was ambiguous and the defendant claimed it meant the plaintiffs were to pay him £1,200 for doing the work. The learned judge said[27]—

20 30 Beav. 450-1.
21 30 Beav. 457.
22 30 Beav. 457-8.
23 See p. 546, *post*.
24 (1884), 13 L.R.Ir. 304.
25 [1900] 1 Ch. 616. See also *Solle* v. *Butcher*, [1950] 1 K.B. 671 (C.A.).
26 [1948] I.R. 306.
27 [1948] I.R. 312.

> I regard this as a case of mutual mistake. I think that it is immaterial that one party knows the document to be inaccurate for the purposes of the application of the principles of law applicable to mutual mistake. What is material is that both parties were agreed upon certain matters and that the completed contract did not correctly represent the substance of their agreement. A unilateral mistake arises where one of two or more parties is not ad idem with the other party or parties, and there is therefore, no real agreement between them. In such a case, recission may be appropriate, but the present is a different case. It is not a case of unilateral mistake in that sense, but to speak of it as a case of mutual mistake may obscure its true character of a common or mutual intention misrepresented by the record of that intention.

Dixon, J., in *Nolan* v. *Nolan*,[28] followed his previous decision in *Monaghan C.C.* v. *Vaughan*, reducing the argument about epithets for mistakes to its true level. He said[29] that—

> It had been submitted . . . that it was not a case of mutual mistake, susceptible of rectification, and that seemed to be so in a limited sense, in as much as no case of rectification could really be regarded as a case of mutual mistake; if it were there would be no contest, for the parties could rectify the instrument themselves.[30] The whole question whether a mistake was mutual or unilateral was largely one of phraseology.

The latest reported authority on this aspect of rectification is *A. Roberts & Co. Ltd.* v. *Leicestershire C.C.*[31] The plaintiffs tendered to build a school for the defendants, the tender being based on completion of the work in eighteen months. The defendants drew up a contract specifying completion in thirty months, but did not draw the plaintiffs' attention to the variation. The plaintiffs executed the contract believing it to specify eighteen months, and later, the defendants executed it, knowing of the plaintiffs' misapprehension. The first ground upon which the plaintiffs based their claim for rectification of the contract was common mistake. Pennycuick, J., said[32]—

> . . . the council and the company were not at one upon the length of the period for completion intended by them respectively to be inserted in the contract, and, accordingly, the company is not entitled to rectification upon the first ground relied upon by it.

[28] (1957), 92 I.L.T.R. 94.
[29] 92 I.L.T.R. 99.
[30] It is true that they could, but there might still be a contest because one of the mistaken parties might find the mistake to his advantage.
[31] [1961] Ch. 555.
[32] [1961] Ch. 570.

However, the learned judge granted rectification on the second ground put forward by the plaintiffs, which he described as follows—

> The second ground rests upon the principle that a party is entitled to rectification of a contract upon proof that he believed a particular term to be included in the contract, and that the other party concluded the contract with the omission or a variation of that term in the knowledge that the first party believed the term to be included. . . .
>
> The exact basis of the principle appears to be in some doubt. If the principle is correctly rested upon estoppel[33] it seems to me that it is not an essential ingredient of the right of action to establish any particular degree of obliquity to be attributed to the defendants in such circumstances. If, on the other hand, the principle is rested on fraud, obviously dishonesty must be established.

What can be Rectified

In the case of a bilateral transaction, rectification at its simplest is seen in the situation where there is, first, an oral agreement between the parties, secondly, a written contract or contract under seal, correctly setting out the terms of the oral agreement, and, finally, a conveyance or some other instrument purporting (but failing) to carry out the written contract. The latter document can be rectified to comply with the written contract.

Problems begin to arise when the elements of the situation are varied slightly. Suppose, first, that the written contract does not correctly set out the terms of the oral agreement, but the final instrument of which rectification is sought, does comply with the terms of the written contract. If it be the case that the prior oral agreement is an enforceable contract, there would seem to be no theoretical or practical objection to rectifying the final instrument (thus, by implication, also rectifying the written contract). The objection on principle to oral evidence contradicting a written contract gives way to the equitable jurisdiction to relieve from the consequences of fraud or mistake. This view is well accepted, being supported, for example, by a string of marriage settlement cases reported within a few years of each other. One such case is *Smith* v. *Ilffe*.[34] There, the settlement was in accordance with the marriage articles. In the events which happened, the husband was dead, there were no children, and the property was out of the

[33] See Snell's *Principles of Equity*, 26th ed. (1966), p. 684.
[34] (1875), L.R. 20 Eq. 666. See also *Cook* v. *Fearn* (1878), 27 W.R. 212; *Edwards* v. *Bingham* (1879), 28 W.R. 89; *Hanley* v. *Pearson* (1879), 13 Ch.D. 545; *Cordeaux* v. *Fullerton* (1879), 28 W.R. 320; *Lovesy* v. *Smith* (1880), 15 Ch.D. 655. These were all decisions of first instance.

control of the settlor wife. Her affidavit, which was uncontradicted, was to the effect that that was not her intention. Bacon, V.-C., ordered rectification of the settlement to accord with that intention.

Uncontradicted evidence on one side is not, however, the commonest state of affairs in litigation. In practice, if the final instrument conforms to the written contract, it may be difficult to prove that both documents are at variance with a prior unwritten agreement. Not only may such evidence, if disputed, be disbelieved, but, even if accepted, may lead to one of two alternative conclusions, namely (a) that the parties may have changed their minds between the oral agreement and the written contract, or (b) that in their oral negotiations the parties never became ad idem. In *Fowler* v. *Fowler*,[35] Lord Chelmsford pointed out that, to be rectified, a deed must fail to embody the final intention of the parties. He said[36]—

> . . . a person who seeks to rectify a deed upon the ground of mistake must be required to establish, in the clearest and most satisfactory manner, that the alleged intention to which he desires it to be made conformable continued concurrently in the minds of all parties down to the time of its execution, and also must be able to shew exactly and precisely the form to which the deed ought to be brought.

If the parties did not agree about what was meant, the Lord Chancellor held, there could be no rectification. This last point is substantially what lies behind the troublesome dictum of James, V.-C., in *Mackenzie* v. *Coulson*[37]—

> Courts of Equity do not rectify contracts; they may and do rectify instruments purporting to have been made in pursuance of the terms of contracts. But it is always necessary for a Plaintiff to shew that there was an actual concluded contract antecedent to the instrument which is sought to be rectified; and that such contract is inaccurately represented in the instrument.

The proposition that the court does not rectify contracts is too wide: it does rectify written contracts to comply with prior oral agreements. On the other hand it is true that the court does not otherwise rectify contracts. That is all that was necessary for the decision in *Mackenzie* v. *Coulson*, where the contract in dispute was an insurance policy. The claimant, who sought to have it rectified, alleged that there had

35 (1859), 4 De G. & J. 250. See also *Bentley* v. *Mackay* (1862), 4 De G.F. & J. 279.
36 De G. & J. 265. See also p. 273.
37 (1869), L.R. 8 Eq. 368, 375. See also *W. Higgins Ltd.* v. *Northampton Corp.*, [1927] 1 Ch. 128; *Frederick E. Rose* (*London*) *Ltd.* v. *William H. Pim Jnr. & Co. Ltd.*, [1953] 2 Q.B. 450 (C.A.).

been a prior agreement for a term not included in the policy. That allegation was denied by the insurer. The Vice-Chancellor, in refusing rectification, did not hold that there was any prior agreement. The failure to establish a prior agreement would dispose of the case. He did hold, however, that if there was a prior agreement, it was not a contract. That, in the light of later cases, would not be fatal to a claim for rectification.

Another variation is introduced if the contract is for the sale of land. The initial oral agreement is binding but unenforceable (until part performed or evidenced in writing). Suppose that the subsequent memorandum in writing or written contract is at variance with the oral contract, and the conveyance follows the earlier document. For a time, the battle over the possibility of rectification swayed back and forth. In *Woollam* v. *Hearn*,[38] Grant, M.R., would not admit evidence to contradict the memorandum in writing. The bill was for rectification of a lease which, in conformity with the memorandum, stated the rent to be £73-10s. a year. The Master of the Rolls dismissed the bill, rejecting the plaintiff's parol evidence that the parties intended a rent of £60. In *Olley* v. *Fisher*,[39] on the other hand, North, J., accepted the view that the written agreement could be rectified and made the subject of an order for specific performance at the same time. He thought this a consequence of Section 24(7) of the Judicature Act, 1873,[40] which provides for the court to grant all remedies any of the parties may appear to be entitled to in respect of any legal or equitable claim properly brought forward by them in any cause or matter, so that, as far as possible, all matters in controversy between the parties may be completely and finally determined, and multiplicity of legal proceedings avoided. All North, J., decided was that evidence of the true agreement could be given, the suit ending thereupon in a compromise. The Statute of Frauds was not pleaded (in any case, it could not have been pleaded because there was part performance). Some years later, in *May* v. *Platt*,[41] Farwell, J., decided, citing *Woollam* v. *Hearn*[42] and *Davies* v. *Fitton*,[43] that a deed conforming with a written agreement would not be rectified so as to accord with some prior intention. Shortly after that, Cozens-Hardy, J., in *Johnson* v. *Bragge*,[44] held that rectification was possible, despite the Statute of Frauds, because an action for rectification was not an action to charge a person upon the

38 (1802), 7 Ves. 211. Ireland: *Davies* v. *Fitton* (1842), 2 Dr. & War. 225.
39 (1886), 34 Ch.D. 367.
40 Now Sect. 44 of the Supreme Court of Judicature (Consolidation) Act, 1925. Ireland: Supreme Court of Judicature (Ireland) Act, 1877, Sect. 27(7).
41 [1900] 1 Ch. 616, 621-2.
42 (1802), 7 Ves. 211. See above.
43 (1842), 2 Dr. & War. 225.
44 [1901] 1 Ch. 28.

contract. The last fling for the contrary view came in the decision of Neville, J., in *Thompson* v. *Hickman*.[45] This case was similar to *May* v. *Platt*,[46] except that the conveyance was in conformity with the terms of an option, not of a contract for sale: this was held to make no difference. The Court of Appeal settled the dispute in *Craddock Bros.* v. *Hunt*.[47] After an oral agreement for the sale of land, a mistake was made in the subsequent written contract. The conveyance having been made in accordance with the written contract, rectification was granted (Younger, L. J., dissenting on the facts and the law) to make it conform to the oral contract. The majority preferred *Olley* v. *Fisher*[48] to *May* v. *Platt*.[49] Lord Sterndale, M.R., with whom Warrington, L.J., agreed,[50] said[51]—

> . . . rectification can be granted of a written agreement on parol evidence of mutual mistake, although that agreement is complete in itself, and has been carried out by a more formal document based upon it. I think the contrary view is based upon an insufficient consideration of the result of rectification. After rectification the written agreement does not continue to exist with a parol variation; it is to be read as if it had been originally drawn in its rectified form . . .

Johnson v. *Bragge*[52] was approved. The rectified written contract satisfied the Statute of Frauds.[53] Both that contract and the conveyance had been rectified to conform to a valid prior contract.

A final situation to be considered is that where there is (1) an oral agreement not amounting to a contract (even an unenforceable one), for example because one of the parties, by law, can contract only by deed, followed by (2) a contract by deed (for example) which misstates the terms of the oral agreement, possibly followed finally by (3) a conveyance which conforms to the deed. The dictum in *Mackenzie* v. *Coulson*[54] to the effect that courts of equity do not rectify contracts would appear to stand against rectification in such cases. And that was the view of Romer, J., in *W. Higgins Ltd.* v. *Northampton Corp.*[55] There was a contract under seal by which the plaintiffs undertook to do some

[45] [1907] 1 Ch. 550.
[46] [1900] 1 Ch. 616. See pp. 534, 538, *ante*.
[47] [1923] 2 Ch. 136, approved by the Privy Council in *United States of America* v. *Motor Trucks Ltd.*, [1924] A.C. 196, on appeal from Ontario. Ireland: *Nolan* v. *Graves*, [1946] I.R. 376, a case of an elaborate fraud that came unstuck. Haugh, J., held that the fact that the contract was executory, while in *Craddock Bros.* v. *Hunt* it was executed, made no difference.
[48] (1886), 34 Ch.D. 367.
[49] [1900] 1 Ch. 616.
[50] [1923] 2 Ch. 159-60.
[51] [1923] 2 Ch. 151.
[52] [1901] 1 Ch. 28.
[53] [1923] 2 Ch. 152.
[54] (1869), L.R. 8 Eq. 368, 375. See pp. 537-9, *ante*.
[55] [1927] 1 Ch. 128.

building for the defendant local authority. Under the terms of the deed, the plaintiffs would get less than they intended: they had been mistaken as to those terms. However, the learned judge found that the deed expressed what the corporation intended: there had been neither mutual mistake nor an error by the plaintiffs induced by the defendants. That put an end to the claim for rectification, but Romer, J., went on to hold that, even if there had been a common mistake, there could be no rectification because there was no contract, before the sealed one, to accord with which anything could be rectified.[56] The case differed in that respect from those under the Statute of Frauds in that oral agreements within the Statute are valid contracts, though unenforceable.[57]

The technical and inequitable nature of this distinction might be acceptable in that particular case, as there was not even a prior oral agreement, but if a prior agreement is proved the court should be able to see that what is carried out is what was agreed and not what was written down by mistake. *Hall-Dare* v. *Hall-Dare*,[58] which was a case of rectifying a deed of disentailment and resettlement, is often regarded as support for that position because of the remark[59] made by Lindley, L.J., that "The deed when altered will really be the deed of the parties . . ." Ross, J., seemed willing to go a good way along these lines in *Collen Bros.* v. *Dublin C.C.*,[60] where builders sought rectification of a contract with a local authority and failed because the action was barred by lapse of time under a local government statute. The learned judge said[61]—

> The meaning of rectification of a written instrument is to carry out the real intention of the parties which has been erroneously expressed. That is what the plaintiffs ask me to do. There are all kinds of technical difficulties. How can you rectify the deed without rectifying the tender ? How can you alter an accepted tender ? These technicalities ought not to be allowed to stand in the way of a Court of Equity, whose primary duty is to struggle to enforce fair dealing between man and man, if it can be done without violating some matter of principle.
>
> But at last I am brought face to face with a difficulty[62] which I regret to say I do not at present see how the plaintiffs can get over.

56 [1927] 1 Ch. 136.
57 [1927] 1 Ch. 137-8.
58 (1885), 31 Ch.D. 251 (C.A.). See also *Meeking* v. *Meeking*, [1917] 1 Ch. 77, where Astbury, J., extended the application of that decision, disagreeing with the view of Wylie, J., in *Re Ottley's Estate*, [1910] 1 I.R. 1.
59 31 Ch.D. 259.
60 [1908] 1 I.R. 503.
61 [1908] 1 I.R. 509-10.
62 I.e., lapse of time.

Younger, J., took a less optimistic view of the possibility of rectification in *Faraday* v. *Tamworth Union*,[63] where the plaintiff surveyor was in dispute with the defendant local authority over the amount due by way of remuneration under a contract for personal services. He said[64]—

> The plaintiff asks for rectification. Now it appears to me, even if there had been mutual mistake on the part of himself and the defendants, that the difficulties in the way of rectification are, in a case like the present, very great, if not insuperable. Admittedly such an agreement as this is only binding on a union like the defendants if it be under their seal. But the defendants have attached their seal to no agreement in a form other than that which they executed; and to rectify that agreement as executed and then make it binding upon them in terms other than those which they have sealed, would appear to me, as at present advised, to have the effect of binding them to an agreement which requires a seal for its validity, but which they have never sealed. It is, however, unnecessary to determine that point in this case, since I am satisfied that there was here no mutual mistake at all.

The parties had never been ad idem. The deed was set aside for a mistake innocently induced by the defendants as to the amount, and the plaintiff recovered on a quantum meruit. Clauson, J., in *Shipley U.D.C.* v. *Bradford Corp.*,[65] inclined the other way. He held that a contract between the two councils bore the construction the plaintiffs contended for and that, if it did not, it would be rectified so as to do so. His decision was affirmed on the point of construction by the Court of Appeal, who did not consider the question of rectification.[66] Clauson, J., pointed out that (1) historically, courts of equity have rectified instruments so as to accord with the expressed agreement of the parties; (2) James, V.-C., in *Mackenzie* v. *Coulson*,[67] intended to say no more than that, prior to the written contract, the parties had not been ad idem; and (3) *Hall-Dare* v. *Hall-Dare*[68] and *Meeking* v. *Meeking*[69] show that rectification has the effect of making the altered deed the deed of the parties from the date of execution.

The latest cases indicate that this view is becoming accepted. In Ireland, Dixon, J., held[70] that he could rectify a sealed contract to make it accord with a prior non-contractual agreement. In England,

63 (1916), 86 L.J.Ch. 436.
64 86 L.J.Ch. 438.
65 [1936] Ch. 375.
66 [1936] Ch. 399n.
67 (1869), L.R. 8 Eq. 368, 375. See p. 537, *ante*.
68 (1885), 31 Ch.D. 251. See p. 540, *ante*.
69 [1917] 1 Ch. 77. See p. 540, *ante*.
70 *Monaghan C.C.* v. *Vaughan*, [1948] I.R. 306, 315-7.

Ungoed-Thomas, J., was of the same opinion in *Carlton Contractors Ltd.* v. *Bexley Corp.*[71] In that case there was an agreement between the plaintiff builders and the defendant corporation that the plaintiffs would build some houses for the defendants. Due to a mistake, the contract under seal omitted some of the terms of the prior non-contractual agreement. The learned judge held that, although the defendants could contract only under seal, the contract could be rectified so as to accord with the prior unsealed agreement. He said[72]—

> What we are concerned with here is not the power to execute an agreement, but the power to express a consensus or an intention. To my mind, the corporation is not limited to expressing its intention or its consensus in the form of a document under seal. For a contract to be effective, there must be a contract under seal, but it is not the contract with which we are concerned here. It is the expression of consensus or intention and that, to my mind, is perhaps the fundamental fallacy in the submission which has been made.

Recission and Cancellation

General

The equitable remedy of recission is that of setting aside a transaction, i.e. declaring it to be avoided. Cancellation is a related process. The court may order a document to be delivered up and cancelled when it is the written expression of a transaction which has been rescinded, or which, in certain other circumstances, is or has become void.[73]

Common grounds for rescission are: (i) fraud; (ii) innocent misrepresentation; (iii) mistake; (iv) substantial misdescription; and (v) non-disclosure in respect of contracts uberrimae fidei. This is not an exhaustive list. Where a party has a defence to an action for specific performance of a contract, he is often also entitled to claim rescission of it, so that, for example, a defect in title[74] or special hardship may, in a proper case, give rise to rescission. Frequently, also, contracts of sale deal expressly with the right to rescind. Condition 10(1) of the Law Society's Conditions of Sale, 1953, provides—

> If a purchaser takes or makes any objection or requisition as to title, conveyance or otherwise which the vendor is unable or, on the ground of unreasonable expense, unwilling to remove or comply with, and does not withdraw the same within ten days after being required in writing to do so, the vendor may . . . rescind the contract by notice in writing delivered to the purchaser or his solicitors.

[71] (1962), 60 L.G.R. 331.
[72] 60 L.G.R. 338.
[73] See pp. 552-5, *post*.
[74] *Manning* v. *Turner*, [1957] 1 W.L.R. 91. Cf. *Harold Elliott and H. Elliott (Builders) Ltd.* v. *Pierson*, [1948] Ch. 452.

While this condition appears to be in absolute terms, it will not protect a vendor who has been fraudulent, dishonest or reckless. In *Baines* v. *Tweddle*[75] the Court of Appeal did not allow a vendor to rescind under this Condition, on the ground of recklessness, where he had contracted to sell free from two mortgages without having inquired of the mortgagees whether they would concur in the sale (in the event, the first mortgagee refused to concur in it).[76]

In all cases where recission is asked for, an apparent agreement has been concluded, and one of the parties wishes to set it aside. If he stands by and takes no action, the agreement will take effect. On the other hand, a void transaction is in a different position. No title will pass under it. Suppose, for example, a contract for the sale of goods which is void as contrary to public policy (e.g., for infringing exchange control regulations). The purchaser acquires no title to the goods, and hence can pass no title to anyone else. If, on the other hand, the contract is voidable (e.g., for fraudulent misrepresentation by the purchaser), the vendor can ask for rescission, but if he does not, title to the goods has passed; and if the purchaser sells them to a bona fide third party, it is too late for the original vendor to rescind. Rescission always depends upon the possibility of restitution.[77]

Fraud

Equity exercises a wide jurisdiction in respect of fraud.[78] In so far as fraudulent misrepresentation is concerned,[79] this is concurrent with the common law jurisdiction, but beyond that the equitable jurisdiction over cases of fraud is exclusive. It is a ground for rescission of a transaction, or may be set up as a defence to an action for specific performance of a contract[80] or to one for damages for breach.[81]

As a judicial process, rescission for fraud is an exclusively equitable remedy. For fraudulent misrepresentation, the common law allows a party to rescind a contract, but there is no common law action for rescission. At common law, fraudulent misrepresentation is the basis of an action for damages in tort or a ground for resisting an action by

75 [1959] Ch. 679, following the Court of Appeal decision in *Re Jackson and Haden's Contract*, [1906] 1 Ch. 412, that vendors could not rescind under a similar clause where, knowing they had no title to them, they contracted without a reservation of minerals.

76 Ireland: for a case of rescission by a purchaser, see *Coleman* v. *Fry* (1873), I.R. 7 C.L. 247.

77 *Hunt* v. *Silk* (1804), 5 East 449; *Sheffield Nickel and Silver Plating Co. Ltd.* v. *Unwin* (1877), 2 Q.B.D. 214; *Erlanger* v. *New Sombrero Phosphate Co.* (1878), 3 App. Cas. 1218, 1278, *per* Lord Blackburn; *Thorpe* v. *Fasey*, [1949] Ch. 649.

78 See ch. ix.

79 See pp. 329-32, *ante*.

80 See pp. 499-501, *ante*.

81 See p. 329, *ante*.

the other party for breach of contract. Lord Blackburn explained the difference in *Erlanger* v. *New Sombrero Phosphate Co.*[82] in these words—

> It is, I think, clear on principles of general justice, that as a condition of a rescission there must be a *restitutio in integrum*. The parties must be put *in statu quo* . . . It is a doctrine which has often been acted upon both at law and in equity. But there is a considerable difference in the mode in which it is applied in Courts of Law and Equity, owing, as I think, to the difference of the machinery which the Courts have at command. I speak of these Courts as they were at the time when this suit commenced, without inquiring whether the Judicature Acts make any, or if any, what difference.
>
> It would be obviously unjust that a person who has been in possession of property under the contract which he seeks to repudiate should be allowed to throw that back on the other party's hands without accounting for any benefit he may have derived from the use of the property, or if the property, though not destroyed, has been in the interval deteriorated, without making any compensation for that deterioration. But as a Court of Law has no machinery at its command for taking an account of such matters, the defrauded party, if he sought his remedy at law, must in such cases keep the property, and sue in an action for deceit, in which the jury, if properly directed, can do complete justice by giving as damages a full indemnity for all that the party has lost . . .
>
> But a Court of Equity could not give damages, and unless it can rescind the contract, can give no relief. And, on the other hand, it can take accounts of profits, and make allowance for deterioration. And I think the practice has always been for a Court of Equity to give this relief whenever, by the exercise of its powers, it can do what is practically just, though it cannot restore the parties precisely to the state they were in before the contract.

Innocent Misrepresentation

Relief for a misrepresentation which, though false, was not made fraudulently, is confined within narrow limits at common law. The misrepresentation must be a term of a contract before relief is given. If it is a condition of the contract, the party injured can rescind (out of court) or, waiving the right to rescind, sue for damages. If the representation is a mere warranty, an action for damages is the only remedy.[83]

[82] (1878), 3 App. Cas. 1278-9. See also McCleary, " Damage as Requisite to Rescission for Misrepresentation " (1937), 36 *Michigan Law Review*, 1 and 227.

[83] For a recent discussion of the principles by the Court of Appeal, see *Oscar Chess Ltd.* v. *Williams*, [1957] 1 W.L.R. 370.

Where the innocent misrepresentation is not a term of a contract, there is no remedy at common law, To fill this gap, at least partially, equity developed a wider juridsiction, giving the remedy of rescission or, in some cases, a defence to an action for specific performance. In order to have such redress for innocent misrepresentation, the person misled must show (1) that the language relied upon imports or contains a representation of some material fact, (2) that it is untrue, and (3) that he was induced to enter into the contract (or other transaction) in reliance upon it.[84]

As Jessel, M.R., pointed out in *Redgrave* v. *Hurd*,[85] the equitable rule can be based on one of two grounds—either that a man is not to be allowed to get a benefit from a false statement which he now admits to be false, or that, even assuming that moral fraud must be shown in order to set aside a contract, you have it where a man, having obtained a beneficial contract by a statement which he now knows to be false, insists upon keeping that contract. *Redgrave* v. *Hurd* is a good illustration of the nature of the equitable jurisdiction. A solicitor had advertised the sale of his surburban house and, with it, a partnership in his practice. In interviews with a prospective purchaser, he represented the practice as worth about £300 a year. There were no properly kept accounts but, after examining such papers as there were, the purchaser decided the business was worth about £200 a year. He agreed to buy the house and to enter into partnership. Shortly afterwards, he found the practice to be worthless. He was sued for specific performance, and counterclaimed for rescission and damages. The Court of Appeal held that the defendant could not recover damages because there had been no deceit, but they granted him rescission of the contract. They also held that it was no answer to a claim for relief for innocent misrepresentation to say that if the purchaser had used due diligence, he would have discovered the true state of affairs.

This categorisation (innocent misrepresentation: rescission but no damages; warranty: damages but no rescission; condition: rescission or damages but not both) has been altered by the Misrepresentation Act 1967.[86] By Section 1, the fact that a misrepresentation inducing a person to enter into an agreement has subsequently become a term of the contract does not stop the person misled from rescinding the contract for innocent misrepresentation. By Section 2(1), where a person has suffered loss by entering into a contract on the faith of an innocent misrepresentation, he has an action for damages unless the

[84] *Brown* v. *Raphael*, [1958] Ch. 636, 641 (C.A.), *per* Lord Evershed, M.R.
[85] (1881), 20 Ch.D. 1, 12-13. See also *With* v. *O'Flanagan*, [1936] Ch. 575 (C.A.).
[86] See also the Misrepresentation Act (Northern Ireland) 1967. There is no equivalent legislation in the Republic of Ireland.

defendant proves that he had reasonable ground to believe and did believe up to the time the contract was made that the facts represented were true. Subsection (2) of the same section provides that where a contract could be rescinded for innocent misrepresentation, in proceedings on the contract damages may be awarded in lieu of rescission, if it would be equitable to do so, having regard to the nature of the misrepresentation and the loss that would be caused by it if the contract were upheld, as well as to the loss that rescission would cause to the other party. Damages may be awarded under subsection (2) whether or not there is liability in damages under subsection (1).[87]

Apart from this statutory introduction of damages, there is an equitable jurisdiction to make a monetary adjustment on rescission. Equitable remedies being discretionary, they may be awarded on terms. An invariable condition of rescission is restitutio in integrum, including an indemnity against all claims which might have arisen out of the plaintiff's conduct while acting under the contract. In *Newbigging* v. *Adam*[88] the plaintiff was induced to enter into partnership with the defendants in consequence of their innocent misrepresentations concerning the value of the business. The Court of Appeal granted rescission of the contract, which meant that the defendants must repay the capital which the plaintiff had brought into the business, and that they were jointly and severally bound to indemnify the plaintiff against the debts and liabilities of the partnership.[89]

There is thought to have been a rule of equity that a contract could not be rescinded for innocent misrepresentation if it had been performed,[90] though performance has never rendered rescission too late in cases of fraud. Denning, L.J., threw doubt on the existence of any such rule, obiter, in *Solle* v. *Butcher*[91] and *Leaf* v. *International Galleries*.[92] It could be regarded, not as a rule, but as an aspect of whether restitutio in integrum was possible in the particular instance. However, in *Long* v. *Lloyd*[93] the Court of Appeal inclined to favour the rule rather than the opinion of Denning, L.J. Section 1 of the

87 See subsection (3). See also section 3, avoiding certain agreements excluding liability for misrepresentation.

88 (1886), 34 Ch.D. 582.

89 The distinction between this type of indemnity in cases of innocent misrepresentation and damages for fraud (of only historical interest in cases governed by the Misrepresentation Act 1967), was explored by Cotton, L.J. (pp. 589-90), with whom Fry, L.J. (p. 596), inclined to agree, and, more elaborately, but somewhat differently, by Bowen, L.J. (pp. 592-5).

90 *Seddon* v. *North Eastern Salt Co. Ltd.*, [1905] 1 Ch. 326; *Angel* v. *Jay*, [1911] 1 K.B. 666 (Div. Ct.). Ireland: *Lecky* v. *Walter*, [1914] 1 I.R. 378.

91 [1950] 1 K.B. 671, 695 (C.A.).

92 [1950] 2 K.B. 86, 90 (C.A.).

93 [1958] 1 W.L.R. 753, 756-60. See also *Senanayake* v. *Cheng*, [1966] A.C. 63 (P.C., Singapore).

Misrepresentation Act 1967[94] now makes it clear that, in future, a right to rescind is not abrogated by performance of the contract.

Individual clauses in contracts have been rescinded when a person has been induced to agree to them by an innocent misrepresentation by the other party as to their effect. In *Curtis* v. *Chemical Cleaning and Dyeing Co.*[95] the Court of Appeal held that the defendants could not rely on a clause exempting them from all liability for damage after their shop assistant had told the customer that only specific liabilities were excluded. The majority of the Court of Appeal (Cairns, J., not dealing with the point) again took that view when an estate agent got a vendor to sign a contract by saying that commission would become due if a sale went through, whereas the document specified payment of commission on introducing a prospective purchaser.[96]

Mistake

An initial difficulty which attends any discussion of rescission[97] on this ground is that of defining " mistake." "... I can find no definition of what ' mistake ' is . . . ," said Lord Esher, M.R., in *Barrow* v. *Isaacs & Son*,[98] and Kay, L.J., added:[99] " Very wisely, as I presume to think, the Courts have abstained from giving any general definition of what amounts to mistake." Mistake is the misapprehension or ignorance of one or both parties of some fact or circumstance material to the conclusion of the transaction in question; and where mistake has legal consequences, giving the party who has suffered from it a remedy or defence, it is because it has amounted to absence of agreement or has affected the consent given or the act done by the party claiming relief.[1]

Mistake is often closely associated with some other factor which is legally relevant. For example, by a misrepresentation, A may induce B to enter into (what is or appears to be) a contract with him. If the mistake made by B is such that there is no agreement between the parties, the apparent contract is void (at common law) for mistake. If, on the other hand, the mistake does not negative consensus ad idem, there may be rescission (in equity) for mistake or rescission (at law or in equity) for fraud or (in equity) for innocent misrepresentation

94 See also Sect. 4; Misrepresentation Act (Northern Ireland) 1967, Sects. 1 and 4.
95 [1951] 1 K.B. 805.
96 *Jaques* v. *Lloyd D. George & Partners Ltd.*, [1968] 1 W.L.R. 625.
97 As to mistake as a defence to an action for specific performance, see pp. 506-7, *ante*, and as a ground for rectification, see pp. 530-42, *ante*.
98 [1891] 1 Q.B. 417, 420.
99 [1891] 1 Q.B. 425.
1 See Keener, " Recovery of Money Paid under Mistake of Fact " (1887), 1 *Harvard Law Review*, 211; Abbot, " Mistake of Fact as a Ground for Affirmative Equitable Relief " (1910), 23 *H.L.R.*, 608.

or damages for misrepresentation or damages or rescission for breach of contract. The distinction between a contract which is void for mistake and one which is voidable (i.e., which can be rescinded) for mistake or misrepresentation has important consequences. A void contract is no contract while a voidable one is valid till rescinded. The equity to rescind may be lost, for example by laches or when a bona fide third party becomes involved. The consequences can be appreciated by contrasting the two cases of *Cundy* v. *Lindsay*[2] and *Phillips* v. *Brooks Ltd.*[3] In *Cundy* v. *Lindsay*, Alfred Blenkarn, who occupied a room near Cheapside, wrote as from 37, Wood Street, Cheapside, ordering goods from a Belfast linen firm, signing the letter in such a way that his name appeared to be Blenkiron & Co. There was a respectable firm, Blenkiron & Co., carrying on business at 123, Wood Street, which had previously dealt with the Belfast manufacturers. The latter thought they were dealing with Blenkiron & Co., and supplied goods which Blenkarn disposed of to an innocent third party. The House of Lords held that there never was any contract between the manufacturers and Blenkarn. Accordingly, no property in the goods passed from the manufacturers, who could recover them from the third party. On the other hand, in *Phillips* v. *Brooks Ltd.*, one North went into the plaintiff's shop and selected jewellery priced at £3000. He wrote out a cheque for £3000 and declared he was Sir George Bullough, giving an address. The jeweller had heard of Sir George Bullough and, having checked the address given by North in a directory, let him take the jewels away. The cheque was dishonoured, but in the meantime North (using the name Firth) had pawned one of the items of jewellery with the defendants. Horridge, J., held that, though there was a mistake induced by fraud, there had been a consensus ad idem because the plaintiff had " intended to contract with the person present, and there was no error as to the person with whom he contracted, although the plaintiff would not have made the contract if there had not been a fraudulent misrepresentation."[4] Accordingly, property in the jewellery had passed under a voidable title to North and the defendants acquired a title, as bona fide purchasers for value without notice, free from the equity to rescind. Whether the presence of the cheat in the latter case and his absence in *Cundy* v. *Lindsay* is a sufficient ground for the distinction may be questioned, but the cases do illustrate the importance of whether a contract is void or voidable. In *Ingram* v. *Little*,[5] where the circumstances were similar to those in *Phillips* v. *Brooks Ltd.*, the Court of Appeal came to the conclusion that

[2] (1878), 3 App. Cas. 459.
[3] [1919] 2 K.B. 243. See also *Lake* v. *Simmons*, [1927] A.C. 487 (H.L., E.); *Dennant* v. *Skinner*, [1948] 2 K.B. 164.
[4] [1919] 2 K.B. 248-9.
[5] [1961] 1 Q.B. 31.

there was no contract and that accordingly the vendors (of a car) could recover it from the innocent third party to whom the rogue had sold it before his cheque was dishonoured. The majority did not disagree with the decision in *Phillips* v. *Brooks Ltd.*, but regarded themselves as dealing with a different fact situation, i.e., with one in which the vendors meant to deal only with the reputable person the purchaser pretended to be (as in *Cundy* v. *Lindsay*). Devlin, L.J., who dissented, would have followed *Phillips* v. *Brooks Ltd.*

At common law, a contract is void for mistake if the mistake is inconsistent with agreement or it is impossible to perform on account of mistake (e.g. where, unknown to both parties, the subject-matter of the contract does not exist), but does not appear to be affected at all if the mistake neither negatives agreement nor precludes performance.[6] In equity, quite apart from misrepresentation, a jurisdiction has been exercised to rescind contracts for mistake.[7] This jurisdiction must be confined to contracts which are not void at law for lack of agreement, for it is impossible to rescind what has never been operative.[8]

Solle v. *Butcher*[9] is the leading modern case on the equitable jurisdiction. A landlord let a flat to a tenant at £250 a year, both parties being under the mistaken impression that structural alterations had taken the premises outside the Rent Acts. The rent of £250 would have been permissible under the Acts had appropriate notices of increase been served, but because of the mistake the landlord served no notice. After paying the agreed rent for a time, the tenant sought a declaration that the standard rent was £140 a year and recovery of past overpayments. The Court of Appeal (Jenkins, L.J., dissenting) held that there had been a mistake of fact and set the lease aside on terms as to payment for occupation already enjoyed, and for the grant of a new lease in accordance with the Rent Acts (including a rent properly increased but not to more than £250 a year). According to Denning, L.J.,[10] with whom Bucknill, L.J., agreed, mistakes giving rise to rescission in the absence of misrepresentation occur when: (1) one party, knowing that the other is mistaken about the terms of an offer, or the identity of a person by whom it is made, lets him remain under his delusion and

6 For a recent criticism of traditional treatments of mistake, see Atiyah and Bennion, " Mistake in the Construction of Contracts " (1961), 24 *Modern Law Review*, 421. See also Atiyah, " Judicial Techniques and the English Law of Contract " (1968), 2 *Ottawa Law Review*, 337.

7 See Grunfeld, " A Study in the Relationship between Common Law and Equity in Contractual Mistake " (1952), 15 *Modern Law Review*, 297.

8 Cf. Atiyah and Bennion, *op. cit.*, 24 *M.L.R.* 439-42, who doubt the existence of the equitable jurisdiction.

9 [1950] 1 K.B. 671. See also *Grist* v. *Bailey*, [1967] Ch. 532; *Bligh* v. *Martin*, [1968] 1 W.L.R. 804; *Gallie* v. *Lee*, [1969] 2 W.L.R. 901. (C.A.); *Magee* v. *Pennine Insurance Co. Ltd.*, [1969] 2 W.L.R. 1278 (C.A.); pp. 535-7, *ante*.

10 [1950] 1 K.B. 692-3.

concludes a contract on the mistaken terms instead of pointing out the mistake; (2) if the parties were under a common misapprehension either as to facts or as to their relative and respective rights, provided that the misapprehension was fundamental and that the party seeking rescission was not himself at fault. Jenkins, L.J., considered[11] that there had been a mistake of law (i.e., as to the effect of a statute) of a kind that was not a ground for rescission.

One of the cases relied on by the majority in *Solle* v. *Butcher* is *Cooper* v. *Phibbs*.[12] A person had taken a lease of a fishery, unaware (as were the lessors) that he was already the owner of it. The House of Lords set the lease aside, upon terms (e.g., connected with payment for occupation of a cottage that did belong to the lessors), on the ground of a common mistake of fact. It may be observed that it is difficult to see how a lease by someone with no estate in the land could be operative at law, but the House of Lords could not have imposed terms had they not been granting the equitable remedy of rescission. A few years after *Cooper* v. *Phibbs*, in an English case,[13] the House of Lords held that there had been no mistake, but Lord Chelmsford, obiter, affirmed the jurisdiction and that mistakes of fact include private rights, which involve matter of law, but that there would be no relief if the mistake were one as to the general law.[14]

Substantial Misdescription

This is a defence to an action for specific performance. In general, rescission is granted when specific performance is refused, but there are cases in which the court refuses specific performance without also granting rescission.[15]

Non-Disclosure in respect of Contracts Uberrimae Fidei

There are certain contracts considered to require the utmost good faith in the negotiations leading up to them because agreement depends upon facts peculiarly within the knowledge of one of the parties. In such cases, in equity, there is imposed upon that party the duty of making full disclosure of all material facts known to him. Failure to make this complete disclosure entitles the other party to have the contract rescinded. The main types of contract falling within this class are: (1) contracts of insurance; (2) contracts for the purchase of shares in a company on its formation; and (3) family arrangements.

11 [1950] 1 K.B. 705.
12 (1867), L.R. 2 H.L. 149, on appeal from Ireland.
13 *Earl Beauchamp* v. *Winn* (1873), L.R. 6 H.L. 223.
14 L.R. 6 H.L. 233-4. See also Bigelow, " Mistake of Law as a ground of Equitable Relief " (1885), 1 *Law Quarterly Review*, 298.
15 See pp. 506-8, *ante*.

All contracts of insurance are uberrimae fidei according to the principles of equity.[16] In the case of marine insurance, disclosure is now a statutory requirement.[17] Both under the statute and under the general doctrine of equity, a material fact is one which would influence the judgment of a prudent insurer in fixing the premium or in determining whether he will take the risk.[18]

In deciding whether or not to buy shares in a newly floated company, or a new issue of shares, investors are generally influenced by the prospectus drawn up by the promoters. At one time, there were suggestions that the doctrine of equity was that a promoter must disclose all material facts, or the shareholder would be able to rescind the contract.[19] Later, it was settled[20] that this was so only if the non-disclosure was such that the prospectus conveyed a false impression. Rigby, L.J., said[21]—

> It is not that the omission of material facts is an independent ground for rescission, but the omission must be of such a nature as to make the statement actually made misleading. In other words, as has often been said before, supression of the truth may contain a suggestion of falsity—may make what is actually stated reasonably untrue.

In the twentieth century, successive statutes—at present the Companies Act, 1948, Section 38[22]—have prescribed the particulars which must appear in the prospectus, the accuracy of which must be vouched for by the promoter and directors.[23]

Family arrangements can take many forms,[24] but they have this element in common: that they affect the distribution of property among members of the same family. It has always been the rule of equity that such an arrangement can be rescinded unless there has been full disclosure by the parties of all material facts known to them.[25]

16 See also p. 552, *post*.

17 Marine Insurance Act, 1906, Sects. 17-19.

18 For a jurisdictional consequence of an insurance contract being voidable, not void ab initio, for non-disclosure, see *Mackender* v. *Feldia A.G.*, [1967] 2 Q.B. 590 (C.A.).

19 See *New Brunswick and Canada Railway and Land Co.* v. *Muggeridge* (1860), 1 Dr. & Sm. 363, 381-2, *per* Kindersley, V.-C. (refusal of specific performance); *Central Railway Co. of Venezuela* v. *Kisch* (1867), L.R. 2 H.L. 99, 113, *per* Lord Chelmsford, L.C. (rescission).

20 *McKeown* v. *Boudard-Peveril Gear Co.* (1896), 74 L.T. 712 (C.A.).

21 74 L.T. 713.

22 Equivalent legislation: Companies Act (Northern Ireland), 1960, Sect. 38; Companies Act, 1963, Sect. 44 (Republic of Ireland).

23 As to damages for misstatements in a prospectus, see p. 329, *ante*.

24 As to the nature of family arrangements, and undue influence in arriving at them, see p. 344, *ante*.

25 *Smith* v. *Pincombe* (1852), 3 Mac. & G. 653; *Greenwood* v. *Greenwood* (1863), 2 De G. J. & S. 28 (both C.A. Ch.).

Delivery Up and Cancellation

Where there existed in equity a ground for rescinding a transaction, and that transaction was expressed in or given effect to by a document, it used to be common for the court to order the document to be delivered up to be cancelled so that it could not be produced as the foundation for a subsequent action in a common law court. An early case where this was done to counteract fraud is *Whittingham* v. *Thornburgh.*[26] The defendant took out a life insurance policy on someone in whose life he had no insurable interest, who was languishing but whom he represented to be healthy, and who died shortly afterwards. The order was that the policy be delivered up and cancelled and that there be a perpetual injunction against a verdict obtained on it at law. Similar orders have been made in cases of guarantees obtained by misrepresentation,[27] a conveyance made under a mistake,[28] an equitable mortgage brought about by undue influence,[29] and various circumstances of fraud on third parties (or what are now classified as agreements contrary to public policy).[30]

Delivery up and cancellation were not ordered only in cases where there were equitable grounds for rescission. Failure to appreciate that has sometimes led to cases being treated by later commentators as cases of rescission when they were cases of cancellation without rescission. One example is cancellation in the light of changed circumstances—which would now probably be regarded as termination of a contract by virtue of the operation of an implied term. In *Lawrence* v. *Brasier*[31] Lord Clarendon, L.C., and Windham, J., ordered the

[26] (1690), 2 Vern. 206. See also *De Costa* v. *Scandret* (1723), 2 P. Wms. 170 (marine insurance policy cancelled for non-disclosure amounting to fraud); *Ward* v. *Duke of Buckingham* (1725), 3 Bro. P.C. 581 (H.L., E.) (receipt); *Bishop of Winchester* v. *Fournier* (1752), 2 Ves. Sen. 445 (promissory note for £8,800, obtained from the plaintiff by fraud or forged, ordered to be delivered up, but not cancelled for the time being). Ireland: *Field* v. *Boland* (1837), 1 Dr. & Wal. 37 (conveyance cancelled for fraud).

[27] *Cooper* v. *Joel* (1859), 1 De G. F. & J. 240; *Blest* v. *Brown* (1862), 4 De G. F. & J. 367 (C.A. Ch.).

[28] *Cooper* v. *Phibbs* (1867), L.R. 2 H.L. 149. See p. 550, *ante*.

[29] *Williams* v. *Bayley* (1866), L.R. 1 H.L. 200.

[30] *Law* v. *Law* (1735), 3 P. Wms. 391 (bond by holder of post with commissioners of excise to pay £10 a year, while holding the post, to the person who secured it for him); *Debenham* v. *Ox* (1749), 1 Vest. Sen. 276 (bond as reward for influence over another's estate for benefit of obligor); *Wynne* v. *Callander* (1826), 1 Russ. 293 (bill of exchange for money lost playing cards); *Earl of Milltown* v. *Stewart* (1837), 3 My. & Cr. 18, 24, *per* Lord Cottenham, L.C.; *Rice* v. *Gordon* (1848), 11 Beav. 265 (surety signed bill of exchange on understanding that another would join as co-surety, but the other did not: bill endorsed to third party: holder given option of cancellation or rectification by erasure of surety's name); *Evans* v. *Bremridge* (1856), 8 De G. M. & G. 100 (C.A. Ch.); *W.* v. *B.* (1863), 32 Beav. 574 (mortgage by father and daughter partly in consideration of father not hindering mortgagee's seduction of daughter).

[31] (1666), 1 Ch. Cas. 72.

delivery up of a bond on the ground of changed circumstances arising out of the civil war. In *Burgess* v. *Eve*[32] Malins, V.-C., said obiter—

> . . . a person who gives a guarantee would have a right to say to the person taking it, " You will continue at your own peril to employ the person on whose behalf I gave the guarantee;" provided that the clerk or other person has been guilty of embezzlement or gross misconduct, or has turned out to be unworthy of the confidence reposed in him by the person giving the guarantee for him. If the employer under such circumstances refused to give the guarantee up, the person giving it would have a right to file a bill in this Court, and in my opinion would succeed in the contest, because the Court would direct the bond to be delivered up to be cancelled.

In *King* v. *King*[33] there was a contract for the sale of land but the vendor was unable to make title. The purchasers had been in possession for eight years without paying any purchase-money or accepting such title as the vendor could convey. Leach, M.R., ordered the delivery up and cancellation of the contract. In *Onions* v. *Cohen*,[34] on the other hand, Page Wood, V.-C., held that the mere fact that the lessor could not make title was no ground for cancelling an agreement for a lease.

A long controversy engaged judges of courts of equity on the question whether a document void at law could be cancelled under the equity jurisdiction. On the one hand, cancellation would seem unnecessary, for the person seeking to make use of the document would fail at law; on the other hand, the continued existence of the document might present a threat of proceedings which could be embarrassing even if the proceedings were likely to fail. In *Ryan* v. *Mackmath*[35] X had given a promissory note in the names of himself and Y. X had no authority to commit Y, therefore the note gave no rights at law against Y. Lord Thurlow, L.C., refused both delivery up and erasure of Y's name on the ground that equitable relief was not necessary for Y's protection. Yet in *Lisle* v. *Liddle*[36] in the Court of Exchequer, Macdonald, C.B., and Thomson, B., apparently without qualms,

32 (1872), L.R. 13 Eq. 450, 458-9, approved in *Phillips* v. *Foxall* (1872), L.R. 7 Q.B. 666, 677-8, by Quain, J., giving the judgment of Cockburn, C.J., Lush, J., and himself, and by Blackburn, J. at pp. 681-2.

33 (1833), 1 My. & K. 442.

34 (1865), 2 H. & M. 354.

35 (1789), 3 Bro. C.C. 15. See also *Hilton* v. *Barrow* (1791), 1 Ves. Jun. 284; *Franco* v. *Bolton* (1797), 3 Ves. 368; *Thornton* v. *Knight* (1849), 16 Sim. 509; *Gray* v. *Mathias* (1800), 5 Ves. 286, where the Court of Exchequer thought equity proceedings a waste of money and that the plaintiff should demur as defendant at law; *Simpson* v. *Lord Howden* (1837), 3 My. & Cr. 97, 108, where Lord Cottenham, L.C., objected to the courts of equity being involved in deciding pure questions oflaw; *Hoare* v. *Bremridge* (1872), L.R. 8 Ch. App. 22 (C.A. Ch.).

36 (1795), 3 Anst. 649.

ordered the delivery up for cancellation of promissory notes even after the defendant had sued on them at law and failed. Lord Eldon was the great supporter of cancelling documents void at law to prevent vexations litigation[37] or to get rid of what he called "a cloud upon the title."[38] After his time the jurisdiction seems to have been accepted on the whole, though seldom resorted to.[39]

After the passing of the Judicature Acts, there would seem to be little scope for cancelling documents, except where they are void at law. In this one case, a person may prefer to get the document out of the way rather than wait and see if it is used to cause him trouble. Even in this type of case, the plaintiff may be equally well served by an action for a declaration.[40] In cases of rescission by the court on equitable grounds, the judgment rescinding the transaction should be enough, for there is no other court in which the defendant in equity can later become the plaintiff at law. In *Walton* v. *Cook*[41] a deed of guarantee was rescinded. Kay, J., did not order cancellation of the deed, but said[42]—

> There must be a declaration to that effect [i.e. rescission], and a memorandum of this judgment may be indorsed on the deed.

There are, however, indications that delivery up and cancellation are not quite dead. In *Brooking* v. *Maudslay, Son, & Field*[43] Stirling, J., held that there was jurisdiction to cancel where a document was voidable in equity or void at law, but not on the ground that there was a defence at law to a claim on a valid document. In this case, applying the last proposition, the learned judge refused to cancel a valid marine insurance policy where there was a defence (of unsea-

37 *Bromley* v. *Holland* (1802), 7 Ves. 3, 16-22; *Kemp* v. *Pryor* (1802), 7 Ves. 237, 248-50; *Jervis* v. *White* (1802), 7 Ves. 413, 414-5; *Lord St. John* v. *Lady St. John* (1805), 11 Ves. 526, 535; *Underhill* v. *Horwood* (1804), 10 Ves. 209, 218-9, reheard as *Ware* v. *Horwood* (1807), 14 Ves. 28, 32-3; *Jackman* v. *Mitchell* (1807), 13 Ves. 581, 586.

38 *Hayward* v. *Dimsdale* (1810), 17 Ves. 111, 112; *Colchester Corp.* v. *Lowten* (1813), 1 V. & B. 226, 244; *Davis* v. *Duke of Marlborough* (1819), 2 Swans. 108, 157; *A.-G.* v. *Morgan* (1826), 2 Russ. 306.

39 In *Jones* v. *Frost* (1818), 3 Madd. 1, 8, Leach, V.-C., said: ". . . and though the Ecclesiastical Court has decreed against the will, as having been obtained by fraud, this Court will not order the will to be delivered up; for being declared a nullity by the proper Court, it can never be made use of." In *Duncan* v. *Worrall* (1822), 10 Price 31, Richards, L.C.B., ordered an insurance policy to be delivered up after an action at law on it had failed, but without costs because he considered the equity proceedings undesirable. In *Peake* v. *Highfield* (1826), 1 Russ. 559, Lord Gifford, M.R., held that the Court of Chancery could try the question whether an instrument was forged and, having decided it was, order it to be delivered up; but in this case there was evidence of due execution, so the issue of forgery was sent for trial at law.

40 See pp. 559-60, *post*.

41 (1888), 40 Ch.D. 325.

42 40 Ch.D. 330.

43 (1888), 38 Ch.D. 636.

worthiness of the vessel) to a particular claim under the policy. He said that if there was a danger of loss of evidence pending the time of defending a future legal claim, the insurers should bring an action for perpetuation of testimony.[44] In *Gun* v. *M'Carthy*[45] Flanagan, J., actually ordered delivery up and cancellation of a lease when he rescinded it for mistake.

Perpetuation of Testimony

The suit for perpetuation of testimony does not lead to an equitable remedy in the sense that it leads to an order for something to be done by a party, but, as it is a separate action, it is convenient to mention it in this chapter. This suit is an ancient Chancery proceeding for the purpose of preserving testimony from loss (for example, by the death of witnesses) before a dispute can be brought to trial.

The general nature of the action to perpetuate testimony was surveyed by Leach, V.-C., in *Angell* v. *Angell*.[46] The learned Vice-Chancellor pointed out that this action can be brought only when the dispute cannot be brought to trial. There are two typical cases: first, where the plaintiff is a remainderman and cannot establish his title by action because he has not, as yet, any claim to possession even if his title is good; and secondly, where the plaintiff is in possession (and so has nothing to claim) but there is an adverse claimant who is delaying taking action while waiting for witnesses to die.[47] He said that on principle an action for perpetuation of testimony could not be brought where the dispute could be the subject of an immediate trial.[48] (In *West* v. *Lord Sackville*[49] the Court of Appeal thought that the possibility of an immediate trial was not a bar to an order for perpetuation of testimony, but a factor which would (and did in that case) influence the court to exercise its discretion against making such an order.) Leach, V.-C., went on to explain the sparing use of this jurisdiction by referring to two of its disadvantages: one is that, if the matter does come on for trial on the basis of the testimony so obtained, a case normally heard on oral evidence will be a trial on written depositions; the other that, by the time his evidence is used, the witness will be beyond the reach of temporal sanctions for perjury (and so, perhaps,

44 See below.
45 (1883), 13 L.R. Ir. 304.
46 (1822), 1 Sim. & St. 83. For other general statements, see the judgments of Lord Eldon, L.C., in *Lord Dursley* v. *Fitzhardinge Berkeley* (1801), 6 Ves. 251, and of Romilly, M.R., in three cases of *Ellice* v. *Roupell* (1863), 32 Beav. 299, 308 and 318. Ireland: *Kelly* v. *Kelly*, [1917] 1 I.R. 51 (O'Connor, M.R.).
47 See *Duke of Dorset* v. *Girdler* (1720), Prec. Ch. 531.
48 See *Brandlyn* v. *Orr* (1738), 1 Atk. 571; *Earl Spencer* v. *Peek* (1867), L.R. 3 Eq. 415. Ireland: *Lyndsay* v. *Lyndsay* (1849), 1 Ir. Jur. Rep. 289.
49 [1903] 2 Ch. 378.

not so careful what he says). The depositions can be used at a subsequent trial only if the witness is dead, sick, incapable of travelling to court or prevented from doing so by accident.[50]

To support an action for perpetuating testimony, the plaintiff must have an interest in disputed property, but, said Lord Eldon, L.C., in *Allan* v. *Allan*[51]—

> . . . it is perfectly immaterial how minute the interest may be; how distant the possibility of the possession of that minute interest: if it is a present interest. . . . On the other hand, though the contingency may be ever so proximate and valuable; yet if the party has not by virtue of that an estate, the Court does not deal with him . . .

Accordingly, no such action could be brought in relation to an estate tail by issue expecting to succeed to it, for they might never in fact so succeed: it is only a spes successionis until the death of the ancestor; but a remainderman may perpetuate testimony.

In 1842 the jurisdiction of the Court of Chancery in this matter was put on a statutory basis,[52] but the principles on which it was exercised remained the same. Nowadays actions to perpetuate testimony are rarer than they were during previous centuries, but they still occur. Among the reasons are shorter periods of limitation (thus curtailing the period for which a person out of possession may delay his claim) and the introduction of actions for a declaration[53] (thus providing a remainderman with an opportunity for bringing an issue of title to trial despite the fact that he can claim no remedy).[54]

Leach, V.-C., in *Angell* v. *Angell*,[55] was at pains to distinguish between perpetuation of testimony and examination of witnesses de bene esse. Whereas a suit for perpetuating testimony is meant for the recording of perishable evidence as to a matter which cannot be brought to trial, examination de bene esse is for the purpose of recording the evidence of a particular witness who is not expected to be available at the trial (for example, because of ill health or impending departure for a distant destination), where trial is pending. According to the learned Vice-Chancellor, the equitable jurisdiction to take evidence de bene esse can be exercised only if a suit to determine the matter in issue has been commenced.[56]

50 *Morrison* v. *Arnold* (1817), 19 Ves. 670, *per* Lord Eldon, L.C. See also *Biddulph* v. *Lord Camoys* (1855), 20 Beav. 402; *Beresford* v. *A.-G.* [1918] P. 33 (C.A.).

51 (1808), 15 Ves. 130, 135-6. See also *Re Stoer* (1884), 9 P.D. 120 (C.A.).

52 5 & 6 Vict., c. 69, applicable to England and Ireland. See now, for England, R.S.C. 1965, O. 39, r. 15.

53 See pp. 559-60, *post*.

54 See the remarks of Stirling, J., in the Court of Appeal in *West* v. *Lord Sackville*, [1903] 2 Ch. 378, 392-3.

55 (1822), 1 Sim. & St. 83.

56 See also *Philips* v. *Carew* (1709), 1 P. Wms. 117; *Shirley* v. *Earl Ferrers* (1730), 3 P. Wms. 77.

PROCEEDINGS QUIA TIMET

Proceedings quia timet are proceedings taken, before any actionable wrong has occurred, to forestall its occurrence. This seems to be an equitable extension of a common law jurisdiction based on writs of prevention.[57] The commonest examples are quia timet injunctions,[58] to restrain a threatened tort, breach of contract, etc., and the appointment of a receiver[59] to prevent a probable dissipation of assets. Quia timet proceedings are also available in other circumstances, mainly in the field of administration of estates and in suretyship cases.

The preservation of a chattel interest which is left to persons in succession is an early reported example of equitable intervention quia timet. If a testator leaves a chattel or money to A for life, with remainder to B, B may sue quia timet in the lifetime of A (i.e., before he is entitled to call for the property) for an order that A give security for the eventual handing over of the chattel or money to B.[60] It seems that B is not entitled to an order unless he can show that, in the absence of security, there is some danger that A will not preserve the subject-matter of the legacy for him.[61] B must also show that he has some title, not a mere spes successionis.[62] In *Hayes* v. *Hayes*[63] there was a devise to A for life, remainder in fee simple to B, the estate being made subject to a liability to pay £500 thereout to C on her attaining the age of 16. Finch, L.K., held that B could sue quia timet for an order that A pay part of the £500. It is enough that B's interest is future: it need not be a remainder. In *Green* v. *Pigot*[64] there was a legacy of £5000 to an infant on reaching majority, with 4% interest in the meantime. Lord Thurlow, L.C., exercising the jurisdiction quia timet to order an executor to set aside a fund to meet a future or contingent legacy of personalty, prescribed investment of the sum in gilt edged securities. Finally, the jurisdiction is not confined to legacies. In *Flight* v. *Cook*[65] A had covenanted to give B two specific funds of £100 each if B survived A. A sold the investment representing one of the funds. Clarke, M.R. (with A's agreement), made an order quia timet in favour of B that A give security for the performance of the covenant.

[57] See Holdsworth, *History of English Law*, vol. 2, p. 344, n. 6.
[58] See pp. 460, 462, 463, 476, *ante*.
[59] See p. 510, *ante*.
[60] *Johnson* v. *Mills* (1749), 1 Ves. Sen. 282, where Lord Hardwicke, L.C., made such an order at the suit of B's creditor, to whom B had assigned his interest in the legacy.
[61] *Fisher* v. *Hughes* (1820), Coop. t. Cott. 329.
[62] *Brown* v. *Dudbridge* (1788), 2 Bro. C.C. 321, where Kenyon, M.R., refused an order at the suit of the next of kin of a legatee who was not shown to be dead; *Fisher* v. *Hughes* (1820), Coop. t. Cott. 329.
[63] (1674), 1 Ch. Cas. 223.
[64] (1781), 1 Bro. C.C. 103.
[65] (1755), 2 Ves. Sen. 619.

Quia timet proceedings in respect of indemnities and guarantees were the subject of an early reported case, *Earl of Ranelaugh* v. *Hayes.*[66] A covenanted to indemnify B against certain debts of fluctuating amount. Lord Guilford, L.K., held that B could have an order quia timet against A to perform his covenant as soon as the creditor made a demand (i.e. before B had to pay anything). From this base a number of rules developed.

One rule is that if the surety for a debt is asked by the creditor to pay it, the surety can insist quia timet on payment by the principal debtor. He need not wait to bring proceedings against the principal debtor until he (the surety) has paid or been sued himself.[67] A co-surety can also get a quia timet declaration of his right to contribution from the other co-sureties before paying anything.[68]

Another rule is that a surety has a right to be discharged if circumstances change so that it is inequitable to rely on the guarantee. In *Padwick* v. *Stanley*[69] Turner, V.-C., held that this was so only if the creditor had a right to sue the principal debtor and refused to do so. It is clear from the decision of Porter, M.R., in *Mathews* v. *Saurin*,[70] an Irish case later followed in England by Swinfen Eady, J.,[71] that that right is not so confined.

A surety cannot make the principal debtor pay, it would appear, if nothing is due from the surety and the amount of the debt is not yet ascertained.[72] In *Bradford* v. *Gammon*[73] Eve, J., thought this immunity extended to all cases in which the creditor had made no demand upon the surety. However, in *Re Anderson-Berry*,[74] where an administrator was threatening to distribute the intestate's estate without providing for contingent liabilities, the Court of Appeal held that the sureties to the administration bond could sue him quia timet for an indemnity. Morton, J., in *Tate* v. *Crewdson*[75] said that the absence of a demand by

[66] (1683), 1 Vern. 189, criticised by Fry, J., in *Lloyd* v. *Dimmack* (1877). 7 Ch.D. 398.
[67] *Wooldridge* v. *Norris* (1868), L.R. 6 Eq. 410; *Ascherson* v. *Tredegar Dry Dock and Wharf Co. Ltd.*, [1909] 2 Ch. 401; *Watt* v. *Mortlock*, [1964] Ch. 84.
[68] *Wolmershausen* v. *Gullick*, [1893] 2 Ch. 514.
[69] (1852), 9 Hare 627.
[70] (1893), 31 L.R. Ir. 181.
[71] *Ascherson* v. *Tredegar Dry Dock and Wharf Co. Ltd.*, [1909] 2 Ch. 401. As to rescession by the surety of his guarantee, see p. 553. *ante*.
[72] *Morrison* v. *Barking Chemicals Co. Ltd.*, [1919] 2 Ch. 325.
[73] [1925] Ch. 132.
[74] [1928] Ch. 290. Ireland: *Hibernian Fire and General Insurance Co. Ltd.* v. *Dorgan*, [1941] I.R. 514, Black J., applying *Re Anderson-Berry* where there was no threat of misappropriation or a devastavit but the administrator was just not getting on with the job.
[75] [1938] Ch. 869, following *Ascherson* v. *Tredegar Dry Dock and Wharf Co. Ltd.*, [1909] 2 Ch. 401. See also *Watt* v. *Mortlock*, [1964] Ch. 84.

the creditor was no bar to the surety's quia timet action against the principal debtor for an indemnity, and that *Bradford* v. *Gammon* could not be supported on that ground.

ACTIONS FOR A DECLARATION

In one sense it can be said that a declaration, like the perpetuation of testimony,[76] is not a remedy. In making a declaration, the court gives an authoritative statement of the legal rights of the party in relation to the matter in issue, but does not order anybody to do or refrain from doing anything. In a sense, too, such actions do not derive from equity. Although they started in the Court of Chancery, they are almost entirely the creature of statute.

Access to a court to have the legal position settled before exposing oneself to the consequences of acting on a particular view of one's rights is clearly a beneficial facility. To take a frequent modern example, should a statutory instrument, purporting to create a criminal offence, be suspected of invalidity, a person affected by it can bring an action for a declaration that it is ultra vires instead of ignoring it and pleading its invalidity upon his subsequent prosecution.

Declaring a party's legal rights is analogous to certain other functions of the Court of Chancery, such as dealing with actions quia timet[77] and construing wills and settlements. However, no general jurisdiction was developed to grant declarations without ordering relief. Occasional attempts have been made to show that the Court of Chancery had inherent jurisdiction to declare rights without granting remedies,[78] but these are really American endeavours to persuade American courts to take the initiative without statutory authority. The most that can be said is that the Court of Chancery could have done it but did not generally do so.[79] According to Jessel, M.R., in the Court of Appeal in *Curtis* v. *Sheffield*,[80] Shadwell, V.-C., used to grant declarations [81] but that was irregular. There are certainly ample dicta[82] that there was no jurisdiction to grant a declaration without relief.

[76] See pp. 555-6, *ante*.
[77] See pp. 557-9, *ante*.
[78] See Triplett, " The Inherent Jurisdiction of Equity to Administer Declaratory Relief " (1964), 35 *Mississippi Law Journal*, 241.
[79] See *Guaranty Trust Co. of New York* v. *Hannay & Co.*, [1915] 2 K.B. 536, 568, *per* Bankes, L.J., in the Court of Appeal; Borchard, " The Declaratory Judgment —A Needed Procedural Reform " (1918), 28 *Yale Law Journal*, 1 and 105; Borchard, *Declaratory Judgments*, 2nd ed. (1941), pp. 137, 215-30; Zamir, *The Declaratory Judgment* (1962), pp. 7-9.
[80] (1882), 21 Ch.D. 1, 3.
[81] See the decision of Shadwell, V.-C., in *Taylor* v. *A.-G.* (1837), 8 Sim. 413.
[82] Knight Bruce, V.-C., in *Elliotson* v. *Knowles* (1842), 11 L.J. Ch. 399, 400, and *Clough* v. *Ratcliffe* (1847), 1 De G. & Sm. 164, 178-9; Wigram, V.-C., in *Ferrand* v. *Wilson* (1845), 4 Hare 344, 385; Lord Cottenham, L.C., in *Grove* v. *Bastard* (1848), 2 Ph. 619, 620-1; and Kindersley, V.-C., in *Jackson* v. *Turnley* (1853), 1 Drew. 617, 626.

The first limited jurisdiction to do that was given to the Court of Chancery in 1850,[83] but that was replaced by a more general jurisdiction conferred by the Chancery Amendment Act, 1852, Section 50.[84] That section enabled the Court of Chancery to give a mere declaration provided there was some relief the plaintiff could have obtained had he chosen to ask for it.[85] Under the Judicature Acts, the jurisdiction to make such declarations passed to all Divisions of the High Court. It was later extended[86] to cases in which there is no relief the plaintiff can claim. The present English rule[87] provides—

> No action or other proceeding shall be open to objection on the ground that a merely declaratory judgment or order is sought thereby, and the Court may make binding declarations of right whether or not any consequential relief is or could be claimed.

Writ of Ne Exeat Regno

This was originally a prerogative writ, issued at the suit of the king, to prevent a subject departing the realm for political reasons. Somehow —no one knows quite how or when[88]—it came to be used in the Court of Chancery, at the suit of a private litigant, to stop a person leaving the jurisdiction when he owed an equitable money obligation. It became the Chancery equivalent of the common law arrest on mesne process, and the defendant could be stopped from leaving the country or allowed to go after providing the equitable equivalent of bail. In *Drover* v. *Beyer*[89] the Court of Appeal said that, to get the writ, the applicant must show two things: (1) that the debt is equitable;[90] and

83 Court of Chancery Act, 1850, Sects. 1, 13-16.

84 That section provided: No Suit in the said Court shall be open to Objection on the Ground that a merely declaratory Decree or Order is sought thereby, and the Court may make binding Declarations of Right without granting consequential Relief. To the same effect was the Chancery (Ireland) Act, 1867, Sect. 155.

85 *Jackson* v. *Turnley* (1853), 1 Drew. 617, 627-8, *per* Kindersley, V.-C.; *Rooke* v. *Lord Kensington* (1856), 2 K. & J. 753, 760-1, *per* Page Wood, V.-C., *Lady Langdale* v. *Briggs* (1856), 8 De G. M. & G. 391, 427-8, *per* Knight Bruce, V.-C.

86 In England, by Rules of the Supreme Court in 1883, held valid by the Court of Appeal in *Guaranty Trust Co. of New York* v. *Hannay & Co.*, [1915] 2 K.B. 536.

87 R.S.C. 1965, O. 15, r. 16. See Sunderland, " A Modern Evolution in Remedial Rights,—The Declaratory Judgment " (1917), 16 *Michigan Law Review*, 69; Jennings, " Declaratory Judgments against Public Authorities " (1932), 41 *Yale Law Journal*, 407; Zamir, *The Declaratory Judgment*.

88 An early reported example is the issue of the writ by Bridgman, L.K., and Twisden, J., in *Reas* v. *Read* (1668), 1 Ch. Cas. 115. See also *Ex parte Brunker* (1734), 3 P. Wms. 312.

89 (1879), 13 Ch.D. 242.

90 See also *Anon.* (1741), 2 Atk. 210; *Pearne* v. *Lisle* (1749), Amb. 75; *Brocker* v. *Hamilton* (1751), Dick, 154; *Ex parte Duncombe* (1774), Dick, 503; *Crosley* v. *Marriot* (1783), Dick. 609; *Atkinson* v. *Leonard* (1791), 3 Bro. C.C. 218; *Jenkins* v. *Parkinson* (1833), 2 My. & K. 5, 13-14, *per* Lord Brougham, L.C.; *Felton* v. *Callis*, [1969] 1 Q. B. 200. Ireland: *Hill* v. *O'Hanlon* (1840), 2 Ir. Eq. Rep. 463; *Alder* v. *Ward* (1843), 5 Ir. Eq. Rep. 367.

(2) that if it were legal, the defendant could be arrested on mesne process. In the words of Cotton, L.J., in *Colverson* v. *Bloomfield*,[91] also in the Court of Appeal (Bowen and Fry, L.JJ., concurring)—

> The Court of Chancery, in granting this writ, merely proceeded by analogy to the process at common law. At common law arrest on *mesne* process was only applicable to legal debts. The Court of Chancery, by analogy, issued a writ of *ne exeat* where the debt was equitable. In my opinion the objection is fatal, that if this had been a legal demand there could have been no arrest at common law, and by analogy we ought not to grant a writ of *ne exeat.*

To the proposition that the debt has to be analogous to a legal debt for which a person could be arrested at common law there are no exceptions; but to the rule that the debt must be equitable there are two: the writ can be had in respect of alimony or a sum due on balance of account.[92]

In addition, the plaintiff must prove that the defendant is indebted to him in a certain sum.[93] He must also prove that the defendant intends to quit the jurisdiction.[94] The writ will then issue if his going abroad will endanger payment: it is not necessary for the plaintiff to prove that the defendant's intention in going abroad is to avoid payment.[95]

The writ is not used much in modern times. That is mainly because common law arrest for debt has been reduced to but a few cases by Section 6 of the Debtors Act, 1869[96] In consequence there can now be few equitable debts analogous to debts for which the debtor can be arrested at law.[97] After 1869, the going abroad must prejudice the plaintiff in recovering judgment, not in enforcing payment.[98] Cases

91 (1885), 29 Ch.D. 341, 342.

92 *Jones* v. *Sampson* (1803), 8 Ves. 593; *Flack* v. *Holm* (1820), 1 J. & W. 405 where (at pp. 413-6) Lord Eldon, L.C., makes a general survey of the law governing the writ.

93 *Rico* v. *Gaultier* (1747), 3 Atk. 501; *Anon.* (1748), 1 Atk. 521; *Parker* v. *Appleton* (1792), 3 Bro. C.C. 427; *Cock* v. *Ravie* (1801), 6 Ves. 283; *Dawson* v. *Dawson* (1803), 7 Ves. 173; *Jackson* v. *Petrie* (1804), 10 Ves. 164, *Haffey* v. *Haffey* (1807), 14 Ves. 261. Ireland: *Hill* v. *O'Hanlon* (1840), 2 Ir. Eq. Rep. 463; *Alder* v. *Ward* (1843), 5 Ir. Eq. Rep. 367.

94 *Etches* v. *Lance* (1802), 7 Ves. 417; *Hannay* v. *M'Entire* (1805), 11 Ves. 54; *Jones* v. *Alephsin* (1810), 16 Ves. 470; *Hyde* v. *Whitfield* (1815), 19 Ves. 342; *Sichel* v. *Raphael* (1861), 4 L.T. 114; *Re Underwood* (1903), 51 W.R. 335. Ireland: *Darley* v. *Nicholson* (1841), 1 Dr. & War. 66.

95 *Tomlinson* v. *Harrison* (1802), 8 Ves. 32. Ireland: *M'Gauran* v. *Furnell* (1837), S. & Sc. 263.

96 Ireland: Debtors (Ireland) Act, 1872, Sec. 7.

97 See *Felton* v. *Callis*, [1969] 1 Q.B. 200, where Megarry, J., reviews fully the modern condition of the writ.

98 *Felton* v. *Callis*, [1969] 1 Q.B. 200.

of this kind can, nevertheless, exist. In *Colverson* v. *Bloomfield*[99] the Court of Appeal refused the writ only on the ground that the debt was not yet payable. There are reported instances after 1869 of it being granted.[1]

ACTION FOR AN ACCOUNT

Whereas at common law sums due from one party to another could be assessed as damages, and simple calculations could be made, in the Court of Chancery a claim for money was normally by an action for an account, and complicated details of accounts could be investigated. A claim by a beneficiary against a trustee is an action for an account, but the scope of the action extended beyond this. It was described by Lindley, L.J., in the Court of Appeal in *London, Chatham and Dover Railway Co* v *South Eastern Railway Co.*[2]—

> Before the *Judicature Acts* a suit for an account could be maintained in equity in the following cases:—(1.) Where the plaintiff had a legal right to have money payable to him ascertained and paid, but which right, owing to defective legal machinery, he could not practically enforce at law. Suits for an account between principal and agent,[3] and between partners,[4] are familiar instances of this class of case. (2.) Where the plaintiff would have had a legal right to have money ascertained and paid to him by the defendant, if the defendant had not wrongfully prevented such right from accruing to the plaintiff. In such a case a Court of law could only give unliquidated damages for the defendant's wrongful act; and there was often no machinery for satisfactorily ascertaining what would have been due and payable if the defendant had acted properly. In such a case, however, a Court of Equity decreed an account, ascertained what would have been payable if the defendant had acted as he ought to have done and ordered him to pay the amount . . .[5] (3.) Where the plaintiff had no legal but only equitable rights against the defendant, and

[99] (1885), 29 Ch.D. 341. See also *Whitehouse* v. *Partridge* (1818), 3 Swanst. 365, 367, *per* Lord Eldon. Ireland: cf. *Waller* v. *Fowler* (1837), S. & Sc. 274.

[1] *Sobey* v. *Sobey* (1873), L.R. 15 Eq. 200; *Lees* v. *Patterson* (1878), 7 Ch. D. 866; *Hands* v. *Hands* (1881), 43 L.T. 750; *Lewis* v. *Lewis* (1893), 68 L.T. 198.

[2] [1892] 1 Ch. 120, 140.

[3] In *Mackenzie* v. *Johnston* (1819), 4 Madd. 373, 375, Leach, V.-C., said: "The Defendants here were agents for the sale of the property of the Plaintiff, and wherever such a relation exists, a bill will lie for an account."

[4] In *Phillips* v. *Phillips* (1852), 9 Hare 471, Turner, V.-C., refused an order between partners because there was no mutual account. He said the remedy should be at law, save in exceptional circumstances, unless each partner has received and paid money on the other's account. Normally, without that situation, the relations between partners would not be too complicated to be dealt with at law.

[5] See *M'Intosh* v. *Great Western Railway Co.* (1850), 2 Mac. & G. 74.

where an account was necessary to give effect to those equitable rights. Ordinary suits by *cestuis que trust* against their trustees and suits for equitable waste[6] fell within this class. (4.) Combination of the above cases.

The jurisdiction to deal with accounts arising out of legal rights depended upon their being so complicated that they could not be taken in a court of law.[7] Accounts are now taken in the Chancery Division in the same way and on the same basis as in the Court of Chancery before.

[6] See *Jesus College* v. *Bloom* (1745), 3 Atk. 262. See also *Bishop of Winchester* v. *Knight* (1717), 1 P. Wms. 406; *Smith* v. *Cooke* (1746), 3 Atk. 378.

[7] See *Taff Vale Railway Co.* v. *Nixon* (1847), 1 H.L.C. 111 (H.L., E.); *North-Eastern Railway Co.* v. *Martin* (1848), 2 Ph. 758; *Fluker* v. *Taylor* (1855), 3 Drew. 183; *Denmark Productions Ltd.* v. *Boscobel Productions Ltd.*, [1968] 3 W.L.R. 841 (C.A.). Ireland: *O'Connor* v. *Spaight* (1804), 1 Sch. & Lef. 305.

INDEX

ACCIDENT, 48, 49
ACCOUNT—
    action for, 562-3
    foreign estate, of, 14
    origin of, 48, 130
ACQUIESCENCE, 28, 33-4, 342, 373, 460, 466
ACTUAL NOTICE—*see* NOTICE.
ADEMPTION—
    following conversion by operation of law, 383
    of legacies by portions, 58, 422-5
    of specific legacies, 288
ADMINISTRATION OF ESTATES—
    ademption of legacies, 58, 288, 383, 422-5
    administrator,
        cum testamento annexo, 263
        intestacy, on, 263, 268
        preference by, 281
        retainer by, 281
    appropriation, power of, 271-2
    assents, 286-7
    assets,
        distribution of, 285-91
        equitable, 265-6
        legal, 265-6
        liability of personal representatives for, 105-6
        marshalling of, 65, 438-9
        order of application of, to debts, 265, 268, 282-5
    bankruptcy rules in administration of insolvent estates, 78-9, 266, 275-82
    business of the deceased carried on by personal represetnatives, 273-4
    chain of representation, 267-8
    Chancery Division, assigned to, 76, 263
    court, by, 264-5
    creditors,
        common law, at, 264-5
        payment of, 274-5
        preference by personal representative, 63, 265, 280, 281-2
    debts, payment of, 274-85
    devise, 287
    disclaimer by executor, 267
    ecclesiastical courts, in, 264
    equity, in, 5-6, 48, 63-4, 150, 264-91
    executor,
        acts before probate, 267
        appointment of, 263
        chain of representation, 267-8
        de son tort, 268
        disclaimer by, 267
        preference by, 63, 265, 280, 281-2
        retainer by, 63, 265, 280-1
        transactions of, with legatee, 341
    foreign estate, 14, 15
    insolvent estates, 78-9, 266-7, 275-82
    intestacy, trust for sale on, 269-70
    Judicature Acts, effect of, 78-9
    legacy,
        ademption of, 58, 288, 383, 422-5
        contingent, 290-1

ADMINISTRATION OF ESTATES—(*contd.*)
legacy,—(*contd.*)
demonstrative, 288
general, 287-8
interest on, 289-91
order of abatement, 288
order of payment, 289
payment of, 285-91
pecuniary, 288
realty, charged on, 287
residuary, 287
satisfaction of —*see* SATISFACTION.
specific, 288
legatee,
at common law, 264
payment to, 285-91
marshalling of assets, 65, 438-9
personal representatives,
administrative powers of, 270-4
administrators, 263, 268, 281
assents by, 286-7
assets, liability for, 105-6
debts, payment of, 274-85
devolution of property on, 267
distribution by, to beneficiaries, 286-91
executors, 63, 263, 265, 267-8, 280-2
trustees, as, 269, 270-1
who are, 263
preference, personal representative's right of, 63, 265, 280, 281-2
Probate judge, vesting of property in, 267
probate of will, 267-8
quia timet proceedings, 557
realty, liability of, for debts, 264
receiver, appointment of, 512
retainer, personal representative's right of, 63, 265, 280-1
ADMINISTRATOR—*see* ADMINISTRATION OF ESTATES.
ADMIRALTY COURT, 74, 75
ADVANCEMENT—
power of, 357
presumption of, 31
AFFIDAVITS—*see* PROCEDURE.
AGENT—*see* PRINCIPAL AND AGENT ; TRUSTEES.
APPEALS—*see* PROCEDURE.
APPOINTMENT—*see* POWER OF APPOINTMENT.
ASSETS—*see* ADMINISTRATION OF ESTATES.
ASSIGNMENT—*see* CHOSES IN ACTION .
ASSOCIATIONS—*see* INJUNCTION.
ASSURANCE POLICY—*see* INSURANCE, CONTRACTS OF.
ATTORNEY, LETTER OF—*see* CHOSES IN ACTION.

BANKER, RELIEF OF, IN RESPECT OF UNAUTHORISED PAYMENTS, 114-17
BANKRUPTCY RULES—*see* ADMINISTRATION OF ESTATES.
BARRISTER AND CLIENT, TRANSACTIONS BETWEEN, 341
BENEFICIARY—
concurrence of, in breach of trust, 31
payment to, by personal representative, 285-91
tracing by, 526-9
transactions of,
with executor, 341
with trustee, 341
trust, rights under, 80
BETH DIN, 295
BILL IN CHANCERY—*see* PROCEDURE.
BILL OF SALE—*see* CHATTELS.

BREACH OF TRUST—*see* TRUST.
BUILDING CONTRACTS—*see* SPECIFIC PERFORMANCE.
BUILDING SCHEME—*see* RESTRICTIVE COVENANT.

CANCELLATION OF DOCUMENTS, 15-16, 48, 76, 542, 552-5
CANON LAW, INFLUENCE OF, 3, 48, 50-1, 54, 482, 484
CAPITAL MONEY—*see* CONVERSION.
CESTUI QUE TRUST—*see* BENEFICIARY.
CHAMPERTY—*see* CHOSES IN ACTION.
CHANCELLOR—
common law, associations with, 52
delegation of petitions to, 3
development of equity by ecclesiastical chancellors, 45, 48
discretion originally unfettered, 3-4
ecclesiastic in Middle Ages, 3-4, 44-5, 48
functions of, 3, 455
Ireland, in, 128-35, 139-40
jurisdiction, origin of, 44-7
office of, 44-8
origin of term, 44
writ system, connection with 3, 45
CHANCERY, COURT OF—
arrears of business in, 72
business of, 5-6
clerks in, 73-4
conflict with common law courts, 51-2
damages, power to award, 75, 463, 466, 483, 496-7, 508
emergence of, 2, 46
English side of, 47
evidence in, 6, 451-2
evolution of equity in, 2-5, 46-72
Ireland, in, 129-35, 137-8, 139, 141
Masters in, 73-4, 131, 454
merger of, in Supreme Court of Judicature, 1-3, 75
prerogative court, as, 52
procedure in, 47, 449-56
reorganisation of, in the nineteenth century, 73-5
separates from the Council, 46
CHANCERY DIVISION—
business assigned to, 75-6, 231, 263
evidence in, 452-3
procedure in, 448, 450-4
CHARGE—
Chancery Division, assigned to, 76
declaration of, unknown at common law, 11
equitable mortgage, by way of, 186
floating, 165, 209
legal mortgage, by way of, 18, 179-81
tracing, to give effect to, 11, 518, 521-4
CHARGEE—
reconversion by, 391
remedies, of, 186, 244, 252
CHARITABLE TRUSTS, 5, 66, 67, 149, 150, 152-9
CHATTELS—
bill of sale, 165, 232-3, 303
constructive notice, unaffected by, 108
mortgage of, 165
restrictive covenants do not run with, 468-9
specific performance of contracts to transfer, 482, 490
CHEQUE, NEGLIGENT PAYMENT OF, 114-17
CHOSES IN ACTION—
assignment of,
champerty in relation to, 293-4, 296
common law, at, 293-6
consideration, how far required for, 309-25, 328
deposit receipts, 325

CHOSES IN ACTION—(*contd.*)
assignment of,—(*contd.*)
equities, subject to, 307-9, 326, 328
equity, in, 5, 296-325
evidence of, 299-300
formalities of, 299-300, 326-8
history of, 293-6
Judicature Acts, effect of, 81, 314, 326-8
litigate, right to, 298-9
maintenance in relation to, 294-6, 298
nature of notice of, 304, 306, 328
notice of, need for, 301-7, 326, 328
possibilities, of, 296-8, 309
priorities of, 300-7, 328
statutory, 326-8
definition of, 292-3
equitable, 296, 309-10
letter of attorney, 294-5
mercantile, 294-6
negotiable instruments, 294, 308
novation in relation to, 294
personal contracts, 298
unassignable, generally, at common law, 293-6
CHOSES IN EQUITY, 296, 309-10
CIRCUIT COURTS IN THE REPUBLIC OF IRELAND, 448
CIVIL BILL COURTS IN IRELAND, 140-1
CLEAN HANDS, PRINCIPLE OF, 30-2, 460
CLERKS—*see* CHANCERY, COURT OF.
CLOGS ON THE EQUITY OF REDEMPTION—*see* MORTGAGES.
CLUBS—
trusts for, 5
injunctions in connection with, 476-7
COMMITTEE OF LUNATIC, ELECTION BY, 405
COMMON INJUNCTION—*see* INJUNCTION.
COMMON LAW—
courts,
conflict with Court of Chancery, 51-2
equitable jurisdiction of, 2-4, 69-70, 75
merger of, in Supreme Court of Judicature, 75-7
fusion with equity, 9, 12-13, 36, 41, 43, 69, 75-127
procedure,
amendment of, 75
chancery procedure, contrasted with, 47
limitations of, 46
relation to equity, 2-4, 51-4, 69-70, 71, 74-127
restriction of growth of, after 1285, 3
rights in rem, 11
rigidity of, 2, 46
tracing at, 9-11, 519
trade competition, gives no remedy against, 7
uses at, 144
COMMON PLEAS, COURT OF, 63, 75, 454
COMPANY DIRECTOR—
formerly liable both at law and in equity, 75
fraud by, 329
injunction, use of, to protect, 476
receiver of his company, may not be, 517
COMPENSATION—
election, in cases of, 395-6, 398-405
specific performance with, 506-7
CONCEALED FRAUD, PLEA OF—*see* FRAUD.
CONFIDENCE, BREACH OF—*see* INJUNCTION.
CONFLICT OF LAWS, 16
CONFLICT OR VARIANCE BETWEEN COMMON LAW AND EQUITY, 77-127

CONSIDERATION—
assignment of choses in action, how far required for, 309-25, 328
deed, unnecessary for enforcement of, at common law, 17, 118
inadequacy of, as a defence to specific performance, 29, 501
incompletely constituted trust, required for enforcement of, 1, 310-11
variation of contract, unnecessary to validate, in equity, 122-5
CONSOLIDATION—*see* MORTGAGES.
CONSTRUCTION OF DOCUMENTS, 25-6
CONSTRUCTIVE NOTICE—*see* NOTICE.
CONSTRUCTIVE TRUST—*see* TRUST.
CONTRACT—
assignment of—*see* CHOSES IN ACTION.
building—*see* SPECIFIC PERFORMANCE.
conversion under—*see* CONVERSION.
deed, by—*see* DEED.
injunction to enforce—*see* INJUNCTION.
penalty clause in —*see* PENALTY, RELIEF AGAINST.
rectification of —*see* RECTIFICATION.
rescission of—*see* RESCISSION.
specific performance of—*see* SPECIFIC PERFORMANCE.
stipulations as to time in, 18, 81-3, 505-6
third party rights under, 38
treatment of, in Court of Chancery, 145-6
uberrimae fidei—*see* RESCISSION.
variation of, without consideration, 122-5
CONTRIBUTION—
amongst joint adventurers, 109
amongst tortfeasors, 83
amongst trustees, 31
CONTRIBUTORY NEGLIGENCE, 83
CONVERSION—
capital money, of, 393-4
contract for sale or purchase, under, 380-4
doctrine of, 6, 65, 375-94
failure of objects of, 386-9
Land Purchase Acts, under, 383-4
Leasehold Reform Act, under, 383
option, under, 381-3
order of court, under, 377-80
origin of doctrine of, 65, 375-6
partnership agreement, under, 377
reconversion, 388-93
statutory trusts, under, 65, 376, 392, 394
trust for sale or purchase, under, 65, 376, 384-6, 392, 394
CORPORATION—*see* INJUNCTION.
COUNCIL—
petitions to, 3, 46
separation of Court of Chancery from, 45-6
COUNTY COURTS—*see* PROCEDURE.
COVENANT —*see* DEED ; RESTRICTIVE COVENANT.
COVIN—*see* FRAUD.
CREDITORS—
administration of estates, in—*see* ADMINISTRATION OF ESTATES.
fraud on—*see* FRAUD.
marshalling as between—*see* MARSHALLING.
receiver, appointment on behalf of—*see* RECEIVER.
CY-PRES DOCTRINE, 153, 158-9

DAMAGES—
adequacy of, as a defence to a claim for an equitable remedy, 29, 32, 454, 458, 459-60, 465, 482, 486, 488, 489, 490
Court of Chancery given power to award, 75
in lieu of injunction, 463, 466
in lieu of rescission, 546
in lieu of specific performance, 483, 496-7, 508
innocent misrepresentation, for, 36, 330, 545-6
liquidated, in relation to penalties, 18-20

DEARLE *v.* HALL, RULE IN, 211, 300-6
DE BENE ESSE, EXAMINATION OF WITNESSES, 556
DEBENTURE HOLDER—*see* RECEIVER.
DEBT—
  administration of estates, in —*see* ADMINISTRATION OF ESTATES.
  assignment of —*see* CHOSES IN ACTION.
  satisfaction of—*see* SATISFACTION.
  set-off—*see* SET-OFF.
DECLARATION, ACTION FOR A, 559-60
DEED—
  common law and equity, variations between, 117-25
  contract under seal,
    discharge of, 120-5
    rectification of—*see* RECTIFICATION.
    specific performance of, 118-9
    valid without consideration, 17, 118
  conversion under trust for sale in—*see* CONVERSION.
  equitable interests, unnecessary for transfer of, 120
  variation of terms of, 120-5
DELIVERY UP OF DOCUMENTS, 48, 542, 552-5
DENNING, LORD, MASTER OF THE ROLLS, 38-42
DEPOSIT RECEIPTS—*see* CHOSES IN ACTION.
DESERTED WIFE—*see* LICENCE.
DEVISE—*see* ADMINISTRATION OF ESTATES ; CONVERSION.
DIRECTOR—*see* COMPANY DIRECTOR.
DISCOVERY OF DOCUMENTS—*see* PROCEDURE.
DOCTOR AND PATIENT, TRANSACTIONS BETWEEN, 341
DOCUMENTS—
  cancellation of, 15-16, 48, 76, 542, 542-5
  delivery up of, 48, 542, 542-5
  discovery of, 49, 75, 131, 452-3
DURESS, 26, 337

EASEMENT—
  equitable, 27-8, 33, 40
  estoppel, by, 28
  injunction to enforce, 469
  licence distinguished from, 94, 100
ECCLESIASTICAL COURTS, 63-4, 143, 145, 148, 150, 152, 153, 154, 263, 264
ELDON, LORD CHANCELLOR, 4, 71-2
ELECTION—
  basis of, 32, 395-6, 398-401, 404-5
  compensation, availability of property for, 401-3
  disability, persons under, 401-3, 405, 408
  express and implied, 405-8
  extensions of doctrine of, 408-11
  history of, 65-6, 396-401
  implied intent theory, 398-401
  infants, incapacity of, 405
  life interest in relation to, 403
  lunatics, incapacity of, 405
  perpetuities, rule against, in relation to, 404
  powers of appointment in relation to, 403-4
  restraint upon anticipation in relation to, 401-3
ENGAGED COUPLES, TRANSACTIONS BETWEEN, 345-6
ENGLISH SIDE OF THE COURT OF CHANCERY, 47
EQUITABLE EXECUTION—*see* PROCEDURE.
EQUITABLE INTERESTS—
  assignment of—*see* CHOSES IN ACTION.
  legal estates contrasted with, 85-6, 106-8
  priorities of—*see* PRIORITIES.
  transfer of, formalities for, 120, 299
  trusts, under—*see* BENEFICIARY
EQUITABLE JURISIDICTION—
  nature of, 5-6
  over foreign contracts, estates, mortgages and trusts, 13-17, 61, 487

EQUITABLE MORTGAGE—*see* MORTGAGES.
EQUITABLE REMEDIES—
account—*see* ACCOUNT.
auxiliary, 6
cancellation of documents—*see* CANCELLATION OF DOCUMENTS.
delivery up of documents—*see* DELIVERY UP OF DOCUMENTS.
discretionary nature of, 29-34, 67, 454, 459-60, 482-3, 484-5, 492-3
foreclosure—*see* MORTGAGES.
injunction—*see* INJUNCTION.
ne exeat regno—*see* NE EXEAT REGNO.
receiver—*see* RECEIVER.
rectification—*see* RECTIFICATION.
rescission—*see* RESCISSION.
restitution—*see* RESTITUTION, SPECIFIC.
sale—*see* MORTGAGES.
specific performance—*see* SPECIFIC PERFORMANCE.
tracing—*see* TRACING .
See also PROCEDURE.
EQUITABLE WASTE—*see* WASTE.
EQUITY—
acts in personam, 9-17, 47, 163, 449, 455
common law in relation to, 2-4, 51-4, 69-70, 71, 74-127
common law courts, in, 2-4, 69-70, 75
conflict or variance with the common law, 51-3, 77-127, 142
does not allow a person to approbate and reprobate, 28, 32, 33, 408
does nothing in vain, 390, 487
early, 44-52
flexibility of, 55, 61
follows the law, 54
fusion with common law, 9, 12-13, 36, 41, 43, 69, 75-127
growth of, 44-72
he who seeks, must come with clean hands, 30-2, 460
he who seeks, must do equity, 32-3, 92, 113, 188, 441
imputes an intention to fulfil an obligation, 412, 417, 429
influence of Roman and canon law on, 3, 48, 50-1, 54, 397, 426, 482, 484
Ireland, in, 128-42
jurisdiction, 5-6, 13-17
justice in relation to, 6-8
leans against double portions, 417
looks to the intent rather than to the form, 17-29, 178-9
maxims of, 54-5
Middle Ages, in, 46
natural justice as, 6-8
nature of, 1-43
of redemption—*see* MORTGAGES.
precedent, guided by, 1-5, 7, 51, 53-5, 71
regards as done that which ought to be done, 85, 92 297, 375
rules of, modern origin of, 58-9
scope of, 5-6
settled principles, now based on, 4-5, 71-2
source of law, as, 1-3, 34-5, 37-42
statutes, treatment of, 26-9, 482-3, 493-7
statutory, 5, 7, 11, 12, 25, 42-3, 78
to a settlement, married woman's, 32, 441-3
trade competition, gives no remedy against, 7
will not allow a statute to be used as an instrument of fraud, 26-9, 493
will not assist a volunteer, 310
ESTATES IN LAND AT LAW AND IN EQUITY, 106-8
ESTOPPEL—
acquiescence as, 33
basis of, 32
easement by, 28
High Trees doctrine, 6, 40-2, 122-5
recital, by, 125-7
rectification, in relation to, 126-7, 536
representation, by, 38-40

ESTOPPEL—(*contd.*)
variation of contract without consideration by, 6, 40-2, 122-5
EVIDENCE—
Chancery Division, in, 452-3
choses in action, of assignment of, 299-300
Court of Chancery, in, 6, 451-2
de bene esse, 556
extrinsic, to rebut presumption of satisfaction of—
debts by legacies, 417
legacies by legacies, 428
legacies by portions, 423
portions by legacies, 421
parol,
in cases of ambiguity, 497, 530
of fraud or mistake, 536, 538-9
See also WITNESSES.
EXAMINATION OF WITNESSES DE BENE ESSE, 556
EXCHEQUER—
assignment of debts due to, 296
Chamber, Court of, 455
Court of, 73, 75
Irish Court of, 129
Jewish, 295
EXECUTION—*see* PROCEDURE.
EXECUTOR—*see* ADMINISTRATION OF ESTATES.
EX PARTE INJUNCTION—*see* INJUNCTION.
EXPECTANCY—*see* POSSIBILITY.

FAMILY ARRANGEMENTS, 344, 550-1
FEOFFEE TO USES, TREATMENT OF, IN EQUITY, 145-7
FIDEICOMMISSUM, 143
FIDUCIARY RELATIONSHIP—
abuse of, 48, 49, 336-52
nature of, 338-49
necessity for, in cases of tracing, 525-6
FLOATING CHARGE, 165, 209
FORECLOSURE—*see* MORTGAGES.
FORFEITURE—
election, not the basis of, 399
relief from, 25
FORMS OF ACTION, 3, 450
FRANCISCAN FRIARS, USES IN FAVOUR OF, 5, 143-4
FRAUD—
catching bargains, 353-6, 487
common law, at, 26, 49, 329-30, 332
concealed, 28-9, 104-5
constructive notice, in relation to, 215-7, 332
creditors, on, 31, 147
equity, in, 6, 26, 49, 60, 329-56
fiduciary relationship, abuse of, 48, 49, 336-52
legal proceedings, in, 332
misrepresentation, 49, 329-32
on a power, 368-74
on the public or third parties, 352-3
priorities, in relation to, 215-7, 332
rescission for, 131, 543-4
statute as an instrument of, 26-9
unconscionable bargains, 26, 333-6, 353-6
undue influence, 6, 26, 32, 49, 337-52
FUSION OF LAW AND EQUITY, 9, 12-13, 36, 41, 43, 69, 75-127

GOODWILL—*see* INJUNCTION.
GOVERNMENT STOCK—*see* SPECIFIC PERFORMANCE.
GUARDIAN AND WARD, TRANSACTIONS BETWEEN, 344-5

HARDWICKE, LORD CHANCELLOR, 59-61
HEIR—
catching bargain with, 353-6
descent of realty to, 263, 375-6
HIGH COURT OF JUSTICE, 3, 75-7, 448, 450-4, 456
HIRE CONTRACTS, PENALTY CLAUSES IN, 24-5
HIRE-PURCHASE CONTRACTS, PENALTY CLAUSES IN, 20-4
HUSBAND AND WIFE—*see* MARRIED WOMAN.

ILLUSORY APPOINTMENT—*see* POWER OF APPOINTMENT.
IMPERFECT GIFT, EQUITY WILL NOT PERFECT, 310-11
IMPLIED TRUST—*see* TRUST.
IMPUTED NOTICE—*see* NOTICE.
INCOMPLETELY CONSTITUTED TRUST—*see* TRUST.
INDUSTRIAL PROPERTY—*see* INJUNCTION.
INFANT—
custody and education of, 83, 150
election by, 405
equity, in, 6, 48, 49, 66, 76
reconversion on behalf of, 390
undue influence over, 342-5
ward of court, 6, 76
wardship assigned to Chancery Division, 76
INFLUENCE, UNDUE—*see* FRAUD.
INJUNCTION—
acquiescence as a defence, 460, 466
associations, in connection with, 476-9
clubs, in connection with, 476-7
common, 15-16, 52, 75, 76, 131, 458-9
common law courts, in, 75
confidence, to prevent breach of, 31-2, 461
contract, to enforce, 471-3
corporations, against, 476
county court, grant by, 459
crime, to restrain, 6, 480
criminal proceedings, to stay, 459
damages, adequacy of, as a defence, 458, 459-60, 465
damages in lieu of, 463, 466
development of, 6, 35-6, 130-1, 459
director of a company, to protect, 476
discretionary nature of, 459-60
easement, to enforce, 469
enforcement of, 459
ex parte, 453, 458
execution, by way of, 456
history of, 459
industrial property, to protect, 473-6
interlocutory, 111, 448, 453, 457-8, 461-2
intimidation, to restrain, 479
Judicature Acts, effect of, 35-6, 83, 110-13, 458, 460-1
labour disputes, in, 35, 477-9
laches as a defence, 460, 466
libel, to restrain, 35, 458, 461-2
licence, to enforce, 37, 97, 103, 470
mandatory, 457, 465, 466, 476
nature of, 457
nuisance, to restrain, 465-7
passing-off, to restrain, 470
perpetual, 457
personal services, to secure, 472-3
professional associations, in connection with, 477
prohibitory, 457
property, to protect, 463-70
public law, in, 35, 479-81
quia timet, 111, 460, 462, 463, 476
restraint of trade, to enforce, 471-3

INJUNCTION—(*contd.*)
restrictive covenant, to enforce, 11-12, 36, 467-9
scope of, 457, 459-63
settlement, to enforce, 469-70
terms, on, 111
tort, to restrain, 6, 35, 36, 111, 461-3, 470, 479
trade unions, in connection with, 477-9
trespass, to restrain, 36, 111, 464-5
trust, to enforce, 469-70
waste, to restrain, 80, 111, 458, 463-4
INNOCENT MISREPRESENTATION—
damages for, 36, 330, 545-6
rescission for, 26, 544-7
INSOLVENT ESTATES—*see* ADMINISTRATION OF ESTATES.
INSURANCE, CONTRACTS OF—
assignment of assurance policies, 326
non-disclosure in, 550-1
INTEREST—
award of, 82-3
legacy, on, 289-91
mortgage money, on, 82, 178, 206
INTERLOCUTORY PROCEEDINGS—*see* PROCEDURE.
INTERROGATORIES—*see* PROCEDURE.
INTESTACY—*see* ADMINISTRATION OF ESTATES.
INTIMIDATION—*see* INJUNCTION.
INVESTMENT—*see* TRUSTEES.

JEWS, INFLUENCE OF, ON ASSIGNMENT OF CHOSES IN ACTION, 295-6
JOINT ADVENTURE—*see* CONTRIBUTION.
JOINT DEPOSIT RECEIPTS—*see* CHOSES IN ACTION.
JOINT MORTGAGE—*see* MORTGAGES.
JOINT STOCK TRADING, 5
JUDICATURE ACTS, EFFECT OF—
administration of estates, 78-9
assignment of choses in action, 81, 314, 326-8
beneficiary's claim against trustee, 80
cancellation of documents 554-5
concealed fraud, 104-5
conflict or variance between law and equity, 77-127
contribution in a joint adventure, 109
courts, organisation of, 75-7
deeds, 117-25
delivery up of documents, 554-5
equitable relief, 113-17
estates, 106-8
injunctions, 35-6, 83, 110-13, 458, 460-1
leases, 84-93
licences, 93-104
merger, 81, 193
mortgagor, suit for possession by, 81, 224
part performance, 496
practice and procedure, 110, 448, 453, 454
receivers, 83, 111, 509, 510, 515
rectification, 538
stipulation as to time, 81-3
waste, 80-1
JURIES—*see* PROCEDURE.
JURISDICTION—*see* EQUITABLE JURISDICTION.
JUSTICIAR, 45

LABOUR DISPUTES—*see* INJUNCTION.
LACHES, 33-4, 197, 342, 460, 466, 504-6, 548
LAND PURCHASE ACTS—*see* CONVERSION.

LEASE—
agreement for, effect of, 85-93
conversion on enfranchisement, 383
deed, necessity for, 84
definition of, 88
Judicature Acts, effect of, 84-93
licence, distinguished from 94, 100
mortgagee or mortgagor, by, 224-32, 235
option in, conversion under, 381-3
writing, necessity for, 84
written, effect of, at law and in equity, 84-93
LEGACY—*see* ADMINISTRATION OF ESTATES ; SATISFACTION.
LEGAL ESTATES, TRANSFER OF, 119-20
LEGATEE—*see* ADMINISTRATION OF ESTATES ; CONVERSION ; SATISFACTION.
LIBEL—*see* INJUNCTION.
LICENCE—
at law and in equity, 37, 93-104
coupled with an interest, 37, 94-5, 97, 100
definition of, 93
deserted wife's, 36, 37-8, 104
easement and profit distinguished from, 94, 100
injunction to protect, 37, 97, 103, 470
interest in land, whether, 102-4
Judicature Acts, effect of, 93-104
lease, distinguished from, 94, 100
occupational, 36
personal, not assignable, 298
revocation of, 37, 94-103
specific performance of contract for, 37, 98, 101
third parties, and, 98, 103-4
LIEN—
Chancery Division, assigned to, 76
nature of, 186
LIMITATION OF ACTIONS—
acquiescence, 28, 33-4, 342, 373
common law, at, 104-5
concealed fraud, 28-9, 104-5
equity, in, 33, 80, 104-5
laches, 33-4, 197, 342, 460, 466, 504-6, 548
trustees, in respect of, 80
LIQUIDATED DAMAGES, 18-20
LITIGATE, RIGHT TO—*see* CHOSES IN ACTION.
LORD CHANCELLOR—*see* CHANCELLOR.
LORDS JUSTICES IN CHANCERY, 73-4, 455
LUNATIC, 49, 66, 129, 391, 405

MAINTENANCE—
tort of, 294-6, 298
trustees' powers of, 357
MANDAMUS, 83, 111, 455, 483
MANDATORY INJUNCTION—*see* INJUNCTION.
MANSFIELD, LORD CHIEF JUSTICE, 9, 68-70
MARINE INSURANCE—*see* INSURANCE.
MARRIAGE SETTLEMENT—*see* RECTIFICATION.
MARRIED WOMAN—
common law, position at, 440
election by, 401-3
equity to a settlement, 32, 441-3
matrimonial home, rights in, 36, 37-8, 104
protection of, 49
reconversion by, 391
restraint upon anticipation, 401-3, 446-7
separate estate of, 5, 32, 58, 63, 150, 443-6
transactions with husband, 345, 348
undue influence over, 345, 348

MARSHALLING—
administration of estates, in, 65, 438-9
basis of, 432
creditors, as between, 65, 432-8
history of, 32, 65, 433
mortgages, of, 432-7
principal and agent, as between, 438
suretyship, in, 437-8
MASTER OF THE ROLLS, 73-4, 132-4, 455
MASTERS IN CHANCERY—*see* CHANCERY, COURT OF.
MASTERS IN THE HIGH COURT, 454
MATRIMONIAL HOME—*see* MARRIED WOMAN.
MEDICAL ADVISER AND PATIENT, TRANSACTIONS BETWEEN, 341
MELIORATING WASTE—*see* WASTE.
MEMORANDUM IN WRITING—*see* WRITING.
MENTAL PATIENT—*see* PATIENT.
MERCANTILE LAW, NEGOTIABILITY UNDER, 294, 308
MERGER OF ESTATES, 81, 193-6
MISDESCRIPTION—*see* RESCISSION ; SPECIFIC PERFORMANCE.
MISREPRESENTATION—*see* FRAUD ; INNOCENT MISREPRESENTATION.
MISTAKE—
common, 49, 532-3, 535
common law, at, 547-9
equity, in, 6, 49, 547-50
fraud, induced by, 49, 329-32, 548
idenity of other party, as to, 548-9
mutual, 530, 534-5
nature of transaction, as to, 549-50
negativing agreement, 547-9
rectification for—*see* RECTIFICATION.
rescission for, 26, 49, 530-42
subject-matter, as to, 550
title, as to, 550
unilateral, 533-6
MONEYLENDER, 32, 113-14
MORTGAGEE—
collateral advantages of, 18, 206-9
covenant by mortgagor to pay, enforcement by, 238, 248-9
entry into possession by, 230-8
foreclosure by, 170, 242-9
in possession, accountability of, 235-8, 261
leases, grant by, 231-2, 235
option given to, to purchase equity of redemption, 205-6
payment of, by person not entitled to redeem, 192-3
possession, right to, 230-2
powers of, when in possession, 235-7
proceeds of sale, duty to apply, 256-7
purchase by, of equity of redemption, 177-8, 205-6, 259-60
purchase by, when exercising power of sale, 254-5
receiver, appointment by, 238-42, 511, 512-4
redemption of prior mortgage by, 189-90
remedies of, to enforce his security, 238-57
sale by,
after foreclosure, 249
duty of care in respect of price, 253-4, 261-2
express power, under, 252, 253
in lieu of foreclosure, 246-7
order of court, under, 192, 253
proceeds of sale, 256-7
statutory power, under, 249-57
who may not purchase, 254-6
trustee, as, 257-62
See also MORTGAGES ; MORTGAGOR.
MORTGAGES—
agreements for, 184-5

MORTGAGES—(*contd.*)
attornment clauses in, 232-5
Chancery Division, assigned to, 76, 231
charge, by,
equitable, 186
legal, 18, 179-81
clogs on the equity of redemption, 18, 61, 176-8, 180, 202-9
collateral advantages, 18, 206-9
common law, at, 166-8
consolidation of, 32, 62, 175-6, 197-202
covenants in restraint of trade in, 207-9
deposit of title deeds, by, 181-4, 186
equitable, 171, 181-6
equitable right to redeem, 61, 166, 168-71, 187-209
equity of redemption,
clogs on, 18, 61, 176-8, 180, 202-9
history of, 61, 166-71
incidents, of, 168-9
nature of, 61, 62, 168-71, 187
purchase of, by mortgagee, 177-8, 205-6, 259-60
foreign land, of, enforced in equity, 13-14
forms of, 18, 166-8, 178-86
fraud in relation to, 212, 215-7
history of, 5, 49, 61, 164-78
joint, 262
legal, 12, 178-81
marshalling, of, 432-7
merger of estates in connection with, 193-6
mortgagee—*see* MORTGAGEE.
mortgagor—*see* MORTGAGOR.
nature of, 61, 164-71
notice in relation to, 214-22
penalty clauses in, 178, 206
priorities of, 12, 62, 171-5, 183, 209-22
redeem, right to,
equitable, 61, 166, 168-71, 187-209
legal, 166, 168, 187
loss of, 196-7
redemption,
duty of mortgagee on, 190-2
interference with, 176-8, 202-9
lapse of time in relation to, 169-70, 196-7
lessee, by, 190
limited owner of equity of redemption, by, 189-90
merger on, 193-6
mortgagor, by, 188-9, 190
postponement of, 203-4
procedure for, 188-9
right of, 168-71, 187-209
sale in lieu of, 192
subsequent mortgagee, by, 189
third party, by, 190
registration of,
company charges register, in, 211, 213
deeds registry, in, 210, 211, 212
land charges, as, 209-12, 214
register of titles, in, 211, 213
tacking,
further advances, 62, 175, 220-2
tabula in naufragio, 62, 172-5, 218-20
MORTGAGOR—
attorned tenant to the mortgagee, 232-5
in possession, status of, 222-3
leases, grant by, 224-30
owner, regarded as, in equity, 18
powers of, when in possession, 223-30

MORTGAGOR—(*contd.*)
  redeem, right to, 61, 166, 168-71, 187-9
  redemption by, 166-71, 187-9
  suit by, for possession, 81
  trustee, as, 259, 260-1
    See also MORTGAGEE ; MORTGAGES.
MOTIONS—*see* PROCEDURE.

NATURAL JUSTICE, 6-8
NE EXEAT REGNO, WRIT OF, 560-2
NEGOTIABLE INSTRUMENTS—*see* CHOSES IN ACTION.
NON-DISCLOSURE—
  rescission of contracts for, 550-1
  specific performance, defence to, 29, 30
NOTICE—
  actual, 214, 215
  choses in action, in connection with, 301-7, 326, 328
  constructive—
    inapplicable to chattels, 108
    nature of, 214, 215-7
  equitable rules of, 5
  imputed, 215
  mortgages, in connection with, 214-22
  restrictive covenants, of, 11-12
NOTTINGHAM, LORD CHANCELLOR, 52-6, 151, 170-7
NOVATION—*see* CHOSES IN ACTION.
NUISANCE—*see* INJUNCTION.

OCCUPATIONAL LICENCE—*see* LICENCE.
OPTIONS—
  conversion by virtue of, 381-3
  mortgagee, of, to purchase equity of redemption, 205-6
  perpetuities, rule against, in relation to, 382
ORIGINATING SUMMONS—*see* PROCEDURE.

PARENT AND CHILD, TRANSACTIONS BETWEEN, 342-4
PART PERFORMANCE—
  basis of doctrine of, 493-4
  Judicature Acts, effect of, 496
  nature of acts constituting, 494-6
  origin of doctrine of, 54, 68, 482
  scope of, 26, 496-7
PARTITION LAND, TRUSTEES' POWER TO, 392
PARTNERSHIP—
  accounts, 562
  agreement, conversion under, 377
  Chancery Division, assigned to, 76
  equity, as a product of, 5
  foreign, winding up of, 14
  land, conversion in relation to, 377
  receiver on behalf of partner, appointment of, 515-7
  specific performance of, 487-9
PASSING-OFF—*see* INJUNCTION.
PATIENT—
  mental,
    election by, 405
    receiver of property of, 516
    reconversion on behalf of, 391
    sale of land of, by order of court, 378-80
    trust for, 5
      See also LUNATIC.
  transactions with doctor, 341
PENAL LAWS AGAINST ROMAN CATHOLICS IN IRELAND, 137
PENALTY, RELIEF AGAINST, 18-25, 178, 206, 454

PERFORMANCE—
    doctrine of, 65-6, 413, 429-31
    part—*see* PART PERFORMANCE.
    specific—*see* SPECIFIC PERFORMANCE.
PERMISSIVE WASTE—*see* WASTE.
PERPETUAL INJUNCTION—*see* INJUNCTION.
PERPETUATION OF TESTIMONY, 130, 555-6
PERPETUITIES—
    charities, in relation to, 153
    election and, 404
    modern rule against, 5, 53, 58, 59
    options, in relation to, 382
    powers of appointment, in relation to, 363-5
PERSONAL REPRESENTATIVES—*see* ADMINISTRATION OF ESTATES.
PERSONAL SERVICE, CONTRACT FOR—
    injunction to enforce, 472-3
    not assignable, 298
    part performance, doctrine of, not applicable to, 493
    specific performance not granted of, 7, 36, 492
PERSONALTY—
    assignments of interests in, 302
    devolution of, in relation to conversion—*see* CONVERSION.
PETITIONS TO COUNCIL, 3, 46
PLEADINGS—*see* PROCEDURE.
PORTIONS—
    ademption of legacies by, 58, 422-5
    Chancery Division, assigned to, 76
    definition of, 417-9
    double, 417, 419
    satisfaction of,
        by legacies, 58, 417-22
        legacies by portions, 58, 422-5
POSSIBILITIES—
    assignment of, 296-8, 309
    catching bargains affecting, 353-6, 487
    specific perforamcne of contract for sale of, 487
POWER—
    appendant, 360
    appointment, of—*see* POWER OF APPOINTMENT.
    collateral, 360
    in gross, 360
    in the nature of a trust, 362-3
POWER OF APPOINTMENT—
    bare, 361-2
    certainty of objects, 361-2
    contract not to exercise, 363
    defective execution of, 366-7
    disclaimer of, 363
    election in relation to, 403-4
    excessive execution, 367-8
    fiduciary, 361-2
    fraud on, 368-74
    general,
        nature of, 357
        rule against perpetuities in relation to, 364
    hybrid, 358
    illusory appointment, 365-6
    nature of, 357-63
    objects,
        certainty of, 361-2
        entitled in default of appointment, 362-3
        self-exclusion, 358
    perpetuities, rule against, in relation to, 363-5
    property, distinction from, 359-60
    release of, 363, 374
    revocation of appointment, 367, 374

POWER OF APPOINTMENT—(*contd.*)
special,
nature of, 357-8
rule against perpetuities in relation to, 364
trust, in the nature of, 361-3
PRACTICE—*see* PROCEDURE.
PRECEDENT, JUDICIAL, 1-5, 7, 61, 53-5, 71
PREFERENCE, RIGHT OF—*see* ADMINISTRATION OF ESTATES.
PRINCIPAL AND AGENT—
accounts, 562
marshalling as between, 438
tracing between, 9-10
transactions between, 338, 346-7
PRIORITIES—
assignments of choses in action, of, 300-7, 328
equitable interests, of, 106-8
legal interests, of, 106-8
mortgages, of, 12, 62, 171-5, 183, 209-22
registration in relation to, 209-14
PROBATE—*see* ADMINISTRATION OF ESTATES.
PROCEDURE—
affidavits, 452
appeals, 73-4, 135-6, 138-9, 141, 454, 455
assignment of cases to Divisions of the High Court, 75-6, 231, 263, 448
bill in Chancery, 47, 450, 451
chambers, in, 454
Chancery Division, in, 448, 450-4
commission, examination of witnesses by, 452
county courts, in, 90, 140-1, 448-9, 459
Court of Chancery, in, 47, 449-56
decree, enrolment of, 454
discovery of documents, 49, 75, 131, 452-3
evidence—*see* EVIDENCE.
execution, 15, 47, 455-6, 460, 483, 491, 509, 510-11, 515
High Court, in, 448, 450-4, 456
interlocutory, 111, 448, 452-3, 457-8, 461-2, 509
interrogatories, 452
judges, opinion of, on points of law, 449, 453
Judicature Acts, effect of, 110, 448, 453, 454
juries, 47, 75, 452, 453
masters, 73-4, 131, 454
motions, 450, 453, 454
originating summons, 450
pleadings, 450-1
rehearing, 56, 454-5
sequestration, 456
subpoena, writ of, 47-9, 130
witnesses—see WITNESSES.
writ of summons, 450
See also EQUITABLE REMEDIES.
PROFESSIONAL ASSOCIATIONS—*see* INJUNCTION.
PROHIBITORY INJUNCTION—*see* INJUNCTION.
PROPERTY—
equitable conception of, 78
injunction, use of, to protect, 463-70
receiver to preserve, during litigation, 510
PURCHASER WITHOUT NOTICE, PROTECTION OF, 1, 11-12, 42, 130, 146, 151, 170-1, 519, 526-7, 530, 548.

QUIA TIMET PROCEEDINGS—
administration of estates, in 557
injunction, 111, 460, 462, 463, 476
receiver, appointment of, 510
suretyship cases, in, 558-9

RECEIVER—
administration of estates, in, 512
appointment of, by the court, 509, 511
creditor, on behalf of, 515
debenture holder, on behalf of, 511, 514-5
execution, appointment by way of, 509, 510-11, 515
executorship, in, 512
Judicature Acts, under, 83, 111, 509, 510, 515
mental infirmity, in cases of, 516
mortgagee, apppointment by, 239-42, 511, 512-4
partner, on behalf of, 515-6
power to appoint, 237-41
powers of, 241-2
property, to preserve, during litigation, 510
settlement, in, 512
shareholders, on behalf of, 514
trust, in, 512
vendor and purchaser, between, 512
who may be appointed, 516-7
RECONVERSION, 388-93
RECTIFICATION—
Chancery Division, assigned to, 76
common mistake, for, 49, 532-3, 535
contract, of, 530, 536-42
conveyance, of, 530
estoppel in relation to 126-7, 536
Judicature Acts, effect of, 538
marriage settlement, of, 530, 532
mistake required, 532-6
mutual mistake, for, 530, 534-5
rescission as an alternative to, 533-5
scope of, 536-42
unilateral mistake, for, 533-6
voluntary settlement, of, 530, 531
REDEMPTION—*see* MORTGAGES.
REGISTRATION—
bills of sale, of, 232-3
charges, of, 211, 213
deeds, of, 28, 210, 211, 212
land charges, of, 12, 27-8, 86, 209-12, 214
mortgages, of, 12, 209-14
notice, effect on, 27-8
restrictive covenants, of, 12, 469
titles, of, 211, 213
REHEARING—*see* PROCEDURE.
REMEDIES—*see* EQUITABLE REMEDIES ; MORTGAGEE.
RENT, PAYMENT OF—
as evidence of tenancy, 85
by mortgagor to mortgagee, 232-4
not part performance, 495
RESCISSION—
Chancery Division, assigned to, 76
damages in lieu of, 546
fraud, for, 131, 543-4
grounds for, 542
innocent misrepresentation, for, 26, 544-7
misdescription, for, 550
mistake, for, 26, 49, 547-50
nature of, 542-3
non-disclosure, for, 550-1
rectification, as an alternative to, 533-5
restitutio in integrum, depends on, 32, 543, 544, 546
terms, on, 546
RESTITUTION—*see* SPECIFIC RESTITUTION.
RESTRAINT OF TRADE, 7, 207-9, 471-3

RESTRAINT UPON ANTICIPATION—
abolition of, 447
election, effect on, 401-3
origin of, 446-7
RESTRICTIVE COVENANT—
building scheme, under, 32-3
injunction, enforcement by, 11-12, 36, 467-9
nature of, 6, 11-12
notice in relation to, 11-12, 469
registration of, 12, 469
restraint of trade—*see* RESTRAINT OF TRADE.
RETAINER—*see* ADMINISTRATION OF ESTATES.
REVERSIONS, SALES OF, 353-6, 487
RIGHT TO LITIGATE—*see* CHOSES IN ACTION.
ROMAN LAW, INFLUENCE OF, 397, 426
RULE AGAINST PERPETUITIES—*see* PERPETUITIES.

ST. GERMAIN, 4, 48-9, 50
SALE—
mortgagee, by, 192, 246-7, 249-57, 261-2
order of court, under, 192, 253, 378-80
reversion, of, 353-6
SATISFACTION—
debts, of, by legacies, 290, 413-17
doctrine of, generally, 412-13
history of, 65-6, 413
legacies, of—
by legacies, 425-8
by portions, 58, 422-5
portions, of, by legacies, 58, 417-22
SEAL—
imports consideration, 17, 118
use of, in deeds, 17, 117-8
SECRET TRUST—*see* TRUST.
SELDEN, JOHN, 4, 50
SEPARATION DEED—
discharge of, 121-2
specific performance of, 489-90
SEQUESTRATION—*see* PROCEDURE.
SET-OFF, 32, 117, 308-9
SETTLEMENT—
family arrangement, by way of, 344
injunction, enforcement by, 469-70
receiver in respect of, 512
strict, 42, 66, 67, 150
voluntary, rectification of, 530, 531
SHARES—
assignment of, 318-24
contracts for allotment of, duty of disclosure, 550-1
receivers to protect, 514
specific performance of contract to purchase, 487
SOLICITOR AND CLIENT, TRANSACTIONS BETWEEN, 338-41
SOLICITOR-TRUSTEE—*see* TRUSTEES.
SPECIFIC PERFORMANCE—
abatement of price, with, 506-7
arbitrator's award, of, 490
available where damages inadequate, 32, 482, 486, 488, 489, 490, 491
building contract, of, 482, 491
chattel, of contract to transfer, 482, 490
Chancery Division, assigned to, 76
cinema seat, of contract for, 37, 98, 101
compensation, with, 506-7
contract under seal, of, 118-9
conversion under contract of sale depends on, 380
damages in lieu of, 483, 496-7, 508

SPECIFIC PERFORMANCE—(*contd.*)
defences,
hardship, 29-30, 501
ignorance, 29
inadequacy of consideration, 29, 501
incompleteness, 497-8
laches, 504-6
misdescription, 506-8
non-disclosure, 29, 30
uncertainty, 499
want of
fairness, 29-30, 356, 499-501
mutuality, 32, 501-3
title, 30, 504
writing, 493-7
development of, 6, 482-5
discretionary, 29-30, 482-3, 484-5, 492-3
enforcement of, 483, 491
executory contracts, applicable only to, 484
expectancy, of contract for sale of, 487
foreign land, of contract relating to, 14, 61, 487
goods, of contract for sale of, 490-1
government stcok, of contract to transfer, 487
land, of contract for sale of, 32, 486-7
lease, of contract for, 36, 85-90, 92
licence, of contract for, 37, 98, 101
limits of, 7
money, of obligation to pay, 32
nature of, 483-5
origin of, 48, 482
part performance, 26, 54, 68, 482, 493-7
partnership articles, of, 487-9
patent contracts, of, 491
personal services, of contract for, 7, 36, 492
scope of, 485-92
separation deed, of, 489-90
stocks and shares, of contract to transfer, 487
terms, on, 506-7
third party, in favour of, 38
volunteer cannot obtain, 17, 492
SPECIFIC RESTITUTION, 67-8, 484
SPIRITUAL ADVISER, UNDUE INFLUENCE BY, 342
STAR CHAMBER, COURT OF, 46, 47, 52, 353
STATUTE OF LIMITATIONS—*see* LIMITATION OF ACTIONS
STATUTES, TREATMENT OF, IN EQUITY, 36-9, 482-3, 493-7
STATUTORY TRUSTS—*see* TRUST.
SUBPOENA, WRIT OF—*see* PROCEDURE.
SUBROGATION, 439
SUPREME COURT OF JUDICATURE, 75, 141-2
SURETIES—
contribution between, 30-1
marshalling between, 437-8
quia timet proceedings by, 558-9

TACKING—*see* MORTGAGES.
TAXATION—
avoidance of, 5, 161-2
evasion of foreign, 31
TENANT IN TAIL—*see* RECONVERSION.
TESTIMONY, PERPETUATION OF—*see* PERPETUATION OF TESTIMONY.
TIME, STIPULATIONS AS TO, 18, 81-3, 505-6
TITLE—
registration of, 211, 213
want of, as defence to specific perforamnce, 30, 504
TORT—*see* INJUNCTION.

TRACING—
bank account, into, 521-6
charge, imposition of, 11, 518, 521-4
Clayton's case, rule in, 521-2
common law, at, 9-11, 519
development of, 38
fiduciary relationship, necessity for, 525-6
identification of property, necessity for, 519
mixed funds, 521-6
nature of, 8, 9-11, 162-3, 518-9
principal and agent, between, 9-10
third party, property in hands of, 526-9
trustee, by, 519
ultra vires payments, 525-6
wrongdoer's hands, property in changed form in, 519-26
TRADE UNIONS—*see* INJUNCTION.
TRESPASS—*see* INJUNCTION.
TRUST—
accounts, 562, 563
beneficiary's rights under, 31, 80
breach of, 80, 130-1
Chancery Division, assigned to, 76
charitable, 5, 66, 67, 149, 150, 152-9
constructive, 57, 150, 520, 527
development of law of, 5, 48, 49, 53, 62-3, 146-63
foreign land, of, 14-15
for sale,
after 1925, 42
conversion, application to, 65, 376, 392, 394
injunction to restrain breach of, 469-70
partition of land held on, 392
statutory,
ademption of legacies on conversion under, 394
intestacy, on, 269-70
history of, 5, 48, 49, 53, 62-3, 67, 130, 143-63
implied in law, 53, 145, 150
incompletely constituted, 1, 310-11
injunction to enforce, 469-70
non-charitable purposes, for, 38
origin of, 5, 48, 143-6
power in the nature of a, 361-3
receivers in connection with, 512
secret, 8, 27
statutory, 269-70, 394
trustees—*see* TRUSTEES.
unit, 5
variation of, 14-15, 35, 38, 161-2
TRUSTEES—
agents, appointment by, 159-60
assignments of beneficial interests, position in respect of, 300-6
bankruptcy of, 512
beneficiary's rights against, 31, 80
breach of trust by, 31, 80, 130-1
contribution between, 31
for sale, may partition unsold land, 392
improper investment by, 512
injunction to restrain, 469-70
investment by, 160-1, 162, 164
limitation of actions against, 80
mortgagees as, 257-62
mortgagors as, 259, 260-1
not liable,
for signing for conformity, 150
to beneficiaries who concur in breach of trust, 31
personal representatives as, 269, 270-1

TRUSTEES—(*contd.*)
powers of,
maintenance and advancement, 357
to appoint agents, 159-60
purchase of beneficiary's interest by, 341
sale of trust property to, 336
solicitor, duty to indemnify co-trustees, 31
tracing by, 519
transactions with beneficiaries, 341
See also TRUST.

UBERRIMAE FIDEI CONTRACTS—*see* RESCISSION.
UNCONSCIONABLE BARGAINS—*see* FRAUD.
UNDUE INFLUENCE—*see* FRAUD.
UNIT TRUSTS—*see* TRUST.
UNSOUND MIND, PERSONS OF—*see* LUNATIC ; PATIENT.
USES, 48, 49, 130, 143-63
See also TRUST.

VARIATION OF TRUSTS—*see* TRUST.
VENDOR AND PURCHASER—*see* RECEIVER.
VICE-CHANCELLOR, 73-4, 455
VOLUNTARY SETTLEMENT—*see* RECTIFICATION.
VOLUNTARY WASTE—*see* WASTE.
VOLUNTEER—*see* CONSIDERATION ; SPECIFIC PERFORMANCE.

WARD—*see* GUARDIAN AND WARD ; INFANT.
WASTE—
account of, 563
equitable, 58, 67, 80-1, 464
equity, in, 67, 80-1
injunction to restrain, 80, 111, 458, 463-4
Judicature Acts, since, 80-1
meliorating, 464
permissive, 80, 463-4
voluntary, 80, 463-4
WILL—
conversion directed by, 387-8
foreign land, of, 15
land, of, introduction of, 144, 148
married woman, by, 440
undue influence procuring, 349
WITNESSES—
evidence of, on commission, 452
examination of, de bene esse, 556
oral evidence by, 451-2
perpetuation of testimony of, 130, 555-6
See also EVIDENCE.
WRITING—
necessity for, under Statute of Frauds, 482, 493-7, 520, 538-9
required for transfer of certain equitable interests, 120